A History of Clinical Psychiatry

The Origin and History of Psychiatric Disorders

Edited by

German E. Berrios & Roy Porter

THE ATHLONE PRESS
London & New Brunswick, NJ

First published in 1995 by
THE ATHLONE PRESS
1 Park Drive, London NW11 7SG
and New Brunswick, New Jersey

This paperback edition first published in the United States 1999

British Library Cataloguing in Publication Data
*A catalogue record for this book is available
from the British Library*

ISBN 0 485 24011 4 hb
0 485 24211 7 pb

Library of Congress Cataloging-in-Publication Data
A history of clinical psychiatry : the origin and history of
  psychiatric disorders / edited by German E. Berrios & Roy Porter.
    p.   cm.
  Originally published: New York University Press, 1995.
  Includes bibliographical references and index.
  ISBN 0-485-24011 4 (hb). -- ISBN 0 485-24211-7 (pb)
  1. Mental illness--Classification--History.   2. Neurobehavioral
disorders--Classification--History.   3. Psychology, Pathological-
-History.   4. Mental illness-Terminology--History.   I. Berrios, G.
E.   II. Porter, Roy, 1946-   .
  [DNLM: 1. Mental Disorders--therapy.   2. Mental Disorders-
-history.   Not Acquired / WM 400 H673 1995a]
RC455.2.C4H57   1999
616.89'009--dc21
DNLM/DLC
for Library of Congress   98-52022
                                                               CIP

Distributed in the United States, Canada and South America by
Transaction Publishers
390 Campus Drive
Somerset, New Jersey 08873

Printed and bound in Great Britain by
Bookcraft (Bath) Ltd

Contents

PART 2
THE FUNCTIONAL PSYCHOSES

PART 3
NEUROSES and PERSONALITY DISORDERS

Preface

This book demonstrates that historians and clinicians working together generate good scholarship. It also wants to show to professional historians that there is a point in researching into the history of mental and neuropsychiatric disorders; and to clinicians that their *knowledge by acquaintance* is essential to the writing of good clinical history. In general, the book's guiding idea is to approach each disease or topic from a clinical (emphasising original observations, clinical samples, and biographical accounts) and a social perspective (including constructivist and contextual explanations).

By *mental disorder* it is meant here 'organic' conditions, psychoses, neuroses, and personality disorders, and by *neuropsychiatric disorder* neurological conditions that include clear psychiatric symptoms. Various factors have governed our selection of topics. The most general concerned disease frequency and/or importance (e.g. disorders such as Prader-Willi syndrome, oneirophrenia, etc. were left out). However, in the case of some common conditions (e.g. clinical disorders of sleep, sexual pathology) it was not possible to find either a clinical or professional historian to do the job. Yet in other cases (e.g. multiple sclerosis, unitary and cycloid psychosis), no professional historian was willing to tackle their social history. To compensate for this, other chapters show an embarrassment of riches: e.g. 'mental retardation' includes four sections, each conveying a *different* perspective: clinico-psychological (Miller), clinico-psychiatric (Berrios), social (Goodey) and social-educational (Thom). When important for historical understanding, the book includes short accounts on individuals: this is the case with the 'psychoses' whose evolution would be impossible to grasp without knowing something about Kraepelin and Wernicke.

To keep the length of the book within manageable proportions, inevitably certain areas of clinical psychiatry have been left unexplored (e.g. psychiatric treatments and sub-specialisms). These may be treated in a future volume. However, the body of knowledge included in this book should provide historians with solid foundations for their macro-concepts, and give clinicians new information on the very diseases they confront and the patients they want to help.

G.E. Berrios and R.S. Porter

Contributors

Dr. German E. Berrios, BA, DPhilSci, MA(Oxon); MD; FRCPsych; FBPsS; DPM. After reading philosophy and psychology at Oxford, he trained in the history and philosophy of science under A. Crombie, C. Webster and R. Harré; and then as a neurologist and psychiatrist at the United Oxford Hospitals. After working as a lecturer to the late Professor Max Hamilton at Leeds University, he went to Cambridge in 1977 where he is a University Lecturer and Honorary Consultant in Psychiatry, and Fellow of Robinson College. He was elected *Fellow* of the Royal College of Psychiatrists in 1983, and *Fellow* of the British Psychological Society in 1988. His clinical research is on the psychiatric aspects of neurological disease and dementia, and his historical work on the formation of the descriptive language of psychiatry. He has published more than 180 papers and book chapters, and 5 books. For 6 years he was the editor of the History and Philosophy of Psychiatry section of *Current Opinion in Psychiatry*. Currently, he is the Honorary Librarian of the RCPsych, and Chairman of its *Special History Group*. He is assistant editor of the *British Journal of Psychiatry*. With Professor Roy Porter, he co-edits *History of Psychiatry*. His *History of Mental symptoms: descriptive psychopathology since the 19th century* (CUP) appeared in 1995.

Prof. Dr. med. H. Beckmann, MD, Professor of Psychiatry is Head of the Department of Psychiatry at Würzburg University. After studying Medicine in Cologne, Heidelberg and Munich he worked at the Munich Psychiatric University Hospital. He spent 1973–1974 at the Psychobiology Section of the National Institute of Mental Health (USA) working with Fred Goodwin. He has been interested in the biochemical and pharmacological aspects of the endogenous psychoses, particularly noradrenaline in depression. During his period as Vice-President of the Central Institute of Mental Health in Mannheim (Germany) he undertook research into the biochemistry of endogenous depression and schizophrenia. He then became interested in the psychopathology and neuroanatomy of these disorders and formed a research partnership with Hermann Jakob at the Neuropathology Department in Heidelberg. He has also done work on the nosology of Karl Leonhard. In 1985, he became Chairman of Psychiatry at the Department of Psychiatry, University of Würzburg where he has continued working on the genetic, morphological, and psychopathological aspects of the endogenous psychoses. He has published around 270 scientific papers and several books, and co-edits several leading scientific journals.

Dr. M. Dominic Beer, MD; MA(Oxon); MB BS; MRCPsych is Senior Lecturer in Psychiatry at the United Medical & Dental Schools (University of London) and Honorary Consultant Psychiatrist at Bexley Hospital, Kent. He read Modern Languages at Oxford and held a post-doctoral research fellowship at the Wellcome Institute for the History of Medicine (London) where he completed his MD

Thesis on *Psychosis: a history of the concept*. His research interests in the History of Psychiatry include the concept of mental illness in European Psychiatry; and in the clinical area the Mental Health of expatriate workers, and intensive care and challenging behaviour psychiatry. He has published on the historical aspects of mental illness in European psychiatry and on the clinical aspects of challenging behaviour.

Edward M. Brown MD practices psychology in Providence R.I. where he is on the Faculty of the Department of Psychology and the Center for Bio-Medical Ethics at Brown University.

Michael J. Clark is a History graduate of New College and Linacre College, Oxford and former Wellcome Research Fellow in the Department of History at Lancaster University. He has published a number of articles and essays on aspects of the history of psychiatry and forensic medicine in the nineteenth and twentieth centuries, and has co-edited a collection of essays entitled *Legal Medicine in History* for Cambridge University Press. Since 1990, he has managed the Wellcome Trust's collections of medical and medical-historical films and videos.

Ann Dally is a psychiatrist who read history at Somerville College, Oxford, then medicine at St. Thomas's Hospital, London, qualifying in 1953. She became well known first for her work on mothers and children, then for opposing the 'official' treatment of drug addicts and the theories on which it is based. This got her into serious trouble with the General Medical Council (see her book *A Doctor's Story*, 1990). Her other recent books are *Inventing Motherhood* (1982) and *Women under the Knife* (1991). Since 1990 she has been working at the Wellcome Institute for the History of Medicine on fantasy surgery after Lister and, more recently, the history of some of the conflicts in psychiatry.

Dr. Tom R. Dening, MD; MRCPsych studied at the University of Newcastle upon Tyne, qualifying in Medicine in 1980. Postgraduate psychiatric training in Cambridge and Oxford. Current appointment (since 1991): Consultant Psychiatrist and Clinical Director, Psychiatric Services for the Elderly, Addenbrooke's NHS Trust, Cambridge; also Associate Lecturer, Department of Psychiatry, University of Cambridge. MD thesis: *The Neuropsychiatry of Wilson's Disease*, Newcastle, 1989. His publications and research interests include neuropsychiatry, descriptive psychopathology, old age psychiatry and history of psychiatry.

Ian Dowbiggin is Assistant Professor of History at the University of Prince Edward Island, Canada. He has published a number of articles on the history of psychiatry and his *Inheriting Madness: Professionalization and Psychiatric Knowledge in Nineteenth-Century* was published by University of California Press in 1991. He is currently working on a book dealing with the relations between the eugenics movement and Anglo-American psychiatry.

Eric J. Engstrom was born in 1961. He took his BA (1984) at Lewis and Clark College in Portland, Oregon and his MA (1990) at the University of Munich, where he wrote his masters thesis on Emil Kraepelin. He is presently a Fulbright Fellow and is researching under the supervision of Konrad H. Jarausch at the University of North Carolina at Chapel Hill a doctoral dissertation on the emergence of the university psychiatric clinic in nineteenth-century Germany.

Dr. Waltraud Ernst is a lecturer at the Department of Sociology and Social Policy, University of Southampton. She has been trained as a clinical psychologist and psychotherapist in Germany, and as a social historian in England. She is a Wellcome University Award holder and focuses in her current research on the history of mental health and healing in colonial India and New Zealand. She has published various articles and a book on psychiatry in British India.

C.F. Goodey has formerly been Tutor in Sociology at Ruskin College, Oxford, and on the teaching staff of both Arts and Social Science faculties of the Open University. He is currently a Leverhulme Fellow, working on the early history of psychological concepts of learning difficulty.

Dr. Renate Hauser, MD; MPhil; PhD is in private practice at Geneva, where she is also affiliated to the Department of History of Medicine of the University. She took her MPhil degree at Cambridge (*Emil Kraepelin and dementia praecox*). Her PhD was on *Sexuality, Neurasthenia and the Law: Richard von Krafft Ebing (1840–1902)*, (London University, 1992). She has contributed to *Sexual Knowledge, Sexual Science. The History of Attitudes to Sexuality* (CUP) edited by Roy Porter and Mikuláš Teich (1994).

Dr. med. S. Herpertz, MD was born on 16th of April 1960 and studied medicine in Bonn. His MD thesis (1986) was on the history of occupational diseases. Between 1989 and 1992, he trained as a Neurologist at the University of Bochum and as a Psychiatrist at Aachen. Since 1993, he has been Senior Psychiatrist at the Clinic of Psychiatry and Psychotherapy of the latter University. His main research interests and publications are on personality disorders, impulse control and self-harm behaviour.

Dr. Andrew D. Hodgkiss, BA (Cantab); MRCPsych studied History and Philosophy of Science as a pre-clinical student at Cambridge University, and has maintained an interest in the history of psychiatry. He is an Assistant Editor of *History of Psychiatry* and recently spent a year as a Fellow at the Wellcome Institute for the History of Medicine, London, working on an historical M.D. thesis on chronic pain. He trained in psychiatry on the Guy's Hospital Rotation and currently works as Senior Registrar in Liaison Psychiatry at Guy's. Research interests include chronic pain, refractory depression and Lacanian psychoanalysis.

Prof. J. Hoenig, MD, FRCP, FRCPsych, FRCP(C) After serving in the RAMC took training at the National Hospital, Queen's Square, London and the Maudsley Hospital. Later he was Reader in Psychiatry at Manchester University; from 1969 to 1981 Foundation Chairman in Psychiatry, Memorial University, Canada; and from 1983 Professor of Psychiatry, University of Toronto. At present, he is Professor Emeritus of U of T. Joint author of *The segregation of the Mentally ill* and joint-translator of *General Psychopathology* and the *Essence of Psychotherapy* by Karl Jaspers. He has published several papers and book chapters on diverse subjects, including schizophrenia.

Prof. Dr. med. P. Hoff, MD, PhD born 1956, studied medicine and philosophy at the Universities of Mainz and Munich, and did post-graduate work at the department of psychiatry and neurology of the University of Munich. He is a Clinical and Forensic Psychiatrist and Psychotherapist. Since 1994, he has been University Lecturer at the University of Munich. His fields of interests are history of psychiatry in the 19th and 20th centuries, general psychopathology and psychiatric diagnosis, philosophical aspects of psychiatric research, especially with regard to the relevance of transcendental philosophy.

Stephen Jacyna is a research officer at the Wellcome Unit for History of Medicine, Manchester.

Prof. Dr. med. Dr. phil. Gundolf Keil born in Silesia, Doctor of Medicine, Doctor of Philosophy, physician and historian (speciality: History of the Middle Ages). He has been Chairman of the Department of History of Medicine at the University of Würzburg since 1973.

Dr. Kenneth S. Kendler, MD graduated from the University of California at Santa Cruz and Stanford University School of Medicine and completed a residency in psychiatry at Yale University School of Medicine. A developing interest in biometrical genetics led him to the Medical College of Virginia, where he is Rachel Brown Banks Distinguished Professor of Psychiatry and Professor of Human Genetics. Since coming to MCV in 1983, he has been Principal Investigator on over a dozen grant-funded projects, of which the most significant are a large-scale family and linkage study of schizophrenia in Ireland and a series of twin/family studies of stress and coping, and mood, anxiety and alcohol disorders in the population-based Virginia Twin Registry. He has published more than 180 articles and several book chapters and has a long-standing interest in the history of psychiatry and psychiatric nomenclature.

Helen King took a first degree in Ancient History and Social Anthropology, and a PhD on ancient Greek gynaecology, at University College London. Research fellowships on ancient medicine at Newnham College Cambridge and University of Newcastle. Current position as Senior Lecturer in History, Liverpool Institute of Higher Education. Her publications include 'Once upon a text: hysteria from Hippocrates' in *Hysteria Before Freud* (S. Gilman, H. King, R. Porter, G. Rousseau, E. Showalter, University of California Press, 1993), and she has written numerous articles on ancient women and on history of gynaecology and midwifery. She is Women's Studies Area Advisor to *Oxford Classical Dictionary*.

Dr. Tom Kitwood is Senior Lecturer in Psychology at the University of Bradford, and Leader of Bradford Dementia Group. His present research is concerned with the social psychology surrounding the dementing process, and his work involves him in constant contact with persons who have dementia and their carers. Recent books include *Concern for Others* (Routledge, 1990), *Person-to-Person: A Guide to the Care of Those with Failing Mental Powers*, with Kathleen Bredin, (Gale Centre Publications, 1991), and *The New Culture of Dementia Care*, as editor and contributor (Hawker Publications, 1995). He has also written numerous articles on dementia and dementia care.

Dr. med. Mario Horst Lanczik, MD Current position: Senior Consultant at the Department of Psychiatry, University of Würzburg. He was born in Nuremberg and studied History, Political Sciences and Philosophy in Heidelberg, and Medicine and Psychiatry at Würzburg. He obtained his MD thesis (*summa cum laude*) on a psychiatric-historic subject at the latter university. His *Habilitation* (1995) was on *Postpartum Psychiatric Disorders*. He is co-founder of the *International Wernicke-Kleist-Leonhard-Society* and of the Section *Women's Mental Health* at the World Psychiatric Association. He was also co-founder of the *German Society of Psychiatry, Psychotherapy and Neurosciences*. Currently, he is co-secretary of the *European Association for the History of Psychiatry*. His research interests and publications are on the classification of psychiatric disorders, psychiatric genetics, psychiatric disorders of women, history of German psychiatry and history of psychiatric hospitals in Germany.

Dr. Christopher C.G. Link, MB ChB, MPhil, MRCPsych, Dip Pharm Med, MFPM, trained as a psychiatrist in Edinburgh and became involved in the clinical development of novel therapies for the treatment of depression and anxiety when he joined Smith Kline Beecham as a Clinical Pharmacologist in 1988. He has published a number of articles on the evaluation of models of anxiety in volunteers and the role of psychomotor test performance and quantitative EEG in predicting the efficacy of new chemical entities in patients. He is currently employed in the Medical Research Department of Zeneca Pharmaceuticals and is involved in researching the clinical properties of atypical antipsychotics.

Tom Lutz is an Associate Professor in the English Department of the University of Iowa. He is the author of *American Nervousness, 1903: An anecdotal history* (Cornell, 1991) and is currently working on a cultural history of complaint in the 1920s.

Dr. John Spencer Madden MB; BCh; BAO; FRCP(ED), FRCPsych; DPM Honorary Research Fellow, Department of Psychiatry, University of Liverpool; Emeritus Consultant, Countess of Chester Hospital; Deputy Editor, *Alcohol And Alcoholism*; member Journal Committee, *British Journal of Psychiatry*; Founding Consultant, Mersey Regional Alcohol and Drug Dependence Service (the second of its nature within the UK); Initial Chairman, Substance Misuse Section, Royal College of Psychiatrists. Single author of *A Guide to Alcohol and Drug Dependence*. Co-Editor of other books and author of articles and chapters on Substance Misuse; author of articles on the History of Psychiatry; co-organiser of nine international conferences on Substance Misuse.

Michael MacDonald received his PhD in history from Stanford University in 1979. He is the author of *Mystical Bedlam: Madness, Anxiety and Healing in Seventeenth-Century England* (Cambridge, 1981). *Sleepless Souls: Suicide in Early Modern England*, with Terence R. Murphy (Oxford, 1990) and numerous articles on social history and the history of psychiatry. He is Professor of History at the University of Michigan.

Dr. Harold Merskey, DM, FRCP(C), FRCPsych, FAPA took degrees in Psychology and Physiology (BA, 1950) and Medicine (BM, BCh, 1953 and DM, 1965). He worked with Erwin Stengel at the University of Sheffield (1961–1964), then at Saxondale Hospital, Nottingham and at the National Hospitals for Nervous Diseases (1967–1976). Since then he has been at the University of Western Ontario where he is now Professor Emeritus. His research interests have been connected particularly with pain, conversion and dissociation and Alzheimer's Disease. He has published some 300 papers and chapters and 8 books, including *Pain: Psychological and Psychiatric Aspects* (with F.G. Spear, 1967); *Classification of Chronic Pain, Descriptions of Chronic Pain Syndromes and Definitions of Pain Terms* (with N. Bogduk: second edition, 1994), and *The Analysis of Hysteria* (second edition, 1995).

Prof. E. Miller, MPhil; BSc; PhD; C Psychol; FBPsS is currently Professor of Clinical Psychology in the University of Leicester. Has had a career that involved working in both universities and clinical service settings. Main research interests have been in clinical neuropsychology, especially the impact of degenerative diseases (Alzheimer's disease, Parkinson's disease, etc.) and also head injury on psychological functioning. Historical interests are particularly in the area of nineteenth century ideas on idiocy.

Dr. M.A. Mohanna, MB BS; MRCPsych was a senior registrar in Psychiatry at Cambridge and is currently a Consultant Psychiatrist at the Peter Hodgkinson Centre, Lincoln. He has done research and published on the history of suicide.

Dr. David B. Mumford, MD, MPhil, MA, MRCPsych is a Consultant Senior Lecturer in the Department of Mental Health of the University of Bristol. He studied theology at Cambridge, Varanasi (India) and Oxford; medicine at Bristol and psychiatry at Edinburgh. He is interested in cross-cultural aspects of psychiatry, particularly somatization and eating disorders, and the interface between religion and mental health. He developed the Bradford Somatic Inventory and has conducted extensive research into somatic symptoms associated with anxiety and depression in Pakistan and Britain. He has also completed historical studies of the language of emotional distress in the Hebrew Bible and Homer's Iliad. He has published many papers on transcultural aspects of psychiatry.

Malcolm Nicolson is Research Fellow at the Wellcome Unit for the History of Medicine, University of Glasgow. He works on the history of diagnostic practice and on several aspects of the history of twentieth-century biomedical science. His publications include: 'Social constructionism and medical sociology: The case of the vascular theory of multiple sclerosis', (with C. McLaughlin) in *Sociology of Health and Illness*, 10: (1988) 234–61.

Brenda Parry-Jones, BA, DAA, Honorary Research Fellow, Department of Child and Adolescent Psychiatry, University of Glasgow, UK.

William Ll. Parry-Jones, MA, MD (Camb), FRCPsych, FRCP, DPM Professor of Child and Adolescent Psychiatry, University of Glasgow and Supernumery Fellow, Linacre College, Oxford. Author of *The Trade in Lunacy* (1972), a study of English private madhouses. Current research interests focus on the history of psychiatric institutions, child and adolescent psychiatry and eating disorders. Keen protagonist for the integration of psychiatric history in clinical medical settings.

Prof. C. Perris, MD, Professor of Psychiatry at the Department of Psychiatry, Umea University, Sweden and Director of the WHO Collaborating Centre for Research and Training in Mental Health at Umea. MD in Italy in 1951 and in Sweden in 1967. Specialist in Neurology and Psychiatry in Italy in 1954, and in Psychiatry in Sweden on 1964. Hon. President of the World Federation of Biological Psychiatry, President of the Swedish Association of Cognitive Psycho-therapy. Member, Hon. Member of several international scientific societies. Books on Electroencephalography, Social Psychiatry, Cognitive Psychotherapy. Has published some 300 articles in International Journals.

Dr. Roy Porter is professor in the social history of medicine at the Wellcome Institute for the History of Medicine. He is currently working on the history of hysteria. Recent books include *Mind Forg'd Manacles. Madness in England from the Restoration to the Regency* (Athlone, 1987); *A Social History of Madness* (Weidenfeld and Nicolson, 1987); *In Sickness and in Health. The British Experience, 1650–1850* (Fourth Estate, 1988); *Patient's Progress* (Polity, 1989) – these last two co-authored with Dorothy Porter; *Health for Sale. Quackery in England 1660–1850* (Manchester University Press); *Doctor of Society: Thomas Beddoes and the Sick Trade in Late Enlightenment England* (London: Routledge, 1991) and *London: A Social History* (Hamish Hamilton, 1994)

Dr. J.I. Quemada, MRCPsych trained in Psychiatry at Cambridge. He has worked as Director of a Brain Injury Unit in Spain. Currently he is a MSc student at the Department of Psychiatry, University of Cambridge researching on the neurobiology of psychomotor change in the affective disorders. His research interests are motor disorders in psychiatric illness and psychiatric aspects of head injury on which he has published papers in international journals.

Univ.-Prof. Dr. med. Henning Saß, MD, PhD was born on 4th of December, 1944. He studied medicine in Kiel, Vienna and Mainz, and did his psychiatric training at the University of Heidelberg. *Habilitation* (1986) was on personality disorders and abnormal behaviour in the social and forensic field. Between 1987–1990 he was Head of the Department of Forensic Psychiatry, University of Munich. Currently he is Head of the Clinic of Psychiatry and Psychotherapy (since 1990) and Dean of the Medical School at the University of Aachen. His research interests and publications are on psychopathology, personality disorders, and forensic psychiatry. He is member of various scientific associations and co-editor of the psychiatric and neurological journal *Der Nervenarzt*.

Dr. F. Schiller, MD Clinical Professor of Neurology, Emeritus; Lecturer, History of Health Sciences, University of California, San Francisco. Born in 1909 in Prague, educated in Austria and later Czechoslovakia, gained his MD from the German University in 1933, and interned there in the Neuropsychiatric Department. Interested in Neurosurgery he worked under Clovis Vincent in Paris, Sir Hugh Cairns in Oxford, and Wilder Penfield in Montreal. Moved to San Francisco and back to Neurology in 1950, eventually with *Kaiser Permanente Medical Group*. The centenary of Broca's aphasia in 1961 started his neuro-historical interests, hence his Broca biography, followed by that of Paul Mobius, co-editorship of *The Founders of Neurology*, and numerous neuro-historical articles.

Edward Shorter is the Hannach Professor of the History of Medicine in the Faculty of Medicine of the University of Toronto. His most recent book is *From Paralysis to Fatigue: A history of psychosomatic illness in the modern era* (1992).

Deborah Thom is a historian who is a Fellow, College Lecturer in History and Social and Political Sciences, and Admissions Tutor at Robinson College, Cambridge. She has completed two ESCRC research projects, one on mental testing and the other on child guidance clinics which are the basis of her forthcoming books on psychology in the education system in Britain, and she has published on women's employment, feminism and psychology and education. Current research pursues further materials on child guidance at the Child Care and Development Group in Cambridge.

Dr. E. Trillat, MD Etienne Trillat trained as a psychiatrist under Julian de Ajuriaguerra and Henri Ey and was actively involved in the great renovation psychiatric movement of the 1950s and 60s which culminated in the transformation of French public psychiatry. He is the author of a large number of papers and dedicated his life to clinical work and the epistemology of psychiatry. During the last 10 years he has been editor of *L'Evolution Psychiatrique*. Attracted by matters historical he has written on Charcot's views on hysteria and on 20th century psychiatry in the *Nouvelle Histoire de la Psychiatrie* (edited by Postel and Quétel). He is also the author of *Histoire de l'Hysterie* (Paris, Seghers, 1986).

Trevor Turner studied Classics at Bristol University (1967–70), and medicine at St Bartholomew's Hospital Medical College in London, qualifying in 1976. Specialising in psychiatry at the Maudsley Hospital, he obtained the Membership examination of the Royal College of Psychiatrists (MRCPsych) in 1981, was Research Lecturer at the Institute of Psychiatry (1985–6), and took up his current appointment as consultant Psychiatrist at St Bartholomew's and

Homerton Hospitals in 1987. He has researched and written on psycho-endocrinology, mental handicap, schizophrenia and community care as well as the history of psychiatry. His MD thesis (1990), a diagnostic analysis of the casebooks of a 19th-century asylum, was published as a monograph supplement to the journal *Psychological Medicine* in 1992.

Dr. Walter Vandereycken, MD; PhD is Professor of Psychiatry at the Catholic University of Leuven and Head of the Department of Behaviour Therapy at the Alexian Brothers Psychiatric Hospital in Tienen. Over the past twenty years, he has been intensively involved in research and treatment of eating disorders. He has widely published on this subject and is the international editor of the journal *Eating Disorders*. With Ron van Deth he wrote *From Fasting Saints to Anorexic Girls – The History of Self-Starvation* (Athlone Press/New York University Press, London/New York 1994).

Dr. Ron van Deth, MA studied psychology at the University in Leiden, and is currently working as a lecturer. He has specialized in the medical and cultural history of eating disorders. In co-operation with Professor W. Vandereycken he has published articles in international journals such as *Psychological Medicine, British Journal of Psychiatry, Journal of the History of Medicine* and *History of Psychiatry*. With the same author, he has written a comprehensive history of anorexia nervosa now translated into Dutch, German, and Italian.

Dr. Simon Wessely, MD, MRCPsych is Reader in Liaison Psychiatry at King's College School of Medicine and the Institute of Psychiatry in London, and Consultant Psychiatrist at King's College and Maudsley Hospital. After training in Medicine at Cambridge and Oxford Universities, and a period in internal medicine in Newcastle-upon-Tyne, he trained in Psychiatry at the Maudsley Hospital and the National Hospital for Nervous Diseases in London. His clinical interests are in liaison psychiatry, and he is Director of the Consultation-Liaison service at King's College Hospital, a busy London Teaching Hospital. His research interests are in clinical epidemiology, and he has over a hundred professional publications on various aspects of the epidemiology of chronic fatigue syndrome, schizophrenia and other topics. His clinical and research interests in chronic fatigue syndrome led inevitably to a fascination with the topic of neurasthenia, and hence the amateur historical essay for this volume.

Introduction

Some terminological clarification is required at the outset. *Descriptive psycho-pathology* deals with the language of description (lexicon, grammar, etc.) used in psychiatry (Berrios, 1995). *Nosology* and *nosography* (Faber, 1923) study the rules by which symptoms cluster together into diseases; and *clinical psychiatry* deals with the diagnosis and treatment of mental disorder. The latter is not a contemplative but a modificatory enterprise. Nosological diagnosis is episte-mologically dependent upon the power of psychopathological descriptions to identify the right symptoms and predict treatment-response and outcome (Berrios and Chen, 1993). To achieve this ideal state, descriptions must be set in stable conceptual frames (Mechelen, et al 1993). However, since it is likely that the biological substratum of mental illness undergoes secular change, a periodic mismatch between descriptions and symptoms should be expected to occur (Berrios, 1994a). A remedy for such semiological instability is to under-take periodic descriptive recalibrations. To these, conceptual-historical analyses and clinical observation are essential.

The history of clinical psychiatry may be defined as the study of the way in which clinical signals and their descriptions have interacted in successive histor-ical periods, and of their psychosocial context. To estimate the extent to which earlier meanings (terms, concepts and behaviours) are preserved when clinical categories are transferred from one discourse to the next, historian and clinician need to know how descriptive and nosographic rules are formulated. For example, can it be assumed that 'mania', 'melancholia' or 'hypochondria' mean in 1995 the same as they did in 1800? How can differences be made explicit? One of the objectives of historical nosography is to decode the rules controlling psychiatric discourse, and make explicit the drafts upon which it is based.

Historical research differs from clinical research in that in the former the question asked and the research technique employed may determine what counts as the 'object' of inquiry and as evidence. Depending on how the object is defined, the historian of, say, 'schizophrenia' will find that earlier centuries offer nothing or a great deal. Current clinical researchers, on the other hand, find their object of inquiry determined by 'operational' definitions (e.g. DSM IV) (APA, 1994). Those very definitions would land the historian in hopeless anachronism.

This does not mean, of course, that the DSM IV definition of schizophrenia cannot be made, itself, the object of historical inquiry. It can (and, incidentally, it should) but the resulting tale will have little to do with the history of *dementia praecox* (as defined by Kraepelin or Morel) or with that of *intellectual insanity* (as defined by Esquirol). It will have, however, much to do with the social factors that led a group of psychiatrists in the North East of the USA to arrive at this definition of the disease (Blashfield, 1982).

A question arises: does the historian need to posit an *invariant element* successfully to 'trace back' the history of a mental disorder? Would the finding of an enduring neurobiological or psychodynamic marker render the psycho-social context less important? (Berrios, 1994b). It would seem that this is a vain hope, as the history of how an apparently invariant condition, such as Alzheimer's disease was constructed, shows (Berrios, 1990). Trans-historical invariants are vulnerable to challenge, particularly from the social construction-ist perspective. After all, it has been argued with plausibility that so-called natural facts and invariants do not and cannot exist independently from the language of description; i.e. facts are not 'given' but 'created'.

Two metaphors seem to control the understanding of historical nosology. One pictures the clinician as cataloguing species (diseases) in a garden (i.e. assuming ontological invariance); the other envisages the clinician as a sculptor carving shapes out of formless matter, i.e. creating 'clinical forms'. The garden approach encourages the search for a 'discoverer' who with his powerful eye overcomes all misleading descriptions. The creationist approach requires that the vision guiding the sculptor be 'contextualized'. The latter activity may range from severe 'social-constructionism' to milder forms of social accounting which leave room for notions such as scientific progress.

The clinical historian must also specify whether the intention is to deal with the history of *terms* (say delirium or mania), or *concepts* (say attentional theories of schizophrenia) or *behaviours*. Whilst not always easy in practice, this distinction is useful, particularly to the beginner. For example, historical seman-tics and etymology (say of the word *melancholia*) are unlikely to provide any information on the history of the actual biological signals involved (say, early awakening, psychomotor retardation or constipation) or on the concepts in-volved. Likewise, what could be called behavioural palæontology, i.e. the study of the actual behaviours throughout time, will say little on the history of the terms or concepts involved.

Together with clinical and statistical research, the history of clinical psychi-atry is essential to the calibration of psychiatric nosology. Calibration here means re-adjustment of descriptions to: 1. changes affecting the biological foundation of symptoms (caused, for example, by genetic mutation), 2. shifts in psychological theory leading to new conceptualizations of behaviour, and 3. variations in the social import of disease. Professional historians have a contri-bution to make not only to psychiatric culture but to clinical knowledge. Building on the belief that mental disorders are complex and distorted reflections of dysfunctional brain sites and states, they should seek to determine which past 'psychiatric' phenomena were noise, and which were actual expressions of biological signals modulated by individual grammars and cultural codes.

Throughout history, psychiatric nosology has shown periods of stability and change. Change attracts much soul-searching but stability is taken for granted. The historian should also ask why some 'diseases' remain in steady state for considerable time. Are biological invariants more responsible for disease stabil-ity than cultural devices such as symbols, myths, or 'mentalities'? Self-styled calibrators of the nomenclature of psychiatry often show ignorance of the conceptual history of mental disorders. In general, professional historians have been more preoccupied with the social history of psychiatry, and this has encouraged the growth amongst clinicians of a 'do-it-yourself', low standard, historical industry. Another objective of this book is to correct this trend.

That psychiatric understanding and creativity are enhanced by knowledge of their history was clear to nineteenth century alienists. Some like Calmeil, Morel, Trélat, Semelaigne, Kirshoff, Winslow, Ireland, Mercier, Bucknill and Tuke wrote special works on psychiatric history. Most of the others, such as Pinel, Heinroth, Esquirol, Guislain, Prichard, Connolly, Griesinger, Lucas, Falret and Dagonet, included historical chapters in their classical textbooks.

But few alienists from this period did as well as Feuchtersleben (1847): 'All professional men labour under a great disadvantage in not being allowed to be ignorant of what is useless . . . every one fancies that he is bound to transmit what is believed to have been known'. He proposed that only the empirical sciences should be allowed to dismiss the past as a mere 'history of errors'. As to the other sciences (which included medical psychology), Feuchtersleben wrote: 'the history of a science [is] properly the science itself'. The new science of psychiatry 'belonged to both spheres' or types of science: 'That part of it which was philosophical contained an abstract of that state of philosophy in every age, while that which is empirical has by no means attained such precision and clearness as to render a knowledge of previous opinions superfluous' (p.23).

In their use of historical information, writers of twentieth century psychiatric textbooks have fared less well. Historical chapters in modern textbooks rarely include (unlike clinical chapters) *references to recent research*; instead, they rehearse the oft-told tale of a mythical continuity of ideas starting with Hippocrates and leading to Areteus, Galen, Platter, Linné, Cullen, Chiarugi, Pinel, Griesinger, Kraepelin, Freud, Jung and Schneider.

Whilst, perhaps, of some help with professional examination questions, this approach misleads psychiatric trainees into believing that everything historical is already known and that the history of psychiatry has ceased to be a field of inquiry. Even worse, it might suggest to them that concepts are no longer important, and that all that matters is 'empirical' research. We believe that a closer collaboration between professional historians and clinicians will put this right, and render the history of clinical psychiatry an independent, exciting and lively psychiatric specialism.

G.E. Berrios and R.S. Porter

REFERENCES

APA (1994) *Diagnostic and Statistical Manual of Mental Disorders* (Fourth Edition) Washington, DC, American Psychiatric Association.

Berrios, G.E. (1990) 'Alzheimer's disease: a conceptual history'. *International Journal of Geriatric Psychiatry*, 5: 355–65.

Berrios, G.E. (1994a) 'The language of psychiatry: a time for a change?' *Hong Kong Journal of Psychiatry*, 4: 5–10.

Berrios, G.E. (1994b) 'Historiography of mental symptoms and diseases'. *History of Psychiatry*, 5: 175–90.

Berrios, G.E. (1995) *The history of mental symptoms. Descriptive Psychopathology since the 19th century*, Cambridge, Cambridge University Press.

Berrios, G.E. and Chen, E. (1993) 'Symptom-recognition and neural-networks'. *British Journal of Psychiatry*, 163: 308–14.

Blashfield, R.K. (1982) 'Feighner et al., Invisible Colleges and the Matthew Effect'. *Schizophrenia Bulletin*, 8: 1–6.

Faber, K. (1923) *Nosography in Modern Medicine*, London, Oxford University Press.

Feuchtersleben, E. von (1847) *The Principles of Medical Psychology* (translated by H.E. Lloyd and B.G. Babington) Sydenham Society, London.

Mechelen, I.V., Hampton, J., Michalski, R.S. and Theuns, P. (eds) (1993) *Categories and concepts*, London, Academic Press.

PART 1
NEUROPSYCHIATRIC DISORDERS

Chapter 1

Delirium and Cognate States

Clinical Section
GE BERRIOS

Delirium (acute confusional state, exogenous psychosis) names a cluster of mental symptoms and behaviours, with fluctuating course and (often) incomplete presentation, occurring in the wake of acute brain disease (Lipowski, 1980; Trzepacz, 1994). Early this century, it was suggested that delirium might be a stereotyped, (wired-in) brain response (Bonhoeffer, 1910). This might explain its transhistorical and transcultural stability (i.e. the fact that psychosocial factors distort little its clinical presentation). During the nineteenth century, from being a state of excited *behaviour* accompanied by fever (phrenitis), delirium became a disorder of consciousness, attention, cognition, and orientation; in this process, the transitional concept of *confusion* played a crucial role. During the same period, *vesanic* and *non-vesanic* (Ball and Ritti, 1882, p.357)[1] 'deliriums' were also separated: the former becoming the current notion of delusion. This chapter explores the way in which this ancient mental disorder was shaped by the conceptual and empirical forces that operated during the nineteenth century and suggests that it was delirium, and not progressive paralysis of the insane, that served as the clinical model for the *current notion of psychosis.*[2]

Historiographic issues
Psychiatric observations culled from the past are not necessarily 'epistemologically' continuous with the present, i.e. the historian must distinguish between 'continuities' pertaining to semantics and etymology (i.e. the history of words), from those related to concepts (i.e. conceptual history) and behaviours (behavioural palæontology) (APA, 1994; Berrios, 1992).[3] Concepts also show discontinuities due to their dependence upon specific models of disease and other ideological factors: for example, the fact that in the pre-Cartesian world no ontological distinction was made between physical and mental disease meant that, in practice, the coexistence of the two caused little theoretical or practical discomfort, i.e. physicians did not feel the need to explain their association. Such need, however, appeared once the Cartesian separation between the thinking and extended substances became established.[4] In response to these changes, nineteenth century psychiatry constructed her own epistemology (Swain, 1977). This borrowed from classical psychology a new view of consciousness (Boring, 1950; Hamilton, 1859) and a methodology of self-observation (introspection) (Lyons, 1986) based on the metaphor of the 'inner eye'.

It is also important to trace the origins of the current assumption that all mental symptoms are by definition generated in the brain. In this regard, it is often forgotten that before 1800 the brain was considered as just another viscus (like lungs or heart), only that housed in the skull (Lanteri-Laura and Bouttier, 1983, p.415). Whilst in general terms it was accepted that the brain was responsible for mental functions such as cognition and memory, it was otherwise for functions such as the emotions or passions which were still thought to be (literally) related to the heart or hypochondria. For example, during the early nineteenth century, Broussais claimed that some insanities might be related to the stomach (Broussais, 1828; Chazaud, 1992). Towards the end of the same century, notions such as sympathy (Hetch, 1884) are still found linking (albeit indirectly) mental states to organs other than the brain.

Equally important is to understand the changes that took place in the grammar of clinical description: symptoms became 'signifiers' of disease, and their meaning was felt to be stable and independent from the observer. These encouraged the development of: 1. a view of delirium based on a wider set of mental symptoms; 2. a notion of 'exogenous psychosis'; and 3. acute delirium which was separated from the concept of 'dementia', which was redefined as an irreversible state defined in purely 'cognitive' terms (Berrios, 1989; 1990a).

DELIRIUM BEFORE THE NINETEENTH CENTURY

Reference to phrenitis and delirium and to an association between physical and mental disease can be found in the Ancient literature. For the Greeks, phrenitis (Sakai, 1991) was a disturbance of thought, mood, and action associated with physical disease: 'The Hippocratic collection is rich in words meaning delirium: 1. those in which mental derangement is the dominant idea, and 2. those in which stress is laid upon delirious talk' (Hippocrates, 1972). Phrenitis, mania, melancholia, and paranoia were the core categories of Greek psychiatry (Roccatagliata, 1973; Simon, 1978). Concepts similar to delirium can also be found in other cultures, for example, Hankoff (1972) has suggested that the Greek term *Kordiakos* was used in the *Talmud* to refer to temporary madness associated with wine drinking – probably a form of delirium tremens.

Since Antiquity, absence of fever separated conventional madness (e.g. mania) from phrenitis. Sydenham (1666) wrote: 'The patient falls into a brain fever, or into what is next door to it. He gets no sleep, he utters frequent exclamations, he uses incoherent language, he looks and talks wildly' (p.66). Willis (1684), and Cullen (1827) (p.166, vol.2) fully agreed with this description. Indeed, these criteria remained central to Western medicine up to the early 19th century (Esquirol, 1814; Middleton, 1780; Sutton, 1813). With his usual historical sense, von Feuchtersleben asked: 'the question: are delirium and insanity identical? has been answered thus: that acute delirium with fever must be distinguished from the chronic variety which is called insanity', however, 'the presence or absence of fever, which is possible in every condition [cannot] decide the matter' . . . 'Delirium is a symptom which indicates the transition of a purely somatic disease into a mental disorder'. In respect to the classification of delirium (here shifting its meaning to delusion) he wrote: 'it is fruitless, as has been frequently done, to consider differences in the object [of the delusion] as a

ground for division [for] they do not express the essence of the disturbance.'
(Feuchtersleben, 1847).

Delirium and intellectual function
In Galen, delirium was co-extensive with *mentis alienatio* (Siegel, 1973) and
thus it remained until the eighteenth century. For example, Quincy (1719)
defined delirium as: 'An incapacity in the organs of sensation to perform their
function in due manner, so that the mind does not reflect upon and judge of
external objects as usual; as is the case frequently in fevers, from too impetuous
a hurry of the blood, which alters so far the secretion in the brain, as to disorder
the whole nervous system.' (p.103). Dr Johnson (1755) wrote that delirious
means 'light headed, raving and doting', 'people about him said he had been for
some hours delirious, but when I saw him he had his understanding as well as
ever I knew'. Quoting Arbuthnot, Johnson considered delirium tantamount to
'alienation of mind': 'Too great alacrity and promptness in answering, specially
in persons naturally of another temper, is a sign of an approaching delirium. In
a feverish delirium there is a small inflammation of the brain'.
   This (intellectualistic) view was challenged by Sutton (1813) who, when
describing delirium tremens (or shaking delirium), played down the old view of
phrenitis: 'As the disease advances, the faculties do not, generally speaking, show
themselves in disorder by any extravagance of thought'. Sutton went on to
suggest that *affective* and *motor disturbance* were, in fact, a central part of the
new syndrome. By the middle of the nineteenth century, the term delirium had
accumulated a long list of medical synonyms (Mayne, 1860, p.261).[5]

Délire, delirium and delusion
For linguistic reasons – particularly troublesome to the French – delirium had a
double meaning in most European countries (Ball and Ritti, 1882). For example,
Pinel (1809) used *délire* to refer both to specific errors of judgement (i.e.
delusion) and to phrenitis (Pinel, 1806).[6] Esquirol (1814) did likewise, and
believed that *délire* was a primary disturbance of perception: 'A person is
delirious when his ideas are not in keeping with his sensations, etc'. 'hallucinations are the most frequent cause of *délire*'. Georget (1820) used the word to
refer both to disorders of intellect and also to 'a disorder . . . resulting from
general illness or illness of the brain', i.e. as *délire aigüe*. Georget composed a
table showing the differential diagnosis between *délire aigüe* and *folie* and
noticed the intermittent and reversible nature of the former. In a posthumous
article, he separated *délire aigüe* (or febrile) from *délire chronique ou sans fiévre*
(tantamount to insanity proper) (Georget, 1835).
   By the 1860s, a differential usage had become established and *délire* mainly
referred to aberrant ideas accompanying delirium. This shift from syndrome to
symptom was consolidated by Lasègue (1852) and Falret (1864, p.354) and
legitimized in Littré's dictionary (1877). In French psychiatry, this created the
need for a term for organic delirium and the term 'confusion mentale' was
charged with this role (see below). These linguistic ambiguities affected less
British and German psychiatry where the early availability of the terms delusion
and *Wahn* helped to separate the symptomatic meaning from the syndromatic
(i.e. the organic syndrome was called delirium or *Verwirrtheit*) (Ey et al, 1952).[7]

Delirium and Insanity
The distinction between delirium and insanity remained an object of dispute up
to the middle of the nineteenth century (Feuchtersleben, 1847). Brierre de
Boismont, in a classical essay (Brierre de Boismont, 1845), claimed that both
shared the same 'moral' (psychological) aetiology and could not be told apart
by post-mortem studies. He asked, 'is it the case that acute delirium is just an
acute form of [ordinary] insanity?' He reported a sample of 11 patients showing
that the fever criterion did not work. Brierre's views crossed the waters, and
twenty years later the *American Journal of Insanity* presented them to American
alienists (Leader, 1864). Griesinger (1861) also quoted Brierre in the second
edition of his textbook. Indeed, the debate on whether acute delirium constituted
a separate form of insanity went on until the end of the century (Ball and Ritti,
1882, p.97; Gowers, 1888). For example, Calmeil (1859) stated that delirium
was caused by peri-encephalitis and that many insanities were also mild forms
of the same lesion; if that was the case, he asked, is it not wrong to consider
delirium and insanity as totally different diseases? Worcester (1889), however,
felt that this 'continuity' view was no longer acceptable.

The enduring nature of this debate is likely to be related to the popularity of
the doctrine of unitary psychosis (Berrios & Beer, this volume; Vliegen, 1980;
Mundt and Saß, 1992). According to this view, clinical differences between all
forms of insanity were explicable in terms of environmental or pathoplastic
effects. Thus, if the insanities were on a continuum, i.e. expressions of one basic
disease, why should delirium not be part of it? A reason for some alienists to
resist this conclusion was clinical tradition; another was that *there were* clinical
differences, for example, in type and distribution of symptoms and outcome
(e.g. there was a higher mortality in delirium: of Brierre's 11 cases, 7 died)
(Brierre de Boismont, 1845).

Only later in the century involvement of consciousness became an *official
criterion* to separate delirium and insanity. This does not mean that earlier
descriptions of delirium did not, occasionally, include reference to confusion or
other disorders of consciousness; indeed, they did: the issue here is that the same
disturbances of consciousness were also attributed to ordinary insanity, and that
no clinical stipulation existed that such disturbances were a hallmark of (organic) delirium. In fact, such stipulation only became possible after the psychoses
had been redefined (Sauri, 1972; Berrios, 1987). Thanks to degeneration theory
(Morel, 1857; Genil-Perrin, 1913), the latter were now considered to be
hereditary i.e. capable of breeding through (which could not be said of delirium);
likewise, insanities with chronic course were identified (i.e. *délire chronique*)
(Magnan, 1866–7; Magnan and Sérieux, 1911; Berrios and Hauser, 1988), and
shown to be different from delirium. Having found two external criteria to
separate delirium from insanity, it only remained to compare their symptoms.

Delirium as a form of dreaming
The idea that hallucinations and delusions (particularly those seen in delirium)
were dreams experienced during wakefulness was popular during the nineteenth
century. This was well expressed by Griesinger (1861): 'The acute febrile
delirium, from which the insanities cannot be specifically distinguished, consists
of active dreams during waking or half-waking' (p.115). In his classical paper

on *Alcoholic delirium is not a delirium but a dream*, Lasègue (1881; 1971) defined dreaming as a half-physiological, half-pathological state accompanied by visual hallucinations superior in sensory quality to those seen in insanity. He believed that alcoholic hallucinosis was gradually 'prepared' by periods of disturbed sleep and dreaming.

But the most popular book on the subject during this period was written by a historian and politician (Paz, 1964; Dowbiggin, 1990). In *Le Sommeil et les Rêves*, Alfred Maury (1878) reprinted some of his own published papers on the subject and discussed the physiology and psychology of sleep. The core of the book he dedicated to the view that hallucinations and delusions were related to dreaming. *Onirisme*, the name that the French gave to this putative mechanism, deserves a historical chapter of its own (Ey, 1954). It was defined as a 'form of automatic mental activity constituted by visions and animated scenes similar to those experienced in dreams' (Porot, 1975, p.461).

Perhaps the best description of *délire onirique* is the one offered by Régis (1906). This great alienist from Bordeaux remarked that although the tendency to compare delirium and dreams was ancient, earlier writers had only used the comparison analogically, and that only Lasègue had actually identified dreaming with alcoholic delirium from the *physiological* viewpoint. Séglas, Legrain, and Régis went on to extend the same explanation to febrile and toxic deliria. Régis described *délire onirique* as a state of somnambulism followed by amnesia and occasionally by fixed ideas, and recalled that it was in 1901 that he first presented his views: 'the typical form of toxic psychosis includes two elements: confusion and delusions . . . mental confusion is related to obtusion, disorientation, mental hebetude, and followed by amnesia and occasionally dementia' . . . 'as far as delusions are concerned, these are oniric in the strict sense of the term, i.e. born and developed during sleep, and formed out of coincidental associations of ideas and fragments of hallucinatory experiences related to old memories' (pp.293–7). Onirism and oniroid states played, until recently, a descriptive and explanatory role in French psychiatry (Ey et al, 1974).

CONFUSION

The term 'confusion' is still used in French (Garrabé, 1989, pp.35–8) and British Psychiatry (Hamilton, 1974)[8] but is no longer present in ICD-10.[9] *Verwirrtheit*, its German counterpart, is infrequent in German-speaking psychiatry and no longer differentiated from *Verworrenheit* (Scharfetter, 1980). The term was dropped from DSM III-R (APA, 1980)[10] and it does not feature in PSE (Wing et al, 1974).

In Roman times, 'confusion' had a 'legal' meaning (Anonymous, 1928), and acquired a 'logical' one during the Medieval Period (when it was defined 'negatively' as an aberration of the logical doctrine of clarity and distinctness of thought) (Abbagnano, 1961). Both usages were parasitical upon the Latin term *confundere*. To these, an 'epistemological' dimension was added during the seventeenth century (Eisler, 1904; Grimm and Grimm, 1956). These quaint meanings are still present in the work of John S. Mill (1898) for whom the 'fallacy of confusion' was an: 'indistinct, indefinite and fluctuating conception of what the evidence is'. In 1813, the word confusion was introduced into medicine as the name for a disease of the eyes (Jourdan, 1813) and in 1851, 'confusion of ideas' was used in a psychiatric context by Delasiauve (1851).[11] From here on, the symptom seems to have been defined in terms of the theory of association, (Claparède, 1903; Warren, 1921) the 'psychological' arm of British empiricism (Hoeldtke, 1967; Bricke, 1974; Billod, 1861).

Verwirrtheit, as well as *Verworren* and *Verwirren* were used to describe states of mental chaos and perplexity (Grimm and Grimm, 1956). At the beginning of the nineteenth century Heinroth, Ideler, and Spielman used these words as synonyms of mental disorder (Wille, 1888) and Griesinger (1861) associated them with dementia (p.345). From then on, interest grew in Germany into the nosological meaning and independence of *Verwirrtheit*. Notable in this respect is the work of Fritsch (1879) suggesting the existence of a symptomatic and an idiopathic form of confusion: the former seen in hysteria and epilepsy; the latter subdivided into its pseudo-aphasic and hallucinatory forms. Fritsch stated that the hallmarks of confusion were clouding of consciousness and impaired judgement. As early as 1874, Meynert became interested in *Verwirrtheit*, but at the beginning he thought that disorientation was *secondary* to the hallucinatory experiences (Meynert, 1881; 1890; Pappenheim, 1975; Lévy-Friesacher, 1983).[12] Wille (1888) defined *Verwirrtheit* as 'an acute, functional disorder of the brain characterized by confusion, hallucinations, delusions, disorder of consciousness, and sometimes stupor'.

Interestingly, the term confusion does not feature in the dictionaries by Tuke (1892) and Power and Sedwick (1892) although it was discussed in Baldwin's a few years later.[13] Thus, it would seem that since the 1860s confusion has referred to a defect in the organization of ideas which is found in delirium, severe depression (for this see below), and other insanities. At the beginning, its presence did not entail organic aetiology, but this was to change after the work of Chaslin (1892; 1895). The 'syndromatic' view of confusion, however, lived on (Bleuler, 1911).

Confusional States

The terms confusion and *Verwirrtheit* (Zeh, 1960) came into common medical use during the 1890s. The delay was due, at least in France, to the belief defended by Baillarger that confusion was a form of melancholia. By the end of the century, melancholia was replaced by the narrower category 'depression' (Berrios, this volume) which did not include confusion as a symptom. Philippe Chaslin (1892) wrote his first paper on the subject precisely during this period. Only two years earlier, Conolly Norman (1890) had published his paper on *Acute Confusional Insanity* including most of the clinical elements that were to be dealt with by the French writer. Norman defined confusional insanity as characterised by rapid onset, impairment of consciousness and hallucinations. Chaslin does not seem to have been aware of Norman's work whose syndrome, nonetheless, survived in British psychiatry up to the present century (Bolton, 1906; Bruce, 1935).

The work of Chaslin

Chaslin's[14] paper of 1892 was an expanded version of a communication presented at the Blois Congress. Influenced by Wille, Chaslin made 'confusion' tantamount to delirium (i.e. used the word in a sense wider than that introduced by Delasiauve). Confusion became the anchor symptom to hallucinations, stupor, delusions and physical symptoms. The syndrome was distinguished from mania, melancholia, *délire chronique*, schizophrenia) and even febrile delirium. He speculated that confusion might be due to 'cerebral weakness' (Chaslin, 1892). Chaslin's paper struck the right chord and a year later, at La Rochelle, a string of supporting communications were presented. Séglas (1894), in his *Salpêtiére* lecture also acknowledged Chaslin's contribution and regretted the fact that Delasiauve's views had fallen into desuetude (due, he claimed, to Baillarger's negative ideas). Séglas agreed with the new meaning given to confusion (or *Verwirrtheit, Amentia* or *Dysnoia*) for it referred 'not to a banal symptom accompanying insanity but to a specific loss of voluntary control upon the intellectual faculties' (i.e. confusion was a manifestation of *mental automatisme*).

Chaslin's great monograph on the subject appeared three years later (Chaslin, 1895). Not surprisingly, he also linked *confusion mentale* to automatism (Delay, 1953; Balan, 1989; Baruk, 1972; Janet, 1889).[15] The term gained international circulation after Régis, together with a very young Hesnard, used it as the title for their contribution to the *Traité International de Psychopathologie* (Régis and Hesnard, 1911). In this work, the authors identified three stages in the history of the concept: a first period up to 1843, during which confusion, dementia and *stupidité* (Berrios, 1981) were conflated; a second period beginning in 1843 with Baillarger's paper (1843), during which (melancholic) stupor encompassed all the confusional states; and a third period, starting in the work of Delasiauve (1851) and completed by Chaslin, Charpentier, Régis, Hannion, Séglas and Marandon de Montyel, who re-defined *confusion mentale* as a separate syndrome.

It was at this stage that Binet and Simon (1911) published their classic review of *confusion mentale* (stung by criticism that they had not included this clinical category in their 1910 review of mental disorders). After stating that confusion was the new *caput mortuum* of medicine, Binet and Simon identify two meanings: confusion, as a symptom, meant 'experiencing obscurity of comprehension' and 'having incoherence of purpose'; confusion, as a disease, included the disease first described by Chaslin and adumbrated by Delasiauve and others. The authors conclude that there was little reason to construct a disease out of what was simply a cluster of symptoms. Lastly, Binet and Simon consider it wrong, both from the psychological and clinical viewpoints, to conflate confusion with dementia. These conditions differed in their mental state: in the former there was obscurity of thinking, due to 'paralysis', in the latter an 'abolition' of the cognitive faculty.

In 1915, Chaslin departed from his original view by conceding that confusion was: 1. a syndrome (not a maladie), 2. a *global* disorder of mental functions (not only of intellect) and 3. always related to organic causes (by this time Bonhoeffer had already published his work on exogenous psychosis).[16] It became clear that a new debate was needed to clear the air. This took place in 1920 (SMP, 1923) where an elderly Chaslin (1920) rose to outline, for the last time, his ideas on confusion. His intervention was motivated by a claim by Toulouse *et al* (1920) that confusion and dementia were, after all, not clinically differentiable because both were disorders of *autoconduction*.[17] These writers had also criticized, in a general way, the lack of structure and sensitivity bedevilling psychiatric interviewing techniques, and proposed the use of standardized techniques and questionnaires (Sommer, 1899; Binet and Simon, 1905; Jaspers, 1910). Chaslin reiterated that the crucial disturbance in confusion was a loosening of synthesis affecting intellectual, affective and volitional functions, and stated (rightly) that Toulouse's mechanism of *autoconduction* was just another name for the old notion of synthesis. Chaslin concluded that the misunderstanding resulted not from real clinical similarities between confusion and dementia but from attributing a prognostic value to the latter. He warned (with some prescience) that such predictions were unwarranted unless seriatim assessments were carried out. One of the offshoots of the 1920 debate (and of Chaslin's defence) was that the diagnostic criteria for delirium (for that is what was being discussed) were written in stone, and linked up with clouding of consciousness (Porot, 1975).

Confusion and Stupor

It is difficult to understand the concept of confusion without dealing, however briefly, with melancholic stupor, i.e. with a state of non-responsiveness that occasionally accompanies depression. Subjects thus affected may show confusion, psychomotor retardation, and delusions and hallucinations. During the nineteenth century, the description of melancholic stupor went through three stages but only the first two are relevant to the history of confusion (Berrios, 1981; 1990b).

The earliest hypothesis concerning melancholic stupor was sensory 'numbness', i.e. that non-responsiveness was due to a temporal abolition of perception. Pinel (1809) favoured this view and hence did not see the need to separate stupor from idiocy. Georget (1820) classified 'stupidity' as a separate genre of insanity characterised by involvement of cognition and introduced a post-hoc criterion: 'The mental content experienced by these patients may be delusional suggesting that stupidity must be separated from both idiotism and dementia'.

The second period is characterised by the view that stupor resulted from an inhibition of higher mental functions rather than peripheral numbness. In his paper on *stupidité*, Etoc-Demazy (1833) concluded that: 1. 'stupidity' is not a genre of insanity but a complication of mania and monomania, 2. symptoms evolve in two stages: diminution of cognition and then suspension of relational functions, 3. none of the symptoms has predictive value in regard to outcome, and 4. *stupidité* and 'dementia' were different syndromes.

The 1840s witnessed the development of a view of stupor based on the analysis of subjective experience. For example, Baillarger (1843) believed that *stupides* were not devoid of mental experiences for they were, in fact, suffering from 'melancholia'. Baillarger concluded that: 1. patients diagnosed as 'stupid' experience delusions and hallucinations, 2. delusions are depressive in content including thoughts of self-harm, 3. illusions and hallucinations cause an internal, 'oniric' world of fantasy, and stupor is analogous to 'dreaming', and 4. 'stupidity' is an advanced state of melancholia (Camuset, 1897).

Baillarger's view did not go unchallenged, particularly because clinical counter-examples of non-melancholic stupors were easily found (such as, for example, cases to be later called catatonic stupor) (Delasiauve, 1851). Sauze (1852), however, supported Baillarger and offered narrow criteria for melancholic stupor (Dagonet, 1872). Baillarger (1853) wrote a second paper making use of Sauze's cases and his views were to predominate in France up to the 1860s when the issue was debated at the *Societé Médico-Psychologique*. This started when Legrand du Saulle (1869) reported the case of Della F, a 32 year old Italian patient who had died in a stuporous state.[18] To deal with the issues raised by this case, Ritti (1883) suggested that stupor be classified into melancholic and symptomatic; the latter becoming a sort of rag-bag which included catatonic states.

In Germany, Griesinger (1861) had subdivided 'melancholic stupor' into one type characterised by rigidity, catalepsy, negativism, clouding, incontinence, fantastic hallucinatory and delusional experiences (recounted after recovery); and another consisting of 'a half-sleeping state without clear dreams or hallucinations' but 'marked abulia and melancholia'. In Scotland, Newington (1874) also distinguished anergic from delusional stupor, and intended these two categories to replace 'acute dementia' and 'melancholic stupor', respectively. 'Melancholia with stupor' or 'melancholia attonita' (Berthier, 1869)[19] remained a source of controversy until Kahlbaum cut the Gordian knot by suggesting that stupor was, after all, the first stage of a new insanity (*vesania catatonica*) (Kahlbaum, 1874; Mora, 1973). At the turn of the century, Kraepelin brought catatonia under the *dementia praecox* umbrella.[20] By this period, the view that stupor, confusion and *obtusion*[21] (Delasiauve, 1851) might involve a change in consciousness began to be discussed.[22] For example, Krafft-Ebing defined stupor as an 'elementary disorder of consciousness' (Krafft-Ebing, 1888; Hoch, 1921).

DISORIENTATION

The symptom disorientation has an interesting conceptual history. Like hallucination or delusion, it is meant to refer to a mental state: but unlike these symptoms it relates to a negative state, to a failure to 'know that' (verbal orientation) and 'know what' (behavioural orientation) (Ryle, 1949). Indeed, since the time of Jackson disorientation has been considered as a 'negative symptom' i.e. as entailing a failure in a hypothetical orientation function (Metzger, 1954).[23] Failure in orientation might thus result from breakdowns in: 1. perception; 2. updating of the internal maps; 3. map-reading; 4. matching of retrieved scripts with incoming information; 5. acting upon any detected mismatch. And also from 'pathological updating', i.e. according to private, delusional reference systems.

Considered as a general symptom rather than as a feature of delirium, disorientation had been discussed already by Meynert, Rieger and Sommer, and Grasset (1901). Wernicke proposed an abstract classification of *Ratlosigkeit* in terms of three modes of consciousness (allo-, auto-, and somato-psychic). Alienists interested in standardised ways of collecting information, such as Rieger and Sommer (1899) suggested that the orientation questions be standardised.[24] Finzi (1899) was able to write a classic paper on disorientation as a symptom. Testing techniques began to be developed, and Bouchard (1926) assessed time evaluation and orientation by asking subjects to 'produce' (by tapping or pacemaking) or to 'reproduce' time, i.e. to judge the duration of a given unit of official time (the relevance of this technique to time orientation has been since called into question) (Benton et al, 1964; McFie, 1950).

The English word 'orientation' derives from the French *orienter* (Klein, 1967) and was first used as a scientific term in astronomy (Oxford English Dictionary). Mott (1899) called 'imperfect orientation' one of the symptoms of cerebral arteriosclerosis. Earlier, disorientation had been reported in association with acute brain syndromes (Dupuytren, 1834; Sutton, 1813) transient memory disturbance (Falret, 1865, p.343; Winslow, 1861), and reduction in mental function (Bercherie, 1980). Janet (1919) used the term 'feeling of disorientation' to describe the loss of appreciation of spatial relationships; and König (1912) characterized as disorientation the confusion observed in Parkinson's disease.

Jaspers (1963) recognised four types of disorientation: amnesic, delusional, apathetic and clouded. Bleuler (1924) drew attention to the phenomenon of psychotic 'double orientation'. Régis (1906) described a subgroup of patients suffering from dementia praecox who exhibited confusion and disorientation. Jung (1964) suggested that because patients with dementia praecox preferentially attend their 'illusions', they *give the impression* of disorientation. Likewise, Bleuler (1950) believed that in dementia praecox there was no 'primary' failure of temporal orientation and so did Kraepelin (1919) although he found that in the stuporous and severely agitated patient 'perception of the environment may be occasionally disordered'.

It would seem, therefore, that these authors did not consider verbal descriptions *alone* as evidence for real time disorientation; but later writers such as Minkowski, (1927; 1926), Schilder (1936) and Seeman (1976) did. With Kurt Schneider (1948) (Conrad, 1960) *clouding of consciousness*[25] became an 'axial' symptom of delirium for the German school; and temporo-spatial disorientation became its clinical (mental state examination) counterpart. The perceptive observation by Chaslin that acute organic states may occur *without* clouding was rescued by the German school when, in the 1950s, it recognized the *Durchgang* or transitional syndrome (Wieck, 1961) i.e. a reversible symptomatic (organic) psychosis without clouding of consciousness.

SUMMARY

At the beginning of the nineteenth century, delirium (*délire*) ambiguously named the acute organic disorder (phrenitis), and also the symptom 'delusion'. The two meanings were gradually separated on the basis of duration, reversibility, presence of fever, and confusion. This latter term was defined first in terms of the doctrine of association of ideas, and later as a disorder of consciousness. 'Confusion' had been considered, until the 1850s, as a type of melancholic stupor. Towards the end of the century, and after the concept of melancholia was replaced by the narrower one of depression, it became a syndrome in its own right.

The symptoms of delirium were considered by some as dreams breaking through into consciousness, and this model was reformulated during the second half of the century as an instance of 'psychological automatism'. On this, the influence of Jackson, via Ribot and Janet, is important. Difficulties in defining clouding of consciousness led to the acceptance of the clinical notion of disorientation. The final separation of the non-vesanic and vesanic deliriums encouraged the creation of the modern notion of psychoses. Indeed, the latter is modelled upon the symptom structure of delirium.

NOTES

1 Vesanic delirium was also called: cold, apyretic, or chronic; the non-vesanic hot, febrile or acute. The distinction was first made by Achilles Foville in 1869 (see Ball and Ritti, 1882, p.357).

2 It has been claimed that the modern concept of mental illness (by which is meant the psychoses) is based on Bayle's 'discovery', i.e. the view that changes in the brain lead to changes in mental functioning. Whilst this may have confirmed the *causal* views implicit in the anatomo-clinical model of disease, it did not provide a *clinical* model, i.e. the view that the psychoses must be characterised by hallucinations, delusions, behavioural disorder, insightlessness, and loss of cognitive grasp and reality-testing. This model was provided by the clinical picture of organic delirium (see Berrios, 1987; Zilboorg, 1941; Leibbrand and Wettley, 1961; Ackerknecht, 1957).

3 For example, the clinical content of the DSM IV categories 'mania' and 'melancholia' has little to do with the behaviours associated with this term before 1800 (see also DSM IV); for mania before 1800 see Berrios, 1992. Thus, when writing on the history of mania, it would be anachronistic to assert a continuity of the disease between Classical times and DSM IV (such a chronicle would only be but the *history of a word*).

4 A good example can be found in the entry on Delirium (*Délire*) in the French Encyclopedia where the author (probably Arnolphe d'Aumont) struggled with the problem: 'The soul is always intact in this state – as it is not susceptible to any disorder; it is not to the soul, therefore, that we must attribute the disorder of judgement that is delirium, but to the state of the organs of the body to which the Creator has pleased to join the soul' (Diderot and D'Alembert, 1754, p.785 in vol.4). For an analysis of the conceptual changes that led to this split between soul and body see: Kenny, 1968; Lain Entralgo, 1978; Sauri, 1969; Bynum, 1976.

5 Such as *Allophasis, Desipientia, Insipientia, Karabitus, Leros, Paracope, Paracusis, Paranæa, Paraphora, Paraphrenesis,* and *Paraphrosyne* (see: Mayne, 1860).

6 This can be illustrated by the confusion caused by the translator of Pinel who rendered *délire* as delirium even when the context makes it clear that Pinel meant delusion (see Pinel, 1806).

7 Such has been the translational confusion that in the first (1950) World Congress of Psychiatry, Honorio Delgado, a Peruvian psychiatrist, proposed that the word 'delusion' be universally used (see Ey et al, 1952, p.100).

8 p.83, in Hamilton (1974): 'unfortunately, this word is used in everyday speech to mean "muddled", "bewildered", or "perplexed" and some English speaking psychiatrists use the word in this sense'. This observation is correct, and the usage in question reflects (as it is explained below) the different

conceptual pedigree of 'confusion' which during the nineteenth century was
not conceptualised as a disorder of consciousness but of association of ideas!

9 It was still present in ICD-9 (World Health Organization (1978).

10 It has not reappeared in DSM IV.

11 The terms *confusion de idées* and *obtusion* were used for the first time by
Delasiauve in 1851 in the context of a famous analysis of the stuporous
states associated with severe lypemania (depression) (Delasiauve, 1851).

12 See for example, his paper at the Vienna Medical Meeting (Maynert, 1881).
In 1890, Maynert proposed a separation of *Verwirrtheit* from the rest of the
psychosis having as its central symptom the experience of bewilderment
(*Ratlosigkeit*) (see Meynert, 1890).

13 Therein confusion is defined both as symptom ('a condition of embarrassment, distraction, or lack of clearness of thought and appropriateness of
action') and as a disease ('a variety of "amentia", called also "confusional
amentia". Another variety is stupidity or *amentia stupida*. A third variety is
hallucinatory acute insanity. . . .') The subtypes were taken from Wille
(p.212) (1888) (see Morselli, 1901).

14 On the life of this great mathematician and alienist see Daumezon (1973).

15 *Automatisme* names a psychological mechanism that since the 1880s has
enjoyed much popularity in French psychiatry. It described the release of
'lower mental functions' from the control of higher ones resulting from
weakening or dissolution. Ribot's interest in Spencer had led him to
Hughlings Jackson, from whom he borrowed the central idea (see: Delay,
1953; Balan, 1989; Baruk, 1972). On this, Janet followed Ribot's ideas
(Janet, 1889). Hence, the hierarchical model of the mind implicit in Chaslin's
definition of confusion is Jacksonian in origin.

16 Karl Bonhoeffer started the view that delirium was a stereotyped response
to any brain insult, and that symptoms did not reflect aetiology (Bonhoeffer,
1910; 1917; Bleuler et al, 1966; Redlich, 1912). On Bonhoeffer see superb
monograph by Neumarker (1990) and Fleck (1956).

17 Auto-conduction was the name for a psychological mechanism that enjoyed
transient popularity in France around the Great War. It meant something
between 'self-deportment' and 'ego self-organization' and involved those
voluntary and involuntary aspects of personality which are supposed to fulfil
an adaptational function.

18 The case was widely reported in the Parisian press, and the ensuing debate
throws light on the uneasy relationship between press, alienists, and the public
during the Second Empire. The central issue was whether Mr Della F. was a
simulator. Although there is little doubt that he was suffering from catatonic
stupor, at the time suspicions were aroused by the fact (common in this
condition) that he occasionally talked to himself or showed defensive movements such as removing the bed cover from his face. The debate that followed,
in which Morel, Moreau, Voisin, Linas, Berthier, and Foville intervened,
shows how rigidly diagnostic criteria were adhered to: because it was assumed
that stupor consisted of a total inhibition of psychological function, no
movement or speech were allowed (see Legrand du Saulle, 1869).

19 Term introduced by Bellini during the 17th century.

20 See Hoenig on 'History of Schizophrenia', this volume.

21 Since the middle of the century (Delasiauve, 1851), *obtusion* had also been used to name the confusional state. However, the term was not synonymous with confusion in that it emphasised a different aspect of the mental state and derived from a different metaphor. Obtusion referred to blurring of consciousness and not to the incapacity to associate ideas.

22 The concept of 'consciousness' became fully 'psychologised' during the nineteenth century, and did so around the metaphor of visual perception. Two versions were available. One regarded consciousness as a super inner eye; the other as an extra-dimension of awareness generated by individual perceptions. The former, being a separate function, was susceptible to being localised in the brain but succumbed to *reductio ad absurdum* (i.e. was there another eye within the eye?). The latter was conceptually economic in that it added no further modules to the collection, but was unlocalisable in the brain.

23 Its role consisting in periodic updating of time and space information.

24 For example Sommer asked: What is your name? Your job? Where are you? Where do you live? What year is it? What month? What date? What day? How long are you here? What town is this? etc.

25 This symptom is a typical example of the ways in which the metaphor of perception has been applied to consciousness. The latter was said to have a focus and a periphery, and both could become disordered. This is the origin of symptoms such as 'narrow, acute, oscillating, or clouded' consciousness. The latter proved particularly difficult to define, and since the 1930s, it was made tantamount to disorientation.

REFERENCES

Abbagnano, N. (1961) *Dizionario di Filosofia*, Turin, Unione Tipografico-Editrice Torinese.

Acknerknecht, E.H. (1957) *Kürze Geschichte der Psychiatrie*, Stuttgart, Enke.

American Psychiatric Association, *Diagnostic and Statistical Manual of Mental Disorders, Fourth Edition*, Washington, DC, American Psychiatric Association, 1994.

Anonymous (1928) 'Confusion'. In *Enciclopedia Universal Illustrada Europeo-Americana*, vol.14, Madrid, Espasa-Calpe, pp.1198–2000.

Baillarger, J. (1853) 'De la Melancolie avec Stupour'. In *Annales Médico-Psychologiques*, 5: 251–76.

Baillarger, J. (1843) 'De l'état désigné chez les aliénés sous le nom de stupidité'. *Annales Médico-Psychologiques*, 1: 76, 256.

Balan, B. (1989) 'Les Fondements Psychologiques de la Notion d'Automatisme Mental chez J.H. Jackson'. *L'Information Psychiatrique*, 69: 610–19.

Ball, B. and Ritti, A. (1882) 'Délire'. In Dechambre, A. and Lereboullet, A. (eds.) *Dictionnaire Encyclopédique des Sciences Médicales*, vol.26, Paris, Masson, pp.315–434.

Baruk, H. (1972) 'Automatisme et troubles des mécanismes de la pensée intérieure dans la psychiatrie française et dans la psychologie interprétative de Freud'. In Bastide, R. (ed.) *Les Sciences de la Folie*, Paris, Mouton.

Benton, A.L., Allen, M.W. van and Fogel, M.L. (1964) 'Temporal orientation in cerebral disease'. *Journal of Nervous and Mental Disease*, 139: 110–19.

Bercherie, P. (1980) *Les Fondements de la Clinique*, Paris, La Bibliotheque d'Ornicar.

Berrios, G.E. (1981) 'Stupor: a conceptual history'. *Psychological Medicine*, 11: 677–88.

Berrios, G.E. (1987) 'Historical Aspects of Psychoses'. *British Medical Bulletin*, 43: 484–97.

Berrios, G.E. (1989) 'Non-Cognitive Symptoms and the Diagnosis of Dementia: Historical and Clinical Aspects'. *British Journal of Psychiatry*, 155: (Suppl.4) 11–16.

Berrios, G.E. (1990a) 'Memory and the Cognitive Paradigm of Dementia during the 19th Century: a Conceptual History'. In Murray, R.M. and Turner, T.H. (eds.) *Lectures on the History of Psychiatry*, London, Gaskell.

Berrios, G.E. (1990b) 'Melancholic Stupor: a conceptual history'. In Stephanis, C.N., Soldatos, C.R. and Rabavilas, T. (eds.) *Psychiatry: A World Perspective*, vol.4, Amsterdam, Excerpta Medica, pp.918–27.

Berrios, G.E. (1992) 'History of the Affective Disorders'. In Paykel, E.S. (ed.) *Handbook of Affective Disorders*, 2nd Edition, Edinburgh, Churchill-Livingstone.

Berrios, G.E. and Hauser, R. (1988) 'The Early Development of Kraepelin's ideas on classification: a conceptual history'. *Psychological Medicine*, 18: 813–21.

Berthier, M. (1869) 'Note sur la stupidité'. *Annales Médico-Psychologiques*, 27: 56–8.

Billod, M. (1861) 'De la Lésion de l'Association des Idées'. *Annales Médico-Psychologiques*, 18: 540–52.

Binet, A. and Simon, Th. (1905) 'Sur la Nécessité d'établir un diagnostic scientifique des états inférieurs de l'intelligence'. *L'Année Psychologique*, 11: 163–90.

Binet, A. and Simon, Th. (1910) 'Définition des principaux états mentaux de l'aliénation'. *L'Année Psychologique*, 16: 61–371.

Binet, A. and Simon, Th. (1911) 'La confusion mentale'. *L'Année Psychologique*, 17: 278–300.

Bleuler, E. (1911) 'Dementia Praecox oder die Gruppe der Schizophrenien'. In Aschaffenburg G. (ed) *Handbuch der Psychiatrie*, Leipzig, Deuticke.

Bleuler, E. (1924) *Textbook of Psychiatry*, New York, McMillan.

Bleuler, M., Willi, J. and Bühler, H.R. (1966) *Akute Psychische Begleiterscheinungen Körperlicher Krankheiten*, Stuttgart, Thieme.

Bolton, L.C. (1906) 'Amentia and dementia: A clinico-pathological study'. *Journal of Mental Science*, 52: 427–90.

Bonhoeffer, K. (1910) *Die symptomatischen Psychosen. Im Gefolge von akuten Infektionen und inneren Erkrankungen*, Leipzig, Deuticke.

Bonhoeffer, K. (1917) 'Die exogenen Reaktionstypen'. *Archiv für Psychiatrie und Nervenkrankheiten*, 58: 58–70.

Boring, E.G. (1950) *A History of Experimental Psychology* (2nd edition), New York, Appleton-Century Crofts.

Bouchard, R. (1926) *Sur l'evaluation du temps dans certains troubles mentaux*, Thèse de Paris, Vigot freres Editeurs.

Bricke, J. (1974) 'Hume's Associationistic Psychology'. *Journal of the History of the Behavioral Sciences*, 10: 397–409.

Brierre de Boismont, A. (1845) 'Du délire aigu'. *Memoires de l'Académie de Médicine*, 11: 477–595.

Broussais, F.J.V. (1828) *De L'Irritation et de la Folie*, Paris, Delaunay.

Bruce, L.C. (1935) 'Physical symptoms of acute confusional insanity'. *Lancet*, i: 550–1.

Bynum, W. (1976) 'Varieties of Cartesian Experience in Early Nineteenth Century Neurophysiology'. In Spicker, S.F. and Engelhardt, Jr, H.T. (eds.) *Philosophical Dimensions of the Neuro-Medical Sciences*, Dordrecht, Reidel, pp.15–33.

Calmeil, L.F. (1859) *Traité des Maladies Inflammatoires du Cerveau*, 2 Vols, Paris, Baillière.

Camuset, (no initial) (1897) 'Review of Chaslin's "La confusion mentale primitive"'. *Annales Médico-Psychologiques*, 5: 317.

Chaslin, Ph. (1892) 'La confusion mentale primitive'. *Annales Médico-Psychologiques*, 16: 225–73.

Chaslin, Ph. (1895) *La Confusion Mentale Primitive*, Paris, Asselin et Houzeau.

Chaslin, Ph. (1915) 'La confusion mentale'. *Annales Médico-Psychologiques*, 6: 276–89; 413–43.

Chaslin, Ph. (1920) 'Quelques mots sur la confusion mentale'. *Annales Médico-Psychologiques*, 6: 356–66.

Chazaud, J. (1992) 'La Folie selon Broussais'. *L'Information Psychiatrique*, 68: 384–90.

Claparède, E. (1903) *L'Association des Idées*, Paris, Doin.

Conrad, K. (1960) 'Die symptomatischen Psychosen'. In Grühle, H.W. and Mayer-Gross, W. (eds.) *Psychiatrie der Gegenwart* vol.2, Berlin, Springer.

Cullen, W. (1927) *The Works of William Cullen*, vol.2, Edinburgh, William Blackwood.

Dagonet, M.H. (1872) 'De la Stupeur'. *Annales Médico-Psychologiques*, 7: 161–95; 359–97.

Daumezon, G. (1973) 'Ph. Chaslin'. *Confrontations Psychiatriques*, 11: 27–39.

Delasiauve, M. (1851) 'Du Diagnostic différentiel de la lypemanie'. *Annales Médico-Psychologiques*, 3: 380–442.

Delay, J. (1953) 'Le Jacksonisme et l'oeuvre de Ribot'. *Études de Psychologie Médicale*, Paris, Presses Universitaires de France.

Diderot and D'Alambert (eds) (1754) *Encyclopédie our Dictionnaire Raissoné de Sciences, des Arts et des Métières*, Paris, Briasson, David, Le Breton, Duran.

Dowbiggin, I. (1990) 'Alfred Maury and the Politics of the Unconscious in nineteenth-century France'. *History of Psychiatry*, 1: 255–88.

Dupuytren, Baron de (1834) 'On nervous delirium'. *Lancet*, i: 919–23.

Eisler (1904) *Wörterbuch der Philosophischen Begriffe*, vol.2, Berlin, Mitler und Sohn.

Esquirol, J.E.D. (1814) 'Délire'. *Dictionnaire des Sciences Médicales*, Paris, Panckoucke.

Etoc-Demazy, G.F. (1833) *De la stupidité*, Paris, Didot le Jeune.

Ey, H. (1954) 'Confusion et délire confuso-onirique. Étude 24'. *Études Psychiatriques*, vol.III, Paris, Desclée De Brouwer, pp.325–428.

Ey, H., Marty, P. and Dublineau, J. (eds.) (1952) *Psychopathologie Générale*, vol.1, Comptes Rendus des Séances, Paris, Hermann, pp.98–104.

Ey, H., Bernard, P. and Brisset, Ch. (1974) *Manuel de Psychiatrie*, 4th Edition, Paris, Masson, pp.307–10.

Falret, J. (1865) 'Amnesie'. In Dechambre, A. (ed) *Dictionnaire Encyclopédique des Sciences Médicales*, vol.3, Paris, Asselin and Masson, pp.725–42.

Falret, J.P. (1864) 'Délire'. *Des Maladies Mentales et des Asiles d'Aliénes*, Paris, Asselin, p.354.

Feuchtersleben, E. von (1845) *Lehrbuch der Ärzlichen Seelenkunde*, Vienna, Gerold, pp.228–9. (English translation by H.E. Lloyd (1847) *The Principles of Medical Psychology*, London, New Sydenham Society.)

Finzi, J. (1899) 'Sul sintoma disorientamiento'. *Rivista di Patologia Nervosa e Mentale*, 4: 347–62.

Fleck, U. (1956) 'Über die Bewußtseinstrübung bei den exogenen Reaktionsformen (Bonhoeffer)'. *Nervenarzt*, 27: 433–40.

Fritsch, J. (1879) 'Die Verwirrheit'. *Jahrbücher für Psychiatrie*, 2: 27–89.

Garrabé, J. (1989) *Dictionnaire Taxinomique de Psychiatrie*, Paris, Masson.

Genil Perrin, G. (1913) *L'Idée de Dégénérescence*, Paris, Leclerc.

Georget, E.J. (1820) *De la Folie*, Paris, Crevot.

Georget, E.J. (1835) 'Délire'. *Dictionnaire de Médicine ou Répertoire Général des Sciences Médicales*, 2nd Edition, vol.10, Paris, Bechet.

Gowers, W. (1888) *A Manual of Diseases of the Nervous System*, vol.2, London, J. & A. Churchill.

Grasset, J. (1901) *Les Maladies de l'orientation et de l'équilibrium*, Paris, Alcan.

Griesinger, W. (1861) *Die Pathologie und Therapie der psychischen Krankheiten für Aerzte und Studirende*, 2nd Edition, Stuttgart, Krabbe.

Grimm, J. and Grimm, W. (1956) *Deutsches Wörterbuch*, vol.12, Leipzig, S. Hirzel.

Hamilton, M. (ed) (1974) *Fish's Clinical Psychopathology*, Bristol.

Hamilton, W. (1859) *Lectures on Metaphysics and Logic*, vol I, Edinburgh, William Blackwood & Sons, pp.129–383.

Hankoff, L.D.S. (1972) 'Ancient descriptions of organic brain syndrome: the "Kordiakos" of the Talmud'. *American Journal of Psychiatry*, 129: 233–6.

Hetch, L. (1884) 'Sympathie'. In Dechambre, A. and Lereboulet, A. (eds) *Dictionnaire Encyclopédique des Sciences Médicales*, vol.13, Paris, Asselin, pp.670–84.

Hippocrates: Works (1972) vol.I (English translation by W.H.S. Jones). Loeb Classical Library, London, William Heinemann.

Hoeldtke, R. (1967) 'The History of Associationism and British Medical Psychology'. *Medical History*, 11: 46–64.

Janet, P. (1889) *L'Automatisme Psychologique*, Paris, Alcan.

Janet, P. (1919) *Les obsessions et la psychasthenie*, (Third Edition) vol.1, Paris, Alcan.

Jaspers, K. (1910) 'Die Methoden der Intelligenzprüfung und der Begriff der Demenz'. *Zeitschrift für die gesamte Neurologie und Psychiatrie*, 1: 402–52.

Jaspers, K. (1963) *General Psychopathology*, (Translated by M. Hamilton and J Hoenig), Manchester, Manchester University Press.

Johnson, S. (1755) *A Dictionary of the English Language*, London, J. and P. Knopton, T. Longman.

Jourdan, (no initial) (1813) 'Confusion'. *Dictionaire des Sciences Médicales*, Paris, Panckouke.

Jung, C.G. (1964) 'The Psychology of Dementia Praecox'. In *The Collected Works*, vol.3, London, Routledge and Kegan Paul.

Kahlbaum, K. (1874) *Die Katatonie, oder das Spannugsirresein*, Berlin, Kirschwald.

Kenny, A. (1968) *Descartes: A Study of his Philosophy*, New York, Random House.

Klein, E. (1967) *A Comprehensive Etymological Dictionary of the English Language*, vol.2, Amsterdam, Elsevier.

König, H. (1912) 'Zur Psychopathologie der Paralysis agitans'. *Archives für Psychiatrie und Nervenkrankheiten*, 50: 285–305.

Kraepelin, E. (1919) *Dementia Praecox and Paraphrenia*, Edinburgh, Livingstone.

Krafft Ebing, R. (1888) *Lehrbuch der Psychiatrie*, Stuttgart, Krabbe. English translation by Hoch, A. (1921) *Benign stupors*, University Press, Cambridge.

Laín Entralgo, P. (1978) *Historia de la Medicina*, Barcelona, Salvat. English translation by Sauri, J.J. (1969) *Historia de las Ideas Psiquiátricas*, Buenos Aires, Carlos Lohle.

Lanteri-Laura, G. and Bouttier, G. (1983) 'L'Evolution des idées sur le système nerveux et le cerveau'. In Postel, J. and Quétel, C. (eds.) *Nouvelle Histoire de la Psychiatrie*, Paris, Privat, pp.413–30.

Lasègue, C. (1852) 'Du délire de persécution'. *Archives Générales de Médicine*, 28: 129–50.

Lasègue Ch. (1881) 'Le délire alcoolique n'est pas un délire, mais in rêve'. *Archives Générales de Médicine*, 2: 573–9 (reprinted in Lasègue, C. (1971) *Ecrits Psychiatriques*, Textes choisis et présentés par J Corraze, Paris, Privat, pp.85–105).

Leader, (1864) 'Acute delirium in 1845 and 1860'. *American Journal of Insanity*, 21: 181–200.

Legrand du Saulle (1869) 'Stupour mélancolique'. *Annales Médico-Psychologiques*, 27: 454–63.

Leibbrand, W. and Wettley, A. (1961) *Der Wahnsinn, Geschichte der Abendländischen Psychopathologie*, Freiburg, Karl Alber.

Lévy-Friesacher, Ch. (1983) *Meynert-Freud: L'Amentia*, Paris, Presses Universitaires de France, pp.37–59.

Lipowski, Z. (1980) *Delirium. Acute Brain Failure in Man*, Springfield, Illinois, Charles C. Thomas.

Littré, E. (1877) *Dictionnaire de la Langue Française*, vol.2, Paris, Librairie Hachette.

Lyons, W. (1986) *The disappearance of Introspection*, London, Bradford Books.

Magnan, V. (1866-7) 'Considérations générales sur la folie'. *Le Progrés Médical*, 4: 1089–91; 1108–12; 5: 187–90; 209–13.

Magnan, V. and Sérieux, T. (1911) 'Délire chronique'. In Marie, A. (ed.) *Traité International de Psychologie Pathologique*, vol.2, Paris, Alcan.

Maury, L.F.A. (1878) *Le Sommeil et les Rêves. Etudes psychologiques sur ces phénomènes et les divers états qui s'y rattachent*, 4th Edition, Paris, Didier.

Mayne, R.G. (1860) *An Expository Lexicon of the Terms, Ancient and Modern, in Medical and General Science*, London, John Churchill.

McFie, J. (1960) 'Psychological testing in clinical neurology'. *Journal of Nervous and Mental Disease*, 131: 383–93.

Metzger, W. (1954) *Psychologie*, (2nd Edition), Darmstadt, Steinkopff.

Meynert, Th. (1881) 'Die akuten (halluzinatorischen) Formen des Wahnsinns und ihr Verlauf'. *Jahrbücher für Psychiatrie*, 2: 181–6.

Meynert, Th. (1890) 'Amentia, die Verwirrtheit'. *Jahrbücher für Psychiatrie und Neurologie* 9: 1–112.

Middleton, E. (1780) *Dictionary of Arts and Sciences: or A Universal System of Useful Knowledge*, London, Hog.

Mill, J.S. (1898) *A System of Logic*, London, Longmans (First Edition 1845).

Minkowski, E. (1926) 'Bergson's conceptions as applied to psychopathology'. *Journal of Nervous and Mental Disease*, 63: 553–61.

Minkowski, E. (1927) *La schizophrenie. Psychopathologie des schizoides et des schizophrenes*, Paris, Desclée de Brouwer.

Mora, G. (1973) *Introduction to the English Translation of Catatonia*, (K L Kahlbaum), Baltimore, Johns Hopkins University Press.

Morel, B.A. (1857) *Traité des Dégénérescences Physiques Intellectuelles et Morales de l'Espèce Humaine*, Paris, Baillière.

Morselli, E. (1901) 'Confusion'. In Baldwin, J.M. (ed.) *Dictionary of Philosophy and Psychology*, London, McMillan, p.212.

Mott, F.W. (1899) 'Arterial degenerations and diseases'. In Allbutt, T.C. (ed.) *A System of Medicine*, vol IV, London, McMillan, pp.294–344.

Mundt, Ch. and Saß, H. (eds) (1992) *Für und wider die Einheitspsychose*, Stuttgart, Thieme.

Neumarker, K.J. (1990) *Karl Bonhoeffer*, Berlin, Springer.

Newington, H.H. (1874) 'Some observations on different forms of stupor'. *Journal of Mental Science*, 20: 372–86.

Norman, C. (1890) 'Acute confusional insanity'. *Dublin Journal of Medical Science*, 89: 506–18.

Oxford English Dictionary, Oxford, Oxford University Press.

Pappenheim, E. (1975) 'On Meynert's amentia'. *International Journal of Neurology*, 9: 310–26.

Paz, M. (1964) 'Alfred Maury, member del'Institute, chroniqueur de Napoléon III et du Second Empire'. *Revue des Travaux de l'Academie des Sciences Morales et Politiques*, 117: 248–64.

Pinel, P. (1809) *Traité Medico-Philosophique sur l'Aliénation Mentale*, 2nd Edition, Paris, Brosson.

Pinel, Ph. (1806) *A Treatise on Insanity*, translated by D.D. Davis. Sheffield, W. Todd.

Porot, A. (1975) *Manual Alphabétique de Psychiatrie*, Paris, Presses Universitaires de France.

Power, H. and Sedwick, L.W. (1892) *The New Sydenham Society's Lexicon of Medicine and the Allied Sciences*, London, New Sydenham Society.

Quincy, J. (1719) *Lexicon Physico-Medicum: or, a new physical Dictionary*, London, Taylor, Taylor and Osborne.

Redlich, E. (1912) 'Die Psychosen bei Gehirnerkrankungen'. In Aschaffenburg, G. *Handbuch der Psychiatrie*, Leipzig, Deuticke.

Régis, E. and Hesnard, A. (1911) 'Les confusions mentales'. In Marie, A. (ed.)

Traité International de Psychopathologie, vol.2., Paris, Félix Alcan.

Régis, E. (1906) *Précis de Psychiatrie*, 3rd Edition, Paris, Doin.

Ritti, A. (1883) 'Stupeur. Stupidité'. In Dechambre, A. (ed.) *Dictionnaire Encyclopédique des Sciences Médicales*, Paris, Asselin, pp.454–69.

Roccatagliata, G. (1973) *Storia della Psichiatria Antica* Milan, Ulrico Hoepli; English translation by Simon, B. (1978) *Mind and Madness in Ancient Greece*, London, Cornell University Press.

Ryle, G. (1949) *The concept of mind*, London, Hutchinson.

Sakai, A. (1991) 'Phrenitis: inflammation of the mind and body'. *History of Psychiatry*, 2: 193–206.

Sauri, J.J. (1972) 'Las significaciones del vocablo psicosis'. *Acta Psiquiátrica Psicológica de América Latina*, 18: 219–23.

Sauze, V. (1852) *De la stupidité, de sa nature psychologique et de son traitement*, Paris, Thèse de Medicine.

Scharfetter, C. (1980) *General Psychopathology*, Cambridge, Cambridge University Press.

Schilder, P. (1936) 'Psychopathology of time'. *Journal of Nervous and Mental Disease*, 83: 530–46.

Schneider, K. (1948) *Beiträge zur Psychiatrie*, Stuttgart, Enke.

Seeman, M.V. (1976) 'Time and schizophrenia'. *Psychiatry*, 39: 189–95.

Séglas, J. (1894) 'De la confusion mentale primitive'. *Archives Générales de Médécine*, 1: 538–49; 665–84.

Siegel, R.E. (1973) *Galen on Psychology, Psychopathology and Function and Diseases of the Nervous System*, Basel, Karger.

SMP (1923) Minutes of three meetings (29 March to 31 May) *Annales Médico-Psychologiques*, (Paris) vol.79.

Sommer, N. (1899) *Lehrbuch der psychopathologischen Untersuchungs-Methoden*, Stuttgart, Enke.

Sutton, T. (1813) *Tracts on Delirium Tremens, on Peritonitis and on the Gout*, London, Thomas Underwood, pp.1–77.

Swain, G. (1977) *Le Sujet de la Folie, Naissance de la Psychiatrie*, Paris, Privat.

Sydenham, T. (1666) *Methodus Curandi Febres*, London, Crook.

Toulouse, Juquelier and Mignard (no initials) (1920) 'Confusion, démence et autoconduction'. *Annales Médico-Psychologiques*, 10th Series, 12: 335–49.

Trzepacz, P.T. (1994) 'The Neuropathogenesis of delirium'. *Psychosomatics*, 35: 374–91.

Tuke, D.H. (1892) *Dictionary of Psychological Medicine*, London, Churchill.

Vliegen, J. (1980) *Die Einheitspsychose*, Stuttgart, Enke.

Warren, H.C. (1921) *A History of the Association Psychology*, New York, Charles Scribner.

Wieck, H.H. (1961) 'Zur klinische Stellung des Durchgangs-syndrome'. *Schweizer Archiv für Neurologie und Psychiatrie*, 88: 409–19.

Wille, L. (1888) 'Die Lehre von der Verwirrtheit'. *Archives für Psychiatrie und Nervenkrankheiten*, 19: 328–51.

Willis, T. (1684) *Practice of Physick*, (translated by S. Pordage), London, T. Dring.

Wing, J.K., Cooper, J.E. and Sartorius, N. (1974) *The Measurement and Classification of Psychiatric Symptoms*, Cambridge, Cambridge University Press.

Winslow, F. (1861) *On obscure diseases of the brain and disorders of the mind*, London, John W. Davies, p.343.

Worcester, W.L. (1889) 'Delirium'. *American Journal of Psychiatry*, 46: 22–7.

World Health Organization (1978) *Mental Disorders: Glossary and Guide to their Classification in accordance with the Ninth Revision of the International Classification of Diseases*, Geneva, WHO.

Zeh, W. (1960) 'Über Verwirrtheit'. *Fortschritte der Neurologie und Psychiatrie*, 28: 187–205.

Zilboorg, G. (1941) *A History of Medical Psychology*, New York, W.W. Norton & Co.

Chapter 1
Delirium and Cognate States

Social Section
LS JACYNA

This essay does not attempt to give a connected account of the concept of delirium in history. Nor does it seek to trace the connexions between this notion and related terms such as confusion and dementia. This task has been undertaken elsewhere.[1] Instead, using chiefly nineteenth-century materials, I have attempted to consider the way that delirium was deployed polemically by psychiatrists in their attempts to construct a professional identity. I also consider how the discourse of delirium reveals psychiatrists' engagement with social and cultural preoccupations of their era.

Numerous medical authors in the eighteenth and nineteenth centuries offered definitions of delirium. Among the most quoted was that offered by J.E.D. Esquirol in 1814. 'A man', Esquirol declared,

> is in delirium when his sensations are not at all in agreement with external objects, when his ideas are not at all in agreement with his sensations, when his judgments and his resolutions are not at all in agreement with his ideas, when his ideas, judgments, and resolutions are independent of his volition.[2]

Several aspects of this definition are noteworthy. The first is its concern with the phenomenological aspects of delirium. Esquirol presumes to enter into the mind of the sufferer and to give an account of his inner experience. The second is the generality of this definition; it comprehends every kind of mental disturbance. While, at least in the popular mind, delirium might most aptly describe the heightened and chaotic intellectual activity of the maniac, for Esquirol it was no less applicable to the depressed, obsessed mind of the melancholic or to the absence of mentation in dementia.[3]

According to this view, delirium was insanity. So prevalent was this amalgamation of the two terms that Etienne-Jean Georget in 1820 felt the need to register a protest. A preoccupation with the intellectual aspects of insanity had, he argued, led to a neglect of other disorders that were no less pathognomonic of insanity: 'one has taken this symptom for madness itself'. In Georget's view the fixation upon delirium was part of a more general prejudice among alienists; they insisted on regarding insanity as 'a lesion of the soul, or the manifestation of the intellectual faculties as taking place without the cooperation of the brain'.[4]

On this psychological or spiritualist model insanity would seem to be a disease apart. While the other disorders with which medical men had to deal had their seats in the organs of the body, the alienist was concerned with a sick soul. There was, however, a paradox inherent in such reasoning. Esquirol, and those who adopted his approach to mental illness, were well aware that delirium, as defined by them, was symptomatic of a wide range of states other than what they considered true insanity. It had one *locus classicus* in brain fever or 'phrenitis' – the symptoms of which included 'watchfulness, acute headache, impatience of light, suffusion of the eyes, and maniacal delirium'.[5] But it was generally acknowledged that a much wider range of morbid and other states could also induce a delirious state. Alexander Crichton arranged the causes of delirium in three categories:

> 1st. Physical, or corporeal causes; such as too great determination of blood to the head, as in fevers, or intoxication, diseased viscera of the abdomen, poisons, excessive discharges, &c.
> 2ndly. Too great, or too long continued exertion of the mental faculties, as in the delirium which often succeed long continued and abstract calculation; and the delirium to which men of genius are particularly subject.
> 3dly. Strong passions, such as anger, grief, pride, love, &c.[6]

In the course of the nineteenth century this classification was considerably extended and refined. The role of rheumatism, heart, kidney and liver disease, of epilepsy, syphilis, scrofula and many other diseases in the production of delirium was discussed at length.[7] Substances other than alcohol – notably hashish – were also recognized to induce a state of delirium.

The close analogy of these states to, if not identity with, insanity presented immediate practical problems of diagnosis to the clinician. Sauveur Morer admitted that occasionally, delirious patients had been sent to asylums who, it later transpired, were 'at the outset of a typhoid fever or of pneumonia.'[8] As well as the damage such misdiagnosis could do to medical credibility, it could also have a dire impact upon the patient; one could well imagine, 'the inconveniences that result both for the patient who, coming to his senses, finds himself locked up in a madhouse, and for the doctor who put him there.'[9]

Moreover, at the level of theory, such facts also posed a problem for proponents of a spiritualist understanding of mental illness. Was not the claim that insanity was the consequence of a 'lesion of the soul' redundant when its leading symptom could be induced by such very material causes as absinth and tapeworm? Conversely, the prevalence of these other forms of delirium offered a serviceable polemical resource to those who wished to insist upon a somatic theory of madness.

The spiritualist could seek to circumvent this difficulty by maintaining a distinction between the 'acute' delirium of fever and other diseases and the 'chronic' delirium of the insane. The delirium of the drunkard was *like* that of the madman, but he was not truly insane. For the somaticist, however, such distinctions were mere sophistry: there was only one delirium albeit with many possible causes; and those who suffered from it were, if only briefly, mad.

The concept of delirium thus constituted throughout the nineteenth century a debatable territory of great theoretical significance. Despite the attempts of Esquirol and other 'psychologists' to establish a special psychiatric sense of the term that relieved delirium of its offensive and threatening connotations, the use of the word in other departments of medicine made it an ideal instrument for those who wished to establish that there was no fundamental distinction between diseases of the mind and other branches of pathology. The physicalist psychiatrist Guillaume Marie Ferrus made the point starkly in the course of a 1855 debate in the Académie de Médecine:

> To introduce the word *delirium* definitively into the vocabulary of alienation is to characterise a great fact and to consecrate a great principle, for, in making use of this same expression for the delirium of ordinary maladies as for maniacal delirium . . . one succeeds in establishing a rapprochement of seat and nature that gives insanity the pathological character which, in our view, it is impossible to deny it; while, on the other hand, the word *folie* generally implied in the past an immaterial malady, a pure affection of the spirit.[10]

A sensitivity to the metaphysical dimensions to these issues was typically French. British medical men arrived at similar conclusions by way of a bluff common sense approach: the brain, one wrote, 'may be the seat of the soul, of the senses, or what not; but it is after all a brain, and nothing but a brain; and, as such, is subject to the same laws which regulate the other material organs of our system'.[11]

Such faith in the possibility of pathological monism – of accounting for the phenomena of mental disease in terms drawn from general medicine, became an article of faith among a vocal body of nineteenth-century alienists. As another participant in the debate on delirium in the Académie de Médecine declared, 'it is blasphemy to say that pathological anatomy and physiology have not illuminated the history of human madness.'[12] The same faith maintained that in the future the same sciences would go still farther to elucidating these obscure phenomena.

It was one thing to make such assertions, quite another to validate them. One obvious site in which to seek the physical correlates of insanity was in the autopsy room; in the course of the nineteenth century innumerable dissections were undertaken with the express aim of discovering the lesions responsible for the symptoms of mental derangement displayed in life. Even Esquirol, albeit half-heartedly, contributed to this enterprise; his pupils took up the challenge with far greater zeal.[13] British alienists too were no less anxiously committed to this quest.

Faith in the existence of an invariable somatic basis for delirium was obliged, however, to deal with the embarrassment that the brains of those who had died insane often displayed no trace of disease. A number of strategies were devised to meet this difficulty. The means available to the observer were, it was argued, inadequate to the task: lesions might rest in the fine texture of nervous tissue or in the subtle chemical changes of its constituents. Great weight was placed upon specific cases that seemed to confirm this hypothesis. Thus in 1869 H. Charlton Bastian reported a case of delirium where microscopic examination revealed aggregations of white corpuscles in the capillaries of the patient's brain. He was quick to point out 'the important bearing which the possibility of the occurrence of minute embolisms of this kind may have in the elucidation of previously obscure forms of so-called functional disease of the nervous system.'[14]

There were attempts also to go beyond these structural considerations by constructing a dynamic model of mental disorder that drew upon the conceptual resources of contemporary neurophysiology. By the second half of the nineteenth century the principle of the morphological and functional continuity of the cerebro-spinal axis was firmly established. It was agreed that the lower nervous centres were governed by the laws of reflex action; the same principles should, therefore, be equally applicable to an understanding of the working of the cerebral hemispheres. 'The reflex phenomena of the spinal cord', declared Ball and Ritti in 1882, 'created the reflex phenomena of the brain'.[15]

On this view, there should be an analogy between the diseases of the lower, purely sensory-motor centres, and those of the ideational centres of the cerebral cortex. Some argued that delirium should be seen as a form of intellectual chorea: the fact that it was often accompanied by 'motor hallucinations' made this analogy the more plausible. More generally, insanity, like other disorders of the nervous system, was to be understood in terms of a breakdown of the functional hierarchy of nervous centres that obtained in health. The 'highest', most complex of these centres mediated voluntary action and exercised supervision and control over the lower ganglia. When these managerial nodes became diseased thought and behaviour suffered accordingly. Delirium was thus due to a lesion of the will; it was intellectual automatism.[16]

Of all nineteenth-century psychiatrists, it was Henry Maudsley who made the most concerted effort to conceptualize mental disorder in terms of the evolution and dissolution of nervous hierarchies. Delirium, he argued, evinced 'the regressive undoing of the structure of doing'. Just as

> in the anatomy of the bodily structure we have the primary *element*; then the *tissue* which is formed of elements; next, the *organ* built up of tissues; and, last, the *organism* or organic whole; so in the structural composition of action we have a like progressive scale of ascent – first, the *elemental reflex movement*; then the union of elementary movements in *associated movements*; next, the composite *purposive movement*, which is the organ, as it were; and, last, the full *voluntary action* of the whole being. When this order of gradual evolution or making suffers a swift and violent resolution or unmaking, then we behold, in acute and confused display, such phenomena of disintegrative will and act as *acute delirious* mania presents.[17]

This acute delirious mania represented an intermediary stage between febrile delirium and 'ordinary mania.' The various forms of delirium did not, therefore, constitute discrete pathological entities; they were merely points upon a continuum characterized by increasing mental disorganization with a concomitant deterioration of motor function. It was not unknown, although it was, Maudsley conceded, rare, for the same case 'to go through the several stages, beginning as ordinary mania, rising by increments of excitement to delirious mania, and ending in delirium, convulsions, and coma.'[18]

Maudsley listed the various exciting causes that might engender delirium; but he emphasized that these irritants did not have a uniform effect on all individuals. A necessary factor in the causation in all cases was 'the native proclivity of the nervous structure.' Certain individuals possessed, in other words, a greater predisposition to delirium than others: their nervous system exhibited 'a lack of compact unity and strength . . ., either in element or in organisation, whereby a cause of no uncommon power or character is able to effect a degree of disorganisation of mental function nearly approaching that which is produced in a more stable structure by a positive toxic agent.'[19] By thus insisting on the reality of a proclivity to madness Maudsley was able to establish a connexion between his theory of delirium and his more general concern with the impact of racial degeneration upon the mental health of populations.[20]

While the opposition between spiritualist and somaticist concepts of insanity is of value in understanding the nineteenth-century debates over the nature of delirium, it should not be accepted uncritically. This antithesis has a mythic quality. It was largely the construct of physicalist psychiatrists of the period concerned to dramatize and ennoble the enterprise they professed to pursue. Thus Georget in 1820 reproached the authors of earlier texts of madness on the grounds that

> these authors, through an extreme circumspection, or perhaps out of fear of finding themselves opposed to philosophic or religious opinions, have described the phenomena of this malady without going back to its cause; they have considered the functional disturbances without the organ which is their seat; the disorders of the intellectual faculties without the brain which is indispensable to their manifestation; so that the symptoms constitute the malady rather than the organic disturbance from which they derive.[21]

Physicalism was thus identified, not only with progress in medicine, but also with the more general advance of liberal ideas in society; psychiatrists presented themselves as in the vanguard of advanced thought. At the same time the somaticization of mental illness served in both France and Britain the more specific interests of a psychiatric profession that was still seeking to establish its claims and prerogatives.

If, however, the gaze shifts from rhetoric to the reality of psychiatric discourse, these sharp contrasts become blurred. For instance, for late nineteenth-century psychiatrists Esquirol, along with Pinel, were the leading exponent of the 'psychological' school which maintained that there were 'no anatomical lesions in madness;' and that 'insanity, properly defined, is absolutely distinct from the delirium of acute diseases.'[22] Esquirol was a 'psychologist' inasmuch as he made use of a theory of the mind derived from the work of Pierre Laromiguière, a contemporary philosopher. He made particular use of Laromiguière's theory of attention to explain the psychic mechanisms of mental derangement. But in so doing Esquirol identified himself with the *idéologue* tradition of Cabanis and Destutt de Tracy, and he emphatically rejected any affiliation with the more recent spiritualist tendency of French philosophy.[23] There was for him no contradiction between an unequivocally 'physiological' approach to mind and its disorders and a willingness to explore the subjective aspects of madness; Esquirol held that such psychological investigations were, indeed, necessary to effective moral therapy.

Similarly, for all his aggressive somaticism, Georget explored the psychological aspects of insanity at length. He maintained that the particular forms of delirium were to be linked to the personality and social position of an individual. The symptoms could either be in character – as when an ambitious person suffered the delusion that he was a king; or in opposition to normal traits – for instance, a normally irreproachable woman might 'become shameless, inviting sexual union by means of gestures and obscene remarks.' Georget also acknowledged the importance of 'moral' antecedents in the aetiology of madness. He held that 'the cause that produced the delirium often determines its character; a woman is betrayed by her lover, abandoned by her husband, and everywhere sees only faithless men, monsters fit only for the torments of hell.'[24]

Georget also expatiated on the physiognomy of the delirious mind. In madness, he reported, the passions were predominant over the other intellectual faculties. Judgment was in abeyance. Moreover, 'there is such an intellectual prostration that the will is null; the patient does not have the strength to decide for one thing rather than for another.'[25]

Regardless of their stance on the corporeality or otherwise of mental disease, nineteenth-century French psychiatrists were deeply concerned with the phenomenology of madness. This was, in turn, typical of a wider cultural preoccupation with the *moi* – in the form and potentialities of the self. For these authors insanity was not reassuringly other: it fascinated because through its distortions it revealed both the lineaments of the healthy mind and the disintegration which the personality could suffer.

The proximity between the sane and insane mind made possible an experimental approach to the phenomenology of madness in which the subject was the psychiatrist himself. None pursued this form of research with more vigour than Jacques-Joseph Moreau de Tours who in 1845 published a study entitled *Du Haschisch et de l'Aliénation Mentale: Études Psychologiques*. Moreau claimed that hashish provided a 'powerful, unique, means of exploring the subject of mental pathology'. By taking this substance he was, in effect, able to induce in himself the symptoms of delirium while retaining the ability to monitor the effects of the drug upon consciousness; he had found the means of initiating himself into the 'mysteries of alienation.'[26]

The principal conclusion Moreau derived from these investigations was that insanity was not merely analogous to but was *absolutely identical* with the dream state.'[27] Despite criticism, this claim attracted strong support among his colleagues. Jules-Gabriel-François Baillarger insisted that it was impossible 'to deny the extreme resemblance between [delirium] and dreams[.] And melancholy accompanied by stupour is it not a sort of nightmare protracted over several months?' Delirium, in short, was nothing but an 'extended dream.'[28] This identification had the effect of underlining the continuities between the pschologically normal and morbid. Delirium was the pathological form of the physiological state of dreaming.

In this discourse the self was an entity at once immersed in the flow of sensation and the interplay of the mind's faculties and yet independent of them. It was a *spiritus rector* that discriminated between the impressions presented to it and manipulated the powers available to it while remaining irreducible to any combinations of these components of mind. It was, Esquirol insisted, 'to the *moi* that all the sensations, all the ideas, all affections of the man refer as long as he exercises reason.' Moreover, 'it is the *moi* that one again meets with in the midst of the most violent delirium, as the essential object [*but*] and last term of the disorder of our ideas.'[29]

Esquirol thus implied that even in the midst of delirium the integrity of the self was preserved – albeit in caricature form. Moreau's experiments tended to a similar conclusion: while hashish might impair all the powers of the mind, it left untouched 'self-consciousness, the intimate sense of individuality.' However bizarre his illusions, the individual remained 'master of himself. Situated beyond its reach, the *moi* dominates and judges the disorders that the perturbating agent provokes in the inferior regions of the intelligence.'[30]

Some alienists hinted, however, at a far more disturbing understanding of madness. François Leuret in 1834 distinguished two forms of 'inspiration' that might impinge upon consciousness: one active, the other passive. In the first the individual

> is aware of the activity of his intelligence and directs it; he is elevated above himself, but there remains continuity in his being; his self of today is still his self of yesterday, his self of always; he has a consciousness of his thoughts and he knows that his thoughts are his own; he wills his actions and takes responsibility for them. In the second, the individual has lost his unity; he is still cognisant, but within him something different from his self also has a will; it speaks, it acts, but rarely in accordance with his consciousness and wishes; he is dominated, he is enslaved, his body is a machine obedient to a power which is not his own.[31]

Baillarger quoted the words of one of his patients to illustrate the experience of such an invasion of an individual's inner space: 'Little by little . . . I discovered the terrible truth. My existence divides itself into two parts. . . . I have compromised my entire *moral being*.'[32]

Insanity might therefore violate the integrity of the *moi*; the self might find itself sharing consciousness with another. The control over mind and body the *moi* normally exercised was lost. The self might even come under the control of the other. This was the ultimate bad dream.

Thankfully, the other was as a rule *au dehors* of the bourgeois mind; delirium was other people. The language of mental pathology afforded a resource for stigmatizing behaviour and beliefs that offended the sensibilities of psychiatrists – whether they spoke in the guise of spokesmen of their profession or articulated the prejudices of their class.

Throughout the nineteenth and in the early part of the twentieth centuries, psychiatrists in France saw it as part of their mission to combat the hold that religion, or superstition as they preferred to call it, exerted over the popular mind. This anticlericalism was particularly intense under Louis Philippe and during the Third Republic.[33]

Alienists often pursued this aim by suggesting that religious belief was itself pathogenic: thus Georget declared that 'the terrors of religion, the fear of eternal damnation, very often give rise to the idea of suicide'.[34] Louis-Florentin Calmeil presented detailed case-histories to establish the connection between religion and mental disturbance. He recounted the case of a woman already prone to melancholy who, 'after having spent an hour in the company of her confessor, . . . declares to her husband and to her . . . parents that she is no less than the mother of Christ.' During the days that followed she sought to play out this role in a variety of bizarre ways. Calmeil took care to underline the point that 'the religious ideas had originated during the conversation that she had with her priest'.[35] The pernicious influence of confessors on the female mind was a perennial concern of nineteenth-century republicans.

Psychiatrists were also anxious to present rational explanations for phenomena that had traditionally been ascribed to supernatural causes.[36] Religious ecstasy and 'demonic' possession were alike placed in the category of mental disturbance. Such delusions were often, Calmeil reported, seen in association with motor disturbances that betrayed their neurological origins. Moreover, religious alienation of this sort often possessed strong erotic undertones. For instance, 'at the beginning of 1836, mademoiselle F*** felt her penchant for devotion increase; more often than before she frequented churches, to seek conversation with pious persons [and] the company of priests. . . . One day mademoiselle F*** experienced deep in her heart a passionate love for her brother.' After an unsuccessful attempt to consummate this love, she fell prey to hallucinations and obsessive ideas.[37]

Calmeil was not content to provide psychiatric accounts only of bizarre religious phenomena. Other forms of behaviour that seemingly breached the constraints of the scientific world-view were treated in similar fashion. Mesmerists, like the theologians, had failed to understand the nervous origins of the morbid behaviour that they themselves encouraged.[38] In 1912 Jean-Baptiste-Henri Thulié tried to complete Calmeil's work by publishing a book that showed all 'mystical' phenomena to be no more than 'pathological manifestations'.[39]

Religion, along with other forms of the 'irrational', was one source of anxiety to the liberal psychiatric mind, another lay in the lower reaches of society. If the one threatened intellectual and political reaction, the other augured anarchy. This form of discourse led alienists to go beyond an exclusive concern with the psychology of the individual and to essay the question of the interaction between mind and society.

A 'sociological' approach to the question of the aetiology of mental disease was nothing new: F.E. Foderé in 1817 echoed George Cheyne when he announced that 'My researches on the relations between, climate, social institutions, and the relative number of the insane, has made me almost certain that England, . . . the most civilized country in the world, . . . is also the nation in which delirium is most prevalent, and which sees it ever increasing.'[40]

Psychiatrists were also sensitive to the way in which social context necessarily impinged upon the form and content of delirium. 'An insane person', according to Maudsley, 'cannot, any more than a sane person, get outside the social and intellectual atmosphere of his time and place; to do that would be nothing less than to get out of his own mental being.' For example, in the Middle Ages 'witches were the terrors to melancholics which the police are now.'[41] Sauveur Morer in 1872 took a similar view of the relation between delirium and social context; but he drew upon more recent history for illustration:

the habits of the individual, the milieu in which he lives, often explains the form of the mental disturbance – witness the prophetesses who have, during the [Franco-Prussian] war, filled the south of France with their foolish predictions; all the inventors of speedy, infallible, but impossible, means of destruction; and those saviours of the nation who required to be hospitalized.[42]

J.V. Laborde also saw an intimate relation between mental pathology and political upheavals. Rather than attributing manifested forms of delirium to such disturbances, however, he sought to ascribe the pattern of societal events to the insanities of the individuals that shaped them. Laborde insisted that

> for more than half a century, ... the popular and working classes, have been afflicted by a malaise which draws them instinctively to seek a better lot: from this movement, out of this collective and irresistable tendency, have arisen all the perturbations, and the few veritable political and social commotions that we have seen arise in this period.[43]

These great social movements were the collective expression of the morbid passions of individual constituents of the lower classes; and foremost among these passions were ambition and pride. In excess, these traits 'approximate more or less to delirium'. The events of 1871 permitted those suffering from this condition to realise their delusions. Laborde cited various cases of this pathology he had himself witnessed in the course of the Paris Commune: for instance, a 'general of the army ... more apt to hold a tool than a sword'. There was an obvious analogy between the pretensions of such upstarts and the 'pathetic contrasts that characterize *ambitious deliria fallen into dementia*'.[44] In other words, 'actual madness' had the potential to play a role in the political realm.[45]

Delirum was thus construed as a fact of nature – as a symptom of mental pathology which was itself derived from lesions of the brain. Its form might depend upon contingent social circumstances; and it might well influence the course of historical events. But it was not itself a product of history. This essay indicates, however, that the content of psychiatrists' thinking, no less than that of their patients, reflected the preoccupations and prejudices of their era. They used the discourse of delirium to elaborate their own sense of the fragility of the self. Moreover, they used the category to stigmatize behaviour that they reprehended or feared.

NOTES

1 Berrios, G.E. (1981) 'Delirium and confusion'. *British Journal of Psychiatry*, 139:439–49.

2 Esquirol, J.E.D. (1814) 'Délire'. In *Dictionnaire des Sciences Médicales, par une Société de Médecins et de Chirurgiens*, Paris, Panckoucke, p.251.

3 Esquirol did not originate this extended sense of delirium: see Goldstein, J. (1987) *Console and Classify: The French Psychiatric Profession in the Nineteenth Century*, Cambridge, Cambridge University Press, pp.45–6.

4 Georget, E.-J. (1820) *De la Folie. Considérations sur cette Maladie: Son Siège et ses Symptômes; la Nature et le Mode d'Action de ses Causes; sa Marche ses Terminaisons; les Différences qui la distingue du Délire Aigu; les Moyens de Traitement qui lui Conviennent; suivies de Recherches Cadavériques*, Paris, Crevot, p.83.

5 Abercrombie, J. (1828) *Pathological and Practical Researches on the Diseases of the Brain and Spinal Cord*, Edinburgh, Waugh and Innes, p.6.

6 Crichton, A. (1798) *An Inquiry into the Nature and Origin of Mental Derangement: Comprehending a Concise System of the Physiology and*

Pathology of the Human Mind. And a History of the Passions and their Effects, London, T. Cadell, vol.1, pp.141–2.

7 For a typical listing see: Sauvet, J.-J. (1849) Considérations sur le Délire, Paris, Rignoux, pp.12–13.

8 Morer, S. (1872) Du Délire dans les Maladies Aigues, Paris, A. Parent, p.24.

9 Pison, H. (1847) Du Délire en Général et de ses Diverses Formes, Paris, Rignaux, p.29.

10 Moreau de Tours, J. (1854–5) 'Du délire au point de vue pathologique et anatomique'. Bullétin de l'Académie Impériale de Médécine, 20:961–2. The quotation is taken from the discussion of Moreau's paper.

11 Galloway, M.B. (1838–9) 'Nature and Treatment of Delirium'. London Medical Gazette, 1:81.

12 Pierre Adolph Piorry in Moreau (1854–5), p.992.

13 Goldstein (1987), pp.250–4.

14 Bastian, H.C. (1869) 'On the plugging of minute vessels in the grey matter of the brain as a cause of the delirium and stupor in severe febrile diseases, and on other symptoms of the typhoid state'. Transactions of the Pathological Society of London, 20:16.

15 Ball, B. and Ritti, A. (1882) 'Délire'. In Dictionnaire Encyclopédique des Sciences Médicales, 26:337.

16 See, for example, Ball and Ritti (1882), p.349.

17 Maudsley, H. (1895) The Pathology of Mind: A Study of its Distempers, Deformities and Disorders. London, Julian Friedmann [reprint], p.271.

18 Ibid., p.274.

19 Ibid., p.275.

20 See: Pick, D. (1989) Faces of Degeneration: A European Disorder, c. 1848–1918, Cambridge, Cambridge University Press, pp.203–16.

21 Georget (1820), pp.vii–viii.

22 Ball and Ritti (1882), p.331.

23 See Goldstein (1987), pp.246–8.

24 Georget (1820), p.98.

25 Ibid., pp.90, 95.

26 Moreau de Tours, J. (1845) Du Hachish et de l'Aliénation Mentale: Études Psychologiques, Paris, Fortin, pp.29–30.

27 Ibid., p.31.

28 Moreau (1854–5), p.940.

29 Esquirol (1814), p.253.

30 Moreau (1845), pp.34–5.

31 Leuret, F. (1834) Fragmens Psychologiques sur la Folie, Paris, Crochard, p.269.

32 Baillarger, J.G.B. (1856) 'La théorie de l'automatisme étudiée dans le manuscrit d'un monomaniaque'. Annales Médico-Psychologiques, 3rd series, 3: 62–3.

33 Dowbiggin, I. (1989) 'French psychiatry and the search for a professional identity: The Société Médico-Psychologique, 1840–1870'. Bulletin of the History of Medicine, 63: 331–55; Goldstein (1987), pp.363–7.

34 Georget (1820), p.114.

35 Calmeil, L.-F. (1845) De la Folie Considérée sous le Point de Vue

Pathologique, Philosophique, Historique et Judiciaire, depuis la Renaissance des Sciences en Europe jusqu'au Dix-Neuvième Siècle; Description des Grandes Epidémies de Délire Simple ou Compliqué, qui ont Atteint les Populations d'Autrefois et Régné dans les Monastères, 2 vols, Paris, Baillière, vol.1, pp.43–4.

36 See: Devlin, J. (1987) *The Superstitious Mind: French Peasants and the Supernatural in the Nineteenth Century*, Yale, New Haven, pp.122–7.

37 Calmeil (1845), vol. 1, pp.58–9.

38 Ibid., vol.2, p.44.

39 Thulié, J.-H.-B. (1912) *La Mystique Divine, Diabolique et Naturelle des Théologiens*, Paris, Vigot, p.381 and passim.

40 Fodéré, F.E. (1817) *Traité du Délire, Appliqué à la Médecine, à la Morale et à la Législation*, 2 vols, Paris, Croullebois, vol.1, p.7.

41 Maudsley (1895), p.189.

42 Morer (1872), p.11.

43 Laborde, J.V. (1872) *Fragments Médico-Psychologiques. Les Hommes et les Actes de l'Insurrection de Paris devant la Psychologie Morbide: Lettres à M. le Docteur Moreau (de Tours)*, Paris, Baillière, p.71.

44 Ibid., pp.72–4.

45 Ibid., p.125.

Chapter 2
Dementia

Clinical Section
GE BERRIOS

To prevent projecting onto the past perspectives that belong to the present, historical method recommends that a historical overview of dementia distinguish between the history of the word and that of the concepts and behaviours nowadays associated with it. This chapter will concentrate on the nineteenth and early twentieth centuries, as it is during this period that the current notion of dementia was constructed. The narrowing down of the clinical scope of 'dementia' started during the 1860s, and culminated in the early 1900s with the consolidation of the 'cognitive paradigm' i.e. the view that dementia only consisted in an irreversible disorder of intellectual functions (Berrios, 1990). Historical analysis shows that this restrictive definition resulted more from theoretical change than observation: this is why the cognitive paradigm has shown to have limited value in the identification of 'early caseness', the explanation of the non-cognitive symptoms of dementia, and the search for brain sites responsible for the disease (Berrios, 1989).

DEMENTIA BEFORE THE EIGHTEENTH CENTURY

Before 1700, terms such as amentia, imbecility, morosis, fatuitas, anoea, foolishness, stupidity, simplicity, carus, idiocy, dotage, and senility (but not dementia) were used to name, in varying degree, states of cognitive and behavioural deterioration leading to psychosocial incompetence. The word 'dementia', as old as the oldest of these (for example, it can be found in Lucretius) simply meant 'being out of one's mind' (Berrios, 1987). Thomas Willis (1684) included what would now be called dementia under *Stupidity* or *Foolishness*, which 'although it chiefly belongs to the rational soul, and signifies a defect of the intellect and judgement, yet it is not improperly reckoned among the diseases of the head or brain; for as much as this eclipse of the superior soul proceeds from the imagination and the memory being hurt, and the failing of these depends upon the faults of the animal spirits, and the brain itself' (p.209). Willis suggested that stupidity might be genetic ('original', as when 'fools beget fools') or caused by ageing ('Some at first crafty and ingenious, become by degrees dull, and at length foolish, by the mere declining of age, without any great errors in living') (p.211), or other causes such as 'strokes or bruising upon the head', 'drunkenness and surfeiting', 'violent and sudden passions', and 'cruel diseases of the head' such as epilepsy.

THE EIGHTEENTH CENTURY

The word 'dementia' first appeared in the vernacular in Blancard's popular *Physical dictionary* (1726) as an equivalent of 'anoea' or 'extinction of the imagination and judgement' (p.21). The earliest adjectival usage ('demented') has been dated by the *Oxford English Dictionary* (OED) to 1644. The OED also dates the earliest substantival usage to Davies's translation of Pinel's (1806) *Treatise of Insanity*. Sobrino's (1791) Spanish-French dictionary offers the following definition: 'demencia = démence, folie, extravagance, égarement, alienation d'esprit' (p.300). It would seem, therefore, that the latin stem 'demens' (without mind) was incorporated into the European vernaculars sometime between the seventeenth and eighteenth centuries, and that after the 1760s, it acquired a medical connotation. Further evidence for this usage can be found in the French Encyclopaedia (Diderot and d'Alambert, 1765):

> Dementia is a disease consisting in a paralysis of the spirit characterized by abolition of the reasoning faculty. It differs from fatuitas, morosis, stultitia and stoliditas in that there is in these a weakening of understanding and memory; and from delirium in that this is but a temporary impairment in the exercise of the said functions. Some modern writers confuse dementia with mania, which is a delusional state accompanied by disturbed behaviour (*audace*); these symptoms are not present in subject with dementia who exhibit foolish behaviour and cannot understand what they are told, cannot remember anything, have no judgement, are sluggish, and retarded. . . . Physiology teaches that the vividness of our understanding depends on the intensity of external stimuli . . . in pathological states these may be excessive, distorted or abolished; dementia results in the third case; abolition may follow: 1. damage to the brain caused by excessive usage, congenital causes or old age, 2. failure of the spirit, 3. small volume of the brain, 4. violent blows to the head causing brain damage, 5. incurable diseases such as epilepsy, or exposure to venoms (Charles Bonnet reports of a girl who developed dementia after being bitten by a bat) or other substances such as opiates and mandragora. Dementia is difficult to cure as it is related to damage of brain fibres and nervous fluids; it becomes incurable in cases of congenital defect or old age . . . [otherwise] treatment must follow the cause.

The legal definition reads:

> Those in a state of dementia are incapable of informed consent, cannot enter into contracts, sign wills, or be members of a jury. This is why they are declared incapable of managing their own affairs. Actions carried out before the declaration of incapacity are valid unless it is demonstrated that dementia predated the action. Ascertainment of dementia is based on examination of handwriting, interviews by magistrates and doctors, and testimony from informants. Declarations made by notaries that the individual was of sane mind whilst signing a will are not always valid as they may be deceived by appearances, or the subject might have been in a lucid period. In regards to matrimonial rights, *démence* is not a sufficient cause for separation, unless it is accompanied by aggression (*furour*). It is, however, sufficient for a separation of property, so that the wife is no longer under the guardianship of her

husband. Those suffering from dementia cannot be appointed to public positions or receive privileges. If they became demented after any has been granted, a coadjutor should be appointed.

These entries summarise well the state of knowledge on dementia during the 1760s. The clinical definition distinguished dementia from mania (a term which, at the time, described any state of acute excitement be it schizophrenic, hypomanic, or organic) and from delirium (which referred, more or less, to what goes on nowadays under the same name). Dementia was reversible and affected individuals of any age. Reference to many aetiologies suggests that a 'syndromal' view of dementia had developed. The legal meaning survived the French Revolution and was enshrined in Article 10 of the Napoleonic Code: 'There is no crime when the accused is in a state of dementia at the time of the alleged act' (Code Napoléon, 1808).

Pinel and the end of the eighteenth century

Pinel was, by ideology and temperament, the last great nosologist of the eighteenth century. In the *Nosographie* (1818; first published: 1798), he dealt with cognitive impairment under amentia and morosis, explaining it as a failure in the association of ideas leading to disordered activity, extravagant behaviour, superficial emotions, memory loss, difficulty in the perception of objects, obliteration of judgement, aimless activity, automatic existence, and forgetting of words or signs to convey ideas. He also referred to *démence senile* (para 116) thus disproving Cohen's point (1983) that 'the term senile dementia was first used by Esquirol' (p.30). Pinel did not emphasise the difference between congenital and acquired dementia.

DEMENTIA DURING THE NINETEENTH-CENTURY

There is a major difference between Pinel's concept of dementia and what was to go under the same name eighty years later. Dementia by then referred to states of cognitive impairment mostly affecting the elderly, and almost always irreversible. The word 'amentia' had changed meaning and named a 'psychosis, with sudden onset following severe, often acute physical illness or trauma' (Meynert, 1890). This section will explore these momentous changes.

French views on dementia

Esquirol

It has been claimed that Esquirol's views on dementia were more advanced than Pinel's (Tomlison and Corsellis, 1984); this is not borne out by an analysis of the primary sources. Esquirol's notion of dementia changed, in fact, between 1805 and 1838. In his thesis on *Des passions* (1805) he used the word (as in *démence accidental, démence melancolique*, etc.) to refer to loss of reason; by 1814, however, he was beginning to distinguish (Esquirol, 1814) between acute, chronic and senile dementia, and to suggest 'composite' types which may included defect states following melancholia, mania, epilepsy, convulsions, scurvy and paralysis. Acute dementia was short lived, reversible, and followed fever, haemorrhage, and metastasis; chronic dementia was irreversible and caused by masturbation, melancholia, mania, hypochondria, epilepsy, paralysis, and apoplexy; senile dementia resulted from ageing, and consisted in a loss of the faculties of the understanding (pp.292–3).

Esquirol's (1838) final thoughts on dementia were influenced by his controversy with Bayle (1822) who had described *chronic arachnoiditis*. This young Frenchman entertained an anatomical ('organic') view of the insanities and had scorned Pinel's views (Bayle, 1826). Esquirol, together with his student Georget, supported the latter's 'descriptivist' approach. His 1838 chapter on dementia includes new terms, clinical vignettes, and postmortem descriptions. He reported 15 cases of dementia (7 males and 8 females) with a mean age of 34 years (sd = 10.9); 7 being, in fact, cases of general paralysis of the insane with grandiosity, disinhibition, motor symptoms, dysarthria and terminal cognitive failure. There also was a 20 year-old girl with a catatonic syndrome (in modern terms), and a 40 year-old woman with pica, cognitive impairment, and space-occupying lesions in her left hemisphere and cerebellum. The type of patient reported illustrates well Esquirol's concept of dementia. For example, *no cases of senile dementia* are included – and although this may reflect the type of patient admitted to the Charenton Hospital – it is more likely that age was not for him a relevant variable. Indeed, 'senile dementia' only appears in early nineteenth century classifications as an afterthought. The same holds true for the 'irreversibility' criterion which was only mentioned in cases of severe brain damage: as to the rest, improvement was expected.

Calmeil

Aware of the importance of clinical description, Calmeil wrote (1835): 'it is not easy to describe dementia, its varieties, and nuances; because its complications are numerous . . . it is difficult to choose its distinctive symptoms' (p.71). Dementia followed chronic insanity and brain disease, and was partial or general. Calmeil was less convinced than Georget that all dementias were associated with alterations in the brain. In regards to senile dementia, he remarked: 'there is a constant involvement of the senses, elderly people can be deaf, and show disorders of taste, smell and touch; external stimuli are therefore less clear to them, they have little memory of recent events, live in the past, and repeat the same tale; their affect gradually wanes away' (p.77). Although a keen neuropathologist, Calmeil concluded that there was no sufficient information on the nature and range of anomalies found in the skull or brain to decide on what caused dementia (pp.82–3).

Guislain

Guislain (1852) defined dementia thus: 'All intellectual functions show a reduction in energy, external stimuli cause only minor impression on the intellect, imagination is weak and uncreative, memory absent, and reasoning pathological . . . There are two varieties of dementia . . . one affecting the elderly (senile dementia of Cullen) the other younger people. Although confused with dementia, idiocy must be considered as a separate group' (p.10). Amongst the 'acquired' forms Guislain included 'vesanic dementias': 'there is nothing sadder than seeing a patient progress from mania or monomania to dementia' (p.19). In his *Lectures* Guislain (1852) also offered an operational definition for 'cognitive failure':

The patient has no memory, or at least is unable to retain anything . . . impressions evaporate from his mind. He may remember names of people but cannot say whether he has seen them before. He does not know what time or day of the week it is, cannot tell morning from evening, or say what 2 and 2 add to . . . he has lost the instinct of preservation, cannot avoid fire or water, and is unable to recognize dangers; has also lost spontaneity, is incontinent of urine and faeces, and does not ask for anything, he cannot even recognize his wife or children. (p.311)

Morel

Criticising older taxonomies, Morel (1860) wrote that in the past the mentally ill: 'had been categorized only in terms of a [putative] impairment of their mental faculties . . .' (p.2). He endeavoured to develop a 'causal' taxonomy, i.e. one based on separating *occasionelle* (e.g. social precipitants) from *determinante* (e.g. genetic factors and brain changes) causes (p.251). Six groups were thus identified: hereditary, toxic, associated with the neuroses, idiopathic, sympathetic, and dementia. Morel believed that:

> if we examine dementia (amentia, progressive weakening of the faculties) we must accept that it constitutes a terminal state. There will, of course, be exceptional insane individuals who, until the end, preserve their intellectual faculties; the majority, however, are subject to the law of decline. This results from a loss of vitality in the brain. . . . Comparison of brain weights in the various forms of insanity shows that the heavier weights are found in cases of recent onset. Chronic cases show more often a general impairment of intelligence (dementia). Loss in brain weight – a constant feature of dementia – is also present in ageing, and is an expression of decadence in the human species. [There are] natural dementia and that dementia resulting from a pathological state of the brain . . . some forms of insanity are more prone to end up in dementia (idiopathic) than others . . . it could be argued that because dementia is a terminal state it should not be classified as a sixth form of mental illness . . . I must confess I sympathise with this view, and it is one of the reasons why I have not described the dementias in any detail . . . on the other hand from the legal and pathological viewpoints, dementia warrants separate treatment. (pp.837–8)

Morel's view that the dementias are a terminal state was in keeping with his 'degenerationist' hypothesis (Pick, 1989). Consequently, he also dealt with dementia in other chapters of his treatise (Morel, 1860). His view was based on the assumption that insanity always predated dementia; he soon realised that this was nonsense, and explained the frequent exceptions by ageing or degeneration. The 'terminal state' hypothesis dissuaded Morel from believing that there were specific brain alterations in dementia.

THE FRAGMENTATION OF THE DEMENTIA CONCEPT

By 1900, senile, arteriosclerotic, and 'subcortical' forms of dementia had been recognised (Berrios and Freeman, 1991). Many clinical forms, however, found no place in this tripartite classification; some had been known for a long time, such as general paralysis of the insane, dementia praecox, and melancholia attonita; others had been recently described, such as the dementias related to alcoholism, epilepsy, brain damage, myxoedema, hysteria, and lead poisoning. Their presence created clinical ambiguity, and this was resolved in various ways: some were considered as independent conditions (e.g. Korsakoff's syndrome and myxoedema), others were hidden under a different name (e.g. dementia praecox became schizophrenia and melancholia attonita stupor); yet others were explained away as 'pseudo-dementias' (e.g. hysteria). The history of some of these states, however, must be picked up *ab initio*.

General paralysis of the insane

Bayle (1822) described under the name *arachnitis chronique* cases of what later was to be called 'general paralysis of the insane'. Whether this 'new phenomenon' resulted from 'a mutation in the syphilitic virus towards the end of the eighteenth century' is unclear (p.623) (Hare, 1959). Equally dubious is the claim that its discovery reinforced the belief of alienists in the anatomo-clinical view of mental disease (Zilboorg, 1941). In fact, it took more than 30 years for general paralysis to gain acceptance as a 'separate' disease. Bayle's 'discovery' was more important in another way, namely, in that it challenged the 'cross sectional' view of disease; in the words of Bercherie (1980): 'for the first time in the history of psychiatry there was a morbid entity which presented itself as a sequential process unfolding itself into successive clinical syndromes' (p.75).

By the 1850s, no agreement had yet been reached as to how symptoms were caused by the *periencephalite chronique diffuse* (as general paralysis was known at the time). Three clinical types were recognised: manic-ambitious, melancholic-hypochondriac, and dementia; according to the 'unitary view', all three constituted stages of a single disease, the order of their appearance depending on the progress of the cerebral lesions. Baillarger (1883), however, sponsored a 'dualist' view: 'paralytic insanity and paralytic dementia are different conditions'. It is clear that the debate had less to do with the nature of the brain lesions than with how mental symptoms and their contents were produced in general: how could the 'typical' content of paralytic delusions (grandiosity) be explained? Since the same mental symptoms could be seen in all manner of conditions, Baillarger (1883) believed that chronic periencephalitis could only account for the motor signs – mental symptoms 'therefore, having a different origin' (p.389). The absence of a link between lesion and symptom also explained why some patients recovered.

The view that general paralysis might be related to syphilis (put forward by Fournier, 1875) was resisted. Indeed, the term 'pseudo-general paralysis' was coined to refer to cases of infections causing psychotic symptoms (Baillarger, 1889). In general, there is little evidence that alienists considered general paralysis as a 'paradigm-disease', i.e. a model for all other mental diseases. It can even be said that the new 'disease' created more problems than it solved (for a discussion of this issue see Berrios, 1985).

Pseudodementia and vesanic dementia

The mechanism and/or concept of 'pseudodementia' was created during the 1880s to deal with cases of 'dementia' that eventually recovered; its most common name at the time being *démence melancolique* (Berrios, 1985). Before then, these cases had been considered as 'vesanic', i.e. as dementias caused by a functional psychosis (Berrios, 1987). Mairet (1883) challenged this compromise by showing that melancholic patients with cognitive impairment may show alterations in the temporal lobe; this led him to hypothesise that these sites were related to feelings, and that nihilistic delusions only appeared when the lesion spread to the cortex. Mairet's cases (some of which would now be called 'Cotard's syndrome') (Cotard, 1882; Berrios and Luque, 1995) showed psycho-motor retardation, refused food, and died in stupor. Another contributor to the understanding of cognitive impairment in the affective disorders was George Dumas (1894) who suggested that it was 'mental fatigue that explained the psychological poverty and monotony of melancholic depressions' and that the problem was not 'an absence but a stagnation of ideas'; i.e. he was, therefore, the first to explain the disorder as a failure in performance.

The word 'pseudodementia', in turn, originated in a different clinical tradition, and was first used by Carl Wernicke to refer to 'a chronic hysterical state mimicking mental weakness' (Bulbena and Berrios, 1986). It was little used until the 1950s, when it was given a lease of life (e.g. Madden et al, 1952; Anderson et al, 1959; Kiloh, 1961). Current usage is ambiguous for it refers to, at least, three different clinical situations: a real (albeit reversible) cognitive impairment accompanying some psychoses, a parody of such impairment, and the cognitive deficit of delirium (Bulbena and Berrios, 1986).

The term 'vesanic dementia' began to be used after the 1840s to refer to the clinical states of cognitive disorganisation following insanity; its meaning, has changed *pari passu* with psychiatric theory. According to the unitary insanity notion, vesanic dementia was a terminal stage (after mania and melancholia); according to degeneration theory, it was the final expression of a corrupted pedigree; and according to post-1880s nosology, a final common pathway to some insanities. Vesanic dementias were reversible, and could occur at any age; risk factors such as old age, lack of education, low social class, bad nutrition, etc. accelerated the progression of the dementia or impeded recovery (p.597) (Ball and Chambard, 1881). By the 1900s, the vesanic dementias became 'pseudodementias'.

Brain changes and ageing

Since the beginning of the nineteenth century, cases had been described of brain 'softening' followed by cognitive failure. Rostan (1823) reported 98 subjects thus affected, thought to be scorbutic in origin, and divided them into simple, abnormal, and complicated (the latter two groups being accompanied by psychiatric changes). Mental symptoms might occur before, during and after the softening itself; thus, senile dementia and insanity might precede the brain changes. Accompanying stroke, Rostan described cognitive failure and attacks of insanity suggesting that these symptoms were 'a general feature . . . not a positive sign of localisation' (pp.214–15). Durand-Fardel (1843) provided an account of the relationship between softening and insanity, warning that softening was used to refer both to a disease (stroke) and to a state of the brain. Psychiatric complications were acute and long term, the former including confusion, depression, irritability, acute insanity, and loss of mental faculties (p.139); the latter had gradual onset, and exhibited an impairment of memory, poverty of thinking, and a regression to infantile forms of behaviour, features which led to 'true dementia' (pp.327–8).

Years later, J.H. Jackson (1875) reviewed the problem: 'softening . . . as a category for a rude clinical grouping was to be deprecated' (p.335); he nonetheless, followed Durand-Fardel's classification, and suggested that after stroke mental symptoms might be immediate or follow after a few hours or months; he recognised that major cognitive failure may ensue, and saw this as an instance of 'dissolution': emotional symptoms being release phenomena (for an analysis of this concept see Berrios, 1991). He believed that anxiety, stress and irritability might be harbingers of stroke.

The concept of arteriosclerotic dementia

Old age was considered as an important factor in the development of arteriosclerosis (Berrios, 1994) and a risk factor in diseases such as melancholia (Berrios, 1991). By 1910, there was a trend to include all dementias under 'mental disorders of cerebral arteriosclerosis' (Barret, 1913). Arteriosclerosis, might be generalised or cerebral, inherited or acquired, and caused by syphilis, alcohol, nicotine, high blood pressure, and ageing. In those genetically predisposed, cerebral arteries were considered as thinner and less elastic. Arteriosclerosis caused mental changes by narrowing of arteries and/or reactive inflammation. The view that arteriosclerotic dementia resulted from a gradual strangulation of blood supply to the brain was also formed during this period; consequently, emphasis was given to prodromal symptoms and strokes were but the culmination of a process started years before. Some opposed this view from the beginning. For example, Marie (1906) claimed that such explanation was a vicious circle as alienists claimed both that: 'ageing was caused by arteriosclerosis and the latter by ageing' (p.358), and Walton (1912) expressed serious doubts from the histopathological point of view. The frequent presence in postmortem of such changes also concerned pathologists who worried that they could not 'safely exclude cerebral arteriosclerosis of greater or less degree in any single case' of senile dementia (p.677) (Southard, 1910). Based on a review of these arguments, Olah (1910) concluded that there was no such thing as 'arteriosclerotic psychoses'. But the 'chronic global ischaemia' hypothesis won the day, and it was to continue well into the second half of the twentieth century. For some it became a general explanation; for example, North and Bostock (1925) reported a series of 568 general psychiatric cases in which around 40 percent suffered from 'arterial disease', which – according to the authors – was even responsible for schizophrenia. The old idea of an apoplectic form of dementia, however, never disappeared.

Apoplectic dementia

'Apoplectic dementia' achieved its clearest enunciation in the work of Benjamin Ball (Ball and Chambard, 1881). 'Organic apoplexy' resulted from bleeding, softening or tumour and might be 'followed by a notable decline in cognition, and by a state of dementia which was progressive and incurable . . . of the three, localised softening (*ramollissement en foyer*) caused the more severe states of cognitive impairment' (p.581). Ball believed that prodromal lapses of cognition (e.g. episodes of somnolence and confusion with automatic behaviour, for which there was no memory after the event) and sensory symptoms were caused by atheromatous lesions. Visual hallucinations, occasionally of a pleasant nature, were also common. After the stroke, persistent cognitive impairment was frequent. Post-mortem studies showed in these cases softening of 'ideational' areas of cortex and white matter. Ball also suggested a laterality effect (p.582) in that 'right hemisphere strokes led more often to dementia whereas left hemisphere ones caused perplexity, apathy, unresponsiveness, and a tendency to talk to oneself' (p.583). Following Luys, he believed that some of these symptoms resulted from damage to corpus striatum, insular sulci, and temporal lobe. During Ball's time attention also shifted from white to red softening. Charcot (1881) wrote on cerebral haemorrhage (the new name for red softening): 'having eliminated all these cases, we find ourselves in the presence of a homogeneous group corresponding to the commonest form of cerebral haemorrhage. This is, par excellence, sanguineous apoplexy . . . as it attacks a great number of old people, I might call it senile haemorrhage' (p.267).

Presbyophrenia and confabulation
The word 'presbyophrenia' was coined by Kahlbaum (1863) to name a subtype of the paraphrenias (insanities occurring during periods of biological change). Presbyophrenia was a form of paraphrenia senilis characterised by amnesia, disorientation, delusional misidentification, and confabulation. Ignored for more than 30 years, the term re-appeared in the work of Wernicke, Fischer, and Kraepelin. Wernicke's classification of mental disorders was based on his theory of the tripartite relational structure of consciousness (outside world, body, and self) (Lanczik, 1988). Impairment of the link between consciousness and outside world led to presbyophrenia, delirium tremens, Korsakoff's psychosis, and hallucinoses. Amongst the features of presbyophrenia, Wernicke included confabulations, disorientation, hyperactivity, euphoria, and a fluctuating course; acute forms resolved without trace, chronic ones merged with senile dementia (Berrios, 1986).

In France, Rouby (1911) conceived of presbyophrenia as a final common pathway for cases suffering from Korsakoff's psychosis, senile dementia, or acute confusion. Truelle and Bessière (1911) suggested, in turn, that it might result from a toxic state caused by liver or kidney failure. Kraepelin (1910) lumped presbyophrenia together with the senile and pre-senile insanities, and (as compared with Korsakoff's patients) believed presbyophrenic patients to be older, free from polyneuritis and history of alcoholism, and showing hyperactivity and elevated mood. Ziehen (1911) wrote that 'their marked memory impairment contrasts with the relative sparing of thinking'. Oskar Fischer (1912) suggested that disseminated cerebral lesions were the essential anatomical substratum of presbyophrenia.

During the 1930s, two new hypotheses emerged. Boestroem (1933) concluded on phenomenological grounds that presbyophrenia could be identified with mania, suggesting an interplay between two factors: cerebral arteriosclerosis and cyclothymic pre-morbid personality. Lafora (1935) emphasised the role of cerebrovascular pathology, and claimed that disinhibition and presbyophrenic behaviour were caused by a combination of senile and atherosclerotic changes. Burger-Pritz and Jacob (1938), however, questioned the view that cyclothymic features were a necessary pre-condition. Bessière (1948) claimed that presbyophrenia was a syndrome found in conditions such as senile dementia, brain tumours, traumatic psychoses, and confusional states. More recently, it has been suggested that presbyophrenia may be a subform of Alzheimer's disease characterised by a severe atrophy of locus coeruleus (Berrios, 1985a).

Alzheimer's disease

Alzheimer's disease has become the prototypical form of dementia. From this point of view, a study of its origins should throw light on the evolution of the concept of dementia. The writings of Alzheimer, Fischer, Fuller, Lafora, Bonfiglio, Perusini, Ziveri, Kraepelin, and other protagonists are deceptively fresh, and this makes anachronistic reading inevitable. However, the psychiatry of the late nineteenth century is a remote country: concepts such as dementia, neuron, neurofibril and plaque were then still in a process of construction and meant different things to different people. A discussion of these issues is beyond the scope of this chapter (for this see Berrios, 1990a).

The neuropathology of dementia before Alzheimer

Enquiries into the brain changes accompanying dementia started during the 1830s but consisted in descriptions of external appearance (Wilks, 1865). The first important microscopic study was that of Marcé (1863) who described cortical atrophy, enlarged ventricles, and 'softening'. The vascular origin of softening was soon ascertained (Parrot, 1873), but the distinction between vascular and parenchymal factors had to wait until the 1880s. From then on, microscopic studies concentrated on cellular death, plaques and neurofibrils.

Alzheimer and his disease

Alzheimer (1907) reported the case of a 51 year-old woman, with cognitive impairment, delusions, hallucinations, focal symptoms, and whose brain showed plaques, tangles, and arteriosclerotic changes. The existence of neurofibrils had been known for some time (DeFelipe and Jones, 1988; Barret, 1911); for example, that in senile dementia 'the destruction of the neuro-fibrillae appears to be more extensive than in the brain of a paralytic subject' (Bianchi 1906, p.846). Fuller (1907) had remarked in June 1906 (i.e. five months before Alzheimer's report) on the presence of neurofibrillar bundles in senile dementia (p.450). Likewise, the association of plaques with dementia was not a novelty: Beljahow (1889) had reported them in 1887, and so had Redlich and Leri a few years later (Simchowicz, 1924); in Prague, Fischer (1907) gave an important paper in June 1907 pointing out that miliary necrosis could be considered as a marker of senile dementia.

Nor was the syndrome described by Alzheimer new: states of persistent cognitive impairment affecting the elderly, accompanied by delusions and hallucinations were well known (Marcé, 1863; Krafft-Ebing, 1873; Crichton-Brown, 1878; Marie, 1906). As a leading neuropathologist Alzheimer was aware of this work. Did he then mean to describe a new disease? The answer is that it is most unlikely he did, his only intention having been to point out that such a syndrome could occur in younger people (Alzheimer, 1911). This is confirmed by commentaries from those who worked for him: Perusini (1911) wrote that for Alzheimer 'these morbid forms do not represent anything but an atypical form of senile dementia' (p.143).

The naming of the disease

Kraepelin (1910) coined the term in the 8th edition of his Handbook: at the end of the section on 'senile dementia' he wrote:

> the autopsy reveals, according to Alzheimer's description, changes that represent the most serious form of senile dementia . . . the *Drusen* were numerous and almost one third of the cortical cells had died off. In their place instead we found peculiar deeply stained fibrillary bundles that were closely packed to one another, and seemed to be remnants of degenerated cell bodies. . . . The clinical interpretation of this Alzheimer's disease is still confused. Whilst the anatomical findings suggest that we are dealing with a particularly serious form of senile dementia, the fact that this disease sometimes starts already around the age of 40 does not allow this supposition. In such cases we should at least assume a "senium praecox" if not perhaps a more or less age-independent unique disease process.

The reception of the new disease

Alzheimer (1911) showed surprise at Kraepelin's interpretation, and always referred to his 'disease' as *Erkrankungen* (in the medical language of the 1900's a term softer than *Krankheit*, the term used by Kraepelin). Others also expressed doubts. Fuller (1912), whose contribution to this field has been sadly neglected, asked 'why a special clinical designation – Alzheimer's disease – since, after all, they are but part of a general disorder' (p.26). Hakkébousch and Geier (1912), in Russia, saw it as a variety of the involution psychosis. Simchowicz (1911) considered 'Alzheimer's disease' as only a severe form of senile dementia. Ziehen (1911) does not mention the disease in his major review of senile dementia. In a meeting of the New York Neurological Society, Ramsay Hunt (Lambert, 1916) asked Lambert, the presenter of a case of 'Alzheimer's disease' that 'he would like to understand clearly whether he made any distinction between the so-called Alzheimer's disease and senile dementia' other than . . . 'in degree and point of age'. Lambert agreed, suggesting that, as far as he was concerned, the underlying pathological mechanisms were the same (Lambert, 1916). Lugaro (1916) wrote: 'For a while it was believed that a certain agglutinative disorder of the neurofibril could be considered as the main "marker" (*contrassegno*) of a pre-senile form [of senile dementia], which was "hurriedly baptized" (*fretta battezzate*) as "Alzheimer's disease" (p.378). He went on to say that this state is only a variety of senile dementia'. Simchowicz (1924), who had worked with Alzheimer, wrote 'Alzheimer and Perusini did not know at the time that the plaques were typical of senile dementia [in general] and believed that they might have discovered a new disease' (p.221). These views, from men who lived in Alzheimer's and Kraepelin's time, must be taken seriously (for a detail discussion of these issues see Berrios, 1990a).

Pick's disease and the frontal dementias

Dementias believed to be related to frontal lobe pathology have once again become fashionable, and authors often invoke the name of Arnold Pick (Niery et al, 1988). However, when the great Prague neuropsychiatrist described the syndrome named after him, all he wanted was to draw attention to a form of localised (as opposed to diffuse) atrophy of the temporal lobe (Pick, 1892). This alteration was to give rise to a dysfunction of language and praxis, and be susceptible to diagnosis during life. Pick believed that lobar atrophies constituted a stage in the evolution of the senile dementias.

The story starts, as it should, before Pick. Louis Pierre Gratiolet (1854) was responsible for re-naming the cerebral lobes after their overlying skull: thus 'anterior' became 'frontal' lobe. He made no assumption as to the function of the 'anterior extremity of the cerebral hemisphere'. 'Phrenologists', however, did and related reflective and perceptive functions (qualitatively defined) to the forehead (Anonymous, 1832) (on the science of Phrenology: see Combe, 1873; Lanteri-Laura, 1970). 'Modular' assumptions (i.e. a one-to-one correlation between mental function and brain site) involving the frontal lobes started only during the 1860s, following reports on dysfunctions of language in lesions of the frontal lobes (Broca, 1861; Henderson, 1986). These claims ran counter to those of Jackson's, that the cerebral cortex was the general seat of personality and mind (Jackson, 1894). Meynert (1885) believed that 'the frontal lobes reach a high state of development in man' but still defined mental disorders as diseases of the 'fore-brain' (by which he meant 'prosencephalon' or human brain as a whole).

In his first report (the case of focal senile atrophy and aphasia in a man of 71) Pick (1892) did not inculpate the frontal lobes nor did he in his second case (Pick, 1901) (a woman of 59 with generalised cortical atrophy, particularly of the left hemisphere). The association with the frontal lobes only appears in his fourth case (Pick, 1906) (a 60 year-old man with 'bilateral frontal atrophy'). Which of these cases should, therefore, be considered as the first of Pick's disease? At the time, in fact, no one thought that Pick had described a new disease; Barrett (1913) considered the two first cases of Pick's as atypical forms of Alzheimer's disease, and Ziehen (1911) did not see anything special in them. During the same period, Liepmann, Stransky, and Spielmeyer had described similar cases with aphasia and circumscribed cerebral atrophy (Mansvelt, 1954); so much so, that Urechia and Mihalescu felt tempted to name the syndrome 'Spielmeyer's disease' (Caron, 1934). This did not catch on, however, and in two classical papers on what he called 'Pick's disease', Carl Schneider (1927; 1929) constructed the new view of the condition by suggesting that it evolved in three stages – the first with a disturbance of judgement and behaviour, the second with localised symptoms (e.g. speech), and the third with generalised dementia. He recognised rapid and slow forms, the former with an akinetic and aphasic subtypes and a malignant course, and the latter with a predominance of plaques (probably indistinguishable from Alzheimer's disease).

THE AFTERMATH

The history of the word 'dementia' must not be confused with that of the concepts or behaviours involved. By the year 1800, two definitions of dementia were recognised and both had psychosocial incompetence as their central concept: in addition to cognitive impairment, the clinical definition included other symptoms such as delusions and hallucinations; irreversibility and old age were not features of the condition, and in general dementia was considered to be a terminal state to all sorts of mental, neurological and physical conditions. The adoption of the anatomo-clinical model by nineteenth century alienists changed this. Questions were asked as to the neuropathological basis of dementia and this, in turn, led to re-adjustments in its clinical description. The history of dementia during the 19th century is, therefore, the history of its gradual attrition. Stuporous states (then called acute dementia), vesanic dementias, and localised memory impairments, were gradually reclassified, and by 1900 the cognitive paradigm, i.e. the view that the essential feature of dementia was intellectual impairment, was established. From then on, efforts were made to explain other symptoms such as hallucinations, delusions, and mood and behavioural disorders as epiphenomena, and as unrelated to whatever the central mechanism of dementia was. There has also been a fluctuating acceptance of the parenchymal and vascular hypotheses, the latter leading to the description of arteriosclerotic dementia. The separation of the vesanic dementias and of the amnestic syndromes led to the realisation that age and ageing mechanisms were important, and by 1900 senile dementia became the prototype of the dementias; by 1970, Alzheimer's disease had become the flagship of the new approach. During the last few years, the cognitive paradigm has become an obstacle, and a gradual re-expansion of the symptomatology of dementia is fortunately taking place.

REFERENCES

Alzheimer, A. (1907) 'Über eine eigenartige Erkrankung der Hirnrinde'. *Allgemeine Zeitschrift für Psychiatrie und Psychisch-Gerichtlich Medizine*, 64: 146–8.

Alzheimer, A. (1911) 'Über eigenartige Krankheitsfälle des späteren Alters'. *Zeitschrift für die gesamte Neurologie und Psychiatrie*, 4: 356–85.

Anderson, E.W., Threthowan, W.H. and Kenna, J.C. (1959) 'An Experimental Investigation of Simulation and Pseudodementia'. *Acta Psychiatrica et Neurologica Scandinavica*, 34, Supplement 132.

Anonymous, (1832) 'An Exposure Of The Unphilosophical And Unchristian Expedients Adopted By Antiphrenologists, For The Purpose Of Obstructing The Moral Tendencies Of Phrenology. A Review Of John Wayte's Book'. *The Phrenological Journal and Miscellany*, 7: 615–22.

Baillarger, J. (1883) 'Sur la Théorie de la Paralysie Générale'. *Annales Médico-Psychologiques*, 35: 18–52, 191–218.

Baillarger, J. (1889) 'Doit-on Dans La Classification Des Maladies Mentales Assigner Une Place á Part Aux Pseudo-paralysies Générales?' *Annales Médico-Psychologiques*, 41: 521–5.

Ball, B. and Chambard, E. (1881) 'Démence'. In Dechambre, A. and Lereboullet,

L. (eds.) *Dictionnaire Encyclopédique des Sciences Médicales*, Paris, Masson, pp.559–605.

Barrett, A.M. (1913) 'Presenile, Arteriosclerotic And Senile Disorders Of The Brain And Cord'. In White, W.A. and Jellife, S.A. (eds.) *The Modern Treatment of Nervous and Mental Diseases*, London, Kimpton, pp.675–709.

Bayle, A.L.J. (1822) *Recherches Sur Les Maladies Mentales*, Paris, Thése de Médecine.

Bayle, L.J. (1826) *Traité Des Maladies Du Cerveau*, Paris, Gabon et Compagnie.

Beljahow, S. (1889) 'Pathological Changes In The Brain In Dementia Senilis'. *Journal of Mental Science*, 35: 261–2.

Bercherie, P. (1980) *Les Fondements De La Clinique*, Paris, La Bibliothéque d'Ornicar.

Berrios, G.E. (1985) ' "Depressive Pseudodementia" Or "Melancholic Dementia". A 19th Century View'. *Journal Of Neurology, Neurosurgery And Psychiatry*, 48: 393–400.

Berrios, G.E. (1985a) 'Presbyophrenia: Clinical Aspects'. *British Journal of Psychiatry*, 147: 76–9.

Berrios, G.E. (1986) 'Presbyophrenia: The Rise And Fall Of A Concept'. *Psychological Medicine*, 16: 267–75.

Berrios, G.E. (1987) 'History Of The Functional Psychoses'. *British Medical Bulletin*, 43: 484–98.

Berrios, G.E. (1989) 'Non-cognitive Symptoms And The Diagnosis Of Dementia. Historical And Clinical Aspects'. *British Journal of Psychiatry*, 154: (suppl 4), 11–16.

Berrios, G.E. (1990) 'Memory And The Cognitive Paradigm of Dementia During The 19th Century: A Conceptual History'. In Murray, R. and Turner, T. (eds.) *Lectures on the History of Psychiatry*, London, Gaskell, pp.194–211.

Berrios, G.E. (1990a) 'Alzheimer's Disease: A Conceptual History'. *International Journal of Geriatric Psychiatry*, 5: 355–65.

Berrios, G.E. (1991) 'Affective Disorders in Old Age: A Conceptual History'. *International Journal of Geriatric Psychiatry*, 6: 337–46.

Berrios, G.E. (1992) 'Positive And Negative Signals: A Conceptual History'. In Marneros, A., Andreasen, N.C. and Tsuang, M.T. (eds.) *Negative Versus Positive Schizophrenia*, Berlin, Springer, pp.8–27.

Berrios, G.E. (1994) 'The Psychiatry of Old Age: A Conceptual History'. In Copeland, J., Abou-Saleh, M. and Blazer, D. (eds.) *The Principles and practice of Geriatric Psychiatry*, Chichester, Wiley, pp.11–16.

Berrios, G.E. and Freeman, H. (eds.) (1991) *Alzheimer and the Dementias*, London, Royal Society of Medicine.

Berrios, G.E. and Luque, R. (1995) 'Cotard's delusion or syndrome? A conceptual history'. *Comprehensive Psychiatry*, 36: 218–23.

Bessière, R. (1948) 'La Presbyophrénie'. *L'Encéphale*, 37: 313–42.

Bianchi, L. (1906) *A Textbook Of Psychiatry*, London, Bailliére, Tindall and Cox.

Blancard, S. (1726) *The Physical Dictionary Wherein The Terms Of Anatomy, The Names And Causes Of Diseases, Chirurgical Instruments, And Their Use, Are Accurately Described*, London, John and Benjamin Sprint.

Bostroem, A. (1933) 'Über Presbyophrenie'. *Archiv für Psychiatrie und Nervenkrankheiten*, 99: 339–54.

Broca, P. (1861) 'Perte De La Parole, Ramollissement Chronique Et Destruction Partielle Du Lobe Anterieur Gauche Du Cerveau'. *Bulletin de la Société de Anthropologie*, Paris, 2: 235–8.

Bulbena, A. and Berrios, G.E. (1986) 'Pseudodementia: Facts and Figures'. *British Journal of Psychiatry*, 148: 87–94.

Burger-Prinz, H. and Jacob, H. (1938) 'Anatomische und klinische Studien zur senilen Demenz'. *Zeitschrift für die gesamte Neurologie und Psychiatrie*, 161: 538–43.

Calmeil, L.F. (1835) 'Démence'. In *Dictionaire de Médicine on Repertoire General des Sciences Médicales*, 2nd. edition, Paris, Bechet, pp.70–85.

Caron, M. (1934) *Etude Clinique De La Maladie De Pick*, Paris, Vigot Fréres.

Charcot, J.M. (1881) *Clinical Lectures on Senile and Chronic Diseases*, London, The New Sydenham Society.

Code Napoléon (1808) *Edition Originale et Seule Officielle*, Paris, L'Imprimerie Impériale.

Cohen, G.D. (1983) 'Historical Views and Evolution of Concepts'. In Reisberg B. (ed.) *Alzheimer's Disease*, New York, The Free Press, pp.29–34.

Combe, G. (1873) *Elements of Phrenology*, Edinburgh, MacLachlan and Stewart.

Cotard, J. (1882) 'Du délire des negations'. *Archives de Neurologie*, 4: 152–70; 282–96.

Crichton-Browne, J. (1874) 'Senile Dementia'. *British Medical Journal*; i: 601–3; 640–3.

DeFelipe, J. and Jones, E.G. (eds.) (1988) *Cajal on the Cerebral Cortex. An Annotated Translation of the Complete Writings*, Oxford, Oxford University Press.

Diderot and d'Alembert (eds.) (1765) *Encyclopédie ou Dictionnaire Raisonné des Sciences, des Arts et des Métieres, par une Societé de Gens de Lettres*, vol.4, Paris, Briasson, David; Le Breton, Durand, pp.807–8.

Dumas, G. (1894) *Les États Intellectuels dans la mélancolie*, Paris, Alcan.

Durand-Fardel, M. (1843) *Traité du Ramollissement du Cerveau*, Paris, Baillière.

Esquirol, E. (1805) *Des Passions*, Paris, Didot Jeune.

Esquirol, E. (1814) 'Démence'. In *Dictionaire des Sciences Médicales, par une Societé de Médicins et de Chirurgiens*, Paris, Panckouke, pp.280–93.

Esquirol, E. (1838) *Des Maladies Mentales*, Paris, Bailliére.

Fischer, O. (1907) 'Miliare Nekrosen mit drusigen Wucherungen der Neurofibrillen, eine regelmaessege Verandaerung der Hirnrinde bei seniler Demenz'. *Monatsschrift für Psychiatrie und Neurologie*, 22: 361–72.

Fischer, O. (1912) 'Ein weiterer Beitrag zur Klinik und Pathologie der presbyophrenen Demenz'. *Zeitschrift für die gesamte Neurologie und Psychiatrie*, 12: 99–135.

Fournier, A. (1875) *Syphilis du Cerveau*, Paris, Baillière.

Fuller, S.C. (1907) 'A Study Of The Neurofibrils In Dementia Paralytica, Dementia Senilis, Chronic Alcoholism, Cerebral Lues And Microcephalic Idiocy'. *American Journal of Insanity*, 63: 415–68.

Fuller, S.C. (1912) 'Alzheimer's Disease (Senium Praecox): The Report Of A Case And Review Of Published Cases'. *Journal of Nervous and Mental Disease*, 39: 440–55; 536–57.

Gratiolet, L.P. (1854) *Mémoires Sur Les Plis Cérébraux De L'homme Et Des Primates*, Paris, Bertrand.

Guislain, J. (1852) *Leçons Orales Sur Les Phrénopathies*, Gand, L. Hebbelynck.

Hakkébousch, B.M. and Geier, T.A. (1913) 'De la Maladie d'Alzheimer'. *Annales Médico-Psychologiques*, 71: 358.

Hare, E. (1959) 'The Origin And Spread Of Dementia Paralytica'. *Journal of Mental Science*, 105: 594–626.

Henderson, V.H. (1986) 'Paul Broca's Less Heralded Contributions To Aphasia Research. Historical Perspective And Contemporary Relevance'. *Archives of Neurology*, 43: 609–12.

Jackson, J.H. (1875) 'A Lecture On Softening Of The Brain'. *Lancet*, ii: 335–9.

Jackson, J.H. (1894) 'The Factors Of Insanities'. *Medical Press and Circular*, ii: 615–25.

Kahlbaum, K.L. (1863) *Die Gruppierung der psychischen Krankheiten*, Danzig, A.W. Kafemann.

Kiloh, L.G. (1961) 'Pseudo-Dementia'. *Acta Psychiatrica Scandinavica*, 37: 336–51.

Kraepelin, E. (1910) *Psychiatrie: Ein Lehrbuch für Studierende und Ärzte*, Leipzig, Johann Ambrosius Barth.

Krafft-Ebing, R. (1873) 'De la Démence Sénile'. *Annales Médico-Psychologiques*, 34: 306–7.

Lafora, G.R. (1935) 'Sobre la Presbiofrenia sin Confabulaciones'. *Archivos de Neurobiologia*, 15: 179–211.

Lambert, C.I. (1916) 'The Clinical And Anatomical Features Of Alzheimer's Disease'. *Journal of Mental and Nervous Disease*, 44: 169–70.

Lanczik, M. (1988) *Der Breslauer Psychiater Carl Wernicke*, Sigmaringen, Thorbecke.

Lanteri-Laura, G. (1970) *Histoire de la Phrenologie*, Paris, Presses Universitaires de France.

Lugaro, E. (1916) 'La psichiatria tedesca nella storia e nell'attualita'. *Rivista di Patologia Nervosa e mentale*, 21: 337–86.

Madden, J.J., Luhan, J.A., Kaplan, L.A. et al. (1952) 'Non-dementing Psychoses In Older Persons'. *Journal of the American Medical Association*, 150: 1567–70.

Mairet, A. (1883) *De la Démence Melancolique*, Paris, Masson.

Mansvelt, J. (1954) *Pick's Disease*, Enchede, Van der Loeff.

Marcé, L.V. (1863) 'Recherches Cliniques Et Anatomo-Pathologiques Sur La Démence Senile Et Sur Les Différences Qui La Separent De La Paralysie Générale'. *Gazette Médicale de Paris*, 34: 433–5; 467–9; 497–502; 631–2; 761–4; 797–8; 831–3; 855–8.

Marie, A. (1906) *La Démence*, Paris, Doin.

Meynert, T. (1885) *Psychiatry. A Clinical Treatise On Diseases Of The Forebrain* (translated by B. Sachs), New York, Putnam.

Meynert, T. (1890) 'Amentia'. In *Klinische Vorlesungen über Psychiatrie auf Wissenschaftlichen Grundlagen, für Studierende und Ärzte, Juristen und Psychologen*, Vienna, Braumüller.

Morel, B.A. (1860) *Traité des Maladies Mentales*, Paris, Masson.

Niery, D., Snowden, J.S., Northen, B. and Goulding, P. (1988) 'Dementia of

Frontal Lobe Type'. *Journal of Neurology, Neurosurgery and Psychiatry*, 51: 353–61.

North, H.M. and Bostock, F. (1925) 'Arteriosclerosis and Mental Disease'. *Journal of Mental Science*, 71: 600–1.

Olah, G. (1910) 'Was kann man heute unter Arteriosklerotischen Psychosen verstehen?' *Psych. Neur. Wochenschr*, 52: 532–3.

Parrot, J. (1873) 'Cerveau. VIII Ramollissement'. In Dechambre, A. and Lereboullet, L. (eds.) *Dictionnaire Encyclopédique des Sciences Médicales*, vol.14, Paris, Mason and Asselin, pp.400–31.

Perusini, G. (1911) 'Sul valore nosografico di alcuni reperti istopatologici caratteristiche per la senilitá'. *Rivista Italiana di Neuropatologia, Psichiatria ed Elettroterapia*, 4: 193–213.

Pick, A. (1892) 'Über die Beziehungen der senilen Hirnatrophie zur Aphasie'. *Prager Medicinische Wochenschrift*, 17: 165–7 (there is a translation of this paper: Berrios, G.E. and Girling, D.M. (1994) Introduction to and translation of *On the relationship between senile cerebral atrophy and aphasia*, by Arnold Pick. *History of Psychiatry*, 1994, 5: 539–49).

Pick, A. (1901) 'Senile Hirnatrophie als Grundlage von Herderscheinungen'. *Wiener klinische Wochenschrift*, 14: 403–4.

Pick, A. (1906) 'Über einen weiterer Symptomenkomplex im Rahmen der Dementia senilis, bedingt durch umschriebene sträkere Hirnatrophie (gemische Apraxie)'. *Monatschrift für Psychiatrie und Neurologie*, 19: 97–108.

Pick, D. (1989) *Faces of Degeneration*, Cambridge, Cambridge University Press.

Pinel, Ph. (1806) *A Treatise On Insanity*, (transl. D.D. Davis), Sheffield, Cadell and Davies.

Pinel, Ph. (1818) *Nosographie Philosophique*, 6th edition, Paris, Brosson (first published: 1798).

Rostan, L. (1823) *Recherches sur le Ramollissement du Cerveau*, 2nd. Edition, Paris, Bechet.

Rouby, J. (1911) *Contribution á l'étude de la presbyophrénie*, Thèse de Médicine, Paris, E. Nourris.

Schneider, C. (1927) 'Über Picksche Krankheit'. *Monatschrift für Psychiatrie und Neurologie*, 65: 230–75.

Schneider, C. (1929) 'Weitere Beiträge zur Lehre von der Pickschen Krankheit'. *Zeitschrift für the gesamte Neurologie und Psychiatrie*, 120: 340–84.

Simchowicz, T. (1911) 'Histologische Studien über die Senile Demenz'. *Histologische und histopathologischen Arbeiten über der Grosshirnrinde*, 4: 267–444.

Simchowicz, T. (1924) 'Sur la Signification des Plaques Séniles et sur la Formule Sénile de l'Ecorce Cérébrale'. *Revue Neurologique*, 31: 221–7.

Sobrino (no initial) (1791) *Aumentado O Nuevo Diccionario De Las Lenguas Española, Francesa Y Latina*, Leon de Francia, J.B. Delamolliere.

Southard, E.E. (1910) 'Anatomical Findings In "Senile Dementia": A Diagnostic Study Bearing Especially On The Group Of Cerebral Atrophies'. *American Journal of Insanity*, 61: 673–708.

Tomlinson, B.E. and Corsellis, J.A.N. (1984) 'Ageing and the Dementias'. In Adams, J.H. et al (eds.) *Greenfield's Neuropathology*, London, Arnold, pp.951–1025.

Truelle, V. and Bessière, R. (1911) 'Recherches sur la Presbyophrénie'. *L'Encéphale*, 6: 505–20.

Walton, G.L. (1912) 'Arteriosclerosis Probably not an Important Factor in the Etiology and Prognosis of Involution Psychoses'. *Boston Medical and Surgical Journal*, 167: 834–6.

Wilks, S. (1865) 'Clinical Notes on Atrophy of the Brain'. *Journal of Mental Science*, 10: 381–92.

Willis, T. (1684) *Practice of Physick*, (Transl. S. Pordage), London, T. Dring, C. Harper and J. Leigh, pp.209–14.

Ziehen, T. (1911) 'Les Démences'. In Marie, A. (ed) *Traité International de Psychologie Pathologique*, vol.2, Paris, Alcan, pp.281–381.

Zilboorg, G. (1941) *A History of Medical Psychology*, New York, Norton.

Chapter 2
Dementia

Social Section – Part I
ROY PORTER

Alongside congenital idiotism, medicine has long required some expression to describe fatuity, mindlessness or mental vacancy. Dementia, or, for some authors, amentia, has been the umbrella term meeting the need for a word broadly defining intellectual, memory and personality impairment. Issues relating to the socio-legal standing of those suffering from mental imbecility are considered in this volume in the papers by Deborah Thom and Christopher Goodey, and I shall not here explore them further. Nor shall I cover specific forms of dementia, such as the state for which Emil Kraepelin (1856–1926) popularized the term dementia praecox, that being examined in the discussion of schizophrenia. This chapter will rather focus on a socio-historical contextualization of senile dementia.

Inevitably associated with the dilemmas surrounding death – medical, religious, moral, personal – senescence has been a perennial problem, theoretical and practical alike, for medicine. Is the ageing process inevitable? Can it be prevented, or at least retarded? Is ageing itself a species of (fatal) disease, necessarily entailing impairment and incapacity? Or is ageing a natural state adventitiously but routinely attended by rising illness risks?

Our culture has fostered certain romantic myths about white-haired people full of years, and particularly about being old in the olden days. In the Antediluvial epoch, the Bible tells us, the Patriarchs lived to a ripe old age, commanding all their faculties: Methuselah survived to 969. It was only after the Deluge that the consequences of original sin were fully experienced, and, as the psalmist sang, 'the days of our years' became 'threescore and ten'. In the good old days, legend insisted, the old assumed patriarchal and matriarchal airs and the community respected the venerable. Age has found various eulogists, none more so than Cicero (106–43BC). In *De Senectute* (45BC), he observed that the old man 'does not do those things that the young men do, but in truth he does much greater and better things'; on a similar upbeat note, he also insisted that 'senile debility, usually called "dotage", is a characteristic, not of all old men, but only of those who are weak in mind and will' – though, somewhat paradoxically, he also wrote, '*senectus ipsa morbus est*' (old age is itself a disease).

But these homely fables probably bore little resemblance to pre-industrial realities. As shown by Georges Minois (1989) and other social historians, little sentimentality was displayed towards the elderly in traditional rural society.

Essential to the labour force, greybeards perhaps commanded esteem so long as they could work; but they worked till they dropped, for feudal, peasant societies could carry few passengers, and, except for the leisured classes, there was little concept of 'retirement'. As Alan Macfarlane (1986) and others have demonstrated, the English social structure did not even possess the extended family to shelter the aged; nor did it prize generous sentiments of family welfare responsibility. English 'individualism' meant that the old often lived not with their children but on their own; in times of need they had to fall back on Poor Law provision, and, especially in the nineteenth century, many ended up in the workhouse, the forerunner (and all too often the prototype) of the old people's home or geriatric ward. There is little evidence that the aged were particularly revered. In *King Lear*, Shakespeare offered a none too flattering portrait of the old and of the treatment they received from their offspring. And in Jaques's 'All the World's a Stage' speech in *As You Like It*, the ultimate of the seven ages of man is the worst, 'second childishness and mere oblivion/Sans teeth, sans eyes, sans taste, sans everything'.

Traditional society embraced realistic rather than romantic philosophies of growing old. As proverbial wisdom reveals, it was widely accepted that the old would not just become physically infirm but would grow crabbed and crotchety, slipping eventually into dotage. Affronted by such degrading views, Samuel Johnson protested: 'There is a wicked inclination in most people to suppose an old man decayed in his intellects. If a young or middle-aged man, when leaving a company, does not recollect where he laid his hat, it is nothing; but if the same inattention is discovered in an old man, people will shrug up their shoulders and say, "His memory is going" '. That much-feared condition was described, at around the same time, by the English philosopher and physician, David Hartley (1705–57), drawing upon his psycho-physiological associationist theories. 'The dotage of old persons', he explained,

> is often times something more than a mere decay of memory. For they mistake things present for others, and their discourse is often foreign to the objects that are present to them. However the imperfection of their memory in respect of impressions but just made, or at short intervals of past time, is one principal source of their mistakes. One may suppose here that the parts of the brain in which the miniature vibrations belonging to ideas have taken place, are decayed in a peculiar manner, perhaps from too great use . . . the sinuses of the brain are probably considerably distended in these cases, and the brain itself in a languishing state; for there seems to be a considerable resemblance between the inconsistencies of some kinds of dotage, and those of dreams. (Hartley, 1834)

Hartley's notion of the encroaching sluggishness of the brain was, of course, a medical commonplace. In his *Iatrica* (1681), William Salmon (1644–1713) reported a case of senility and concluded that 'age may be partly a cause of such decay of the intellectuals'. A similar image underpinned later conceptualisations – now discredited – of dementia as the product of 'hardening of the arteries' or arteriosclerosis. Some eminent figures, of course, experienced such a 'decay of the intellectuals' at first hand. Jonathan Swift (1667–1745) – whose *Gulliver's Travels* (1726) depicts Lemuel Gulliver in a ghastly encounter with the senile

Struldbruggs, who do not die but merely grow older and more debilitated – himself suffered mental impairment from middle age, bitterly commenting upon his plight in verse, by imagining his 'friends' gloating over his decrepitude:

Tho' it is hardly understood
Which way my death can do them good,
Yet thus, methinks, I hear 'em speak:
'See, how the Dean begins to break!
Poor gentleman, he droops apace!
You plainly find it in his face.
That old vertigo in his head
Will never leave him till he's dead.
Besides, his memory decays:
He recollects not what he says;
He cannot call his friends to mind:
Forgets the place where last he din'd;
Plyes you with stories o'er and o'er;
He told them fifty times before. . . .

(On the Death of Dr Swift)

Old age thus was an object of fear. All agreed with Edward Young (1683–1765) that, 'there is a great difference between *middle* and *old age*. Hope is quartered on the middle of life, and fear on the latter half of it'. 'In my esteem age is not estimable', judged Lord Byron (1788–1824), who never lived to change his views.

Over the *longue durée* of European history, in other words, there was general recognition that ageing was frequently attended by waning mental powers. Perhaps for that reason, there was no special need for a distinctive medical notion of ageing as a disease, or the prominencing of specific theories of senile dementia. In pre-modern society, old age was hardly 'medicalized'.

That is, of course, not to imply that doctors had not pondered the difficulties and diseases of the old, or that there were no medical concepts respecting senescence. From the earliest Greek writings, medical attention had been accorded to the elderly, and, from Hippocrates to the nineteenth century, medico-philosophical debates raged on gerontological issues. Why did ageing happen? Was it due to some failing of a vital force (*vis vitalis*) or a vital flame, or was it the consequence of what Aristotle (384–322BC) construed as a waning of innate heat? Or was ageing rather a by-product of some mechanical attrition of the parts, and hence an inescapable wearing-out process? If any of these possibilities, then ageing seemed a natural process. Other authors, by contrast, contended that ageing was itself a disease or a pathological operation, responding, perhaps, to adventitious accumulation of body poisons. If such were the case, then hopes might legitimately be entertained for its avoidance or at least arrest: if a disease, old age might be amenable to prevention or cure. Over the centuries, such possibilities underwrote prolongevist projects. In the Middle Ages, Roger Bacon (1210–1293) had speculated, in *On the Cure of Old Age and the Preservation of Youth*, on the prospects of extending life. Within the established traditions of the 'six non-naturals', personal hygiene and dietetics, many Renaissance writers offered advice on health maintenance and expounded regimens for longevity. Amongst notable gerontocomi, Luigi Cornaro (1484–1566) and Santorio Santorio (1561–1636) maintained that abstemiousness, moderation in eating and drinking, and emotional tranquillity could secure a life-span of at least a hundred years, capped by a demise that was a gentle, pain-free, disease-free ebbing of vitality. The Renaissance era also witnessed widespread discussion of the 'fountain of life' and of a possible alchemical or Rosicrucian 'elixir of life'; Paracelsus (1493–1541) suggested one might live to 600.

A slightly different strain of prolongevist thought becomes visible with Francis Bacon's (1561–1626) *History Natural and Experimental of Life and Death* (1623); for Bacon was confident that the new science would discover fresh ways of preserving the vital heat. In the Enlightenment era, *philosophes* like Erasmus Darwin (1731–1802), Condorcet (1743–94), and Godwin (1756–1836) confidently predicted that medico-scientific and intellectual advance would together eradicate ageing, and effect a kind of secular immortality. The nineteenth century saw numerous rejuvenation schemes, not least Brown-Sequard's (1817–1894) and Voronoff's (1866–1951) endocrinologically-based advocacy of testicular implants and glandular grafts.

Alongside gerontological debates about the physiology of ageing, questions were raised in respect of the diseases of old age. Galen (c.130–200), who believed that the decline associated with old-age began around 56, being due, in humoral terms, to evaporation of corporeal heat and moisture, offered many observations on diseases of the old. He took note of chronic arthritis, podagra, asthma, catarrh, congestion of the lungs, apoplexy, paralysis, tremor, convulsions, cough, digestive disturbances, spinal deformities and so forth; and amongst them he listed 'dementia', meaning decay of intellectual power, memory, recognition and speech abilities.

Stemming from the Latin 'demens' (out of one's mind), 'dementia' was used by the Roman medical writer, Celsus (fl. 1st cent. AD) in his *De medicina* and enjoyed a certain limited circulation in medical circles thereafter. Galen's reference to dementia ensured it a place in medieval and Renaissance disease terminology. As Berrios has noted (1987), Richard Cosin referred in 1592 to dementia as 'a passion of the minde, bereaving it of the light of understanding: or when a mans perceivance and understanding of all things is taken away, and may be englished distracted of wit'. That was one of a number of contemporary observations. The French surgeon, Ambroise Paré (1510?–1590), was well aware that ageing was sometimes accompanied by dementia. 'Extreme old age, which extends to eightie, or a hundred yeares', he reflected, 'it is so cold and drie, that those which arrive by that decrepit age are troublesome, harsh, touchy, froward, crabby, and often complaining'. Moreover, according to André Du Laurens' (1558–1609) *Discourse of the Preservation of the Sight; of Melancholic Diseases; of Rheums and of Old Age* (1597), 'melancholike men, which are cold and drie, become old in shorter time'. In the light of du Laurens's association of senescence and depression, it is no surprise that Robert Burton (1577–1640) had much to say about the mental disorders of the old. His *The Anatomy of Melancholy* (1621) suggested that old age was a disease in itself, explaining it in terms of the standard humoral theory that melancholy was the consequence of an excess of black bile acting on the body, particularly the brain. Whereas the principles of vitality were radical heat and radical moisture, black bile was cold and dry; it was thus inescapable that Burton and his contemporaries should link ageing and melancholy as the betrayers of true vitality. In a psychologically penetrating insight, he noted that 'such as have lived in action all their lives, had great employment, much business, much command, and many servants to oversee, and leave off exabrupt . . . resign up all of a sudden . . . are overcome with melancholy in an instant'.

As Berrios (1987) has demonstrated, the idea of dementia became well-established in medical discourse during the seventeenth and eighteenth centuries, being viewed as a mode of melancholy and associated with old age. Nevertheless, it was not until the nineteenth century that dementia assumed any centrality in psychiatric thinking. As incidence of the condition has grown during the last two centuries, medical interest in its cause, nature and treatment has correspondingly increased. There are powerful socio-cultural reasons for such a transformation.

Most basic is the fact of rising longevity, a trend evident from around 1850 and increasingly remarkable during the twentieth century. In 1841, the average life expectation in early industrial England was 40.3 years. This does not, it goes without saying, mean that nobody attained the age of 70, 80, or 90 – ages when senile dementia would begin to become noticeable. What it meant is that such people formed an insignificant percentage of the population, in an era when diseases of infancy and childhood were mighty killers, and childbearing and heavy labour killed adults prematurely. During the last century and a half, life expectations in all developed countries have approximately doubled; in 1988, the British life expectation was 75 years. In some advanced nations, life expectations for women now exceed eighty, with men not far behind, and these are still rising. Tens of millions in the great industrial nations can now expect to live well beyond the psalmist's statement. In 1900 three million Americans were 65 or older; nowadays there are 27 millions (11% of the population); that percentage is expected to double by 2030. Better living standards and medicine have prolonged life, and can ensure survival, but they have not, in general, conquered the chronic and degenerative diseases typical of old age. One survey has suggested that about 20% of British octogenarians suffer from some kind of dementia. The elderly population will continue to grow, and so, it seems, will incidence of senility.

Moreover, social change has made dementia more visible. With the decline of family support systems, the elderly are increasingly herded together in old people's homes, geriatric and terminal wards in hospitals, and in districts specializing in care of the elderly. There they are tended by professionals, who, for reasons good and bad, are less likely to treat them less as individuals and more apt to view them as psycho-medical cases. As old age becomes professionalized and medicalized, dementia's conspicuousness magnifies its growing reality.

These contemporary socio-institutional changes are not exactly new. They mirror and accentuate processes accelerating from the nineteenth century. For it was then that the ageing, and, in particular, 'problem' old people, began for the first time to be swept from the secret recesses of the family bosom into large public institutions: the new lunatic asylums that were becoming ubiquitous throughout the civilized world, in England the workhouse or the workhouse infirmary, in France, mammoth *hôpitaux généraux* like the Parisian Bicêtre and Salpêtrière, which in the nineteenth century could contain, sardine-like, up to 4000 old men and women respectively. Given such extraordinary concentrated institutions, it is little surprise that the specialties of gerontology and geriatrics developed precociously in France, from around 1840, under the promotion of psychiatric doctors. 'The Salpêtrière may rightly be considered', Grmek (1958) has maintained, 'an [sic] nucleus of the first geriatric scientific institution'.

The growth of large institutions standardly encourages professionalization and specialization, tendencies early interpreted by Rosen (1944) and recently surveyed by Bynum (1994). A glance at such processes will contextualize the new nineteenth-century involvement with psychogeriatrics. In the ultra-competitive world of bourgeois occupations, nineteenth century medical men were under enormous pressure to stake their claims and secure their place in the sun. Medicine was asserting its unique vocation and doctors sought tighter professional organization and public privileges. Teaching and research assumed greater institutionalization in the university and through the laboratory. With new ladders of advancement and the expansion of research schools and scientific circles, professional *esprit de corps* rose commensurably, entailing a certain displacement of the patient – newly reduced to the status of an object of 'the medical gaze'. All such changes had profound implications for the image and the treatment of the old, senile and demented.

Becoming over-populated, insecure, yet ambitious, medicine fractured into proliferating sub-disciplines; new specialties multiplied, vying for funds and fame. Obstetrics and gynaecology staked out the terrain of women's medicine, and became linked in complex ways to surgery and psychiatry. Neurology took shape as a specialty and splintered into further subdivisions; pathology branched out on its own, and forged alliances with many other disciplines. Public health came of age, and coalitions between the social sciences and the emergent specialties of organic chemistry and bacteriology forged modern epidemiology. As Goldstein (1987) has shown, psychiatry blossomed, colonizing its own special locations, above all, the lunatic asylum and the university polyclinic. Everywhere, heightened medical division of labour led to rival research schools, national groups, and sub-specialisms vaunting individual cognitive claims: in some cases, basic science, in others, clinical experience, or laboratory experimentation, keyed to the microscope.

In this fierce, dog-eats-dog environment of growth, change and alliance, certain groupings of pathological anatomists and neurologists emerged, notably in France, claiming special expertise in neurological research. Above all, the Salpêtrière became the focus for study of degenerative conditions, affording unique opportunities because of its almost limitless research material. In the first half of the nineteenth century such figures as Rostan (1790–1866), Cruveilhier (1791–1874), Prus (1793–1850) and Durand-Fardel (1815–99) were associated with the Salpêtrière and engaged in studies of the ageing; in 1840, Prus published his path-breaking *Recherches sur les maladies de la vieillese*. It was this tradition that led to the *Démence Mélancolique*, the remarkable monograph published in 1883 by Albert Mairet (1852–1935).

Mairet shared the general neuropathological aim of mapping the distinct varieties of neurological abnormalities, but his special claim to distinction lay in his claim to have distinguished 'melancholic dementia' from other organic dementias. Melancholic dementia, as depicted by Mairet, consisted in 'a state of confusion of mind of which the patients were aware'; 'they complain of inability to disentangle their thoughts' and 'their memory becomes impaired for recent events'. Charcot (1825–93) engaged in debate with Mairet. Charcot stressed that the typical diseases of old age included senile marasmus, atrophy of the brain, heart disturbances and calcification of the blood vessels.

French studies of dementia became inseparable in the *fin de siècle* era from the fortunes of degenerationist theory. Originally associated with the French psychiatrist, Morel (1809–1873) – who believed that mental illness was degenerative brain disease, hereditary and progressive – and then espoused in the last decades of the century by numerous leading physicians, intellectuals, psychiatrists, moralists, criminologists and politicians from Vienna to New England, degenerationism argued that modernity was morbidly self-destructive in its socio-cultural traits. The elite were amongst the victims of exhausted nerves, because, as illustrious American nerve-doctors like George Beard (1839–83) and Silas Weir Mitchell (1829–1914) argued, career strains in the business rat-race devitalized high-flyers; brain-fagged by stress and tension in the cockpit of commerce, they cracked, ending up nervous wrecks, their psychological capital overtaxed. But all of society was affected. The factory's production-line and its division of labour; the *anomie* accompanying enormous, atomized towns and the lonely crowd; the dissolution and fragmentation of once stable household units, employment, rural communities, and organized religion; the vapid and vicarious excitements of Megalopolis, and its accompanying destitution, alcoholism, prostitution and venereal disease – all these (according to degenerationists) were inherently psychopathological manifestations, that were spawning a degenerate *classe dangereuse* of drunks, syphilitics, paralytics, defectives, atavists, and, in the end, senile dements. Worse still, the interbreeding of misfits and profligates – and it was widely assumed that degenerates, driven by perverted sexual appetites and lacking self-control, might procreate disproportionately – would lead, over the generations, to the swamping of the healthy by the residuum. Society would grow more disgenic through internal psycho-physiological decay. The perfect proof of such a view appeared the senile individual. Through the analogy of ontogeny recapitulating phylogeny, such a person was said to have undergone in a single lifetime the deterioration processes society itself was believed to suffer over the course of many. Such parallels were thought especially plausible because so many dements were judged to be suffering from the consequences of tertiary syphilis or general paresis. If melancholy were a characteristic stage along the downhill path of mental illness, dementia was its climax, or rather nadir. In the popular mind at least, degenerationist psychiatry seemed to be forecasting that all degenerate roads led to dementia. These were not absolutely new ideas in the *fin de siecle*. Esquirol (1772–1840) had contended that depression 'degenerates not infrequently into dementia', while his English follower, James Cowles Prichard (1786–1848) maintained that 'senile decay is occasionally the consequence of various disorders affecting the brain, such as long continued mania, or melancholia'. But the theory and mood of degenerationism, allied to the dark side of evolution, imparted after the 1860s a special gloom to such convictions. Influenced by

Morel, Henry Maudsley (1835–1918) saw dementia as rampant, interpreting it as the 'natural termination of mental degeneration, whether going on in the individual or through generations; and it is accordingly in the great majority of cases chronic, and secondary to some other form of mental disease'. 'Senile dementia', suggested C.P. Pickett (1868–1907), author of *Acute Combined Degeneration of the Spinal Cord* (1907) and *Paresis* (1907), 'is that mental impairment which is a direct expression of cerebral deterioration from old age'.

Towards the close of the last century, in other words, a diagnostic entity – senile melancholia – was 'framed', thanks partly to Mairet's ideas and partly to degeneration theory. It portrayed a condition in the elderly characterized by depression and fatuity. Depressive states in the elderly were taken as evidence for organic deterioration. Maudsley believed that severe depression amongst the old was caused by decay of the brain, prognosticating that 'in no case is the forecast favourable'. A slight twist on these notions was offered by E.H. Douty (1861–1911). He postulated that it was patients exceptionally aware of their deteriorating bodily and mental capacities who, by consequence, developed melancholia. 'Senile melancholia', he judged, '(with very few exceptions) terminates either in the mind's own grave, dementia, or more frequently in the general dissolution'. Through the category of senile melancholia, pessimism peaked regarding the mental and emotion aspects of the ageing process. By 1900, an extremely dismal vision of the condition was prominent, highlighting intimate links between ageing, physical and mental deterioration and melancholy despair. The late nineteenth-century obsession with general paresis of the insane further clinched the matter. Sooner or later, the implication seemed to be, all who had committed youthful sexual indiscretions would pay the price by growing demented. Famous instances were to hand, such as Alphonse Daudet (1840–97) and Guy de Maupassant (1850–93). It is no surprise that institutional psychiatry was taking such a pessimistic, defeatist view. For asylums had been filling up with a never-ending stream of apparently incurable and untreatable elderly demented patients.

Another emergent branch of medicine, however – itself further testimony to medical specialization – was beginning to advance more optimistic views. Certain physicians associated with the newly-developing specialties of gerontology and geriatrics were arguing more hopefully that old age would not necessarily lead to dementia, given proper facilities and treatment; a few even suggested that the condition of the demented might be improvable. In the USA, a key figure in building optimism was the Austrian-born emigré, Ignatz Nascher (1863–1915), the leading booster of geriatrics as a specialty. In his *Longevity and Rejuvenescence* (1909), Nascher proposed (in terms revealing with exceptional clarity the new specialist subdivisions) that 'geriatrics . . . is a term I would suggest as an addition to our vocabulary to cover the same field, in old age, that is covered by the term "paediatrics" in childhood . . . to emphasize the necessity of considering senility and its diseases apart from maturity and to assign to it a separate place in medicine'. Rather poignantly Nascher was personally concerned with psychogeriatrics, since his wife grew senile. His final paper, called 'The Aging Mind', was based in part on personal observation of her progressive mental disintegration. Despite such advocates, gerontology and geriatrics have proved somewhat equivocal specialisms. They lack dramatic success stories;

often tarred with the brush of deteriorating and indigent patients, they have never commanded high prestige.

The medicalization of old age in what may broadly be called 'psychogeriatrics' has given rise to fierce internal and intraprofessional struggles, focusing on the question of whether senile dementia is caused by ageing or by disease. Central has been the conceptualization of Alzheimer's disease, called by Lewis Thomas (b. 1913), 'the disease of the century', an indirect challenge to the degenerationist conceptualization of senile melancholy, with its tendency to conflate ageing, depression, and dementia.

On these issues doubt and dissent were expressed around 1900, as the views of the doyen of early twentieth-century psychiatry, Emil Kraepelin (1856–1926) make clear. Kraepelin was impressed by the linking of melancholy dementia with senescence. Yet he did not subscribe to the denegerationist view. Rather he slotted the concept of senile melancholy into his theories about bipolar disorder, interpreting the life-course after the age of twenty as marked by a growing disposition to melancholy, accentuated in time by experience of failing vitality and inadequacy. Ageing and depression were indeed connected, but this was in part because, with age, life grew more arduous and the individual less adaptable.

Kraepelin did not dispute that depression could be an early stage of senile dementia; but it was not an invariable symptom. When melancholy in an elderly patient was attended by inability to 'retain impressions', senile dementia should be suspected. But he disputed belief that depression inescapably degenerated into dementia. Kraepelin was thus open to the possibility that dementia was not a life stage but a definite disease. That was the idea advanced by his younger colleague, Alois Alzheimer (1864–1915).

The son of a small-town Bavarian notary, Alzheimer received his medical training from 1882 at the universities of Berlin, Würzburg, and Tübingen, and trained in neuropathology at the Städische Irrenanstalt in Frankfurt, before joining Kraepelin at Heidelberg. There, and later at Munich, he offered classical descriptions of various kinds of neuropathology, including Huntington's chorea and general paresis of the insane.

Alzheimer's views challenged the degenerationist ideas of senility popular amongst the French. In 1906, he spelt out the clinical and neuropathological evidence that represented the origins of what we now know as Alzheimer's disease, showing the now familiar senile plaques and neurofibrillary tangles in the brain of a 51-year old demented woman. Alzheimer contended that the dementia common amongst the old was not essential and intrinsic to ageing. It was not growing old *per se* that produced the organic alterations that constituted the pathological state of senescence. Alzheimer also dismissed the idea that dementia was a general condition; rather it was a specific disease.

Alzheimer's position has received support from accumulating evidence that Alzheimer-like conditions occur not just amongst the old but amongst the middle-aged too. Though the apparent spread of pre-senile dementia amongst the over-40s seems to strengthen the case for Alzheimer's disease, the issues involved in adjudicating such claims (is senile dementia the same as Alzheimer's disease?) remains contested, and personal, political and ideological forces are deeply implicated.

One attraction of Alzheimer's position is that it alleviates gloom, by removing the degenerationist assumption that the normal outcome of ageing is some form of senility. Medical imperialism has doubtless also been important, at least, as Beach (1987) and Fox (1989) have shown, in the USA. Battling against entrenched psychogeriatric interests, supporters of the Alzheimer position – not least, ambitious neuroscientists, angling for research funds and prestige – have been able enormously to enlarge the scope of 'their' disease category, through the claim, in effect, that you don't have to be old to join the club. Promoters of Alzheimer's position have avoided being 'ageist': when viewed as a distinct disease, Alzheimer's is not age-specific: all may be at risk. Alzheimerian senility has been recast from a relatively rare phenomenon to what has been called the 'fourth or fifth most common cause of death in the United States'. In medical politics, such formulations have undoubted advantages in struggles for leverage and funds.

Supporters of the Alzheimer concept have been successful in mobilizing an influential lobby in the USA, aiming to raise consciousness of the disease as a major social and health problem. They have fostered the prospect that, identified as a specific disease, research will progress and a cure may be found – views attractive not only to biomedical egos but also to such institutions as the National Institute on Aging (NIA), terrified of the growing problems of an ageing population and its attendant soaring medical costs.

Over-simplification must be avoided. As always in such cases, the alliances and trade-offs between science, healing and self-interest are complex and difficult to unravel. Genuine concern amongst medical scientists to alleviate the plight of sufferers goes hand in glove with individual prestige, fund raising and the launching of research projects. But the growing prominence of the Alzheimer concept over the last half-century appears to reflect at least one deep-seated tendency in the history of Western medicine, the urge to medicalize conditions, specifically by bestowing names upon them. It is a desire seemingly shared by medical scientists, clinicians, governments and the public alike. Once a problem – such as the psychiatric aspects of old age – is called a disease, in some senses it ceases to be part of the human condition and gets turned into a technicality: a paradox is reduced to a problem. Western perfectibilism is gratified (diseases can be cured); professional pride is appeased; and hope is offered to the suffering. Senile dementia presents a telling instance of the alluring gains apparently to be won from the medicalization of life.

REFERENCES

Beach, T.G. (1987) 'The history of Alzheimer's Disease: three debates'. *Journal of the History of Medicine*, 42: 327–49.
Berrios, G.E. (1985) ' "Depressive pseudodementia" or "melancholic dementia": A 19th century view'. *Journal of Neurology, Neurosurgery and Psychiatry*, 48: 393–400.
Berrios, G.E. (1987) 'Dementia during the 17th and 18th centuries: a conceptual history'. *Psychological Medicine*, 17: 829–37.
Berrios, G.E. (1988) 'Melancholia and depression during the 19th century: a conceptual history'. *British Journal of Psychiatry*, 153: 298–304.

Berrios, G.E. and Freeman, H.L. (eds.) (1992) *Alzheimer and the Dementias*, London, Royal Society of Medicine Services Limited.

Bynum, W.F. (1994) *Clinical Medicine and Basic Science in Nineteenth Century Society*, Cambridge, Cambridge University Press.

Comfort, A. (1964) *Ageing: The Biology of Senescence*, London, Routledge & Kegan Paul.

Fox, P. (1989) 'From senility to Alzheimer's Disease: the rise of the Alzheimer's Disease Movement'. *The Millbank Quarterly*, 67: 58–102.

Freeman, J.T. (1979) *Aging, its History and Literature*, New York, Human Sciences Press.

Goldstein, J. (1987) *Console and Classify: The French Psychiatric Profession in the Nineteenth Century*, Cambridge, Cambridge University Press.

Grmek, M. (1958) *On Ageing and Old Age*, The Hague, Monographiae Biologicae.

Iqbal, K., Wisneiwski, H. and Winblad, B. (eds.) (1989) *Alzheimer's Disease and Related Disorders*, New York, Liss.

Jackson, S.W. (1986) *Melancholia and Depression: From Hippocratic Times to Modern Times*, New Haven, Yale University Press.

Macfarlane, A. (1986) *Marriage and Love in England: Modes of Reproduction, 1300–1840*, Oxford, Basil Blackwell.

Minois, G. (1989) *History of Old Age: From Antiquity to the Renaissance*, Cambridge, Polity Press.

Roccatagliata, G. (1986) *A History of Ancient Psychiatry*, Westport, Conn., Greenwood Press.

Rosen, G. (1944) 'The specialization of medicine with particular reference to ophthalmology', Ph. D. thesis, Columbia University.

Willmuth, L.R. (1979) 'Medical views of depression in the elderly: historical notes'. *Journal of the American Geriatrics Society*, 27: 494–9.

Chapter 2
Dementia

Social Section – Part II
TOM KITWOOD

For some years now the category 'dementia' has maintained a relatively stable and uncontested meaning in psychiatry. The accepted general definitions[1] all point to a deterioration of an individual's mental functioning as compared to previous levels; and here they focus particularly on impairments of cognition (memory, orientation, comprehension, judgment, etc.), when there is no 'clouding of consciousness'. These definitions also specify that dementia is associated with irreversible pathological processes in nerve tissue.

The story of how dementia has come to be thus narrowed down is a convoluted one, as the first section of this chapter has demonstrated. Even in its modern and restricted meaning, however, dementia is a far more problematic category than has generally been recognized, and the much-cherished distinction between so-called 'organic' and 'functional' mental disorders is by no means clear. This can be illustrated by reference to four topics: the prevalence of dementia, research on psychological and social factors associated with the dementing process, the rise of the 'Alzheimer culture' at a popular level, and approaches to dementia care. This part of the chapter will focus entirely on the 20th century, and attention will be directed principally to the primary degenerative dementias of old age; here the part played by social and cultural factors is both crucial and readily accessible to view.

THE PREVALENCE OF DEMENTIA

With the ageing of the populations of the more affluent societies of the world, the problem of the so-called 'rising tide' of dementia has become paramount in the planning of services for those in later life. However, despite enormous effort and expenditure, figures for both incidence and prevalence remain elusive. The most-cited of all prevalence studies is that of Kay et al (1964). A total of 758 persons over 65 were interviewed, and of these 6.2 per cent were assessed as having 'chronic brain syndrome': roughly equivalent, in contemporary terms, to severe and moderately severe dementia. Since that time there have been numerous surveys giving prevalence figures among the over 65's ranging from around 2 per cent to 20 per cent overall, and around 1 per cent to 8 per cent for severe dementia (Ineichen, 1987). Only one cross-cultural study with really sound methodology has been carried out thus far, that of Gurland et al (1983) in New York and London. Higher prevalence rates were found in New York than in London at all ages, and for all degrees of severity.

To some extent the anomalies in reported prevalence figures can be explained in terms of a standard empiricist methodology. For example, the samples have generally been relatively small as judged by epidemiological standards, typically numbering a few hundred persons. Refusal rates tend to be rather high, of the order of 20 per cent (although some studies do not report the figure). There is also the fact that no study is truly comprehensive. Those which are based on community survey methods leave out individuals who are already in long-stay institutional care; those which are based on medical and social provision leave out persons who have not yet made use of existing services.

Other aspects of the prevalence data, however, render the category of dementia much less robust than is commonly assumed. First and foremost there is the fact that the criteria for diagnosing a dementing illness are far from clear. Clinical judgments take many aspects into account simultaneously, and involve implicit decisions as to how to weigh cognitive and non-cognitive factors. The standardized tests which are most reliable (Blessed et al, 1991) deal mainly with cognitive impairments, and here much depends on which aspects of cognition are prioritized. Tests which emphasize defective memory (which is relatively simple to measure) tend to give higher prevalence rates, blurring the boundaries between dementia and 'benign senescent forgetfulness' (Kral, 1962). The problems are particularly severe in the assessment of mild dementia.

The interpretation of prevalence data is made more complex by the fact that a person who is depressed may show symptoms very like those of a dementing illness: this fact has led to the creation of the further, and even more problematic, diagnostic category of pseudodementia (Arie, 1983; Ames et al, 1990). Finally, there is the unresolved question of the difference in prevalence between New York and London. Psychiatry at present accepts the possibility that the explanation might lie with environmental factors of a physical kind. It seems resolutely opposed, however, to considering that social-psychological factors might be involved. One clear hypothesis would be that stress and its accompanying biochemical and immunological changes can have a causative role in some dementing conditions. Since these ideas are entirely compatible with what is known in neurochemistry, it can only be a gross prejudice which would exclude them a *priori*.

PSYCHOLOGICAL AND SOCIAL FACTORS IN THE DEMENTING PROCESS

In the current framing of dementia there is no serious dispute over the idea that the pattern of an individual's symptoms is related to his or her pre-morbid personality, or that the existence of a dementia might be 'unmasked' by critical events. To go beyond this, however, and suggest that psychological and social factors might be causally implicated in dementia, is generally forbidden (see, for example, Gilhooly, 1984).

This has not always been the case. Not long after the research which laid the foundations for the disease categories of today, it was recognized that the correspondence between indices of dementia and those of neuropathology was not always high; the most serious anomalies were those persons who went through the entire course of a dementing illness, and yet whose brains showed no degenerative changes beyond those typical of 'normal' persons of the same age.[2] The suggestion, therefore, was made by a succession of workers in the field that neuropathology did not provide a sufficient explanation, and that other types of causative factor should also be sought. From around 1925 to 1975 various hypotheses were advanced about ways in which psychological, social and neurological factors might interact with each other in causing a dementing illness.

Probably the most important mid-century work on this topic is that of David Rothschild. Drawing on his clinical work, and particularly on 'extreme' case studies, he insisted that the dementia sufferer (like the stroke victim) should not be regarded as the passive carrier of a disease process; factors of a personal kind must be considered in every case (Rothschild and Sharpe, 1941). This theme is repeated many times in the post-war literature. Williams et al (1942), for example, presented primary data which associated 'senile psychosis' with a loss or lack of social integration and the means of independence. Wilson et al (1955) reviewed a considerable body of research and concluded that 'senility' has many of the features typical of a psychosomatic disorder.

Oakley (1965), using relatives' accounts, found an association between dementia and the obsessional personality (roughly equivalent, in his terms, to Freud's 'anal character'). Morgan (1965) attempted to use psychoanalytic ideas, suggesting that dementia is a form of defence against impending death. Folsom (1968), the founder of 'reality orientation', claimed that dementia can be understood as a valid reaction to such negative experiences in old age as isolation and disempowerment. Similar ideas were put forward by Meacher (1972), in his study of the institutionalization of old people. A significant conceptual development was the work of Barnes, Sack and Shore (1973), who viewed the dementing process as an iterative generation of dependency and lowered self-esteem, leading to a state of vegetation. Amster and Kraus (1974) found a high incidence of crucial life events to be associated with the onset of dementia.

Some of the work cited here is over-speculative, and some studies contain such serious methodological flaws that they can easily be dismissed, (Meacher, for example, paid no attention at all to the direct effects of neurological impairment). There has, however, been no rebuttal of the case that a full account of the dementing process requires research into psychological and social factors, some of which may be causal. Recently that case has been taken up again. Gilleard (1989), for example, has shown that 'losing ones mind' takes a very different aspect if mind itself is understood as social rather than individual. Kitwood (1989, 1990) has elaborated a view of dementia as a dialectical interplay between neuropathology and the 'malignant social psychology' that often bears down on those who are elderly and mentally frail. Sabat and Harré (1992) have questioned the idea of 'loss of self' in dementia, on social-psychological grounds. The significant point here is that while an immensely powerful research programme grounded in the biomedical sciences has been consolidated over two decades and more, nothing comparable has developed in the psycho-social field, although the logic of evidence strongly requires it. If this fact is to be explained, we must look at the cluster of interests that gave rise to the modern conception of 'Alzheimer's Disease'.

THE 'ALZHEIMER CULTURE'

Twenty five years ago the name of Alois Alzheimer was known to only a small handful of specialists, and the main dementias of old age were generally labelled as 'senility'. Today Alzheimer is a household word, often carrying dreadful connotations; Alzheimer's Disease Societies have been established in virtually every country of the developed world, and in several of those that are fast developing. There is also a world-wide federation, Alzheimer International. How has this extraordinary transformation come about?

The crucial initiatives were taken in the USA between 1960 and 1980, at a time when there was the potential for mobilizing vast resources for biomedical research (Fox, 1989). No additional information was needed to convert senility into Alzheimer's Disease, nor was there a shift from one scientific paradigm to another. It was a consequence, rather, of a set of pragmatic and political decisions, mainly in the attempt to attract funding for research in neuroscience, following the conspicuous success of lobbying around the issues of heart disease and cancer. The 'Alzheimer culture' came into being essentially out of a confluence of the interests of research groups and the concerns of family carers. This fact is reflected in the two types of discourse that still predominate in Alzheimer Society newsletters: the one technical, giving information about research findings, and the other sentimental, describing carers' lived experience.

The neurological interest arose primarily from the application of electron microscopy to fresh brain tissue, where it soon became evident that much new knowledge would be forthcoming. Brain biopsies were needed, and those with a primary degenerative dementia were judged to be appropriate subjects (Terry, 1963). This and other work generated a surge of interest in the brains of dementing persons, and a new research lobby began to emerge. A key figure here was Robert Katzman, who entered this field in the early 1970's. Since there had been only limited success in making senility a focus of widespread concern, he made two crucial proposals in 1974. The first was that senility should thenceforward be re-named as Alzheimer's Disease: that is, taking over the term that had previously been applied only to certain pre-senile dementias. The second was to use epidemiological data to proclaim the disease as the fourth largest cause of death in the USA (confounding the categories 'dying from' and 'dying with' a dementia). In this way the needed focus was created, and with it a new medical-moral panic. In the same year coincidentally, the National Institute of Aging was established. Katzman reiterated his thesis several times in subsequent years (e.g. Katzman, 1976).

A key conference was held in 1977, co-sponsored by the National Institute of Neurological and Communicative Disorders and Stroke (NINCDS), the National Institute for Mental Health (NIMH), and the NIA. It was here, apparently, that the idea of forming a new voluntary organization was first openly proposed, to heighten public awareness and create a pressure for research on the disease that the NIA could call its own. The Alzheimer's Disease and Related Disorders Association came into being not long after; with it the 'disease of the century' began to gain public recognition, and a vast increase in research funding (Lockett, 1983). Alzheimer societies soon followed in other parts of the world. Senility was no longer an acceptable term. Accompanying the new formulation was an implicit taboo on considering the possible causal role of psychological and social factors.

This recategorisation came to provide a major new resource for interpreting life history. The troubles, inadequacies and confusions of human existence, especially in later life, could now be re-framed as manifestations of the insidious advance of Alzheimer's Disease (Gubrium and Lynnott, 1985). Many biographies have been written along these lines (for example, Roach, 1985). The paradigm of this re-framing is that of the life of Rita Hayworth, the former Hollywood actress. The medicalization of senility may have sharpened the work of medical scientists and practitioners; but it has also generated a pervasive (and perhaps unjustified) pessimism, as epitomized in such images as 'the poison that waits'[3] or 'the living death' (Woods, 1989).

DEVELOPMENTS IN DEMENTIA CARE

During the earlier part of this century there were no specific prescriptions for the care of those suffering from a dementing illness. When their behaviour became intolerable they, like others classed as insane, were to be taken into institutions, there to remain until their death. The creation of 'Alzheimer's Disease' as a broad category did little to promote better care practice. According to the new ideology caregivers would attend mainly to physical needs, while standing witness to the sufferer's tragic undoing, as he or she went through the 'stages of dementia' as variously described (eg Reisberg, 1984).

Over the last 30 years or so there has accumulated a portfolio of intervention tactics viewed as appropriate to dementia care. This includes Behaviour Modification, Reality Orientation, Reminiscence, Stimulation, Validation Therapy, Resolution Therapy, Art Therapy, Music Therapy and even Psychodynamic Psychotherapy (see, for example, Jones and Miesen, 1992.) If any historical trend can be observed here it is a move away from behavioural approaches, towards engaging with the dementing person's subjectivity, and the enhancing of his or her agency. All the most recent developments, such as Resolution Therapy (Stokes and Goudie, 1990) have been along these lines. Caregivers, for their part, often seem to live with a kind of 'doublethink'. On the one hand they hold to the disease formulation, with its dire implications. On the other, they use a different, and more optimistic set of beliefs in their actual practice (Roth, 1980). The various intervention tactics provide rudiments of a theory appropriate to dementia care, but no more (Mace and Rabins, 1989).

The oldest, and perhaps the best known, of the interventions is Reality Orientation (Taulbee and Folsom, 1960). Its origins lie in the attempt to rehabilitate severely disturbed war veterans, not in geriatric work. The method as typically used involves the continual presentation of 'correct' information, often of a fairly banal kind, and sometimes actual classes modelled on an old-time primary school. Folsom himself, it must be said, never advocated this kind of one-sidedness, and attempted to address such issues as the patient's general well-being and self-worth. Reality Orientation has been reconstructed a number of times (Holden and Woods, 1988), and as it has moved away from a narrowly cognitive frame the earlier and more holistic emphases have begun to reappear.

Validation Therapy also is of long standing, originating in part as a reaction to some of the crudities performed in the name of Reality Orientation (Feil, 1962). The purported aim is to help the 'confused old-old' to resolve long-standing intra-psychic conflicts, rather as in psychoanalysis. To validate, literally, means to make strong or robust; thus in this context it implies accepting the subjective reality of another's experience, especially his or her feelings. Feil offers a set of specific techniques for those with various degrees of confusion. For a long time it was not clear whether the approach was deemed relevant to dementia, and although the answer is now clearly positive, there has been no attempt to take serious account of the effects of neurological impairment.

Evidence is now appearing which suggests that individuals can stabilize in a dementing illness, and that the stages of dementia are not an ineluctible path (Kitwood and Bredin, 1992); there is even some ground for claiming that a changed social-psychological environment may have benign neurological consequences (Karlsson et al, 1988). However, evidence for the specific efficacy of the intervention tactics listed above is extremely slight. The methodological problems are notoriously difficult to resolve; and where effects do occur, these are attributable as much to general arousal of interest, and greater social involvement, as to the intervention per se. Belief in the efficacy of a specific 'therapy' may rest, to some extent, on observations too subtle to be measured by standard techniques. But also, and possibly more significant, caregivers need some framework within which to work with hope; and this is certainly not provided by the Alzheimer ideology.

THE DISEASE THE PERSON AND THE FUTURE

Even within its contemporary and restricted meaning, dementia is a deeply paradoxical category. The figures on prevalence show enormous variability, reflecting in part the arbitrariness with which a dementing condition is demarcated from 'normality'. Psychological and social factors which, if properly adduced, might help to rationalize some of the most serious anomalies, are excluded from serious consideration. A disease, or a group of diseases, has been proclaimed to the world, but without meeting the accepted criteria of a disease entity: the symptoms are vague, the course is unclear, and the links with pathology are far less robust than medical science normally demands. Tactics in care practice have grown up largely without reference to psychiatry, and carers often hold to two sets of beliefs simultaneously, neither of them well justified by evidence. The present construction of dementia, then, is far from being the direct and logical consequence of biomedical science. It should be seen, rather, as a feat accomplished often in the face of countervailing evidence, and made possible by a unique conjuncture of social interests and economic opportunity. There is a powerful web of social forces which keeps the construction in place. The question now is whether those forces can withstand new pressures, as the century comes to its close: of disillusionment with medical science, of sharper theoretization, of so-called care in the community, and of rising anger with inadequate provision.

NOTES

1 See, for example, the definition of dementia profferred by DCM III (Lipowski, 1984) and by the NINCDS – ARDRDA Working Group (McKhann et al, 1984).
2 This finding has been corroborated repeatedly, and still poses major problems for those who hold to exclusively biomedical views. (See, for example, Tomlinson et al, 1970, and Homer et al, 1988).
3 This is the title of a BBC Horizon programme first shown in 1988.

REFERENCES

Ames, O., Dolan, R., and Mann, A., (1990) 'The distinction between dementia and depression in the very old'. *International Journal of Geriatric Psychiatry*, 5: 195–8.
Amster, L.R. and Kraus, H.H. (1974) 'The relationship between life events and mental deterioration in old age'. *International Journal of Aging and Human Development*, 5: 51–5.
Arie, T. (1983) 'Pseudodementia'. *British Medical Journal*, 286: 1300–2.
Barnes, E.R., Sack, A. and Shore, H. (1973) 'The cycle of dementia'. *Gerontologist*, 13: 513–27.
Blessed, G., Black, S.E., Butler, T. and Kay, O.W.K. (1991) 'The diagnosis of dementia in the elderly: a comparison of CAMCOG (the cognitive section of CAMDEX), the AGECAT program, DSM-III, the Mini Mental State Examination and some short Rating Scales', *British Journal of Psychiatry*, 159: 193–8.
Feil, N. (1962) *Validation: the Feil Method*, Cleveland, Edward Feil Productions.
Folsom, J.C. (1968) 'Reality orientation for the elderly patient'. *Journal of Geriatric Psychiatry*, 1: 291–307.
Fox, P. (1989) 'From senility to Alzheimer's Disease: the rise of the Alzheimer's Disease movement'. *The Millbank Quarterly*, 67: 58–102.
Gilhooly, M. (1984) 'The social dimensions of senile dementia'. In Hanley, I. and Hodge, J. (eds.) *Psychological Approaches to the Care of the Elderly*, London, Croom Helm.
Gilleard, C. (1989) 'Losing one's mind and losing one's place: a psychosocial model of dementia'. Address to the British Society of Gerontology, 10th Annual Conference.
Gubrium, J.R. and Lynnott, R.J. (1985) 'Alzheimers disease as biographical work'. In Peterson, W.A. and Quadagno, J. (eds.) *Social Bonds in Later Life*, Beverley Hills, Sage.
Gurland, B., Copeland, J., Kuriansky, J., Kellerer, M., Sharpe, I. and Dean, L.L. (1983) *The Mind and Mood of Aging: Mental Health Problems of the Community Elderly in New York and London*, London, Croom Helm.
Holden, U. and Woods, R. (1988) *Reality Orientation: Psychological Approaches to the Confused Elderly*, New York, Churchill Livingstone.
Homer, A.C., Honavar, M., Lantos, P.L., Hastie, I.R., Kellett, J.M. and Millard, P.H. (1988) 'Diagnosing dementia: do we get it right?' *British Medical Journal*, 297: 894–6.
Ineichen, B. (1987) 'Measuring the rising tide: how many dementia cases will there be by 2001?' *British Journal of Psychiatry*, 150: 193–200.

Jones, G.M.M. and Miesen, B.M.L. (eds.) (1992) *Care-giving in Dementia: Research and Applications*, London, Routledge.

Karlsson, I., Brane, G., Melin, E., Nyth, A.L. and Rybo, E. (1988) 'Effects of environmental stimulation on biochemical and psychological variables in dementia'. *Acta Psychiatrica Scandinavica*, 77: 201–13.

Katzman, R. (1976) 'The prevalence and malignancy of Alzheimer's Disease'. *Archives of Neurology*, 33: 217–18.

Kay, O.W.K., Beamish, P. and Roth, M. (1964) 'Old age mental disorders in Newcastle upon Tyne: Part I, A Study of Prevalence'. *British Journal of Psychiatry*, 110: 146–58.

Kitwood, T. (1988) 'The technical, the personal and the framing of dementia'. *Social Behaviour*, 3: 161–79.

Kitwood, T. (1989) 'Brain, mind and dementia: with particular reference to Alzheimer's Disease'. *Ageing and Society*, 9: 1–15.

Kitwood, T. (1990) 'The dialectics of dementia: with particular reference to Alzheimer's Disease'. *Ageing and Society*, 10: 177–96.

Kitwood, T. and Bredin, K. (1992) 'Towards a theory of dementia care: personhood and well-being'. *Ageing and Society*, 12: 269–87.

Kral, V.A., (1962) 'Senescent forgetfulness: benign and malignant'. *Canadian Medical Association Journal*, 86: 257–60.

Lipowski, Z.J. (1984) 'Organic mental disorders – an American perspective'. *British Journal of Psychiatry*, 144: 542–6.

Lockett, B. (1983) *Aging, Politics and Research: Setting the Political Agenda for Research on Aging*, New York, Springer.

Mace, N. and Rabins, P.V. (1989) *The 36 Hour Day: A Family Guide to Caring for Persons with Alzheimer's Disease, Related Illnesses and Memory Loss in Later Life*, New York, Warner Books.

McKhann, G., Drachman, D., Folstein, M., Kalzman, R., Price, D. and Stadlan, E.M. (1984) 'Clinical diagnosis of Alzheimer's Disease: Report of the NINCDS – ADRDA Working Group under the auspices of the Department of Health and Social Services Task Force on Alzheimer's Disease'. *Neurology*, 34: 939–44.

Meacher, M. (1972) *Taken for a Ride: Special Residential Homes for Confused Old People: A Study of Separatism in Social Policy*, London, Longmans.

Morgan, R.F. (1965) 'Note on the psychopathology of senility: senescent defence against the threat of death'. *Psychological Reports*, 16: 303–6.

Oakley, D.P. (1965) 'Senile dementia: some aetiological factors'. *British Journal of Psychiatry*, 114: 414–19.

Reisberg, B. (1984) 'Stages of cognitive decline'. *American Journal of Nursing*, 84: 225–8.

Roach, M. (1985) *Another Name for Madness*, Boston, Houghton Mifflin.

Roth, M. (1980) 'Senile dementia and its borderlands'. In Cole, J.O. and Barrett, M.D. (eds.) *Psychopathology in the Aged*, New York, Raven Press.

Rothschild, D. and Sharpe, M.L. (1941) 'The origin of senile psychoses: neuropathological factors and factors of a more personal nature'. *Diseases of the Nervous System*, 2: 49–54.

Sabat, S.R. and Harré, R. (1992) 'The construction and deconstruction of self in Alzheimer's disease'. *Ageing and Society*, 12: 443–61.

Stokes, G. and Goudie, F. (1990) 'Counselling confused elderly people'. In Stokes, G. and Goudie, F. (eds.) *Working with Dementia*, Bicester, Winslow Press.

Taulbee, L. and Folsom, J. (1960) 'Reality orientation for geriatric patients'. *Hospital and Community Psychiatry*, 17: 133–5.

Terry, R. (1963) 'The fine structure of neurofibrillary tangles in Alzheimer's Disease'. *Journal of Neuropathology and Experimental Neurology*, 22: 629–42.

Tomlinson, B.E., Blessed, G. and Roth, M. (1970) 'Observations on the brains of demented old people'. *Journal of Neurological Science*, 11: 205–42.

Williams, H.W., Quesnel, E., Fish, V.W. and Goodman, L. (1942) 'Studies in senile and arteriosclerotic psychoses: relative significance of extrinsic factors in their development'. *American Journal of Psychiatry*, 98: 712–15.

Wilson, D.C. (1955) 'The pathology of senility'. *American Journal of Psychiatry*, 111: 902–6.

Woods, R. (1989) *Alzheimer's Disease: Coping with a Living Death*, London, Souvenir Press.

Chapter 3
Stroke and other Vascular Disorders

Clinical Section
TR DENING

The history of stroke and cerebrovascular disorders is obviously of most interest to psychiatrists in considering the conceptual origins of modern views of vascular dementias. This review will therefore take a deliberately psychiatric perspective and will discuss the related mental disorders in more detail than the more mechanical, hard-wired neurological sequelae. However, to approach the vascular dementias requires some understanding of the development of ideas about strokes.

APOPLEXY AND STROKE[1]

The clinical concept of apoplexy, falling to the ground with loss of senses and voluntary motion (Cooke, 1820), remained stable from antiquity until the mid 19th century. Apoplexy was then redefined in pathological terms as effusion of blood (Jackson, 1875), but subsequently disappeared altogether.

The syndromes produced by strokes, such as hemiplegia and unconsciousness, were recognised by classical authors, and Aretaeus of Cappadocia described the contralateral localisation of lesions and weakness (Schiller, 1970). However, concepts of pathophysiology were less well developed. Galen held that blood was produced by the liver, passing to the right side of the heart from where it either went to the lungs for impurities to be exhaled or flowed across the interventricular septum and then to the brain. At the base of the brain the network of vessels (*rete mirabile*) converted the 'vital spirit' in the blood to 'animal spirit' which flowed through the nerves (Spillane, 1981). Galen (after Hippocrates) attributed apoplexy to the accumulation of phlegm in the cerebral arteries, interfering with the flow of animal spirits.

Anatomical knowledge progressed more rapidly than physiology during the 16th and 17th centuries, particularly with the work of Vesalius, Wepfer and Willis. The identification of the circle of collateral arteries and the notion of arterial circulation enabled the first steps in understanding the origins of stroke. Wepfer was probably responsible for recognition of the importance of cerebral haemorrhage as a cause of apoplexy, and both he and Willis were aware of the relevance of arterial disease and risk factors such as age and irregular pulse (Fields and Lemak, 1989). Haemorrhage remained a dominant concept in the pathophysiology of stroke at least until Rostan in the 1820s, and perhaps even thereafter.

The 18th century witnessed the rise of pathology and attempts at clinico-pathological correlations. Morgagni subdivided apoplexies into sanguinous and serous forms; the former being cerebral haemorrhages, the latter probably including infarcts. Morgagni erroneously regarded the fluid-filled cavities of serous apoplexy as its cause (Cooke, 1820; Schiller, 1970). Baillie (1793; fifth edition 1818) recognised that diseased cerebral arteries were more liable to rupture[2] but he did not apparently consider the possibility of vascular occlusion.

Rostan (1820, second edition 1823) developed the notion of serous apoplexy into the concept of softening (*ramollissement*)[3]. He described a first stage of the illness, with non-specific symptoms such as headache and dizziness, after which apoplexies might occur, generally progressing to a fatal outcome. Pathologically, softening could be classified according to consistency, colour, site, extent and number of lesions. In particular, yellow or greenish softening was typically found after apoplexies. He was not clear as to the cause of softening and did not link it specifically to arterial disease, but he did challenge the view that all such cases were due to inflammation. Considerable controversy followed, notably with Lallemand (1830)[4], but Rostan's ideas proved influential in Britain, e.g. with Abercrombie (1828) and Carswell (1838). Abercrombie may have been the first to associate softening with arterial occlusion, suggesting that it was a process analogous to gangrene, i.e. usually caused by impaired circulation but sometimes by inflammation. Carswell (1838) was ambivalent and rather sceptical as to whether arterial occlusion did lead to softening, but then included a plate of an illustrative case.

Rokitansky in 1840 published the next major contribution, demonstrating the association between cerebral haemorrhage and cardiac disease, notably left ventricular hypertrophy. He also drew attention to the relationship between fatty changes in arterial walls and cerebral haemorrhages, and offered a pathological classification of softening, though he was uncertain of the cause of yellow softening. Schiller (1970) has described how Virchow subsequently transformed the modern view of stroke by emphasising the role of thrombosis and embolism in causing cerebral infarction. Miller Fisher (1951) drew attention to the importance of emboli from arteriosclerotic plaques in the internal carotid artery.

THE VASCULAR DEMENTIAS

The establishment of a concept of dementia arising from vascular changes required not just the processes outlined above but also a relatively stable concept of dementia, which developed through the 19th century (Berrios and Freeman, 1991), with the ascendancy of the cognitive component probably starting with Guislain (1833).

Through the 19th century, the effect of apoplexy on intellectual processes was increasingly recognised. For example, Rostan (1823) and Guislain (1833) listed intellectual impairment among the prodromal symptoms; while Durand-Fardel (1843) felt that such changes were among the most interesting features of apoplexy, and could progress to '*une véritable démence*'.

British and German authors were influenced by these developments. Prichard (1835), whose book was dedicated to Esquirol, advocated the term 'incoherence' rather than 'dementia' or '*démence*', for a syndrome including not just forgetfulness but also emotional disturbance, repetitive ideas, extravagance, impaired judgement and perceptual disorders. Indeed, the cardinal feature of incoherence was the failure of connections between ideas, rather than memory loss *per se*.

Incoherence could be either primary, arising from the agency of excitatory causes on previously healthy persons, or secondary to other disorders, e.g. mania, apoplexy, epilepsy or fevers. However, there was no mention of the connection between arterial disease and apoplexy. Bucknill and Tuke (1858), in contrast, were interested in arterial disease and cerebral blood flow. They felt that cerebral congestion and also lack of blood flow were more important than inflammation. They complained that microscopy could demonstrate pathology in vessel walls, but did not show the pathophysiology or the state of cell nutrition. They considered but rejected the suggestion that small vessel changes might be secondary to primary neuronal disease. Cerebral haemorrhage might result in no mental symptoms or might produce mania, swiftly followed by dementia. Ultimately, their account seems confused, since they also stated that *ramollissement* was not found any more frequently in the brains of the insane than in normals, and there was no excess of cerebral arterial disease. Forbes Winslow (1849, 1861),[5] unlike Bucknill and Tuke, considered aphasia to be a type of memory disorder. Winslow emphasised a range of prodromal symptoms, including headache, amnesia or hypermnesia, melancholy, excitement, fatigue, vertigo, irritability and a sensation of cold. Apoplexy could be related to heart disease, and he appeared to think that the direct impulse from an enlarged left ventricle could cause cerebral haemorrhage. More importantly, cerebral arterial disease caused reduced blood flow because of frictional effects of atheroma and narrowing. He distinguished between acute and chronic (white) softening, though in fact the clinical picture suggested for each was very similar. Softening often occurred as the result of excessive anxiety or mental overactivity, so rest and relaxation were advocated as preventive measures.

In the view of Griesinger (1861) apoplexy (like epilepsy) could, besides paralysis, be followed by insanity; sometimes mania but usually dementia. The resulting insanity could follow immediately after the apoplexy, or later, following further brain degeneration. Griesinger felt that the importance of heart disease had been overestimated, but arterial diseases were much more important, leading to local anaemia through vascular narrowing, inflammation and changes in brain nutrition. Atheroma was common in the brains of the insane, often in the smaller arteries.

Marcé (1863),[6] in an influential paper, contrasted the clinical and pathological features of senile dementia (*démence sénile*) with general paralysis. He recognised that dementia was not an inevitable consequence of ageing and that senile dementia was an imprecise term covering a variety of disorders, but with a distinct range of clinical features. Clinically, there were three stages. The onset in most cases followed apoplexy (an acute softening) or resulted from chronic progressive softening. In some cases, haemorrhage could be followed by good recovery without intellectual decline, but usually there was impaired recent memory, repetitive speech, personality change and motor weakness. The second stage was characterised by further decline, including monotonous speech, impoverished vocabulary, abnormal eating behaviour, and typical physiognomy and gait. At this stage, behaviour disorders requiring supervision or hospital were common. The picture could be complicated by maniacal or melancholic symptoms due to cerebral congestion. The third stage led to incontinence and immobility, with death through cerebral congestion or haemorrhage, or other complications such as chest infections or pressure sores. Pathologically, cognitive symptoms were related to cortical lesions, with atrophy of gyri and atheromatous degeneration of nervous tissue and blood vessels. Senile dementia arose from general vascular disease, leading to reduced blood flow and cell loss, as well as an increased risk of vascular rupture and haemorrhage.

Hughlings Jackson (1875) was also interested in the relationship between cerebral softening and mental symptoms. He argued that softening was a pathological term, describing a localised phenomenon caused by arterial disease. Softening was often misapplied as a description for a clinical picture with mixed mental and physical symptoms. Softening itself would only give rise to focal paralytic symptoms or speech disturbances, and could not cause general mental disorders, such as delirium or intellectual and emotional deterioration. Such general mental disorders could only arise from general disturbances, e.g. of nutrition or blood flow. The relationship between mental symptoms and softening was thus indirect, and either could precede or follow the other. Later mental symptoms, diminished abstract reasoning and 'sense of justice' (personality change), were often related to subsequent brain atrophy.

By the 1870s, arterial disease, and in particular occlusion rather than haemorrhage, was seen as the principal cause of senile dementia. For example, Crichton Browne (1874) found atheromatous changes in 75 per cent of cases, and attributed aetiological significance to the impeded blood supply. As to the cause of dementia in the remainder, he was non-committal, describing 'diminished functional activity' but offering no explanation of the term. Thus, the syndrome of senile dementia had apparently heterogeneous (vascular and presumably degenerative) aetiology. However, if an apoplectic stroke then occurred, the case was classified as having an organic dementia (organic here meaning focal structural damage).

However, the term apoplectic dementia (démence apoplectique) seems to have originated with Ball and Chambard (1881), who described apoplexies of organic origin caused by haemorrhage, softening or tumour, almost always followed by cognitive impairment. They also followed Rostan by emphasising prodromal symptoms such as headache, vertigo, drowsiness and hallucinations. These were followed by features of senile dementia with agitation or incongruous acts, and then later by the apoplectic attack, followed by further intellectual decline. Very rarely, cases had preserved intelligence even after an apoplexy. Ball and Chambard also described laterality effects, left hemisphere lesions producing more intellectual and emotional disturbance (discussed further by Nicolson, this volume).

As German psychiatry moved into the ascendancy, the work of Alzheimer and Binswanger was crucial. Binswanger (1895) approached the field from the investigation of 'general progressive paralysis' (allgemeine progressive Paralyse). This he regarded as heterogeneous with no pathognomonic features, and he distinguished two categories: subcortical encephalitis[7] and atheromatous degeneration of the brain. Alzheimer (1895)[8] borrowed the French picture in describing 12 cases of 'arteriosclerotic atrophy'. Prodromal symptoms (headache, irritability, fatigue, dizziness) were often followed by impaired memory, or cases could present straightaway with apoplexy, leading to typical mental and physical changes. In two later papers Alzheimer (1899 and 1902) developed a four-part classification of arteriosclerotic cerebral disorders. In addition to arteriosclerotic atrophy and subcortical encephalitis, he proposed perivascular gliosis and senile cortical devastation (Rindenverdung: a combination of senile and arteriosclerotic changes). Although Alzheimer claimed that each of the four entities had its own distinct clinical and pathological picture, the latter two were defined pathologically and do not seem to have caught on. Subcortical encephalitis has since had fluctuating fortunes. The most penetrating criticism of arteriosclerotic dementia was by von Olah (Marr, 1910), who argued that it was wrong to give an anatomical term to a clinically-defined disease and that the relationship between the symptoms and cerebral arteriosclerosis was too inconsistent to infer causation.

After Ball, and especially after Alzheimer, two effects occurred. Firstly, the demarcation of apoplectic/arteriosclerotic dementia allowed senile dementia to pursue a non-vascular course. This was assisted by the division of old age mental disorders (senile psychoses) into dementia proper and the late-life forms of other states such as melancholia and mania. It was convincingly argued (Walton, 1912) that these latter disorders were not at all related to arteriosclerosis.

Secondly, it is possible to derive either one or two syndromes from Ball's apoplectic dementia or Alzheimer's arteriosclerotic atrophy. The subdivision occurs if cases with prodromal symptoms are viewed as distinct from those presenting with the onset of apoplexies. These descriptions are somewhat ambiguous as to whether the prodroma could occur without frank apoplexies.

VASCULAR DEMENTIAS: BINARY AND UNITARY VIEWS

The binary view of apoplectic dementia was represented for example by Ballet (1903) in a discussion of organic dementias (*démences organiques*). Organic dementias were to be distinguished from those of toxic, psychoneurotic and psychotic origin, and there were two main subtypes: localised and diffuse encephalopathies. Localised forms included haemorrhage and softening, tumours, abscesses, gummas, (multiple) sclerosis and diffuse meningo-encephalitis; whereas diffuse forms included all forms of cerebral arteriopathy including senile dementia. Senile dementia, 'the clinical expression of the atrophic involution of the nervous system in the decline of life' was characterised by atheroma of the cerebral arteries, fatty degeneration of capillaries and diffuse atrophy of cortical cells. Usually, senile dementia had an insidious onset, with a slow progressive course, though more rapid evolution with somatic symptoms also occurred. Important features were poor memory, irritability, insomnia and daytime drowsiness, apathy and nocturnal agitation.

Similarly, Ziehen (1911), in an influential account, distinguished between senile, arteriosclerotic and apoplectic forms of dementia (other types including meningitic, toxic, traumatic, vesanic, epileptic and hebephrenic or précoce). Senile dementia was due to senile involution, resulting directly from loss of neurones or indirectly from disease of cerebral blood vessels. The frequency of generalised arteriosclerosis and heart disease in dementia sufferers, and of strokes in their relatives, were emphasised. Therefore, for Ziehen, senile dementia was often, but not always, of vascular origin. However, it differed from arteriosclerotic dementia because, in senile dementia, there was also a direct loss of grey matter independent of arteriosclerosis. The clinical picture in arteriosclerotic dementia differed subtly from senile dementia, but headaches, vertigo, tinnitus and feelings of physical and mental weakness were more common with arteriosclerosis. Other mental symptoms were also prominent, notably depression with hypochondriacal features and anxiety. Severe cases could develop delirious (*délirantes*) states with delusions, hallucinations and disorientation. Overall, the degree of cognitive impairment was less severe than in senile dementia. The apoplectic forms of dementia belonged to the group of dementias arising from localised lesions.[9]

Thus, Ziehen conceived of a senile dementia, not solely vascular in nature, and distinct forms of arteriosclerotic and apoplectic dementia. Subsequent authors do not seem to have pursued the subtle distinction he made between haemorrhagic, thrombotic and embolic dementias. A later example of a binary view of vascular dementias was provided by Wiersma (1930), writing about the psychology of dementia. He did not seem to regard senile dementia as due to vascular disease. In discussing arteriosclerotic dementia, he emphasised the importance of neurasthenic symptoms (fatigue, irritability, insomnia), also depression and preserved insight in the face of memory loss. The course of the illness was progressive with frequent deteriorations due to (slight) haemorrhages or thromboses. However, apoplectic dementia could arise either without this preliminary stage or else as the result of a larger apoplexy superimposed on the arteriosclerotic picture. Apoplectic dementia was characterised clinically by emotionalism and focal neurological signs such as aphasia.

Kinnier Wilson (Wilson and Bruce, 1954) used an earlier term 'cerebral arteriosclerosis' (attributed by Ziehen (1911) to Dupré). He did not believe that arterial disease accounted for the whole of senile dementia, as there was an inconstant relationship between the degree of vascular pathology and the degree of senility. Wilson distinguished between early and advanced (severe) forms of the disease. The early picture ('arteriopathic neurasthenia') included such symptoms as headache, giddiness, fatigue, somnolence, impaired memory, irritability and emotional overaction. Focal symptoms, usually apoplectiform attacks, could occur, but often never did. The severe/advanced form was more rapidly progressive, with changes in personality and behaviour including confusion, excitement, restlessness and wandering, and delusions. Hypochondriacal and suicidal preoccupations were said to be common, and focal neurological symptoms and signs were to be expected. The two forms thus corresponded to the notion of separate arteriosclerotic and apoplectic syndromes.

In addition, Wilson (echoing Hughlings Jackson) offered perceptive criticism of the relationship between lesions and symptoms in cerebral arteriosclerosis, arguing that vascular narrowing, ischaemia or diminished blood flow could not be the sole causes. He suggested that those toxic factors which lead to generalised arterial disease might also directly affect neurones, and that secondary factors such as renal failure might also contribute.

What I have referred to as the binary view of vascular dementias was largely a European perspective, directly reproducing the views of Alzheimer for about half a century, but with little empirical data in its support. It is also worth noting that, although the second edition of Wilson's Neurology appeared as late as 1954, it was largely written during Wilson's lifetime, i.e. before 1937; and was only completed by his son-in-law acting as amanuensis. In other words, this account probably reflects a dated perspective.

An alternative theme can be traced which makes no subdivision of vascular dementias. This unitary view was initially largely American, and continued via English language journals. For example, Southard (1910) studied 42 cases dying with a clinical diagnosis of senile dementia. His main interest was in cerebral atrophy rather than arteriosclerosis, but all cases had some degree of cerebro-vascular disease. However, in only 20 cases, those with sclerosis of terminal arteries, was the arteriosclerosis considered significant. There was no attempt to subdivide cases with arteriosclerotic dementia. Furthermore, Southard's view of senile dementia was that it was caused either by general visceral atrophy or by specific metabolic or toxic disease affecting brain tissue, rather than by vascular disease. He quoted Alzheimer as favouring this stance.

Barrett (1913) published an important description of cerebral arteriosclerosis, in which he clearly regarded post-apoplectic and arteriosclerotic dementias as synonyms. He set out the Alzheimer classification of the four clinico-pathological types, but qualified it by stating that pure forms were uncommon owing to the variability of focal lesions. He then described the clinical syptomatology as a unity. The predominant features were progressive cognitive impairment, espe-cially memory loss, with focal neurological disturbances. Onset was generally gradual; even when an apoplexy occurred early, some evidence of previous mental symptoms could be found. Fatigue, emotional lability, character change, irrita-bility, episodes of confusion and preserved insight were common. Somatic symptoms, notably headache and dizziness were also emphasised. This symptom-complex has remained influential to the present day, except the notion of mental changes predating stroke, which has fallen from favour.

Barrett's influence upon Rothschild (1941) is obvious. Rothschild published a series of articles based on clinico-pathological studies of dementia between 1934 and 1947. His views on the differentiation of senile and arteriosclerotic psychoses (dementia) were summarised in a paper of 1941, comparing 31 cases of senile dementia with 29 cases of arteriosclerotic dementia. Only one clinical syndrome of arteriosclerotic dementia was described, characterised by early symptoms such as headache, dizziness, convulsions and apoplexies, with com-plaints of weakness, fatigue and somatic discomfort. Emotional lability and sudden episodes of confusion were common. In arteriosclerotic dementia the onset was more likely to be acute or subacute than in senile dementia, and life expectancy was also somewhat shorter. Rothschild pointed out that the patho-logy often showed evidence of both disease processes, but that the clinical picture was not usually mixed in this way. He was also impressed by the frequency of cardiac hypertrophy in cases of arteriosclerosis, which he took (in keeping with psychobiological and psychosomatic influences) as evidence of a connection between cardiac and psychological robustness (Rothschild, 1942).

These New England views of arteriosclerotic dementia were re-imported to Europe by Mayer-Gross in a review of Recent Progress in Psychiatry, though this author was understandably sceptical about the psychobiological theorising. Roth (1950) also had a unitary view of arteriosclerotic psychosis. The Mayer-Gross textbook (third edition edited by Slater and Roth, 1969) was used as the basis for the symptom-complex of multi-infarct dementia (Hachinski et al, 1974 and 1975), which superseded arteriosclerotic dementia from the mid 1970s.

Multi-infarct dementia was based on the view that all vascular dementia was a question of strokes, and that there was no evidence for general ischaemia or 'toxic' processes. Its originators were critical of the vague diagnostic criteria for arteriosclerotic dementia, and generated the Hachinski Ischaemic Scale, a clinical instrument for the differentiation of multi-infarct and degenerative dementias. The scale was probably more reliable than what preceded it, but more recently its psychometric properties and validity have been called into question (Dening and Berrios, 1992).

The concept of multi-infarct dementia rested on its historical base in a strangely hybrid way. By rejecting all non-stroke contributions, it was therefore in line with older formulations of apoplectic dementia, e.g. the thrombotic dementia of Ziehen (1911) or even Crichton Browne's (1874) organic dementia. Yet the list of symptoms for its diagnosis included several elements from the wider arteriosclerotic syndrome (as described say by Barrett, 1913), such as somatic symptoms, depression and emotional incontinence. Some symptoms were included but weighted in opposing directions, e.g. Rothschild (1941) felt that arteriosclerotic dementia caused more personality impairment than did senile dementia, and Barrett (1913) stressed the usually gradual onset of arteriosclerotic dementia. In effect, Hachinski and colleagues managed to entangle the concept of apoplectic dementia with the symptom complex of arteriosclerotic dementia. Clearly strokes and focal neurological features are related to multi-infarct dementia, but the significance of the other 'arteriosclerotic' features was much less clear.

CONTEMPORARY PLURALISM

More recently, there has been a softening (pun intended) of the hard-line multi-infarct position, now reflected in official classificatory systems. DSM-III-R (APA, 1987) included multi-infarct dementia as the only form of vascular dementia. One of the four features necessary for its diagnosis was stepwise deterioration, a criterion for which there has never been much empirical support (Zubenko, 1990). The heavy emphasis upon memory disorder in the diagnosis of DSM-III-R dementia has also been criticised as inappropriate for vascular dementia (Hachinski, 1992).

The inevitable movement away from this extreme position was punctuated and stimulated by several notable contributions. For example, Marshall (1988) discussed the possibility of diffuse cerebral ischaemia due to low blood flow, and Erkinjuntti (1987) contrasted the clinical pictures of cortical and subcortical multi-infarct dementia, questioning whether these presentations should be regarded as two disorders or one. Loeb (1990) elegantly criticised the limitations of multi-infarct dementia and considered the need for a new classification of vascular dementias. A Swedish collaborative group (Wallin, 1990) proposed a classification with six subcategories. A similar taxonomy, together with diagnostic criteria for research studies was published by an international group (Roman et al, 1993). Proposed categories were multi-infarct dementia, strategic single-infarct dementia, small-vessel disease with dementia, hypoperfusion, haemorrhagic dementia, and dementia arising by other mechanisms.

The current International Classification of Diseases (ICD-10; WHO, 1992) reflects the influence of these views. Vascular dementia (F01) is divided into six: vascular dementia of acute onset (equivalent to strategic infarct dementia in the Swedish system), multi-infarct dementia, subcortical vascular dementia (which combines such elements as the lacunar state and Binswanger's disease), mixed cortical and subcortical dementia, other and unspecified vascular dementias. Whether hypoperfusion (ischaemic/hypoxic) dementia falls within the subcortical category is not clear. However, it may be this degree of demarcation is excessive as up to 40 per cent of cases cannot be confidently assigned to a subtype (Wetterling et al, 1993).

However, by contrast, in DSM-IV (APA, 1994), the category is renamed vascular dementia (formerly multi-infarct dementia) (290.4), but it remains unitary and is dominated by the multi-infarct concept, e.g. it is described as having 'typically' an acute onset and stepwise course. No subdivision by pathophysiological mechanism is included, nor is this area included in the appendix which sets out areas for future study.

There are thus some signs of conceptual convergence, but the unitary view is still around, and it is unclear how much subdivision can be supported by the available evidence. Also, should vascular dementia be classified according to its pathophysiology (e.g. Brun, 1994) or according to its extent and the location of lesions within the brain (O'Brien, 1994)? The area is important because many of the likely risk factors, such as hypertension, cardiac disease, smoking and diabetes are potentially treatable (Skoog, 1994). Finally comes a proposal to abandon the notion of vascular dementia and replace it with vascular cognitive impairment (Hachinski, 1994). In Hachinski's view, neither 'dementia' nor 'vascular' are entirely accurate: many patients have specific impairments falling short of full-blown dementia, and vascular causes should be subdivided according to the underlying physiological mechanisms rather than considered to be a unitary phenomenon. Vigorous debate is likely to continue into the next millennium.

NOTES

1 This brief, rather linear view of the history of stroke inevitably overlooks the developing conceptual context in which the advances in understanding took place. A comprehensive account requires discussion of such fundamental concepts as the relationship between brain function and structure, cerebral localisation, models of nervous tissue, brain changes with ageing, arterial disease and blood pressure. There would also be several promising avenues for inquiry leading from the main route of the story. These include the history of other disorders of vascular origin, e.g. migraine (Pearce, 1986); subarachnoid haemorrhage; the identification of the syndromes due to occlusion of individual arteries by Foix and others (Caplan, 1990); other, now obsolete, categories of vascular disorder (e.g. cerebral hyperaemia:

Blustein, 1986, Roman, 1987); and the development of surgery and other treatments for cerebrovascular disease (Drake, 1985, Fields and Lemak, 1989).

2 This suggestion did not receive immediate acceptance. Cheyne (1812) could find no cases where rupture of a large artery had caused extravasation of blood. He felt that apoplexy resulted when the arterial impulse was transmitted with excessive force to the periphery, i.e. this was less likely to occur with diseased arteries.

3 The term *'ramollissement'* was used earlier by Cruveilhier (1816), though applied to splenic infarcts.

4 Lallemand managed to write a whole book on this subject without any mention of Rostan at all. Nor was it simply that the views of Rostan predominated easily. Twenty years later, Durand-Fardel (1843) also argued for inflammation as the cause of apoplexy, dismissing the alternative hypotheses of arterial occlusion, senility and scurvy. Although he deplored how Rostan's work had been neglected, he was also sceptical about the specificity or the importance of the prodromal symptoms described by Rostan.

5 The 1849 monograph was the text of a lecture delivered in Brighton. Obscure Diseases of the Brain was originally intended as the introduction to a treatise on brain softening. In the event, it appears that the latter work was not published.

6 Nowadays, perhaps incorrectly, more renowned for his work on puerperal disorders.

7 Encephalitis subcorticalis chronica progressiva by now almost deserves its own monograph. See Förstl et al (1991) for English translation of Binswanger's seminal 1894 paper. The decline of Binswanger's disease after about 1920 may have been related to a lack of clinico-pathological data and especially to the lack of a discernible clinical syndrome. The paper cited here was the transcript of a paper given in Dresden in September 1894, and followed by Alzheimer (1895).

8 An English translation by Förstl and Levy (1991) is available.

9 Ziehen not only distinguished between senile, arteriosclerotic and apoplectic dementias, but also divided the latter into haemorrhagic, thrombotic and embolic subtypes. Cerebral haemorrhages often did not cause appreciable dementia but Ziehen was increasingly aware of subtle impairments in many cases. Furthermore, in some patients, haemorrhages were followed by progressive dementia, although the reasons for this were not understood. Typical cases with haemorrhagic dementia had relative sparing of memory but the 'liquidity of their representations' was impaired, e.g. they were often slow in thinking and mental processing, with consequent 'mental narrowing', though less severe than the apathy associated with senile dementia. Haemorrhagic dementia was distinguished clinically from senile and arteriosclerotic dementia by means of the history: the haemorrhage had to precede the mental changes. Thrombotic dementia was similar to haemorrhagic but more common and generally more severe, more often associated with transient delirium at the time of the event or subsequently at night. The dementia resembled arteriosclerotic dementia, and aphasia and apraxia were commonly seen. Embolic dementia was very rare, and resembled the haemorrhagic form.

REFERENCES

Abercrombie, J. (1828) *Pathological and Practical Researches on Diseases of the Brain and the Spinal Cord*, Edinburgh, Waugh & Innes.

Alzheimer, A. (1895) 'Die arteriosklerotische Atrophie des Gehirns'. *Allgemeine Zeitschrift für Psychiatrie*, 51: 809–12.

Alzheimer, A. (1899) 'Beitrag zur pathologischen Anatomie der Geistesstörungen des Greisenalters'. *Neurologisches Centralblatt*, 18: 95–6.

Alzheimer, A. (1902) 'Die Seelenstörungen auf arteriosklerotische Grundlage'. *Allgemeine Zeitschrift für Psychiatrie*, 59: 695–711.

American Psychiatric Association (1987) *Diagnostic and Statistical Manual of Mental Diseases*, third edition, revised, Washington, American Psychiatric Association.

American Psychiatric Association (1994) *Diagnostic and Statistical Manual of Mental Diseases*, fourth edition, Washington, American Psychiatric Association.

Baillie, M. (1818) *The Morbid Anatomy of Some of the Most Important Parts of the Human Body*, fifth edition, London, Nicol, Nicol & Cox.

Ball, B. and Chambard, E. (1881) 'Démence apoplectique'. In *Dictionnaire Encyclopédique des Sciences Médicales*, edited by Dechambre, A., Lereboullet, L., Paris, Masson, pp.581–5.

Ballet, G. (1903) *Traité du Pathologie Mentale*, Paris, Octave Doin, pp.1244–58.

Barrett, A.M. (1913) 'Presenile, arteriosclerotic and senile disorders of the brain and cord'. In *The Modern Treatment of Nervous and Mental Diseases*, edited by White, W.A. and Jelliffe, S.E., London, Henry Kimpton, pp.675–709.

Berrios, G.E., and Freeman, H.L. (1991) 'Dementia before the twentieth century'. In *Alzheimer and the Dementias*, edited by Berrios, G.E. and Freeman, H.L., London, Royal Society of Medicine, pp.9–27.

Binswanger, O. (1895) 'Die Begrenzung der allgemeinen Paralyse'. *Allgemeine Zeitschrift für Psychiatrie*, 51: 804–9.

Blustein, B.E. (1986) 'The brief career of "cerebral hyperaemia". William A. Hammond and his insomniac patients, 1854–90'. *Journal of the History of Medicine and Allied Sciences*, 41: 24–51.

Browne, J.C. (1874) 'Clinical lectures on mental and cerebral diseases: V. Senile dementia'. *British Medical Journal*, i: 601–3.

Brun, A. (1994) 'Pathology and pathophysiology of cerebrovascular dementia: pure subgroups of obstructive and hypoperfusive etiology'. *Dementia*, 5: 145–7.

Bucknill, J.C. and Tuke, D.H. (1858) *A Manual of Psychological Medicine: Containing the History, Nosology, Description, Statistics, Diagnosis, Pathology, and Treatment of Insanity*, London, Churchill.

Caplan, L.R. (1990) 'Charles Foix: the first modern stroke neurologist'. *Stroke*, 21: 348–56.

Carswell, R. (1838) *Pathological Anatomy: Illustrations of the Elementary Forms of Disease*, London, Longman, Orme, Brown, Green & Longman.

Cheyne, J. (1812) *Cases of Apoplexy and Lethargy: With Observations upon the Comatose Diseases*, London, Thomas Underwood.

Cooke, J. (1820) *A Treatise on Nervous Diseases: Volume 1. On Apoplexy, Including Apoplexia Hydrocephalica, or Water in the Head; with an Account of the Opinions of Ancient and Modern Physiologists, Respecting the Nature and Uses of the Nervous System*, London, Longman, Hurst, Rees, Orme & Brown.

Cruveilhier, J. (1816) *Essai sur l'Anatomie Pathologique en Général, et sur les Transformations et Productions Organiques en Particulier*, Paris, Crochard.

Dening, T.R. and Berrios, G.E. (1992) 'The Hachinski Ischaemic Score: a re-evaluation'. *International Journal of Geriatric Psychiatry*, 7: 585–9.

Drake, C.G. (1985) 'Earlier times in aneurysm surgery'. *Clinical Neurosurgery*, 32: 41–50.

Durand-Fardel, M. (1843) *Traité du Ramollissement du Cerveau*, Paris, Ballière.

Erkinjuntti, T. (1987) 'Types of multi-infarct dementia'. *Acta Neurologica Scandinavica*, 75: 391–9.

Fields, W.S. and Lemak, N.A. (1989) *A History of Stroke: Its Recognition and Treatment*, New York, Oxford University Press.

Fisher, C.M. (1951) 'Occlusion of the internal carotid artery'. *Archives of Neurology and Psychiatry*, 65: 346–77.

Förstl, H., Howard, R. and Levy, R. (1991) 'Binswanger on Binswanger's disease'. *International Journal of Geriatric Psychiatry*, 6: 529–35.

Förstl, H. and Levy, R. (1991) 'Arteriosclerotic brain atrophy'. *International Journal of Geriatric Psychiatry*, 6: 129–30.

Griesinger, W. (1861) *Die Pathologie und Therapie der psychischen Krankheiten für Arzte und Studirende*, second edition, Stuttgart, Krabbe.

Guislain J (1833) *Traité sur les Phrénopathies, ou Doctrine Nouvelle des Maladies Mentales, basée sur l'Etude des Causes, de la Nature, des Symptomes, du Pronostic, du Diagnostic et du Traitement de ces Affections*, Brussels, Etablissement Encyclographique.

Hachinski, V. (1992) 'Preventable senility: a call for action against the vascular dementias'. *Lancet*, 340: 645–8.

Hachinski, V. (1994) 'Vascular dementia: a redefinition'. *Dementia*, 5: 130–2.

Hachinski, V.C., Lassen, N.A. and Marshall, J. (1974) 'Multi-infarct dementia: a cause of mental deterioration in the elderly'. *Lancet*, ii: 207–10.

Hachinski, V.C., Iliff, L.D., Zilhka, E., du Boulay, G.H., McAllister, V.L., Marshall, J., Ross Russell, R.W. and Symon, L. (1975) 'Cerebral blood flow in dementia'. *Archives of Neurology*, 32: 632–7.

Jackson, J.H. (1875) 'A lecture on softening of the brain'. *Lancet*, ii: 335–9.

Lallemand, F. (1830) *Recherches Anatomico-pathologiques sur l'Encéphale et ses Dépendances*, Paris, Béchet Jeune.

Loeb, C. (1990) 'Vascular dementia'. *Dementia*, 1: 175–84.

Marcé, L.V. (1863) 'Recherches cliniques et anatomo-pathologiques sur la démence sénile et sur les différences qui la séparent de la paralysie générale'. *Gazette Médicale de Paris*, 34: 433–5; 467–9; 497–502; 631–2; 761–4; 797–8; 831–3; 855–8.

Marr, H.C. (1910) 'Epitome: What is meant at the present day by the term "arteriosclerotic psychoses"? ' *Journal of Mental Science*, 56: 532–3.

Marshall, J. (1988) 'Vascular and multi-infarct dementia: do they exist?' In *Vascular and Multi-infarct Dementia*, edited by Meyer, J.S., Lechner, H., Marshall, J., Toole, J.F., Mount Kisco, NY, Futura, pp.1–3.

Mayer-Gross, W. (1944) 'Arteriosclerotic, senile and presenile psychoses'. In

Recent Progress in Psychiatry, edited by Fleming, G.W.T.H., London, Churchill, pp.316–27. (also referenced as *Journal of Mental Science*, 90: 316–27)

O'Brien, M.D. (1994) 'How does cerebrovascular disease cause dementia?' *Dementia*, 5: 133–6.

Pearce, J.M.S. (1986) 'Historical aspects of migraine'. *Journal of Neurology, Neurosurgery and Psychiatry*, 49: 1097–1103.

Prichard, J.C. (1835) *A Treatise on Insanity and Other Disorders Affecting the Mind*, London, Sherwood, Gilbert & Piper.

Roman, G.C. (1987) 'Cerebral congestion: a vanished disease'. *Archives of Neurology*, 44: 444–8.

Roman, G.C., Tatemichi, T.K., Erkinjuntti, T., Cummings, J.L., Masdeu, J.C., Garcia, J.H., Amaducci, L., Orgogozo, J-M., Brun, A., Hofman, A. et al (1993) 'Vascular dementia: diagnostic criteria for research studies'. *Neurology*, 43: 250–60.

Rostan, L. (1823) *Recherches sur le Ramollissement du Cerveau*, second edition, Paris, Béchet, Gabon, Crévot.

Roth, M. (1950) 'Problems of old age and the senile and arteriosclerotic psychoses'. In *Recent Progress in Psychiatry*, volume 2, edited by Fleming, G.W.T.H., London, Churchill, pp.379–415.

Rothschild, D. (1941) 'The clinical differentiation of senile and arteriosclerotic psychoses'. *American Journal of Psychiatry*, 98: 324–33.

Rothschild, D. (1942) 'Neuropathologic changes in arteriosclerosis and their psychiatric significance'. *Archives of Neurology and Psychiatry*, 48: 417–36.

Schiller, F. (1970) 'Concepts of stroke before and after Virchow'. *Medical History*, 14: 115–31.

Skoog, I. (1994) 'Risk factors for vascular dementia: a review'. *Dementia*, 5: 137–44.

Slater, E. and Roth, M. (1969) *Clinical Psychiatry*, third edition, London, Balliere, Tindall & Cassell.

Southard, E.E. (1910) 'Anatomical findings in senile dementia: a diagnostic study bearing especially on the group of cerebral atrophies'. *American Journal of Insanity*, 61: 673–708.

Spillane, J.D. (1981) *The Doctrine of the Nerves: Chapters in the History of Neurology*, New York, Oxford University Press.

Wallin, A. (1990) 'Konsensus om demenssjukdomar (I): klassifikation och utredning'. *Läkartidningen*, 87: 3856–65.

Walton, G.L. (1912) 'Arteriosclerosis probably not an important factor in the etiology and prognosis of involution psychoses'. *Boston Medical and Surgical Journal*, 167: 834–6.

Wetterling, T., Kanitz, R.D. and Borgis, K.J. (1993) 'Clinical evaluation of the ICD-10 criteria for vascular dementia'. *European Archives of Psychiatry and Clinical Neuroscience*, 243: 33–40.

Wiersma, E.D. (1930) 'Psychology of dementia'. *Journal of Mental Science*, 76: 1–42.

Wilson, S.A.K. and Bruce, A.N. (1954) 'Cerebral arteriosclerosis'. In *Neurology*, second edition, London, Butterworth, pp.1402–12.

Winslow, F. (1849) *On Softening of the Brain Arising from Anxiety and Undue Mental Exercise and Resulting in Impairment of Mind*, Monograph 2, Journal of Psychological Medicine and Mental Pathology, volume 2, London, Churchill.

Winslow, F. (1861) *On Obscure Diseases of the Brain and Disorders of the Mind*, second edition, London, Davies.

World Health Organization (1992) *The ICD-10 Classification of Mental and Behavioural Disorders*, Geneva, World Health Organization.

Ziehen, T. (1911) 'Les démences'. In *Traité International de Psychologie Pathologique*, volume 2, edited by Marie, A., Paris, Félix Alcan, pp.281–381.

Zubenko, G.S. (1990) 'Progression of illness in the differential diagnosis of primary dementia'. *American Journal of Psychiatry*, 147: 435–8.

Chapter 3
Stroke and other Vascular Disorders

Social Section
MALCOLM NICOLSON

Cerebrovascular accidents are currently a major cause of mortality and morbidity in the Western world (Hartunian et al, 1980). Acute stroke is one of the commonest causes of admission to hospital and, overall, stroke currently consumes more resources from health-care budgets than any other physical disease (Baum and Roberts, 1981; Adelman, 1981). Mortality from acute stroke is about 50 per cent, and, of those who survive the acute phase, about half will need some degree of long-term continuing care (Melville and Renfrew, 1961; Royal College of Physicians, 1990). While the incidence of stroke may be presently declining from a historical peak earlier in the twentieth century (Malmgren et al, 1987; Whishnant, 1984), it is probable that cerebrovascular disease has been a major cause of brain damage and functional impairment throughout human history.

The sudden onset, dramatic effects, and serious consequences of stroke have long made the condition an object of especial interest to physicians (Schiller, 1970; Fields and Lemak, 1989; Quest, 1990). From Classical times, moreover, interest in stroke has been heightened by an appreciation that the study of the condition might shed light on the relation between mental and physical processes and on the nature of conscious action. Several of the ancient Greek authors, including Hippocrates, Galen and Aretaeus of Cappadocia, wrote on 'apoplexy' (McHenry, 1969), leaving careful descriptions of its clinical features and behavioural manifestations. Unlike Aristotle, who regarded the heart as the principal organ of the body and the seat of consciousness, Galen believed that voluntary power and sensation derived from the brain. He, therefore, associated the impairment of those functions with damage to the brain, an opinion he was able to support with some clinical and experimental evidence. Galen followed Hippocrates in attributing apoplexy to the accumulation of phlegm in the arteries of the brain, resulting in obstruction of the passage of 'animal spirits' to the ventricles. A detailed comment upon the effect of such obstructions on the victim's mental state is to be found in the works of the 5th century author, Caelius Aurelianus (Licht, 1975).

During the more recent period, the study of stroke damage and its effects had a central role in two of the historical trends most formative of modern medicine, namely the localisation of disease to anatomical lesions and the localisation of brain function. However, it might also be argued that, despite the social, economic and historical significance of their condition, the chronic victims of cerebrovascular disease have been granted only a somewhat problematic status within modern medicine. It is a paradox that cerebrovascular disease manages simultaneously to be at the centre and 'on the periphery' (Kaufman and Becker, 1986) of health care.

Investigation of the pathological anatomy of stroke is very nearly as old as systematic post-mortem dissection itself, being first instigated by Gregor Nymman, who published a monograph on apoplexy in 1619 (McHenry, 1969). Johannes Wepfer published a more detailed study in 1658. One may trace the roots of our modern understanding of the cerebrovascular circulation in disease back to Wepfer's work (Donely, 1909; Clarke, 1974; Isler, 1989). Wepfer adhered to the Classical opinion that ascribed the powers of sense and motion to the presence of 'animal spirits' in the brain and nervous system. In his view, animal spirits were manufactured in the substance of the brain from 'vital spirits' transported there, along the carotid and vertebral arteries, from the heart. Wepfer was the first author to propose cerebral haemorrhage as a cause of apoplexy. He also suggested that the disorder could arise if the arteries supplying the brain were occluded by 'fibrous masses' or blood clots. Apoplexy, in Wepfer's usage, was however a somewhat wider concept than the modern category of stroke – a circumstance which explains his belief that the damage caused by blockage or rupture could impair bodily function both ipsilaterally and contralaterally.

One of the greatest eighteenth-century exponents of pathological anatomy was the Italian physician and anatomist, Giovanni Morgagni (1682–1771) (Jarcho, 1948). Morgagni devoted one of the five books which make up his *magnum opus, De Sedibus et Causis Morborum*, to the investigation of the pathology of the head and brain (Morgagni, 1761). Many cases of apoplexy are described. Morgagni marshalled much evidence to demonstrate that damage to the cerebral hemispheres produced paralysis on the opposite side, a dictum which he credited to his mentor, Antonio Valsalva. Morgagni prided himself upon his ability to predict the site of the lesion within the cerebrum by consideration of the patient's gross behaviour following the attack. He claimed, moreover, that Valsalva had been able to ascertain, by noting changes in the victim's respiratory or intestinal function, whether the cerebellum was affected.

It was the practice of many eighteenth-century anatomists to pronounce upon what would be found within the body, before any incision was made. It should be remembered that autopsy was often, in this period, a public event, the dissector being surrounded by students, colleagues and even interested lay people. Successful predictions displayed the erudition of the anatomist and thus enhanced his status and authority within the individualistic environment of eighteenth-century medicine (Jewson, 1974; Nicolson, 1989). Apoplexy cases, with their relatively obvious and circumscribed lesions and their generally well-defined deficits, provided Morgagni and his colleagues with material which was readily exploitable in this respect. The evidence provided by stroke damage played, moreover, a central role within Morgagni's general enterprise of locating the sites of disease within the solid structures of the body. And *De Sedibus* formed an important starting point for a further project of localisation, which would not have been possible without the success of the first, namely the ascribing of specific functions to particular sites within the brain.

Relatively little more was added to pathological concepts of stroke until the invention, in the nineteenth century, of techniques of fixing, slicing and staining brain tissue. For virtually the whole of the nineteenth century, scientific investigation of the brain was dominated by an on-going debate as to the mode of brain function – between, on the one hand, the field theorists, who held that the entire brain, or at least the cerebral hemispheres, acted as a single functional unit, and, on the other, the localisation theorists, who held that specific functions are controlled by specific parts of the brain (Harrington, 1991; Swazey, 1970; Leigh Star, 1989). In the first half of the century, the debate was broadly polarised between the advocates of phrenology and the supporters of the more orthodox equipotentiality theories of Pierre Flourens. But in the latter decades, dominant ideas of the nature of the brain and its relation to the mind began to change, from the earlier holistic sensorium notions to more materialist and analytical conceptions.

The first outright opponent of the principle of homogeneity was Paul Broca (Schiller, 1979), who correlated acquired inability to speak with localised damage to the base of the third frontal convolution of the left hemisphere. Broca drew much of his evidence from the brains of stroke victims (Churchland, 1986), as did many of the other nineteenth- and early twentieth-century localisation theorists. Evidence was, of course, also gained from stimulation and ablation experiments upon animals and from human brains damaged by injury and by other diseases such as tumours and infections. Stroke lesions have, however, the advantage of generally being more discrete and more stable throughout the remaining life of the subject than other forms of damage to the human brain (Gardner, 1977). They are also more common. Experiments upon animal brains, moreover, can shed little direct light on the distinctively human characteristics of language, personality, and creativity. Strokes thus have functioned, for neuroscientists and psychologists, as natural experiments on the human brain.

Historically it has always been malfunction, that is to say disease, which has revealed the existence of the various physiological process of the body and thus constituted them as objects of investigation. As Canguilhem (1966) put it, it is only in the loss of the organic innocence of health that the knowledge of health is made possible. Thus brain injury is an avenue to the physical basis of mind (Gardner, 1977; also Sacks, 1985). And much of what stroke has told us about the character and constitution of cognition and other mental activities has been extra-ordinary and counter-intuitive. The scalpel of the stroke lesion has often forced us to distinguish between abilities which would otherwise have been thought of as being so closely related as to be inseparable or even identical.

One of the most famous and interesting of nineteenth-century stroke case-histories is that of Monsieur C., initially described by J. Dejerine in 1892 and commented on, more recently, by Geschwind (1962) and Gardner (1977). In 1887, Monsieur C. suffered a stroke after which he largely retained his intellectual capacities. He was able to express himself, to distinguish objects and persons but he could not read, being unable to recognise letters. He could see well enough in other respects and could copy the shapes of letters, which he appeared to regard as abstract designs. Even more surprisingly, Monsieur C. could write. He was able to compose his own sentences or transcribe material dictated to him – but he could not read what he wrote. He suffered from alexia, print blindness. Such fascinating case-histories evidently tell us something quite fundamental about how the brain functions – even if it is not always obvious quite what.

In the late twentieth century, a localised view of brain function has become generally accepted. Moreover, modern techniques of visualising the contents of the living skull with X-ray computerised tomography, with nuclear magnetic resonance imaging and, most recently, with positron emission tomography have meant that we no longer have to wait until death occurs to ascertain the exact site and extent of a patient's injury (Phelps, 1991). Our ability to correlate functional or cognitive deficit with specific lesions is more developed than ever before. Nevertheless, our understanding of the functional architecture of the brain, not to mention the general principles of its operation, is still very far from complete. Indeed, despite views occasionally advanced to the contrary (Slezak, 1989), how the human nervous system works, and how it adapts behaviour to environment, remain, as Millikan (1984) put it quite recently, 'matters of sheerest speculation'.

Recently considerable attention has been paid to whether and how the emotions and other affective aspects of human psychological function can be associated with localised structures in the brain. Here too the study of stroke-damaged individuals has had a role to play. Several investigators have argued that there is some relation between the site of the stroke lesion and the subsequent affective state of the patient. Gainotti (1972), for instance, reported that left hemisphere brain injury was associated with depressive mood changes while right hemisphere brain injury was associated with apathy, cheerfulness and a tendency to minimise difficulties. Earlier, Anderson and Havnik (1950) argued that the intrahemispheric location of the lesion was important in determining the psychopathological manifestations of brain injury. With the advent of CT scanning, there has an attempt to establish these associations in a more precise and rigorous manner. Robinson *et al* (1984) studied a selected group of patients with single stroke lesions of either the right or left hemisphere and no predisposing factors for psychiatric disorder. They found that the severity of depression was significantly increased in patients with left anterior lesions as opposed to any other lesion location. In addition, in patients with left anterior lesions, the severity of depression correlated significantly with the proximity of the lesion to the frontal pole. In patients with right anterior lesions the reverse was the case. Robinson and his co-authors suggested that their results indicated that lesion location had a graded effect upon severity of mood change after cerebrovascular disease.

It should be noted that these conclusions have not been universally accepted. House (1987) reviewed the evidence and concluded that both the location and the degree of brain damage were only weakly associated with subsequent emotional problems. Depression after stroke was, he argued, largely determined by social factors. However the existence of controversy merely highlights the fact that the precise nature of brain localisation remains an on-going area of research. It is, moreover, in this area of depressive illness that the paradox of stroke is very obvious. The pathological basis of mood change after stroke constitutes an important focus of basic scientific research but yet depression among stroke victims has been accorded relatively little priority as a clinical or health-care problem.

Isaacs, Neville and Rushford (1976) pointed out that many stroke victims became depressed and frustrated and noted that this group of patients received little in the way of medical recognition or long-term support. Similar studies with similar conclusions were undertaken more recently by Brocklehurst *et al* (1981) and by Thompson *et al* (1989). Long-term care for stroke patients has been recognised for some time as being inadequate (Kings Fund Forum, 1988) and psychological and psychiatric help and care would seem to be a neglected area within this neglected area. When Sidney Licht edited his important collected volume on *Stroke and Its Rehabilitation* (1975) he was unable to find a clinician who could deliver a chapter on mental problems in rehabilitation. Recently, it is true, interest has been growing in the problems posed by stroke both to victims and to the health-care services (Wade, 1991). In 1992, two major conferences on stroke took place in Scotland, one under the auspices of the Royal College of Physicians and Surgeons of Glasgow and the other under the auspices of the Royal College of Physicians of Edinburgh and the Chief Scientist's Office. In both an attempt was made to survey the whole field of stroke care – the presentations covered pathology, epidemiology, acute care, primary and secondary prevention, surgical intervention, and economic aspects as well as long-term care and rehabilitation. However, at both meetings, discussion of the psychological or psychiatric problems associated with stroke and of the particular therapeutic challenges that these pose was conspicuous only by its absence. Yet it is a common observation of workers in the field of stroke rehabilitation (pers. com.; Hyman, 1971; Wade et al, 1987) that patients are often prevented from fully participating in, and benefiting from, their programme of rehabilitation by depression and/or other psychological problems. One might also contrast the stroke provision with the psychological counselling given to cardiac patients, who are sometimes in adjacent units of the same hospital. At the moment the burden of psychological caring for stroke victims lies largely with nursing staff, with informal carers (Muller, 1988), and with voluntary and self-help groups, such as 'stroke clubs' (Millard, 1976). But it would seem that many family and other lay carers feel that they are not provided with sufficient information on the possible emotional, psychological and social effects of stroke upon the persons for whom they are responsible (Wahrborg, 1991; Anderson, 1992).

It should also be acknowledged that it is only lately that those observers of the medical scene whose specialism ought to be taking the broader view – namely the medical sociologists – have themselves begun to study chronic illness at all systematically (Anderson and Bury, 1988; Bury, 1991). However, even in the light of our relatively limited knowledge of the psychological and social impact of chronic disease, it is clear that the effects of stroke upon the subjective experience of self in daily life are likely to be very severe indeed. Stroke is sudden in onset, allowing no time for preparation or anticipatory coping. It would seem to fit very neatly therefore within Bury's (1982) characterisation of the onset of chronic disease in terms of 'biographical disruption'. The course of underlying vascular disease may be uncertain, leaving the stroke victim feeling vulnerable to further attacks. Similar uncertainty has been identified as a major source of anxiety and coping difficulty in other chronic conditions (Scambler, 1989). Diseases which, like stroke, produce obvious handicap tend to be potent sources of stigma and suspicion (Robinson, 1988; Hyman, 1971). Furthermore, because of their impaired mobility stroke victims may suffer from social isolation with concomitantly increased risk of depressive illness (House, 1987; Folstein et al, 1977).

Anderson (1988) focussed attention on the welfare of the main supporters of stroke patients and provided sensitive measurements of the deterioration of quality of life experienced by both partners. A more recent book by the same author, *The Aftermath of Stroke* (Anderson, 1992) describes the results of an major interview-based investigation of the long-term experience of cerebrovascular damage, and of the impact upon carers. (This very welcome publication also provides an excellent introduction to the literature on the consequences of stroke.) Anderson concludes that it is the patient's emotional and social behaviour, rather than her or his physical disability, which determines how burdensome family, friends and neighbours find the duty of care to be. Anderson's study reveals the lack of a coherent policy for the support of the carers of stroke patients. He concludes, moreover, that there would seem to be little medical awareness of the need for active treatment of emotional distress among the victims of stroke.

The interview subjects for the Anderson study were drawn from the largely working-class population of the hard-pressed Greenwich health district in London. There is a need for similar studies from other areas to allow a more general understanding of the social condition of stroke patients and their carers to be constructed.

Perhaps one reason for the relative lack of interest in the longer term social and psychological problems associated with cerebrovascular disease is that the prognosis of stroke has generally been regarded very pessimistically indeed. The Hippocratic dictum that 'It is impossible to cure a severe attack of apoplexy and difficult to cure a mild one' may be found more or less reiterated in the medical textbooks of the nineteenth and twentieth centuries. However in the last decade or two, a mood of greater optimism has gradually emerged. This improvement in attitude was first stimulated by developments in stroke care and rehabilitation, which confirmed the possibility of much functional improvement, even after quite severe strokes (Licht, 1975). Some of this improvement was, of course, intrinsic and, thus, largely independent of any treatment. Other improvements were however the result of learning to cope with, and adapt to, functional impairment and could undoubtedly be facilitated by specialised rehabilitation therapy. Also increased understanding of the epidemiology and aetiology of cerebrovascular disease has stimulated interest in the primary prevention of stroke, with particular attention being given to the risk factors of smoking, hypertension, cardiac disease and, possibly, excessive salt consumption.

While surgical intervention, in the form of carotid endarterectomy, has an established role in stroke prevention, there is at the moment no treatment which has been fully proved to be of real value during the acute phase of the disease. Recently however there have been a number of promising developments in this field (Forbes, 1991) and several therapeutic strategies were under clinical trial as this essay was being written. It may, for instance, prove possible to mitigate the tissue damage caused by ischaemic stroke by the administration of thrombolytic agents and/or free radical scavengers. However, if the value of this form of acute stroke treatment is proven and it comes into general use, it will be very likely be highly resource dependent. Implementing innovations in acute stroke treatment will probably demand the setting-up of specially staffed and equipped stroke units, to which patients can be assigned as soon as possible after their attack. These units will require ready access to a number of expensive technical aids, especially CT scanning. The CT scanner allows the physician to differentiate quickly and surely between strokes of ischaemic and haemorrhagic origin. Appropriate intervention is dependent upon this discrimination since the drug treatment indicated for ischaemic stroke is diametrically opposite to that for haemorrhagic stroke.

Cerebrovascular disease therefore challenges the provision of health care in several ways. In this sense it encapsulates a major dilemma of modern medicine, that of achieving a balance of priority and resource allocation between prevention, acute care and long-term care. It is to be hoped that future developments in acute therapy do not merely reinforce the paradox of stroke, that they do not obscure or deny the requirements of chronic patients and their carers. And within the context of rehabilitation and long-term provision, it is to be hoped that patients' needs for social, psychological and psychiatric support, as well as physical care and treatment, are recognised as being central to, rather than 'on the periphery' of, stroke medicine.

REFERENCES

Adelman, M.S. (1981) 'National survey of stroke: economic impact'. *Stroke*, 12 (Suppl 1): 69–78.

Andersen, A.L. and Hanvik, I.J. (1950) 'The psychometric localisation of brain lesions: the differential effect of frontal and parietal lesions on MMPI profiles'. *Journal of Clinical Psychology*, 6: 177–80.

Anderson, R. (1988) 'The quality of life of stroke patients and their carers'. In *Living with Chronic Illness: The Experience of Patients and their Families*, (ed. Anderson, R. and Bury, M.) London, Unwin Hyman.

Anderson, R. (1992) *The Aftermath of Stroke: The Experience of Patients and Their Families*, Cambridge, Cambridge University Press.

Anderson, R. and Bury, M. (eds.) (1988) *Living with Chronic Illness: The Experience of Patients and their Families*, London, Unwin Hyman.

Baum, H.M. & Robins, M. (1981) 'National survey of stroke: survival and prevalence'. *Stroke*, 12 (Suppl 1): 59–68.

Brocklehurst, J.C., Morris, P., Andrews, K., Richards, B. and Laycock, P. (1981) 'Social effects of stroke'. *Social Science and Medicine*, 15: 35–9.

Bury, M.R. (1982) 'Chronic illness as biographical disruption'. *Sociology of Health and Illness*, 4: 167–82.

Bury, M.R. (1991) 'The sociology of chronic illness: a review of research and prospects'. *Sociology of Health and Illness*, 13: 451–68.

Canguilhem, G. (1966) *Le Normal et le Pathologique*, Paris. Translated (1989) as *The Normal and the Pathological*, by C.R. Fawcett with R.S. Cohen, New York, Zone Books.

Churchland, P.S. (1986) *Neurophilosophy: Towards a Unified Science of the Mind-Brain*, Cambridge, MA, MIT Press.

Clarke, E. (1974) 'Cerebrovascular system – historical aspects'. In *Radiology of the Skull and Brain: Angiography*, (ed. Newton, T.H. and Potts, D.G.) vol.2, Book 1.

Donley, J.E. (1909) 'John James Wepfer: a Renaissance student of apoplexy'. *Bulletin of the Johns Hopkins Hospital*, 20: 1–9.

Fields, W.S. and Lemak, N.A. (1989) *A History of Stroke: Its Recognition and Treatment*, New York, Oxford University Press.

Folstein, M.F., Maiberger, R. and McHugh, P.R. (1977) 'Mood disorder as a specific complication of stroke'. *Journal of Neurology, Neurosurgery and Psychiatry*, 40: 1018–20.

Forbes, C.D. (1991) 'Acute stroke care – opportunities for limiting brain damage'. *Scottish Medical Journal*, 36: 163–4.

Gainotti, G. (1972) 'Emotional behavior and hemispheric side of the lesion'. *Cortex*, 8: 41–55.

Geschwind, N. (1962) 'The anatomy of acquired disorders of reading'. In *Reading Disability*, (ed. J. Money) Baltimore, Johns Hopkins University Press.

Gardner, H. (1977) *The Shattered Mind: The Person after Brain Damage*, London, Routledge & Kegan Paul.

Gurdjian, E.S. and Gurdjian, E.S. (1979) 'History of occlusive cerebrovascular disease: I, From Wepfer to Moniz'. *Archives of Neurology*, 36: 340–3.

Harrington, A. (1991) 'Beyond Phrenology: Localization theory in the modern era'. In *The Enchanted Loom: Chapters in the History of Neuroscience*, (ed. P. Corsi) New York and Oxford, Oxford University Press.

Hartunian, N.S., Smart, C.N. and Thompson, M.S. (1980) 'The incidence and economic costs of cancer, motor vehicle injuries, coronary heart disease and stroke: a comparative analysis'. *American Journal of Public Health*, 70: 1249–60.

House, A. (1987) 'Depression after stroke'. *British Medical Journal*, 294: 76–8.

Hyman, M.D. (1971) 'The stigma of stroke. Its effects on performance during and after rehabilitation'. *Geriatrics*, 26: 132–41.

Isaacs, B., Neville, Y. and Rushford, I. (1976) 'The stricken: the social consequences of stroke'. *Age and Ageing*, 5: 188–92.

Jarcho, S. (1948) 'Giovanni Battista Morgagni: his interests, ideas and achievement'. *Bulletin of the History of Medicine*, 22: 503–24.

Jewson, N. (1974) 'Medical knowledge and the patronage system in eighteenth-century England'. *Sociology*, 8: 369–85.

Kaufman, S. and Becker, G. (1986) 'Stroke: health care on the periphery'. *Social Science and Medicine*, 22: 983–9.

Leigh Star, S. (1989) *Regions of the Mind: Brain Research and the Quest for Scientific Certainty*, Stanford, Stanford University Press.

Licht, S. (1975) 'Brief history of stroke and its rehabilitation'. In *Stroke and its Rehabilitation*, (ed. S. Licht) Baltimore, Waverly.

McHenry, L.C. (1969) *Garrison's History of Neurology*, Springfield, Illinois, Thomas.

Malgren, R., Warlow, C., Bamford, J. and Sandercock, P. (1987) 'Geographical and secular trends in stroke incidence'. *Lancet*, 2: 1196–9.

Millard, J.B. (1976) 'Stroke clubs. Their value to patients and relatives'. *Chest, Heart and Stroke Journal*, 26: 46.

Millikan, R.G. (1984) *Language, Thought and other Biological Categories: New Foundations for Realism*, Cambridge, MA, MIT Press.

Morgagni, G.B. (1761) *De Sedibus et Causis Morborum per Anatomen Indagatis*, Venice. Translated (1769) as *The Seats and Causes of Diseases Investigated by Anatomy*, by B. Alexander, London, Cadell.

Muller, D. (1989) *Psychological Effects of Stroke: a Guide for the Carer*, London, Chest, Heart and Stroke Association.

Nicolson, M. (1988) 'The metastatic theory of pathogenesis and the professional interests of the eighteenth century physician'. *Medical History*, 32: 277–300.

Phelps, M.E. (1991) 'The evolution of positron emission tomography'. In *The Enchanted Loom: Chapters in the History of Neuroscience*, (ed. P. Corsi), New York and Oxford, Oxford University Press.

Quest, D.O. (1990) 'Stroke: a selective history'. *Neurosurgery*, 27: 440–5.

Robinson, I. (1988) *Multiple Sclerosis*, London, Routledge.

Royal College of Physicians, (1990), 'Stroke: toward better management – summary and recommendations'. *Journal of the Royal College of Physicians, London*, 24: 15–17.

Sacks, O. (1985) *The Man Who Mistook His Wife for a Hat*, London, Duckworth.

Scambler, G. (1989) *Epilepsy*, London, Routledge.

Schiller, F. (1970) 'Concepts of stroke before and after Virchow'. *Medical History*, 14: 115–31.

Schiller, F. (1979) *Paul Broca: Founder of French Anthropology, Explorer of the Brain*, Berkeley and London, University of California Press.

Slezak, P. (1989) 'Scientific discovery by computer as empical refutation of the strong programme'. *Social Studies in Science*, 19: 563–600.

Swazey, J.P. (1970) 'Action propre and action commune: the localisation of cerebral function'. *Journal of the History of Biology*, 3: 213–34.

Thompson, S.C., Sobolew-Shubin, A., Graham, M.A. and Janigian, A.S. (1989) 'Psychosocial adjustment following a stroke'. *Social Science and Medicine*, 28: 239–47.

Wade, D.T. (1991) 'Epidemiologically based needs assessment: Stroke (acute cerebrovascular disease)'. Unpublished review paper, copies available from author, Rivermead Rehabilitation Centre, Abington Road, Oxford, OX1 4XD.

Wade, D.T., Legh-Smith, J. and Langton-Hewer, R. (1987) 'Depressed mood after stroke'. *British Journal of Psychiatry*, 151: 200–5.

Wahrborg, P. (1991) *Assessment and Management of Emotional and Psychosocial Reactions to Brain Damage and Aphasia*, Kibworth, Far Communications.

Whishnant, J.P. (1984) 'The decline of stroke'. *Stroke*, 15: 160–8.

Chapter 4

Parkinson's Disease (Paralysis Agitans)

Clinical Section
GE BERRIOS

This chapter explores the history of the psychiatric aspects of Parkinson's disease (PD), a 'disease' whose unity has been periodically called into question. The view that PD is but a collection of disorders variously sharing features such as tremor, rigidity, akinesia, and dysautonomy is currently fashionable (Editorial, 1992). Since the last century, this syndrome or 'construct' has been called parkinsonism (Duvoisin, 1987) and is now known to result from damage to pigmented cells in the substantia nigra and sympathetic ganglia. The cause is unknown in a substantial proportion[1] of cases hence the name 'idiopathic'[1] or Parkinson's disease proper. There is no evidence that this group – defined by exclusion – is homogeneous either (Schwab and England, 1968).[2] It could be said that PD is a prototypical construct kept alive by alternatively defining it on the basis of clinical presentation or of low frequency neuropathological markers (Lewy bodies). Unfortunately, the two definitions are known not to coincide: those with the symptoms may not have Lewy bodies, and those with the latter not the disease.

These features make PD into an ideal historical subject as it offers the possibility of separately studying the history of terms (Parkinson's disease, *paralysis agitans*, etc.), behaviours (tremor, akinesia, rigidity), and concepts and hypotheses. It also offers an opportunity to understand the way in which diseases were taken over by medical specialisms. This is the case with PD which, in spite of its clear psychiatric component, has been firmly kept within neurology. Indeed, to maintain the *status quo*, such component was either denied or played down well into the present century.

Paralysis *and* Scelotyrbe *during the 18th century*
It would be difficult to understand the contribution of James Parkinson (after whom the disease was named by Charcot in 1862) without knowing of the medical concepts he used and reacted against. Parkinson called his disease 'shaking palsy' (*paralysis agitans*) (Morris, 1989). At the end of the eighteenth century, the medical meaning of 'paralysis' was wide: Sauvages had defined it as a loss of motion and/or *sensation (Motus aut tactus, vel utriusque, in uno tantum artu debilitas)* (Cullen, 1803, p.23, para. 169) as had Vogel (*Sensus motusve aut utriusque defectus in singulari parte externa*) (Cullen, 1803, p.91, para. 126). These definitions were still official teaching for medical students at the beginning of the nineteenth century (Anonymous, 1803).[3] By 1819, things

had changed little and paralysis was still defined as 'the abolition or weakening of *sensation* and voluntary movement – or of only one of these faculties – in one part of the body' (Chamberet, 1819). Long after Parkinson's death, Roche (1834) still defined paralysis as a 'diminution or total loss of motility or *sensation*'. However odd this view of paralysis might sound to modern medical ears,[4] it is the definition that Parkinson had in mind when writing on his disease.

RE-READING PARKINSON'S DEFINITION

Sufficient information has been published on the life of James Parkinson (1755–1824) to need iteration (Critchley, 1955; Tyler and Tyler, 1986), and little in his political and literary biography will help to understand his choice of words or clinical bias (Parkinson, 1817). His definition of 'shaking palsy', quoted *ad nauseam*, is: 'Involuntary tremulous motion, with lessened muscular power, in parts not in action and even when supported; with a propensity to bend the trunk forwards, and to pass from a walking to a running pace: *the senses and intellects being uninjured*' (p.1).

Two of these claims merit re-reading: 'lessened muscular power' and 'the senses and intellects being uninjured'. Nineteenth century medics interpreted 'lessened muscular power' as actually meaning *paresis* and this caused some debate;[5] after the 1860s, the same terms were interpreted as meaning 'inability to exercise (normal) muscular power on account of rigidity'. Interestingly enough, it is likely that Parkinson actually meant *paresis*!

Likewise, his second claim has been interpreted as meaning that the 'disease' was not accompanied by insanity (injured *senses*) or dementia (*intellects*) (Jellife and White, 1929). Crucial from a psychiatric viewpoint is what did Parkinson mean by 'senses'. An historical – as opposed to an anachronistic – reading of the text suggests that he meant 'sensory modalities' (i.e. functions such as vision or touch) rather than 'reason'. This would be in keeping with the logic of his medical argument, i.e. of his wanting to demonstrate that his disease was *not just another form of paralysis* (and hence involved the 'senses', as strokes often did). Parkinson believed that PD was a *different form* of paralysis characterized by tremor (*agitans*) and festination (*scelotyrbe*) but not by *sensory impairment*: 'having made the necessary inquiries respecting these two affections . . . which appear to be characteristic symptoms of the disease, it becomes necessary, in the next place, to endeavour to *distinguish this disease from others*', (Parkinson, 1817, p.27). Indeed, there was little reason (whether medical or historical) for his wanting to define a physical disease by saying: 'by the way, it is not accompanied by insanity!'[6] This reading would also tally with the fact that one of his cases, the Count of Lordat, *was in fact affected by severe mental disorder*.[7]

In regard to the word 'intellects' it is likely that Parkinson actually meant cognition, for elsewhere he says: 'the unimpaired state of the intellects', (Parkinson, 1817) (p.45). His wanting to deny the presence of cognitive symptoms also makes sense (for the reasons given above), for at the time intellectual impairment *was considered to be part* and parcel of 'paralysis' (Chamberet, 1819, see p.251). Indeed, none of the nine patients mentioned by Parkinson (mean age = 60 years) was reported as having dementia; this would make sense for subjects with early onset PD and with short rate of survival. It would also be in keeping with the suggestion that dementia only began to be reported as a complication of PD after the 1850s, when anti-muscarinic agents were introduced as treatment (Miller et al, 1987).[8]

The right interpretation of Parkinson's claims will have to wait for the discovery of new evidence. It is also a pity that Parkinson never seems to have finished his monograph. Analysis of its structure suggests that it was meant to have *two parts*, dedicated to justifying the two main claims in his definition; in the event, he seems to have completed only the *first part* (i.e. Chapter 2) which dealt with tremor and festination. The second part, where he might have planned to justify his claim about the 'senses and intellects', was never completed.

HISTORY OF THE MAIN SYMPTOMS

Parkinson's interest in tremor and festination (to the detriment of akinesia and rigidity) poses an interesting historical problem. One obvious explanation is that his patients *did not show these signs* (indeed, of his 9 cases only five seemed fully to have met diagnostic criteria!); another explanation is that by the beginning of the nineteenth century, the 'conceptualisation' of rigidity and akinesia had not yet been completed. This seems to be the view of Schiller, who in a superb paper, suggests that the separation of rigidity from 'spasms' only took place after the 1860s (Schiller, 1986; Barbeau, 1958). The same could be said of akinesia (inability to move not due to impairment of voluntary motor mechanisms) which does not seem to have been separated from paralysis until *after* Parkinson's monograph (Ajuriaguerra, 1975).

On the other hand, much had been written on tremor before Parkinson's time; indeed, he used this knowledge deftly. For example, from the time of Galen it was known that there were static and dynamic tremors; during the eighteenth century, Van Swieten called the former *palpitatio* (and believed that it was a convulsive phenomenon), and the latter *tremor* (and related it to paralysis) (Demange, 1887, p.61). Cullen claimed that tremor was always 'symptomatic to palsy, asthenia or convulsions and therefore not be treated of by itself' (Anonymous, 1803, p.338); (Cullen, 1803, p.282). Parkinson complained that although 'tremor has been adopted, as a genus, by almost every nosologist; but always unmarked, in their several definitions, by such characters as would embrace this disease' (Parkinson, 1817, p.2). He then described the natural history of tremor in his own disease: insidious onset, slight sense of weakness, fatigue, and then gradual interference with task such as writing and eating (Parkinson, 1817, pp.3–7).

Up to the middle of the nineteenth century, tremors remained in the words of Romberg (1853), 'the bridge which conducts from the region of convulsions to the paralyses' (p.230), i.e. Van Swieten's hypothesis was still valid. Romberg (1853) included tremors under 'neuroses of motility' and dealt with prototypical examples: mercurial tremor, *tremor potatorum* (alcoholic), senilis, febrilis, and paralysis agitans (pp.231–5). In 1841, Hall re-introduced the term 'paralysis agitans' and (surprisingly early) reported slight delirium and lethargy as occasional symptoms of the disease (Hall, 1841). A few years later, Charcot complained that since 1817 PD had been neglected in France, and went on to demonstrate various subtypes of tremor. He also distinguished between intentional and rest tremor but acknowledged that this had been known to Galen and Van Swieten (Charcot, 1886, pp.158–160). He quoted Gubler's view of tremor as being an *astasie musculaire* and attributed to Ordenstein (1868) the final separation between multiple sclerosis and PD (Cohn, 1860; quoted in Charcot, 1886, p.161).[9] In 1877, Jackson put forward a cerebellar hypothesis of tremor by making use of his negative-positive dichotomy, and suggested that tremor and rigidity were on a continuum:

> in health, the cerebellar influx is fully antagonised; in the early stages of paralysis agitans it is intermittently antagonised – the movement constituting each single tremor occurring betwixt the cerebral impulses; and in the late stages it is not antagonised at all, and there is such a stream of cerebellar impulses that rigidity occurs. We have cerebral paresis with cerebellar tremor; later, cerebral paralysis with cerebellar rigidity! (Jackson, 1931, p.454)

SEPARATION OF PD FROM THE NEUROSES

Until the time of Charcot (Lereboullet and Bussard, 1884), PD was still classified as a 'neurosis'. In practice, this meant that, as Axenfeld (1883) put it (after reviewing all available information on lesions): 'PD must provisionally remain in the class of the neuroses given that it is not characterised by an identical and constant lesion' (p.699). Charcot (1886) thought likewise: 'paralysis agitans is at the moment a *névrose* in the sense that we cannot identify any characteristic lesion' (pp.161–162). However, the notion of 'neuroses' was rapidly changing during this period, and the new science of neurology was being populated by conditions in which 'constant' focal lesions were identified as responsible for motor and sensory symptoms. The rest of diseases remained as 'neuroses' (see list in Axenfeld), *including the insanities*. Physiology offered a partial solution which was to re-define 'lesion' in 'functional' terms, i.e. give up the idea that there had to be structural damage. This change allowed PD (as it did epilepsy) to be incorporated into neurology *without having a 'constant' anatomical lesions*.

EARLY NEUROPATHOLOGY AND AETIOLOGY

Not everyone was happy with the view that PD was a neurosis. For example, Meynert suggested that it might be associated with a disorder of the basal ganglia (Meynert, 1871; Schiller, 1967). Blocq and Marinesco (1893) reported a case of unilateral Parkinsonism caused by destruction of Substantia Nigra by a tuberculoma. Based on this and other pathological findings, Brissaud (1899) also favoured the *Locus Niger*. Lewy (1913) reported the first important series (60 cases) showing lesions in Striatum and Globus Pallidus and described the inclusion bodies which have since carried his name.[10] Tretiakoff (1919) described three cases of encephalitis lethargica with inflammatory lesions in the Substantia Nigra. Gringer (1926) found pallidal necrosis in a subject, with a combination of parkinsonian and catatonic features, who had attempted suicide with carbon monoxide. In the wake of Critchley's 1929 paper, Keschner and Sloane (1931) described lesions of Substantia Nigra in association with arteriosclerotic Parkinsonism. (The more recent history of PD is beyond the scope of this chapter; for this see Rose, 1989.)

No definite views on aetiology were expressed during the earlier period, but psychological causes such as emotional shock and excessive bodily fatigue featured prominently, together with physical factors such as exposure to cold and wet, and wounds and injuries involving peripheral nerves (Bristowe, 1894; Lereboullet and Bussard, 1884).

THE PSYCHIATRY OF PD

A crucial question is why did it take so long for psychiatric symptoms to be accepted as part of PD? There may be various reasons for this: one, that patients did not live for long enough to show them; another, that everyone followed Parkinson's injunction and refused to accept that when present, psychiatric symptoms were actually *part of the disease*; yet another, that there were sociological reasons for such refusal.[11] Be that as it may, it was only well into the twentieth century that it was accepted that PD may be accompanied by personality changes, insanity, depression, and cognitive impairment.

Benjamin Ball and the insanity of PD

In 1881, Benjamin Ball (1882)[12] read a paper 'On the relations between insanity and paralysis agitans' before the Mental Disease Section of the International Medical Congress in London (Report, 1881). Therein, he stated: 'Few reports have been published concerning the psychological complications of Parkinson's disease and psychosis has not been one of them' (p.23). He reported a case from the literature who developed hallucinations following treatment with potassium bromide,[13] and another two with irritability and depression.[14] He disagreed with the view that the association was coincidental: 'I think otherwise; a large number of Parkinsonian patients present psychological disorders extending from simple irritability to psychosis; far from being an exception I would say that a slight degree of cognitive impairment (*perturbation intellectuelle*) is the rule' (p.24).

The ensuing debate illustrates the empirical attitude characteristic of British medicine at the time. Bucknill protested that only 'statistical evidence' could substantiate the putative association, and Tuke stated that the cases reported by Ball were just Kahlbaumian Catatonias[15] accompanied by severe motor disturbance! Huggard (Report, 1881) described a patient of his with both PD and recurrent mania (Ball included this case in his paper of 1882), and Atkins (1882) reported another with hallucinations. Mercier sided with Ball and made the important observation that the motor disorder of PD might conceal the psychological disorder. In his summing up, Ball exhorted the audience to report new cases.

His request did not go unheeded. Parant (1883) described a case with nocturnal delusions, and another with sensory changes that induced the patient to believe that his extremities were larger than normal. In a later work, Parant (1892) regarded as exaggerated Ball's claim that psychiatric disorders were the rule rather than the exception, and suggested that a causal link (mediated by the cortex) existed between the neurological and psychological manifestations of

PD. This view reveals that alienists had to move away from the spinal theory of PD (popular at the time) in order to make plausible claims about the 'psychiatric' dimension to the disease (which most sited on the cortex).

Régis and his classification

The debate continued, and Régis (1906) identified two opposing views: some like Charcot and Brissaud believed that the association between psychiatric symptoms and PD was artifactual; others such as Ball, Parant, Régis, Luys, Roger, and Bechet, claimed that the symptoms were part of the disease. Régis (1906) distinguished two types of psychological symptoms: 'Elementary psychological disturbances and delusional or psychotic states' (p.784). The former included mood disorder, intellectual apathy, hypersensitivity, irritability, asthenia, torpidity, lethargy, nightmares, and deterioration of mental functions; the latter, 'depression with delusions of ruin, guilt, hypochondria and suicidal ideation . . . [the patients] exhibit a dissociation between their subjective experience of illness and its expression [that is] Pierret's paramimia' (p.785).[16] Occasionally, dementia, confusion, oniric states[17] and nocturnal hallucinosis were found. Régis did not consider the possibility that some of these symptoms resulted from intoxication with *hyoscyamus* or *atropine*, the drugs prescribed for Parkinson's disease during this period (Marchand, 1909). Dutil (1903) also supported the view that mental symptoms were important in PD, but rejected an explanation based on degeneration theory, on the grounds that patients improved from their delusions.

Similar claims were made in Germany. König (1912) reported five female patients showing irritability, hypochondria, depression, and short-lived psychotic states characterized by paranoid hallucinatory and melancholic features and suicidal ruminations. In a series of 282 patients, Mjönes (1949) reported that 40 per cent exhibited neurotic and affective disorders, depressive illness, schizophrenia-like psychosis, and confusional states.

The 'Reactivity' hypothesis

Not everyone agreed with the view that mental symptoms were frequent or indeed part of the disease, and (particularly neurologists) favoured a 'reactivity' mechanism. Gowers (1893), for example, wrote: 'The intellect may be unaffected throughout, except by the irritability which usually accompanies the physical restlessness, or by mental depression, which is chiefly the *natural result of the physical ailment*' (p.648). Years later, Wilson (1954) repeated this without paying any attention to the work done in the interim!: 'mental symptoms are mostly limited to depression and irritability, the *natural outcome, perhaps, of an incurable disease*, anything beyond these is to be ascribed to accompanying arteriosclerosis or some incidental condition . . . on the intellectual side there may be noted some bradyphrenia or slowness of thought yet it is probably *more apparent than real*' (p.933). Vulpian (1886) was equally clear: 'Intelligence remains unchanged to the very end, likewise it can be ascertained that there is no thought disorder, delusions or hallucinations' (p.657). Brissaud (1893) also claimed that patients keep their intellect to the very end but made an interesting point, namely, that they become 'selfish in their approach to life, only taking but not giving' to the point that carers eventually get fed up; when this happens the patient sulks, feels abandoned, and can become paranoid (*délire de la suspicion*).

Other French neurologists, however, were more open and included mental symptoms in their description. For example, Charcot (1886) himself wrote that 'at a given moment, intellect becomes blurred and memory is lost' (p.179); and Marchand (1909) that: 'patients frequently present irritability, affective disorder and cognitive impairment' (p.493). Claude (1922) was even more explicit, and quoted the work of Ball and Parant (p.603). Thus, the 1881 London meeting encouraged the view that psychiatric symptoms were part of PD. Further support accrued from the kaleidoscopic nature of cases with parkinsonism and mental disorder seen in the wake of the encephalitis lethargica epidemics (Von Economo, 1931; Leader, 1981).

THE EPIDEMICS OF ENCEPHALITIS LETHARGICA

The association between parkinsonian and mental symptoms observed during the post-encephalitic state led to a revision of general views on both the nature of mental symptoms and of motor disorders in psychiatry. Von Economo (1931) believed that 'delusional ideas might have to be given a lesser role' in diagnosis (p.192). Post-encephalitic states often showed rigidity without tremor, akinesia, compulsive behaviour, akathisia, blepharospasms, tics, torticollis, oculogyric crisis, attacks of hyperapnoea with forced expiration, seborrhoea, sialorrhoea, distrophia adiposo genitalis, disturbance in temperature control, and psychic torpor. Some of these features had not been described before in relation to parkinsonism. Similar symptoms were later on reported in patients taking neuroleptic medication (Delay and Deniker, 1968; Petit et al, 1979).

The epidemics of encephalitis lethargica which occurred at the end of the First World War was not a new phenomenon (Von Economo, 1931). An epidemics of 'nona' had already taken place in Northern Italy towards the end of the nineteenth century (Editorial, 1890) and Von Economo (1931) believed it to be similar to the one he named in 1917. A decade after the Italian epidemics, Kleist reported cases 'with a psychosis of delirium, slight fever and hyperkinesis, which in turn passed into state of akinetic Parkinsonian rigidity' (Von Economo, 1931, p.8). It is also of interest to notice that the second case reported by Ball (1882) was that of a 32 year-old *Italian* with akinesia, dysarthria, and peripheral vasomotor disturbance.

The epidemics of 1917–1921 caused far more post-encephalitic cases than earlier ones (Brill, 1974, p.154). It has also been suggested that the increased incidence of Parkinsonism observed after the First World War might have resulted from subclinical infections affecting a large proportion of cases during this period (Poskanzer and Schwab, 1963). However, this conclusion, and the assumptions upon which it was based, have been challenged on statistical (Selby, 1968; Pallis, 1971) and clinical (Martin et al, 1973) grounds. It has been claimed that symptoms apparently pathognomonic of post-encephalitic parkinsonism may be present in the idiopathic and so-called arteriosclerosis types of PD. However, the distinctive psychiatric sequelae is still used to characterise the post-encephalitic form (Leader, 1981). Nonetheless, the earlier belief that post-encephalitic parkinsonism was associated with lesions predominantly in

Substantia Nigra, and the idiopathic form with striatal impairment, has been replaced by a unitary view (Denny-Brown, 1962; Adams and Victor, 1977).

BRADYPHRENIA AND ARTERIOSCLEROTIC PARKINSONISM

Critchley (1929) published a classical paper on arteriosclerotic parkinsonism. Parkinsonism he defined as a 'symptomatic variety of paralysis agitans' (p.23). He suggested that there was no major clinical difference between the idiopathic and arteriosclerotic varieties, and on this he sought the support of Souques (1921) and Foix and Nicolesco (1925) who also believed that the important aspect of PD was not the cause itself but the site of the lesion. Critchley concluded that an arteriosclerotic insult to the basal ganglia would cause the same clinical syndrome. However, he had observed that incomplete forms were common and that affected subjects ranged from showing an immobility of expression and short-stepping gait to severe cerebello-pallidal syndromes. Akinesia was particular common but tremor rare; onset was often sudden and age of onset late. Some cases were associated with marked intellectual impairment. During the 1960s, when the reaction came against all forms of 'arteriosclerotic' aetiology, some called Critchley's syndrome into question (Eadie and Sutherland, 1964; Pallis, 1971).

Critchley's paper also drew attention to bradykinesia and bradyphrenia, phenomena which until then had only been mentioned in French neuropsychiatry. Bradyphrenia was defined as 'a failure in mental elasticity' or 'mental viscosity' (pp.50–51). This concept (*bradykinésie*) had already been proposed by Rene Cruchet in 1921 (Verger and Cruchet, 1925, p.7) to refer to 'post-encephalitic states of slowness affecting the starting and execution of voluntary actions without there being either paralysis or trouble with coordination' (p.19). Bradyphrenia, on the other hand, was described by F. Naville (1922) to refer to a specific type of post-encephalitic mental slowness with impaired initiative but normal praxia, memory and cognition. This author suggested that bradyphrenia ought to be differentiated from dementia praecox, dementia, and brain damage. These states have become fashionable in current neuropsychiatry in regard to so-called subcortical dementia, and other states with putative frontal lobe involvement.

THE PARKINSONIAN PERSONALITY

During the 1920s and 30s, psychosomatic medicine enjoyed a period of popularity, and some suggested that PD might be caused by psychological factors. For example, Jelliffe considered oculogyric crisis (then mainly associated with post-encephalitic Parkinsonism) to be a form of 'substitutive action', i.e. 'a looking away' from a threatening reality (Jelliffe, 1932, p.215). This was challenged by Kubie (1933) and a debate ensued (Jelliffe, 1935). Jelliffe also believed that compulsive post-encephalitic respiratory disorders resulted from a neurotic defect (Jelliffe, 1926) and that rigidity was a reflection of 'unconscious hostility' (Jelliffe, 1940). Sands (1942) suggested that states of chronic emotional tension render subjects prone to PD and Schwab et al (1951) that chronic anxiety caused irreversible neuronal change. Booth (1948) characterized PD patients as showing 'urge towards action, industriousness and motor activity, striving for independence, authority, and success within a rigid, usually moralistic behaviour pattern ... the symptoms appear when the personality attitude cannot be carried on successfully'; the author based his views on a sample of 66 uncontrolled PD patients (of varied aetiology) studied by means of the Rorschach Test.

NEUROSES IN PD

The study of this association was only possible after PD ceased to be considered as a 'neurosis' and the 'five neuroses' had become established, i.e. after the Second World War. Mjönes (1949) reported that many of his cases showed 'psychoneurosis' and psychogenic mental depression. Anxiety, depression, hypochondriacal preoccupations, and dysphoria have also been reported following surgery for PD (Asso et al, 1969). Sensory symptoms such as formication[18] and temperature changes (Snider et al, 1976) may, however, lead to pseudo-hypochondriacal complaints.

Obsessional-compulsive symptoms featured prominently among the sequelae of encephalitis lethargica. Von Economo (1931) observed compulsive behaviour and ruminations and Mayer Gross and Steiner (1921) reported similar symptoms during the acute stage. Schilder (1929) suggested that the disease 'liberated motor impulses' but only one of his seven cases presented with a 'marked degree of akinesis and paralysis agitans posture'. Grimshaw (1964) also reported three encephalitic cases with obsessional features in support of an organic theory of obsessional symptoms; this author observed that German authors had often 'found symptoms similar to obsessions in post-encephalitic Parkinsonism'.

AFFECTIVE DISORDER IN PD

Ball (1882) wrote: 'The psychiatric complication takes the form of depression. Frequently, it constitutes a real lypemania[19] accompanied by suicidal behaviour, hallucinations, and stupor' (p.31). Régis (1906) iterated this view: 'Patients first show depressive features, sadness, painful resignation and intellectual apathy ... then they develop melancholic psychosis with delusions of ruin, guilt, hypochondria and suicide' (p.785). Five female PD patients reported by König (1912) also suffered from severe depression and showed hypochondriacal and paranoid features. In a study of 201 cases of post-encephalitic parkinsonism, Neal (1942) found 17 cases with depression and 8 with hypomania. Indeed hypomania had been reported earlier (Report, 1881) but believed to be uncommon (Souques, 1921).

As has been mentioned above, the early British neurological literature considered affective disorder to be an 'understandable' response to the motor disability. It is, therefore, important to know whether authors have ever ascertained whether 'severity' of depression is proportional to duration or severity of PD. Mjönes (1949) found that depression was out of proportion with the neurological deficit. More recently, it has been suggested that depression only develops in vulnerable personalities and bears no relation to illness severity (Warburton, 1967). The debate continues but its analysis brings us perilously near to the present.

SCHIZOPHRENIA AND PD

Since the 1880s, insanity (characterized by delusions and hallucinations) has been considered as an occasional feature of PD. The finding that encephalitis lethargica may also be accompanied by a schizophrenia-like state reinforced this view. However, the early literature shows that some of the visual hallucinations reported in PD occurred in the presence of clouding of consciousness and might have been due to anticholinergic toxicity (Warnes, 1967; Johnson et al, 1981). When symptoms occur in clear consciousness, the question arises as to whether they are related to schizophrenia-like states. Such reports are uncommon. For example, Patrick and Levy (1922) found none in a series of 146 cases; and in 282 patients, Mjönes (1949) only identified 2.1 per cent with 'schizophrenic' symptoms. In a period of ten years, Hollister and Glazener (1961) reported 8 cases of schizophrenia-like illness (some antedating the onset of Parkinson's disease) among 36 hospital cases of PD subjects; unfortunately, some of these patients received maintenance neuroleptics for their chronic schizophrenia, so the PD diagnosis is not safe.

Most schizophrenic symptoms (from hallucinatory states to delusional, psychomotor, and personality deterioration) have been reported in post-encephalitic states (Dimitz and Schilder, 1921; McCowan and Cook, 1928). For example, paranoid-hallucinatory states may be as frequent as 20 per cent (Steck, 1926; 1931; Hall, 1929). In this regard, Davison and Bagley (1969) have concluded:

schizophrenia-like psychoses have long been accepted as sequelae of encephalitis lethargica, but no firm data on their actual incidence have been located; *parkinsonism is commonly associated with the psychosis*; opinion is divided on the degree of resemblance of the psychosis to schizophrenia; and there is no good evidence of personality or genetic predisposition to schizophrenia in patients with post-encephalitis psychoses. (pp.131–32)

Doubts have also been voiced as to the genuine nature of these schizophrenic states. For example, Schilder (1929) believed that psychotic states with insight and without personality splitting did not constitute schizophrenia. The diagnostic use of complex categories such as insight and splitting, however, is unwarranted in this context. In regards to this debate, Von Economo (1931) commented: 'Many psychiatrists are of the opinion that the main difference between schizophrenia and these post-encephalitic states is the fact that the disturbance of motility and psycho-motorium in the former are caused *secondarily*, i.e. they are purely psychological and based on delusions, whereas in post-encephalitic process the primary cause rests in anatomical lesion of the basal ganglia' (p.132). 'The question may be asked whether after our experience with encephalitis lethargica this position should not be revised. . . . The old, but not antiquated, conception of Meynert, that in these forms of dementia praecox not only the cerebral cortex but also the deep grey masses of the brain-stem are affected, may have to be adopted and adapted, with the conclusion that these disturbances of motility and changes in personality and character are primarily caused by specific anatomical alterations' (p.162).

At least one recent author has sided with this view, and claimed that schizophrenia is an epiphenomenon of encephalitis lethargica (Hunter, 1972).

After explaining that catatonic symptoms, 'before they made neurological sense in the wake of lethargic encephalitis, were endowed with psychological meaning and regarded as physical expression of an abnormal mental or emotional state' (p.363) the late Richard Hunter concluded: 'the concept of psychosis or schizophrenia is a historical accident. The abnormal mental state is not the illness, nor even its essence or determinant, but an epiphenomenon. Had the epidemic of encephalitis broken out only ten years earlier, or had its manifestations in endemic form been recognised for what they were, psychiatry would look very different today' (p.364). Hunter also claimed that a study of long-stay mental hospital patients labelled 'schizophrenic' confirmed that some 60–70 per cent had motor signs corresponding to an extrapyramidal disorder (Jones and Hunter, 1969). Unfortunately for his hypothesis, outbreaks of encephalitis had already occurred before 1917. This fact, however, should not obscure Hunter's central point, namely, that psychology alone is not sufficient to explain the motor disturbance of catatonia (Ajuriaguerra, 1975; Berrios, 1981; Saß, 1981). Indeed, combinations of catatonia and parkinsonism have been reported (Bromsberg, 1930; Farran Ridge, 1926), reflecting perhaps a common substratum.

PD, DEMENTIA AND THE WORK OF WITOLD AUBRUN

Given the currency of the view that cognitive impairment is common in both early and late onset PD, the historian must ask why it was not observed earlier in the history of the disease. As mentioned above, one reason might have been that subjects died too early to show dementia; other that the (untreated) physical manifestations of the disease masked mental changes; yet another that dementia was considered to be a manifestation of senility; and yet another that treatments have been a factor in the presentation of dementia.

It was only during the early 1860s that Charcot reported 'blurring of intellect and loss of memory'. This point is of some interest as it historically coincides with the early usage of anti-muscarinic agents (Bourgeot, 1926). For the rest of the century, most writers, including neurologists, refer to intellectual weakness during the *terminal stage* of the illness (and one wonders how often these patients were already in delirium). No psychometric studies seem to have been carried out until after the First World War. The reason for this is not necessarily a lack of instruments or psychometric methodology for both were available by the 1910s.[20]

Under the supervision of Guillain (of Guillain-Barré syndrome fame) and Piéron, Witold Aubrun (1937) wrote a doctoral thesis on the cognitive state of parkinsonians.[21] This work is interesting on two accounts: first, it is one of the earliest experimental studies of cognitive functions in PD, and secondly, it makes use of 'normed' psychometric instruments. Although by current standards the work is flawed, it is nonetheless path-breaking. It also paid attention to patient selection (i.e. made use of entry criteria); for example, it excluded elderly subjects to avoid contamination with 'senile dementia'. Aubrun used a structured interview which he rigorously applied to 20 cases. The protocol included questions on perception, state of consciousness, cognitive function, attention, remote memory, and recent memory (Ziehen's test, a form of paired learning), orientation, praxia, mood, personality, and sleep. A physical examination and blood tests were also carried out.

A full psychological assessment was performed by means of Piéron's 'Psychological battery for professional orientation' which included eleven sections, and for which French norms existed. On the basis of the wealth of data obtained, the author concluded that parkinsonian patients *were cognitively impaired*. Unfortunately, retrospective analysis of his sample has proven difficult, for no raw scores were included in the publication.

SUMMARY

This chapter has only dealt with the history of the psychiatric complications of PD. It started by offering an alternative interpretation to Parkinson's definition that there are no mental symptoms in PD. The work of Ball, Parant, Régis and others was described and considered as important to the eventual acceptance of the fact that psychiatric symptoms are part of the definition of PD. A separate analysis was carried out of the historical development of specific mental disorders, and of the contribution of factors such as encephalitis lethargica, arteriosclerotic parkinsonism, bradykinesia, bradyphrenia, and anti-muscarinic medication.

NOTES

1 The problem with negative (i.e. idiopathic) definitions is that they depend on the sensitivity and power of current and future tests i.e. the more refined the detection procedure, the smaller the 'idiopathic' group.

2 Parkinsonism may be caused by toxic, vascular, immunological, and tumoural factors and by neuroleptic drugs (see Schwab and England, 1968).

3 For example, the Edinburgh *vademecum* read: paralysis is 'a sudden loss of tone and vital power in a certain part of the body' . . . 'in the slighter forms of the disease, it only affects a particular muscle' 'in the higher degrees of the disease the paralytic affection is diffused over a whole limb . . . and sometimes it affects a whole side of the body, in which case it is called hemiplegia' . . . 'Sometimes there occurs a total loss of sense while motion is entire'.

4 The explanation for this wide definition is that 'paralysis' was then used as a clinical (*pars per toto*) generalization of the symptoms of apoplexy and hence both loss of motor and sensory function had to be included. Evidence for this view can be found in Middleton's Dictionary: 'palsy in medicine is a disease wherein the body, or some of its members, lose their motion, and sometimes their sensation of feeling. This disease is never acute, is often tedious, and in old people, almost incurable; and the patient for the most part drags a miserable life. For the vigour of his mind, together with his memory, are lost or vastly impaired; he totters and shakes, and becomes a dismal sight; as if no longer a man, but an animal half dead' (Middleton et al, 1780).

5 Bourneville, the editor of Charcot's *Leçons* tells (Appendix II, vol.1, p.394) that in his lecture of 19th November 1876, Charcot criticised the term 'paralysis' as inappropriate, on the basis that muscle power was well

preserved, and suggested *Maladie de Parkinson* instead. Charcot confirmed this in a letter to a Dr. Nunn dated 5th May 1884 (see also Critchley, 1955, p.x). Not everyone agreed. William Gowers (1893) believed that paralysis agitans was adequate and that there was no need to use an eponym.

6 Parkinson had experience with mental illness. For years, he was the visiting physician to the Hoxton madhouse and would not have hesitated to use the word 'insanity' (rather than the more ambiguous one *uninjured senses*) (see Morris, 1986).

7 'A more *melancholy object* I never beheld. The patient, naturally handsome, middle-sized, sanguine man, of cheerful disposition, an active mind, appeared much emaciated, stooping and *dejected*' (p.40) (Parkinson, 1817).

8 Anti-muscarinic treatment may have prolonged life, thus allowing the dementia to appear, or more likely to have caused itself the cognitive impairment.

9 Charcot was referring here to the work of his protégé Ordenstein published in 1868. In a footnote, however, Charcot felt forced to accept that it had not been Ordenstein, after all, who had first proposed the difference between the two conditions: 'Cohn, nonetheless, had already noticed that in two cases with multiple plaques in brain and spinal cord, tremor only appeared when the patients wanted to carry out a movement but never during rest or sleep'.

10 See charming historical account written by Lewy (1942) when visiting Pennsylvania for the 1940 meeting of the *Association for Research in Nervous and Mental Disease*.

11 For example, Axenfeld felt that the lesions 'should be in the spinal cord' (Axenfeld, 1886, p.699). Thus, insanity could not be part of a disease which did not affect the brain.

12 Benjamin Ball (1834–1893) was of British extraction and the first incumbent to the chair of Mental Diseases (1877) at Sainte-Anne, the famous French psychiatric establishment.

13 The case had been published by Althaus in 1870.

14 Published by Nichol in 1875.

15 Kahlbaum described 26 cases exhibiting 'a brain disease with a cyclic, alternating course, in which the mental symptoms are, consecutively melancholia, mania, stupor, confusion and eventually dementia. One or more of these symptoms may be absent from the complete series of psychic "symptoms-complexes". In addition to the mental symptoms, locomotor neural processes with the general character of convulsions occur as typical symptoms' (Kahlbaum, 1874, p.83).

16 Paramimia is defined as a lack of congruence between ideas and gestures (see pp.194–211 in Dromard, 1909). Pierret led a group of French neuropsychiatrists interested in the analysis of facial expression in both neurological and psychiatric disease (for details see Régis, 1906, pp.116–18).

17 The 'oniric' state was an important descriptive and explanatory concept in French psychiatry. It referred to hallucinatory and other 'automatic' behaviours resulting from the break-through of dream activity during wakefulness (see chapter on history of delirium, this book).

18 Formication refers to tactile hallucinations of ants crawling under the skin (see Berrios, 1982).

19 Lypemania was a term coined by Esquirol to refer to depression (see chapter on the history of affective disorders).
20 See chapters on delirium and dementia for information on the influence of the work of Binet and Simon, Jaspers, Tolouse and others.
21 Aubrun also wrote a paper on emotional reactions in PD subjects (Aubrun, 1937a).

REFERENCES

Adams, R.D. and Victor, M. (1977) *Principles of Neurology*, New York, McGraw-Hill.

Ajuriaguerra, J. de (1975) 'The concept of Akinesia'. *Psychological Medicine*, 5: 129–37.

Anonymous (1803) *The Edinburgh Practice of Physic, Surgery and Midwifery*, vol.2, Medicine, London, Kearsley.

Asso, D., Crown, S., Russell, J.A. and Logue, V. (1969) 'Psychological aspects of the stereotactic treatment of Parkinsonism'. *British Journal of Psychiatry*, 115: 541–3.

Atkins, R. (1882) 'A case of Paralysis Agitans in which Insanity occurred'. *Journal of Mental Science,* 28: 534–6.

Aubrun, W.P.A.J. (1937) *L'Etat Mental des Parkinsoniens. Contribution a son Etude Expérimentale*, Paris, Baillière.

Aubrun, W.P.A.J. (1937a) 'Résponses aux emotions-chocs chez les parkinsoniens'. *Année Psychologique,* 37: 140–71.

Axenfeld, A. (1883) *Traité des Névroses*, 2nd Edition, Paris, Baillière.

Ball, B. (1882) 'De l'insanité dans la paralysie agitante'. *L'Encéphale*, 2: 22–32.

Barbeau, A. (1958) 'The understanding of involuntary movements: An historical approach'. *Journal of Nervous and Mental Disease*, 127: 469–89.

Berrios, G.E. (1981) 'Stupor revisited'. *Comprehensive Psychiatry*, 22: 466–78.

Berrios, G.E. (1982) 'Tactile hallucinations: conceptual and historical aspects'. *Journal of Neurology, Neurosurgery and Psychiatry*, 45: 285–93.

Blocq, P. and Marinesco, G. (1893) 'Sur un cas de tremblement parkinsonian hemiplegique symptomatique d'une tumeur du péduncule cérébrale'. *Comptes Rendus Société Biologique de Paris*, 45: 105.

Booth, G. (1948) 'Psychodynamics in Parkinsonism'. *Psychosomatic Medicine*, 10: 1–12.

Bourgeot, H. (1926) *Contribution a l'étude de la Belladona et en particulier de ses alcaloïdes totaux dans les etats parkinsoniens*, thèse a la Faculté de Médecine et de Pharmacie de Lyon, Lyon, Bosc.

Brill, H. (1974) 'Post-encephalitic states or conditions'. In Arieti, S. (ed.) *American Handbook of Psychiatry*, New York, Basic Books, pp.152–65.

Brissaud, E. (1893) *Leçons sur les maladies du système Nerveux*, (First Edition), Paris, Masson.

Brissaud, P. (1899) *Leçons sur les Maladies Nervouses*, vol.2, 2nd Edition, Paris, Masson.

Bristowe, J.S. (1894) 'Paralysis Agitans'. In *Quain's Dictionary of Medicine* vol.2, London, Longmans, Green and Co.

Bromsberg, W. (1930) 'Mental symptoms in Chronic encephalitis'. *Psychiatric Quarterly,* 4: 537–66.

Chamberet, N. (1819) 'Paralysis'. In *Dictionaire des Sciences Médicales,* vol.39, Paris, Panckouke.

Charcot, J.M. (1886) *Oeuvres Complètes,* vol.1, Paris, Delahaye.

Claude, H. (1922) *Maladie du Systéme Nerveux,* vol.2, Paris, Baillière.

Cohn, (no initial) (1860) 'Ein Beiträg zur Lehre der Paralysis Agitans'. *Wienner Medizinischen Wochenschrift,* (in Charcot, 1886, p.161).

Critchley, M. (ed.) (1955) *James Parkinson 1755–1824,* London, MacMillan.

Critchley, M. (1929) 'Arteriosclerotic Parkinsonism'. *Brain* 52: 23–83.

Cullen, W. (1803) *Synopsis Nosologiae Methodicae,* Sixth Edition, Edinburgh, Creech.

Davison, K. and Bagley, C.R. (1969) 'Schizophrenia-like psychoses associated with organic disorders of the central nervous system: A review of the literature'. In Herrington, R.N. (ed.) *Current Problems in Neuropsychiatry,* British Journal of Psychiatry, Special Publication No4, Kent, Headley Brothers.

Delay, J. and Deniker, P. (1968) 'Drug-induced extrapyramidal, syndromes'. In Vinken, P.J. and Bruyn, G.W. (eds.) *Handbook of Clinical Neurology,* vol.6, Diseases of the Basal Ganglia North-Holland, Amsterdam, pp.248–66.

Demange, E. (1887). 'Tremblement'. In Dechambre, A. and Lereboullet, L. (eds.) *Dictionnaire Encyclopédique des Sciences Médicales,* vol.97, Paris, Masson, pp.59–77.

Denny-Brown, D. (1962) *The Basal Ganglia and their Relation to Disorders of Movement,* London, Oxford University Press.

Dimitz, L. and Schilder, P. (1921) 'Über die psychischen Störungen bei der Encephalitis Epidemica des Jahres 1920'. *Zeitschrift für Neurologie und Psychiatrie,* 68: 298–340.

Dromard, G. (1909) *La Mimique chez les Aliénés,* Paris, Alcan.

Dutil, A. (1903) 'Troubles Psychiques dans la Maladie de Parkinson'. In Ballet, G. (ed.) *Traité de Pathologie Mentale,* Paris, Doin, pp.872–5.

Duvoisin, R. (1987) 'History of Parkinsonism'. *Pharmacological Therapy,* 32: 1–17.

Eadie, M.J. and Sutherland, J.M. (1964) 'Arteriosclerosis in Parkinsonism'. *Journal of Neurology, Neurosurgery and Psychiatry,* 27: 237–40.

Editorial (1890) 'La Nona, the so-called new disease'. *British Medical Journal,* i: p.748.

Editorial (1992) 'Parkinson's disease: one illness or many syndromes'. *Lancet,* 339: 1263–4.

Farran Ridge, C. (1926) 'Some symptoms referable to the Basal Ganglia occurring in Dementia Praecox and Epidemic Encephalitis'. *Journal of Mental Science,* 72: 513–23.

Foix, Ch. and Nicolesco, J. (1925) *Les Noyaux Gris Centraux,* Paris, Masson.

Gowers, W. (1893) *A Manual of Diseases of the Nervous System,* 2nd Edition, vol.2, London, Churchill.

Gringer, R.R. (1926) 'Parkinsonism following carbon monoxide poisoning'. *Journal of Nervous and Mental Disease,* 64: 18–28.

Grishaw, L. (1964) 'Obsessional disorders and neurological illness'. *Journal of Neurology, Neurosurgery and Psychiatry,* 27: 229–31.

Hall, M. (1841) *On the Diseases and Derangements of the Nervous System*, London, Baillière.

Hall, S.B. (1929) 'Mental Aspects of Epidemic Encephalitis'. *British Medical Journal*, i: 444–6.

Hollister, L.E. and Glazener, F.S. (1961) 'Concurrent paralysis agitans and schizophrenia'. *Diseases of the Nervous System*, 22: 187–9.

Hunter, R. (1972) 'Psychiatry and Neurology. Psychosyndrome or Brain disease'. *Proceedings of the Royal Society of Medicine*, 66: 359–64

Jackson, J.H. (1931) *Selected Writings*, London, Hodder and Stoughton, pp.452–8.

Jelliffe, S.E. (1926) 'Post Encephalitic respiratory disorders. Psychopathological considerations'. *Journal of Nervous and Mental Disease*, 64: 503–27.

Jelliffe, S.E. (1932) 'Psychopathology of forced movements in oculogyric crises'. *Nervous and Mental Disease Monograph*, Series No 55.

Jelliffe, S.E. (1935) 'The Psychopathology of the oculogyric crises and its funeral by Dr. Lawrence S. Kubie'. *Psychoanalytic Quarterly*, 4: 360–6.

Jelliffe, S.E. (1940) 'The Parkinsonian body posture: Some considerations on unconscious hostility'. *Psychoanalytic Review*, 27: 467–79.

Jelliffe, S.E. and White, W.A. (1929) *Diseases of the Nervous System*, 5th Edition, London, Lewis.

Johnson, A.L., Hollister, L.E. and Berger, P.A. (1981) 'The anticholinergic intoxication syndrome: Diagnoses and treatment'. *Journal of Clinical Psychiatry*, 42: 313–17.

Jones, M. and Hunter, R. (1969) 'Abnormal movements in patients with chronic psychiatric illness'. In Crane, G.E. and Gardner, P. (eds.) *Psychothropic Drugs and Dysfunctions of the Basal Ganglia: A Multi-disciplinary Workshop*, U.S. Public Health Service Publication. No1938, Washington, Government Printing Office, pp.53–64.

Kahlbaum, K. (1874) *Die Katatonie*, Berlin, Kirschwald.

Keschner, M. and Sloane, P. (1931) 'Encephalitic, Idiophatic and arteriosclerotic Parkinsonism'. *Archives of Neurology and Psychiatry*, 25: 1011–14.

König, H. (1912) 'Zur Psychopathologie der Paralysis Agitans'. *Archiv für Psychiatrie und Nervenkrankheiten*, 50: 285–305.

Kubie, L.S. (1933) 'On the Psychopathology of Forced Movements and the Oculogyric crises of Lethargic Encephalitis'. *Psychoanalytic Quarterly*, 2: 622–6.

Leader, (1981) 'Encephalitis lethargica'. *Lancet*, ii, 1396–7.

Lereboullet, L. and Bussard, T. (1884) 'Paralysie agitante'. In Dechambre, A. and Lereboullet, L. (eds.) *Dictionnaire Encyclopédique des Sciences Médicales*, vol.72, Paris, Masson, pp.614–54.

Lewy, F.H. (1913) 'Zur pathologischen Anatomie der Paralysis Agitans'. *Deutsches Zeitschrift für Nervenheilkunden*, 50: 50–54.

Lewy, F.H. (1942) 'Historical introduction: The basal ganglia and their diseases'. In *The Diseases of the Basal Ganglia*, Baltimore, Williams and Wilkins, pp.1–20.

Marchand, L. (1909) *Manuel de Neurologie*, Paris, Doin.

Martin, W.E., Young, W.I. and Anderson, V.E. (1973) 'Parkinson's Disease: A genetic study'. *Brain*, 96: 495–506.

Mayer-Gross, W. and Steiner, G. (1921) 'Encephalitis Lethargica in der Selbsbeobachtung'. *Zeitschrift für Neurologie und Psychiatrie*, 73: 422–75.

McCowan, P.K. and Cook, L.C. (1928) 'The mental aspects of Chronic Epidemic Encephalitis'. *Lancet*, i, 1316–20.

Meynert, T. (1871) 'Beiträge zur differentiel Diagnose des paralytischen Irreseins'. *Wiener Medizinische Praktizieren*, 12: 645–7.

Middleton, E., Turnbull, W., Ellis, T. and Davison, J. (eds.) (1780) *The New Complete Dictionary of Arts and Sciences*, London, Alex Hogg.

Miller, E., Berrios, G.E. and Politynska, B.E. (1987) 'The Adverse Effect of Benzhexol on Memory in Parkinson's Disease'. *Acta Neurologica Scandinavica*, 76: 278–82.

Mjönes, H. (1949) 'Paralysis Agitans, clinical and genetic study'. *Acta Psychiatrica Scandinavica* (Suppl) 54: 1–95.

Morris, A.D. (1989) 'A Discussion of Parkinson's Essay on the Shaking Palsy'. In Rose, C. (ed.) *James Parkinson. His life and Times*, Boston, Birkhäuser, pp.131–48.

Morris, A.D. (1989) 'The madhouse doctor'. In Rose, C. (ed.) *James Parkinson. His life and times*, Boston, Birkhäusen, pp.96–113.

Naville, F. (1922) 'Etudes sur les complications et les séquelles mentales de l'encéphalite épidémique'. *L'Encéphale*, 17: 369–75.

Neal, J.B. (1942) *Encephalitis: A Clinical Study*, New York, Grune and Stratton.

Ordenstein, L. (1868) *Sur la Paralysie Agitante et la Sclérose en Plaques Généralisées*, Thèse de Paris, Paris, Mortimer.

Pallis, C.A. (1971) 'Parkinsonism: natural history and clinical features'. *British Medical Journal*, 3: 683–90.

Parant, V. (1883) 'La paralysie agitante examinée comme cause de folie'. *Annales Médico-Psychologiques*, 10: 45–66.

Parant, V. (1892) 'Paralysis Agitans'. In Tuke, D.H. (ed.) *Dictionary of Psychological Medicine*, Churchill, London.

Parkinson, J. (1817) *An Essay on the Shaking Palsy*, London, Sherwood, Neely, and Jones.

Patrick, H.T. and Levy, D.M. (1922) 'Parkinson's Disease. A clinical study of 146 cases'. *Archives of Neurology and Psychiatry*, 7: 711–20.

Petit, M., Lepine, J.P. and Lesieur, Ph. (1979) 'Chronologie des effets extrapyramidaux des neuroleptiques et système dopaminergique nigrostriatal'. *L'Encéphale*, 5: 297–316.

Poskanzer, D.C. and Schwab, R.S. (1963) 'Cohort analysis of Parkinson's Syndrome: Evidence for a single aetiology related to a subclinical infection about 1920'. *Journal of Chronic Diseases*, 16: 961–74.

Régis, E. (1906) *Précis de Psychiatrie*, 2nd Edition, Paris, Doin.

Report (1881) Mental Diseases Section (International Medical Congress, London) *Journal of Mental Science*, 27: 457–60.

Roche, L.Ch. (1834) 'Paralysie'. In *Dictionaire de Médicine et de Chirurgie Pratiques*, vol.12, Paris, Baillière, p.364.

Romberg, M.H. (1853) *A Manual of the Nervous Diseases of Man*, (translated by E.H. Sieveking) vol.2, London, Sydenham Society.

Sands, I.J. (1942) 'The type of personality susceptible to Parkinson disease'. *Journal of Mount Sinai Hospital*, 9: 792–4.

Saß, H. (1981) 'Problem der Katatonieforschung'. Nervenarzt, 52: 373–82.

Schilder, P. (1929) 'Zur Kenntnis der Psychosen bei chronischer Encephalitis Epidemica nebst Bemerkung under die Beziehung organischer Strukturen zur den psychischen Vorgangen'. Zeitschrift für Neurologie und Psychiatrie, 118: 327–49.

Schiller, F. (1967) 'The Vicissitudes of the Basal Ganglia'. Bulletin of the History of Medicine, 41: 515–38.

Schiller, F. (1986) 'Parkinson's rigidity: the first hundred-and-one years 1817–1918'. History and Philosophy of Life Sciences, 8: 226–36.

Schwab, R.S., Fabing, H.D. and Prichard, J.S. (1951) 'Psychiatric Symptoms and syndromes in Parkinson's Disease'. American Journal of Psychiatry, 107: 901–7.

Schwab, S. and England, A.C. (1968) 'Parkinson syndromes due to various specific causes'. In Vinken, P.J. and Bruyn, G.W. (eds.) Diseases of the Basal Ganglia. vol.6. Handbook of Clinical Neurology, Amsterdam North-Holland, pp.227–47.

Selby, G. (1968) 'Parkinson's Disease'. In Vinken, P.J. and Bruyn, E.W. (eds.) Handbook of Clinical Neurology, vol.6, North Holland, Amsterdam, pp.173–211.

Snider, S.R., Rahn, S., Isgreen, W.R. and Cote, L.J. (1976) 'Primary sensory symptoms in Parkinsonism'. Neurology, 26: 423–9.

Souques, M.A. (1921) 'Formes Cliniques des syndromes parkinsoniens'. Revue Neurologique, 28: 562–87.

Steck, H. (1926) 'Les syndromes extrapyramidaux dans les maladies mentales I and II'. Schweizer Archiv für Neurologie, 19: 195–233; 20: 92–136.

Steck, H. (1931) 'Les syndromes mentaux post-encephaliques'. Schweizer Archiv für Neurologie, 27: 137–73.

Tretiakoff, C. (1919) Contribution a l'étude de l'anatomie patholologique du locus niger, Paris, Thèse de Paris.

Tyler, K.L. and Tyler, H.R. (1986) 'The secret life of James Parkinson'. Neurology, 36: 222–4.

Verger, H. and Cruchet, R. (1925) Les États Parkinsoniens et le Syndrome Bradykinétique, Paris, Baillière.

Von Economo, C. (1931) Encephalitis Lethargica: Its Sequelae and Treatment, (translated by K.O. Newman), Oxford, Oxford Medical Publications.

Vulpian, A. (1886) Maladies du Système Nerveux, (moëlle épinière), vol.2, Paris, Doin.

Warburton, J.W. (1967) 'Depressive symptoms in Parkinsonism patients referred for Thalamotomy'. Journal of Neurology, Neurosurgery and Psychiatry, 30: 368–70.

Warnes, H. (1967) 'Toxic psychosis due to antiparkinsonian drugs'. Canadian Psychiatric Association Journal, 12: 323–6.

Wilson, S.A.K. (1954) Neurology, 2nd Edition (edited by Bruce, A.N.), vol.2, London, Butterworth.

Chapter 4

Parkinson's Disease (Paralysis Agitans)

Social Section
ROY PORTER

Examination of key features of Parkinson's disease, its incidence and theorization, affords a window upon the contours of modern medical science. Today Parkinson's disease is well-known and readily identified by its characteristic symptoms: a tremor, notably in the hand, with a 'pill-rolling' quality; disorders of gait and movement (a certain hurry, 'push', or festination); and abnormal postural fixation (sometimes apparently showing absence of will, or 'aboulia'). It is named in honour of James Parkinson (1755–1824), an English general practitioner active in London. Parkinson naturally called the condition by another name: the 'shaking palsy'. For much of the nineteenth century learned medicine made use of a Latin term: *paralysis agitans*, the eponym becoming common only in the last quarter of the century, its first textbook mention in English being in Julius Althaus's (1833–1900) *Diseases of the Nervous System* (1877). It is referred to in an edition of Fagge's (1838–83) *Principles and Practice of Medicine* (1886), in which a footnote intriguingly observed that 'abroad it is commonly known as Parkinson's disease'. Sir William Gowers (1845–1915) referred to Parkinson's disease in his *Manual of the Diseases of the Nervous System* (1888), while expressing his preference for Parkinson's original term; for its part Daniel Hack Tuke's (1827–95) magisterial *A Dictionary of Psychological Medicine* (1892) spoke of 'paralysis agitans' and barely mentioned Parkinson.

An instructive contrast may be drawn between the milieu of Parkinson and his humble 'shaking palsy', and that of the *fin de siècle*, by which time specialists had made strides in plotting the disorder onto the neurological map. Parkinson and his *Essay on the Shaking Palsy* (1817) reflect a 'vernacular' medical environment of yesteryear. The author himself, an apothecary's son, was anything but an elite physician or a career medical scientist, though he was certainly involved in scientific pursuits. Having studied under John Hunter (1728–93), Parkinson became a surgeon-apothecary, or as we would say, family doctor, in Hoxton in London's East End. For long, however, it seemed as though, if he were ever to win fame, it would be for something other than stamping his name upon a disease. During the French Revolutionary and Napoleonic eras, he was active as a metropolitan agitator, radical pampheteer and member of the London Corresponding Society, a political society dedicated to furthering the rights of man; at one stage he was questioned by the Privy Council for his involvement in the 'popgun plot', an alleged conspiracy to assassinate George III

(1738–1820). Parkinson published numerous anti-government tracts, mainly under the pseudonym of 'Old Hubert'. In later years, he also became a distinguished geologist, authoring *Organic Remains of a Former World* (3 vols, 1804–11), a pioneering palaeontological text, while also contributing to the debate on custodial care for the insane in his *Observations on the Act for Regulating Madhouses* (1811). And, perhaps most characteristically, he brought out works of medical popularization, involving kitchen medicine, hygiene and domestic tips for common folk, like *The Villager's Friend and Physician, or a Familiar Address on the Preservation of Health and the Removal of Disease on its first Appearance, Supposed to be Delivered by a Village Apothecary, with Cursory Observations on the Treatment of Children, on Sobriety, Industry, etc, Intended for the Promotion of Domestic Happiness* (1804).

Parkinson was thus no hobnobbing high-society physician or career scientist but a man of the people. And the concept of palsy upon which he drew was a familiar part of the common consciousness. 'He had the shaking Palsey in his handes', John Aubrey (1626–97) had written, over a century earlier, about his aged friend, the philosopher, Thomas Hobbes (1588–1679):

> which began in France before the year 1650 [when Hobbes was in his early sixties], and haz growne upon him by degrees, ever since, so that he haz not been able to write very legibly since 1665 or 1666, as I find by some letters he hath honoured me withall. Mr Hobbs wase for severall yeares before he died so Paralyticall that he wase scarce able to write his name.

In the *Essay on the Shaking Palsy*, Parkinson related his views to an earlier medical literature concerning chorea, scelotyrbe, palsy and twitching, drawing respectfully upon such authorities as Sylvius de le Boë (1614–1667), Gerard van Swieten (1700–1772) and Boissier de Sauvages (1706–1767), while emphasizing that the 'disease does not accord with any which are marked in the systematic arrangements of the nosologists'. Sifting the symptomatologies of paralysis agitans offered in the nosological writings of Linnaeus (1707–78), Vogel (1750–1837), Cullen (1710–90), and MacBride (1726–78), Parkinson delineated what he termed the 'pathognomonic symptoms' (tremor coactus and scelotyrbe festinans), so as to distinguish the disorder 'from other diseases with which it may be confounded'. He also examined its 'proximate' and 'remote causes', and, in the concluding chapter, evaluated prospects of a cure (he was mildly encouraging). Overall, the thrust of Parkinson's little book – it ran to just sixty-six pages – lay in establishing 'the real shaking palsy' as nosologically distinct from other infirmities involving tremor, including those consequent upon old age and alcohol, tea- and coffee-abuse. In other diseases, he noted, referring to Thomas Kirkland's (1722–1792) *Commentary on Apoplectic and Paralytic Affections* (1792),

> if the trembling limb be supported, and none of its muscles be called into action, the trembling will cease. In the real Shaking Palsy the reverse of this takes place, the agitation continues in full force whilst the limb is at rest and unemployed: and even if sometimes diminished by calling the muscles into employment.

Early in his essay, Parkinson had identified the chief 'pathognomonic symptoms of this malady' to be 'tremulous agitations, and the almost invincible propensity to run, when wishing only to walk'. He made much of the 'propensity to bend the trunk forwards, and to pass from a walking to a running pace'. As Clifford Rose (1989) has noted, Parkinson's listing is revealing; for his portrait of the shaking palsy lacks what would today be considered an essential component: awareness of muscle rigidity. Why was this? It is perhaps because Parkinson probably did not touch his patients. And why was *that*? It would have been because physical examinations were rather rare in those days. For one crucial divide between the 'pre-modern' and the 'modern' medical era is that traditional physicians did not routinely undertake systematic physical examinations. In a consultation the practitioner would listen to the patient tell his 'history' – a process that might be lengthy. He would also make a certain physical scrutiny of the body; but, by today's standards, this would not only be extremely perfunctory but would be conducted primarily by the eye not by touch, paying attention to skin discolouration and lesions, to eye colour and so forth. The pulse would also be taken, though the assessment would be qualitative rather than by timing beats. Physicians would also listen to coughs and eructations, and they might examine faeces and urine. Nevertheless, physical examination was quite secondary. For one thing, pre-modern medicine had no diagnostic technology to aid and objectify the senses. Stethoscopes, ophthalmoscopes and so forth were not introduced until the nineteenth century, and then not without foot-dragging from patients and practitioners alike. For another, training of the senses, apart from the eye, for diagnostic purposes was rudimentary. As late as 1800, only a rather advanced doctor would tap the body with his finger (percussion), listening for tell-tale evidence of fluid in the internal cavities (auscultation). Prudishness and professional dignity probably constrained physical examinations, but by and large the reason why traditional physicians did not touch their patients was because they did not think much was to be learned that way. A couple of generations later, physical examination had become one of the major aids to the neurologist. Therein lies one reason why neurologists of the 1870s like Charcot (1825–93) had become familiar with parkinsonian rigidity.

Parkinson enjoyed a certain reputation in Britain after his death, Marshall Hall (1790–1857), Stokes (1804–78) Graves (1796–1853) and others all mentioning his work with respect. In *Diseases and Infirmities of Advanced Life* (1863), David Maclachlan (1807–1870) praised 'Mr Parkinson whose interesting essay must ever be referred to as giving a faithful account of the symptoms of the disease from beginning to the end, and is still the best work on the subject'. But study of the ailment made greater progress in France, where, oddly, his reputation may have been higher. It was the aim of a succession of eminent French neurophysiologists to study tics, tremors, and all the other tell-tale signs of nervous disorders and develop a full differential taxonomy. Thus Armand Trousseau (1801–1867), physician at the Parisian Hôtel Dieu, remarked in his *Lectures on Clinical Medicine* (1859) how 'some authors of eminence' had 'not without some reason' confused paralysis agitans with chorea festinans, before outlining their authentic difference. Calling for an energetic research drive, Trousseau insisted 'we must pay great attention to the alterations which Parkinson, Oppolzer and Lebert have described'.

The research drive Trousseau demanded was aided by the mushroom growth of university clinics, hospitals, lunatic asylums and similar institutions. The site inspiring the most energetic investigation was the Salpêtrière in Paris, where the greatest neurological investigator of the age, Jean-Martin Charcot, was Clinical Professor of the Nervous System. Despite a common misconception, Charcot never was an alienist or psychiatrist in the tradition of Pinel (1745–1826) and Esquirol (1772–1840), nor was he exclusively preoccupied with hysteria. He was an ardent and wide-ranging neurologist, committed to deploying patho-anatomical techniques to reduce to neurological order the chaos of fiendishly complex symptom-clusters. Conditions like 'epilepsy, hysteria, even the most inveterate cases, chorea, and many other morbid states', he granted in his *Leçons sur les maladies du système nerveux* (1877), 'come to us like so many Sphynx', defying 'the most penetrating anatomical investigations'. The 'Napoleon of the neuroses' aimed to pin down nervous phenomena to organic lesions, and thereby to normalize general paralysis, neuralgias, seizures, epileptiform fits, spastic symptoms, tabes dorsalis, and, probably his special favourite, hysteria (which, he wished to show, partook of the general characteristics of neurological disorders). Charcot pursued massive clinical neuropathological scrutiny, exam-ining motor and sensory symptoms, bizarre visual abnormalities, tics, migraine, epileptiform seizures, aphasia, sonambulism, hallucinations, word blindness, alexia, mutism, contractures, hyperaesthesias and numerous other deficits. Clinical observation, he was confident, would reveal the natural histories of extended families of related neurological deficits: hemilateral anaesthesias, pharyngeal anaesthesias, *grandes paroxysmes*, palpitations, chorea, St Vitus Dance, tertiary neurosyphilitic infections and temporal lobe epilepsy. 'These diseases', he insisted, 'do not form, in pathology, a class apart, governed by other physiological laws than the common ones'. Whereas Parkinson was a lone general practitioner writing a pamphlet, Charcot, with the backing of his colleagues and students and with unlimited access to clinical material, mobilized a research industry.

Small surprise, then, that Charcot left a masterly depiction of paralysis agitans, giving, for instance, a particularly good account of the quirky parkin-sonian hand tremor whereby the thumb moves over the fingers 'as when a pencil or paper ball is rolled between them: . . . [or] in crumbling a piece of bread'. In his Salpêtrière lectures, he attended closely to the nuances of tremors, distin-guishing case types in which 'tremor is only shown when an intensive movement is made', from other clusters in which 'tremor is a constant symptom, from whom it rarely departs except du. 'ng sleep'. In thereby being perhaps the first clearly to distinguish multiple sclerosis from paralysis agitans, Charcot paid due honour to Parkinson. The history of paralysis agitans or 'la maladie de Parkinson', he noted, 'does not reach far back. The first regular description of it only dates from 1817; it is due to Dr Parkinson, who published it in a little work entitled *Essay on the Shaking Palsy*'.

A master of rhetoric and diplomacy, Charcot excelled in the subtle arts of self-promotion and the belittling of rivals. From Parkinson's day, he pro-nounced, 'paralysis has often been mentioned in England and Germany; but in France it was almost unheard of until these latter years' (i.e., his own times). Amongst the French, he remarked, it had first been described by See (1818–96), who, in his memoir on chorea, had distinguished it from chorea minor or St Vitus' Dance. Discussing chorea, Trousseau had then 'succinctly tabulated the principal characters of paralysis agitans'. And Trousseau's work had in its turn paved the way for Charcot's own investigations, begun in 1861, and undertaken collaboratively with Vulpian (1826–87). 'We were struck by the insufficiency of the details to be found in existing works . . . and, uniting these with the accounts given by foreign authors, we traced a tolerably complete history of paralysis agitans, considering the period. From that date', he triumphantly concluded, 'this disease obtained the right of domicile in classic works'. In short, the well-connected and ambitious Clinical Professor of the Nervous System created a pedigree for paralysis agitans that, in a slightly patronizing manner, gave a crumb of credit to Parkinson as a forerunner while staking his own claim to be the definitive codifier of the disorder, heaping credit upon himself for first ('if I mistake not') drawing the distinction between sclerosis and paralysis agitans.

Parkinson exemplified clinical investigation in the solitary manner; Charcot embodied the 'mass production' of neurology becoming entrenched by the final decades of the nineteenth century. Continuing these trends, the present century has experienced two further noteworthy twists to Parkinson's disease. First, parkinsonism of various kinds became, from mid-century, an all too common side-effect of medically-prescribed drugs like phenothiazine and the major tranquilizers operating on the basal ganglia. As Richard Hunter (1923–83) and Ida Macalpine (1899–1974) noted, such preparations produce an artificial state, mimicking 'natural' parkinsonism through creating an 'increase of rigidity, tremor and flexion, loss of associated movements . . . and sometimes fits, agitation, and perplexed motor restlessness'. It is an ironic unintended consequence of modern medicine's efficacy that the pharmaceuticals employed may occasionally serve to blur the distinction between disease and medicine – or in other words, 'iatrogenesis' has become an intrinsic feature of contemporary medicine.

The second modern phenomenon deserving mention is the great sleeping-sickness epidemic that began in 1916 and lasted just over a decade, creating a 'new' sort of parkinsonism with an unambiguous and definite cause. Unlike regular parkinsonism which afflicts the elderly (Thomas Hobbes became palsied in his sixties), post-encephalitic parkinsonism struck individuals of all age-groups, often in far more severe and spectacular forms than in any manifestations of the standard, idiopathic illness.

In the winter of 1916–17, a new malady appeared in Vienna and elsewhere, spreading swiftly, over the next three years, to become pandemic (parallels suggest themselves with the 'Spanish flu', both outbreaks being expedited by wartime disruption). Its manifestations varied profoundly, and physicians initially offered a lucky-dip of diagnoses ranging from epidemic delirium, epidemic schizophrenia and epidemic disseminated sclerosis, to poliomyelitis and rabies. In the end, thanks to the investigations of the Greek-born neuropathologist, Constantin von Economo (1876–1931), who showed via autopsy that victims' brains had been damaged in a standard pattern, and that they contained a sub-microscopic, filterable virus capable of transmitting the disease to monkeys, the identity of this horrifying disorder was established. It was termed by Von Economo encephalitis lethargica. The pandemic killed or disabled nearly five million, until it vanished, as mysteriously as it arrived, in the late 1920s. A substantial minority of the victims died in the acute stages, sometimes reduced to coma so deep as to preclude arousal. Survivors often failed to regain their wonted vivacity, and many sufferers eventually assumed all-too-familiar features of parkinsonism but in extreme forms, turning into 'living statues', who would remain motionless for years on end.

As he recounts in *Awakenings* (1976), the British-born neurologist Oliver Sacks (1933–), working at the Mount Carmel Hospital, New York, experimentally tried the new 'wonder drug' for parkinsonism, L-dopa (designed to counter dopamine deficiency), on some encephalitis lethargica survivors in the years between 1969 and 1972. The consequences were sensational, for virtually all parkinsonism patients displayed some sort of 'awakening' on being given the drug. The effects of these treatments were so remarkable that Sacks represented them as a 'drama' verging on the miraculous. 'Health, disease, care – these are the most elemental concepts we have, the only ones adequate to bear the discussion', he has reflected:

> When we give L-DOPA to patients, we see first an emergence from sickness
> – an AWAKENING; then a relapse, and a multiplication of problems and
> troubles – TRIBULATION; finally, perhaps, the patient reaches a sort of
> 'understanding' or balance with his problems – this we can call ACCOMMO-
> DATION. It is in terms of this sequence – Awakening . . . Tribulation . . .
> Accommodation – that we can best discuss the consequences of L-DOPA.

L-dopa treatment had the most astounding effect upon chronically disabled post-encephalitic sufferers, crippled not just with parkinsonism but with other disabilities too. These patients often exhibited significant and speedy reduction not only of their parkinsonism but of other ailments: spasms, chorea, depression, apathy, torpor, tics, catatonia. Disorders not routinely considered to have a dopamine-substrate or to be responsive to L-Dopa seemed to vanish along with the parkinsonism, and such patients returned, temporarily, to fullish health.

Sacks traced the physiological recovery effected by L-dopa; but he was no less concerned with transformations in mind and personality accompanying the 'awakenings'. Relief was often sudden (Sacks compared it to 'passing flatus, eructation, or emptying of the bladder'). Stiffness, spasm and swellings disappeared, and the patient quickly 'relaxed' and was at ease. Yet those commenting on the relief of the 'pressure' of their parkinsonism, Sacks contended, were 'clearly not speaking in physical terms, but in ontological or metaphysical terms which correspond to their experience'. And every patient's experience was unique. Rose R. awoke, not to 1970 but to 1926, and to *her* 1926 not anyone else's; Magda B. experienced hallucinations of her husband; she positively felt his presence, his absence, and his adulteries. 'How absurd', Sacks has commented, 'to call such phenomena "side-effects"!' Far from being marginal, these experiences were central. They afforded crucial insights into a personal dimension of illness too often neglected by medicine, the 'nature of ontological or "inner" space in these patients; and in all of us'.

Sacks argued such 'awakenings' pointed to the dynamic inner affinity of sickness with health, or of a 'false self' with the real self, or of a disease-world with a well-world:

The automatic return of real being and health with the drainage of disease shows that disease is not a thing-in-itself, but parasitic on health and life and reality: an ontological ghoul, living on and consuming the grounds of the real self ('draining the *da-sein*', in Binswanger's term). It shows the dynamic and implacable nature of our experience.

In *Awakenings*, and elsewhere, notably in the autobiographical *A Leg to Stand On* (1984), Sacks, unusually for a neurologist, has sought to enter into the thought-worlds of the sick. He has aimed to trace the existential meanings of maladies, and, in some cases, patients' confrontations with terrible disability or death. Especially in *The Man who Mistook his Wife for a Hat* (1985), he has explored the compensatory benefits sometimes accruing to those suffering severe neurological deficits. It is his conviction that all such experiences – 'the terrors of suffering, sickness and death, of losing ourselves and losing the world' – are fundamental to our nature as fully human beings:

> Our sense that there is something the matter, that we are ill or in error, that we have departed from health, that we are possessed by disorder and no longer ourselves – this is basic and intuitive in us; and so too is the sense of coming to or awakening, of resipiscence or recovery, being restored to ourselves and the world: the sense of health, of being well, fully alive, in-the-world.

In endeavouring to retrieve, analyse and cherish the microcosm of the sick, Sacks has drawn upon existential philosophers from Nietzsche (1844–1900) onwards, and upon works of fiction and imagination. Arguing that metaphysics as well as mechanics is integral to medicine, he has posed elemental questions of the interplay between human beings and their diseases, drawing attention to some reflections of the poet and divine, John Donne's (1572–1631), regarding the strange conspiracies entered into with sickness:

> We are not onely passive, but active, in our owne ruine; we do not onely stand under a falling house, but pull it downe upon us; and we are not onely executed, but wee are executioners, and executioners of ourselves.

It has been Sacks's aim to confront modern neuroscience – the specialism created by practitioners such as Charcot – with a key question: the relations between sickness, suffering and science. In his view, Sigmund Freud's (1856–1939) case histories constitute, beyond question, extraordinary instances of suffering and healing that body forth 'meaning and experience'. But such psychotherapeutic insights seem, to Sacks, to have been largely ignored by routine scientific medicine. 'The history of neurology', he notes, 'has nothing, or almost nothing of this sort to offer. It is as if some absolute and categorical distinction had been made between the nature of neurotic and neurological illness, the latter being seen as arrays of "facts" without design or connection'. This, he believes, is a deplorable state of affairs. It is not, however, the predetermined order of things, rather a cultural accident resulting from the priorities, principles and protocols of modern medicine. In the course of the last two centuries, the patient as person has been tending to 'disappear', Jewson (1976) has argued, being reduced to a mechanism (a body) subject to disease (invasive micro-organisms). The rise of diagnostic technology, the religion of statistics, numbers and objectivity, the increasingly scientific self-image of the medical profession, and a powerful commitment to drug therapies ('a pill for every ill') have all midwived the 'medical model', and its subsequent extension from general medicine to psychiatry. One branch of psychiatry, Freudian psychoanalysis, committed itself wholeheartedly to the therapeutic strategy of the 'talking cure'. But the exorbitancy of Freudian claims provoked an equal and opposite reaction amongst organic psychiatrists, with their conviction that the experiences of patients are, at bottom, no more than epiphenomenal: listening to patients and talking with them may be humane gestures, but they are not the essence of psychological medicine as science and treatment.

It may be instructive to point the contrast. 'Today', complained Richard Hunter and Ida Macalpine in their history of Colney Hatch Hospital (1974), training their artillery on the Freudians,

> neurotic types are . . . postulated who react to adversity by developing neurosis. It is assumed that mental pathology derives from normal psychology and can be understood in terms of faulty inter or intrapersonal relationships and corrected by re-education or psychoanalysis of where the patient's emotional development went wrong. Despite all efforts which have gone into this approach and all the reams devoted to it, results have been meagre not to say inconclusive, and contrast sharply with what medicine has given to psychiatry and which is added to year by year. [This is because] Patients are victims of their brain rather than their mind. To reap the rewards of this medical approach, however, means a reorientation of psychiatry, from listening to looking.

To clinch their case against a psychotherapeutics preoccupied with talk and other superficial, secondary phenomena rather than with neuroscience grounded in the diagnostics of signs, Hunter and Macalpine cited instances of asylum patients from earlier centuries, once routinely (mis)diagnosed as cases of 'melancholia' or depression, who could confidently be identified nowadays as having been stricken with parkinsonism. 'Early parkinsonism', they comment,

> is still of all extrapyramidal syndromes the most likely to be missed because psychomotor impoverishment and anergy are judged by their mental component and labelled endogenous depression. Photographs of many patients called melancholic in the old casebooks of Colney Hatch show unmistakable signs of parkinsonism. Their hang-head posture and what appeared as painful facial expression were interpreted as a feeling state, or the abnormal play of facial muscles as responding to inner voices or hallucinations. Bowed head, furrowed brow, fixed gaze, bent arms, rigid posture, and trembling hands made patients appear – and doubtless feel – anxious and sad. This is why in former times catatonia was called picturesquely *melancholia attonia* because patients appeared thunder-struck in a posture.

Two sides of a radical dispute over psychiatric principles and methods here confront each other. On the one hand, there is the organic position, exemplified by Hunter and Macalpine. In their opinion, the humanistic 'moral therapies' of earlier generations, and the Freudian psychodynamics that succeeded them, made the mistake of interpreting as emotionally and behaviourally determined modes of mental disorder cases that clinicians could nowadays confidently ascribe to neuropathy. They noted, for instance, that the blepharospasm or blinking tic characteristic of encephalitic parkinsonism, commonly found in mental hospitals in the interwar years, and numerous other facial tics and spasms, used to be called 'mannerisms', and were interpreted as signs of abnormal emotional disturbance or evidence of hallucination. These could today be satisfactorily reascribed as motorneuron problems.

All this is doubtless diagnostically correct. But it does not detract from Sacks's charge that medicine should, additionally, attend to the authentic experiences of all such patients, whatever the aetiology. 'Why should diseases be exceptions?', Sacks demands,

> And why especially such extraordinary illnesses as Parkinsonism and post-encephalitic 'syndromes', which have such profound (if generally unre-garded) analogies to neurotic illness? If ever an illness and a 'cure' called out for a dramatic and biographic presentation, the story of Parkinsonism and L-DOPA does so.

In the handling of neurological disorders like parkinsonism, scientific advance is evident. But the social historian of medicine will also point to unresolved debates within neuroscience, in respect of scientific status and humanistic orientation. These debates can never finally be 'resolved'. In Sacks's pleas for the voice of the parkinsonism patient we surely hear echoes of Parkinson's own political radicalism.

REFERENCES

Critchley, M. (ed.) (1955) *James Parkinson, 1755–1824*, London, Macmillan.

Gardner-Thorpe, C. (1988) *James Parkinson, 1755–1824*, Exeter, Dept of Neurology, Royal Devon and Exeter Hospital.

Hunter, R. and Macalpine, I. (1974) *Psychiatry for the Poor, 1851. Colney Hatch Asylum, Friern Hospital 1973: A Medical and Social History*, London, Dawsons.

Jewson, N. (1976) 'The disappearance of the sick man from medical cosmology, 1770–1870'. *Sociology* 10: 225–44.

Keppel-Hesselink, J.M. (1983) 'Some historical aspects of Parkinson's Disease. The progression of insights in the period 1817–1868'. *Janus* 70: 263–79.

Klawans, H. (1990) *Newton's Madness*, London, The Bodley Head.

Morris, A.D. (1989) *James Parkinson, his Life and Times*, Boston, Birkhauser.

[Parkinson, J.] (1795) *A Sketch by Old Hubert*, London, Burks.

Parkinson, J. (1801) *Medical Admonitions to Families Respecting the Preservation of Health, and the Treatment of the Sick, also a Table of Symptoms Serving to Point out the Degree of Danger, and to Distinguish one Disease from another*, 4th ed., London, C. Whittingham for H. D. Symonds.

Parkinson, J. (1802) 'The way to health', extracted from *The Villager's Friend and Physician*, London, C. Whittingham for H. D. Symonds.

Parkinson, J. (1803) *The Town and Country Physician*, Philadelphia, J. Humphreys.

Parkinson, J. (1804) *The Villager's Friend and Physician, or a Familiar Address on the Preservation of Health and the Removal of Disease on its First Appearance, Supposed to be Delivered by a Village Apothecary, with Cursory Observations on the Treatment of Children, on Sobriety, Industry, etc, intended for the Promotion of Domestic Happiness*, 2nd ed., London, C. Whittingham.

Parkinson, J. (1817) *An Essay on the Shaking Palsy*, London, Sherwood, Neely and Jones.

Pearce, J. M. S. (1989) 'Aspects of the history of Parkinson's Disease'. *Journal of Neurology, Neurosurgery and Psychiatry* spec. supplement pp.6–10.

Rose, F. C. (1989) 'Parkinsonism since Parkinson'. In Morris, A.D. (ed.) *James Parkinson, his life and times*, Boston, Birkhauser, pp.176–87.

Sacks, O. (1976) *Awakenings*, Harmondsworth, Penguin Books.

Sacks, O. (1984) *A Leg to Stand on*, London, Duckworth.

Sacks, O. (1985) *The Man who Mistook his Wife for a Hat*, London, Duckworth.

Stern, G. (1989) 'Did Parkinsonism occur before 1817?' *Journal of Neurology, Neurosurgery and Psychiatry*, spec. supplement pp.11–12.

Tyler, K.L. (1987) 'A history of Parkinson's Disease'. In Koller, W.C. (ed.) *Handbook of Parkinson's Disease*, New York, Dekker, pp.1–34.

Chapter 5

Chorea and Huntington's Disease

Clinical Section

FRANCIS SCHILLER

Eponyms are a happy hunting ground for historians. How well deserved was or is a particular eponymic designation? That question appeals to the critical faculty, given the almost regular incidence of forerunners. Another search is for the life and labours of the person so honored. There exists a dictionary of eponyms, [Ruffner, 1977], a folio which lists 130,000 persons and 20,000 things on 730 pages. While attributors from all the sciences have at times been 'mesmerized' by some discoverer or practitioner and have applied his name to a law or fact, medicine (not to speak of botany) has probably supplied an inordinate number of eponyms, and neuropsychiatry can claim an outstanding portion. They may come in handy as abbreviations for lengthy descriptive terms, even when historical justice forced more than one name on some particular sign, syndrome or disease. Habit or euphony often win over other considerations. 'Charcot-Marie-Tooth disease' may be preferred to 'peroneal muscular atrophy' or confer an extra mark of erudition to the user. One of the oldest examples is the 'Hippocratic facies' of the cachectic characterizing a symptomatic appearance. An anatomical model referring to antiquity is the 'vein of Galen', another such dating from the early enlightenment comes to us as the 'circle of Willis', and there is 'Bell's palsy'. Sir Humphrey Rolleston (1937) pointed to the injustice committed against Trousseau who had described what goes under the names of Graves and of Addison; he also mentioned nine describers of toxic goiter, the neglect of Hippocrates for the sake of Cheyne-Stokes, etc.

The above mentioned dictionary lists three Huntingtons in addition to the subject of this chapter: a geographer, an engineer, and a preacher with 'Huntingtonians' his followers. The disease named after our George Sumner Huntington (1850–1916), described by him and published in 1872, is also often called 'Huntington's chorea' (Huntington, 1872).

'In the whole range of medical terminology there is', according to William Osler (1849–1919), 'no such *olla potrida* as chorea, which for a century has served as a sort of nosological pot into which authors have cast indiscriminately affections characterized by irregular purposeless movements' (Osler, 1894). It is not even clear why, when, and by whom the simple term *chorea* was introduced into the literature. The Greek dictionary tells you that the word means 'dance, especially choral dance with music'. Does the medical vocabulary owe the term to Paracelsus (1493–1541)? Possibly, for there is no evidence that it was used before him. He divided what had long been known as the 'dancing mania' into *chorea imaginativa, lasciva*, and *naturalis* or *coacta*. The first referred to a psychiatric problem: waves of mass hysteria resulting in groups of mostly young people holding hands and exerting their limbs to the point of utter exhaustion: the 'St. Vitus dance'. Such psychosomatic epidemics featuring wild muscular activity of face and limbs were already recorded in 1027 and 1237; most notorious was one at Aix-la-Chapelle (Aachen) in 1374 and finally one in Strasbourg, 1418 (Barbeau, 1958). Not far removed or clearly distinct in the 16th century was Paracelsus' *chorea lasciva* which added a sexual connotation to the dance. Paracelsus' third, 'natural' or 'forced, involuntary' variety was based on his organic concept of an 'internal pruriency in blood vessels producing laughter, joy, dancing'. Above all, he wrote, 'we will not, however, admit that the saints have the power to inflict diseases and that these ought to be named after them . . . idle talk . . . nonsensical gossip' (Hecker, 1846). In the instance of chorea lasciva he was referring to St. Vitus. Why the dancing mania was in any way related to this saint has in itself remained a mystery. Why should this Sicilian adolescent, martyrized as early as 303, have 'asked God', according to Hecker, 'to deliver from dancing those who keep his day (June 15th) sacred?' Besides, the 'disease' was at times called St. John's passion, also after St. Anthony and St. Modestus.

Divesting chorea of its association with hysterical crowds, if not of its eponym, Thomas Sydenham (1624–89) fairly briefly described similar symptoms affecting single patients of an age close to that of the martyrized Sicilian boy. The involuntary nature of the abnormal movements was to Sydenham 'a kind of convulsion'. 'St. Vitus dance', he echoed Paracelsus in a footnote, was 'a name still absurdly enough retained, though a remnant of superstitious folly'.

> It first shows itself by a certain lameness, or rather unsteadiness of one leg, which the patient draws after himself like an idiot, and afterwards affects the hand of the same side, which is being brought to the breast or any other part, cannot be held in the same posture or movement, but it is distorted, or snatched by a kind of convulsion into a different posture and place, notwithstanding all his efforts to the contrary . . . this disorder appears to me to proceed from some humour thrown upon the nerves. . . . If a glass of liquor be put into his hand to drink, he uses a thousand odd gestures before he can get it to his mouth. . . . As soon as he has happily reached his lips, he throws it suddenly in his mouth, and drinks it very hastily, as if he only meant to divert the spectators. . . . (Sydenham/Wallis, 1788)

(The analogy with some gestures in modern ballet, e.g. Nijinsky, is suggestive (Ostwald, 1990).)

To contrast the historical, mostly German, epidemics against the present and individually afflicted youngsters the former 'disease' was called *chorea Germanorum* and *chorea major*, while Sydenham's clinical variant became *chorea minor*, sometimes *chorea Anglorum*, and finally Sydenham's chorea.

About one hundred years after Sydenham, François Boissier de Sauvages (1706–1767), in his epoch-making *Nosologia Methodica . . . juxta Sydenhami mentem & Botanicorum Ordinem* (Sauvages 1768), revived the Galenic term *skelotyrbe* (limb disorder) to apply both to chorea and what after 1817 was to become the 'shaking palsy' or 'Parkinson's disease'. In an earlier draft Sauvages quotes Schenkius senior with a case of Chorea Sancti Viti Brittanica that showed the features of adult age, chronicity, as well as insanity, if not the heredity, of the Huntington syndrome:

> A certain woman in her fifties, living in our neighborhood, and rather insane, had for a long time been disturbed by a similar affection: a convulsive instability of either one of her legs and arms, moving about involuntarily and with ridiculous distortions of her face. (Sauvages, ?1732)

A treatise on 'Chorea or St. Vitus Dance' of 1810 by Etienne Michel Bouteille (1732–1816) said in its preface 'Everything is out of the ordinary in this Disease, its name ridiculous, its symptoms strange, its character equivocal, its cause unknown, its treatment problematic'. No wonder that Osler chose these words as the motto for his monograph on the subject near the end of the century (Osler, 1894). In Bouteille's experience there always is a slight degree of intellectual weakness in these youngsters, sometimes even a first degree of imbecility – an impression not generally shared (Blache, 1843). By 1850 Sydenham's chorea began to be associated with rheumatism and rheumatic heart disease (G. Sée, 1850). At the same time it was possible to conceive chorea 'psychosomatically' as 'insanity of the muscles' which one author considered better than 'delirium of the sensori-motor ganglia' (Broadbent, 1869).

It is on this background that we must appreciate the fact how toward the end of the 19th century the majority of the medical profession felt motivated to apply a new eponym – Huntington's – to a variant of chorea, differing in several aspects from Sydenham's. But while most researchers chosen for eponymic fame have been members of the academic establishment, George Sumner Huntington (1850–1916) was a life-long humble country practitioner in New York State. Both his father and his grandfather had also practiced medicine in East Hamptom, Long Island. George was the 7th generation of immigrant New Englanders, arriving in 1633 from Norwich, England. A hereditary factor, we might say – as in the disease he described – but a positive one here, played a role in George Huntington's discovery. For as he much later revealed in the speech he was invited to give on the subject by the New York Neurological Society in 1909, it was at the age of eight

> riding with my father on his professional rounds, I saw my first case of 'that disorder' which was the way the natives always referred to the dreaded disease. I recall it as vividly as though it had occurred but yesterday. It made the most enduring impression on my boyish mind, an impression every detail of which I recall today, an impression which was the first impulse to my choosing chorea as my virgin contribution to medical lore. Driving with my father through a wooded road leading from East Hampton to Amagansett, we suddenly came upon two women, mother and daughter, both tall, thin, almost cadaverous, both bowing, twisting, grimacing. I stared in wonder almost in fear. What could it mean? My father paused to speak to them, and we passed on. Then my Gamaliel-like instruction began; my medical education had its inception. From this point, my interest in the disease has never wholly ceased. (Huntington, 1910)

And ever so modestly he closed his address by saying:

It must also be remembered that, without the facts and observations handed down to me by my grandfather, Dr. Abel Huntington, and my father, Dr. George Lee Huntington, the medical lives of whom both were spent in East Hampton, Long Island, and whose memory is still cherished there by the few remaining who once knew them – I never could have formulated a picture of the salient characteristics of the disease so true and so complete as to make of it a so-called classic. As in old Greece the pupil sat at the feet of his teacher, so your essayist sat at the feet of these two, and whatever of honour, whatever of praise, whatever of scientific worth there is, is due much more to them, than to him to whom has come this unsought, unlooked for honour.

His mother was also well educated, a paternal aunt an acknowledged author, one younger brother became a physician. Among his developing interests and talents there was both music and painting. From adolescence he sang in the local Presbyterian Church choir, played the piano and flute; he sketched or painted natural objects in the quiet and dignified beauty of this coastal settlement, inhabited by mostly virtuous middle class or indigent New Englanders. He would hunt and fish or paint or just sit on the beach or in the woods and develop a thorough knowledge of the local fauna and flora. Another hobby was making ship models. He obtained a classical education from a graduate of the University of Edinburgh who had been Lord High Sheriff there. Besides some interest in geology and mineralogy his reading was soon concentrated on medical matters, including the clinical notes of his father and grandfather. He first studied at home, then attended and graduated from Columbia University in New York, with a thesis on opium, in the spring of 1871. At the same time he began to write his paper on chorea. Later that year he opened his own practice in Pomeroy, Ohio. It was in the following February, 1872, that he read the paper that was to immortalize his name before the obscure provincial Meigs and Mason Academy at Middleport, also in Ohio State. Two month later it received publication in the Medical and Surgical Reporter of Philadelphia. (The MS showed pencilled corrections by his father.) Another two years, aged 24, he was married to the daughter of the local judge; they had five children. True to the family tradition he would take one of them along on his horse and buggy house calls, pointing out all kinds of interesting objects on the way. Realizing that his professional chances were better in East Hampton than in Pomeroy he moved back there. But becoming increasingly subject to disabling attacks of asthma he never considered city life and finally settled in the Catskill mountains of New York in a place called La Grangeville, happy with his home life and a numerous practice albeit yielding a very modest income. Some of this came in foodstuffs; fees amounted to 50 cents for an office call; house calls were $1 to $1.50 depending on the miles driven; maternity cases and consultations came to $5. All in all his biographers depict Dr. Huntington as mild mannered and easy going, devoted to his patients, his family and to religion, but with a good sense of humor, including practical jokes. An anecdote tells of his once putting a long strip of adhesive on a lacerated scalp, then crossing it with another such, telling the inebriated subject that this sign of the cross would make him well. As the drunk burst into curses against church and state, Dr. Huntington applied another long strip of adhesive, 'making the letter H which stands for Hell, and that is where you are going just as fast as rum can take you' (Stevenson, 1934).

The only paper the 22 year old George Huntington was ever going to see published was the one that catapulted him to eponymic fame. It bore the simple title 'On Chorea', and occupied the first page of the April 13 issue under the general heading 'Original Department, Communications' (Huntington, 1872). Double spaced it was four pages long. About two thirds consisted of a well referenced historical account and a vivid description of the clinical manifestations of Sydenham's chorea. 'And now', Huntington continued with some emphasis, 'I wish to draw your attention more particularly to a form of the disease which exists, so far as I know, almost exclusively on the East end of Long Island. It is peculiar in itself and seems to obey certain fixed laws'. By contrast he could not remember ever seeing a case of common chorea in the practice of his father in whose opinion the disease was altogether rare.

> The hereditary chorea, as I should call it, is confined to certain and fortunately a few families . . . spoken of by those in whose veins the seeds of the disease are known to exist, with a kind of horror, and not at all alluded to except dire necessity . . . attended generally by all the symptoms of common chorea, only in an aggravated degree, hardly ever manifesting itself until adult or middle life . . . often occupying years in its development, until the hapless sufferer is but a quivering wreck of his former self. . . . (It is) believed, more common among men than among women. . . . There are three marked·peculiarities in this disease: 1. Its hereditary nature. 2. A tendency to insanity and suicide. 3. Its manifesting itself as a grave disease only in adult life.

Regarding heredity Huntington did not believe it could skip a generation, 'as for instance in phthisis or syphilis' – writing at a period when the latter were still believed to be hereditary, not infectious. As to insanity:

> In all the families, or nearly all in which the choreic taint exists, the nervous temperament greatly preponderates. . . . [Hence] the tendency to insanity, and sometimes that form of insanity which leads to suicide . . . is marked. . . . As the disease progresses the mind becomes more or less impaired . . . in others both mind and body gradually fail until death relieves them of their sufferings. At present I know of two married men, whose wives are living, and who are constantly making love to some young lady, not seeming to be aware that there is any impropriety in it. They are suffering from chorea to such an extent that they can hardly walk, and would be thought, by a stranger, to be intoxicated. They are men of about fifty years of age, but never let an opportunity to flirt with a girl go past unimproved. The effect is ridiculous in the extreme.
>
> 3. Its third peculiarity is its coming on, at least as a grave disease, only in adult life. I do not know of a single case before the age of thirty or forty years, while those who pass the fortieth year without symptoms of the disease are seldom attacked. It begins as an ordinary chorea might begin, by the irregular and spasmodic action of certain muscles, as of the face, arms, etc. These movements gradually increase, when muscles hitherto unaffected take on the spasmodic action until every muscle in the body becomes affected (excepting the involuntary ones), and the poor patient presents a spectacle which is

anything but pleasing to witness. I have never known a recovery or even an amelioration of symptoms in this form of chorea; when once it begins it clings to the bitter end. No treatment seems to be of any avail, and indeed nowadays its end is so well known to the sufferer and his friends, that medical advice is seldom sought. It seems at least to be one of the incurables . . . I know nothing of its pathology. I have drawn your attention to this form of chorea, gentlemen, not that I considered it of any great practical importance to you, but merely as a medical curiosity, and as such it may have some interest. (Huntington, 1872)

This important graphic, and elegant presentation, topped by becoming modesty, was duly registered in the same year by Kussmaul and Nothnagel in the *Jahresbericht der gesamten Medizin* published by Virchow and Hirsch (1872). Otherwise no public notice was taken of this 'medical curiosity' before the eighteen-eighties, even then only sporadically and sometimes reluctantly. Jendrassik while dealing with the subject in the 1911 *Handbuch der Neurologie* commented that

Although G. See had already emphasized the heredity in such cases (*Mem. Acad. Med.* 1856, vol.XIV, p.343) and in 1816 Thilenius (no reference given; he was a spa physician in Ems, 1776–1818), also Rufs in 1834 had made similar observations, it is Huntington's merit. . . . His description was not sufficiently taken notice of until Landouzy in France and Ewald in Germany drew attention to it. (Landouzy, 1873; Jendrassik, 1911)

By contrast in the French multivolume dictionary of the medical sciences of 1880 Raymond discussing 'St. Vitus Dance' wrote that

an often reported observation of the Huntingtons proves nothing; physicians from father to son on Long Island they had occasion to observe choreic accidents in successive generations of the same family. Their description of each case is less than summary. . . . If this fact may furnish a good argument in favor of mental heredity it proves little as far as chorea is concerned . . . Dispositions are transmitted; among them we must count rheumatisms. . . . (Raymond, 1880)

Peretti, in a German article on hereditary chorea published in 1885 also refers to Huntington's 'repeatedly quoted observation' as an example for this 'on the whole rare' combination. Insanity as such is hereditary, he says, too, as are hysteria, epilepsy, dystrophia muscularis progressiva (Erb) and Thomson's disease (myotonia congenita, Strümpell) As to the pathological mechanism Peretti relies on Meynert who in the same year had ascribed chorea to 'irradiations from the nucleus caudatus and nucleus lentiformis' added to cortical impulses (Peretti, 1885). In the same year Clarence King, in his doctoral thesis on hereditary chorea at the University of Buffalo, analyzed four generations with the Huntington features. He was uncertain about the pathology: brain or spinal marrow? (King, 1885) J.C. McLearn's case published in the 1885 *Lancet* was of a 56 years old man, with poor memory and irritability associated with chorea of 15 years standing; he was the father of a fidgety son (McLearn, 1885) – Often quoted was the Rinderknecht family, suffering from what by now became termed as 'Huntington's chorea'; here an affected daughter had married a man having the same problem (Hubber, 1887).

The two leading European neurologists of the period, Charcot and Gowers, were, perhaps significantly, unimpressed. Presenting a typical case in 1888 at one of his Tuesday lectures Charcot rhetorically asked: Was here really a separate, autonomous disorder? Was it more frequent in Germany? (He did not mention New England.) In France nobody was very interested. In his opinion 'Huntington's chorea does not represent a distinct, well delineated, or specific pathologic entity. . . . [It is] ordinary chorea with an exceptional presentation of late onset and chronicity in selected families'. After showing his patient's telling family tree he continued

> This is Huntington's disease which, according to me, and I repeat it once again, is only a variety, an aspect of ordinary chorea.

He did not go into the psychiatric aspects (Charcot, 1887).

Gowers in his extensive neurological classic, also of 1888, mentions Huntington's name only in a footnote, saying nevertheless that 'a remarkable form of hereditary chorea (affecting many generations) has been described in Long Island, N.Y. (a favorite haunt of tetanus)'. He did not deny hereditary influences in chorea, referring to collected records showing a 45 per cent such incidence in 439 cases of rheumatism (p.956). Adult, senile and permanent cases of chorea were rare; they presented some peculiarities, a second class (p.972). He also mentioned that

> in some cases there has been progressive dementia . . . maniacal excitement. Hence many cases of senile chorea have been reported from asylums for the insane . . . changes in the nerve cells have been found by some recent observers . . . hyaline swelling and degeneration in the central ganglia (Meynert) (p.974). . . . Choreic movements have been produced by organic disease in so many parts of the brain that no connection can be drawn from such cases to the probable seat of the morbid process (p.975). . . . It was formerly thought that the corpus striatum is the part primarily diseased. . . . We now know that this is impossible . . . we know of no anatomical arrangement by which the gray matter of the corpus striatum can influence the cortex. . . . However . . . choroid movements have been caused by disease of the thalamus . . . (p.977). (Gowers, 1888)

(It must be remembered that during the last three decades of the 19th century Fritsch and Hitzig and others had temporarily dethroned the basal ganglia in favor of the cerebral cortex as the source of motricity.)

Two years after Huntington's publication, and apparently unaware of it, Camillo Golgi (1843–1926) applied his histologically epoch-making silver stain to a case of '*chorea gesticulatoria* associated with mental alienation' and found significant atrophy of the basal gangilia and thalamus (Golgi, 1903). In 1885 Theodor Meynert in Vienna (1833–1893) also associated chorea in general with these nuclei (Meynert, 1885). Hughlings Jackson (1835–1911) had earlier associated embolism of the corpus striatum with hemichorea. Another tentative contribution to the pathology of 'chorea progressiva hereditaria' was in 1890 provided by Hermann Oppenheim (1858–1919). Together with a collaborator he found 'small round cortical cells much diminished in the lower superficial layer' of the cerebral cortex, as well as a somewhat enigmatic 'tumorlike formation in the left lenticular nucleus', considered 'irrelevant' for what looked like 'disseminated encephalitis' (Oppenheim & Hoppe, 1890). The final verdict was briefly provided by Alois Alzheimer (1864–1915) in 1911. There were some characteristic structural changes in the cortex, 'no doubt'. Yet these were 'a doubtful cause as other cortical changes are not accompanied by chorea'. The cause 'probably' was 'the severe degenerative process in the corpus striatum: both nucleus caudatus and nucleus lentiformis'. These areas showed severe loss of neurons and a larger increase in glial cells without fibers, changes also present in the region subthalamica (Alzheimer, 1911).

The lack of enthusiasm which Huntington's American contribution encountered in Europe may have been more than accidental. In any case it was probably William Osler's endeavor and repute more than anyone else's which established the syndrome and eponym internationally. In the 1890's Osler had become interested in the puzzling subject of chorea: after 15 pages in the *Journal for Nervous and Mental Diseases* of 1893 (Osler, 1893) he published a short monograph on it (Osler, 1894). This he dedicated to W.R. Gowers, 'the most brilliant British exponent of the complex science of neurology'.

The term, Osler says, has been freely used: for habit spasms and the various forms of tic, the so-called symptomatic chorea, the chronic, the hereditary, the congenital, and the spastic forms, and the pre- and postthemiplegic disorders of motion. . . . One malady alone in this group may be separated as an independent affection, the so-called Huntington's chorea (Osler, 1894). In his earlier paper Osler had written:

> Nothing illustrates so pointedly the widespread interest now taken in diseases of the nervous system than the rapid manner in which facts accumulate about obscure and rare affections. Twenty years have passed since Huntingdon(sic), in a postscript to an everyday sort of article on chorea minor, sketched most graphically, in three or four paragraphs, the character. . . . In the whole range of descriptive nosology there, is not, to my knowledge, an instance in which a disease has been so accurately and so fully delineated in so few words. (Osler, 1893)

Osler distinguished four groups of chorea: 1) in infants up to 3 years with spastic diplegia; 2) affecting any age including the elderly, described by Herringham in 1888, chronic and incurable, not hereditary, but preceded or accompanied by 'dementia or mania'; 3) Huntington's; 4) Chronic chorea minor with recovery.

Small wonder also that the hunt was on to catch forerunners, again occasionally coupled with a rejection of the Huntington eponym. Wharton Sinkler of Philadelphia in 1889 called it 'Undesirable: on general grounds, and because Huntington was not the first to describe this peculiar form of hereditary chronic chorea' (Sinkler, 1889). Nor was it peculiar to Long Island. For 30 years before Huntington there had been a popular textbook: Dunglison's *Practice of Medicine* of 1842; it contained a letter dated May 5, 1841, 'In obedience to your kind request', sent from Franklin, New York, by Rev. C.O. Waters, M.D. Occupied as a minister and teacher as well as physician in a number of Eastern states, Waters reported five generations of a family in Bedford, Westchester, suffering from the 'fidgets. . . . a spasmodic action of all or nearly all the voluntary muscles of the system . . . involuntary and more or less irregular – popularly called the "magrums" ' (Waters, 1848). Another mention in the same textbook was of Dr. Charles Rollin Gorman (1817–1879) who in his Inaugural Dissertation had described similar cases, stressing the 'influence the *moral* is known to exert over the *physical*' (Gorman, 1848). Thirdly there had been Irving Whitall Lyon's paper of 1863, possibly dealing with the same families as Dr. Waters; he medicalized Waters' 'magrums' into 'megrims' without mentioning any mental symptoms (Lyon, 1863). 'Very chronic chorea, incurable until death, frequently complicated by paralysis and dementia with proven pathology at autopsy' was described in 1868 by Julius Sanders in Berlin, but no heredity mentioned (Sanders, 1868). In 1898 Frank Hallock of Cromwell, Connecticut supported Sinkler's negative attitude and suggested the term *dementia choreica* (Hallock, 1898). *Choreophrenia* was another such suggestion in 1940 (Bertha & Kolmer, 1940).

Probably the first forerunner was John Elliotson, M.D., F.R.C.P., (1791–1868) better known as the controversial innovator introducing phrenology and mesmerism to the London medical profession, as well as the use of the stethoscope, also onetime President of the Royal Medical and Surgical Society and Professor of London University, a brilliant lecturer at St. Thomas's and Guy's Hospital. As early as 1832, in the first issue of *The Lancet*, he published an article on 'St. Vitus Dance', saying it all. He pointed to the occasional case in which this disease was

> united with other diseases of the nervous system and be chronic, last for life . . . in adults frequently connected with paralysis or idiotism, and will perhaps never be cured. . . . It then appears to arise for the most part from something in the original constitution of the body, for I have often seen it hereditary. (Elliotson, 1832)

Next in this continued research for forerunners a Norwegian medical historian (Stevens, 1972) discovered a health report to the government of that country of 1859, by Johann Christian Lund; it had not reached the medical literature. It referred to two families in Saersdalen suffering from the 'twitches' or the 'inherited disease', subsiding only during sleep and associated with dementia or 'fatui'. Four consecutive generations were traced, stricken at various degrees (Orbeck, 1961).

Huntington's rule that consecutive generations were always affected was contradicted by Ernst Remak in 1891; he observed the reappearance of the disease after missing one generation. He also suggested that 'rather than speak of Huntington's we would prefer to call it chorea chronica' (Remak, 1891). Another Berlin neurologist writing 'On Chorea Hereditaria' in the same issue of *Neurologisches Centralblatt*, although quoting Huntington among others, found no 'essential difference to Sydenham' (Jolly, 1891). It may be going too far to include among the forerunners a case referred to by Romberg (1795–1853). In his germinal neurological textbook of 1846 he mentions a

> 20 year old girl, recently described by Julius Bier [a former pupil of his], affected with chorea, whose grandmother had died insane, and whose mother was at every confinement subject to eclampsia and yet continues to suffer from

daily attacks of catalepsy. . . . [The daughter showed] evident choreic movements. . . . for three months . . . accompanied by mental excitement. . . . [making it] necessary to tie her down to her bed. . . . Six weeks later . . . discharged cured. (Romberg, 1846)

Finally, we may recall the 18th century case of Sauvages–Schenkius quoted earlier (Sauvages, ?1732).

By 1908 the time seemed right for a new journal called *Neurographs* to honor Huntington and his discovery. Pocket-sized, the journal seems to have lived only to 1915, with four issues gathered in one volume. Edited by William Browning, M.D., Ph.D., it was published in Brooklyn by one Albert T. Huntington (significantly?). Its No. 2 volume was the 'Huntington Number' containing much of the foregoing and two portrait photographs. The included bibliography stretching from 1842–1908 was by now swollen to well over 200 items. Browning's editorial stressed the fact that despite world-wide interest comparatively little personal appreciation has been shown locally. While

operations, methods and instruments in considerable number are known by the names of their American originators or describers . . . in the list of diseases very few are thus designated. Neurasthenia may occasionally be termed Beard's disease . . . dermatitis herpetiformis . . . Duhring's disease. . . . There are arguments against custom . . . Many attempts have been made, notably in this country, to elide this word. . . . But . . . somehow, despite attacks and without effort on anyone's part to retain the eponym; the term, 'Huntington's chorea' is continued. In reality it is the most scientific, because the simplest and most distinctive of any name yet applied to this condition and the one that is known and used in medical circles everywhere. There is another favorable side to the use of this. It balances up with the nomen often used for ordinary chorea . . . Sydenham's and Huntington's chorea. . . . It can be Latinized, as is done abroad, into *chorea Huntingtonii*, . . . [to] satisfy the fastidious scientist who is not a pedant. . . . [Earlier American observers] remained more obscure than the pre-Columbian discoverers of America. (Browning, 1908)

One of the two foreign contributors to this issue of *Neurographs* (if we may exclude William Osler, the Canadian, as the third) was the famous Prof. Dr. Adolf Strümpell of Breslau (1853–1925). He had observed only 'about' half a dozen cases, two of whom he described in detail. He pointed out that the 'late manifestation of hereditary disease is a rare phenomenon' and that psychiatric symptoms had not been 'very outstanding' in his material, or 'altogether absent' (Strümpell, 1908). The second foreign contribution, by M. Lannois and J. Paviot of Lyon dealt with the histopathology of the disease. With Nissl staining they found chromatolysis and deformity of nerve cells, interspersed with small intensely and homogeneously stained blue bodies. The changes were found in the cortex, even more so in the basal ganglia, characteristic of infection or intoxication, indistinguishable from the changes found in cases of non-hereditary chorea (Paviot & Lannois, 1908).

The psychiatric abnormalities were detailed by A. Ross Diefendorf of Yale University, also known for his English adaptation of Kraepelin's standard Clinical Psychiatry. Diefendorf had studied 75 case histories, 14 of which were his personal observations. One of them, a 56 year old female patient was also suffering from frequent epileptic seizures since the age of 17; her 'slight simple mental deterioration started at 52 with loss of memory, paralysis of thought, etc'. Choreic manifestations developed one year later; another two years later she was 'profoundly demented, not even knowing her own name; extreme paralysis of thought, total apathy . . . and great energy'. This patient had not what Diefendorf called 'crazy symptoms', i.e. delusions. These were present in 14; none, he wrote, suffered from hallucinations (but see below). Irritability with passionate outbursts, violence and destructiveness were common, also 'despondency, gloominess, ennui, with suicidal tendency not based on insight, some were intemperate, immoral, tramps, lacking insight, resembling dementia praecox, or paralytica'. He also mentioned hebephrenia and paranoia. On the whole he felt that the movement abnormality was more disabling then the mental aberration – the latter usually appearing first. Only in one case both developed coincidently; in one other, now 70 years old and choreic for 20 years no mental symptoms had appeared at all, a rare fact observed by several other authors (e.g. Huber, 1887). Three of his cases were

> most like that of the anxiety psychosis with distinct intermissions. Here, also, the onset was gradual with increasing apprehensiveness, delusions of self-accusation, of condemnation, of punishment, occasional hallucinations of hearing [sic; see above] considerable agitation and frequent suicide attempts.

Only one of these three showed 3 periods of 'disturbance of thought or attention, or clouding of consciousness' at intervals from six months to two years, lasting up to 5 years (Diefendorf, 1908).

A good deal of interest also developed in the epidemiology, genealogy, finally the genetics of the condition. The first report of a black Huntington family appeared in 1890 (Bower, 1890). The patient seen was a 36 year old barber whose mother, two sisters and one brother were similarly affected. A 'hard drinker', but otherwise 'mentally unimpaired', he had started to 'twitch' six years earlier. His case was complicated by the fact that aged 28, two years before the onset of chorea, he had been struck with a sudden paraplegia lasting three months. The author commented that any kind of chorea (including Sydenham's) was rare in the negro race.[1] To this day the question whether the gene has invariably been imported to other continents by white colonists – especially from north-western Europe – has found no completely satisfactory answer. Cases among non-whites were reported from Rhodesia and other South-African countries (Samuels & Gelfand 1978; Glass & Saffer 1979; Hayden 1981); in Trinidad a family definitely mixed from English, Negro, Spanish and Indian stock was said to have been brought by a Brahmin priest from the Madras area (Beaubrun, 1963), and it has been observed in the Punjab (Chuttani, 1955). A special case is Zulia, a state of Venezuela: On the western shore of its Lake Maracaibo there were in 1973 no less than 28 Huntington patients, i.e. an excessive prevalence of around 7 per thousand. According to legend the culprit was a Spanish sailor who abandoned ship to mate with a local woman (Avila-Giron, 1973). No source, legendary or other, suggests the origin of the condition in Japan, a country with a very low prevalence – 3.8 per million – in the Aichi district (Kishimoto et al, 1957; Nayarabashi, 1973; Hayden, 1981, p.35).

Much research has shown that not only did Dr. Huntington's own family arrive in 1633 in Boston Bay, but also, three years earlier, the ancestors of his cases. The latter have been traced to Bures, a village in East Anglia. All wished to escape the religious persecution and political turmoil of 17th century England. While the Huntingtons became respected citizens in their new country, some of those affected with the 'magrums' suffered, aside from their slowly and distressingly killing disease, the fate they had tried to escape: execution on account of their grimacing being taken as a 'blasphemous imitation of the savior', or so Cotton Mather had put it (Vessie, 1932; Maltsberger, 1961; Critchley, 1973).

In this context, finally, the first if vague mention of genetics was made by Smith Ely Jelliffe of New York, in the Huntington number (Jelliffe, 1908):

> All in all my figures seem to show a very close approximation to the results of Mendelian crossing as more recently brought out by Farabee, Drinkwater, Bateson and Punnett (*Proc. Roy. Soc. Med. Epidemiological Section Feb. 28, 1908*), but until I have been able to fill out my family trees I am unwilling to present any conclusions.

To this it might be added that Punnett introduced his talk on the subject 'with some trepidation', mentioning 'the rediscovery of Mendel's paper a few years ago' (in 1900 after a dormancy of 34 years), as well as the 'rapid progress' in this field, only to encounter a good deal of disbelief and criticism by some members of the Royal Society of Medicine (Punnett, 1908). Naturally hundreds of papers have appeared since, dealing with the inheritance of this autosomal dominant disease. By 1983 it was linked to chromosome 4 (Gusella et al).

NOTES

1 Fairly recent studies (Folstein, 1989) also found major affective disorders to be a rare feature in black Huntington patients.

REFERENCES

Alzheimer, Alois (1911) 'Über die anatomische Grundlage der Huntingtonschen Chorea und der choreatischen Bewegungen überhaupt'. *Neurol. Zentralbl.* 30: 891–2.

Avila'-Giron, Ramon (1973) 'Medical and social aspects of Huntington's chorea in the State of Zulia, Venezuela'. In Barbeau, A., Chase, T.N. and Paulsen, G.W., *Huntington's Chorea, 1872–1972. Advances in Neurology*, vol.I, New York, Raven, pp.262–6.

Barbeau, André (1958) 'The understanding of involuntary movements. An historic approach'. *J. Nerv. Ment. Dis.*, 127: 459–89.

Beaubrun, M.H. (1963) 'Huntington's chorea in Trinidad'. *West Indian. Med. J.*, 12: 39–46.

Bertha, H. & Kolmer, H. (1940) 'Über psychopathologische Erscheinungen bei der Chorea Huntington (Choreophrenie)'. Dtsche. Zschr. Nervenheilk., 151: 26–46.

Blanche, J.G.M. (1843) *Dictionnaire de Médecine*, 2nd ed., vol.VII, Paris, Bichet.

Bower, J.L. (1890) 'Notes on some cases of chorea and tremor'. *J. Nerv. Ment. Dis.*, 15 (3): 131–42.

Broadbent, W.H. (1869) 'Remarks on the pathology of chorea'. *Brit. Med. J.*, 1: 345–7, 369–71.

Browning, William, (1908) 'Editorial. The Huntington Number'. *Neurographs*, 1: 55–85.

Charcot, Jean Martin (1888) *Charcot the Clinician. The Tuesday Lectures*, Transl. Goetz, Christopher G., 1987, New York, Raven Pr. pp.80–101.

Chuttani, P.N. (1955) 'Huntington's Choria in the Punjab'. *J. Assoc. Physicians*, India, 3: 401.

Critchley, Macdonald (1973) 'Great Britain and the early history of Huntington's chorea'. In Barbeau, A., Chase, T.N. and Paulsen, G.W. (eds.), *Huntington's Chorea, 1872–1972. Advances in Neurology*, New York, Raven Pr. vol 1, pp.13–17.

Diefendorf, A. (1908) 'Ross: Mental symptoms in Huntington's chorea'. *Neurographs*, 1: 128–36.

Elliotson, John (1832/3) 'St. Vitus dance'. *Lancet*, 1: 162–4.

Folstein, Susan L. (1989) *Huntington's Disease. A Disorder of Families*, Baltimore, John Hopkins Pr. pp.88–105.

Glass, J. & Saffer, D.S. (1979) 'Huntington's chorea in a Black family'. *S. Afr. Med. J.*, 56: 685–8.

Golgi, Camillo (1903) 'Sulle alterazioni degli organi centrali nervosi in un caso di corea gesticulatoria associata ad alienazione mentale'. *Opera Omnia*, Milano, vol.3, pp.867–99.

Gorman, Charles R. (1848) In Dunglison, Robley, *The Practice of Medicine*, Philadelphia, Lea & Blanchard, 3rd Ed., vol.II, p.218.

Gowers, William. R. (1888) *A Manual of Diseases of the Nervous System*, Philadelphia, Blakiston, p.956 (footnote), p.972 ff.

Gusella J.F., Wexler N.S. et al. (1983) 'Apolymorphic DNA marker genetically linked to Huntington's disease'. *Nature*, 306: 234–8.

Hallock, Frank K. (1898) 'A case of Huntington's chorea with remarks upon the propriety of naming the disease "dementia chronica"'. *J. Nerv. Ment. Dis.*, 25: 851–64.

Hayden, M.R. *Huntington's Chorea*, New York, Springer, pp.1–30.

Hecker, J.F.C. (1846) 'The dancing mania'. *The Epidemics of the Middle Ages*, Tr. Babington, B.G., London, Sydenham Soc. pp.87–174.

Herringham, W.P. (1888) 'Chorea in the adult, and in the old'. *Brain*, 11: 134–9.

Huber, A. (1887) 'Chorea hereditaria der Erwachsenen (Huntingtonsche Chorea)'. *Virchow Arch.* 108: 267–85.

Huntington, George (1872) 'On Chorea'. *Med. & Surg. Reporter*, 26: 317–21.

Huntington, G. (1910) 'Recollections of Huntington's chorea as I saw it in East Hampton, Long Island during my boyhood'. *J. Nerv. Ment. Dis*, 37: 255–7.

Jelliffe, Smith Ely (1908) 'A contribution to the history of Huntington's chorea. A preliminary report'. *Neurographs*, 1: 116–24.

Jendrassik, Erno (1911) 'Die hereditären Krankheiten'. In Lewandowsky, M., *Handbuch der Neurologie*, vol.II, p.321.

Jolly, F. (1891) 'Ueber chorea hereditaria'. *Neurol. Centralbl.*, 10: 321–6.

King, Clarence (1885) 'Hereditary chorea'. *N.Y. Med. J.*, 41: 468–70.

Kishimoto, K., Nakamura, M. and Sotokawa, Y. (1957) 'Population genetics study of Huntington's chorea in Japan'. *Amer. Rep. Res. Inst. Environ. Med.*, 9: 195–211.

Kussmaul, Adolf and Nothnagel, Hermann: In Virchow, R. & Hirsch: *Jahresbericht über die Fortschritte der Gesamten Medizin*, 1866–93.

Landouzy, L. (1873) *Gaz. Méd. Paris*, 44: 329.

Lannois, M. and Paviot, J. (1908) 'La nature de la lésion histologique de la chorée de Huntington'. *Neurographs*, 1: 105–12.

Lyon, I.W. (1863) 'Chronic hereditary chorea'. *Amer. Med. Times*, 7: 289–90.

McLearn, J.C. (1885) 'A case of chorea of fifteen years standing in a man aged fifty-six'. *Lancet*, 337–8.

Maltsberger, John T. (1961) 'Even unto the twelfth generation – Huntington's chorea'. *J. Hist. Med.*, 16: 1–17.

Meynert, Theodor (1885) 'Ueber Irradiationszustände im Gehirn'. *Jahrbucher fur Psychiatrie*, vol.VI, p.77.

Narabayashi, H. (1973) 'Huntington's chorea in Japan: review of literature'. In Barbeau, A., Chase, T.N. and Paulsen, G.W. (eds.) *Huntington's Chorea 1872–1972. Advances in Neurology*, vol.I, New York, Raven Pr., pp.253–9.

Oppenheim, H. and Shoppe, H.H. (1890) 'Zur pathologischen Anatomie der Chorea progressiva hereditaria'. *Arch. f. Psychiat. Nervenhk.*, 25: 617–36.

Orbeck, Alf L. (1961) 'An early description of Huntington's Chorea'. *Med. Hist.*, 3: 165–8.

Osler, William (1893) 'Remarks on the varieties of chronic chorea, and a report upon families of the hereditary form with an autopsy'. *J. Nerv. Ment. Dis.*, 20 (XVII): 97–112.

Osler, William (1894) *On Chorea and Choreiform Affections*, London, Lewis, Chapter 7.

Ostwald, Peter (1991) *Vaslav Nijinsky, a Leap into Madness*, New York, Carol.

Peretti, Joseph (1885) 'Ueber hereditäre choreatische Bewegungsstörungen'. *Berlin. kl. Wschr.*, 22: 824–7, 858–862.

Punnett, R.C. (1908) 'Mendelism in relation to disease'. *Proc. Roy. Soc. Med.* 135–68.

Raymond, (1880) 'Danse de Saint Guy'. *Dictionnaire Encyclopédique des Sciences Médicales*, Paris, Masson, p.465.

Remak, Ernst (1891) 'Typische chorea hereditaria nach Epilepsie'. *Neurol. Zbl.*, 3: 326–9, 361–7, 376–8.

Rolleston, Sir Humphrey (1937) 'Medical eponyms'. *Ann. Med. Hist.*, 9: 1–12.

Romberg, Moritz Heinrich (1846) *A Manual of the Nervous Diseases of Man.* Tr. H. Sieveking, 1853, London, Sydenham Soc. vol.2, p.60.

Ruffner, James A. (ed.) (1977) *Eponyms Dictionaries Index*, Detroit, Mich., Gale.

Samuels, B.L. and Gelfand, M. (1978) 'Huntington's chorea in a Black Rhodesian family'. *S. Afr. Med. J.*, 54: 648–57.

Sanders, Julius (1868) 'Chorea minor'. *Arch. f. Psychiat.*, II: 226–7.

Sauvages, François Boissier de la Croix de (1768) *Nosologia Methodica Sistens Morborum Classes juxta Sydenhami mentem & Botanicorum ordinem.* Amsterdam, de Tournes, vol.I, pp.590–1.

Sauvages, François Boissier de la Croix de (1732) *Nouvelles Classes de Maladies*. Avignon, d'Auville, p.268.

Sée, Germain (1850) 'De la chorée et des affections nerveuses en général, avec leurs rapports avec les diathèses et principalement avec le rheumatisme'. *Mem. Acad. Méd.* 14: 343.

Simon, Jules (1867) 'Chorée'. *Nouveau Dictionnaire de Médecine et de Chirurgie pratiques*. Paris, Bailliere, pp.525–56.

Sinkler, Wharton (1889) 'Two additional cases of hereditary chorea'. *J. Nerv. Ment. Dis.*, 14: 86–91.

Stevens, David L. (1972) The history of Huntington's chorea. *J. Roy. Coll. Phycns.*, 6: 271–82.

Stevenson, Charles S. (1934) 'A biography of George Huntington, M.D'. *Bull. Inst. Hist. Med.*, 2: 35–76.

Strümpell, Adolf (1908) 'Zur Casuistik der chronischen Chorea'. *Neurographs*, 1: 98–105.

Sydenham, Thomas (1788) *The Works of Thomas Sydenham on Acute and Chronic Diseases*. ed. George Wallis. London, Robinson, vol.2. pp.327–9.

Vessie, P.R. (1932) 'On the transmission of Huntington's chorea for 300 years- the Bures family group'. *J. Nerv. Ment. Dis.*, 76: 553–73.

Waters, C.O. (1848) In Dunglison, Robley, *The practice of Medicine. A Treatise of Special Patholgy Pathology and Therapeutics.*, 3rd Ed. Philadelphia, Lea & Blanchard, pp.216–18.

Chapter 5
Chorea and Huntington's Disease

Social Section
ROY PORTER

The elucidation of Huntington's disease since the time of George Sumner Huntington (1850–1916), elegantly told in the companion chapter by Professor Schiller, testifies to the progress of modern medicine in its various departments – neurology, biochemistry, genetics. Huntington's chorea as a recognizably distinct disorder goes back around a century and a half. There was a gradual build-up of sightings. In 1841, C.O. Waters, a doctor from Franklin, New York, described a highly convulsive affliction popularly known as 'the magrums', common in the southeastern part of the state. Waters drew attention to its strikingly hereditary nature. He pointed out the cessation of the movements during sleep, the speech impediments attending the condition, its insidious onset and progressive course; and underscored the fact that the disease 'rarely – very rarely indeed – makes its appearance before adult life', but, after onset, 'in all cases it gradually induces a state of more or less perfect dementia'. Here was a reasonably satisfactory characterisation of what was later dubbed Huntington's disease.

Another instance was recorded nearly twenty years later. Johan Christian Lund (fl. 1859), a district physician in Saetersdal, Norway, reported cases of what he termed chorea St Vitus or St Vitus's dance, disorders long familiar, which, he noted, seemed to recur locally as an hereditary disease:

> It is commonly known as the 'twitches', occasionally as the 'inherited disease'. It usually occurs between the ages of 50 and 60, generally starting with less obvious symptoms, which at times only progress slowly, without becoming violent, so that the patient's normal activities are not particularly hindered; but more often after a few years they increase to a considerable degree, so that any form of work becomes impossible and even eating becomes difficult and circuitous. The entire body, though chiefly the head, arms and trunk, is in constant jerking and flinging motion, except during sleep, when the patient is usually motionless. A couple of the severely affected patients have, during the last days of their lives, become demented.

A third description appeared two years later in an article entitled 'Chronic Hereditary Chorea' (1863), by Dr Irving Whitehall Lyon (1840–96), house physician at Bellevue Hospital, New York. Lyon stated that he had been 'familiar from childhood with a variety of chorea . . . unlike in its origin to anything described in our standard textbooks', that is, chorea minor; it was, nevertheless, he insisted, truly a type of chorea, since it consisted of 'irregular action of the voluntary muscles when stimulated by the will', and was marked by 'obstinent chronicity'. He also underscored its hereditary characteristics, observing 'it is confined almost exclusively to certain families ... and the children of parents affected with this disorder are very liable to become the subject of the manifestations, and in turn transmit it to their offspring'.

Some new disorder was thus in the air, but it could not even begin to be *Huntington*'s disease until, on February 15th, 1872, George Huntington addressed the Meigs and Mason Academy, Middleport, Ohio, on the subject of what Thomas Sydenham (1624–89) had designated 'chorea minor'. Only at the close of his talk did he draw attention to hereditary chorea, which he portrayed as a subset of the Sydenhamian condition, though it was 'peculiar in itself and seems to obey certain fixed laws'. Huntington did not know about, or at least did not mention, the earlier accounts. He pointed out its adult onset, the tendency to insanity and suicide, and its congenital nature: 'When either or both of the parents have shown manifestations of the disease ... one or more of the offspring invariably suffer from the disease, if they live to adult life'.

There is no need here to chronicle advances in understanding the disease since Huntington's classic paper; it is a story that may largely be told in terms of the internal dynamics of medical science as investigative technique and clinical practice. These have now yielded a well-documented clinical picture of the syndrome and a satisfactory explanatory framework (genetically transmitted neuronal defects). In respect of actual and potential sufferers, informed decisions, e.g., about childbearing risks, can now be made on the basis of expert evidence: see for example the graphic chapter in Klawans (1990). Yet even technical developments in laboratory and clinical medicine make fuller sense when contextualized within broader cultural expectations and socio-historical trends; and various aspects of Huntington's disease since Huntington catch the social historian's eye. For one thing, it is suggestive that Huntington himself, born in East Hampton, at the eastern end of Long Island, was, like his grandfather and father before him, an obscure country practitioner. 'On Chorea' was his only published paper; he subsequently remained a country generalist. With present career patterns, is it credible that a comparable rural practitioner could make a similar break-through? In the Victorian era, however, such contributions were common. It was not at all unusual for ordinary family practitioners, working solo, to engage in medical investigations – indeed to achieve high-order discoveries, treading in the footsteps of Edward Jenner (1749–1823), the Gloucestershire pioneer of smallpox vaccination. Perusal of the early volumes even of a new specialist journal like *Brain* (founded in 1878) reveals that a substantial proportion of contributors were private physicians entirely without official or hospital appointments or institutional laboratory facilities. James Mackenzie (1853–1925), one of the most innovative investigators of heart disease earlier this century, was, for much of his career, a Lancashire general practitioner. Only since the First World War have increased medical funding and the forging of clinical science granted specialists virtual monopoly of research opportunities and glory.

But, as the founding of *Brain* six years after Huntington's lecture equally suggests, the research pace was quickening, partly through the efficacy of medico-scientific journals in network creation. If Huntington's chorea was slow to be identified, or at least labelled, a remarkable stream of papers rapidly followed Huntington's publication. In the fifteen-year span between 1872 and 1887, as Dr Schiller shows, at least thirty-one studies were devoted to the subject, including papers by such eminent investigators as Landouzy (1845–1917), Golgi (1843–1926), Bourneville (1840–1909), Charcot (1825–93) and Meynert (1833–1892). Investigation moved from the countryside into the clinic, hospital and university laboratory.

And, over the decades, conceptualization of the disorder shifted as medical preoccupations themselves changed. In the late Victorian era, Huntington's condition was widely interpreted as a degenerative disorder, in line with prevalent theories of degeneration and later eugenics. In the present century, growing theorization of metabolic disorders has transformed understanding of constitutional diseases, with great attention being paid to hereditary disorders due to inborn errors of metabolism. Recent success in unravelling Huntington's disease has depended upon striking advances in biochemical and neurological research, in turn helping to crown these specialties in glory.

An intriguing contrast may thus be drawn. A condition with a demonstrably long history was not, it seems, isolated for specific attention, and certainly not for a special appellation, until the second half of the nineteenth century. Thereafter, research advanced rapidly, both quantitively and qualitatively. Intriguing general questions are raised by this paradox. Why do diseases become 'visible' at particular times? – does every disease have its day? How far is such visibility due to discerning individual practitioners, and how far to the *Zeitgeist*? How is it that scattered physicians independently produced almost identical observations at roughly the same time? What role is played by the affixing of an eponym in stimulating or giving coherence to research? And why, for example, did the disorder become Huntington's not Waters' or Lund's? After all, the other depictions included the same elements as Huntington's, stressing that the condition was serious, chronic, beginning in adulthood with slight choreic movements and progressing until the patient became a quivering, demented wreck.

These questions cannot be resolved here, but it is worth airing the issues surrounding the historical understanding of diseases or what the eminent American medical historian, Charles Rosenberg (1989), has termed the business of 'framing disease'. Diseases, Rosenberg does not doubt, are real entities in nature; but in some important sense they do not *exist* for medicine until they have been identified, named and classified. To that extent, as well as being 'natural', diseases are also socio-medically 'constructed' or, in his preferred term, 'framed' – though he is surely right to observe that there is no advantage in making a big play about *social* constructivism. The term 'social history of medicine', he explains, 'is as tautological as that of the "social construction" of disease; every aspect of medicine's history is necessarily "social" – that acted out in laboratory or library as well as at the bedside'. To pit social against scientific factors would mean a silly cold war of words.

The 'framing disease' issue is not a trivial pursuit indulged by ivory-towered philosophers of history. For it helps explain why physicians have been so preoccupied with probing the history of diseases. When doctors scrutinize the medical records of previous centuries (case-books, hospital records, diagnostic manuals, and so forth), there may be two aims in view; broaching accurate retrospective identifications for conditions formerly undiagnosed or mistakenly diagnosed; and/or hoping to uncover shrewd clinical descriptions of syndromes penned before these were officially named and designated. A thriving cottage industry, for example, seeks to unearth from hospital and clinical case-notes credible depictions of schizophrenics a full century before the classic formulations of Kraepelin (1856–1926) and Bleuler (1857–1939). The motives for such after-the-event diagnosis have included matters of practical epidemiological importance; but there have also been other agendas, overt and hidden. The capacity retrospectively to diagnose once mysterious or misidentified complaints *avant la lettre* – for example, the great 'plague' of Athens, recorded by Thucydides (c.460–400BC); a problem that has attracted mountains of scholarship – may gratify the ego at the same time as offering confirmation of medical progress. But something else is at stake, substantiation of a key tenet of psychological medicine.

A certain strand of medical sociology, drawing upon the work of Thomas Szasz (b. 1920) and of 1960s radical anti-psychiatry, has queried the reality of mental illness. Much so-called psychiatric illness, critics allege, was in truth but the expression, in diverse forms, of suffering and protest; and various supposed psychiatric disorders, like nymphomania, have been labels affixed by health professionals for tightening of social control. Mental disease was thus in large degree a social artefact (a more extreme version of Rosenberg's position, just discussed). In the levelling and countering of such charges, the historical record has naturally formed a key battleground. For if it can be shown through case analysis that patients in former centuries were definitely suffering from diseases presenting nowadays, the logical inference would be that such disorders display a natural incidence relatively unconstrained by socio-cultural determinants and independent of observer prejudice. Thus if early nineteenth-century asylum doctors accurately described schizophrenic traits, long before the disorder itself was framed and named, would not that be a particularly powerful refutation of critics who deny schizophrenia's objective reality? Eighteenth-century natural philosophers were keen to assert the action throughout the Universe of basic laws of nature like gravity, since they would thereby be accorded an unlimited cognitive empire over which their writ would be unchallengeable; in a parallel manner, psychiatrists have felt reassured by apparent confirmations of the objective occurrence of clinical syndromes in time and space. For medical science it has been crucial to establish the historical stability of illnesses, physical and psychiatric alike. Thus the great French neurologist, Jean-Martin Charcot (1825–93) declared in ringing tones that '*l'Hystérie a toujours existé, en tous lieux et en tous temps*'. That was a bold enunciation of a creed, one perhaps betraying Charcot's private anxieties that critics may have been right to allege that his dramatic demonstrations of hysteria at the Salpêtrière were not natural facts but artifacts of clinical practice.

Huntington's disease offers an arresting instance of this phenomenon. Being 'framed' only recently, it leaves a vast historical *longue durée* in which sleuths might expect to unearth earlier manifestations, unwittingly described or camouflaged under other clinical names. And it also raises complicated questions of the relationship between Huntington's disease specifically and chorea in general (Huntington's own lecture, it will be remembered, was principally on chorea minor). So it is worth asking: when clinicians and neurologists interested in chorea and allied disorders involving involuntary and disruptive motion have peered back into the past, what have they 'found', and how have they framed their historical narratives?

Monotonously but instructively, such (pre-)histories standardly revert to a common source event: the striking phenomenon of the dancing sicknesses frequently chronicled during the medieval era. Records of dancing manias go back at least to the twelfth century, but they become common after the Black Death (1348–50). In 1374 a band of Germans arrived in Aix-la-Chapelle (Aachen), formed a circle and, according to the chronicler, began to dance compulsively. Screaming and foaming at the mouth, and having 'lost all control over their senses' after cavorting 'in a wild delirium', they finally collapsed exhausted. Onlookers joined in and the dancing fever spread, becoming a kind of epidemic that finally engulfed the whole region. During the next half-century further outbreaks were recorded, especially in German-speaking lands and the Low Countries. The eruptions in Strasbourg in 1418 were particularly severe. The idea also grew up that music was a remedy, though it may simply have exacerbated the phenomenon. In this respect, the northern dancing mania joined hands with the contemporary phenomenon of tarantism on the far side of the Alps. When Italians were seized with convulsions and fell into trances, folk wisdom supposed that their condition was due to the bite of the tarantula, and the prescribed remedy was violent, ecstatic group dancing, accompanied by wine and music, to induce the perspiration that would carry off the spider's poison. For several centuries tarantella players were summoned to save the lives of those bitten.

Stories like these of medieval dancing manias and tarantism have been retailed for centuries in the literature of psychological medicine, often with dark hints of connexions with demoniacal possession and the witch-craze. Bruyn (1968) is correct to note that

> Traditionally, nearly every recent writer on the subject [of involuntary limb motions] has sought the historical sources of choreatic movements in the strange phenomenon of an epidemic dance psychosis which originated in the fourteenth century and which has become known as 'St Vitus dance', a term which first came into use in the early seventeenth century. Obvious as this may seem, since choreatic disorders are described as 'St Vitus dance' by the laity of this day, it is to be doubted if it is correct, choreomania certainly differs widely from chorea. Study of pertinent works on the subject (Hecker, 1832; Bouteille, 1810; Wicke, 1844; Brandis, 1818; Nicolas, 1883; Haeser, 1865; Davidson, 1867/68; Zdralek, 1868; Witkowski, 1879; Sée, 1850; Sauvages, 1772) will show that following a dance epidemic in 1021 in Kolbig and the Black Death which swept over the European countries from 1348 onwards, a widespread dance epidemic started in Untenheim in 1374, within some weeks spreading to Cologne and Aachen and from there to Utrecht, Liège, Tongeren and Metz. It had been customary in those times of the Plague to have a 'St John the Baptist festival' if the year had been free of the dreaded

disease. The wear and tear of the Crusades, the toll levied by the Black Death, and the persecution of the Jews instigated by the Emperor Charles IV (in spite of the papal prohibition) under the pretext that they poisoned the wells, had made the people nervous and confused. In addition to this, the rivers Rhine and Main flooded large areas of land in February 1374. The first wild, religious, mass-psychotic St John's dance occurred in 1374. The dance mania spread to other countries (France: 'danse de St Guy', Italy: 'tarantulismo', 'stellio', 'astaragazza', Baglivi 1699) and in Strasburg the epidemic exploded again in 1518 (not in 1418 as was pointed out by Witkowski). About the middle of the sixteenth century the term 'chorea' seems to have been accepted for denoting dance mania; we know that Paracelsus (1493–1541) distinguished chorea naturalis s. coacta due to natural somatic causes, chorea lasciva (due to voluptuous desire), and chorea imaginativa s. aestimativa (caused by imagination), and that Bayro used the word 'chorea' Sancti Viti' seems to have come into use to denote the epidemics and similar individual manifestations.

It is worth pondering this lengthy and weighty statement, because it details such an extraordinary roll-call of physicians, over several centuries, who have felt driven to trace choreatic movements back to the dansomaniacs. The explanatory process has generally involved a certain circularity. On the one hand, ancient instances of bizarre behaviour are interpreted in the light of later medical expertise, while, on the other, to close the explanatory loop, modern disorders, through association with a fantastic past, are endowed with a historical pedigree and a voyeuristic fascination.

Scrutiny of writings on chorea-like phenomena suggests a succession of evolutionary stages in their preoccupations. Medical authors before the mid-seventeenth century were very close to the phenomenon – not necessarily to the 'dance craze' *per se* but certainly to menacing outbursts of collective hysterical and disruptive behaviour associated with radical religious sects. Not surprisingly, therefore, their main concern lay in something akin to diagnostics. Were convulsionaries sick? Or were they diabolically possessed? Should they be treated by the Church or by physicians? Should they be punished? Was the condition curable or preventable? With varying aims, medical men confirmed, complemented or confounded the tenets of the ecclesiastics. And that is evident in the terminology they deployed. Early modern physicians like Felix Plater (1536–1614) and Daniel Sennert (1572–1637) used such phrases as 'Viti Saltus', St Vitus's dance, or 'chorea Sancti Viti'. In other words, their medical nomenclature was contingent upon prior religious formulations. St. Vitus himself was, according to folk myth, an early fourth century Christian missionary who, in A.D. 303, miraculously escaped alive from being boiled in oil. For rather obscure reasons, belief grew up that sufferers with the dancing malady and other spastic afflictions could be cured by a visit to his shrine in the Alsatian village of Zabern.

St Vitus's dance was thus a revealing term for the physicians to employ. It acknowledged the religious force field governing conceptualization of the condition, and it carried undertones of divine healing (St Vitus would cure). But it could also convey a powerful anti-religious charge. Especially for Protestants, the enigmatic St Vitus, and healing by saints in general, were tarred with the same brush as the Shakers and Convulsionaries: Robert Burton (1577–1640) insisted in his anti-catholic *Anatomy of Melancholy* (1621) that veneration of saints was a form of melancholy delusion. Paracelsus (1493–1541) had earlier protested against diseases being attributed to the devil or being named after a saint. He rejected the notion that Saint Vitus's intervention could cure the affliction, preferring hydrotherapy, solitary confinement and fasting; he even abandoned the name, calling such afflictions varieties of 'chorea'.

In line with Paracelsus's stand, a shift seems to have been occurring in the latter part of the seventeenth century, notable in the writings of Thomas Sydenham. Discussing St Vitus's dance, Sydenham did not even mention the earlier demoniacal associations or the medieval manifestations. In *Schedula monitoria* (1686) he wrote of 'Chorea of St. Vitus':

> This disorder is a kind of convulsion which seizes children of both sexes from the tenth to the fourteenth year; it manifests itself by a halting or unsteadiness of one of the legs which the patient draws after him like an ideot. If the hand of the same side be applied to the breast, or any other party of the body, the child can't keep it a moment in the same posture, but it will be drawn into a different one by a convulsion, notwithstanding all his efforts to the contrary. Before the child who hath this disorder can get a glass or cup to his mouth he useth abundance of odd gestures; for he does not bring it in a straight line thereto, but his hand being drawn sideways by the spasm he moves it backwards and forwards till at length the glass accidentally coming nearer his lips he throws the liquor hastily into his mouth and swallows it greedily, as if he meant to divert the spectators.

Sydenham thus focused upon musculoskeletal manifestations and upon establishing an organic aetiology in clinical cases that he may well have seen first-hand.

In the age of reason, as choreomania ceased to be a palpable threat and faded into a memory, physicians mounted discussions of St Vitus's dance to serve didactic purposes. Richard Mead (1673–1754) was one of many Enlightenment physicians trenchantly dismissive of all facets of the phenomenon as traditionally understood: dancers, priests and earlier doctors alike – all were guilty of superstition. For Mead, disease was necessarily, of its nature, mechanical and susceptible to rational explanation. Taxonomists like Boissier de Sauvages (1706–1767) and William Cullen (1710–1790) naturalized St Vitus's dance by detailing its varieties and emplacing it snugly within their larger nosological systems. Sauvages distinguished five different forms of chorea: scelotyrbe Viti (corresponding to Sydenham's chorea); scelotyrbe festinans (agreeing with what later became known as parkinsonism); scelotyrbe instabilis, including the ataxias and (possibly) Huntington's chorea; scelotyrbe intermittens; and scelotyrbe verminosa, as described by Gaubius (1705–1780). Similar tendencies continued in later examinations, but with a further twist. In writing about chorea's prehistory, many nineteenth-century physicians showed, in addition to the 'univeralism' Charcot exhibited, a new attention to evaluating the verdicts of earlier medical writers. In other words, interest in the *history of medicine* was beginning to take its place alongside concern for the *natural history of disease*.

Medical erudition, antiquarianism and bibliography had much to say about the early history of chorea, sometimes to the accompaniment of much scholarly scolding: 'The name chorea', pronounced the *Encyclopaedia Medica* (1916), with a wag of the finger, 'has unfortunately been applied to a number of entirely different complaints'.

In the twentieth century, the medieval dansomaniacs have retained their exemplary status within medicine's historical mythology: for the latest airing in the literature, see Park and Park (1990); but the rationale has once again changed. Such phenomena have mainly been debated during the last generations in context of psychodynamics. Partly in the light of social psychology and partly thanks to Freudian doctrines, the terminology of 'neurosis', 'mass hysteria' and 'collective neurosis' has been bandied about for explaining tarantism and ecstatic behaviour. Popular Freudian accounts have, in turn, been challenged, thanks to today's scepticism towards purely psychogenic behavioural theories and the speculative excesses of psychohistory; Mary Matossian (1989) has counter-argued that the collective frenzies of the past may best be explained as the outcome of spoiled or toxic foodstuffs (ergotism). And neurologists like Harold Klawans (1990) have hinted at continuing suspicions that Huntington's disease or some form of chorea may have been implicated in the dancing mania.

There is no convincing evidence – in the bulk of cases we will never know for certain. But a few reasonably well-documented cases may be cited in which phenomena identified several centuries ago as demoniacal can reliably be associated with Huntington's disease. Certain American Huntington's sufferers have been traced back to seventeenth-century ancestors in Bures (Suffolk), who migrated to the New World in the 1630s. No fewer than seven of the daughters or grand-daughters of the family in question were accused, in the New World, of witchlike activities, one of them, Mercy Disborough, becoming a *cause célèbre* and being subjected in 1692 to the traditional water trial. It is plausible to suggest that signs of Huntington's chorea exhibited by these family members played some part in sparking the charges of witchcraft levelled against them. In the case of Elizabeth Knapp, for instance, the local preacher wrote: 'this pore and miserable object . . . was observed to carry herselfe in a strange and unwonted manner, sometimes she would give sudden shriekes . . . and then would burst forth into immoderate and extravagant laughter . . . as sometimes shee fell onto ye ground with it'. He described what appear to have been plain manifestations of chorea: 'shee was violent in bodily motions, leapings, strainings and strange agitations'. He concluded that she was a demoniac, possessed by a Devil who 'began by drawing her tongue out of her mouth most frightfully to an extraordinary length and greatnesse, and many amazing postures of her bodye'. It would be wrong to assume that all accused witches, or even any substantial proportion of them, suffered from neurological disorders. But cases like these suggest that the concurrence was not unknown; and the disease may truly have reinforced belief in diabolism.

REFERENCES

Bruyn, G.W. (1968) 'Huntington's Chorea: historical, clinical and laboratory synopsis'. In Vinken, P.J. and Bruyn, G.W. (eds.) *Handbook of Clinical*

Neurology, vol.6, Amsterdam, North-Holland Publishing Company, pp.298–378.

Critchley, M. (1964) 'Huntington's Chorea. Historical and geographical considerations'. In *The Black Hole and Other Essays*, London, Pitman Medical Publishing Co Ltd, pp.210–19.

Critchley, M. (1973) 'Great Britain and the early history of Huntington's Chorea'. In *Advances in Neurology*, vol.1. New York, Raven Press, pp.13–17.

DeJong, R.N. (1973) 'The history of Huntington's Chorea in the United States of America'. In *Advances in Neurology*, vol.1. New York, Raven Press, pp.19–27.

Huntington, G. (1872) 'On Chorea'. *The Medical and Surgical Reporter*, 26: 320–1.

Klawans, H. (1990) *Newton's Madness*, London, The Bodley Head.

Matossian, M.K. (1989) *Poisons of the Past: Molds, Epidemics and History.* New Haven, Conn., and London, Yale University Press.

Orbeck, A.L. (1959) 'An early description of Huntington's Chorea'. *Medical History*, 3: 165–8.

Park, R.H.R. and Park, M.P. (1990) 'Saint Vitus' Dance: vital misconceptions by Sydenham and Bruegel'. *Journal of the Royal Society of Medicine*, 83: 512–15.

Rosenberg, C.E. (1989) 'Disease in history: frames and framers'. *Millbank Quarterly*, Suppl. 1: 67: 1–15.

Russell, J.F. (1979) 'Tarantism'. *Medical History*, 23: 404–25.

Shechter, D.C. (1975) 'St Vitus' Dance and rheumatic disease'. *New York State Journal of Medicine*, 75: 1091–1102.

Chapter 6
Epilepsy

Clinical Section
GE BERRIOS

The history of epilepsy has received attention from historians, and Temkin's book (Temkin, 1971) remains a classic in the field. This chapter will only explore the history of the relationship between mental symptoms and epilepsy, particularly since the nineteenth-century. Up to the 1840s, the severe presentations of epilepsy were treated in mental asylums. Thus, in one of the most complete reviews on epilepsy published towards the end of the century, the author wrote: 'In fact, alienists have been the ones who have shown more interest in epilepsy' (Burlureaux, 1887, p.121). This was to change, particularly in the wake of Jackson's work, when epilepsy ceased to be a 'psychiatric' disease. This created a difficulty in regard to the status of its psychiatric manifestations which had then to be called 'complications' (Pond, 1973; Guerant et al, 1962; Lamperière, 1955; Lecce and Caraffa, 1964; Bruens, 1973). Studying these events will help to understand how neurology and psychiatry came to diverge, and also current obscurities affecting the 'psychiatry of epilepsy'. Work is made difficult by the fact that, since the last century, and whether due to genetic mutations, new medication, or level of care, the clinical presentation of some mental symptoms is said to have changed (Hare, 1974).

THE BEGINNINGS

At the beginning of the nineteenth century, the old Cullean category of 'neuroses' encompassed both the insanities and epilepsy (López Piñero, 1983) and convulsions and unconsciousness were the defining features of the latter. For example, Cullen defined epilepsy as *Musculorum convulsio cum sopore* (Cullen, 1803, p.299). Thus definitions from this period are out of phase with current ones, and the historian must be careful not to equate the two. By the beginning of the nineteenth century, the clinical scope of epilepsy began to expand and its re-definitions became progressively more 'psychiatric' in content, this process culminating with the notion of 'masked epilepsy' in which convulsions and unconsciousness did not seem necessary any more to make the diagnosis of epilepsy.

By the end of the nineteenth century, however, the bubble had burst and a much narrower, 'neurological' definition ensued out of the work of Jackson, Gowers, Hitzig and others. Factors relevant to this process included the narrowing of the concept of neurosis, the introduction of some forms of statistical analysis, the availability of data arising from longitudinal cohorts and private practice, the redefinition of delirium, and the creation of the new category of 'psychoses'. Neo-Baconianism and the philosophy of observation had encouraged the development of new descriptive categories (units of analysis) and this led to the acceptance of subjective experiences (as reported by the patient) as valid indices of disease (Berrios, 1884; Riese, 1960). As it is repeatedly mentioned in this book, the objective of early nineteenth century medicine was the search for a focused anatomical 'lesion' that might explain the disease (Laín Entralgo, 1978; Foucault, 1973; Ackerknecht, 1967).

FRENCH VIEWS

Esquirol
It was during that period of expansion that Esquirol (1815) felt able to write: 'Epilepsy, when compounded by insanity, never gets better'. This conclusion, one of twelve he listed, was to control thinking on the association between epilepsy and insanity for decades. Esquirol found that four-fifths of his female epileptic inpatients were affected by monomania, mania, dementia, fury, idiocy and character disorders. None of these categories fully tallies with current usage of these terms. Esquirol's view on the range of epileptic manifestations includes generalized attacks, 'vertigo' (later to be called absence or petit mal epilepsy), and other disorders of movement and awareness (Esquirol, 1838). His classification of epilepsy into essential, sympathetic, symptomatic, and simulated was based on the pre-nineteenth century view that epilepsy was not exclusively associated with the brain (Masland, 1973). *Essential* epilepsy resulted from cerebral lesions or from 'moral' (psychological) causes. Thus, Esquirol was still able to diagnose patients with no identifiable lesion as having epilepsy. *Sympathetic* epilepsy arose from digestive, cardiovascular, lymphatic, and genital lesions; *symptomatic* epilepsy included seizures caused by infections; *simulated* epilepsy encompassed hysterical seizures and malingering. On the basis of his classifications, Esquirol identified 46 cases of 'feigned epilepsy' in a sample of 385 hospitalized 'epileptics'. Two hundred and seventy-nine patients suffered from psychiatric disorder: 50 patients had post-ictal cognitive impairment, 12 patients monomania, 30 mania, 34 aggressive behaviour, 145 dementia, and 8 idiocy. Esquirol's conclusion that four fifths of his cohort were affected by mental disorder is one of the earliest *statistical* claims in favour of an association between epilepsy and mental disorder.

Esquirol did not distinguish between inter-ictal and peri-ictal disorders; his itemized psychiatric categories are, in the main, clinical variations of post-ictal confusion, and the group categorized as 'dementia' included patients suffering from early brain damage, mental handicap, and obscure degenerative conditions (Bouchet and Cazauvieilh, 1825–26). Esquirol concluded that psychiatric disorder was more likely to occur following epilepsy of early onset, or high seizure frequency and *vertigo*.

Bouchet and Cazauvieilh
Esquirol's view that mental disorder worsened the prognosis of epilepsy did not go unheeded, and in 1825, in one of the earliest issues of the *Archives Générales de Médicine*, Bouchet and Cazauvieilh published the result of their enquiry into

the nature of the association between epilepsy and insanity. Of the 47 cases on which they had post-mortem data, the authors personally studied twenty-eight. Clear conclusions cannot be drawn from this material as the language of description is variable and no allowance is made for ante- and post-mortem changes. Eighteen patients suffered from both epilepsy and psychiatric disturbance and ten from insanity alone. The age of the patients in the combined diagnoses group ranged from 21 to 77 years (mean = 35; SD = 16) and the duration of their illness from three to 31 years. Dementia (i.e. cognitive impairment) was the most common psychiatric disturbance (66.6 per cent). All patients had grand mal fits, and in seven patients absences had also been present. The mean age of the patients in the insanity group was 47.7 (SD = 11); seven (70 per cent) of these patients had a diagnosis of dementia, and two (20 per cent) exhibited uncal involvement.

The most remarkable finding (but alas one that just misses statistically significance) is that seven patients (38 per cent) in the combined diagnosis group exhibited *uncal* involvement. Twenty-eight years later Bouchet (1853) described yet another 43 patients, 12 of whom also had '*induration des cornes d'Ammon*'. Their ages ranged from 14 to 71 years (mean = 35, SD = 14); four patients had been mentally retarded, two patients had dementia, and one was insane. When Sommer (1880) published his famous study of 90 cases on the association between epilepsy and Ammon's horn sclerosis, he made sure to include all of Bouchet's cases. Neither of these authors remarked on the possible association between hippocampal sclerosis and mental disorder.

Bouchet and Cazauvieilh suggested that 'vertigo' was an 'imperfect' form of grand mal epilepsy and believed it might predict the development of psychiatric disorder. They concluded that 'phlegmasia of the brain' caused both conditions; but while epilepsy resulted from involvement of the white matter, insanity was the outcome of grey matter involvement. Analysis of their post-mortem reports, however, does not support this conclusion; it is more likely that their interpretation was determined by the generalized theoretical view that insanity was a disease of the cortex.

Bouchet and Cazauvieilh also wrote that past research 'had been based on the assumption that epilepsy was the cause of insanity. We shall try to analyse all the possibilities of the relationship'. With prescience they wanted to deal with a very specific type of patient: 'Many patients do not become psychotic until a number of years have passed: In some cases the psychosis appears after the fourth or fifth admission separated by intervals in which they are well'.

Other French alienists

After Bouchet and Cazauvieilh the view was held in France that no fundamental difference existed between epilepsy and psychosis. Indeed, theirs should be considered as the first strong claim that epilepsy and insanity shared a common neuropathology. Whether the patient showed one or the other depended on whether the same pathological process affected white or grey matter. This is the way in which later specialists understood their contribution: 'The authors tried to demonstrate the relationship between epilepsy and insanity . . . suggesting that both were . . . due to phlegmasia (inflammation) of the brain, the one of the white, the other of the grey matter' (Garimond, 1878). This interesting view is in keeping with early and middle nineteenth-century neurophysiology, namely, that the highest motor station was sited in subcortical regions, and that grey matter or cortex was reserved for consciousness and the mind (Young, 1970). These assumptions, however, did not save the clinical facts: they could not explain, for example, why grand mal seizures (accompanied by loss of consciousness and hence reflecting 'cortical involvement') were not always complicated by insanity. Furthermore post-mortem studies showed that cortical pathology was often absent in grand mal epilepsy.

Calmeil (1824), on the other hand, was inclined to the view that epilepsy was a brain disease *without* specific locus. He confirmed Esquirol's claim about the incurability of insane epileptics, noted that worsening of the psychiatric disorder may lead to a reduction of seizure frequency, and replaced vertigo by 'absence'. He also believed that melancholia could only develop if there was no cognitive impairment and that mania was extremely rare. Hysterical seizures, he observed, do not lead to dementia.

Georget (1835) defined epilepsy as a 'disease of the brain whose nature was intermittent, chronic, and apyretic, and that was characterized by convulsive attacks, generally of short duration, accompanied by sudden and complete loss of consciousness', and refused to accept the existence of 'sympathetic epilepsy'.

Thus, by this period, claims were accumulating that considered epilepsy as a disease of the white matter, a form of neurosis, and a possible cause of psychiatric disorders (particularly dementia). Age of onset, frequency, and type of seizure were all considered as relevant to the development of mental disease. Peri-ictal and inter-ictal mental disorders, however, were not systematically differentiated and clinical conclusions were only based on impressionistic and uncontrolled observations of long-term hospital patients. The main reported psychiatric complications were dementia and confusion, but since the meaning of these categories was changing at the time (Berrios, 1981; Berrios and Freeman, 1991) no conclusion can be drawn as to the real nature of the mental disorders observed.

MOREL AND THE 'MASKED EPILEPSY' CONCEPT

Morel put forward the radically new concept of 'épilepsie larvée' or 'masked epilepsy' (Morel, 1860). He argued that epilepsy manifested itself either as convulsions and absences or in 'abnormal mental states' or abnormal behaviour. A diagnosis of 'masked epilepsy' could, therefore, be made in the absence of a history of convulsions. It is sufficient, he claimed, to recognize clinical features such as a paroxysmal nature and pre-morbid personality. To advance his notion of 'masked epilepsy', Morel used the concept of *epileptic character*. This great French alienist, better known for his work on degeneration, was an experienced asylum doctor, and is likely to have looked after many epileptics with personality disorder. Adjectives used to describe the 'epileptic character' form a long list: sticky, obsequious, explosive, unpredictable, over-religious, irritable, vindictive, and so on. Lecce and Caraffa (1964) have shown that most of these terms appeared during Morel's time. The problem with such a rich descriptive set is that, when used carelessly, it generates many false positives (i.e. many without the disease are diagnosed as having epilepsy).

Morel's concept was never fully accepted in French Psychiatry, and in the event, an important debate about its significance took place at the *Société*

Médico-Psychologique (Société Médico-Psychologique, 1873). Critics (like Fournet) insisted that insanity and epilepsy were independent diagnoses, and pointed at the clinical fallacy of diagnosing as epileptic a patient who had never had a seizure. Morel (who, unfortunately, died in 1873 before the debate was over) offered diagnostic 'signes': 1) marked instability of character, 2) increased motor activity, 3) 'polymorphous' delusions, 4) sudden, explosive behaviour, 5) episodic repetition of stereotyped insanity, and 6) sudden shouting.

It also had its defenders. For example, Legrand (1877) wrote that 'he had personally participated in the construction of that condition, and to judge by the interest shown by many authors, science should not hesitate now to award to l'épilepsie larvée its letters patent' (p.104). In spite of this spirited defence, the diagnosis of 'masked epilepsy' continue declining, and its obituary was written by Garimond (1878) who showed that it had given rise to too many conceptual difficulties, and had both negligible explanatory power and limited clinical value.

THE CONTEXTUAL CHANGES

Evolution of the Concept of Neurosis
The persistent failure to identify relevant anatomic changes in the neuroses led to a reassessment of the concept of 'lesion' (López Piñero, 1983). The rediscovery of the reflex arc (Fearing, 1930; Liddell, 1960; Canguilhem, 1975, 1977), with its prompt application to matter clinical, and the rapid growth of physiology (Schiller, 1968) led to the development of the concept of 'functional lesion'. Pathologic phenomena such as inflammation and irritation (Broussais, 1828) acquired explanatory value by being considered as pathogenic mechanisms mediated by the nervous system. Hall (1841), for example, put forward a 'reflex theory' of epilepsy: 'I have already suggested, indeed, that all convulsive diseases are affections of the true spinal marrow . . . [which is] the centre of a peculiar series of excitomotor phenomena, physiological and pathological'. (Toward the end of the century, similar mechanisms were invoked for 'neurasthenia' which was also seen as a form of 'brain irritation'.) (Savill, 1906; Cobb, 1920; Carlson, 1970) (see also chapter on the history of neurasthenia, this book).

Towards the end of the century, this 'physiological' re-interpretation of the concept of lesion inevitably led to a 'psychologisation' of the neuroses (López Piñero and Morales Meseguer, 1970; Bercherie, 1983). From the clinical viewpoint, however, its most immediate effect was that it led to separating all 'neurotic' conditions with specific and localized lesions, i.e. the ones that were to become the core of the new specialty of neurology (López Piñero, 1883; Riese, 1959; McHenry, 1969; Riese, 1945). Cullen's definition of neuroses was partially responsible for this. For him, neuroses were 'praeternatural affections of sense and motion which do not depend upon a topical affection of the organs but upon a more general affection of the nervous system' (Cullen, 1784). The anti-localization bias (Carlson and Simpson, 1969), contained in this definition could not but clash with the principles of the anatomico-clinical school (López Piñero, 1983). Toward the end of the nineteenth century, the number of 'neuroses' had dwindled back to the original 'nervous diseases' of Sydenham and Willis (Hare, 1991); the only new member in this group being the 'obsessive neurosis' (Berrios, 1985).

The 'Numerical Method'

Head-counting and percentages were a common evidential method of the anatomico-pathologic school (Shryock, 1961). In 1814, Laplace (1921) published his calculus of probabilities and later on suggested that it might apply to medical research (Keynes, 1929; Gigerenzer et al, 1989). Descriptions by counting thus became important to the analysis of the symptoms of epilepsy. Louis, the great French physician, led the movement to introduce statistics into medicine, and his views influenced researchers on both sides of the channel (Ackerknecht, 1967). Works from this period on neurology (Hall, 1841) and epilepsy (Herpin, 1852; Reynolds, 1861) often acknowledged Louis's work. The conclusions drawn by these great men rarely achieved 'statistical significance' but were suggestive enough to create clinical trends, some of which have lingered on to the present day (Ey, 1954).

The New Psychopathology

As it is mentioned in other chapters of this book, the first half of the nineteenth century saw the development of languages specialized in the description of mental symptoms (Berrios, 1984; Lanteri-Laura, 1983). The new philosophy of observation made possible a detailed description of symptoms which replaced global accounts of madness. This also led to the introduction of subjective information (i.e. of patients' experiences [Riese, 1960; Moreau de Tours, 1850]). This, in turn, created the need for psychological theories to understand and structure introspective data: this was satisfied by a combination of faculty psychology and associationism (Berrios, 1988). This acceptance by alienists of the 'subjective' as legitimate data was another factor in the eventual divergence of neurology from psychiatry. During this period, the language of causal explanation may appear confusing to the casual observer. Stressful life events, post-mortem findings and (after the 1850s) hereditary factors, were listed together. The pre-eminence of organic factors during this period created the impression that all that mattered was a brain lesion. This is an inaccurate view of how alienists conceived of the causes of disease. Principal and mediating causes were distinguished with much emphasis put on the former. Organic lesions, in fact, were considered as *mediating* factors and the interest that alienists showed in them should not be interpreted as a rejection of psychological accounts. Failure to find any lesions led, toward the end of the century, to reduced interest in the 'lesion principle'. Kraepelin was interested in experimental psychology and Freud's work did not emerge in a vacuum: both reflect a process of psychologisation started earlier in the century (Bercherie, 1983; Levin, 1978).

SEPARATING EPILEPSY FROM INSANITY

Herpin and Reynolds

Herpin's monograph (1852) was the first to challenge the view that epilepsy and insanity were closely associated. The great French physician described 38 cases collected from his private practice (20 females and 18 males) with a length of illness ranging from a few days to 20 years (the majority were, however, of recent onset). For 15 cases Herpin reported positive response to treatment (usually zinci oxidum). This surprising rate of success may have been due to the fact that he included in the sample transitory seizure disorders such as febrile convulsions (indeed, four patients were aged under 12 months!). Herpin concluded: 'However common this sad complication [i.e. insanity] is in the asylum, we have found only one case in our series . . . which we can claim constitutes a natural cross section of the epileptic population . . . the type of epilepsy observed in the hospitals is far more severe than that examined here'. Herpin's second series of 300 cases, and dedicated to Louis, was only published posthumously (Herpin, 1867). In this book, he developed the clinical concept of 'incomplete seizure' and reported cases exhibiting bizarre subjective experiences of the kind that Jackson and Steward (1899) were to describe much later as 'dreamy states'. Jackson intimated that he had come across Herpin's book only after his own work on the subject had been completed.

It followed the classic monograph by Reynolds (1861) dedicated to W.H. Walshe (another of Louis' students). Reynolds conceived of epilepsy as a physiological disturbance favouring the medulla oblongata as the most likely 'organ affected' (p.245). He defined epilepsy as a chronic disease characterized by occasional loss of consciousness with or without muscular contraction (p.12) and suggested that the term be used to refer only to the *idiopathic* form (i.e. when no pathologic alteration could be identified). The source of Reynolds' cases is not altogether clear (they are likely to have been a mixture of private and hospital patients). He studied the 'mental condition of 62 epileptics during the interval of their attacks' and found that 38 per cent were free from any 'failure', 32 per cent showed a slight degree of memory defect for 'trifling events', and 18 per cent suffered from impairment of memory and of the 'faculty of apprehension'. Reynolds believed that insanity and 'mania' were rare complications.

He concluded that epilepsy: (1) did not necessarily give rise to mental disorder, (2) a severe degree of mental impairment was the exception rather than the rule, (3) women were more prone to manifesting mental symptoms than men, (4) the most common mental impairment involved memory and judgement, (5) depression was more common in men, and (6) other disorders (e.g. insanity) were rare (Reynolds, 1861, p.46). In regard to risk factors, he discounted early onset (if anything, he believed the opposite to be the case) and severity and type of attacks. He suggested, however, that frequency of attacks might be relevant to cognitive impairment (based, perhaps, on his observation that this complication was seen in subjects surviving status epilepticus).

Reynolds' views on symptoms and their mechanisms were influential among Queen Square neurologists, particularly Jackson and Gowers. For example, it is not commonly known that he is, in fact, the source of Jackson's much quoted concepts of 'positive' and 'negative' symptom (Reynolds, 1858; Berrios, 1985; 1991) Jackson's views on epilepsy will not be dealt with here in any depth as it has deserved historical notice elsewhere. Suffice it to say that he re-structured the condition in terms of his evolutionist and hierarchical model of the brain. Indeed, epilepsy was his favoured disease (López Piñero, 1973; Dewhurst, 1982).

Falret
In 1860, Falret reviewed the nature of the link between epilepsy and insanity. He denied claims that all epileptic cases must have psychiatric complications although he accepted that: 'Epilepsy is a condition of the brain which often

brings in its wake mental disorder' (Falret, 1860). His concern was threefold: sharpen clinical description of the mental state of epileptics; detect associations with other epileptic phenomena; and, develop criteria for forensic work.

The first problem that Falret tried to solve was one of definition. Before Kraepelin's synthesis, many clinical states qualified as 'insanities'. The fleeting presence of hallucinations, delusions, bizarre behaviour, and obsessions was then sufficient to construct yet another form of insanity. Little was done about searching for any deep structure that might underlie the various symptom clusters nor was there any interest in the longitudinal history of disease. Definitions of insanity-types merely consisted of descriptions of kaleidoscopic mixtures of symptoms with no guarantee that the next episode would resemble the previous one. This was also the case in regard to the 'epileptic insanities': before Falret, writers rarely bothered to distinguish peri-ictal phenomena (e.g. acute confusional states) from lasting inter-ictal states. This is likely to have resulted from the fact that during the period in question the notion of acute confusion or delirium had not yet been separated from the non-confusional insanities (see chapter on delirium in this book). Indeed, the acute organic psycho-syndrome was then considered as yet another form of insanity (Chaslin, 1895).

Falret classified epileptic insanities into three groups: 1) peri- and intra-ictal mental phenomena; 2) inter-ictal changes in personality; and 3) long-term insanities. He described the latter thus: 'Finally, there are those phenomena of longer duration constituting true madness, whose onset should be described as either associated with or independent from any seizural manifestations'. Falret also dealt with the medico-legal implications of his views, and supported Zachias' rule that insanity pleas should be valid only within three days (either before or after) a genuine seizure. Like Falret, Billod (1843) and Delasiauve (1852) also tried to impose clinical order on this field.

THE BRITISH VIEW

Jackson
The impact of the French debate was felt in Britain. In a paper in the famous but short-lived *West Riding Lunatic Asylum Medical Reports* Jackson wrote:

> I believe that according to some, I believe most alienist physicians, that degree of it which is called epileptic mania, although it usually occurs after a fit, does not always do so. It sometimes 'replaces' a fit. A patient who is subject to ordinary epileptic attacks may on this hypothesis have as it were instead a paroxysm of mania. There is what is called the masked epilepsy described by Falret (sic) . . . I used to adopt the hypothesis of masked epilepsy. But I do not now think it possible that a nervous discharge at all comparable in degree to that which causes convulsion would cause epileptic mania . . . I now think that another hypothesis is preferable. I think it probable that there is a transitory epileptic paroxysm in every case. (Jackson, 1875)

Clouston and Maudsley
Jackson's view did not go unchallenged. Clouston crisply wrote: 'I do not agree with Hughlings Jackson, that in cases of petit mal and slight convulsions, the explosion, not finding vent in a motor form, is more apt to extend up into mental

centres' (Clouston, 1887). The great Edinburgh alienist was, however, well aware of the link between the two conditions:

> When I speak of epilepsy causing insanity and mental symptoms, you must clearly understand that the whole series of symptoms, bodily and mental, may in some cases be the combined result of a general disturbance of function or disease of the brain, neither the convulsions being the primary disease, nor the mania, but both being equally effects of the same cause. It is usual for the epileptic insanity not to follow at once the first appearance of fits. Most commonly years elapse before it comes on.

Clouston's explanation of the nature of the association is, however, close to that of Bouchet sixty years before: 'It will be observed that all those relationships point to a close connection between the locus in quo of epilepsy and the seat of mental disturbance. The fact that they are related to each other in such various ways is the strongest proof of the nearness of their pathological seat' (Clouston, 1887, p.402).

Maudsley, in the 1879 edition of the *Pathology of Mind*, accepted the notion of 'masked epilepsy' and emphasised the chronic paranoid forms: 'In the less acute and more partial forms of epileptic insanity there are commonly chronic hallucinations; the person hears distinctly a voice which insults him or commands him peremptorily to do some deed' (Maudsley, 1879). By the turn of the century, the problem had not yet been resolved. In Tuke's Dictionary there are two entries on the topic: one, by James Anderson from the National Hospital, is a rambling attempt to develop Jackson's views (Anderson, 1892); the other, by George Savage offers a fairer summary of what was actually going on at the time. Savage included a description redolent of Landolt's views: 'Patients, having been relieved or cured of the fits, have from that time begun to degenerate mentally and we have elsewhere described cases in which epileptiform, if not epileptic, fits have been followed by mental improvement' (Savage, 1892).

Gowers

Gowers' book on epilepsy appeared in 1881. In the style of Reynolds he reported 1085 patients and – in marked difference with Continental authors – he only occasionally called upon earlier authorities. Gowers was interested in cases with cognitive impairment and on the mechanisms leading to this complication. He suggested that memory deficit might be caused by the epileptic lesion itself, rather than by the seizure, and that the early development of dementia may be related to duration and early onset of illness and (probably) presence of petit mal epilepsy. He ruled out fit frequency as relevant, but suggested that a combination of risk factors might be more important than any single one. Gowers had little interest in the non-cognitive psychiatric complications of epilepsy, and his book marks the full incorporation of epilepsy into neurology.

THE QUESTION OF THE 'COMBINED PSYCHOSES'

As a reaction to the conflation of epilepsy and insanity attempted by Morel, during the 1880s French alienists leaned, once again, towards the 'random combination hypothesis'. Thus, Magnan in his 1880 paper on 'the coexistence of various forms of insanity in the same individual' tackled the problem of the link in a different way: 'Some patients suffer from both epilepsy and partial madness, mania or melancholia. These two conditions remain independent although they can influence and modulate each other' (Magnan, 1880). This view is as important in the solution it puts forward as in the questions it raises. In fact, Magnan went on to ask: 'Can two psychoses co-exist in the same individual?' If so, would they influence each other in their symptomatic manifestations? If not, why not? What is so specific or unique about psychoses that two cannot be found in the same person at the same time?

Two assumptions are implicit in these questions: one that there is more than one psychosis, the other that the psychoses must be stable over time. Indeed, Magnan did assume both; before Kraepelin, he saw his category of *délire chronique* as a form of psychosis that ran true to form (Magnan, 1887). Likewise, he used heredity (in fact, degeneration) as an explanation. As Meeus said years later: 'The co-existence of two psychoses in the same patient was considered by Magnan to be due to double inheritance. One of the parents transmitting epilepsy and the other insanity' (Meeus, 1908).

GERMAN VIEWS

Nineteenth century German views on the relationship between epilepsy and mental disorder are not different from those debated in France and Britain. For example, Griesinger (1867) believed that the two states were closely related: 'the numerous points of contact and transition of the motory [sic] convulsive forms comprehended under this name [epilepsy], to the more profound derangements of the psychical functions, are manifested partly in the symptoms which precede, accompany, and follow the attack'. Amongst those mental disorder preceding the attack Griesinger mentioned confusion, sadness, anger, and hallucinations; during the attack, alterations of consciousness; and after the attack, mania and melancholia. He also described inter-ictal disorders: 'But a very great number of epileptics are in a state of chronic mental disease even during the intervals between the attacks'.

These views percolated through only partially into the medical literature of the period. For example, Niemeyer's (1876) popular *Textbook of Practical Medicine* only referred to postictal states: 'there are instances in which every attack, or else each severe one or rapidly recurrent succession of them, is followed by mental derangement, and other disorders of innervation. The former may consist of well-marked fits of mania . . . in other instances the fit is succeeded by a condition usually called partial insanity: for example, the patient may have an irresistible inclination to run . . . in other cases, the patient may be in an irritable mood . . . sometimes the memory and mental acuteness are impaired for some days . . .' (p.360). Kraepelin's (1904) views differ little from those expressed above, except, perhaps, in the exaggerated emphasis he put on the role of alcohol in the development of mental complications (pp.48–57). By the end of the century, views on epilepsy in Germany had become associated with heredity and degeneration theory. A good illustration of this is the discussion in Weygandt's (1902) contribution to *Lehmann's Medizinische Handatlanten* where a full review is offered of German views on epilepsy, particularly those of Kraepelin, Aschaffenburg, Schultze, and Buchholz. The chapter is profusely illustrated with photographs and clinical vignettes, mostly of epileptics with psychiatric disorders and mental retardation. Weygandt quoted figures purporting to support the hereditary hypothesis: 90 per cent of epilepsies were supposed to be 'hereditary', 33 per cent of epileptics to descend from alcoholics; degeneration is specifically mentioned as the constitutional basis for the disorder (1902, pp.258–94).

German views on epileptic insanity are also well illustrated in the debate on the *Frage der kombinierten Psychosen* (Gaupp, 1903). This dealt with the question of whether: (1) psychoses could become grafted upon mental sub-normality or acquired brain lesion, 2) two psychoses could co-exist in the same individual, and 3) such co-existence was in space or time. German alienists accepted the view that psychoses were found combined with each other at rates higher than chance (Samt, 1875). Their main concern related, therefore, to the mechanisms involved. Buchholz wrote that epilepsy paved the way for insanity by weakening the resistance of the brain (Buchholz, 1895). Ziehen opted for a psychological account claiming that delusions in epileptic insanity resulted from the accumulation of insane experiences which occurred during ictal episodes (Ziehen, 1902, p.542). This view has since been mistakenly attributed to Pond (Betts et al, 1976, p.178).

Krafft-Ebing was one of the first to address the problem of the 'combined psychoses' and deal with the question of psychoses grafted upon pre-existing mental retardation, and with the issue of co-existence during which the psychoses were assumed to preserve their individuality (Krafft-Ebing, 1888). Along the same lines, Ziehen (1902) described the *zusammengesetzte Psychosen* to which he dedicated a chapter of his *Psychiatrie*. 'Composite psychoses' were mixtures of 'simple states' such as mania, melancholia, stupor and paranoia; whether 'periodic' (like manic-depressive psychosis) or 'non-periodic' (like Kahlbaum's catatonia), the 'simple' states were supposed to co-exist within the same episode. Wernicke believed that 'composite psychoses' were more common than 'simple forms', and called *gemischten Psychosen* those forms in which the psychoses had lost individuality as a result of pathoplastic interactions (Wernicke, 1900). It is against this ever-growing proliferation of insanities, that Kraepelin carried out his synthetic effort by creating, in fact, two 'supercomposite insanities', dementia praecox and manic depressive insanity. This he did by making full use of the 'combinatorial' hypothesis and by developing a structural view of insanity that transcended clinical features and relied on integrating factors such as natural history, prognosis and aetiology.

Equally relevant is the contribution of Erwin Stransky, the Viennese psychiatrist, who in 1906 published his *Zur Lehre der kombinierten Psychosen* (Stransky, 1906) where the view is rejected that the concept of 'combined psychoses' should be applied to any symptom cluster. He defined the former: 'As a combination of two unrelated psychoses occurring simultaneously or in sequence with symptoms that have no known connection with each other, e.g. the combination of manic-depressive insanity and paranoid illness or the former with dementia praecox'. In a review, Meeus (from the Gheel Colony) reinforced this view: 'I cannot see any theoretical contradiction in the fact that, in the same individual or brain psychoses clinically different can succeed each other at short or long intervals' (Meeus, 1908).

THE AFTERMATH

By the early 1900s, most explanations pertaining to the combination of epilepsy and psychosis had been considered. The 'chance combination' was explored by Herpin and explained as resulting from sampling biases, and by Magnan as resulting from aleatory genetic combinations. The view that the link was real had also been studied. Griesinger and Clouston claimed that insanity produced psychoses; others held the converse: Buchholz that epilepsy weakened the brain; Ziehen and Gaupp that the constant alterations of consciousness caused by epilepsy disrupted reality testing, and Jackson that both disorders had a common cause. The debate as to which of these accounts corresponds to the clinical facts has continued to this day.

Indeed, other accounts have since been added. Early this century, Glaus (1931), reported that the incident of epilepsy in schizophrenia was, in fact, *lower* than in the general population and concluded that the two conditions must be antagonistic. It has been claimed that this view provided Sakel and Meduna (1937) with a rationale for their belief that induced seizures might alleviate the psychosis (Lennox has since quoted Sakel as rejecting this account). Yet another more recent hypothesis has been that anti-convulsant medication plays a role in the development of psychotic complications.

During the 1950s, opinion moved in the direction of nineteenth century beliefs. Bartlet (1957), Pond (1957) and Dongier (1959) suggested that there was, after all, an increased incidence of mental disorder in epilepsy. In 1963, Slater and co-workers published their work showing that a schizophrenia-like psychosis was associated with temporal lobe epilepsy (different from run-of-the-mill schizophrenia in that it had no higher genetic load than a control population). This was characterized by warm and appropriate affect, and did not lead to deterioration (Slater and Beard, 1963). Although occasionally challenges are levelled against the existence of a true relationship between epilepsy and mental disorder (Stevens, 1966) efforts have been made during the 1970s to ascertain the facts. For example, Flor Henry (1976) and Betts (1974) offered some evidence for such, and also for a 'laterality effect', namely that schizophrenia-like psychosis might be more frequent in dominant hemisphere pathology. The debate continues (Diehl, 1989).

REFERENCES

Ackerknecht, E.H. (1967) *Medicine at the Paris Hospital*, 1794–1848, Baltimore, Johns Hopkins University Press.

Anderson, J. (1892) 'Epilepsies and Insanities'. In Tuke, D.H. (ed.) *A Dictionary of Psychological Medicine*, London, Churchill, pp.440–50.

Bartlet, J.E.A. (1957) 'Chronic psychosis following epilepsy'. *American Journal of Psychiatry*, 114: 338–43.

Bercherie, P. (1983) *Genèse des Concepts Freudiens: Les Fondements de la Clinique*, vol.2., Paris, Navarin Editeur.

Berrios, G.E. (1981) 'Delirium and Confusion during the 19th century: A conceptual history'. *British Journal of Psychiatry*, 139: 439–49.

Berrios, G.E. (1984) 'Descriptive Psychopathology: Conceptual and historical aspects'. *Psychological Medicine*, 14: 303–13.

Berrios, G.E. (1985) 'Obsessional disorders during the 19th century. A conceptual history'. In Bynum, W., Porter, R. and Shepherd, M. (eds.) *The Anatomy of Madness*, vol.1, London, Tavistock Publications, pp.166–87.

Berrios, G.E. (1985) 'Positive and negative symptoms and Jackson'. *Archives of General Psychiatry*, 42: 95–7.

Berrios, G.E. (1988) 'Historical background to abnormal Psychology'. In Miller, E. and Cooper, P. (eds.) *Adult Abnormal Psychology*, Edinburgh, Churchill Livingstone, pp.26–51.

Berrios, G.E. (1991) 'Positive and negative signals: a conceptual history'. In Marneros, A., Andreasen, N.C. and Tsuang, M.T. (eds.) *Negative versus Positive Schizophrenia*, Berlin, Springer, pp.8–27.

Berrios, G.E. and Freeman, H. (eds.) (1991) *Alzheimer and the Dementias*, London, Royal Society of Medicine.

Betts, T.A. (1974) 'A follow up study of a cohort of patients with Epilepsy admitted to Psychiatric care in an English city'. In Harris, P. and Maudsley, C. (eds.) *Epilepsy*, Edinburgh, Churchill-Livingstone, pp.326–36.

Betts, T.A., Merskey, H. and Pond, D.A. (1976) 'Psychiatry'. In Laidlaw, J. and Richens, A. (eds.) *A Textbook of Epilepsy*, Edinburgh, Churchill-Livingstone, p.178.

Billod, M. (1843) 'Recherches et considérations relatives à la symptomatologie de l'Epilepsie'. *Annales Médico-Psychologiques*, 2: 381–423.

Bouchet, C. (1853) 'Sur l'Epilepsie'. *Annales Médico-Psychologiques*, 5: 209–50.

Bouchet, C. and Cazauvieilh, G. (1825–1826) 'De la Epilepsie considéré dans ses rapports avec l'aliénation mentale: Recherches sur la nature et le siége de ces deux maladies'. *Archives Générales de Médecine*, 9: 510–42; 10: 5–50.

Broussais, F.J.V. (1828) *De l'irritation et de la folie*, Paris, Delaunay.

Bruens, J.H. (1973) 'Psychoses in Epilepsy'. In Vinken, M.J. and Bruyn, G.W. (eds.) *Handbook of Clinical Neurology*, Amsterdam, North Holland Publishing Co. vol.17: The Epilepsies, pp.593–609.

Buchholz, E. (1895) *Über die Chronische Paranoia bei Epileptischen Individuen*, Habilitationsschrift, Halle.

Burlureaux, M. (1887) 'Epilepsie'. In Dechambre, A. and Lereboullet, L. (eds.) *Dictionnaire Encyclopédique des Sciences Médicales*, vol.35, Paris, Masson, pp.120–221.

Calmeil, L.F. (1824) *L'Epilepsie etudiée sous le rapport de son siege et de son influence sur la production de l'aliénation mentale*, Thèsis, Université de Paris.

Canguilhem, G. (1975) 'Le concept de réflexe au XIXe siècle'. In *Etudes d'Histoire et de Philosophie des Sciences*, Paris, Vrin, pp.295–304.

Canguilhem, G. (1977) *La Formation du Concept de Réflexe aux XVIIe et XVIIIe siècles*, Paris, Vrin.

Carlson, E.T. (1970) 'The nerve weakness of the 19th century'. *International Journal of Psychiatry*, 9: 50–4.

Carlson, E.T. and Simpson, M.M. (1969) 'Models of the nervous system in 18th century Psychiatry'. *Bulletin for the History of Medicine*, 43: 101–15.

Chaslin, Ph. (1895) *La Confusion Mentale Primitive: Stupidité, Démence aigüe, Stupeur Primitive*, Paris, Asselin et Houzeau.

Clouston, T.S. (1887) *Clinical Lectures on Mental Diseases*, London, J. & A. Churchill.

Cobb, I.G. (1920) *A Manual of Neurasthenia*, London, Baillière Tindall.

Cullen, W. (1803) *Synopsis Nosologiæ Methodicæ*, 6th Ed, Edinburgh, W. Creech, p.299.

Cullen, W. (1784) *First Lines of the Practice of Physic*, Fourth Edition, vol.3., Edinburgh, Creech, p.122.

Delasiauve, F.J.F. (1852) 'D'une forme mal décrite de délire consecutif a l'epilepsie'. *Annales Médico-Psychologiques*, 9: 491–508.

Dewhurst, K. (1982) *Hughlings Jackson on Psychiatry*, Oxford, England, Sandford Publications.

Diehl, L.W. (1989) 'Schizophrenic syndromes in Epilepsies'. *Psychopathology*, 22: 64–140.

Dongier, S. (1959) 'Statistical study of clinical and electroencephalographic manifestations of 536 psychotic episodes occurring in 561 Epileptics between clinical seizures'. *Epilepsia*, 1:117.

Esquirol, J.E.D. (1815) 'Epilepsie'. In *Dictionnaire des Sciences Médicales*, Paris, Panckouke.

Esquirol, J.E.D. (1838) *Des Maladies Mentales*, Paris, J.B. Baillière.

Ey, H. (1954) 'Epilepsie'. *Études Psychiatriques*, vol.3, Paris, Desclée de Brouwer, pp.519–652.

Falret, J. (1860–1861) 'De l'état mental des epileptiques'. *Archives Générales de Médicine*, 16: 661–79; 17: 461–91; 18: 423–43.

Fearing, F. (1930) *Reflex Action: A Study in the History of Physiological Psychology*, Baltimore, Williams & Wilkins Co.

Flor, Henry P. (1976) 'Epilepsy and Psychopathology'. In Granville-Grossman, K. (ed.) *Recent Advances in Clinical Psychiatry*, vol 2, Edinburgh, Churchill-Livingstone, pp.262–95.

Foucault, M. (1963) *Naissance de la Clinique*, Paris, Presses Universitaires de France.

Garimond, T. (1878) 'Contribution à l'histoire de l'Epilepsie'. *Annales Médico-Psychologiques*, 19: 5–37; 181–217.

Gaupp, R. (1903) 'Zur Frage Kombinierten Psychosen'. *Centralblatt für Neurologie und Psychiatrie*, 6: 766–87.

Georget, E.J. (1835) 'Epilepsie'. In *Dictionnaire de Médecine ou Repertoire Général des Sciences*, Second Edition. vol.12, Paris, Bechet, pp.172–91.

Gigerenzer, G., Swijtink, Z., Porter, T., et al (1989) *The Empire of Chance*, Cambridge, Cambridge University Press.

Glaus, A. (1931) 'Ueber Kombinationen von Schizophrenie und Epilepsie'. *Zeitschrift für die Gesamte Neurologie und Psychiatrie*, 135: 450–500.

Gowers, W.R. (1881) *Epilepsy and Other Chronic Convulsive Disorders*, London, Churchill.

Griesinger, W. (1867) *Mental Pathology and Therapeutics*. (Translated by C.L. Robertson and J. Rutherford), London, New Sydenham Society, pp.403–6.

Guerrant, J., Anderson, W.W., Fisher, A., et al (1962) *Personality in Epilepsy*, Springfield, Ill, Charles C. Thomas.

Hall, M. (1841) *On the Diseases and Derangement of the Nervous System*, London, Baillière Tindall.

Hare, E. (1991) 'The history of "Nervous Disorders" from 1600 to 1840, and a comparison with modern views'. *British Journal of Psychiatry*, 159: 37–45.

Hare, E. (1974) 'The changing content of Psychiatric illness'. *Journal of Psychosomatic Research*, 18: 283–9.

Herpin, T. (1852) *Du Pronostic et du Traitement Curatif de l'Epilepsie*, Paris, J.B. Baillière, p.468.

Herpin, T. (1867) *Des Accés Incomplets d'Epilepsie*, Paris, Baillière.

Jackson, J.H. (1875) 'On temporary mental disorders after Epileptic Paroxysms'. *West Riding Lunatic Asylum Medical Reports*, 5: 240–62.

Jackson, J.H. and Stewart, J.P. (1899) 'Epileptic attacks with a warning of a crude sensation of smell and with the intellectual aura (dreamy state) in a patient who had symptoms pointing to gross organic disease of the right temporo-sphenoidal lobe'. *Brain* 22: 534–41.

Keynes, J.M. (1929) *A Treatise on Probability*, London, MacMillan.

Kraepelin, E. (1904) *Lectures on Clinical Psychiatry* (Translated by T. Johnstone), London, Baillière, Tindall and Cox, pp.48–57.

Krafft-Ebing, R. von (1888) *Psychiatrie*, vol.3 Stuttgart, Enke.

Laín Entralgo, P. (1978) *Historia de la Medicina*, Barcelona, Salvat.

Lamperière, T.H. (1955) 'Histoire de l'évolution des idèes sur la mentalité Epileptique'. *Histoire Médicine*, 5: 69–75.

Lanteri-Laura, G. (1983) 'La sémiologie psychiatrique: Son evolution et son état en 1982'. *L'Evolution Psychiatrique*, 48: 327–63.

Legrand du Saulle, H. (1877) *Etude Médico-Légale sur les Epileptiques*, Paris, Delahaye.

Laplace, P-S. (1921) *Essai Philosophique sur les Probabilités*, Paris, Gauthier-Villars.

Lecce, C. and Caraffa, T. (1964) 'Concetto di "Epileptoide" e di "Epileptoidismo" dalle origini ai tempi nostri'. *Rivista Neurobiologica*, 10: 123–45.

Levin, K. (1978) *Freud's Early Psychology of the Neuroses. A Historical Perspective*, Hassocks, Harvest Press.

Liddell, G.T. (1960) *The Discovery of Reflexes*, Oxford, England, Clarendon Press.

López Piñero, J.M. (1973) *John Hughlings Jackson (1835–1911): Evolucionismo y Neurología*, Madrid, Editorial Moneda.

López Piñero, J.M. (1983) *Historical Origins of the Concept of Neurosis*. (Translated by Berrios, D.), Cambridge, England, Cambridge University Press.

López Piñero, J.M. and Morales Meseguer, J.K. (1970) *Neurosis y Psicoterapia: Un Estudio Histórico*, Madrid, S.A. Espasa-Calpe.

Magnan, J.J.V. (1880–81) 'De la coexistence de plusieurs délires de nature differente chez le méme aliéne'. *Archives Neurologique*, 1: 49–59.

Magnan, J.J.V. (1887) 'Considérations générales sur la Folie'. *Le Progrès Médical*, 2nd. 5: 190–7.

Masland, R.L. (1973) 'The Classification of the Epilepsies: A Historical Review'. In Vinken, M.J. and Bruyn, G.W. (eds.) *Handbook of Clinical Neurology*, Amsterdam, North Holland Publishing Co. vol.17; The Epilepsies, pp.1–29.

Maudsley, H. (1879) *The Pathology of Mind*, London, Macmillan.

McHenry, L.C. (1969) *Garrison's History of Neurology*, Springfield Ill., Charles C. Thomas.

Meduna, L. (1937) *Die Konvulsiontherapie der Schizophrenie*, Halle, Marhold.

Meeus, F. (1908) 'Epilepsie et délire chronique: Contribution a l'étude des psychoses combineés'. *Annales Médico-Psychologiques*, 7: 353–82.

Moreau de Tours, J.J. (1850) *La Psychologie Morbide dans ses Rapports avec la Philosophie de l'Histoire, ou de l'Influences des Neuropathies sur le Dynamisme Intellectuel*, Paris, Masson.

Morel, B.A. (1860) 'D'une forme de délire, suite d'une sur excitation nerveuse se rattachant a une varieté non encore décrite d'épilepsie (épilepsie larveé)'. *Gazette Hebdomadaire Médicine Chirurgie*, 7: 773–5; 819–21; 836–41.

Niemeyer, F. von (1876) *A Text-book of Practical Medicine* (translated by G.H. Humphreys and C.E. Hackley), 8th Edition, vol.2, London, Lewis, p.360.

Pond, D.A. (1957) 'Psychiatric aspects of Epilepsy'. *Journal of Indian Medical Profession* 3: 1441–50.

Reynolds, J.R. (1858) 'On the pathology of convulsions with special reference to those of children'. *Liverpool Medical Chirurgical Journal*, 1: 1–14.

Reynolds, J.R. (1861) *Epilepsy. Its Symptoms, Treatment and Relation to Other Chronic Convulsive Disorders*, London, John Churchill.

Riese, W. (1945) 'History and principles of classification of nervous diseases'. *Bulletin of the History of Medicine*, 18: 465–512.

Riese, W. (1959) *A History of Neurology*, New York, MD Publications.

Riese, W. (1960) 'The impact of the 19th century thought on Psychiatry'. *International Record of Medicine*, 173: 7–19.

Samt, P. (1875) 'Epileptische Irreseinsformen'. *Archive für Psychiatrie un Nervenkrankheiten* 5: 393–444; 6: 110–216.

Savage, G.H. (1892) 'Epilepsy and Insanity'. In Tuke, D.H. (ed.) *A Dictionary of Psychological Medicine*, London, Churchill, pp.452–6.

Savill, T.D. (1906) *Clinical Lectures on Neurasthenia*, London, Henry J. Glaisher.

Schiller, J. (1968) 'Physiology's struggle for independence in the first half of the 19th century'. *History of Science*, 7: 64–89.

Shryock, R.H. (1961) 'The history of quantification in medical science'. *Isis*, 52: 215–37.

Slater, E. and Beard, A.W. (1963) 'The Schizophrenia-like psychosis of Epilepsy'. *British Journal of Psychiatry*, 109: 95–112.

Societé Médico-Psychologique (1873) De L'Epilepsie Larvée. *Annales Médico-Psychologiques*, 5 series, 9, 139; 155; 281; 301; 490; 493.

Sommer, W. (1880) 'Erkrankung des Ammonshorns als ätiologisches Moment der Epilepsie'. *Archiv für Psychiatrie und Nervenkrankheiten*, 10: 631–75.

Stevens, J.R. (1966) 'Psychiatric complications of psychomotor Epilepsy'. *Archives of General Psychiatry*, 14: 461–71.

Stransky, E. (1906) 'Zur Lehre der kombinierten Psychosen'. *Allgemeine Zeitschrift für Psychologie*, 63: 73–102.

Temkin, O. (1971) *The Falling Sickness*, 2nd Edition, John Hopkins University Press, Baltimore.

Trélat, U. (1861) *La Folie Lucide*, Paris, Delahaye.

Wernicke, K. (1900) *Grundriss der Psychiatrie*, Leipzig, Thieme, p.459.

Weygant, W. (1902) *Atlas und Grundriss der Psychiatrie*, München, J.F. Lehmann, pp.258–94.

Young, R.M. (1970) *Mind, Brain and Adaptation in the 19th Century*, Oxford, Clarendon Press, p.111.

Ziehen, T.H. (1902) *Psychiatrie*, Leipzig, A. Barth, p.542.

Chapter 6
Epilepsy

Social Section
ROY PORTER

The socio-cultural history of epilepsy falls within, and provides a key example of, two principal themes in medical history. It offers a rich instance of sacred/secular contrasts in aetiology and therapeutics. In early or so-called primitive societies, maladies were commonly attributed to supernatural powers (sometimes divine but generally diabolical) as part of animistic or magical cosmologies that personalized the Universe. Spirits or demons were standardly blamed as sources of diseases, visiting individuals or groups with afflictions, perhaps to avenge sacrilege or profanation. Relief of such maladies was to be attained through propitiation and sacrifice, or at least through the use of remedies themselves considered sacred. Nineteenth-century philosophers, notably Auguste Comte (1798–1857), contended that the road to civilization was a long trek from 'theological' interpretations of the order of things, through a 'metaphysical' stage, culminating finally in contemporary empirical or 'positivist' science. The history of the 'falling sickness' broadly bears out Comte's scheme; but the sequence of steps outlined must not be taken in a rigidly unilinear or deterministic sense. As will be noted below, long after leading Greek physicians proposed somatic theories of epilepsy, praeternatural explanations and magical therapeutics continued to be influential.

Second, epilepsy offers interesting confirmation of positions outlined by Susan Sontag. In *Illness as Metaphor* (1978), Sontag maintained that certain sorts of disorders – notably those that are fatal, incurable or attended by humiliating symptoms – acquire a moralistic colouring and a stigmatizing potential. Random and meaningless calamity is insupportable; this compels the invention of meanings for disease and the construction of illness narratives rationalizing and thereby reducing the terror of lethal disease. Through victim-blaming procedures, the sufferer may be held responsible, or may shoulder blame, for his or her condition, judged as precipitated by some character flaw. In the most negative variants, the victim brings the disease 'punishment' upon him or herself, in a process representing a medical analogue of the catastrophe of Classical tragedy: an instance would be the so-called 'cancer personality'. In a more positive register, serious illness may be regarded as the partner and proof of superior gifts, holiness, genius, a talent for love or sacrifice: in such a case, physical weakness is counterbalanced by personal strengths; greatness has both costs and rewards. In her essay, Sontag concentrates on insanity, tuberculosis and cancer – and more recently, in *AIDS as Metaphor* (1989), on sexually transmitted diseases; but her interpretation also throws light on epilepsy, a disease commanding an extensive folklore on account of its shocking violence and the traditional impotence of the medical profession when confronting it: 'epilepsy may be called the reproach of physicians', judged the great English clinician, William Heberden (1710–1801) in his *Medical Commentaries* (1802), 'for it was well known before the writing of the most ancient medical books and as yet no certain method of cure has been discovered'. So long as epilepsy remained beyond the doctors' power, it bred a lush mythology.

The early peoples of the Near East and the Nile were familiar with the seizures and swoonings characteristic of epilepsy. Babylonians and Assyrians ascribed such fits to demons. In later centuries, Islamic lore sometimes attributed them to the blow of a ghost. In the Ottoman Empire, an epileptic paroxysm was said to betray an illicit sexual affair; a jealous spirit was believed to have surprised its rival, seizing him or her by the throat and attempting to choke the party – hence the lapse into unconsciousness. Classic Hindu mythology had a special demon who caused convulsions: Grahi, or 'she who seizes'; in modern Indian lore, a dog-demon is accused of possessing the afflicted.

The supernatural has loomed large in European attitudes to epilepsy. It would, in general, be a mistake to imagine that Christianity's triumph stifled Graeco-Roman medical theories: the medical learning of Antiquity, preserved through the Arabs, was readily transplanted into the soil of medieval Christendom. Nevertheless, supernatural explanations were frequently advanced for certain diseases, for instance Bubonic plague. Epilepsy was another.

For this there was ample scriptural warrant. When Christ healed a child suffering convulsions, the episode was represented as the casting out of a demon: 'a spirit taketh him and he suddenly crieth out; and it teareth him that he foameth again and bruising him hardly departeth from him' (Luke 9:39). Christ was involved with another epileptic when approached by a father who pleaded, 'Master, I have brought unto thee my son, which hath a dumb spirit, and wheresoever he taketh him, he teareth him: and he foameth and gnashes his teeth and pineth away' (Mark 9:14–29). Noting Jesus's handling of 'unclean spirits', leading churchmen later regarded both the cause and cure of the falling sickness as lying beyond the physical body. St Basil (c.330–379) denied that seizures were produced by natural causes alone. Some, in his view, were sent by God as punishments, while others were Satan's curse. Within medieval Christendom, epileptics were rejected and dreaded, under supposition that some at least were demoniacs. In popular belief, epileptics might have the 'evil eye'; thus it was thought possible that contact (even at a distance) with an epileptic could be infectious. As late as the eighteenth century, epilepsy was still regarded by some as a preternatural affliction, Jean Westphal (d.1722), author of *Pathologia Daemoniaca* (1707), terming it *morbus daemoniacus*. Another contributing to the perpetuation of the demonic disease notion was the Swiss demonologist, Jean-Joseph Gassner (1727–79), himself an epileptic.

Corresponding to transcendental aetiologies, religious cures were recommended. Within Catholicism, patron saints were invoked, as is evident from the terms *morbus Sancti Valentini* and *morbus Sancti Ionni* for the falling sickness. It was widely believed that St Valentine, St Sebastian and St Vitus assisted epileptics; other local saints considered to offer protection were St Eunemond of Lyons, St Nymphase of Cahors and St Mathieu of Sens. A fable connected with

St John supposedly explained a Berkshire custom of using offertory rings as a cure. Medieval epilepsy treatments often combined folk cures, classical medicine, and the ecclesiastical rite of casting out devils. The English physician, John of Gaddesden (1280?–1361) recommended reading the Gospel over an epileptic patient – advising that he should at the same time be covered with peony and chrysanthemum amulets, or even the hair of a white dog. Thaumaturgical medicine has also sometimes been extended to epilepsy. Following Edward the Confessor's precedent, English kings sometimes used the royal touch to treat the falling sickness (there is a parallel in Pliny the Elder's (c AD 23–79) observation that a sufferer might be healed if touched by the right thumb of a virgin). Religious cures took myriad forms. In Spain, sleeping in a churchyard or in the church itself (not during service!) were considered restorative.

Alongside Christian cures, magical treatments proliferated, drawing upon the principles of suggestion, sympathy and antipathy, in hope of vanquishing the mysterious disorder. The Romans, who thought the *morbus daemoniacus* or *morbus daemonius* was caused by devils, devised charms and rituals to drive away the evil spirits responsible. They also associated epilepsy with the evil eye. Prominent during the next thousand years amongst the mass of techniques developed for combatting the evil eye was spitting. Belief in epilepsy's contagiousness endured through the Middle Ages and beyond. A pseudo-Salernitan verse cited by Bernard de Gordon (d.c.1320) specified epilepsy amongst the eight diseases thought to be communicable, the others being bubonic plague, phthisis, scabies, erysipelas (*ignis sacer*), anthrax, trachoma, and leprosy. Sympathetic magic lore judged foul smells effective for driving away epilepsy demons. Black slaves in the American Deep South daubed epileptics with putrid possum fat; the equally revolting skunk fat remedy was grounded upon the same rationale.

As with treatments of other terrifying maladies, *materia medica* deriving from the human body were thought especially potent. Human blood was often used. Pliny recorded that epileptics drank the blood of gladiators mutilated in the stadium: 'They think it most valuable to sip the blood, still warm, still flowing, from the wounded themselves and thus to imbibe the breath of life immediately from the fresh opening'. Such practices had medical approval. Scribonius Largus (cAD1–50), Aetius (fl. c.500) and Alexander of Tralles (525–605) all urged human blood as a remedy against the falling sickness, and its use is documented well into the eighteenth century. Other bodily parts were also commended: pulverized human skull was said to be particularly approved in France.

Perhaps the most distinctive folk cure for epilepsy has been mistletoe. The parasite was probably selected because of its anomalous nature; mistletoe was widely cited in folklore as simultaneously ominous but auspicious, poisonous but pharmaceutical. Sir James Frazer (1854–1941) lent a sympathetic ear to Pliny's explanation for the efficacy of mistletoe as a specific against epilepsy:

> As the mistletoe cannot fall to the ground because it is rooted on the branch of a tree high above the earth, it seems to follow as a necessary consequence that an epileptic patient cannot possibly fall down in a fit as long as he carries a piece of mistletoe in his pocket or a decoction of mistletoe in his stomach.

According to medieval legend, it was King David who had discovered the plant's virtue. Keeping watch over his father's flocks, the young David saw a woman collapse in a spasm. Praying that a remedy might be revealed to him, an angel appeared and announced: 'Whoever wears the oak mistletoe in a finger ring on the right hand, so that the mistletoe touches the hand, will never again be bothered by the falling sickness'. Mistletoe rings long remained popular as prophylactics, but the plant was used in a variety of ways. Some took powders or infusions made from the dried leaves and berries. In central Europe, the stalk was hung round children's necks to prevent seizures, while in Scandinavia countryfolk warded off seizures by carrying a knife with a handle cut from oak mistletoe. Nor was it only popular culture that championed mistletoe's powers. The noted sixteenth-century Parisian physician, Jean Fernel (1497–1588) recommended a mixture of mistletoe, powdered human skull and peony seeds gathered when the Moon was waning. Robert Boyle (1627–1691), founder member of the Royal Society of London, was convinced of the efficacy of mistletoe against epilepsy, a view repeated by the botanist John Ray (1628–1705) and the Leiden medical professor, Herman Boerhaave (1668–1738). The most shameless promoter of mistletoe, however, was the quackish London physician, Sir John Colbatch (1670–1728), whose popular *A Dissertation Concerning Mistletoe: A Most Wonderful Specifick Remedy for the Cure of Convulsive Distempers* (1719) ran through six editions before his death.

Horrifying and seemingly without a certain cure, it was inevitable that in its *grand mal* form the falling sickness would gather an aura of the supernatural and occult. Nevertheless, a counter-tradition had been at work ever since the dawn of 'rational' or 'scientific' medicine. Hippocrates (c.460–c.357BC), or rather one of the body of anonymous Hippocratic authors, denied that epilepsy was supernatural. As in *On Airs, Waters, Places* so also in *On the Sacred Disease*, the Hippocratic writer disclaimed the notion that there was any such entity as a divine malady. All diseases arose from natural causes, he contended; none could more plausibly be attributed to the deities than any other. Indeed, the very notion of divine intervention in human health attracted Hippocratic scorn. The writer ironically catalogued the different gods supposed by miscellaneous necromancers to cause the distinct forms of epileptic seizure: if the convulsive patient behaved in a goatlike way, or ground his teeth, or if his right side were convulsed, the cause supposedly lay in Hera, the mother of the gods. If the victim made horselike movements, then Poseidon was the appropriate god. Hecate, the goddess of sorcery, was responsible if the sufferer experienced night terrors, delirium, jumping out of bed and frightful apparitions; and so forth. What evidence, asked the author, was there for any of these fantastic old wives' tales? The malady had been called divine only because it baffled human understanding. 'Men regard its nature and cause as divine from ignorance and wonder', the Hippocratic writer maintained, 'and this notion is kept up by their inability to comprehend it'. But such reasoning was the slippery slope to folly, for all manner of diseases, like malaria, defied ready understanding, and if a condition 'is reckoned divine because it is wonderful, instead of one there would be many diseases which would be sacred'.

Underlying the Hippocratic onslaught against the very idea of a 'sacred disease' was a powerful, idealist and elitist perception of professional identity. In early Greece, there was no official state sanction of, or legal safeguarding for the medical art. Anybody was free to practice in the medical market-place. Under such circumstances, the followers of Hippocrates strove in various ways – witness the Hippocratic oath – to distance themselves from other healers they disparaged as tantamount to quacks. Those impostors and shady healers 'who first referred this disease to the gods', the author complained,

> appear to me to have been just such persons as the conjurors, purificators, mountebanks, and charlatans now are, who give themselves out for being excessively religious, and as knowing more than other people. Such persons, then, using the divinity as a pretext and screen of their own inability to afford any assistance, have given out that the disease is sacred, adding suitable reasons for this opinion, they have instituted a mode of treatment which is safe for themselves, namely by applying purifications and incantations and enforcing abstinence from baths and many articles of food which are unwholesome to men in diseases.

The Hippocratic strategy was thus systematically to differentiate themselves, methodologically and metaphysically, from those dabbling in divination. The Hippocratic author had, therefore, to specify an alternative, *natural*, theory of the aetiology of epilepsy. This was effected in terms of the doctrine of the humours. The young were stricken when excessive exposure to heat, perhaps the result of the sudden onset of south winds, resulted in production of surplus quantities of phlegm. In the old, epilepsy was .chiefly bred in the winter, especially by temperature fluctuations. In either case the disturbance centred on the brain; that organ secreted a cold phlegm (pituita) which, passing down to the blood vessels, encountered the 'pneuma' or principle of life, the resulting obstruction triggering convulsions. Another possible cause, the author suggested, was sudden acute fear, a view destined to have a prominent future both in medicine and the popular imagination alike.

The Hippocratic account of epilepsy was thus exemplary: *On the Sacred Disease* plucked disease from the heavens and brought it down to earth. Historians of medicine have commonly regarded the Hippocratic denial as, symbolically at least, constituting the foundation of scientific medicine, by its programmatic denial of supernatural aetiology. By systematically asserting that health and sickness were governed by the natural order of things, by saying, in effect, that all bodily changes were to be explained solely in terms of the inherent laws of the soma, understood in its natural environment, the Hippocratic author set the agenda for rational medicine.

The Hippocratic corpus left an explanatory legacy: epilepsy was a humoral disorder. Its tenets were taken over by Aristotle (384–322BC) in *De Partibus Animalium*, and, several centuries later, in large part by Galen (c.130–c.200), who emphasized that epilepsy was seated in the brain. Galen's humoral approach remained influential through the Middle Ages into the early modern era. One dissenter, predictably, was Paracelsus (1493–1541), who challenged the Hippocratic-Galenic view that epilepsy was caused by fluid blocking the ventricles.

The new anatomical inquiries associated with the seventeenth century Scientific Revolution opened up prospects of advances in the physical understanding of epilepsy. In particular, pioneering investigations into brain anatomy by Thomas Willis (1621–75), notably in his *De Cerebri Anatome* (1664), encouraged neurological interpretations of that and analogous convulsive disorders. In the short term, however, these bore little fruit, since Willisian cerebral physiology remained largely speculative. It was only in the nineteenth century that the mutually fruitful interplay of pathological anatomy, vivisection experiments on animal reflexes, and localization theories laid the foundations for a solid grasp of the relations between seizures and the brain abnormalities responsible for irregular electrical discharges. John Hughlings Jackson (1835–1911) questioned the conventional wisdom that cortical functions were undifferentiated, connecting local indications with specific brain centres. He also defined the epileptic neuron, those nerve cells whose excessive discharges precipitated paroxysms. In Germany, Gustav Fritsch (1838–1927) and Edward Hitzig (1838–1907), and in Britain, David Ferrier (1843–1928), experimentally deployed electrical stimulus to make the link between brain control points and physical functions.

Functional localization theory paved the way for brain mapping for surgical purposes, an advance coming to fruition in 1884 when Victor Horsley (1857–1916) conducted the first surgical operation on a patient suffering epileptiform fits. Taking the synoptic view, we may say that if, in the fourth century BC, the 'professionalization' of medicine as a somatic pursuit created the concept of epilepsy as disease, in the nineteenth century in turn the professionalization of a biomedical specialty, neurology, facilitated its scientific coming of age: late nineteenth-century physicians rejoiced that their new neurological skills had finally set epilepsy onto a scientific footing. *Les Démoniques dans l'Art* (1887), jointly written by Jean-Martin Charcot (1825–93) and his colleague, Antoine Richer (1849–1933), was a bold attempt to prove, through an overarching historical survey, that those whom benighted ages had mistaken for mystics, prophets and demoniacs were sufferers from classic neurological conditions like epilepsy and hysteria.

One possibly ambiguous consequence of this tide of neurological research was that it tended to conflate – or, at least, perpetuate the conflation of – epilepsy with mental disorder; after all, both the falling sickness and lunacy had long been associated with the Moon, a view finally scotched by Moreau de Tours (1804–84). Epileptics were frequently herded with the insane in madhouses, though moves were made in the nineteenth century to set up distinct asylums for epileptics. In 1815 Esquirol (1772–1840), the celebrated French psychiatrist renowned for studies of *petit mal* and 'absence', organized a special sanatorium for epileptics. He aimed to keep epileptics segregated from the mentally disturbed, lest the latter should acquire the condition by a mode of psychological 'contagion' (an echo of a view we have encountered already): epileptics were thus even more 'dangerous' than lunatics. By 1860, exclusive institutions had been built in France and Germany; in 1891, the first American hospital dedicated to epileptics was founded in Gallipolis, Ohio. The greater concentration permitted by segregation and specialization stimulated collection of further clinical data.

There had, of course, been a prolonged custom of singling out epileptics, like lepers, as 'unclean' and in need of being kept apart from society. Epilepsy was popularly viewed as condign punishment for some terrible sin or flaw. In classical times, Aretaeus (cAD150–200) had already noted that epilepsy was 'reckoned a disgraceful form of disease; for it is supposed that it is an infliction on persons who have sinned against the Moon'. In the Enlightenment, the Swiss physician, Tissot (1728–97), developed the notion that epilepsy could be the consequence of the solitary vice; even in the 1880s, William Gowers (1845–1915) was still attributing epilepsy to masturbation. And the mutual associations of epilepsy and insanity proved doubly stigmatizing, above all within the framework of the 'degnerationist' psychiatry gaining ground from the mid-nineteenth century and feeding into eugenics. The leading Italian criminologist, Cesare Lombroso (1836–1909), argued for the 'integral connection between epilepsy and crime', seeing both epilepsy and criminality as deriving from hereditary psycho-physiological handicaps, peculiarities and perversions. Lombroso drew attention to 'atavistic abnormalities' in the skulls of convicts and degenerates, and associated epilepsy with 'atavistic behaviour'. Similar views were held in Britain by Henry Maudsley (1835–1918). Certain twentieth-century social psychiatrists gave a new lease of life to Lombrosian views by adopting the notion that 'disturbed people' were 'epileptic equivalents', interludes of violent behaviour being regarded as analogous to uncontrollable *grand mal* seizures.

Such ideas betray the survival of deep-rooted prejudices against epileptics; yet there is also another side, that which Sontag has seen as the glamorization of the illness. A powerful tradition has purported to see affinities between epilepsy and greatness. In this view, epilepsy could be a 'sacred' disorder, one that even elevated the sufferer during the fit to godlike status, as is indicated by the Latin tag, *morbus deificus*. Priests and seers have often been said to be stricken by epileptiform seizures, while, in certain cultures, notably the Siberian, epileptics have been respected as shamans, teenage boys suffering from seizures becoming neophytes into the role of medicine man. Within medieval Christendom, epileptics were sometimes looked upon as divinely possessed and spiritually gifted. Foaming at the mouth suggested heavenly speech and so the gift of tongues.

Epilepsy was, furthermore, believed to accompany genius or superhuman traits. According to Aristotle, Hercules suffered from the sacred disease, which was sometimes thereafter called *morbus Herculeus*. Euripides's play, *The Frenzy of Hercules*, showed Hercules afflicted with seizures through associating with the gods. And claims have been advanced, usually on rather slender evidence, that various heroes were epileptic, notably Alexander the Great (356–323BC), Julius Caesar (c.102–44BC), Saint Paul (AD3–c.64), Mohammed (c.570–632), Petrarch (1304–74), Peter the Great (1672–1725) and Napoleon Buonaparte (1769–1821). The most famous and best authenticated epileptic ruler, of course, was Julius Caesar. 'And when the fit was on him', Shakespeare has Cassius observe, 'I did mark how he did shake; 'tis true this god did shake. His coward lips did from their colour fly, and that same eye whose bend doth awe the world did lose his lustre; I did hear him groan'. In most of the cases just mentioned, the evidence is too slim to support a firm conclusion, but what is noteworthy is the keenness of popular desire to associate the 'falling sickness' with extraordinary individuals, eminent conquerors, and religious reformers – to say nothing of writers, artists, and scientists like Buffon (1707–88), Flaubert (1821–80), Dostoevski (1821–81), Helmholtz (1821–94), and Van Gogh (1853–90).

Mythologization of the epileptic genius peaked in the nineteenth century. The Romantic movement, as Sontag and others have pointed out, provided a secular reworking (a 'natural supernaturalism') of many traditional Christian parables. Formerly regarded as a literally divine 'inspiration', genius became a function of the individual's psychical and physiological make-up. Religious notions of sin and redemption were recast, *inter alia*, in terms of the Romantic artist, doomed to suffer for his almost blasphemous creativity (God alone had the right to create). These themes reached their highest degree of self-awareness in the case of Dostoevski (1821–81). A well-attested epileptic, the Russian novelist construed his condition in a way that perceptively bridged the demonological/theological and the clinical/rationalistic explanations of the affliction – one that also blurred the divide between the factual and the fictional. In Dostoevski's mind, epilepsy was inseparable from a passion for religious renewal – it is noteworthy that he had no notion of its demonological dimension.

Dostoevski wrote with great perspicacity about the ecstatic aura, a rare event during which some temporal lobe epileptics, in ecstatic moments before a seizure, find their entire attention converging on transcendental themes like God and death. It is portrayed with enormous particularity in *The Idiot* (1868), where it is given a religious interpretation. Gastaut (1978) has cast doubt upon Dostoevski's authentic experience of the aura; Voskuil (1983) has upheld it.

Dostoevski's case history is particularly well-recorded, as he wrote extensively about his own seizures, and such accounts are supplemented by records from his wife, friends and physicians. In the manner depicted by Sontag, Dostoevski gave meaning to his personal epileptic history by attributing its origins to his jail sentence and Siberian exile. Certainly the first diagnosis was made in Siberia. But in reality Dostoevski had been suffering seizures for the whole of the previous decade. His friend Grigorowitch recorded an episode in 1846 when, out walking, the writer spotted a passing funeral procession, tried to flee, but was struck down with a severe seizure and long remained unconscious. Other paroxysms followed. One night, probably in the same year, a friend saw Dostoevski's face change dramatically and a terrified look came into his eyes. 'Where am I?', the writer then supposedly asked, dashing to the window to get some air, 'his face twisted, his head bent to one side, and his body shaking convulsively'. In her *Childhood Recollections*, Sophia Kovalevskaia (1850–91) reported Dostoevski's account of what he then chose to remember as his first attack, consequent upon Siberian exile. The writer was talking with friends, discussing God. Suddenly, he exclaimed: 'God exists, He exists', just as a church bell began to toll for midnight mass: 'I felt the heaven was going down upon the earth and that it had engulfed me', Kovalevskaia reports Dostoevski as saying,

> I have really touched God. He came into me myself, yes God exists, I cried, and I don't remember anything else. You all, healthy people . . . can't imagine the happiness which we epileptics feel during the second before our fit. Mohammed, in his Koran, said he had seen Paradise and had gone into it. All these stupid clever men are quite sure that he was a liar and a charlatan. But no, he did not lie, he really had been in Paradise during an attack of epilepsy; he was a victim of this disease like I was. I don't know if this felicity lasts for seconds, hours, or months, but believe me, for all the joys that life may bring, I would not exchange this one.

The novelist set down further description of his aura in a letter where he asserted that 'during a few moments I feel such a happiness that it is impossible to realize at other times, and other people cannot imagine it'. His feeling of oneness was 'so strong and so sweet' that he would exchange 'perhaps even one's whole life' for 'a few seconds of this enjoyment'.

Dostoevski thus portrayed the aura as creating a feeling of extreme ecstasy and 'harmony with the world and himself'. He happily subscribed to the 'myth' of creative and blessed malady. How far such feelings were the psycho-physiological effects of epilepsy itself, and how far the upshot of pre-existent myths of the epileptic genius and the sacred disease, it is impossible to unravel.

Epilepsy continues to be a serious problem, though medicine has made substantial progress. Its clinical symptoms have been systematized, its location identified, its nature clarified, and with effective medication and occasional surgery, its effects can be controlled; most epileptics are able to function adequately in society. The ancient stigmas attaching to epilepsy are fading: does that mean there will be no more Dostoevskis?

REFERENCES

Alström, C.H. (1950) 'A study of epilepsy in its clinical, social and genetic aspects'. *Acta Psychiatrica et Neurologica Supplimentum 63*, Stockholm, Munksgaarel.

Berrios, G.E. (1979) 'Insanity and epilepsy in the nineteenth century'. In Roth, M. and Cowie, V. (eds.) *Psychiatry, Genetics and Pathography, a Tribute to Eliot Slater*, London, Gaskell Press, pp.161–71.

Berrios, G.E. (1984) 'Epilepsy and insanity during the early nineteenth century: A conceptual history'. *Archives of Neurology*, 41:978–81.

Crawfurd, R. (1917) 'The blessing of cramp-rings: a chapter in the history of the treatment of epilepsy'. In Singer, C. (ed.) *Studies in the History and Method of Science*, Oxford, Clarendon Press, pp.167–87.

Dougherty, T.M. (1956) 'Epilepsy: the history of folklore in its treatment'. *Journal of the Kansas Medical Society*, 57:304–18.

Gastaut, H. (1978) 'Fyodor Mikhailovitch Dostoevsky's involuntary contribution to the symptomatology and prognosis of epilepsy'. *Epilepsia*, 19:186–201.

Kanner, L. (1939) 'The folklore and cultural history of epilepsy'. *Medical Life*, ns 37:167–214.

Kanner, L. (1939) 'Mistletoe, magic and medicine'. *Bulletin of the History of Medicine*, 7:875–936.

Kanner, L. (1939) 'The names of the Falling Sickness, as introduction to the study of the folklore and cultural history of epilepsy'. *Human Biology*, 2:109–27.

Murphy, E.L. (1959) 'The Saints of epilepsy'. *Medical History*, 3:303–11.

Pasternak, J.L. (1981) 'An analysis of social perceptions of epilepsy: increasing rationalization as seen through the theories of Comte and Weber'. *Social Science and Medicine*, 151:223–9.

Politzer, H. (1963) 'Dostoevsky and the epilepsy of the modern world'. *Ciba Symposium*, 11:106–15.

Sontag, S. (1978) *Illness as Metaphor*, New York, Farrar, Straus & Giroux.

Sontag, S. (1989) *AIDS as Metaphor*, Harmondsworth, Allen Lane.

Temkin, O. (1945) *The Falling Sickness; a history of epilepsy from the Greeks to the beginnings of modern neurology*, Baltimore, Johns Hopkins University Press; revised edn 1971.

Voegele, G.E. and Dietze, H.J. (1964) 'An historical reflection on the medico-social aspects of epilepsy'. *Delaware State Medical Journal*, 36:131–6.

Von Storch, E.P. (1930) 'An essay on the history of epilepsy'. *Annals of Medical History*, ns 2:614–50.

Chapter 7
Multiple Sclerosis

Clinical Section
GE BERRIOS and JI QUEMADA

Historical analysis shows that the current view of multiple sclerosis (MS) remains close to that painted by Vulpian (1886), Charcot (1877) and Kurtzke (1888). This stability notwithstanding, the disease seems to have remained 'hidden' for more than 20 years in Cruveilhier's work. Historical accounts portray MS as having been intermingled with other myelitis and paraplegias including clinical phenomena such as progressive locomotor ataxia (Duchenne, 1883; Vulpian, 1879), tabes dorsalis (Schiller, 1976), and Friedreich's ataxia (Ladame, 1890). Indeed, early in the 20th century, MS was still being classed as a disease of the spinal cord! (Dejerine and Thomas, 1902). More surprising is the fact that MS was also confused with paralysis agitans (Ordenstein, 1868) and general paralysis (Targowla, 1924). The historian may well ask, therefore, what in MS has now become clear that was once obscure? The question does not ask for the role of biological markers, for the disease was disentangled on *descriptive grounds alone*. It concerns the development of an ever subtler language for the description of motor and sensory symptoms. The answer also depends on what is taken to be the 'essence' of disease, i.e. whether it be its symptoms, or their pattern of temporal and spatial distribution. The question is particularly pressing to those keen on determining priorities. For example, it has recently been suggested that the symptoms of MS were first described by Olliver D'Angiers in 1824, the lesions by Carswell in 1838, and their combination by Cruveilhier circa 1841 (Compston, 1988). In giving priority to the Scotsman this author opts for the concept of lesion as providing the definition of MS.

A Working model
One solution is to conceive clinical nosology as resulting from an interaction between a descriptive (verbal or numerical) language and a biological process (emitting signals in the shape of symptoms and signs) (Berrios, 1984). The language of description both influences, and is influenced by, the observer's perception (in a literal sense); the latter, in turn, is controlled by theory. So, description can be said to be an active theoretical interface. It can be further suggested that the content, rate, and direction of any change affecting descriptors and signals, is determined by different sets of factors (Berrios, 1996). Consequently, changes in the definition of a disease may result from changes in the language or in the biological signal. The widespread belief that only the

former is the case is pre-Darwinian in origin and based on a creationist view of biological invariance (Berg, 1956; Larson, 1971; Stevens, 1984). In the case of MS, one could ask, have the changes resulted from modifications in its descriptors or in its biological expression, which, may have biased, for example, lesion deployment? In can be concluded, that the question of why a disease was not 'discovered' earlier cannot be settled by reference to the history of its clinical discourse alone; indeed, even within relatively short periods, biological variation must be taken into consideration. The purpose of this chapter is to deal with the history of the 'mental symptoms' of MS. However, it will make a brief incursion into its neurological history. For example, the fact that MS was only 'described' during the middle of the 19th century needs explanation; and if it is to be claimed that MS has now achieved the zenith of its description, then, this newly acquired invariance also needs explanation.

The historical hypothesis to be discussed here states that the clinical boundaries of MS (as set up by Charcot and his contemporaries) were too narrow (in that, for example, they did not include mental symptoms in the definition of the disease). The reasons for this narrowness will be discussed as will be the arguments used to explain away the presence of mental symptoms. It will also be argued that the *neurological* description of MS was made possible by: a) conceptual changes relating to the role played by the spinal cord, and b) shifts in the way in which the relationship between lesion and symptom is conceived. The second part of the chapter will be dedicated to the historical analysis of the neuropsychiatric aspects of the disease, particularly to how this can be improved by the application of certain conceptual and statistical techniques.

THE HISTORICAL BACKGROUND

The *clinical* boundaries of MS were drawn during the 19th century in response to the tension created by dichotomies such as brain anatomy v. physiology, motor v. sensory, role of brain v. role of spinal cord, symptom v. syndrome, tremor v. disorganized movement; and by problems such as the *definition* of paralysis, and ataxia. Of these, only the role of the spinal cord will be touch upon in this chapter. On the other hand, the *anatomical* boundaries of MS were determined by changing views on the concept of 'sclerosis' (this latter problem falls beyond the scope of this chapter and will not be treated further).

MS and the spinal cord

In spite of a few dissenting voices, the Galenic (Siegel, 1973) centrifugal model of the spinal cord prevailed well into the 1830's (Clarke and Jacyna, 1987; Clarke and O'Malley, 1968) when it was replaced by a centripetal or convergent view, according to which the spinal cord acted as an *afferential* transmitter of environmental and bodily information. Animal research showing a marked degree of spinal cord autonomy (Neuburger, 1981), and theoretical support from comparative anatomy (Agassiz and Gould, 1870) (showing that such autonomy was even greater in some lower species) also contributed to this shift.

This led to the development of an integrated conception of the spinal cord as a chain of 'ganglia', crowned by the magnificent ganglion that was the brain. It followed that motor and sensory deficits could have spinal origins and were not necessarily the result of brain pathology. The 'autonomy' view found its most pointed expression in Marshall Hall's (1836) notion of 'eccentric epilepsy' supposed to result from 'excitor nerves of the true spinal cord'. Another consequence concerns the 'semantics' of description, i.e. the view that signs and symptoms convey information about localized lesions or structural changes (what has been called the 'anatomo-clinical' model) (Foucault, 1963; Ackerknecht, 1967; López Piñero, 1983) rather than about some occult general property of the central nervous system (e.g. irritation) (Cook, 1858; Gross, 1979). Better symptom-descriptions followed and encouraged the search for modular psychological functions which might correspond to specific lesions (Fodor, 1983; Shallice, 1988). Faculty psychology played an important role in these developments (Berrios, 1988) and also in the growth of phrenology (Young, 1970), and in the drive towards brain localization (Hécaen and Lanteri-Laura, 1977; Tizard, 1959).

These changes were crucial to the development of the concept of neurological disease. Without the notion of localized CNS lesion, and of modular function, neurological and 'systemic' disease blended hopelessly in the primeval garden of 'neuralpathology' (an 18th century medical hypothesis according to which all diseases were related to changes in the general properties of the CNS) (Rath, 1954; Riese, 1949). Cullen's (1827) overgeneral concept of neuroses was a direct result of this view for these disorders resulted from 'general changes in motion and sensation'. 18th century beliefs in the existence of lesions affecting 'general aspects of the CNS' were challenged early in the following century (Gross, 1979). For example, Foville (1834) felt able to describe the neuroses as diseases 'whose organic nature is unknown' although he continued including under this class mental illness, asthma, whooping cough, blindness, etc. However, before the 'anatomo-clinical model' could work properly, lesion 'locus' needed re-definition. This was achieved by Bichat and others, and marks the beginning of the modern history of morbid anatomy (Albury, 1977; Maulitz, 1987). Lesions were defined as perceivable and localizable anatomical changes. This did away with the old metaphysical notion of disease. From then on, organs first, and then cells, were to be considered as the carriers of disease (Charcot, 1881).

As mentioned above, this re-definition of CNS disease in terms of a localized lesion led to the development of neurology as a separate speciality. But the process did not always go smoothly. In cases with circumscribable lesions such as strokes (Schiller, 1970), brain tumours, and even general paralysis of the insane, there was little difficulty. In others, however, particularly when lesions were beyond the power of resolution of the technology of the period such as Parkinson's disease (Charcot, 1877a) or Epilepsy (Berrios, 1984a), there was classificatory consternation. MS belongs to an intermediate group in which the problem was, in a way, an 'embarrassment of riches', i.e. it exhibited an excess of lesions but these were (apparently) deployed at random, and consequently, there was a collection of signs and symptoms.

Vulpian (1886) and Charcot (1877) are important in this respect. They showed that the symptomatic heterogeneity of MS was only apparent, and that biases in lesion deployment, and hence symptom-pattern, were identifiable. It must be remembered that their work was carried out during a period when

inferential statistics, pattern recognition techniques, and the very idea of ana-
lyzing representative patient cohorts, were not yet available. Vulpian and
Charcot resorted to what can be called an 'ideal types' strategy, much in the
same way as Jaspers (Schwartz and Wiggins, 1987) did in regards to mental
diseases the following century. This approach is based on the belief that the
shape of a disease is dictated by its high symptom-density areas. Prior to its
application, however, it was required that 'units of analysis' (to define 'symptom
density') were identified. This was not easy for them as the concepts of paralysis
(Chamberet, 1819), (for a discussion of 'paralysis' during the 19th century see
chapter 4, clinical section), sensory deficit, and tremor (Charcot, 1890) were in
a state of flux (dictated by advances in neurophysiology). Once the question of
the motor and sensory physiology of the spinal cord was settled (this occurred
in the 1840's) (Walker, 1839; Rice, 1987), the field was ready for a stable
definition of MS to emerge.

MS, together with progressive locomotor ataxia, are good examples of
another historical phenomenon, namely a shift in emphasis in regards to what
is thought to constitute the 'essence' of a neurological disease (what Duchenne
called a 'morbid species') (Poore, 1883). During the 1850's, the candidates were
'lesion' and 'stable symptom-cluster'. In the event, the latter predominated.
Commenting on Duchenne's views, Poore (1883) wrote: 'the coarser features of
this disease are sufficiently often associated to constitute a morbid entity, an
espèce morbide as Duchenne calls it, and the name which he gave to this new
species has been of great clinical value, and has enabled the pathologist to
determine those minute changes in the spinal cord upon which the symptoms
depend'. But, then, Poore warned: 'it must be remembered that it is no more
possible to draw rigid lines of demarcation in pathology than in other departments of natural science. "Morbid species" fuse imperceptibly together, the
divisions are artificial, and the separation of the symptoms into phenomena and
epiphenomena is artificial also'. Lastly, in regards to the fact that in clinical
practice combinations of morbid species were often met with (e.g. locomotor
ataxia and MS) Poore wrote: 'when a pathological process has once started, who
shall assign a limit to its operations? It may be true, nay, is true, that the
hardening process which we call sclerosis very often limits its operations to one
or other of the columns of the spinal cord, and travels apparently along the path
of least resistance'.

Sometimes there was not a lesion to speak of, such as in paralysis agitans. In
these cases, a tight symptom-description (the morbid species) was all that there
was available and had to suffice. Incidentally, this view also gave succour to
alienists, as it encouraged them to accept the existence of psychiatric entities
(which were only theoretically 'organic') on the basis of a tightness of symptom-
cluster.

THE HISTORY OF MS

A view on how MS was 'discovered' became official by the end of the 19th
century, and was formulated by Vulpian (1886) and Charcot (1877) who
themselves had played a role in the action. The received view was consolidated
by repetition in all the textbooks of the period (Gowers, 1893; Marie, 1895;

Dupré, 1903; Dejerine and Thomas, 1902). Whether the hero was Carswell (Monro, 1895) or Cruveilhier (Dejerine and Thomas, 1902; Ritter, 1966) depended on what side of the channel the writer was on. The irony here was that although Carswell was a Scotsman he did most, if not all, of his morbid anatomy in France (Maulitz, 1987). The debate has continued to this day (Compston, 1988). After the pathological work of Carswell and Cruveilhier (and Rokitansky, Türck, Frerichs, and Rindfleisch) (McAlpine et al, 1955; Marie, 1895), that of clinicians came to the scene. Thus, at Charcot's instigation, Ordenstein (1868) worked on the differential diagnosis between MS and PD, and Bourneville and Guérard (1869), followed by Jaccoud, Vulpian and Marie completed the clinical description.

Problems with the official version

For all its neatness the conventional view (Kurtzke, 1988; McAlpine et al, 1955; Compston, 1988; Jelliffe and White, 1929; Timme, 1950; Guillain, 1959; Ombredane, 1929) leaves some questions unanswered: why did Cruveilhier's description remain unattended for more than two decades? Why was the differential diagnosis with paralysis agitans (PA) (Charcot, 1877), tabes dorsalis (Duchenne, 1883) and Friedreich's ataxia (Ladame, 1890) so difficult to make? In regard to the first question the answer cannot simply be lack of diffusion as Cruveilhier's beautifully illustrated 'Anatomical Pathology' was well known in medical circles (Flamm, 1973). In respect to the second question, it must be remembered that earlier neurological classifications (Hall, 1836; Romberg, 1853; Roche, 1834) followed the old principle of grouping diseases according to symptoms, e.g. spasms, tremors, acineses, and paralysis (the latter including both disorders of movement and of *sensation*) (Roche, 1834; Anonymous, 1841). For example, under tremors Romberg (1853) discussed mercurial intoxication, alcoholic, senile and febrile tremor, and paralysis agitans; and Todd (1856) included paralysis agitans under 'peripheral paralysis'. Since, like any other, the definition of MS needed to be based on a cluster of symptoms, it found no place in any of these classifications, nor was there any need to separate it from other diseases with overlapping semiology such as paralysis agitans or locomotor ataxia.

THE MENTAL SYMPTOMS OF MS

Conceptual and historiographical issues

When searching for the moment in which certain mental symptoms are first described as associated with a neurological disease (be this MS, epilepsy, Parkinson's or Wilson's disease), the historian must take at least four factors into consideration: a. when in the *natural history* of the condition are the mental symptoms likely to appear? (if late, and the disease used to be a killer, then earlier reports are unlikely to include mental symptoms), b. the likely aetiology of mental symptoms (reactive, organic, precipitated by medication?), c. had those particular symptoms been already described at the time? (for example, had the concept of depersonalization already become stable?), and d. what mental symptoms were sought for and in fashion during the period in question (fashion, as much as frequency or clinical importance, determines symptom-perception).

MENTAL SYMPTOMS IN THE HISTORY OF MS UP TO THE GREAT WAR

Earlier accounts of MS do not include mental symptoms (Firth, 1948). However, of the woman Dargès, a patient described in his *Atlas*, Cruveilhier (1835–42) wrote: 'She would smile and greet me with effusion; but on addressing her, she would be taken over by an emotion difficult to describe (at the time the symptom "emotional incontinence" had not yet been coined). She would blush, laugh, weep, and her limbs and trunk would start shaking'. In 1835, after 6 years of hospitalization, Dargès died aged 37; she had spent the last few years in the 'urinary incontinence' ward. Her neurological symptoms included left-sided weakness, tremor, dysarthria, difficulty with swallowing, and ambliopia, but no cognitive impairment. She was thought to have a brain tumour, but post-mortem only showed 'grey transformation' of brain, optic nerves and corpus callosum. Retrospectively, Vulpian (1886) concurred with the diagnosis of MS (p.703). (It has been suggested that Dargès' diagnosis might have been pseudobulbar palsy) (Compston, 1988).

However, as early as 1853, Valentiner discussed mental symptoms in a paper on 'brain and spinal sclerosis' that included a report of 15 cases (13 borrowed from the literature, including those of Cruveilhier's). Early in his disease, one of Valentiner's patients showed excitement, religious fervour, grandiosity, and periods of severe depression; then an 'indifference set in as the disease progressed'. Another patient showed marked 'cognitive impairment'. Valentiner concluded that mental symptoms are .'common when there is brain involvement'. Charcot (1877) gave a more comprehensive description: 'There is a marked enfeeblement of the memory; conceptions are formed slowly; the intellectual and emotional faculties are blunted in their totality. The dominant feeling in the patients appears to be a sort of almost stupid indifference in reference to all things. It is not rare to see them give way to foolish laughter for no cause, and sometimes, on the contrary, melt into tears without reason. Nor is it rare, amid the state of mental depression, to find psychic disorders arise which assume one or other of the classic forms of mental alienation' (pp.194–5). He illustrated his description with cases from the literature: 'One of the patients of Valentiner, usually subject to melancholia, was, from time to time, seized with ambitious mania' . . . 'Mademoiselle V. was seized with genuine fits of lypemania [Esquirol's term for major depression]. She had hallucinations of sight and hearing' . . . 'she was convinced that we wanted to poison her . . .' (p.195).

Vulpian (1886) distinguished between early and late MS, and believed that during the former 'cerebral functions – unless a complication sets in are intact' (p.704). This changed with the progress of the disease. Vulpian was, in fact, an early sponsor of the 'reactivity' hypothesis (for a discussion of the 'reactivity' hypothesis see Berrios and Quemada, 1991): 'the distress caused by the progression of the disease is sufficient to cause permanent sadness intellectual weakness and dementia'. He complemented this view by stating: 'however, cerebral lesions can also cause similar mental changes: memory and intelligence fail, the face becomes expressionless, and the sadness becomes lypemania. But even in the cerebrospinal form of the disease mental troubles are far from being frequent; or if present they are mild . . .' (pp.707–8). Vulpian's suggestion that mental symptoms were infrequent and mostly reactive was to become the official neurological view. It was, however, in clear contrast to Charcot's view who, as it is well known, showed 'psychiatric' inclinations.

Following Vulpian, Marie (1895) wrote: 'it cannot be argued that [mental symptoms] are not present . . . but this does not mean that all reported observations are correct. Far from it. I can quote cases with marked mental symptoms who on post-mortem showed in fact diffuse sclerotic changes' [i.e. did not have MS]. Bastian (1886) also pointed out that dementia, or a subacute maniacal state, might be seen during the late stages of the disease (p.651), and Gowers (1893) wrote in his epigrammatic style

> slight mental change is common; considerable alteration is very rare. There may be failure of memory, but specially frequent is an undue complacency and contentment, which, under the increasing disability, is distinctly unnatural. This morbid complacency is rather more frequent in women than in men, and in young adults than in later life. Hysterical and emotional disturbance may also occur even in men. Very rarely mental disturbance is considerable enough to amount to chronic insanity. (p.552)

In Germany, Spiegel (1881) concurred based on an analysis of 34 cases: 'psychological impairment is found in MS, but is neither as frequent nor as severe as some authors have thought'. And so did Müller (1904) in his great book on MS where he emphasized the rarity of psychiatric disorder and suggested that, when present, it mainly consisted in a memory problem which could be found in about 25 per cent of subjects. Phillipe and Cestan (1903) studied 11 cases up to post-mortem and cast doubt on the suggested high frequency of mental symptoms as reported, for example, by Danneberger (1901) in his MD thesis from Giessen University, where he had studied about 104 cases; Phillipe and Cestan (1903) suggested that the diagnosis of MS was unclear in a number of his patients, some of whom were probably suffering from general paralysis of the insane. Others followed Charcot's 'high frequency view'. Mendel, Ziehen (Ombredane, 1929) and Dannenberger (1901) himself lent their support, as did others who even offered psychometric and statistical evidence for their claims (see below).

The turn of the century was also the period when clinicians came to realize that MS might be confused with hysteria. Thomas Buzzard (1890), in a work redolent of Slater's 1965 paper, wrote: 'I am convinced that a very large number of cases of an early stage of disseminate sclerosis – the stage in which there are probably patches of sub-acute interstitial myelitis – continue to be diagnosed either as examples of hysteria or of voluntary simulation' (p.19). This worry is also illustrated by the debate between LHermitte and Halberstadt (1906) and Lapointe on whether the case L.B., presented at *la Société Médico-Psychologique* on 25 February 1906, had MS or hysteria. Raymond and Touchard (1909), in turn, drew attention to the fact that MS could also be confused with general paralysis of the insane.

To summarize what has been said so far, by the turn of the century, and before the large neuropsychiatric series had been reported, anecdotal observation convinced clinicians that, during the late stages of MS, three types of symptoms might appear: cognitive, described in terms of memory and intellectual impairment (and loss of insight with regard to the seriousness of the disease); affective, including sadness, occasionally depression, and emotional incontinence; and more rarely insanity (psychosis). Both organic and reactive mechanisms were suggested to account for the origin of these symptoms, and there was disagreement as to their absolute frequency.

It is convenient to be reminded that these observations were made possible by the fact that, after the 1860's, patient cohorts, and a language of description (imported from psychiatry) had become available. Once described, the mental symptoms of MS were accepted by most. For example, Duchenne (1883) made use of the presence of mental symptoms to differentiate between progressive locomotor ataxia, MS and other conditions (p.18); and so did Friedreich in regards to hereditary ataxia (Ladame, 1890).

The beginning of psychometry and statistical analysis
Around the turn of the century the debate was helped by the reporting of larger samples. Berger's (1905), for example, included 206 cases, 10% of whom were described as showing 'emotional incontinence'; and 12% dementia. Seiffer (1905) (under the direction of Ziehen) published a detailed report of 10 cases (nine with psychiatric disorder) on the basis of whom he claimed that psychiatric complications were frequent. In spite of the fact that case–selection invalidates any claim concerning absolute prevalence, the level of psychometry and clinical assessment utilized in Seiffer's paper is high (for example, it included objective memory tests a la Ebbinghaus). Four patients were found to have memory problems (cases 3, 4, 8 and 10), and 6 affective disorder (cases 2, 5, 6, 7 and 9). Seiffer also made the suggestion that the 'dementia' of MS was mainly characterized by a memory defect. This was challenged by Ross (1915) in his study of cases of MS with mental symptoms at the *Royal Edinburgh Asylum*.

Raecke (1906) (working under Siemerling) reported 37 patients of which the 13 with recent onset showed no major psychiatric problem; as to the rest, 15 did exhibit cognitive impairment and the other 9 a variety of psychiatric disorders; the author included three very detailed cases reports. Duge (1914) (working under Westphal and Nonne) reported 10 cases, 9 of whom had cognitive impairment characterized by a reduction of either memory (Gedächtnisschwache) or power of recollection (Erinnerungsvermögens). The distinction between retrograde and anterograde amnesia was, therefore already known, by the psychiatrists of this period. Redlich (1912) in his classical book on 'Psychoses in cerebral disease' (a volume in Aschaffenburg's series which also included Bleuler's and Bonhoeffer's monographs) exhaustively reviewed the literature and concluded that 'real depression was rare in MS', but that dementia, characterized by a severe defect of memory, was common in 'the late stages of the condition' (pp.405–22). A major French review by LHermitte and Guccione (1910) attempted to explain what they called the 'polymorphous' nature of the mental symptoms of MS in terms of the random pattern of lesions in MS. To the question 'do these symptoms belong to MS or are they epiphenomena of the disease?' (p.264) they answered that: 'the mental symptoms are related to the cortical localization of the plaques' (p.265).

The same type of argument led Euzière (1909), in a theoretical review, to set the questions which were to control research well into our own day: 'Why is it that MS has a higher rate of psychiatric complications than other neurological disorders? Is it because its widespread lesions have a higher probability of triggering "predispositions"? Is it that MS itself only develops when such predispositions are present? *This last hypothesis seems the more acceptable*; if so, the high frequency of cases showing a combination of mental symptoms and MS must be taken as evidence for Strumpell's view, namely, that MS has genetic origin' (our emphasis pp.755–6).

Summary and Conclusions
This first part of the chapter briefly mentioned the historiographical issues that get in the way of research into the history of the association between mental symptoms and MS. It also offered the briefest of accounts of the neurological development of MS as a full history would have been outside the scope of a book on the history of psychiatry. It suggested that the development of the concept of MS was influenced by conceptual changes relating to the physiology of the spinal cord, to the definition of 'lesion', and to relationship between lesion and sign. In regard to mental symptoms it has been explained that there were two schools: those who believed that they pertained to the disease and those who defended the reactivity hypothesis. Up to the First World War, the biased nature of clinical vignettes, the absence of large series, and of statistical techniques, prevented an adequate assessment of the problem.

MENTAL SYMPTOMS IN MS: FROM THE GREAT WAR TO OMBREDANE.
Three features characterize research into the neuropsychiatry of MS during this period: reporting of larger series, improved methodology, and the influence of psychoanalysis, and of Bonhoeffer's views on the indifferentiability of psychiatric syndromes in terms of their underlying disease.

The New York meeting
A useful introduction to this part of the analysis is the report of the famous 1921 meeting on MS held by the *Association for Research in Nervous and Mental Disease* (Dana et al, 1922) whose list of participants included Percy Bailey, Sanger Brown, Charles Dana, Smith Ely Jelliffe, and Bernard Sachs. It dealt with historical, epidemiological, clinical, and aetiological aspects of MS, and its conclusions became the guiding text for the rest of the decade. The chapter on mental symptoms had two sections: a descriptive presentation by Sanger Brown and Thomas Davis, and a psychodynamic section by Jelliffe. Brown and Davis (1922) who also published an expanded version of their presentation elsewhere (Brown and Davis, 1922a), organized their review under the following headings: euphoria (frequent albeit mild), states of mental depression (uncommon and probably reactive), mental deterioration (very rare), hallucinations (auditory and without insight are not unusual), trends (schizophrenia-like states), personality (little change apart from the euphoria), and course of the mental symptoms (oscillation according to the acuteness of the disease). Both organic (plaques) and reactive (stress plus personality) mechanisms were suggested as explanation for the presence of the mental symptoms. They were asked why had they considered euphoria as organic and depression as 'reactive', and Brown replied that euphoria *seemed* organic for it was also present in general paralysis of the

insane and in arteriosclerotic dementia. Taylor, the then Professor of Neurology at Harvard, asked whether in the case of euphoria there might, in fact, be frontal lobe (plaques) involvement. Brown, probably aware of Taylor's recent paper on the topic (Taylor, 1921) replied that correlations of this nature were not yet possible. Indeed, Taylor himself had written: 'a precise determination of lesions from symptoms or of symptoms from lesions is not possible on account of the peculiar type of degeneration in the disease, particularly the long persistence of axons, the resistance of cells, and the multiplicity of lesions which confuses the clinical picture' (p.581).

During the second half of the psychiatric session Jelliffe (1922) talked on 'Emotional and psychological factors in MS' and emphasized the 'reactivity' hypothesis, which he explained in psychodynamic terms. For example, he interpreted sexual hallucinations as being compensatory phenomena in impotent patients. He also discussed the role of psychological factors in the development of some forms of MS. The 'reporteur' summed up Jelliffe's conclusions: 'a study of the unconscious factors in organic disease therefore becomes of paramount importance' . . . 'he [Jelliffe] would advocate this in MS because he believes there will be found, in certain types of disease, certain vascular alterations, which produced the plaques' (p.89). It followed a lively debate whose central point related to the question of why did Jelliffe feel that his theory did not apply to other organic diseases. By drawing conclusions that Jelliffe was unable to explain, some also tried to reduce his position *ad absurdum*. Jelliffe was, however, well acquainted with the (European) literature on MS as attested by the superb review included in his own Textbook. In this work Jelliffe and White (1929) suggested in regard to mental symptoms in MS: 'these are not constant nor prominent, and are for the most part absent, yet careful analysis shows them to be much more frequent than is usually thought' (p.602). They proposed that there might be a primary and secondary form of MS, and that psychogenic factors were relevant to course and plaque distribution.

The Paris meeting

A similar 'stock-taking' exercise took place in Paris in May 1924, and its proceedings appeared in the *Revue Neurologique* the same year. Henri Claude (1924), then the upcoming star of French neuropsychiatry, delivered a paper on the diagnosis of MS and supported the 'low frequency view' of mental symptoms: 'these have been mentioned, and I should like to say something about this. Guillain has rightly said that mental symptoms occupy a second plane in MS. I should like to add that I have never had admitted in my psychiatric ward someone who also had MS. The literature is full of reports about all kinds of psychiatric disorders complicating this disease. It is likely that many of these result from diagnostic error' (p.727). Claude went on, however, to state that minor changes in mood, and symptoms such as puerilism, euphoria, attentional difficulties, depression and apathy were not uncommon in advanced MS. But for some reason he did not see fit to include these amongst the 'serious mental complications' ('*troubles mentaux véritablement graves*'). The latter, he believed, were only to be found in some varieties of MS such as Westphal's 'pseudo-sclerosis' (which might have been, in fact, a form of Wilson's disease), 'diffuse sclerosis', as described by Krankl-Hochwardt, and in 'white matter sclerotic leuco-encephalitis' as described by LHermitte. Claude concluded that the severe dementias described by Seiffer and Redlich (see above) belonged, in fact, in this latter category (p.728) (Claude, 1924).

Other papers on the psychiatric aspects of MS were also presented at the Paris symposium. For example, Etienne et al (1924) suggested that subjects with the cerebellar form of MS were more prone to cognitive deficits; Targowla (1924) reviewed the value of tests that might differentiate MS from general paralysis of the insane; and Söderberg (1924) and Dubois (1924) explored the association between hysteria and MS, the latter of the two men concluding that differential diagnosis was difficult because the two coexisted (p.739).

The 1920's also saw the publication of three important papers, and a book on MS and its mental symptoms. Böhmig (1925) reported a comparative statistical analysis of three more or less contemporary series taken from 3 cities: 115 cases collected in Hamburg between 1910–1920, 113 cases from Halle between 1905–1924, and 50 cases from Chemnitz between 1912–1924. The proportions of psychiatric cases (including emotional incontinence) in the three series together were: 1.9, 7, and 4 per cent, respectively (p.284). During this period also appeared the often quoted paper by Cotrell and Wilson (1926) which was one of the first to discuss *methodological* issues such as how to obtain representative samples, the use of reliable techniques to collect information (e.g. using semi-structured interviewing technique), etc. In fact, the data were collected by Cotrell, an American *psychiatrist* working under Kinnier Wilson. One hundred (more or less) successive cases were studied, and the information analyzed by means of percentages. Operational definitions were included, particularly with regards to affective symptomatology. No real attempt was made to evaluate subjects from the *cognitive* point of view, although one of the clinical conclusions relates to this type of symptom. Other conclusions were based on aetiological speculation. The authors found that more than 70% of the subjects were affected by a degree of *euphoria* or feeling of physical well being not in keeping with the severity or duration of the disease. They concluded that these changes were probably organic in nature, that there was no much evidence for psychogenic mechanisms, and that cognitive impairment was extremely rare. This work was soon to be matched by another important study by André Ombredane (1929). Because it is almost unknown in the history of MS, the latter will be described in some detail.

Ombredane's thesis
André Georges Ombredane was a *normalien* trained as a psychiatrist under Claude, Dumas and Foix. In 1929, aged 31, he published his great book on *Les troubles mentaux de la sclérose en plaques'*. By then he had already co-authored more than ten papers with Targowla, Alajouanine, and others. His publications continued unabated into the 1950's but he never wrote on MS again. For example, he authored an important book on Aphasia (Ombredane, 1951) and monographs on educational psychology reporting research on Congolese children (Ombredane, 1954; 1956; 1957). After spending some time as an associate professor at *L'Ecole de Hautes Etudes*, he was elected to the Chair in Psychology at the Free University of Brussels.

Ombredane was aware of three methodological pitfalls that might threaten his study: a) selection bias (p.43), b) that some of the mental symptoms of MS can not be easily fitted into conventional psychiatric categories (p.19), and c) the need to use a gold standard for the diagnosis of MS. He decided to undertake a 'random' (p.329) collecting of '50 MS patients from the various hospitals of the city' (p.43); used the Wasserman test to exclude patients with neurosyphilis, and used a structured psychometric evaluation. To the 50 cases he added another 10 culled from the literature. All 60 cases are described in his book in exquisite detail.

The statistical analysis of historical samples
Ombredane's series presents the historian, not only with information about the state of psychiatric research in Paris in the late 1920's, but also with a database susceptible to modern statistical techniques. This approach one of us (GEB) has called 'statistical history of psychiatry'. However, it is not easy to undertake and its success depends on the quality of the data. There are also semantic and diagnostic problems: the older the database, the more difficult it is to analyze. In general, good operational definitions are needed (of symptoms) rather than of diseases, and only robust variables must be studied. One of the authors (JIQ) rated all cases; the other (GEB) rated every fifth case. A Kappa Coefficient (Thompson and Walter, 1988) = or>0.65 was sought for all symptoms (except for 'sensory deficit' which was persistently about 0.62). The following 15 variables were rated: age, sex, age of onset and duration of MS, and presence of motor and sensory deficits (with laterality at onset), changes in optic discs, speech disorder, urinary incontinence, depression, euphoria, psychosis (e.g. schizophrenia-like disease, persistent unexplained hallucinatory state), and suicidal behaviour. The proportion of missing data was low.

To 'illustrate' some psychiatric disorders absent from his data, Ombredane 'borrowed' 21 cases from the literature (9 French and 11 German). Statistical comparison (Kolmogorov-Smirnov two-sample test) (Siegel, 1956) of his 39 'personal' cases with the 21 'borrowed ones' showed that Ombredane's cases were older and had a lower rate of psychosis. For methodological reasons it was decided to analyze separately the cases that Ombredane had studied himself.

Subjects and methods
A prospective sample of 39 cases, collected (as randomly as possible) from various hospitals in Paris, and evaluated by one researcher (AO) was analyzed. Clinical diagnosis of MS had been made by a 'consultant neurologist', and patients were only included who had a negative Wasserman test. The same structured interview was used in all cases. Its first section evaluated 'affective function' and included 4 parts: the first asked 17 questions concerning 'emotional content' (e.g. Do you become depressed easily? Is this affected by what you may see, hear, read?); the second asked 9 questions relating to cognitions relating to mood (e.g. are your thoughts constantly unpleasant, sad, etc.); the third contained 10 questions assessing 'physical factors'; and the fourth was dedicated to evaluating 'emotional incontinence'. The second section of the interview assessed cognitive function under 9 headings: attention; memory for old information (episodic memory); for general facts (semantic memory); and

for retention of new facts; orientation; comprehension; imagination; arithmetic ability; and reasoning. Data were analysed by means of the SPSS PC + V2 statistical package (Norusis, 1986). Kappa coefficients were calculated by hand.

Results

Only the most salient results are reported here (for full results see Berrios and Quemada, 1990a). Cognitive and motor impairment were significantly worse in the females. A correlational matrix (with Bonferroni correction for multiple correlations) confirmed a positive correlation between sex and cognitive (r = 0.45) and motor impairment (r = 0.42). Not surprisingly, there was a correlation between age and age of onset (r = 0.81), and between depression and suicidal behaviour (r = 0.46) and euphoria (r = 0.48). To summarize information, an *exploratory* principal components analysis (Kim, 1978) with varimax rotation was carried out. Six factors with an eigenvalue>1 were extracted accounting for 70 per cent of the variance. Four of these factors were recognized clinically and named as Neurological, Affective, Cognitive and Chronicity. Lastly, to ascertain whether the 39 patients could be classified into clinically recognizable sub-groups, a Cluster Analysis (single linkage or nearest neighbour method) (Aldenderfer and Blashfield, 1984) was implemented. 26 patients were grouped into 3 clusters. *Cluster 1* included patients who were younger, female, with shorter illness, less suicidal and no psychosis; *cluster 2* subjects who were older, had older age of onset, more incontinence, and more motor and sensory impairment; *cluster 3* included subjects with less cognitive and depressive illness, and with less incontinence.

Discussion

Some of the conclusions put forward by Ombredane were used as supporting evidence by later researchers (Saethre, 1932; Sugar and Nadell, 1943; Sai-Halász, 1956; Pratt, 1951; Borberg and Zhale, 1946; Ross and Reitan, 1955). Surridge (1969) has claimed that 'Ombredane's work exerted considerable influence on the Continent. One of the reasons for this was that [he] provided supporting evidence for the view already widely publicised by Runge that euphoria was simply a concomitant of intellectual deterioration' (p.750). The same author also described Ombredane's study as 'extremely careful' and showing that 'disturbance of affect occurred in 30 of the 36 cases with intellectual deterioration'. On the other hand, Ross and Reitan's (1955) commented that 'the procedure used by Ombredane did not provide a quantitative basis for group comparisons'. It must be asked therefore whether Ombredane's data did, in fact, support his own conclusions, particularly because he did not use any inferential statistical technique.

Ombredane identified three categories of disorder: 1) 'sclerotic mental state', which included mood (74 per cent) and cognitive (72 per cent) impairment, 2) dementia, and 3) psychosis. He concluded that 'the mental symptoms were related less to the existence and distribution of plaques than to a *diffuse toxic state*'. Since only 3 of his patients had a post-mortem examination it is difficult to see how he reached this conclusion. Some of his subjects exhibit both 'mood' and 'cognitive' disorder but he did not compare these patients with those in his sample who did not show the combination. Textual analysis shows that

Ombredane's claim, that 30 of his 36 *intellectually impaired* patients had also 'affective disorder', is *meaningless* for he rated 'fatigue' (p.330) as a form of cognitive impairment, and 'fatalism' (p.63) as a form of affective disorder. Indeed, if the data are parsed out according to current definitions for both depression and cognitive impairment *no significant correlation between these variables is found* (r = − 0.13). In regard to Runge's point (Surridge, 1969) that depression occurred early, and euphoria later in the disease, Ombredane's data show no correlation between duration of illness and Euphoria (r = − 0.10) or depression (r = 0.02). There was, however, a significant negative correlation between depression and euphoria (r = − 0.48; p<0.01) suggesting that these two mental states tended not to co-exist in the same subject.

Conclusions

This chapter illustrates two historical methodologies: conceptual and statistical analysis of historical data. The first part showed that the concept of MS was formed: a) following the idea of 'morbid species' (i.e. of being a more or less stable set of signs and symptoms); b) in relation to a particular type of lesion (plaques) and to its peculiar distributional features, namely, the existence of multiple and progressive lesions showing temporal and spatial patterns; and c) according to conceptual changes affecting the notion of nervous disease. The history of the neuropsychiatry of MS was divided into two stages: from the beginnings up to the Great War, and from then to the work of Ombredane. The second period is characterized by a new sophistication of analysis, of use of evaluative techniques, and of anatomo-pathological correlations. Mental symptoms have tended to be excluded from the operational definition of the disease. This fact was due less to empirical (statistical or clinical) evidence than to the fact that during the middle of the 19th century only motor and sensory deficit states (related to identifiable localized lesions) qualified as relevant for the characterization of neurological diseases. From then on the *onus probandi*, in respect to the relevance of mental symptoms, fell upon the shoulders of alienists. Vulpian's 'reactivity' explanation can be interpreted as an attempt to deal with this problem. The argument that mental symptoms were not frequent enough could not work because they are, in fact, more frequent than some of the neurological symptoms themselves.

Lastly, the statistical method in the history of psychiatry was used to show how a particular patient database, collected 65 years ago, can be analyzed with profit. It found that: a) some of Ombredane's conclusions (later to be influential) were unwarranted by his data; and b) that the database enshrined hidden information, whose early availability might have changed the direction of research into the neuropsychiatry of MS.

REFERENCES

Ackerknecht, E.H. (1967) *Medicine at the Paris Hospital 1794–1848*, Baltimore, The Johns Hopkins Press.

Agassiz, L. and Gould, A.A. (1870) *Outlines of Comparative Physiology touching the Structure and Development of the Races of Animals, Living and Extinct*, London, Bell & Daldy, pp.42–9.

Albury, W.R. (1977) 'Experiment and explanation in the physiology of Bichat and Magendie'. *Studies in the History of Biology*, 1: 47–131.

Aldenderfer, M.S. and Blashfield, R.K. (1984) *Cluster Analysis*, London, Sage Publications.

Anonymous, (1841) 'Paralysie'. In Fabre, D. (ed.) *Dictionnaire des Dictionnaires de Médicine Française et Étrangers*, Paris, On Souscrit au Bureau de la Gazette des Hopitaux, vol.6, pp.157–60.

Bastian, H.C. (1886) *Paralyses. Cerebral, Bulbar and Spinal*, London, Lewis.

Berger, A. (1905) 'Eine Statistik über 206 fälle von multipler Sklerose'. *Jahrbuch für Psychiatrie*, 25: 168–88.

Berrios, G.E. (1984) 'Descriptive psychopathology: conceptual and historical aspects'. *Psychological Medicine*, 14: 303–13.

Berrios, G.E. (1984) 'Epilepsy and insanity during the early 19th century'. *Archives of Neurology*, 41: 978–81.

Berrios, G.E. (1988) 'Historical background to abnormal psychology'. In Miller, E. and Cooper, P.J. (eds.) *Adult Abnormal Psychology*, Edinburgh, Churchill Livingstone, pp.26–51.

Berrios, G.E. (1990) 'Memory and the cognitive paradigm of dementia. The 16th Squibb Lecture'. In Murray, R.M. and Turner, T.H. (eds.) *Lectures on the History of Psychiatry*, London, Gaskell, pp.194–211.

Berrios, G.E. (1996) 'Descriptive Psychiatry and psychiatric nosology during the 19th century'. In Wallace, E. (ed.) *History of Psychiatry*, Yale, Yale University Press, (in the press).

Berrios, G.E. & Quemada, J.I. (1990) 'Depressive illness in multiple sclerosis: clinical and theoretical aspects of the association'. *British Journal of Psychiatry*, 156: 10–16.

Berrios, G.E. & Quemada, J.I. (1990a) 'André G. Ombredane and the psychopathology of multiple sclerosis: a conceptual and statistical history'. *Comprehensive Psychiatry*, 31: 438–46.

Böhmig, W. (1925) 'Statistische Bemerkungen zur Klinik der multiplen Sklerose'. *Monatsschrift für Psychiatrie und Neurologie*, 58: 277–88.

Borberg, N.C. and Zahle, V. (1946) 'On the psychopathology of disseminated sclerosis'. *Acta Psychiatrica et Neurologica Scandinavica*, 21: 75–89.

Bourneville, D.M. and Guérard, L. (1969) *De la Sclérose en Plaques Disséminées*, Thèse de la Faculté de Médecine, Paris, Delahaye.

Brown, S. and Davis, T.K. (1922) 'The mental symptoms in Multiple Sclerosis'. In Dana, C.L., Jelliffe, S.E., Riley, H.A. et al (eds.) *Multiple Sclerosis, An Investigation by the Association for Research in Nervous and Mental Diseases*, New York, Hoeber, pp.76–82.

Brown, S. and Davis, T.K. (1922) 'The mental symptoms of multiple sclerosis'. *Archives of Neurology and Psychiatry*, 7: 630–4.

Buzzard, T. (1890) 'On the simulation of hysteria by organic disease of the nervous system'. *Brain*, 13: 1–44.

Chamberet, T. (1819) 'Paralysie'. In Adelon, Alibert, Barbier et al (eds.) *Dictionnaire des Sciences Médicales par une Société de Médicins et de Chirurgiens*, vol.39, Paris, C. L. F. Panckoucke, pp.243–60.

Charcot, J.M. (1877) *Lectures on the Diseases of the Nervous System*, (translated by G. Sigerson), London, New Sydenham Society, pp.157–222.

Charcot, J.M. (1877) *Lectures on the Diseases of the Nervous System*, (translated by G. Sigerson), London, New Sydenham Society, pp.129–56.

Charcot, J.M. (1881) *Clinical Lectures on Senile and Chronic Diseases*, London, The New Syndenham Society, pp.3–7.

Charcot, J.M. (1890) 'Tremblements et mouvements choreiformes'. In *Ouvres Complètes*, vol.9, Paris, Bureaux du Progrès Médicale, pp.215–28.

Clarke, E. and Jacyna, L.S. (1987) *Nineteenth-century Origins of Neuroscientific Concepts*, Berkeley, University of California Press, pp.29–57.

Clarke, E. and O'Malley, C.D. (1968) *The Human Brain and Spinal Cord. A Historical Study illustrated by Writings from Antiquity to the Twentieth Century*, Berkeley, University of California Press, pp.291–322.

Claude, H. (1924) 'Quelques remarques sur le diagnostic de la Sclérose en plaques'. *Revue Neurologique*, 31: 727–30.

Compston, A. (1988) 'The 150th anniversary of the first depiction of the lesions in multiple sclerosis'. *Journal of Neurology, Neurosurgery and Psychiatry*, 51: 1249–52.

Cook, W.M. (1858) *A treatise on the principles and practice of physio-medical surgery*, Cincinnati, Moore, Wilstach, Keys, pp.17–24.

Cottrell, S.S. and Wilson, S.A.K. (1926) 'The affective symptomatology of disseminated sclerosis'. *Journal of Neurology and Psychopathology*, 7: 1–30.

Cruveilhier, J. (1835–1842) *Anatomie Pathologique. Ou descriptions, avec figures lithographieés et coloriées, des diverses altérations morbides dont le corps humain est susceptible*, vol.2, Paris, Baillière.

Cullen, W. (1827) *The works of William Cullen* (edited by J. Thomson), vol.1, Edinburgh, William Blackwood.

Dana, C.L., Jelliffe, S.E., Riley, H.A. et al (eds.) (1922) *Multiple Sclerosis (disseminated sclerosis)*, New York, Hoeber.

Danneberger, N. (1901) *Zur Lehre von den Geistesstörungen bei multipler Sklerose*, Inaugural Diss. Gießen.

Dejerine, J. and Thomas, A. (1902) *Traité des maladies de la moelle èpinière*, Paris, Baillière, pp.171–92.

Dubois, C. (1924) 'Sclèrose en plaques et hystèrie'. *Revue Neurologique*, 31: 739.

Duchenne, G.B.A. (1883) 'Progressive Locomotor Ataxy'. In Poore, G.V. (ed.) *Selections from the clinical works of Dr. Duchenne (de Boulogne)*, London, New Sydenham Society, pp.1–35.

Duge, M. (1914) 'Ein Beitrag zur Kenntnis der Psychosen bei der multiplen Sklerose des Gehirns und Rückenmarks'. *Deutsche Zeitschrift Nervensheilkunde*, 51: 459–512.

Dupré, E. (1903) 'Sclérose en plaques'. In Ballet, G. (ed.) *Traité de Pathologie Mentale*, Paris, Baillière, pp.1198–1201.

Etienne, D., Cornil, M. and Mathieu, L. (1924) 'A propos de la symptomatologie et du diagnostic de la Sclérose en plaques'. *Revue Neurologique*, 31: 730–1.

Euzière, T. (1909) 'Les troubles psychiques dans la sclérose en plaques'. *Archives Générales de Médecine*, 72: 746–56.

Firth, D. (1948) *The Case of Augustus D'Este*, Cambridge, Cambridge University Press.

Flamm, E.S. (1973) 'The neurology of Jean Cruveilhier'. *Medical History*, 17: 343–55.

Fodor, J. (1983) *The modularity of the mind*, Cambridge, MIT Press.
Foville, A.L. (1834) 'Nèvrose'. In Andral, Begin, Blauding et al (eds.) *Dictionnaire de Médicine et de Chirurgie Pratiques*, vol.12, Paris, Baillière, pp.55–63.
Gowers, W.R. (1893) *A manual of diseases of the nervous system*, vol.2, London, Churchill, pp.543–61.
Gross, M. (1979) 'The lessened locus of feelings: a transformation in French physiology in the early nineteenth century'. *Journal of the History of Biology*, 12: 231–71.
Guillain, G. (1959) *J M Charcot 1825–1893. His life-his work* (translated by P. Bailey), London, Pitman Medical, pp.111–13.
Hall, M. (1836) *Lectures on the Nervous system and its diseases*, London, Sherwood, Gilbert and Piper, p.143.
Hécaen, H. and Lanteri-Laura, G. (1977) *Evolution des connaissances et des doctrines sur les localisations cerebrales*, Paris, Desclée de Brouwer.
Jelliffe, S.E. and White, W.A. (1929) *Diseases of the Nervous System*, London, Lewis, pp.589–608.
Jelliffe, S.E. (1922) 'Emotional and psychological factors in multiple sclerosis'. In Dana, C.L., Jelliffe, S.E., Riley, H.A. et al (eds.) *Multiple Sclerosis, An investigation by the Association for Research in Nervous and Mental Diseases*, New York, Hoeber, pp.82–95.
Kim, J.O. (1978) *Introduction to Factor Analysis*, London, Sage Publications.
Kurtzke, J.F. (1988) 'Multiple sclerosis. What's in a name?' *Neurology*, 38: 309–16.
Ladame, P. (1890) 'Freidreich's ataxia'. *Brain*, 13: 467–537.
Larson, J.L. (1971) *Reason and Experience. The Representation of Natural Order in the work of Carl von Linné*, Berkeley, University of California Press.
LHermitte, J. and Guccione, A. (1910) 'De quelques symptomes et lésions rares dans la sclérose en plaques'. *L'Encéphale*, 5: 257–75.
LHermitte, J. and Halberstadt, N. (1906) 'Troubles mentaux dans la sclérose en plaques'. *Annales Médico-Psychologiques*, 64: 448–57.
López Piñero, J.M. (1983) *Historical Origins of the Concept of Neurosis* (translated by D. Berrios), Cambridge, Cambridge University Press.
Marie, P. (1895) *Lectures on Diseases of the Spinal Cord* (translated by M. Lubbock), London, New Sydenham Society, pp.102–3.
Maulitz, R.C. (1987) *Morbid appearances. The Anatomy of Pathology in the early Nineteenth Century*, Cambridge, Cambridge University Press.
McAlpine, D., Compston, N.D. and Lumsden, C.E. (1955) *Multiple Sclerosis*, Edinburgh, Livingstone, pp.1–6.
McHenry, L.C. (1969) *Garrison's History of Neurology*, Springfield, Charles C Thomas, p.279.
Monro, T.K. (1895) *A History of the Chronic Degenerative Diseases of the Central Nervous System*, Glasgow, Alex MacDougall, pp.79–82.
Müller, E. (1904) *Die multiple Sklerose des Gehirns und Rückenmarks, ihre Pathologie und Behandlung*, Jena, Fisher.
Neuburger, M. (1981) *The Historical Development of Experimental Brain and Spinal Cord Physiology before Flourens*, (translated and edited, with

additional material by E. Clarke), Baltimore, Johns Hopkins University Press, pp.185–208.

Norusis, M.J. (1986) *SPSS/PC + V2.0. Base Manual*, Chicago, SPSS Inc.

Ombredane, A. (1929) *Les Troubles Mentaux de la Sclérose en Plaques*, Paris, Presses Universitaires de France, pp.23–41.

Ombredane, A. (1951) *L'Aphasie et la Élaboration de la Pensée Explicite*, Paris, Presses Universitaires de France.

Ombredane, A. (1954) *La Exploration de la Mentalité des Noirs Congolais au moyen d'une Preuve Projective: le Congo TAT*, Bruxelles, Duculot.

Ombredane, A. (1956) *Etude Psychologique des Noirs Asalampasu*, 2 vols, Bruxelles, Duculot.

Ombredane, A. (1957) *Etude Psychotechnique des Baluba*, Bruxelles, Duculot.

Ordenstein, L. (1868) *Sur la Paralysie Agitante et la Sclérose en Plaques Généralisées*, Paris, Martinet.

Phillipe, T. and Cestan, R. (1903) *Les Troubles Mentaux de la Sclérose en Plaques*. Mémoire présenté à L'Académie de Médecine, Paris.

Poore, G.V. (1883) *Selections from the Clinical Works of Dr. Duchenne (de Boulogne)*, London, New Sydenham Society, pp.35–6.

Pratt, R.T.C. (1951) 'An investigation of the psychiatric aspects of disseminated sclerosis'. *Journal of Neurology, Neurosurgery and Psychiatry*, 14: 326–36.

Raecke, N. (1906) 'Psychische Störungen bei der multiplen Sklerose'. *Archiv für Psychiatrie und Nervenkrankheiten*, 41: 482–518.

Rath, G. (1954) 'Neauralpathologische Anschauungen in 18. Jahrhundert'. *Deustche Medizinischen Journal*, 5: 125–7.

Raymond, F. and Touchard, C. (1909) 'Sclérose en plaques débutant par des troubles mentaux simulant la paralysie générale'. *Revue Neurologique*, 17: 224–8.

Redlich, E. (1912) *Die Psychosen bei Gehirnerkrankungen*, Leipzig, Deuticke, pp.405–22.

Rice, G. (1987) 'The Bell-Magendie-Walker controversy'. *Medical History*, 31: 190–200.

Riese, W. (1949) 'An outline of a history of ideas in neurology'. *Bulletin of the History of Medicine*, 23: 111–36.

Roche, L.Ch. (1834) 'Paralysie'. In *Dictionnaire de Médicine et de Chirurgie pratiques*, vol.12, Paris, Baillière, pp.464–7.

Romberg, M.H. (1853) *A Manual of the Nervous Diseases of Man* (translated by E.H. Sieveking), vol.2, London, Sydenham Society.

Ross, A.T. and Reitan, R.M. (1955) 'Intellectual and affective functions in multiple sclerosis'. *Archives of Neurology and Psychiatry*, 73: 663–77.

Ross, D.M. (1915) 'The mental symptoms in disseminated sclerosis'. *Review of Neurology and Psychiatry*, 13: 361–73.

Saethre, H. (1932) 'Psychische Störungen bei multipler Sklerose'. *Acta Psychiatrica et Neurologica Scandinavica*, 7: 511–43.

Sai-Halasz, A. (1956) 'Psychic alterations in disseminated sclerosis. A General, statistical and Rorschach-Test study in 200 patients'. *Monatsschrift für Psychiatrie und Neurologie*, 132: 129–54.

Schiller, F. (1970) 'Concepts of stroke before and after Virchow'. *Medical History*, 14: 115–31.

Schiller, F. (1976) 'Venery, the spinal cord, and tabes dorsalis before Romberg: the contribution of Ernst Horn'. *Journal of Nervous and Mental Disease*, 163: 1–9.

Schwarz, M.A. and Wiggins, O.P. (1987) 'Diagnosis and Ideal Types: a contribution to psychiatric classification'. *Comprehensive Psychiatry*, 28: 277–91.

Seiffer, W. (1905) 'Über psychische, insbesondere Intelligenzstörungen bei multipler Sklerose'. *Archiv für Psychiatrie und Nervenkrankheiten*, 40: 252–303.

Shallice, T. (1988) *From Neuropsychology to Mental Structure*, Cambridge, Cambridge University Press.

Siegel, R.E. (1973) *Galen on Psychology, Psychopathology, and function and diseases of the nervous system*, Basel, Karger, pp.239–43.

Siegel, S. (1956) *Nonparametric Statistics for the Behavioral Sciences*, New York, McGraw-Hill, pp.127–36.

Slater, E.T.O. (1965) 'Diagnosis of hysteria'. *British Medical Journal* i: 1395–9.

Söderberg, G. (1924) 'Sclèrose en plaques et pithiatisme'. *Revue Neurologique*, 31: 736–8.

Spiegel, M. (1881) *Über die psychischen Störungen bei der multiplen Sklerose*, Berlin, medicinischen Diss.

Sugar, C. and Nadell, R. (1943) 'Mental symptoms in multiple sclerosis'. *Journal of Nervous and Mental Disease*, 98: 267–80.

Surridge, D. (1969) 'An investigation into some psychiatric aspects of multiple sclerosis'. *British Journal of Psychiatry*, 115: 749–64.

Targowla, R. (1924) 'Sur le diagnostic différentiel de la sclèrose en plaques et de la paralysie générale. Intérêt du syndrome humoral'. *Revue Neurologique*, 31: 734–6.

Taylor, E.W. (1921) 'Multiple sclerosis: the location of lesions with respect to symptoms'. *Archives of Neurology and Psychiatry*, 7: 561–81.

Thompson, W.D. and Walter, S.D. (1988) 'A reappraisal of the Kappa coefficient'. *Journal Clinical Epidemiology*, 41: 949–58.

Timme, W. (1950) 'Multiple sclerosis. Historical aspects'. In *Multiple Sclerosis and the Demyelinating diseases*, Research Publications, Association for Research in Nervous and Mental Diseases, vol.28, Baltimore, Williams and Wilkins, pp.3–11.

Tizard, B. (1959) 'Theories of brain localization from Flourens to Lashley'. *Medical History*, 3: 132–45.

Todd, R.B. (1856) *Clinical Lectures on Paralysis and Certain Diseases of the Brain, and other Affections of the Nervous System*, 2nd Edition, London, John Churchill.

Valentiner, W. (1856) 'Über die Sklerose des Gehirns und Rückenmarks'. *Deutsche Klinik*, 8: 147–9; 158–9; 167–70.

Vulpian, A. (1879) *Maladies du Système Nerveux, Maladies de la Moelle* (recueillies et publies by Bourceret), vol.1, Paris, Doin, pp.240–55.

Vulpian, A. (1886) *Maladies du Système Nerveux (moelle pinire)*, vol.2, Paris, Doin, pp.676–749.

Walker, A. (1839) *Documents and Dates of Modern Discoveries in the Nervous System*, London, John Churchill.

Young, R.M. (1970) *Mind, Brain and Adaptation in the Nineteenth Century*, Oxford, Clarendon Press.

Chapter 8
Pain Disorders

Clinical Section
ANDREW HODGKISS

INTRODUCTION

Most accounts of the clinical history of pain start from the premise that recent interest in psychological and psychiatric aspects of physical pain represent a rediscovery of 'insights' lost long ago. For example, Price (1988) states that while Aristotle regarded pain as a 'Passion', the opposite of pleasure, 'the advent of post-renaissance scientific thinking has tended to obscure this dimension of pain. Beginning with Descartes and continuing to the present, a mechanistic approach toward the analysis of pain has prevailed . . . pain being subsumed within the framework of sensory systems'. Price goes on to name Müller's doctrine of specific nerve energies as an important example of this 'reductionist error'. Similarly Diamond and Coniam (1991) argue that post-cartesian physiologists did not take account of pain occurring in the absence of tissue damage and ignored emotional responses to pain.

Gibson (1982), citing Merskey and Spear (1967), dates the loss of psychological insight rather later:

> The enlightened view of the essential nature of pain which was current in the first half of the nineteenth century became obscured later on by findings in neuroanatomy and neurophysiology which generated confidently expressed theories about pain that were mechanistic in nature.

For these authors the work of Noordenbos (1959), Beecher (1959) and Melzack & Wall (1965) emphasising 'higher' influences on pain perception was a rediscovery of 'insights' obscured by nineteenth century neurosciences.

Dally (1991) has argued that psychiatric interest in physical pain is a very recent phenomenon (post 1960) and can be seen as an attempt to boost the prestige of the profession.

This chapter challenges the views above and argues against a reading of contemporary psychiatric involvement with pain patients as professional opportunism (or, at best, a new fad). Evidence will be presented of continuous discussion of psychological aspects of pain in European medical writings from 1800 to 1914. In particular, it will be argued that a clinical syndrome of 'chronic pain without lesion' was recognised and theorised throughout this period.

The most useful secondary sources on the clinical history of psychological and psychiatric aspects of pain are Merskey & Spear (1967), Keele (1957) and Rev

(1993). Texts by Foucault (1973), López Piñero (1983) and Starobinski (1990) are central to the organisation of this chapter.

The choice of primary sources is problematic. Following pain in over a century of medical texts yields too much material yet it would be an anachronistic and ahistorical to pursue 'somatoform pain disorder', 'psychogenic pain' or 'appreciation of psychological aspects of pain'. It may be helpful to study a problem of a single episteme – namely chronic pain without lesion after the birth of the anatomo-clinical method (Foucault, 1973). Once Bichat's concept of structural lesion was widely accepted, disease was reduced to abnormal tissue detectable in vivo as clinical signs and post mortem as 'morbid appearances' (Maulitz, 1987). Pinel was among the first to emphasise a group of syndromes in which no lesions could be found and borrowed Cullen's term 'Neurosis' to name them (López Piñero, 1983). Chronic pain without lesion (CPWL) was an important example of this problematic group of conditions. Following textual references to CPWL over time is one way to access discussion of psychological aspects of pain.

CPWL – RECOGNITION, TERMINOLOGY AND CLASSIFICATION

A syndrome of CPWL was widely recognised and theorised in nineteenth century medical writings. While terminology varied a good deal, the phenomena described were rather stable over time. A few examples will suffice – further evidence from British medical texts may be found in Hodgkiss (1991).

Travers (1826) picked out 'pain unattended by any other sign of inflammation' (i.e. turgor, calor, rubor) as one category of 'Local Irritation'. Three years later Tate (1829) preferred to consider CPWL as one variety of 'Hysteria'. He emphasised the excessive disability associated with such pain and regarded left sided pain as pathognomonic. Briquet's 'Treatise on Hysteria' of 1858 (Mai and Merskey, 1980) supported this view. On examining 430 cases at the Charité he found pain in the epigastrium, left chest and left of the spine to be invariable clinical features of Hysteria.

Teale's 'Neuralgias' of 1830 and Swan's case histories of 1834 emphasised the constancy, severity and chronicity of CPWL as well as the excessive disability and low spirits associated with the syndrome. Swan drew attention to the risk of opiate dependence in such patients.

Brodie's 'Lectures' of 1837 are devoted to the problem of CPWL which he termed 'Nervous Pain' and classified as a 'Local Hysteria'.

In the 1870's Tuke and Wilks saw CPWL as a pathognomonic hallucination pointing to the diagnoses of Hysteria or Hypochondria. Wilks emphasised the severity, chronicity and left sided predominance of such pain and the excessive disability and opiate dependence associated with it. Anstie's account of 'Neuralgia' (1871) described the boring/burning character of CPWL.

Freud and Breuer's 'Studies on Hysteria' of 1895 includes several cases of CPWL – notably Fraulein Elizabeth von R., Frau Cäcilie and Frau Emmy von N.

In 1907 the French psychiatrists Dupré & Camus classified CPWL as a 'Cenestopathic State'. They described the constancy and chronicity of such pain, its incompatibility with neurological distribution, its non-relief by analgesics, the associated psychiatric disorder (notably depression) and the poor prognosis.

These examples support the view that CPWL was rather widely noted throughout the nineteenth century. It seems to have fallen to surgeons and physicians to care for such patients initially and only late in the century were psychiatrists involved. This is consistent with previous accounts of the professional context in which nervous patients were seen in the nineteenth century. (Bynum, 1985 and Mayou, 1989). Reynolds (1990) has described the intimate relationship between developing professional boundaries and the shifting meaning of the term 'functional' over this period.

The phenomenological stability of CPWL over time is notable. Trimble (1989) and Berrios (1984) have suggested that such stability is evidence of biological constancy or organicity underlying a syndrome. It is difficult to account for the repeated observation of a left sided predominance of pain, for example, in any other terms.

THEORETICAL RESPONSES TO CPWL: CONTEXTS AND EXAMPLES

Theories of CPWL are most easily understood within certain conceptual contexts. These might include histories of the concepts 'neurosis', 'pain pathways', 'cenesthesia' and 'ideodynamism'.

Neurosis

López Piñero (1983) has reviewed the history of the concept of neurosis. Pinel defined the neuroses by the absence of Bichatian, structural lesion early in the anatomoclinical episteme. Anatomoclinicians such as Teale, Swan, Brodie and Anstie sought structural lesions at a spatial distance from pain to account for chronic pain without lesion at the site of the pain. Such 'Referred Pain' could be explained neuroanatomically in simple cases (e.g. pain in the little finger on knocking the elbow was explained by the course of the ulnar nerve). More distant relationships between pain and lesion drove Brodie to invoke Marshall Hall's new concept of 'Reflexion' and Anstie to employ Müller's term 'Radiation' (Hodgkiss, 1991).

Broussais proposed functional lesions to account for symptoms without structural lesion. Travers (1826) provides one example of such 'speculative functionalism' applied to CPWL. He borrowed Broussais's term 'Irritation' to refer to an obscure functional or dynamic process, similar to inflammation but resulting in no morbid appearances, that could explain CPWL.

Functional localisers such as Foville and Jaccoud criticised speculative functionalism, insisting that functional lesions must be localised to the nervous system in neuroses. Tate's writing on CPWL is one example of 'functional localisation'. Following Bell and Magendies' recent experiments on spinal nerve roots, he proposed that irritation confined to 'the upper dorsal portion of the spinal marrow' caused CPWL.

To generalise, two strands of opinion ran through nineteenth-century discussion of neurosis. Some clung to Pinel's early definition and assumed that the category would shrink to nothing as improved investigative technology revealed new lesions; while others, following Georget, thought that there would always be somatic symptoms inexplicable by lesion. Charcot's description of certain positive clinical features in neurosis, such as belle indifférence, is one example of the attempt to describe the psychopathology of neurosis. Freud could have written up the tendency of hysterics to reveal past histories of sexual abuse in childhood under transference in descriptive terms. Instead, he regarded it as aetiological. This confusion of descriptive psychopathology, dynamic psychopathology and aetiological theory still colours the DSMIV approach to Pain Disorder (see below).

Pain Pathways

While early attempts to localise psychological faculties in the body, for example Gall's work (Bynum, 1976), were based on teleological premises (the designed universe), Bell's work was grounded in the premises of anatomoclinical method. Foucault (1973) has described how Bichat's concept of lesion 'welded' the symptom to the body and this was a conceptual prerequisite for Bell's search for a physical locus for sensibility in the body. His work on facial expression in madness is another example of his effort to make visible the mental (Donnelly, 1983).

Rice (1987) has summarised how Bell's 'Idea of a New Anatomy of the Brain' of 1811 – that the cerebrum mediated operations of the mind (i.e. sense and motion) while the cerebellum was concerned with vital functions – led him to perform and interpret spinal root sectioning experiments on stunned rabbits. Magendie operated on live puppies and observed the delayed effects of root sectioning in the alert animal. His use of puncture and strong pressure facilitated the publication in 1822 of the first clear statement that the posterior roots were 'sensible', the anterior 'motor'.

Johannes Müller is often read as a neuroscientist who reduced the rather open eighteenth century concept of 'sensibility' (Mullan, 1988) to the narrow, quantifiable 'sensation' of psychophysics and neurophysiology, so heralding a century of neglect of higher aspects of pain. Müller's 'Elements of Physiology' (1842) shows that he did not regard pain as a primary sense, such as vision, but as one of several 'sensations of feeling and touch'. Müller distinguished 'sensation' (a knowledge of certain conditions of the nerves of sense) from 'perception in the mind' which, he wrote, depends on interpretation in the light of past ideas then projection of the percept to the exterior. For Müller the mind had, at the very least, an intensity-modulating function with respect to conditions of the nerves of sense.

Weber (1846) distinguished senses with and without external referents – vision and pain respectively. He thought pain might arise through overstimulation of any nerve of sense and had no special anatomy.

Despite these influential views, later workers such as Schiff and Brown-Séquard did attempt to find 'pain pathways' so that in 1886 Gowers could write: 'it is almost certain that the anterolateral ascending tract constitutes the path for sensibility to pain'.

While a tradition may be traced from Bell to Gowers and beyond there are clues within this corpus that psychological aspects of pain were not ignored. Müller's emphasis on attention and memory in pain perception was cited approvingly in Tuke's 'Illustrations of the Influence of the Mind upon the Body' some thirty years later. Weber's account of sensations lacking external referents summing to constitute the 'Gemeingefühl' (or 'cenesthesia') is best read as German romantic psychiatry rather than as reductionist neuroscience.

Cenesthesia

Starobinski (1990) has reviewed the history of cenesthesia. He pointed out that Aristotle's equation of pain with pleasure as 'Bodily Passions' was not overturned by Descartes who advocated three categories of perception relating to external objects, the body and the soul. In 1794 the German romantic psychiatrist Reil maintained this tripartite division, labelling perception of ones own body 'Cenesthesia' (synonymous with 'Gemeingefühl'). In his view phenomena such as CPWL represented disorders of cenesthesia, uncorrected by judgement.

Clark's (1988) review of 'Morbid Introspection' in nineteenth-century British psychological medicine indicates how influential such thinking was. He suggests that Carpenter, Holland, Carter, Lewis, Tuke and Maudsley shared the view that excessive absorbtion in ones subjective, internal world of bodily sensations gave rise to pains and other hallucinations characteristic of hysteria and hypochondria. Developing 'outside interests' was regarded as protective against such conditions.

Perhaps the most striking examples of Reil and Weber's influence are the accounts of CPWL to be found in the writings of a number of French psychiatrists in the first two decades of the twentieth century. Dupré, Camus and Maillard theorised some CPWL in terms of disordered cenesthesia while Blondel (1914) thought symptoms arose when there was insufficient verbalisation of cenesthesia. Blondel's model was close to the contemporary concept of 'alexithymia' (Taylor 1984).

Ideodynamism

Ideodynamism – symptoms caused by ideas – came to the fore in discussions of hysteria and hypnosis in France and in Britain in the late nineteenth century (Merskey, 1979, 1983; Clark, 1981; Harris, 1985; Williams, 1985; Harrington, 1988).

Reynolds (1869), cited by Charcot, wrote the first clear account of the pathogenicity of ideas for perhaps a century. Most British nerve doctors of the day, notably Hughlings Jackson, believed psychic and physical states were autonomous in health – 'psychophysical parallelism'. In mental illness Jackson regarded the psychopathology as a mere epiphenomenon of the physical dissolution in the nervous system. As such, the content of psychopathology was of no interest while the form might be useful as a localising sign. Reynolds advocacy of ideodynamism was a radical departure from this position.

Charcot noted that a patient's beliefs and ideas about disease could determine the nature and localisation of symptoms in hysteria and hypnotic trance. However, his version of ideodynamism was psychophysiological – he insisted

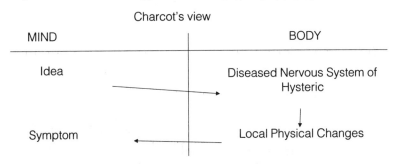

Charcot's view

that only constitutionally vulnerable hysterics could be so affected and that local physical changes were induced in the territory of an idea.

In contrast, Bernheim in France and members of the Society for Psychical Research in Britain argued that hypnosis need not be a pathological phenomenon and was possible in the healthy. They placed greater emphasis on the content of psychical phenomenon and advocated a thoroughgoing psychological model of ideodynamism:

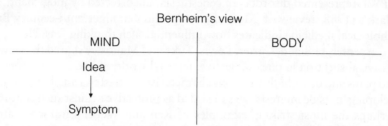

Bernheim's view

MIND	BODY
Idea	
↓	
Symptom	

Hyperaesthesia and anaesthesia were phenomena central to the Paris-Nancy debate between Charcot and Bernheim in the 1880s. Members of the Society for Psychical Research were involved in experiments provoking pain in healthy subjects by suggestion, and even transferring such pain between such subjects in the 1870's and 1880's.

Freud and Breuer's subtly different responses to CPWL reflected their positions regarding ideodynamism. While Freud placed it at the centre of the 'Project for a Scientific Psychology' of 1895, deriving his first axiom from the clinical phenomenon of hysterical conversion, Breuer, in his theoretical contribution to 'Studies on Hysteria' of the same year, emphasised that much hysterical pain was not ideogenic. For example, Breuer regarded the pain of ovarian neuralgia as unique to neurotics but not necessarily ideogenic (psychoneurotic).

Breuer's psychophysiological account of ideogenic pain followed Charcot – the overexcited, diseased nerves of the hysteric were central to the phenomenon, acting to enliven traumatic reminiscence.

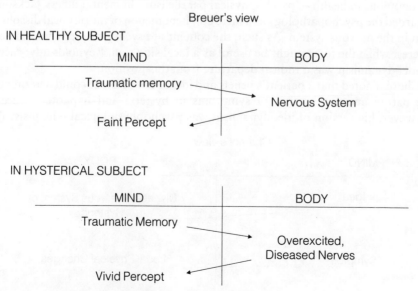

Breuer's view

IN HEALTHY SUBJECT

MIND	BODY
Traumatic memory	Nervous System
Faint Percept	

IN HYSTERICAL SUBJECT

MIND	BODY
Traumatic Memory	Overexcited, Diseased Nerves
Vivid Percept	

Freud's discussion of pain in the 'Project' is more complex. To explain how a reminiscence could assume the vivid phenomenological quality of pain (Schmerz), as opposed to discomfort (Unlust), he was forced to invoke a third class of ω neurones (in addition to perceptual φ and mnemic ψ neurones). A principal function of the 'ego' in this early work was inhibition of pointless affect whenever a traumatic memory was evoked. The healthy ego achieved such inhibition through a network of side routes in ψ which dissipated the energy of 'key ψ neurones' bearing the traumatic memory. The hysterical ego defended by substituting energy from the traumatic memory to a symbolically associated one. This merely changed the cue for pointless affect from a traumatic memory to another stimulus and so the defence failed.

In Freud's 'Project' the hysteric is defined by a pathological psychical defence rather than an overexcited nervous system. Following Bernheim, Freud took psychic content seriously. However, he was at one with Charcot and Breuer in favouring a diseased nervous system underlying the psychopathology. In 1895 Freud's ideodynamism was psychophysiological.

CONCLUSION

A review of nineteenth-century theorisation of CPWL reveals that both anatomoclinicians and ideodynamists worked within a causal theory of pain. Such a theory defines pain as that which arises from certain specified causal states (Smith and Jones, 1986). Lesion or idea were the favoured causal states in the texts reviewed here. However the phenomenology of pain perception, for example the effects of attention, memory and emotion, were emphasised by Müller and many later authors.

In DSM IV (1994) 'Pain Disorder' is defined by a number of criteria which suggest that a narrow causal theory of pain underpins the nosology. Lesion may be present or absent while 'psychological factors' must be at play in the aetiology. The phenomenology of pain perception is not discussed, resulting in the problematic situation of a psychiatric diagnosis without any abnormalities of descriptive psychopathology (Murphy, 1990). Indeed, if there is depressed mood DSMIV insists that a Mood Disorder rather than Pain Disorder should be diagnosed. This preservation of presumed 'psychogenesis' in the absence of detailed psychopathology risks neglecting nearly two centuries of work toward defining the positive clinical features of neuroses.

REFERENCES

Primary Sources
Anstie, F.E. (1871) *Neuralgia and the Diseases that Resemble It*, London, Macmillan.
Bell, C. (1811) *Idea of a New Anatomy of the Brain*, London.
Blondel, C. (1914) 'La Conscience Morbide'. Summarised in *The Troubled Conscience and the Insane Mind*, (1928) London, Kegan Paul.
Brodie, B.C. (1837) *Lectures Illustrative of Certain Nervous Affections*, London, Longman.
Dupré, E. and Camus, P. (1907) 'Les Cénestopathies'. *L'Encephale*, 2: 616–31.

Freud, S. (1895) *A Project for a Scientific Psychology*, Standard Edition, volume 1.

Freud, S. and Breuer, J. (1895) *Studies on Hysteria*, Standard Edition, volume 2.

Gowers, W.R. (1886) *Manual of Diseases of the Nervous System*, London, Churchill.

Magendie, F. (1822) 'Experiences sur les fonctions des racines des nerfs rachidiens'. *J. Physiol. exp.* 1: 277–9.

Müller, J. (1842) *Elements of Physiology*, trans. Baly, W., London, Taylor & Walton.

Reynolds, J.R. (1869) 'Remarks on paralysis and other disorders of motion and sensation, dependent on idea'. *British Medical Journal*, 2: 483–5.

Swan, J. (1834) *A Treatise on Diseases and Injuries of the Nerves*, second edition, London, Longman.

Tate, G. (1831) *A Treatise on Hysteria*, second edition, Philadelphia, Carey & Hart.

Teale, T.P. (1830) *A Treatise on Neuralgic Diseases*, Philadelphia, Carey & Hart.

Travers, B. (1826) *An Inquiry concerning that Disturbed State of the Vital Functions usually denominated Constitutional Irritation*, New York, Stevenson.

Tuke, D.H. (1872) *Illustrations of the Influence of the Mind upon the Body*, London, Churchill.

Weber, E.H. (1846) 'Der Tastsinn und das Gemeingefühl'. In *Weber: The Sense of Touch* (1978) trans. Ross, H.E. and Murray, D.J., London, Academic Press.

Wilks, S. (1883) *Lectures on Diseases of the Nervous System delivered at Guy's Hospital*, second edition, London, Churchill.

Secondary Sources

American Psychiatric Association (1994) *Diagnostic & Statistical Manual of Mental Disorders*, Washington, DC, A.P.A. pp.458–62.

Beecher, H.K. (1959) *Measurement of Subjective Responses*, Oxford, Oxford University Press.

Berrios, G.E. (1984) 'Descriptive Psychopathology: conceptual and historical aspects'. *Psychol Med*, 14: 303–13.

Bynum, W.F. (1976) 'Varieties of Cartesian experience in early nineteenth-century neurophysiology'. In Spicker and Engelhardt (eds.) *Philosophical dimensions of the neuromedical sciences*, Dordrecht Holland, Reidel.

Bynum, W.F. (1985) 'The nervous patient in eighteenth- and nineteenth-century Britain: the psychiatric origins of British Neurology'. In Bynum, Porter and Shepherd (eds.) *The Anatomy of Madness, vol.1*, London, Tavistock.

Clark, M.J. (1981) 'The Rejection of Psychological Approaches to Mental Disorder in Late Nineteenth-Century British Psychiatry'. In Scull (ed.) *Madhouses, Mad-Doctors and Madmen*, London, Athlone Press.

Clark, M.J. (1988) 'Morbid introspection, unsoundness of mind, and British psychological medicine c. 1830–1900'. In Bynum, Porter and Shepherd (eds.) *The Anatomy of Madness, vol.3*, London, Tavistock.

Dally, A. (1991) The Significance of Pain in Psychiatry. Work in Progress Meeting, Wellcome Institute for the History of Medicine, London (10.12.91).

Diamond, A.W. and Coniam, S.W. (1991) *The Management of Chronic Pain*, Oxford, Oxford University Press.

Donnelly, M. (1983) *Managing the Mind: a study of medical psychology in early nineteenth-century Britain*, London, Tavistock.

Foucault, M. (1973) *The Birth of the Clinic*, London, Tavistock.

Gibson, H.B. (1982) *Pain and its Conquest*, London, Peter Owen.

Harrington, A. (1988) 'Hysteria, hypnosis and the lure of the invisible'. In Bynum, Porter and Shepherd (eds.) *The Anatomy of Madness, vol.3*, London, Tavistock.

Harris, R. (1985) 'Murder under hypnosis in the case of Gabrielle Bompard'. In Bynum, Porter and Shepherd (eds.) *The Anatomy of Madness, vol.2*, London, Tavistock.

Hodgkiss, A.D. (1991) 'Chronic pain in nineteenth-century British medical writings'. *History of Psychiatry*, 2: 27–40.

Keele, K.D. (1957) *Anatomies of Pain*, Oxford, Blackwell Scientific Publications.

López Piñero, J.M. (1983) *Historical origins of the concept of neurosis*, Cambridge, Cambridge University Press.

Mai, F.M. and Merskey, H. (1980) 'Briquet's *Treatise on Hysteria*: a synopsis and commentary'. *Arch. Gen. Psychiatry*, 37: 1401–5.

Maulitz, R.C. (1987) *Morbid Appearances: the anatomy of pathology in the early nineteenth century*, Cambridge, Cambridge University Press.

Mayou, R. (1989) 'The History of General Hospital Psychiatry'. *Br. J. Psych*, 155: 764–76.

Melzack, R. and Wall, P.D. (1965) 'Pain Mechanisms: a new theory'. *Science*, 150: 971–9.

Merskey, H. (1979) *The Analysis of Hysteria*, London, Baillière Tindall.

Merskey, H. (1983) 'Hysteria: the history of an idea'. *Can. J. Psychiatry*, 28: 428–33.

Merskey, H. and Spear, F.G. (1967) *Pain: psychological and psychiatric aspects*, London, Baillière, Tindall & Cassell.

Mullan, J. (1988) *Sentiment and Sociability: the language of feeling in the eighteenth century*, Oxford, Clarendon Press.

Murphy, M.R. (1990) 'Classification of the Somatoform Disorders'. In Bass (ed.) *Somatisation: physical symptoms and psychological illness*, Oxford, Blackwell Scientific Publications.

Noordenbos, W. (1959) *Pain*, Amsterdam, Elsevier.

Price, D.D. (1988) *Psychological and Neural Mechanisms of Pain*, New York, Raven Press.

Rey, R. (1993) *History of Pain*, trans. Wallace, L., Cadden, J. and Cadden, S., Paris, Editions La Découverte.

Reynolds, E.H. (1990) 'Structure and Function in Neurology and Psychiatry'. *Br. J. Psych.*, 157: 481–90.

Rice, G. (1987) 'The Bell – Magendie – Walker Controversy'. *Med. Hist.* 31: 190–200.

Smith, P. and Jones, O.R. (1986) *The Philosophy of Mind: an introduction*, Cambridge, Cambridge University Press.

Starobinski, J. (1990) 'A Short History of Bodily Sensation'. *Psychol. Med.*, 20: 23–33.

Taylor, G.J. (1984) 'Alexithymia'. *Am. J. Psychiatry*, 141: 725–32.

Trimble, M. (1989) 'Pseudosyndromes', Sandoz Lecture, Queen Square.

Williams, J.P. (1985) 'Psychical research and psychiatry in late Victorian Britain'. In Bynum, Porter and Shepherd (eds.) *The Anatomy of Madness, Vol.1*, London, Tavistock.

Chapter 8
Pain Disorders

Social Section
ANN DALLY

There are many ways of looking at pain. Like 'punishment', the word comes from the Greek ποινη *poine*, meaning money paid in atonement, a ransom paid for the shedding of blood and the Latin *poena*, punishment. Only in the last century has there been a concerted attempt to separate physical from mental pain and this seems to have been achieved or perhaps exploited, largely by the medical profession in response to popular demand. The separation is crucial to understanding the history of pain in psychiatry. British psychiatry has long been reductionist in an attitude valuable for research based on measurement but incompatible with the popular view that an important task of the psychiatrist is to treat mental pain.

It is common belief that during the nineteenth century, and still more during the twentieth, the task of relieving pain passed from the priest to the doctor, and that whereas physical pain is now relieved by the surgeon or physician, mental pain belongs to the psychiatrist. But did the psychiatrist take over this role? Is it true and if so, how far and how and why? What part has pain, mental and physical, played in the theory and practice of psychiatry? Little information about this is readily available in modern psychiatric literature.

Michael Balint was a doctor who probably did more than anyone to offer a comprehensible model for understanding how the mind influences the body and the part that doctors play in this.[1] He pointed out that every doctor has a set of fairly firm beliefs as to which illnesses are acceptable and which not; how much pain, suffering, fear and deprivation a patient should tolerate and when he has the right to ask for help or relief. These beliefs are hardly ever stated explicitly but they are nevertheless very strong.

> [E]very doctor has a vague, but almost unshakably firm, idea of how a patient ought to behave when he is ill. Although this idea is anything but explicit and concrete, it is immensely powerful and influences . . . practically every detail of the doctor's work with his patients. *It was almost as if every doctor had revealed knowledge of what was right and what was wrong for patients to expect and to endure, and further, as if he has a sacred duty to convert to his faith all the ignorant and unbelieving among his patients.*[2]

Balint had considerable influence on a number of general practitioners who recognised that standard diagnoses and treatments in both medicine and psychiatry did not help a substantial minority of their patients. With the aid of a few psychoanalytically minded psychiatrists, he encouraged GPs to explore mental pain and helped them to understand and alleviate it, but he had little influence on psychiatrists in general. There is a Balint Society and journal but his ideas have remained a minority interest. Few modern students study him and the library of the Royal Society of Medicine in London has now consigned his important (and well-thumbed) book to the basement. Psychiatry has developed other ideas about pain.

Pain, suffering, fear and deprivation. These are symptoms of *mental* pain. One could add to them grief, misery, anguish, distress. Yet these have played little part in psychiatric theory and this may be an important reason for public dissatisfaction with psychiatrists. Until about ten years ago, pain was seldom mentioned in connection with psychiatry. Nowadays it *is* mentioned, but only within certain rather narrow and specific limits.

The Concise Oxford Dictionary defines pain as 'Suffering or distress of body (from injury or disease) or mind'. This junction of what we now try to divide is the classical and traditional definition and can be traced through history. Pain was generally regarded as an inevitable part of life, universally present in mankind, and little effort was made to relieve it. In ordinary speech we still use the same words for both physical and mental pain and show no signs of wishing to separate them. But psychiatrists do separate them and one can see the advantage of so doing. The traditional meaning of 'pain' is so wide and so diffuse that it is difficult to encompass. Reducing the subject to something that can be defined and measured is easier and produces more concrete results, even if it distorts the picture.

Public attitudes to pain have changed during the last 250 years. At one time this happened so fast that it seemed to some that the *physiology* of pain had changed during the nineteenth century.[3] There was a shift in attitude from the belief that pain was a punishment for sin and should be borne with fortitude with the aid of the Church to the belief that it was something to be conquered and cured and that this conquest was for *doctors* to achieve, a belief and attitude that is still common today.

Although there have been attempts to overcome pain as long as there has been civilisation, there seems to have been no great effort to do this until the mid-nineteenth century. There was, for instance, little interest in or acceptance of analgesia and anaesthesia, despite the fact that they were known. God put Adam to sleep when he created Eve from his rib. Opium was known to virtually all civilisations. Paracelsus prepared ether or some such anaesthetic, which he called 'sweet vitriol' and said: 'it quiets all suffering without any harm, and relieves all pain, and quenches all fevers and prevents complications in all illnesses' but he dared not use it on humans for fear of offending the Church.

The Church was powerful in imposing attitudes towards pain. There was no Christian tradition that pain should be relieved. This can be seen, for instance, in the mid-nineteenth century debates about chloroform in childbirth. Pain was not regarded as a physical malfunction but as part of the universe, perhaps God's punishment. For some believers, such as Descartes, pain was a self-protective mechanism that taught the soul to avoid further damage to the body.

The nineteenth century was an age of secularisation and of increasingly humanitarian sentiments. Inevitably ideas about pain were part of these. In general, there was *de*creasing emphasis on a world made bad by sin and *in*creasing emphasis on a world made bad by *suffering* and *pain*. Progress in civilization (a powerful belief at the time) came to mean reduction of the sum of human suffering. Diminishing pain more than increasing happiness. Pain came to be seen as passive, something that happened to victims, for which they deserved the best treatments and cures that medicine might bring. It no longer seemed rational to face pain as it came and it seemed sensible and possible to escape it. Expectations rose of a *pain-free* existence which would have been impossible before. This idea was helpful to the rising medical profession. But even a hundred years later it seems to have had little direct influence on psychiatry, which developed more with these things as a background than as problems to be solved.

Many nineteenth century writers avoided the wider issues involved in the study of pain. They narrowed the field of study and found a focus for attention and measurement. Moreover, since most of the patients who suffered from pain without lesion were *women*, it raises the whole question of women, pain and psychiatry in the nineteenth century. However, some of the older psychiatric writers showed interest in chronic pain without a lesion to explain it[4] and some of the older psychiatric writers discussed pain more freely. In 1879 Henry Maudsley, describing insanity, wrote 'There are great diversities in the character of what we confound under the general name of pain as well as in the character of those manifold modifications of sensibility which fall short of pain so much complained of in some forms of mental disorder'.[5] He does not elaborate on this. Perhaps he was wary of getting involved in mental pain. He also described in detail the painful sensations experienced by melancholics, which he regarded as one of the worst features of the illness. He postulated 'a neuralgic storm of anarchic sensations' unlike and worse than the pains of physical illness such as cancer.

Reductionist forces were already at work. The article on pain in Quain's Medical Dictionary for 1894 is totally physiological.[6] After about that date, the subject is not even mentioned in most textbooks and histories of psychiatry and until recently there has been little discussion about it in psychiatric texts of the twentieth century. To mention just a few of these picked at random, there is no reference to pain in any of the psychiatric books I used as a student, or in Stafford-Clark's textbook for students, published in 1964, or in a huge Dictionary of Psychiatry from the 1960s, in Winnicott's collected papers, Kurt Schneider's *Clinical Psychopathology*, published in a number of editions in the forties and fifties, or Anthony Clare's *Psychiatry in Dissent*, published in 1976. Historical works that do not discuss it include Tuke's *History of the Insane in the British Isles*, Hunter and McAlpine's *Three Hundred Years of Psychiatry*, or Ellenburger's *Discovery of the Unconscious*. Of those that *do* mention pain, Fish's *Clinical Pathology*, published in 1967 and revised by Max Hamilton in 1974 says only:

> Twisting and tearing pains may be complained of by chronic schizophrenics. Sometimes the somatic hallucinations are described in a bizarre way, when the patient complains that his organs are torn out, the flesh ripped away from his body and so on.[7]

Slater and Roth[8] mention it only in increased sensibility to pain, insensitivity to pain and morbid craving for pain in severe subnormality. Sargant and Slater[9] suggest that relieving depression diminishes anginal pain, and discuss 'modified narcosis and combined treatment with ECT and antidepressants' in 'intractable pain', adding:

> the results have not been very rewarding. However, one or two patients with intractable pain, not responding to leucotomy, have been helped after years and years of misery, and leucotomy has been avoided in other cases of intractable pain. One is tempted to think that the depressive state has been the underlying cause of the pain, even though it did not respond to the leucotomy.[10]

These authors encourage the use of leucotomy in intractable physical pain and also say they have had patients who had leucotomy for *tic douloureux* or post-herpetic neuralgia.

> In some of our patients suffering from these conditions there has only been rather temporary relief; but though the patient, if asked, will say that his pain is as bad as ever, he may still live a more normal life, complain less and look less pinched and harassed.[11]

In books published in that era, the only account of pain that I found helpful to the practitioner was in a textbook for *nurses*, first published in 1964.

> Pain is used by some patients as a means of communication, an appeal for love and sympathy, an expression of resentment, an excuse for a sense of failure and impotence . . . . Emotional attitudes and past experiences play an important part in the way a patient feels and reacts to pain. A soldier may not even feel a severe wound received in the heat of battle. But at another time a minor wound evokes severe pain. Some patients over-react when a particular part of the body is damaged. And sometimes an injury which should be painful produces pleasurable sensations. This is most obvious in sado-masochism. Personality plays a part in pain reaction. Introverts have a lower threshold for pain than extraverts, although the latter tend to complain more readily. Depressed patients frequently express their misery solely through complaints of pain; the most common sites are head, abdomen, chest, limbs and face, in that order.[12]

Then came the era of increased physiological work on physical pain and its neurological pathways. Pain as a physiological problem had long been with us, but now there was discussion of 'the gate theory', a new and impressive physiological theory about the mechanism of physical pain. The books now began to display complicated diagrams, though these can also be found in nineteenth century works. All these books discuss pain in terms of neurology. Typical of this period, *The Oxford Companion to the Mind*, published in 1987[13], has a section on pain written by R. Melzack, a neurophysiologist. It cites five references, all of them by Melzack! This is typical of the reductionism that has dominated the study and understanding of pain. It does, however, give an overview of how psychiatrists *now* think of pain, as something to be studied by physiological means in order to *control* it, often in special clinics for the purpose, run by psychiatrists. All this is echoed at greater length in the University College Hospital *Textbook of Psychiatry*[14], which devotes a whole column of its index to the subject of pain. So what happened to mental pain and those wider issues that were discussed by our forbears? And how has the situation in psychiatry changed?

In 1951 the iconoclastic psychiatrist Thomas Szasz pointed out that students of pain have been almost exclusively preoccupied with what Bertrand Russell called 'public data', which can be shared by several observers, rather than with 'private data', though knowledge about pain is not accessible without it.[15] This is the way research has gone and is also the core of the problem. Psychiatry shares with so-called 'scientific medicine' a profound distrust for subjective data. Yet psychiatrists have not been very successful in separating organic from psychogenic pain.

An important event in the history of pain in relation to psychiatry occurred in 1964, when Erwin Stengel, professor of Psychiatry in Sheffield, delivered the 39th. Maudsley Lecture[16] before the Royal Medico-Psychological Association (soon to become the Royal College of Psychiatrists). The lecture is important partly because it represents the standard psychiatric view of the time but chiefly because it was the standard text on the subject for many years. It was reprinted and circulated throughout the country to all clinical tutors in psychiatry, the only paper on the subject that *was* thus circulated, and copies of it were also given to all examiners in the Diploma of Psychological Medicine and later for the examination for the Membership of the Royal College of Psychiatrists. It was the guide to what they should expect the candidates to know. So you could say that for many years it was the blueprint on pain for British psychiatrists. After the usual formalities, thanks for the honour and so on, Stengel announced:

Lay persons asked to list doctors according to their concern with the treatment of pain are likely to rank the psychiatrist last, if at all.

He had also discovered, by means of a questionnaire, that only 23 out of 83 medical students thought that pain played a very important part in psychiatry – even though they were allowed to include mental pain if they wished. This optional clause seems a little peculiar in itself. He continues,

I shall concern myself with *physical pain only* and *not with so-called mental pain*, a vague concept referring to distress not related to the body . . . [T]he relief of pain has always been regarded as one of the doctor's noblest tasks.

Then he adds, interestingly and perhaps significantly:

The belief that it plays relatively little part in psychiatry might be one of the many reasons why the psychiatrist has not enjoyed the same prestige as other doctors.

'*Enjoyed the same prestige*'. This was an important concept at the time. There were many discussions going on regarding the founding of the Royal College of Psychiatrists and one of the purposes in founding that College was to raise the status of psychiatry.

Stengel continued with another prophetic statement:

It seems that with the expansion of the scope of psychiatry, pain has become a common feature in many conditions we are called upon to treat, often after our colleagues the physicians and surgeons have failed.[17]

Looking to the future and the coming drive to expand psychiatry, it seems that Stengel could see pain as a potentially rewarding area. Supporting this argument he concluded the lecture by opposing 'the generally held belief that the relief of pain does not play an important part in the psychiatrist's work'. On the contrary, he says *'the psychiatric approach is indispensable in the study and treatment of pain, whatever its origin. It could not be otherwise, because pain is essentially a mental state.'*

I used the word 'prophetic'. Those discussions took place in an atmosphere of expanding knowledge in the era of the new psychotropic drugs but it soon became obvious that the differences between one drug and another were often minor and commercial rather than clinically useful. Then, at the end of 1961, came the tragedy of thalidomide, a popular and successful tranquilliser that was found to be causing hideous deformities in unborn children. The incident had a sobering effect on many who had been enthusiastic about psychotropic drugs. By the time the Royal College of Psychiatrists received its Royal Charter, in 1971, progress in psychiatry was slowing down. Only an occasional new drug coming onto the market was more effective than the old ones and the side-effects and complications of drug therapy were becoming apparent, as were the imperfections of older, drastic treatments such as ECT and lobotomy. So where could psychiatry expand under its new College?

One thing that had been achieved by the major tranquillizers was the control of many cases of psychosis. Many more patients with serious mental illness could be managed and treated in general hospitals, where new posts were now created for psychiatrists. For example, one London teaching hospital, probably typical, had only one consultant psychiatrist on its staff until 1961. In that year it appointed a second and by 1980, having taken over a few peripheral hospitals, it had over 60. So what was there for all these psychiatrists to do in the nineteen eighties? What better than to take Stengel's advice and take over the problems of pain, which were endemic in general hospitals? This was done and soon there was a host of doctors called 'liaison psychiatrists' who work in general hospitals and deal mostly with problems of pain in non-psychiatric patients. New clinics sprang up – liaison clinics, pain clinics and so on. Psychosomatic medicine, an old and somewhat outmoded concept, was taken over by the psychiatrists, and its commonest problem was pain. Not all psychiatrists were happy about these developments and some were distinctly disenchanted. Typically, one senior consultant said:

> 'Liaison' psychiatrists go round patients in other specialties and 'deal with' their problems. Nowadays a patient with pain that could perfectly well be dealt with by any competent clinician has to have his own 'liaison psychiatrist'.[18]

Thus in its recent attempts to embrace problems of physical pain, psychiatry has increased its strength and its hold on medicine and its dedication to physical rather than mental pain. It has also increased the disenchantment that many feel, even within its ranks.

Before I finish, I'd like to look briefly at what happened to pain in psycho-analysis, which one might expect to concern itself with pain, particularly the mental pain that psychiatry so positively excluded.

The relationship between psychoanalysis and psychiatry in Britain is complicated. It is also different from other countries. The present situation stems from the decision of the British Psychoanalytical Society not to join the National Health Service in 1948, a decision that many analysts came to regret while politicians were only too thankful (the idea of free psychoanalysis for everyone on the NHS sent shivers down many governmental spines). Anyway, that decision relegated psychoanalysis to a marginal position, but it still plays a part and has influence.

Freud distinguished between physical pain (*Schmerz*) and the pain associated with instinctual tension, which he called *Unlust*, literally *unpleasure*, but there is not a great deal of psychoanalytical work on the subject of pain. In the literature, much less attention has been given to pain than to anxiety. Freud himself could find no philosophical or psychological theory that could inform him about the meaning of pleasure and unpleasure.

> This is the most obscure and inaccessible region of the mind, and since we cannot avoid contact with it, the least rigid hypothesis, it seems to me, will be the best. We have decided to relate pleasure and unpleasure to the quantity of excitation that is present in the mind but is not in any way 'bound'; and to relate them in such a manner that unpleasure corresponds to an *increase* in the quantity of excitation and pleasure to a diminution.[19]

In the literature, the subject becomes complicated and difficult to understand. One of Freud's followers summed it up:

> If one puts Freud's earlier theories on the production of pain alongside his latest views on the development of anxiety, one feels that one is approaching a situation in which pain and anxiety are the same thing and all instinct-tension threatens to become anxiety-tension.[20]

A common psychoanalytical concept about *physical* pain that is useful practice is the idea that the sufferer may '*need*' his symptoms, though this idea arouses anger in some people. Szasz calls such a person '*homo dolorosus*', a person who has 'decided' to make a career of pain. Szasz describes him thus.

> [A] pain situation in which the usual medical approach fails is exemplified by the severely depressed and agitated person who complains of annoying bodily feelings, such as itching, headaches, lack of appetite, insomnia, backache and so forth. Such a person has adopted – fully or partly, permanently or temporarily – the career of being sick and in pain. He does not want his pains allayed or relieved. What is the physician's task in the situation? *Whose* pain should he control: the patient's? that of his relatives, tortured by the patient's complaints? Or his own, generated by his inability to help the patient?[21]

Pain is now a psychiatric industry, providing work for thousands of psychiatrists. It provides or aims to provide what the public clearly wants, freedom or *relief* from pain in a world that regards pain as unnecessary but in which some of the worst forms of physical pain, for example from cancer, are actually increasing. There is now an International Association for the Study of Pain. Its first World Congress was held in Florence in 1975, the year the journal *Pain* was launched. But the study of pain is still largely confined to physical pain, including so-called 'psychogenic' physical pain, and to value-judgments as to whether or not patients are reacting to it 'normally' or 'excessively'. The wider issues are ignored. Perhaps they have to be in order to have something to measure and to study in a laboratory.

NOTES

1 Michael Balint (1957) *The Doctor, His Patient and the Illness*, London, Pitman.
2 Balint, *op. cit.*, p.216. Italics, Balint's.
3 Moulin, Daniel de (1974), 'A Historical-Phenomenological Study of Bodily Pain in Western Man', *Bulletin of the History of Medicine*, 48, 540–70.
4 For a full account of this, see A.D. Hodgkiss, (1991), 'Chronic Pain in Nineteenth Century British Medical Writings', *History of Psychiatry*, 2: 27–40.
5 Henry Maudsley (1895) *Pathology of Mind*, 2nd. edn., New York, Appleton.
6 Quain, R., (ed.), (1882) *A Dictionary of Medicine: including general pathology, general therapeutics, hygiene, and the diseases peculiar to women and children*, (2 vols.), London, Longmans Green. Article written by T. Buzzard.
7 Max Hamilton (1974) *Fish's Clinical Psychopathology*, revised reprint, Bristol, John Wright and Sons, 1974, p.26.
8 Slater, E., and Roth, M. 1969, *Clinical Psychiatry*, 3rd. edn., London, Baillière, Tindall & Cassell.
9 William Sargant and Eliot Slater (1944–72), *Physical Methods of Treatment in Psychiatry*, 1944–72, Edinburgh and London, Churchill.
10 *ibid.*, p.92.
11 *ibid*, p.123.
12 HPeter Dally and H. Harrington (1980, [1964]) *Psychology for Nurses*, Hodder & Stoughton, London, 4th. edn., p.122.
13 Richard L. Gregory (1987) *The Oxford Companion to the Mind*, Oxford, Oxford University Press.
14 H.H.O. Wolff, A. Bateman and D. Sturgeon. (eds.) (1990) *Textbook of Psychiatry: an integrated approach*, London, Duckworth.
15 Szasz, T. (1957), *Pain and Pleasure: a study of bodily feelings*, London, Tavistock Publications.
16 Erwin Stengel (1965) *Pain and the Psychiatrist*, The Thirty-Ninth Maudsley Lecture delivered before the Royal Medico-Psychological Association, 20 November, 1964. *British Journal of Psychiatry*, 111, 795–802.
17 *ibid.*, p.796.
18 Personal communication.
19 Freud, S. (1920), *Beyond the Pleasure Principle*, Standard Edition, volume 18, London, Hogarth Press, 1955, pp.7–8.
20 M. Brierley (1951) 'Affects in Theory and Practice', in Brierley, M., *Trends in Psychoanalysis*, London, Hogarth Press, p.48. Reprinted with minor alterations from the *International Journal of Psychoanalysis*, 1937, xviii, p.256.

21 T. Szasz (1974) 'A Psychiatric Perspective on Pain and its Control', in F.D. Hart (ed.) (1974) *The Treatment of Chronic Pain*, Lancaster, Medical and Technical Books, p.43.

Chapter 9

Mental Retardation

Clinical Section – Part I
EDGAR MILLER

Writing about the history of idiocy (or mental retardation) presents a number of problems. It is a largely undeveloped field which means that there is very little in the way of earlier work to offer any guidance or orientation. In addition, it is more than usually confused with regard to terminology. Over the past two centuries a very varied range of terms has been used to designate those who, in today's terminology, might be described as exhibiting 'mental retardation', 'learning disabilities', or 'mental handicap'. In addition to describing those afflicted as 'idiots' the terms employed have included 'imbeciles', 'feeble minded', 'solitaries', 'morons', 'aments' and even as suffering from 'fatuity'. 'Cretin' was also occasionally used as a generic term in some contexts to refer to a much wider range of afflicted individuals than would meet the standard clinical criteria for cretinism.

This chapter will use 'idiocy' as the main defining term. This is for two reasons. Firstly, it is by far the most commonly used term for much of the period under consideration which runs from the beginning of the nineteenth century until the early years of the twentieth. Secondly, it emphasises the point that whilst the concept referred to by 'idiocy', or many other more-or-less synonymous terms, has shown some stability over time, this stability is far from complete. There has been some appreciable variation in what is understood by these appellations. The adult or child described as 'severely mentally retarded' (US) or 'severely learning disabled' (UK) in the 1990s might well have been labelled as an 'idiot' in the 1850s but the implications of these labels would not be entirely the same at the two different times. Contrary to expectations, the 1850s label of 'idiocy' would not necessarily imply a less optimistic outcome than would be indicated by the equivalent descriptions during much of the twentieth century.

At the beginning of the nineteenth century idiocy was largely understood to be the result of a lack of sensory input to the mind. As John Thelwall[1] put it in 1810, the mind 'is contracted in its sphere of activity by physical privation'. The mind needs some sort of input to stimulate it into action and for the mental faculties to work upon. This input is lacking in idiocy.

This view of idiocy dominated much of the nineteenth century work on the treatment and training of idiots by authorities such as Seguin and Guggenbuhl. Their programmes laid a heavy emphasis on sensory training. Later of course, the underlying problem in idiocy was seen as lying rather deeper than mere sensory deprivation. However, it is interesting to note that a strong theme in modern psychological conceptualisations of idiocy is that the major problem lies at the 'input' end of the system. Not that there is assumed to be sensory deprivation in the sense implied by Thelwall but rather that afflicted individuals are unable to adequately process and derive proper meaning from the incoming information that is provided by the senses.[2]

THE DEFINING CHARACTERISTICS OF IDIOCY

From at least medieval times onwards most definitions of idiocy have included two elements. These are, firstly, the lack of, or failure to develop intellectual functions to a normal degree. Secondly, that this situation is apparent early in life. Where there has been some departure from these two features it has been in the direction of allowing that idiocy can be acquired rather later in life than early childhood. Pinel[3] implied that adults could, amongst other things, become idiotic due to 'excessive intemperance and venery'. Howe[4] considered that young 'ladies and gentlemen' had developed idiocy as a result of masturbation. Nevertheless, such views do not appear commonly in the writings of recognised authorities in the nineteenth century. Where they do arise, the implication is usually that such cases do not constitute the majority of idiots.

Nineteenth century writers tended to add further characteristics to the basic criterion of intellectual failure manifest in early life. A common opinion was that idiocy was necessarily associated with some physical manifestations or deformities as well. This often went beyond the view, largely speculative at that time and especially clearly expressed by Seguin[5] that the nervous system is implicated. In some instances thinking even went so far as to claim that idiocy was essentially but one manifestation of a much wider physical abnormality. Down[6] wrote in 1871 that 'It became clear to me that idiocy and imbecility were not simply disturbances of brain power, – were not simply nerve lesions in the narrowed acceptance of the term, – but were profound diseases involving almost every organ and system of organs in the body'.

Not only was it recognised that idiots might have unusually small or large or deformed heads (as in microcephaly or hydrocephalus) but the presence of a high arched palate was regarded by some as a sine qua non of idiocy. Down[7] initially asserted that palatal deformities were a universal feature of idiocy but later modified this view to argue that this was only an invariant feature of those types of idiocy he classified as 'genetous' (congenital). Some other leading authorities followed Down in stressing the examination of the palate when investigating possible cases of idiocy.[8]

An interesting feature of work on idiocy from about the mid-nineteenth century onwards, is that when claims of this kind were made there was a marked tendency for others to test out the assertion by collecting systematic data to give a statistical picture of the prevalence of the alleged feature. A good example of this is provided by Shaw[9] who in 1876 reported extensive investigations of the palates of residents in Leavesdon Hospital and found that he could detect no association between idiocy and a high arched palate. In fact he commented that two microcephalic sisters turned out to have the lowest height of palate that he had measured 'including persons of high intellect'.

A final and possibly surprising aspect of the concept of idiocy in the nineteenth century was the view that at least some cases might be curable. The work of Seguin[10] on the training of idiots was influential. This was followed by very encouraging and dramatic reports of the alleged successes achieved by Guggenbuhl at his institution for cretins on the Abendberg in Switzerland where 'cures' were definitely claimed. Many influential people, such as Charles Dickens, made the pilgrimage to the Abendberg and wrote glowing accounts of Guggenbuhl's work.[11] Guggenbuhl's work had considerable impact in both Europe and North America and led to institutions for cretins and idiots being established elsewhere with some of these leading to further claims that 'cures' had been achieved.

A consequence of this was a rather more optimistic period in the mid-nineteenth century when cure was regarded as possible in some cases, although certainly not the rule. This optimism is evident even in the report of the English Commissioners in Lunacy of March 1865 which stated:

> The benefits to be derived, even in idiot cases apparently hopeless, from a distinctive system, and from persevering endeavours to develop the dormant powers, physical and intellectual, are now so fully established, that any argument on the subject would be superfluous. The soundness and importance of such views are generally recognised and appreciated, and benevolent efforts are being made in several quarters to carry them into practical operation.[12]

Unfortunately, Guggenbuhl's immense reputation suffered a massive setback when it was later found that standards at his institution had deteriorated considerably.[13] Views on the ability to cure or even beneficially influence the course of idiocy then started to decline, possibly reaching a nadir in the late nineteenth and early twentieth centuries.

CLASSIFICATION

Up to the early part of the nineteenth century it was generally recognised that idiocy was a matter of degree although it was not common to distinguish particular levels. By mid-century with accounts like those of Seguin and Howe, different levels of impairment were separately identified. Howe,[14] for example, had three levels consisting of idiots, fools and simpletons in ascending order of intellectual ability. In general such distinctions have persisted into and throughout the twentieth century. The value of dividing the total 'idiot' population in this way was nevertheless queried by a few. Down[15] questioned this form of classification on the grounds that such distinctions were difficult to make in practice with no clear dividing point between one level and the next.

Another way of subclassifying idiocy is in terms of supposed clinical types and presumed causal mechanisms. Cretinism was well recognised throughout the period with microcephaly and what would today be described as hydrocephalus also being distinguished since the marked variations in head size were easily recognised. Down[16] in 1866 described a 'Mongolian' form of idiocy as well as claiming to find other 'ethnic' variants. The twentieth century has seen a steady growth in the identification of different clinical conditions associated with 'idiocy'.

The immediately preceding discussion relates to specific clinical conditions. However, broader distinctions were also made into such categories as congenital and acquired idiocy.[17] This classification was maintained by other authorities and even extended. Ireland[18] had several different categories including genetous (or congenital), microcephalic, hydrocephalic and traumatic idiocy as well as cretinism, thus offering a mixture of the general and specific. In the early twentieth century Barr[19] opted for 'congenital', 'developmental' and 'accidental' idiocy whereas Tredgold[20] had only two main classes which were 'intrinsic' (or hereditary) and 'extrinsic' (or environmentally caused).

Although the general tendency was to distinguish between idiocy, on the one hand, and madness on the other, not all authorities were entirely clear about this. There were those who regarded idiocy very much as a variety of madness. This view was also buttressed by the fact that idiots were commonly admitted to asylums for the insane for much of the nineteenth century and even after. (Specialised institutions for idiots started to be created from the 1840s in both Europe and America although their original emphasis was in dealing with children. Facilities taking adults followed much later.)

It is interesting that the English legal situation in the early years of the nineteenth century was still based on the distinction between idiocy and madness made in the early fourteenth century in the reign of Edward II.[21] Medical discussions of madness in the early nineteenth century differed with regard to whether they included idiocy as a form of madness.[22] In particular, there was a trend to classifying idiocy with dementia based on a tradition which goes at least as far back as Cullen.[23]

As the nineteenth century progressed idiocy was increasingly distinguished from dementia. Esquirol's comment of 1845 to the effect that 'A man in a state of dementia is deprived of advantages which he formerly enjoyed; he was a rich man, who has become poor. The idiot, on the contrary, has always been in a state of want and misery'[24] was often cited in support of the distinction between these two things.[25]

CAUSATION

The first systematic attempt to consider the causation of idiocy appears to be that of Samuel Gridley Howe in 1848. Howe was the chairman of a group of commissioners asked to report on the state of idiocy in the Commonwealth of Massachusetts. Part of this report, published in Edinburgh a decade later,[26] consists of an account of causation heavily laced with moralistic overtones. Howe firmly states:

The moral to be drawn from the existence of individual idiots is this, – he, or his parents, have so far violated the natural laws, so far marred the beautiful organism of the body, that it is an unfit instrument for the manifestation of the powers of the soul. The moral to be drawn from the prevalent existence of idiocy in society is, that a very large class of persons ignore the conditions on which alone health and reason are given to men, and consequently they sin in various ways; they disregard the conditions which should be observed in intermarriage; they overlook the hereditary transmission of certain morbid tendencies, or they pervert the natural appetites of the body into lusts of divers kinds, – the natural emotions of the mind into fearful passions, – and thus bring down the awful consequences of their own ignorance and sin upon the heads of their unoffending children.

Apart from alleging that parents, and even the idiots themselves, may be directly responsible for the unfortunate situation, Howe clearly identifies the predominant causal explanation considered throughout the period in question, which is the operation of hereditary mechanisms. Rather crude and unsophistic-ated views about the hereditary transmission of idiocy persisted until well into the twentieth century as indicated by Goddard's classic study of the Kallikak family in 1912.[27]

Of course genetic factors are now known to underlie many forms of mental retardation and it is not intended to trace the discovery of the various genetically transmitted conditions, such as tuberous sclerosis, here. Discussion will be confined to certain alleged mechanisms which might underlie hereditary trans-mission and which attracted considerable attention in the second half of the nineteenth and early twentieth centuries.

In the passage cited above, Howe mentions consanguineous marriages as one factor predisposing to idiocy. The idea that such things as cousin marriages may predispose to the production of idiot offspring almost certainly antedates Howe. Nevertheless his account of the causes of idiocy proved immensely influential and may well have been at least partly responsible for the more critical later examinations of the influence of cousin marriages.

Later authorities like Down, Shuttleworth and George Darwin[28] examined the question more critically by ascertaining the proportion of institutional inmates whose parents had been cousins and, in some instances, comparing this proportion with the rate of cousin marriages in the general population. This work failed to reveal a clearly raised incidence of cousin marriages in the way that had been expected, although there were authorities who continued to allow that cousin marriages might predispose to idiocy under some circumstances. For example, when both partners came from an afflicted family and so might both carry the taint of idiocy.[29]

In addition, other explanatory concepts with links to heredity were also used in the latter half of the nineteenth century. These were 'atavism', 'diasthesis' and 'degeneracy'. Diasthesis consists of a general tendency to problems of the nervous system. According to Ireland[30] 'idiots frequently are born in families in which there is a decided neurotic tendency, as manifested by the appearance of insanity, imbecility or epilepsy'.

A related and much overworked concept which can be seen as an extreme version of diasthesis is that of 'degeneracy'. This was a widely used and generally ill-defined concept in the late nineteenth century, particularly inspired by Morel's book of 1857.[31] Morel specifically identified cretinism as a manifesta-tion of degeneracy. It is interesting that Howe's account of the causation of idiocy, originally appearing in 1848 in the form of a report to the Massachusetts legislature, antedated Morel's widely influential book by a few years. Howe anticipated the general notion of degeneracy in the following passage:

that among certain classes of miserably paid and poorly fed women, the physical system degenerates so rapidly that the children are feeble and puny, and but few live to maturity; that the grandchildren are still more puny; until, in the third or fourth generation, the individuals are no longer able to perpetuate their species, and the ranks must be filled up by fresh subjects from other walks of life, to run the same round of deterioration.[32]

Degeneration was an idea that was quite extensively used in other contexts. It also had a respectable scientific pedigree. Lankester,[33] a distinguished zoologist, argued for degeneration on the basis of the Darwinian concept of evolution. He suggested that evolutionary trends can lead to degeneration as well as to advance (he cites the loss of limbs in some lizards as an example of degeneration). The corollary of this argument was that the same can happen to man.

At its crudest the notion of degeneration implies that a mild abnormality such as a cleft palate or an overanxious personality may appear in one generation, to be followed in the next by something rather more far reaching like madness or scrofula, and with complete idiocy, or some other equally dreadful affliction emerging in the third. At this stage the degenerate line dies out (at least in Morel's conception of degeneracy). Morel[34] in 1857 defined degeneracy 'as a marked departure from the original type tending more or less rapidly to the extinction of it'.

Degeneracy was most often invoked as an explanation for the occurrence of idiocy in the mid to late nineteenth century with detailed discussions of degeneracy persisting up to the end of the century. By the early twentieth century degeneracy had started to disappear from the writings of the more established authorities. For example, it receives a small and extremely cautious mention in the first edition of Tredgold's 'Mental Deficiency'[35] and the same is true of Barr.[36] Sherlock's[37] book of 1911 offers only the lingering residue of the notion of degeneracy. This is, of course, not to deny that the general idea of degeneration persisted into the twentieth century in the notions of less sophisticated commentators on the problems of idiocy.[38]

A degenerative tendency in a family could allegedly be precipitated by a wide range of factors. These included such things as tuberculosis, abuse of alcohol and diabetes. Microcephaly was regarded by some as a degeneration to a monkey-like state and this theory is discussed in some detail by Ireland[39] in 1877 who rejected it. The classic manifestation of degeneracy as an explanatory concept in relation to idiocy came from Down in 1866 with his 'ethnic' classification of idiots.[40] He identified cases at the Earlswood Asylum in Surrey with the apparent physical characteristics of Malays, Ethiopians, and Red Indians. He especially drew attention to the Mongolian (or Kalmuc) type and this rapidly became recognised as a form of idiocy. For example, in 1876 Fraser and Mitchell[41] were reporting cases of 'Kalmuc' idiocy found in Scotland.

Down considered that 'Mongolian idiocy' was present in about 10% of the cases that he saw and claimed that it was always congenital. 'They are, for the most part, instances of degeneracy arising from tuberculosis in the parents'.[42] His thinking appears to have been very much along the lines that other manifestations of the human race are inferior to the Caucasian (which presumably reached its apotheosis as far as he was concerned in the English!) and that groups like the Mongols are at an evolutionary earlier stage. The Mongolian idiot represents a degeneration to this more primitive type. (It is interesting to note, that Down also specifically argues that the occurrence of 'Mongolian' and other 'ethnic' types shows that the human race is essentially unitary and this caused him to reject some manifestations of what today would be described as racism.) It was Down's own son, Reginald Langdon Down who in 1909 was one of the first to point out that the features of so-called Mongolian idiots were only 'accidental and superficial' in their resemblance to real Mongolian people and to express considerable scepticism that they were an example of degeneration in the sense assumed by his father.[43]

Another commonly invoked causal factor was the abuse of alcohol and many authorities noted the apparent frequency of inebriation among the parents of idiots.[44] Down even asserted that idiocy was especially likely to occur when the father was drunk at the time of conception.[45] Again this was a view that did not pass without challenge, even by those who were more-or-less contemporaries. Shuttleworth[46] was one who denied that the parents of idiots were unusually intemperate and furthermore also pointed out that a considerable proportion of the children of drunkards were not idiots.

Finally it is worth noting that a whole range of other things were considered as potentially causal. The mother's experiences during pregnancy were long thought to be one possible cause of idiocy[47] and attention was drawn to the potential hazards of the birth process. In particular, Down[48] pointed out that there was a considerable excess of males amongst idiots who happened to be first born children and noted that pressure on the cranium during birth would be greater in males due to their larger heads. The use of laudanum to put children to sleep was also regarded as another potential factor.[49]

MANAGEMENT AND TREATMENT

For much of the nineteenth century it was considered that idiocy was modifiable and that idiots were trainable. The first writer who had great influence in this area was Seguin although he came from a background which had already seen major contributions to the training and education of handicapped children, particularly those with sensory handicaps, as exemplified by the work of Condillac and Itard.[50]

Seguin[51] in his so-called 'psycho-physiological training' stressed that training the senses and motor functioning was the royal road to improving the functioning of idiots. As described above, this is related to an earlier idea about the nature of idiocy whereby it is presumed that poor perceptual and discriminatory processes have a major role in producing idiocy. This is on the grounds that the individual's mental apparatus cannot act intelligently without the necessary sensory material with which to work.

The figure who made the greatest impact in the mid-nineteenth century was Johann Jakob Guggenbuhl (1816–1863).[52] Guggenbuhl's work has already been mentioned in a different context but it is worth describing again in a little greater detail. Having obtained some land from a Swiss philanthropist on the Abendberg, near Interlaken in Switzerland, Guggenbuhl set up an institution for the care of children with cretinism in 1842. He emphasised a good diet, baths and physical exercise, a variety of medications and training procedures designed to develop the sensory systems. The Abendberg rapidly achieved considerable international fame and a stream of influential visitors who included the Countess Ida Hahn-Hahn, Samuel Gridley Howe and Charles Dickens. Like many of the visitors, to the Abendberg, Dickens sang its praises in print.[53] Institutions based on that of Guggenbuhl were started in a number of other countries, including Britain, Germany, and the USA.

Eventually, more critical views prevailed and Guggenbuhl's claims[54] of what amounted more-or-less to cures were challenged. Following a visit from the British minister to Berne in order to see the few English patients at the Abendberg, a formal complaint was lodged in 1858 about the poor condition of the children and the state of disorder in the institution. Guggenbuhl himself was not there at the time. Two Swiss physicians, Vogt and Verdat, conducted an inquiry which led to quite damning criticisms including, amongst other things, a denial that any 'cures' had ever been achieved.

After Guggenbuhl's fall, optimism about what could be achieved by the training and education of idiots declined. In the early twentieth century, the standard texts do, of course mention training and education.[55] Nevertheless the expectations as to what can be achieved by these activities were not great and some of the accounts are quite perfunctory, almost as if this was something that the author felt had to be included but in which he had little interest or confidence. It is not until the great expansion of research into learning processes that took place in the decades immediately after the Second World War that there was increasing expectation that appropriate training could be effective enough to make a real impact on the way that the mentally retarded could function.[56] By this time, the biomedical underpinnings of retardation were understood in much more detail and the social climate was also changing so as to be more accepting of those with severe handicaps.

A few other aspects of management and related issues are worth mentioning. Howe's account of the causes of idiocy[57] is written in a high moral and religious tone very much in line with what has been described as the 'cult of curability' or 'cult of perfectibility'.[58] This was a view of the world which had its main impact prior to the mid-nineteenth century, especially in the USA, and which saw problems like idiocy as being due to the failure of people to follow God's laws. This might be by the marriage of those who were related, by over-indulgence in alcohol, masturbation, or in any other way going against the principles by which the world and those in it were considered to have been constructed by the Creator. To the extent that people could actually live a Godly life, so problems like idiocy and madness would be reduced.

Various physical interventions were also advocated in the late nineteenth and early twentieth centuries. One theory of the causation of microcephaly was that there might be premature closing of the fontanelle and ossification of the cranial sutures thus arresting the development of the brain. In 1878 Fuller in Montreal first tried to modify this situation surgically be performing a craniectomy. Within the following 15 years or so similar operations had been performed in a number of different countries with poor results and even some mortalities. The operation appears then to have fairly rapidly fallen into disfavour.[59]

Another surgical intervention was 'asexualization'. The combination of viewing idiocy as largely hereditary coupled with an alleged exaggerated sexuality led to the belief that restraining the sexual activities of idiots is an important preventative measure. Unlike the European countries some American states actually passed laws fuelled by these views. Legislation passed in Connecticut in 1895 stated 'No man and woman either of whom is epileptic, or imbecile, or feeble-minded, shall inter-marry, or live together as husband and wife when the woman is under forty-five years of age'.[60] Some authorities went further and advocated operations designed to asexualize those considered to be idiots or feeble-minded. Operations were performed at a number of institutions and Pennsylvania came close to passing an act in 1901 making it lawful to perform an 'operation for the prevention of procreation' on idiots and imbeciles deemed to be 'non-improvable' by appropriate medical authority. Barr remained a strong supporter of the introduction of such legislation.[61]

COMMENT

As was indicated at the beginning, the history of idiocy has been substantially neglected. This chapter offers a relatively brief glimpse of a largely uncharted area. It is hoped that it has identified some of the key features of the terrain although it is expected that more detailed explorations will inevitably lead to some modifications of the map that is offered here in outline.

The nineteenth century saw the concept, referred to here as idiocy, undergo some significant changes. The middle of this century represented a time characterised by some optimism. Idiocy was considered curable, at least in some instances, by proper training and treatment. Adherence to God's laws might even result in a reduction of the incidence of idiocy by cutting out major causes such as consanguineous marriages, breeding from debased stock, the abuse of alcohol, masturbation, and so on. The later years of that century as well as the early years of the twentieth were much more pessimistic in tone with a more optimistic picture beginning to emerge again in the decades following the Second World War.

The history of idiocy is particularly interesting as a manifestation of wider issues in nineteenth century thought. To take but one example, the idiot was the ultimate degenerate and therefore idiocy fitted well into the pervasive influence of the notion of degeneration in the latter half of the nineteenth century.

Also worth noting are the attempts by those working in the field to test out aspects of the then 'received wisdom' by empirical means. Examples of this are the collecting of detailed data on palatal measurements to determine whether idiocy was really characterised by a high arched palate as some had claimed. Similarly, several later nineteenth century investigators looked at the frequency of cousin marriages to see if these were especially frequent in the parents of idiots as would be predicted by the idea that consanguineous marriages were an appreciable cause of idiocy. In this work it is possible to see investigators struggling to use statistical data to answer scientific questions in an era that lacked appropriate statistical techniques other than working out averages.

If nothing else, it is hoped that this chapter will have demonstrated that the history of idiocy is as worth pursuing as the history of madness. How society viewed this most extreme of deviant groups provides an interesting mirror through which to identify aspects of more general trends in thought.

NOTES

1 Thelwall, J. (1810) *Imperfect Development of the Faculties, Mental and Moral,* London, Richard Taylor and Co.

2 For a summary of recent thinking on this point see: Miller, E. and Morley, S.J. (1986) *Investigating Abnormal Behaviour,* London, Weidenfeld & Nicolson.

3 Pinel, P. (1806) *A Treatise on Insanity,* London, Cadell and Davis.

4 Howe, S.G. (1858) *On the Causes of Idiocy,* Edinburgh, Maclachlan and Stewart.

5 Seguin, E. (1866) *Idiocy and its Treatment by the Physiological Method,* New York, William Wood & Co.

6 Down, J.L.H. (1871–2) 'On the relation of the teeth and mouth to mental development'. *Transactions of the Odontological Society,* 4: 268–88. (References to Down can be confusing since he originally used 'Down' as his surname and then changed to 'Langdon Down' in his later publications. The earlier usage is followed here for consistency but other publications may refer to, or index this same person as 'Langdon Down'.)

7 Down, J.L.H. (1862) 'On the condition of the mouth in idiocy'. *Lancet,* 1: 186; Down, J.L.H. (1887) *On some of the Mental Affections of Childhood and Youth,* London, J. & A. Churchill.

8 For example: Ireland, W.W. (1882) 'On the diagnosis and prognosis of idiocy and imbecility'. *Edinburgh Medical Journal,* 27: 1072–85.

9 Shaw, T.C. (1876) 'On the measurement of the palate in idiots and imbeciles'. *Journal of Mental Science,* 22: 196–201.

10 Whose most influential book, at least in the English speaking world, was: Seguin, E. (1866) *Idiocy and its Treatment by the Physiological Method,* New York, William Wood & Co.

11 A large number of accounts could be cited from both professional and more general sources of which the following are fairly typical examples: Anonymous (1848) 'Schools and asylums for the idiotic and imbecile'. *American Journal of Insanity,* 5: 19–33; Dickens, C. (1853) 'Idiots'. *Household Words,* 7: 313–17.

12 Cited by: Duncan, P.M. and Willard, W.A. (1866) *Manual for the Classification, Training and Education of the Feeble-minded, Imbecile, and Idiotic,* London, Longman.

13 Kanner, L. (1959) 'Johann Jakob Guggenbuhl and the Abendberg'. *Bulletin of the History of Medicine,* 33: 489–502.

14 Howe, S.G. (1858) *On the Causes of Idiocy,* Edinburgh, MacLachlan and Stewart.

15 Down, J.L.H. (1887) *On some of the Mental Affections of Childhood and Youth,* London, J. & A. Churchill.

16 Down, J.L.H. (1866) 'Observations on an ethnic classification of idiots'. *London Hospital Reports,* 3: 259–62.

17 Down, J.L.H. (1887) *On some of the Mental Affections of Childhood and Youth,* London, J. & A. Churchill.

18 Ireland, W.W. (1877) *On Idiocy and Imbecility,* London, J. & A. Churchill.

19 Barr, M.W. (1905) *Mental Defectives: Their History, Treatment and Training,* London, Rebman Limited.

20 Tredgold, A.F. (1908) *Mental Deficiency (Amentia)*, London, Baillière, Tindall and Cox.

21 Collinson, D. (1812) *A Treatise on the Law concerning Idiots, Lunatics and other persons non compos mentis*, London, W. Read.

22 Differing views on this issue are expressed, amongst others, by: Arnold, T. (1782) *Observations of the Nature, Kinds, Causes, and Prevention of Insanity, Lunacy or Madness*, Leicester, G. Ireland; Connolly, J. (1830) *An Inquiry Concerning the Indications of Insanity*, London, John Taylor; Rush, B. (1812) *Medical Inquiries and Observations upon the Diseases of the Mind*, Philadelphia, Kimber & Richardson; Uwins, D. (1833) *A Treatise on those Disorders of the Brain and Nervous System which are usually considered and called Mental*, London, Renshaw & Rush.

23 Cullen, W. (1800) *Nosology or, a Systematic Arrangement of Diseases by Classes, Orders, Genera, and Species; with the Distinguishing Characters of each, and outlines of the Systems of Sauvages, Linnaeus, Vogel, Sagar, and MacBride*, Edinburgh, William Creech.

24 Esquirol, J.E.D. (1845) *Mental Maladies: A Treatise on Insanity*, Philadelphia, Lea and Blanchard.

25 For example: Bateman, F. (1882) *The Idiot: His Place in Creation, and his Claims on Society*, London, Jarrold & Sons.

26 Howe, S.G. (1858) *On the Causes of Idiocy*, Edinburgh, MacLachlan and Stewart.

27 Goddard, H.H. (1912) *The Kallikak Family: A Study in the Heredity of Feeble-mindedness*, New York, The MacMillan Company.

28 Darwin, G.H. (1875) 'Marriages among first cousins in England and their effects'. *Journal of the Statistical Society*, 38: 153–82.

29 For example: Tredgold, A.F. (1908) *Mental Deficiency (Amentia)*, London, Bailliere, Tindall and Cox.

30 Ireland, W.W. (1877) *On idiocy and imbecility*, London, J. & A. Churchill.

31 Morel, B.A. (1857) *Traite des Degenerescences Physiques, Intellectuelles et Morales de l'Espece Humaine*, Paris, JB Bailliere. For a recent account of the general use of the concept of degeneration in the second half of the nineteenth and early twentieth centuries see: Pick, D. (1989) *Faces of Degeneration*, Cambridge, Cambridge University Press.

32 Howe, S.G. (1858) *On the Causes of Idiocy*, Edinburgh, MacLachlan and Stewart.

33 Lankester, E.R. (1880) *Degeneration: a Chapter in Darwinism*, London, MacMillan & Co.

34 Morel, B.A. (1857) *Traite des Degenerescences Physiques, Intellectuelles et Morales de l'Espece Humaine*, Paris, JB Bailliere.

35 Tredgold, A.F. (1908) *Mental Deficiency (Amentia)*, London, Bailliere, Tindall and Cox.

36 Barr, E.B. (1905) *Mental Defectives: Their History, Treatment and Training*, London, Rebman Limited.

37 Sherlock, E.B. (1911) *The Feeble Minded*, London, MacMillan & Co.

38 For example: Schwartz, K. (1908) 'Nature's corrective principle in social evolution'. *Journal of Psycho-Asthenics*, 13: 74–90.

39 Ireland, W.W. (1877) *On Idiocy and Imbecility*, London, J. & A. Churchill.

40 Down, J.L.H. (1866) 'Observations on an ethnic classification of idiots'. *London Hospital Reports*, 3: 259–62.
41 Fraser, J. and Mitchell, A. (1876) 'Kalmuc idiocy: report of a case with autopsy'. *Journal of Mental Science*, 22: 169–79.
42 Down, J.L.H. (1866) 'Observations on an ethnic classification of idiots'. *London Hospital Reports*, 3: 259–62.
43 Langdon Down, R. (1906) 'Some observations on the Mongolian type of imbecility'. *Journal of Mental Sciences*, 52: 188–90.
44 Good examples are Bateman, F. (1882) *The Idiot: His Place in Creation, and his Claims on Society*, London, Jarrold & Sons; Howe, S.G. (1858) *On the causes of idiocy*, Edinburgh, MacLachlan and Stewart.
45 Down, J.L.H. (1887) *On some of the Mental Affections of Childhood and Youth*, London, J. & A. Churchill.
46 Shuttleworth, G.E. (1877) 'Intemperance as a cause of idiocy'. *Journal of Mental Science*, 23: 372–7.
47 Amongst many who mentioned this possible cause were: Howe, S.G. (1858) *On the Causes of Idiocy*, Edinburgh, Maclachlan and Stewart; Down, J.L.H. (1873) 'Some of the causes of idiocy and imbecility'. *British Medical Journal*, 2: 432.
48 Down, J.L.H. (1873) 'Some of the causes of idiocy and imbecility'. *British Medical Journal*, 2: 432.
49 Stevens, E. (1850) 'Use of opium in childhood'. *American Journal of Insanity*, 7: 89.
50 For the background to this see: Lane, H. (1977) *The Wild Boy of Aveyron*, London, George Allen & Unwin Ltd.
51 Seguin, E. (1866) *Idiocy and its Treatment by the Physiological Method*, New York, William Wood & Co.
52 For further details see the account of Guggenbuhl's life and work by Kanner, L. (1959) 'Johann Jakob Guggenbuhl and the Abendberg'. *Bulletin of the History of Medicine*, 33: 489–502.
53 Dickens, C. (1853) 'Idiots'. *Household Words*, 7: 313–17.
54 Guggenbuhl, J.J. (1845) *Extracts from the First Report of the Institution on the Abendberg, near Interlachen, Switzerland; for the Cure of Cretinism*, London, Printed pamphlet (No publisher given).
55 For example: Berry, R.J.A. and Gordon, R.G. (1931) *The Mental Defective: A Problem in Social Inefficiency*, London, Kegan Paul, Trench, Trubner & Co.; Ireland, W.W. (1877) *On Idiocy and Imbecility*, London, J. & A. Churchill; Tredgold, A.F. (1908) *Mental Deficiency (Amentia)*, London, Bailliere, Tindall and Cox.
56 See: Miller, E. and Morley, S.J. (1986) *Investigating Abnormal Behaviour*, London, Weidenfeld & Nicolson.
57 Howe, S.G. (1858) *On the Causes of Idiocy*, Edinburgh, MacLachlan and Stewart.
58 Luchins, A.S. (1992) 'The cult of curability and the doctrine of perfectibility: social context of the nineteenth-century American asylum movement'. *History of Psychiatry*, 3: 203–20.
59 For a more detailed description see: Barr, M.W.(1905) *Mental Defectives: Their History, Treatment and Training*, London, Rebman Limited.

60 Cited by: Barr, M.W. (1905) *Mental Defectives: Their History, Treatment and Training*, London, Rebman Limited.
61 Barr, M.W. (1905) *Mental Defectives: Their History, Treatment and Training*, London, Rebman Limited.

Chapter 9
Mental Retardation

Clinical Section – Part II
GE BERRIOS

Existing historical work on the *concept* of mental retardation (as opposed to its management) is limited, particularly in its association with the notion of mental illness. Whether undertaken by Séguin (1846), Barr (1904), Kanner (1964), Lewis (1961), or Scheerenberger (1983), historical accounts appear as *pre-sentistic.*[1] And yet a contextualised historical analysis should offer a unique opportunity to study the combined operation of concepts such as cognition, mental disorder, development, and psychometry (Netchine, 1973; Pichot, 1948; Lang, 1965; Mahendra, 1985); indeed, on a wider canvas, it may even throw light on the history of child psychiatry (Walk, 1964; Gontard, 1988; Duché, 1990), infantile psychosis (Gineste, 1983), and the vexed question of the definition of man as a rational or cognitive being.[2] Most of this work, however, has not yet been carried out. So, this chapter will limit itself to mapping the process whereby the *concept* of mental retardation was constructed in European *psychiatric* thinking during the first half of the 19th century. Historical changes after the 1860s will be barely mentioned.

MATTERS HISTORIOGRAPHICAL

The *biographical* approach has been extensively used in this context, and the ghosts of Pereira, Itard, Esquirol, Belhomme, Guggenbühl, Séguin, Howe, and Morel comfortably inhabit most of the historical works mentioned above. This technique, however, works only when it avoids anachronistic interpretation: otherwise, as in Séguin (1846),[3] it can be unduly harsh with earlier figures, because no attempt is made to determine the boundary conditions within which they made their claims.

Likewise, little effort is made to separate the history of: 1. the *words* used for naming phenomena (semantic history), 2. the *behaviours* in question (behavioural palæontology), and 3. the *concepts* created throughout the ages to *understand* such behaviours (conceptual history). Confusing these three levels has led to historical error such as, for example, the claim that it was Esquirol who first *distinguished* idiocy from dementia (Scheerenberger, 1983). The assumption behind this historical approach is that, whatever the name or conceptual interpretation used, the behaviours in question – because they are biologically determined – have existed for a long time (Clarke, 1975; Rushton, 1988). History tells that their *medicalisation* probably started by the 17th century (Lewis, 1961; Cranfield, 1961; James, 1991), and their *psychiatrisation* by the 19th century. This is probably the reason why Esquirol – who was writing from the point of view of mental alienism – is credited with creating the notion of idiocy.

This brief historiographical excursion is meant to provide some conceptual tools with which the early 19th century debate on the boundaries of mental retardation can be usefully analysed.

MENTAL RETARDATION BEFORE THE 19TH CENTURY

Clear operational distinctions between idiocy and dementia have, in fact, existed since before the 19th century. For example, they were used by Medieval Courts (Clarke, 1975) where idiocy is already associated with qualifiers such as congenital and irreversible. By the 17th century, legal definitions even included *tests* (based on the assessment of everyday behaviour, such as handling money) to decide on the level of mental retardation of a particular individual.[4] From a *medical* viewpoint, these definitions were first sharpened by Thomas Willis (Cranfield, 1961) and later by Vicenzo Chiarugi (1987) both of who distinguished between insanity, dementia, and mental retardation. There was also an awareness that the latter was congenital and irreversible (James, 1991).

Cullen

To understand recent changes in the meaning of mental retardation one must take up the story at the time of Cullen (1827) whose class II, *neuroses* had as its Order IV the *Vesaniae*, defined as: 'lesions of the judging faculty without fever or coma'. This rubric included four genera: *Amentia, Melancholia, Mania*, and *Oneirodynia*. Amentia, the category relevant to mental retardation, was defined as: 'imbecility of the judging faculty with inability to perceive or remember', and classified into three species: congenital, senile, and acquired – the latter two corresponding roughly to dementia (pp.316–17). Under Amentia, Cullen (1803) brought together a number of 18th century nosological categories: *Amentia, Stupidity, Morosis* and Fatuity (Vogel), *Amentia* and *Amnesia* (Sauvages and Sagar), and *Morosis* and *Oblivio* (Linné).[5] *Amentia congenita* is particularly important to the subsequent history of mental retardation because it was specifically defined by Cullen 'as a condition present from birth' and which included *Amentia morosis* and *microcephala*, both types of idiocy. Indeed, the Latin term amentia was translated into the vernacular by Cullen's students as *folly* or *idiotism* (Vademecum, 1803).

French views
Pinel
Apart from being the translator of one of the French versions of Cullen's Nosology,[6] Pinel composed a Nosography himself. His Class IV, *Neuroses*, included neuroses affecting the senses, cerebral function, locomotion, voice, nutritive function, and generation (Pinel, 1818). *Idiotisme* appears as one of the categories classified under the *Névroses des fonctions cérébrales*, where it is defined as an 'abolition, more or less absolute, of the functions of understanding and feeling' which may be acquired or congenital (*originaire*) (pp.132–3). Pinel

did not deviate from this definition which he linked to the views expressed by the '*auteur of Synonymes français*' on a '*échelle de graduation de la raison*' (pp.132).[7] Thus, in 1801, Pinel defined *ideotism* as 'total or partial obliteration of the intellectual powers and affections: universal torpor: detached half articulated sounds; or entire absence of speech from want of ideas: in some cases, transient and unmeaning gusts of passion' (Pinel, 1806) and continued defending the view that it was acquired or congenital. The same was repeated in the second and last edition of the *Traité* (Pinel, 1809, pp.181–90).

Thus, Pinel's conception of idiotism can be described as fully medical (for example, it was included in his nosography), psychiatric (it featured together with mania, melancholia and dementia), and based upon his notion of disorder of reason or the intellectual faculty.[8] Like Cullen (he also considered idiotism as a synonym of Amentia), Pinel proposed that this condition may be either acquired or congenital. However, for the first time, he used the word *Démence* (Berrios, 1987) to refer to Cullen's acquired amentias, and included a discussion of *cretins* (Pinel, 1809, pp.188–90) which shows his awareness of the variety of cases that might fall under the category idiotism.

Esquirol

This great French alienist had the advantage of writing in the context of the much reduced psychiatric nosological system created by Pinel, and in the wake of the French Revolution, whose progressivism required that the distinction between idiocy and dementia (as we have seen already present in Cullen) was emphasized. In his later writings on *L'idiote* Esquirol seems, however, to have been influenced by Georget (see below), although he does not mention him by name. Thus, whilst in his entries to the Panckoucke Dictionary, Esquirol (1814, 1817) stated that mental retardation *was* a disease,[9] in their 1838 reprinting he made changes, the most important being, perhaps, his addition of a criticism of the *célèbre professeur* Pinel for 'not distinguishing between idiocy and dementia' and his claim that: 'idiocy is not a disease but a state in which the intellectual faculties are never manifested or *developed* for lack of education' (Esquirol, 1838, p.284). In spite of the fact that chronology indicates that the developmental view originated in Georget, it is difficult to be positive about the origin of this idea. After all, this young man – who was close to his teacher (he is said to have died in Esquirol's arms) could have borrowed it from him. Esquirol seems also to have left a door open to the possibility, in some cases, of mental retardation resulting from pure cultural influence: for example, he discusses this in relation to the *cagots*[10] who were supposed to have a higher rate of mentally retarded children.

Influenced by faculty psychology, Esquirol (1838) provided a *psychological account* of dementia and idiocy. He considered the latter as a *disorder of intellect*, and hence, as a problem with which alienists ought to be concerned. He *did not*, however, consider idiocy as a form of insanity (*folie*) for this was, at the time, narrowly defined in terms of *délire*,[11] Esquirol, however, saw no difficulty in considering it as a mental illness (*maladie mentale*). This did not reflect therapeutic pessimism: indeed, imbued by the optimism of the French Revolution, he had encouraged Itard in his quest to educate the boy of Aveyron.[12]

But those who followed Esquirol, particularly after the 1850s, when the doctrine of *degeneration* began to take hold,[13] did not share in his optimism. There is little doubt that it was this fatalism, and all the negative consequences it engendered, that fuelled the challenge to the view that idiocy was yet another form of mental illness. This questioning, born out of the altruism of educators – such as Séguin (1846) and others – was motivated by practical reasons as it was felt that accepting the 'psychiatric' view would lead to suffering and hardship amongst the mentally retarded (pp.69–71). Current arguments concerning the separation between idiocy and mental illness are, therefore, redolent of those rehearsed during the 19th century. The problem then, as now, was not totally created by semantic confusion. There was, in fact, a substantive point, to wit, whether or not mental retardation was on a *continuum* with normal subjects. This was interpreted by some to mean that mental retardation *per se*, was not a form of mental illness for the mentally retarded, like anyone else, *might develop* mental illness. The fact was also known that the more severe the idiocy, the more frequent was the presence of psychiatric or neurological disease (Marcé, 1862, pp.487–521).

Georget and the developmental hypothesis

An important departure of the 'disease concept' took place when Georget (1820) defined idiocy as 'failure in the *development* of the intellectual faculties'. Aware of his own originality Georget went on to state: 'idiocy *should not be made into a type of insanity (délire)* for a failure to develop cannot be properly considered as a disease *(maladie)*' ... 'idiots must be classified as monsters *(monstres)*' (my emphasis) (Davaine, 1874; Talbot, 1898). The expression of such an unorthodox view by a man barely aged 25 at the time needs explanation, particularly as he was a disciple of Esquirol who considered idiocy and imbecility as forms of *aliénation mentale*, and who, in general, paid little attention to the developmental aspects of mental disorder.

Onésime Édouard Séguin

By the middle of the century, French views on mental retardation had divided between those who continued supporting the medical views of Esquirol and those who, like Séguin (soon to emigrate to America) took an anti-medical stance. For example, in the full review that appeared in Fabre's (1849) popular encyclopaedia, the anonymous author starts its narrative with Esquirol and then quotes Belhomme and Séguin (the latter in his more medical or *physiological* vein) (pp.553–76). The same can be said of Guislain (1852) – another popular author of the period – who in his *Leçons* accepted the conventional distinction between idiots and imbeciles, but also argued that he saw no reason to make of this group a different variety of mental illness (p.343). Views on mental retardation during this period, however, are dominated by the work of Séguin.

A rather controversial figure, a lawyer turned educator and then physician, Séguin was also interested in metrication and thermometry (on which subjects he wrote with enthusiasm) (Martin, 1981). During the 1848 revolution, he sided with the *républicains de la veille*, and in the France of Louis Napoléon he is said to have felt (groundlessly) 'insecure'. In 1850, he decided to 'escape' to the USA (Pichot, 1948). An account of his views on *idiotisme* appeared in 1838 in joined authorship with Esquirol (*Résumé de ce que nous avons fait pendant 14 mois*).

A year later, he published a second work (*Conseils à Monsieur O **** sur l'éducation de son enfant idiot*). Three minor publications followed before his great book of 1846. Therein Séguin (1846) claimed that he had found 'in his soul the resources' needed to develop a theory which was not only important for 'idiocy but for education' (p.2). It is unlikely, however, that these ideas were original.[14] Likewise, for all his aggressive comments on the medical approach,[15] he remained ambivalent on the question of whether mental retardation was a form of mental illness.[16]

The medical view, however, remained unaltered. For example, when Foville (1874) wrote his review, he repeated the old concepts, except that, under the new Morelean banner, emphasised the degenerative taint (p.354). The same can be said of Chambard (1888) who, in his full review of the topic confirmed the medical approach, and stated that both idiocy and imbecility should be discussed under the rubric of *mental dysgenesis* (p.508). Thus, it is not surprising that when Ball (1890) published his great work on mental disorder he called these states morphological insanities (*folies morphologiques*) (p.934).

German Views
Hoffbauer
During the first half of the 19th century, perhaps the best example of German thought on this issue is to be found in the work of Hoffbauer (1827),[17] who dealt with the issue of legal responsibility in the mentally retarded and the deaf and dumb. He considered feeblemindedness (*Verstandschwäche*) as a form of pathology of intellect which could affect its level (imbecility-*Blödsinn*) or extension (stupidity-*Dummheit*). Both subtypes, in turn, could be congenital or acquired; in other words, mental retardation proper or dementia (pp.42–85).

Heinroth
Heinroth is another influential German writer whose views on idiocy must be discussed.[18] He made idiocy (*anoia*) into a *Genus* of mental disorder (*Störungen des Seelenlebens*) and divided it into four subtypes. He characterised idiocy as a disorder in which: 'the senses, especially the higher senses, cannot comprehend or grasp, and the intellect cannot collect any ideas from the sensations. The spirit is quite empty and is merely vegetating. The animal feelings and instincts, such as hunger or the sexual instinct, are however, stronger, and the patient can easily be excited into anger, which may become rage' (Heinroth, 1975, p.195). The distinction between the four subtypes of idiocy was made in terms of accompanying symptoms: *anoia simplex* was the pure form; *anoia melancholica*, was accompanied by agitation and partial insight into the condition; *anoia abyole*, by lethargy, inactivity and lack of responsiveness; and *anoia catholica*, which was the more severe form (pp.195–9). Heinroth (1975) referred to Hoffbauer with approval: 'Idiocy has been subdivided into several grades for the purpose of forensic medicine. The description of these fine differences must be credited, in the first place, to Hoffbauer' (p.198).

Griesinger
The third German writer worth mentioning here is W. Griesinger (1861) whose work has, on occasions, been described as sponsoring a 19th century form of

unitary psychosis (Vliegen, 1980, pp.13–17). This is because he seemed to suggest that melancholia, mania and dementia were clinical states which could appear successively in the same individual, thereby reflecting the fact that he was suffering from a disease characterised by a march of organic events starting with neurophysiological depression (*Depressionzunstände*) and proceeding to excitation (*Exaltationszustände*) to end up in weakness (*Schwächezustände*) (pp.22–59). Idiocy fitted well into Griesinger's clinical cascade and was made, together with chronic insanity (*partielle Verrückheit*), confusion (*Verwirrtheit*) and stupor or terminal dementia (*apathische Blödsinn*) the central example of *psychischen Schwächezustände*. Whilst the other three states were *acquired*, and constituted what, nowadays, would be called the defect states,[19] idiocy was congenital: 'By the term idiocy (*Idiotismus*), we understand conditions in which the state of mental weakness exists from birth or early infancy, and in which psychological development has been impeded or prevented' (p.352). Griesinger postulated a strong organic and hereditary hypothesis for such states of mental weakness, considering all social explanations as 'shallow' (*flache Auffassung*) (p.356). His account is interesting for it shows, as it had done Cullen's the previous century, that – although there was awareness of the congenital nature of mental retardation – theoretical and social considerations led to its being conflated with acquired defect states such as dementia. It also sets in perspective the relevance of Esquirol's 'discovery'.

Von Feuchtersleben
The fourth German-speaking writer to be mentioned here is von Feuchtersleben (1847), who dealt with idiocy in 1845:

Idiocy proceeds, as a psychopathy,[20] proximately from *anaesthesia*, weakness of attention, *amnesia*, and want of images. It represents, in some measure, an approximation of the human character to that of animals, and is characterized by an incapacity of judging, or even, in its higher degree, of contemplating. The alteration is more prominent in the direction of thought than in that of feeling and will, though, in the higher degrees, both feeling and will are also wanting (*Abulia*, Heinroth) . . . the lowest degree, which Hartman calls stupidity, is characterised by an incapacity of comprehending, judging, and concluding, even in affairs of what is called common sense . . . the higher degree, idiocy *sensu strictiori*, shows total incapacity for mental activity. (p.301)

This wider definition of mental retardation includes changes in all mental functions.

British Views
Prichard
James Cowles Prichard, the great British alienist and anthropologist (Stocking, 1973), wrote an important book on mental disorders in which the influence of Continental views, particularly Esquirol's, can be detected. Prichard (1835) did not consider idiotism or mental deficiency as a form of insanity, and hence treated these states in a separate chapter (pp.318–27). Idiotism he defined as: 'a state in which the mental faculties have been wanting from birth, or have not

been manifested at the period at which they are usually developed. Idiotism is an original defect, and is by this circumstance, as well as by its phenomena, distinguished from that fatuity that results from disease or from protracted age' (p.318). Prichard quotes Esquirol, Fodéré, and Georget, discusses cretinism at length, and supports Esquirol's continuity view: 'there is no exact line of demarcation between idiotism and a degree of weakness which is generally termed imbecility' (p.324); but goes one step further in linking these states to normality: 'There are different degrees and varieties of mental deficiency, which scarcely amount to what is termed either idiotism, or, in general language, imbecility. Persons so affected are commonly said to be weak in character, stupid, or of mean capacity' (p.326).

Bucknill and Tuke (1858) also criticised Esquirol's pessimism: 'it would no longer be right to speak of the faculties of the idiot being doomed to remain stationary' (p.93), and found contradiction between what he lists in a table showing that decrease in the size of the heads of idiots and what he states in the text (p.100).

THE SECOND HALF OF THE 19TH CENTURY

Views on mental retardation during the second half of the 19th century are characterised by a transformation of the categorical approach: for example, quantitative bridges begin to be established between normal children and the mildly retarded. This required a major change in theory. Thus, Netchine (1973) has suggested that, up to this period, whilst mental retardation itself was graded into sub-categories, there was no general quantitative dimension to include the various levels of normality (pp.100–7). This was to occur only after the important work of Sollier (1891) (sadly neglected) and that of Binet and Simon (often quoted) who introduced the first workable concept of intellectual coefficient.

Paul Sollier

Sollier trained under Bourneville at Bicêtre, and was for a while in charge of the Pathological Museum. His aim was to deal with the general psychological characteristics of idiocy rather than with specific or rare cases. He complained that writings on this category were 'poor' (piii, Sollier), in France 1891 as compared with America or England. The first problem he encountered was that 'idiocy is not a clinical entity . . . that the idiot is an abnormal being but that its abnormality varies in many dimensions . . . [on the other hand] he is not a separate category but merges with the milder forms of the disorder' (pp.2–3). To sort this out he suggests that it might be possible to 'measure their mental state by seeking to compare it to a particular age in the normal child' (p.3). (This view is often attributed to Binet and Simon.) Sollier finds an important obstacle: 'for this principle to apply it would be needed that the cause of idiocy was the same in each case . . . unfortunately this is not the case' (p.3). To collect his data, Sollier made use of a modified version of a structured interview schedule developed by Voisin (1843) which included sections on instincts, feelings and affections, perceptual functioning, psychomotor skills, intellect, and physiological and psychological functions. In spite of discussing quantification, Sollier's book includes no numerical data; indeed, it is not even clear how many cases were studied. His principles as much as his conclusions, however, are modern in outlook and break with categorical thinking, to the point that Binet and Simon did not need to think out a justification for their work.

Binet and Simon

Binet and Simon (1905),[21] closely followed Sollier's view that there was a 'need to establish a scientific (quantitative) diagnosis of the states of lower intelligence'. One year before Binet's death, they published his final manifesto on the nosology of l'arriération. After remarking upon the fact that alienists had neglected the study of these conditions, Binet and Simon (1910) criticised both classifications based on pathological-anatomy (à la Bourneville)[22] and Sollier's view that imbecility was not accompanied by brain changes (p.350). They re-affirmed the value of grouping subjects according to quantitative criteria but criticised Régis and Kraepelin for not providing adequate operational definitions for their groups. Lastly, Binet and Simon commented negatively on suggestions by psychologists that only one mental function was primarily disorder in mental handicap, stating that, in fact, all are (p.351). During the 1930s, new ingredients were added to the definition of mental retardation, particularly Lewis' (1933) notion of 'sub-cultural deficiency' (p.303). Current views, well reflected in the criteria of DSM IV, include quantitative criteria, genetics, physical disability, behavioural adaptation, and social competence. This form of Chinese menu system has improved the reliability of the descriptors but does not guarantee validity nor does it offer a theory to unify the various strands involved in the clinical expression of mental retardation. What is worse, it does not offer a conceptual framework to tackle the question: is mental retardation a form of mental illness?

CONCLUSIONS

The view that mental retardation was a defect of *intellectual* function different from insanity or dementia became well established during the first half of the 19th century. It was also during this period that mental retardation became burdened with an important ambiguity, to wit, the question of whether it was necessarily a form of mental illness. This was not only due to definitional confusions. In fact, encouraged by faculty psychology, and the categorical view of idiocy, 19th century alienists felt entitled to claim that most forms of mental retardation were diseases. But following protestations by educators and anti-medical men such as Séguin, a compromise developed during the second half of the century which suggested a human-variation type of continuum between normality, imbecility and idiocy (leading to the claim that members of the latter two groups could not be considered as mentally ill). This hypothesis was heuristic in that it encouraged the development of a quantitative view which first with Sollier, and then Binet and Simon, led to the creation of the abstract notion of intellectual coefficient. Since early in the 19th century, however, there had also been awareness of the possibility that the frequency of neurological and psychiatric pathology increased *pari passu* with the depth of the mental retardation. The tensions that this observation created within the continuum model were not solved during the 19th century, and might not have been alleviated even today.

NOTES

1 By 'presentistic' it is meant here a style of historiography that assumes that current views on reality are necessarily superior to earlier ones, and that the past was but a preparation for the present. This view is partially related to what – in a different context – Herbert Butterfield (1931) called 'the Whig interpretation of history'.

2 See for example Sir Frederic Bateman's (1897) evocative title: *The idiot: his place in creation and his claims on society*; or the debate initiated by Georget (1820) that the mentally handicapped were a type of monster. On the concept of monster and its relationship to the definition of man see Davaine (1874). After the 1860s, the notion of monstrosity became entangled with degeneration theory, see Talbot (1898). The same ideological background inspired the debate on a classification of idiots based upon the physiognomic features of the 'great Caucasian family' which led to the coining of mongolism: see Down (1866), Schachter (1943).

3 The English version of this rare book, written by Séguin and his son for the American market did not include a large and telling section entitled: *Définitions de l'Idiotie antérieures à mes travaux* (pp.23–71), in which the French writer describes and criticises earlier definitions and classifications.

4 See 17th century definition: 'He that shall be said to be a sot and idiot from his birth, is such a person who cannot count or number twenty, and tell who was his father or mother' (Bucknill and Tuke, 1858, p.94); see also Neugebauer (1989).

5 Cullen's contemporaries were already aware of the fact that his category *Amentia* resulted from lumping together a number of previous disparate clinical states. For example, the great Italian nosologist Chiarugi stated: 'in his nosology, Cullen combined them in the same way' (Chiarugi, 1987).

6 See Cullen (1785). This translation seems to have been a financial failure due, apparently, to the fact that E. Bosquillon, the Royal lecturer, published another the same year.

7 It is not easy to identify the work Pinel refers to. However, it is likely to be Morin's (1802) *Dictionnaire Universel des synonymes de la langue française*.

8 Although influenced by Cabanis and the French ideologues, Pinel used a common sense form of faculty psychology which he is likely to have borrowed from Dougald Stewart. On Pinel's psychological influences see Riese (1969), Staum (1980), Postel (1981), d'Istria (1926).

9 Esquirol (1814) dealt with the notions of *idiotism* and *imbécillité* in the context of *démence* (pp.280–94). In this work he quoted Pinel (1809): 'dementia should not be confused with imbecility or idiotism. The faculty of reasoning in the imbecile is undeveloped and weak; the dement has lost his . . . idiots and cretins are not able to have sensations, memory or judgement and show only few animal instincts; their external shape shows that they are not organised to think' (p.284). In the same entry, he stated that *imbécillité* was a species of *aliénation mentale*. The entry on *Idiotisme* appeared three years later (Esquirol, 1817) and was reprinted in an expanded form (Esquirol, 1838, pp.283–397).

10 *Les cagots*, referred to by Michel as one of the accursed races (*races maudites*), include groups of peoples who, since the Medieval period, were

ostracised into areas of Northern Spain and Western France, and forbidden to enter into social contact with the rest of the population (see Lagneau, 1869). Whether through inbreeding or social isolation and lack of education, it is claimed that mental retardation was highly prevalent in this group. Esquirol (1838) claimed that this improved once their ostracism ended (pp.370–2).

11 The French term *délire* (like the German *Wahn*) names a complex psychiatric phenomenon which is not totally rendered into English by the word 'delusion'. This has caused much difficulty over the years.

12 Nothing else will be said in this chapter about the boy of Aveyron and its relevance to the conceptual debate on idiocy and its treatment in early 19th century France. Particularly important works on this topic are: Malson (1964), Lane (1977), Sánchez (1982) and Swain (1976).

13 The notion of degeneration was introduced into psychiatry by Morel in 1857. Literature on this topic is now very large; for three different historical approaches see: Genil-Perrin (1913), Huertas (1987) and Pick (1989).

14 For a good analysis of the Saint-Simonian and 'moral treatment' origins of his method, see: Kraft (1961).

15 He started his medical training only in 1843, and had to quit the Bicêtre Hospital after entering into conflict with its physicians. His writing on the education of the idiot were praised by the *Académie des Sciences* and ignored by the *Académie de Médicine*. This may partly explain his anti-medical stance (Martin, 1961). Likewise, Séguin was displeased about a certificate issued by Esquirol and Guersant: 'The undersigned have the pleasure of acknowledging that Mr. Séguin has started with success the training of a child almost mute and *seemingly* retarded . . .' The use of the word 'seemingly' irked Séguin who felt that this betrayed Esquirol's belief in the incurability of idiocy (Séguin, 1846, p.14). In the same work, Séguin mounted a savage attack on Esquirol and his disinterest in idiocy (Séguin, 1846, see pp.24–30). This text was omitted from the American translation (Séguin, 1866).

16 For example, he wrote: 'I hereby formally accuse physicians . . . of having confused idiocy with other analogous chronic conditions, of confusing it with concomitant pathological states that are not part or consequence of idiocy, of not dedicating sufficient time to their study'. Séguin goes on to say that physicians entertain too theoretical a view, that their definitions are negative, and that there is too much emphasis on the intellectual defect (Séguin, 1846, pp.69–71).

17 J.C. Hoffbauer (1766–1827) was a professor of Philosophy and Law at Halle University from which he had to retire early on account of deafness. He collaborated with the German alienist Reil. The French translation of Hoffbauer's work (1827) was made by A.M. Chambeyron with notes by Esquirol and Itard. This curious translation included critical notes from both translator – a disciple of Esquirol – and the great man himself. Many of these miss the point and deride Hoffbauer's interesting efforts to carry out a psychological analysis – in terms of Faculty Psychology – of the subtypes of feeblemindedness (see, for example, pp.43–4). Chambeyron and Esquirol seemed to have preferred the clinical and frequential method which was irrelevant to Hoffbauer's needs. An intriguing historical point is also made

by Chambeyron and Esquirol in a table comparing Hoffbauer's classification of mental disorder with ongoing French views: 'imbecility, idiocy and dementia are *confused* by the Germans under the general heading of feeblemindedness which they divide into imbecility and stupor' (my emphasis). It was wrong of them to generalise to all 'Germans' alienists as some (e.g. Heinroth) thought otherwise (see below).

18 Historical misreading has created the myth that Heinroth believed that 'the ultimate cause of mental disturbance is sin' (Alexander and Selesnick, 1966, p.141). For a timely correction see Cauwenbergh (1991).

19 He wrote: 'Under this section are included morbid states which, although different in detail, form a sort of natural group. With some exceptions to be mentioned later, they look like each other in that they do not constitute primary, but secondary (*consecutives*) forms of insanity, and that they are remnants of the [acute] types already considered when these are not cured'. (Griesinger 1861, pp.322–3).

20 A clarification is indicated here: circa 1845, the term 'psychopathy' simply meant mental disorder, and had nothing to do with the usage it was to acquire after 1890 (on this see Berrios (1993)).

21 Binet has received far more attention than Simon. For a general introduction on the former see Wolf (1973) and Schneider (1992).

22 Désiré Magloire Bourneville (1840–1909), a protégé of Charcot's, spent most of his career at Bicêtre, where he became the leading French specialist in mental retardation.

REFERENCES

Alexander, F.G. and Selesnick, S.T. (1966) *The History of Psychiatry*, New York, Harper and Row.

Ball, B. (1890) *Leçons sur les maladies mentales*, second edition, Paris, Asselin et Houzeau (first edition 1880).

Barr, M.W. (1904) *Mental defectives, their history, treatment and training*, Philadelphia, Blackiston's Son & Co.

Bateman, Sir F. (1897) *The idiot; his place in creation and his claims on society*, second edition, London, Jarrold & Sons.

Berrios, G.E. (1987) 'Dementia during the seventeenth and eighteenth centuries: a conceptual history'. *Psychological Medicine*, 17: 829–37.

Berrios, G.E. (1993) 'European views on personality disorders: a conceptual history'. *Comprehensive Psychiatry*, 34: 14–30.

Binet, A. and Simon, Th. (1905) 'Sur la nécessité d'établir un diagnostic scientifique des états inférieurs de l'intelligence'. *L'Année Psychologique*, 11: 163–90.

Binet, A. and Simon, Th. (1910) 'L'Arriération'. *L'Année Psychologique*, 16: 349–60.

Bucknill, J.C. and Tuke, D.H. (1858) *A Manual of Psychological Medicine*, London, John Churchill.

Butterfield, H. (1931) *The Whig interpretation of History*, London, Bell.

Cauwenbergh, L. (1991) 'J. Chr. A. Heinroth (1773–1843): psychiatrist of the German Romantic era'. *History of Psychiatry*, 2: 365–83.

Chambard, E. (1888) 'Idiotie'. In Dechambre, A. and Lereboullet, L. (eds.) *Dictionnaire Encyclopédique des Sciences Médicales*, vol.51, Paris, Masson, pp.507–27.

Chiarugi, V. (1987) *On Insanity and its Classification*, Translation of G. Mora, Canton, Watson, p.230 (First edition: 1793).

Clarke, B. (1975) *Mental Disorder in Earlier Britain*, Cardiff, University of Wales Press, pp.56–81.

Cranfield, P.F. (1961) 'A seventeenth century view of mental deficiency and schizophrenia: Thomas Willis on "stupidity and foolishness"'. *Bulletin of the History of Medicine*, 35: 291–316.

Cullen, W. (1785) *Institutions de Médicine pratique*, 2 vols, French Translation of Ph. Pinel, Paris, Duplain.

Cullen, W. (1803) *Synopsis Nosologiæ Methodicæ*, Edinburgh, W. Creech.

Cullen, W. (1827) *The Works of William Cullen MD*, vol.1, Edinburgh, William Blackwood.

D'Istria, F.C. (1926) 'La Psychologie de Bichat'. *Revue de Metaphysique et de Morale*, 23: 1–38.

Davaine, C. (1874) 'Monstres. Monstruosité'. In Dechambre, A. and Lereboullet, L. (eds.) *Dictionnaire Encyclopédique des Sciences Médicales*, vol.61, Paris, Masson, pp.201–64.

Down, J.L. (1866) 'Observations on an ethnic classification of idiots'. *London Hospital Reports*, 3: 259–62.

Duché, D.-J. (1990) *Histoire de la Psychiatrie de l'enfant*, Paris, Presses Universitaires de France.

Esquirol, E. (1817) 'Démence'. In *Dictionnaire des Sciences Médicales*, vol.8, Paris, Panckoucke, pp.280–94.

Esquirol, E. (1838) *Des Maladies Mentales considérées sous les rapports médical, hygiénique et médico-légal*, Paris, Baillière, pp.283–397.

Fabre, Dr. (ed.) (1849) *Bibliothéque du Médicin-Practicien*, vol.9, Paris, J.B. Baillière.

Feuchtersleben, Baron von E. (1845) *Lehrbuch der ärztlichen Seelenkunde*, Wien, Carl Gerold (English translation by Lloyd, H.E. and Babington, B.G. (1847) *The Principles of Medical Psychology*, London, Sydenham Society).

Foville, A. fils (1874) 'Idiotie, Imbecillité'. In Anger, B. et al (ed.) *Nouveau Dictionnaire de Médicine et de Chirurgie pratiques*, vol.18, Paris, Baillière, pp.363–75.

Genil-Perrin, G. (1913) *Histoire des Origines et de l'Évolution de l'Idée de Dégénérescence en Médicine Mentale*, Paris, A. Leclerc.

Georget, E.J. (1820) *De la Folie. Considérations sur cette maladie*, Paris, Crevot.

Gineste, T. (1983) 'Naissance de la psychiatrie infantile (destins de l'idiote, origine des psychoses)'. In Postel, J. and Quetel, C. (eds.) *Nouvelle Histoire de la Psychiatrie*, Paris, Privat, pp.499–516.

Gontard, A. (1988) 'The Development of Child Psychiatry in 19th century Britain'. *Journal of Child Psychology and Psychiatry*, 29: 569–88.

Griesinger, W. (1961) *Die Pathologie und Therapie der psychischen Krankheiten*, Stuttgart, Krabbe, (First edition 1845).

Guislain, J. (1852) *Leçons orales sur les phrénopathies*, vol.1, Gand, Hebbelynck.

Heinroth, J.C. (1975) *Textbook of Disturbances of Mental Life. Or Disturbances of the Soul and their Treatment*, vol.1, Baltimore, Johns Hopkins University Press (First German Edition 1818).

Hoffbauer, J.C. (1827) *Médicine Légale Relative aux Aliénés et aux Sourds-muets ou les Lois Appliquées aux Désordres de l'Intelligence* (translated by Chambeyron A.M. with notes by Esquirol and Itard) Paris, Baillière (First German Edition 1808).

Huertas, R. (1987) *Locura y Degeneración: Psiquiatría y sociedad en el positivismo francés*, Madrid, Consejo Superior de Investigaciones Científicas.

James, F.E. (1991) 'Some observations on the writings of Felix Platter (1539–1614) in relation to mental handicap'. *History of Psychiatry*, 2: 103–8.

Kanner, L. (1964) *A History of the care and study of the mentally retarded*, Springfield, Illinois, Charles C Thomas.

Kraft, I. (1961) 'Edouard Seguin and the 19th century moral treatment of idiots'. *Bulletin of the History of Medicine*, 35: 393–418.

Lagneau, G. (1869) 'Cagots'. In Dechambre, A. and Lereboullet, L. (eds.) *Dictionnaire Encyclopédique des Sciences Médicales*, vol.11, Paris, Masson, pp.534–57.

Lane, H. (1977) *The Wild Boy of Aveyron*, London, George Allen & Unwin.

Lang, J.L. (1965) 'Situation de l'infance handicapée'. *Esprit*, 33: 588–99.

Lewis, A. (1961) 'The study of defect'. *American Journal of Psychiatry*, 117: 289–305.

Lewis, E.O. (1933) 'Types of mental deficiency and their social significance'. *Journal of Mental Science*, 79: 298–304.

Mahendra, B. (1985) 'Subnormality revisited in early 19th century France'. *Journal of Mental Deficiency*, 29: 391–401.

Malson, L. (1964) *Les Enfants Sauvages*, Paris, Union Générale d'Editions.

Marcé, L.V. (1862) *Traité Pratique des Maladies Mentales*, Paris, Baillière.

Martin, J. (1981) *Une Biographie Française (1812–1850) d'Onésime Édouard Séguin, Premier Thérapeute des Enfants Arriérés, d'après ses Écrits et les Documents Historiques*, Thèse de Médecine, Saint Antoine, Paris.

Morin, B. (1802) *Dictionnaire Universel des Synonymes de la Langue Française publiées jusqu'à ce jour*, 3 vols, Paris, Benoît Morin.

Netchine, G. (1973) 'Idiotas, débiles y sabios en el siglo XIX'. In Zazzo, R. (ed.) *Los Débiles Mentales*, Fontanella, Barcelona, pp.77–117 (translation of *Les Débilités Mentales*, Colin, Paris, 1969).

Neugebauer, R. (1989) 'A doctor's dilemma: the case of William Harvey's mentally retarded nephew'. *Psychological Medicine*, 19: 569–72.

Pichot, P. (1948) 'French Pioneers in the Field of Mental Deficiency'. *American Journal of Mental Deficiency*, 53: 128–37.

Pick, D. (1989) *Faces of Degeneration: A European Disorder, c1848–1918*, Cambridge, Cambridge University Press.

Pinel, Ph. (1806) *A Treatise of Insanity* (translation of D.D. Davis), Sheffield, W. Tood, p.172, (First edition: (1801) (Year IX) *Traité Médico-Philosophique sur l'aliénation mentale ou la manie*, Paris, Richard, Caille et Ravier).

Pinel, Ph. (1809) *Traité Médico-Philosophique sur l'Aliénation Mentale*, Paris, Brosson, pp.181–90.

Pinel, Ph. (1818) *Nosographie Philosophique ou la Méthode de l'Analyse*

Appliquée a la Médicine, Paris, vol.1, 6th Edition, J.A. Brosson, (First Edition 1798).

Postel, J. (1981) *Genèse de la Psychiatrie*, Paris, Le Sycomore.

Prichard, J.C. (1835) *A Treatise on Insanity*, London, Sherwood, Gilbert and Piper, pp.318–27.

Riese, W. (1969) *The Legacy of Philippe Pinel*, New York, Springer.

Rushton, P. (1988) 'Lunatics and idiots: mental disability, the community, and the poor law in North-East England, 1600–1800'. *Medical History*, 32: 34–50.

Sánchez, R. (1982) 'Comentarios del Traductor'. In *Jean Itard, Victor de L'Aveyron*, Madrid, Alianza, pp.99–251.

Schachter, M. (1943) *Mongolism*, Madrid, Morata.

Scheerenberger, R.C. (1983) *A History of Mental Retardation*, Brookes, Baltimore.

Schneider, W. (1992) 'After Binet: French Intelligence Testing, 1900–1950'. *Journal of the History of the Behavioral Sciences*, 28: 111–32.

Séguin, E. (1846) *Traitement Moral, Hygiéne et Éducation des Idiots et des Autres Enfants Arriérés*, Paris, Baillière.

Seguin, E. (1866) *Idiocy and its Treatment by the Physiological Method*, New York, Wood & Company.

Sollier, P. (1891) *Psychologie de l'idiot et de l'imbécile*, Paris, Alcan.

Staum, M. (1980) *Cabanis*, Princeton, Princeton University Press.

Stocking, G.W. (1973) Introduction in Prichard, J.C. *Researches into the Physical History of Man*, Chicago, Chicago University Press, pp.ix–cvxiii.

Swain, G. (1976) 'The Wild boy of Aveyron de H. Lane'. *L'Evolution Psychiatrique*, 41: 995–1011.

Talbot, E.S. (1898) *Degeneracy, its Causes, Signs and Results*, London, Walter Scott, Ltd.

Vademécum (of the London Hospitals) (1803) *The Edinburgh Practice of Physic, Surgery, and Midwifery*, vol.2, London, Kearsley, p.451.

Vliegen, J. (1980) *Die Einheitspsychose. Geschichte und Problem*, Stuttgart, Enke.

Voisin, F. (1843) *De l'Idiotie chez les Enfants*, Paris, Baillière.

Walk, A. (1964) 'The pre-history of Child psychiatry'. *British Journal of Psychiatry*, 110: 754–67.

Wolf, T.H. (1973) *Alfred Binet*, Chicago, Chicago University Press.

Chapter 9
Mental Retardation

Social Section – Part I
CF GOODEY

I

Mental handicap is a generic term covering a vastly disparate range of behaviours, ways of living, feeling and thinking which rarely have anything in common. Its unity, its reason for existence, consists in its being the justification of particular social practices of segregation, exclusion or termination.

For the historian as academic, working within a fixed discipline such as the history of psychiatry, it is the marginality of all marginalities. If the issue were madness, then someone who was a convinced positivist would probably be capable of seeing the opposite point of view, while remaining unpersuaded. However, to suggest that mental handicap is at its most fundamental level socially constructed would be beyond comprehension, even for argument's sake. The opponent would have the impossible task of persuading us that the world may be validly conceived as the person with a mentally handicapping condition conceives it: at the extreme, what if anything does a person with the severest learning difficulties conceive? In fact the issue has rarely been discussed by anti-positivists. The view of madness as pathology pure and simple can tacitly be displaced to congenital incurable deficiency instead; silence on this topic is what enables them to argue against a monolithic rationality from a covertly monolithic and rational point of view, situating them at the opposite end of a scale of academic intelligence from the severest mentally handicapped individual. As the physiognomist Johann Caspar Lavater put it, 'The idiot-born cannot without a miracle become a philosopher'. On the other hand Alfred Binet, the very inventor of the formalised psychometric testing of deficiency, pointed out that intelligence in any sense could be defined only as a battery of performances that are selected arbitrarily.

This kind of ambivalence is also what makes interpreting the concrete historical material awkward. On the one hand, positive sightings of historical individuals recognizable to us as our 'mentally handicapped' ought to be, and actually are, easier to verify (if extremely sparse) than of the 'mad'. On the other hand, we have only to compare the variations in assessment criteria and in the selection of inmates in today's concentration-zones (residential institutions, special schools, etc.) within a unified political culture such as Britain or the USA to realise how unstable the concept is. It has also been subject to very short-term historical shifts. A majority of the individuals shut away as 'feeble-minded' at the height of the first wave of mass segregation, as recently as the turn of this last century, would today be ordinary citizens; one could not assert this so confidently about the 'mad' of that time.

Trying to write a social history of the real-life idiot is thus something of a fool's errand. The history of the concept itself, however, is another matter. There is a consistent resource of historical texts that have been exploited and re-worked to fuel the practices of social exclusion on grounds of intellectual incompetence; although the kinds of exclusion that have been made in the past have varied, the same textual resources often continue to be used with modern mental handicap. They are characterised by a set of underlying descriptions and explanations: the excluded individual as a deviation on the slow or deficient side of a mean; as incurable and ineducable; as congenital; as accident or inheritance. I shall deal with these textual resources in turn before discussing the roots of early modern social practice.

In Western medicine, intellectual soundness has often been cast as a median point beyond which 'mental activity' can either be too fast or too slow, in excess or in deficit. The first extant text to discuss pathological mental states via this antithetical pairing is by the Greek philosopher and medical theoretician Empedocles, in the fifth century BC. A century later the same model is invoked in a more detailed form in a text ascribed to Hippocrates, *On Regimen*. As well as describing speed and sloth, excesses and deficiencies, this work offers a kind of materialist explanation for them. The 'mind' itself, the psyche, consists in a balance of elemental particles of fire and water. If water predominates, the psyche moves too slowly (and if fire, too fast) to engage optimally with the sensations it receives from the external environment. We could compare explanations of epilepsy in terms of excessive biochemical activity in the brain with chromosomal abnormalities where there is a shortfall or deficiency in the movement of neurons across synapses. In addition, the Hippocratic author tabulates three discrete levels of severity on each of the two sides, fast and slow, of the median point of intellectual soundness; this degree of meticulous neatness would not be achieved again until the nineteenth century.

The fast/slow, excessive/deficient criterion of Hippocrates passed into the Peripatetic school of philosophy and indirectly into Galenic medicine. The Galenists saw amentia, stultitia and fatuitas as signs of imbalance (towards coldness and humidity) in the four 'humours' that they took to constitute the human subject, and of an under-supply of the 'animal spirits' that they understood as nourishing the intellect. This 'slow' pathology became the framework for the description of melancholia, which was closely related to mania as either a sub-class or its antithesis. With the revival of interest in Hippocrates that took place in late Renaissance Italy, the new Latin translation of *On Regimen*, a standard text in medical education, facilitated a new reading of the doctrine of the mean. The expression of the slow pathology in terms of 'the senses meeting their objects only spasmodically' (Hippocrates) and of its effects on attention, memory and judgement, gradually became part of a new antithesis, where the excess speed of madness (in which by contrast the mind 'rushes on to too many objects') was opposed to a slow condition that borrowed its 'idiocy' terminology from legal definitions of incurability and congenitality applied to mental competence. Although this expanded terminology establishes itself very quickly, it is not clear for a long time how the practice of institutions such as Bedlam distinguishes between a 'melancholic' sloth/

deficiency and that of a separable kind of idiocy related to the juridical concept.

There is another textual tradition that uses an analogous criterion, and has affinities with modern cognitive psychology. Its first appearance, though the context seems to suggest it is a reference back to earlier materialist thought, is in Plato, whose dialogue *Theaetetus* discusses the ignorance and incorrect belief of philosophers and, along the way, possible organic explanations for them. Imagine the mind is a wax tablet, says Plato. (The wax tablet is what his lecture class would have been scratching their notes on, the ancient equivalent of a blank sheet of paper or a computer.) Imprints that penetrate clearly and deeply enough into the wax will last, and the individual with this kind of mind will be quick to learn and have a retentive memory. Unclear imprints due to excesses or deficiencies in the mental wax's impressionability will produce people who 'when they see, hear or think of anything, cannot quickly assign things to the right imprints, but are slow about it, and because they assign them wrongly they usually see and hear and think amiss'. The term in Greek that Plato coins for this condition means 'learning difficulty'. In fact the passage is partly ironic, since Plato is criticising everyday notions of human intelligence in a culture where it was assessed by the rhetorician's criterion of verbal agility. The theme is taken up more seriously in Aristotle's influential text *On Memory* and by the neo-Platonists of later antiquity; it is via this route that the language of 'impressions' becomes familiar in medieval psychology and a modern everyday metaphor. But it is rarely encountered in this kind of pathological context until the early seventeenth century, when writers such as Pierre Gassendi revived materialist explanations of mind and mental disorders in the debate with Descartes.

The criterion of the mean is one where philosophy tends to dominate over medicine as such. The opposite ought to be the case with the criterion of curability/incurability and the closely associated one of congenitality. However, although these play an important part in Greek medicine, they are rarely applied there to mental pathology. The entire Hippocratic corpus has just one reference to a condition of stupidity that exists from birth. Writers on obstetrics from later antiquity such as Soranus knew that hypotonia, hydrocephalus etc. were signs of generalised weakness in the new-born infant, but did not associate this with incurable learning difficulties. What this indicates may be less aetiological ignorance than the absence of an allotted social or juridical dungeon for idiots in that society; it was not an important factor in the classification of human difference. Aretaeus of Cappadocia, in the second or third century AD, is the first medical writer with an extant text giving 'incurable' mental pathology as a generic category. His only illustration of it is senile dementia, but it is obvious (to us) that the category could also be illustrated by people who are born with incurable difficulties, or who acquire them early in life.

This particular distinction, hardly touched on by medicine, is given full force by feudal property law. Its juridical category of 'born fool', who is distinguished from the person credited with 'lucid intervals', looks not dissimilar to our mentally handicapped person. But in fact the picture of feudal legislation on intellectual incompetence viewed over the whole period is disjointed and puzzling. Different psychological conditions (and such distinctions themselves are not easily verified) do not yet necessarily match the curable/incurable divide.

And it was not always assumed that to be born a fool meant that you would always remain that way; you may have been a 'natural', i.e. created by God in that state, but He could get you out of it too. The puzzles go away if we focus clearly on one central point: that the fundamental assessment criterion is not this or that condition describable in psychological terms, but purely and simply the (in)capability of administering one's own property. (The assessment of propertyless fools is part of an altogether different agenda.) The general category 'fool', whatever its other fluctuations, defines people with no rights or restricted ones as to their inherited property and its administration. According to an Irish legal text (Hancock, 1865), 'A child is a fool until the age of seven, and a fool of half sense until the age of fourteen'. This primitive mental age score, just like the modern IQ score, is not a psychological assessment at all, not even one that is vitiated by being historically and culturally relative because of its attachment to the administrative needs of a particular society; it *is* the act of administration itself and no more, a warehousing of souls determined by the needs and disabilities of a particular society, its lack of ability to cope with certain humans. Categorisation following assessment, having appeared first in the terminology of a theological notion of human nature (the legal phrase *idiota* derives from Canon Law), then becomes part of the history of medical jurisprudence; but this should correctly be understood as jurisprudence pure and simple, as a theory for the administration of property that happens to fly a medical flag of convenience.

In the early fourteenth century, the legal procedures began to be standardised by the issue of a statute of King's Prerogative, which entailed the issue of various kinds of writ based on assessment criteria connected with congenitality and incurability (Neugebauer, 1978). The monarch now made claims over the property of all categories of incompetent, including those rights that previously had reverted to the family; the statute also allowed the monarchy to use the profits of the estates of 'natural' or born fools for itself, but not those of the person who had lucid intervals or might even recover permanently. A devolved system of guardianship and tutelage emerged from this in the Tudor period, with separate rights and duties tied to the binary distinction. The assessment of mental competence in the Court of Wards was still the business of juries and (later) of magistrates rather than of expert medical witnesses, and was based on criteria (the ability to count, know one's name, the date, etc.) that are still familiar. Juries appear to have been reluctant to approve the more severe category. Battles between family guardians and monarch, who would of course have a vested interest in proving the more remunerative category, lasted long enough to become an issue in the struggle between king and parliament in early seventeenth-century England, where the juridical category encounters and influences the shifting medical antithesis of the Hippocratic revival.

Inheritability, like curability, interests ancient writers almost exclusively in respect of bodily disorders. Its importance for mental states, at least in medical terms, is rarely prominent earlier than the late seventeenth century. This awakening interest transposes into medical science contemporary changes in property relationships and patterns of the distribution of power. To whole strata in the fluidity of the immediate post-revolutionary society in England and the continuing crisis of its political constitution, the social order was embedded in the order of 'nature' still, but also dependent for its existence on their maintenance of their own uncertain positions in it. They could not simply assume that they were born to such positions; they had to use something we would call intelligence, secular reason, to maintain social and their own stability, and acknowledge that they might be overtaken by people of possibly greater intelligence below them in the social order. The same discourse that had begun in the early seventeenth century as an ideology of educating the sons of gentry to avoid the 'folly' of self-indulgence and to master the management of their estates gradually became re-routed towards the medical diagnosis of distinct psychological conditions. The intelligence needed to manage one's patrimony became, instead, intelligence *as* patrimony. The late-century medical practitioner Thomas Willis in his *De anima brutorum* clearly felt the need to point out that in addition to fools begotten by fools there is also the quite distinct category of 'changelings', who can be born to 'a wise man and very ingenious'. The underlying concept is Aristotle's, for whom degrees of monstrosity corresponded inversely to the degree of resemblance to one's parents, but Willis's concerns are up-to-date and urgent. This curiosity about inheritance recurs in the mid-nineteenth century and has remained extraordinarily high among clinicians ever since.

II

To trace the social construction of mental handicap with a historical point of arrival in the early modern period, we need a knowledge of all the foregoing descriptive frameworks. But these texts immediately prompt the question as to how real individuals with learning difficulties are related to the whole human community or species; this is a relationship whose very basis for existence presents itself to us as problematical. To help explain the questions of social practice, we can refer to the title of a recent magnum opus on the history of North American slavery, 'Without Consent or Contract'. This phrase describes the slave's social status: remove the social and legal constraints from slaves (regardless of incidental assumptions about their intellectual inferiority) and presto, you have people *with* the power of consent and contract. Remove the same constraints from the person constitutionally incapable of those powers (if such there be, as we assume), and nothing happens: no such transformation takes place. The question then for the historian must be to find the particular problematically human type for whom, given the self-defined 'species' boundaries demarcated for itself by a whole society, crossing those boundaries towards inclusion is an existential impossibility. In societies where consent and contract have not been the cornerstone of complex social arrangements, when we apply the kinds of criteria I have so far discussed it is not necessarily the mentally handicapped person in our sense whom we shall find left outside. In the matter of social inclusion, then, there is an element of variability, even choice. Whom will I have in my polis? Whom do I want to exclude – who is the greatest threat to it? If there is a general problematic behind the myriad temporary and local interweavings among the texts of all the lawyers, medical theorists and entrepreneurs, logicians, patients, zoologists, priests, etc. who wrote the idiot into civil society, then this is it: the superficially human thing that cannot lead the life of a citizen, in *this* society of *these* citizens, is a necessary nightmare.

It is often assumed that in other societies infanticide and exposure have been practised. This assumption reflects modern values better than it matches historical evidence: palaeopathology shows that there were nomadic groups in prehistory who transported with them people who had severe and multiple congenitally disabling conditions (including intellectual ones) which our own society lacks the ability to cope with. Selection for inclusion entails certain rituals. The Athenian Greeks practised a ceremony five days after birth called amphidromia, in which the father ran round the hearth with the new-born baby after a discussion with the midwife as to whether or not the infant looked fit to be reared within the family. The medieval church acted as arbiter of community or species membership in its function of deciding whether or not an infant was human enough to risk its being baptised. The major preoccupation here was with anatomy and physical appearance, though both the Talmudists and Lutherans extend this to all kinds of unusual difference (Luther thought that 'changelings' were possessed by the devil and should be drowned).

The significant shift that occurred in the late seventeenth century came to inform the rituals of our current institutions. The texts on this subject of the physician and philosopher John Locke are symptomatic and influential. He criticised the influence of neo-Aristotelian theologians on species definition, especially that of humans. According to Locke, we are not capable of knowing objectively 'real' species boundaries; for us (if not for God) distinct species exist merely to the extent that we have distinct ideas of and names for them. So there was no need for agonising at the time of baptism, is it 'really' human or is it beast? The infant of dubious physical appearance, the anatomical 'monster', has enough morphological distinctiveness to form a species on its own – all that is needed, all that is possible, is for intelligent people to assent to this and to a name for the species. Moreover, defining an infant's species membership by its outward physical appearance missed out what was, for all those interested in the differences between humans and other animals, a more important possibility. Why not hypothesise a species whose physical appearance was indistinguishable from that of humans but whose intellectual capacities might be different, less, or non-existent – in short, an *intellectual* monster?

Such a species already had an agreed species name, the changeling or idiot of the kind currently being discussed by Willis. It is no accident that his account occurs in a work about the reasoning powers of animals; he already understands the question of idiocy in a comparative sense. But his explanation of its causes owes much to the materialist anti-Aristotelianism of earlier in the century. For Locke, the distinguishing marks of the sub-species were not to be sought in physiological causes which he was sure could not be verified experimentally. The difference lay in the efficiency with which its members sorted 'ideas'. The act of comparing or putting together ideas has resonances of the cognitive 'matching' model of sense impressions resuscitated by Gassendi; it is transferred by Locke to a purely mental realm in which ideas are not the end-result of some hypothetically material process but are 'objects of understanding'. He introduces the Hippocratic fast/slow criterion of intellectual pathology into the realm of pure ideas, conjoining it with the standard neo-Aristotelian faculty psychology of the time, which compartmentalised intellectual abilities and ranked them in a hierarchical order. However, Locke's version of intellectual ability in general, or 'natural reason', features not just as evidence in the natural or visible world of God's own reason, as it had in the Aristotelian tradition, but also as the responsibility of the individual species-member who possesses it. To the extent that reason was at least partly non-divine and therefore not necessarily unitary, it enabled him to envisage discrete kinds of *non*-reason and thus discrete kinds or sub-kinds of human such as the idiot definable purely in these terms. The route towards classification and exclusion by psychological criteria is open. The mad, according to Locke, had not 'lost' the faculty of reasoning at all; they have ideas, but they join them together wrongly or too quickly and so make wrong propositions. The idiot, however, scarcely puts ideas together or 'reasons' at all: 'The defect . . . seems to proceed from want of quickness, activity, and motion, in the intellectual faculties. . . . [They] cannot distinguish, compare and abstract'.

It is from the incapacity for 'abstract' thinking that the modern idiot classification flows. Anyone familiar with modern textbook descriptions and clinical assessments of individuals with learning difficulties can testify to the ubiquitous ritual currency of 'ability to generalise/think abstractly' as a condition for social inclusion and species membership. Though quite meaningless, it certainly demonstrates the debt that developmental and educational psychology, presiding gloomily over the permutation of modern discourses about the abilities of the mentally handicapped, claim to owe more or less directly to Locke. But he himself meant something very precise indeed by 'abstraction'. It is the ability to *sort*, by finding the most useful way of naming and classifying species which all intelligent people would assent to; the idiot is incapable of abstraction and is thus by definition incapable of sorting the distinct ideas that correspond to species. That is why the idiot is not a species member. In this circular definition of what it is to be human, idiots are implicitly penned away with non-human animals; when he wants to define the specific difference between humans and other animals, he coins the famous dictum, 'Brutes abstract not'.

The inspiration for this description of idiocy appears fleetingly in the daily notebooks Locke kept as a practising physician; only later is it expounded in wider philosophical terms. However, the textual history begs the question, *why* would Locke or someone like him, in that time and place, be more anxious about idiots than about monsters? Fluctuating optimism about human reason did not sit easily with his espousal of toleration and liberty. Individual differences among humans in respect of their 'natural reason' did not matter as long as it was considered merely as a way in which an invisible God revealed himself and His own reason to the world, since *His* reason was unique. But to the extent that this picture began to admit a human reason that was grounded in an aggregate of human individuals, and a multiplicity of potentially competing wills, then this set a greater value on the problematic of a unitary secular reason here on earth and of humans being able to agree and assent to it. The individual who is incurably incapable of assent and who (unlike the mad person) is incapable even of the 'faculties' that are its prerequisite, is thus not the discovery or invention of a psychological type by a great physician-philosopher; rather, idiocy is the area lying beyond the precise line within which 'man' and the human have been circumscribed, with clauses stipulating what it means to be a believer and a citizen. Idiocy in this sense and the nascent social order are a monozygous development.

It seems as if the very emergence of a concept of the human ('concept of man') inevitably depends upon its boundaries being drawn short. In the century following they are increasingly defined by intellectual competence. But in fact the necessary compatibility between a concept of man and a practice of exclusion is not merely a modern phenomenon. The only ancient school of thought with something like a concept of the human, the Stoics, also made an especially intense demarcation between understanding and ignorance, and simply made all ignorance coterminous with insanity; Roman law has fairly detailed clauses on mental incompetence and the management and inheritance of property which reflect this position. It is not surprising that conversely some otherwise less 'human' conceptual traditions display a relaxed and non-discriminatory attitude to species membership where human unreason is concerned. This is the position of Aristotle himself (regardless of what neo-Aristotelians and other commentators have claimed he actually said). It is also true of those medieval theologians who continue to find ways of arguing for the inclusion of *lethargia* and other non-reasoning mental states or individuals within their definition of the species 'rational animal'. This is not for them an ivory-tower question. Here too there is exclusion intimating a kind of *social* exclusion, but it is administered instead to heretics and ideological rivals, the principle being the same: we exclude those whose intellectual difficulties are, as we think, severer than ours and threatening to our own reason. We owe the word 'fool' to the Latin term for a bellows, an intellectual opponent who is full of air – a windbag; 'dunce' to the philosopher Duns Scotus in his obsolescence; etc. In the mid-seventeenth century Descartes was still using the principle that even idiots have souls (that is to say are reasoners, not automata) to justify the intensity of the species differences between humans and other animals: it is true of the person with a 'captive mind' and even 'the stupidest children or the child with a diseased brain'. This is in diametric contrast to Locke's use of the argument about animals. Descartes's contemporary, Thomas Hobbes, not only denied the customary Renaissance notion of lumping the uneducated among the brutes, he also took pains to insist on the common humanity of people who were constitutionally incapable of learning or society; but he also displays the beginnings of a dilemma, disapplying his 'common humanity' argument precisely when he needs to be more specific about the ability to enter into contract in the context of contemporary political and juridical relationships.

Space does not permit us to examine how specific social practices and psychological theories in the early modern period are imbricated so as to form an exclusion of sub- or questionably human types. In the eighteenth century there are two ways of approaching idiocy theoretically that run alongside each other. One tradition sees it primarily as a purely mental state demanding classification (like the various types of madness) by analogy with the nosology of bodily diseases. Another develops a materialist psychology of idiocy, couched in more narrowly medical terms of hypothetical explanations about the workings of the 'nerves'; this starts out from Gassendi and is particularly strong in France, although it includes Willis and the English psychologist David Hartley. The two traditions are not incompatible, and in fact it becomes possible to discuss idiocy in terms of both. In both cases, it is the very device of psychological description that tightens the screws of exclusion on the concept of 'man'. Where Locke, as he lays bare the context of social anxiety, is merely exploring possibilities and still emphasising the ideas more than the human types who embody them, the emergent practices of psychology start to take social exclusion tacitly for granted: the demands and abilities of a new kind of citizenship are already sealed within them.

In this process, certain philosophical and medical arguments become re-entwined. The essence of the human and the nature of the human had previously tended to be part of separate discussions. 'Essence' and (non-)membership of species were problems for logic and metaphysics; in theory at least, any example would do to illustrate problems of classification whether it be reasoners and non-reasoners, real gold and fool's gold, black and albino crows, etc. The 'nature' of any creature, however, was discussed in terms of its creation by God and, gradually, of a biological notion of creation, without as yet any classificatory implications for borderline cases: exceptions do not seriously test the rule. But the distinction between essence and nature tended eventually to become lost, and sciences such as medicine increasingly adopted the quasi-*logical* taxonomy of *natural* items, including human ones, that we take for granted today. Indeed, the psychological classification of individuals is an edifice built with medieval logic as its scaffolding, not to mention assorted late-classical bricks such as memory, attention, etc. Just as Ray and Linnaeus produced plant and animal taxonomies, so by the end of the eighteenth century psychiatric theory was beginning to spawn taxonomies of intellectual pathology. These were displayed in nosological format alongside diseases of the body, in Britain by physicians such as William Cullen, and later Sir Alexander Crichton and (my personal favourite) John Good, for whom our type of intellectual difference comes under Class 4 (Neurotica), Order 1 (Phrenica), Genus 6 (Moria or Fatuity), Species 2 (Moria demens), Variety 3 (Anoea or Idiotism). The detailed description of this state still depended largely on criteria derived from faculty psychology, though the compartmentalised capabilities (perception, memory, judgement etc.) are constantly subject to a wayward process of re-assortment, as they had been from the time of their source in Aristotle's *On the Soul*.

More importantly for the social role of idiots, in this heady brew of philosophy and theoretical medicine there was also a general undercurrent of the age, a burgeoning sense of nature as progression over time. Out of the old concept of the cosmos as a kind of spatial structure, in which humans ranked 'below' the angels and 'above' the other animals on a vertical axis, there was beginning to emerge the outline of an evolutionary or horizontal axis, on which humans came 'after' the brutes and 'before' the saintly or intellectual perfection that was their destiny and goal. Identifying any condition that might be perceived to contradict this teleological picture of human intellect therefore became gradually more urgent. Eventually the existence of such conditions would come to be seen as a hindrance to progress, and liquidation would appear on the agenda of mid-nineteenth century scientific 'ablism' (of which the contemporary scientific 'racism' was merely one aspect). In the previous century, the early development of this outlook was bound up with the 'Argument from Design' for the existence of God. Diderot cites idiocy as a way of refuting the argument that the intelligent-seeming design of the universe indicates the existence of a creator who had patterned it with an end in view for humans. A century later Charles Darwin, struggling against the overwhelming implications of a non-teleological evolutionary theory for his own faith (grounded, as for most Victorian theologians, in the Argument from Design), came to question the existence of an intelligent and omnipotent designer of the universe on the specific grounds that if He existed, idiots would not.

The optimistic obverse to these anxieties about progress was that they provided a motive to educate the idiot if at all possible. Earlier suggestions of this had been few. Willis thought that the only mentally handicapping condition that might be curable was *lethargia*, which by his time usually indicated the results of encephalitis. Locke encountered one such child in his medical practice, and his so-called theory of education owes much to this case (Gorn, 1967); nevertheless, an optimist in all other respects concerning the development of children, Locke simply remains nonplussed and disturbed by it. The first flush of enthusiasm for educating does not begin until the generation that learned its optimism from the seminal French physician Philippe Pinel, particularly in the post-revolutionary societies of France and the USA. The movement was led in France by Itard (the alleged educator of the 'wild boy of Aveyron') and Esquirol, and in the USA by Samuel Gridley Howe, who studied in France and later brought Eduard Séguin, Itard's protégé and a founder of institutional 'special' education, to the new world. By the second half of the nineteenth century the optimism is already waning considerably, and today the educational prognosis given by clinicians for mentally handicapping conditions remains conventionally very pessimistic, even though it is regularly contradicted by the pedagogic experiences of teachers, therapists and parents.

III

Let us finish by mentioning the early history of the over-riding urge that drives modern clinical research: the scientific detection of idiocy based on empirical investigation of the body, with the physician as Sherlock Holmes. Its early development is piecemeal. Medical science could not discover the aetiologies until it had invented the classification. Madness was always a disease with physiological explanations as long as Galenism held sway, but the idiot classification in a recognizably modern sense arrived only as Galenism was disappearing. Willis had used cerebral anatomy to try to explain intellectual disabilities, including the 'stupidity' and 'foolishness' of changelings, and he sought to establish empirical evidence and an iconography for differences in brain structure. On the whole, the physical correlates of early idiocy had been sought, if at all (and that was very rarely), in morphology. In comparison with physically congenitally disabled people (such as the anatomically 'monstrous'), idiots fared relatively well by the scale of values of Renaissance natural philosophy, which held anatomy rather than psychology to be the evidence for God's intelligence in designing humans. Paracelsus associated the intellectual difficulties of 'cretins' not just with their facial features but with a malfunctioning thyroid, but he was something of an exception. The fifteenth-century physician John Metham noted that rounded ears, excessively narrow nasàl passages and tapering shoulders (all characteristic of trisomy-21) signified foolishness and 'a man dysposyd to no kunnyng' – this in a work, *The Days of the Moon*, conventionally offering astrology as its explanatory framework. Epicanthic folds around the eyes and a large gap between the first and second toes are characteristic of the same condition: we see them depicted in the infant Jesus at the same period by the painter Andrea Mantegna. Ironically, Mantegna is an important precursor of the tradition of characterological draughtsmanship that Lavater in the late eighteenth century was to use negatively in his attempt to establish a taxonomy of relationships between physical appearance and mental pathology. Before Lavater's iconography of mental 'imbecility' appeared, physiognomic associations between mental states and morphology are sparse and rarely aimed at anything recognizable as idiocy.

If the early history of inferring idiocy from physiological signs is patchy, it is because there is no unified social practice to steer its development. As late as the start of the nineteenth century, phrenologists such as Spurzheim conceded that there could be no hard and fast demarcation between idiots and, as it were, real humans simply by the criterion of bumps on the skull *or* of differing intellectual capabilities, because sometimes they looked or performed differently but sometimes they did not. In the last resort, to be an idiot was not yet *necessarily* a bad thing. Later developments in empirically based and physiologically oriented knowledge, combined with new technologies which come with exclusion already imprinted within them, have dictated otherwise.

REFERENCES

Aretaeus (1856) *The Extant Works of Aretaeus the Cappadocian* (ed. Francis Adams), London, The Sydenham Society.

Aristotle (1936) 'On Memory and Recollection' (translated by W.S. Hett). In *The Loeb Classical Library: Aristotle VIII*, London, Heinemann, p.295.

Binet, Alfred (1912) *L'Année Psychologique* XVIII, Paris, Beaunis.

Burt, Cyril (1925) *Mental and Scholastic Tests*, London, LCC Education Committee.

Crichton, Alexander (1798) *Inquiry into the Nature and Origin of Mental Derangement*, London, T. Cadell.

Cullen, William (1769) *Synopsis Nosologiae Methodicae*, Edinburgh, W. Creech.

Darwin, Charles (1986) 'Letter to Asa Gray'. In *Culture and Society in Britain 1850–1890*, (ed. J.M. Golby), Oxford, Oxford University Press, p.46.

Descartes, René (1913) 'Letter to Henry More, 5 February 1649'. In *Oeuvres Complètes* V (ed. Ch. Adam & P. Tannery), Paris, Ministère de l'Instruction publique.

Descartes, René (1925) *Discours de la méthode. Texte et commentaire* (ed. Étienne Gilson). Paris, Vrin, p.96.

Diderot, Denis (1966) 'D'Alembert's Dream'. In *Rameau's Nephew and D'Alembert's Dream* (translated by L. Tancock), Harmondsworth, Penquin.

Empedocles (1917). In Theophrastus, *De sensu* 11. Translated as *Theophrastus and the Greek Physiological Psychology before Aristotle* by G.M. Stratton, London, Allen and Unwin, p.83.

Good, John (1822) *The Study of Medicine*, London.

Gorn, Janice L. (1967) 'The strange "case" of Edward Clarke, Jr.: attending physician – John Locke, Gent'. In *Educational Theory* 17/4.

Hancock, W.N. et al (1865) *Ancient Laws of Ireland*, Dublin.

Hartley, David (1749) *Observations on Man*, London, J. Johnson.

Hippocrates (1931) On Regimen I.35 (translated by W.H.S. Jones). In *The Loeb Classical Library: Hippocrates IV*, London, Heinemann, p.281 ff.

Hobbes, Thomas (1983) *De cive. The Latin Version* (ed. Howard Warrender), Oxford, Oxford University Press.

Howe, Samuel Gridley (1858) *On the Causes of Idiocy*, Boston, Massachusetts Commission on Lunacy.

Lavater, Johann Caspar (1789) *Physiognomy* III.xxxvi.186 (translated by Thomas Holcroft), London, G.G.J. and J. Robinson.

Locke, John (1975) *An Essay concerning Human Understanding* (ed. Peter Nidditch), Oxford, Clarendon Press.

Metham, John (1916) *The Works of John Metham* (ed. Hardin Craig), London, Early English Text Society.

Neugebauer, Richard (1978) 'Treatment of the mentally ill in medieval and early modern England'. In *Journal for the History of the Behavioural Sciences*, 14, p.158 ff.

Plato (1921) 'Theaetetus' (translated by H.N. Fowler). In *The Loeb Classical Library: Plato VII*, London, Heinemann, p.197.

Soranus (1956) *Gynaecology* (translated by O. Temkin), Baltimore, Johns Hopkins Press.

Spurzheim, Johann Caspar (1825) *Phrenology*, London, Treuttel, Wurtz and Richter.

Willis, Thomas (1672) *De anima brutorum*, Oxford, R. Davis. Translated (1683) as *Two Discourses concerning the Soul of Brutes*, by Samuel Pordage, London, Thomas Dring.

Chapter 9
Mental Retardation

Social Section – Part II
DEBORAH THOM

The need to identify, educate and control the mentally handicapped was seen as more pressing in both Europe and the USA as urbanisation, literacy and a cash economy developed at the end of the eighteenth century. Ideas of a human nature implicit in the work of Rousseau and other Enlightenment thinkers included ideas of perfectibility to be found in the thinkers on the new philosophy like Condorcet, who argued that to assume an innate character, given by biology to a person or type was to 'make nature herself an accomplice in the crime of political inequality'. Changes in philosophy and education which affected few children like the work of Seguin and his mentor Itard, lead to the belief that all children were educable. They believed, following Locke, that learning could be impressed on the empty brain of a child rendered idiot through absence of human company, and thus most in need of filling. This belief in sensory training was to be characteristic of programmes of education for those classified as idiots. These programmes remained at the level of the body, unlike the other disciplines of the soul imposed upon the criminal and the insane. The idiot was to be encouraged by stimulus of the senses and the development of instinctual learning to be trained to work as a way of rendering him (and it usually is him) social.

The eradication of idiocy was not a widespread demand until the upheaval of European revolutions, the 1830s and 1840s. It is this period when the need to define, classify and not to treat but to control by creating a specialised institution begins to affect the general provision for idiots in the creation of philanthropic or state controlled asylums for the mentally handicapped. Such institutions were set up in the 1840s in most of the Protestant countries of Europe, after originating in Catholic France. In the United States the writings of Itard and Seguin were speedily translated. The creation of a relevant institution expanded the number of potential inhabitants for it, while raising the question of who they should be.

The act of segregating idiots, aments or the feebleminded – as they were variously called – thus predated the worst excesses of hereditarian argument on the aetiology of mental handicap. Cesare Lombroso asserted that various combinations of specific oddities in parts of the face indicated, by manifesting 'the stigma of degeneration', the presence of decline in the population as a whole being shown in the faces of degenerates (Lombroso, 1911). Mental handicap was assumed to be observable to the informed in both the face and demeanour of the handicapped. Such an observation indicated a trend in populations in general to deteriorate if inferior qualities were allowed to reproduce unchecked. Added to this way of describing a population was the concept of race. Race was believed to exist genetically and was assumed to reflect an ordered hierarchy in which the civilised races, busy conquering the more 'backward' were like superior people in the hierarchy of individuals. In part this reflected the expansion of Empire and its Christian justifications. Some writers attributed various forms of handicap to the tendency of phylogeny to recapitulate ontogeny, that is that the handicapped manifest characteristics of inferior non-European races to which they are degenerating – the most notable example of this argument being the description of trisomy 21 as mongolism by the association between the condition and 'mongoloid' racial characteristics such as the fold in the eyelid.

When Langdon Down wrote his influential paper, 'Observations on the ethnic classification of idiots' he was able to argue comfortably that the characteristics of other inferior races were to be found in those who could not function adequately as he saw it in the white Anglo-Saxon world which he inhabited. At the same time others more interested in the concept of 'mental ability' began to investigate whether there was such a thing as intellectual ability, intelligence or genius. They also looked to populations. Mackenzie has described how the development of population statistics was motivated by an anxiety about the condition of a population feared to be in decline because of differential ability and differential fertility (Mackenzie, 1981). Galton advanced the notion that certain characteristics of mind were distributed in a Gaussian curve, as Quetelet had demonstrated they were for the body (Quetelet, 1846). But he attacked the assumption of many of his contemporaries, particularly Lombroso, that the 'problem people', or deviants from the norm, were a distinct type to be observed – he took some composite pictures of criminals to see if the generic face was visibly distorted and concluded that on the contrary the composite thus created was a noble and dignified collective face (Galton, 1869). Galton's life has been described as one devoted to measurement and certainly his contribution lay as much with this concept of a continuum as in the hereditarianism he also refined and extended. His substitution of a continuous curve of ability for a notion of a type of the disabled simply refined concepts of treatment and custody: it did not attack them.

In order to understand the actions of states and professional groups which are the bodies most responsible for developing and refining the discourse of mental ability and disability, we need also to think about the language of 'common-sense' or everyday discourse. It is quite clear that the word idiot was acceptable in a non-technical sense to most Britons in the nineteenth century – Karl Marx used it to describe the incapacity of rural workers to unite and act to change their conditions. The concept of idiocy became a stigma when it was used as a technical term to isolate, to identify the non-productive or those who disturbed the peace of a working day. (Although earlier idiots had been separated from lunatics in the Idiots Act of 1866, designed to keep idiots from lunatic asylums.) When both handicap and criminality were lumped together under the notion of degeneracy as they were in the very different systems of mensuration of Lombroso, Broca and Galton the problem of being labelled an idiot became more than merely technical for those so-called defectives. Idiots were to be locked up, to have the general extension of civil rights characteristic of advanced industrial societies denied them and in particular denied the right to reproduce. It is questionable how many of the real disadvantages consequent upon being labelled an idiot, a moron, a cretin, an ament or a debile were felt by people before legal distinction was made on the basis of notions of responsibility, how much was a consequence not of the denial of legal status, but of the denial of reproduction inherent in the discussions about sex so characteristic of nineteenth century discussions of social problems. The confusion between the biological and the mental is never greater than it is in the discussions on mental handicap.

Doctors began to formulate their own technical explanations of mental handicap at a time of great anxiety about the impact of degeneration on the health of future generations, particularly as seen in the stunted physique and educational difficulties of large numbers of children in increasingly extensive school systems. G.E. Shuttleworth published his first summary manual on *Mentally Deficient Schoolchildren* to communicate to his profession the experience of 25 years in two Training Institutions for Imbeciles and to support, explicitly, the programme of Seguin for the 'physiological education of the senses' (Shuttleworth, 1895). This book, which was into its fifth edition by 1921, was intended to demonstrate the primacy of medicine in assessing and treating cases of mental defect. By the time this fifth edition appeared there were two Mental Deficiency acts in the United Kingdom and the United States, many special schools for children classified as ineducable and a few specialist medical officers with claims to be able to identify mental handicap and procedures for treating the condition. There was also a new professional group with an interest in the mentally handicapped, the psychologists.

Once again with psychologists, as with doctors, therapy and measurement followed on from the ideas of diagnosis and etiology not, as is often argued, the other way around. A doctor, Francis Warner, had been able to assess children for the London School Board by what he claimed were visible signs of ineducability (Warner, 1888). Alfred Binet was asked by the French government to find a means of diagnosing children who were failing in the education system, and he developed the battery of test questions which related children to their chronological peers by establishing a mental age as a measure of the degrees by which a child was behind the average. However Binet's notion of mental age was not intended to be seen as a quality independent of the act of measurement, 'We have nothing to do with either his past history or his future; consequently we shall neglect his etiology' (Binet, 1905 cit Gould, 1981) and the conclusion of his programme was to develop an educational means of training this sort of untrained mind. In 1908 he wrote of the child who was behind, 'he needs to be exercised in mental orthopedics, in other words he needs to learn how to learn'. Binet's work reveals the twin concerns of those who discussed mental handicap – he argued that it could be measured but he also argued that it could be cured, in that such children could be helped; and in this respect he differed from those of his contemporaries and successors who took the concept of measurable intelligence and allied it with theories of degeneration and the assumption that this measurable quality was a permanent thing, innate in the individual. In 1908, the German psychologist Stern took the concept mental age, which became decreasingly useful as children aged, and turned it into a ratio – the intelligence quotient. Thus the two years difference in mental age between a two-year old and a four-year old was seen as greatly more significant than that between fourteen and sixteen. It also tied the measurement into the assumption of normal distribution of intelligence in the population. The concept of IQ entered popular discourse much later but it was well in place among professionals by the outbreak of European war in 1914. It was to become an acceptable part of public policy through its use by the United States military in processing conscript soldiers in 1917 when the US entered the war. None of the European armies used the concept, although the various laws already in place exempted all men from conscription if defined as defective.

The assumption of the heritability of intelligence, the association of mental 'defect' with large families and anxieties over the state of Imperial populations meant that concern over mental deficiency was to lead to legislation in both Britain and the USA and to the creation of specialised institutions for the care of the 'mentally defective'. The definition in the British mental deficiency legislation was a catch-all one indicating the circular nature of most such definitions: the people defined as defective were those defined as in need of care in an institution for the defective. This was explicitly stated in the description of the 'moral defective', which was the fourth category of mental defective under the act alongside idiots, 'who cannot guard themselves against common dangers'; imbeciles, 'incapable of managing their own affairs'; and the feeble minded whose defect was less severe but who, 'require care, supervision and control for their own protection or the protection of others'; the moral defectives were classified as permanently defective 'coupled with strong vicious or criminal propensities on which punishment has had little or no deterrent effect'. Neither this legislation nor most of the sterilisation laws of those states which had them in fact included any sum of measured intelligence as the defining feature of the mental defective (Kevles, 1986).

The governmental body in the U.K. responsible for these unfortunates was called the Board of Control. It was both control of their fertility and control of their behaviour that the institutions were meant to provide. As far as can be seen they did not offer a programme of constructive mental exercise so much as the maintenance of life in the institution. Certification as defective resulted in a sentence for life in that any release into the community was always on license and permission had to be sought, and annually renewed, for work, travel and, most contentious of all, for marriage. Local authorities supervised the admission of children into mental deficiency institutions and their custody as legal guardians was maintained by committee. The crucial officer in this process was the School Medical Officer who was, as certificating officer, responsible for the assessment and classification of children as part of the regular scheme of examination of all children at seven and upon report by parents or other people before the age of seven. Thus was placed upon a doctor's expertise the assumption that a child could be defined in this way by mental capacity for life. The Chief Medical Officer at the Board of Control and the Board of Education were at this time one and the same and, as Sutherland has shown (Sutherland, 1984), the development of a mass primary school system in Britain after 1880 had as much to do with this process as the professional claims of medicine. The theory of mental defect, offering as it did little hope for change and certainly none for cure, was of course one of the reasons for this. Doctors were encouraged by the Board's recommendation to use Binet-Simon tests but this was not enforced; in 1913, for example, the Chief Medical Officer argued, 'The Binet tests which are recommended in the Board's schedule, are, it should be remembered, tentative, and not yet standardised for English use'. Shuttleworth argued in 1921 that they were still resting 'upon a more or less empirical basis' but pointed out that they had been used for this purpose in Belgium, France, Denmark, Germany and the United States. There is clear evidence of a culture of testing for mental deficiency which spread across Europe despite Binet's explicit arguments that the purpose of diagnosis was to take remedial action based upon the individual's specific difficulties. In general, though, the institutionalisation of mental defectives preceded the development of standardised testing systems in other countries as in Britain.

World recession affected the treatment and care of 'defectives' in the years between the wars. A stronger eugenics influenced European and American governments and professionals in which the aim of eliminating the 'unfit' dominated over the aim of improving the 'fit'. In the United States twenty seven states had passed a law encouraging the sterilisation of the mentally defective by 1928. In Britain the Wood Committee and the Brock Committee discussed introducing similar legislation in Britain but, although some such operations were carried out, it was discounted after a discussion in Parliament which affirmed the civil liberties of the handicapped and the absence of any firm definition of mental defect upon which such a policy could be based. In Britain this debate sparked off a profound interest in the nature and delineations of mental handicap, in particular through the work of Lionel Penrose, who was the medical officer of the 2,000 person Colchester institution. He studied the inmates of this vast hospital and concluded in his 1938 report to the Medical Research Council (who had funded the study) that the number of cases of mental defect whose parents were themselves defective was greatly outnumbered by those who were not. In *The Biology of Mental Defect* (Penrose, 1948, revised 1954) he argued against any measure which presupposed the accuracy of intelligence quotients, 'It is absurd and unfair to apply an all-or-none measure to a continuous distribution, like that of intelligence'. In Denmark abortion and sterilisation had been introduced but remained voluntary and the take-up was slight; while in the United States some 15,000 men and 8,000 women had been so sterilised. The 1933 National Socialist policy of sterilisation of the mentally defective was by no means unique, although the policy of murdering the mentally defective was. Discussions on such a policy had been carried on in the USA but were decisively rebuffed by Kanner in 1942 (Kanner).

The twentieth century then sees the spread of legislation and institutions which accept an assumption of ineducability, which in some cases will attempt also to prevent the spread of mental defect by not just segregating but also sterilising. In the 1920s and 1930s the belief in the heritability of intelligence was at its most widespread and engendered the most punitive policies towards the 2–4 per cent of the population defined as defective. Voluntary organisations developed which campaigned for the welfare of the feeble-minded and the sophistication of accounts of etiology. Burt reversed Binet's disclaimer of a test demonstrating anything about past or future when he described the psychologist's special scientific method as enacted in the psychological clinic as being no less than a survey of the past (primarily genealogy but also life history and family profile), the present (meaning both social circumstances in home and school and the clinical encounter) and future, which was the information gathered from tests, which identified potential as well as achievement, and the knowledge of unconscious dynamics of dreams and drawings (Burt, 1925).

Potts has argued that doctors were responsible for the establishment of a disease model of handicap and a 'fusion of clinical and social judgments' (Potts, 1983). Psychologists were perhaps as responsible for the reification of an artefact, the placing a child along a Gaussian curve in relation to its peers, and turning it into a diagnosis, a low IQ. But both were responding to a more general understanding that this group, however defined, presented a single problem to the rest of the community. Yet a large number of the inhabitants of institutions in the inter-war years were there because of the epidemic of encephalitis lethargica of 1919–1922. These sufferers of a disease had suffered the consequence of behavioural disorder and falls in measured intelligence, averaging 16 points of IQ and therefore representing some quite major losses of points scored in tests. Yet their care and treatment appears to have differed little from those segregated as 'defective' for having a baby under age or simply out of wedlock, or those who had some of the conditions in which defect was visible – Down's syndrome, microcephaly, cretinism, idiopathic epilepsy with epiloia. The assumptions were thus increasingly administrative ones – that segregation was desirable and that that was the fundamental treatment of the problem – not treatment of the individual.

The inter-war period had seen direct state intervention to eradicate mental handicap by eradicating the mentally handicapped in Germany, Poland and Austria. In other European states there was intense anxiety about the declining fertility of the majority and the large families of the very poor which lead to fears of the declining birth-rate lowering the 'national intelligence'. The most extreme version of this case in the U.K. was argued by R.B. Cattell when he commented that the current trend was towards a 'race of sub-men' (Cattell, 1937). The model of hereditary transmission was crude and not universally accepted but there was enough anxiety to encourage the formation of the Royal Commission on the Population in 1943. A sub-section of their report recorded the views of psychologists that a decline in intelligence was possible but not inevitable when the upturn in the birth-rate made such discussion seem redundant. Investigation in Scotland demonstrated that the national intelligence had not declined, but risen (Mackintosh, 1947). Mental deficiency was increasingly categorised along with other attributes of the 'social problem group' who were seen as responsible for prostitution, crime, alcoholism and degeneracy by way of their high fertility – but the effect on the treatment, in custody, of those so defined was unaffected by these debates. Incidence varied across the country not just with the availability of institutional care but with the tolerance of the local community.

Post war provision for the mentally handicapped, as they were increasingly known, was affected by disputes within genetics and education. European societies reconstructing welfare systems focussed on children and nearly all children became the subject of compulsory medical inspection on entry to school, which resulted in institutional segregation for those defined as handicapped. Socialist societies had particular problems with this group if they followed the Stalinist scientific community line on the inheritance of acquired characteristics all the way – since all human beings were therefore educable and segregation minimised the chances of collaborative educational work. Stalin's 1936 decree on pedology had condemned psychometry as a deviation and psychologists were discouraged from practicing measurement. However the incarceration of the handicapped continued despite the change of philosophy and professional practice, since it remained associated with mental hospital models of treatment. These discussions were mediated in Western Europe by their association with psychologists who worked on the theories of Luria and other ideas of the acquisition of humanity through the acquisition of language. In the 1950s discussion over genetics and the occasional case of 'wild' children was muted but in the late 1960s the question of the heritability of IQ reemerged in association with race in Jensen's critique of compensatory education programmes in the USA (Jensen, 1969). The Clarkes, who had collaborated on successive versions of a book called *Mental Deficiency, the Changing Outlook* in the UK were leading figures in discussions about the psychology of individual difference and subsequent discussions about custodial care, summed up the problems that were created by the examination of incidence and treatment in the 1954–1957 Royal Commission on the Law relating to Mental Illness and Mental Deficiency which suggested that defect and idiot would no longer be used, and would be replaced by the concept of subnormality. The Clarkes referred severely to the 'ludicrous over-simplification' of the discussions of before the First World War; less severely they criticised the 1957 report for assuming any correlation between character and low intelligence (Clarke, 1958, p.17). They were especially critical of the association between subnormality and psychopathy. Yet the 1957 Act which followed the commission was to include for the first time an IQ score as a component of the assessment which would lead to classification as defective; in 1954 the World Health Organisation similarly insisted that the score should be a part of, but not the sole, classification of deficiency while including Tredgold's notions of social competence.

Late 20th century discussions have begun to move away from segregation and control into notions of community care. Education has begun to extend lower down the scales of measured IQ. Abortion and birth control have affected both the number of children women have and the incidence of certain detectable genetic conditions which include mental handicap. Debate over the balance between the interests of individuals and society remains open in democracies – as does the question of resources to be allocated to this group.

REFERENCES

Binet, A. (1905) 'The development of intelligence in children'. *L'Annee Psychologique*, vol. xii, pp.191–248. Trans. 1916, Kite, E.S. *The development of intelligence in children*, Publication of the Vineland Training School, repub. 1973 New York, Arno Press.
Burt (1925) *The Young Delinquent*, London, University of London Press.

Cattell, R.B. (1937) *The Fight for Our National Intelligence*, London, P.S. King and Son.

Clarke, A.M. and Clarke A.D.B. (1958) *Mental Deficiency, the Changing Outlook*, London, Methuen.

Galton (1869) *Hereditary Genius*, London, Macmillan.

Gould, S.J. (1981) *The Mismeasure of Man*, New York, W.W. Norton.

Jensen, A. (1969) 'How much can we boost IQ and educational achievement' *Harvard Educational Review*, 33:1–123.

Kanner, L. (1942) 'Exoneration of the feeble-minded'. *American Journal of Psychiatry*, 99:17.

Kevles, D.J. (1986) *In the Name of Eugenics*, Penguin, Harmondsworth.

Langdon Down, J.H. (1887) *Mental Affections of Children and Youth*, London, J.A. Churchill.

Mackintosh, D. (1947) *The Trend of Scottish Intelligence*, London, University of London Press.

Mackenzie, D.A. (1981) *Statistics in Britain, 1865–1930*, Edinburgh, University Press.

Macnicol, J. (1989) 'Eugenics and the campaign for voluntary Sterilization between the Wars'. *Social History of Medicine*, vol. 2, no. 2, Aug., pp.147–69.

Penrose, L.S. (1954) *The Biology of Mental Defect*, London, Sidgwick and Jackson.

Potts. P. (1983) 'Medicine, Morals and Mental Deficiency: the contribution of doctors to the development of special education in England'. *Oxford Review of Education*, vol.9, no.3, pp.181–96.

Rose, N. (1989) *The Psychological Complex*, London, Routledge and Kegan Paul.

Sutherland, G. (1984) *Ability, Merit and Measurement*, Oxford, Clarendon.

Warner, F. (1888) 'A Method of Examining Children in Schools as to their Development and Brain Condition'. *British Medical Journal*, 22 Sept., pp.659–60.

PART 2
THE FUNCTIONAL PSYCHOSES

Chapter 10
Kraepelin

Clinical Section – Part I
P HOFF

INTRODUCTION

Kraepelin's psychiatry is often discussed in a rather undifferentiated way so that a number of prejudices may arise. For example, Kraepelin is sometimes regarded as a dogmatic materialist, who stands for nothing but the strong version of 'brain psychiatry' (*'Gehirnpsychiatrie'*), others only refer to his diagnostic dichotomy between 'dementia praecox' (schizophrenia) and manic-depressive illness without taking into account his basic assumptions on psychiatry as a clinical science. In this study, I want to combine a comprehensive overview over Kraepelin's understanding of psychiatric research in general with a discussion of the important clinical entities, as they were interpreted by him throughout the nine editions of his textbook of psychiatry.

BIOGRAPHICAL NOTE

Emil Kraepelin was born on the 15th of February, 1856, as the son of a music teacher and singer in Neustrelitz (Mecklenburg-Vorpommern). In his early years his brother Karl, who was eight years older than him and who later became director of the Museum for Natural History in Hamburg, encouraged Kraepelin's interest in the natural sciences and especially in botany. He studied medicine in Leipzig and Wuerzburg from 1874 until 1878. Already during his medical studies in Wuerzburg Kraepelin had been working as a guest student at the psychiatric hospital under the directorship of Franz Rinecker (1811–1883). He began his professional life working with Bernhard von Gudden (1824–1886) in 1878 at the District Mental Hospital in Munich, where he stayed until 1882. Kraepelin then moved to Leipzig, where he was a co-worker of Paul Flechsig (1847–1929) and Wilhelm Erb (1840–1921). He was promoted to university lecturer here in 1883.

In Leipzig, his personal and scientific relationship to Wilhelm Wundt (1832–1920) began, which was to later be extremely important for the further development of his concept of psychiatric research. Encouraged by Wundt, Kraepelin wrote his 'Compendium of Psychiatry' in 1883, which became the precursor of the nine editions of the 'Lehrbuch der Psychiatrie' ('Textbook of Psychiatry'), published between 1883 and 1927. Kraepelin stayed in contact with Wundt until Wundt's death in 1920 by visiting him several times and by correspondence. In many of his publications he emphasized and acknowledged the importance of this relationship for himself.

In 1884 Kraepelin married Ina Schwabe. After a short period of employment in Leubus (Silesia) and Dresden, Kraepelin was appointed professor of psychiatry at the university of Dorpat (Baltic) where he stayed from 1886 until 1891. In 1891 he took over the psychiatric hospital of the university in Heidelberg in the same capacity. Here, as a second area of particular interest, as well as his experimental psychological work, Kraepelin focussed especially on clinical psychopathological research based on data about the course of illness, aiming at defining nosological boundaries. His work on this concept is often considered to be his main contribution towards psychiatry. However, Kraepelin gave impulses in many research directions: psychopharmacology and transcultural psychiatry were given scientific significance for the first time, and he also worked in the fields of forensic psychiatry, psychiatric genetics and epidemiology as well as neuropathology.

From 1903 until 1922 Kraepelin was ordinary professor of psychiatry in Munich. In 1904 he opened the new building of the psychiatric hospital of the Ludwig Maximilian-University, the main part of which is still in use nowadays. In spite of the contrary situation due to the First World War, in 1917 Kraepelin founded the 'Deutsche Forschungsanstalt fuer Psychiatrie' ('German Psychiatric Research Institute') in Munich to encourage and benefit psychiatric research as far as possible. This institution received considerable financial support from the Rockefeller Foundation and from an American banker and antiquary, James Loeb (1867–1933), whom Kraepelin had treated for some time for an affective disorder (Weber, 1991). During his time in Munich, Alois Alzheimer (1864–1915), Franz Nissl (1860–1919), Korbinian Brodmann (1868–1918), Walter Spielmeyer (1879–1935), August Paul von Wassermann (1866–1925) and Felix Plaut (1877–1940) – to mention only a few – were among his co-workers at the university hospital or the 'Forschungsanstalt'. Later – after Kraepelin's death – the 'Deutsche Forschungsanstalt' was taken over by the Max Planck-Society, being renamed 'Max-Planck-Institute for Psychiatry'.

Emil Kraepelin died, probably of pneumonia, in Munich on the 7th of October, 1926.

EMIL KRAEPELIN'S BASIC CONCEPT OF PSYCHIATRIC RESEARCH

Before discussing Kraepelin's position, two important 19th century psychiatrists have to be mentioned briefly, Griesinger and Kahlbaum.

It had definitely been Wilhelm Griesinger (1817–1868) who had marked the 'turning point' in the development of psychiatric conceptualization by postulating a thorough clinical and pathophysiological research based on the hypothesis that 'mental illness is a somatic illness of the brain'. But it must be stressed that Griesinger's theory was by no means as simple as this one statement, which is so often quoted without integrating it into its original context. Griesinger definitely held a very differentiated view on the problem of somato- and psychogenesis, although favouring the first in the case of what we would call 'endogenous psychoses' or – more modestly – 'psychoses of unknown etiology' nowadays (Griesinger, 1845; Wahrig-Schmidt, 1985; Verwey, 1985).

Another author seems to have been of even more significance for Kraepelin: Karl Ludwig Kahlbaum (1828–1899). Continuing the traditions of French psychopathology as represented for example by J. Falret and A.L.J. Bayle, Kahlbaum developed a clinically orientated research method in the second half of the 19th century in Germany, especially taking the course of illness into consideration (Lanczik, 1992). This was believed to be a victory over the speculative concept of the so-called 'romantic medicine' and even more so an argument for a critical distance to the position of the harsh and unreflected 'somaticists', who were no less dogmatic than some of the 'psychicists'. Kahlbaum's description of catatonia is a well-known example of his nosological approach, whereas his nosological system itself, employing many completely new terms, was not accepted in general and has not gained any significance for the development of 20th century psychopathology and nosology (Kahlbaum, 1863, 1874).

But – and this was going to be the most impressive part of his theory for Kraepelin – Kahlbaum clearly recognized the methodological differences between pathological-anatomical and clinical-psychopathological work. With 'progressive paralysis of the insane' as an example he explained the way he wanted to take from the syndrome-course unit to the – postulated – etiologically based disease unit. Kraepelin took up Kahlbaum's basic ideas and expanded them.

In general, any basic scientific concept necessarily rests on certain philosophical foundations. If regarding Kraepelin as a decidedly 'unphilosophical' psychiatrist, as it often happens, one might be astonished to read the following passage in his memoirs, where he describes the winter term 1874/75 at the university of Leipzig – he was 19 years of age:

> At the same time, I started learning philosophy and joined the academic-philosophical society, which was successfully headed by Avenarius at that time. I also got to know the very much older colleagues, Kehrbach, Vaihinger, Eduard Meyer and Moritz Wirth, who were members of the society. (Kraepelin, 1987, p.3)

And, as for the next year, 1876, while studying in Würzburg:

> In the summer of 1876, the state examinations seemed to be a long way off and I eagerly read the philosophical works of Kant, Hume, Locke, Berkeley, Hobbes, Schopenhauer, de la Mettrie and so on. An older friend of mine, Rieck, had to write his philosophical thesis on 'Studies on the concept of necessity', which gave me particular incentive to work on the origin of the concept of causality. (Kraepelin, 1987, p.4)

These formulations might suggest a developing interest in the questions involved; but in Kraepelin's psychiatric work we do not find thorough discussions of, for example, Kant's relevance for psychiatry, not even comments on the philosophy of Richard Avenarius (1843–1896), whom he obviously met in Leipzig and who later developed the concept of empiriocriticism. This theory was part of the positivistic and neo-Kantian movement in the second half of the 19th century with its strict opposition to metaphysics, its orientation on empirical data and – a highly typical example of 'Zeitgeist' – its profound confidence in the ideas of development and progress. All these aspects can be found in Kraepelin's writings, too, but generally in a more or less implicit manner and definitely not in a philosophical context.

On the other hand, it is nearly impossible to overestimate Wundt's influence on Kraepelin. Wundt's aim was to establish psychology as a kind of natural science which relied on experimental data. He criticized the highly speculative approach of the philosophy of nature, as, for example, developed by Schelling or Schleiermacher, but he also did not agree with materialism or with association psychology sensu Herbart (Wundt, 1880). There has been a lively controversy in the literature about whether or not Wundt directly stands in the tradition of English empiricism, as represented by J. St. Mill (1806–1873) and Herbert Spencer (1820–1903) (Arnold, 1980; Boring, 1950; Danziger, 1990; Titchener, 1921; Pauleikhoff, 1987; Schneider, 1990). The majority of recent studies deny this kind of dependency and emphasize Wundt's profound knowledge of and appreciation for the so-called German idealism, especially in the Kantian version. And indeed, Wundt's insisting on one of the central functions of 'consciousness', 'apperception', as he calls it, in part reminds of Kant's transcendental epistemology: for Wundt, apperception is the psychological function which intentionally connects sensory data and forms the personal knowledge about them. So, without this apperception, which is an active mental process, not a mere sensorial input or a simple additive association, there would – according to Wundt – be no knowledge and no science at all.

At least in his earlier writings, Wundt favored a parallelistic point of view in the mind-body-problem. And he postulated a certain kind of causality within mental life as well. But this forms a line of causality of its own and must not be mixed up or, even worse, identified with physical causality. Experimental research – and that Wundtian idea was obviously the most fascinating one for the young Kraepelin – may successfully be used in natural sciences as well as in psychology without ignoring the epistemological differences between the two fields. As a practical consequence, Wundt founded the world's first laboratory for experimental psychology in Leipzig in 1879 and Kraepelin became one of his co-workers there (see Kraepelin, 1987, pp.22ff).

In his later work, particularly when it comes to the philosophical foundation of his monumental ten-volume '*Völkerpsychologie*', Wundt broadened his views significantly: he developed a voluntaristic, not to say idealistic concept which has been criticised from a materialistic perspective as falling behind his previous views of psychology as a natural science (Arnold, 1980; Wundt, 1900–1920).

In my view, Wundt's philosophy and psychology may well be understood as a profound effort to combine Kant's critical impetus against metaphysical speculation and materialism with a kind of psychology which understood itself as an empirical, but non-reductionistic study of man. His roots in Kant's philosophy and his very specific, very personal development of classical philosophical concepts – these two aspects led to a highly complex theory which was not free of contradictions and was therefore very likely to be misinterpreted.

What did Kraepelin make out of this complex Wundtian '*Weltanschauung*'? He modified it by extracting what he regarded to be useful for the foundation of empirical research in psychiatry. That is the reason why Wundt's psychology, viewed through the 'filter' of Kraepelin's texts, seems so much more unified and straight than it really is. Kraepelin simplified and in a certain way 'smoothened' Wundt's concept, but he did not falsify it.

In general, Kraepelin adopted philosophical theories more or less implicitly. Contrary to the steadily changing clinical aspects of his nosology, he did not call into question the philosophical implications in detail once they had become an integrative part of his theory of psychiatry as a science. By doing so, Kraepelin was very likely to underestimate the implicit difficulties and contradictions within the philosophical theories themselves and – metaphorically speaking – 'imported' these problems into psychiatry (Hoff, 1992b).

Given this attitude towards philosophy, it is obvious that one has to be very cautious in simply attaching one of the common philosophical categories to Kraepelin's thinking. But, nevertheless, if looking at the basic ideas underlying his psychiatry, be they implicit or not, we have to distinguish the following four major concepts: 1. Realism; 2. Parallelism; 3. Experimental approach; 4. Naturalism. I will now discuss these points in some detail, since they all gain significance for his clinical concepts.

1. Realism

Again, there is no definitive statement by Kraepelin himself on realism as a theory. But what he wrote on science in general and on psychiatry in particular, tells us, that he – philosophically speaking – was a realist. However, one will hardly be able to philosophically qualify this kind of realism in more detail: he does not discuss the ideas of empiricism or positivism apart from just mentioning Locke and Hume – in his memoirs, not in his psychiatric writings (!) – although especially positivism gained much influence during the last decades of the 19th century. In addition, in the beginning of our century there was a broad philosophical discussion about the epistemological consequences of realism. Some of the exponents, like Oswald Külpe (1862–1915), Hans Driesch (1867–1941) and Erich Becher (1882–1929) were decidedly interested in psychology and psychiatry; two of them, Külpe and Becher, were Kraepelin's colleagues at the university of Munich. But although Kraepelin – according to the historical information available at present – did not interfere in this debate, there can be no doubt that he did believe in an independently existing 'real world', including other people and their healthy or disturbed mental processes. And when, which happens very seldom, Kraepelin declares that we have access to all objects only via consciousness, this must not be misunderstood as an idealistic or transcendental point of view. Instead, it is a typical Wundtian position, stressing the importance of mental processes in generating knowledge. These processes themselves, however, are not believed to be apriorical, as Kant had suggested, but aposteriorical and subject to empirical, particularly psychophysiological research:

> Anything is primarily existing for us as an inner experience. We call the form of these inner experiences 'consciousness'; our mental life represents the string of subsequent conscious processes. (Kraepelin, 1921, p.1, translated by P.H.)

In different places of his work Kraepelin points out, that the psychiatric researcher objectively has to describe, what really exists and what nature presents to him – the formulations differ, but the essence is a strictly realistic philosophy:

The raw material of experience, which is provided by sensory perception and clarified by attentiveness, forms the basis of all further mental acts and therefore of man's whole set of ideas. . . . The less perfectly and the more falsified our information about the external world is perceived, the more incomplete and unreliable will be the idea, developed in man's consciousness, of the external world surrounding him, of his own mind and of his mind's relation to the external world. (Kraepelin, 1899, pp.126–7, translated by P.H.)

The consequences for psychiatric nosology are evident: such a realism will lead to the concept of natural disease entities which exist completely independently from the researcher. The scientist describes what he finds – or, in a stronger formulation, he describes 'given things'. His own activity in constructing scientific hypotheses or diagnostic systems tends to be underestimated.

Kraepelin often speaks of the 'essence' of a disease process ('*das Wesen des Krankheitsvorganges*'). This might lead to the assumption, that his understanding of 'essence' is similar to Husserl's or, as an important representative of anthropological psychiatry, Ludwig Binswanger's. But this is not at all the case, since there can be no doubt about the fundamental discrepancies between Kraepelin's and Husserl's philosophical approach. Given this theoretical incompatibility, it is all the more remarkable that anthropologically oriented authors often refer to and accept the clinical relevance of Kraepelin's dichotomy of endogenous psychoses (e.g. Binswanger, 1957, 1960).

2. Parallelism

Kraepelin held the position of psychophysical parallelism. Like Wilhelm Griesinger, whom he admired for his highly critical position against speculative psychiatric theories, he disapproved of reductionistic materialism which declares mental events identical with neurophysiological processes. Kraepelin speaks about two kinds of phenomena, somatic and psychological, which are decidedly different, but closely connected:

We strictly adhere to the principle, that a regular parallelism between somatic and mental processes is existing. Without this principle, scientific psychiatry would definitely be impossible. However, it is important, always to keep in mind, that this connection is not exhaustively understood by the assumption of a simple causal relationship. (Kraepelin, 1887, pp.17–18, translated by P.H.)

Kraepelin defended the existence of mental phenomena against all kinds of what he repeatedly calls 'brain mythologies'. Some of his remarks on this issue do not lack polemic undertones, for example when he ironically criticizes

the position of naive materialism . . ., which believes that psychiatry's and psychology's work is completely done by studying the physical basis of our mental life. This position by no means only belongs to outdated epochs of our historical development; it still often underlies – more or less consciously – the ideas of our contemporary psychiatric authors. This is proven by expressions like 'moral fibre systems', 'logic of brain process', 'cortical conclusions', 'foci of emotions of innervation', 'stocks of memories' and the like. (Kraepelin, 1887, p.12, translated by P.H.)

But contrary to Wundt himself (Wundt, 1894), Kraepelin, although calling himself a parallelist, did not enter on the philosophical controversy about that concept. In particular, he did not critically differentiate between parallelism and interactionism and did not realize that any strictly defined parallelism makes it more than doubtful if mental life can still be regarded as an independent sphere and not just as standing in a 1:1 relationship with the somatic level; and that, of course, means (causal) determinism.

As a consequence of his somewhat ambigious position with regard to the mind-body-relationship, there indeed is an implicit tendency towards monism in Kraepelin's writings, particularly when considering his ideas about psychology as a natural science. But, to avoid severe misunderstandings, it should be emphasized that this 'monistic tendency' was definitely not a metaphysical one and especially not comparable with Ernst Haeckel's understanding of monism.[1] Keeping in mind his pragmatic attitude towards philosophy, one might speak of a weak version of methodological monism, insofar as he decidedly favored quantitative methods brought forward especially by the natural sciences. But, again, Kraepelin does not explicitly apply the term 'methodological monism', nor does he refer to philosophers who had thoroughly evaluated that concept, e.g. Friedrich Albert Lange (1828–1875) (Verwey, 1985). It may be assumed that it was Wundt's basical concept which prevented Kraepelin from moving even closer in the direction of the materialistic and monistic point of view. In conclusion, Kraepelin's theory of the mind-body-relationship, although called parallelistic by himself, is not free from certain ambiguities and therefore may have created more questions than it answered.

3. Experimental approach

The psychological experiment should become a major scientific tool not only for the understanding of disturbed mental processes, but also of healthy mental life – one has only to remember Kraepelin's lifelong efforts to improve his 'work curve'. Both Wundt and Kraepelin realized the difference between a physical and a psychological experiment, but the experimental design for both areas did not differ significantly. The following quotations demonstrate Kraepelin's emphasis on the experimental approach and – more generally – his scientific optimism, which is so typical for the way, many scientists in the second half of the 19th century saw themselves:

> One would be astonished, however, if suddenly any knowledge which was gained by systematical application of psychological experiments was dismissed from our science. (Kraepelin, 1920a, p.359, translated by P.H.)

In cases of psychoses occuring during imprisonment, one can – as Kraepelin argues –

> follow the development of persecutory ideas under the pressure of adverse life events with the clarity of the experiment. (Kraepelin, 1915, p.1760, translated by P.H.)

And, in an even stronger version:

> The methods developed by experimental psychology provide us with the

means to define a more precise concept of the alterations of mental life, as nature produces them by its harmful influences. (Kraepelin, 1918, p.187, translated by P.H.)

Kraepelin seems to have considered the experimental approach a kind of guarantee for the scientific status of psychiatric research. Therefore, it is obvious that he rated the experimental approach higher than mere description of clinical phenomena, although the latter method was nevertheless regarded to be indispensable, especially if combined with follow-up examinations. Introspection, however, was discussed critically, not to say suspiciously by Kraepelin, as were the theoretical and practical aspects of psychoanalysis – an important topic which cannot be further analyzed here.

In summary, Kraepelin developed and maintained a skeptical attitude towards subjective, especially biographically determined aspects of mental disorders, which could not be studied experimentally.

4. Naturalism

In his early writings – especially on forensic psychiatry – Kraepelin clearly expresses his opinion that there are no such things as apriorical ideas, freedom of the will or unchangeable moral values. Anything is depending on the time and the specific sociocultural situation in which it is used. For Kraepelin, man is nothing but a part of nature, and anything man can do, is a product of this natural existence – Kraepelin as an exponent of the evolutionary approach:

> In this context morality completely loses its absolute value, and it becomes a product of cultural and historical development; it is no longer something existing outside mankind, but is linked to the concept of human society; it is conceptualized as developed within and founded on manifold human relations. (Kraepelin, 1880, p.3, translated by P.H.)

As for the field of religion, Kraepelin even speaks of 'the idea of God, which is developing with psychological necessity' (Kraepelin, 1880, p.5, translated by P.H.).

Later in his life, Kraepelin became somewhat more cautious concerning this matter, but there is no reason to believe that he substantially changed his mind. This naturalistic, 'anti-metaphysical' point of view of course made Kraepelin feel sympathetic with Darwinistic and biologistic concepts, although – which should be stressed once more – he always declined simplified monistic theories as for example represented by Ernst Haeckel (1834–1919), Jakob Moleschott (1822–1893) and Ludwig Büchner (1824–1899). His naturalism, of course, is one of the topics where Kraepelin definitely left the platform of Wundtian psychology and philosophy, although he never discussed this fact. The controversy on whether, philosophically speaking, categories are apriorical structures or products of an evolutionary process, is still going on (Hundert, 1992; Vollmer, 1992).

The conclusion of this chapter may sound paradoxical, but especially the example of such an influential psychiatrist as Emil Kraepelin, although he was not interested in 'classical' philosophical matters, proves the significance of philosophical ideas in psychiatry.

NOSOLOGY

a. In general

Kraepelin's basic nosological assumptions are closely related to the philo-sophical concepts that have just been discussed in detail. His nosology shows a remarkable stability over time, although, on the clinical level, he did of course change the details of his diagnostic system over and over again. But, on the basic level, from the 2nd to the 9th edition of his textbook, i.e. from 1887 to 1927 (40 years!), Kraepelin does not change the central postulate, that the 'essential' features of all psychotic disorders will once be definitely classified in a 'natural' system, no matter which scientific method is applied: anatomy, etiology and symptomatology, if once developed sufficiently, will converge in the same 'natural disease entities', as illustrated by figure 1.

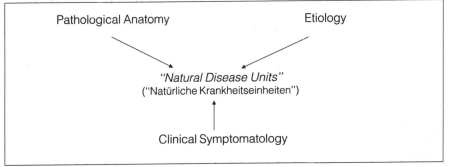

Figure 1: Basic Assumptions of Kraepelinian nosology

This very strong and optimistic hypothesis is limited to a certain extent in three of Kraepelin's most important theoretical papers, written between 1918 and 1920. They were published during the last quarter of his career, i.e. after four decades of psychiatric research: 'Ends and means of psychiatric research' (1918) ('*Ziele und Wege der psychiatrischen Forschung*'), 'Research in the manifesta-tions of mental illness' (1919) ('*Die Erforschung psychischer Krankheits-formen*') and 'Clinical manifestations of mental illness' (1920) ('*Die Erscheinungsformen des Irreseins*'). Ignoring these publications would mean to identify Kraepelin's position with the one held in the eight edition (4 vol., 1909–1915) of his textbook. And this, as I will show, is not justified.

In the above mentioned papers Kraepelin took into account contemporary arguments as for example Birnbaum's differentiation between pathogenetic and pathoplastic factors (Birnbaum, 1919) or Gaupp's hypothesis on the possibility of psychogenic delusions (Gaupp, 1920), and he did acknowledge the value of defining certain syndromes as a medium level between symptoms and disease entities. But – and this is quite typical for Kraepelin – he did not abandon his concept of underlying distinct disease entities. He admitted his methodological doubts, whether it will be possible to realize his optimistic plans as easily as he had predicted in the textbook; but Kraepelin did not have principle doubts.

The most relevant paper in the present context is 'Clinical manifestations of mental illness' ('*Die Erscheinungsformen des Irreseins*') from 1920. His theory now reads as follows: three levels have to be differentiated in psychiatric research. The first is the level of clear-cut natural disease entities, called 'disease processes' (I). They are activating what Kraepelin calls 'preformed reaction sets of the organism' (II). These 'sets' are believed to be biologically or psychologically preformed and potentially active in *any* human being, but they are not as specific as the disease entities and not as *un*specific as clinical symptoms. They show individual variation and there may be a certain amount of overlap between them, as opposed to the disease processes at the basic level.

Interestingly enough, in the 1920 paper Kraepelin does not speak of or, maybe, even avoids to speak of 'syndromes'; instead, referring to Bonhoeffer directly, he differentiates three 'registers' with altogether 10 different psychopathological manifestation types. These registers are situated 'between' level II and III. Register 1 includes – in Kraepelin's terms – the delirious, paranoid, emotional, hysterical and instinctive type of manifestation; register 2 consists of the schizophrenic and – presumably – hallucinating type with voices talking with each other, and register 3 includes the encephalopathic, oligophrenic and spasmodical type. The psychopathological phenomena on level II are not specific for the underlying disease process; there is, as Kraepelin deplores, an 'unpleasantly broad' area of overlap.

After being activated by the underlying distinct disease processes, the preformed reaction sets – via the above mentioned typical 'registers' – lead to the clinical picture (III), which in addition is influenced by so many other pathoplastic factors that it nearly completely lacks specificity as for etiology or pathogenesis.

Referring to degeneration theory, which had great, not to say dominating influence in psychiatry at that time (Hermle, 1986; Pick, 1989), Kraepelin compared mental illness with earlier stages of ontogenesis or phylogenesis and suggests a kind of 'vertical' grouping, which in a way reminds of Karl Jaspers' theory ('*Schichtenregel*'): in Kraepelin's view, the destructive power of the underlying disease process increases from register 1 to 3; furthermore, the psychopathological features of register 3 have a higher diagnostic priority, since a clearly defined organic psychosis may well be associated with features of register 1 or 2, but in a psychogenic disorder clinical phenomena of register 3 are 'regularly missing'. Furthermore, Kraepelin discusses in some detail that mental illness at least partly may be interpreted as an ontogenetic or even phylogenetic regression; consequently, he draws a parallel between mental illness and psycho(patho)logical phenomena in children, in so-called primitive cultures and even in animals.

The following scheme gives an overview:

Disease Processes (Level I)
activate
"Preformed reaction sets of the organism" (Level II)
via three typical psychopathological "registers" lead to
Clinical picture (Level III)

Figure 2: The differentiated nosological position of the later Kraepelin

In Kraepelin's view, the unspecifity of level III was the main reason for the failure of most of 19th century nosological systems. This Kraepelinian concept shows parallels to Hoche's syndrome doctrine and especially to Bonhoeffer's work, although Kraepelin himself does not discuss this coincidence (Hoche, 1912; Bonhoeffer, 1910).

It may be assumed that it was personally rather difficult for Kraepelin to accept the necessity of restricting his very optimistic earlier view. This can be shown by many formulations like 'we will have to get accustomed to the idea that . . .', 'under these circumstances we are forced to believe. . . .' But he does keep up his main thesis:

> Nevertheless, as I believe, we will have to maintain the fundamental differences between the processes of illness. (Kraepelin, 1920b, p.26, translated by P.H.)

To sum up, in his later work Kraepelin significantly altered his nosological system as for *clinical details*, he even revoked earlier concepts after new data on symptomatology and course of illness became available, and he often added new aspects to earlier descriptions – examples are melancholia, paraphrenia, paranoia. One can trace the development of these concepts through the different editions of the textbook. But on the *basic level* he maintained his hypothesis of the existence and scientific recognizability of natural disease entities in spite of many critical comments by contemporary authors.

Kraepelin's nosology is often called 'unidimensional' (e.g. by Kretschmer). If one takes into account the above mentioned papers, one must conclude that only if his orientation on distinct disease units is called unidimensional, the term is justified. But on the methodological level, the level of practical clinical research, Kraepelin did accept several 'dimensions', otherwise it would be difficult to explain his widespread influence on so many psychiatric disciplines. Therefore, in my view it is not justified to view Kraepelin only as a dogmatic nosologist, who, at the end of his career, more or less unwillingly had to give up his basic hypotheses.

As for the development of the diagnostic categories in Kraepelin's work, it is not suitable here to go through all the different groups and subgroups separately. Instead, I will split this highly complex development into three periods and briefly delineate the main theoretical concepts and their practical consequences for diagnosis and nosology.[2]

b. The early period
This period, lasting from 1880, the beginning of Kraepelin's psychiatric career, to about 1891, when he took over the chair of psychiatry in Heidelberg, can be characterized as the search for a reliable and valid psychiatric system between clear-cut naturalistic beliefs and the methodological framework of experimental psychology sensu Wundt. During these years, Kraepelin published the 'Compendium of Psychiatry' (i.e. the first edition of his textbook) in 1883 and the second and third editions in 1887 and 1889, respectively.

As for nosology, he slowly moved away from earlier 19th century concepts that he criticised as unreliable and ill-defined from a clinical and, especially, prognostic point of view. In these years, however, the term '*dementia praecox*' was not yet used. Kraepelin described a group of clinically heterogenous paranoid and hallucinatory psychoses that tend to become chronic; this group that he called 'Wahnsinn' resembles what will later be called schizophrenic psychoses developing a residual state. On the other hand, he introduced 'Verruecktheit' as a chronic psychosis, too, which – contrary to 'Wahnsinn' – has a better prognosis and does not typically lead to residual states. Although comparable to some extent, this early concept of 'Verruecktheit' must not be identified with the later term paranoia, especially as developed in the eighth edition.[3] The affective psychoses were split into the three groups of melancholia, mania and periodical or 'circular' psychosis.

c. The middle period

In this period, lasting from about 1891 to 1915, Kraepelin published the fourth (1893) to the eighth (last volume 1915) edition of his textbook. Here, his thinking reached its most systematical and influential position as for its clinical and scientific implications: Kraepelin significantly broadened his clinical experience and self-consciously created a nosological system. It is in these years that he finalized his concept of natural disease entities as discussed above.

The main clinical result of this period – first clearly proposed in the sixth edition of 1899 – was the well-known dichotomy of endogenous psychoses, i.e. the separation of dementia praecox (schizophrenia) with – as he saw it – a poor prognosis and manic-depressive illness with a good, or at least better, prognosis.

As for dementia praecox, he supposed an organic defect as the basis of the illness, leading to the destruction of cortical neurons, possibly by a process of 'auto-intoxication'. The patient's individual personality may promote the development of the psychotic illness, but it is not a central factor; contrary to most of the other nosological areas, 'degeneration' was believed to be of much less etiological importance in dementia praecox. Clinically, he described the hebephrenic, catatonic and paranoid form of the illness (1899). In the eighth edition he even differentiated 10 subtypes (1913). 'Paraphrenia' was conceptualized as a psychosis with acute and heterogenous clinical symptomatology including the development of lasting deficits, but its separation from typical cases of dementia praecox was justified by the absence of massive disturbances of volition and by a much lesser degree of affective flattening.

In manic-depressive illness, the etiology of the disease process was said to be much more unclear in comparison to dementia praecox. Kraepelin proposed a genetically determined irritability of 'normal' affects in patients with affective psychosis, so that the psychosis itself emerges from certain predisposing 'basic states' ('Grundzustände'). The concept of degeneration was an integrative and central part of this hypothesis. In this period Kraepelin integrated the several types of circular or recurrent affective illness into the concept of manic-depressive insanity ('Manisch-depressives Irresein') (6th edition, 1899).

The Kraepelinian concept of paranoia was modified several times in these years (Bräunig, 1990; Hoff, 1994; Kendler, 1988). After the very broad concept of 'Verruecktheit' of the early editions, which was of restricted clinical use, he significantly narrowed it, especially in the 5th edition of 1896. Here, paranoia was defined as a severe and chronic delusional illness without constant deficits of volition and without significant alterations of the patient's personality. The existence of abortive or benign cases was denied up to the 7th edition. In the

8th edition (1915) this very rigid concept was broadened again, but not as much as in the early versions. Kraepelin now accepted cases with low severity and a comparably good prognosis, but he maintained the strict separation of dementia praecox and paranoia.

Disorders of personality – in a very broad sense – in Kraepelin's view resulted from a circumscript retardation of psychical development. This concept – highly typical for the way of thinking within the lines of degeneration theory – argued that these patients never reached a 'normal' or mature level of affective and cognitive functioning. Since this deficit was thought to be present in all patients with personality disorders it made no sense to differentiate between clear-cut disease processes as, for example, in the case of dementia praecox and manic-depressive psychosis.

d. The later period

In these years, from about 1916 to 1926, Kraepelin reacted to several comment-aries and criticisms of his nosology, for example Hoche's syndromatic theory (Hoche, 1912), Birnbaum's analysis of the 'inner structure' of psychotic states (Birnbaum, 1919) and Kretschmer's suggestion to supplement the Kraepelinian system by a multidimensional approach (Kretschmer, 1919). Kraepelin therefore tried to develop an internal broadening of his system. He reformulated his disease concept as discussed above, combining a more differentiated view of pathogenesis and the role of individual psychological factors with an unchanged position on the existence of 'natural disease entities'. In comparison to this differentiation and improvement in the theoretical basis of his nosology, the changes of the clinical nosology were small.

CONSEQUENCES FOR PSYCHIATRY – FROM KRAEPELIN TO 'NEO-KRAEPELINIANISM' AND DSM-IV/ICD-10

Kraepelin's psychiatry became so influential, because it offered a pragmatical, clinically and prognostically oriented nosology, developed by a self-confident author who focussed on rather straight-forward quantitative and naturalistic research methods and claimed to abandon speculative aspects from psychiatry as much as possible (Aschaffenburg, 1929; Avenarius, 1979; Bendick, 1989; Berrios and Hauser, 1988; Boroffka, 1988; Braceland, 1957; Fish, 1968; Gross, 1929; Hoenig, 1968; Hoff, 1985, 1988, 1994; Janzarik, 1979; Kick, 1981; Lauter, 1965; Mayer-Groß, 1929; Schneider, 1956; Spielmeyer, 1927). As shown above, this anti-speculative impetus brought about the danger of under-estimating qualitative, 'subjective' aspects and, generally speaking, philosoph-ical foundations that psychiatry necessarily has, whether the single author wishes to discuss that issue or not. This again is important for present-day researchers, who call themselves 'Neo-Kraepelinians' and intend to adopt Kraepelinian principles in modern biological psychiatry (Blashfield, 1984).

Two examples show the relevance of this consideration:
1. In recent years, many authors postulated a 'denosologization' of psychiatric research especially in biological studies (e.g. van Praag et al, 1987). Their idea is to avoid nosological prejudices that will hamper research by restricting the interpretation of data only to the limits of 'classical' concepts, especially the

Kraepelinian dichotomy of endogenous psychoses. There might well be, they argue, valuable biological findings that show quite another distribution in psychiatric patients than one would expect within the framework of classical nosology. This argument, in itself, is quite right. But when criticising psychopathology's tendency to create nosological dogmas, one should not make the same mistake by replacing these dogmas by a nosology that is *only* biologically based, leaving psychopathology aside as unscientific. Nosological prejudices or dogmas do exist in psychopathological approaches as well as in biological ones, and they both severely obstruct research.

2. Modern operationalized diagnostic systems, which are supported by 'neo-Kraepelinian' authors, in my view must avoid to adopt Kraepelin's – rather implicit – kind of ontology of mental illness uncritically. With respect to this problem, the authors of DSM-IV, for example, warn the users of the diagnostic system not to take the diagnostic categories as definite or natural entities, but as conventions which need further clinical verification (Faust and Miner, 1986; Hoff, 1992a; Klerman et al, 1984; Saß, 1990; Schwartz and Wiggins, 1986). This is of special relevance for forensic practice, since in this context diagnostic systems are sometimes misinterpreted as collections of natural constants, quasi automatically leading to diminished or even completely missing criminal responsibility (e.g. pathological gambling or kleptomania).

10 THESES ON KRAEPELINIAN PSYCHIATRY

1. Kraepelin's nosology aimed at detecting mental illnesses, as they are 'created' by nature, i.e. 'natural disease entities'. This basic idea remained unchanged, although in his later programmatic papers, published between 1918 and 1920, he tried to implement new concepts like Kretschmer's and Birnbaum's.

2. Kraepelin's well-known psychiatric nosology is linked with several philosophical assumptions, which he seldom discusses explicitly.

3. While constantly improving and widening his descriptive approach in clinical psychopathology and nosology, Kraepelin did not deepen his reflection on the theoretical foundations.

4. As for the mind-body-problem, Kraepelin, following Wundt, held the position of parallelism. He was not a materialist.

5. Kraepelin's highly optimistic view of the future possibilities of his naturalistical, experimental and quantitative research program made him widen psychiatric concepts into quite different areas, for example jurisdiction and social politics (Engstrom, 1991). This important topic, however, is beyond the focus of the present article.

6. There are striking parallels between the basic questions of Kraepelin's approach on the one hand and the actual biologically oriented psychiatric research strategies on the other hand. This fact makes the historical research on Kraepelin practically relevant for present-day psychiatry.

7. 'Neo-Kraepelinianism' is not a homogenous theory. It is an influential and rather heterogenous set of concepts, trying to create a fundamentum for biological research in clinical psychiatry. It is necessary for 'neo-Kraepelinian' authors to fully and critically discuss Kraepelin's position, because by applying shortened and simplified approaches they will be at risk to repeat Kraepelin's theoretical prejudices.

8. Although 'neo-Kraepelinian' authors clearly favor operationalized psychiatric diagnoses, the theoretical basis of these diagnostic systems – like DSM-IV or ICD-10 – is no direct result of Kraepelin's concept. The philosophical foundations are too different, e.g. naturalism in Kraepelin vs. logical empiricism in DSM-IV and ICD-10. In the present context, the most important aspect is that Kraepelin's tendency to underestimate individual psychological features – mediated by his rather unreflected philosophical realism or 'objectivism' – and to view mental illnesses as 'real things', existing independently from the researcher and the patient – keyword: 'reification' –, should not be copied by the users of modern operationalized diagnostic systems, because this – from a psychopathological perspective – would severely obstruct their clinical and research value.

9. Whereas Kraepelin's aim was to unify psychiatry clinically and scientifically – especially by applying quantitative methods as in natural sciences –, in present-day psychiatry just the opposite is happening: different theoretical and therapeutical concepts are developed and discussed quite separately, sometimes nearly isolated from one another. Attempts to create integrative approaches, that are not mere compromises, but substantial psychiatric concepts on a high scientific level, are still in their beginnings.

10. Paradoxically, Kraepelin, although not interested in philosophical debates, is a convincing example for the thesis, that psychiatry and philosophy are necessarily closely linked and that their reciprocal misjudgement will create scientific prejudices that are of negative impact for psychiatric therapy (e.g. unreflected materialism).

NOTES
1 This topic will be taken up again in the context of Kraepelin's naturalism (see III.4.).
2 For a detailed discussion of this topic see Hoff (1994).
3 The fact that Kraepelin sometimes uses the terms 'Paranoia' and '*Verruecktheit*' synonymously in the early editions has brought about misunderstandings of his concept of paranoia.

REFERENCES
Arnold, A. (1980) *Wilhelm Wundt – Sein philosophisches System*, Berlin, Akademie.
Aschaffenburg, G. (1929) 'Der Einfluß Kraepelins auf die Kriminalpsychologie

und Kriminalpolitik'. *Archiv für Psychiatrie und Nervenkrankheiten*, 87:87–95.

Avenarius, R. (1979) 'Emil Kraepelin, seine Persönlichkeit und seine Konzeption'. In Janzarik, W. (Hrsg) *Psychopathologie als Grundlagenwissenschaft* Stuttgart, Enke. S. 62–73.

Bendick, C. (1989) *Emil Kraepelins Forschungsreise nach Java im Jahre 1904. Ein Beitrag zur Geschichte der Ethnopsychiatrie. Arbeiten der Forschungsstelle des Instituts für Geschichte der Medizin der Universität zu Köln*, Band 49, Köln.

Berrios, G.E. and Hauser, R. (1988) 'The early development of Kraepelin's ideas on classification: a conceptual history'. *Psychological Medicine*, 18:813–21.

Binswanger, L. (1957) *Schizophrenie*, Pfullingen, Neske.

Binswanger, L. (1960) Manie und Melancholie. Pfullingen, Neske.

Birnbaum, K. (1919) 'Der Aufbau der Psychose. Ein klinischer Versuch'. *Allgemeine Zeitschrift für Psychiatrie und psychisch-gerichtliche Medizin*, 75:455–502.

Binswanger, L. (1957) *Schizophrenie*, Pfullingen, Neske.

Binswanger, L. (1960) *Manie und Melancholie*, Pfullingen, Neske.

Blashfield, R.K. (1984) *The Classification of Psychopathology – Neo-Kraepelinian and Quantitative Approaches*, New York, London, Plenum Press.

Bonhoeffer, K. (1910) *Die symptomatischen Psychosen im Gefolge von akuten Infektionen und inneren Erkrankungen*, Leipzig Wien, Deuticke.

Boring, E.G. (1950) '*A history of experimental psychology*', 2nd edition, New York, Appleton-Century-Crofts.

Boroffka, A. (1988) 'Emil Kraepelin (1856–1926) and Transcultural Psychiatry: A Historical Note'. *Transcultural Psychiatry Research Review*, 25:236–9.

Braceland, F.J. (1957) 'Kraepelin, his system and his influence'. *American Journal of Psychiatry*, 113:871–6.

Bräunig, P. (1990) 'Der Paranoia-Begriff Kraepelins'. *Fundamenta Psychiatrica*, 4:58–63.

Danziger, K. (1990) *Constructing the subject: Historical origins of psychological research*, Cambridge, Cambridge University Press.

Engstrom, E.J. (1991) 'Emil Kraepelin: psychiatry and public affairs in Wilhelmine Germany'. *History of Psychiatry*, 2:111–32.

Faust, D. and Miner, R.A. (1986) 'The empiricist and his new clothes: DSM-III in perspective'. *American Journal of Psychiatry*, 143:962–7.

Fish, F. (1968) 'Kraepelin's nosology'. *British Journal of Psychiatry*, 114:356.

Gaupp, R. (1920) 'Der Fall Wagner. Eine Katamnese, zugleich ein Beitrag zur Lehre von der Paranoia'. *Zeitschrift fuer die gesamte Neurologie und Psychiatrie*, 60:312.

Griesinger, W. (1845). *Die Pathologie und Therapie der psychischen Krankheiten*, Stuttgart, A. Krabbe.

Gross, A. (1929) 'Kraepelins Bedeutung für die Anstaltspsychiatrie'. *Archiv für Psychiatrie und Nervenheilkunde*, 87:50–67.

Hermle, L. (1986) 'Die Degenerationslehre in der Psychiatrie'. *Fortschritte der Neurologie und Psychiatrie*, 54:69–79.

Hoche, A.E. (1912) 'Die Bedeutung der Symptomenkomplexe in der Psychiatrie'. *Zeitschrift für die gesamte Neurologie und Psychiatrie*, 12:540–51.

Hoenig, J. (1968) 'Kraepelin and his approach to nosology'. *British Journal of Psychiatry*, 114:125–6.

Hoff, P. (1985) 'Zum Krankheitsbegriff bei Emil Kraepelin'. *Nervenarzt*, 56:510–13.

Hoff, P. (1988) 'Nosologische Grundpostulate bei Kraepelin – Versuch einer kritischen Würdigung des Kraepelinschen Spätwerkes'. *Zeitschrift für klinische Psychologie, Psychopathologie, Psychotherapie*, 36:328–36.

Hoff, P. (1992a) 'Neuere psychiatrische Klassifikationssysteme und ihre Bedeutung für die forensische Psychiatrie'. *Gesundheitswesen*, 54:244–50.

Hoff, P. (1992b) 'Emil Kraepelin and Philosophy. The Implicit Philosophical Assumptions of Kraepelinian Psychiatry'. In Spitzer, M., Uehlein, F.A., Schwartz, M.A. and Mundt, Chr. (Hrsg) *Phenomenology, Language and Schizophrenia*, Berlin Heidelberg New York, Springer. S. 115–25.

Hoff, P. (1994) *Emil Kraepelin und die Psychiatrie als klinische Wissenschaft. Ein Beitrag zum Selbstverständnis psychiatrischer Forschung*, Berlin Heidelberg New York, Springer.

Hundert, E.M. (1992) 'The Brain's Capacity to Form Delusions as an Evolutionary Strategy for Survival'. In Spitzer, M., Uehlein, F.A., Schwartz, M.A. and Mundt, Chr. (Hrsg) *Phenomenology, Language and Schizophrenia*, Berlin Heidelberg New York, Springer. S. 346–54.

Janzarik, W. (1979) 'Die klinische Psychopathologie zwischen Griesinger und Kraepelin im Querschnitt des Jahres 1878'. In Janzarik, W. (ed) *Psychopathologie als Grundlagenwissenschaft*, Stuttgart, Enke, S. 51–61.

Kahlbaum, K. (1863) *Die Gruppierung der psychischen Krankheiten und die Eintheilung der Seelenstörungen. Entwurf einer historisch-kritischen Darstellung der bisherigen Eintheilungen und Versuch zur Anbahnung einer empirisch-wissenschaftlichen Grundlage der Psychiatrie als klinischer Disciplin*, Danzig, Kafemann.

Kahlbaum, K. (1874) *Die Katatonie oder das Spannungsirresein. Eine klinische Form psychischer Krankheit*, Berlin, Hirschwald.

Kendler, K.S (1988) 'Kraepelin and the diagnostic concept of paranoia'. *Comprehensive Psychiatry*, 29:4–11.

Kick, H. (1981) 'Der Forschungsansatz Kraepelins aus der Sicht seiner klinischen Praxis'. *Fortschritte der Neurologie und Psychiatrie*, 49:259–64.

Klerman, G.L., Vaillant, G.E., Spitzer, R.L., and Michels, R. (1984) 'A Debate on DSM-III'. *American Journal of Psychiatry*, 141:539–53.

Kraepelin, E. (1880) *Die Abschaffung des Strafmasses. Ein Vorschlag zur Reform der heutigen Strafrechtspflege*, Stuttgart, Enke.

Kraepelin, E. (1883–1927) *Psychiatrie*. Nine editions: 1883, Leipzig, Abel; 1887, Leipzig, Abel; 1889, Leipzig, Abel; 1893, Leipzig, Abel; 1896, Leipzig, Barth; 1899 (2 vol.), Leipzig, Barth; 1903/1904 (2 vol.), Leipzig, Barth; 1909/1910/1913/1915 (4 vol.), Leipzig, Barth; 1927 (2 vol.), Leipzig, Barth.

Kraepelin, E. (1887) *Die Richtungen der psychiatrischen Forschung*, Leipzig, Vogel.

Kraepelin, E. (1918) 'Ziele und Wege der psychiatrischen Forschung'. *Zeitschrift für die gesamte Neurologie und Psychiatrie*, 42:169–205.

Kraepelin, E. (1919) 'Die Erforschung psychischer Krankheitsformen'. *Zeitschrift für die gesamte Neurologie und Psychiatrie*, 51:224–46.

Kraepelin, E. (1920a) 'Wilhelm Wundt'. *Zeitschrift für die gesamte Neurologie und Psychiatrie*, 61:351–62.

Kraepelin, E. (1920b) 'Die Erscheinungsformen des Irreseins'. *Zeitschrift für die gesamte Neurologie und Psychiatrie*, 62:1–29.

Kraepelin, E. (1921) *Einführung in die psychiatrische Klinik*, 4th ed, 3 vol, Leipzig, Barth.

Kraepelin, E. (1987) *Memoirs*. Edited by H. Hippius, G. Peters, D. Ploog, Berlin, Springer.

Kretschmer, E. (1919) 'Gedanken über die Fortentwicklung der psychiatrischen Systematik'. *Zeitschrift für die gesamte Neurologie und Psychiatrie*, 48:370–7.

Lanczik, M. (1992) 'Karl Ludwig Kahlbaum (1828–1899) and the emergence of psychopathological and nosological research in German psychiatry'. *History of Psychiatry*, 3:53–8.

Lauter, H. (1965) 'Kraepelins Bedeutung für die Kulturpsychiatrie'. *Transcultural Psychiatry Research Review*, 2:9–12.

Mayer-Groß, W. (1929) 'Die Entwicklung der klinischen Anschauungen Kraepelins'. *Archiv für Psychiatrie und Nervenkrankheiten*, 87: 30–42.

Pauleikhoff, B. (1987) *Das Menschenbild im Wandel der Zeit. Ideengeschichte der Psychiatrie und der klinischen Psychologie*, Band 3, Pressler, Hürtgenwald.

Pick, D. (1989) *Faces of Degeneration: A European Disorder 1848–1918*, Cambridge, Cambridge University Press.

Praag, H.M. van, Kahn, R.S., Asnis, G.M., Wetzler, S., Brown, S.L., Bleich, A. and Korn, M.L. (1987) 'Denosologization of biological psychiatry or the specificity of 5-HT disturbances in psychiatric disorders'. *Journal of Affective Disorders*, 4:173–93.

Saß, H. (1990) 'Operationalisierte Diagnostik in der Psychiatrie'. *Nervenarzt*, 61:255–8.

Schneider, Chr M. (1990) *Wilhelm Wundts Völkerpsychologie. Entstehung und Entwicklung eines in Vergessenheit geratenen, wissenschaftshistorisch relevanten Fachgebietes*, Bonn, Bouvier.

Schneider, K. (1956) 'Kraepelin und die gegenwärtige Psychiatrie'. *Fortschritte der Neurologie und Psychiatrie*, 24:1–7.

Schwartz, M.A. and Wiggins, O.P. (1986) 'Logical empiricism and psychiatric classification'. *Comprehensive Psychiatry*, 27:101–14.

Spielmeyer, W. (1927) 'Kraepelin und die naturwissenschaftlich-medizinische Forschung in der Psychiatrie'. *Zeitschrift für die gesamte Neurologie und Psychiatrie*, 108:10–20.

Titchener, E.B. (1921) 'Wilhelm Wundt'. *American Journal of Psychology*, 32:161–78.

Verwey, G. (1985). *Psychiatry in an anthropological and biomedical context – Philosophical presuppositions and implications of German psychiatry 1820–1870*, Dordrecht, D. Reidel.

Vollmer, G. (1992) 'Ist evolutive Selbstorganisation zu Leben und Bewußtsein doch denkbar?' *Fichte-Studien*, 4:53–67.

Wahrig-Schmidt, B. (1985) *Der junge Wilhelm Griesinger im Spannungsfeld zwischen Philosophie und Physiologie*, Tübingen, Narr.

Weber, M.M. (1991) 'Ein Forschungsinstitut für Psychiatrie. Die Entwicklung

der Deutschen Forschungsanstalt für Psychiatrie München 1918–1945'.
Sudhoffs Archiv, 75:74–89.

Wundt, W. (1880). *Grundzüge der physiologischen Psychologie* (2nd ed.),
Leipzig, Engelmann.

Wundt, W. (1894) 'Über psychische Causalität und das Princip des psy-
chophysischen Parallelismus'. *Philosophische Studien*, 10:1–124.

Wundt, W. (1900–1920) *Völkerpsychologie. Eine Untersuchung der Ent-
wicklungsgesetze von Sprache, Mythus und Sitte*, 10 Bände, Leipzig, Engelmann.

Chapter 10
Kraepelin

Clinical Section – Part II
GE BERRIOS and R HAUSER

The Kraepelinian classification of the psychoses governs twentieth century psychiatric thinking and neurobiological research (e.g. Den Boer et al, 1995; Marneros and Tsuang, 1990). Alternative nosologies, such as the one proposed by Wernicke-Kleist-Leonhard (Beckmann and Lanczik, 1990) (see Chapter 11 and 16, this book) have not been able to compete in equal terms. Other nosologies, such as that based on the unitary psychosis view, are mere curiosities (Berrios and Beer, 1994; Vliegen, 1980) and others such as Magnan's have fallen into desuetude (Pichot, 1982).

The fact that current psychiatry lives in a Kraepelinian world is to many not a historico-conceptual event, but a fact of nature. Because the *raison d'être* of psychiatry is not the construction of conceptual systems but the efficient treatment of mental illness, it is of the essence that this naïve approach be tempered by a more contextualized and historical understanding of Kraepelin's contribution. The young psychiatrist must be brought up with the view that it should be possible to develop alternative nosologies with superior *reliability* (i.e. conceptual stability) and *validity* (i.e. better fit with neurobiological facts). This section offers a brief analysis of the origin of Kraepelin's ideas[1] and briefly explores the reception of Kraepelin's ideas in France.

KRAEPELIN AND HIS HISTORIANS

A curious fact about Kraepelinian scholarship is disagreement concerning what he said and constructed. Some have caricatured his approach: for example, Zilboorg (1941) once made the groundless claim that for Kraepelin 'a mentally sick person seems to have been a collection of symptoms' (p.452). Even sympathetic historians seem to echo this view: 'what was felt to be lacking in Kraepelin's description of the clinical picture was the "psyche". The symptoms were symptoms of the underlying disease process. The patient's life history, his premorbid personality, even his own experience of the illness had no assigned place in the scheme of things. They were an irrelevancy' (Hoenig, 1983, p.549). Other writers have produced hagiographic comment and said little on the construction of Kraepelin's thinking (Lange, 1926; Wirth, 1927; Mayer, 1956; Braceland, 1956; Kolle, 1957; Kahn, 1956; Havens, 1956; Wender, 1963; Leader, 1968; Bruch, 1969). Yet others have seen Kraepelin as the empiricist *à outrance*, for example, Avenarius (1979) has claimed that for Kraepelin 'theory was only the handmaid of praxis' (p.63).

These claims do not altogether match Kraepelin's complex combination of empiricism, a priori theorizing, and sentimental humanism: 'to what extent and by what clinical methods can we more clearly understand the manifestations of madness? The symptoms and signs that correspond to the underlying disease are extraordinarily varied. This implies that the *antecedent conditions* must have been complex. Even where clear-cut external agents are involved (e.g. a head injury or poisoning) there is an interplay of forces at work: the nervous system of the affected individual, the deficits inherited from past generations and *his own personal history*' . . . 'these preconditions are specially important when considering forms of the illness which do not arise from external injury, but from *circumstances of the individual concerned*' . . . 'it seems absurd to propose that syphilis causes patients to believe that they are the proud possessors of cars' . . . 'rather *the general desires of such people* are reflected in these delusions' . . . 'if these observations approximate the truth we will have to look for the key to the understanding of the clinical picture primarily in characteristics of the individual patient, *his expectations play a decisive role*' (our italics) (all translations are the authors') (Kraepelin, 1920, pp.2–3). An accurate assessment of Kraepelin's views has been offered by a great historian of psychoanalysis: 'Kraepelin has become the whipping boy of many present-day psychiatrists who claim that his only concern for his patients was to place diagnostic labels on them, after which no more was done to help them. In fact, however, he took the greatest care that every one of his patients should have the best treatment available at the time' (Ellenberger, 1970, p.285).

In spite of the prolix nature of Kraepelin's writings, there has also been debate on what he actually said. For example, in 1968 there was an interesting exchange about the extension and relevance of his nosological criteria. As against claims made by Professor Fish (1967; 1968), Hoenig (1968) stated that Kraepelin based his distinction between the two major psychoses on clinical picture and not incurability. Alexander Walk (1968) sided with the latter. Evidence to be presented in this chapter should suggest that both sides were right. There are two aspects to Kraepelin's work: *methodological* (dictated by the logic of his research and which included the theoretical criterion of incurability) and *clinical* (the empirical dimension including the descriptive criterion of 'symptom-picture'). The two converged on the *Zählkarten* (which contained both cross-sectional and longitudinal information) and which allowed Kraepelin to divide up his patient cohort according to 'incurability' and 'deterioration'. He then correlated within each group the original symptom-presentation and outcome.

Hence, in as much as he was referring to the methodological criterion, Fish (1968) was right in saying that Kraepelin 'used the criterion of incurability to establish his concept' (p.356). In as much as they were referring to the clinical criterion, Hoenig (1968) and Walk (1968) were right in saying that Kraepelin 'rested his concept of *dementia praecox*' on a clinical picture (p.644). The debate, however, should not have stop there for in his *Erscheinungsformen des Irreseins*, Kraepelin (1920) acknowledged the existence of damaging clinical overlaps between the main two psychoses (Berrios and Beer, 1994). Kahn (1956) once suggested that this change of heart might have been a late reaction to Hoche's (1912) powerful paper.[2]

After only eight years of training (including a period in experimental psychology under Wundt), and at age thirty, Kraepelin acceded to his first chair.[3] The Dorpat professorship had been vacated by Emminghaus (1845–1904), a friend and sponsor of Kraepelin's, who later also helped him to obtain the Heidelberg chair. Kraepelin's (1887) inaugural lecture, entitled 'The Directions of Psychiatric Research', was a defence of academic psychiatry and contained a veritable research programme. Therein he announced his intention of combining psychiatric research and patient care: in regards to the former, he was to collect a valid patient cohort and seek the 'laws' that linked brain anatomy and psychological data.[4] In his quest for stable descriptions of disease he resorted to operational definitions: 'I tried to organize the confusing manifestations of disease in my patients by describing their behaviour as exactly as possible . . .' (Kraepelin, 1983, p.35). He expressed dissatisfaction with ongoing classifications because groupings were not distinct enough.[5] In Dorpat, he also 'was led to consider the importance of the course of the illness with regard to the classification of the mental disorders' (Kraepelin, 1983, p.49). Ten years later he was able to announce that he had 'found a new way of looking at mental illness'. He referred to the 'traditional' view as 'symptomatic' and to his own as 'clinical' (Kraepelin, 1896).

The Dorpat sample

At Dorpat, Kraepelin became the director of an 80-bedded University Clinic, and had opportunity to explore the course of many conditions. There was a further advantage: in contrast to German legislation that dictated that all patients had to be legally detained (*bezirksaerztliche Einweisung*), Russian regulations allowed for the admission of 'informal' or voluntary patients. Hence, his Dorpat samples included more milder and fresher cases and less chronic organic mental disorders. In collaboration with Daraszkiewicz, Kraepelin was able to study many clinical histories in detail. The observation that behavioural dilapidation was *acquired* suggested that it might be secondary to a degenerative process (Kraepelin, 1983).[6] However, a further (and crucial) cultural variable was in operation. Kraepelin's clinic at Dorpat (now *Tartu* in Estonia), served a non-German speaking community whose main languages were Werro-Estonian and Reval-Estonian.[7] Only one thirteenth of the population spoke German, and to this group belonged the upper classes who sought medical treatment in Germany. Kraepelin had to use an interpreter (Kraepelin, 1983) and it is suggested in this chapter that this linguistic barrier created his long-lasting interest in the behavioural (e.g. psychomotor) signs of insanity.

At least since 1879, Kraepelin (1983) had been aware of Kahlbaum's (1863) distinction between the *form* (or 'essence') of a disease and its *presentations* (phenomena). As late as 1889, he also seems to have been critical of Kalhbaum's concepts on the grounds that they were 'too abstract and might lead to a form of unitary psychosis'. However, around this time Kraepelin relinquished his overtly 'narrow' interpretation of Kahlbaum's views. It is known that Daraszkiewicz, his bright assistant and author himself of a superb monograph on Hebephrenia (1892), was attracted by the views of Kahlbaum and Hecker. Kraepelin duly acknowledged his influence.

In 1891, upon returning to Germany to take up his appointment at Heidelberg,[8] Kraepelin decided to test Kahlbaum's longitudinal approach. He also surrounded himself with a larger academic team which allowed the realization of another of Kahlbaum's injunctions, namely that specialized monographs were essential to stimulate growth.[9] Kraepelin (1897) started a *Research Programme* (the phrase is his) whose objective was to follow up a patient cohort and analyze statistically the results. It started in 1891, and was based on a systematic collection of all cases, so to avoid the 'interesting cases' bias (Kraepelin, 1919; Grayson, 1987). Within four weeks of admission, patients were allocated a diagnosis and a prognosis (in *separate* notes). Follow up was pursued with energy and patients were asked to attend out-patients or their mental state was periodically checked up if they had been transferred to country asylums. Clinical information was recorded in especially designed index cards (the famous '*Zählkarten*').

However, Kraepelin still had to contend with the fact that at Heidelberg patient samples were biased in the direction of severity and chronicity. There were three reasons for this: patients in Baden could only be judicially admitted; his Clinic could not refuse admissions; and there was a tendency for patients to accumulate in the wards as the long stay facilities at Pforzheim and Emmendingen (to which patients could, in theory, be transferred) were always full. Kraepelin requested that another long term hospital be built, that he should be given the right to reject patients, and to admit voluntary cases.[10]

Kraepelin was unsuccessful, and this might have contributed to his decision to leave Heidelberg (Janzarik, 1979). His reaction, however, was a constructive one in that he started to explore issues pertaining to deterioration and defect. Data in hand already suggested to Kraepelin (1983) that a large proportion of patients, whatever their clinical presentation, ended up in a state of dementia:

> It gradually dawned on me that many patients, who initially presented a picture of mania, melancholia or amentia showed progressive dementia. In spite of individual differences they began to resemble one another. It seemed as if the earlier clinical differences had little bearing on the course of the illness. This evolution was similar to what was known with regards to paralysis. Thus, I could not resist concluding that only one illness process might be affecting many of the institutionalized patients that developed dementia. The process might be slow or quick and sometimes accompanied by delusions, hallucinations and excitement. On some occasions there might be a sad (or an elated) mood – whatever its presentation, it always led to the destruction of the personality.

Having reached this conclusion, Kraepelin sought to identify indicators for the degenerative process. He thus used 'deterioration' as a discriminating criterion to divide up his sample and then identify any clinical differences that the patients might have presented *ab initio*.[11]

Collecting information in the same card facilitated the search for correlations between early presentation and later changes. The way in which Kraepelin developed his views on prognosis can be mapped in the successive editions of the *Lehrbuch* and in lectures he gave on the topic. Early results allowed

Kraepelin to formulate two clinical concepts: 'degenerating psychological process' and '*dementia praecox*'. Introduced in the 4th edition (1893) of the *Lehrbuch*, the concepts were defined thus: 'The common feature of those illnesses which we group under the name of degenerating psychological processes is the rapid development of a lasting state of psychological weakness' and 'what we call dementia praecox is the sub-acute development of a peculiar, simple condition of mental weakness occurring at a youthful age' (p.435). In a paper on 'Remission in Catatonia', read at a meeting of the Psychiatric Society in November 1895, Kraepelin (1896a) criticised the views of Kahlbaum and others on the relative good prognosis of Catatonia. He reported 63 cases of which only 24 had improved, and of these 14 had been re-admitted within 5 years. More importantly, the 24 had not actually been symptom-free during the interval (he presented a detailed follow-up of 10). In March 1896, appeared the important 5th edition of the *Lehrbuch* including a description of Kraepelin's method: 'what convinced me of the superiority of the clinical method of diagnosis (followed here) over the traditional one, was the *certainty with which we could predict (in conjunction with our new concept of disease)* the future course of events (his italics). Thanks to it the student can find his way more easily in the difficult subject of psychiatry' (Kraepelin, 1896).

At the 1896 Heidelberg meeting of the German Psychiatrists Association, Kraepelin (1897) expressed the view that he had achieved one of his aims. Therein, he stressed the importance of making 'valid' diagnoses, and rhetorically asked the 'Dorpat question' (how to differentiate essential from accidental symptoms?). He stated that the only external criterion available for symptom classification was illness course, and that longitudinal observation and ascertainment of terminal state allowed the clinician to differentiate between essential and accidental symptoms. He reported the results of his correlational work, based on the follow-up cards, and listed two groups of symptoms: those common to all the psychoses but unable to predict outcome such as 'sensory deceptions', hallucinations and affective pathology and those present only in some psychoses but able to predict deterioration such as 'flight of ideas, orientation failures, perceptual disturbances, motor excitement and inhibition' (p.841) (Kraepelin, 1897).[12]

Meschede, Siemerling, Mendel, Grashey and Jolly opposed Kraepelin's views. Jolly, a former editor of the *Archiv für Psychiatrie* and a respected Berlin alienist, criticised the idiosyncratic use by Kraepelin of the concept of 'prognosis' as a key to diagnosis on the ground that this 'contradicted the general principles of pathology'. He also made the interesting point that at any rate the criterion was logically weak as the course of illness depended upon factors such as severity of lesion, host resistance, context and treatment, none of which could be considered as an 'essential' aspect of the disease. Jolly was a strict adherent of the established anatomico-pathological model according to which a classification of diseases had to be based upon anatomical criteria (López Piñero, 1983).

In principle, Kraepelin might have agreed as during this period of his life he still believed in the possibility of identifying pathological mechanisms (Hoff, 1985). In practice, however, he was beginning to use the concept of diagnosis in a 'functional' way and had decided to postpone any hope of basing it on anatomy. To achieve his short-term objective of finding a valid classification, he needed to abandon the view that anatomy was the royal road to the 'essence of diagnosis'. There is some evidence for this change of mind: Aschaffenburg, Kraepelin's main collaborator at Heidelberg, described it epigramatically: 'a wrong diagnosis is not an incorrect diagnosis but one that has "no-purpose" i.e. does not empower the clinician to make any educated guess as to the future of his patient'.[13]

Kraepelin (1897) was aware of some of the undesirable consequences of using descriptive criteria alone: 'no one will regret it more than I if (by using such an approach) *dementia praecox* temporarily became too large a category. So I would gratefully receive suggestions as to how to split this group into clinical subtypes' (p.263). Years later Kraepelin (1919a) wrote:

> Future observation of many cases will tell whether or not the attempt to widen or narrow the 'form' of the illness was justified. It is to be expected that the clinical boundaries of the disease groups drawn by us will change in due course. Such changes will continue until more knowledge, concerning the correlation of observations through the accumulation of experiences, has been reached. (p.235)

FRENCH REACTION TO KRAEPELIN'S NOSOLOGY

By 1900, France was almost alone amongst European countries in having an organized and autochthonous nosology, and there were very few points of contact between French clinical groupings and Kraepelin's. French alienists were divided in their reaction. Younger ones showed enthusiasm and amongst this can be mentioned the masterly monograph by Deny and Roy (1903) introducing Kraepelin's concept of *Démence précoce* to French psychiatry. More traditional men such as Marandon de Montyel (1905) reacted violently, particularly against the view that dementia praecox always led to defect (*La démence précoce de M. Kraepelin . . . n'est ni démence, ni précoce*) (p.247). The same author also criticised the fact that the 'Germans had not been able to offer an adequate clinical characterization' of the new disease. In his reply, Mongeri (1905) made the point that Kraepelin had actually provided a clinical picture and not based his classification on outcome alone. He also contradicted Marandon's claim that 'Kraepelin's disease' was after all 'identical' to Magnan's *folie degenerative*.[14] Victor Parant (1905) also criticised Kraepelin on account of the 'wooliness of his suggested clinical pictures'. The views underlying the notion of '*dementia praecox* are artificial, groundless, and lack confirmation both from the semiological and anatomo-pathological viewpoints. They arbitrarily bring together independent clinical states and are contrary to clinical experience' (pp.240–1). It was left to Monod (1905) and later to Mairet and Margot (1920) to present Kraepelin's views in a fairer manner. These efforts notwithstanding, the concept of schizophrenia has remained partially incompatible with French native views on the chronic psychoses (Pichot, 1982; 1984; Allen, 1990).

SUMMARY

Kraepelin's methods and ideas between 1886 and 1896 are important to understand the development of his nosology. He endeavoured to identify a clinical picture and create a taxonomy for the psychoses. Longitudinal analysis allowed him to use outcome groups as symptom discriminators. Kraepelin's statistical analysis, however simple, generated a view of disease which was light years ahead from what had been the trend earlier in his century.[15] It will always be motive of wonder to know how further might Kraepelin have gone had he used modern statistical techniques.[16] By trying to do away with systematic biases, Kraepelin also gave new meaning to the notion of reliability and made possible the development of clinical databases. The cohorts of patients he helped to constitute were in fact good enough to provide the empirical evidence against his own findings. Thus, Lange utilized these data to challenge the categorical prognosis (negative and positive, respectively) that Kraepelin had associated with *dementia praecox* and manic depressive (Vaillant, 1964).

Kraepelin's contribution to the development of the concept of psychosis is undeniable. He lived during a period of rampant empiricism and he did not waste the many clinical opportunities at his disposal. The concept of psychosis was formed at the cross-roads of four dimensional notions: psychoses-neuroses, unitary-multiple, organic-functional and exogenous-endogenous (Berrios, 1987); and his work had something to say on each of these. His categorical mind had a truly Kantian bent (Dörner, 1969) which he probably learned from Wundt (Klein, 1970; Mischel, 1970; Leary, 1978). In the end, he imposed an enduring categorical structure upon psychiatric nosology, buttressed to a certain extent, by empirical data. We are still governed by it (Berrios, 1995).

NOTES

1 The authors have greatly benefited from recent important work in this area (Hoff, 1992; Engstrom, 1990; Allen, 1990; Blashfield, 1984).

2 On Hoche's ideas, see Berrios and Dening (1991); Dening and Berrios (1991).

3 Kraepelin was fifteen when Bismark acceded to power. He was also deeply affected by the defeat of France, the excesses perpetrated by the Prussian Army, and the attack on the Roman Catholic church by Prussian Liberals. He was still at school in Neustrelitz when Virchow (one of his heroes and a left liberal deputy) coined the term *Kulturkampf* and claimed that the fight against the Roman Church had assumed 'the character of a great struggle for civilization in the interest of humanity' (Craig, 1978). Politically a conservative, and an admirer of Bismarck (Alexander and Selesnick, 1966), Kraepelin (1921) wrote a paper on the *Personality of Bismarck* (establishing a parallel between the Chancellor and himself!). In the wake of the German debacle, Kraepelin (1919) tried to 'exonerate the ruling élite of Wilhelmine Germany . . . and endorsed the legitimacy of aristocratic and authoritarian Wilhelmine rule' (Engstrom, 1992, p.225). During his time science took its lead from Bismarckian politics; for example, without knowing about the latter it would be difficult to understand the brain localization debate: 'localization both represented bureaucratic order and was a means for promoting that order in concrete ways. It gave crucial support to the argument that mental illnesses were diseases of the brain, thereby bringing insanity more firmly within the boundaries of medicine' (Pauly, 1983, p.146). Kraepelin was a convinced localizationist: he paid homage to Hitzig (Kraepelin, 1918) and wrote with admiration of Gudden (Kraepelin, 1983;

pp.16–17). Kraepelin seems to have played his political cards successfully. His career progressed well apart, perhaps, from his contretemps with Flechsig in 1882.

4 Before Dorpat, Kraepelin had realized that patient recruitment had to be based on clinical description alone, and that the state of neuropathology did not even allow to 'differentiate between the cortex of a patient with GPI and of a normal subject, let alone identify a disease by its pathological features' (Kraepelin, 1983, p.18).

5 On this he agreed with Karl Kahlbaum (1863) who had put forward an 'empirico-clinical approach' to classification and emphasized the importance of the 'illness course' and made a distinction between the cross-sectional (synchronic) and longitudinal (diachronic) concepts of disease. The 'essence' of the disease (and is unclear what the 'ontological' import of his use of the word 'essence' actually is) was to be found in its natural history and temporal profile. It must not be forgotten that up to this period, 'time' (i.e. the temporal dimension) was not part of the definition of psychiatric illness (Lanteri-Laura, 1972; Del Pistoia, 1971). Kahlbaum hinted at the distinction between acute and chronic states. This was to crystallize only in the French concept of *délire chronique* (Lanteri-Laura, 1986) and in Kraepelin's work. Kahlbaum's (1863) views were not supported by empirical evidence. Kraepelin sought to test them by asking what 'aspects' (or symptoms) carried information with regards to the 'essence' of a disease. He hoped that, once identified, such symptoms could be used as criteria to generate a classification that was, for the first time, based *in re*. He put it succinctly: 'It is true that at present we cannot yet find a way out of the maze of clinical pictures. Our present situation is that we are unable to select from a vast number those elements or signs which may be essential or characteristic in the concrete case' (pp.20–1) (Kraepelin, 1887) . . . 'I thought that it may be possible to find similar courses of disease and uniform diseases by retrospective observation . . .' (Kraepelin, 1983, p.49). To summarize, circa 1886 the central issue for Kraepelin was to find 'essential' signs of disease on which to base both diagnosis and classification.

6 Whether this conclusion was also encouraged by their belief in 'degeneration theory' (Zubin et al, 1985) is difficult to know although it would be fair to say that most late nineteenth century alienists were influenced by this view. However, its influence should not be overemphasized for there also were critics of the doctrine (Genil-Perrin, 1913). In the specific case of Kraepelin, it is likely that his views were mainly governed by empirical observation. Given that at the time the concept of dementia was still in a state of flux (Berrios and Freeman, 1991), Kraepelin's observation is important.

7 Werro-Estonian was most commonly spoken but was also less literary and inflexional than Reval-Estonian (Anonymous, 1878).

8 He also took over what was a very well organized psychiatric clinic (built in 1878) and a laboratory (Janzarik, 1979). The building was near a railway station and this also facilitated patient attendance and follow up.

9 For example, at the 1892 Karlsruhe meeting, Kraepelin spoke with enthusiasm about monographs as a genre (Kraepelin, 1894).

10 He was opposed by 'Institutional' psychiatrists (e.g. Schuele from Illenau)

who were intent on diverting funds towards asylums and also on reducing the power of the University Departments. On the struggle between Academic Departments and Government psychiatric services see Jaspers (1963).

11 Rapid accumulation of data forced him to streamline procedures, and from 1893 on diagnosis and prognosis were entered in the cards soon after the first interview (Kraepelin, 1897; 1983).

12 This view, that only some symptoms carry information on the course of the disease, is still alive in current psychiatry particularly in relation to the so called positive and negative symptoms (Berrios, 1985; 1987a).

13 With respect to correlation between anatomy and symptoms, Rieder (1974) has suggested that Kraepelin insisted on a 'one-to-one correlation between aetiology, pathology and symptomatology' (p.199). This claim is based on a free translation by A.R. Diefendorf (Kraepelin, 1907) that overemphasizes the point. There is no evidence from any direct source that Kraepelin ever entertained such a one-to-one correlation.

14 Interestingly, during his two visits to Constantinople, Kraepelin had been a guest of Mongeri's (a psychiatrist trained in France) (Kraepelin, 1983).

15 For example, Esquirol's (1838) head-counting technique (Berrios, 1988) or Griesinger's cascade model that soon led a form of unitary psychoses (Rennert, 1968).

16 Galton had already suggested ways of improving correlational analysis but it is unlikely that Kraepelin knew of these although he had met Galton in a trip to London (Kraepelin, 1983, p.62). He only thought of employing a statistician during the planning of the Munich Institute (Kraepelin, 1983, p.218).

REFERENCES

Allen, D.F. (1990) *Autour du Palais Somptueux. Contribution à l'étude du mot 'schizophrénie'*, Memoire de DEA, Paris, University of Paris VII.

Anonymous (1878) 'Esthonia'. In *Encyclopaedia Britannica*, Ninth Edition, vol.VIII, Edinburgh, Adam and Charles Black.

Alexander, F.G. and Selesnick, S.T. (1966) *The History of Psychiatry*, New York, Harper and Row.

Avenarius, R. (1979) 'Emil Kraepelin, seine Perösnlichkeit und seine Konzeption'. In Janzarik, W. (ed.) *Psychopathologie als Grundlagenwissenschaft*, Stuttgart, Enke, pp.62–73.

Beckmann, H. and Lanczik, M. (eds.) (1990) 'Leonhard Classification of Endogenous Psychoses'. *Psychopathology*, 23: 189–341.

Berrios, G.E. (1985) 'Positive and negative symptoms and Jackson'. *Archives of General Psychiatry*, 42: 95–7.

Berrios, G.E. (1987) 'Historical aspects of psychoses: 19thC issues'. *British Medical Bulletin*, 43: 484–98.

Berrios, G.E. (1987a) 'Outcome prediction and treatment response in schizophrenia'. *Practical Reviews in Psychiatry*, 2: 7–9.

Berrios, G.E. (1988) 'Historical background to abnormal Psychology'. In Miller, E. and Cooper, P. (eds.) *Adult Abnormal Psychology*, Edinburgh, Churchill and Livingstone, pp.26–51.

Berrios, G.E. (1995) 'Conceptual problems in diagnosing schizophrenic disorders'. In Den Boer, J.A., Westenberg, H.G.M. and Van Praag, H.M. (eds.) *Advances in the Neurobiology of Schizophrenia*, Chichester, John Wiley, pp.7–26.

Berrios, G.E. and Dening, T. (1991) 'Alfred Hoche and DSM-III-R'. *Biological Psychiatry*, 29: 93–5.

Berrios, G.E. and Freeman, H. (eds.) (1991) *Alzheimer and the Dementias*, London, Royal Society of Medicine.

Berrios, G.E. and Beer, D. (1994) 'The notion of Unitary Psychosis: a conceptual history'. *History of Psychiatry*, 5: 13–36.

Blashfield, R.K. (1984) *The Classification of Psychopathology. Neo-Kraepelinian and Quantitative Approaches*, New York, Plenum Press.

Braceland, F.J. (1956) 'Kraepelin, his system and his influence'. *American Journal of Psychiatry*, 113: 871–4.

Bruch, H. (1969) 'One hundred years of psychiatry (Kraepelin) fifty years later'. *Archives of General Psychiatry*, 21: 257–8.

Craig, G.A. (1978) *Germany 1866–1945*, Oxford, Clarendon Press.

Daraszkiewicz, L. (1892) *Über Hebephrenie, insbesondere deren schwere Form*, Dissertation, Dorpat, Laakmanns.

Del Pistoia, L. (1971) 'Le problème de la temporalité dans la psychiatrie française classique'. *L'Evolution Psychiatrique*, 36: 445–74.

Den Boer, J.A., Westenberg, H.G.M. and Van Praag, H.M. (eds.) (1995) *Advances in the Neurobiology of Schizophrenia*, Chichester, John Wiley.

Dening, T.R. and Berrios, G.E. (1991) Introduction to 'The significance of symptom complexes in psychiatry'. *History of Psychiatry*, 2: 329–33.

Deny, G. and Roy, P. (1903) *La démence précoce*, Paris, Baillière et fils.

Dörner, K. (1969) *Bürger und Irre*, Frankfurt am Main, Europäische Verlagsanstalt.

Ellenberger, H.F. (1970) *The discovery of the Unconscious. The history and evolution of dynamic psychiatry*, London, Allen Lane.

Engstrom, E.J. (1990) *Emil Kraepelin: Leben und Werk des Psychiaters im Spannungsfeld zwischen positivistischer Wissenschaft und Irrationalität*, Master's Thesis, Munich, Ludwig-Maximilians-Universität München.

Engstrom, E.J. (1992) Introduction to 'Psychiatric observations on contemporary issues'. *History of Psychiatry*, 3: 253–6.

Esquirol, E. (1838) *Des maladies mentales*, 2 vols, Paris, Baillière.

Fish, F. (1967) 'Recent developments in schizophrenia: a review'. *British Journal of Psychiatry*, 113: 1321.

Fish, F. (1968) 'Kraepelin's nosology'. *British Journal of Psychiatry*, 114: 356.

Genil-Perrin, G. (1913) *L'Idée de Dégénérescence*, Paris, Leclerc.

Grayson, D.A. (1987) 'Can categorical and dimensional views of psychiatric illness be distinguished?' *British Journal of Psychiatry*, 151: 355–61.

Havens, L.L. (1956) 'Emil Kraepelin'. *Journal of Nervous Mental Disease*, 141: 16–28.

Hoche, A. (1912) 'Die Bedeutung der Symptomenkomplexe in der Psychiatrie'. *Zeitschrift für die gesamte Neurologie und Psychiatrie*, 12: 540–51. (Translation by R.G. Dening and T.R. Dening as 'The significance of symptom complexes in psychiatry'. *History of Psychiatry*, 1991, 2: 334–43.)

Hoenig, J. (1968) 'Kraepelin and his approach to nosology'. *British Journal of Psychiatry*, 114: 125–6.

Hoenig, J. (1983) 'The concept of schizophrenia Kraepelin-Bleuler-Schneider'. *British Journal of Psychiatry*, 142: 547–56.

Hoff, P. (1985) 'Zum Krankheitsbegriff bei Emil Kraepelin'. *Nervenarzt*, 50: 8–13.

Hoff, P. (1992) *Emil Kraepelin und die Psychiatrie als klinische Wissenschaft. Ein Beitrag zum Selbsvertändnis psychiatrischer Forschung*, Habilitationschrift, Munich, Ludwig-Maximilians-Universität München.

Janzarik, W. (1979) '100 Jahre Heidelberger Psychiatrie'. In Janzarik, W. (ed.) *Psychopathologie als Grundlagenwissenschaft*, Stuttgart, Enke, pp.1–18. (Translated by R.G. Dening and T.R. Dening as '100 years of Heidelberg psychiatry'. *History of Psychiatry*, 1992, 3: 5–27.)

Jaspers, K. (1963) *General Psychopathology*, (translated by Hoenig, J. and Hamilton, M.), Manchester, Manchester University Press.

Kahlbaum, K. (1863) *Die Gruppirung der psychischen Krankheiten und die Eintheilung der Seelenstrungen*, Danzig, A.W. Kafemann.

Kahn, E. (1956) 'Emil Kraepelin'. *American Journal of Psychiatry*, 113: 289–94.

Klein, D.B. (1970) *A History of Scientific Psychology*, London, Routledge & Kegan Paul.

Kolle, K. (1957) *Kraepelin und Freud. Beitrag zur neuren Geschichte der Psychiatrie*, Georg Thieme, Stuttgart.

Kraepelin, E. (1887) *Die Richtungen der psychiatrischen Forschung. Vortrag, gehalten bei der bernahme des Lehramtes an der Kaiserlichen Universität Dorpat*, Leipzig, Vogel.

Kraepelin, E. (1893) *Lehrbuch der Psychiatrie*, 4 Auflage, Leipzig, Abel Meixner.

Kraepelin, E. (1894) 'Die Abgrenzung der Paranoia'. *Allgemeine Zeitschrift für Psychiatrie*, 50: 1080–1.

Kraepelin, E. (1896a) 'Über remissionen bei Katatonie'. *Allgemeine Zeitschrift für Psychiatrie*, 52: 1126–7.

Kraepelin, E. (1896) *Lehrbuch der Psychiatrie*, 5th edition, Leipzig, Barth.

Kraepelin, E. (1897) 'Ziele und Wege der klinischen Psychiatrie'. *Allgemeine Zeitschrift für Psychiatrie*, 53: 840–8.

Kraepelin, E. (1907) *Textbook of Psychiatry*, (7th Edition) translated by Diefendorf, A.R. (abstracted), London, MacMillan.

Kraepelin, E. (1918) 'Hundert Jahre Psychiatrie. Ein Beitrag zur Geschichte menschlicher Gesittung'. *Zeitschrift der Neurologie*, 38: 161–275.

Kraepelin, E. (1919) 'Die Erforschung psychischer Krankheitsformen'. *Zeitschrift für die gesammte Neurologie und Psychiatrie*, 51: 224–46.

Kraepelin, E. (1919) 'Psychiatrische Randbemerkungen zur Zeitgeschichte'. *Süddeutsche Monatshefte*, 16: 171–83.

Kraepelin, E. (1920) 'Die Erscheinungsformen des Irreseins'. *Zeitschrift für die gesammte Neurologie und Psychiatrie*, 62: 1–29. (Translation by Beer, D. as 'The manifestations of Insanity'. *History of Psychiatry*, 1992, 3: 509–29.)

Kraepelin, E. (1921) 'Bismarcks Persönlichkeit. Ungedruckte persönliche Erinnerungen'. *Süddetischen Monatshefte*, 19: 105–22.

Kraepelin, E. (1983) *Lebenserinnerungen*, Springer, Berlin.

Lange, J. (1926) 'Emil Kraepelin'. *Naturwissenschaften*, 14: 1255–6.

Lanteri-Laura, G. (1972) 'La chronicité dans la psychiatrie moderne française'. *Annales,* (Paris) No 3, 548–68.

Lanteri-Laura, G. (1986) 'Acuité et pathologie mentale'. *L'Evolution Psychiatrique,* 51: 403–16.

Leader (1968) 'Emil Kraepelin (1856–1926): psychiatric nosographer'. *Journal American Medical Association,* 203: 978–9.

Leary, D.E. (1978) 'The philosophical development of the conception of psychology in Germany, 1780–1850'. *Journal of the History of the Behavioral Sciences,* 14: 113–21.

López Piñero, J.M. (1983) *Historical Origins of the Concept of Neurosis.* Translated by Berrios, D., Cambridge, Cambridge University Press.

Mairet, A. and Margot, J. (1920) *La Démence Précoce,* Paris, Dubois.

Marneros, A. and Tsuang, M.T. (eds.) (1990) *Affective and Schizoaffective Disorders,* Heidelberg, Springer.

Mayer, W. (1956) 'Emil Kraepelin'. *American Journal of Psychotherapy,* 10: 273–6.

Marandon de Montyel, E. (1905) 'Les formes de la démence précoce'. *Annales Médico-Psychologiques,* 2: 246–60.

Mischel, T. (1970) 'Wundt and the conceptual foundations of Psychology'. *Philosophy and Phenomenological Research,* 31: 1–26.

Mongeri, L. (1905) 'Les formes de la démence précoce'. *Annales Médico-Psychologiques,* 2: 261–5.

Monod, G. (1905) *Les Formes Frustres de la Démence Précoce,* Paris, Rousset.

Parant, V. (1905) 'D'une prétendue entité morbide dite démence précoce'. *Annales Médico-Psychologiques,* 1: 229–41.

Pauly, P.J. (1983) 'The political structure of the brain: cerebral localization in Bismarckian Germany'. *International Journal of Neuroscience,* 21: 145–9.

Pichot, P. (1982) 'The diagnosis and classification of mental disorders in French-speaking countries: background, current view and comparisons with other nomenclatures'. *Psychological Medicine,* 12: 475–92.

Pichot, P. (1984) *A Century of Psychiatry,* Paris, Dacosta.

Rennert, H. (1968) 'Wilhelm Griesinger und die Einheitspsychose'. *Wissenschaftliche Zeitschrift der Humboldt Universität,* 17: 15–16.

Rieder, R.O. (1974) 'The origins of our confusion about schizophrenia'. *Psychiatry,* 37: 197–208.

Walk, A. (1968) 'What Kraepelin really said'. *British Journal of Psychiatry,* 114: 643–4.

Wender, P.H. (1963) 'Dementia Praecox: the development of the concept'. *American Journal of Psychiatry,* 119: 1143–51.

Wirth, W. (1927) 'Emil Kraepelin zum Gedächtnis'. *Archiv gesammte Psychologie,* 58: 1–32.

Vaillant, G.E. (1964) 'An historical review of the remitting schizophrenias'. *Journal of Nervous and Mental Disease,* 138: 48–56.

Vliegen, J. (1980) *Die Einheitspsychose. Geschichte und Problem,* Stuttgart, Enke.

Zilboorg, G. (1941) *A History of Medical Psychology,* New York, Norton.

Zubin, J., Oppenheimer, G. and Neugebauer, G. (1985) 'Degeneration theory and the stigma of schizophrenia'. *Biological Psychiatry,* 20: 1145–8.

Chapter 10
Kraepelin

Social Section
ERIC J ENGSTROM

Upon his return to Germany from the Russo-German university of Dorpat in the spring of 1891 Emil Kraepelin (1856–1926) stood on the verge of what was to become perhaps the most productive and ultimately significant period in his life. After spending five years on the geographic fringe of German academic life, Kraepelin found himself occupying the chair in psychiatry at Heidelberg, one of the most prestigious universities in the Wilhelmine empire. It was here in the years prior to the appearance of the fifth edition of his influential textbook (1896) that Kraepelin laid the foundations for his nosology, in particular the distinction between dementia praecox and manic depressive insanity.

In tracing the origins of Kraepelin's nosology historians of psychiatry have traditionally focused their attention on scientific and theoretical debates within the discipline.[1] They have hence implicitly assumed that the categories which Kraepelin delimited had emerged from largely autonomous, internal forces specific to psychiatric research and theory. Kraepelin's nosology has been viewed more or less as the product of his own 'objective' empirical studies in the clinic and of an hermetic discourse within psychiatry.

It is only very recently that attempts have been undertaken to investigate the clinical reality behind the development of this psychiatric taxonomy and to consider its emergence in an institutional context.[2] This is not to suggest that theoretical developments were solely the product of a particular historical situation or that they had very little impact on Kraepelin's research. In fact, theory played an important part in the reorientation of his research in the 1880s and 1890s. However, any explanation of Kraepelin's nosology remains deficient to the extent that it either ignores or dismisses the influence of personal, social, and institutional determinants and constraints on the construction of psychiatric theory. Even if one argues that Kraepelin's categories were immune from external influences and that they truly reflected deeper, ahistorical, biological fact, there can nevertheless be little doubt that the realities of Kraepelin's clinic formed *conditions of possibility* of the construction of those categories. Regardless of whether his nosology was rooted more in biological fact or in social norms, Kraepelin (and by inference every psychiatrist) worked under social and institutional constraints which profoundly shaped the direction, method, and meaning of his research.

When Kraepelin returned to Germany from Dorpat in 1891 to assume his position as professor of psychiatry and clinic director in Heidelberg he found psychiatric care in the German state of Baden still laboring under the burden of a debilitating feud between the university clinics and the state asylums. For years the asylum director in Illenau, C.F.W. Roller (1802–1878), had succeeded in delaying the construction of a university clinic which he envisioned as threatening his authority and influence among officials in the state capital in Karlsruhe.[3] When the Heidelberg clinic finally was opened shortly after Roller's death in 1878 its statutes reflected his concern that the university clinic might become too powerful and autonomous within the state system of care for the insane in Baden. Thus, while on the one hand the clinic was part of the university and hence subject to the authority of the Ministry of Justice, Culture and Education, on the other hand the clinic had been conceived as a health care institution of the state of Baden and was situated within the jurisdiction of the far more powerful Ministry of the Interior.[4] Although the clinic enjoyed relative financial autonomy, it was fully integrated into the state-wide system of care for the insane. The clinic had in effect a double role to play: it was at once a university run hospital in which teaching and research were high priorities as well as a public hospital subject to strictly regulated policies of admission, transfer, and discharge.[5]

The system of care for the insane in Baden[6] divided the state into three districts, two of which were served by the university clinics in Heidelberg and Freiberg while the third was administered by the asylum in Illenau. These three institutions admitted patients directly. In addition there were two further institutions (Emmendingen and Pforzheim) which were not responsible for a specific geographic district, but rather were designed exclusively to relieve pressures on the clinics. Emmendingen accepted transfer patients who could be engaged in productive work while Pforzheim was responsible for accepting the long-term, chronically ill patients. The smooth functioning of this system depended upon two variables: first, the institutions admitting patients directly needed to have sufficient space in reserve to accomodate new patients and, second, Emmendingen and Pforzheim required the capacity to accept transfers from the three admitting institutions.[7] The explosion of the mental patient population in the late nineteenth century placed great strains on the orderly functioning of the system and further aggravated tension between the university clinics and the asylums.[8]

Kraepelin's presence in Heidelberg did nothing to alleviate these tensions and if anything the conflict worsened during his tenure of service.[9] In 1891 Kraepelin directed a letter to the Ministry of Justice, Culture and Education in which he voiced his objection to the standing policy of transferring patient records between Heidelberg and Emmendingen. In a letter dated 26 December 1891 Kraepelin suggested that, upon the transfer of patients, admission files not follow the patient, but rather remain in the admitting institution. Kraepelin argued that

> we have the first claim to holding those files since they are the product of our administrative labor and that it should rather be the responsibility of the directorate of E[mmendingen] to acquire the data of interest to it from the files which we would gladly place at its disposal.[10]

Kraepelin supported his argument by stressing both the administrative and the scientific interest which the clinic had in the admission files. For the clinic the files were of

> fundamental administrative importance, not to mention the specific medical, scientific, and practical interest, whereas for the directorate of E[mmendingen] they are of absolutely no administrative and only very subordinate medical importance.[11]

Kraepelin's concern for patient files must be viewed in the context of his growing interest in the temporal course of mental diseases and the potential which studying their longitudinal development might harbor for isolating specific illnesses and grouping them into nosological categories.[12] To this end he had pondered, while still in Dorpat, a research agenda which drew on the ideas of Kahlbaum (1828–1899) and which stressed clinical observation in an attempt to supplant synchronic with diachronic diagnostic criteria.[13] He speculated that by investigating the entire course of a disease he might succeed in isolating specific nosological categories. It was, however, not until Kraepelin was called to Heidelberg in 1891 that he began systematically to collect his clinical observations. It was only there that he found the conditions (in particular the ability to keep track of patients as they moved from one institution to the next) which he deemed suitable for rigorous clinical investigation.[14] Thus, over the next five years, and indeed for much of the rest of his life, Kraepelin meticulously traced the histories of countless patients. It was on the basis of these histories that he constructed the disease categories which appeared in the vanguard fifth edition of his textbook Psychiatrie. In the preface to that textbook he wrote that the fifth edition represented a

> decisive step from a symptomatic to a clinical view of insanity. The necessity of this shift in perspective was impressed upon me by practical needs and is illustrated above all in the delimitation and ordering of clinical cases (Krankheitsbilder). The importance of external clinical signs (Krankheitszeichen) has necessarily and everywhere been subordinated to considerations of the conditions of origin, the course, and the terminus which result from individual disorders. Thus, all purely 'symptomatic categories' (Zustandsbilder) have disappeared from the nosology.[15]

Patient cards (Zählkarten) were an essential tool in the construction of Kraepelin's nosology as well as a reflection of his emphasis on clinical observation and longitudinal analysis. These cards provided excerpts of the patient history and outlined the 'essential characteristics of the clinical picture'.[16] They were supposed to avoid technical jargon and give as objective an account of the clinical facts as possible.[17] Upon admitting a patient, a card would be prepared on which a diagnosis and future course of the disease could be recorded. Even after the patient had left the clinic the cards would continue to be updated as to the course of the illness until a final outcome could be determined.[18] That the patient not be lost from sight upon leaving the clinic was crucial to the success of Kraepelin's research project. But one of the consequences of the project was that Kraepelin's yearly visits to the other mental institutions in Baden to check up on transferred patients further exacerbated tensions between the university clinics and the asylums.[19]

In spite of these tensions, the relationship between Kreapelin's clinic and the asylums remained tolerable through the early 1890s. The opening of Emmendingen in 1889 had alleviated some of the pressures on the system in Baden. Nevertheless, by the mid-1890s the number of patients had risen dramatically, driving up the temperature in the simmering conflict between Kraepelin and his colleagues in the asylums. As early as 1893 there had been instances of patient log jams which, according to Kraepelin, 'threatened significantly to disrupt the smooth functioning of our clinic'.[20] And by June of 1896 Kraepelin was complaining to Karlsruhe that 'the extent of overcrowding in our clinic [had] long since reached an entirely unacceptable level' and that an 'extraordinarily large number of unruly, violent and cumbersome [patients]' had collected in the clinic.[21] In closing his letter Kraepelin called for a reform of the system of care for the insane in Baden.

Barely three weeks later Kraepelin's patience had come to an end and in a letter dated 12 July 1896 he sparked a controversy which raged for months between himself and the state Office of Administration (*Verwaltungshof*) in Karlsruhe.[22] The Office of Administration was ultimately responsible for overseeing the admission and transfer of patients throughout Baden. The dispute was touched off by the Office of Administration's rejection of a transfer application submitted by the directorate of the Heidelberg clinic (i.e. Kraepelin) and its request that the directorate supply a cogent justification for the transfer. The intervention of the Office of Administration was, in Kraepelin's eyes, an insult to his professional and medical integrity:

> the Office of Administration is predominantly a *lay agency*, which, given even the most detailed description of the disease, could at most judge the purely formal justification of our transfer request, but not its medical [justification]. . . . How are we supposed to prove such things to a *lay agency* and what purpose would such a proof have![23]

Hardly one to wait for directives from Karlsruhe, Kraepelin proposed a reform in the practice of distributing patients and the introduction of a questionnaire in order to pass necessary information on to the institution receiving the transferred patient. Furthermore, he demanded that 'our clinic immediately be given the capacity to free up space rapidly in the event of an emergency'.[24]

Kraepelin's exhortations prompted the immediate and vociferous outcry of the directorate of Illenau, the Ministry of the Interior, and the Office of Administration.[25] In its position paper of 8 September 1896 the Office of Administration pointed out that the Heidelberg directorate was required to supply an 'obvious and exhaustive' justification of its transfer applications and that the directorate was '*very well aware*' of the problem of overcrowding in the state system.[26] The government's chief medical advisor rejected Kraepelin's criticisms and suggested that the size of the Heidelberg district be reduced in order to alleviate the overcrowding there.[27] Finally, the Ministry of the Interior also dismissed Kraepelin's complaints, seconding the suggestion of the medical council that the clinic's admission district be curtailed while simultaneously accusing the clinic's director of

deeming the statutes of the institution unscientific and ignoring them and of disputing the authority of the Office of Administration as a lay agency incompetant to distribute the sick among the individual institutions. . . .

Irrespective of divergent scientific opinion, the directorate of the clinic cannot be allowed to ignore those [statutes] at its whim; even in this instance [the directorate] shall rather be able to justify its applications in accordance with the official statutes.[28]

For a scientist of Kraepelin's mettle this rebuttal was intolerable and it prompted him, upon his return from vacation in Italy in the spring of 1897, to write an extensive memorandum concerning the transfer of mental patients out of the university clinic.[29] He again expressed the opinion that only the psychiatrists in the clinic and not the Office of Administration could 'truly and accurately judge' issues concerning the transfer of patients and that the current regulations were 'utterly useless in both fundamental and practical terms'.[30] Kraepelin again called for the introduction of a questionnaire and warned of impending 'tragedies' which would 'in the not so distant future convince even the most die-hard skeptic'.[31] In order to relieve the pressure on his clinic Kraepelin suggested that he be allowed to transfer patients from Heidelberg to Illenau (i.e. to one of the admitting institutions rather than Emmendingen or Pforzheim) or that his applications for transfer to Emmendingen and Pforzheim be given priority.[32]

What most piqued Kraepelin's anger was, however, the suggestion that the admission district of the Heidelberg clinic be restricted.[33] Kraepelin did his best to discourage efforts along these lines by pointing out the entirely different functions of the clinic and the asylum. For example, according to Kraepelin's conception of a clinic, if long-term patients 'were not to have their health acutely endangered then they must in all cases be allowed to remain only briefly [in the clinic]'.[34] Long-term patients were to be transferred as soon as possible to the appropriate asylum, where their needs could be better attended to than in a clinic. From Kraepelin's perspective the problem of overcrowding was more one of proper patient distribution within and among the existing institutions than of excessive admissions in the Heidelberg district.

A further argument against the reduction of the Heidelberg district focused on the pedagogical function of the clinic. Kraepelin protested vehemently that

> every reduction in the number of our yearly admissions below the level of about 250 cases would gravely compromise the quality of psychiatric education.[35]

Kraepelin categorically rejected every attempt to reduce the number of admissions to the clinic because this would inevitably lead to a reduction in the spectrum of patients available for use in the classroom. In fact, he contended that his clinic could easily cope with double the current number of admissions.[36] Only an extension of the existing system of care and not a reduction in the size of Heidelberg's district, 'the realization of which we will never and under no circumstances lend our hand', could alleviate the problems of overcrowding and prevent the 'debilitation of our classroom material [Lehrmaterial, i.e. patients, EJE]'.[37]

Kraepelin was successful in heading off attempts to reduce the size of the Heidelberg district, but his protests did not succeed in improving conditions in his clinic.[38] Instead the situation continued to deteriorate throughout the

1890s[39] so that he began calling for the 'decoupling of university clinics from the state system of care for the insane'.[40] Kraepelin argued that the addition of psychiatry to the state medical board examination in Baden in 1896 as well as the clinic's more general educational mission required that the directorate be granted greater flexibility:

> As soon as the instruction of all doctors in psychiatry has been required by the state, the clinic must be granted such autonomy in the selection of its patient material [*Krankenmaterial*] as the to enable it satisfactorily to fulfill its scientific and educational duties. The clinic should be an ideal institution in which [doctors] experience, in both scientific and practical terms, the best which is presently attainable.[41]

For Kraepelin the autonomy necessary to accomplish the clinic's scientific and educational mission was, again, not a question of reducing admissions to the clinic, but rather of allowing the directorate to chose the patients it wished to admit and granting it the authority to ensure the transfer of patients which it deemed superfluous to the realization of the clinic's aims. Indeed it was precisely this issue of the clinic's autonomy that in 1902/3 prompted Kraepelin to leave Heidelberg and accept a position in Munich, where the university clinic was less hampered by admission requirements and transfer restrictions.[42]

Kraepelin's struggle against the reduction in the size of the Heidelberg district as well as his call for the decoupling of the clinic from state care for the insane must be viewed in the context of his own research agenda. The construction of nosological groups according to the criteria of a disease's course required not only access to admission files and the use of *Zählkarten*, but also the broadest selection and largest number of patient histories possible. Only then was a satisfactory comparison and hence a reliable grouping of individual cases possible. Kraepelin's research agenda (as well as the exigencies of teaching) was contingent upon an abundant supply of patients who could be tracked as they moved through the state system of psychiatric care and whose symptoms could be recorded on *Zählkarten*. From this perspective its becomes clear why Kraepelin was at once unwilling to accept any reduction of the Heidelberg admission district that might have relieved the overcrowding in his clinic and, simultaneously, avidly encouraging a greater number of admissions.[43] The clinic was to serve as a funnel into which the greatest possible number of patients were to be admitted, diagnosed, and then distributed to varying secondary institutions. While high rates of admission may have aggravated already crowded clinical conditions, Kraepelin welcomed additional patients to the extent that they provided him with fresh research and classroom 'material', fortified his stance in the struggle for clinical autonomy against the state bureaucracy, and above all facilitated the demarcation of disease categories.

When Kraepelin finally presented the auspicious results of his clinical research to the annual meeting of the Association of German Psychiatrists in Heidelberg in 1896 he had already collected a thousand patient histories.[44] But the sharpness of the boundaries between the nosological categories he had isolated depended upon the number of cases investigated; and for Kraepelin 1000 cases were far too few to arrive at a final categorization. Thus, he stressed that there was still much work to be done in order gradually to uncover the unknown [disease] patterns, if necessary to construct groupings, [and] to extend or restrict old ones as the increased knowledge of clinical experience demands.[45]

Thus, by implication, the pace at which psychiatric knowledge advanced stood in direct proportion to the rate of admissions to the university clinic. This consideration represented an important motivating factor behind Kraepelin's battles with government bureaucrats in Karlsruhe, so that what appeared to be a conflict arising out of the overcrowded situation in the Heidelberg clinic was at the same time a struggle over institutional and scientific autonomy. From each of these perspectives it would appear that Kraepelin had little interest in the reduction of admissions to his clinic. On the contrary, he passionately argued for the expansion of clinic admissions in order to acquire additional cases for his expressly quantitative research method. As one of his colleagues noted

> [Kraepelin] could not investigate enough cases, following their emergence, course, and outcome; he was forever preoccupied with the reworking of the thousands upon thousands of patient histories which had passed through his hands, pursuing each detail and continually grouping and regrouping what he had discovered.[46]

The development of the nosology which emerged from this passionate desire to organize was conditional upon an expressly quantitative research agenda requiring the use of *Zählkarten* to track the course of mental diseases over time and to allow for their grouping into nosological categories. This agenda was, in turn, subject to institutional policies of admission and transfer as well as to Kraepelin's struggle for clinical autonomy within the state system of psychiatric care in late nineteenth century Baden.

NOTES

1 See for example Birnbaum (1928), de Boor (1954), Leibbrand and Wettley (1961), Pauleikhoff (1983).
2 Berrios and Hauser (1988) and Engstrom (1990).
3 On the feud cf. Wilmanns (1929) and Janzarik (1978).
4 Janzarik (1978), 96.
5 Riese (1977), 226.
6 Cf. M. Fischer (1902/3), 89–92, 102–4, 111–16. Cf. also Kraepelin (1983), 116–18.
7 Fischer (1902/3), 92.
8 On overcrowding in Baden see Fischer (1911/12).
9 Kraepelin (1983), 67f; Wilmanns (1929), 18. Janzarik states that Kraepelin was an opponent of regional psychiatry as practiced in Baden, cf. Janzarik (1978), 98.
10 Emil Kraepelin to Ministry of Justice, Culture and Education, 26 December 1891, Nr. 2000, Archive of the psychiatric clinic of the University of Heidelberg (subsequently cited as PKUH), VIII/4.
11 Ibid.
12 Kraepelin (1983), 67; Kraepelin (1896), v.

13 Hauser and Berrios (1988), 815.
14 Mayer-Gross (1929), 32.
15 Kraepelin (1896), v.
16 Kraepelin (1983), 142.
17 Mayer-Gross (1929), 34.
18 Kraepelin (1983), 67.
19 Ibid.
20 Emil Kraepelin to Ministry of Justice, Culture and Education, 22 April 1893, Nr. 868, PKUH VIII/4.
21 Emil Kraepelin to Ministry of Justice, Culture and Education, 20 June 1896, Nr. 1328, PKUH I/1.
22 Emil Kraepelin to Ministry of Justice, Culture and Education, 12 July 1896, Nr. 1577, PKUH VIII/4.
23 Ibid.
24 Ibid.
25 Wilmanns, 18; also Kraepelin (1983), 118.
26 Report of the grand-ducal Office of Administration, 8 September 1897, Nr. 36818, PKUH VIII/4.
27 Statement of the Medical Advisor for psychiatric affairs, 26 December 1896, PKUH VIII/4. The suggestion of reducing the size of the Heidelberg district was also made by the director of the asylum in Illenau, Schüle (1840–1916). Cf. Wilmanns (1929), 19.
28 Finding of the grand-ducal Ministry of the Interior, 2 January 1897, Nr. 37593, PKUH VIII/4.
29 Emil Kraepelin's report to the Ministry of Justice, Culture and Education, 6 May 1897 PKUH VIII/4.
30 Ibid., 1 and 3.
31 Ibid., 4.
32 Ibid., 8f.
33 Kraepelin (1983), 117f.
34 Report of Emil Kraepelin to the Ministry of Justice, Culture and Education, 6 May 1897, 7, PKUH VIII/4.
35 Ibid.
36 Ibid., 8.
37 Ibid., 10.
38 Wilmanns (1929), 19.
39 In the 'July crisis' of 1900, for example, patient log jams again occurred. In a two-and-a-half week period Kraepelin flooded the Ministry for Justice, Culture and Education with no less than eight reports. Cf. General State Archives Karlsruhe, 235/3899.
40 Emil Kraepelin to Ministry of Justice, Culture and Education, 2 August 1899, PKUH I/1.
41 Ibid.
42 Emil Kraepelin to Medical Faculty of the University of Heidelberg, 7 July 1903, University of Heidelberg Archives III, 4a, Nr. 174b; also Kraepelin (1983), 126 and Wilmanns (1929), 20. In his negotiations with the Bavarian Ministry of Culture Kraepelin secured assurances that procedures of admission and transfer at the Munich clinic would be rapid and unbureaucratic:

'It would be . . . of the utmost importance, to ensure from the very beginning that a smooth and rapid discharge of those patients suitable for long-term care in an asylum take place and that [the clinic] never be forced to admit patients beyond the number of beds available'. Emil Kraepelin to Ministry of Culture, 30 June 1903, Central Bavarian State Archives, MK 11287.

43 Kraepelin reports in his memoirs how the regional asylums criticized how the 'clinics continually complained about over-crowding and yet wanted substantially to expand the admissions capacity'. Kraepelin (1983), 117.

44 'Bericht zur Jahressitzung des Vereins der deutschen Irrenaerzte in Heidelberg' (1897), 842.

45 Ibid., 844. Kraepelin described in detail the way in which he used patient cards to construct and delimit specific diseases in E. Kraepelin, 'Ziele und Wege der psychiatrischen Forschung', Zeitschrift fuer die gesamte Neurologie und Psychiatrie 42 (1918), 181f.

46 Felix Plaut, cited in K. Kolle (1957), 23.

REFERENCES

Berrios, G. and Hauser, R. (1988) 'The Early Development of Kraepelin's Ideas on Classification: A Conceptual History'. Psychological Medicine, 18: 813–21.

Bericht zur Jahressitzung des Vereins der deutschen Irrenärzte in Heidelberg [Report on the annual meeting of the Society of German Psychiatrists]. (1897) Allgemeine Zeitschrift für Psychiatrie, 53: 840–4.

Birnbaum, K. (1928) 'Geschichte der Psychiatrischen Wissenschaft' [History of Psychiatric Science]. In Handbuch der Geisteskrankheiten [Handbook of Mental Illness] (ed. Bumke, O.) Berlin, Springer.

Blasius, D. (1986) Umgang mit Unheilbarem: Studien zur Sozialgeschichte der Psychiatrie [Handling the Incurable: Studies in the Social History of Psychiatry], Bonn, Psychiatrie Verlag.

de Boor, W. (1954) Psychiatrische Systematik: Ihre Entwicklung in Deutschland seit Kahlbaum [Psychiatric Systems and their Development in Germany since Kahlbaum], Berlin, Springer.

Dörner, K. (1969) Bürger und Irre: Zur Sozialgeschichte und Wissenschaftssoziologie der Psychiatrie. Frankfurt, Europäische Verlagsanstalt. Translated (1981) as Madmen and the Bourgeoisie: A Social History of Insanity and Psychiatry, by Neugroschel, J. and Steinberg, J., Oxford, Basil Blackwell.

Engstrom, E. (1990) Emil Kraepelin: Leben und Werk des Psychiaters im Spannungsfeld zwischen positivistischer Wissenschaft und Irrationalität [Emil Kraepelin: Life and Work between Positivist Science and Irrationalism], Unpublished master's thesis, University of Munich.

Fischer, M. (1902/3) 'Die Irrenfürsorge in Baden' [The Care for the Insane in Baden]. Psychiatrisch-Neurologische Wochenschrift, 4, 89–92, 102–4, 111–16.

Fischer, M. (1911/12) 'Statistisches aus dem Badischen Irrenwesen' [Statistics on Insanity in Baden]. Psychiatrisch-Neurologische Wochenschrift, 13: 47–9.

Gross, A. (1929) 'Kraepelins Bedeutung für die Anstaltspsychiatrie' [Kraepelin's Significance for Asylum Psychiatry]. Archiv für Psychiatrie und Neurologie, 87: 50–67.

Hoff, P. (1985) 'Zum Krankheitsbegriff bei Emil Kraepelin' [Emil Kraepelin's Concept of Disease]. *Nervenarzt,* 56: 510–13.

Janzarik, W. (1978) '100 Jahre Heidelberger Psychiatrie' [100 Years of Psychiatry in Heidelberg]. *Heidelberger Jahresbücher,* 22: 93–113.

Kolle, K. (1957) *Kraepelin und Freud: Beitrag zur neueren Geschichte der Psychiatrie* [Kraepelin and Freud: A Study in the Recent History of Psychiatry], Stuttgart, Thieme.

Kraepelin, E. (1896) *Psychiatrie: Ein Lehrbuch für Studierende und Aerzte* [Psychiatry: A Textbook for Students and Physicians], (5th ed.), Leipzig, J.A. Barth.

Kraepelin, E. (1918) 'Ziele und Wege der psychiatrischen Forschung' [Trends in Psychiatric Research]. *Zeitschrift für die gesamte Neurologie und Psychiatrie,* 42: 169–205.

Kraepelin, E. (1983) *Lebenserinnerungen,* Berlin, Springer.

Leibbrand, W. and Wettley, A. (1961) *Der Wahnsinn: Geschichte der Abendländischen Psychopathologie* [Madness: A History of Occidental Psychopathology], Munich, Karl Alber.

Mayer-Gross, W. (1929) 'Die Entwicklung der klinischen Anschauungen Kraepelins' [The Development of Kraepelin's Clinical Views]. *Archiv für Psychiatrie und Nervenkrankheiten,* 87: 30–42.

Pauleikhoff, B. (1983) *Das Menschenbild im Wandel der Zeit: Ideengeschichte der Psychiatrie und der Klinischen Psychologie* [Perspectives on Humanity: A History of Psychiatric Ideas and Clinical Psychology], Hürtgenwald, Guido Pressler.

Riese, R. (1977) *Hochschulbetrieb auf dem Weg zum wissenschaftlichen Großbetrieb: Die Universität Heidelberg und das badische Hochschulwesen, 1860–1914* [The Academy in Transition: The University of Heidelberg and Higher Education in Baden, 1860–1914], Stuttgart, Klett.

Wilmanns, K. (1929) 'Die Entwicklung der badischen Irrenfürsorge mit besonderer Berücksichtigung der Universitäts-Kliniken' [The Development of Care for the Insane in Baden with Special Emphasis on University Clinics]. *Archiv für Psychiatrie und Nervenkrankheiten,* 87: 1–23.

Chapter 11
Wernicke

Clinical Section
MARIO HORST LANCZIK, HELMUT BECKMANN and GUNDOLF KEIL

INTRODUCTION

Since the eighteenth century neurology began to influence scientific psychiatry. Albrecht von Haller (1708–1777) and William Cullen (1710–1790) were among the most significant representatives of a new neurologically orientated psychopathology (Lanczik and Beckmann 1991). Haller's differentiation between reduced and increased neural excitability fostered the origin of neuropathological and neurophysiological explanations of mental illness. Psychiatry took over the terms irritability and excitability and distinguished between increased or diminished psychic irritability. Cullen's ideas of sadness, fear and depression assumed a depression of the brain vessels with a resulting atonia or diminished excitability of nerve fibres. The term depression in its historical origins for example was not a psychopathological phenomenon, i.e. a functional change in the organic substrate (Schmidt-Degenhard, 1983). Later on Cullen's pupil John Brown (1735–1788) simplified Cullen's ideas and differentiated between sthenic and asthenic forms of mental illness (Brown, 1795; Leibbrand and Wettley, 1961).

With Paul Broca (1824–1880) cerebral localization theories received new impetus in the nineteenth century. In 1861 Broca described the motor aphasia. In 1867, Theodor Meynert (1833–1892) pointed out that brain areas associated with motor function are mostly located in the frontal parts of the brain, whereas those mostly involved in sensation are located in the posterior parts (Meynert, 1867/68; Papez, 1953). John Hughlings Jackson (1834–1911) suggested that focal seizures might be an expression of cortical irritation affecting the brain areas described by Meynert (Lennox, 1953). Eduard Hitzig (1838–1907) then showed how electrical stimulation of dog's brain resulted in muscle jerking in the contralateral side (Hitzig, 1874; Kuntz, 1953). Thus discoveries of Broca, Meynert, Jackson and Hitzig seemed to contradict the early view of Jean Marie Flouren's (1794–1867) that the brain is a homogeneous organ, and to establish a theory of cerebral localization. At this stage, Wernicke appeared on the scene (Walker, 1957; Stender, 1968; Marx, 1970).

LIFE AND WORK

Carl Wernicke was born on 15 May 1848 in Tarnowitz in Silesia. He was the son of a civil servant and grew up in modest circumstances (Lanczik and Keil,

1991). After graduating in medicine at Breslau University he worked as an assistant to Heinrich Neumann (1814–1884) – one of the protagonists of the concept of unitary psychoses (Neumann, 1859; Lanczik, 1989) – in the Department of Psychiatry in Breslau and to Carl Westphal (1833–1889) – one of the protagonists of neuropsychiatry and Griesinger's successor – at the Charité in Berlin. Neumann gave him the chance to go to Vienna for six months, where he studied under the neuroanatomist-psychiatrist Meynert.

In *The Aphasic Symptom Complex*[1] (1874) Wernicke described his discovery of the sensory speech centre, and this brought him world-wide reputation. In 1876, he received his venia legendi with a thesis entitled *On the Primordial System of Convolutions in the Human Brain*.[2] During his work under Westphal in Berlin Wernicke wrote his famous three volume *Textbook of Diseases of the Brain*[3] which appeared between 1881 and 1883, and in which he presented a description of the anatomy, pathology and ontogenesis of the brain, which formed the basis of his reputation as a neurologist.[4] But this was to change in his work in Breslau. In 1885 Wernicke was called upon to succeed Neumann as an associate professor of neurology and psychiatry at the University of Breslau. The two subjects had been combined in Germany since the time of Griesinger. In his scientific work in Breslau Wernicke focussed on psychiatry as his main point of interest. In 1900, the first edition of Wernicke's *Basic Psychiatry*[5] appeared. In his studies on neurology Wernicke acknowledged his teachers, but his *Basic Psychiatry* 'is written almost as if a science of psychiatry did not yet exist' Theodor Ziehen (1862–1950) wrote in 1905. Taking as a model his views on the mechanism of aphasia, Wernicke attempted to establish a relationship between psychopathological symptoms and cerebral pathology.

After declining the offer of a professorial appointment in Vienna, in 1904 he moved to the chair of psychiatry in Halle an der Saale in Saxony. He died a year later, in 1905, as a consequence of a fatal accident while cycling in the Thuringian Forest (Goldstein, 1957; Kleist, 1970).

'THE APHASIC SYMPTOM COMPLEX' – THE BASIS FOR HIS NEUROPSYCHIATRIC CONCEPT

Wernicke's work, *The Aphasic Symptom Complex*, which stands as an important pillar of support to modern clinical neurology, was also decisive in his development as a psychiatrist. The key to his approach is revealed in the subtitle: *A Psychological Study with an Anatomical Basis*.[6]

The fact, that aphasic states could be found in which there was no brain lesion of the type described by Broca meant that there had to be a second type of localization. Following the postulate of Meynert that the frontal brain contains the *impressions of action*[7] and the temporal brain the *remembered images*,[8] Wernicke searched in the temporal region for the centre for sensory speech. His achievement was threefold. Firstly, he recognized the fact that the region described by Broca was not the only speech centre. Secondly, following the discovery by Meynert (1867) that the *Nervus acusticus* was connected to the cortex by a bundle of fibres – the origin of these nerve fibres he called the *sound image*[9] – Wernicke asserted that these sound images of speech were located in (what is now called) the *secondary auditory centre* of the *Gyrus temporalis superior.* Thirdly, he realized that the location described by Broca only acted as a *motor speech centre.*

Based on the *psychic reflex arc*[10] (Griesinger, 1867) and using *sensory aphasia* as an example, Wernicke described the *psychic reflex process.*[11] According to Wernicke, sensory impressions reach the brain via the so-called *projection system.*[12] These sensory impressions are then stored in the memory in *projection fields*[13] as *remembered images* in the same way that impressions received from moving muscles are stored as *impressions of action.* The combination is of *remembered images* and the so-called *action of will*[14] which immediately follows a stimulus. According to his views, *actions of speech*[15] are also an *action of will.* These *reflex movements* can be interrupted at various locations: for example, by destroying the *projection fields* – in the present case the location of *action speech images* meaning the motor speech centre – or by interrupting the nerve fibres linking the *projection fields* to the Nervus acusticus, the motor speech path. Individual symptoms are determined by localization of the damage. Wernicke was thus able to distinguish Broca's *motor aphasia* from *sensory aphasia.* In addition, he suggested the existence of a *conduction aphasia* caused by destruction of the connecting association system.

Between the sensory and motor *projection fields* Wernicke identified a new centre, the so-called *centre of ideas,*[16] which is connected to the *projection fields* via transcortical paths belonging to the association system. Wernicke did not localize this centre in great detail (Liepmann, 1911) – although his critics have claimed he did – but speculated that it must be located in other regions of the cortex and that it must radiate to various cortical areas. Thought processes would take place in the centre, itself made out of bundles of nerve fibres. Thus, he considered the substrate of thought to be localized in the nerves and – applying the knowledge of brain physiology acquired by Hitzig – he concluded that pathological reduction, increase or perversion of excitability or conductivity of ganglion cells must be involved in mental illness.

If one calls to mind the organization of the *psychic reflex process* then Wernicke's thesis concerning the relationship between mental disorders and malfunctioning of the association areas becomes clearer. The *reflex process* includes a

	→	psychosensory path between the *sensory projection field* and the *centre,*
an	→	intrapsychic path, meaning the association paths within the *centre,*
and the	→	psychomotor path between *centre* and *motor projection field.*

When types of change in excitability mentioned above are combined with the three speculative paths the following combinations result:

1. anaesthesia, hyperaesthesia and paraesthesia of the *psychosensory path.*
2. afunction, hyperfunction and parafunction of the *intrapsychic path.*
3. akinesis, hyperkinesis and parakinesis of the *psychomotor path.*

In a lecture on the classification of psychiatric symptoms given at Breslau University in 1891, Wernicke presented examples of a 'natural taxonomy' for

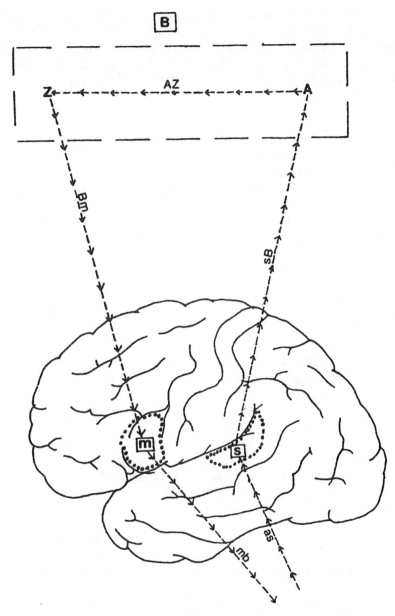

Figure 1: Wernicke's psychic reflex arc – in the present example the location of the actions of speech

as : sensory nerves, for example the n. acusticus;
s : sensory projection field;
sB : psychosensory path (transcortical);
B : centre of ideas;
AZ : intrapsychic path;
Bm : psychomotor path (transcortical);
m : motor projection field;
mb : motor nerves mb: motor speech path

mental disorders: in *logomania* he believed the disorder was to be found in the psychosensory path of the psychic reflex arc – as in hallucination – or else in the intrapsychic path as, for example, in mania. Imbecility, too, he considered to arise intrapsychically by a complete breakdown of the thinking process. He explained catatonic symptoms in terms of a malfunctioning of the psychomotor path.

THE 'SEJUNCTION' THEORY

On the basis of this association theory, Wernicke developed the idea that pathological disorders of the central nervous system – which included mental illness – were caused by interruptions in the continuity of the association pathways. He called these *sejunctions*. The same views he applied to pathological psychic processes which he called *irritable symptoms*.[17] Irritable symptoms resulted either from the malfunction itself or from a build-up of energy – according to the principles of mechanics – in the ganglion cells, caused by the interrupted flow. This led to an increased tension in the nerve cells. The location of the *sejunction process*[18] would determine the *irritable symptom*. Hallucinations were thus explained in terms of a discharge of the increased excitation. Other pathological processes in the brain, including psychopathological processes, were, however, associated with the malfunction itself.

WERNICKE'S CLASSIFICATION OF PSYCHOSES

Wernicke's teacher Neumann had suggested that there are no individual syndromes in psychiatry, and that the various forms of mental illness were only expressions of one and the same basic disorder (Neumann, 1859; Henseler, 1959). Wernicke considered this view as pessimistic and suggested that the classification of mental illnesses should not await for major pathological-anatomical discoveries in brain anatomy. Classification was necessary even for practical purposes, so he endorsed Karl Ludwig Kahlbaum's (1828–1899) call for the outlining of *syndromes* on the basis of clinical observation (Kahlbaum, 1863; Hecker, 1871; Katzenstein, 1963; Lanczik, 1992). In 1957 Goldstein wrote that one may miss descriptions of clinical entities in Wernicke's psychiatry. This is not accidental. Wernicke considered the time not yet ripe for distinction of separate psychiatric diseases. Thus, he was and remained always an ardent adversary of Emil Kraepelin (1856–1926), whose pure clinical method he considered not sufficiently scientific (Wernicke, 1906; Goldstein, 1957). Neurological discoveries suggested, in his opinion, that classification should take into account localization (Wernicke, 1899). It must be remembered that his definition of psychoses was different from that commonly held at the time: he believed that psychoses were all psychic deviations arising from a disorder in nervous function (Wernicke, 1906).

Wernicke considered the cortex to be the organic substrate of consciousness, and hence the latter had to be associated, according to the division into sensory and motor *remembered images* with certain defined cortical regions. In 1899, he defined consciousness as the sum of impressions derived from three sources, environment, self and body, and according to which group was involved he classified the psychoses into

	→	allopsychoses,
	→	autopsychoses,
and	→	somatopsychoses,

respectively.

Autopsychoses resulted from having false impressions of oneself; allopsychoses from having false impressions of the environment; and somatopsychoses from having a distorted experience of one's own body (Wernicke, 1906).

Localization is not disregarded in this classification. The objective of classifying psychic illnesses is to establish which aspect of consciousness is involved, then to examine symptoms with respect to motor behaviour which may result from disorders in psychosensory, intrapsychic and psychomotoric pathway. Only then ought the cause of the illness and its course to be considered. Wernicke makes use of delirium tremens to explain his model (Wernicke, 1899). In this condition the symptoms are those of an exogenous psychoses and hence indicate a disorientation in environment (i.e., an allopsychoses). The symptoms can be conceptualized as follows:

1. optical and tactile hallucinations
   → psychosensory hyperaesthesia
2. illusions
   → *psychosensory paraesthesia*
3. lack of local orientation ability
   → *psychosensory anaesthesia*
4. motor agitation
   → *psychomotoric hyperkinesia*
5. anxiety
   → *psychosensory paraesthesia*

Melancholia and mania are likewise examples of autopsychoses and are associated with symptoms of *intrapsychic afunction* or *hyperfunction*, respectively. Hyperchondriacal psychoses are included under the *somatopsychoses*.

THE SIGNIFICANCE OF WERNICKE'S NEUROPSYCHIATRIC CONCEPT AND HIS CRITICS

A number of neurological syndromes have been named after Carl Wernicke. His localization theories are recognized in neurology, neurosurgery and neuropsychology, but are less popular in modern psychiatry. He considered neurology and psychiatry as inseparable, but his teachings in psychiatry remain largely unknown. Almost inevitably Wernicke's theories attracted criticism from his contemporaries. For example, Karl Jaspers (1883–1969) was later to dub this materialistic perspective 'brain mythology' (Jaspers, 1922). Wernicke would be an individual who, after establishing some links between psychological disorders and various regions of the brain, extrapolated this model to the whole field of psychiatry. Jaspers even compared Wernicke with Sigmund Freud (1856–1939) by stating that both made generalizations beyond the facts and produced only abstract constructions. Wernicke and Freud were, incidentally, both students of Meynert in Vienna.

Wernicke was defended by his followers, particularly Liepmann, who made clear that Wernicke's model was not dependent upon actual anatomical localization, but on an analysis of psychological processes which could then be empirically correlated with central nervous system functions (Liepmann, 1911). Wernicke's model only required that the specified psychological processes could be mapped on the *projection system* of unknown locality. Thus, Wernicke's psychiatry was brain pathology that is, cerebral pathophysiology and not pathological anatomy. Since Wernicke, however, the site localization has become an essential principle in psychiatry and the debate is about sites and their extension and as to whether localization is map-like or mosaic-like, Liepmann resumed in 1911. Wernicke's psychopathological descriptions, in particular his accounts of motility disorders such as akinesis, hyperkinesis and parakinesis, constitute undisputed achievements (Leonhard, 1966; Leonhard, 1972). They best reflect his view that mental illness should be conceived as a neurological phenomenon.

WERNICKE'S SUCCESSORS IN GERMAN NEUROPSYCHIATRY

Wernicke's views and his terminology reveal an original and independent mind. His influence can be seen in the work of a whole generation of neurologists. Only a few continued to work along the lines he suggested in psychiatry. But with some justification, however, one can speak of a *Wernicke school* or *Breslau school of neuropsychiatry*. Karl Bonhoeffer (1868–1948) succeeded Wernicke at the Department of Psychiatry in Breslau. In his work on the form of *acute exogenous reaction*[19], Bonhoeffer postulated that acute organic brain symptoms are not descriptively bound to a particular aetiology (Bonhoeffer, 1917; Neumärker, 1990).

Otfrid Foerter (1873–1941), the founder of neurosurgery in Germany, was also a student of Wernicke (Wartenberg, 1953).[20] The latter's work on aphasia was the starting point for Karl Heilbronner (1869–1914) and Hugo Liepmann (1863–1925) who investigated apraxia, asymbolia and the significance of focal disorders to mental illness (Goldstein, 1953).

The studies of Karl Kleist (1879–1960) on psychomotor disorders in the mentally ill identified him as a student of Wernicke in Halle, and as his true successor in neuropsychiatry. Kleist became a Professor of Psychiatry in Rostock and Frankfurt am Main. He followed the same model, in that he attempted to understand clinical observations from the neuropathological point of view.

From Wernicke to Kleist and Leonhard – on the way to the development of the most differentiated nosology of endogenous psychoses

Kleist opposed Kraepelin's dichotomous classification of the endogenous psychoses and, like Wernicke, he postulated the existence of a variety of endogenous psychoses (Kleist, 1953; Teichmann, 1990).

Karl Leonhard (1904–1988), took over from Kleist the separation of the phasic and cycloid psychoses and differentiated between *unsystematic* and *systematic schizophrenias*. Leonhard, who died in 1988, was the last contemporary psychiatrist to retain the nosological categories of catatonia and hebephrenia (Leonhard, 1979; 1986). He delineated 35 different types of endogenous psychoses and he tried to validate them in terms of symptoms, prognosis and heredity; he outlined seven categories of catatonia and four of hebephrenia.

Wernicke had adopted Kahlbaum's principle of categorizing mental disorders in terms of the neurological concept of function, i.e., hyper-, hypo- and parafunction. In keeping with Wernicke and Kleist (1908, 1909, 1953) who regarded schizophrenia in terms of neurological impairment, Leonhard (1936, 1948) maintained that the condition had its origins in the selective loss of cerebral function. This produced either evidence of specific mental dysfunction or symptoms of cerebral irritation, both of which lent the psychosis its characteristic clinical picture. Leonhard's work echoed Wernicke's scheme of classifying mental and brain diseases along lines suggested by neurology. In creating their classification the neuropsychiatric school of Wernicke, Kleist and Leonhard concentrated on the cardinal symptoms of the disease (Teichmann, 1990). This meant that they looked for symptoms which reflected a loss of function or a specific focus of cerebral irritation. Their failure to find a corresponding physical basis for psychopathological phenomena seriously weakened their theoretical position. As a consequence their work has been dismissed as merely speculation (for example, see Pauleikhoff, 1983). In contrast to Kraepelinian psychiatry (Hoff, 1988), the work of Wernicke and his followers has much less influence until the eighteenth century.

The nosology of Wernicke, Kleist and Leonhard was flawed by its abstract notion of anatomical function: as a result it had little impact on the devising of modern classifications. However, this appears to be unfair: it was Kleist, Leonhard and Neele (1949) who first proposed the subdivision of affective illness into unipolar and bipolar categories. This deserves to be more widely known, and, indeed, so do many aspects of historical development of psychiatric nosology (Lanczik, 1992). Leonhard wrote that the history of psychiatry would have taken a different course had Wernicke not died so young.

NOTES

1 Der aphasische Symptomenkomplex.
2 Über das Urwindungssystem des menschlichen Gehirns.
3 Lehrbuch der Gehirnkrankheiten.
4 His work on central hemiplegia also dates from this period.
5 Grundriß der Psychiatrie.
6 Eine psychologische Studie auf anatomischer Basis.
7 Bewegungsvorstellungen.
8 Erinnerungsbilder; i.e., past sensory experiences.
9 Klangbilder.
10 Psychischer Reflexbogen.
11 Psychischer Reflexvorgang.
12 Projektionssystem.
13 Projektionsfelder.
14 Willensbewegung.
15 Sprachbewegungen.
16 Begriffszentrum.
17 Reizsymptome.

18 Sejunctionsvorgang.
19 Akuter exogener Reaktionstyp.
20 For nearly two years Foerster was physician to Lenin at Moscow.

REFERENCES

Broca, P.P. 'Perte de la parole; ramollissement chronique et destruction partielle du lobe anterieur gauche de cerveau'. *Bull. Soc. Anthrop.*, Paris, 2: 235–8.

Brown, J. (1795) *The Elements of Medicine*, London.

Goldstein, K. (1953) 'Hugo Karl Liepmann 1863–1925'. In Haymaker, W. *The Founders of Neurology*, Springfield, Thomas, pp.326–9.

Goldstein, K. (1953) 'Carl Wernicke (1848–1905)'. In Haymaker, W. *The Founders of Neurology*, Springfield, Thomas, pp.406–9.

Griesinger, W. (1867) *Die Pathologie und die Therapie der psychischen Krankheiten für Aerzte und Studierende*, 2nd. ed., Stuttgart, Krabbe.

Hecker, E. (1871) 'Zur Begründung des klinischen Standpunktes in der Psychiatrie'. *Archiv für pathologische Anatomie, Physiologie und Klinische Medizin*, 25: 202.

Henseler, H. (1959) *Die analytische Medizin des Psychiaters Heinrich Wilhelm Neumann*, Diss. med., University of Munich.

Hoff, P. (1988) 'Zum Krankheitsbegriff Emil Kraepelins'. *Nervenarzt*, 58: 510–3.

Hitzig, E. (1874) *Untersuchungen über das Gehirn*, Berlin, Hirschwald.

Jaspers, K. (1922) *Allgemeine Psychopathologie*, 3rd. ed., Berlin, Springer.

Kahlbaum, K.L. (1863) *Die Gruppirung psychischer Krankheiten und die Eintheilung der Seelenstörungen*, Danzig, Kafemann.

Katzenstein, R. (1963) *Karl Ludwig Kahlbaum und sein Beitrag zur Entwicklung der Psychiatrie*, Diss. med., Zürich.

Kleist, K. (1908) *Untersuchungen über die Kenntnis der psychomotorischen Bewegungsstörungen bei Geisteskrankheiten*, Leipzig, Brandstetter.

Kleist, K. (1909) *Weitere Untersuchungen an Geisteskrankheiten mit psychomotorischen Störungen*, Leipzig, Brandstetter.

Kleist, K. (1953) 'Die Gliederung der neuropschiatrischen Erkrankungen'. *Monatsschrift für Psychiatrie und Neurologie*, 125: 526–54.

Kleist, K. (1970) 'Carl Wernicke (1848–1905)'. In Kolle, K. (ed.) *Große Nervenärzte*, vol. 1, Stuttgart, Thieme.

Kuntz, A. (1953) 'Eduard Hitzig (1838–1907)'. In Haymaker, W., *The Founders of Neurology*, Springfield, Thomas, pp.138–42.

Lanczik, M. and Keil, G. (1991) 'Carl Wernicke's localization theory and its significance for the development of scientific psychiatry'. *History of Psychiatry*, 2: 171–80.

Lanczik, M. (1992) 'Karl Ludwig Kahlbaum (1828–1899) and the emergence of psycho-pathological and nosological research in German psychiatry'. *History of Psychiatry*, 3: 53–8.

Lanczik, M. and Beckmann, H. (1991) 'Historical aspects of affective disorders'. In Feighner, J.P. and Boyer, W.F. (eds.) *Diagnosis of depression. Perspectives in Psychiatry*, vol. 2, Chichester, Wiley, pp.1–16.

Leibbrand, W. and Wettley, A. (1961) *Der Wahnsinn. Geschichte der abendländischen Psychopathologie*, Freiburg, Alber.

Lennox, W.G. (1953) 'John Hughlings Jackson (1835–1911)'. In Haymaker, W., *The Founders of Neurology*, Springfield, Thomas, pp.308–11.

Leonhard, K. (1936) *Die defektschizophrenen Krankheitsbilder*, Leipzig, Thieme.

Leonhard, K. (1948) *Grundlagen der Psychiatrie*, Stuttgart, Enke.

Leonhard, K. (1966) 'Hatte Wernicke mit seiner Lokalisationslehre Unrecht?'. *Journal of Neurological Sciences*, 3: 434–8.

Leonhard, K. (1972) 'Die Aufteilung der endogenen Psychosen in der Forschungsrichtung von Wernicke und Kleist'. In Kisker, K.P., Meyer, J.-E., Müller, M. and Strömgren, E. (eds.) *Psychiatrie der Gegenwart*, vol. II/1, Berlin, Springer, pp.183–212.

Leonhard, K. (1979) *The Classification of Endogenous Psychoses*, 5th ed., New York, Irvington.

Leonhard, K. (1986) *Aufteilung der endogenen Psychosen und ihre differenzierte Nosologie*, Berlin, Akademie.

Liepmann, H.K. (1911) 'Über Wernickes Einfluß auf die klinische Psychiatrie'. *Monatsschrift für Psychiatrie und Neurologie*, 30: 1–32.

Marx, O.M. (1970) 'Nineteenth-century medical psychology. Theoretical problems in the work of Griesinger, Meynert and Wernicke'. *ISIS*, 61: 335–70.

Meynert, Th. (1867/68) 'Der Bau der Grosshirnrinde und seine örtlichen Verschiedenheiten'. *Vierteljahresschrift für Psychiatrie*, 1: 77–93, 88–113.

Neele E. (1949) *Die phasischen Psychosen nach ihrem Erscheinungs- und Erbbild*, Leipzig, Barth.

Neumärker K.-J. (1990) *Karl Bonhoeffer. Leben und Werk eines deutschen Psychiaters und Neurologen in seiner Zeit*, Leipzig, Hirzel.

Neumann, H. (1859) *Lehrbuch der Psychiatrie*, Erlangen, Enke.

Papez, J.W. (1953) 'Theodor Meynert (1833–1992)'. In Haymaker, W., *The Founders of Neurology*, Springfield, Thomas, pp.64–7.

Pauleikoff, B. (1983) *Das Menschenbild im Wandel der Zeit. Ideengeschichte der Psychiatrie und klinischen Psychologie*, vol. I–II, Hürtgenwald, Pressler.

Schmidt-Degenhard, M. (1983) *Melancholie und Depression*, Stuttgart, Kohlhammer.

Stender, A. (1968) 'Über die Forschungstätigkeit von Eduard Hitzig (1838–1907) und Carl Wernicke (1848–1905) in Berlin'. *Deutsches Medizinisches Journal*, 19: 335–9.

Teichmann, G. (1990) 'The influence of Karl Kleist on the nosology of Karl Leonhard'. In Beckman, H. and Lanczik, M. *Leonhard classification of endogenous psychoses, Psychopathology*, 23: Suppl. 4–6, 267–76.

Walker, A.E. (1957) 'The development of the concept of cerebral localization in the nineteenth century'. *Bulletin for the History of Medicine*, 31: 99–121.

Wartenberg, R. (1953) 'Otfrid Foerster (1873–1941)'. In Haymaker, W. *The Founders of Neurology*, Springfield, Thomas, pp.422–5.

Wernicke, C. (1874) *Der aphasische Symptomenkomplex. Eine psychologische Studie auf anatomischer Basis*, Breslau, Max Cohn & Weigert.

Wernicke, C. (1876) 'Über das Urwindungssystem des menschlichen Gehirns'. *Arch. Psychiat.*, 6: 298–326.

Wernicke, C. (1881–1883) *Lehrbuch der Gehirnkrankheiten für Ärzte und Studierende*, vol. I–III, Kassel and Berlin, Theodor Fischer.

Wernicke, C. (1899) *Über die Klassifikation der Psychosen*, Breslau, Schlettersche Buchhandlung.

Wernicke, C. (1906) *Grundriß der Psychiatrie in klinischen Vorlesungen*, 2nd ed. (1st ed. 1900), Leipzig, Georg Thieme.

Ziehen, Th. (1905) 'Carl Wernicke'. *Monatsschrift für Psychiatrie und Neurologie*, 18. Suppl.

Chapter 12
Unitary Psychosis Concept

Clinical Section
GE BERRIOS and D BEER

The term 'unitary psychosis', a rendition of the German *Einheitspsychose*,[1] is the name for a collection of views which have in common the assertion that there is only one psychosis.[2] To reach this conclusion, it is variously assumed: a. that clinical differences between traditional 'psychoses' are fully due to the pathoplastic effect of personality, life events or observer bias; and b. that the single psychosis is the clinical expression of an underlying *invariant* conceived as 'organic' (e.g. Neumann), 'psychological' (e.g. Freud) or 'structural' (e.g. Ey or Llopis). Cross-sectional versions of the doctrine must explain why, given that personal and environmental factors change, psychoses may remain the same from episode to episode; longitudinal versions (as per Griesinger) provide the mechanism by means of which the 'invariant' may change clinical presentation within the same individual.

During the 'pre-statistical' period, 'unitarians' (the name given here to the sponsors of the doctrine) favoured arguments such as that the mind can not be split into faculties, or that 'intermediate cases' were common, or that all diagnoses are longitudinally unstable. After the statistical revolution of the 1930s, factor analysis, cluster analysis and discriminant function analysis have been increasingly used to show that boundaries between the psychoses are unreliable; mathematical naiveté, unfortunately, led many to assume that failures to obtain bimodal distributions were tantamount to proving their case.[3]

HISTORIOGRAPHIC PITFALLS

Writing the history of this doctrine is not easy. Unitarians have rarely made their assumptions explicit, or have changed their mind and contradicted themselves; furthermore, there is little continuity in the unitarian doctrine itself, and the assumptions made by Reil, Neumann, Griesinger, Hoche, Bonhoeffer or Crow are closely tied up with the science and ideology of their time. There is also the question of the object referred to by the doctrine. If anachronistic reading is to be avoided, one must not readily assume the existence of an 'invariant' or 'trans-epistemic' object (whether a neurobiological lesion or a psychological archetype) which unitarians have striven to capture. Even concepts such as 'ruling ideas' (used by Vliegen (1980) in his important book) must be avoided, as must the assumption that unitarians are necessarily anti-nosological: Menninger probably was so, but not Griesinger, Llopis, or Ey who *believed* in the medical model but disagreed with the idea that there could be many psychoses. The best work on the unitary psychosis doctrine is still in the German and Spanish languages (Mundt and Saß, 1992; Vliegen, 1980; Wyrsch, 1956; Pauleikhoff, 1986; Masi, 1981; Lanczik, 1989; Llopis, 1954; Rennert, 1968; Valenciano, 1970).

MEDICAL NOSOLOGY AND TAXONOMY

Classifications of insanity entail a taxonomic theory and a concept of disease (Aschaffenburg, 1915; Temkin, 1965; Sartorius et al, 1990). Classical medical taxonomy included strategies for the description and *grouping* of symptoms, syndromes, diseases and lesions (on historical aspects of classification see: Pichot, 1984; Verga, 1876; Riese, 1945; Guiraud, 1950; Rémond, 1902; Desruelles et al, 1934; Lewes, 1988; on modern aspects see: Overall and Woodward, 1975; Sadler et al, 1994; Schwartz and Wiggins, 1987; 1986; Reuchlin, 1984; Andreasen and Spitzer, 1980; Corning and Steffy, 1979). So-called *natural* classifications, particularly in psychiatry, depend on description, so rules for symptom-recognition are needed, and indeed they were developed during the nineteenth century. But symptom-description is also influenced by 'non-cognitive' forces so that the older the psychiatric discourse, the harder its understanding. The nineteenth century feels more 'accessible', but this may be because the historian still shares in the same 'discourse'. Periods of taxonomic change offer privileged windows; one such is the early nineteenth century, when the anatomo-clinical model of disease was introduced (Ackerknecht, 1967). According to this view, signs and symptoms were to be considered as 'signals' emitted by biological lesions (localisable in the internal space of the body).

Pre-1800 Psychiatric Taxonomy

The eighteenth century witnessed the apotheosis of one type of medical taxonomy and the stirrings of another. Following Sydenham's injunction (1848) physicians classified diseases 'in the manner of botanists' (López Piñero, 1983), indeed, many were both (Berg, 1956; Faber, 1923; Fischer-Homberger, 1970). Diseases, like plants, were classified in terms of privileged features (Larson, 1971), i.e. in the 'top-to-bottom' or 'downwards' mode. Two assumptions needed to be made: a. the object to be classified (whether plant or disease) was a 'complete' and immutable entity, and b. privileged features were part of a universal design. (In pre-Darwinian periods such design issued from the divine hand; afterwards, from that of evolution.) 'Natural' classifications reflected the natural order; 'artificial' ones, practical needs (Hoppe, 1978; Raven et al, 1971; Stevens, 1984).

During the latter part of the eighteenth century a second view was suggested by Adanson (Baillon, 1864), the great French botanist of Scottish descent. Influenced by Aristotelian ideas, he believed that more 'natural' groupings might be identified if no 'feature' was privileged or 'weighted' in any way. For example, plants (or diseases) might be exhaustively described and patterns sought out. This 'bottom-to-top' or 'upwards' approach assumes that clusters are determined by feature density. For reasons which are beyond the scope of this work,

Adanson was not influential, although it has been claimed that his work led to the development of numerical taxonomy (Adams, 1964; Vernon, 1988).

Battie (1703–1776)
Battie's (1758) top-to-bottom classification, on the other hand, combines clinical and aetiological criteria, and shows how its results caused embarrassment to the 'sensationalist' hypothesis of perception (the dominant approach at the time). Battie started with the assumption that the 'medullary' substance of the brain was the seat of 'sensation', and that sensations were produced by stimuli (pressure) impinging upon it. Imaginary sensations are caused 'by an internal disorder of the nervous substance' (p.43) or by the 'nervous substance being, indeed, in like manner disordered, but disordered *ab extra*; and therefore chiefly to be attributed to some remote and accidental cause' (pp.43–4). Each mechanism gave rise to a different madness: 'the first species, until a better name can be found, may be called original, the second may be called consequential madness' (p.44). It would be anachronistic to interpret him as offering an early version of the late nineteenth century dichotomy of endogenous-exogenous or of the twentieth century ones of functional-organic and primary-secondary. He was just applying to abnormal sensations a model taken from Hartley (Hartley, 1834; Ober, 1976; Smith, 1987) and Condillac (Riese, 1968; Le Roy, 1937).

Battie said little about the mechanism involved in 'original madness' and concentrated on 'consequential' madness where the problem was to explain why only some external (*ab extra*) stimuli gave rise to 'delusive' (insightless) sensations. Battie suggested a way round based on the 'quality' of the sensation, i.e. a delusive sensation may occur when *per chance* the stimulus is identical with one causing a real sensation: 'which force necessarily implies impulse and pressure in delusive sensation in the same manner and order as it does in the perception of objects really corresponding thereto' (Battie, 1758, p.44). But do all subjects thus duped develop delusions? Apparently not, and he soon realised that explanations only based on the 'quality' of the sensation were not adequate. So he resorted to personality characteristics and concurrent factors:

> What this particular sort and degree of pressure is, which is capable of creating delusive sensation, we are not able to ascertain; because *the different circumstances of the unknown subject* acted upon will make the nervous effects variable and oftentimes contrary, notwithstanding the action of the known cause considered *per se* is in all respects the same (our emphasis). (pp.45–6)

Cullen (1710–1790)
Cullen (1827) suggested that mental disorders might be classified on the basis of anatomical, functional, symptomatic, and outcome features. Cullen, a downward taxonomist, used principles already present in Sauvage, Linneus, Vogel, Sagar and McBride (Cullen, 1803; Bowman, 1975). In regard to anatomical criteria he wrote: 'there have occurred so many instances of this kind, that I believe physicians are generally disposed to suspect organic lesion of the brain to exist in almost every case of insanity' . . . 'this, however, is probably a mistake; for we know that there have been many instances of

insanity from which the persons have entirely recovered' (Cullen, 1827, p.175) ... 'Such transitory cases, indeed, render it probable, that a state of excitement, changeable by various causes, had been the cause of such instances of insanity' (p.176). Cullen believed that 'physiological' lesions might be important. In regard to classifications, he stated: 'having thus endeavoured to investigate the cause of insanity in general, it were to be wished that I could apply the doctrine to distinguishing the several species of it, according as they depend upon the different state and circumstances of the brain, and thereby to the establishing of scientific and accurately adapted method of cure. These purposes, however, appear to me to be extremely difficult to be attained. . . .' Thus, only symptomatic classifications seemed possible.

Cullen criticised classificators:

> The ingenious Dr Arnold has been commendably employed in distinguishing the different species of insanity as they appear with respect to the mind; and his labours may hereafter prove useful, when we shall come to know something more of the different states of the brain corresponding to these different states of the mind; but at present I can make little application of his numerous distinctions.

And then stated a view that sounds 'unitarian':

> It appears to me that he [Dr Arnold] has chiefly pointed out and enumerated distinctions, that are mere varieties, which can lead to little or no variety of practice: and I am specially led to form the latter conclusion, because these varieties appear to me to be often combined together, and to be often changed into one another, in the same person; in whom we must therefore suppose a general cause of the disease. (pp.76–7, Cullen, 1827)

Kant (1724–1804)

Kant is a typical example of the eighteenth century armchair classificator. His writings on mental disorder are surprisingly little known, in spite of the fact that it has been suggested that they were influential in German psychiatry (Dörner, 1969). Reference will only be made here to the classification included in his *Anthropologie* and not to earlier writings (Kant, 1974) where Kant attempted a downwards classification.

Kant (1974) assumed that mental disorders result from impairment of the brain, but believed that classification had to be based on what 'faculty of the mind is involved' (p.220). Dysfunction of the mental faculties dealing with reality-unreality, judgement, and reason, led to different mental disorders: 'I should like to classify all [diseases of the mind] according to the three following categories: perturbation of experience which I want to call confusion (*Verruckung*); dysfunction of judgement which I call delusion (*Wahnsinn*); and impairment of reason which I call mania (*Wahnwitz*). All other manifestations of brain disease may be, it seems to me, classified as variations in degree or as combinations of these three [basic] disorders or as their combination with emotions' (pp.220–1). Kant's classification is a good example of a botanical top-to-bottom approach, uncomplicated by clinical experience.

Pinel (1745–1824)
There is less elegance and insight in Pinel's nosography. He identified three stages in the formulation of a new disease: a) recognition of symptoms (Pinel quoted on this Landre-Beauvais, 1813), b) observation of clusters and symptom-covariance, particularly during the acute stage of the disease, and c) distinction between simple and complex diseases, the latter showing (and in this he followed Cullen) 'in their course two or three different symptom-clusters' (Pinel, 1818). Pinel espoused a less organic view of insanity than Cullen. His experience at Bicêtre had 'convinced him that the common sources of mental alienation related to sadness and loss' (p.53) and hence 'non-febrile insanity, far from resulting from brain lesions, [may be] triggered by unbridled passions'. Pinel had no difficulty in accepting symptomatic classifications. It must be kept in mind, however, that his use of terms such as mania, melancholia and dementia is different from the present, and unless casenotes are studied, it is not possible always to determine what sort of patient he was talking about.

CLASSIFICATION AND NOSOLOGY DURING THE 19TH CENTURY
Nineteenth century alienists were confronted with the task of classifying objects whose definition was in a state of flux. There were changes at all levels: symptom description (including for the first time subjective information), temporal context (acute vs. chronic disease), outcome (reversible versus irreversible), causality (psychological vs. physical), lesion type (anatomical vs. physiological) and localization (brain sites vs. diffuse location). In the wake of these changes, the insanities started their transformation from monolithic entities to multiple categories defined as symptom-clusters (Berrios, 1984).

The anatomo-clinical model
The single most important factor was, perhaps, the development of the 'anatomo-clinical' view (Ackerknecht, 1967; López Piñero, 1983; Laín Entralgo, 1978) according to which disease was a collection of signals resulting from lesioned sites. When the quest for anatomical lesions failed, the model encouraged the search for physiological and psychological lesions (à la Freud). The anatomo-clinical model also encouraged the refinement of surface descriptors (i.e. of 'semiology').

Clinical descriptors
'Symptom and sign' are categories already present in Hippocratic medicine. During the eighteenth century 'signs' (of a disease) and 'features' (of a plant) played the same role in classification. The rules governing their combination, however, were clearer for plants than for diseases. Medical classifications at the time often consist in mere lists of 'symptoms' reified as diseases. After the 1820s, rules of combination were created based on new anatomical and physiological knowledge. The old insanities were broken up and the resulting fragments became veritable 'units of analysis' or building blocks which could partake in the definition of more than one disease. There is no better illustration of this than Landré-Beauvais' semiology (1813): 'it is not sufficient faithfully to list the signs of disease, it is also required to offer them in the sort of order that shows

up their relationship to physiology and nosography' (p.xx). He considered *sémiotique* as a new science dealing with the language of medical description: 'as sciences progress, terms to name more objects multiply in number and its language becomes more appropriate' (pp.xxiii–xxiv). He distinguished between phenomenon, symptom and sign and saw the latter as carrying information on occult changes (lesions) in the body (in this chapter called biological signal).

Changes in the concept of insanity

Before 1750, insanity tended to be considered as an all-or-none, metaphysical state relating to the body in an abstract way. The mind was fully alienated and there was little machinery for accounting for partial insanities, in spite of the fact that such states have been suggested by both medics and lawyers (Walker, 1968). The wide acceptance of this 'holistic' view is hidden by the fact that pre-1800 insanity was defined (since John Locke) in intellectual terms. For example, although forms of partial madness seem to be included in Kant's classification (see above), in real life the insane were considered as having 'lost their reason'. It seems also clear that there were no concepts to distinguish 'remission', 'improvement' and 'cure'. For example, the concept of 'lucid interval' (Haslam, 1809, pp.45–9) was created so that the belief in a continuous underlying state of insanity could be preserved.

THE NINETEENTH CENTURY AND AFTER

The collapse of eighteenth century classifications was due less to theoretical failure than to lack of clear symptom- and disease-description; both these elements were sharpened during the nineteenth century (King, 1982). To start off with, psychiatric taxonomy benefited little from these advances, and mental disorders continued being classified on theoretical principles (such as faculty psychology) up to the time of Esquirol. It is not by chance, therefore, that the zenith of the 'unitarian' doctrine occurred in a period when in Germany both Cartesianism and faculty psychology were resisted by *Naturphilosophie* and holistic notions that wanted body, mind and spirit to be studied in conjunction. For example, the 'ganglion system' (the white matter of the nervous system) featured centrally in Reil's views. He conceived of the body as a hollow sphere with one surface facing the outside world and the other closeting the soul. The body contained the nerves or ganglia; there was no real centre to this system, which resembled a monarch-less Republic (Vliegen, 1980, p.4).

German-speaking Psychiatry prior to Kraepelin

German unitarians agreed on the view that classifications of insanity were neither feasible nor useful, but on little else. It must not be forgotten that they lived in the pre-Kraepelinian universe in which there could be no preoccupation about whether dementia praecox and manic depressive insanity were the same disease!

Reil (1759–1813)

Reil subscribed to a philosophy of integration (Lewis, 1967; 1965; Harms, 1960; Heller, 1975). For example, in regard to brain function, he took an anti-localizationist position. He believed, however, that insanity had an organic basis: 'the nervous system, more precisely the brain, is diseased in madness' (Reil, 1805, p.470). Although a 'disease of the nerves' (p.365), madness was different 'from other nervous diseases, i.e. those of the imagination, memory, attention, or consciousness' (p.288). Reil was writing before the anatomo-clinical view had become predominant, and hence had no real 'lesional' language in which to express his organic view: 'classification is impossible for the pathologist and the psychologist can classify only according to phenomena' (p.365).

Nonetheless, and perhaps due to his great interest in 'psychological treatments' (Harms, 1960), Reil contributed little to descriptive psychopathology. He believed that mental illness was caused by 'irritation' of the brain, a theory also sponsored by Autenrieth who himself believed that mental disorders were related to each other as the links in a morbid chain (*transmotio morborum*). Hypochondriasis and melancholia might lead to idiocy or dementia.[4] His unitarian views were expressed in two ways. In regard to 'activation' levels, Reil wrote: 'In mania (*Tobsucht*), rage (*Raserei*), insanity (*Wahnsinn*), and melancholia (*Melancholie*), brain irritability is increased; in Idiocy (*Narrheit*) reduced. Dementia (*Blödsinn*) results from a paralysis (*Lahmung*) of the brain' (Reil, 1805, p.477). Thus, different mental disorders resulted from changes in the levels of brain energy. This view was developed by Griesinger, and reached Janet. But Reil also expressed his unitarianism in the abstract psychological language of the late eighteenth century by claiming that mental disorders resulted from pathological splits in *Gemeingefühl*[5] (Harms, 1960; Starobinski, 1981, pp.254–61; Reil, 1803).

Zeller (1804–1877)
Zeller learned of Reil's Ganglion Theory from Esquirol in France and Autenrieth in Germany, and subscribed to the Romantic belief that 'Man is body and soul at the same time' (Vliegen, 1980). In 1834, Zeller was confident enough to claim that the insanities were but stages of a common disease: 'in the course of one case all the main forms of mental disorder may occur' (Zeller, 1837, p.344). Organic and psychological aetiologies of mental disorder unworriedly combine in his work. In regard to the former, he wrote 'the organic basis of all mental disorders is indicated by the physical illness which antedates the mental disorder' (Zeller, 1840, p.135); as to the latter or 'moral' causes, he believed that 'pain' was the universal source of morbidity. Under 'pain' he included experiences induced by remorse, guilty conscience, failures in friendship, and poverty. He believed that 'cases are rare in which the mental disorder is caused by purely organic problems of the central nervous system'. Thus, 'adverse circumstances and physical disease may conspire to produce mental disorder after mood, mind and soul have been affected . . . possibly by hereditary factors' (Zeller, 1843, p.300). Psychological causes, pain and organic changes combined caused melancholia. Irritations and aggravations led to mania, paranoia, and finally dementia. All four types of madness were but stages in the same pathological process.

Jacobi (1775–1858)
Karl Wigand Maximilian Jacobi, the son of the great spiritualist philosopher F H Jacobi (Focke, 1859), held a *somatic* view of insanity (Marx, 1990–1; Kirkby, 1992; Hagner, 1992). He was involved in hospital organization, and showed interest in the English administrative system. Kraepelin noticed his

support for neuropathology (Kraepelin, 1962, pp.42–3). But Zilboorg (1941) was wrong in exaggerating Jacobi's anti-psychological stance. He did not deny the existence of mental symptoms but considered them as non-specific, change-able in time and space, and as providing a poor basis for classification: 'the signs which are given such weight by others (e.g. Esquirol) as being indicative of mental illness are deceptive' (Jacobi, 1830, p.131); 'the symptoms of melancholia are found in more than twenty diseases' (Jacobi, 1830, p.107; Griesinger, 1865, p.14); 'the form of the mental illness changes without the underlying disease lifting. It can come and go quickly because the latter undergoes a modification' (Jacobi, 1830, p.129).

Jacobi put forward a unitary view of mental illness based on the belief that the resolution power of neuropathology and psychology was limited: 'in my view, there are no mental illnesses which are independent . . . all are caused by an organic disturbance and should be seen as organic illnesses inasmuch as the psychic manifestations are determined by the organism' (Jacobi, 1830, pp.24–25). 'Mental illnesses are merely symptoms of the illnesses which cause them. Their manifestations and course depend upon them' (Jacobi, 1830, p.118).

Feuchtersleben (1806–1849)
In his *Principles of Medical Psychology*, this insightful physician dealt with the problem of classifying mental disorders:

> Many ingenious, acute, profound attempts have been made to classify the diseases of the personality; they are all good but all unsatisfactory. . . . I cannot, however, refrain from again classifying these classifications for you, at least in a general way for your historical information. The grounds of their divisions may form the basis of mine. These are in the main five: 1. According to the so-called faculties of the mind. Amongst these we may reckon those of Kant, Hartmann, Heinroth, Ritgen, Stark, &c. These faculties, or rather direction, of the mind cannot however be empirically separated, 2. according to the provinces of the nervous system, or also of other organic systems profoundly affected. Amongst these may be reckoned those of Töltenyi, Grohmann, Buzzorini, Blumröder, Sinogowitz, &c.; but the predominance of these provinces and systems cannot be empirically shown in the individual forms; 3) according to temperaments. The divisions of Dietz and Windbüchler come from this head. A cause founded on predisposition does not, however, suffice for classification; 4) according to quantitative, gradual, opposing, or mixed proportions. Among these I reckon those of Eschemayer, Fantonetti, Tschallener, Flemming, &c.; but the logical constraint causes unnatural separations and connections among the natural groups; and 5) according to the phenomena or symptoms. Under this head I reckon those of Pinel and of most French and English authors, of Reil, Linnich, Ideler &c; but it cannot be properly called a division . . . or we must call it a provisional division, till we know its internal foundation. (pp.248–9)

The elegance and accuracy of this analysis can be hardly improved.

Griesinger (1817–1868)
Griesinger criticised the 'ganglion system' view, and rejected the notion that

physical disease not affecting the brain might lead to madness. Mental diseases were brain diseases which *were caused themselves by psychological factors*. Levels of nervous or psychological energy were central to his theory. Mania was the mental counterpart of the convulsive state; dementia, of the lameness caused by brain and spinal palsy. Like Zeller, Griesinger considered melancholy to be the fundamental disorder leading in due course to disturbances of thought and of will (mania, partial madness, confusion) and then dementia. He went further than Zeller in the belief that mood disorder was an entity *per se*, and in this respect he prepared the ground for the Kraepelinian view. Although his earlier writings suggested that he believed in unitary psychosis, later views go against this. He wrote 'From our observations there are two groups of insanities: firstly, the affective ones, secondly the primary disturbances of perception and will, arising not from a problem of mood but from false thinking and will' (Griesinger, 1861). But in 1864, in his superb inaugural lecture at the University of Zurich, he started developing a new classification based on both organic and psychological criteria. By then he had read Kahlbaum's book on classification: 'This excellent work must be received with favour as witness of the current tendency to try new classifications and abandon the old ones. The simple classification I am proposing today is in keeping with clinical observation, responds to different needs and has only few points of coincidence with the ideas exposed by my honourable friend' (Griesinger, 1865, p.14). Three years after this publication Griesinger was dead, and never was to develop these ideas in any depth.

Neumann (1814–1884)

Heinrich Neumann joined the unitarians with his notion of the *Einheit der Psychosen* (Lanczik, 1989). His anti-taxonomic position was the expression of idiosyncratic views on mental illness: 'Insanity [*Wahnsinn*] is a state of lack of productivity in which the sufferer creates a world which is in contradiction to that of other human beings, and which is not amenable to correction. He gets less and less intellectual pabulum so that his capacity is exhausted and his creativity diminishes' (Neumann, 1859, p.168). Herbartian echoes (Ribot, 1876; Stout, 1888) are clear in his pathogenetic ideas: 'confusion is to be defined as a loosening of associations, and dementia as a disintegration of conscious intellectual life and dissolution of mental elements' (Neumann, 1859, p.168). And again: 'in health, there is a ready differentiation between sensation, thought and wish. In mental illness, there is confusion, the subject may have sensations without the corresponding nerves being stimulated, this is called a hallucination' (Neumann, 1859, p.111). The pathogenic mechanism that Neumann called 'metamorphosis' consisted of a *disturbance of consciousness* leading to misinterpretation of sensations. Excesses of stimulation caused irritation and mania, and led to drops in psychic energy and to an increased likelihood of hallucinations.

His views on taxonomy and diagnosis were at odds with the growing medicalization of insanity in his time, and reflect his late hour acquaintance with *Naturphilosophie*: 'true diagnosis has nothing to do with nomenclature. The former is concerned with the individual case, the latter is a product of abstraction ... it may be comforting to classify by external symptoms but it does not provide true knowledge [of the phenomena] ... diagnosis has to do with understanding, not with a group of signs' (Neumann, 1859, pp.75–6). Neumann dispensed with Zeller's 'primary form' of mental illness in favour of a continuum from health to disease.

This very view was later to be taken up by twentieth century unitarians such as Menninger. Neumann's continuum ranged thus: health – sleeplessness – illusions – exaggerated sensitivity – illness – madness – confusion – and terminal dementia. He wrote: 'every classification of mental illness is artificial. We should throw it all overboard . . . there is only one form of mental illness, that is insanity [*Wahnsinn*], which does not have different forms but different stages' (Neumann, 1859, p.167).

Neumann, however, left open the future possibility of classifying according to causes: 'classification is only possible when there are "genera", but these do not exist in the absence of "generation" [aetiology]. The only diseases with generation are those characterized by contagiousness. Thus, as far as mental illness is concerned, there are only individual diseases' (Neumann, 1859, p.75); 'one cannot classify except on the basis of physical disease . . . fever, delirium, and mental illness can [therefore] be considered as different from each other' (Neumann, 1859, p.181).

Kahlbaum (1828–1899)
The principle that differences in symptoms reflect differences in causes and hence provide the foundation for a classification was developed by Kahlbaum, one of the greatest alienists of the 19th century (Lanczik, 1992), and the strongest known influence on Kraepelin (Berrios and Hauser, 1988). Initially influenced by the view that all insanities were stages of one disease, he progressed on to offer a classification which included many. Kahlbaum divided mental illness into four categories of vesania: 'an idiopathic mental disorder with the whole range of mental life clearly affected to some degree', i.e. *vesaniae acuta, typica* (which included Neumann's four stages), *progressiva* and *catatonica* (Kahlbaum, 1863). He believed in the separation of clinical pictures (which he called the 'Elementary forms of the disease process') but as emerging from only one (unitary) vesania.

French-speaking psychiatry
At the beginning of the nineteenth century, Pinel (1818; 1801) set the pattern for psychiatric classifications in France. Georget and Esquirol (de Caprariis, 1971) modified his views somewhat, but the real challenge came in 1853 with Baillarger's classical *Essai sur une classification des differents genres de folie* (Baillarger, 1853). Like his predecessors, he opted for a symptomatic taxonomy but based on a different criterion, namely, insight. Baillarger believed it to be nonsense to talk of partial and total delusions (*délires partial et générale*) (as Esquirol and Georget had done) (Baillarger, 1853, p.549).

Although the frondous pre-1800 nosologies had been left behind, some of its principles were still in operation, namely those of categorical groupings and privileged symptoms (Renouard, 1846). It is not surprising, therefore, that when, as late as 1860, the *Société Médico-Psychologique* of Paris held its debate on classification, some of the discussants appealed to the old principles (see below).

Guislain (1797–1860)
It has been claimed that Joseph Guislain, the Belgian alienist, was a 'unitarian', and that he influenced Zeller (Vliegen, 1980, p.9). Guislain entertained a psychological view of the causation of mental illness. In 1852 he wrote: 'all the phenomenology[6] of the mental diseases, all their forms of presentation may be found combined . . . or they change into each other with some symptoms disappearing and others reappearing' (Guislain, 1852, p.96). Guislain's terminology was quaint. He suggested that at the basis of mental illness there was *phrenalgia* (pain of the mind) which could range from melancholia to simple suffering. Given the right 'irritants', melancholia could be transformed into other brain diseases (*phrenopathies*) such as mania, paraphrenia, epilepsy, delirium, and dementia (*Noasthenie*).

Morel (1809–1873)
Few years later, symptomatic taxonomy itself came under attack when Morel (1860) suggested the first aetiological classification. This led to a famous debate at the *Société Médico-Psychologique* where Delasiauve[7] together with Falret, Brierre, and the non-alienists Maury (Dowbiggin, 1990) and Bouchez (Biéder, 1986), defended the symptomatic approach. Morel, who had not planned to intervene, made a spirited defence of the aetiological criterion. A third course was chosen by Garnier who put forward a unitarian view, based on the observation (made already by Cullen and Pinel), that the insanities changed one into another (AMP, 1861, p.327).

Morel proposed six groups: hereditary (four classes), by intoxication (alcoholism, pellagra, etc.), neuroses (hysterical, hypochondriacal and epileptic insanity), idiopathic, sympathetic, and dementia. At the time, his classification was criticized for being a taxonomy 'of [putative] causes of insanity but not of its clinical pictures' (Foville, 1872, p.17). In 1872, Foville (fils) presented his own nomenclature and classification; in this important paper he identified the 1860s as the time when the shift from symptomatic to causal taxonomy had started. He mentioned Skae and Batty Tuke as two British alienists supporting a causal taxonomy, and noticed that Morel's (aetiological) classification did, in fact, depend on symptoms and pathogenic mechanisms (Foville, 1872, p.17).

Degeneration theory and classification
After 1857, degeneration theory (Genil-Perrin, 1913; Pick, 1989) became an important factor in the reorganization of French psychiatric classifications. Although hereditary taint had been mentioned in relation to insanity before that time, it was Morel's work that made it fully fashionable. Overtly Lamarkian (not Darwinian), and inspired by the concept of the original sin, his notion of degeneration included the claim that mental illness affecting one generation could visit the next in an ever worsening degree. Thus, melancholia or mania led to dementia and eventually idiocy. Two mechanisms were involved: transmission and degradation of the tainted seed.

Anachronistically interpreted, degeneration theory offered alienists a credible 'genetic' hypothesis. Since the expression of the hereditary taint was not only behavioural but physical, 'stigmata' (signs) of degeneration could also be recognized such as deformed teeth, ears, head, etc. (Talbot, 1898; Saury, 1886).

Mechanisms for initiating and maintaining the process of degeneration were searched, and alcoholism and masturbation were found to play a prominent role. After few generations, sterility ended the deteriorating chain.

Degeneration theory seemed to entail a longitudinal form of 'unitary psychosis'. The same 'invariant' was passed on from generation to generation, although on each occasion it caused a 'different' clinical picture. Why did the same metamorphosis not occur within the life span of the same individual (as Griesinger had suggested)? Morel never explained. Furthermore, degeneration theory seemed to be in contradiction with the (cross-sectional) taxonomic view put forward by Morel himself in 1860, according to which each disease had a different cause.

Valentin Magnan completed the incorporation of degeneration theory into psychiatry by cleansing it from its overtly religious and moral overtones, and rendering it palatable to the strong anti-religious world of late nineteenth century France (Bing, 1983, p.354). He placed the degeneration process firmly *in the brain*.

Towards the end of the century, Roubinovitch (1896)[8] compared German and French psychiatric classifications and concluded that differences were due to intellectual tradition. Indeed, symptom overlapping and mental conditions were the same on both sides of the cultural divide.

BRITISH ECHOES: Monro and Sankey

British psychiatrists were not given to offering new classifications and in general echoed continental efforts. On occasions men like Yellowless reduced this *ad absurdum* by suggesting that each symptom should be considered as a disease. In 1857, Henri Monro[9] published a paper on the classification and forms of insanity in which he echoed vitalistic and unitarian views then fashionable in the Continent: 'Madness is to be characterised very much by the results of too much, and too little . . . what is required for cure is to restore this lost equilibrium. . . . I believe it is a right thing to esteem emotional insanity rudimentary to notional, and notional to intelligence. . . . In laying down this rule, I do not mean to say that all cases of more complete insanity must have passed through the more rudimentary forms' (Monro, 1857, p.197). Monro was here using the English names for melancholia, mania and dementia.

In 1866, W.H.O. Sankey published his *Lectures on Mental Disease*. A reviewer (Anonymous, 1860) noticed that Sankey's views had much in common with Neumann's in that he felt that there were 'no different species of insanity, but that all the phenomena observed are the symptoms of the disease (insanity), which commences with a stage of depression [melancholia] and passes through those of delusion and excitement to mental torpor and decay'. This was also redolent of Griesinger's views.

KRAEPELIN (1856–1926) AND THE 20TH CENTURY

Kraepelin dismissed Zeller's unitarian view as 'speculative and clinically unfruitful', and based his nosology on brain lesion, course and symptoms: 'we need facts not theories'. He kept detailed clinical notes and performed genuine 'longitudinal' studies (Berrios and Hauser, 1987). By 1899, he had reached the conclusion that there were only dementia praecox and manic-depressive insanity. This view has dominated psychiatry for nearly a century. Griesinger and others had hinted at this, but Kraepelin's originality resided in choosing to base his classification on clinical course, response to treatment, and prognosis.

Kraepelin was aware of the difficulties involved, and already in 1887 had noted that mental disorders merged into one another. By 1918, in 'Ends and means of psychiatric research', Kraepelin began to use the word 'syndrome' (Kraepelin, 1918; Hoff, 1985), and in his magnificent 1920 paper on 'The Manifestation of Madness' (Kraepelin, 1920) he abandoned the view that symptoms could be pathognomonic: 'It is incorrect to attribute signs to specific disease processes . . . symptoms are not limited to a distinct disease process but occur in the same form in response to different morbid insults'. Indeed, Kraepelin, cast doubt on the distinction between dementia praecox and manic-depressive illness: 'We shall have to get used to the fact that our much used clinical check-list does not permit us to differentiate reliably between manic-depressive illness and *dementia praecox*'.

As opposed to Kraepelin's dichotomous classification, Wernicke (Liepmann, 1911; Lanczik, 1988; Donalies, 1971) started to develop, based on his own speculative pathophysiology, a taxonomy of the psychoses that included many groups (Burckard, 1931). His untimely death brought these ideas to an abrupt halt although Kleist, and later Leonhard, tried to develop his views further (Leonhard, 1957; Beckman and Lanczik, 1990).

20TH CENTURY UNITARIANS
During the 1940s, the unitarian doctrine resurfaced in Europe and the USA. Valenciano (Valenciano, 1960, p.114) has listed the factors that might explain its re-appearance:

1. Kraepelin's change of heart in regards to the specificity of symptoms and diseases;
2. The failure to find a specific organic basis, and clear descriptive boundaries for the psychoses;
3. The long term effect of Bonhoeffer's views concerning the non-specificity of psychiatric syndromes, and of Hoche's criticism of Kraepelin's dichotomy;
4. Specht's view that the only difference between 'exogenous' and 'endogenous' psychoses related to severity and rapidity of onset (i.e. less severe and slow onset psychoses were likely to be recognized as 'endogenous');
5. The application of evolutionist, Jacksonian, and psychodynamic views to psychopathology;
6. The influence of holistic and Gestalt models, particularly in brain localization studies.

Bonhoeffer, Hoche, and Kretschmer
The view that symptom-patterns carried information on aetiology was challenged by Bonhoeffer (Jossmann, 1949). Influenced by the anti-localizationistic fashion, he suggested that the brain was endowed with few stereotyped mental reactions, triggered by a variety of noxae (Bonhoeffer, 1910). Auguste Hoche

(1912) contributed to the debate with an important paper on symptom-complexes. Although he never expressed a unitarian view, his notion of syndrome emphasised description and dismissed over-searching for causes (whether organic and psychological). Diseases might just be collections of syndromes with no structure to themselves. The search for 'entities', Hoche called 'the hunt after a phantom'. He drew attention, however, to the role of 'cerebral properties' in the modulation of symptom-complexes; rather unfairly, Jaspers accused Hoche of psychiatric nihilism. A sort of unitarian view was also implicit in Kretschmer's body-types (Kretschmer, 1936). Character depended on body build and endogenous psychoses were not 'isolated entities' but 'constitutional episodes'. Because environmental triggers (key events) were part of the pathogenic equation, endogenous and psychogenic illness were not independent from one another. Kretschmer rejected off-hand Hoche's notion of symptom-complex in favour of 'living illness pictures'. He believed that dementia praecox and manic-depressive insanity were not really independent: 'they are not separate, but flow into each other'. Kretschsmer's views could be seen as a resurrection during the early twentieth century of the romantic unity of body and soul (Vliegen, 1980, p.40).

UNITARIANISM AFTER THE SECOND WORLD WAR

Conrad (1905–1961)

Klaus Conrad (Cutting, 1989) was an early Kraepelinian whose own clinical observations convinced him that symptoms and diagnosis were unstable. For example, subjects started as manic or depressive might develop delusions and deterioration of personality. He also observed that cyclothymic patients produced children with schizophrenia more often than expected. By 1959, he questioned Kraepelinian dualism and spoke of varied manifestations of one endogenous 'circle of illness' (Conrad, 1958). Less severe presentations of psychoses would lead to reversible forms; severe ones to deterioration. In a magnificent lecture before the German Psychiatric Society, Conrad analyzed in depth the concept of nosological unity in psychiatry (Conrad, 1959). He also claimed a link between the endogenous and exogenous psychoses: 'What connects the exogenous and endogenous? Different noxae attack the same structure, physiological mechanism, biochemical metabolism, or physiochemical relationship' and may include 'physical exhaustion or heightened emotion' (Conrad, 1958). Alteration in emotions led to depression and delusions and madness started. These claims are redolent of the heyday of unitarianism according to which all forms of insanity could be seen in the same patient.

Llopis (1906–1966)

Observations of pellagra psychosis during the Spanish Civil War, led Llopis to formulate his theory of 'The Axial Syndrome common to all psychoses' (Llopis, 1946). According to this view, there were only quantitative differences between endogenous and exogenous psychoses (Llopis, 1954). Symptoms resulted from disorders in the 'content' and 'state' of consciousness. The former were caused by localized brain lesions; the latter by generalized brain 'excitement' and 'irritation' (Llopis, 1970). Consciousness was a Janus-like structure facing both external and internal worlds. Misinterpreted sensations become pathological 'contents' if there is a degradation of insight: like Zeller and Neumann, Llopis believed in degrees of impairment. On the other hand, pathology of 'state' of consciousness would be proportional to the potency of the 'irritant'.

For Llopis, however, changes in mood and affect *per se* were not to be considered as manifestations of disease: the person may say that they are happy or sad but as long as *insight* is preserved there is no psychiatric disorder. Illness ensues as insight is lost. Normally, dreaming provides humans with 'as if' experiences, but as long as these can be separated from 'real' perceptions there is no psychosis. Psychiatric disturbances ensue as this capacity is gradually lost. Llopis suggested that all syndromes are 'quantitative gradations of a single fundamental disorder' (Colodrón, 1991).

Ey (1900–1977)

Ey (1954) defined psychosis as a *mouvement de regression* to archaic and primitive forms of mental life and based his evolutionary model of illness on Lamarck's 'graded increase in intellectual ability' in the animal kingdom (Lamarck, 1984). Ey supported the existence of a *monopsychose* with all clinical types resulting from variations in the same mechanism (*il y a une certaine unite dans la desorganisation de l'étre psychique*) (Albernhe and Roux, 1990). Categories such as exogenous/endogenous and organic/functional were superfluous, as was the notion of mental disease itself. There were only 'reactions' reflecting degrees of functional 'dissolution' (à la Jackson) (Ey, 1962; Evans, 1972; Berrios, 1991). Ey was a neo-Romantic in the Zeller-Neumann mould who understood psychopathology as an evolutionary drama (Ey, 1954).

Ey was not the only French-speaking psychiatrist to ponder over psychiatric taxonomy. The *Société Médico-Psychologique* debated classifications (once again!) in April 1940 when Vie (1940) offered a spirited defence of the need to classify; opposing views were heard from Minkowski, Laignel-Lavastine, Ferdiére, Bonhomme, and Delmas. In 1963, Ellenberger mounted a major attack on classifications drawing attention to 'unconscious and irrational factors influencing classifiers' (Ellenberger, 1963, p.242).

Menninger

Unitarians found some echo in the USA. After introducing Kraepelinian dualism, the Swiss émigré Adolph Meyer went on to develop the overinclusive and confused notion of mental 'reaction' (Gelder, 1991). The psychoanalyst Karl Menninger, already antipathetic to medical diagnosis, also argued against classification (Menninger et al, 1958). He claimed that he did not object to taxonomy per se, as a 'scientific tool', but worried lest it led to an impersonal approach to patient care. He preferred to see illness as a continuum from health to sickness. Severity of disease he defined in terms of social dysfunction. Although he did not dispense with terms such as manic or schizophrenic, he preferred his own terminology which included four orders of mental problems: nervousness, neurosis, episodic and explosive discharges and syndromes of persistent and severe disorganisation. For him 'there were no natural mental disease entities' (Menninger et al, 1958).

Rennert

In three important articles, Rennert (1964; 1965; 1968) supported the view that a common disease process operated in all psychoses, and that personality factors accounted for the differences. He also introduced a probabilistic or statistical dimension in favour of unitarianism (Masi, 1981). There was only one psychosis but it appeared as if there were many, for symptoms had different distribution in the population. Symptom-combinations showing high density would be, understandably, interpreted as being a separate disease. Differential densities were not, however, determined by the brain but by social and pathoplastic factors. Rennert also believed that an endogenous-morbid factor was not necessary.

Janzarik

Janzarik (Mundt, 1992) proposed that the more evolved an organism, the more prone it is to insanity. In man, the 'shackles of instinctive behaviour are loosened' and the emotions freed (Janzarik, 1988). 'Psychic dynamics' is released from its biological chains and causes psychosis when mental structures become dismantled. The 'type' of psychosis will be determined by the structure that has been impaired by the flow of the 'dynamics'. (Psychosis is rare in children because this process takes longer.)

'Preconditions' for the psychosis are to be found in the structures themselves. The 'dynamics' goes through stages of 'reduction', 'expansion', 'unsteadiness' and 'emptiness' (more or less corresponding to Griesinger's melancholia, mania, madness, and dementia). Human beings carry in them a propensity to insanity. Deviations from normality or the presence of organic illness may release the 'dynamics' and induce insanity. Reductions in the 'dynamics' may cause mood disorder. Psychotic patients treated with neuroleptics may develop post-psychotic depression after their positive symptoms have remitted. For him the unitarian view is more a *Leitidee* than a nosological reality (Janzarik, 1969).

Kendell and Crow

The views of two recent British writers may be interpreted as unitarian. Kendell used statistical techniques to cast doubt on the existence of clinical boundaries between neurotic and psychotic depression (Kendell, 1968), and schizophrenia and mania (Brockington and Kendell, 1979; Kendell and Gourlay, 1970; Kendell and Brockington, 1980). His work highlights the importance of descriptor reliability and validity, and of pattern recognition techniques. Crow's interpretation of genetic finding led to temporary unitarian conclusions: 'psychosis is a continuum extending from unipolar, through bipolar affective illness and schizoaffective psychosis, to typical schizophrenia, with increasing degrees of defect' (Crow, 1986; 1987). Crow based his view on three arguments: absence of a convincing bimodal separation between the two psychoses (as per Kendell), evidence for common aetiological determinants, and putative genetic link between the psychoses.

SUMMARY

This chapter has traced the history of the unitary psychosis doctrine and shown that it is not homogeneous. It has also shown that the debate between unitarians and classificators has taken place on various battle grounds: earlier exchanges revolved around clinical and logical argument; more recent ones around statistical and genetic analysis. The debate continues.

NOTES

1 The term has been translated into Spanish as *psicosis única* or *psychosis unitaria,* and into French as *Monopsychose* and *Psychose unique.*

2 During the nineteenth century, the term 'insanity' (*folie, pazzia, locura,* or *Wahnsinn*) was replaced by 'psychosis' (Berrios, 1987). This was more than a terminological change and reflected a shift in the conception of mental disorder (i.e. the abandonment of pre-nineteenth century views of insanity as states of total irrationality).

3 During the 1970s, a useful debate erupted about the power of these statistical techniques; it eventually led to a healthier return to questions of validity and the search for 'markers' of disease (Eysenck, 1970; Kendell, 1976; Garside and Roth, 1978; Everitt, 1981).

4 At the time, this term meant 'psychological dilapidation' and had no necessary relationship to old age, cognitive status, or irreversibility (see History of Dementia, this volume).

5 This term referred to the general bodily sensation of commonality and integration serving as background to all other experiences.

6 Guislain was fond of neologisms; he also introduced into French psychiatry the term 'phenomenology' to refer to the symptomatic presentation of the psychosis.

7 Delasiauve, like Forbes Winslow in England, edited his own Journal and mostly kept aloof from his National Society.

8 At the request of his chief, Joffroy, Roubinovitch wrote this little classic of French psychiatry.

9 His views were to be influential in the development of Jackson's notion of positive and negative symptom (see Berrios, 1985).

REFERENCES

Ackerknecht, E. (1967) *Medicine at the Paris Hospital 1794–1848,* Baltimore, Johns Hopkins Press.

Adams, J.N. (1964) 'A Critical Evaluation of Adansonian Taxonomy'. *Developmental and Industrial Microbiology,* 5: 173–9.

Albernhe, T. and Roux, J. (1990) *La Pensée de Henri Ey,* Paris, Scripta.

AMP (1861) 'Debate on Classification'. *Annales Médico-Psychologiques,* 7: 128–77; 316–32; 456–500; 648–57.

Andreasen, N.C. and Spitzer, R.L. (1980) 'Classification of psychiatric disorders'. In Van Praag, H.M. (ed.) *Handbook of Biological Psychiatry,* Part 1, New York, Dekker, pp.378–95.

Anonymous (1860) Review of 'Lectures on Mental Diseases'. *Journal of Mental Science,* 6: 243–6.

Aschaffenburg, G. (1915) *Die Einteilung der Psychosen,* Leipzig, Deuticke.

Baillarger, J.G.F. (1853) 'Essai sur une classification des differents genres de folie'. *Annales Médico-Psychologiques*, 5: 545–66.

Baillon, T. (1864) 'Adanson'. In Dechambre, A. and Lereboullet, L. (eds.) *Dictionnaire Encyclopédique des Sciences Médicales*, vol.1, Paris, Masson, pp.689–91.

Battie, W. (1758) *A Treatise on Madness*, London, J. Whiston.

Beckman, H. and Lanczik, M. (1990) (eds.) 'Leonhard Classification of Endogenous Psychoses'. *Psychopathology*, 23: 193–341.

Berg, F. (1956) 'Linné at Sauvages. Les rapport entre leurs systèmes nosologiques'. *Lychnos*, 16: 31–54.

Berrios, G.E. (1987) 'Historical aspects of psychoses: 19th century issues'. *British Medical Bulletin*, 43: 484–98.

Berrios, G.E. (1984) 'Descriptive Psychopathology: Conceptual and Historical Aspects'. *Psychological Medicine*, 14: 303–13.

Berrios, G.E. (1985) 'Positive and Negative symptoms and Jackson'. *Archives of General Psychiatry*, 42: 95–7.

Berrios, G.E. (1991) 'Positive and Negative Signals: A conceptual History'. In Marneros, A., Andreasen, N.C. and Tsuang, M.T. (eds.) *Negative Versus Positive Schizophrenia*, Berlin, Springer, pp.8–27.

Berrios, G.E. and Hauser, R. (1988) 'The Early Development of Kraepelin's ideas on Classification: A conceptual History'. *Psychological Medicine*, 18: 813–21.

Biéder, J. (1986) 'Un Précurseur de la démocratie chrétienne et de l'Europe á la Société Médico-Psychologique: Philippe-Joseph-Benjamin Buchez'. *Annales Médico Psychologiques*, 144: 109–15.

Bing, F. (1983) 'La Théorie de la dégénérescence'. In Postel, J. and Quetel, C. (eds.) *Nouvelle Histoire de la Psychiatrie*, Paris, Privat, pp.351–6.

Bonhoeffer, K. (1910) *Die symptomatischen Psychosen*, Leizig, Deuticke.

Bowman, I.A. (1975) *William Cullen (1710–1790) and the Primacy of the Nervous System*, PhD Dissertation, Indiana University (History of Science).

Brockington, I.F. and Kendell, R.E. (1979) 'The distinction between the affective psychoses and schizophrenia'. *British Journal of Psychiatry*, 135: 243–8.

Burckard, E. (1931) 'Les Conceptions Psychiatriques de Wernicke'. In *Travaux de la Clinique Psychiatrique de la Faculté de Médicine de Strasbourg*, Strasbourg, Universitaire D'Alsace No 9, pp.45–141.

Caprariis, E. de (1971) 'La Scuola psichiatrica parigina del primo Ottocento e la nosografia di Esquirol'. *Minerva Medica*, 62: 1439–48.

Colodrón, A. (1991) 'Bartolomé Llopis (1906–1964)'. *History of Psychiatry*, 2: 219–24.

Conrad, K. (1959) 'Das problem der "nosologischen Einheit" in der Psychiatrie'. *Nervenarzt*, 30: 488–94.

Conrad, K. (1958) *Die Beginnende Schizophrenie*, Stuttgart, Thieme.

Corning, W.C. and Steffy, R.A. (1979) 'Taximetric strategies applied to psychiatric classification'. *Schizophrenia Bulletin*, 5: 294–305.

Crow, T.J. (1986) 'The continuum of psychosis and its implication for the structure of the gene'. *British Journal of Psychiatry*, 149: 419–29.

Crow, T.J. (1987) 'Psychosis as a continuum and the virogene concept'. *British Medical Bulletin*, 43: 754–67.

Cullen, W. (1803) *Synopsis nosologiae methodicae*, 6th Edition, Edinburgh, W. Creech.

Cullen, W. (1827) *The works of William Cullen*, edited by J. Thomson, vol.1, London, Blackwood.

Cutting, J. (1989) 'Gestalt theory and psychiatry: discussion paper'. *Journal of the Royal Society of Medicine*, 82: 429–31.

Desruelles, M., Léculier, P. and Gardien, M.P. (1934) 'Contribution à l'histoire des classifications psychiatriques'. *Annales Médico-Psychologiques*, 92: 637–75.

Donalies, C. (1971) 'Zur Systematik in der Psychiatrie vor Wernicke, Kraepelin und Bonhoeffer'. *Psychiatrie Neurologie Medizinische Psychologie*, (Leipzig) 23: 411–19.

Dörner, K. (1969) *Bürger und Irre*, Frankfurt am Main, Europäische Verlagsanstant.

Dowbiggin, I. (1990) 'Alfred Maury and the Politics of the Unconscious in Nineteenth-Century France'. *History of Psychiatry*, vol.1, 255–87.

Ellenberger, H. (1963) 'Les illusions de la classification psychiatrique'. *L'Evolution Psychiatrique*, 28: 221–48.

Evans, P. (1972) 'Henry Ey's concepts of the organisation of consciousness and its disorganisation: An extension of Jacksonian Theory'. *Brain*, 95: 413–40.

Everitt, B.S. (1981) 'Bimodality and the nature of depression'. *British Journal of Psychiatry*, 138: 336–9.

Ey, H. (1954) 'La classification des maladies mentales et le problème des psychoses aigües. Etude N.20'. In *Etudes Psychiatriques*, vol.3, Paris, Desclée de Brouwer, pp.11–45.

Ey, H. (1962) 'Hughlings Jackson's Principles and the Organo-Dynamic Concept of Psychiatry'. *American Journal of Psychiatry*, 118: 673–82.

Eysenck, H.J. (1970) 'The classification of depressive illness'. *British Journal of Psychiatry*, 117: 241–50.

Faber, K. (1923) *Nosography in Modern Internal Medicine*, London, Oxford University Press.

Feuchtersleben, Baron E. von (1847) *Principles of Medical Psychology*, translated by Lloyd, H.E. and Babington, B.G., London, Syndenham Society.

Fischer-Homberger, E. (1970) 'Eighteenth century nosology and its survivors'. *Medical History*, 14: 397–403.

Focke, Dr. (1859) Obituary Notice. *Journal of Mental Science* 5: 289–97.

Foville, Ach. (fils) (1872) 'Nomenclature et classification des maladies mentales'. *Annales Médico-Psychologiques*, 30: 5–35.

Garside, R.F. and Roth, M. (1978) 'Multivariate statistical methods and problems of classification in psychiatry'. *British Journal of Psychiatry*, 133: 53–67.

Gelder, M. (1991) 'Adolf Meyer and his influence on British psychiatry'. In Berrios, G.E. and Freeman, H. (eds.) *150 Years of British Psychiatry: 1841–1991*, London, Gaskell, pp.419–35.

Genil-Perrin, G. (1913) *L'Idée de Dégénérescence en Médicine Mentale*, Paris, Leclerc.

Griesinger, W. (1865) 'La Pathologie Mentale au Point de vue de L'Ecole Somatique Allemande'. *Annales Médico-Psychologiques*, 23: 1–31.

Griesinger, W. (1861) *Die Pathologie und Therapie der Psychischen Krankheiten*, Stuttgart, Krabbe.

Guiraud, P. (1950) 'Evolution de la Nosographie Clinique'. In *Psychiatrie Générale*, Paris, Le Françoise, pp.17–34.

Guislain, J. (1852) *Leçons orales sur les phrenopathies*, vol.1, Hebbellynk, Gand.

Hagner, M. (1992) 'The Soul and the Brain between Anatomy and Naturphilosophie in the early Nineteenth Century'. *Medical History*, 36: 1–33.

Harms, E. (1960) 'Johann Christian Reil'. *American Journal of Psychiatry*, 116: 1037–9.

Hartley, D. (1834) *Observations on Man, his Frame, his Duty, and his Expectations*, London, Tegg (first edition 1749).

Haslam, J. (1809) *Observations on Madness and Melancholy*, London, Callow.

Heller, R. (1975) 'J.C. Reil's Training Scheme for Medical Auxiliaries'. *Medical History*, 19: 321–32.

Hoche, A. (1912) 'Die Bedeutung der Symptomenkomplexe in der Psychiatrie'. *Zeitschrift für die gesamte Neurologie und Psychiatrie*, 12: 540–51. ('The significance of symptom complexes in Psychiatry' (1991), introduction by Dening, T. and Berrios, G.E., translation by Dening, R.G. and Dening, T. *History of Psychiatry*, 2: 329–43.)

Hoff, P. (1985) 'Zum Krankheitsbegriff bei Emil Kraepelin'. *Nervenarzt*, 56: 510–13.

Hoppe, B. (1978) 'Der Ursprung der Diagnosen in der botanischen und zoologischen Systematik'. *Sudhoff's Archiv*, 62: 105–30.

Jacobi, M. (1830) *Sammlungen für die Heilkunde der Gemüthskarankheiten*, 1st edition, Bonn, Elberfeld.

Janzarik, W. (1969) 'Nosographie und Einheitspsychose'. In Huber, G. (ed.) *Schizophrenie und Zyklothymie. Ergebnisse und Probleme*, Stuttgart, Thieme.

Janzarik, W. (1988) *Strukturdynamicsche Grundlagen der Psychiatrie*, Stuttgart, Enke.

Jossmann, P.B. (1949) 'In Memoriam; Professor Karl Bonhoeffer 1868–1948'. *American Journal of Psychiatry*, 106: 159–60.

Kahlbaum, K. (1863) *Die Gruppirung der psychischen Krankheiten und die Eintheilung der Seelenstörungen*, Danzig, Kafemann.

Kant, I. (1974) *Anthropology from a Pragmatic Point of View*, (translated by Gregor, M.J.), The Hague, Martinus Nijhoff (first edition 1797).

Kendell, R.E. (1976) 'The classification of depression. A review of contemporary confusion'. *British Journal of Psychiatry*, 129: 15–28.

Kendell, R. and Gourlay, J. (1970) 'The clinical distinction between the affective psychoses and schizophrenia'. *British Journal of Psychiatry*, 117: 261–70.

Kendell, R.E. and Brockington, I.F. (1980) 'The identification of disease entities and the relationship between schizophrenic and affective psychoses'. *British Journal of Psychiatry*, 137: 324–31.

Kendell, R.R. (1968) *The Classification of Depressive Illnesses*, Oxford, Oxford University Press.

King, L.S. (1982) *Medical Thinking*, Princeton, Princeton University Press, pp.105–27.

Kirkby, K.C. (1992) 'Proving the Somaticist Position: J.B. Friedreich on the Nature and seat of Mental Disease'. *History of Psychiatry*, 3: 237–52.

Kraepelin, E. (1920) 'Die Erscheinungs formen des Irreseins'. *Zeitschrift für die Gesamte Neurologie und Psychiatrie*, 62: 1–29.

Kraepelin, E. (1918) 'Ziele und Wege der psychiatrischen Forschung'. *Zeitschrift für Gesamte Neurologie und Psychiatrie*, 42: 169–205.

Kraepelin, E. (1962) *One Hundred Years of Psychiatry*, London, Owen (First Edition 1818).

Kretschmer, E. (1936) *Physique and Character*, New York, Harcourt (First Edition 1925).

Lain Entralgo, P. (1978) *Historia de la Medicina*, Barcelona, Salvat.

Lamarck, J.B. (1984) *Zoological Philosophy*, Chicago, University of Chicago Press (First Edition, 1809).

Lanczik, M. (1989) 'Heinrich Neumann und seine Lehre von der Einheitspsychose'. *Fundamenta Psychiatrica*, 3: 49–54.

Lanczik, M. (1988) *Der Breslauer Psychiater Car Wernicke*, Sigmaringen, Thorbecke.

Lanczik, M. (1992) 'Karl Ludwig Kahlbaum (1828–1899) and the emergence of psychopathological and nosological research in German Psychiatry'. *History of Psychiatry*, 3: 53–8.

Landre-Beauvais, A.J. (1813) *Séméiotique, ou Traité des Signes des Maladies*, 2nd edition, Paris, Brosson.

Larson, J.L. (1971) *Reason and Experience. The Representation of Natural Order in the Work of Carl von Linné*, Berkeley, University of California Press.

Le Roy, G. (1937) *La Psychologie de Condillac*, Paris, Boivin & Cie.

Leonhard, K. (1957) *Aufteilung der Endogenen Psychosen*, 1st edition, Berlin, Akademie-Verlag.

Lewes, F.M.M. (1988) 'Marc d'Espine's Statistical Nosology'. *Medical History*, 32: 301–13.

Lewis, A. (1965) 'J.C. Reil: Innovator and Battler'. *Journal of the History of the Behavioral Sciences*, 1: 178–90.

Lewis, A. (1967) 'J.C. Reil concepts of brain function'. In *The State of Psychiatry*, London, Routledge and Kegan Paul, pp.18–28.

Liepmann, H. (1911) 'Über Wernickes Einfluß auf die Klinische Psychiatrie'. *Monatsschrift für Psychiatrie und Neurologie*, 7: 1–32.

Llopis, B. (1954) 'La psicosis única'. *Archivos de Neurobiologia*, 17: 3–39.

Llopis, B. (1946) *La Psicosis Pelagrosa*, Barcelona, Científico Médica.

Llopis, B. (1970) *Introducción Dialéctica a la Psicopatología*, Madrid, Morata.

López Piñero, J.M. (1983) *Historical Origins of the Concept of Neurosis*, (translated by Berrios, D.), Cambridge, Cambridge University Press.

Marx, O. (1990–91) 'German Romantic Psychiatry: Part I and II'. *History of Psychiatry*, 1: 351–82; 2: 1–26.

Masi, C. (1981) 'Histoire des psychoses "endogenes"'. *L'Information Psychiatrique*, 57: 57–72.

Menninger, K., Ellenberger, H., Pruyser, P. and Mayman, M. (1958) 'The unitary concept of mental disease'. *Bulletin Menninger Clinic*, 22: 4–12.

Monro, H. (1857) 'On the classification and forms of insanity'. *Asylum Journal of Mental Science*, 3: 193–218.

Morel, B.A. (1860) *Traité des Maladies Mentales*, Paris, Masson.

Mundt, Ch. (1992) 'The Life and Work of Professor Werner Janzarik'. *History of Psychiatry*, 3: 1–4.

Mundt, Ch. and Saß, H. (eds.) (1992) *Für und wider die Einheitspsychose*, Stuttgart, Thieme.

Neumann, H. (1859) *Lehrbuch der Psychiatrie*, Erlangen, Enke.

Oberg, B.B. (1976) 'David Hartley and the Association of Ideas'. *Journal of the History of Ideas*, 37: 441–54.

Overall, J.E. and Woodward, J.A. (1975) 'Conceptual validity of a phenomenological classification of psychiatric patients'. *Journal of Psychiatry Research*, 12: 215–30.

Pauleikhoff, B. (1986) *Endogenen Psychosen als Zeitstörungen*, Stuttgart, Pressler.

Pichot, P.J. (1984) 'The French approach to psychiatric classification'. *British Journal of Psychiatry*, 144: 113–18.

Pick, D. (1989) *Faces of degeneration*, Cambridge, Cambridge University Press.

Pinel, Ph. (1801) (An IX) *Traité Médico-Philosophique sur L'Aliénation Mentale ou la Manie*, 1st edition, Paris, Richard, Caille et Ravier (second edition in 1809 by Brosson).

Pinel, Ph. (1818) *Nosographie Philosophique*, (6th edition), Paris, Brosson (pp.xxxviii–xxxix).

Raven, H., Berlin, B. and Breedlove, D.E. (1971) 'The Origins of Taxonomy'. *Science* 174: 1210–13.

Reil, J.C. (1803) *Rhapsodieen über die Anwendung der psychischen Curmethode auf Geisteszerrüttungen*, Halle, (1968 re-impression, Amsterdam, Bonset).

Reil, J.C. (1805) *Über die Erkenntnis und kur der Fieber*, vol.4, Nervenkrankheiten, Halle.

Rémond, M. (1902) 'Essai sur la classification en Psychiatrie'. *Gazette des Hopitaux*, 75: 973–6; 983–7.

Rennert, H. (1964) 'Aufteilung der Psychosen und Einheitspsychose'. *Nervenarzt*, 35: 263–71.

Rennert, H. (1965) 'Die Universalegenese der endogenen Psychosen'. *Fortschritte Neurologie Psychiatrie*, 33: 251–62.

Rennert, H. (1968) 'Wilhelm Griesinger und die Einheitspsychose'. *Wissenschaftsliche Zeitschreift Humbolt Universitäts Berlin*, 17: 15–16.

Renouard, P.V. (1846) *Histoire de la Médicine*, vol.2, Paris, Baillière.

Reuchlin, M. (1984) 'Contribution to the theoretical problems of classification in the observational sciences'. *Psychopathology*, 17: 149–57.

Ribot, Th. (1876) 'La Psychologie de Herbart'. *Revue Philosophique*, 2: 68–85.

Riese, W. (1945) 'History and principles of classification of nervous diseases'. *Bulletin of the History of Medicine*, 18: 465–512.

Riese, W. (1968) 'La Méthode Analytique de Condillac et ses Rapports avec l'oeuvre de Pinel'. *Revue Philosophique*, 158: 321–36.

Roubinovitch, J. (1896) *Des variétés cliniques de la Folie en France et en Allemagne*, Paris, Doin.

Sadler, J.Z., Wiggins, O.P. and Schwartz, M.A. (eds.) (1994) *Philosophical perspectives on psychiatric diagnostic classification*, Baltimore, Johns Hopkins University Press.

Sartorius, N., Jablensky, A., Regier, D.A., Burke, J.D. and Hirschfeld, R.M.A. (eds.) (1990) *Sources and Traditions of Classification in Psychiatry*, Toronto, Hogrefe & Huber.

Saury, H. (1886) *Etude Clinique sur la Folie Héréditaire (Les dégénérés)*, Paris, Delahaye et Lecrosnier.

Schwartz, M.A. and Wiggins, O.P. (1986) 'Logical empiricism and psychiatric classification'. *Comprehensive Psychiatry*, 27: 101–14.

Schwartz, M.A. and Wiggins, O.P. (1987) 'Diagnosis and ideal types: a contribution to psychiatric classification'. *Comprehensive Psychiatry*, 28: 277–91.

Smith, C.U.M. (1987) 'David's Hartley's Newtonian Neuropsychology'. *Journal of the History of the Behavioral Sciences*, 23: 123–36.

Starobinski, J. (1981) 'Bréve histoire de la conscience du corps'. *Revue Française de Psychanalyse*, 2: 261–79.

Stevens, P.F. (1984) 'Metaphors and typology in the development of Botanical Systematics 1690–1960'. *Taxon*, 33: 169–211.

Stout, G.F. (1888) 'The Herbartian Psychology'. *Mind*, 13: 321–38; 473–98.

Syndenham, T. (1848) *The works of Thomas Sydenham MD*, (translated by Latham, R.G.), vol.1, London, Sydenham Society.

Talbot, E.S. (1898) *Degeneracy. Its Causes, Signs and Results*, London, Walter Scott.

Temkin, O. (1965) 'The history of classification in the medical science'. In Katz, M.M., Cole, J.O. and Barton, W.E. (eds.) *The Role of Methodology of Classification in Psychiatry and Psychopathology*, Washington, US Department of Health, pp.11–25.

Valenciano, L. (1970) 'La Tesis de la Psicosis única en la Actualidad'. In Llopis, B. *Introducción Dialéctica a la Psicopatología*, Morata, Madrid, pp.113–59.

Verga, D. (1876) 'Projet d'une classification uniforme des maladies mentales, au point de vue de la statistique'. *Annales Médico-Psychologiques*, 34: 140–4.

Vernon, K. (1988) 'The founding of numerical taxonomy'. *British Journal of History of Science*, 21: 143–59.

Vie, M.J. (1940) 'Sur l'existence d'éntites morbides en psychiatrie'. *Annales Médico-Psychologique*, 98: 347–58.

Vliegen, J. (1980) *Die Einheitspsychose*, Stuttgart, Enke.

Walker, N. (1968) *Crime and Insanity in England. vol.1: The Historical Perspective*, Edinburgh, Edinburgh University Press.

Wyrsch, J. (1956) *Zur Geschichte und Deutung der endogenen Psychosen*, Stuttgart, Thieme.

Zeller, A. (1837) *Beilage zum Medizinischen Correspondenzblatt des Würtenbergischen Arzlichen Vereins*, vol.7, No30, Stuttgart.

Zeller, A. (1840) *Beilage zum Medizinischen Correspondenzblatt des Würtenbergischen Arzlichen Vereins*, vol.10, No17, Stuttgart.

Zeller, A. (1843) *Beilage zum Medizinischen Correspondenzblatt des Würtenbergischen Arzlichen Vereins*, vol.13, No38, Stuttgart.

Zilboorg, G.W. (1941) *A History of Medical Psychology*, Norton & Co, New York.

Chapter 13
Schizophrenia

Clinical Section
J HOENIG

The history of schizophrenia is in many ways very complex, with great uncertainties and still many open questions. The beginning of the history however is definite and unequivocal. It began exactly 100 years ago in 1893 when Emil Kraepelin (1855–1926) first introduced it as a diagnostic entity in his textbook of psychiatry under the name of dementia praecox (Kraepelin, 1893). Kraepelin had begun publishing his textbook in 1883, but *dementia praecox* was not mentioned in the first 3 editions. Only the 4th edition introduces the term in the group of the degenerative processes. The 4th edition was not the end of this development, only the start. Various conditions like '*Verrücktheit*' or '*Wahnsinn*' were still maintained as separate diagnoses to be subsumed into *dementia praecox* in later editions. Kraepelin's views never stood still. The foreword to each edition explains almost apologetically that

> As the previous classifications proved untenable a radically new grouping became necessary. . . .
> If there is an excuse for these changes, I would mention my striving to stick as much as possible to my own experience, even though that is as yet rather inadequate. (Kraepelin, 1887)

The 4th edition appeared shortly after Kraepelin's appointment to the chair in Heidelberg in 1892 having just returned from Dorpat in Estonia, at the time part of Germany, where he had held the chair in psychiatry. The new post enabled him, he says in his foreword (Kraepelin, 1893), to 'turn all my attention to the collection of clinical observations'.

The degenerative processes included 3 headings: *Dementia praecox*, Katatonia and Dementia paranoides.

> What these clinical pictures . . . have in common is the unusually rapid development of a lasting state of psychic weakness [*Schwächezustand*] the beginning of which can be clearly recognized by certain accompanying symptoms. In contrast to the other psychoses which also end in '*Schwachsinn*' the mental debility here is clearly seen right at the start or at least shortly after. (Kraepelin, 1893, p.435)

The rapid deterioration apart, the clinical pictures of those 3 conditions are indeed rather different. The name dementia praecox refers at this stage to one group only, which corresponds more or less to what Hecker (1843–1909) (1871) had called Hebephrenia, a rapidly progressive deterioration of psychic functions affecting mainly adolescents (Hebe meaning adolescence). The prognosis is invariably bad. Hecker had described mainly relatively milder forms of the illness. Daraszkiewiez (1892) had submitted a dissertation on a group of more severe cases. The thesis had been submitted in Dorpat, Kraepelin's place of work, just before leaving for Heidelberg.

A condition similar to what Hecker called Hebephrenia had been described by the french psychiatrist Augustin B. Morel (1809–1873) (1852) who had used the name *Dementia praecox*. The name had also been used by the Prague physician A. Pick, (1851–1924) (1891) and was now adopted by Kraepelin. Morel who had also introduced the concept of dégénérance clearly influenced Kraepelin and led to the inclusion of dementia praecox, alias Hebephrenia, in the group of the degenerative processes.

The concept of dégénérance had a very specific meaning which had its roots in religious ideas. The perfect man, also perfect in health, was the divinely created Adam. After the fall and consequent expulsion from paradise his condition became flawed. He became prone to sin, and the human condition and society and its ways went from bad to worse. With this his health degenerated. Not only that, but the illness was passed on to the next generation and in doing so became worse with each successive generation, leading finally to sterility and the extinction of the line. Morel's ideas had a tremendous impact on European thought. In the hands of Valentine Magnan (1835–1912) (1885) these ideas were secularized. It was no longer sin and fall from grace that gave the impetus to the degeneration but the corruption of social life. The idea that the conditions in the world are going from bad to worse, and are the cause of the deterioration in human health, particularly mental health, is still often heard today. It is a kind of culturo-somatic concept of disease. It served as a model for any kind of illness of unknown etiology, but had and still has its widest application in the group of psychiatric disorders.

In that form, even the secularized form of Magnan, the concept of dégénérance did not survive without modification, but the idea was fruitful. As Karl Jaspers (1883–1969) put it in the historical overview in his General Psychopathology:

> Morel and Magnan understood not so much as a sharp concept, as intuitively the importance of heredity and of degeneration; they saw the types of degenerative mental illnesses and with it the basic differentiation between the endogenous and exogenous psychoses. (Jaspers, 1959, p.712)

Morel's and Magnan's ideas had their influence on such german writers as Heinrich Schüle (1840–1910) and Richard von Krafft-Ebing (1840–1902) now largely stripped of their metaphysical aspects, and it is in that context that Kraepelin created his own *dementia praecox* concept.

The third and perhaps most important stimulus for Kraepelin's thinking about the psychosis came from Kahlbaum (1828–1899). Karl Ludwig Kahlbaum (1863) wanted to overcome the contemporary attempts to arrive at a nosology by describing cross sectional clinical pictures of illnesses. In order to comprehend and classify the bewildering variety of mental illnesses, he stressed the importance of observing the patient over a lifetime. He wanted to base his illness categories on the longitudinal history of the symptoms. He was hoping in this way to discover actual illness entities, nosological categories. He takes the, at the time, commonly accepted categories of melancholia, mania, moria and dementia, and shows that over time, these syndromes change one into others in the same patient.

> Thus it cannot be doubted that in the socalled forms of the psychic illnesses as they have been know through the ages, we do not see the forms of various disease entities, but only the forms of their various stadia or better still the forms of various symptomcomplexes anyone of which the illness can adopt during different periods of its course . . . therefore the symptom complexes cannot form the basis for diagnosis. (Kahlbaum, (1878), p.1133)

That thinking leads Kahlbaum to look at the onset, the actual course that is the sequence of the various syndromes, and at the outcome, and with this he arrives at a new classification of the actual illnesses as conceived by him. He finds that each type of course – e.g. succession of different syndromes as opposed to a syndromatically unchanging course – tends to be associated with a different outcome.

> With this we have recognized another very important clinical fact: The psychic illnesses with a changing course are complex or relatively total psychic disorders with a tendency to end in dementia, to degenerate psychically, whereas the earlier described forms with a constant unchanging course can be conceived as relatively partial psychic disorders which do not tend towards psychic degeneration. (p.1137)

In order to further clarify his new approach Kahlbaum argues for the creation of a new terminology, uncontaminated by earlier usages which unfortunately tend rather to confuse matters. This however need not concern us here.

Kahlbaum was probably not the first or only one to look to the course and outcome of morbid states to arrive at disease entities. Already Morel (1860) had tried to link cause or origin, course and outcome. In internal medicine the demand to take the entire course sharply into focus had been made by Rudolf Virchow, (1821–1902). Hecker (1871) had succeeded with an even more precise formulation of this view. But Kahlbaum's determined use of this approach began as it were a new era in Germany and beyond.

Kahlbaum (1874) published his monograph on Katatonia (*Das Spannungsirresein*), an illness he conceived primarily as a neuropsychiatric disorder, characterized by various motor abnormalities and stupor. (A better term for the latter might be akinetic mutism.) The name chosen for the condition – tonia – refers to an abnormality in muscle tone, a hypertonus. The description of the abnormal movements including mannerisms, fidgeting and stereotypes are all described in, as it were, neurological terms.

> Katatonia is a cerebral illness with a cyclically changing course in which psychic symptoms represent in turn the picture of melancholia, mania, stupescence, confusion and finally of dementia (deterioration). One or more of these pictures may occur. Besides these psychic symptoms abnormal processes in the motor nervous system show themselves as essential symptoms with the general characteristics of hypertonus [*Krampf*]. (p.68)

The Morel-Kahlbaum-Hecker stimulus has provided for Kraepelin the idea of heredity, the name, and two 'diagnostic' groups, Hebephrenia, still called Dementia praecox, and Katatonia. To this Kraepelin (1896) added a third group, Dementia paranoides, a rapidly deteriorating form of what would today be labelled paranoid schizophrenia. In subsequent editions of his textbook earlier diagnostic terms like *Verrücktheit*, *Wahnsinn* and some others were gradually omitted, and the name of *dementia praecox* was now used for the entire group while the name hebephrenia was reinstated in its old meaning.

Kraepelin thought of this new dementia praecox with its 3 subtypes as a disease entity. He expected future research to demonstrate the pathology and the cause to confirm the nosological validity. He was of course aware that a number of somatic or toxic conditions could produce a similar clinical picture, but this would be only a dementia praecox*like* condition outside the periphery of the core illness.

At the same time Kraepelin (1913) never quite lost sight of the fact that the clinical types which were here put together as one illness were so diverse in appearance. Even as late as in the 8th edition in 1913 he writes:

> Although there still are in many details far reaching differences of opinion, the conviction is gaining ground more and more, that *dementia praecox* is by and large a distinct disease entity; and that we are justified in regarding at least the main group of the outwardly often very diverse clinical pictures brought here together as the expression of a uniform morbid process. (p.668)

An expression of this unease is perhaps that he keeps subdividing dementia praecox into more and more different types. In the 8th edition the index mentions 10 types.

> The detailed clinical presentation of the vast area of *dementia praecox* encounters considerable difficulties, because the definition of the several morbid pictures can only be achieved artificially. There are no doubt a range of frequently recurring forms, but between them are numerous transitions making it impossible to provide sharp definitions and to assign every case unequivocally to a particular type. (p.761)

One condition which Kraepelin (1913) always kept outside dementia praecox is paraphrenia with its own 4 subtypes. In some ways paraphrenia appears to be the successor to what used to be '*Verrücktheit*' also called 'paranoia'. (It is not exactly what is now called 'paranoia'.)

> All these clinical pictures which cannot always be clearly separated one from the other have in common is a pronounced presence of delusions, the paranoid colouring of the clinical picture. In addition there are also mood abnormalities but not, even in the latest stages of the illness, that blunting and indifference which in *dementia praecox* are often the earliest symptoms. . . . Disorders of volition which normally accompany *dementia praecox* in so many diverse forms, appear here only occasionally in the mildest form. (p.973)

A follow up study carried out by Kolle (1931) found that prolonged follow up observation of cases of paraphrenia makes a differentiation from dementia praecox impossible.

PSYCHIATRIC NOSOLOGY BEFORE KRAEPELIN

The introduction of *Dementia praecox* – as well as the creation of the manic-depressive illness – has so transformed the clinical practice and research, that it is difficult to imagine the time before that. Although there are several excellent works on the history of Psychiatry up to the end of the 19th century – and beyond – there are no histories of schizophrenia. Leibbrand and Wettly (1963) published a 'History of Madness' [*Der Wahnsinn*] which contains much that is of relevance, but is not exclusively concerned with schizophrenia. One of the few such histories is by Hans Walter Gruhle (1880–1958) in vol. IX of the Handbuch der Geisteskrankheiten (Handbook of Mental Illnesses) edited by O. Bumke (1877–1950) (1932). That volume contains chapters on many aspects of schizophrenia and remains an excellent source book for schizophrenia research. It reads remarkably modern. Unfortunately it is not known widely enough outside the German speaking world and to my knowledge has never been translated. The clinical section – the biggest chapter – was written by Wilhelm Mayer-Gross (1889–1961) and its contents have to a limited extent become known to British psychiatry through the 'Textbook of Psychiatry' by Mayer-Gross, Slater and Roth (1969). There has been a recent publication 'The Concept of Schizophrenia: Historical Perspective' edited by J.G. Howells (1991), who himself also contributed an introduction and two chapters. The book is a collection of papers on the history of schizophrenia, never published before. The pre-Kraepelinian period, covering mainly the 19th century is written by U.H. Peters (1991), the director of a clinic associated with the University of Cologne, Germany.

Gruhle (1932) begins his historical chapter by saying:

> The history of schizophrenia is really the history of the psychoses in general, because from the entirety of what in the beginning of psychiatric science was subsumed under such names as mental illness, psychic illness [*Seelenkrankheit*], delusional illness, derangement of mind, alienation ... the exogenous psychoses became more and more separated, and the actual nucleus of mental derangement left was just schizophrenia. (p.1)

Peters similarly does not attempt to actually trace a history of the illness, but describes rather the dominant influences of the times, the Zeitgeist, on psychiatric thinking. Significantly, he chooses as illustrative influences on the so-called romantic psychiatry of the early 19th century a poet, Novalis (1772–1801) and a novelist, E.T.A. Hoffman (1776–1822). In fact there cannot be a history of pre-Kraepelinian schizophrenia, because the concept did not exist. What Gruhle and Peters attempt is to trace certain aspects of Kraepelin's *dementia praecox* back to their sources: they include the French tradition of excellent case descriptions, based on close observations of patients; the French insistence on basing their classification on causal concepts; Morel's views on degeneracy, which led to the recognition of heredity; the recognition of the brain as the 'organ of psychic disorders' by Wilhelm Griesinger (1810–1868) (1845); the distinction between cross-sectional syndromes and their unsuitability for nosology, and longitudinal case studies, to establish disease entities as emphasized by Kahlbaum (1863) and Hecker; and the syndromatic entities of catatonia by Kahlbaum (1874) and hebephrenia by Morel (1852) and Hecker (1871); and finally the origin of the term *dementia praecox* by Morel (1852) and Pick (1891).

These do not represent a linear growth of the concept. They were elements there for all to see, but it fell to Kraepelin to use them to create de novo his dementia praecox. It testifies to his genius that he could see those elements and use them in the creation of his new clinical entity. Berrios and Hauser (1988) have taken that creative period in Kraepelin's life and work under a magnifying glass and have brought to light much interesting and illuminating material.

The psychiatric classification or nosology of the 19th century strikes us as bewildering. The divers views presented in large numbers – are often more philosophical than clinical. Gruhle describes these attempts as 'naive'. The terminology is idiosyncratic, new terms were constantly introduced, and one and the same term given varied applications. And yet it is astonishing how much these authors knew which makes reading them still profitable and illuminating.

Herman Emminghaus (1845–1904) (1878) in his excellent '*Allgemeine Psychopathologie*' [General Psychopathology] describes the contemporary state as follows:

> One still speaks generally about depression or melancholia, about mania or furor [*Tobsucht*], about *Wahnsinn, Verrücktheit* or disintegration [*Blödsinn*] and links these terms to ideas of certain empirical-psychological syndromes. The terms however are not always used in the same sense. Furor describes symptomatically divers, even contradictory states, *Wahnsinn* and *Verrücktheit* are used promiscuously, *Verrücktheit* and *Blödsinn* are often not strictly differentiated. . . . In addition this contrived nosological system, called aptly a 'pigeonhole system' [*Fachwerk*] by Kahlbaum, is unable to accommodate certain more complex psychopathological entities and although they do exist in fact, the system has to ignore them or treat them as irrelevancies . . . and this brings it into stark conflict with the everyday observations. (p.236)

To this dismal state could be added that perusal of the illustrative case histories shows that many cases fit one or more of the categories as well as the one they were meant to represent.

Looking at the classifications used by various authors, one is struck by certain similarities as well as differences in the French, German and English textbooks.

The diagnostic categories which are always included are those of melancholia and mania which had been established already in antiquity, and were brought into their modern form by Jean Pierre Falret (1794–1870) (1854) and J.G.F. Baillarger (1806–1891) (1854) who also established the acceptance of folie circulaire i.e. manic depressive psychosis. They were considered to be disease entities. The other categories show a marked variability in the anglophone textbooks. The authors struggle to make what they can of those German words *Verrücktheit* (according to Langenscheidt's dictionary 'screwball'), *Wahnsinn* (explained by Peters, 1991) *Blödsinn, Amentia, Schwächezustand* etc. In France, classifications, although not uniform, appear to have more common ground (Pelicier, 1991). But what would now be regarded as belonging to schizophrenia is not unified there either but appears amongst J.E. Esquirol's (1772–1840) (1838) monomanias, the Folies dégénérances and other categories.

KRAEPELIN AND FURTHER DEVELOPMENTS

Kraepelin continued to further develop his views in each subsequent edition of his textbook. In the 5th edition in 1896 Dementia praecox with its main types of Hebephrenia, catatonia and dementia paranoides, is classified as a form of the degenerative disorders. In later editions dementia praecox is subsumed under the metabolic disorders. Various until then not understood psychoses when examined as to their endstates were included in dementia praecox, as they were indistinguishable from the endstate of that illness. Gruhle (1932), very much involved in these developments, says in the face of the increasing variety of clinical syndromes now included,

> The Heidelberg workers never gave up the inner resistance against their own efforts to unite so many diverse matters in one concept. (p.23)

Kraepelin's view at first did not find much acceptance outside the circle of his co-workers, and in fact encountered much resistance. This did not change until the appearance of Eugen Bleuler's (1857–1939) book 'Dementia praecox or the Group of Schizophrenias' in 1911. This book, and the greatly enlarged 8th edition of Kraepelin's textbook of 1913, broke the deadlock and brought a general acceptance not just in Germany but in the world – except in France. Some of this French reservation appears to persist to the present. Pelicier (1991), Professor of Psychiatry in Paris, France, writes:

> Between the first edition of his textbook of psychiatry in 1883 and the edition of 1896, Kraepelin had locked European psychiatry into a terrifying system: every clinical picture had its place, every patient's destiny was predetermined. The psychiatric hospital was like the firmament of Kepler in which the positions and movements of stars and planets are determined. French psychiatrists, like those in other countries, were impressed by the Kraepelinian system, but they tried more and more to defend their traditional nosography. (p.132)

Kraepelin and Bleuler had the same case material in mind. Bleuler disliked the name *Dementia praecox* and felt it was misleading; there is no dementia in the sense of Dementia senilis, and so he co-opted Schizophrenia in the title. Carl Schneider (1891–1946) (1930) in his monograph on the Psychology of Schizophrenics says,

> Gradually the new name was adopted by us without subscribing to Bleuler's theoretical concepts. (p.1)

Bleuler had never intended to oppose Kraepelin's views. M. Bleuler (1903–1994) (1988) has recently said about his father:

> Nowadays it is sometimes stated that Bleuler had wanted to present the concept of schizophrenia as contradicting that of Kraepelin. There can be no talk of that, on the contrary, Bleuler felt himself to be almost a student of Kraepelin and greatly admired his psychiatric knowledge. He wanted to expand Kraepelin's work, not to disprove it. This of course did not prevent him from introducing his own ideas into the concept of schizophrenia. (p.1324)

And yet Kraepelin's *Dementia praecox* and Bleuler's schizophrenia are not the same. One of the first to subject the two to a close comparative scrutiny was Gruhle (1913). He went into great detail, but perhaps the main points of difference can be seen to be the following.

1. Whereas Kraepelin gives descriptions and examples of all the symptoms of dementia praecox his approach is purely observational and empirical, and he avoids any kind of theorizing about them. Bleuler on the other hand is guided by a theory. He postulates an as yet unknown cerebral disease process which expresses itself by the primary symptoms in the clinical picture, such as perhaps thought blocking and dissociation of ideas. The secondary symptoms which include most of the remaining up to now described symptoms, like hallucinations, delusions, certain thought disorders and abnormal affects, are not directly linked to the disease process but are due to, as it were, haphazard life experiences. Bleuler's distinction looks particularly misconceived to our hindsight, as it is precisely the 'psychogenic' symptoms which respond to the neuroleptic treatment whereas the disease-near basic symptoms are largely unaffected. In the actual clinical picture Bleuler distinguishes between basic symptoms by which he means obligatory symptoms found in every case, and facultative symptoms which need not be present in every case, and can also appear in other illnesses. Thus Bleuler introduces a structure into the symptoms. Kraepelin dismisses all that as pure speculation.

2. The second most important difference is the application of psychoanalytic ideas by Bleuler, who was in close contact with Freud, Karl Abraham (1877–1925) and C.G. Jung (1875–1961), the last two on the staff of his clinic (M. Bleuler, 1988). Bleuler 'understood' the content of the symptoms which ordinarily made no sense, but lend themselves to interpretation by reference to unconscious complexes. Bleuler and Jung took this 'understanding' beyond the symptom content and applied it to the very existence of the symptom and even of the entire illness (Hoenig, 1983). Kraepelin responds to this with impatience and sarcasm.

> I must confess openly that with the best will I cannot go along with the ideas of that 'Metapsychiatry' which, just like a complex, soaks up all the sober clinical method of observation. (p.938)

A paradoxical situation had come about: Kraepelin had, as he thought, established a disease entity without being able to name a single obligatory symptom, whereas Bleuler had the obligatory primary symptom but spoke of a 'Group of schizophrenias'. This dilemma still exists and bears on the definition of the circumference of the illness i.e. the decision which particular case falls into the diagnosis and which has to be excluded. The DSM-III-R (1987) for instance, following Kraepelin states that no single symptom is found in all cases.

Bleuler's approach led to an enlargement of the circumference, particularly with the introduction of 'latent schizophrenia'.

> There is such a thing as latent schizophrenia and I almost believe that is the most frequent occurring form even though it comes under treatment the least often. To describe the features of latent schizophrenia is probably not worth while. All the symptoms and symptom combinations which can be found in

the fully developed illness can appear here in nuce. Irritable, strange, moody, lonely, excessively punctual people arouse suspicion, amongst other things, to be schizophrenic. One often finds hidden one or another catatonic or paranoid symptom, and various such habits becoming more pronounced in later life proof that all forms of the illness can run a latent course. (Bleuler, 1911, p.196)

This had unforeseen consequences, not just for schizophrenia research but for the medico-legal position of such patients. In 1933 the German government, for the purification of the race, had introduced sterilisation laws for patients with hereditary diseases, and who is or is not schizophrenic assumed vast importance for the individual. Mainly in view of this, the followers of Bleuler's view, mainly Swiss psychiatrists, revised these concepts (Wyrsch, 1966). Such dangers are by no means a matter of the past but still existed in countries of the Sowjet block (Smulevitch, 1989).

KURT SCHNEIDER 1887–1967

The work of Kurt Schneider, his first and second rank symptoms of schizophrenia, gained influence, particularly in British psychiatry, when his 'Clinical Psychopathology' was translated into English by Marian W. Hamilton (1959). Mellor (1970) used the symptoms for empirical, statistical research and Wing et al (1974) based the 'Present State Examination', a statistical diagnostic tool, largely on the first rank symptom list as described by Schneider.

Schneider's work itself is based on the new approach to psychiatry created by a group of workers, mainly in Heidelberg, during the first quarter of our century (Hoenig, 1982). The group included Gruhle, Wilmanns, Homburger, Ranke, Mayer-Gross and Jaspers. An attempt was made to overcome the sterile dichotomy of 'schools' which flourished in Germany and the rest of Europe during the 19th century, into the 'organicist' and 'psychicists'. Kraepelin's approach was in line with the organicists who had gained dominance. Jaspers (1957) writes about that state of affairs:

Freuds influence was limited to small circles. Psychological approaches were regarded to be subjective and futile, not scientific . . . . The cause for confusion appeared to lie in the nature of the subject itself. The subject of psychiatry was man, not just his body; his body even least of all, but rather his psyche, his personality, man himself. (p.10)

Bleuler's application of psychoanalytic views to the understanding of schizophrenia had overshot the target. Jaspers (1963) in his General Psychopathology, which had first appeared in 1913 i.e. two years after Bleuler's work and one year after Kraepelin's much enlarged 8th edition, attempted to clarify the situation by precisely defining the methodology which allowed the study of the patient as a person (Hoenig, 1991). The meaningful study of the patients' life by the method of empathy represents the basic approach. Where this empathy fails, where it reaches its limits, where the meaning is no longer discernable, the patient's inner experience, the symptom, can be described and points to a 'process' which has broken into the patient's life, disrupting the meaningful cohesion of the personality. This 'new' element cannot be 'understood' but has to be 'explained'. These two methods of comprehending the patient's condition, meaningful understanding and causal explanation, became the cornerstone of the new psychopathology.

This methodology introduces a subjective method. It is the psychiatrist who 'understands', the psychiatrist who encounters the limits of this 'understanding'. This turn to the subjectivity of the diagnostic approach was taken to perhaps an extreme degree by the Dutch psychiatrist H.C. Rümke (1893–1967) (1941) who introduced the concept of 'praecox feeling'. He writes in a recently translated paper (1991),

> What is the praecox feeling? I feel that this term is preferable to 'schizophrenic colouration' as it implies that a feeling induced in the clinician is the final and most important diagnostic guideline. As it plays such an important role in diagnosis, it deserves some further analysis. (p.336)

He calls it 'the nuclear symptom of schizophrenia'. Rümke's diagnostic conclusions may not be accepted by most but they illustrate that turn to the subjective method of 'understanding'. Psychoanalysis too, had drawn attention to the importance of subjectivity in the study of the patient, but the emphasis was on its elimination by the training analysis. It was regarded as something that could interfere with a proper understanding of the patient. In Jaspers' psychopathology it becomes an instrument of investigation.

Psychiatry placed, as the discipline is, in both the biological sciences and the humanities, is always exposed to the Zeitgeist, the prevailing philosophies. The new turn inwards betrays here perhaps a parallel to the cultural movements of 'modernism' and 'postmodernism', i.e. a progressive shift from the observed to the observer. Lefebre (1957) pursuing these ideas writes:

> Jaspers shifts psychology as it were a step 'beyond' the present psychologies, just as with his phenomenology he went 'beyond' the usual procedures. By returning beyond the object of the psychologist to the thinking subject, he moors psychology within the psychologist. From this follows that the 'ultimate' in psychology for Jaspers is the way in which the psychologist thinks of a psychic fact. (p.477)

Based on these methodological principles are Schneider's, the clinician's, 1st rank symptoms of schizophrenia. They represent a clinical reality arrived at by a strict method (Hoenig, 1984), a fact not perhaps fully appreciated by various investigators like Carpenter et al (1974) when testing statistically the validity of Schneider's (1959) claim that

> Wherever such experiences (the 1st rank symptoms) can be established with certainty, and no underlying physical illness can be found, we speak clinically in all modesty of schizophrenia. (p.133)

C.P. Peters (1991) traces the development of the concept of schizophrenia from Kraepelin – mentioning briefly the 19th century anticedents – to Schneider and the impact on present day psychiatry. The widening differences in the concept of that illness in Europe and the USA during the post 2nd World War era was tested as to its practical diagnostic consequences in the Cross-national Project for the Study of the Diagnosis of Mental Disorders in the United States and the United Kingdom (1974). The study showed that in the U.S. more patients were diagnosed as schizophrenic. This was followed by the International Pilot Study of Schizophrenia by the World Health Organization (1973). Peters then traces the various steps which led to the DSM-III-R criteria for that diagnosis, trying to establish core symptoms based on symptom description.

The history of the concept of schizophrenia has not written its final chapter. Up to now the diagnosis still rests on psychopathological criteria. By the nature of psychopathology it cannot provide pathognomonic symptoms. Furthermore no uncontested single obligatory symptom has yet been found. The problem is really to define the circumference of the illness. The arbitrary and unclinical limitation of the diagnosis to the 16–45 years age group used in DSM-III-R has not brought greater diagnostic certainty about which particular cases must be in - or excluded. The uncertainties dictate tentativeness. In the clinic this means caution and often 'wait and see'. In research it means that definition of what kind of case is included in any study cannot be left for granted.

Acknowledgment.
I am very grateful to Inge Hoenig for the enormous help she gave me in the preparation of this essay.

REFERENCES

Baillarger, J.G. (1854) 'Note sur un genre de folie'. *Gazette Hepdomadaire de Medicine et de Chirurige*, 2: Feb.

Berrios, G.E. and Hauser, R. (1988) 'The early development of Kraepelin's ideas on classification'. *Psychological Medicine*, 18: 813–21.

Bleuler, E. (1911) *Dementia praecox oder Gruppen der Schizophrenien*, Leipzig, Deutike.

Bleuler, M. (1988) 'Zur Entstehung und Bedeutung von Eugen Bleulers Werk "Dementia praecox oder Gruppe der Schizophrenien" '. *Schweizer Rundschau Med. (Praxis)*, 77: 48: 1322–6.

Carpenter, W.T., Strauss, J.S. and Bartko, J.J. (1974) 'Uses of signs and symptoms for the identification of schizophrenic patients'. *Schizophrenia Bulletin*, 11: 37–49.

Cross-National Project (1974) 'The diagnosis and psychopathology of schizophrenia in New York and London', *Schizophrenia Bulletin*, 11: 80–102.

Daraszkiewics, L. (1892) *Über Hebephrenie, insbesondere deren schwere Form*, Dissertation, Dorpat.

DSM III R (1987) Diagnostic and statistical manual, Washington, American Psychiatric Association.

Emminghaus, H. (1878) *Allgemeine Psychopathologie zur Einführung in das Studium der Geistesstörungen*, Leipzig, Vogel.

Esquirol, J.E.D. (1838) *Mental Maladies: A Treatise on Insanity*, (in French 1838). Translated by Hunt, E.K. (1845) Philadelphia, Lea & Blanchard.

Falret, J.P. (1854) 'De la Folie circulair'. *Bulletin de l'Academie, NAT med*, Paris, 19: 382–95.

Griesinger, W. (1845) *Die Pathologie und Therapie der psychischen, Krankheiten*, Stuttgart, Krabbe.

Gruhle, H. (1913) 'Bleulers Schizophrenie und Kraepelins Dementia praecox'. *Zeitschrift f.d. gesamte Neurologie und Psychiatrie*, 17: 114–33.

Gruhle, H. (1932) 'Geschichtliches'. In Bumke, O. (ed.) *Handbuch der Geisteskrankheiten*, vol. IX, Berlin, Springer.

Hecker, E. (1871) 'Begründung des klinischen Standpunktes in der Psychiatrie'. *Virchows Archiv*, 52: 203–18.

Hecker, E. (1871) 'Die Hebephrenie', *Virchows Archiv*, 52:394–429.

Hoenig, J. (1982) 'Kurt Schneider and anglophone psychiatry'. *Comprehensive Psychiatry*, 23: 391–400.

Hoenig, J. (1983) 'The concept of schizophrenia, Kraepelin-Bleuler-Schneider'. *British Journal of Psychiatry*, 142: 547–56.

Hoenig, J. (1984) 'Schneider's first rank symptoms and the tabulators'. *Comprehensive Psychiatry*, 25:77–87.

Hoenig, J. (1991) 'Jaspers' view on schizophrenia'. In Howells, J.G. (ed.) *The Concept of Schizophrenia: Historical Perspectives*, Washington, American Psychiatric Press, Chapter 5, pp.75–92.

Howells, J.G. (1991) *The Concept of Schizophrenia: Historical Perspective*, Washington, American Psychiatric Press.

Jaspers, K. (1957) 'Philosophische Autobiographie'. In Karl Jaspers (ed.) *Schlipp. P.A.*, Stuttgart, Kohlhammer. Translated as 'The philosophy of Karl Jaspers', La Salle, Open Court, 1957.

Jaspers, K. (1959) *Allgemeine Psychopathologie*, 8th ed., Berlin, Springer. Translated by Hoenig, J. and Hamilton, M.W. (1963) *General Psychopathology*, Manchester University Press.

Kahlbaum, K. (1863) *Gruppierung der psychischen Krankheiten*, Danzig, Kafemann.

Kahlbaum, K. (1874) *Die Katatonie oder das Spannungsirresein*, Berlin, Hirschwald.

Kahlbaum, K. (1878) 'Klinisch-diagnostische Gesichtspunkte der Psychopathologie'. *Sammlung Klinischer Vorträge*, 126: 1127–46.

Kolle, K. (1931) 'Paraphrenie und Paranoia'. *Fortschritte der Neurologie-Psychiatrie*, 3: 319–34.

Kraepelin, E. (1887) *Psychiatrie*, 2nd ed., Leipzig, Abel.

Kraepelin, E. (1893) *Psychiatrie*, 4th ed., Leipzig, Abel.

Kraepelin, E. (1896) *Compendium der Psychiatrie*, 5th ed., Leipzig, Barth.

Kraepelin, E. (1913) *Psychiatrie*, 8th ed., Leipzig, Barth.

Krafft-Ebing, R.V. (1904) *Textbook of Insanity*, translated by Chaddock, C.G., Philadelphia, Davis.

Lefebre, L.B. (1957) 'Die Psychologie von Karl Jaspers'. In Karl Jaspers (ed.) *Schlipp P.A.*, Stuttgart, Kohlhammer, pp.465–92.

Leibbrand, W. and Wettly, A. (1961) *Der Wahnsinn*, Freiburg, Alber.

Magnan, V. (1885) 'Les delirants chroniques et le dégénérés'. Gazett des Hospitaux, 22 et 26 avril.

Mayer-Gross, W., Slater, E. and Roth, M. (1969) Clinical Psychiatry, London, Cassell.

Mellor, C.S. (1970) 'First rank symptoms of schizophrenia'. *British Journal of Psychiatry*, 117:15–23.

Morel, B.A. (1852) *Etudes Cliniques: Traite Theoretique et Practique des Maladies Mentales*, Paris, Masson.

Morel, B.A. (1860) *Maladies Mentales*, Paris, Masson.

Pelicier, Y. (1991) 'France'. *History of Psychiatry*, ii:119–35.

Peters, C.P. (1991) 'Concept of Schizophrenia after Kraepelin and Bleuler'. In Howells, J.G. (ed.) *The Concept of Schizophrenia: Historical Perspectives*, Washington, American Psychiatric Press, Chapter 6, pp.93–107.

Peters, U.H. (1991) 'The German classical concept of schizophrenia', Chapter 4:59–73. In Howells, J.G. (ed.), *The Concept of Schizophrenia: Historical Perspective*, Washington, American Psychiatric Press.

Pick, A. (1891) *Über primäre Demenz im jugendlichen Alter*, Berlin, Fischer.

Rümke, H.C. (1991) 'The nuclear symptom of schizophrenia and the praecox feeling'. *History of Psychiatry*, 1: 331–41.

Schneider, Carl (1930) *Die Psychologie der Schizophrenen*, Leipzig, Thieme.

Schneider, K. (1962) *Klinische Psychopathologie*, 6th ed. Stuttgart, Thieme. Translated from an earlier edition by M.W. Hamilton (1959) London, Grune & Stratten.

Schüle, H. (1886) *Klinische Psychiatrie*, Leipzig, Vogel.

Smulevitch, A.B. (1989) 'Slowly progressive schizophrenia – myth or clinical reality?' *British Journal of Psychiatry*, 155:166–77.

Wing, J.K., Cooper, J.E. and Sartorius, N. (1974) *The Measurement and Classification of Psychiatric Symptoms*, New York, Cambridge University Press.

World Health Organization (1973) The international pilot study of schizophrenia, Geneva, World Health Organization.

Wyrsh, J. (1966) 'Das Problem der schizophrenen Person'. *Psychiatria Neurologia (Basel)* 151:129–49.

Chapter 13
Schizophrenia

Social Section
TREVOR TURNER

In 1992 it became possible, for the first time in Britain at least, to telephone a National Schizophrenia Hotline. In part this was due to a series of articles in The Times, during the winter of 1985/6. Written by Marjory Wallace (1987), who won a journalism award, they drew to the public's attention the problems of people with schizophrenia in the post-asylum world of community care. A new organization, calling itself Schizophrenia – A National Emergency (SANE) was the linking factor. Born amidst the embarrassments and debates generated by images of lonely psychotics, on the streets, in the prisons, or in bleak boarding house casements, it has become the latest in a long line of pressure groups campaigning on behalf of the mentally ill. Such organisations, from the Alleged Lunatics' Friend Society (Hervey, 1986) or the Mental After Care Association (founded 1879), to MIND and the Mental Health Foundation, have constantly struggled against stigma, an easily distracted public concern, and sceptical belief-systems fearful for the loss of a distinctive morality. Somewhere between their versions and the official descriptions of schizophrenia as an illness lies its social history, but different attributions and changing aetiologies have constantly obscured its meaning and its social role. The victims, victims' relatives, learned researchers, day-to-day clinicians, social commentators, ordinary journalists and a matrix of go-betweens have talked and written at length, using various definitions in various languages. That the term is very much of the 20th century, a child of the Freudian world view, and confined to that century in terms of strict chronology, is perhaps best demonstrated by the opening sentence of the 1951 'Autobiography of a Schizophrenic' (Anon, 1951), 'I must have been an ultra-sensitive boy'. Another later writer, also describing herself as a 'schizophrenic', has even insisted, 'I believe that I have been a schizophrenic since I was a child' (Gibson, 1982).

Any attempts at an historical narrative of schizophrenia, its own story, must acknowledge a most uncertain beginning. There is an unresolved debate as to whether schizophrenia existed before the 18th century (Hare, 1988; Jeste et al, 1985); but for the sake of simplicity this essay will assume that the term and its meaning, linguistic, social, and diagnostic, are inextricably part of the 20th century. The word itself was invented by Eugen Bleuler (1856–1939) as an explanation for a related series of psychic symptoms (Bleuler, 1911) that largely overlapped the Dementia Praecox of Emil Kraepelin (1855–1922). Vying with its predecessor over the early part of the century, by the Second World War it had become a dominant motif of professional descriptions of psychosis. Thus Slater (1975), describing the 'large and lucrative practice to be derived from neurotic and mentally disturbed patients' in 1931, suggested that the consultants involved 'had no understanding of anxiety states and depressive illnesses, let alone *schizophrenia* (*dementia praecox* it was called then) but they did not think this was at all necessary'. Yet by 1937 the index of the Journal of Mental Science no longer included dementia praecox, a process delayed in America until about 1951, when 'see schizophrenia' is to be found under the Dementia Precox heading in Volume 17 of 'The Reader's Guide to Periodical Literature' (H W Wilson & Co, New York).

This dichotomy was not merely semantic. Bleuler's version, based around the four As (Ambivalence, Autism, Affective disturbance and impaired Associations) had introduced a recoverable element, related to a psychological and even psychodynamic aetiology, that was deemed lacking in the pessimistic term 'dementia'. Definitions continued vague, as neurological, biochemical, genetic and psychodynamic causations attracted a shifting support. Thus by 1948 a powerful Hollywood melodrama 'The Snake Pit' ('somehow nobody's favourite movie') could portray the hopelessness and terror of a crowded asylum alongside a Freudian rescue cure of shining optimism. It was also possible for the American psychiatric profession to hold a view of schizophrenia that was much broader and more loosely defined than elsewhere, such that the WHO International pilot study (1973) found a significantly higher prevalence of the disorder in the USA. Tighter operational definitions, leading to the Research Diagnostic Criteria (Spitzer et al, 1978), and then DSM III, have brought the USA, so to speak, back into line. This has allayed fears, for the present, and among the professionals, of a natural and irredeemable unreliability in the diagnostic process, but such fears have nevertheless become an inseparable incubus, part of the meta-understanding, of schizophrenia in the public purview.

Alongside this internal, technical development, the popular view of what is meant by schizophrenia has also changed. The notion of a 'split personality', a Jekyll and Hyde persona, has intruded on the more diffuse Bleulerian construction. How this happened is difficult to trace, although the earliest such use as recorded in the Oxford English Dictionary is from T S Eliot, in 'The use of poetry and the use of criticism', in 1933. He wrote, 'For a poet to be also a philosopher he would have to virtually be two men; I cannot think of any example of this thorough schizophrenia'. This Janus-like version has broadly developed to become a cliche of the toilet graffitologist, the cinema of developmental anguish and upmarket political journalism. Thus we have 'You are never alone with schizophrenia', and related statements, scrawled in public, while 'Psycho' and 'The Three Faces of Eve' were deemed part of a schizophrenia cycle of films. The Observer Newspaper (1992) has proposed that 'at the heart of the Tory campaign there is schizophrenia and Major is not capable of making such duality plausible'. The co-existence of Republican presidents and a Democrat congress in the USA has been termed 'political schizophrenia' (The Independent on Sunday, 1992).

Within this continuing perception there have been other orthodoxies ranging from an insistent psychoanalytic argument centred around a failure of ego development, to the Laingian attributions of failed family care and schizophrenogenic mothers. There has also been, because of the constant failure of psychiatrists either to define with clarity or to produce an irreducible causal agent, a persisting scepticism that the condition even existed. The ripest form of this belief came in the work of Thomas Szasz who called schizophrenia 'the sacred symbol of psychiatry' (1976). In this invited address, to a symposium on 'What is Schizophrenia?', he stated that there was 'no such thing' as this 'alleged disease'. He was prepared to acknowledge differences in behaviour and speech in 'so-called schizophrenic' individuals. However, he demanded recognition, by the 'dominant intellectual, economic, moral and political institutions of society' of 'the differences between disease and disagreement'. The latest academic version of this position (Boyle, 1991) sees schizophrenia as a scientific delusion, based on a false accumulation of data inappropriate to a nosological entity. Such jealous doubts reflect, perhaps, the thwarted desire of the profession of Psychology to have a more dominant role in defining and treating those regarded as suffering from mental illness. This yearning for a return to a new 'moral treatment', a feeling that saying the right thing or selecting the right interpretation remains central to any notion of therapy, has become another unconscious attribute of schizophrenia's polyglot meaning.

Such critiques have also been reflected in the adversarial processes of the law courts, where the announcement of schizophrenic symptoms has been seen as excuse-mongering by muddleheaded doctors, most notoriously in Britain in the trial of Peter Sutcliffe, nicknamed the 'Yorkshire Ripper'. Despite concordance between prosecution and defence psychiatrists as to the accused's mental state, the Judge in the trial persisted in pursuing the charge of murder, as opposed to manslaughter. The jury did, in the end, return a murder verdict. Such was the public and political pressure, that several appeals to the Home Secretary were needed before Sutcliffe, overtly psychotic before and during his imprisonment, was transferred to a Special Hospital. Yet this episode only reflected a norm in the public headlines around schizophrenia. Examples include: 'Mental patient found dead in shallow stream'; 'Schizophrenic Barbara Jackson was found'; 'Man stabbed Police Officer' ('A voice blamed for death'); 'Schizophrenic was drunk and disorderly'; 'Tragedy of a brilliant student' (who 'dropped his high-powered computer job after mixing with Buddhists, became schizophrenic and was found burned to death in the grounds of St Francis Hospital'); 'Axeman who heard voices sent to Broadmoor'; 'Son "evil force" killer' ('a schizophrenic computer engineer strangled his crippled mother . . .'); 'Brick hurled by schizophrenic broke window'; 'Don't give me pity' ('schizophrenic seeks only understanding'); 'Schizophrenic man sets fire to Hospital Church'; 'Man did not pay for meal' ('schizophrenic Clive Staples ate a meal in the Worthing Pizza Hut then told the Manager he had no money to pay') (NSF 1989).

Such public phraseology, associating the term with violence, death and incarceration, remains a constant and fearful public format. Reich (1980) has also elaborated on the tendency of terms like 'crazy, mad, paranoid and even schizophrenic' to 'identify and exclude people who are annoying, discomforting and different', seeing diagnosis as 'discreditation, the attribution of a person's views, politics, actions or conclusions to a mind gone sick' and even a 'weapon'. Yet despite these considerable assaults it is quite clear that with all its internal difficulties, its ill-defined qualities, its neologistic origins and its pejorative sense of being a label, schizophrenia has grown up and become an indispensable part of the sociology of illness. It has been at times the Verdun of the psychiatric enterprise, often reduced to apparent rubble under supernatural, religious or moral bombardment. Yet over 80 years after its birth it is endowed with two specialist Journals, (Schizophrenia Research and Schizophrenia Bulletin), specific voluntary organisations (e.g. National Schizophrenia Fellowship, (NSF), American Schizophrenia Association (ASA)) and acceptance as a disease worthy of a General Hospital rather than sterilised isolation in an out-of-town asylum. Even in 1945 'the label of schizophrenia' was rejected (as having too much clarity and legal refutability) for the recalcitrant, possibly treasonous, Ezra Pound (1885–1972) whose 'history and productivity were so clearly at variance with the diagnosis' (Torrey, 1984, p.197) The notion that 'schizophrenics can recover' (Williams, 1960) has moved on even further from such certainty of formulation, with an increasing public acceptance that treatment and positive outcome may not be mere platitudes.

Tracing out the lives in society of those who have been deemed schizophrenic, from their own point of view, also shows considerable variations in approach. The forceful neurological perspective (Hunter and Macalpine, 1974) suggested 'a common set of abnormal motor and mental experiences which they rationalise or elaborate into similar delusional systems', thus 'autobiographies of the insane are basically made up of the same elements' (p.229). A less dismissive review of 37 books by 'former mental patients' (Sommer and Osborne, 1960 and 1961) found writing 'that ranged from beautiful to clumsy, with a median above the average mark', and at least 17 of these authors had been told they were officially schizophrenic. Most had 'come down in the world before entering hospital', and divorce rates were high. It seems that 'family rejection', rather than being an especial schizophrenic problem, was greater amongst alcoholics. Chronological analysis showed a striking increase in the publication of books by paranoid schizophrenics in the 1950's, which group was however more likely to use little-known publishers and to have no 'Foreword' by another person. Difficulties in gauging reality; a sense of uniqueness as to one's own symptoms (none of the quoted authors attempted a comparison of their experiences with other autobiographies); a mixture of extravagant praise for attendants alongside claims of brutal treatment; the 'hellish' time of Christmas; the disturbing effects of ambiguous designs and patterns in the wards; such were the generalities that await further systematic review in the post-modern era. Peterson (1982) has, meanwhile, collected a range of historical and 20th century accounts, and a useful bibliography, appending little in the way of comment so as to emphasize the authors' own voices. Perhaps the least polemicized, an excerpt from Mark Vonnegut's 'Eden Express', has the most succinct account of the process of being dealt with as a schizophrenic. 'I didn't know it was just a normal day with a normal father and a normal friend of his son taking his son who had gone crazy to the sort of place you normally take someone who's gone crazy' (p.323).

It is also possible, with the eye of an impressionistic faith, to view the word 'schizophrenia' through a periodical literature that has commented on, anguished over, and publicised the word in a range of formats. The term was created in a world of Insanity (e.g. 'Insanity and Marriage', Wilcox, 1902), lunacy reports and feeble-mindedness, with shellshock waiting in the wings. By the 1920's asylum treatment (e.g. Lomax, 1922), crime and punishment (Lodge, 1924), the mental hygiene movement and debates about psychoanalysis were dominant themes. Fears of an alarming increase in insanity were widespread, such that one commentator could suggest that, unless something was done 'there will not be a sane man or woman left in North America in two hundred years' (Kendall, 1929). The same writer chose to highlight, in this regard, dementia praecox 'about which we read so much in connection with the suicides of university students', and suggested the time may come when 'mental examinations will be as much a matter of routine as visits to the dentist'. In the 1930's a notion of the 'schizophrenic personality' (Faris, 1934) and even 'The Age of Schizophrenia' (Barber, 1937) were in the public domain, as were the new treatments of insulin shock ('bedside miracle') and even brain surgery. The multiple diagnoses, therapies and opinions given to the dancer Nijinsky (Ostwald, 1991) summarize nicely this period. Thus Bleuler's early, bleak advice (p.197) to Romola (Nijinsky's wife) to take her child away and get a divorce ('I am helpless. Your husband is incurably insane'), was followed by Professor Wagner-Jauregg's assurance that 'as long as a schizophrenic patient has periods of agitation there is hope for improvement towards normalcy' (p.259). By 'relentlessly visiting clinics, research laboratories and mental institutions' Romola met Dr Sakel, and persuaded him to assess Nijinsky (pp.295–7) for insulin-shock treatment in 1937, and the dancer received in all 228 such 'shocks'. But Ostwald wisely comments that 'more and more patients with unclear or borderline conditions were being called schizophrenic, thus making them eligible' for this approach (p.297), and concludes that 'nothing really helped' (p.342).

Most dominant in this world was the asylum, the brooding background to intense Jungian relationships in Phyllis Bottome's (1934) novel 'Private Worlds'. Evoked with a mixture of awe and nostalgia and despair (e.g. Rollin, 1990; Parfitt, 1985) and visualised in the popular mind by images of large anonymous buildings where silent people were attended by white-coated nurses, there was a general acceptance that those legally defined as 'insane' should reside there. An inability to socialise appropriately or indulge one's pleasures safely (e.g. Evelyn Waugh's (1943) black short story 'Mr Loveday's Little Outing'), a primary schizoid tendency so to speak, was deemed an essential part of the problem. 'In social intercourse you get a normal brain stimulus without severe mental application. The average lunatic does not supply this' (Le Pelley, 1912), thus 'the mental case being out of gear with life, and in a state of senseless rebellion, the question of discipline becomes of paramount importance', and 'they have no interests outside themselves'.

These asylum buildings became associated with a range of legal issues, questions of morality, and the problems of continuing care. Brain disorder, heredity, the family, sterilisation, immigration, alcohol and crime were all closely associated. Even modern art (Current Opinion 71: 81–2, July 1921, 'Modern Art as a Form of Dementia Praecox') and occultism (Literary Digest 67; 99–102, October 16, 1920, 'After War Occultism and Insanity') added their lurid overtones. Self-confession could enhance this feeling, such that the anonymous 'Jungle of the Mind' (1922) was sub-titled 'Notes on a Disfranchisement'. The author of this disjointed piece hinted that 'the keen sense of others' was perhaps 'one test of the normal' (p.332). Likewise in his more formal sociological paper, Faris (1934) could write of 'cultural isolation and the schizophrenic personality' and even suggested the cause of schizophrenia lay 'in the nature of the social relations of the person'. In the same Journal in the same year, Dollard (1934) saw schizophrenics 'as sociologically sick . . . there is a problem in how the culture took on with them', commenting on Harry Stack Sullivan's revision of the Hospital milieu as in itself a mode of treatment (an exception to the general rule). Underlying this was an important economic difference between the care of people with schizophrenia and those with physical disorders. 'In lung cancer or coronary thrombosis death removes treatment failures from the scene, whereas chronic schizophrenics do not get well and do not die; they accumulate in public institutions' (Williams, 1961).

By the late 1930's it was becoming increasingly possible for schizophrenics to hit the headlines (e.g. 'Schizophrenia: Diabetes insulin shock relieves insane', Newsweek, January 23 1937), thanks to insulin, other shock treatments, operations and hormonal theories. Less apparent during the war – although 'three-day schizophrenia' as 'combat disease' (Science Newsletter 43, 364, 1943) demonstrated its acute recoverable version – during the late 1940's the scandal in the USA of 'snake pit' hospitals led to an insistent curative zeal. Whether locked up, 'Spellbound' (Alfred Hitchcock's 1945 film using dream sequences designed by Salvador Dali), given a ten minute brain operation or attached to a little black box, things were being done in its name. By the 1950's parental behaviour, chemical acidosis and split personality were back in vogue, even though Newsweek could insist (June 30, 1951) 'schizoids are different'. It was also possible to read a 'Mother's Story' (McCall's 80, July 1953) and admit 'they called me crazy and I was!' (Saturday Evening Post 227: 17–19, January 29, 1955). The term was an accepted ikon, undergoing sensible research (e.g. Stevenson, 1957) susceptible to syringes, a pharmacologically treatable condition. Unfortunately it could also be linked to 'toads and mushrooms' (Fabing, 1957), 'Schizoid Spiders' (Time 69: 83, May 6, 1987) and phrases like 'trouble leads men to drink and women to schizophrenia' (Science Digest 44: 30–31, August 1958). In a critique of fads and abuses related to psychoanalysis (Gengerelli, 1957) it could even be casually stated that 'these days the average reader runs across the word *schizophrenia* in nearly every novel or play'.

By the 1960's and early 1970's there developed a more critical viewpoint towards psychiatry ('the troubled science'), and its loose terminologies. The family's role (e.g. the 1971 film 'Family Life' by Ken Loach), the open-door policies and the 'myth of mental illness' (Szasz, 1961) were in vogue. Schizophrenia was deemed a mere label and to this day struggles to unstick itself therefrom. The 'Mary Barnes' myth, of a schizophrenic helped to regress back into a faeces-smearing childhood and to grow again within the caring replacement family of the Kingsley Hall commune, achieved paperback and theatrical acceptability, although Sedgwick (1982) has robustly criticized the 'Laingian psychosis' as an 'elaborately staged artefact' (p.124).

Therapy, nurture not nature, and existential analysis were all the rage. There were still scientific cul-de-sacs, like the 'pink spot' test, and 'Taraxein'; there were lurid news stories such as 'I am a Second Hitler; schizophrenic attacks children and teachers in Cologne school' (Newsweek 63: 42, January 22, 1964); there were trans-cultural adventures, showing for example the positive use of native healers in Nigeria (Randal, 1968) even though 'male schizophrenics will say quite openly that their mothers are witches'. But for the great mass of those troubled in mind, in their families, in the crumbling asylums or in their bare bedsits, little changed internally. Louise Wilson (1968) could still write of 'This stranger, my Son' and reach a popular audience, with the 'tormented journey of a lost boy'. The review in The Times Literary Supplement (3 April, 1969 p.373) used phrases such as 'a frighteningly widespread and mysterious disease', 'Oedipal attachment', 'constantly deferred hope', 'terrifying fits of violence and rage' and 'tragic situations'. Mark Vonnegut (1974) even wrote of why he wanted to bite RD Laing, even though 'he said so many nice things about us'. Not because schizophrenics were apparently 'the only sane members of an insane society, our insights are profound and right-on, we are prophetic, courageous explorers of inner-space, and so forth', nor because 'having your mental health depend on the socio-political, religious etcetera health of America' was a questionable privilege. But as Vonnegut pointed out, 'schizophrenics are mystics who do not have the luxury of vacations', and so he admitted that when ill (crazy) 'my perceptions are so screwed up I can barely see or hear someone standing right in front of me, let alone make any sense of what they are saying or manage enough control over my body, mind and voice to make some appropriate response, which in the case of RD, would be biting him'. He felt progress would come 'from biochemists, not poets'.

Over the last 20 years however, schizophrenia has gradually followed Vonnegut's advice, and a biological model, something viral or biochemical or chemical, or bits of all three, has consensually emerged. As a form of comfort, a rejection of the scapegoating of the parents, this has achieved acceptance, but cultural variations persist. 'From adolescent insanity to dopamine disease' is one version, but 'living with schizophrenia' remained hard work. Thus 'having a schizophrenic child or parent is wearing both physically and emotionally. Many families felt guilty because they were sure they had done something wrong' (Cohen, 1977). There has been Torrey's 'Schizophrenia and Civilization' (1980) suggesting a distinct relationship between the disorder and modern times, and according to a leading London newspaper 'Schizophrenia rules in the land of the rising yen' (Observer, 1992). In 1965 the heroic television psychoanalyst Dr Roger Corder ('The Human Jungle – Struggle for a Mind') could cure a woman's nervous breakdown by getting the father to confess 'She's not my daughter – she's my shame, your shame'. The case had been dismissed in the early part of the show ('Oh come now, she's a paranoid schizophrenic'), as related to a 'mysterious family', therefore 'get the Social Workers onto it'. By the 1980's a British TV series, Maybury, was much more didactic, biological, practical, less the Dr Kildare (i.e doctor as hero) than St Elsewhere's or Casualty (organised teamwork). By 1992 a popular Home Health Fact File on Schizophrenia could give straightforward question-and-answer advice. Thus to the question 'When should I see my doctor?', came the answer 'If someone in your family exhibits bizarre behaviour, seems unable to think straight, and seems out of touch with reality, consult your doctor, who may arrange for them to see a specialist or be hospitalised for observation'.

Is it possible to summarise these themes and variations, or is the notion of schizophrenia too diffuse to clarify? It is a unique distinction of 20th century thought to have defined nearly 1% of its population in terms of a disease entity, yet to remain perplexed by the indistinct nature of its nosological enterprise. Such classifications have led to fears of the therapeutic state, and the rejection of medicine, as exampled by 'Medical Nemesis' (Illich, 1975). Early in the century such people were carefully separated from the notion of being mystics – whose hallucinations do not let them apparently 'fall into the association of these schizophrene types' (de Sanctis, 1927, p.231) – and have largely been seen as a burden, a problem, a form of dependency. Socially sterilised, sent to gas chambers particularly early in Nazi Germany (Meyer, 1988) they have nevertheless been felt to have 'the malady of dictators' in Barker's trenchant, discursive overview of 'The Age of Schizophrenia' (1937). This diatribe on the failings of the pre-war world has many modern echoes, insisting that the opposite pull of emotions and intellect was the signifying event of 20th century culture. For this generation of mankind 'schizophrenia is almost its only salvation' given that it was 'schooled in Genesis' but 'suddenly confronted by Darwin'. Barber also suggested 'it is easier to avoid schizophrenia than to cure it', and would have us begin social development with the children, trying to avoid inflicting them with 'habit-patterns which they will some day have to change'. Yet by 1989, over 50 years on, a 'new, comprehensive guide for sufferers and their families' could merely admit to the 'considerable uncertainty about the nature of schizophrenia' (p.41) while still 'fervently' wishing doctors would forget 'those meaningless interim diagnoses' (e.g. personality disorder) and get on with early treatment (Hemmings, 1989).

But in presenting some kind of public version of schizophrenia there have been troubling research studies, on 'rehabilitation', on social withdrawal, and on the close relationship between social environment and the general poverty of personal affect. Debates have even been engendered around the notion of doing nothing, since one study showed that the average schizophrenic spends 8.2 hours a day 'doing nothing' (Wing & Brown, 1961). Was 'doing nothing' a symptom of illness, or could this be seen as an acceptable way of getting through the 20th century? More evolutionary notions have been expressed (Stevenson, 1957), in that 'schizophrenia is to a great extent a penalty of our social sins'. According to this author, 'prevention may have to await a transformation of our society which will reduce our competitiveness and increase the flow of love to a previously unobtained rate'. And whether evaluated in the busy inner cities of Europe and North America, or in the simpler agrarian villages of the Third world, the sheer similarity in form and prevalence of schizophrenia has regularly contrasted with its apparent outcome, which always seems better in simpler societies (Jablensky & Sartorius, 1975). Whatever the social history of schizophrenia really is, and it rarely comes into consideration in official Social Histories, perhaps it is pointing to a new, non-religious, yet binding ethic. A society able to honour *AND* care for those deemed to have schizophrenia may have no further need to go on searching for the city of God.

NB This piece is dedicated to my uncle R., who suffered a 'nervous breakdown', apparently after driving a car involved in an accident with a child. Diagnosed as schizophrenic, he spent over 20 years in mental hospitals despite a lobotomy and other treatments. Emerging in the early 1960's, he lived with another ex-patient in a small Council house crammed with unnecessary furniture and other chattels, and at least 20 cats. His occasional visits were relaxed, discursive and a little awkward. On one occasion, setting off to leave in his worn grey flannels and off-white gym shoes, he advised me 'not to take life so seriously'.

REFERENCES

Anonymous (1922) 'The Jungle of the Mind – Notes on a disfranchisement'. *Atlantic Monthly*, 130: 328–38.

Anonymous (1951) *Autobiography of a Schizophrenic*, Bristol, J Baker and Son.

Barber, L.C. (1937) 'The Age of Schizophrenia'. *Harper's Magazine*, 176: 70–8.

Bleuler, E. (1911) *Dementia Praecox or the Group of Schizophrenias* (translated by Zinkin, J., 1950), New York, International Universities Press.

Bottome, P. (1937) *Private Worlds*, London, Penguin Books.

Boyle, M. (1990) *Schizophrenia. A scientific delusion?* London, Routledge.

Cohen, D. (1977) 'The Trials of Living with a Schizophrenic'. *Psychology Today*, 10: 102.

de Sanctis, S. (1927) *Religious Conversion. A bio-psychological study*, London, Kegan Paul, Trench, Trubner & Co.

Dollard, J. (1934) 'The psychotic person seen culturally'. *American Journal of Sociology*, 39: 637–48.

Fabing, H.D. (1957) 'Toads, Mushrooms and Schizophrenia'. *Harper's Magazine*, 214: 50–5.

Faris, R.E.L. (1934) 'Cultural isolation and the schizophrenic personality'. *American Journal of Sociology*, 40: 155–64.

Gengerelli, J.A. (1957) 'Dogma or Discipline?' The Saturday Review, 40: 9–11, 40.

Gibson, M. (1982) Foreword. In *Living and Working with Schizophrenia*, (edited by Seeman, M.V.), Milton Keynes, Open University Press.

Hare, E.H. (1988) 'Schizophrenia as a recent disease'. *British Journal of Psychiatry*, 153: 521–31.

Hemmings, G. (1989) *Inside Schizophrenia*, London, Sidgwick and Jackson.

Hervey, N. (1986) 'Advocating, or folly: the Alleged Lunatics' Friend Society; 1845–63'. *Medical History*, 30: 245–75.

Hunter, R., and Macalpine, I. (1974) *Psychiatry for the Poor*, London: Dawsons.

Illich, I. (1975) *Medical Nemesis. The expropriation of health*, London, Calder and Boyars.

Independent on Sunday, The (1992) 'Singing the blues in the 'burbs' (March 15, p.10).

Jablensky, A. and Sartorius, N. (1975) Editorial. 'Culture and Schizophrenia'. *Psychological Medicine*, 5: 113–24.

Jeste, D.R., Carman, R., Lohr, J.B. and Wyatt, R.J. (1985) 'Did schizophrenia exist before the eighteenth century?' *Comprehensive Psychiatry*, 26: 493–503.

Johnstone, E.C. (1991) Editorial Preface. In 'Disabilities and Circumstances of Schizophrenic Patients – A Follow-up Study'. *British Journal of Psychiatry*, 159 (Supplement 13): 5–6.

Kendall, C. (1929) 'The Threat of Insanity'. *The North American Review*, 227: 353–60.

Le Pelley (1912) 'Treatment of Insanity'. *Westminster Review*, 178: 174–84.

Lodge, O. (1924) 'Crime, Punishment and Insanity'. *Contemporary Review*, 126: 162–8.

Lomax, M. (1922) 'The problem of insanity and its asylum treatment'. *Fortnightly Review*, 111: 270–81.

Meyer, J-E. (1988) 'The fate of the mentally ill in Germany during the Third Reich'. *Psychological Medicine*, 18: 575–81.

National Schizophrenia Fellowship (1989) *Slipping Through the Net*, London, NSF.

Observer, The (1992) 'Schizophrenia rules in land of the rising yen', (May 24, p.16).

Ostwald, P. (1991) *Vaslav Nijinsky – A Leap into Madness*, New York, Lyle Stuart.

Parfitt, D. (1985) 'Asylum 1929'. *British Journal of Clinical and Social Psychiatry*, 3: 3–5.

Randal, J. (1965) 'Witch Doctors and Psychiatry'. *Harper's Magazine*, 231: 56–61.

Reich, W. (1980) 'The Force of Diagnosis'. *Harper's Magazine*, 260: 20–32.

Rollin, H. (1990) *Festina Lente – A Psychiatric Odyssey*, London, The Memoir Club, British Medical Journal.

Sedgwick, P. (1982) *Psycho Politics*, London, Pluto Press.

Slater, E. (1975) 'Psychiatry in the thirties'. *Contemporary Review*, 226: 70–5.

Sommer, R. and Osmond, H. (1960) 'Autobiographies of former mental patients'. *Journal of Mental Science*, 106: 648–62 and (1961) Addendum: *Journal of Mental Science*, 107: 1030–2.

Spitzer, R.L., Endicott, J. and Robins, E. (1978) 'Research Diagnostic Criteria'. *Archives of General Psychiatry*, 35: 773–82.

Stevenson, I. (1957) 'Schizophrenia: What we are finding out about our worst mental illness'. *Harper's Magazine*, 215: 59–64.

Szasz, T.S. (1961) *The Myth of Mental Illness*, New York, Hoeber-Harper.

Szasz, T.S. (1976) 'Schizophrenia: The Sacred Symbol of Psychiatry'. *British Journal of Psychiatry*, 129: 308–16.

Torrey, E.F. (1980) *Schizophrenia and Civilisation*, London, Aronson.

Torrey, E.F. (1984) *The Roots of Treason*, New York, Harcourt, Brace, Jovanovich.

Vonnegut, M. (1974) 'Why I want to bite R.D. Laing'. *Harper's Magazine*, 248: 90–2.

Vonnegut, M. (1982) 'Extract from "The Eden Express". ' (1975). In *A Mad People's History of Madness*, (ed. Peterson, D.), Pittsburgh, University of Pittsburgh Press, p.312–26.

Wallace, M. (1987) *The Forgotten Illness. The Times Campaign on Schizophrenia*, London, Times Newspapers Ltd.

Waugh, E. (1943) 'Mr Loveday's Little Outing'. In *Work Suspended and Other Stories*, London, Chapman & Hall.

Wilcox, J. (1902) 'Insanity and Marriage'. *Westminster Review*, 158: 199–209.

Williams, G. (1961) 'The Rejection of the Insane'. *The Atlantic Monthly*, 208: 79–83.

Williams, G. (1962) 'Schizophrenics can recover'. *The Atlantic Monthly*, 209: 27–31.

Wing, J.K. and Brown, G.W. (1961) 'Social treatment of chronic schizophrenia: A comparative survey of three mental hospitals'. *Journal of Mental Science*, 107: 847–61.

Wilson, L. (1968) *This stranger, my son. A mother's story*, London, John Murray.

World Health Organization (1973) *The International Pilot Study of Schizophrenia*, vol.1, Geneva.

Chapter 14

Delusional Disorder

Clinical Section

KENNETH S KENDLER

INTRODUCTION

The description of delusional disorder in DSM-IV begins:

> The essential feature of Delusional Disorder is the presence of one or more non-bizarre delusions that persist for at least 1 month. A diagnosis of Delusional Disorder is not given if the individual has ever . . . [met symptomatic criteria] for schizophrenia. Auditory or visual hallucinations, if present, are not prominent. . . . Apart from the direct impact of the delusions, psychosocial functioning is not markedly impaired and behavior is neither obviously odd or bizarre. If mood episodes occur concurrently with the delusions, the total duration of these mood episodes is relatively brief compared to the total duration of the delusional periods. The delusions are not due to the direct physiological effects of a substance (e.g. cocaine) or a general medical condition. (American Psychiatric Association, 1994)

The goal of this essay is to begin to develop a history of the descriptive psychopathologic tradition (Berrios, 1984) that has influenced our current thinking about the syndrome. We use DSM-IV as a focus because it presents one of the most widely used operationalized criteria for delusional disorder. The nosologic history of delusional disorder or paranoia is inextricably intertwined with the history of the nosology of the psychotic disorders as a whole (Berrios, 1987). Since this is a subject far too complex to treat in a short essay, our goal is more modest. In addition, as an active clinical researcher, and only an amateur historian, with unfortunately common linguistic limitations, the depth of scholarship that I can bring to bear on this immense subject is limited. Therefore, I have conceptualized this essay as a series of 'sketches' of the history of delusional disorder, through a clinician's eyes. In contrast to Lewis's review (1970), which examined the history of the term 'paranoia', we will here focus on the development of the clinical construct. The social and political issues that impacted on the history of delusional disorder (de Saussure, 1946), some of which are discussed in the paper by Dowbiggin in this volume, are not here considered.

ESQUIROL

Although widely different from modern conceptualizations in a number of important ways, Esquirol's concept of monomania represents a logical starting point for a recent history of the concept of the delusional disorders. Esquirol (1772–1840) first proposed the term monomania in 1810 (Goldstein, 1987; Mora, 1972). The syndrome has been characterized as 'an idée fixe, a single pathological preoccupation in an otherwise sound mind' (Goldstein, 1987), or, more succinctly, as 'partial insanity' (Berrios, 1987). Esquirol began his section on monomania in his textbook (Esquirol, 1845) (published first in 1838 and translated into English in 1845) with the following more detailed description:

> Monomania and lypemania [distally related to the modern concept of melancholia] are chronic cerebral affections, unattended by fever, and characterized by a partial lesion of the intelligence, affections or will. At one time, the intellectual disorder is confined to a single object, or a limited number of objects. The patients seize upon a false principle, which they pursue without deviating from logical reasonings, and from which they deduce legitimate consequences, which modify their affections, and the acts of their will. Aside from this partial delirium, they think, reason and act like other men. (Esquirol, 1845)

This quote introduces a central conceptual issue in the history of delusional disorders – that this condition is *limited* in its impact. Esquirol describes this limitation in three inter-related ways. First, the disturbance is limited to one major psychological faculty. This is in contrast to the more pervasive dysfunction seen in 'mania' or 'dementia', as he conceptualized them. Second, the abnormality can be understood as the 'logical' consequences of a single 'false principle'. That is, much of the disorder can be conceptualized as arising, in an understandable manner, from a single or small set of errors of reasoning, logic or perception. Third, from an objective behavioral perspective, aside from the areas associated with their disorder, individuals with monomania 'think, reason and act like other men'. Esquirol gives a poignant description of this clinical phenomenon, using the term 'partial delirium', which was broadly synonymous with monomania:

> Partial delirium is a phenomenon so remarkable, that the more we observe it, the more are we astonished, that a man who feels, reasons and acts like the rest of the world, should feel, reason and act no more like other men upon a single point?

Esquirol goes on to describe subtypes of monomania. The subtype he termed 'intellectual' monomania (as opposed to 'affective' and 'instinctive') appears to be most relevant to the history of the concept of delusional disorder. However, he rarely distinguished between subtypes in his subsequent discussion.

Esquirol described the course of monomania as variable but tending toward a favorable outcome, often with remissions and relapses. Monomania can take a more unfavorable course, which, he notes, is often complicated by paralysis. This suggests that a proportion of the cases considered as monomania by Esquirol were probably in the early phases of central nervous system syphilis. When monomania becomes chronic, he notes that deterioration often occurs and reasoning, affect and action, which were previously intact, lose their 'logical and natural connection'. 'Incoherence' of ideas and actions then ensues.

Esquirol described monomania as usually associated with an elevated mood, and increased physical and mental activity. He wrote in his text, 'Among monomaniacs, the passions are gay and expansive. . . . They are active, petulant, [and] inexhaustible in their loquacity' (Esquirol, 1845).

In addition to Esquirol's textual description of monomania, his textbook contains a substantial number of his case histories. A review of these provides a more 'clinical' sense of the syndrome than can be obtained from his syndromic descriptions. One is immediately impressed at the symptomatic diversity of cases of monomania as diagnosed by Esquirol. Quite early in his chapter, he briefly notes a case of a young woman who 'had received instruction, and who believed that she controlled the sun, moon and clouds'. One of his first detailed cases, 'M. de R'. demonstrates a late-onset hallucinatory psychosis occurring after the onset of deafness. His first case of erotic monomania was a 32-year-old woman whose illness began with a simple delusion that a man of high rank was in love with her. However, she soon came into hallucinatory communication with her lover and began experiencing pains induced in her by her relatives 'although they were several leagues distant from her'. These more 'fantastic' or 'bizarre' delusions are clearly outside the realm of those which would today be considered typical of delusional disorder.

Two cases merit closer attention, the first of which is Mr. 'M', the second case in the main section of Esquirol's chapter on monomania. At 34, he had a major financial reversal shortly after which his personality changed and he began to be preoccupied with his physical health, especially his digestion. Two years later, he came to the conclusion that he was being poisoned. He visited friends to get away, but soon became convinced that they too were poisoning him. Esquirol first treated him at this point and quickly produced a cure. However, shortly thereafter, on reading a newspaper article about the pretended dauphin, Mr. M formed the conviction that he was the true dauphin, the son of Louis XVI. He again came into treatment with Esquirol, who observed him to be polite although consistently and gently protesting that he was not ill. He wrote frequently with 'the greatest facility, want[ing] neither force nor beauty' to the French people and the minister of police. He also wrote poetry and painted. Esquirol ends the case history with a section of one of his letters, commenting on its 'coherency of reasoning'.

The second case, also called Mr. 'M', in Esquirol's section on erotic mono-mania, developed the belief that a famous actress was in love with him. He followed her, always attended her performances, and repeatedly visited her home at night with the hope of seeing her through the window. He took her violent rebuffs as further evidence of her love for him. Taking leave from his work, he became entirely preoccupied with this relationship. On examination by Esquirol, he noted that aside from his delusion, he reasoned very well and was quite coherent, able to parry at every turn Esquirol's attempts to point out the irrationality of his beliefs.

These two cases are remarkable for the degree to which they resemble those classic cases of paranoia described at the end of the 19th century. It is clear, however, that conceptually, Esquirol's diagnosis of monomania was quite different from later views on paranoia in including a wide array of psychotic syndromes. However, Esquirol's view did appear to anticipate later conceptions in one key point: that this was a syndrome of *limited* insanity – that one could be delusional in only a circumscribed area of functioning, leaving intact other domains of reason, judgement and will.

DELUSIONAL DISORDER IN THE MID-19th CENTURY

The conceptualization of psychotic disorders in Europe underwent a fundamental shift during the course of the 19th century with the eventual emergence of a single predominant 'anatomo-clinical' or 'neurological' orientation (Berrios, 1984; 1987). We can only say a few words about the complex history of delusional disorder during this time. (For a very interesting 19th century perspective on this history see the review by Seglas [Seglas, Noyes, 1888a, b, c, d]). Several authors, including Kraepelin himself, noted that marked expansion and contraction of the diagnostic concept of paranoia (Lewis, 1970; Kraepelin, 1921). At times, paranoia, or its immediate predecessor, *verrücktheit*, was used to describe nearly all cases of delusional and even hallucinatory insanity. For much of the century, particularly in France, the delusional disorders were viewed largely in the context of degeneration theory (Dowbiggin, 1985) and embroiled in debates about the forensic implications of the concept of limited insanity (de Saussure, 1946). Much discussion focused on the etiologic nature of the delusions in the delusional psychoses. Were they predominantly expressions of disordered affect or disordered judgement? This debate continued into the twentieth century (Bleuler, Ricksher, 1912). For a brief review of what came to be known as the 'paranoia question' in the late 19th century, see Lewis (1970).

VON KRAFFT-EBING

I chose to examine the views of Krafft-Ebing (1840–1902) (hereafter KE) on delusional disorder for two reasons. First, both in the review of Seglas (Seglas, Noyes, 1888a), and especially in the English translation of his textbook (*A Textbook of Insanity Based on Clinical Observations*) (Krafft-Ebing, 1905), we have detailed descriptions in English of his views on this diagnostic category. Second, KE was working and writing in the last several decades of the 19th century, thus providing us with an important sample of the nosologic approach to delusional disorder in the psychiatric German speaking world just prior to its dominance by Kraepelin, but after the 'epistemological shift' in the mid-19th century.

From the first edition of his textbook, KE placed paranoia among the 'psychic degenerations', emphasizing that this disorder occurs 'exclusively in tainted individuals', the most common source of the taint being hereditary. The conceptual connection with the French perspective is obvious. He goes on to describe the chief clinical characteristics of the syndrome. First, the main symptoms are delusions. In contrast to delusions in certain other disorders (chiefly his 'primary hallucinatory insanity'), the delusions in paranoia are, according to KE, systematized and methodical. He records that persecutory delusions are most common, but also notes grandiose delusions, delusions of jealousy and erotomanic delusions can occur. Second, KE emphasizes the restricted range of abnormalities in psychological functioning. Judgement and reason are, in general, intact. The intellect is not damaged. Neither the psycho-motor nor the emotional spheres are perturbed. He notes

> on superficial observation, one is struck by the clearness and logic of such patients. (p.369).

Third, he notes that affected individuals appear to be reasoning correctly from 'false premises'. All their feelings and actions can be understood as reactive manifestations to these delusions. The patient's '. . . logical powers, acting correctly, create an entire system of delusions' (p.371).

Fourth, hallucinations are also quite common. Some cases can occur without prominent hallucinations, but these seem, according to KE, to be in the minority. In his case 24, the delusions appeared to first arise as a result of the derogatory content of auditory hallucinations.

Fifth, KE notes that the development of the disorder often reflects the affected individual's underlying personality. He writes

> an originally suspicious, retiring, solitary individual one day becomes perse-cuted; a rough, irritable, egotistic person, defective in his notions of justice, becomes a querulous paranoiac; a religious eccentric becomes the victim of religious paranoia.

While emphasizing that paranoia is fundamentally an organic or constitutional disorder, he does note that 'the development of the disease is ordinarily gradual, growing, so to speak, out of the abnormal personality'. He describes in detail the premorbid personality common in cases of persecutory paranoia as

> from childhood on, peculiar, quiet, retiring, uncommunicative, easily injured, irritable, suspicious and not infrequently inclined to hypochondria. (p.382)

Sixth, KE describes the expected course of paranoia in some detail. The disease itself is 'always chronic'. However, remissions with insight frequently occur, but are always followed by a relapse. 'Intermissions . . .', he comments, 'are not to be confounded with recovery'. The disorder, however, does not progress and 'never . . . ends in dementia'. In the terminal states 'powers of judgement are left unaffected'.

KRAEPELIN

Even in English translation, we have a number of sources to review Kraepelin's nosologic approach to paranoia (Kraepelin, 1904a; 1904b; 1907; 1916; 1921). We can only briefly review them here. For a more detailed examination, see (Kendler, 1988). Kraepelin (1856–1926) started the section on paranoia in the 7th edition of his famous textbook (Kraepelin, 1907) as follows:

> Paranoia is a chronic progressive psychosis . . . characterized by the gradual development of a stable progressive system of delusions, without marked mental deterioration, clouding of consciousness or disorder of thought, will or conduct.

For Kraepelin the delusions in paranoia were always 'built out into a coherent system' (Kraepelin, 1907). The delusions were always 'systematized, mentally worked up, and uniformly connected, without gross internal contradictions' (Kraepelin, 1921). Furthermore, the delusion was not bizarre, for

with all the improbability and uncertainty of its foundations, (it) does not contain any apparent absolute impossibilities. (Kraepelin, 1921)

In clear contrast to *dementia praecox*, delusions in paranoia are never 'incoherent' or 'nonsensical'.

Like KE, Kraepelin held that the psychic abnormalities in paranoia were restricted in range. Despite their chronic delusions, cases with paranoia were characterized 'by perfect preservation of clear and orderly thinking, willing, and acting'. Unity of personality was preserved despite years of illness. Activity and conduct, although often influenced by delusional beliefs, were not themselves disturbed. This central concept is best illustrated by Kraepelin in the following passages from his famous case of paranoia in his 'Clinical Lectures':

Striking disturbances in the emotional deportment of the patient, and especially in the deportment of the will, are wanting throughout. There is at most a certain touchiness . . . but otherwise the patient is in neither a morbidly cheerful nor gloomy mood, nor is he emotionally dull or indifferent, but in a natural way takes interest in the events and persons of his surroundings. . . . His outward bearing and behavior are entirely unexceptional and without remark, and are free from mannerisms, automatic obedience and negativism. (Kraepelin, 1904b)

While *dementia praecox* influences nearly all areas of psychic functioning, Kraepelin viewed paranoia as deriving from a specific defect in the psychological capacity of 'judgement'.

In his earlier writings, Kraepelin, like KE, emphasized that hallucinations, especially of hearing, were always present in paranoia, but rarely clinically predominant. However, he changed his view about this over time, concluding by his 8th edition that 'genuine' hallucinations did not occur in paranoia. This change may have been influenced by Kraepelin's increasing interest in his new category of paraphrenia, which was, from a descriptive perspective, somewhere mid-way between paranoid *dementia praecox* and paranoia. Kraepelin may have felt more comfortable placing the forms of paranoia with prominent hallucinations into this new category, thereby reducing the clinical variability of paranoia.

Kraepelin discussed at length the course of paranoia. In his early writings, he emphasized chronicity and absence of genuine recovery. 'The prognosis of the disease is very poor, as no case of genuine paranoia ever recovers', he wrote in this 6th edition (Kraepelin, 1904a). While social impairment is relatively common, however, 'genuine weakmindedness' does not develop even after decades of illness. In his eighth edition, Kraepelin, influenced by several reports of remitting forms of paranoia (Gierlich, 1908; Friedman, 1908), broadened his view on the possible course and outcome of paranoia. He recognized that the delusions could fully remit, although he continued to assume that the 'latent' paranoia remained.

Finally, Kraepelin's early view of paranoia was entirely in keeping with the prevailing 'anatomo-clinical' view of psychiatric disease. Like KE, he considered paranoia to be an endogenous disease, always developing 'on a defective constitutional basis'. He felt that there was a firm dividing line separating paranoia, an endogenous disease, from a variety of 'psychogenic' delusional states due largely to environmental precipitants.

By the time of the writing of his 8th edition, however, his views had changed somewhat. From a disease model focused entirely on an underlying 'morbid process', Kraepelin, not fully consistently, tentatively suggested two additional aetiologic models for paranoia. First, he suggested that paranoia, like hysteria, could be better understood as an abnormal personality development. Paranoia could be viewed as

> essentially a matter of abnormal development which takes place in persons of psychopathic disposition under the influences of the ordinary forces of life. Apparently, we do not have to do with a special disease process, but with a sort of 'psychic malformation'. (Kraepelin, 1916)

This conceptual model contrasted strongly with Kraepelin's view of dementia praecox, which was clearly seen as a degenerative neurologic-like disease. Second, Kraepelin also felt that the dividing line between paranoia and psychogenic delusions was in fact quite unclear. In classic paranoia, internal causes are predominant, while in psychogenic delusional states, external causes play the critical role. However, so many in-between conditions arise that

> paranoia and psychogenic delusion formation may, perhaps, be regarded as the end-links in a chain in which all possible intervening links are represented. (Kraepelin, 1971)

GAUPP AND KRETSCHMER – THE TÜBINGEN SCHOOL

R. Gaupp (1870–1953), who had studied with Kraepelin, was appointed professor of Psychiatry in Tübingen in 1906. One of his great interests was in studying the individual character of the symptoms and development of psychosis as a method of clarifying diagnostic heterogeneity (Gaupp, 1974a). The application of what was called 'understanding' psychiatry to the problem of delusional disorder was aided by the famous case of the mass-murderer Ernst Wagner. Gaupp's son summarizes the impact of this case as follows:

> It was decided in Tübingen to demonstrate that delusional psychoses do exist which are not necessarily 'process' disorders and therefore cannot be classified as schizophrenia: such disorders can be viewed much more as a misdevelopment of the psyche which is both psychologically understandable and a direct result of experiences in persons of abnormal psychopathic personality. (Gaupp, 1974a)

In a number of papers published over nearly three decades, two of which have been translated into English (Gaupp, 1974b; Gaupp, 1974c), Gaupp wrote in detail about Wagner, who is described as a classic case of paranoia in the Kraepelinian tradition. He displayed chronic persecutory and referential delusions with a complete preservation of personality, intellect and will. The delusions began after he performed an act of sodomy while drunk. For twelve years after this incident, despite being convinced that he was the nearly continuous object of public ridicule, he functioned normally as a husband, father and school teacher. Then, in a carefully planned act of revenge, he set fires to the sleeping village where he had resided and killed 8 and wounded 12 of the fleeing inhabitants before being overwhelmed. One of the issues of this case, which we will not focus on here, was whether all cases of paranoia in fact had 'mild' schizophrenia. Gaupp argued vigorously against this position and even presented Wagner late in his life at a public meeting to demonstrate that he had not 'a trace of schizophrenia'.

For our purposes, we are more interested in Gaupp's clinical nature and etiologic formulation of paranoia, and especially its elaboration by his student and successor in Tübingen, Ernst Kretschmer (1888–1964) (Hafner, 1990). Kretschmer published his now famous work 'The Sensitive Delusion of Reference' in 1918 and a partial translation of the fourth edition (originally published in 1966) into English is now available (Kretschmer, 1974).

The syndrome of the 'Sensitive Delusion of Reference' (hereafter SDR), as described by Kretschmer, has many similarities to paranoia as articulated by Kraepelin. SDR is characterized by persecutory, referential and/or erotic delusions in individuals with a previously sensitive personality. Most of the delusions appear to be of a relatively ordinary or nonbizarre quality (although one of the many delusions expressed in his case of Helene Renner was rather bizarre – that the police were conducting 'pregnancy experiments' on her while she slept). Hallucinations can occur but are rarely prominent. Affect and volition are unimpaired. The outcome of SDR is, in most cases, favorable. He emphasizes 'the preservation of the fully intact personality even in severe cases'.

Of greater interest to us was his etiologic model for SDR. He clearly rejected the disease model for this syndrome. Rather, he saw SDR as emerging from an abnormal personality subjected to a specific kind of stress. To be pathogenic, this stress must 'attack' the personality at a particularly vulnerable point for delusions to develop. An example might be an individual with a high level of religious scruples who masturbates with great guilt and is then caught masturbating in a public bathroom. This development would occur in a manner which is completely psychologically understandable. Kretschmer's formulation is similar to that expressed by the psychiatrist-philosopher Jaspers who distinguished, as early as 1910, between psychologically understandable delusional states and those which were 'ununderstandable' and therefore must be due to a somatic 'process' (Lewis, 1970). Kretschmer went even further than that in claiming that SDR was amenable to psychotherapeutic influences.

CONCLUSIONS

How has the current clinical concept of delusional disorder, as articulated in the DSM-IV (American Psychiatric Association, 1994), arisen? Our review suggests that from relatively early in the 19th century, although operating within a fundamentally different epistemological framework, French psychiatry had articulated a concept of limited or partial insanity. Although differing in particulars, all the clinicians we have examined agreed in the existence of a syndrome characterized by delusions which, in contrast to other delusional syndromes, is *not* associated with major abnormalities in volition, affect or behavior. This central construct is reflected in DSM-IV criteria B and D, which exclude from the diagnosis of delusional disorder individuals with schizophrenia or those whose delusions are possibly a result of a major mood disorder.

Nearly all the clinicians reviewed, including Esquirol, commented on the clinical impression forcefully conveyed to any individual who has cared for such patients – while clearly deluded, they appear, in all other ways, to be basically normal. This striking contrast – between clearly deficient reality testing in one area of their mental life and evident normality in so many others – is reflected in DSM-IV criterion C for delusional disorder: 'Apart from the delusion(s) or its ramifications behavior is not markedly impaired and behavior is not obviously odd or bizarre'.

Our small group of clinicians also all commented, in different ways, on the quality of the delusions in delusional disorder. Two major themes emerged. First, compared to other psychotic states (many of which would probably currently be considered within the syndrome of schizophrenia), the delusions of individuals with delusional disorder were well organized, coherent and systematized. Esquirol himself noted that delusions in monomania usually derive in a logical fashion from a single set of false beliefs or perceptions. Second, the nature of the beliefs tends to deviate little from the fears or wishes commonly experienced by the psychologically healthy. This is in contrast to the fantastic and bizarre delusions often seen in other psychotic states. Kraepelin perhaps captured this concept best when he wrote that the content of the delusions in paranoia show

> although in morbidly developed form, . . . a remarkable agreement with those fears, wishes, and hopes, which even in normal individuals proceed from the feeling of uncertainty and the endeavor after happiness. (Kraepelin, 1921)

The DSM-IV criteria for delusional disorder attempt to capture the second of these two aspects of the delusions in delusional disorder by requiring, in criterion A, that they be

> nonbizarre . . . involving situations that occur in real life, such as being followed, poisoned, infected, loved at a distance, or deceived by one's spouse or lover, or having a disease.

One area of continued uncertainty in the clinical construct of delusional disorder is the role of hallucinations. Both KE, and Kraepelin early in his career, commented on the frequent occurrence of hallucinations. Kraepelin's final formulation of paranoia excluded cases with prominent hallucinations. Kretschmer only comments that hallucinations can occur but are rarely prominent. This controversy continues. In DSM-III (American Psychiatric Association, 1980) the criteria for what was then termed paranoid disorder excluded any case with 'prominent hallucinations'. In DSM-III-R, (American Psychiatric Association, 1987) this exclusion was relaxed somewhat and applied only to auditory or visual hallucinations. This change was made to allow the common experiences of olfactory hallucination in the 'olfactory reference syndrome' (Pryse-Phillips, 1971) (individuals noting a foul smell emanating from a bodily orifice that is smelled by others) and of tactile hallucinations in delusions of parasitosis (the belief and feeling of 'bugs' crawling on or just under the skin) (Skott, 1978). This approach was made more specific in DSM-IV (American Psychiatric

Association, 1994) with the note appended to criterion B that 'Tactile and olfactory hallucinations may be present in Delusional Disorder if they are related to the delusional theme'.

Perhaps the most interesting aspect of the history of delusional disorder is not, however, reflected in the DSM nosologies. This disorder has, over time, tended to challenge etiologic models for psychosis, especially after the triumph of the clinico-anatomic model for psychosis in the late 19th century. Although strongly committed to the neurologic model, KE's case descriptions convey a considerable sensitivity to the psychological evolution of this condition – and how it appears to develop on the fertile soil of certain personality types. Kraepelin found it even more difficult to conceptualize this psychotic syndrome within his neurologic framework. Delusional disorder was not, apparently, a disease, in the way in which Kraepelin conceptualized, for example, dementia praecox. In particular, patients with delusional disorder did not demonstrate the deterioration which, for Kraepelin, was one of the central characteristics of dementia praecox. Rather, Kraepelin came to view paranoia from a very different perspective – as a form of 'personality development'.

Gaupp and Kretschmer took this position further, developing a psychogenic model for delusional disorder and arguing that the condition was treatable by psychological therapies. This represented part of a trend in 20th century European psychiatry, particularly developed in Scandinavia, to regard a major subgroup of psychotic disorders as fundamentally 'reactive' or 'psychogenic' in nature (McCabe, 1975).

I cannot avoid a brief clinical speculation about the struggles to fit delusional disorder into etiologic models for psychosis which is no doubt influenced by the clinical traditions in which I was trained. These difficulties might be impelled by the striking clinical impression consistently made by such patients, particularly in contrast to the more 'severe' psychotic syndromes we now term schizophrenia. Individuals suffering from schizophrenia 'feel' pervasively impaired so that it is not difficult to believe that a 'disease' is at work. Patients with delusional disorder 'feel' very different and far more 'normal'. Faced with such patients, the clinician frequently struggles to understand how reality testing could become so impaired in one specific area, while other emotive, cognitive and volitional aspects of their life are apparently so intact.

REFERENCES

American Psychiatric Association (1980) *Diagnostic and Statistical Manual of Mental Disorders, Third Edition*, Washington, DC, American Psychiatric Association.

American Psychiatric Association (1987) *Diagnostic and Statistical Manual of Mental Disorders, Third Edition, Revised*, Washington, DC, American Psychiatric Association.

American Psychiatric Association (1994) *Diagnostic and Statistical Manual of Mental Disorders, Fourth Edition*, Washington, DC, American Psychiatric Association.

Berrios, G. (1984) 'Descriptive psychopathology: conceptual and historical aspects'. *Psychological Medicine*, 14: 303–13.

Berrios, G.E. (1987) 'Historical aspects of psychoses: 19th century issues'. *British Medical Bulletin*, 43: 484–98.

Bleuler, E. (1912) 'Affectivity, suggestibility, paranoia' (trans. Ricksher, C.). In *N.Y. State Hospitals Bulletin, vol. IV No.4* (ed. Ferris, A.W.), Utica, NY, State Hospitals Press, pp.481–601.

de Saussure, R. (1946) 'The influence of the concept of monomania on French medico-legal psychiatry (from 1825 to 1840)'. *Journal of the History of Medicine and Allied Sciences*, pp.365–97.

Dowbiggin, I. (1985) 'Degeneration and hereditarianism in French mental medicine 1840–1900: psychiatric theory as ideological adaptation'. In *The Anatomy of Madness: Essays in the History of Psychiatry. Volume 1, People and Ideas* (ed. Bynum, W.F., Porter, R. and Shepherd, M.), London, Tavistock Publications, pp.188–232.

Esquirol, E. (1845) *Mental Maladies. A Treatise on Insanity*. Translated from the French, with additions, by Hunt, E.K., M.D. Philadelphia, PA, Lea and Blanchard.

Friedman, M. (1908) 'Contributions to the study of paranoia'. In *Studies in Paranoia* (ed. and tr. Jelliffe, S.E.), New York, Journal of Nervous and Mental Diseases Publishing Company, pp.1–24.

Gaupp, R. (1974a) Robert Gaupp, 1870–1953. In *Themes and Variations in European Psychiatry: An Anthology* (ed. Hirsch, S.R. and Shepherd, M.), Charlottesville, University Press of Virginia, pp.119–20.

Gaupp, R. (1974b) 'The scientific significance of the case of Ernst Wagner'. In *Themes and Variations in European Psychiatry: An Anthology* (ed. Hirsch, S.R. and Shepherd, M.), Charlottesville, University Press of Virginia, pp.121–33.

Gaupp, R. (1974c) 'The illness and death of the paranoid mass murderer, schoolmaster Wagner: a case history'. In *Themes and Variations in European Psychiatry: An Anthology* (ed. Hirsch, S.R. and Shepherd, M.), Charlottesville, University Press of Virginia, pp.134–50.

Gierlich, N. (1908) 'Periodic paranoia and the origin of paranoid delusions'. In *Studies in Paranoia* (ed. and tr. Jelliffe, S.E.), New York, Journal of Nervous and Mental Diseases Publishing Company, pp.1–24.

Goldstein, J. (1987) *Console and Classify: The French Psychiatric Profession in the Nineteenth Century*, New York, Cambridge University Press.

Hafner, H. (1990) 'Ernst Kretschmer 1888–1964'. *Psychological Medicine*, 20: 487–92.

Kendler, K.S. (1988) 'Kraepelin and the diagnostic concept of paranoia'. *Comprehensive Psychiatry*, 29: 4–11.

Kraepelin, E. (1904a). *Clinical Psychiatry: A Text-Book for Students and Physicians*. (Abstracted and adapted from the sixth German edition of Kraepelin's 'Lehrbuch der Psychiatrie' by Diefendorf, A. Ross, MD), New York. The Macmillan Company.

Kraepelin, E (1904b) *Lectures on Clinical Psychiatry*, London, Balliere, Tindall & Cox.

Kraepelin, E. (1907) *Clinical Psychiatry: A Text-Book for Students and Physicians*. (Abstracted and adapted from the seventh German edition of Kraepelin's 'Lehrbuch der Psychiatrie' by Diefendorf, A. Ross, MD), New York, The Macmillan Company.

Kraepelin, E. (1916) 'Kraepelin on "Paranoid conditions" ' (tr. H.I. Gosline). *Alienist Neurol,* 37: 184–210.

Kraepelin, E. (1921) *Manic-Depressive Illness and Paranoia,* Edinburgh, E. & S. Livingstone.

Kraepelin, E. (1971) *Dementia Praecox and Paraphrenia,* Huntington, NY, Krieger Publishing.

Krafft-Ebing, R. (1905) *Text-book of Insanity: Based on Clinical Observations. For Practitioners and Students of Medicine.* (Authorized translation from the last German edition by Charles Gilbert Chaddock, MD), Philadelphia, F.A. Davis Company.

Kretschmer, E. (1974) 'The sensitive delusion of reference'. In *Themes and Variations in European Psychiatry: An Anthology* (ed. Hirsch, S.R. and Shepherd, M.), Charlottesville, University Press of Virginia, pp.153–95.

Lewis, A. (1970) 'Paranoia and paranoid: a historical perspective'. *Psychological Medicine,* 1: 2–12.

McCabe, M.S. (1975) 'Reactive Psychoses: A Clinical and Genetic Investigation'. *Acta Psychiatrica Scandinavica, Supplement 259,* pp.13–129.

Mora, G. (1972) 'On the bicentenary of the birth of Esquirol (1772–1840), the first complete psychiatrist'. *American Journal of Psychiatry,* 129:562–7.

Pryse-Phillips, W. (1971) 'An olfactory reference syndrome'. *Acta Psychiatrica Scandinavica,* 47: 484–510.

Seglas, J. (1888a) 'Paranoia: systematized delusions and mental degenerations: an historical and critical review' (tr. W. Noyes). *Journal of Nervous and Mental Disease,* 13: 157–71.

Seglas, J. (1888b) 'Paranoia: systematized delusions and mental degenerations: an historical and critical review' (tr. W. Noyes). *Journal of Nervous and Mental Disease,* 13: 285–300.

Seglas, J. (1888c) 'Paranoia: systematized delusions and mental degenerations: an historical and critical review' (tr. W. Noyes). *Journal of Nervous and Mental Disease,* 13: 366–73.

Seglas, J. (1888d) 'Paranoia: systematized delusions and mental degenerations: an historical and critical review' (tr. W. Noyes). *Journal of Nervous and Mental Disease,* 13: 225–8.

Skott, A. (1978) *Delusions of infestation: Dermatozoenwahn – Ekbom's Syndrome.* (Reports from the Psychiatric Research Centre, St. Jorgen Hospital, University of Goteberg, Sweden), Kungalv, Sweden, Gotab.

Chapter 14
Delusional Disorder

Social Section
I DOWBIGGIN

As is the case with most clinical concepts, the social history of delusional states, or Delusional (Paranoid) Disorder (DPD), is complex and can only be traced in its entirety in a monograph-length study. However, by focusing on a distinct chapter in its history we can identify factors that shaped its clinical definition and also played a role in the formulation of other psychiatric categories.

The APA DSM-III defines 'delusional (paranoid) states' as a pathological disorder chiefly characterized by 'the presence of a persistent, nonbizarre delusion'. It is distinguishable from schizophrenia or mood disorders when there is evidence that it was not caused and maintained by an organic condition. Typical delusions feature erotic, grandiose, jealous, persecutory, and hypochondriacal themes. DPD is 'relatively uncommon', tends to strike 'slightly' more women than men, and allows patients to function in social and occupational settings better than schizophrenia.[1]

In contrast to a disease like hysteria, DPD has had a rather short history.[2] Before the nineteenth century those who exhibited the symptoms of what we today call DPD or paranoia were normally diagnosed as suffering from 'melancholy'.[3] While some physicians began talking about 'paranoia' or something resembling delusional states in the early nineteenth century, it was not until the second half of the nineteenth century that the concept began to enlist the support of Western psychiatrists. Most of its supporters before the twentieth century were either German or French physicians. Although both the Germans and French developed nationally idiosyncratic definitions of delusional states, they all borrowed heavily from the trend in clinical psychiatry which stressed the observation of the full range of symptoms displayed by a patient over the entire course of his/her disease.

It was during the late nineteenth century, when the clinical approach began to dominate institutional psychiatry, that French clinicians introduced a disease concept that is a recognizable forerunner of DPD. They called it either 'chronic delusional insanity' (*'délire chronique'*), 'chronic progressive insanity', or 'systematized progressive insanity', and although they sometimes disagreed over its exact course and symptoms, they meant essentially the same thing. When Emil Kraepelin's (1856–1926) nosological views began to spread, French psychiatrists tenaciously hung on to the notion of chronic delusional states and tended to be wary about *dementia praecox* and, later, schizophrenia. This trend, originating between 1909 and 1911, has characterized French psychiatry throughout most of the twentieth century.[4] A close look at the French debate over delusional states around the turn of the twentieth century tells us not only something about the history of DPD, but also a great deal about the nature of the psychiatric enterprise itself.

The French contributions to the history of DPD began as the popularity of the clinical concept of 'monomania' faded after the mid-nineteenth century. Around 1810 the psychiatrist J.E.D. Esquirol (1772–1840) did away with the category of 'melancholy' and replaced it with 'monomania', which he used to describe mental states that featured impairment of intelligence, affect, and volition, but no impairment of logical reasoning. Then he divided monomania into a wide variety of monodelusional subcategories, including melancholy itself (or 'lypemania'), and partial insanities based on delusions of persecution and grandeur. Esquirol's followers eagerly employed the monomania diagnosis, mostly because it legitimized growing psychiatric involvement in legal proceedings and because it was congruent with the liberal political attitudes of many physicians. Since monomania could be used to describe the mental state of some criminals, psychiatrists could – and did – argue that their expertise was essential in order to identify the limits of legal responsibility.[5]

French psychiatrists dropped their allegiance to monomania in the 1840s and 1850s as resistance to Esquirol's classification scheme mounted. An important reason for this change was the increasing scepticism of French judges about the monomania defence.[6] Many were also dissatisfied with the way physicians were inventing countless types of monomania. Thus, in only a few short years significant revisions were made to Esquirol's theories. Jules Baillarger (1809–1890) and J.P. Falret (1794–1870) introduced what later came to be called 'manic-depressive psychosis' or 'bipolar disorder' (1854), and B.A. Morel (1809–1873) used the term 'démence précoce' to describe the symptoms of schizophrenia (1853). Charles Lasègue (1816–1883) took another important step away from Esquirol's system by formulating a diagnostic concept which he called '*délire de persecution*'. Lasègue's great achievement was to isolate from the swirl of symptoms asylum clinicians encountered in everyday practice a group of patients suffering from a partial insanity characterized by pronounced and systematic delusions of persecution.[7]

Other psychiatrists who helped to dismantle the diagnosis of monomania were Henri Legrand du Saulle (1830–1886) and Jules Falret (1824–1902). At the same time, German psychiatrists were working independently to construct the concept of 'paranoia' that was roughly similar to the French varieties of partial insanity or systematized insanity. All these contributions to the clinical history of DPD stressed basically the same delusional condition which coincided with an apparently clear consciousness and formally correct thinking. However, it was equally true that 'the words and concept they denoted were given so many shades of meaning that . . . the diagnostic application varied enormously, and there was general discontent' throughout the psychiatric community.[8]

In France, Valentin Magnan (1835–1916) made the most ambitious attempt to make sense out of the many different interpretations. Magnan was probably the most famous French psychiatrist of the *fin-de-siècle*, competing for the cultural limelight with his counterpart from the Salpêtrière, the neurologist J.M. Charcot. Late nineteenth-century French psychiatrists were ardent builders of nosological systems designed to classify all mental and nervous disorders, and Magnan, chief psychiatrist at the Sainte-Anne asylum in Paris, was arguably the best example of this trend from his generation.[9] Beginning in 1881 he devoted himself increasingly to the classification of mental diseases. Like Kraepelin he placed great weight on the course and outcome of disease. Magnan's main complaint was that many psychiatrists had confused what he thought were two distinct categories. The first category was what he called 'chronic delusional insanity' (CDI), and the second was hereditary degeneracy. Although antisocial behaviour and delusions of persecution could be symptoms of both diseases, the differential diagnosis between the two was based on clear clinical criteria, he argued. CDI was incurable and ordinarily began in adults 'of undoubted intelligence' between the ages of 35 and 45. Patients diagnosed as hereditary degenerates, on the other hand, had higher rates of recovery yet showed earlier signs of mental abnormality, sometimes during childhood. Whereas the family histories of degenerates revealed that they had inherited their mental weakness, evidence of hereditary precedents for CDI patients was weak.[10]

Yet another major difference between CDI and hereditary madness, according to Magnan, was that the former followed a progressive course culminating in dementia, while the latter often did not. By adding a stage that ended in dementia Magnan was going beyond the four stages Jules Falret had proposed in 1872 for systematic delusions of persecution. As Magnan wrote,

the insanity of the degenerate may either end abruptly in dementia or it may rapidly disappear altogether, or, after a longer or shorter term of remission, it may reappear either in its original form or wearing an entirely different aspect. Chronic progressive insanity . . . progresses slowly but fatally, . . . and is without any hope of cure, or even of a comparatively durable remission.[11]

Magnan's effort to stake out the frontiers between CDI and hereditary degeneracy drew considerable attention from his psychiatric colleagues in France. Between 1885 and 1888 the Paris-based *Société médico-psychologique* debated Magnan's ideas, first his views on degeneracy and then his views on CDI. The *Société* was the leading psychiatric learned society of nineteenth-century France and its journal, the *Annales médico-psychologiques*, was widely read throughout the French and international psychiatric communities.[12] The nature and course of these debates say a great deal about the ways in which psychiatrists of the late nineteenth-century perceived the boundaries among the various abnormal mental conditions. They also say something about the ways personal rivalries and nationalistic feelings affected the diagnostic approaches of psychiatrists.

Magnan's campaign to distinguish degeneracy from CDI met with mixed success. To defenders of degeneracy theory like Jules Séglas (1856–1939), it made no sense to carve a clinical group from hereditary degeneracy. As Séglas argued, if one looked closely at the clinical records of CDI patients one found more and more similarities with the symptoms of degenerate patients. Indeed, he noted, some degenerates ultimately became demented. For Séglas it was better to retain the broad applicability of hereditary degeneracy than to splinter it into smaller clinical groups.[13] His comments reflected the fact that degeneracy theory had assumed the status of an orthodoxy among late nineteenth-century French psychiatrists who often viewed it chauvinistically as a distinctly French contribution to the science of mental medicine.[14] Magnan's efforts to limit its scope were bound to encounter opposition from its supporters.

Other psychiatrists disagreed with Magnan, but for different reasons. They did not like the way Magnan had eliminated Lasègue's '*délire de persecution*' and had absorbed it into CDI. To psychiatrists like Jules Christian (1840–1907), '*délire de persecution*' was a distinct disease in itself with 'characteristic symptoms whose precision all observers have acknowledged'. To Christian, dementia was rarely and 'only accidentally' the terminal stage of CDI.[15]

Another opponent of Magnan's classification was Benjamin Ball (1833–1893), who held the Chair in Mental Diseases at the Paris Faculty of Medicine. That Ball should have spoken out against Magnan at the *Société médico-psychologique* from 1886–1888 was no surprise, for both men had been candidates for the Chair in Mental Diseases when it had first been proposed in 1875. Magnan and many other psychiatrists had made their disapproval known when Ball was appointed in 1877.[16] One source of dissatisfaction for Magnan and his followers was that Ball was more of an academic physician than an 'alienist', that is, a public asylum doctor. They felt that Magnan's failure to land the position was typical of the condescension shown towards alienists by the members of the Faculty of Medicine. This led to bad feelings between the two men and their respective camps, and relations became particularly strained when Ball gave his inaugural lectures at Sainte-Anne, Magnan's bailiwick.

When the two men locked horns at the *Société médico-psychologique* a few years later, Ball claimed Magnan's school was made up of 'theologians' who 'begin by defining a dogma, and once having defined the dogma, they then search for proof'. The next step, he continued, was to condemn every contrary observation as a 'heresy, or instead, to use medical terminology, as a "diagnostic error." With this kind of approach, a sort of local orthodoxy is easily constructed under whose feet dissidents are crushed'.[17]

But the worst part of Magnan's clinical style, Ball alleged, was that by substituting CDI for the more modest diagnosis of '*délire de persecution*', Magnan was erasing the name of Lasègue from medical history. This was not entirely fair, for in his historical accounts of CDI Magnan always cited Lasègue's early work as crucial. Ball was perhaps overly sensitive about Magnan's treatment of Lasègue's theories because Lasègue had been Ball's chief sponsor of his candidacy for the Faculty of Medicine Chair. In any case, Ball, like Christian, could see no reason to replace Lasègue's '*délire de persecution*' with Magnan's CDI; he thought basing a diagnosis mainly on the evolutionary course of a disease ignored the symptomatological inconsistency of CDI and led to absurdities, like the recognition of two kinds of typhoid fever, one that ended in death and one in a cure.

Resistance to Magnan's views could also be traced to the perception that he had more than his share of personality flaws. Emmanuel Régis (1855–1918), a private asylum physician and Professor of Medicine at the University of Bordeaux, had begun his career as a psychiatrist at Sainte-Anne and served there as Ball's *chef de clinique* in the early 1880s. Ball and Régis agreed on most things for, as Ball wrote, Régis's psychiatric ideas were 'in accord with the instruction I have given for many years in the asylum of Sainte-Anne'.[18] Régis was actually more sympathetic than Ball towards Magnan's description of CDI, challenging only Magnan's theory that it featured a fourth stage of dementia. But he plainly disliked Magnan the man. As Régis wrote bitterly in 1894 to an American correspondent,

> the grand master of injustice and scientific vanity is M. Magnan, who has introduced deplorable morals among [French alienists]. Magnan only thinks of himself in psychiatric matters and wipes the slate clean of everything that anyone else does or has done, both within and outside France. Above all he professes a particular disdain for those of his compatriots who do not share his ideas absolutely and he shows this disregard by not citing them in his writings. Never has my name in particular appeared in one of M. Magnan's publications. . . . That is the reward for my loyalty and my scientific probity.[19]

While personal dislike and professional rivalry may account for some of the opposition to Magnan's CDI, his seemingly cordial relations with German psychiatrists at a time when national chauvinism was increasingly characterizing French psychiatry made him even more unpopular in his native land. Although Magnan's psychiatric theories reflected the clinical glory of 'the French psychiatric school', his follower Paul Garnier (1848–1905) told the *Société médico-psychologique* in 1888; they also appeared to win the support of foreign psychiatrists, holding out the hope that 'an international entente' in psychiatry could be achieved.[20] But it is not at all clear that turn-of-the-century French psychiatrists wanted an 'entente' with foreign psychiatrists, especially from Germany. Some were angered by the failure of various German psychiatrists to include references to Lasègue's contributions in their discussions of paranoia.[21] Others like Régis believed that the time had come for French psychiatry to stop borrowing ideas and methods from German psychiatry. In the second edition (1894) of his *Practical Manual of Mental Medicine* he wrote:

> Up to within a few years, indeed, each country has, so to speak, studied mental disorders by itself alone, having in this regard its own special traditions, its own particular views, clinical and therapeutic methods, and even its own terminology. The result has been a lack of unity of effort and a hindrance to progress.[22]

Yet, twelve years later in the third edition, in a remarkable *volte-face*, he advised French psychiatrists to cease borrowing German methods and ideas. Pro-German trends in French psychiatry had engendered a kind of 'snobism', he insisted, that over-estimated what came from abroad and under-estimated the value of 'French science' and its 'incomparable qualities of precise observation, order, method, and clarity'.[23] In 1911, he rejoiced that the new generation of French psychiatrists was 'still not too contaminated by the nebulous, indecisive, and changing theories of Germany'.[24] Thus, in an era punctuated by calls in France for political '*revanche*' against Germany, many French psychiatrists were becoming decidedly Germanophobe in medical matters as well.

The fate of Magnan's CDI was sealed by the French psychiatric reaction to Kraepelin's views. In the 1890s, as successive editions of Kraepelin's *Textbook of Psychiatry* appeared in print, increasing psychiatric credence was given to the notion of a mental disease called *dementia praecox* which encompassed a wide range of delusional states that culminated in dementia. However, leading French clinicians like Gilbert Ballet (1853–1916), Paul Serieux (1864–1947), and Ernest Dupré (1862–1921) resisted this trend by trying to expand the number of nonschizophrenic delusional states. This French restriction of *dementia praecox* and schizophrenia has become what one recent observer has called 'the hallmark of French psychiatric diagnosis and classification' in the twentieth century, one that has 'probably' led French physicians to 'rather consistently overestimate' the 'prevalance of non-schizophrenic delusional states'.[25]

Some observers claimed that this antiKraepelinian attitude on the part of French psychiatrists was a reaction to the often 'loose' and 'indiscriminate use of the word dementia'.[26] But it was also due to the same antiGerman sentiments cited earlier, and translated into a lively suspicion of popular concepts in German psychiatry, like paranoia and *dementia praecox*. As one French psychiatrist wrote in 1910, 'German ideas' in psychiatry like 'la grande conception !!! de la démence praecox' were 'all the rage (*à la mode*)', but all they did, he argued, was 'mask a great ignorance of mental diseases'.[27] Magnan's CDI, which included the all-crucial fourth stage of dementia, was perhaps too reminiscent of Kraepelin's *dementia praecox* to be acceptable to French psychiatrists around the turn of the century. Magnan's classification scheme may have looked too much like Kraepelin's nosology which had thrown all French varieties of delusional paranoid states into either one of two large categories: one, manic-depressive psychosis; or two, *dementia praecox*, which terminated in incurable dementia.

These personal, political, and intraprofessional factors explain why Magnan's own version of CDI encountered opposition, yet two more questions remain: why did he try to disassemble a clinical concept – hereditary degeneracy – which he had done so much to popularize? And why did he then promote another concept that anticipated by some twenty years a major shift in French psychiatric perception?

The answer to both questions may be in part that Magnan, whatever his personal failings, was not only less jingoist than his colleagues but also more faithful to the clinical task of delimiting mental diseases on the basis of cause, course, duration, and outcome. Perhaps he, earlier and more clearly than most of his fellow Frenchmen in psychiatry, saw the clinical limitations of degeneracy theory and recognized the need to reorganize fundamentally the classification of mental diseases. Magnan differed from Kraepelin in that he split the latter's *dementia praecox* into two categories, CDI and hereditary degeneracy, but he still showed the German psychiatrist's interest in reducing the copious list of emotional disorders in the late nineteenth century, a list about which psychiatrists were becoming increasingly uneasy.[28]

Magnan may also have been tempted to strike out in bold new clinical directions *à la Kraepelin* because of his institutional position. His growing interest in a disease that stressed chronicity, incurability, and antisocial behaviour could have been the result of his experience since 1867 as head psychiatrist of Sainte-Anne, whose *'service de l'admission'* was virtually the 'psychiatric clinic' of all Paris, according to his biographer.[29] The vast majority of insane Parisians committed by the civil authorities were processed at the special infirmary at the Paris Prefecture of Police and transferred to Sainte-Anne, so

Magnan saw his share of dangerous and violence-prone *aliénés*. Magnan's encounter since the late 1860s with the criminally insane of Paris may have convinced him of the need to reform the classification of mental diseases in order to account for the seemingly growing number of cases which featured criminal behaviour and protracted delusional thinking mixed with apparent reason, yet which also featured little in the way of hereditary predisposition. The line linking criminality and delusional insanity was firmly drawn in the eyes of French psychiatrists: as Régis wrote, 'The greater part of the crimes committed outside of the asylums by the insane, and nearly all those committed within them, are to be credited to' CDI patients.[30] Thus, it is hardly a coincidence that many of those French physicians who like Magnan publicized the existence of delusional insanity – doctors like Lasègue, Legrand du Saulle, Garnier, and Dupré – spent part of their careers at the special infirmary of the Paris Prefecture of Police.

The fact that many of the patients he admitted had been repeatedly hospitalized must have made Magnan more disposed to diagnose constitutional incurability due to delusional insanity than to resort to the somewhat more hopeful diagnosis of degeneracy. In contrast to 'the possible or probable curability of the psychosis of the degenerate',[31] there were cases like the sixty-five-year-old man with pronounced delusions of persecution who had first been admitted to Sainte-Anne in 1873 and had returned five times by 1895 after numerous brushes with the law, 'always with the same type of symptoms gradually evolving'.[32] Since by Magnan's own admission it was sometimes easy to confuse CDI with degeneracy, this variety of clinical evidence was likely to cause him to see distinctions between the two categories at a time when his colleagues, not yet infected with his therapeutic pessimism, and still wedded to the comparatively optimistic diagnosis of degeneracy, did not. In this regard, too, Magnan was slightly ahead of other French psychiatrists who were loath to diagnose incurability so readily.

Magnan's encounter with this kind of mental patient suggests as well that medico-legal considerations were not far from his mind. Magnan – like almost all French psychiatrists deeply committed to psychiatric involvement in legal proceedings – began in the 1880s to rethink the matter of medical diagnosis and its relevance to physicians' testimony as experts in determining criminal responsibility. Article 64 of the 1810 French penal code had authorized French judges to use their discretion in determining the sanity of the accused and they had accordingly relied on physicians to establish if defendants had been demented at the time of the crime. But in 1832 the code was amended to take into consideration 'extenuating circumstances' which made it possible for judges and juries to impose a lesser sentence than the one stipulated in the code. After this, judicial dependence on psychiatric evidence increased dramatically. By the end of the nineteenth century – and despite some opposition from French judges – medicine had successfully invaded the courtroom.

From this perspective, Magnan's clinical description of CDI was particularly suited to 'succeed in irrefutably demonstrating the morbid character of the actions' of patients who, though adept at disguising their delusions and hallucinations, 'finally ... [took] the law into their own hands and committ[ed] some criminal offense'. 'It may generally be proved', Magnan contended, that a person whose intelligence appears unimpaired and who, up to the very last, performed his usual work, may be the subject of hallucinations and of systematized delusions of long standing. It may be possible to piece together the previous history of the insanity of the patient, the occurrence of the period of persecution after a preceding stage of incubation, and the slow and silent development of the affection. It is important to throw light upon the relation existing between the criminal act and the hallucinatory phenomena, from which ascertained data the nature of the affection may be diagnosed and the irresponsibility of the patient confirmed.[33]

In other words, the diagnosis of CDI provided the legal expert with a fairly clear and reliable clinical picture that enabled him to argue persuasively that lurking beneath the apparently sound mind of the criminal was a certifiable pathological condition.

Magnan's stress on the medicolegal significance of CDI is historically important in view of the fact that the differentiation of chronic delusional states undertaken by French psychiatrists between 1909 and 1911 followed closely on the heels of what Robert A. Nye has called 'a crisis in public and judicial confidence in expert medical testimony' in the years 1905–1909. The growing anxiety in official circles and among the respectable classes of France in the early twentieth century about the seemingly rising tide of crime and violence translated into a widespread scepticism about the ability of public officials like psychiatrists to defend society. In 1905 a circular from the Minister of Justice required two new questions of expert medical witnesses in criminal cases, one of which asked physicians to determine the responsibility of the defendant at the time of the infraction. When courtroom psychiatrists initially showed themselves reluctant to undertake this new task – satisfying themselves with the traditional challenge of defining the nature of mental illness – and when sensational new criminal cases cast further doubt on the competence of medical witnesses, there was talk in the French press of foregoing with medical expertise. While there was little likelihood that this would happen, psychiatry saw the controversy as a challenge to justify its traditional role in criminal justice. Thus, between 1906 and 1910 there was a 'great number of serious efforts to define serious scientific criteria of responsibility'. In order to prove that they were not the weak links in a system of repression based on 'social defence', psychiatrists ceased asking whether or not an individual deserved punishment for his crime or cure for his illness. Instead they began to urge eugenic solutions to prevent mental illness and the crime it supposedly engendered, and they focused on the danger criminal defendants posed to society. Responsibility in criminal cases, in other words, rested simply on the degree to which an individual threatened the health and order of the community. That these two phenomena were often conflated testified to the cultural obsession in early twentieth-century France with deviance of any kind.[34]

The clinical accent on the dangerousness, the incurability, and the dissimulation of patients suffering from CDI refracted the concerns of a profession that in 1906–1908 was anxious to undo any damage to its stature and prestige. Within a cultural climate of 'social defence' against all forms of deviance, a mental disease that made a criminal look more dangerous *because* of his mental

debility testified to the social responsibility of psychiatry, its committment to
'the penal repression' of paranoia rather than the determination of the degree
to which the patient was responsible for his crime. Indeed, as the psychiatrist
Georges Genil-Perrin wrote in 1926, paranoics presented so much danger to
society that the question of extenuating circumstances was really incidental to
the far graver question of what society could do to protect itself from their
crimes. Eugenics and 'internment' were two possibilities. The latter rarely had
a curative effect, he conceded, but that mattered little because delusional insanity
was unlike any of the other psychoses for which there was remedial hope. What
did matter was the patient's 'harmfulness to society'. Therefore, Genil-Perrin's
advice to the courts and to medical experts when it came to the 'penal repression'
of paranoia was hardly surprising: *'no half measures'* (his emphasis). To his
mind, 'attentuated responsibility' and 'attentuated penalty' were things that
perhaps mattered to jurists but not to 'scientific' psychiatrists pledged to defend
society from the delusionally insane.[35] Therefore, the clinical construction of
chronic delusional insanity in early twentieth-century French psychiatry was tied
concretely to the professional perception that its medicolegal role was under
attack and was based on psychiatrists' wish to appear tough on crime. As Robert
A. Nye has written,

> [t]he shift in concern from the welfare and rehabilitation of the individual to
> the protection of the family and the social order was a trait that psychiatry
> had in common with scores of other professions and disciplines and with the
> French intellectual elite.

Nothing demonstrated this characteristic better than the definition of chronic
delusional insanity, which told the respectable classes of *fin-de-siècle* France that
psychiatry too believed 'there were no individual pathologies; there were [only]
social pathologies of which individuals were the signs'.[36]

All these factors indicate that the development of the French theory of
delusional states after the turn of the century was due primarily to the urban,
legal, penal, and Paris-based experience of clinical psychiatry. This conclusion
casts doubt on Georges Lanteri-Laura's explanation for the growing emphasis
in late nineteenth-century French psychiatry on chronic mental diseases such as
delusional insanity. He argues that the diagnosis of chronic disease in general
appeared in asylums that by the latter third of the century had ceased to be
hospitals based on optimistic expectations of cure. A good example of this
phenomenon were the provincial asylums of France whose financial capacity to
treat socially respectable patients (about 1/6 of the total asylum population)
increasingly depended on a workforce of indigent patients engaged in agricultural labour. The growing psychiatric fondness for a diagnosis of chronic disease
after mid-nineteenth century, Lanteri-Laura maintains, was based on the need
of provincial asylums for cheap and plentiful labour: an asylum that included a
sizeable number of chronically ill patients may not have been brimming with
therapeutic confidence, but it could pay its bills.[37]

Based on the evidence presented in this paper, Lanteri-Laura's thesis needs
to be revised. What is certain is that a host of factors shaped the clinican's
'gaze', making it extremely difficult to know, as Berrios notes in his paper on
personality disorders, which of the many shifting descriptions of DPD were

'man-made' and which were due to changes in the very nature of the conditions observed.[38] The aim of this chapter was not to sort out these distinctions. Instead, its aim was to shed some light on the history of DPD by concentrating on phenomena such as Valentin Magnan's role in the decline of the theory of degeneracy and the influence of national partisanship on the construction of psychiatric diseases. It has also drawn attention to the way medicolegal considerations have shaped the clinical history of psychiatry, a topic that scholars like Roger Smith, Jan Goldstein, and Ruth Harris have explored recently.[39] Most of all, however, the hope is that by unravelling some of the complexity surrounding the clinical history of one psychiatric disorder it has contributed to the promising and growing scholarly interest in the history of psychiatry.

NOTES

1 American Psychiatric Association, (1987) *Diagnostic and Statistical Manual of Mental Disorders*. Third Ed. (revised) Washington, American Psychiatric Association, pp.199–202. For more on the clinical definition of DPD over time, see the piece by Kenneth S. Kendler in this volume.

2 For incisive remarks about both the history of and literature on hysteria, see Mark S. Micale, (1990) 'Hysteria and its Historiography: The Future Perspective', *History of Psychiatry*, 1: 33–124; (1993) 'On the "Disappearance" of Hysteria: A Study in the Clinical Deconstruction of a Diagnosis', *Isis*, 84: 496–526.

3 Stanley W. Jackson, (1986) *Melancholia and Depression: From Hippocratic to Modern Times*, New Haven and London, Yale University Press.

4 P. Pichot, (1982) 'The Diagnosis and Classification of Mental Disorders in French-Speaking Countries: Background, Current Views and Comparison with other Nomenclatures', *Psychological Medicine*, 12: 475–92; idem., (1979) 'Les bouffées délirantes et les délires chroniques: Deux concepts nosologiques français', *Annales médico-psychologiques*, 137: 52–8. Hereafter cited as *Amp*. See also Stephen F. Signer, (1991) 'De Clérambault's Concept of Erotomania and its Place in His Thought', *History of Psychiatry*, 2: 409–17.

5 Jan Goldstein, (1987) *Console and Classify: The French Psychiatric Profession in the Nineteenth Century*, Cambridge, Cambridge University Press, pp.152–96. For French legal medicine in the late nineteenth century, see Ruth Harris, (1989) *Murders and Madness: Medicine, Law, and Society in the Fin-de-siècle*, Oxford, Oxford University Press.

6 Goldstein, *Console and Classify*, pp.189–96.

7 Charles Lasègue, (1852) 'Du délire de persecutions', *Archives générales de médecine*, 28: 129–50.

8 Aubrey Lewis, (1970) 'Paranoia and Paranoid: A Historical Perspective', *Psychological Medicine*, 1: 2–12; p.4. See also Vasantkumar L. Tanna, (1974) 'Paranoid States: A Selected Review', *Comprehensive Psychiatry*, 15: 453–70.

9 Paul Serieux, (1918) *Valentin Magnan: Sa vie et son oeuvre (1835–1916)*, Paris, Masson. See also René Semelaigne, (1930–1932) *Les pionniers de la*

psychiatrie française avant et après Pinel, 2 vols., Paris, Baillière, vol. 2, pp.210–22.

10 Valentin Magnan, 'Chronic Delusional Insanity of Systematic Evolution', trans. A. Marie and J. MacPherson, *American Journal of Insanity*, 51, 1895: 37–57; 175–98; 524–38; 52, 1896: 397–415. Hereafter cited as Magnan, *AJI*.

11 *Ibid.*, 52, 1896: p.403.

12 Ian Dowbiggin, (1991) *Inheriting Madness: Professionalization and Psychiatric Knowledge in Nineteenth-Century France*, London and Berkeley, University of California Press, especially pp.32–7; 76–92.

13 J. Séglas, (1888) 30 January 1888 meeting of the *Société médico-psychologique, Amp.*, 7e série, v. 7: 338–42; 27 February 1888 meeting of the *Société, Ibid.*, pp.453–5.

14 Georges Genil-Perrin, (1913) *Histoire des origines et de l'évolution de l'idée de dégénérescence en médecine mentale*, Paris, Leclerc.

15 J. Christian, (1888) 26 March 1888 meeting of the *Société, Amp.*, 7e série, v. 8, p.485.

16 Semelaigne, *Les Pionniers*, v. 2, p.202.

17 B. Ball, (1888) 28 May 1888 meeting of the *Société, Amp.*, 7e série, v. 8, pp.112–15.

18 B. Ball, (1894) 'Introduction' to Emmanuel Régis, *Practical Manual of Mental Medicine*, Second French ed. Trans. H.M. Bannister, Utica, NY, Utica State Hospital Press, p.vi.

19 E. Régis to G. Alder Blumer, 25 August 1894, G. Alder Blumer Papers, Isaac Ray Historical Library, Butler Hospital, Providence, RI, Box 27. Hereafter cited as BP.

20 P. Garnier, (1888) 30 July 1888 meeting of the *Société, Amp.*, 7e série, v. 8, pp.464–5.

21 B. Ball, (1888) 28 May 1888 meeting of the *Société, Amp.*, 7e série, v. 8, p.115.

22 Régis, *Practical Manual of Mental Medicine*, p.xv.

23 Emmanuel Régis, (1906) *Précis de Psychiatrie*, Third ed., Paris, Octave Doin, p.v.

24 E. Régis to G. Alder Blumer, 14 May 1911, BP, Box 31.

25 P. Pichot, 'Diagnosis and Classification in French-Speaking Countries', p.490.

26 G. Alder Blumer, (1907) 'The History and Use of the Term Dementia', *American Journal of Insanity*, 63: 337–47.

27 Victor Parant to G. Alder Blumer, 31 March 1910, BP, Box 31.

28 For an example of the medical dissatisfaction with the state of psychiatric nosology in the late 1880s, see the remarks of P. Garnier, (1888) 30 July 1888 meeting of the *Société, Amp.*, 7e série, v. 8, pp.454–65.

29 P. Serieux, *Magnan*, p.156.

30 E. Régis, *Practical Manual of Mental Medicine*, p.227.

31 Magnan, (1896) 'Chronic Delusional Insanity', *AJI*, 52: p.403.

32 *Ibid.*, (1895) 51: p.52.

33 Magnan, (1896) 'Chronic Delusional Insanity', *AJI*, 52, pp.411–12.

34 Robert A. Nye, (1984) *Crime, Madness and Politics in Modern France: The*

Medical Concept of National Decline, Princeton, Princeton University Press, especially pp.247–64.

35 Georges Genil-Perrin, (1927) *Les paranoiaques*, Paris, Norbert Maloine, especially pp.444–74.

36 Nye, *Crime, Madness, and Politics*, p.232.

37 Georges Lanteri-Laura, (1972) 'La chronicité dans la psychiatrie française moderne', *Annales E. S. C.*, 27e année, no. 3: 548–68.

38 See G. Berrios (1993) 'European views on personality disorders: A conceptual History'. *Comprehensive Psychiatry*, 34: 14–30.

39 See Ruth Harris, *Murders and Madness*; Jan Goldstein, *Console and Classify*; Roger Smith, (1981) *Trial by Medicine: Insanity and Responsibility in Victorian Trials*. Edinburgh, Edinburgh University Press.

Chapter 15
Mood Disorders

Clinical Section
GE BERRIOS

The group of conditions nowadays called 'affective disorders' has resulted from the convergence of certain *words* (e.g. 'affective' and its cognates), *concepts* (theoretical notions accounting for 'mood' related experiences), and *behaviours* (observable changes in action and speech associated with neurobiological changes yet to be fully elucidated). The evolution of these elements has been asynchronous and each has a different history; in fact, their convergence only took place during the early part of the twentieth century. Since there is no reason to expect that such convergence is necessarily 'written in the nature of things', it is postulated here that its explanation belongs more to history than to science. If the 'convergence hypothesis' is correct, then those who believe that the history of clinical conditions such as 'mania' and 'melancholia' (as *currently* defined) starts with the Greeks are mistaken. Indeed, such anachronistic approach would only chronicle the *history of the pertinent words*.

One of the problems confronting the historian is that the phrase 'affective disorders' refers to a family of subjective and objective behavioural disturbances. In current English-speaking psychiatry, for example, it names the depressive and manic syndrome, combinations thereof, and occasionally some of their accompanying anxiety symptoms (Zerssen, 1988). 'Affective' (the operative word), has itself a long and noble history and is part of a panoply of terms which include emotion, passion, feeling, sentiment, mood, affective equivalent, dysthymia, cyclothymia, dysphoria, etc. Although these terms name overlapping subjective states, they have different semantic provenance.

Basically, it is unclear whether they all refer to some fundamental unitary mental function or to combinations of functions (Berrios, 1985). Sentiment, emotion and passion have been customarily distinguished from mood, affect and feeling in terms of criteria such as duration, polarity, intensity, insight, saliency, association with an inner or outer object, bodily sensations, and motivational force. They are defined as short-lived, more or less intense feeling states, which appear related to a recognizable object (Ribot, 1897); emotion and passion (the latter of which is an intense version of the former) are assumed to be accompanied by bodily changes and hence to possess motivational properties (Leeper, 1948). Mood and affect, on the other hand, are defined as longer lasting and more or less objectless states capable of providing a background feeling tone to the individual (Owens and Maxmen, 1979).

Upon this baseline of mood, short-lived emotions or ideas of congruous (*synthymic*) or incongruous (*catathymic*) value can be superimposed (Bash, 1955). The tone and consistency of experiences ordinarily called 'mood and affect' are probably controlled by neuroendocrinological variables, and subject to both genetic and environmental control. In clinical practice, patients suffering from an affective disorder are expected to 'describe' their feeling state, in spite of the fact that some aspects of their illness (e.g. psychotic symptoms) may prevent them from behaving as rational observers. This, in addition to the fact that they may be experiencing novel and strange sensations, make their so-called 'privileged' observer's position precarious. The fact that psychiatrists are successful in identifying mood states is reassuring, not least to the historian, and suggests that a well structured descriptive system is in operation, for example, that doctor and patient share systems of signals of cultural and/or evolutionary origin (Krueger, 1928; Mantegazza, 1878; Gruber, 1981; Darwin, 1872). A complete history of the affective disorders should include an analysis of the words involved in the naming of feeling states (Berrios, 1985).

THE AFFECTIVE DISORDERS

Our current notions of depression and mania date from the second half of the nineteenth century and emerged from the transformacion of the old notions of melancholia and mania. The ideological changes that made them possible included the availability of faculty psychology and of the anatomoclinical model of disease, and the inclusion of subjective experiences into the symptomatology of mental disorders (Berrios, 1987; 1988; 1988a). The concept of mania was first narrowed down, and the residue re-defined (under the influence of faculty psychology) as a primary disorder of affect and action. The pre-nineteenth century notion of melancholia was equally refurbished: this was facilitated by Esquirol's concept of lypemania which emphasized the affective nature of the disorder (Esquirol, 1820). Once the right conceptual conditions were given, the new clinical versions of mania and melancholia combined into the new concept of alternating, periodic, circular or double form insanity (Foville, 1882; Ritti, 1876; Mordret, 1883). This process culminated with Kraepelin's concept of 'manic-depressive insanity' which included most forms of affective disorder under the same umbrella (Kraepelin, 1921).

The transformation of melancholia into depression
'Melancholia' wrote John Haslam (1809): 'the other form in which this disease (madness) is supposed to exist, is made by Dr. Ferriar to consist in "intensity of idea". By intensity of idea I presume is meant, that the mind is more strongly fixed on, or more frequently recurs to, a certain set of ideas, than when it is in a healthy state' (pp.32–3). Haslam's perception was correct. Up to the period of the Napoleonic Wars, melancholia was but a rag-bag of insanity states whose only common denominator was the presence of few (as opposed to many) delusions. In practice, this means that cases of schizophrenia might have been so catalogued. Sadness and low affect (which were no doubt present in some cases) were not considered as definitory symptoms. Indeed, states of non-psychotic depression, of the type that nowadays would be classified as DSM IV 'Major Depressive Episode with melancholic features' would not have been

called 'melancholia' at all. During the eighteenth century these states were classified as 'vapours', (Cheyne, 1733), 'spleen', or 'hypochondria', i.e. what Cullen called 'Neuroses', and Sydenham and Willis, the previous century, had called 'Nervous disorders' (Hare, 1991).[1]

The term depression

To search for the origins of the term and the concept of 'depression' the historian does not need to go beyond the middle of the nineteenth century (Jackson, 1986). After the 1820s, conceptual changes determined that 'melancholia' could no longer be: 1. a subtype of mania, 2. a primary disorder of intellect, and 3. irreversible. What emerged was a form of partial insanity defined as a primary disorder of emotions whose features (clinical and aetiological) reflected loss, inhibition, reduction, and decline. Thus constituted, 'melancholia' was re-named 'depression', a term that had been popular in middle nineteenth century cardiovascular medicine to refer to a reduction in function (Berrios, 1988a). The word was first used analogically as 'mental depression'; soon after the adjective 'mental' was dropped. By 1860, it appears in medical dictionaries: 'applied to the lowness of spirits of persons suffering under disease' (Mayne, 1860).

The first edition of Régis' (1885) Manual (which was to go through many editions) defined depression as: 'the state opposed to excitation. It consists in a reduction in general activity ranging from minor failures in concentration to total paralysis' (p.77). Physicians preferred the word depression to melancholia or lypemania, perhaps because it evoked a 'physiological' explanation. For example, Sir William Gull (1894) used it as early as 1868 in his article on 'hypochondriasis': 'its principal feature is mental depression, occurring without apparently adequate cause' (p.287). By the end of the century, 'depression' was defined as: 'a condition characterized by a sinking of the spirits, lack of courage or initiative, and a tendency to gloomy thoughts. The symptom occurs in weakened conditions of the nervous system, such as neurasthenia and is specially characteristic of melancholia' (Jastrow, 1901 p.270). In his popular manual, Savage (1898) defined melancholia as a 'state of mental depression, in which the misery is unreasonable' (p.151). Adolph Meyer (1901) also campaigned in favour of the new word.

Thus constituted, depression was gradually enlarged by the addition of a number of symptoms and states that ranged from stupor or 'melancholia attonita' (Berrios, 1981) to nihilistic delusions (Cotard, 1882; Berrios and Luque, 1995). Kraepelin legitimized the term by using it in a adjectival manner, and amongst the 'depressive states' he included melancholia simplex, stupor, melancholia gravis, fantastic melancholia and delirious melancholia (Kraepelin, 1921). British psychiatry took longer to catch up, and the same group of disorders continued sailing as 'melancholia'; witness to this is the famous 'Nomenclature of Diseases' drawn up by a Joint Committee appointed by the Royal College of Physicians of London (RCP, 1906). Therein 'melancholia' was classified as a 'disease of the nervous system' (code 146) exhibiting acute, recurrent or chronic states. The Committee advised that 'the variety when known should be returned according to the following' categories: agitated, stuporous, hypochondriacal, puerperal, climacteric, senile and from acute or chronic disease or from injury (p.37).

There was some disagreement concerning the taxonomic position of the new melancholia (or depression). Because its symptoms were often found in other insanities, the new disease was classified as a: 1. stage in the development of a unitary psychosis (Griesinger, 1861), 2. separate disease, self-contained or part of a cycle including euphorias and/or stupor (Baillarger, 1854), 3. development of the subject's personality (Montassut, 1938), i.e. an exaggeration of acquired vulnerabilities (Freud, 1963), and 4. manifestation of a tainted pedigree (as per degeneration theory (Saury, 1886). These hypotheses were not considered as exclusive, and the manner of their combination engendered much debate. This is partly explained by the fact that the logic of justification and falsification which operated amongst nineteenth (and early twentieth) century alienists was based on the marshalling of single cases and of counter-examples. Although the notion of 'law of error' (Gaussian distribution) (Hilts, 1967) was already available, it had not yet penetrated the methodology of psychiatry. So, case reports exhibiting minor deviations from the idealized type created difficulty and forced alienists to declare them as new forms.

In the 8th edition of his Textbook, Kraepelin (1921) cut the Gordian knot by creating an overinclusive notion which comprised all forms of depression and mania, even including the notion of 'involutional melancholia'. This omnibus concept was characterized by: a) a periodic course, b) good prognosis, and c) endogenicity (i.e. not related to precipitants); all three criteria demanded standards of clinical description and observation which at the time were difficult to achieve. They also led to surprising conclusions, for example, that some paranoias, neurasthenias or (even) changes in bowel habit (without other accompanying features) may be hidden forms of manic-depressive illness (Kraepelin, 1921). These less recognizable Kraepelinian views, are rarely mentioned nowadays, perhaps because of selective reading: only those amongst his clinical statements are quoted which are intelligible to current psychiatrists. In Kraepelin, the concept of affective disorder can be said to be at its most overinclusive: indeed, the history of the affective disorders after 1910 is no more than the analysis of the fragmentation of the Kraepelinian notion.

In the period between Esquirol and Kraepelin seven assumptions accumulated in regards to the affective disorders (Berrios 1985, 1987, 1988, 1988a): 1. they were to be a 'primary' pathology of affect (Bolton, 1908), 2. had stable psychopathology (Foville, 1882), 3. had brain representation (Ritti, 1876), 4. were periodic in nature (Falret, 1854; Baillarger, 1854), 5. were genetic in origin (Foville, 1882), 6. appeared in individuals with recognizable personality predisposition (Ritti, 1876), and 7. were endogenous in nature (Kraepelin 1921; Chaslin, 1912). These beliefs originated from clinical observation, logical reasoning, and ideology, and not surprisingly, each has a different conceptual history.

The classification of the affective disorders
During the nineteenth century, the need to re-classify the affective disorders had various origins (Berrios, 1987). There was the taxonomic impetus driving the whole of medicine; an internal need to tidy up the nosology of psychiatry; the influence of faculty psychology (the search for the primary disorders of affect); the ever looming presence of degeneration theory; and, late in the century, the need to identify homogeneous clinical groups for neuropathological study,

particularly in relation to the differential diagnosis between melancholia and dementia (Berrios, 1995a; Dumas 1894; Mairet, 1883).

The first point to understand is that what was involved in this taxonomic drive was not just diseases changing pigeonhole. The magnitude of the transformation is so large that, without a metalanguage and a metaperspective, it cannot be fully appreciated.[2] From the vantage point of the twentieth century, pre-1800 concepts of insanity are only apparently intelligible. Up to the eighteenth century, insanity (lunacy, madness, vesania) was opaque in various ways; the hardest to understand being the fact that it predicated of the insane a state of existence (rather than of mind) which was *sub specie aeternitatis*.[3] The obvious problem with this view is to explain clinical remissions. For this, the notion of 'lucid interval' was created which accounted for 'normal' behaviour without abandoning the view that the person remained mad at a deeper level.[4] This ontological belief is concealed from our view by the fact that medical practitioners in earlier times 'contextualised' their description of madmen by talking about 'life-events', 'onset', 'lucidity', and specific individuals. Madness itself was only given a temporal context during the nineteenth century, when 'time' became, for the first time, a dimension of mental disorder.

The time dimension rendered madness into a longitudinal process. This view achieved full development in the work of Kahlbaum (Katzenstein, 1963) and later in Wernicke (Lanczik, 1988 and Chapter 11, this book) and Kraepelin (Berrios and Hauser, 1988 and Chapter 10, this book). Evidence for this is the preoccupation, up to the time of Kahlbaum, about what 'subsisted', 'endured' and gave identity to mania, melancholia, or dementia: Were the symptoms themselves? The level of psychological energy (as, for example, in Griesinger)? The mental faculty involved (regardless of the symptoms)? The brain lesions? Due to the incipient state of neuropathology, first symptoms, and later faculties were chosen to play this *ontological* role. The danger with taking symptom-combinations seriously is that it leads to a proliferation of new 'diseases'. So, faculties became popular as is the case of Esquirol's taxonomy; and in a way, we still have a classification based on the original disorders of intellectual, affective, and volitional functions.

The addition of the time-dimension refined the process. First Kahlbaum, and then Kraepelin (who followed him closely) postulated that, to be a disease, symptom-clusters persisted in time (i.e. had a disease-course), and had brain representation. The first criterion was easier to comply and drastic enough to reduce the number of insanities described. It was drastic enough in Kraepelin's hands to override clinical description and create two new super-diseases. But Kraepelin's nosology could not escape the curse of 'intermediate' cases, to the point that, as an old man, he grew sceptical and relinquished the dichotomy (Kraepelin, 1920). The taxonomic problem presented differently to the French for their psychiatry was under different conceptual pressures, particularly that of degeneration theory which led to different nosological groups, and to an emphasis on hereditary insanity (Roubinovitch, 1896).

An important cause for this classificatory chaos was the failure of the anatomo-clinical model of disease which left alienists with mere symptom descriptions (Berrios, 1984). Nineteenth century alienists had inherited a simple classification of madness: phrensy, mania, melancholia, and dementia were all neatly defined, albeit on purely theoretical grounds (Pinel, 1809). In their effort to 'naturalise' madness they rejected the old theory and only succeeded in causing a fragmentation of the traditional categories themselves. The only gain was that they could 'observe' symptoms in a new light, and naturalistic observation entered the classificatory equation. So, when new theoretical categories of insanity appeared in the market[5] they had to tally with the reality of observation. To what extent alienists implemented this desideratum, however, remains to be seen.

Nineteenth century France

During the first half of the nineteenth century classificatory fashions originated in France had a commanding influence on the rest of Europe. Pinel was perhaps the last great man to use melancholia and mania in the old, classical sense. Esquirol, Georget, Billod, Baillarger, Falret, Marc, Morel, Linas, Ritti, and Magnan, implemented changes in these categories. Their work, however, had not yet been completed when the Kraepelinian view took France by storm splitting the ranks of her alienists (Ey, 1954; Rouart, 1936). Some, like Deny and Camus (1907) supported the notion of an overinclusive manic-depressive insanity; others stuck to the old views and the debate continued well into the 1930s.

Pinel

Pinel (1809) defined melancholia as an insanity characterized by a circumscribed number of delusions (*délire exclusif*). His clinical conception of the condition, however, was wide:

> Melancholia frequently remains stationary for many years without its central delusion changing in character, and without causing much physical or psychological change. It can be seen in patients with this condition detained at Bicêtre for twelve, fifteen, twenty, or even thirty years, that they are still victims of the delusions that originated their admission . . . some having a more mobile character, and after observing the agitated behaviour of some lunatics, develop a manic state . . . others, after many years undergo a sort of internal revolution, and their delusions change. One of these patients, already advanced in years, had believed for years that he had been imprisoned by his parents who wanted his fortune, more recently however, he began to fear that we wanted to poison him. (pp.167–8)

Pinel thus included under melancholia all forms of chronic psychosis, including schizophrenia.

Esquirol and *lypémanie*

But this was soon to change. Under the influence of faculty psychology, and believing that melancholia was a primary disorder of emotions, Esquirol (1820) criticised the old usage: 'the word melancholia, consecrated in popular language to describe the habitual state of sadness affecting some individuals should be left to poets and moralists whose loose expression is not subject to the strictures of medical terminology' (p.148). Prichard (1835) had a similar view, and Rush (1812) after criticising Cullen's usage, advised against the use of the word 'melancholia' coining, instead, *tristimania*.

But of all these new terms, it was 'lypemania' that survived the longest. Esquirol (1820) defined it as 'a disease of the brain characterized by delusions which are chronic and fixed on specific topics, absence of fever, and sadness which is often debilitating and overwhelming. It must not be confused with mania which exhibits generalized delusions and excited emotions and intellect nor with monomania that exhibits specific delusions and expansive and gay emotions, nor with dementia characterized by incoherence and confusion of ideas resulting from weakening' (pp.151–2). Esquirol (1820) even reported a clinical and epidemiological profile for the new disease: rates for lypemania were found to increase between May and August (p.159) and the age group most affected was that between 25–45 (p.161), in 110 of 482 cases 'heredity' seemed to have played a role, common causes included domestic crisis, grief and disturbed relationships (p.166), and about a third of his cohort died, often of tuberculosis.

The term lypemania had its critics. Delasiauve (1856) called it too 'élastique and apart from being less imprecise was no different in terms of content from the old term melancholia' (p.382). Delasiauve was here referring to the fact that Esquirol had kept 'circumscribed delusions' (a vestige of the old intellectualistic notion) as a *defining criterion*. Delasiauve was right for it is clear from studying Esquirol's case reports that paranoia and delusional disorders were included under lypemania (Sérieux and Capgras, 1909, p.293). Delasiauve (1856) suggested that the boundaries of lypemania be narrowed further to refer only to: 'an exaggeration and persistence of feelings of depression' (p.384). But the highest point in the history of lypemania is reached in the work of Billod who subdivided it and refined its psychopathology. Billod accepted that lypemania had to be defined on the basis of sad delusions and disordered affect, and suggested a four-fold classification: lypemania with sad delusions and sadness; sad delusions and no sadness; sad delusions and mixed or alternating affective disorder (this included the bipolar states); and no sad delusions and sadness. This contrived symmetry allowed the recognition of about sixteen subtypes (Billod, 1856). Some of these have since disappeared (e.g. ironic or religious lypemania) others (e.g. hypochondriacal, stuporous, or irritable lypemania) still sail current seas under different names.

The word 'lypemania' did not catch on in Germany, Austria, Switzerland or Great Britain, where the word 'melancholia' was maintained. Prichard paid no attention to the term and Griesinger (1861), who regularly quoted Esquirol, did not take notice either. Feuchtersleben (1847) mentioned the term once, but did not acknowledge its origins; Bucknill and Tuke did, but continued using melancholia on the excuse that Esquirol himself had stated that the terms could be used interchangeably (p.147). Lypemania is an example of what historians may want to call a 'bridge' category: it only served to catalyse the transition between the old notion of melancholia (as a primary disorder of intellect) to the new one (as a primary disorder of affect).

Baillarger, Falret, and the combined states
In 1851, Jules Falret described, in one of his lectures at the *Salpêtrière*, a condition which he called *forme circulaire de maladie mentale*, consisting in 'a period of excitation followed by one of weakness ordinarily longer' (Falret, 1851). In 1854, Baillarger read a paper before the *Académie de Médicine* where

he reported seven cases of what he called *folie a double forme* and which consisted 'in the succession of two regular periods, one of excitation and the other of depression' (Baillarger, 1854). Few days after this paper had been read, Falret (1854a) published the excerpt of his course including his earlier clinical description and claimed priority for the 'discovery'; 2 weeks after Baillarger's paper, he also managed to get time to read his own paper before *L'Académie de Médicine* (Falret, 1854) (for a full account of this episode see Pichot, 1995).

As Ritti (1883) showed in his superb monograph, suggestions that patients may show combined depressive and manic periods were not knew, and had been in the air for a long time. The issue of priorities cannot be resolved and is in any case irrelevant. No doubt both Baillarger and Falret were talking about forms of manic-depressive illness, as were others before, and indeed afterwards. Thus, Billod (1856) coined the term *à double phase*, and Delaye and Legrand du Saulle, *folie alterne* (Ritti, 1883). However, the full concept of manic depressive illness, as a separate illness, did not crystallize in France until 1883. In 1880, and in an effort to solve the ongoing debate, *L'Académie de Médicine* decided to call for entries (as it had done before in relation to other clinical problems) on 'the form of insanity called circular, double form, or alternating'. A. Ritti was awarded the first prize, and A.E. Mordret (1883) the second; both monographs appeared the same year, and together created the conceptual basis for the disease that was to feature as the centre-piece in Kraepelin's manic-depressive 'circle'.

Nineteenth century Germany

It has been customary to accept the view (e.g. Bolton, 1908), started by Deny and Camus (1907), that during most of the nineteenth century the German contribution to the history of the affective disorders was negligible, and that it only became important after the work of Krafft-Ebing, Weygandt, Kraepelin and Dreyfus. This view is anachronistic in that it judges 'importance' from the perspective of the present.

Under the influence of German Romanticism, writers such as Reil, Heinroth and Griesinger expressed views on the affective disorders which reflect the growing importance of 'affect' and 'passions' in the development of mental illness (Berrios, 1985). For example, Heinroth (1975) wrote:

the origin of the false notions of patients suffering from melancholia . . . is being erroneously attributed to the intellect . . . here the intellect is not at fault . . . it is the disposition which is seized by some depressing passion, and then has to follow it, and since this passion becomes the dominating element, the intellect is forced by the disposition to retain certain ideas and concepts. It is not these ideas or concepts which determine the nature and the form of the disease. (pp.190–1)

Writings by German alienists from this period also reflect an anti-Cartesian approach, for example, by classifying the insanities in terms of the 'single principle of cerebral development, both physical and psychological' (Roubinovitch, 1896).

Griesinger

The concepts of melancholia and mania are more difficult to elucidate in the work of Griesinger. In spite of his great influence and reputation, Griesinger had limited clinical psychiatric experience (Wahrig-Schmidt, 1985), and hence based his definitions on borrowed cases and views. His beliefs on the mechanisms involved in the affective disorders came from various sources: a) Herbartian association-ism, which allowed him to identify 'the elementary symptoms (units of analysis) of insanity', b) Broussais' notion of 'irritation' and his belief that mental disorder could result from increases or decreases in psychological energy or vitality, and c) the 'unitarian' view, i.e. that there was one form of insanity which could change in its symptomatic expression through time (Rennert, 1968). Thus, although Griesinger's clinical description of melancholia has a 'modern' ring, it should not be forgotten that it belongs to a different conceptual world in which there were no independent psychiatric diseases but only successive symptom clusters reflect-ing the oscillations of a vital principle (Griesinger, 1861).

Kahlbaum

The views of Kahlbaum (1863) on melancholia and mania are confusing because he included both syndromes under the term *dysthymia* (which he attributed to Carl Friedrich Flemming) (Bronisch, 1990).[6] Flemming, one of the great leaders of German asylum psychiatry (Kolle, 1963) published a book on 'The pathology and therapy of the psychoses' including a chapter on syndromes resulting from the primary disorder of the emotions (Flemming, 1859 pp.56–80).

In 1863, Kahlbaum put forward an original classification, based on a longi-tudinal concept of disease (Katzenstein, 1963). The third group in this classifi-cation was the *Vecordias* (defined as idiopathic disturbances of mental life, with onset after puberty, and with more or less specific symptoms). These were subdivided, according to faculty psychology, into disturbance of intellect (*para-noia*), volition (*diastrophia*) and emotions (*dysthymia*). The latter included *dysthymia melna* and *elata* according to whether there was a predominance of sad affect (*Vorwalten trauriger Affecte*) or elated affect (*freudiger Affecte*) (Kahlbaum, 1863 p.134). In regard to melancholia, Kahlbaum said: 'In our view melancholia is not a disease but a syndrome (*ein Symptomenkomplex*)' (Kahlbaum, 1863 p.97).

Krafft-Ebing

Krafft-Ebing (1879) is said to have used a 'modern voice' to define and classify melancholia and mania. As Bercherie (1980) has perceptively noticed, Krafft-Ebing's taxonomic principles are based on a series of dichotomies. Firstly, the psychoses are divided into those with and without intellectual retardation; then the latter into those with (organic) or without (functional) identifiable brain pathology; thirdly, the functional psychoses are split into those developing in degenerates (i.e. those with family loading of mental illness: psychoneurosis) and in 'normals'; finally, the psychoneurosis are divided into melancholia, mania, acute and hallucinatory insanity. Melancholia, Krafft-Ebing defined as a 'painful inhibition of psychological functions' and mania an exalted facilita-tion. This classification reigned supreme in Germany until the time of Kraepelin.

Kraepelin and 'involutional melancholia'

The views of Kraepelin are too well known to be rehearsed again (Jackson, 1986; Rouart, 1936; Ey, 1954). However, there is still confusion in regards to the history of involutional melancholia (Arnaud, 1899; Dana, 1904; Gaupp, 1905; Berger, 1907; Ducost, 1907; Phillips, 1912a; Fishbein, 1949; Gibson, 1918; Treadway, 1913; Cordeiro, 1973; Ey, 1954). Thus, let us first quote a standard definition: 'The term customarily refers to agitated depressions occurring for the first time in life after the age 45–50, in contrast to manic-depressive illness which manifest itself at an early age' (Post, 1965 p.103). The conventional story is that, up to the 7th edition of his textbook, Kraepelin considered involutional melancholia as a separate disease, and that when confronted by the evidence collected by Dreyfus (1907), he decided to include it, in the 8th edition, under the general heading of manic-depressive insanity (Kendell, 1968, Sérieux, 1907; Post, 1965; Jackson, 1986). Indeed, this account was first presented by Kraepelin (1921) himself:

> The fact that states of depression are specially frequent at the more advanced ages, had already before this forced the supposition on me, that the processes of involution in the body are suited to engender mournful or anxious moodiness; it was one of the reasons which caused me to make a special clinical place for a portion of these forms under the name melancholia. After the purely clinical foundations of this view were shaken by the investigations of Dreyfus, our representation also now lets the causal significance of age appear in a light somewhat different from my former view. (p.169)

The story is, however, more complex and it is unlikely that the finding of Dreyfus alone caused Kraepelin's change of heart. For example, Thalbitzer (1926) claimed that his own work had also been influential (p.41).

In fact, in the 8th edition, Kraepelin (1921) abandoned not only involutional melancholia but the entire group of 'senile psychoses'. More to the point, the reasons which in the first place led him to consider involutional melancholia as a separate disease had been many: depression became more frequent with age, in older age groups, psychomotor agitation was more frequent than retardation, outcome worsened with age, and melancholia often became complicated by 'mental weakness', that is cognitive impairment (p.190). In the 8th edition, twice did Kraepelin (1921) feel obliged to justify his change of opinion. Firstly, he mentioned Dreyfus (see above); secondly, he stated that further experience had taught him that 'the argument in favour of the separation of melancholia were not sound' (p.191) for 'dementias could be explained by the appearance of senile or arteriosclerotic disease; that other cases, after very long duration of illness, some of them displaying manic symptoms, had they still recovered. The frequency of depressive attacks in advanced age we have come to recognize as an expression of a general law which governs the change of colouring of the attack in the course of life. Lastly, the substitution of anxious excitement for volitional inhibition has proved to be behaviour which we meet with in advancing age in those cases also which decades previously had fallen ill in the usual form' (Kraepelin, 1921, p.191). This account was confirmed years later in his autobiography (Kraepelin, 1983, p.74).

Dreyfus and his monograph

By quoting Dreyfus (1907)[7] in the 8th edition, Kraepelin burdened the young man (who was only 26 when he started the research) with the responsibility of having been the overt cause of his change of heart. To test the hypothesis that involutional melancholia had a bad prognosis (i.e. did not recover), Kraepelin asked Dreyfus to find out what had happened to all the cases he had diagnosed as 'melancholia' in 1892, i.e. whilst he was head of the Heidelberg Clinic. At the time, 'melancholia' was used by Kraepelin as a shorthand for 'involutional melancholia'; the rest he called 'depressive states'. Dreyfus completed the follow-ups in 1906, so the longest was about 14 years. He included 85 cases of which he described 44 in great detail, sometimes even transcribing daily medical entries from the index episode. In more than half of the total sample, Dreyfus managed personal follow-ups. A statistical analysis of Dreyfus' data (for details see Berrios 1991) shows that only 43 subjects improved, and that the only significant correlation of outcome was with age! ($r = 0.30$; $p<0.01$). When the sample is partialled out by sex, the correlation disappears for the males; in the females goes up to $r = 0.39$ ($p<0.01$). The rate of recovery seems to have been much higher for the younger group (Kraepelin, 1921; Brush, 1897). Thus, Dreyfus' conclusion that the natural history of involutional melancholia was no different from that of depression affecting younger subjects is not warranted by his data (he did not include a control group). Indeed, he did not notice that in his patients good outcome was correlated with lower age.

The great synthesis suggested by Kraepelin in the 8th edition of his textbook created as many problems as it solved. The history of the affective disorders in Europe and other parts of the world since his work can fairly be described as attempts at solving the various clinical problems and contradictions that his views created (Deny, 1909; Lange, 1928; Rocha, 1906; Soukhanoff and Gannouchkine, 1903; Rouart, 1936; Ey, 1954).

American Views

For example, these issues were discussed in a famous meeting of the New York Neurological Society on 1st November 1904, with the participation of great men such as Dana, Starr, Collins, Meyer, Parsons and Diefendorf.

Dana (1904) reported a personal series of 400 hundred cases of melancholia and divided them into two groups. One included cases with onset during 'involution or change of life'; this form was chronic and incurable, and was characterized by 'hypochondriacal and obsessive ideas, dysthesia, somatic delusions, hallucinations, self-accusations and at times suicidal ideas and impulses' (p.1032). A second group included cases starting in early life with no 'definite picture' which, according to Dana, Kraepelin wanted to classify under the manic-depressive umbrella. Dana believed that this latter group could also show the clinical features of the 'involutional type' but that in spite of these it often had good prognosis. Dana's was not the first large American series of melancholics to be reported. Brush (1897), from the Sheppard Asylum in Baltimore, read a paper at the 1897 Meeting of the British Medical Association describing 100 cases of acute melancholia and emphasizing the high incidence of physical disease. The same year, Weir Mitchell (1897) reported a series of 3000 cases of melancholia which he studied to test the hypothesis that cases were more 'apt to relapse in the spring or summer'. He found no evidence of seasonal changes.

European views remained predominant in the USA during this period. Smith Ely Jelliffe (1911) read a paper before the 66th Meeting of the American

Medico-Psychological Association on 'Cyclothemia (sic), the mild forms of manic depressive psychoses and the manic depressive constitution' and not once quoted an American colleague. On these mild forms, however, British psychiatrists had a great deal to say during the first 30 years of the twentieth century (see below).

Nineteenth century Great Britain
Prichard
British psychiatric taxonomy took an important step forward in the work of James Cowles Prichard. Although influenced by French views, Prichard showed originality in spite of the fact that, once again, he might not have had a great deal of clinical psychiatric experience (Stocking, 1978). Prichard (1835) classified melancholia as a subtype of 'moral insanity' (in fact, a disorder of the emotions): 'the faculty of reason is not manifestly impaired, but a constant feeling of gloom and sadness clouds all the prospects of life' 'this tendency to morbid sorrow and melancholy, as it does not destroy the understanding, is often subject to control when it first arises, and probably receives a peculiar character from the previous mental state of the individual' (p.18). Mania, in turn, was defined by Prichard (1835) in wider terms, as a form of 'raving madness' and on this he followed closely pre-nineteenth century views. There is little doubt that his clinical description does include, nonetheless, cases of acute psychotic mania, organic delirium and schizophrenia. Mania was for Prichard a harbinger for 'chronic and advanced states of madness' (p.79).

Bucknill and Tuke
In their 'classification', Bucknill and Tuke (1858) limited themselves to listing psychiatric conditions. Melancholia and mania are described as separate entities, but not classified as subtypes of 'emotional insanity' (except the subsyndrome that they called 'melancholia without delusions') (p.178). This listing of conditions without attempting to organise them according to some high level principle is a curious (and healthy) departure from contemporary fashion which, since the time of Pinel, and certainly of Esquirol, had dictated a threefold grouping for all insanities. Bucknill and Tuke listed six forms of melancholia: simple (non-psychotic), complicated (psychotic), acute, chronic, remittent and intermittent. Mania, in turn, was considered as a general form of madness, as Prichard had done before.

Maudsley
Maudsley's views (1895) on mania and melancholia, loosely follow the British tradition. He called melancholia 'insanity with depression' and made it tantamount to Bucknill and Tuke's 'simple melancholia' (i.e. non-psychotic depression). He also described a second group called 'melancholia with delusions' which more or less corresponds to the current concept of psychotic depression: 'in this form of depression the sad feeling is accompanied by a fixed sad idea or by a set of fixed sad ideas which crystallize, so to speak, out of or about it' 'out of the melancholic gloom emerge dimly and shape themselves by degrees positive delusions of thought' (p.188). In this category he included melancholia with stupor, acute delirious melancholia, and hypochondriacal melancholia, and

discussed symptoms such as suicide, homicide, and hallucinations. Maudsley's analysis of mania was symmetrical to that he afforded to melancholia. Mania was 'insanity with excitement' and included mania without delusion or simple mania where: 'there is an extraordinary excitement, without positive derangement, of feeling and thought: quickened thought flushed with elated and aggressive feeling', (p.234) and 'recovery not taking place, what other issues has acute mania? The next most common event is that it becomes chronic, the excitement subsiding but the derangement continuing' (p.262). Nodding in the general direction of the Continent, Maudsley concluded with regards to alternating recurrent insanity (*Folie Circulaire*): 'there is still one issue more of acute or rather subacute mania which it remains to take notice of – where it ends by being transformed, its seeming ending being but the beginning of an opposite – complexioned disorder. When the acute symptoms are past . . . the patient falls instead into an abject melancholy depression' (p.276).

The 1906 'Nomenclature of Diseases'

This pre-Kraepelinian view of melancholia and mania came to an end in Great Britain towards the turn of the century, after the rapid acceptance of the Kraepelinian view (Bolton, 1908). This acceptance was officialized in the fourth edition of the 'Nomenclature of Diseases' drawn up by the Joint Committee of the Royal College of Physicians of London (RCP, 1906) whose psychiatric members were George Savage and Percy Smith. 'Mania: Acute, recurrent and chronic' (code 145) appears as a separate disorder including seven subtypes (a to g): 'hysterical, puerperal, epileptic, alcoholic, senile, from other acute and chronic disease or from injury, and delirious'. 'Melancholia: acute, recurrent or chronic' (146) also appears under a different heading with seven subtypes (a to g): 'agitated, stuporous, hypochondriacal, puerperal, climacteric, senile, and from other acute or chronic disease or from injury'. Finally, 'Circular insanity, alternating insanity' (147) is included without subdivisions. This classification lasted until the great British debate of the 1920s.

Aetiological views

Little has been written on late nineteenth century British aetiological views on the affective disorders. This section will limit itself to listing the most popular hypotheses. G.M. Robertson (1890), then a senior assistant at the Morningside Asylum (later to become Professor of Psychiatry at Edinburgh), published in 1890 a provocative paper suggesting a 'modular' approach: 'what explanation is there of the existence of these symptoms of melancholia . . . in answering this question we must know that we are investigating a function of an organ which has become diseased; the function being the production of depressed or painful emotion' (p.53). Influenced by Darwin and Romanes, Robertson went on to identify a number of symptoms of melancholia (e.g. catalepsy) which he considered as the expression of vestigial behaviours.

Ten years later, John Turner (1900) asked another important question: 'very perplexing to the student of insanity is the question as to how states of exaltation or depression arise. . . . To what changes in the nervous system do they correspond? . . . Are these changes localized in different parts of the nervous system in mania and melancholia?' (p.505). Turner decided against the modular view and adopted a Jacksonian stance (for an account of Jackson's views see Berrios, 1985b): 'whilst both melancholia and mania are associated with a dissolution of the nervous system, in the former case the reduction takes place along sensory lines of the reflex nervous arc, and in the latter along motor lines' (Turner, 1900, p.506).

But, perhaps, the most accomplished paper on 'the cerebral localization of melancholia' was written by Bernard Hollander (1901) who, after reviewing the literature concluded that: 'a certain relation exists between the central area of the parietal lobe, namely, the angular and supramarginal gyri, and melancholic states of mind' (p.485).

Great Britain and the Continent

It has been shown that until the turn of the century, views on the affective disorders in France, Germany and Great Britain were more or less uniform. This is not very surprising as free communication existed between alienists from these nations (Tuke, 1892). Most European alienists shared the belief that mania and melancholia: a. resulted from a primary pathology of the emotions, b. could be combined in various ways, c. resulted from cerebral disease, d. were inherited, and e. could recover. Kraepelin's synthesis, although resisted in France, reinforced this uniformity.

The commonality of views lasted well into the 1920s, when some differences began to appear which originated from the selective attention that alienists from each country paid to aspects of the affective disorders. The British continued worrying about clinical description, severity and classification; the French about inheritance and environmental triggers; and the Germans, influenced by Kretschmer's original thinking, debated a great deal the question of constitution and personality factors. As an illustration of the internal debates that led to national differences we shall explore the British debate on classification.

Early twentieth century Great Britain

During the 1920s, British views began to depart from those held in the Continent. This resulted from uncertainties concerning the nosological position of what was called 'neurotic, reactive, exogenous, psychogenic or constitutional' affective disorders. The view that these might need including with the rest of manic-depressive insanity was based on a number of arguments: a. clinical observation, b. challenge to Kraepelin's dichotomous view, c. the growth of the psychodynamic hypothesis that there might be a 'continuity' between all forms of depression, and d. the influence of Meyerian psychiatry.

As we have seen, during most of the nineteenth century the classification of mania and melancholia (whatever their definition) had not been that difficult. Symptom pattern, presence or absence of delusions, course, and whether or not the two were combined proved sufficient taxonomic criteria. As we have also seen, the cases requiring classification were collected from the most severe end of the affective disorders (i.e. hospitalized patients). These classifications were, therefore, not encumbered by legions of minor and non-psychotic affective disorders which, up to the First World War, were mainly seen in private consulting rooms (Hopewell-Ash, 1934; Ross, 1923) under the diagnosis of hypochondria, hysteria, neurasthenia, agoraphobia or psychasthenia. Indeed, clinical analysis of cases under these rubrics (Sollier, 1893; Soukhanoff, 1909) shows that a good proportion of them would now be diagnosed as depressions and non-psychotic manic-depressive states. Apart from the social changes which led to differential patterns of care (e.g. the foundation of the Maudsley hospital with its emphasis on 'neurotic' out-patients), one of the most important factors in the rekindling of the classificatory debate in Great Britain was the dismembering of 'neurasthenia'; the reasons for this are beyond the scope of this chapter (see Chapter 20, this book) but suffice it to say that not all the cases this fragmentation set asunder could be taken over by its successor, another 'bridge' disease called psychasthenia (Janet, 1903). These cases were to constitute the large group that Montassut (1938) called in his masterly monograph 'constitutional depressions'. In addition, the impact of psychodynamic ideas was beginning to be felt (Newcombe and Lerner, 1981) particularly in relation to mechanisms such as 'reactivity', and the issue of the relationship between personality and depression. A good illustration of this influence is to be found in the British debate over the clinical place of the minor or 'neurotic' depressions.

Mapother

In 1926, Edward Mapother, then superintendent of the Maudsley Hospital (Petrie, 1940) presented a controversial paper in the Nottingham Meeting of the British Medical Association (Mapother, 1926). He stated that his problem was 'what meaning should be attached to the term "manic depressive psychosis" '. He believed that 'the range of the term was a matter of convention; at present there is no agreement, and no one with the authority to impose it' (p.872). In a Meyerian fashion he continued: All would probably agree that under the heading are included cases of functional mental disorder which show as their predominant features one of a contrasting pair of anomalous types of reaction: '1. The depressive reaction, and 2. the manic reaction'. He asked whether all cases with these symptoms should be included or only some, as some 'cases merge into those where constitutional symptoms of one kind or the other are pretty constantly present'. With scepticism he added: 'it is unproven and improbable that any mental syndrome is due to a specific cause, and consequently there is no more likelihood of a constant course in mania or depression than in jaundice' (p.872). He challenged the distinction between neuroses and psychoses which had 'really grown out of practical differences particularly as regards certification and asylum treatment', and concluded that since a distinction could not be made, it was nonsense to try and differentiate between neurotic (anxiety neurosis) and psychotic depression.

E. Farquhar Buzzard, who was chairing, disagreed on the view that these two conditions could not really be distinguished, as did Thomas A. Ross, from the Cassel Hospital, who stated that: 'if Dr. Mapother would carefully study mental states he would find that they would lead him to perceive fundamental differences between the psychoses and the psychoneuroses' (p.877) and added that these doubts originated from the fact that 'only a small section of the psychoneurotic group found their way to the Maudsley Hospital'!

Then, it was the turn of a young Scottish psychiatrist, then working under Ross, called Gillespie (Henderson, 1945) who rose to say that he was surprised about Mapother needing that a 'meaning should be attached to the term manic-depressive psychosis' and that 'the failure [by Mapother] to mention clinical criteria he would have regarded as an accident, were it not for his later remark that details of mental state were utterly unreliable' (Mapother, 1926, p.878) and that 'this tendency more or less unconscious to depreciate clinical differentiation gave the key to Dr. Mapother's subsequent surprising classification of all psychoneurosis as a subdivision of the manic depressive psychosis', 'the truth was that the latter was essentially a clinical conception, and that an attempt to define something that had been differentiated on purely clinical grounds in terms of the academic psychology after McDougall was likely to fail'. Gillespie then flew his own colours: 'The task of psychopathology at present was not so much the discovery of a physical basis – that was not psychopathology, and smacked of the pseudo-physiologizing of the latter half of the nineteenth century – but the unravelling of the meaning and origin of mental symptoms as such . . . it was to be regretted that Dr. Mapother had made no mention of McCurdy's work on the manic depressive psychosis . . . [whose] work did much to upset what might be called the "psychiatrist's fallacy" – that thought always followed emotion. Emotion probably more often followed thought' (Mapother, 1926, p.879). These statements by Gillespie, of importance to the history of the affective disorders in Great Britain, deserve further exploration.

Gillespie and the Cambridge Connection

Robert Dick Gillespie (1897–1945) had trained under D.K. Henderson in Glasgow, and A. Meyer in Baltimore; after a meteoric career he succeeded Sir Maurice Craig at Guy's. In his relatively short life he wrote with originality on fatigue, sleep, hypochondria and depression. In 1926, there was a good reason for Gillespie mentioning McCurdy. In fact, these two great men were to collaborate between 1927 and 1929, whilst Gillespie held the Pinsent-Darwin Research Studentship in Mental Pathology at Cambridge.

McCurdy (1886–1947) was a Canadian psychologist and psychiatrist who first trained as a biologist at Toronto University, and then as a physician at Johns Hopkins (Banister and Zangwill, 1949). After doing postgraduate work in neuropathology under Alzheimer in Munich, he returned to New York as a psychiatric assistant to August Hoch (McCurdy edited Hoch's *Bening stupors*, 1921). It is suggested in this chapter that the change of heart on the nature of the affective disorders shown by Gillespie (1929) between the Nottingham debate and the publication of his classical paper on the 'Clinical differentiation of types of depression' was due to McCurdy's influence.

In this seminal paper, Gillespie reviewed the literature in detail, particularly the work of Kraepelin, Lange, Cimbal and Kretschmer, searching for depressive states that might be dependent on special features of personality or identifiable environmental factors. He also reported 25 cases which he classified into reactive (14), autonomous (7) and involutional (4). He stated that the three could be distinguished in terms of family history, symptoms, personality, and response to life events. These criteria, in fact, he had borrowed from McCurdy (1925). In view of this, Kendell's (1968) comments that Gillespie provided no 'justification for his assumption that classification on the basis of reactivity was more useful or more valid than that based on another criterion' is, perhaps, too harsh.

Gillespie's paper must be read in conjunction with McCurdy's book, where both conceptual and therapeutic justifications (not statistical, for at the time such an evidential methodology was not yet part of medicine) are provided.

Buzzard and the 'milder forms'

Sir E. Farquhar Buzzard (1930) (knighted since chairing the BMA Nottingham meeting of 1926), returned to the issue of milder depressives without cyclothymia: 'We frequently see depressed patients who do not give this history of preceding elation or depression. A source of anxiety may be ascertained and its importance as an aetiological factor has to be measured. The sequence of events suggests that anxiety precipitated or caused depression' (p.881). Buzzard identified some distinguishing features:

> Having referred to the difficulty of diagnosis in the milder forms – and the milder the form, the more difficult the diagnosis . . . let me emphasize those [clinical points] which I have come to regard as most helpful: 1. the type of depression, 2. the loss of all natural and accustomed interests, 3. the self-reproach, 4. the preservation of sleep, 5. the history of hypomanic phase, 6. the coincident physical disturbances, and 7. the family history, particularly of suicide and alcoholism. (pp.882–3)

In the ensuing discussion H. Critchton-Miller 'regretted the title of the discussion . . . the term "manic-depressive psychosis" may be correct enough for use in mental hospitals but it suggests too much. The term "cyclothymia", on the other hand, covered the subject under discussion including the milder forms' (p.883). He emphasized how important it was to know the subject's pre-morbid personality, and criticized Kretschmer's for his over-simplistic distinction between 'cycloids' and 'schizoids'. Critchton-Miller was interested in the 'physiological aspects' of the disease:

> In the first place periodicity appears to be a physiological rather than a psychological quality . . . in the second place there is great similarity between the euphoria of alcoholic intoxication and the exaltation of the cyclothymic . . . thirdly, there is similarity between the depression associated with chronic intestinal absorption and the depressed phase of cyclothymia . . . fourthly the commonest example of cyclothymia occurs in some women in relation to the monthly cycle. (p.886)[8]

He concluded that 'the problem is not one for the psychologist, but for the biochemist'.[9]

Next, George Riddoch emphasized stress and the psychological aspects of the disease, and Henry Yellowlees felt that Kraepelin's taxonomy and psychology were out of date, and that the real clinical issue here was to differentiate the milder forms from neurasthenia; he concluded that they were talking about a physical disease and that psychological treatments were not indicated. W.R. Reynell agreed, and Helen Boyle (the only lady doctor to intervene in the debate) put forward an eclectic view based on Golla's endocrinological work (thyroid disorders) and Stoddart's psychodynamic theory. E.B. Strauss, who had spent some time at Marburg working under Kretschmer (whose translator into English he was to become), defended the views of his teacher, and emphasized the notion of 'reactive depression' which he defined as: 'a condition precipitated by an intolerable situation in the patient's life. It is allied to true neurasthenia, prison psychosis, and the like. Whether the condition is entirely exogenous or whether a current conflict stirs up and allies itself to unconscious mechanisms, may be debated by psychoanalysts' (in Buzzard, 1930 p.895).

The 'milder forms' in the Continent
A similar debate (although couched in different words) took place in France and Germany. It concerned the diagnosis and aetiology of the 'milder forms' of affective disorders. As mentioned above, the Kraepelinian synthesis had been based on the description of asylum cases, and had left out a large group of disorders composed of protracted griefs, dysphorias, minor depressions, anxiety disorders, and neurasthenias. Clinical decisions as to the nature of this group became important in the context of out-patient and private practice.

In comparison with his major contribution to the clinical and nosological aspects of the affective disorders, Kraepelin had been reticent on the role played by other modulatory factors, such as the 'personality'. On this the French were far more advanced (Binet, 1892; Ribot, 1884). After 1900, psychodynamic models and treatments became increasingly important: to these views, France was, perhaps, the most permeable of the three nations (Hesnard, 1971). As has been hinted above, the breaking up of the old group of 'neuroses' (e.g. neurasthenia and psychasthenia) (Berrios, 1985c) set asunder a large number of clinical states which (as the British debate showed) began to be considered as the 'milder' forms of manic-depressive illness. To many, this solution was not satisfactory as illustrated in the work of Courbon (1923), Rouart (1936), Benon (1937), and Montassut (1938). The British debate flared up in the 1930s, as a result of the work of Aubrey Lewis (1934, 1938) this has been well analyzed by Kendell (1968) and is not treated further here.

SUMMARY
This chapter has explored the origin of the 'depressive' states, and the way in which these were combined with mania by the middle of the nineteenth century. It has also mapped the manner in which this process unfolded in German, French, and British psychiatry. Finally, it has studied the history of involutional melancholia and statistically evaluated the empirical evidence on which Kraepelin based his decision to include this syndrome under the heading of manic depressive insanity. The relative unity of approach to melancholia and mania shown during most of the nineteenth century came to grief after the 1910s. A number of factors were responsible for this divergence. There was, first of all, a major increase in the size and variance of the patient database. To asylum patients (with chronic and severe illnesses often complicated by physical disease) cases were added from private practice, out-patients, the disintegration of the neurasthenia group; and those described as 'depressed' by the practitioners of psychoanalysis. During the 1920s, these 'milder' forms were diagnosed as manic-depressive, 'reactive', 'psychoneurotic' and 'personality' disorders. Current diagnostic categories have not yet fully escaped the influence of these early views.

NOTES

1 For Cullen's views, see chapter 12 on 'Unitary Psychosis' (this book); see also chapter 18 on 'Somatoform Disorders' (this book).

2 By *metalanguage* is meant here a language of description that can embrace previous discourses, and hence can operate one step removed from the process of change; by *metaperspective* is meant a notional vantage-point placed outside the temporal perspective. Metalanguage and metaperspective are, in a way, *desiderata* and not *real* options but are meant to illustrate the difficulties involved in trying to explain, from within *the current nosological and taxonomic discourse*, what the perception of mental disorder was in earlier times (see Berrios, 1995).

3 By this is meant 'something' which, once acquired, was not susceptible to come and go. In other words, insanity seem to lay outside time.

4 There is also the oft-told anecdote of the lunatic who, after behaving rationally in front of the mob, was given his freedom against Pinel's strongest advice. Once freed, he re-assumed his madness and had to be restrained. Although this is told to illustrate Pinel's great clinical acumen, the issue is, *how did he know?* My view is that he did not draw a conclusion based on probabilistic knowledge pertaining to a particular diagnosis; he simply based his prediction on the (ontological) belief that 'once a lunatic always a lunatic'; and this is the nearest one can get to understanding pre-1800 views on madness (see Haslam, 1809).

5 These were: a. total vs. partial, b. acquired vs. inherited, c. acute vs. chronic, d. anatomical vs. functional, e. reversible vs. irreversible, f. exogenous vs. endogenous, g. personality-related vs. not personality related, and h. form vs. content. In due course, the affective disorders were analysed vis-à-vis each of these dichotomies.

6 It is unclear when the word *dysthymia* was first used in a language other than Greek. The term δυσθυμίη is already found in Hippocrates (Aphorisms, VI, XXIII) although W.H.S. Jones translated it as 'depression' (Hippocrates, 1931 p.184). It is also inaccurate to say – as Hirschfield (1990) has done (quoting Jackson (1986)) – that 'Kahlbaum described depression in individuals with history of mania which he deemed "dysthymia". The origin of the DSM-III usage, on the other hand, seems to relate to a decision by R. Spitzer (T. Bronisch, personal communication).

7 Dreyfus, a Swiss psychiatrist, was born in Basle in 1879 and died in Zürich in 1957. He trained in Würzburg, Gießen and Heidelberg. In 1905, he came to work with Kraepelin in Munich. He then moved to Frankfurt where he was promoted in 1916 to a University Lectureship. He remained in this city until 1934, when he had to escape to Switzerland.

8 Crichton said this in spite of the reports to the contrary by Mitchell 1897.

9 The term 'cyclothymia' had been in use since the late nineteenth century; see: Bagenoff, 1911; Jelliffe, 1911, Soukanoff, 1909; Deny, 1908.

REFERENCES

Arnaud, S. (1899) 'La senescenza precoce nei melancolici'. *Rivista di Patologia Nervosa e Mentale*, 4: 362–7.

Bagenoff, T. (1911) 'La cyclothymie'. In Marie, A. (ed.) *Traité International de Psychologie Pathologique*, vol.2, Paris, Alcan, pp.709–22.

Baillarger, J.F. (1854) 'De la folie à double-forme'. *Annales Médico-Psychologiques*, 6: 367–91.

Banister, H. and Zangwill, O.L. (1949) 'John Thompson McCurdy (1886–1947)'. *British Journal of Psychology*, 40: 1–4.

Bash, K.W. (1955) *Lehrbuch der Allgemeinen Psychopathologie*, Stuttgart, Thieme.

Benon, R. (1937) *La mélancolie*, Paris, Marcel Vigné.

Bercherie, P. (1980) *Les Fondements de la Clinique*, Paris, Editions du Seuil.

Berger, K. (1907) 'Über die Psychosen des Klimakteriums'. *Monatschrift für Psychiatrie und Neurologie*, 22: 13–52.

Berrios, G.E. (1981) 'Stupor: a conceptual history'. *Psychological Medicine*, 11: 677–88.

Berrios, G.E. (1984) 'Descriptive Psychopathology: conceptual and historical aspects'. *Psychological Medicine*, 14: 303–13.

Berrios, G.E. (1985) 'The psychopathology of affectivity'. *Psychological Medicine*, 15: 745–58.

Berrios, G.E.(1985a) ' "Depressive pseudodementia" or "melancholic dementia": a nineteenth century view'. *Journal of Neurology, Neurosurgery and Psychiatry*, 48: 393–400.

Berrios, G.E. (1985b) 'Positive and negative symptoms and Jackson: a conceptual history'. *Archives of General Psychiatry*, 42: 95–7.

Berrios, G.E. (1985c) 'Obsessional disorders during the nineteenth century'. In Bynum, W.F., Porter, R. and Shepherd, M. (eds.) *The Anatomy of Madness*, vol.1, London, Tavistock, pp.166–87.

Berrios, G.E. (1987) 'Historical aspects of the psychoses: nineteenth century issues'. *British Medical Bulletin*, 43: 484–97.

Berrios, G.E. (1988) 'Melancholia and depression during the nineteenth century: a conceptual history'. *British Journal of Psychiatry*, 153: 298–304.

Berrios, G.E. (1988a) 'Depressive and manic states during the nineteenth century'. In Georgotas, A. and Cancro, R. (eds.) *Depression and Mania*, New York, Elsevier, pp.13–25.

Berrios, G.E. (1991) 'Affective disorders in old age: a conceptual history'. *International Journal of Geriatric Psychiatry*, 6: 337–46.

Berrios, G.E. (1995) *The history of mental symptoms: descriptive psychopathology since the 19th century*, Cambridge, Cambridge University Press.

Berrios, G.E. and Hauser, R. (1988) 'The early development of Kraepelin's ideas on classification: a conceptual history'. *Psychological Medicine*, 18: 813–21.

Berrios, G.E. and Luque, R. (1995) 'Cotard's delusion or syndrome?: A conceptual history'. *Comprehensive Psychiatry*, 36: 218–23.

Billod, E. (1856) 'Des diverses formes de lypémanie'. *Annales Médico-Psychologiques*, 2: 308–38.

Binet, A. (1892) *Les Altérations de la Personnalité*, Paris, Alcan.

Bolton, J.S. (1908) 'Maniacal-depressive insanity'. *Brain*, 31: 301–18.

Bronisch, T. (1990) 'Dysthyme Störungen'. *Nervenarzt*, 61: 133–9.

Brush, E.N. (1897) 'An analysis of one hundred cases of acute melancholia'. *British Medical Journal*, ii, 777–9.

Bucknill, J.C. and Tuke, D.H. (1858) *A Manual of Psychological Medicine*, London, John Churchill.

Buzzard, Sir E.F. (1930) 'Discussion on the diagnosis and treatment of the milder forms of the manic-depressive psychosis'. *Proceedings of the Royal Society of Medicine*, 23: 881–95.

Chaslin, Ph. (1912) *Eléments de Sémiologie et Clinique Mentales*, Paris, Asselin et Houzeau.

Cheyne, G. (1733) *The English Malady*, London, Strahan.

Cordeiro, J.C. (1973) 'Etats délirants du troisième age'. *L'Encéphale*, 62: 20–55.

Cotard, J. (1882) 'Du délire des négations'. *Archives de Neurologie*, 4: 152–70; 282–96.

Courbon, P. (1923) 'De la dualité étiologique de la manie et de la mélancolie'. *L'Encephale*, 18: 27–31.

Dana, C.L. (1904) 'A Discussion on the classification of the melancholias'. *Medical Record*, 66: 1033–5.

Darwin, C. (1872) *The Expression of the Emotions in Man and Animals*, London, John Murray.

Delasiauve, L. (1856) 'Du diagnostic différentiel de la lypémanie'. *Annales Médico-Psychologiques*, 3: 380–442.

Deny, G. (1908) 'La cyclothymie'. *La Semaine Médicale*, No 15, pp.169–71.

Deny, G. (1909) 'Représentation schématique et nomenclature des différentes formes de la psychose maniaque-dépressive'. *L'Encéphale*, 4: 363–6.

Deny, G. and Camus, P. (1907) *La Psychose Maniaque-dépressive*, Paris, Baillière.

Dreyfus, G.L. (1907) *Die Melancholie. Ein Zustandsbild des manisch-depressiven Irreseins*, Jena, Gustav Fischer.

Ducost, M. (1907) 'De L'involution présénile dans la folie maniaque-dépressive'. *Annales Médico-Psychologiques*, 65: 299–303.

Dumas, G. (1894) *Les Etats Intellectuels dans la Mélancolie*, Paris, Alcan.

Esquirol, J.E. (1820) 'Mélancolie'. In *Dictionnaire des Sciences Médicales par une Société de Médicins et de Chirurgiennes*, Paris, Panckoucke.

Ey, H. (1954) 'Les psychoses périodiques maniaco-depressives'. Etude No25 in *Etudes Psychiatriques*, vol.3, Paris, Desclée de Brouwer, pp.429–518.

Falret, J. (1851) 'Marche de la Folie', *Gazette des Hôpitaux*, 14th January, pp.19–23.

Falret, J.P. (1854) 'Mémoire sur la folie circulaire'. *Bulletin de l'Académie de Médicine*, 19: 382–415.

Falret, J. (1854a) *Leçons Cliniques de Médecine Mentale faites a la Salpêtrière. 1re Partie: Symptomatologie générale des Maladies Mentales*, 1 vol, Paris, Baillière.

Feuchtersleben, Baron von E. (1847) *The Principles of Medical Psychology*, London, Sydenham Society.

Fishbein, I.L. (1949) 'Involutional melancholia and convulsive therapy'. *American Journal of Psychiatry*, 106: 128–35.

Flemming, C.F. (1859) *Pathologie und Therapie der Psychosen*, Berlin, August Hirschwald.

Foville, A. (1882) 'Folie à double forme'. *Brain*, 5: 288–323.

Freud, S. (1963) 'Trauer und Melancholie'. *Gesammelte Werke*, vol.10, Frankfurt, Fischer, pp.152–70. (First publication, 1917).

Gaupp, R. (1905) 'Die Depressionszustnde des höheren Lebensalters'. *Münchener Medizinische Wochenschrift*, No22, pp.1531–7.

Gibson, E.T. (1918) 'A clinical summary of 106 cases of mental disorder of unknown etiology arising in the fifth and sixth decades'. *American Journal of Insanity*, 75: 221–49.

Gillespie, R.D. (1929) 'The clinical differentiation of types of depression'. *Guy's Hospitals Reports*, 79: 306–44.

Griesinger, W. (1861) *Die pathologie und Therapie der psychischen Krankheiten*, Stuttgart, Adolphe Krabbe.

Gruber, H.E. (1981) *Darwin on Man*, Chicago, University of Chicago Press.

Gull, W.W. (1894) *A Collection of the Published Writings of W W Gull*, (edited by T. Acland), 2 vols, London, New Sydenham Society.

Hare, E. (1991) 'The History of "Nervous Disorders" from 1600 to 1840, and a "comparison" with modern views'. *British Journal of Psychiatry*, 159: 37–45.

Haslam, J. (1809) *Observations on Madness and Melancholia*, 2nd edition, London, Callow.

Heinroth, J.C. (1975) *Textbook of Disturbances of Mental Life*, 2 vols, translated by J. Schmorak, Baltimore, the Johns Hopkins University Press.

Henderson, D.K. (1945) 'Robert Dick Gillespie'. *American Journal of Psychiatry*, 102: 572–3.

Hesnard, A. (1971) *De Freud à Lacan*, Paris, Les Editions ESF.

Hilts, V.L. (1967) *Statist and Statistician: Three Studies in the History of Nineteenth Century English Statistical Thought*, PhD Dissertation, Harvard University.

Hippocrates, (1931) *Hippocrates*, vol.4, London, Heinemann.

Hirschfield, R.M.A. (1990) 'Personality and dysthymia'. In Burton, S.W. and Akiskal, H.S. (eds.) *Dysthymic disorders*, London, Gaskell, pp.69–77.

Hoch, A. (1921) *Bening stupors*, Cambridge, Cambridge University Press.

Hollander, B. (1901) 'The cerebral localization of melancholia'. *Journal of Mental Science*, 47: 458–85.

Hopewell-Ash, E.L. (1934) *Melancholia in Everyday Practice*, London, Bale.

Jackson, S.W. (1986) *Melancholia and Depression*, New Haven, Yale University Press.

Janet, P. (1903) *Les Obsessions et la Psychasthénie*, Paris, Alcan.

Jastrow, J. (1901) 'Depression'. In Baldwin, J.M. (ed.) *Dictionary of Philosophy and Psychology*, vol.1, London, McMillan.

Jelliffe, S.E. (1911) 'Cyclothemia. The mild forms of manic-depressive psychosis and the manic-depressive constitution'. *American Journal of Insanity*, 67: 661–75.

Kahlbaum, K. (1863) *Die Gruppirung der psychischen Krankheiten und die Eintheilung der Seelenstrungen*, Danzig, A W Kafemann.

Katzenstein, R. (1963) *Karl Ludwig Kahlbaum. Und sein Beitrag zur Entwicklung der Psychiatrie*, Zürich, Juris.

Kendell, R.E. (1968) *The Classification of Depressive Illnesses*, London, Oxford University Press.

Ketal, R. (1975) 'Affect, mood, emotion and feeling: semantic considerations'. *American Journal of Psychiatry*, 132: 1215–17.

Kolle, K. (1963) 'Carl Friedrich Flemming'. In Kolle, K. (ed.) *Grosse Nervenärzte*, vol.3, Stuttgart, George Thieme, pp.61–8.

Kraepelin, E. (1920) 'Die Erscheinungsformen des Irreseins'. *Zeitschrift für die gesamte Neurologie und Psychiatrie*, 62: 1–29.

Kraepelin, E. (1921) *Manic-depressive Insanity*, Edinburgh, E & S Livingstone.

Kraepelin, E. (1983) *Lebenserinnerungen*, Berlin, Springer.

Krafft-Ebing, R. (1879) *Lehrbuch der Psychiatrie*, Stuttgart, Enke.

Krueger, F. (1928) 'Das Wessen der Gefühle'. *Archiv für die gesamte Psychologie*, 65: 91–128.

Lanczik, M. (1988) *Der Breslauer Psychiater Carl Wernicke*, Sigmaringen, Thorbecke.

Lange, J. (1928) 'Die endogenen und reaktiven Gemütserkrankungen'. In vol.2, Bumke, O. (ed.) *Handbuch der Geisteskrankheiten*, Berlin, Springer, pp.120–70.

Leeper, R.W. (1948) 'A motivational theory of emotion to replace emotion as a disorganized response'. *Psychological Review*, 55: 5–21.

Lewis, A. (1934) 'Melancholia: a clinical survey of depressive states'. *Journal of Mental Science*, 80: 277–378.

Lewis, A. (1938) 'States of depression'. *British Medical Journal*, ii, 875–8.

Mairet, D. (1883) *De la Démence Mélancolique*, Paris, Masson.

Mantegazza, P. (1878) *Fisionomia e mimica* (English translation: *Physiognomy and Expression*, no date, London, Walter Scott).

Mapother, E. (1926) 'Discussion on manic-depressive psychosis'. *British Medical Journal*, ii, 872–9.

Maudsley, H. (1895) *The Pathology of Mind. A study of its Distempers, Deformities and Disorders*, London, MacMillan.

Mayne, R.G. (1860) *An Expository Lexicon of the Terms, Ancient and Modern in Medical and General Science*, London, Churchill.

McCurdy, J.T. (1925) *The Psychology of Emotion. Morbid and abnormal*, London, Kegan Paul, Trench, Trubner & Co.

Meyer, A. (1901) 'Melancholia'. In Baldwin, J.M. (ed.) *Dictionary of Philosophy and Psychology*, vol.2, London, McMillan, pp.61–2.

Mitchell, S.W. (1897) 'An analysis of 3000 cases of melancholia'. *Transactions of the Association of American Physicians*, 12: 480–7.

Montassut, M. (1938) *La Dépression Constitutionnelle*, Paris, Masson.

Mordret, E. (1883) *De la Folie à Double Forme*, Paris, Baillière.

Newcombe, N. and Lerner, J.C. (1981) 'Britain between the Wars: the historical context of Bowlby's theory of attachment'. *Psychiatry*, 44: 1–12.

Owens, H. and Maxmen, J.S. (1979) 'Mood and affect: a semantic confusion'. *American Journal of Psychiatry*, 136: 97–9.

Petrie, A. (1940) 'Edward Mapother'. *Journal of Mental Science*, 106: 747–9.

Phillips, J. (1912) 'Involutional conditions'. In Mott, F.W. (ed.) *Early Mental Disease*, The Lancet, Extra Numbers No2, London, Wakley & Son, pp.90–2.

Phillips, J. (1912a) 'Psychoses associated with senility and arteriosclerosis'. In Mott, F.W. (ed.) *Early Mental Disease*, The Lancet Extra Numbers No 2, London, Wakley & Son, pp.146–8.

Pichot, P. (1995) The birth of the bipolar disorder. *European Psychiatry*, 10:1–10.

Pinel, Ph. (1809) *Traité Médico-Philosophique sur l'Aliénation Mentale*, Paris, Brosson.

Post, F. (1965) *The Clinical Psychiatry of late Life*, Oxford, Pergamon Press.

Prichard, J.C. (1835) *A Treatise on Insanity and Other Disorders Affecting the Mind*, London, Sherwood, Gilbert and Piper.

Régis, E. (1885) *Manuel Pratique de Médecine Mentale*, Paris, Doin.

Rennert, H. (1968) 'Wilhelm Griesinger und die Einheitpsychose'. *Wissenschaftliche Zeitschrift der Humboldt-Universität*, 17: 15–16.

Ribot, Th. (1897) *The Psychology of Emotions*, London, Walter Scott.

Ribot, Th. (1884) *Les Maladies de la Personnalité*, Paris, Alcan.

Ritti, A. (1876) 'Folie à Double Forme'. In Dechambre, A. (ed.) *Dictionnaire Encyclopédique des Sciences Médicales*, Paris, Masson, pp.321–39.

Ritti, A. (1883) *Traité Clinique de la Folie a Double Forme*, Paris, Doin.

Robertson, G.M. (1890) 'Melancholia, from the physiological and evolutionary points of view'. *Journal of Mental Science*, 36: 53–67.

Rocha, D. (1906) 'La psychose maniaque-dépressive'. *Annales Médico-Psychologiques*, 64: 250–62.

Ross, T.A. (1923) *The Common Neurosis*, London, Arnold.

Rouart, J. (1936) *Psychose Maniaque Dépressive et Folies Discordantes*, Paris, Doin.

Roubinovitch, J. (1896) *Des Variétés Cliniques de la Folie en France et en Allemagne*, Paris, Doin.

RCP (1906) *Royal College of Physicians of London: The Nomenclature of diseases*, Fourth edition, London, His Majesty's Stationary Office.

Rush, B. (1812) *Medical Inquiries and Observations upon the Diseases of the Mind*, Philadelphia, Kimber & Richardson.

Saury, H. (1886) *Etude Clinique sur la Folie Héréditaire*, Paris, Delahaye et Lecrosnier.

Savage, G. (1898) *Insanity and the Allied Neuroses*, London, Cassell.

Sérieux, P. (1907) 'Review of Dreyfus's book'. *L'Encéphale*, 2: 456–8.

Sérieux, P. and Capgras, J. (1909) *Les Folies Raisonnantes. Le Délire d'Interprétation*, Paris, Alcan.

Sollier, P. (1893) 'Sur une forme circulaire de la neurasthénie'. *Revue de Médicine*, 13: 1009–19.

Soukhanoff, S. and Gannouchkine, P. (1903) 'Etude sur la mélancolie'. *Annales Médico-Psychologiques*, 61: 213–38.

Soukhanoff, S. (1909) 'La cyclothymie et la psychasthénie'. *Annales Médico-Psychologiques*, 67: 27–38.

Stocking, Jr., G.W. (1978) Introduction. In Prichard, J.C. *Researches into the Physical History of Man*, Reprinted, Chicago, The University of Chicago Press, pp.ix–cx.

Thalbitzer, S. (1926) *Emotions and insanity*, London, Kegan Paul, Trench, Trubner & Co.

Treadway, W.L. (1913) 'The presenile psychoses'. *Journal of Nervous and Mental Disease*, 40: 375–87.

Tuke, D.H. (ed.) (1892) *Dictionary of Psychological Medicine*, 2 vols, London, Churchill.

Turner, J. (1900) 'A theory concerning the physical conditions of the nervous system which are necessary for the production of states of melancholia, mania, etc'. *Journal of Mental Science*, 46: 505–12.

Wahrig-Schmidt, B. (1985) *Der junge Wilhelm Griesinger*, Tübingen, Gunter Narr.

Zerssen, D. (1988) 'Definition und Klassifikation affektiver Störungen aus historischer Sicht'. In Zerssen, D. von and Müller, H.J. (eds.) *Affektive Störungen*, Berlin, Springer, pp.3–11.

Chapter 15
Mood Disorders

Social Section
ROY PORTER

To the social historian, the common pairing of depression with mania, both in psychiatry and in the popular mind, points to extra layers of meaning setting the realities of medical science and the clinical record in fuller contexts. It should first be noted that with melancholy and mania – unlike, say, schizophrenia – disease categories are encountered that were 'framed and named' (Rosenberg, 1989) at the dawn of learned medicine, concepts destined to root and blossom over the centuries. Numerous Greek medical writers offered recognizable profiles of the two conditions. The fullest early clinical descriptions were advanced by Galen's (130–199) contemporary, Aretaeus (c AD 150–200). Born in Asia Minor, Aretaeus studied in Alexandria before going to Rome to practice medicine. His accounts of melancholia and mania are contained in the first book of *De Causis et Signis Morborum*. 'The patients are dull or stern: dejected or unreasonably torpid, without any manifest cause: such is the commencement of melancholy', Aretaeus observed:

> and they also become peevish, despirited, sleepless, and start up from a disturbed sleep. Unreasonable fears also seize them. . . . They are prone to change their mind readily, to become base, mean-spirited, illiberal, and in a little time perhaps simple, extravagant, munificent not from any virtue of the soul but from the changeableness of the disease. But if the illness becomes more urgent, hatred, avoidance of the haunts of men, vain lamentations are seen: they complain of life and desire to die; in many the understanding so leads to insensibility and fatuousness that they become ignorant of all things and forgetful of themselves and live the life of inferior animals.

As Berrios (1988) has insisted, it would be anachronistic to conflate the medical concept of melancholia with popular and more modern meanings of the term, evoking as they do a wistful poetic sadness, as in John Keats's (1795–1821) ode 'On Melancholy' (1809). For within post-Aretaean medical theories, melancholia was standardly regarded as a severe mode of mental disturbance. Sorrow and dejection were essential elements, but, from Antiquity to the Renaissance, melancholia involved powerful emotions linked to hallucinations and sensations of suspicion, mistrust, anxiety and trepidation – as Robert Burton's (1577–1640) *Anatomy of Melancholy* (1621) readily shows. Delusory elements had already been well-drawn in Antiquity. 'The patient may imagine he has taken another form than his own', Aretaeus commented:

one believes himself a sparrow; a cock or an earthen vase; another a God, orator or actor, carrying gravely a stalk of straw and imagining himself holding a sceptre of the World; some utter cries of an infant and demand to be carried in arms, or they believe themselves a grain of mustard, and tremble continuously for fear of being eaten by a hen; some refuse to urinate for fear of causing a new deluge.

As demonstrated by Speak (1990), these tropes – the man too terrified to urinate, the patient convinced he was made of glass and liable to shatter at any moment – remained in circulation at least until the eighteenth century.

For Aretaeus, depression was a serious condition. The delusions, obsessions and *idées fixes* of the melancholic could be deeply destructive. 'The melancholic isolates himself, he is afraid of being persecuted and imprisoned, he torments himself with superstitious ideas, he hates life . . . he is terror-stricken, he mistakes his fantasies for the truth . . . he complains of imaginary diseases, he curses life and wishes for death'.

Alongside melancholia, Aretaeus depicted mania, marked by its un-controllability. Mania found vent in various kinds of excess, in 'furor, excitement and cheerfulness'. In serious forms of *furor*, the sick person 'sometimes kills and slaughters the servants'; in less severe instances, he might become grandiose: 'without being cultivated he says he is a philosopher . . . and the incompetent [say they are] good artisans'. Mania was often euphoric: the sufferer 'has deliriums, he studies astronomy, philosophy . . . he feels great and inspired'.

Rationalist by temper, Aretaeus paid particular attention to the collective outbursts of cultic activity that had stained Greek history and were still flourishing in the Roman Empire. He analysed religious mania involving pos-session by a god (divine furor), especially amongst those adhering to goddess cults such as that of Cybele (Juno). Amongst devotees in 'enthusiastic and ecstatic states', processions were held, and, as with the Corybants of old, believers 'would castrate themselves and then offer their penis to the goddess'. All this, Aretaeus considered, betrayed 'an insanity . . . in an ill, drunken and confused soul'. At the height of orgiastic delirium, he observed, fanatics 'some-times do harm to themselves and beat themselves . . . they think that their god wants them to suffer . . . it is a sort of divine furor'. In compensation, zealots experienced sensations of inner transformations they believed derived from divine inspiration, feeling elated and euphoric, and worshipping the god of ecstacy and the dance.

Aretaeus also linked mania with intoxication, brought about by 'ingestion of wine, mandrake or black henbane'. Mania in general was the product of excessive heat, conducted through the blood and originating in the heart, the seat of innate vital heat and sympathetically connected with the brain. The origin of mania thus lay in the heart which inflamed the mind. The significance of such views will become apparent.

It has been noted by sleuths of 'anticipations' that Aretaeus was aware of bipolar disorders. Roccatagiata (1986) has thus stated that Aretaeus identified cyclothymia as a form of mental disease presenting phases of depression alternating with mania. In a sense that is correct. 'Some patients after being melancholic have fits of mania', Aretaeus observed, 'so that mania is like a variety of melancholy'. Aretaeus described conditions in which, in certain cases, 'melancholy is the commencement and a part of mania', whereas in others a person previously vivacious and euphoric suddenly 'has a tendency to melancholy; he becomes, at the end of the attack, languid, sad, taciturn, he complains that he is worried about his future, he feels ashamed'. After the depressive phase, such patients might revert to a hyperactive, manic mode: 'they show off in public with crowned heads as if they were returning victorious from the games; sometimes they laugh and dance all day and all night'. Sometimes mania lapsed not into melancholy but into dementia. 'There are patients suffering from a serious form of mania, who after an illness become insensitive; their intelligence degrades, they sink into the utmost imbecility, they forget themselves and spend the rest of their lives like brutes'.

It is thus in some respects true that Aretaeus had an inkling of manic-depressive disorders. He certainly depicted a complex picture of melancholia involving wild mood swings: 'In certain cases melancholy seems to be a demi-mania . . . the patients are always obsessed with the same idea . . . but the patient can be depressed and gay at the same time'. Melancholy involved a dry and cold brain, mania a dry and hot brain: these were two poles. And, if we choose, we may cast our eyes forward from Antiquity to the nineteenth-century French psychiatrists – Falret (1794–1870), Baillarger (1809–90), and Kahlbaum (1828–99) – whose work on circular or double insanity helped to create the category *manic-depressive psychosis* – and find them referring back to Aretaeus as a forerunner or totemic authority. So did Kraepelin (1856–1926), who was deeply influenced by Falret and who offered the classic formulation of manic-depressive psychosis in the sixth edition of his *Textbook of Psychiatry* (1899). Yet we must avoid hindsight and mischaracterisation.

Accounts of madness advanced in the Middle Ages and the Renaissance bear striking similarities to those developed in Antiquity. The terms melancholia and mania (or simply 'madness') dominated conceptualizations. Denis Fontanon (d. 1547), a professor at Montpellier argued *à propos* of mania in his *De Morborum Interiorum Curatione Libri Tres* (1549):

> This disease occurs when the brain suffers either by itself or by reason of sympathetic reaction. It occurs sometimes solely from the warmer in-temperatura of the brain without a harmful humour, and this is like what happens in drunkenness. It occasionally arises from stinging and warm humours, such as yellow bile, attacking the brain and stimulating it along with its membranes. It sometimes even originates in incorrupt blood which may even be temperate but which harms the brain by its quantity alone.

Fontanon explored the varieties of mania, explaining their disparate features and causes. It was a good sign, he thought, if laughter were mixed with mania; whereas when the mixture of blood and choler (yellow bile) was 'burned', that is especially heavy and thickened, that was a truly dangerous indication, for there would be 'brutal madness (furor) and this is the most dangerous mania of all'.

Fontanon's younger Montpellier contemporary, Felix Plater (1536–1614), similarly depicted mania as excess. As in melancholia, its victims would 'imagine, judge, and remember things falsely'. Unlike the melancholy man, the maniac would also 'do everything unreasonably':

> Sometimes they are the authors of relatively modest words and deeds which are not accompanied by raving but more frequently, changed into rage, they express their mental impulse in a wild expression and in word and deed. Then they come out with false, obscene and horrible things, exclaim, swear, and with a certain brutal appetite, undertake different things, some of them very unheard of for men under any circumstances, even to the point of bestiality, behaving like animals. Some of them seek sexual satisfaction particularly intensely. I saw this happen to a certain noble matron, who was in every other way most honorable, but who invited by the basest words and gestures men and dogs to have intercourse with her. Add to these, cases where they try to do violence to themselves and to others: they pull their hair out, tear their clothes and sometimes injure their own bodies some way or other by biting. Unless they are tightly bound by bonds and chains, which however they strive with every effort to break, and are kept under guard and locked up (where they will often try as hard as they can to break down doors or escape from their prison by digging), they will attack bystanders, and, like beasts, try to scratch, bite, strangle and kill them.

Plater's depiction of melancholia highlighted anxiety and delusion. Melancholy, he emphasized, echoing Aretaeus, was 'a kind of mental alienation, in which imagination and judgement are so perverted that without any cause the victims become very sad and fearful'. The disorder was a castle of delusion built upon false images.

A final instance may be cited of the shaping of early modern ideas of insanity by the twinning of melancholy and mania. After the rebuilding of Bethlem Hospital in London in the 1670s, a pair of sculptures was commissioned, carved by Caius Gabriel Cibber (1630–1700), to straddle the main gateway. One figure depicted a raving maniac, naked, muscle-bound, tense, fierce, restrained by chains, a figure more brutish than human. The other seems to portray a melancholic, lethargic, morose, with his hand tellingly hidden from sight; in traditional iconography, a hidden hand symbolized one that was doing no work, and, traditionally, it was thought that the Devil 'made work' for idle hands, thus implying connections between melancholy and diabolical possession. As Gilman (1982) and Kromm (1984) have emphasized, the Renaissance iconography of insanity prominenced paired but contrasted maniacal and melancholic types.

Two images, the maniac and the melancholic, have thus been much in evidence. Various explanations could be offered, in addition to the claim clinicians would advance that such types are true-to-life expressions of underlying psychopathologies ever visible to the discerning physician. For one thing, Classical medicine possessed immense intellectual authority down into the eighteenth century. Enjoying the prestige of academic learned medicine, the theories of ancient physicians rightly carried, many asserted, greater weight than the observations of fallible eyes; reason and philosophy were often commended over mere 'empiricism'. The medical profession itself was profoundly hierarchical and authoritarian. Under such circumstances, doctrines promulgated by Classical writers readily assumed a medical reality of their own. It is instructive to find the disease descriptions of Aretaeus still looming large, for both substantive and ceremonial reasons, in such eighteenth-century volumes as William Pargeter's (1760–1810) *Observations on Maniacal Disorders* (1792).

The authority of Classical medical theorizations helps explain the persistence of the stereotyping of mania and melancholy. For these two conceptions were deeply entrenched within the humoral medical system adumbrated in Antiquity and influential for the next two thousand years. Broadly speaking, humoralism saw the body's state in terms of rhythms of development and change, determined by the major fluids constrained within the skin-envelope, health or illness resulting from their balance. Classically, these crucial vitality-sustaining juices were blood, choler (or yellow bile), phlegm, and melancholy (or black bile – Greek *melaina kole* – a bitter toxic, gall-like humour produced in the intestine or spleen). The different humours served disparate life-sustaining ends. Blood was the liquor of vitality. Choler or bile was the gastric juice, indispensable for digestion. Phlegm, a broad category comprehending all colourless secretions, was a lubricant and coolant. Visible in substances like sweat and tears, it was most evident when in excess – at times of cold and fever, when it appeared through the mouth and nose. The fourth great fluid, black bile, or melancholy, was more problematic. A dark liquid almost never found neat, it was reckoned responsible for darkening other fluids, as when blood, skin or stools turned blackish.

Between them, the four major fluids accounted for the tangible phenomena of physical existence: temperature, colour and texture. Blood made the body hot and wet, choler hot and dry, phlegm cold and wet, and black bile produced cold and dry sensations. Parallels were drawn with the great elementary substances in the universe at large. Being hot and animated, blood was like fire; choler was like air, being warm and dry; phlegm suggested water (cold and wet), and black bile (melancholy) resembled earth (cold and dry). Such analogies further suggested and meshed with other facets of the natural world, such as astrological forces and seasonal variations. Cold and wet, winter had affinities with phlegm; it was the time people caught cold; and so forth. Each fluid also had its distinctive colour – blood being red, choler yellow, phlegm pale and melancholy dark. These hues were responsible for body coloration, giving the vital clue as to why distinct races were white, black, red, or yellow, and why certain individuals were lighter, swarthier, or ruddier than others.

Humoral balance also explained the spectrum of dispositions and temperaments, or what would, in later centuries, be called personality and psychology. Thus a person generously endowed with blood would present a florid complexion and have a 'sanguine' temperament, being lively, energetic and robust, though perhaps given to hot-bloodedness. Someone cursed with surplus choler or bile might be choleric or acrimonious – in other words, marked by an acid tongue. Likewise with phlegm (pale, and phlegmatic, and cool in character) and black bile (a person with swarthy looks and a saturnine disposition). There was, in short, infinite explanatory promise in such rich holistic linkages of physiology, psychology and bearing, not least because it suggested plausible bridges between inner constitutional states ('temper') and outer physical manifestations ('complexion'): something not just intuitively convincing, but quite indispensable, so long as science had little direct, independent access to events beneath the skin.

Humoral thinking had ready explanations for the lapse from health into illness, both physical and psychological (though these were never contrasted as opposites in the humoral system, with its holistic disposition).

All was well when the vital fluids peacefully co-existed in a proper balance. Illness resulted when one of them accumulated (became 'plethoric') or dried up. If, perhaps through faulty diet, the body made too much blood, 'sanguinous disorders' followed – or, in a modern idiom, blood pressure rose – and one grew overheated and feverish. One might, by consequence, suffer haemorrhage, have a seizure, apoplectic fit, or a heart attack. Deficiency of blood or poor blood quality, by contrast, meant loss of vitality, while blood loss due to wounds would lead to fainting or death. In the psychiatric domain, excesses both of blood and of yellow bile could lead to mania; a surplus of black bile resulted in melancholy or depression.

Fortunately these imbalances were capable of correction, through sensible lifestyle, or by medical or surgical means. The person whose liver 'concocted' a surfeit of blood or whose blood was thought to be polluted – both could cause mania – should undergo blood-letting (for long a favourite therapeutic intervention in Europe's lunatic asylums). Change of diet could help. Raving madmen would be put on a 'diluting' and 'cooling' diet, with green vegetables, barley water and milk puddings. Enormously detailed recommendations, in respect of diet, exercise, life-style and so forth, were spelt out in such works as the *Anatomy of Melancholy* (1621) by Robert Burton, with its gloomy portrait gallery of taciturn, solitary, and deluded melancholics. Burton's therapeutic recommendations ran the gamut of remedies suggested since the Ancients: exercise, distractions, travel, purgatives, bloodletting, diet, sexual moderation, and so on. Amongst other means, Burton urged music therapy for depression, a recommendation common since Old Testament times – in the first book of Samuel it is stated:

> And it came to pass, when the evil spirit from God was upon Saul, that David took the harp, and played with his hand: so Saul was refreshed, and was well, and the evil spirit departed from him. [1 Sam. 16:23]

Burton's mammoth work concluded with the admonition, 'Be not solitary, be not idle', advice the author himself had evidently only half-followed.

The significance of the humoral system lies in the fact that it provided a comprehensive intellectual explanatory scheme, embracing the natural and the human, the physical and the mental, the healthy and the pathological, and drawing upon simple archetypal elements (hot/cold, wet/dry, etc.) It was capable of technical elaboration by the physician while also comprehensible to the layman. Within its concrete and easy-to-visualize grid, it was simple to piece together the elements to form a picture of mania: clear 'spaces' and 'positions' existed for them (literally viewed in terms of up and down, high and low) within the commonsensical plan. And the humoral latticework encouraged the conceiving of contraries and oppositional thinking. In a scheme in which healthiness lay in the equilibrium of antitheses, and disorders lay in extremities, mania almost demanded the existence of an equal but opposite pathological state, depression. In other words, so long as humoralism was in the saddle, shaping the consciousness of the educated world, notions of mania and melancholy, representing hot and cold, wet and dry, 'red' and 'black' conditions respectively, were likely to remain ingrained, cognitively, graphically, emotionally, and perhaps even subliminally.

Plunging into more speculative waters, it might further be argued that the imaging of bipolarity, the manic-depressive disorder, does not only draw upon the schematization presented by the humoral grid but is further dependent upon subconscious or archetypal, religio-mystical myths of polarity. Ideas that the individual comprises some sort of amalgam or struggle of opposites (body and soul, good and evil, the divine and the diabolic, male and female) run deep in Western culture, encouraged by philosophical dualisms deriving from Platonic and Pauline sources and reinforced by Cartesian philosophy. Concepts of alternating manic and depressive illness phases are easily embraced by a culture proclaiming the opposition of body and soul, and the reality of psychomachy, God struggling with Satan for possession of the soul. Later cultural beliefs, such as the Romantic notion of the *Doppelgänger* and the idea, fashionable in the *fin de siècle* era, of Jekyll-and-Hyde 'doubles', to say nothing of the image of interpenetrating masculine and feminine personality components postulated from alchemy through to the Jungian *animus* and *anima*, are all highly compatible with manic-repressive bipolarity.

Space limitations preclude systematic chronological documentation of the theories of mania and depression; it would in any case be unnecessary, since Jackson (1987) offers a magisterial account not just of depression but of mania too. But a few key themes are worth singling out. It seems noteworthy, for one thing, that mania proper (though maybe not the monomanias) has attracted less detailed cultural attention than its twin, melancholy. The maniac has, of course, been an object of profound public concern. Both formerly and nowadays, violent and dangerous characters fill the public imagination, not least in films like *Psycho* or *The Silence of the Lambs*. Popular culture tends to see the psychopath as the paradigm case of the insane or disturbed individual, generating belief that the insane *en bloc* need to be safely 'locked away'. Nevertheless, broadly speaking, the maniac has been a two-dimensional figure in art and literature, a cardboard caricature of rather limited subtlety. And this is because he has generally been construed in essentially negative terms, as 'other' or 'alien'. Above all, from Antiquity through to the seventeenth century – some like Scull (1989) would contend far beyond – the madman was envisaged as a monster, to be treated as an animal, with coercive measures like chains and whips. The maniac was beyond discourse and society, bereft of reason and humanity. In various ways he was unhuman; allegedly maniacs did not catch regular diseases or suffer from heat or cold. 'It would be almost too shocking to portray the real features of this terrible complaint', William Pargeter characterized the maniac,

> yet, in order to a conception of it, they ought in some measure to be contemplated. Let us then figure to ourselves the situation of a fellow creature destitute of the guidance of that governing principle, reason – which chiefly distinguishes us from the inferior animals around us, and gives us a striking superiority over the beasts that perish. View man deprived of that noble endowment, and see in how melancholy a posture he appears. He retains indeed the outward figure of the human species, but like the ruins of a once

magnificent edifice, it only serves to remind us of his former dignity, and fills us with gloomy reflections for the loss of it. Within, all is confused and deranged, every look and expression testifies internal anarchy and disorder. The wretched victim now tortured with ideal woes – his distempered fancy transforms his best friends into the bitterest enemies, and he views them with implacable aversion or with disdain – he swells with pomp, or shrinks with terror, sometimes breathing menaces against his opposers, and sometimes trembling with apprehensions of their displeasure. He now relapses into sullen insensibility – the delirium again returns, and he raves with all the vehemence of exasperated fury – far from attending to his own preservation, he is incapable of using the least effort for his safety – reduced to the mental weakness of a child, he is indebted to the friendly care and precaution of others for his very existence. Without this necessary interposition, the wretched sufferer would but too frequently execute deliberate vengeance on himself, and thus end his miseries and his life together. What then can be more melancholy – what misfortune more afflictive, than to labour under the pressure of this dreadful malady?

The maniac thus became unthinkable, unspeakable. Gilman (1982; 1985; 1988) has argued that societies feed off images of their opposites. In order to forge a cohesive self-identity and a psychological sense of security, in order to expel fears and hatreds, deflecting and projecting them elsewhere, the dominant culture constructs maps of reality, that operate through the principles of inclusion and exclusion, polarizing the world into insiders and outsiders, natives and foreigners, men and women, white and black, straight and gay. Amongst the many groups scapegoated and anathematized by such 'us and them' mentalities, 'maniacs' have been prominent. For the polarity between the 'wild man' or animal and the civilized man packs ideological power. This, however, has entailed the cultural construction of the maniac as primarily a negation.

By contrast, the melancholic type has been not inhuman but intriguing. The depressive has been seen in positive terms, often accorded an eminent social role. In such characterisations, intellectual roots are of importance. From the Greeks, mental peculiarity could be construed as a mark of distinction. Notably in the *Phaedrus*, Plato (c.428–348BC) spoke of the 'divine fury' of the poet, and Aristotle (384–322BC) was to paint the portrait of the melancholy genius. Such views were perpetuated in the Renaissance by Ficino (1433–99) and numerous other humanists; it was a commonplace that to dub a poet 'mad' was to pay him a compliment. Michael Drayton (1563–1631) thus praised Kit Marlowe (1564–93):

> For that fine madness still he did retain,
> Which rightly should possess a poet's brain.

In the early modern period, melancholics were often regarded as gifted, special. There were religious melancholics believed to be in receipt of prophetic voices from on High – or, alternatively, suffering from Satanic possession. There were poets, painters, artists and intellectuals whose melancholy begat the individuality that attested their divine gifts and genius. And, at least in fiction and on the stage, there were melancholy malcontents like Prince Hamlet, dressed all in black, difficult, disdainful, dangerous. Yet, for Hamlet or for Jaques in *As You Like It*, there was another side, something bittersweet to be savoured in a contemplative sorrow (Jaques spoke of sucking 'melancholy out of a stone'). Given man's mortality and the mutability of things, and the dog-eats-dog ferocity of politics in the world of Machiavelli – so argued Robert Burton in his almost obsessional *Anatomy of Melancholy* (1621) – only a great oaf would not meet life's changes and chances with sober sadness. Melancholy madness was thus the only reasonable response of an intelligent man to a crazy world:

> When I go musing all alone,
> Thinking of divers things fore-known,
> When I build Castles in the air,
> Void of sorrow and void of fear,
> Pleasing my self with phantasms sweet,
> Methinks the time runs very fleet.
> All my joys to this are folly,
> Naught so sweet as Melancholy.
>
> When I lie waking all alone,
> Recounting what I have ill done,
> My thoughts on me then tyrannise,
> Fear and sorrow me surprise,
> Whether I tarry still or go,
> Methinks the time moves very slow.
> All my griefs to this are jolly,
> Naught so sad as Melancholy.

Cultural images of the melancholy man underwent considerable change after the mid-seventeenth century. On the one hand, religious melancholy ceased to be an acceptable ideal. After the bloodshed of the witch-craze, the Thirty Years' War on the Continent and the English Civil War, public opinion turned against Ranters, Shakers and all the lunatic fringe of religious zealots spawned by the Reformation. Propertied, powerful and polite interests discredited the so-called revelations of visionaries, and declared the possessed merely crackbrained, victims of the spleen or other morbid conditions. Social retrenchment, the scientific revolution and the dawning of the Enlightenment together disconfirmed religious madness, and transformed the old category of religious melancholy into a wholly negative, psychopathological image, a state of self-deception or -delusion, caused (so argued physicians like George Cheyne (1671–1743) and Richard Blackmore (d.1729)), by organic illness, the vapours or hypochondria. Amongst progressive Enlightenment physicians, 'humoral medicine' itself in turn came under fire. Inspired by the new 'mechanical philosophy', anatomists conceptualized the body as a machine. Heightened attention was paid to the nervous system, envisaged as a kind of hydraulic circuitry of pipes and fibres governing sensation and motion. Within such Enlightenment models, psychiatric disorders could be attributed to the nerves or the brain. As originally coined by William Cullen (1710–90), 'neurosis' meant a disorder of the nervous system. The intellectual basis of the traditional concept of melancholy had thus been kicked away.

At the same time, a newly eligible mode of melancholy was emerging in the age of sensibility and the Romantic era. Amongst social and artistic elites, it became rather fashionable to parade as a hyper-sensitive soul, one whose cerebral organization was too delicate, whose nerves were too highly strung, to cope with a high-pressure urban milieu. For a fashionable man-about-town like James Boswell (1740–95), who wrote a newspaper column under the pen-name 'The Hypochondriack', it became the done thing to put on a show of depression, because torment and suffering were hallmarks of a beautiful soul, proofs of superior sensibility. Far more vulnerable to genuine depression, Samuel Johnson (1709–84) called him a silly ass for flirting with such dangerous nonsense.

Fashionable melancholy had an exquisite future ahead of it. On both sides of the Atlantic, eminent Victorians revelled in hypochondria (mainly a male condition), hysteria (strictly for the ladies), and the 'blue devils' (a form of dyspepsia, validating invalidism). By 1900, it was trendy to be 'neurasthenic', much as nowadays, in superior Manhattan circles, one might lose caste unless engaged in 'analysis interminable' with a chic psychoanalyst.

In particular, as Shorter (1992) has argued, elite depression became closely associated with women – and with 'effeminate' males. Traditional images of both mania and depression had been man-centred. The homicidal maniac was male, but so was the traditional poet, artist or malcontent. Both the Bethlem statues were male. From the eighteenth century, however, and especially with the foregrounding of the image of the hysteric, melancholy became feminized. The novels of Mary Wollstonecraft (1759–97) popularized the image of a heroine becoming victimized and crazed through being too sensitive to survive in a heartless world. Female maniac figures assumed prominence in fiction, notably in the personage of Bertha Mason, the first Mrs Rochester – the original madwoman in the attic – in Charlotte Bronte's (1816–55) *Jane Eyre* (1847). As Elaine Showalter (1987) has documented, depressive, hysterical, suicidal and self-destructive behaviour have become deeply associated, since early-Victorian times, with images of womanhood: in the psychiatric profession, in the public mind, and amongst women themselves. The old links between writing, genius and melancholy were traditionally fixed upon male intellectuals like John Milton (1608–74), author of *Il Penseroso* (1632), or Matthew Green (1696–1737), author of *The Spleen* (1737). During the last hundred and fifty years, they have undergone a sex-change, clustering around female writers like Emily Dickinson (1830–86), Virginia Woolf (1882–1941), Sylvia Plath (1932–63), Anne Sexton (1928–74), and Janet Frame (1924-).

In modern times, the linking of melancholy with superiority has assumed two further twists. The Romantic movement renewed interest in the mad genius that had been cultivated by Renaissance Platonism but dampened by the age of reason. From Blake (1757–1827), through Hölderlin (1770–1843) to Schumann (1810–56), poets and composers either gloried in their transcendental visions or believed that madness was the inevitable price of creativity. Then, in the last third of the nineteenth century, degenerationist psychiatry turned the tables. Leading spokesmen for the 'degenerationist' position, notably Cesare Lombroso (1835–1909), or, in Britain, Theo Hyslop (1864–1933), began to contend that the 'madness' of artists and writers (i.e., their Bohemian disregard for conventional respectabilities) revealed them as sociopaths, moral cripples, and, generally, undesirables. In a more sympathetic move, enlightened asylum psychiatrists began to discover and cherish the art of the insane.

The close of the nineteenth century brought a further extraordinarily fruitful development. A new possibility opened up for the hordes of neuropaths, neurasthenics, hysterics and hypochondriacs who had emerged in Biedermeier and Victorian bourgeois society and filled the clinics and health spas of affluent Europe and America: Freudian psychoanalysis. Since the eighteenth century, the depressed person had been depicted as attention-seeking. From the appearance of Freud (1856–1939), neurosis offered the possibility of being infinitely fascinating.

Freudian psychoanalysis forms a significant marker. For the fact that Freud's mature explanatory system was wholly psychogenic, and his own admission that the free association psychotherapeutics of the couch might succeed with neurotics but not with psychotics, together helped to suggest, at least in the public mind, a *de facto* distinction between depression, or neurosis, indicated as a functional disorder, and psychosis (embracing old mania), as organic. This division carries some stamp of cultural legitimacy in the West. But not so everywhere. As Kleinman (1986) has emphasized, sufferers in Communist China from what we would term depression have characteristically been compelled to represent their condition in physical terms (lethargy, back pain, neuralgia and so forth), since only organic disorders escape the taints of malingering and even political deviancy.

This cross-cultural instance is revealing. It demonstrates, as Shorter has noted (1992), how that which is psychiatrically thinkable in patient/doctor encounters is deeply mediated by cultural values. Ours is a society profoundly fascinated by polar opposite visions of insanity; on the one hand, the maniac, out of control, subhuman, and on the other hand, the neurotic. The one is intriguing because he is so alien, the other fascinating because he is our self. Cultures evidently need such repertoires of stereotypes.

REFERENCES

Belmaker, R.H. and van Praag, H.M. (eds.) (1980) *Mania: an Evolving Concept*, Lancaster, MTP Press.

Berrios, G. (1988) 'History of depression and mania during the 19th century'. In Gorgotas, A. and Cancro, R. (eds.) *Depression and Mania*, New York, Elsevier, pp.13–25.

Berrios, G. (1988) 'Melancholia and depression during the 19th Century. A conceptual history'. *British Journal of Psychiatry*, 153: 298–304.

Diethelm, O. (1970) 'Mania: a clinical study of dissertations before 1750'. *Confinia Psychiatrica*, 13: 26–49.

Gilman, S.L. (1982) *Seeing the Insane*, New York, Brunner, Mazel.

Gilman, S.L. (1985) *Difference and Pathology*, Ithaca and London, Cornell University Press.

Gilman, S.L. (1988) *Disease and Representation. From Madness to AIDS*, Ithaca, Cornell University Press.

Jackson, S.W. (1986) *Melancholia and Depression: From Hippocratic Times to Modern Times*, New Haven, Yale University Press.

Kleinman, A. (1986) *Social Origins of Distress and Disease: Depression, Neurasthenia and Pain in Modern China*, New Haven, Yale University Press.

Kleinman, A. and Good, B. (eds.) (1985) *Culture and Depression: Studies in the Anthropology and Cross-cultural Psychiatry of Affect and Disorder*, Berkeley, University of California Press.

Kleinman, A. and Becker, J. (eds.) (1990) *Psychosocial Aspects of Depression*, Hillsdale, NJ, Erlbaum Associates.

Knoff, W.F. (1975) 'Depression: a historical overview'. *The American Journal of Psychoanalysis*, 35: 41–6.

Kromm, J. (1984) *Studies in the Iconography of Madness, 1600–1900*, Ph.D. dissertation, Emory University.

Miller, K. (1985) *Doubles*, Oxford, Oxford University Press.

Oppenheim, J. (1991) *Shattered Nerves, Doctors, Patients and Depression in Victorian England*, New York, Oxford University Press.

Pargeter, W. (1792) *Observations on Maniacal Disorders*. Reading: for the author, 1792; reprint, London, Routledge, 1988.

Rao, A.V. (1969) 'History of depression – some aspects'. *Indian Journal of History of Medicine*, 2: 46–56.

Rigney, B.H. (1978) *Madness and Sexual Politics in the Feminist Novel*, Madison, Wisconsin, University of Wisconsin Press.

Roccatagliata, G. (1986) *A History of Ancient Psychiatry*, Westport, Conn., Greenwood Press.

Rosenberg, C.E. (1989) 'Disease in history: frames and framers'. *Millbank Quarterly*, suppl. 1: 67: 1–15.

Sass, L.A. (1992) *Madness and Modernism: Insanity in the Light of Modern Art, Literature and Thought*, New York, Basic Books.

Scull, A. (1989) 'The domestication of madness'. In Scull, A. (ed.) *Social Order/Mental Disorder: Anglo-American Psychiatry in Historical Perspective*, London, Routledge, pp.54–79.

Shorter, E. (1992) *From Paralysis to Fatigue. A History of Psychosomatic Illness in the Modern Era*, New York, Free Press.

Showalter, E. (1986) *The Female Malady: Women, Madness, and English Culture, 1830–1980*, New York, Pantheon Press, 1986; London, Virago, 1987.

Speak, G. (1990) 'An odd kind of melancholy: reflections on the glass delusion in Europe (1440–1680)'. *History of Psychiatry*, 1: 191–206.

Chapter 16
Leonhard and the Cycloid Psychoses

Clinical Section
C PERRIS

The term 'cycloid psychosis' is one of the many eponyms (Table 1), that in the course of the years has been proposed to denominate syndromes of a supposed 'endogeneous' nature and of psychotic severity, which are regarded as neither 'typically' schizophrenic, nor 'typically' manic-depressive. They are usually characterized by the simultaneous occurrence in the same patient of symptoms from both the 'schizophrenic' and the 'affective' range, both during a given episode and during different episodes. However, no long-lasting and clear-cut 'schizophrenic' or 'manic-depressive' symptomatology is at any time identifiable in patients presenting the disorder. On the contrary, their symptomatology is highly polymorphous and rapidly changing, also within each single episode (Perris, 1988).

The term cycloid psychoses has been assigned a prominent place in the psychiatric literature concerning the classification of 'endogeneous' psychoses

Table 1. Some of the eponyms occurring in the literature to indicate (roughly) similar psychotic conditions as those included by Leonhard in his concept of cycloid psychoses.

Degenerationspsychosen
Mania
Expansive autopsychose durch autochtone ideen
Motilitätspsychose
Homosexual panic
Mischenpsychosen
Metabolische psychose
Benigh stupor
Randpsychosen, degenerationspsychosen, phasophrenies
Schizo-affective psychosis
(Atypische psychosen), (Randpsychosen), zykloiden psychosen
Schizophreniform psychosis
Acute exhaustive psychosis
Oneirophrenia
Legierung psychosen
Schizomanie
Bouffée délirantes
Emotionspsychosen, oneiroiden emotionspsychosen
Atypical psychoses
Psychogenic psychoses
Benign schizophreniform psychosis
Atypische phasenhafte familienpsychosen
Periodische (rekurrente) schizophrenia

mostly by the late Karl Leonhard, who in successive editions of his treatise: 'Aufteilung der endogenen Psychosen', first published in Germany in 1957, and, much later translated into English (1979), has given a thorough clinical description of these morbid conditions and commented upon their possible hereditary nature. However, the diagnostic label 'cycloid psychosis' has not been comprised in any of the international classification systems, currently in use, nor has been regarded, with a few notable exceptions (see Perris, 1984 for a recent review), as designation of a separate diagnostic category. On the other hand, the working draft of the coming 10th edition of the International Classification of Diseases prepared by the World Health Organisation and presently in the phase of field trials, takes into account 'cycloid psychoses' under the more comprehensive heading 'Acute and transient psychotic disorders'.

The scope of the present article is to trace the historical roots of the concept of 'cycloid psychoses' as conceived by Leonhard and, in doing so, to give a short characterization of their clinical manifestations. A more comprehensive account of the clinical characteristics of these psychoses, including a set of workable diagnostic criteria has been published elsewhere (Perris, 1986, 1988). The reader interested in those aspects is referred to the previous articles, where additional information concerning family studies, prognosis, and epidemiology is also given.

Historical sources: The concepts of 'degeneration' and 'degenerative psychoses'.

Very likely, it was Magnan (1893) who inspired by the Darwinian concept of 'degeneration' previously introduced by Augustin Morel (1860), described for the first time in some detail a particular, recurrent psychopathological condition ('*syndromes épisodiques de les dégénérées*', '*bouffée delirante des dégénérées*') characterized by a sudden onset, a polymorphous symptomatology, and a recurrent course in successive generations of 'degenerate' families. Such a concept, no longer linked to the obsolete 'degenerative hypothesis', is still alive in the French classification of psychiatric disorders in which a disorder labelled 'bouffée delirante, Magnan type' is taken into account (Pichot, 1982). Magnan's description appealed to Wernicke (1900) and to his closest pupils in Germany, who were not prepared to accept Kraepelin's compulsory dichotomy of the major 'endogeneous' psychoses into only dementia praecox and manic-depressive insanity. In fact, the concept was translated into German as '*autochthone Degenerationspsychosen*' (i.e. not depending upon external events), and several papers were published in the early 1900 in which the nosological autonomy of these psychoses was maintained.

Both Bonhoeffer (1907) and Birnbaum (1923) soon described recurrent psychotic episodes, mainly of a paranoid type occurring especially in criminals, which they labelled '*degenerative Phantasten*', '*vorübergehende Wahnbildung auf degenerativer Basis*', '*wahnhafte Einbildung bei Degenerierten*'. These psychotic episodes presented similar clinical characteristics to those described earlier by Magnan, t.i., a sudden onset, a polymorphous symptomatology, and a proneness to recur. They were attributed by Bonhoeffer to a 'constitutional lability', and regarded as separate as well from manic-depressive and epileptic psychotic process, and from dementia praecox as from 'exogeneous' psychotic reactions attributed to a 'reactive lability'.

A further development of the concept of degenerative mental disorders took place in a series of articles by Schröder (1918, 1920, 1926), and Kleist (1921). Even Kleist distinguished '*autochthone-konstitutionelle Psychosen*' (t.i., constitutional psychoses occurring without the influence of external factors) in which he hypothesized the occurrence of still unknown somatogenic factors, probably of endocrinological nature resulting in an 'endogeneous breakdown' ('endogeneous-labile constitution') and 'constitutional-reactive' psychoses, t.i., 'psychogenic' or 'hysterical' psychoses.

Schröder (1920) stressed the polymorphism of the clinical picture of the ('autochthonen') degenerative psychoses and described, in particular, the possible occurrence of akinetic or hyperkinetic manifestations, the occurrence of symptomatological patterns resembling hebephrenia, and that of conditions with the clinical characteristics of an acute hallucinosis. He pointed out in addition, that the duration of single episodes was usually short, but that it could stretch for years in single patients. Schröder also stressed that the prognosis of the single episodes was favourable, and regarded a favourable long-term outcome as one of the most important characteristics of this type of disorder.

In suggesting a provisional classification of the 'degenerative insanities', Schröder divided them into 'habitual states' (e.g., character disorders, perversities) and 'acute psychoses'. Under this last heading he comprised the hysterical and the manic-depressive psychoses, and a 'rest group' comprising the degenerative psychoses. On the same occasion (the Annual Congress of the German Psychiatric Association in 1920), Schröder criticized the Kraepelinian concept of 'mixed' states and pointed out that instances of degenerative psychoses could be erroneously regarded as mixed states.

In a later paper, Schröder (1926), aware of the criticism levelled against the whole concept of 'degeneration' that had extended to the conception of degenerative psychoses commented: 'albeit one should be more concerned with (the essence) of a problem rather than with its name, a bad name has a detrimental effect on the problem'. Hence, he agreed to repudiate the term degenerative psychoses and suggested, as a more appropriate alternative, the denomination '*metabolic psychoses*'. Important to notice is the fact that the attribute '*metabolic*' was used by Schröder in its strict etymological meaning, t.i., 'prone to change' (from the Greek verb *metaballein*) to stress even more the polymorphous and ever changing symptomatological characteristics of those psychotic conditions. However, the label '*metabolic*' never did gain acceptance, and the term '*degenerative psychoses*' survived for a few additional years. For example, in a comprehensive classification, comprising three main subgroups and five different subgroups, proposed by Otto Binswanger in 1928.

Other sources: The concepts of motility symptom complex and that of amentia.
Another important source of Leonhard's conception of cycloid psychoses can be found in Wernicke's (1900) description of 'motility symptom complex', and in the concept of 'amentia' (and especially 'Ratlosigkeit', currently translated into English with 'perplexity', see below) as used by Meynert (1890) and retained by Kraepelin in his Textbook (Kraepelin, 1913).

Wernicke regarded motility disturbances observable in psychotic patients as a 'symptom-complex' that could occur in different disorders, also in the course of manic-depressive insanity. Later on, on the other hand, Kleist (1911), one of Wernicke's most influential pupils, maintained the independence of a group of 'motility psychoses' from other psychotic conditions and proposed the following classification:

1. Recurrent hyperkinetic motility psychosis,
2. Long-lasting psychomotoric agitation states,
3. Cyclic motility psychoses with a short phase of agitation and a longer one of akinesia, and
4. Akinetic motility psychosis (long-lasting stupor).

In his later paper on the degenerative psychoses, earlier mentioned, Kleist (1921) included the motility psychoses as separate entities in the main group of degenerative disorders.

Also the concept of 'motility psychosis' generated a debate. Pohlisch (1925), in fact, presented a comprehensive investigation of this psychotic condition and defended its autonomy, whereas Ewald (1925), on the other hand, rejected the nosological independence of motility psychosis and strongly maintained that it was nothing but an atypical form of manic-depressive insanity. The reader has to be reminded at this juncture, that Eugen Bleuler had admitted some uncertainty as to the correct classification of recurrent psychotic motility disorders, and that this opinion was still reported in the 10th edition of his 'Lehrbuch' (1960) edited by his son Manfred.

Meynert's concept of '*Verwirrtheit*' (less pregnantly translated into English as 'confusion'), refers to a symptom complex of altered consciousness (Jaspers, 1913/1963) mainly characterized by 'incoherence of thought'. In its accelerated form ('*erregte Verwirrtheit*'), this incoherence, according to Jaspers, is distinguished from flight of ideas by the absence of intruding associations. In its less severe form, this type of 'confusion' may manifest itself as '*Ratlosigkeit*' (t.i., 'wondering perplexity') often accompanied by the delusional experience of significance ('*ratlose Bedeutungspsychose*'), and by false perceptions. A detailed description of the 'perplexity psychoses' was made by Ritter and Kleist (1956) whereas a thorough analysis of the essence and meaning of the symptomatology of perplexity was published by Störring (1939).

One early and most comprehensive study of 'motility psychosis' and 'confusion psychosis' was published by Fünfgeld (1936), who reported on clinical and family data of 39 patients with motility psychosis and 27 patients with confusion psychosis, and defended their nosological separation from manic-depressive insanity as well as from schizophrenia. According to Fünfgeld, motility psychosis appeared to be characterized by a bipolar course comprised of shifts between an increased motility (hyperkinesia) characterized by '*pseudo-expressive*' movements, and a reduced motility (akinesia) akin to stupor. Fünfgeld pointed out that instances of pure akinesia were very rare, and that an affective expressive component could be noticed in the akinetic patients as well, thus allowing a distinction from (schizophrenic) catatonic stupor. Even confusion psychosis, in the patients studied by Fünfgeld, showed bipolar shifts between an acceleration of thought, incoherence ('*Erregung*') and stupor ('*gehemmte Verwirrtheit*'). This author also verified that the clinical picture of both forms was polymorphous and comprised both hallucinatory and delusional experiences. He also found, that both conditions most often had a sudden onset, a short duration, and a fairly good long-term prognosis. Incidentally, the conclusions reached by Fünfgeld emphasizing the separation of motility- and confusion psychosis from schizophrenia, also on the basis of family data had an important sociopolitical significance at that time because a law had been passed in Germany by the Nationalsocialist Government, concerning the sterilization of schizophrenic patients. Hence, patients diagnosed as motility- or confusion psychotics were able to avoid such disgrace.

Other psychotic conditions relevant for the development of the concept of cycloid psychoses.
A further morbid condition, originally described by Wernicke (1900) under the name '*expansive Autopsychose*' and later renamed by Kleist (1928) '*akute Eingebungspsychose*' ('acute revelation psychosis'), has also contributed to the building up of the concept of cycloid psychoses.

An '*Eingebungspsychose*' is described as an acute psychotic condition characterized by the experience of a sudden 'revelation' ('*Eingebung*'), or a sudden awareness of the order of the universe, and of an oceanic feeling of closeness to a 'Super Power', most often in a religious context. Patients affected by it, experience a feeling of having been particularly selected in order to save mankind. The revelation psychosis, as we shall see presently, has been included, with its counterpole of 'anxiety' as one subgroup in one of Leonhard's earliest characterizations of the cycloid psychoses (Leonhard, 1939).

The cycloid psychoses.
The term '*zykloiden Psychosen*' was first used by Kleist (1926, 1928) to group together most of the morbid conditions mentioned so far and also, many other conditions that he had previously classified under the headings 'delusional affective psychoses' (t.i., '*perplexed signification psychosis*', '*ecstatic inspiration psychosis*', '*anxious-ecstatic delusional psychosis*', etc.), and '*affective psychoses*' (e.g., '*agitated-stuporose anxiety psychosis*'). It should be stressed, however, that the last mentioned psychotic disorders had been already distinguished from the 'mood psychoses' which comprised mania, melancholia, and manic-depressive insanity, and from the 'amential psychoses' (some of the former degenerative psychoses) which comprised the 'excited-stuporose confusion psychosis', and the 'hyperkinetic-akinetic motility psychosis'. Kleist (1928) disavowed as inappropriate the term '*Randpsychosen*' ('marginal psychoses') that he had previously used to designate those conditions which he now relabelled cycloid, and stressed the risk of confusing degenerative psychoses with schizophrenia if the benign characteristics of the former were not made explicit.

In the classification proposed in 1928, Kleist distinguished between '*typical*' and '*atypical*' '*autochthone Anlagepsychosen*' and included among the former the circular mania and melancholia, paranoia, and the epileptic psychoses, and among the latter the cycloid, the paranoid and the epileptoid psychoses. From this distinction derives the use by some authors (e.g. the Japanese Kurosawa, 1961 and Mitsuda, 1967) of the label 'atypical psychoses' as interchangeable with that of 'cycloid psychoses'. In his later, and more comprehensive classification

Table 2. Leonhard's final classification of the main groups of 'endogeneous' psychoses. Subgroups of the unipolar affective psychoses and of systematic schizophrenia are not included. (abridged)

| Affective psychoses | | Cycloid psychoses | Non-systematic Schizophrenia | Systematic Schizophrenia(*) |
Bipolar	Unipolar(*)			
Manic-depressive	Manic	Anxiety-Happiness psychosis	Affect-laden paraphrenia	Hebephrenic type
	Depressive	Confusion psychosis	Cataphasia	Paranoid type
(*) Both with several sub-groups		Motility psychosis	Periodic catatonia	Catatonic type

of neuropsychiatric illnesses, Kleist (1953) placed the cycloid psychoses in the group of 'bipolar phasophrenias' to stress even more their principal course characteristics.

Leonhard, one of Kleist's most distinguished followers, used in his earlier family studies (Leonhard, 1934) the term 'atypical psychoses' in accordance with Kleist's earlier classification, or the denomination of the particular subgroup with which he was concerned (e.g., 'Angst-Eingebungspsychose' in an article published in 1939). Both he, and other of Kleist's pupils (for example, Neele, 1949) maintained that those conditions were characterized by a homotypical family loading, and stressed that they should be regarded as genotypically separate from schizophrenia as well as from manic-depressive insanity. Furthermore, Leonhard (1939) emphasized, as Bonhoeffer (1907) and Kleist (1928) had done before him, the necessity of distinguishing anxious-ecstatic syndromes of an endogeneous nature from similar psychopathological conditions of an exogeneous (symptomatic) type. Later on in his textbook, Leonhard (1957) presented a comprehensive classification of the endogeneous psychoses in which cycloid psychoses were divided into three distinct subgroups and given a proper place (Table 2). In this classification, which in the textbook has been supplemented with a large number of case reports, he retained confusion psychosis and motility psychosis of which he stressed their bipolar characteristics (e.g., 'excited-retarded confusion psychosis', and 'akinetic-hyperkinetic motility psychosis'), and added a third subgroup, the 'anxiety-happiness psychosis' which results by the combination under the same bipolar heading of two other psychotic disorders, namely the 'anxiety psychosis' and the 'revelation psychosis' previously regarded separated by Wernicke and by Kleist (Table 3).

Apparently the principles on which this classification is based comprise symptomatology, course, prognosis, and end state. In fact, the severity of the disorder, including a poor outcome, is assumed to increase from the affective to

Table 3. Evolution of the conception of 'Angst-Glück Psychose' ('Anxiety-happiness psychosis') in three different classifications

Wernicke	Kleist	Leonhard
Angst Psychose ⟶	Angst Psychose ⟍	
		Angst-Glück Psychose
Expansive Auto-psychosis durch autochtone Ideen ⟶	Akute expansive Eingebungspsychose ⟋	

the cycloid psychoses and from these to the nonsystematic, and finally the systematic schizophrenias. Apparently, a certain correspondence in symptomatology can, also, be detected when considering the three last mentioned groups.

The three subtypes of cycloid psychosis are conceived by Leonhard as being 'bipolar' disorders. It should be observed, however, that the concept of 'bipolarity' does not completely correspond in this case to the same characteristics of the manic-depressive psychosis. In fact, bipolar manifestations in patients suffering from cycloid psychosis are expected to occur more frequently within one and the same episode than as distinct episodes of different polarity as is most frequently the case with mania and depression. Common to all three forms, according to Leonhard, is the fact that they show a phasic course (hence, the denomination of 'cycloid' used as an analogy to the attribute 'cyclic' applied to manic-depressive psychosis) followed by complete recovery, even when the patient has suffered from several episodes. Leonhard admits, however, that single cases can show some degree of defect in the long run, but he emphasizes that this is the exception more than the rule. Own research results, and results by other research workers reviewed by Perris (1988, see also Jönsson, 1992) support Leonhard's observations.

Undoubtedly, Leonhard regarded the cycloid psychoses as disease entities, endogeneous in nature, t.i., strongly determined by a homotypical heredity taint and with a consistent symptomatology, a typical course, and a favourable outcome, and his major emphasis has always been on the necessity of differentiating them from more malign psychotic disorders. However, unlike Kleist, Leonhard has never insisted that the occurrence of cycloid psychoses could be traced to localized brain dysfunctions, a conception which had characterized the Wernicke's school. Apparently, he has never considered that cycloid psychoses could be confused with manic-depressive psychosis, since the diagnostic discussion has always been focused on a distinction from schizophrenia and not on that from manic-depressive psychosis.

In conclusion, from what has been reported in this article, it is evident that the concept of cycloid psychosis has developed from those of degenerative psychoses, amentia, and the motility symptom complex which were largely used towards the turn of the Century, independently from (and – at least in part – in opposition to) the Kraepelinian classification of 'endogeneous' mental disorders.

Initially interpreted within the framework of Morel's Darwinian conception of degeneration, the 'degenerative psychoses' were later divided into those supposedly based on a constitutional lability and those supposedly reactive to external events. Within the group of degenerative psychoses, manic-depressive insanity has been consistently distinguished from the other forms, which comprise the group of recurrent psychoses which were later on labelled 'cycloid' by Kleist and Leonhard. The group of cycloid psychoses has not been identified by its proponents with that of the mixed psychoses and its autonomy has been maintained on clinical as well as on the basis of family studies. Thus schizoaffective psychoses, as they are sometimes understood (i.e., as an admixture of schizophrenia and manic-depressive psychosis) might be said to represent a further evolution of the concept of mixed psychoses, whereas the concept of 'reactive psychosis' represents a further evolution of the reactive degenerative psychoses (cf the concept of bouffée delirante reactive in the French classification). Hence, neither of these last mentioned concepts should be confused with that of cycloid psychosis that represents (in part) a further evolution of the 'autochthonous' (constitutional) degenerative psychoses. Leonhard, in fact (personal communication, 1983) has never regarded the concept of schizoaffective psychosis as interchangeable with that of cycloid psychosis. He stated, in fact, that the term 'schizoaffective' was an impossible term, difficult to delimit since it covered too many different conditions, some of which could be cycloid psychoses. His suggestion was that the concept 'schizoaffective' could be related more to the nonsystematic schizophrenias than to the cycloid psychoses.

There are several possible explanations why Leonhard's classification for a long time did not have a major international impact. First of all, it was presented for the first time in 1957, i.e., when Kraepelin's and Bleuler's conceptions had already been universally accepted for a long time, and the interest for the identification of 'new' disorders had faded out. Secondly, because almost all of Leonhard's original writings have been in German, hence, less accessible to a larger audience. Finally, because Leonhard's connection with Kleist and Wernicke easily evoked the idea that his classification too could have been inspired by assumed brain localization principles which had become obsolete. A notable exception has been Japan, where the concept of 'atypical' psychoses, as it has been mentioned earlier in this article, has been largely used by Mitsuda and his pupils.

More recent investigations, however, carried out on the basis of Leonhard's conception of cycloid psychoses have supported the clinical, and predictive validity of this particular type of psychotic conditions (see Perris, 1988; Maj, 1990; Beckman, Fritze, & Lanczik, 1990; and Jönsson, 1992 for detail), and speak in favour of the heuristic value of keeping them separate from the other major psychoses.

REFERENCES

Beckman, H., Fritze, J. and Lanczik, M. (1990) 'Prognostic validity of the cycloid psychoses. A prospective follow-up study'. *Psychopathology*, 23:205–11.

Binswanger, O. (1928) 'Die klinische Stellung der Degenerationspsychosen. Zugleich ein Versuch ihrer Gliederumg'. *Schweizerische Archiv für Psychiatrie und Neurologie*, 83: 299–325.

Birnbaum, K. (1923) *Der Aufbau der Psychosen*, Berlin.

Bleuler, E. (1960) *Lehrbuch der Psychiatrie*, 10th ed., Berlin, Springer.

Bonhoeffer, K. (1907) *Klinischer Beitrag zur Lehre von den Degenerationspsychosen*, Halle, Marhold.

Ewald, G. (1925) 'Über die Motititätspsychose'. *Archiv für Psychiatrie und Nervenkrankenheit*, 76: 233–52.

Fünfgeld, E. (1936) *Die Motititätspysychosen und Verwirrtheiten*, Berlin, Karger.

Jaspers, K. (1913/1963) *Allgemeine Psychopathologie*. Translation: *General psychopathology*, Manchester, University of Manchester Press.

Jönsson, S. (1992) *Cycloid and schizophrenic syndromes. A comparative study of a preneuroleptic sample using multivariate techniques*, Lund University Medical Dissertations, Lund, Sweden.

Kleist, K. (1911) 'Die klinische Stellung der Motilitätspsychosen'. *Zeitschrift der Gesamte Neurologie und Psychiatrie*, 3: 914.

Kleist, K. (1921) 'Autochthone Degenerationspsychosen'. *Zeitschrift der Gesamte Neurologie und Psychiatrie*, 69: 1–11.

Kleist, K. (1926) 'Über zykloide Degenerationspsychosen, besonders Verwirtheits- und Motilitätspsychosen'. *Archiv für Psychiatrie*, 78: 100–15.

Kleist, K. (1928) 'Über zykloide, paranoide und epileptoide Psychosen und über die Frage der Degenerationspsychosen'. *Schweizerische Archiv für Neurologie und Psychiatrie*, 23: 3–37.

Kleist, K. (1953) 'Die Gliederung der neuropsychischen Erkrankungen'. *Monatsschrift der Psychiatrie und Neurologie*, 125: 526–54.

Kraepelin, F. (1913) *Psychiatrie*, – vol.III, 8th ed., Leipzig, Barth.

Kurosawa, R. (1961) 'Untersuchung der atypischen endogenen Psychosen (periodische Psychosen)'. *Psychiatrie, Neurologie und medicinische Psychologie*, 13: 364–70.

Leonhard, K. (1934) 'Atypische endogene Psychosen im Lichte der Familienforschung'. *Zeitschrift der Gesamte Neurologie und Psychiatrie*, 149: 520–62.

Leonhard, K. (1939) 'Das ängstlich-ekstatische Syndrom aus innerer Ursache (Angst-Eingebungspsychose) und äusserer Ursache (Symptomatische Psychosen)'. *Allgemeine Zeitschrift der Psychiatrie*, 110: 101–42.

Leonhard, K. (1957) *Aufteilung der endogenen Psychosen*, 1st–4th ed., Jena, Akademie. Translation: *The Classification of Endogenous Psychoses*, 5th ed., New York, Halsted 1980.

Leonhard, K. (1979) *The Classification of Endogeneous Psychoses*, New York, Wiley & Sons.

Magnan, V. (1893) *Leçons Cliniques*, 2nd ed., Paris, Bataille.

Maj, M. (1990) 'Cycloid psychotic disorder: Validation of the concept by means of a follow-up and family study'. *Psychopathology*, 23: 196–204.

Meynert, (1890) *Klinische Vorlesungen über Psychiatrie auf wissenschaftlichen Grundlagen für Studierende und Ärzte, Juristen und Psychologen*, Vienna, Braumüller.

Mitsuda, H. (1967) *Clinical Genetics in Psychiatry*, Tokyo, Igako Shoin.

Morel, B.A. (1860) *Traité des Maladies Mentales*, Paris, Masson.

Neele, E. (1949) *Die phasischen Psychosen nach ihrem Erscheinungs- und Erbbild*, Leipzig, J.A. Barth Verlag.

Perris, C. (1986) 'The case for the independence of cycloid psychotic disorder from the schizoaffective disorders'. In Marneros, A. and Tsuang, M.T. (eds.) *Schizoaffective Psychoses* pp.272–308, Berlin-Heidelberg, Springer.

Perris, C. (1988) 'The concept of cycloid psychotic disorder'. *Psychiatric Developments*, 1: 37–56.

Pichot, P. (1982) 'The diagnosis and classification of mental disorders in French-speaking countries: background, current views and comparison with other nomenclatures'. *Psychological Medicine*, 12: 475–92.

Pohlisch, K. (1925) *Der hyperkinetische Symptomenkomplex und seine nosologiscvhe Stellung*, Berlin, Karger.

Ritter, M.R. and Kleist, K. (1956) 'Psychosen der Ratlosigkeit'. *Archiv für Psychiatrie und Zeitschrift der Gesamte Neurologie*, 195: 163–85.

Schröder, P. (1918) 'Ungewöhnliche periodische Psychosen'. *Monatsschrift der Psychiatrie und Neurologie*, 44: 261–87.
Schröder, P. (1920) 'Degeneratives Irresein und Degenerationspsychosen'. *Zeitschrift der Gesamte Neurologie und Psychiatrie*, 60: 119–26.
Schröder, P. (1926) 'Über Degenerationspsychosen (Metabolische Erkrankungen)'. *Zeitschrift der Gesamte Neurologie und Psychiatrie*, 105: 539–47.
Störring, G.E. (1939) *Wesen und Bedeutung des Symptoms der Ratlosigkeit bei psychischen Erkrankungen*, Leipzig, Thieme.
Wernicke, C. (1900) *Grundriss der Psychiatrie*, Leipzig, Thieme.

PART 3

NEUROSES AND PERSONALITY DISORDERS

Chapter 17

Conversion Disorder and Hysteria

Clinical Section

E TRILLAT

The history of hysteria stretches back over more than 2,000 years. Along with epilepsy, it is the oldest illness in the history of medicine; the first description of it being found in the works of Hippocrates. Actually, only a few lines in the treatise 'Illness in Women'[1] are given to this ailment which appears under the title 'suffocation by the matrix'. The womb was envisaged as a tiny capricious autonomic animal given to moving around in the woman's body. These movements caused serious harm. In the absence of coition, the matrix dried out and became lighter; it then tended to move upwards. The resultant compression of the thoracic cage obstructed the respiratory tracts and brought on suffocation accompanied by a series of symptoms:- rolling of the eyes, cold and livid skin, vomiting, cerebral disturbances, loss of speech etc. Treatment was inspired by the pathogenic concepts. To prevent the rise of the organ, the woman's body had to be tightly bandaged; since the little animal could be driven away by unpleasant smells, she was made to inhale noxious substances whilst, to draw it down, they proceeded to fumigate the vulva with pleasant smells.

From the reign of Augustus to the fall of the Roman Empire, a host of doctors (mostly Greek) made important modifications to Hippocrates' ideas. The semiology of the ailment stayed as outlined by the Master of Cos, (suffocation, spasms, loss of voice and speech, falling, heaviness in the head, sometimes loss of consciousness). But they sought to define the boundaries between this suffocation by the matrix and other illnesses. Celsius, who practised in the reign of Tiberias considered that it was distinguished from epilepsy only by negative signs; no rolling of the eyes, no convulsions, no foam on the lips.[2]

During the 1,000 years that followed, hysteria disappeared as a medical concept. Hippocratic medicine, by fighting superstition, belief in the supernatural and magic had attempted to base the art of caring for the sick on observation of natural phenomena. With the spread of Christianity, the naturalistic view of medicine disappeared – though this change owed much more to developments in fashions and mentalities than to the hostility of the the new church. This found much more to combat in the pagan cults and Christian heresies than in the inheritance of naturalistic medicine. However, the art of caring was to be founded on the new belief in one God, and illness was looked on as a divine punishment. There was a return to theurgical medicine which gradually took over from the pagan practices. The term 'hysteria' disappeared; the thing itself emphatically did not. In the middle of the fourth century, St. Martin, bishop of Tours and a great healer, became famous for his miraculous cures. A number of these were performed on ailments which, in the Ancient world, were considered as belonging to hysteria; paralysis, loss of voice, blindness and seeming death.

The heritage of Ancient times was taken up by the Arab scientists. In the work of Avicenna, one finds descriptions of suffocation by the matrix; also in the work of Constantine Africanus, a monk of Monte Cassino. Greek, Roman, Arab and Byzantine texts began to spread into the West from the eleventh century onwards, thanks especially to the Salerno School and it was a scientist from that very university, Trotula of Salerno[3] who in the twelfth century took up again the descriptions of hysteria left by Galen.

In the thirteenth century, schools of medicine were set up throughout Europe. Universities were created at Montpellier, Paris, Lyons, Bologna, Padua, Naples, Oxford, Cambridge, Lisbon. Scholars who were at one and the same time philosophers, doctors, mathematicians and astronomers discovered the ancient texts. The descriptions of the different forms of mania and melancholia left by Arethius of Cappadocia were studied again.

But it was not until the Renaissance that one saw the question of hysteria resurface and this was thanks to the witchcraft trials. For the scholars it was no longer a case of re-copying and translating dusty parchments; it was a case of leaving the libraries for the arena of clinical application.

Johan Weyer (1515–1588), a pupil of Cornelius Aggrippa, published his 'De praestigiis Daemonum' (Of the Trickery of Demons) in 1564 after time spent in Africa and the East where he witnessed the 'miraculous' exploits of sorcerers and magicians. He took up the defence of women accused of being possessed by the devil or worse, accused of sorcery. Without in any way denying the power of the devil, he made use of medical arguments. The effects attributed to the devil by the theologians were, according to Weyer, due to an accumulation of black bile in the brain. The devil who has a predeliction for black, took up residence in this black bile and dominated the woman. Thus Weyer established a compromise between the power of the church and medical knowledge. Conclusion: these women were not criminals, they were ill or spiritually sick.

In the great sorcery trials when priests were called into question, doctors were called in to present diagnoses of known illnesses which could be mistaken for demonic possession (melancholia, epilepsy, hysteria). The diagnosis of hysteria was proposed when there were contorsions, suffocation or loss of consciousness. When the demonic possession was accompanied by self-accusation, they veered towards melancholia. The ending of sorcery trials marked a victory for the doctors over the theologians. These criminal trials where the doctors were called as experts led them to stifle clinical description; to reconstruct a nosography and shore up the constructions with aetiological hypotheses . . . the disturbance of secretions and, already, fermentations which caused vapours.

On the subject of hysteria, in the classical age one sees the characteristics of the illness become more precisely defined, acquiring an identity (although during the Renaissance a little in the shadow of melancholia). The root cause of the illness was the subject of bitter argument which lasted into the nineteenth century. There were those who remained faithful to the uterine theory; the specialists in feminine illness. Jean Varandée in his 'Treatise on Feminine illness' (1666) attributed hysteria to vapours caused by the fermentation of female semen. Thirty years later, Lange took up the same theory. These theories of vaporisation were inspired by early research in chemistry and the physics of gases. They were to find their defenders right up to the beginning of the nineteenth century (Louyer-Villermay, 1802; H. Landouzy, 1846, both of them partisans of the theory of uterine origin).

In the other camp were those who attributed a cerebral origin to hysteria. The theory did not abandon vapours, but these became a harmful by-product of animal spirits. As the brain was the seat of understanding and the master of organised movement, the cerebral hypothesis easily accounts for the symptoms of hysteria (loss of consciousness and motor problems). Charles Lepois, known as Carlos Piso, in a work which appeared in 1618[4] attributed hysteria to disorder in the whole nervous system. He added that emotional upsets, sorrows and joys bring on the disease by contraction of the cervical membranes. In support of this thesis he naturally enhanced the importance of neurological symptomology in hysteria.

Thomas Willis considered that hysteria also resulted from a crisis in the brain and the nerves. One of his treatises is given to this question.[5]

In his 'Dissertation in the form of a letter to William Cole'[6], Thomas Sydenham put hysteria back into the main body of pathology. Referring to the distinction made by Arethius of Cappadocia, he divided pathology into acute and critical illnesses. The latter were also separated into two groups:- those which one might call regular or essential and the other kind which obey no rule. Hysteria and hypochondria fell into the second class. These two disorders had their seat in the brain, and their pathogen was animal spirits whose turbulence caused vapours. Hysteria was irregular, both in symptoms and in development; it could be clothed in any of the symptoms of chronic illness. This was the famous picture of hysteria as a chameleon. It was after Sydenham's work that hysteria acquired the unfortunate reputation of being a deceptive illness. How then does one distinguish the authentic illness from the counterfeit? First by its unpredictable development; but also by close attention to the circumstances which are its trigger. For the disorders often appear as a consequence of fear, sorrow or adverse circumstances. From Charles Lepois onwards, the psycho-affective dimension of hysteria began to be taken into account. Sydenham came to consider that hypochondria also emanated from the brain, and that since the two diseases had the same root, they were, in fact, one. It was the same illness manifest through different symptoms; hysteria in woman corresponding to hypochondria in man.

Vapours were used as an explanation in both cases, whether they were thought to be produced by fermentation of the female semen (uterine/iatro-chemical theory) or by decomposition of animal spirits (cerebral/iatro-physical theory) and thus arose the question of the diffusion of these vapours either upwards or downwards. Since William Harvey's discovery of the circulation of blood in 1628, the idea of diffusion through the arteries (previously thought to be empty) had been abandoned. That left the nerves and it was supposed that the vapours could be diffused through cracks in the nerves. Now, in 1764, Robert Whytt[7] showed that the nerves are full and there is no space that would permit the circulation of a fluid or a gas. Whytt, abandoning vapours spoke henceforward of an 'illness of the nerves', a term introduced by Hermann Boerhaave under whom he studied.

William Cullen, a contemporary of Whytt, was to replace this term with

'Neurosis'[8]. Hysteria was to belong from now on to the family of neuroses, understood as an illness of the nerves. We shall see how, in the course of the nineteenth century, the semantic content of this term was reversed.

When the idea of a uterine origin was abandoned and the neurologists claimed victory over the gynaecologists, hysteria became de-sexualised to the point where it was no longer considered a female prerogative. Descriptions of cases of the illness in men began to appear and hysteria was no longer deemed an expression of sexual imbalance.

The term 'vapour' no longer referred to a chemical or physical theory; rather it described a vague malaise, dizziness, a brief faint, spurts of high spirits or sadness which had no apparent cause. More rarely one found convulsions like a mild form of the classic fit. Vapours were no longer the product of fermentation of the semen or decomposition of animal spirits; they arose from leisure, ballroom assignments or a licentious imagination. They were those wasting diseases and swoons which attacked women of leisure, worn out by sleepless nights, slimming diets and quack remedies. The origin of these vapours should be sought in social behaviour rather than in the medical field.

At the beginning of the nineteenth century, one might have thought that the debate on the root cause of hysteria was dead. Oddly enough, it was re-opened owing to the Romantic Movement which sought to rehabilitate the image of woman . . . sensitive, fragile and caring; to thus highlight feminine sexuality in contrast to the masculine. The discrete character of each sex throws doubt on the possibility of uniting hysteria and hypochondria in the heart of the same illness. Frederick Hoffmann, in 1735, was already separating what Sydenham had, fifty years earlier, joined together; his argument was based on clinical and developmental observations. Hoffmann thought hysteria an acute illness whilst hypochondria was chronic. The symptoms of the two were different; the features of hysteria were predominantly physical whilst those of hypochondria tended to be mental. If the two illnesses were different, they could not have the same basis and, in a rear-guard battle, authorities were again seen defending the uterine theory (Philippe Pinel, 1798; Louyer-Villermay, 1802; Dubois (d'Amiens), 1833). These authorities were opposed by Etienne-Jean Georget who held to a cerebro-spinal origin (1820).

Between the Romantic era and the clinical-anatomical approach of hospital medicine, space should be made for Paul Briquet (1796–1881) who was an intern at the La Charité Hospital. In his treatise of 1859[9], he set out a huge number of observations of hysteria – 430 in all, 7 of them male. He underlined the rôle of emotions in the build-up to the attack, but went further. Not only were the symptoms provoked by the emotions, they were a copy of those emotions and sometimes even an exaggerated version of outbursts of human passions. The delusional episodes which were so frequent during attacks were like dreams in which the sufferer re-lived the traumatic event. Because there were many hysterics in the same ward, Briquet was brought up against the question of imitation and contagion; phenomena already noted in schools and religious institutions.

In the nineteenth century, the story of hysteria is tightly bound up with that of hypnosis, the roots of one being secular, of the other, sacred. In the preceding centuries naturalistic medicine was seen to be opposed to faith healing. In the nineteenth century the debate centred around the opposition of exorcism and hypnosis.

Joseph Gassner, a priest/exorcist, (1727–1778), had become famous for his miraculous healings. Dr. Franz-Anton Mesmer, who claimed to have discovered a fluid emanating from his person, was invited to put Gassner's practices to the test. On Nov. 23 1775, he obtained the same results as the exorcist by simple palpation. This demonstrated that the power to heal was natural rather than supernatural.

On Nov. 13 1841, an obscure surgeon, from Manchester, James Braid[10], obtained the same artificial sleep which the magnetisers produced with their 'fluid' by simply staring fixedly at the subject. Braid was to give the name 'Hypnotism' to the state of modified consciousness which the magnetisers called lucid sleep or somnambolism. In 1843, he published the results of his researches, calling on a body of knowledge drawn from the collected work of the magnetisers. Hypnosis allowed the symptoms pertaining to hysteria (anesthesia paralysis, catalepsy) to be reproduced in a healthy man. In the same manner, Braid pointed out the effects of suggestion during a cataleptic state. His work was introduced into France by Azam in 1859. And thus the affinity between exorcism, magnetism and hypnosis was established.

Charcot became interested in hysteria in 1870. He began by making a clinical inventory of the symptoms. He distinguished between the permanent symptoms (the local hysteria of the English authors); anaesthesia, paralysis, contractions, sensory loss, and the convulsive attack with its four phrases on the other hand. The first two phases are like the early stages of an epileptic attack. The others, more emotional, connected with the passions, often re-play traumatic experiences.

From 1877 onwards, under the influence of Claude Bernard, Charcot was to be concerned with experiments with hysterics. After the work of V. Burq,[11] he studied the effect of metals on hysteric anaesthesia: then the effect of magnets and finally of electricity. He concluded that all these physical agents were capable of making the permanent symptoms disappear. The English authors, Hugh Bennet and Hack Tuke, interpreted the phenomena differently. They considered that the disappearance of the attacks was due, not to physical agents, but to the psychological effect, to a sort of auto-suggestion called 'positive expectation'. They said that simply fixing the subject's attention on the appearance of the desired phenomenon was sufficient to bring it about.

From the 1880's onwards, hypnosis replaced the use of electricity in experiments. Charcot discovered (like Braid) that hypnosis with its two stages (catalepsy – lethargy) allows the reproduction of all the symptoms of actual hysteria and goes beyond this in that the symptoms artificially induced under hypnosis may persist after awakening. In 1882, thanks to Charcot, hypnosis, which had been barred from the Académie des Sciences made its official début there.[12]

The coming of industrialisation and the spread of the railways were at the root of many traumas with neurological symptoms. The English authors were the first to be confronted with this pathology. Now these problems were absolutely comparable with those observed in hysterics. Thus arose the question of 'traumatic neuroses'. In 1866, Ericksen reported fourteen cases of nervous illness caused by railway accidents. He attributed them to an 'inflammation of the marrow hence the name "Railway-Spine" '. In 1885, Page cited 150 cases.

The mental state of the subjects was related to that of patients who had been hypnotised. These were the 'Railway-Brains'. In Germany, Oppenheim and Thomson described, under the name of 'Traumatic neuroses', analogous cases whose symptoms were entirely similar to those of hysteria. As from 1885, Charcot described a dozen cases of traumatic hysteria occurring in men. Experimenting with hysterics in the hypnotic state, he showed that the smallest shock can provoke paralysis persisting into the waking state. Hence the idea that traumatic hysteria in men might be due to a kind of auto-hypnosis by whose agency the idea of trauma could take hold like a parasite whilst the subject was in a state of modified consciousness.

It was at that time, in 1885–86 that Freud spent two periods as Charcot's assistant. These ideas were in the air and he was to remember them. Freud's first paper to the Medical Society immediately after his return to Vienna, (Oct. 15 1886) concerned a case of traumatic hysteria in the male. The *Studies on Hysteria*, written in collaboration with Josef Breuer, appeared in 1895 two years after the death of Charcot.[13] For Freud, it was the starting point of his theory of hysteria and the womb from which all the major concepts of psychoanalytical theory have sprung:- Repression, Psychic Reality, the Subconscious. In this field, Freud held that abandoning hypnosis for the free association method was a modification of technique which had decisive impact both on effecting a cure and on theoretical development. Hypnosis did not allow the obstacles which were preventing subconscious memories from surfacing to be brought to light. In the hic et nunc, the subject will erect defences and these defences are of the same type as the forces which have, in the past, caused the repression of the trauma, and forced it into the subconscious; the defences cause the conscious mind to be excluded. As they are common to three neuroses (hysteria, obsession and phobia), these three can be grouped under the name Psychoses of Defence.[14] But in each of these neuroses the defences have their unique mechanisms. In hysteria there is a disparity between the affect (equivalent to the measure of stimulation) and the representation of the affect. The energy detached from the representation re-bounds on the nervous system. The devitalised representation passes into the subconscious and the stimulation which is thus released passes into the nervous system. The 'conversion symptoms' the new name for permanent symptoms are thus produced.

As for the hysterical fit itself, it will occur in cases where the stimulation stays connected to the representation. The patient gets rid of the unacceptable representation by means of the fit; this is the abreaction.

In the last years of the 19th century, psychoanalytic nosography made Defence neuroses the opposite of current neuroses.[15] The latter included the anxiety neurosis and the neurasthenia in the work of George Beard.[16] The origin of these current neuroses is not to be found in a childhood conflict, but in inadequate sexual satisfaction at the present time. A concept which recalls Galen's theories about hysteria and hypochondria.

As we have seen, in Cullen's work the word neurosis meant illness of the nerves. With Freud the word now refers to a psychological or psychical illness. This semantic inversion was the fruit of Freuds reflexion on organic and hysteric symptoms.[17] According to Charcot, hysteria was a neurosis in Cullen's sense (as epilepsy had formerly been); a neurosis in which the neurological attack was functional or dynamic. Freud showed (in an article actually written in French) that even an attack on the function of the nervous system would have to be obedient to the anatomical distribution of the nerves. Now, in hysteria, the topography of the disturbances does not correspond to anatomy, but to the subject's conception of the attack on the function.

At the beginning of this century, outside a very confidential circle of experts in Freudian theory, hardly anyone mentioned hysteria. Even the word had become suspect, having too often been associated with deception or trickery. Besides which the occurrence of the disease became rarer. The hysterics who clogged up the public wards in the hospitals disappeared, no-one knew why. Hypnosis was abandoned even by those who were its strongest advocates. The idea that Charcot had built, the unified concept of the neuro-logical origins of hysteria was greatly harmed by his pupil, J. Babinski.[18] Freud's theories were rejected by the established Scientific Societies because of their sexual connotations. The theories of Janet,[19] drawn from Associationism were discredited because they rested on the practice of hypnosis (rejected by everyone). So it was preferred to submerge the idea of hysteric illness in a grouping of functional problems gathered together under the label 'psycho-neuroses'. A rather vague appeal was made to some emotive origin; emotion being the crucible where the synthesis of psychical and somatic could take place.

On the clinical level, the gamut of hysteric symptoms was widened to encompass the whole of functional pathology. It was a throw-back to Sydenham and his 'irregular diseases'. Besides which there was less interest in the symptoms, as always labile, fugitive and deceptive, than in the hysteric personality. A characterology and typology of this hysteric personality began to be built up.

The bloodbath of the First World War was to change everything! The outbreaks which everyone thought had disappeared were to re-surface and Sandor Ferenczi could say that the pathology of this war was a veritable museum of hysteric symptoms. The arguments of the 1880's on the subject of traumatic hysteria resurfaced; the respective rôles of emotion (psychic factors) and disturbance (physical factors) were discussed. According to most authorities, this pathology, with its neurological expression arose from emotional shock (always assuming that it was genuine). The treatment was psychotherapy, made more persuasive if necessary by the use of electric shocks (torpillage) (lit. torpedoing). Other authorities thought that the cause was neurological lesions, a result of shell-shock. There was no definite clinical sign which would permit a decision either way. The disciples of Freud attributed the pathology to either conversion hysteria or phobic neurosis.[20]

Numerous cases of dream-like délire or of post traumatic mental confusion were also described. These cases, considered by the Germans to be hysteric psychoses, contributed to the resurrection of the old discussions on hysteric insanity.

In 1919, the epidemic of lethargic encephalitis (von Economo) brought arguments in favour of there being an organic component in certain hysteric disorders.[21,22] It is true that among the longer or shorter lasting after-effects of the illness, one found disorders reminiscent of those classed as hysteric; convulsions, mutism, feelings of passion, twisting spasms etc. Besides this, the close connexion between hysteric catalepsy and lethargy and the similar encephalitic conditions had to be taken into account. This interpretation which attributed a major rôle to the brain (diencephale) was to be contested by most neurologists since, after Charcot's death, hysteria was not considered to belong to neurology. Hysteria was therefore pushed out into the mists of the Psyche and became more and more a synonym for pretence.

Having been thrown out of Neurology, Hysteria could only look for home with Psychiatry. But there the niche was already filled. The neurological expression of certain hysteric symptoms seemed no different from the motor disorders of Kahlbaum's catatonia or those pertaining to Kraepelin's hebepreno catatonia. The result was that they were absorbed by Dementia Praecox and, later, by Schizophrenia.

The symptoms which found psychical expression had been described in the 19th century under the heading 'hysteric madness' or 'neuropathic madness'. These consisted of bouts of dream-like confusion with mystic/sexual themes, themes of demonic possession or bodily transformation. These bouts occurred again during the First World War with its revival of traumatic happenings. All this acute pathology, formerly connected with hysteria was absorbed into the Bleuler's acute forms of schizophrenia, or into the 'acute delusional psychoses' of the French authorities or the 'twilight states' as the Germans called them. In the last few decades attempts have been made to restore a certain autonomy to this pathology on the basis of structural analysis and inspired by the work of Breuer and Freud.

Hysteria today has been rejected by Neurology and partially absorbed by Psychiatry; we may ask 'What remains?' Psychoanalytical theory has been extended to cover neuroses and psychosomatic medicine has taken its place in general pathology; this leads to a need for the re-classification of hysteria within medicine as a whole. Little now remains of the considerable number of 19th century symptoms. The old permanent symptoms described by Charcot and re-interpreted by Freud have kept their clinical identity under the term conversion symptoms even though the framework of Defence Neuroses to which they belonged has become obsolete. They are easy to identify in relation to neurological attacks. The hysteric fit itself has kept its identity in relation to epilepsy.

But what has happened to the functional disorders attributed to hysteria since Sydenham? What is the nature of the pathology which describes the relationship of organic pain and psychosomatic illness? Where are the boundaries between hysteria and psychosomatic illness? The question remains unresolved and the answer should perhaps be sought less from the symptoms themselves than from the methods used in researching and cataloguing those symptoms.

More generally, and to conclude, if one acknowledges that psychoanalysis was born of Freud's encounter with hysteria, one can wonder if analytic theory and practice have not pushed hysteria to the very edges of Hippocratic medicine.

It is true that Freud's initial formulation could be considered as a paradigm of Hippocratic illness since hysteria made a coherent pattern, having an aetiology, a clinical table and a pathogenesis. By renouncing the idea of a genuine sexual trauma, Freud transferred the pathogenic impetus from something actually experienced to the all-powerful realm of psychical Reality. This had the effect of dissolving the medical paradigm. One has to see that psychical Reality and actual reality are mutually exclusive. Moreover, on the level of praxis, the founding of clinical practice in psychoanalysis on the analysis of transference and counter transference is completely alien to Hippocratic thought. One could just as well say that the clarification of the oppositions met in the course of the history of hysteria (sacred/secular, functional/organic, psychoanalysis/medicine) arises from a meditation on the theory of knowledge and on the methods used for gathering the facts which appears to offer a naïve observation and one which admits to being, a priori, rather lacking.

NOTES

1 Hippocrates, *Oeuvres complètes*. trad. Littré. Paris, Baillière, 1839, 1881.

2 For a more detailed account of hysteria in classical times see Chapter by Helen King (this book).

3 Trotula of Salerno, (1940) *De passionibus mulierum*, Los Angeles, Ward Ritchie Press.

4 Lepois, Ch., (1618) *Selectiorum observationem et consiliorum de praetervisis hactenus morbis*, Ponte ad Montuculum.

5 Willis, Th., (1682) *Adfectionum quae dicuntur hystericae et hypocondriacae*, in orera omnia, Amstelodimi, Wetstemius.

6 Sydenham, Th. (1682) *De variolis et morbo hysterico et hypochondriaco.* (Works of Th. Sydenham, Sydenham Society London 1850).

7 Whytt, R. (1764) *Observations on the Nature, Cause and Cure of those Disorders which have been commonly called Nervous, Hypochondriac or Hysteric*, Edinburgh, Becket and Du Hondt.
   Whytt, R. (1767) *Les Vapeurs et les Maladies Hypocondriac et Hystériques*, vol.2, Paris.

8 Cullen, W. (1777) *First Lines of the Practice of Physics*, Edinburgh, *Eléments de Médecine Pratique*, vol.2., Paris, Greech.

9 Briquet, C. (1859) *Traité Clinique et Thérapeutique de l'Hystérie*, Paris, Baillière.

10 Braid, J. (1843) *Neurypnology*, London, Churchill.

11 Burq, V. (1853) *Métallothérapie*, Paris, Baillière.

12 Charcot, J.M. (1882) *Sur les états nerveux déterminés par l'hypnotisation chez les hystériques*, C.R. hebdo. Acad Sc., 94:403–5.

13 Freud, S. and Breuer, J. (1895) *Studies on hysteria*. S.E.2.

14 Freud, S. (1894) 'Neuro-psychoses of Defence'. *S.E. 3*, pp.43, 61.

15 Freud, S. (1898) 'Sexuality in the Aetiology of the Neuroses'. *S.E. 3*, pp.261, 285.

16 Beard, G. (1880) A Practice Treatise on Nervous Exhaustion, London, Lewis.

17 Freud, S. (1893) 'Quelques considérations pour une étude comparative des paralysies motrices, organiques et hysteriques'. *Arch. de Neurologie.* 26:29, 43.

18 Babinski, J. (1901) 'Définition de l'hystérie', in Oeuvres Scientifique, Paris, Masson 1934, 457–64.

19 Janet, P. (1894) *L'état mental des hystériques*, Paris, Rueff.

20 Ferenczi, S. (1921) Psycho-Analysis of War Neuroses, London, The Intern PSA.

21 Marinesco, G. (1928) 'Les méchanismes neurologiques de certains troubles hystériques'. *Journ de Psychologie*, 25: 546, 576.

22 Van Bogaert, L. (1945) *L'hystérie et les fonctions diencéphaliques*, Congrès des Aliénistes et Neurologistes, Paris, Masson, pp.167–229.

Chapter 17
Conversion Disorder and Hysteria

Social Section
HELEN KING

To study the history of hysteria is to tread the shifting boundaries of male and female, mind and body, doctor and patient, gynaecologist and psychiatrist – even life and death. The repeated challenges to the diagnosis itself make their own assumptions about the continuity, and thus the history, of the condition: should we follow Abse (1987) and say that 'east and west, hysteria continues unabated in various guises', or Trillat (1986), who in his recent history of hysteria concludes 'L'hystérie est morte, c'est entendu'? In classical and Renaissance medicine, where the disorder called 'suffocation of the womb' has been seen as a proto-hysteria, the boundaries discussed were between the categories of 'suffocation of the womb' and 'epilepsy', or 'suffocation of the womb', 'uterine fury' and 'lovesickness': how, if at all, were these conditions to be distinguished from each other in terms of symptoms, cause and therapy? In our own century, the questions have hinged on whether or not the label 'hysteria' continues to have any diagnostic validity: it has been proposed that the diagnosis is merely 'a disguise for ignorance and a fertile source of clinical error . . . not only a delusion but also a snare' (Slater, 1965), and that, in a high proportion of patients given the diagnostic label, this in fact covers over an underlying but undetected organic illness (Shorter, 1984; Marsden, 1986; Risse, 1988). Hysteria then becomes the point at which medicine fails; indeed, what was 'the great neurosis' for the Parisian neurologist Jean-Martin Charcot in the late nineteenth century (Micale, 1989b) becomes, in the title of a book published by Krohn in 1978, 'the elusive neurosis'.

The diagnosis seems to have peaked in the nineteenth century, although it is impossible to say whether more people then had it, or more people were *said* to have had it than in other periods (Porter, 1993). Its origins, however, remain obscure. It is still commonly believed, and disseminated in the English-language history of the condition (Veith, 1965), that something recognisable as hysteria was first described in early Egyptian papyri and first named in the Hippocratic writings of the fifth and fourth centuries BC. However, Merskey and Potter (1989) have now shown that the Egyptian connection does not exist, while King (1993) demonstrates not only that the name 'hysteria' is never used in the Hippocratic texts, but also that the classical Greek writers describe a large number of different conditions, with a common origin in the movement of the womb to another part of the body, but with a wide range of symptoms according to the organ most affected by the womb's pressure. The picture of hysteria most familiar from the nineteenth century – that of Charcot's four-stage epileptiform fit, the *grande attaque d'hystéro-epileptique* with its climax in the *arc-en-cercle* posture – simply does not feature in early Egyptian and Greek medicine.

The classical Greek explanatory device of the wandering womb should perhaps have disappeared from medical science with the early discovery of the ligaments – then called 'membranes' – anchoring the womb in the abdominal cavity, attributed to Herophilus of Chalcedon in the third century BC (von Staden, 1989). However, from perhaps as early as the second century BC, the category of *hysterike pnix* – 'suffocation of the womb' – is found in medical writings, referring specifically to a mobile womb which, searching for moisture, puts pressure on the organs of breathing. The patient – always female, since a womb is the prerequisite – lies as if dead, without breath or pulse, and may inadvertently be buried alive. Aretaeus (Adams, 1856), writing in the second century AD, knew of the anchoring membranes, yet still described the womb – 'a living thing inside another living thing' – as moving up the body with great ease; in an early example of a medical writer arguing for a direct relationship between hysteria and women's social roles, he described the womb as 'the seat of womanhood' and suffocation of the womb as occurring more frequently in those whose way of life was 'somewhat wayward' rather than in those whose way of life was 'firmly based' (King, 1993). However, another second century writer, Soranus (Temkin, 1956), whose ideas circulated widely in the late antique and early medieval worlds (Green, 1985), explicitly denied in his *Gynaecology* that the womb moves, attributing the symptom of suffocation to inflammation of the membranes.

Most influential of the second century AD writers for the history of hysteria was the great – and prolific – physician, Galen of Pergamum. In his treatise *On the affected parts* (Siegel, 1976) he discussed what he called 'the so-called hysterical' symptoms: these appeared in the form of the patient lying motionless with an almost imperceptible pulse, or in paroxysms and contracture of the limbs. It must be pointed out that, when Galen argues that these are not really 'hysterical', he means that they do not arise from the direct influence of the womb, the *hystera*, which is unable to move far enough to cause the symptoms because it is held down by its anchoring membranes. Instead, he proposes that the symptoms are caused by tension in the membranes due to the retention of menstrual blood or of 'female seed', believed by some ancient medical writers to be the female contribution to generation. These retained substances produce cold, noxious vapours which travel up the body and poison it. Different symptoms result from different types of retained matter, and the cure in any case is evacuation of the offending substance. In a story repeated for centuries, Galen told of a widow whose womb was 'drawn up' and who passed some thick 'seed' after a midwife applied the 'customary remedies' – details are not given – by rubbing them into her upper thighs: masturbation as a medical treatment was thus sanctioned, it being left to later writers of the ancient world to specify the aromatics to be used.

There was thus disagreement in the period of the Roman Empire as to whether or not the womb moved; however, nobody denied that it was in some sense the origin of the symptoms, whether through direct pressure, 'sympathy' with other organs, or the production of vapours. In the encyclopaedists of the fourth to the seventh centuries AD, despite disagreement over the precise causal mechanism, a consistent picture of the sufferer was constructed and repeated: she loses her power of speech and her senses, her limbs are 'drawn together', her pulse becomes irregular and she stops breathing. At the same time a set of remedies for what continued to be called suffocation of the womb became standardised: foul odours at the nostrils, sweet scents at the vagina or even injected into the womb in order to entice the errant organ back into its proper place; shouting at the patient and making her sneeze in order to gain evidence that she was still alive. When Greek medical writings were incorporated into Arabic medicine from the ninth century onwards, although the influence of Galen dominated, womb movement was fully reinstated (King, 1993).

What of the patient in these early texts? In the Hippocratic writings, movement of the womb could affect all sorts of women, due to their softer and spongier flesh with its gaps through which menstrual blood could travel (King, 1987); childless women were particularly susceptible, but older women not having intercourse and young widows also suffered, as indeed did pregnant women. Galen's 'star patient' is the widow who passes thick seed, but in the Arabic writers the typical patient is a virgin whose blood, thought to be thicker than that of an older, sexually active woman, is more likely to stagnate in the womb.

Once the patient is defined as a woman who is outside the norm of marriage and childbirth, whether virgin or widow, intercourse – or its simulation – becomes the cure of choice. A suffocated/suffocating womb comes to be seen as a womb protesting about being kept from its proper social and medical function; this recalls Plato's fourth century BC description of the womb in his *Timaeus* 91a–d, in which it is a living creature which, if it remains unfruitful beyond the appropriate time, travels around the body blocking passages and causing disease.

It may thus be argued that, at the very heart of hysteria, we find a statement about the nature of woman and her proper social role. Ancient medical writers may debate whether a virgin or a widow is more likely to be troubled by the movement of her womb; but, however such movement is conceptualised, the cure comes to be the normal expression of her abnormal sexuality in marriage and childbearing. A wayward womb should be redirected to its proper task. Here it is valuable to look at the label 'hysteria' itself, unknown to the classical Greeks who used the simple adjective *hysterikos*, 'coming from the womb', as a statement describing the unseen part of the body from which the visible bodily symptoms originated. The Greek word *hystera*, womb, from which 'hysteria' was coined in the Renaissance (King, 1993), is related to *hysteros*, coming last, and *hysterēma*, deficiency or defectiveness (Fredriksen, 1979). Linguistically, the label thus conjures up the eighth century BC poet Hesiod's influential telling of the myth of Pandora, the first woman, a late arrival in a male world, who brings with her the evils of disease, old age, and hard agricultural work (King, 1987). The hysterical personality has been seen as emotionally manipulative, sexually provocative and deceitful: all traits which western civilisation has linked to the female ever since the gods created Pandora with a beautiful appearance concealing what Hesiod described as 'the mind of a bitch'. Her belly/womb is equally voracious for the products of men's agricultural labour and the seed of their bodies. The label 'hysteria' also echoes Aristotle's even more influential account of woman as 'a deformed male', constitutionally forever unable to catch up with the model for the human race, the adult man. For Aristotle, woman is constitutionally cold, unable to muster the heat necessary to convert blood into semen (Clark, 1975). The womb thus becomes the seat of the difference – and defectiveness – of woman. The nineteenth century idea that women are biologically 'not quite whole' (Mitchinson, 1986) thus has a long pedigree based on Aristotle's authority.

The idea of the uterine origin of 'suffocation of the womb' and then of hysteria has proved highly resistant to change. Up until the seventeenth century, with the support of the ancient medical authorities, the belief continued that the origin of hysterical suffocation lay in the womb, and this was reinforced by the idea that women naturally had an excess of blood which needed to be controlled by menstruation, careful diet and occasional venesection. However, some writers of this period shifted the focus from the womb to the brain, spleen or head, and eventually to the whole person (Boss, 1979; Wright, 1980). For Thomas Sydenham, writing in the 1680s, hysteria was the most common of all diseases; working through the nerves, by both 'mental emotions' and 'bodily derangements', it could imitate any disease (Rousseau, 1993). Since its seat was no longer the womb, it could even affect sedentary or studious men, as well as women.

However, in the eighteenth century, when nerve damage from diet, lack of exercise or strong emotion was thought to influence both body and mind through the medium of 'sympathy' (Brain, 1963; Wright, 1980), it was once again argued that women were more likely to suffer from hysteria than were men, because the membranes covering women's nerves were thought to be more delicate, making them more susceptible to pain and fear (Risse, 1988). The nervous system came to be seen as feminine, with the muscles as masculine (Jordanova, 1989; Showalter, 1993). Thus the shift from the womb to the nerves in the end did little to challenge the idea that hysteria affected women. In addition, it was argued that too much blood could irritate the nerves: thus, once more, women's natural excess of blood, obvious from their monthly bleeding, was used as a reason for their greater tendency towards hysteria.

In the nineteenth century there were several competing theories of hysteria's causation, linked not only to the emergence of psychoanalysis but also to the rise of the other medical specialisms which vied for its control (Jacyna, 1987; Moscucci, 1990). In gynaecology, as anatomical and physiological discoveries laid even greater emphasis on the extent of women's 'difference' both from men and from the females of other species (Porter, 1993), the ovaries or the clitoris sometimes tended to take over the womb's ancient role as the focus of femininity (Mitchinson, 1986; Jordanova, 1989). If a womb, a clitoris or ovaries were to be proved essential to hysteria, then gynaecology's claim to the condition would be unassailable. But gynaecology was not the only specialism with an interest in hysteria. Neurology continued to fight for its rights, the idea that men too could have hysteria being restated with particular force by the neurologist Charcot. He argued, against other late nineteenth century medical writers, that hysteria originated in a flaw in the nervous system activated by an emotional or physical trauma; thus both sexes could suffer from it. Nevertheless, Micale (1992) has shown that the assumption that it was a female disorder survived in

Charcot's work; the vast majority of his patients were women, and gender assumptions lay behind Charcot's descriptions of his female patients' hysteria as having been triggered by emotional experiences, while his male patients' symptoms were activated by physical trauma.

The label 'hysteria', with its history of multiple resonances with the womb and with inferiority, simply will not stick to a male patient. Showalter (1993) has shown how the application of the label to the male makes him seem unmanly, leading to attempts to find other names for similar symptoms in a male patient: for example, 'neurasthenia', or the highly respectable 'shell shock'. As well as a gender distinction, there are also racial undertones to hysteria. There was very little British psychiatric writing on hysteria in the late nineteenth century, Clark (1981) has argued, because it was not seen as a real disease – or because it was seen as a disease to which the 'emotional races' only were subject (Micale, 1992). Gilman (1993) has shown how, at the end of the nineteenth century, male Jews were regarded as particularly likely to suffer from hysteria.

Where a patient who is, almost by definition, female meets the professional male physician, the patient/doctor relationship is expressed in what may be seen as its purest form: the patient exhibiting traditionally female traits of passivity and helplessness, the doctor reinforcing his maleness by his active and powerful intervention. Yet this is only one of the many forms taken by the patient/doctor relationship in the context of late nineteenth and early twentieth century hysteria, where we may see acted out what Roy Porter has recently described as 'a wildly new, and deeply aberrant script of doctor-patient interplay' (Porter, 1993). On the one hand, we may detect barely-contained fury on the part of doctors confronted with a patient suffering from hysteria. This may be illustrated with the words of a doctor writing in 1908, when a common symptom was the 'drawing up' or contracture of a limb:

> As Vance cut off the plaster cast from a 14-year old girl whose leg had 'drawn up' a year previously, she cried, 'It is going to draw up; it is going to draw up', at which Vance said severely, 'If it does draw up, I will break your d____d little neck'. (Shorter, 1986)

Similar sentiments appear in the work of late nineteenth century Canadian physicians cited by Mitchinson (1986):

> I am in the habit of regarding a hysterical woman in the same light as a skittish, unmanageable horse; and just as I catch the one by means of a handful of oats, so I do not hesitate to entrap the woman by much the same means.

and

> When you are called to treat a young girl with a hysterical attack . . . Administer an emetic. I have found that a woman who is well under the action of an emetic has not the opportunity to do anything else than be thoroughly nauseated.

These extracts illustrate the other side of this fury and contempt, the attempt by the doctor to establish complete control over the recalcitrant patient. This manifests itself in various forms: for example, in Robert Carter's taming and shaming of the patient with what he called 'tertiary·hysteria', who was thought to produce the symptoms deliberately in order to gain attention and sympathy (Carter, 1853; Kane and Carlson, 1982; Porter, 1993); in the total isolation, bed rest and boredom of Weir Mitchell's infamous 'rest cure' for the often hysteriform neurasthenia (Weir Mitchell, 1904; Poirier, 1983); and, perhaps best known today, in Freud's hostility towards Dora (Bernheimer and Kahane, 1985).

Yet in the midst of this struggle between doctor and patient, Hunter (1983) and Gay (1988) have argued that, at least in the cases of hysteria which mark the origin of psychoanalysis, the patient may be seen as the dominant partner. In Breuer's relationship with Anna O. in 1880–2, the patient treated herself by talking through her past emotional experiences (Rosenbaum and Muroff, 1984): Freud described Cäcilie M. as his 'teacher'. But this conclusion only applies to the star patients; nineteenth century hysteria was by no means a disorder exclusive to the educated classes, but was a common diagnosis in the dispensaries and asylums where the poor were treated (Risse, 1988; Porter, 1993).

The diagnosis of hysteria thus allowed at least some patients to explore the patient/doctor boundary. A related pair of categories challenged by hysteria is that of mind/body since, as has already been seen, hysteria moves between the organic and the psychological. In the Hippocratics, the origin is emphatically organic: the womb's movement causes a range of symptoms. An interest in the reciprocal influence of mind and body in relation to hysteria continued through the medieval period and renaissance (Merskey, 1983). Underlying this interest is a question which challenges the role of doctors of all kinds: can the body, alone, account for all bodily symptoms (Porter, 1993)? If not, then why have physicians at all? Hence, perhaps, the repeated attempts to find *some* physical explanation for the dramatic physical symptoms which hysteria can manifest. Freud's approach, suggesting that hysteria represents the transformation of remote and repressed sexual memories into bodily symptoms, takes it out of the domain of the physician: the cure is to bring the memories into consciousness.

It is striking that so many descriptions of hysteria place the symptoms at opposite – or at both – ends of various spectrums: thus muscle tone is either flaccid, or convulsive, while speech is either absent or takes the form of an outpouring of expletives or meaningless sounds. The hysteria patient, it seems, goes to extremes. It is the linguistic disturbances of hysteria, rather than the epileptiform fit, which have moved to the fore in recent feminist readings of the condition: thus hysteria, Hunter (1983) has argued, is women's language, the language of the body expressing what cannot be said verbally due to the conventions of the day. For the nineteenth century, that language is preserved in the photographic record of Charcot's patients at the Salpêtrière (Didi-Huberman, 1982), who pose for the camera. These images may seem a particularly voyeuristic intrusion into the life of the patient, but the condition requires an audience: there are no solitary hysterics (Porter, 1993). But who teaches the patient the language? Feminist readings of hysteria argue that the treatment of hysteria and related conditions across the ages represents the worst form of misogynism (Fischer-Homberger, 1979); in the nineteenth and early twentieth centuries, it was diagnosed by men in women acting contrary to gender roles, by their demands for the vote, education, or divorce (Showalter, 1985). Yet, in accepting that they are indeed 'hysterical', women can turn men's language back against them, in order to gain the respite afforded by the 'sick role'. Hysteria thus, paradoxically, becomes a form of resistance (Smith-Rosenberg, 1972): a proto-feminism (Showalter, 1993). But hysteria is also the eternal mimic: able to act out any set of symptoms, its actors learn their roles from the doctor who expects to find the condition in certain patients, or who even conveniently displays its image on his wall, as Freud had an etching of Charcot's star patient's performance hanging in his consulting room in Vienna (Micale, 1989b).

Hysteria has thus travelled from the womb's movement to the women's movement, from the label which marks the female sex as biologically inferior to a banner to be paraded with pride. In medical writing, however, it remains an enigma (Micale, 1990): if, as historical study suggests, hysteria is a single heading under which different generations have written their own lists of symptoms, then it must be asked whether it is any longer appropriate to locate it in any medical domain.

REFERENCES

(A wide-ranging bibliography of works on the history of hysteria is given in Micale [1990] and [1995].)

Abse, D. W. (1987) *Hysteria and Related Mental Disorders* (2nd edition), Bristol, Wright.

Adams, F. (1856) *Aretaeus: Of the Causes and Symptoms of Acute Diseases,* London, Sydenham Society.

Bernheimer, C. and Kahane, C. (eds.) (1985) *In Dora's Case: Freud-hysteria-feminism,* New York, Columbia University Press.

Boss, J.M.N. (1979) 'The seventeenth-century transformation of the hysteric affection, and Sydenham's Baconian medicine'. *Psychological Medicine,* 9: 221–34.

Brain, W.R. (1963) 'The concept of hysteria in the time of William Harvey'. *Proceedings of the Royal Society of Medicine,* 66: 317–24.

Carter, R.B. (1853) *On the Pathology and Treatment of Hysteria,* London, John Churchill.

Clark, M.J. (1981) 'The rejection of psychological approaches to mental disorders in late nineteenth century British psychiatry'. In Scull, A. (ed.) *Madhouses, Mad-doctors, and Madmen: The Social History of Psychiatry in the Victorian Era,* Philadelphia, University of Philadelphia Press.

Clark, S.R.L. (1975) *Aristotle's Man,* Oxford, Clarendon Press.

Didi-Huberman, G. (1982) *Invention de l'Hystérie: Charcot et l'iconographie photographique de la Salpêtrière,* Paris, Macula.

Fischer-Homberger, E. (1979) *Krankheit Frau und andere Arbeiten zur Medizingeschichte der Frau,* Bern, Hans Huber.

Fredriksen, P. (1979) 'Hysteria and the Gnostic myths of creation'. *Vigiliae Christianae,* 33: 287–90.

Gay, P. (1988) *Freud: a Life for our Time,* New York, Norton.

Gilman, S. (1993) 'The image of the hysteric'. In Gilman, S., King, H., Porter, R., Rousseau, G.S. and Showalter, E. (eds.) *Hysteria Beyond Freud,* Berkeley, University of California Press.

Green, M.H. (1985) *The Transmission of Ancient Theories of Female*

Physiology and Disease through the Early Middle Ages, Unpublished PhD thesis, Princeton University.

Hunter, D. (1983) 'Hysteria, psychoanalysis, and feminism: the case of Anna O'. *Feminist Studies*, 9: 464–88.

Jacyna, L.S. (1987) *Nineteenth Century Origins of Neuroscientific Concepts*, Berkeley, University of California Press.

Jordanova, L. (1989) *Sexual Visions: Images of gender in science and medicine between the eighteenth and twentieth centuries*, Hemel Hempstead, Harvester.

Kane, A. and Carlson, E. (1982) 'A different drummer: Robert B. Carter on nineteenth century hysteria'. *Bulletin of the New York Academy of Medicine*, 58: 519–34.

King, H. (1987) 'Sacrificial blood: the role of the *amnion* in Hippocratic gynecology'. *Helios*, 13.2: 119–26.

King, H. (1993) 'Once upon a text: hysteria from Hippocrates'. In Gilman, S., King, H., Porter, R., Rousseau, G.S. and Showalter, E. (eds.) *Hysteria Beyond Freud*, Berkeley, University of California Press.

Krohn, A. (1978) 'Hysteria: the elusive neurosis'. In *Psychological Issues* nos.45/46, New York, International Universities Press.

Marsden, C.D. (1986) 'Hysteria – a neurologist's view'. *Psychological Medicine*, 16: 277–88.

Merskey, H. (1983) 'Hysteria: the history of an idea'. *Canadian Journal of Psychiatry*, 28: 428–33.

Merskey, H. and Potter, P. (1989) 'The womb lay still in ancient Egypt'. *British Journal of Psychiatry*, 154: 751–3.

Micale, M. (1989a) 'Hysteria and its historiography: a review of past and present writings I'. *History of Science*, 27: 223–61.

Micale, M. (1989b) 'Hysteria and its historiography: a review of past and present writings II'. *History of Science*, 27: 319–51.

Micale, M. (1990) 'Hysteria and its historiography: the future perspective'. *History of Psychiatry*, 1: 33–24.

Micale, M. (1992) 'Hysteria male/hysteria female: reflections on comparative gender construction in nineteenth century France and Britain'. In Benjamin, M. (ed.) *Science and Sensibility: Essays in the history of gender, science and medicine in nineteenth century Britain*, Oxford, Basil Blackwell.

Micale, M. (1995) *Approaching Hysteria: Disease and its interpretations*, Princeton, Princeton University Press.

Mitchinson, W. (1986) 'Hysteria and insanity in women: a nineteenth-century Canadian perspective'. *Journal of Canadian Studies*, 21: 87–105.

Moscucci, O. (1990) *The Science of Woman: Gynaecology and Gender in England, 1800–1929*, Cambridge, Cambridge University Press.

Poirier, S. (1983) 'The Weir Mitchell rest cure: doctors and patients'. *Women's Studies*, 10: 15–40.

Porter, R. (1993) 'The body and the mind: the doctor and the patient: negotiating hysteria'. In Gilman, S., King, H., Porter, R., Rousseau, G.S. and Showalter, E. (eds.) *Hysteria Beyond Freud*, Berkeley, University of California Press.

Risse, G. (1988) 'Hysteria at the Edinburgh Infirmary: the construction and treatment of a disease, 1770–1800'. *Medical History*, 32: 1–22.

Rosenbaum, M. and Muroff, M. (eds.) (1984) *Anna O.: Fourteen contemporary reinterpretations*, New York, Free Press.

Rousseau, G.S. (1993) '"A Strange Pathology": Hysteria in the Early Modern World'. In Gilman, S., King, H., Porter, R., Rousseau, G.S. and Showalter, E. (eds.) *Hysteria Beyond Freud*, Berkeley, University of California Press.

Shorter, E. (1984) 'Les désordres psychosomatiques sont-ils "hystériques"? Notes pour une recherche historique'. *Cahiers internationaux de Sociologie*, 76: 201–24.

Shorter, E. (1986) 'Paralysis: the rise and fall of a "hysterical" symptom'. *Journal of Social History*, 19: 549–82.

Showalter, E. (1985) *The Female Malady: Women, Madness, and English culture, 1830–1980*, New York, Pantheon.

Showalter, E. (1993) 'Hysteria, feminism and gender'. In Gilman, S., King, H., Porter, R., Rousseau, G.S. and Showalter, E. (eds.) *Hysteria Beyond Freud*, Berkeley, University of California Press.

Siegel, R.E. (1976) *Galen On The Affected Parts*, Basel and New York, S. Karger.

Slater, E. (1965) 'Diagnosis of "hysteria"'. *British Medical Journal*, 1395–9.

Smith-Rosenberg, C. (1972) 'The hysterical woman: sex roles and role conflict in nineteenth-century America'. *Social Research*, 39: 652–78.

Temkin, O. (1956) *Soranus' Gynecology*, Baltimore, Johns Hopkins Press.

Trillat, E. (1986) *Histoire de l'hystérie*, Paris, Eds Seghers.

Veith, I. (1965) *Hysteria: The History of a Disease*, Chicago, University of Chicago Press.

Von Staden, H. (1989) *Herophilus. The Art of Medicine in Early Alexandria*, Cambridge, Cambridge University Press.

Weir Mitchell, S. (1904) 'The evolution of the rest treatment'. *Journal of Nervous and Mental Disease*, 31: 368–73.

Wright, J.P. (1980) 'Hysteria and Mechanical Man'. In *Journal of the History of Ideas*, 41:233–47.

Chapter 18
Somatoform Disorders

Clinical Section
GE BERRIOS and D MUMFORD

The common feature of the *Somatoform Disorders* (APA, 1994): 'is the presence of physical symptoms that suggest a general medical condition (hence, the term *somatoform*) and are not fully explained by a general medical condition, by the direct effects of a substance, or by another mental disorder (e.g., Panic Disorder). The symptoms must cause clinically significant distress or impairment in social, occupational, or other areas of functioning. In contrast to Factitious Disorders and Malingering, the physical symptoms are not intentional' (i.e., under voluntary control) (p.445). Thus, this clinical category includes conditions once called somatization disorder, conversion disorder, hypochondriasis, pain disorder and body dysmorphic disorder (dysmorphophobia). This chapter will only deal with the history of hypochondriasis and dysmorphophobia (other categories are dealt with elsewhere in this book).

Until recently, 'hypochondriasis' denoted a 'morbid preoccupation with one's body or state of health, either mental or physical' (Kenyon, 1976). DSM IV defines it as 'a preoccupation with fears of having, or the idea that one has, a serious disease based on the person's misinterpretation of bodily symptoms'. The preoccupation must last at least six months and persist despite appropriate medical evaluation and reassurance. It should cause clinically significant distress or impairment in social, occupational, or other important areas of functioning (p.465). The term hypochondriasis, however, goes back to Classical times when it referred to emotional disorders believed to originate in organs below the costal margin.

The word 'somatisation' was only coined in the 20th century although it also refers to phenomena described in previous centuries under other names. 'Somatisation disorder', on the other hand, is currently defined as 'history of many physical complaints beginning before age thirty years that occur over a period of several years and result in treatment being sought or significant impairment in social, occupational, or other important areas of functioning' (APA, 1994, p.449).

Lastly, 'the essential feature of Body Dysmorphic Disorder' (historically known as dysmorphophobia) is a preoccupation with a defect in appearance. The defect is either imagined, or, if a slight physical anomaly is present, the individual's concern is markedly excessive. The preoccupation must cause significant distress or impairment in social, occupational, or other important areas of functioning. The preoccupation is not better accounted for by another mental disorder (e.g., dissatisfaction with body shape and size in Anorexia Nervosa) (APA, 1994, p.466).

To make sense of the evolution of all these clinical categories, the history of the *words* (etymology) will have to be distinguished from that of the *clinical phenomena* involved (behavioural palæntology) and from that of the *concepts* periodically formulated to explain them.

The origins

In the earliest Greek literature, the epics of Homer (8th century BC), the *heart* was regarded as the seat of the emotions, intellect and will (Mumford, 1993). The primacy of the head and brain became a tenet of the Hippocratic school in the 5th century BC. Plato's *Timaeus* (circa 360 BC) regarded the abdominal organs as the source of disordered emotions, in turn affecting both the heart and the brain (Warrington, 1965). *Hypochondrium* was used by Hippocrates to refer only to an *anatomical* locus (for example, his post-partum Case IV in Epidemics I: 'suffered in the stomach and the right ὑποχόνδριον') (p.192) (Hippocrates, 1923). [1] Ladee (1966) noticed that the first description of a disease associated with the hypochondria was made by Diocles Carystius circa 350 BC 'who assumes the cause to be a disorder of the digestive organs' (p.7). Diocles, however, was 'severely criticized by Galen for having failed to mention the mental symptoms in his otherwise extensive account of the syndrome' (Siegel, 1973, p.192). [2]

Classical writers established an association between an anatomical locus (hypochondria or praecordia), a physiological theory (humoural), and at least two clusters of 'symptoms': one pertained to digestive symptomatology, flatulence, etc. (as in Diocles); the other to melancholia (as in Paulus de Aegina). Lest anachronistic anticipations blur the understanding of the reader, it is important to remark that during this period melancholia had little or nothing to do with depressive illness (Berrios, 1988).

However, by the early 17th century, centos such as Robert Burton's *Anatomy of Melancholy* still mentioned hypochondriacal or flatuous melancholia, whose symptoms include 'besides fear and sorrow, sharp belchings, fulsome crudities, heat in the bowels, wind and rumblings in the guts, vehement gripings, pain in the belly and stomack' (p.269). [3]

HYPOCHONDRIA AS A NERVOUS DISORDER

Thomas Willis (1621–1675)

Willis refuted the idea that the uterus or the humours were responsible for every inexplicable or unusual somatic symptom. He regarded both hypochondriasis in men and hysteria in women as disorders of the brain:

> as we have shown before that the passions vulgarly called hysterical do not always proceed from the womb, but often from the head's being affected: so though it has been vulgarly held that the affects called hypochondriacal are caused for the most part by Vapours arising from the spleen, and running hither and thither; yet in truth those distempers are for the greatest part convulsions and contractions of the nervous parts. (p.307)

In addition to flatulence, indigestion, pain and other gastrointestinal symptoms, Willis was referring here to others which are redolent of panic disorder: 'more over, the diseased are wont to complain of a trembling and palpitation of the heart, with a mighty oppression of the same, also frequent failings of the spirits, a danger of swooning come upon them, that the diseased always think death at hand . . . fluctuation of thoughts, inconstancy of mind, a disturbed fancy, a dread and suspicion of everything'. But also, (and this is one of the earliest references one finds to valetudinarian complaints): 'an imaginary being affected with diseases of which they are free, and many other distractions of the spirit . . . wandering pains, also cramps and numbnesses with a sense of formication seize likewise almost all the outward parts: night sweats, flushing of blood . . .' (Willis, 1685, pp.308–9).

Thomas Sydenham (1624–1689)

Sydenham noted that symptoms 'which cannot be accounted for on the common principle of investigating diseases' were often preceded by 'disturbances of the mind' which he regarded as 'the usual causes of this disease'. He noted that these symptoms were often accompanied by depression, panic, anger or despair; sufferers were 'enemies to joy and hope'. Like Willis, he linked hysteria and hypochondriasis: 'since, however much antiquity may have laid the blame of hysteria upon the uterus, hypochondriasis (which we impute to some obstruction of the spleen or viscera) is as like it, as one egg is to another' (p.85) 'the affection which I have characterized in females as hysteria and in males as hypochondriasis, arises (in my mind) from a disorder (ataxy) of the animal spirits' (Sydenham, 1850, p.90). As Dewhurst (1966) rightly interpreted: 'an imbalance of the animal spirits which, after upsetting the mind-body relationship, brought on further disorders of the weakest and more vulnerable organs' (p.46).

Sydenham comments on the remarkable frequency and the numerous forms under which hysteria and hypochondriasis appear, 'resembling most of the distempers wherewith mankind are afflicted'. 'Unless the physician be a person of judgement and penetration', it was easy to confuse these hysterical symptoms with symptoms of physical disease. Such symptoms included: severe pain 'attacking the external part of the Head, between the pericranium and the cranium'; vomiting; 'terrible convulsions much like the epilepsy'; and 'so violent a palpitation of the Heart, that the patient is persuaded, those about her must needs hear the heart strike against the ribs'. Sydenham's descriptions of hysterical symptoms were widely quoted by his contemporaries (Williams, 1990).

One of the earliest Continental writers indirectly to inquire into the 'biological' basis of hypochondriasis was Théophile Bonet, the great Swiss pathologist and precursor of Morgagni (Dechambre, 1869). In his celebrated *Sepulchretum anatomicum* (1689), he included about 30 cases in which he reported abdominal anomalies (Ladee, 1966). Almost a hundred years later, John Baptist Morgagni (1769), in Letter 62 of his *The Seats and Causes of Diseases*, reported the case of a 58 year-old physician whose 'hypochondriac disorder' had accelerated his death (Book III, p.517).

The 'English malady'
In the *Elizabethan Malady*, Lawrence Babb (1951) wrote: 'the melancholic malady may be due to any of the foregoing circumstances which engender black bile. It may be due also to functional failure in any one of a group of abdominal organs known collectively as the *hypochondria*, or *hypochondries*. When melancholia is a consequence of disorder in any hypochondriacal organ, it is called *hypochondriacal melancholia*' (italics in original) (p.26). 'Hypochondriacal melancholy is notable among melancholies for the fact that it furnished the late seventeenth century and the eighteenth century with a set of terms. Before the time of Queen Anne, *melancholy*, as the name for morbid depression, had been largely replaced by *hypochondria, spleen, hysteria*, and *vapors*, all four terms denoting the same disorder' (italics in original) (p.28).

The 18th century is rich in books on hypochondria and a sizeable proportion are English. Although from a strict clinical point of view, what Cheyne called the 'English malady' (see below) may not correspond altogether to hypochondriasis, it shows as Porter (1991) has remarked, that environmental factors began to be considered as important in the development of a set of symptoms that since Willis had been considered as also associated with 'neurologie' (Bynum, 1985). However, as the 18th century wears off, a trend can be noticed (particularly amongst the Scottish physicians) to consider hypochondria as a specific disturbance of the nerves (López Piñero, 1983).

Sir Richard Blackmore (1653–1729)
When discussing hypochondriasis, 18th century physicians continued to challenge the Galenist theory of 'vapours' and tò search for a theory to replace it. Blackmore, physician to William III and Queen Anne, set out his views in *A treatise of the spleen and vapours: or, hypochondriacal and hysterical affections* (1725). He regarded pains and other sensory symptoms in various parts of the body, as well as the disturbed mind and imagination, as equivalent in 'hysterick women' and 'hypochondriacal men' (in this he was, of course, following Sydenham). Blackmore ruefully observes that 'patients are unwilling their Disease should go by its right Name' because the public regard their symptoms as an 'imaginary and fantastick Sickness of the Brain, filled with odd and irregular ideas', and such persons often become 'an Object of Derision and Contempt'. He affirms that, whatever the cause, their 'Sufferings are without doubt real and unfeigned'.[4]

Bernard de Mandeville (1670–1733)
De Mandeville's *A treatise of the hypochondriak and Hysterick passions* is likely to reflect less a capital of direct clinical experience than de Mandeville's acquaintance with the literature on the subject.[5] Written in the then fashionable style of a dialogue, the book describes the exchanges between Philopirio (a physician representing de Mandeville's views) and Misomedon, a *hypochondriacus confirmatus* who consulted him after twelve years of gastrointestinal symptoms and countless episodes of bleeding and purging. From the perspective of this chapter, the second dialogue is the most important for it discusses the aetiological theories of Diocles, Sylvius, Willis, Sydenham, Highmore, Platter, Tulp and Baglivi. For example, after quoting at length Thomas

Willis' 'analogy between the body and a still' and his views on the role of the spleen he says: 'You see, Misomedon, how your witty men give every thing a gloss' (p.93). De Mandeville proceeds then to put forward his own view that hypochondria results from a disorder of the stomach and its ferments: 'that the disorders of the chylifications are chiefly the cause of the distempers in question, I shall endeavour to prove' (p.121).

Nicholas Robinson (1697–1775)
In contrast to Blackmore's psychological theories, Robinson (1729), a governor of Bethlem Hospital, wanted to account 'mechanically' for mental as well as bodily diseases. He argued that because mind without brain was inconceivable, psychological processes were simply expressions of physical events in 'the Nerves and Fibres that compose the Brain'. 'Every Change of the Mind, therefore, indicates a Change in the bodily Organs; nor is it possible for the Wit of Man to conceive how the Mind can, from a cheerful, gay Disposition, fall into a sad and disconsolate State, without some Alterations in the Fibres, at the same Time'.

In relation to 'those Disorders we call the Spleen, Vapours, and Hypochondriack Melancholy', Robinson argued: 'Neither the Fancy, nor Imagination, nor even Reason itself, the highest Faculty of the Understanding, can feign a Perception, or a Disease that has no foundation in Nature; . . . cannot feel Pain or Uneasiness in any Part, unless there be Pain or Uneasiness in that Part: The affected Nerves of that Part must strike the Imagination with the Sense of Pain, before the Mind can conceive the Idea of Pain in that Part'.[6]

George Cheyne (1671–1743)
Other medical authors were ready to entertain social, intellectual and environmental causes. Writing from personal experience of depressive illness, Cheyne in *The English Malady: or, a Treatise of Nervous Diseases of all Kinds, as Spleen, Vapours, Lowness of Spirits, Hypochondriacal, and Hysterical Distempers, etc.* (1733) claimed that persons of greater intelligence and upper social class were most often affected. He blamed the 'English Malady' on

> the Moisture of our Air, the Variableness of our Weather, (from our Situation amidst the Ocean) . . . the Richness and Heaviness of our Food, the Wealth and Abundance of the Inhabitants (from their universal Trade) the Inactivity and sedentary Occupations of the better Sort (among whom this Evil mostly rages) and the Humour of living in great, populous and consequently unhealthy Towns. . . . These nervous Disorders being computed to make almost one third of the Complaints of the People of Condition in England.

HYPOCHONDRIA AS A 'NEUROSES'

Robert Whytt (1714–1766)
Whytt was an original writer. In his *Observations on the nature, causes and cure of those diseases which are commonly called nervous, hypochondriac or hysteric* (1765), he defended the view that 'sympathy' (an old notion used to explain

how bodily components came to be co-ordinated) was based on a network of nerves, and hence was a function of the brain. This has been aptly summarized by French (1969): 'since sympathy presupposes feeling, nerves are the mechanism of feeling, and all nerves originate in the brain and spinal marrow . . . all sympathy was to be referred to the brain' (p.34).

Following Sydenham, Whytt believed that hysteria and hypochondria were identical but the former affected females and the latter males. Nervous disorders in general, resulted from 'a too great delicacy and sensibility of the whole nervous system' or 'an uncommon weakness, or a depraved or unnatural feeling, in some of the organs of the body'. Hysteria and 'hypochondria' resulted from a combination of these two types of causes and were but the expression of pathological sympathy.

William Cullen (1712–1790)

Cullen sponsored a version of 'neuralpathology' (the view that all diseases were diseases of the nervous system). Not much has been written on Cullen's psychiatric views although he is quoted *ad nauseam* for having coined the term neurosis (Bowman, 1975). Cullen's taxonomic approach was synthetic in that he blended into larger groups the often over-detailed nosological conditions of his predecessors. This also applies to his views on hypochondriasis. As the anonymous writer of the popular *Edinburgh Practice of Physic* wrote in 1803:

> although some of the nosological writers, particularly Sauvages, have considered this genus as consisting of different species, Dr Cullen is of the opinion that there is only one idiopathic species, the *hypochondriasis melancholica*. He considers not only the hypochondriasis hysterica, phthisica and asthmatica, but also the biliosa, sanguinea, and pituitosa, as being only symptomatic; but he views the true melancholic hypochondriasis as being a proper idiopathic disease, perfectly distinct from hysteria, with which has often been confounded. (p.358) (see also Cullen, 1803, pp.291–2)

The symptoms of hypochondriasis, according to Cullen were: dyspepsia, indigestion, pain under the ribs, palpitations, sleepless nights . . . and occasionally 'depression of spirits and apprehension of danger'. Amongst the causes the following can be listed: 'plethora and preternatural thickness of the blood, suppression of customary evacuations, high and full diet, together with a sparing quantity of drink; and hereditary disposition; indolence; atony of the intestines and violent passions of the mind' . . . 'the hypochondriacal affection, when left to itself, is more troublesome than dangerous' (Anonymous, 1803).

I. Kant (1724–1804) and *Grillenkrankheiten*

Kant's theoretical analysis of the nature and classification of mental illness had some influence on 19th century thought and hence it must be briefly mentioned. In his *Anthropologie* he divided the disorders of mood (*Gemütskrankheiten*) into 'cricket disease (*Grillenkrankheit*) (*Hypochondrie*) and disordered mood (*gestörte Gemüt*) (*Manie*)': 'the former is named thus for its analogy to listening in the quiet of the night to a cricket chirping which disturbs our attention and prevents us from sleeping' (p.101). Kant defines hypochondriasis as a disease in which 'certain internal physical sensations (*innere körperliche Empfindungen*) which are not the expression of a real disease cause nonetheless great anxiety about having one' (p.101). Kant goes on to say that human beings have this characteristic of easily magnifying a sensation by concentrating on it: 'this is how hypochondria causes the patient to imagine that he is physically ill though he may know that the illness is his fantasy' (*Einbildungen sind*) (p.101). This psychological explanation was to influence Feuchtersleben during the middle of the 19th century.

V. Chiarugi (1759–1820)

The publication by Chiarugi (1987) of *Della Pazzia in genere, e in specie* in 1793 facilitated his election to the chair of dermatology and mental pathology at the University of Florence. In volume III of this work, he deals with the question of the relationship between melancholia and hypochondria: 'one could also doubt whether "hypochondria" ever forms a distinct species from melancholia. In this case, the firm belief in an unavoidable danger to life or in the existence of a very serious disease occupies the fantasy of the patient so strongly that no amount of reasoning is sufficient to remove the sadness and the fear' . . . 'but there are also people affected by hypochondria who do not regress towards the state of true melancholia' (p.213). Clearly, Chiarugi hedged his bets and accepted that both forms were possible.

Philippe Pinel (1745–1826)

Although Pinel lived into the first quarter of the 19th century, his medical outlook belongs to an earlier period, and from the point of view of psychiatry he is best considered as one of the last great classifiers of the 18th century (Postel, 1981). He was also one of the translators of Cullen into French. His *Nosographie Philosophique* first appeared in 1798 and changed not a great deal in subsequent editions. His analysis of hypochondria is lively and critical of earlier writers: 'it is difficult to gain a clear idea of hypochondria and not to confuse it with either hysteria or melancholia'.

Boerhave, the Leyden school, Fracassini, Sauvages, and the 'English authors' are all found wanting. Of the latter he wrote:

> One may consult with avidity the English authors Sydenham, Cheyne, Whytt who have the great advantage of frequently observing cases of hypochondria, disease which often occurs in England, and which has been very well described by them. But instead of using the analytical method and consider it as an independent condition, they confuse it by emphasising its complications. Stahl is the only one who has tackled it properly: He is the only one who has tried to separate it from all other nervous diseases and demonstrate with clarity its independent nature. (p.84, vol 3 Pinel, 1813)

Interestingly enough, when it comes to dealing with the symptoms, causality and treatment of hypochondria, Pinel says very little which had not been stated before (see pp.87–9). In the editions that appeared after 1801, he recommended the work of Louhier Villermais (sic) (*Recherches historiques et médicales sur l'Hypochondrie*).

Hypochondria and the nineteenth century
By the end of the 18th century, the term 'hypochondriasis' was losing favour, since it did not fit easily with the new theories of nervous origin of functional somatic symptoms. For example, Benjamin Rush (1745–1813), who had trained in Britain, upon his return to the USA wrote that he wished he could find a better term than hypochondriasis: firstly, 'it would be equally proper to call every form of madness hypochondriasm' . . . 'for they are all accompanied by abdominal symptoms'; and secondly the name 'has unfortunately been supposed to imply an imaginary disease' and 'is always offensive to patients who are affected with it' (Rush, 1812). Rush himself preferred the term 'tristimania', and argued that it differed from hysteria in its symptomatology, notably in its 'extremes of high and low spirits'. Early in the century, however, others began to narrow the term to refer to valetudinarian preoccupations. One example is Jean-Pierre Falret who in 1822 used 'hypochondriasis' to refer to morbid preoccupation with physical health or fear of disease (Veith, 1965).

By the beginning of the 19th century, there was a new generation of asylum-based doctors specializing in severe mental illness. The emergence of psychiatry as a speciality in Britain, France and Germany led, towards the end of the century, to a growing split from neurology and the study of psychosis became distinct from the study of neurosis (Micale, 1990). General physicians still found themselves treating large numbers of patients with somatic symptoms with no evidence of physical disease. They preferred to call these disorders by a variety of new names, reflecting current theories about its nervous origin: neurosis, spinal irritation, cerebral irritation, neurospasm, and neurasthenia. However the debate between physicians who looked for physical causes for neurosis (somatogenesis) and those who regarded neuroses as psychological disorders (psychogenesis) ran on throughout the 19th century (López Piñero, 1983). The 19th century can also be considered as the century that emphasized the organic disorders and the insanities (psychoses). Hence, although important monographs were still published on hypochondriasis, it is noticeable that psychiatric textbook writers treated it in the context of other diseases.[7]

E. von Feuchtersleben (1806–1849) and 'cœnæsthesis'
This great Viennese physician is one of the first 19th century textbook writers to suggest that hypochondriasis resulted from pathological common feeling: 'hypochondriasis, as a state of disease, whose description, owing to the mutability of the phenomena, whose reduction to one principle, and whose treatment, have always been the *vexa medicorum*, is in its essence nothing but a cœnæsthesis abnormally heightened in all directions' (Feuchtersleben, 1847, p.222). There were two forms of hypochondriasis (*sine* and *cum materie*) according to whether cœnæsthesis (*Gemeingefühl*) originated from psychological heightening (a persistent attention to sensations) or from an organic increase in the sensitivity of the nerves, respectively.[8] Feuchtersleben commented that whilst Dubois d'Amiens (1833) (on this great man's contribution to the topic see: Place, 1986) considered an organic increase in sensitivity to be the *only* cause of hypochondriasis, 'in nature, however, there appears a circle between psychical and physical causes'. The debate on whether imagination or real

sensation was the primary component continued during the 20th century in relation to the development of delusional parasitosis (Berrios, 1985).

HYPOCHONDRIA AS A FORM OF 'INSANITY'

Since the 17th century, hypochondria had been a 'nervous disorder' (Hare, 1991). During the 18th century, changes in aetiological theory led to a gradual broadening of this class to the point that most clinical conditions (including insanity and organic delirium) became 'neuroses' under Cullen's 'neuralpathology' theory (López Piñero, 1983). During the following century, the implementation of the *anatomo-clinical model of disease* (Ackerknecht, 1967), and of the new descriptive psychopathology (Berrios, 1984) caused progressive attrition on the class 'neuroses'. As diseases were found to have specific lesions they were re-classified away from the neuroses.

Thus, by the second half of the 19th century, the group was becoming as small as it had once been during the 17th century. The over generality of the noble Cullean definition of neuroses as *sensus et motus laesi, sine pyrexia idiopathica, et sine morbo locali* (p.293) ('preternatural affections of sense and motion, which are without pyrexia as a part of the primary disease') (Cullen, 1827, p.1) made little sense in the new world of specificities, and to accommodate clinical phenomena such as hypochondria writers either proposed a new definition (anatomical lesion became functional or psychological lesion) or assimilated it into the insanities in the hope that anatomical lesions might eventually be found.

The latter was the preferred line. For example, the ever popular 1849 volume on mental illness of *La Bibliothèque du Médecin-Practicien* edited by Fabre includes a clear message as to the change of status of hypochondria: 'today, and like all the other monomanias (partial insanities), hypochondria is generally and with reason considered as being caused by a disorder of brain function'. But when reviewing the pathological anatomy of the condition, the author ruefully states: however, 'in the case of hypochondria this section is kept only for reasons of organization. For, in the rare cases in which it has been possible to carry out postmortems in subjects who have actually died whilst hypochondriacal (rather than on account of a complication of the disease) no lesion has been found to explain the disorder. Amongst recent authors, Broussais has been the only one to report "gastric inflammation" only to recant later' (Fabre, 1849, p.629). Indeed, Broussais (1828) had suggested that there was a 'reciprocal influence between emotions and visceral irritations: for example, in the same way that fear causes palpitations, the latter – when caused by any physical cause – might trigger the memory of fear. This may explain the frequency of sensations in hypochondriacs who have developed chronic gastritis' (p.462).[9]

Hypochondria was re-conceptualized as a form of insanity. Louyer Villermay was one of the first to suggest three stages: 'during the first, the disorder only involves the organs of the abdomen; in the second it extend to the chest and the head, and in the third and last the involvement of brain functions becomes predominant'. This view was challenged by Georget who stated that it 'had no basis other than the opinion of its author' (Fabre, 1841). Dubois d'Amiens also suggested a three-stage model but the criterion was no longer differences in organ involvement but severity. Thus, in the third stage there was 'chronic inflammation of most organs . . . and recovery was almost impossible' (Fabre, 1841, p.91).

At the very end of the century George Savage (1892), still felt that he had to write: 'the word hypochondriasis has a very wide meaning, and includes forms of insanity, as well as many disorders which cannot properly be so-called. Under this name we shall have to describe a nervous disorder varying from slight over-sensitiveness to insanity with marked delusions and actively suicidal tendencies' (p.610).

C.F. Michéa (1815–1882)

Michéa's work[10] summarizes well French views on hypochondriasis during the first half of the 19th century as developed by four classical authors: Georget, Louyer Villermay, Falret, and Dubois d'Amiens. Michéa recognized well the importance of developing an operational definition: 'if in all clinical questions it is essential to understand the importance of the words involved, in the case of hypochondria it is doubly so'. He felt that 'hypochondria' was a confusing anachronism but accepted that a young psychiatrist had little chance to operate a terminological change: 'unless it was supported by a célèbre authority' (p.573). Ideally, 'the definition of a disease should imply adequate knowledge of its localization and intimate nature' (p.574) but this is far from the case in hypochondria. Usefully, he also collected the international synonymy.[11]

By defining hypochondria as a sad monomania (monomanie triste), Michéa committed himself to the view that the condition was a form of depression in which there was 'an exaggeration or exaltation of the instinct of preservation (biophilie) and hence a better name would be nécrophobomanie' (p.575). The neologism never caught on. He agreed with the view that there were an idiopathic and secondary form and that only the former was the true hypochondria. He also followed Dubois d'Amiens in his three-stages analysis of the evolution of the disorder: 'the first stage is characterized by mental changes such as delusions and pure monomania . . . the second includes functional disorders and neuroses of some organs . . . the third includes anatomical changes (lésions de tissu)' (p.577). He replaced Dubois' six groups with a five-fold classification: hypochondriac, pneumo-cardiac, encephalic, genital, and organopathic (p.583).[12]

B.A. Morel (1809–1873)

Although better known for his work on degeneration, Morel was a fine clinician and nosologist and in 1860 offered the first French classification of mental disorders based on aetiological principles. True hypochondria was for him a form of insanity (folie hystérique) that resulted from la transformation de certaines névroses (p.264). There was a hypocondrie simple which affected 'those who worried excessively about their health and were le désespoir des médecins' (p.266). It could become a veritable delusional syndrome in which case the valetudinarian symptoms always 'occupied the forefront of the condition' (p.709). This disorder was often hereditary: 'I have seen hereditary insanity become complicated by hypochondriacal phenomena' (Morel, 1860, p.525).

W. Griesinger (1817–1868)

Griesinger (1861) wrote: 'the hypochondriacal states represent the most moderate form of insanity, and have features which essentially distinguish them from the other forms of melancholia' (p.215) 'the hypochondriac may reason correctly – setting out from false premises, but this does not negate the fact that hypochondria is a mental disorder, any more than because hypochondria often accompanies or complicates various chronic diseases seated in different organs, it ought on that account to be confounded with these diseases' (p.216). Griesinger's effort to integrate hypochondria into the continuum of insanity is a manifestation of this support for the unitary approach to insanity (Berrios and Beer, 1994).

In regards to explanations, he followed Kant and Feuchtersleben:

> it is evident that hypochondria may arise in two different ways. In the first place, as a secondary cerebro-spinal irritation, in consequence of internal, but often slight, diseases (of the intestine, the liver, the genital organs, and even kidney), which give rise more to a feeling of general discomfort . . . in the second place, however, hypochondria may also arise via a direct psychological route (*psychischem Wege entstehen*), in as much as through external circumstances the ideas may be so constantly directed to the state of the general health, or of one particular organ, as to induce morbid sensations. (p.221)

J.L. Luys (1828–1897), hypochondria and interoceptive hallucinations

This great French neuropsychiatrist, who has been accused of gullibility (particularly in his later work on hysteria, hypnosis, and the action of drugs at the distance (Escalard, 1983)) put forward the interesting suggestion that the inner sensations which gave origin to hypochondriasis were veritable proprioceptive hallucinations (*hallucinations viscérales*): 'hallucinations that originate from disorders of visceral sensibility determine the various forms of hypochondria' . . . 'these are delusional types which are first intermittent and then become continuous. Patients may claim that their throat is closed, that are edentulous, that their stomach is blocked, that they have no bowels and cannot go to the toilet, etc'. . . 'these complaints should be considered as veritable interoceptive hallucinations mostly resulting from the gastrointestinal regions; thoracic ones are rare' . . . 'when these hallucinations become associated with those from external senses, the prognosis is sombre because spreading of the irritation to the cortex can be suspected' (Luys, 1881, pp.420–1).

A. Foville (1831–1887) and J. Cotard (1840–1889)

Achilles Foville (*fils*) and Jules Cotard wrote entries on hypochondria for Jaccoud's and Dechambre's dictionaries, respectively. Although both analysed the same domain of national and international literature, they draw different conclusions. This can only be partially explained by the fact that these men were in almost opposite poles of the French ideological divide. Foville (1874) offers a longer historical introduction and defines 'simple hypochondria as a non-psychotic disorder, a habitual state of non-motivated anxiety concerning physical health . . . which can be found alone or as a complication in other conditions' (pp.159–60). Cotard (1888) subscribes to Littré's definition that 'it is a nervous disease that affects thinking and makes patients believe that they have imaginary diseases and can render them depressed'. Foville was less interested in the 'old gastrointestinal symptoms'. Cotard focused on these in order to explain the disease which, is characterized by an exaggerated psychological response, not only visceral pains are amplified but normal sensations cause anxiety . . . it is less a veritable hyperaesthesia than a dysaesthesia, i.e. a hyperesthesia linked to a blunting of sensation (*léger degré d'obtusion sensorielle*) . . . but it is mainly in the cortical elaboration of the sensation where sensations are transformed into extraordinary notions that can be the beginning of insanity. (pp.141–2)

R. Krafft-Ebing (1840–1902) and mild paranoia

The great German psychiatrist followed Griesinger's lead in regards to the nosological status of hypochondria: 'the debate on whether hypochondria is a neurosis or a psychosis should be, all things considered, decided in favour of the latter' . . . 'concerning the place of hypochondria amongst the psychoses, there are differences of opinion. Griesinger regards it as a mild form of melancholia' (p.552). Krafft-Ebing (1893) then explained the mechanisms involved: 'hypochondria may be called a neurosis of the general feeling (*Gemeingefühlneurose*), with effects on the psychological sphere'. The important psychological manifestations of hypochondriacal neuropsychosis (*hypochondrische Neuro(psycho)se*) are 'a facilitated power of apperception (*Apperceptionsfähigkeit*) of the psychological organs, as a result of which the exciting processes (often causal) in the nerves of other organs become conscious. At the same time they become coloured by lively feelings of displeasure' . . . 'the state of consciousness of the patient may extend from ideas of severe disease to the most absurd interpretations of sensations that are actually experienced' . . . 'With Merklin, we are justified in calling hypochondria, on account of these facts, a mild form of paranoia' (p.553).[13]

Twentieth century

Sigmund Freud (1856–1939) classified hypochondriasis as an actual neurosis (in which somatic factors played a predominant causal role). In a classic paper, Gillespie (1928) pointed out that the term hypochondriasis was poorly defined and its meaning fluctuated wildly. He proposed a set of strict clinical criteria: a variety of paraesthesias, a preoccupation of patients with themselves and their bodily functioning, a conviction that they were ill, a refusal to be reassured to the contrary, and a failure to respond to psychotherapy.

Meanwhile the concept of cœnesthesia regained currency in France, denoting an aggregate of general somatic sensations: 'the deep but more or less indefinite awareness that we have of our own bodies and the general tone of functional activity' (Dupré, 1913). Cœnestopathic states (Dupré, 1913) were 'disorders of the primary elements of bodily sensation, i.e., the distressing feelings which emanate from one or other of the cœnesthesic areas'. 'It is not an emotional illness, but simply a change in the normal quality of physical feeling in certain parts of the body . . . in people whose sensory capacity is disordered'.

Stekel and 'somatization'

The word 'somatization' (*somatisieren*) was coined by the Viennese psychoanalyst Wilhelm Stekel (1868–1940). His concept of somatization had close affinities with Freud's conversion hysteria. Stekel had worked with Freud in Vienna (he was one of four founder-members of the Wednesday Society in 1902) until they parted company in 1912. The following entry appears in the glossary of *Peculiarities of Behavior* (English edition, 1925): 'Somatization: Conversion of emotional states into physical symptoms; see Conversion'. A further glossary entry reads: 'Conversion: Transposition of repressed emotions into physical manifestations'.

As mentioned above, Freud had classified conversion hysteria as a 'psychoneurosis', in contradistinction to hypochondriasis, neurasthenia and anxiety neurosis which he regarded as 'actual neuroses'. Freud held that psychoneuroses were the result of unconscious conflicts, whereas actual neuroses were predominantly physical in nature, the result of dammed-up sexual energy. He was reluctant to apply psychoanalytic explanations to bodily disorders which were not mediated by the voluntary nervous system, or which did not involve the apparatus of emotional expression.

By contrast, Stekel argued that every state of morbid anxiety was 'psychically determined' and that neurasthenia as Freud had defined it did not exist. 'In every case of actual neurosis I found the psychical cause, and came to the conclusion that every neurosis is caused by a psychic conflict' (Stekel, 1923). He laid down as a general principle that 'all neuroses are psychic diseases'. Stekel claimed that 'many cases diagnosed by other physicians as heart-trouble, asthma, stomach trouble . . . were caused by mental conflicts'. Physicians overlooked these facts because they had not understood the 'organic language of the soul'. 'This phrase means that neurotics have a wonderful ability to express their mental states in a symbolic language of the bodily organs'.

Stekel provides two examples of somatization in his book, *Patterns of Psychosexual Infantilism* (English edition, 1953). One was a man who presented with a swollen knee, which Stekel believed symbolised the swollen head of his father who died after a fall. 'The inflammatory condition of his knee is like a memento; it constantly reminds him not to forget his father'. The other case was a man who had experienced pain in the groin and back for 24 years since the death of his father, who had suffered similar pain from a hernia.

Franz Alexander and 'psychosomatic specificity'
Stekel believed that there were 'certain areas of predilection' for the organic expression of psychic conflicts. The thesis of psychosomatic specificity was pursued by Franz Alexander and his colleagues at the Chicago Institute for Psychoanalysis in the 1930s. They regarded seven conditions as archetypal psychosomatic disorders: essential hypertension, neurodermatitis, bronchial asthma, rheumatoid arthritis, duodenal ulcer, ulcerative colitis and hyperthyroidism. Much of their research consisted of attempts to show that sufferers from these conditions experienced specific psychological conflicts or exhibited specific types of personality (Alexander and French, 1948).

Unlike Stekel, Alexander himself believed that there were two fundamentally different types of somatic symptom-formation, viz. conversion as in hysteria, and vegetative neurosis (for example, peptic ulcer). The hysterical conversion symptom is an attempt to relieve an emotional tension by some symbolic expression, whereas the vegetative neurosis is not a substitute expression but a physiological concomitant of emotion, which becomes chronically established when the conflict remains unresolved (Lewis, 1967).

The term 'somatization' 1940–1980
The word 'somatization' does not appear in any of the standard British psychiatric textbooks, nor in the British psychoanalytic literature during this period. British psychoanalysts continued to use Freud's terminology of conversion hysteria. It was in North America that the term 'somatization' came into limited use from the 1940s as a synonym for conversion hysteria, which suggests that Stekel had a wider readership there than in Britain. Among works on psychosomatic illness, 'somatization of emotions' is discussed by Menninger (1947), Sontag (1948) and Chrzanowski (1959). In 1968 Lipowski proposed his definition of somatization as a tendency to experience, conceptualise and/or communicate psychological states or contents as bodily sensations, functional changes, or somatic metaphors. This definition broadens the scope of the concept, but retains the implicit notion of a conversion of psychological contents into bodily sensations or bodily metaphors.

In the *British Journal of Psychiatry* during the 1970s there were many papers reporting on aspects of psychiatry in Africa, India, and the Middle East. Without exception these authors comment on the high proportion of psychiatric patients in these countries who present with somatic symptoms, but nowhere does the term 'somatization' appear. In 1977 Kleinman published his influential paper *Depression, somatization and the 'new cross-cultural psychiatry'* which established the term 'somatization' within the transcultural psychiatric literature. Kleinman defines somatization as the 'expression of personal and social distress in an idiom of bodily complaints with medical help-seeking'.

'Somatization disorder' and 'hypochondriasis' in DSM-III
The publication of the third edition of the American Psychiatric Association's *Diagnostic and Statistical Manual of Mental Disorders* in 1980 initiated extensive changes in psychiatric nomenclature. The DSM-III nosological scheme of 'somatoform disorders' consists of four entities: somatization disorder, conversion disorder, hypochondriasis and atypical somatoform disorder.

The term 'hysteria' was abandoned and a new syndrome 'somatization disorder' was created. This is defined by DSM-III as 'a chronic but fluctuating disorder which begins early in life, and is characterized by recurrent and multiple somatic complaints for which medical attention is sought but which are not apparently due to any physical illness'. This new category of somatization disorder owes its status to the St. Louis school (Nemiah, 1985), to which they gave the eponym Briquet's syndrome.

A separate diagnostic category 'hypochondriasis' also appeared among the group of somatoform disorders. DSM-III hypochondriasis is characterized by the fear or belief that one has a serious disease; physical signs or symptoms for which there is no medical explanation; the ineffectiveness of appropriate reassurance; and a duration of more than 6 months. The symptoms must not occur only during panic attacks and must not be delusional.

These diagnostic categories in DSM-III generated continuing controversy about their boundaries. The definition of 'somatization disorder' was criticised because it arbitrarily separated a group of patients who lie at one end of the spectrum of severity (Katon et al, 1991); they belong to a much larger population of patients who present with somatic symptoms, and who may also meet criteria for mood disorders or anxiety disorders. The definition of 'hypochondriasis' excluded many patients who are preoccupied with their physical health, for example with a diagnosed physical ailment (especially in terminal illness), grief reactions, depressive disorders and schizophrenia (Barsky et al, 1992). Patients meeting criteria for DSM-III hypochondriasis may in fact simultaneously meet criteria for anxiety and depressive disorders or somatization disorder.

BODY DYSMORPHIC DISORDER

The term 'dysmorphophobia' was coined in 1886 by Enrico Morselli (1891) to refer to complaints whose common denominator was a negative attitude towards bodily, particularly facial disfigurement. Such an attitude was indistinctly conceptualized by the author as 'phobia', 'obsession' or 'fixed idea' (all three terms used in their pre-1895 sense). Since then, both the *concepts* and *behaviours* brought under such terminological umbrella have changed and the ensuing confusion has led some modern authors to suggest that the term dysmorphophobia – unjustly blamed for such changes – ought to be jetissoned. To deal with the 'neurotic' end of the disorder, the new term *body dysmorphic disorder* was introduced by DSM III-R, whilst cases exhibiting 'delusional' intensity were classified under *delusional (paranoid) disorder, somatic type*. As mentioned above, DSM IV has kept the category but added the extra-criterion of 'clinically significant distress or impairment' in psychosocial functioning. ICD-10 includes under *hypochondriacal disorder* both body dysmorphic disorder and non-delusional dysmorphophobia, and under *other persistent delusional disorder* the so-called delusional dysmorphophobia.

Pre-nineteenth century issues
Since Classical times, writers have been concerned about those who thought little of themselves, whether of their mind or body. For example, Robert Burton (1883) in his *Anatomy of Melancholy* dedicated space to ancient arguments used to convince those with physical handicaps or battle disfigurement that 'the body matter little': 'deformities or imperfections of our bodies be they innate or accidental torture many men: yet this may comfort to them, that those imperfections of the body do not a whit blemish the soul, or hinder the operations of it, but rather help and much increase it' (p.379). It is doubtful whether such advice ever worked.[14]

The nineteenth century
The nineteenth century was not immune to similar concerns. Alienists took seriously those patients who worried about facial deformity and depending upon the severity of their complaint, considered them as hypochondriacal or melancholic in origin.

Enrico Morselli (1852–1929)
When Morselli began to work in this field he had already been out of Modena Clinical School for twelve years. Trained under Canestrini, he learned phrenology at the instigation of Gaddi, the great anthropologist, who believed that this

discipline was the most scientific of all psychiatric specialisms. Morselli trained as a psychiatrist at the mental hospital of Reggio Emilia under Livi. He won a scholarship to the Instituto di Studi Superiori of Florence where he worked with the physiognomist Paolo Mantegazza. In 1880, he went to Turin and worked both at hospital and University. Therein he delivered the lectures he was to include in his *General Anthropology* and also wrote his famous book on suicide. In 1881, he founded the *Rivista di Filosofia scientifica* which became the organ of the Italian positivism. In Turin, he built up a private practice for the rich, and this was probably the main source of patients for his work on dysmorphophobia as, in general, such complaints were unheard of in the asylums for the insane. In 1885, he published his *Manuale di semejotica delle malattia mentali* which was to become a popular textbook of descriptive psychopathology. In 1890, Morselli moved to Genoa by which time he grew unhappy with neuropathological explanations as shown in the second volume of his *Semejotica*, published in 1894 where he emphasized the role of emotions in the generation of mental symptoms. But during the early 1880s, when collecting his 'dysmorphophobic' patients, Morselli was still infatuated with the brain. There is little doubt that this interest had to do with his training in physical anthropology.

Morselli defined dysmorphophobia as *an idea ossesiva, desolante, della deformitá corporea* and classified it as either 'rudimentary paranoia' or 'abortive monomania'. This makes sense in terms of the 1880s European debate on the clinical extension of these two categories. Such an idea threatened the sense of 'personal integration' of the individual and could be either primary or secondary according to whether it was a defence against a direct injury or a manifestation of a deeper psychological disturbance.

The clinical phenomenon (but not the word) was widely discussed during the early part of the twentieth century. Fears of ugliness were studied by Kaan (1892) in his book on neurasthenia and obsession. Hartenberg (1901) referred to similar worries in his book on timidity; and Dupré (1913) explained the condition in terms of a disturbance of proprioceptive information. Janet (1903) called it 'feelings of shame of the body' and considered it as a form of *psychasthenia*.

The term 'dysmorphophobia' took time to catch on. It probably first came into English in the translation of Tanzi's (1909) *Textbook of mental diseases* when it is mentioned in the section on obsessive ideas linked to Morselli's name (p.150). It was legitimated by Kraepelin (1915) in his chapter on *Die Zwangsneurose* (*Dysmorphophobie*; p.1861, vol.4).[15] Kraepelin also discussed the clinical phenomenon under *Ereuthophobie* (p.1862). Many other terms have since been coined to deal with the same theme: shame of the body, psychosis of ugliness, hypochondria of beauty, madness of introspection, etc. It is unlikely that such new terms had advanced our knowledge of the disorder.

The word has been used on and off since the beginning of the century; and better than anything else, the statistical analysis of cases reported throughout should give an idea of usage patterns. A review by Berrios and Kan (1996) of 150 historical papers, yielded about 300 cases. Of these, the authors analysed 160 on the basis of 23 robust variables: age, sex, marital status, age of onset of illness, precipitant events, presence of: psychotic symptoms, depression, anxiety or obsessional disorder apart from the main symptom, family history of psychiatric illness, premorbid history of psychiatric illness or personality disorder, sexual difficulties, treatment offered: drugs or psychotherapy, outcome, course of the condition, whether the symptom remained true to form or changed into another recognizable disorder, suicidal behaviour, nature of the dysmorphophobia: organs or symptoms, and whether or not the patient was in useful employment.

The sample included 83 males and 77 females, their mean age being 29.46 (SD: 12 years) and mean age of onset being 21.8 (SD: 10); patients thus coming to see the doctor an average of eight years after onset of their condition. 43 subjects were married and 107 were unmarried or divorced. In 46 per cent of the sample, reports stated the presence of depression, in 21 per cent of psychosis, in 81 per cent of anxiety, and in 60 per cent of obsessive disorder (overlaps were frequently reported). In 41 per cent of the cases, there was family history of some form of mental illness, 53 per cent had personal history of psychiatric illness, and 81 per cent were described as having some form of premorbid personality disorder. Only 18 per cent reported some form of 'sexual disorder'. As far as treatments were concerned, 55 per cent received some form of medication and 38 per cent psychotherapy. Three types of outcome were recorded: good 35 per cent, partial response 36 per cent and no response 18 per cent (there was 10 per cent of missing data).

The course of the illness was divided into three groups: continuous 41 per cent, relapsing 31 per cent and full remission only 18 per cent (8 per cent of missing data). In 82 per cent of the cases, the illness was true to form. Only 11 per cent of the cases made any suicidal attempts or threats, in 44 per cent the dysmorphophobia involved an organ which was psychodynamically relevant such as the nose, breasts or genitalia, in 55 per cent other organs, and in only 28 per cent functions as opposed to organs were involved. During the illness, 61 per cent of subjects managed to be in useful occupation.

The following correlations proved significant: 1. The younger the subject the higher the chance of being treated with medication $(0.28, p < 0.01)$; 2. Women were given more psychotherapy than men $(0.34, p < 0.001)$; 3. Marriage seemed a protective factor $(0.36, p < 0.001)$; 4. The longer the disease, the higher the chance of receiving drugs, the shorter, of being offered psychotherapy $(0.25, p < 0.01)$; 5. Patients who were reported as 'psychotic' had more sexual difficulties $(0.23, p < 0.01)$, complained more often of an impairment of a function $(0.25, p < 0.01)$; and had worse outcome $(0.33, p < 0.001)$; and 6. Presence of anxiety was a very good prognostic indicator $(0.19, p < 0.01)$ and tended to be associated with somatic complaints which were psychodynamically relevant $(0.27, p < 0.001)$.

Gender comparison showed that females complained more often about organs which were psychodynamically significant $(p < 0.01)$, and males about bodily functions $(p < 0.01)$. Bad outcome cases included a significantly higher number of cases with psychotic features $(p < 0.006)$, sexual problems $(p < 0.009)$ and unemployment through illness $(p < 0.01)$ and were treated more often with drugs $(p < 0.0005)$ than bad outcome cases. To ascertain whether DSM III (1980) caused any major effects on clinical *description* cases were compared which had been reported before (pre) and after (post) 1980 (96 and 64 cases, respectively). The only significant differences between the two samples were: Pre-1980 cases had earlier onset $(p < 0.01)$, more diagnosis of psychosis $(p < 0.01)$, more sexual problems (p <0.001), more somatic symptoms with psychodynamic significance (p <0.001) and more unemployed subjects (p <0.001); they also received less drug treatment (p <0.001) and their outcome was far worse than in the post-1980 sample (p <0.001). These results show that changes in diagnostic criteria have altered little the 'phenomenology' of dysmorphophobia and that they have been more important to what can be called its historical nosology, i.e. shifts have only taken place in aetiological speculation.

Summary
The history of the somatoform disorders must be split into that of its constituting sub-groups as there is no yet known 'biological invariant' to keep them together. The blurred nature of the boundaries between hypochondriasis, somatization, and conversion disorders highlights the difficulty of defining disease entities in this area of psychiatry. It is essential therefore to distinguish the history of the word, the concept and the behaviours. The aetiological theories and behaviours attached to the Classical notion of hypochondria were challenged during the 17th century when the latter became a 'nervous disorder'. During the 19th century, this process was completed in that new behaviours (valetudinarian preoccupations) and new concepts (proprioceptive hallucinations, delusions, visceral hypersensitivity, etc.) were attached to the word hypochondria that by then was but an empty shell. From a nosological point of view, emphasis was put on the idiopathic (rather than the secondary) form of the disorder, and as the Cullean notion of neurosis disappeared, hypochondriasis was alternatively considered as a form of insanity, a subtype of melancholia or a monomania. Towards the end of the century, it became associated with the rising notion of neurasthenia, and after the Freudian revolution it tended to be given a pure psychological interpretation.

'Dysmorphophobia' was coined last century to refer to negative attitudes to the body and self that are likely to have existed from the beginning of mankind. The concepts used to explain these behaviours (e.g. phobias, delusions, fixed ideas, obsessions) have periodically changed and it is likely that this will continue in the future. The history of these disorders shows that the behaviours involved are surprisingly stable but probably aetiologically heterogeneous.

NOTES

1 The word *hypochondrium* temporarily disappeared from the anatomical lexicon during the time of Celsius who used *praecordia* to mean: '1. The lower chest in front of the heart; 2. the region over the diaphragm, and 3. the upper abdomen below the ribs (*hypochondria*)' (Celsus, 1935, p.100). The same is the case with Caelius Aurelianus (1950): 'also pain in the head, pressure on the chest (*praecordiorum etiam tension*), and fixity of gaze or frequent blinking' (p.20).

2 The Platonic scheme lies behind the concept of 'hypochondriac melancholy' of Galen (circa AD 130–200). This was one of three forms of melancholia (the accumulation of 'black bile') which affected abdominal organs below the costal margin, especially the stomach. The principal symptoms were flatulence, abdominal pain, belching and associated psychological

symptoms. In Graeco-Roman medicine, 'black bile' was not merely a material substance, but also a psychic force (Galen, 1916, Book II, Chapter IX). The theory of humours thus enshrined a psychosomatic concept of the emotions (Gardiner et al, 1937). Galenic humoral pathology held sway until the study of anatomy by renaissance physicians focused attention on organs rather than humours. The failure to find the anatomical channels for the humours to flow between the organs led to a discrediting of the Galenist theory of the emotions, and to the use of new terms such as 'the spleen' and 'vapours' (Fischer-Homberger, 1983).

3 At the same time, Burton quotes Crato's prescient remark that: 'in this hypochondriacal or flatuous melancholy, the symptoms are so ambiguous that the most well trained physicians cannot identify the part involved' ('*In hypochondriaca melancholia adeo ambigua sunt symptomata, ut etiam exercitatissimi medici de loco affecto statuere non possint*') (Burton, 1883, p.269).

4 However, Blackmore ridiculed the notion that these somatic symptoms could be caused by fumes or vapours rising up from the lower to upper regions of the body. For one thing, 'there are no Passages, or proper Conveyances, by which these Streams and Exhalations may mount from the inferior to the superior Parts . . . .' He offers a psychological explanation for these symptoms: 'Terrible ideas, formed only in the Imagination, will affect the Brain and the Body with painful Sensations . . . .' He was well aware of the problem of differential diagnosis of psychiatric disorders: 'The Limits and Partitions that bound and discriminate . . . Hypochondriack and Hysterick Disorders, and Melancholy, Lunacy and Phrenzy, are so nice, that it is not easy to distinguish them, and set the Boundaries where one ends, and the other begins'. However, although hypochondriasis and hysteria 'sometimes affects the intellectual Faculties', they seldom result in 'a State of Lunacy'.

5 De Mandeville was a colourful Dutch physician (living in London) better known for his socio-political tract the *Fable of the Bees*. Without a large practice, he seems to have been something of a man-about-town who on occasions had to resort to the financial support of his fellow-country men.

6 Robinson advocated drastic physical cures: 'the most violent Vomits, the strongest purging Medicines, and large Bleeding, are to be often repeated'. He reproached those physicians who played safe: 'It is Cruelty in the highest Degree, not to be bold in the Administration of Medicines, when the Nature of the Disease absolutely demands the Assistance of a powerful Remedy'. By contrast, Cheyne argued for a better diet, and avoidance of 'Gluttony and Intemperance in fermented Liquors'. He cited the example of Sir Isaac Newton who 'confin'd himself to a small Quantity of Bread . . . with a little Sack and Water'.

7 For example Esquirol (1838) dedicates no special chapter to the topic but makes it feature in the differential diagnosis of *lypémanie* (the transitional term for depressive illness) (Berrios, 1988). Guislain (1852) wrote: 'sometimes, melancholia is characterized by intense valetudinarian preoccupations . . . the patient worries about having non-existent diseases . . . this is called melancholic hypochondria . . . hypochondria can be bodily and mental, the

latter being melancholic hypochondria proper' . . . 'the former is uncommon in mental hospitals but is often found in the community. These patients only come to hospital when severely ill' (pp.120–1). Axenfeld (1883), the author of the last great book on 'neuroses' (in the old sense) did not dedicate a section to hypochondria, dealing with it in the chapter on neurasthenia: 'is nervousness different from hypochondria? it is evident that it is not if we refer to the descriptions of the ancients; however, if hypochondria is defined as nosomania (*nosomanie*) then it would be different' (p.896). And at the very end of the century, the great Jules Séglas (1895) lectured that the 'other name for non-delusional melancholia is moral hypochondria (*hipocondrie morale*)' (p.283).

8 Feuchtersleben equated *Hypochondriasis sine materie* with 'a fancied cricket disease': 'Kant derives this name from the attention which is excited through the disturbance caused by the nocturnal chirping of the house-cricket. I believe that the term *grillenfangen* has always been used to indicate, *per analogiam*, the employment of an idle imagination concentrated on itself'.

9 Likewise, Jean Baptiste Parchappe (1841), in his wonderful collection of postmortem reports, included the case of a married 51 year old carpenter who developed an affective disorder in reaction to the insanity of his wife. This was accompanied by abdominal pains and hypochondriacal complaints. On post-mortem he was found to have 'large cortical plaques and softening of the brain' (pp.36–7).

10 In the 1843 essay competition of the *L'Académie Royale de Médecine*, the young Michéa was awarded the 'encouragement medal' for his entry on *L'Hypocondrie*. The same year, the work was published in the *Mémoires* of the Academy, and in 1845 as a book.

11 'French: *maladie vaporeuse, imaginaire*; English: hypochondriac passion, low spirits, vapours; German: *Milzkrankheit, Grillenkheit* (sic); Belgian: *zwaarmoedigheid*; Danish: *modsot*; Swedish: *miaeltsinka*; Italian: *ipocondria*; Spanish: *hipocondria, pasion hipocondriaca*; Portuguese: *molestia hipocondriaca*; Polish: *hypochondrya*' (p.574).

12 Hypochondria had a bad outcome: transformation into insanity, involuntary death or suicide (pp.604–5), and to its development contributed: heredity, nervous temperament and constitution (the 19th century terms for personality) (Berrios, 1993), sex (more frequent in males), age (onset between 30 and 40 years), climate (low temperature and 'elevation of the sun'), season, civil status (with Lepois he believed that hypochondria was a disease of priests!), education, ideology, social conditions, profession, slothfulness, loneliness, violent emotions, ethnic group, tendency to read medical books, masturbation, etc. (pp.607–37). The paper finished with few comments on treatment.

13 These quotations reflect well the synthetic approach to hypochondriasis taken by Kraff-Ebing and his emphasis on the fact that it was a form of insanity. He introduces into the explanation the mechanism of apperception which since Leibniz had become important to the understanding of subconscious processes. This mechanism both fixated attention on, and magnified, the panoply of proprioceptive sensations that constitute the *Gemeingefühl* thereby causing psychological hyperaesthesia (*psychische Hyperästhesie*).

14 Marilou Bruchon-Schweitzer (1990), in her *Une Psychologie du Corps* identifies the nocive belief that 'what is beautiful must be good' as one of the more pervasive ones in Western culture.
15 Kraepelin did not mention Morselli by name, thus giving the impression to some that he had coined the word himself. For example, Koupernik (1962) has fallen into this trap.

REFERENCES

Ackerknecht, E. (1967) *Medicine at the Paris Hospital 1794–1848*, Baltimore, Johns Hopkins Press.
Alexander, F. and French T.M. (eds.) (1948) *Studies in Psychosomatic Medicine*, New York, Ronald Press.
American Psychiatric Association (1980) *Diagnostic and Statistical Manual of Mental Disorders*, 3rd ed. (DSM III) Washington DC, APA.
American Psychiatric Association (1994) *Diagnostic and Statistical Manual of Mental Disorders* 4th ed., Washington DC, American Psychiatric Association.
Anonymous (1803) *The Edinburgh Practice of Physic, Surgery, and Midwifery*, vol.2, Medicine, London, Kearsley.
Axenfeld, A. (1883) *Traité de Névroses*, 2nd edition, improved upon by H. Huchard, Paris, Baillière.
Babb, L. (1951) *The Elizabethan Malady. A Study of Melancholia in English Literature from 1580 to 1642*, East Lansing, Michigan State College Press.
Barsky, A.J., Wyshak, G. and Klerman, G.L. (1992) 'Psychiatric comorbidity in DSM-III-R hypochondriasis'. *Archives of General Psychiatry*, 49: 101–8.
Berrios, G.E. (1984) 'Descriptive Psychopathology: Conceptual and Historical Aspects'. *Psychological Medicine*, 14: 303–13.
Berrios, G.E. (1985) 'Delusional Parasitosis and Physical Disease'. *Comprehensive Psychiatry*, 26: 395–403.
Berrios, G.E. (1988) 'Melancholia and depression during the 19th century. A conceptual History'. *British Journal of Psychiatry*, 153: 298–304.
Berrios, G.E. (1993) 'European views on personality disorders: a conceptual history'. *Comprehensive Psychiatry*, 34: 14–30.
Berrios, G.E. and Beer, D. (1994) 'The notion of Unitary Psychosis: a conceptual history'. *History of Psychiatry*, 5: 13–36.
Berrios, G.E. and Kan Chung Sing (1996) 'Dysmorphophobia: a conceptual and statistical history'. In Sánchez, L. and Hollander, E. (eds.) *Controversies on Dysmorphophobia* Washington, APA Press, (in the press).
Blackmore, R. (1725) 'A treatise of the spleen and vapours: or, hypocondriacal and hysterical affections'. In Hunter, R. and Macalpine, I. (1963) *Three Hundred Years of Psychiatry, 1535–1860*, London, Oxford University Press.
Bowman, I.A. (1975) *William Cullen (1710–90) and the Primacy of the Nervous System*, Indiana University Ph.D. Thesis, History of Science, Xerox University Microfilms, Michigan, Ann Harbor.
Broussais, F.J.V. (1828) *De l'Irritation et de la Folie*, Paris, Delaunay.
Bruchon-Schweitzer, M. (1990) *Une Psychologie du Corps*, Paris, Presses Universitaires de France.

Burton, R. (1883) *The Anatomy of Melancholy*, London, Chatto and Windus (First edition 1621).

Bynum, W.F. (1985) 'The nervous patient in eighteenth and nineteenth century Britain: the psychiatric origins of British Neurology'. In Bynum, W.F., Porter, R. and Shepard, M. (eds.) *The Anatomy of Madness*, vol.1, London, Tavistock, pp.89–102.

Caelius Aurelianus (1950) *On Acute Diseases and on Chronic Diseases*. Edited and translated by I.E. Drabkin, Chicago, the University of Chicago Press.

Celsus (1935) *De Medicina*, vol.1, translated by W.G. Spencer, London, Heinemann.

Cheyne, G. (1733) *The English Malady: or, a Treatise of Nervous Diseases of all Kinds, as Spleen, Vapours, Lowness of Spirits, Hypochondriacal, and Hysterical Distempers, etc.*, London, J. Strachan.

Chiarugi, V. (1987) *On Insanity and its Classification*, translated by G. Mora, Canton, USA, Science History Publications.

Chrzanowski, G. (1959) 'Neurasthenia and hypochondriasis', In Arieti, S. (ed.) *American Handbook of Psychiatry*, New York, Basic Books.

Cotard, J. (1888) 'Hypocondrie'. In Dechambre, A. and Lereboullet, A. (eds.) *Dictionnaire Encyclopédique de las Sciences Médicales*, vol.51, Paris, Masson pp.136–57.

Cullen, W. (1803) *Synopsis Nosologiæ Methodicæ*, 6th edition, Edinburgh, W. Creech.

Cullen, W. (1827) *The Works of William Cullen*, 2 vols., edited by J. Thomson, Edinburgh, William Blackwood.

Dechambre, A. (1869) 'Bonet (les deux fréres)'. In Dechambre, A. and Lereboullet, A. (eds.) *Dictionnaire Encyclopédique de las Sciences Médicales*, vol.10, Paris, Masson pp.65–6.

Dewhurst, K. (1966) *Dr. Thomas Syndenham (1924–1689)*, Berkely, University of California Press.

Dubois, E.F. (d'Amiens) (1833) *Histoire Philosophique de l'Hypocondrie et de l'Hystérie*, Paris, Cavelin, Librairie de Deville.

Dupré, E. (1913) 'Les Cénestopathies'. *Mouvement Médical*, 23: 3–22.

Escalard, B. (1983) *Un Méconnu de l'Hystérie. Jules Luys (1828–1897)*, Thèse de Medecine, Université de Caen.

Esquirol, J.E.D. (1838) *Des Maladies Mentales*, 2 vols., Paris, Baillière.

Fabre, D. (ed.) (1841) 'Hypocondrie'. In *Dictionnaire des Dictionnaires de Médecine*, vol.5, Paris, Béthune et Plon, pp.89–96.

Fabre, D. (ed.) (1849) 'Maladies de l'encephale, maladies mentales, maladies nerveuses'. In *Bibliothèque du Médecin-Practicien*, vol.9, Paris, Baillière.

Falret, J.P. (1822) *De l'Hypocondrie et du Suicide*, Paris, Croullebois.

Feuchtersleben, Baron E. von (1847) *The Principles of Medical Psychology*. Translated by H.E. Evand and B.G. Babington, London, Sydenham Society.

Fischer-Homberger, E. (1983) 'Hypochondriasis'. In Shepherd, M. and Zangwill, O.L. (eds.) *Handbook of Psychiatry*, vol.1, Cambridge, Cambridge University Press.

French, R.K. (1969) *Robert Whytt: the Soul and Medicine*, London, The Wellcome Institute of the History of Medicine.

Foville, A. (fils) (1874) 'Hypocondrie'. In Jaccoud, T. (ed.) *Noveau*

Dictionnaire de Médecine et de Chirurgie Pratiques, vol.18, Paris, Baillière, pp.151–75.

Galen (1916) *On the Natural Faculties*, translated by A.J. Brock, London, Heinemann.

Gardiner, H.M., Metcalf, R.C. and Beebe-Center, J.G. (1937) *Feeling and Emotion. A History of Theories*, New York, American Book Company.

Gillespie, R.D. (1928) *Hypochondria: its Definition, Nosology and Psychopathology, Guy's Hospital Reports*, 78: 408.

Griesinger, W. (1861) *Die Pathologie und Therapie der psychischen Krankheiten*, 2nd edition, Stuttgart, Krabbe.

Guislain, J. (1852) *Leçons Orales sur les Phrénopathies, ou Traité Théorique et Pratique des Maladies Mentales*, 3 vols., Gand, L. Hebbelynck.

Hare, E. (1991) 'The history of "nervous disorder" from 1600 to 1840 and a comparison with modern views'. *British Journal of Psychiatry*, 159: 37–45.

Hartenberg, P. (1901) *Les Timides et la Timidité*, Paris, Alcan.

Hippocrates (1923) *Hippocrates, Vol 1, Epidemics I*, Transl. W.H.S. Jones, Loeb Classical Edition, London, Heinemann.

Hunter, R. and Macalpine, I. (1963) *Three Hundred Years of Psychiatry, 1535–1860*, London, Oxford University Press.

Janet, P. (1919) *Les Obsessions et la Psychasthénie*, Third edition, Paris, Alcan (First Edition, 1903).

Kaan, H. (1892) *Der neurasthenische Angstaffekt bei Zwansvorstellungen und der primordiale grubelzwang*, Liepzig, Deuticke.

Kant, I. (1800) *Anthropologie in pragmatischer Hinsicht abgefaßt*, 2nd edition, Königsberg, Friedrich Nicolovius.

Katon, W., Lin, E., von Korff, M. et al (1991) 'Somatization: a spectrum of severity'. *American Journal of Psychiatry*, 148: 34–40.

Kenyon, F.E. (1965) 'Hypochondriasis: a survey of some historical, clinical and social aspects'. *British Journal of Medical Psychology*, 38: 117–33.

Kenyon, F.E. (1976) 'Hypochondriacal states'. *British Journal of Psychiatry*, 129, 1–14.

Kleinman, A. (1977) 'Depression, somatization and the "new cross-cultural psychiatry" '. *Social Science and Medicine*, 11: 3–10.

Koupernik, C. (1962) 'La psychose de laideur ou dysmorphophobie'. *Entretiens de Bichat (médecine)*, pp.321–6.

Kraepelin, E. (1915) *Ein Lehrbuch für studierende und Ärzte*, vol 4, Klinische Psychiatrie, Leipzig, J.A. Barth.

Krafft-Ebing, R. v (1893) *Lehrbuch der Psychiatrie*, Fifth edition, Stuttgart, Enke.

Ladee, G.A. (1966) *Hypochondriacal Syndromes*, Amsterdam, Elsevier.

Lewis, A. (1967) 'Aspects of psychosomatic medicine'. In *Inquiries in Psychiatry: Clinical and Social Investigations*, London, Routledge and Kegan Paul.

Lipowski, Z.J. (1968) 'Review of consultation psychiatry and psychosomatic medicine, III: theoretical issues'. *Psychosomatic Medicine*, 30: 395–422.

López Piñero, J.M.L. (1983) *Historical Origins of the Concept of Neurosis*. (Translated by Berrios, D.) Cambridge, Cambridge University Press.

Luys, J. (1881) *Traité Clinique et Pratique des Maladies Mentales*, Paris, Delahaye at Lecrosnier.

Mandeville, B. de (1711) *A Treatise of the Hypochondriack and the Hysterick Passions. Vulgarly call'd the hypo in men and vapours in women*, London, Dryden Learb.

Menninger, W.C. (1947) 'Psychosomatic medicine: somatization reactions'. *Psychosomatic Medicine*, 9: 92–7.

Micale, M.S. (1990) 'Hysteria and its historiography: the future perspective'. *History of Psychiatry*, i: 33–124.

Michéa, F. (1843) 'Du siége, de la nature intime, des symptomes et du diagnostic de l'hypocondrie'. *Mémoires de l'Académie Royale de Médicine*, 2: 573–654.

Morel, B.A. (1860) *Traité des Maladies Mentales*, Paris, Masson.

Morgagni, J.B. (1769) *The Seats and Causes of Diseases*, 3 vols., London, A. Millar and T. Cadell.

Morselli, E. (1891) 'Sulla dismorfofobia e sulla Tafefobia due forme non per anco descritte di Pazzia con idee fisse'. *Bolletino della R. Accademia Medica di Genova*, 6: 100–19.

Mumford, D.B. (1993) 'Somatization: a transcultural perspective'. *International Review of Psychiatry*, 5: 231–42.

Nemiah, J.C. (1985) 'Somatoform disorders'. In Kaplan, H.I. and Sadock, B.J. (eds.) *Comprehensive Textbook of Psychiatry*, 4th edition, Baltimore, Williams & Williams.

Parchappe, J.B. (1841) *Traité Théorique et Pratique de la Folie*, Paris, Béchet et Labé.

Pinel, P. (1813) *Nosographie Philosophique ou la Méthode de l'Analyse Appliquée à la Médicine*, 5th edition, 3 vols., Paris, Brosson (first edition 1798).

Place, J.L. (1986) 'L'Hypocondrie. Éloge de Dubois d'Amiens'. *L'Evolution Psychiatrique*, 51: 567–86.

Porter, R. (1991) Introduction. In *George Chayne: The English Malady*, London, Tavistock/Routledge, pp.ix–li.

Postel, J. (1981) *La Genèse de la Psychiatrie. Les Premiers Écrits de Philippe Pinel*, Paris, Le Sycomore.

Robinson, N. (1729) 'A new System of the Spleen, Vapours, and Hypochondriack Melancholy: wherein all the decays of the nerves, and lownesses of the spirits, are mechanically accounted for'. In Hunter, R. and Macalpine, I. (1963) *Three Hundred Years of Psychiatry, 1535–1860*, London, Oxford University Press.

Rush, B. (1812) *Medical Inquiries and Observations upon the Diseases of the Mind*, reprinted 1962, New York, Hafner.

Savage, G. (1892) 'Hypochondriasis and insanity'. In Tuke, D.H. (ed.) *A Dictionary of Psychological Medicine*, vol.1, London, J. & A. Churchill.

Séglas, J. (1895) *Leçons Cliniques sur les Maladies Mentales et Nerveuses*. Collected by H. Meige, Paris, Asselin and Houzeau.

Siegel, R.E. (1973) *Galen on Psychology and Psychopathology*, Basel, Karger.

Sontag, L.W. (1948) 'Determinants of predisposition to psychosomatic dysfunction and disease: problem of proneness to psychosomatic disorder'. In Dunbar, F. (ed.) *Synopsis of Psychosomatic Diagnoses and Treatment*, London, Henry Kempton.

Stekel, W. (1923) *Conditions of Nervous Anxiety and their Treatment*, New York, Dodd, Mead & Co.

Stekel, W. (1925) *Peculiarities of Behavior*, volume I–II, London, Williams & Norgate.

Stekel, W. (1953) *Patterns of Psychosexual Infantilism*, London, Peter Nevill.

Sydenham, T. (1850) *The works of Thomas Sydenham M.D.* Translated by G. Latham, 2 vols., London, Printed for the Sydenham Society.

Tanzi, E. (1909) *A Textbook of Mental Diseases*. Translation by W.F. Robertson and T.C. MacKenzie, London, Rebman.

Veith, I. (1965) *Hysteria: the History of a Disease*, Chicago, University of Chicago Press.

Warrington, N. (1965) *Plato's Timeaus*, edited and translated with an introduction, London, Dent.

Whytt, R. (1765) *Observations on the Nature, Causes and Cure of those Diseases which are commonly called Nervous, Hypochondriac or Hysteric*, Edinburgh, Becket & Du Hondt.

Williams, K.E. (1990) 'Hysteria in seventeenth century case records and unpublished manuscripts'. *History of Psychiatry*, i: 383–401.

Willis, Th. (1685) *The London Practice of Physick*, London, Thomas Basset.

Chapter 18
Somatoform Disorders

Social Section
EDWARD SHORTER

Psychosomatic illnesses, or disturbances in the mind-body relationship, cover a wide area of medicine. Merskey has suggested the following categories: (1) conversion symptoms, such as hysterical aphonia; (2) hypochondriasis, the fear of disease or the quasi-delusional belief in non-existing disease; (3) increased concentration on an independent lesion (called here although not by Merskey 'illness behavior'); (4) psychophysiological effects, such as muscle-tension headaches or irritable bowel syndrome; (5) an anatomical or biochemical lesion in which mental factors are somehow involved, such as a peptic ulcer (Merskey, 1991).[1]

In writing a history of psychosomatic illness, one might distinguish between the history of the term itself, and changes over time in the presentation and diagnosis of its various forms.

HISTORY OF THE TERM 'PSYCHOSOMATIC'

Although physicians have always been aware of the mind's influence on the body, the first systematic inquiry into disorders of their relationship began with the German psychiatrists of the early nineteenth century. These researchers were divided into two schools, one stressing the primacy of the mind itself in causing mental disease, the other stressing the role of the body. Both schools employed psychosomatic concepts. Among the 'psychic' school, Johann Heinroth (1773–1843), professor of psychiatry at Leipzig, described in 1818 'psycho-somatic' sources of insomnia (Margetts, 1950). Among the organicists, Johannes Friedreich (1796–1862), professor of psychiatry at Würzburg, believed in a close reciprocal relationship between mind and body, particularly in somatic causes of mental disease (Friedreich, 1836). Thus the concept psychosomatic, as well as the term itself, became early installed in medicine. Sporadic references to 'psychosomatic' persisted throughout the nineteenth and early twentieth century (Lipowski, 1984).

Sigmund Freud himself (1856–1939) introduced the term 'conversion' in the sense of 'hysterical conversion' into the literature in 1894 (Freud, 1894, p.63). Although Freud was never very interested in physical symptoms as such, mind-body disturbances came to be of great importance in the literature of the psychoanalytic movement. An early contribution was Alfred Adler's (1870–1937) work on 'organ inferiority', which spoke of 'psychophysical relations'

(Adler, 1907). Among Freud's more faithful followers, the first to come to grips systematically with the unconscious mind as a source of physical symptoms was, from 1917 on, the Baden-Baden sanatorium owner Georg Groddeck (1866–1934)[2] (Groddeck, 1917; Will, 1984). As Groddeck wrote in 1921, 'Until now, the organic side of human life has been tabu for psychoanalysis'. It was Groddeck who wrote of hemorrhage, for example, as a symptom 'selected by the unconscious' (Groddeck, 1921, p.254). Yet Groddeck, in his time, was little cited.

Psychoanalytically-oriented physicians in the 1920s tended to refer to 'psychophysical relationships', or the 'psychogenesis of organic symptoms'. Only with the work of the Viennese internist Felix Deutsch (1884–1964) – especially after his lecture in 1927 to a congress on medical psychology – did the word 'psychosomatic' become firmly anchored in psychoanalytical discussions of physical symptoms (Deutsch, 1927; Flagg, 1966).

In the 1920s an important Viennese group, consisting of Adler, Deutsch, Oswald Schwarz (1883–?), Paul Schilder (1886–1940) (Schilder, 1925) and Rudolf Allers (1883–1963) (Allers, 1925), described the psychogenesis of physical symptoms. Psychoanalytic writing, however, made its greatest impact upon North America not via Vienna, but via Berlin. In 1920 Max Eitingon (1881–1943) founded in Berlin a psychoanalytical outpatient clinic for the treatment of psychoneuroses and somatoform illnesses (Eitingon, 1923). In 1927 the clinic became supplemented by Ernst Simmel's (1882–1947) inpatient sanatorium Schloss Tegel. Both these facilities became a proving ground for psychoanalytic theories about psychosomatic illness (Shorter, 1992, pp.259–60).

Among the young psychoanalysts trained in this Berlin setting was Franz Alexander (1891–1964), who migrated from Berlin to Chicago in 1930. It was above all Alexander's work after 1930 that codified the notion that 'psychosomatic illness' consisted of a specific list of disorders situated in the autonomic nervous system, including peptic ulcer, irritable bowel syndrome ('mucous colitis'), bronchial asthma, essential hypertension, various skin diseases, thyrotoxicosis, and rheumatoid arthritis (Alexander, 1934; Alexander, 1943; Alexander, 1950). In his early work Alexander used the phrase 'psychophysiological interrelations' rather than psychosomatic (Alexander, 1932, p.201). He advocated a cautious, multi-causal approach to this list, but other writers were less circumspect in attributing these and other medical disorders to the action of the mind (see for example Halliday, 1943). Alexander also became known for the doctrine of 'psychosomatic specificity', asserting that certain kinds of emotional states became lodged in certain organ systems (Alexander, 1950). Finally, Alexander gave the study of mind-body disturbances a psychoanalytic stamp when he and other like-minded physicians founded in 1939 the journal *Psychosomatic Medicine*. The 'Alexander school', its base Alexander's Chicago Institute for Psychoanalysis, went on to strike the dominant note in psychosomatic research in the 1940s and – 50s.[3]

A second strand in psychosomatic research was holistic medicine, which originated within scientific medicine in the patient-as-a-person movement of the late nineteenth and early twentieth centuries.[4] The holistic approach attempted to diagnose and manage the patient in the context of his or her overall life history and pattern of stress, not just within the pathology of the organ system involved, or within the narrow framework of psychoanalysis. In Europe holistic medicine goes back to the great clinicians of the end of the nineteenth century, such as Hermann Nothnagel (1841–1905) of Vienna and Karl von Noorden (1858–1944) of Vienna and Frankfurt. The Heidelberg internist Viktor von Weizsäcker (1886–1957), sympathetic to psychoanalysis, specifically urged the treatment of 'the whole individual' (des ganzen Menschen) (Weizsäcker, 1925).

In the United States, holistic medicine flowered partly under the shelter of the psychoanalytic movement and partly outside of it. The major bridge figure between holistic medicine and the indigenous American tradition of psycho-analysis (i.e. not the variety imported from Berlin and Vienna in the 1930s) was Columbia psychiatrist Helen Flanders Dunbar (1902–1959). Inspired by her earlier associations with Felix Deutsch and other analysts, Dunbar searched for relationships between the patient's entire emotional life and the presentation of psychoneurotic symptoms. She also became known for an extensive review of the literature she wrote in 1935 (Dunbar, 1935; Powell, 1977). Dunbar rejected the search for 'specificity' that characterized the work of the Alexander school and concentrated instead upon supportive management of patients within internal-medicine services.

Under the influence of Adolf Meyer (1866–1950), professor of psychiatry at Johns Hopkins University, this second strand in psychosomatic research liber-ated itself entirely from the psychoanalytic movement (see, for example, Meyer, 1916). In the United States, Meyer's 'psychobiological' approach represented a continuation of the holistic movement within medicine. Meyer's writings would be picked up again in the 1970s and – 80s by researchers on psychosomatic illness attempting to go beyond the psychoanalytic paradigm[5] (for example, Engel, 1977).

After the 1960s psychoanalytically-oriented psychosomatics began to go out of favor, even though medical interest in mind-body problems in general continued strong. Growing disbelief in the doctrine of psychosomatic 'specificity' contributed to the decline (Buck and Hobbs, 1959; Lipowski, 1968). Also, awareness grew that symptoms referrable to the autonomic nervous system (vegetative) and the somatosensory nervous system (voluntary) were highly intertwined, and that it made little sense to insist dogmatically upon the distinction between 'psychosomatic illness' and 'hysteria' (Engel, 1968). Finally, psychiatry in the 1970s and after lost belief in the credibility of psychoanalytic doctrines as a whole (Bayer and Spitzer, 1985).

Official efforts of the American Psychiatric Association to clarify the notion of psychosomatic illness have produced something of a muddle. The word psycho-somatic itself did not appear in the APA's diagnostic manual of 1980, which instead used the amorphous category 'psychological factors affecting physical condition' (DSM-III, p.303). In addition, DSM-III devised a list of specific 'somatoform' diagnoses, such as somatization disorder, conversion disorder, and psychogenic pain disorder, that overlapped and were difficult to distinguish from each other (DSM-III, 1980, pp.241–52). A revised version of this manual in 1987 merely added a further diagnostic category ('body dysmorphic disorder') to the group of somatoform disorders without resolving the underlying problems (DSM-III-R, 1987, pp.255–6). As the official diagnostic categories for dealing with psychosomatic illness proved unsatisfactory, many clinicians turned to a concept outside the official nosology: 'somatization' as a process.

The term somatization was initially proposed by Viennese psychoanalyst Wilhelm Stekel (1868–1940) sometime before 1924, essentially as a synonym for conversion disorder, or hysteria (Stekel, 1924). Although other writers had used it occasionally thereafter, somatization started to be widely adopted in the 1970s as a result of the work of Z.J. Lipowski (1924-) (Lipowski, 1968). Building specifically upon the holistic tradition of Meyer and Dunbar (Lipowski, 1984), Lipowski defined somatization as, 'a tendency to experience and communicate somatic distress and symptoms unaccounted for by pathological findings, to attribute them to physical illness, and to seek medical help for them'[6] (Lipowski, 1988, p.1359). The definition embraced all physical symptoms, whether in the autonomic or voluntary nervous systems, produced by the action of the mind. Lipowski's definition therefore restored the original meaning of psychosomatic as any disturbance of the mind-body relationship.

CONVERSION DISORDERS

By conversion disorder is meant physical symptoms of a psychogenic nature that affect either the sensory or the motor branches of the voluntary nervous system (the nervous system responsible for movement of muscles and for skin sensation but not for internal sensation or the control of organs). Psychogenic cutaneous anesthesia, for example, affects the sensory side of the nervous system, psychogenic paralysis or pseudoepilepsy the motor side of the nervous system. A young person who awakens one morning unable to walk, and two weeks later is cured by therapy with magnets, would be a classic example of a conversion disorder (Shorter, 1992, pp.95–128). One might distinguish between the actual history of these disorders and the history of changes in their diagnosis.

It is useful to bear in mind that the entire range of conversion symptoms exists in a kind of cultural 'symptom pool', or list of available symptoms, that has been present in the collective memory of western society since the Middle Ages (on the Middle Ages see Sigal, 1985). Thus psychogenic epilepsy, aphonia, paralysis, blindness, pain, fatigue, paresthesia and so forth have always been available to individuals in western society, handed down in oral tradition and in medical folklore from one generation to the next. Yet in given periods some items in this pool are drawn upon more often than others. Which items in the symptom pool are picked up most widely in a given society will depend on that society's larger notion of what constitutes genuine organic illness. Few patients wish to present symptoms that are not 'legitimate', or that will be seen as evidence of silliness or playacting. Accordingly, as concepts of what represents legitimate illness change, the nature of conversion symptoms will change as well.

The history of conversion symptoms in western society may be divided into three main phases:
(1) The pre-1800 phase, in which psychogenic seizures constituted the most commented-upon form of conversion symptom.
(2) 1800 to the First World War, in which seizures continued to be common, but in which important new motor symptoms such as psychogenic paralysis of the lower limbs appeared as well.
(3) The First World War to the present, in which the dominant form of conversion symptom shifted from the motor side of the nervous system to the

sensory. Paralysis receded greatly, to be replaced by such sensory symptoms as psychogenic pain and fatigue.

Given the role of medical diagnosis in legitimating some symptoms and de-legitimating others, shifts in diagnostic fashions have exerted a major influence upon these patterns. Before the middle of the eighteenth century, the impact of academic medical views upon popular life was minimal, for the majority of the European population almost never came into contact with university-trained physicians, receiving health care instead from such paramedical tradespeople as midwives, corncutters and herbalists. Views about the body as inhabited by demons were probably responsible for suggesting many individuals into symptoms of fits and convulsions.

After 1800, with the growing power of medicine to reach into popular life,[7] fashions in medical diagnosis began to exert a major suggestive influence upon people. Medicine entertained three distinct paradigms for diagnosing symptoms that were considered to be nervous or hysterical:

(1) The reflex paradigm, popular from the 1820s until the 1860s and after (depending on the country). In reflex doctrine, every organ in the body was thought capable of influencing every other organ, including the brain, via reflex pathways running along the spine. Thus an 'irritated' uterus, colon or stomach could cause spinal irritation, hysteria, and other nervous states. Reflex doctrine particularly encouraged the formation of motor symptoms, because a sensory impulse from the periphery gave rise, via the reflex arc in the spine, to a motor response. Based on an incomplete understanding of the recently discovered reflex arc, reflex doctrine overestimated the influence of the bodily reflexes.

Among reflex theorists might be mentioned London physicians Marshall Hall (1790–1857) (Hall, 1836) and Thomas Laycock (1812–1876) (Laycock, 1840), in France Charles Negrier (1792–1862) (Negrier, 1858) and Pierre-Adolphe Piorry (1794–1879) (Piorry, 1835), and in Germany Moritz Romberg (1795–1873) (Romberg, 1840) and Benedict Stilling (1810–1879) (Stilling, 1840). All argued that peripheral 'irritation' in women affected the brain, resulting in functional nervous symptoms. These theories gave rise to an orgy of local treatment of organs thought to be irritated, particularly in women, such as the spine, the vagina and the cervix, later to an epidemic of unnecessary surgery on the uterus, ovaries and clitoris. It is likely that medical expectations of motor symptoms led to the actual presentation of such symptoms, as the patients consciously or unconsciously sought to avoid ridicule by offering only symptoms that could be construed as evidence of genuine organic disease.

(2) The central nervous paradigm, present throughout the nineteenth and early twentieth centuries but strongly ascendant in the years 1880 to the First World War, insisted upon invisible but real lesions in the central nervous system as the cause of 'functional' nervous symptoms. Scorning peripheral reflexes, this paradigm postulated such cerebral states as under-stimulation, over-irritation, or hyperemia, as the primary causes of nervous complaints.

Hand in hand with this paradigm shift in medical theory went practical improvements in physicians' ability to differentiate psychogenic from neurogenic nervous symptoms, such as the Babinski reflex (1896). It is possible that these two developments together – an emphasis upon cerebral conditions combined with improved diagnostic acumen – might have encouraged a shift from motor symptoms to sensory symptoms. Motor symptoms had now become medically less plausible, and were also easier to rule out as organic. Sensory symptoms had become medically legitimated as the presumed result of real but invisible brain pathology, and were more difficult to disprove as 'hysterical'. Who, after all, could 'prove' that a patient was not tired or not in pain? By contrast, it was much easier to establish that the patient did not have an upper motor neuron lesion.

Associated with the triumph of the central nervous paradigm in the second half of the nineteenth century in England were London neurologist Thomas Dixon Savill (1856–1910) of the West End Hospital for Diseases of the Nervous System in London (Savill, 1909), as well as the whole school of neurology at the National Hospital for the Paralysed and Epileptic at Queen-Square in London. In France the great neurologist Jean-Martin Charcot (1825–1893) of the Salpêtrière Hospital in Paris (Micale, 1990) embodied the new paradigm, as did Wilhelm Griesinger (1817–1868), professor of psychiatry in Berlin (Griesinger, 1861).

One particular diagnosis derived from the central nervous paradigm seems to have had a quite startling suggestive effect in shaping patients' symptoms: neurasthenia. Literally meaning 'tired nerves', or 'nervous exhaustion', neurasthenia as a diagnosis was initially popularized in 1869 for medical use by the New York neurologist George Beard (1839–1883) (Beard, 1869). Beard's later book on the subject was translated into numerous languages and exerted perhaps the greatest impact of any nineteenth-century American medical publication on international medicine (Beard, 1880). The relationship in the nineteenth century between the diagnosis of neurasthenia and the increase in complaints of fatigue symptoms was a complex one (Abbey and Garfinkel, 1991; Wessely, 1990; Shorter, 1992, pp.277–85). Yet it is likely that Beard's popular new disease-label played at least some role in the shift from motor to sensory.

With the transition in medical paradigms from reflex to central-nervous, the historic shift from traditional motor symptoms to modern sensory ones was virtually complete. In the years after 1880, to be sure, a third medical paradigm – the psychogenic paradigm – would assert itself as an explanation of psychosomatic symptoms. This was associated initially with the Bernese neurologist Paul Dubois (1848–1918) (Dubois, 1904) and the Parisian neurologist Joseph Babinski (1857–1932) (Babinski, 1901), later with the psychoanalysts. Yet patients proved highly resistant to the insights of this paradigm, and through most of the twentieth century they would prefer to attribute their psychosomatic symptoms to dysfunctions of the 'nerves'. The present author has argued that the pattern of psychosomatic illness in the 1990s, wholly unlike the pattern around 1800, closely resembled that around 1900 (Shorter, 1992, pp.295–320).

HYPOCHONDRIASIS

Hypochondriasis qualifies as a psychosomatic condition, not merely because the patient is apprehensive of illness but because he or she is often highly symptomatic as well, magnifying unexceptionable bodily sensations into a quasi-delusional perception of illness. Before the nineteenth century, symptoms referrable to the abdomen, especially in males, were often termed hypochondria (beneath the ribs) (Fischer-Homberger, 1970, pp.22–4). In modern descriptions dating from the end of the eighteenth century, hypochondria means a mental disorder revolving about physical sensations. Among early writers London physician James Sims (1741–1820) described in 1799, 'the hypochondriac disease': '. . . the sufferers . . . having their mind almost entirely taken up with the state of their health, which they imagine to be infinitely worse than it is, constantly auguring death, or the most dreadful consequences from even the most trifling ailments' (Sims, 1799, p.392).

Little is known about historical variation in the incidence or nature of hypochondriasis. The phenomenon does, however, seem to have increased over the years, at least as a kind of delusional system in psychiatric patients. Several studies of psychotic depression suggest that delusions and hallucinations relating to the body have become more frequent. At the university psychiatric clinic in Basel, only 17 per cent of the depressed patients in 1878–1914 expressed 'hypochondriac ideas', 24 per cent in 1915–30 and 23 per cent in 1940–51. For men the rise was from 17 per cent in the first period to 27 per cent in the last (Orelli, 1954). At the Royal Edinburgh Asylum the percentage of depressed patients expressing delusional ideas about disease rose from 7 per cent in 1892 to 29 per cent in 1942–43. This occurred in the context of a large decline in delusional depression generally (Eagles, 1983), so it is all the more interesting that the 'hard core' group shifted to concerns about the body (instead of concerns about 'persecution' or whether strangers were taking an interest in them).

A quintessentially modern theme in the history of hypochondriasis concerns unshakable illness attributions, disease labels that patients give themselves and to which they cling despite medical reassurance. Of course in all times and places individuals have grasped at self-diagnoses, as seen by the faddishness of 'colitis' within the Parisian upper-classes of the late-nineteenth century (Munthe, 1929, pp.32–4). But only after the 1960s did these quasi-delusional illness attributions begin to seize large groups of the population. Beliefs in food allergies, insidious environmental toxins, and occult viral infections and immune dysfunctions have become very common in the last three decades of the twentieth century. Many individuals become convinced that they are experiencing the symptoms of chronic fatigue syndrome, myalgic encephalomyelitis, twentieth century disease (also known as total allergy syndrome), fibromyalgia, yeast hypersensitivity, Lyme disease, and numerous others (Stewart, 1990; Wessely and Powell, 1989). Aronowitz writes of the 'market for somatic labels [that] exists in the large pool of "stressed out" or somatizing patients who seek to disguise an emotional complaint or to "upgrade" their diagnosis from a nebulous one to a legitimate disease' (Aronowitz, 1991, p.97). Such patients find solace in self-support groups and in the care of physicians sympathetic to the diagnosis, which has the effect of entrenching the symptoms so that the sufferers may end up chronically disabled (Shorter, 1992).

'ILLNESS BEHAVIOR' OF VARIOUS KINDS

All individuals who experience medical symptoms concentrate upon, or perceive, the signals their bodies give them. Such concentration occurs no less in organic disease than in psychosomatic conditions. Yet sometimes the concentration in organic illness is disproportionate, disabling and pathological, out of congruence with the cultural norms for dealing with that particular malady. Such responses to organic illness fall within the compass of the psychosomatic, even though a lesion is present. But how to classify them? And in psychosomatic illness itself how should such concentration be classified?

In understanding individuals' responses to illness of all kinds, David Mechanic has proposed the notion 'illness behavior' (1962). According to Mechanic, illness behavior refers 'to the ways in which given symptoms may be differentially perceived, evaluated, and acted (or not acted upon) by different kinds of persons'. But Mechanic made no distinction between illness of psychological origin and that of organic origin.

Given that the etiology of somatogenic symptoms is quite different from the psychogenic variety, even though the patient perceives the two kinds of symptoms as identical, some kind of nosological differentiation seems appropriate in classifying illness behavior. Merskey calls the patient's response to symptoms of an organic nature 'increased concentration upon an independent lesion' (Merskey, 1991). As for the patient's response to psychogenic symptoms, Pilowsky has proposed the term 'abnormal illness behavior' (Pilowsky, 1969). (Psychogenic is understood in terms of Pilowsky's definition, 'physical symptoms for which no organic explanation can be found'.)

To bring medical terminology into conformity with the vocabulary Mechanic and Pilowsky are developing, it is suggested here that the patient's response to symptoms of organic disease be designated 'somatic illness behavior'. Pilowsky's term 'abnormal illness behavior' has embedded itself in the literature and should be retained for the patient's response to symptoms of psychological origin.

Here we encounter an urgent need for further historical research. Both 'somatic' and 'abnormal' illness behavior represent the least well researched of all dimensions of psychosomatic illness. What was the psychological response of patients to organic ailments in the eighteenth and nineteenth centuries?[8] How does that differ in contrast to today? How do these responses differ from psychological responses to 'hysteria' and the like? From systematic, random, nationwide surveys, it is clear that between the 1920s and 1980s the population of the United States became significantly more sensitive to bodily symptoms of all kinds, reporting both organic diseases and non-specific symptoms more commonly in the latter period than the former (Shorter, 1985, pp.213–15). May this increased sensitivity to bodily symptoms serve as an index of increasingly severe 'illness behavior' in both domains of that phenomenon? The subject is a challenging one and awaits further investigation.

PSYCHOPHYSIOLOGICAL EFFECTS

There is no doubt that the action of the mind can derange the body's physiological functions. Among psychosomatic illnesses, tension headache and irritable bowel syndrome are probably the commonest examples of such effects.

The history of headache is among the most obscure in disease biography. There is some evidence of an increasing incidence of tension headaches within the twentieth century, at least in relation to classic conversion symptoms. Merskey writes, 'There is reason to believe that pain becomes more common as a conflict-solving symptom when the classical hysterical symptoms decline in frequency. The latter are increasingly rare in developed societies' (Merskey, 1981, p.113; Merskey, 1979). Within psychiatric settings today, pain is easily the commonest of the psychogenic physical symptoms (Lloyd, 1986). Although it is not clear that the level of 'stress' has truly increased over the years, each society believing itself to labor under great stress, it is possible that muscle-tension headaches have in fact risen as pain becomes an increasingly acceptable medical symptom.

The argument is often made that functional gastrointestinal disorders (those not having an anatomical basis) have also risen, a consequence of driving 'hysteria' from the voluntary nervous system to the autonomic nervous system (Brisset, 1970). The present writer has suggested that this argument is probably incorrect (Shorter, 1993). If irritable bowel syndrome be taken as a quintessential example of 'profound somatization', there is little evidence for such a flight of hysteria to the internal organs. A search of the older literature reveals many cases of what one might retrospectively diagnose as irritable bowel syndrome (Kämpf, 1785; Howship, 1820). While this proliferation of anecdotes does not, in and of itself, demonstrate that IBS was as common then as now, it cautions against the casual assumption that current rates are the highest ever. In sum, changes in the frequency of psychophysiological effects remain a dimly understood aspect of the history of psychosomatic illness. But little is gained in postulating, on the basis of abstract psychoanalytical speculation, an increase in the frequency of physiological disorders that themselves may well turn out to be timeless.

AN ORGANIC LESION OF A PSYCHOGENIC NATURE

This category has been included for the sake of completeness. Some authorities argue for the psychogenesis of such conditions as peptic ulcer disease (Murphy, 1982, pp.213–18). Recent research has failed to confirm these hypotheses (Soll, 1990). It is likely that the striking rise of peptic ulcer disease in twentieth-century males was a result of increasing tobacco consumption rather than of some alteration in mother-child relationships or infant-feeding patterns. In 1964 the US Surgeon General implicated smoking in the pathogenesis of peptic ulcers (US Department of HEW, 1964, pp.337–41). Indeed peptic ulcer disease should probably be removed from the classic list of psychosomatic conditions and, like hypertension, be assigned to the class of diseases exacerbated by stress but whose etiology is, essentially, organic. The present writer would prefer a definition of 'psychosomatic' that excludes entirely conditions involving organic lesions.

NOTES

1 Merskey suggested a sixth category, 'secondary effects of volitional activity', giving as examples, injuries in accident-prone individuals, obesity, or cachexia from anorexia nervosa. A detailed discussion of this important category, which might include deaths from heart disease and carcinoma as well, would exceed space limitations. An account of eating disorders is found elsewhere in this volume.

2 This priority is often claimed for other figures in the psychoanalytic

movement, such as Sándor Ferenczi, the Budapest analyst who in 1919 wrote 'The Phenomena of Hysterical Materialization' (Ferenczi, 1919). Yet Ferenczi's writings on the subject represent merely scattered *pensées*, and were without influence upon further events.

3 See for example one of the classic American psychosomatic textbooks, Edward Weiss and O. Spurgeon English, *Psychosomatic Medicine* (1943), which specifically acknowledges Alexander and other mainline analysts in the preface.

4 See for example the work of Harvard internist Francis Weld Peabody, *The Care of the Patient* (Peabody, 1927). See also Shorter (1991), pp.41–3.

5 George Engel has proposed the notion of a 'biopsychosocial model' in dealing with holism. In his key paper on this subject, Engel, trained as a psychoanalyst, made only glancing reference to Freud and the analytic tradition, and gave Meyer equal billing (Engel, 1977).

6 Somatization in this sense refers to the process producing somatoform (psychosomatic) symptoms, a process going beyond the APA's narrowly defined diagnosis of 'somatization disorder'.

7 This growing social influence of medicine has been called by some scholars 'medicalization' (Huerkamp, 1985).

8 For a first cut at this question, see Porter and Porter (1989).

REFERENCES

Abbey, Susan and Garfinkel, Paul (1991) 'Neurasthenia and Chronic Fatigue Syndrome: the role of culture in the making of a diagnosis'. *American Journal of Psychiatry*, 148:1638–46.

Adler, Alfred (1907) *Studie über Minderwertigkeit von Organen*. Berlin. Eng. trans. (1917) *Study of Organ Inferiority and its Psychical Compensation*, New York.

Alexander, Franz (1932) *The Medical Value of Psychoanalysis*, New York.

Alexander, Franz (1934) 'The influence of psychologic factors upon Gastro-Intestinal disturbances: a symposium'. *Psychoanalytic Quarterly*, 3: 501–39.

Alexander, Franz (1943) 'Fundamental concepts of psychosomatic research: psychogenesis, conversion, specificity'. *Psychosomatic Medicine*, 5: 205–10.

Alexander, Franz (1950) *Psychosomatic Medicine: Its Principles and Applications*, New York, Norton.

Allers, Rudolf (1925) *Grundformen der Psychotherapie* [Basic Forms of Psychotherapy]. In Schwarz, (1925): pp.427–51.

Aronowitz, Robert A. (1991) 'Lyme Disease: the social construction of a new disease and its social consequences'. *Milbank Quarterly*, 69: 79–112.

Babinski, Joseph (1901) 'Définition de l'hystérie' [Definition of hysteria]. *Revue Neurologique*, 9: 1074–80.

Bayer, Ronald and Spitzer, Robert L. (1985) 'Neurosis, Psychodynamics and DSM-III'. *Archives of General Psychiatry*, 42: 187–96.

Beard, George (1869) 'Neurasthenia, or nervous exhaustion'. *Boston Medical and Surgical Journal*, 80: 217–21.

Beard, George (1880) *A Practical Treatise on Nervous Exhaustion (Neurasthenia): Its Symptoms, Nature . . .*, New York, Wood.

Brisset, Charles (1970) 'Hystérie et psychosomatique: Les rapports de la structure et de l'histoire' [Hysteria and Psychosomatic illness. Their structural relationship and history]. *L'Evolution Psychiatrique*, 35: 377–404.

Buck, Carol and Hobbs, G.E. (1959) 'The problem of specificity in psychosomatic illness'. *Journal of Psychosomatic Research*, 3: 227–33.

Deutsch, Felix (1927) 'Psychoanalyse und innere Medizin' [Psychoanalysis and internal medicine], in Wladimir Eliasberg, (ed.) (1927) *Bericht über den II. allgemeinen ärztlichen Kongress für Psychotherapie in Bad Nauheim, 27. bis 30. April 1927*, Leipzig, pp.53–9.

DSM-III (1980) American Psychiatric Association. *Diagnostic and Statistical Manual of Mental Disorders*, 3rd. ed. Washington, American Psychiatric Assocation.

DSM-III-R (1987) American Psychiatric Association. *Diagnostic and Statistical Manual of Mental Disorders*, 3rd. ed. revised, Washington, American Psychiatric Association.

Dubois, Paul (1904) *Les Psychonévroses et leur Traitement Moral*, Paris. Eng. trans. *The Psychic Treatment of Nervous Disorders*, London, 1905.

Dunbar, Helen Flanders (1935) *Emotions and Bodily Changes: A Survey of Literature on Psychosomatic Interrelationships, 1910–1933*, New York.

Eagles, John M. (1983) 'Delusional depressive in-patients, 1892 to 1982'. *British Journal of Psychiatry*, 143: 558–63.

Eitingon, Max, 1923. *Bericht über die Berliner psychoanalytische Poliklinik* [Report on the Berlin Psychoanalytic Outpatient Clinic], Leipzig.

Engel, George L. (1968) 'A reconsideration of the role of conversion in somatic disease'. *Comprehensive Psychiatry*, 9: 316–26.

Engel, George L. (1977) 'The need for a new medical model: a challenge for biomedicine'. *Science*, 196:129–36.

Ferenczi, Sándor (1919) 'The phenomena of hysterical materialization'. Reprinted in Ferenczi (1926), *Further Contributions to the Theory and Technique of Psycho-Analysis*, London, pp.89–104.

Fischer-Homberger, Esther (1970) *Hypochondrie: Melancholie bis Neurose: Krankheiten und Zustandsbilder*, Bern, Hans Huber.

Flagg, Glenn W. (1966) 'Felix Deutsch', in Franz Alexander et al, (eds.) *Psychoanalytic Pioneers*, New York, Basic Books, pp.299–307.

Freud, Sigmund (1894) 'Die Abwehr-Neuropsychosen' [The defensive neuropsychoses]. *Sigmund Freud Gesammelte Werke*, vol.1, Frankfurt, Fischer, reprint 1952.

Friedreich, Johannes Baptist (1836) *Historisch-kritische Darstellung der Theorien über das Wesen und den Sitz der psychischen Krankheiten* [Historical-Critical Account of the Nature and Seat of Psychic Diseases], Leipzig, Wigand.

Griesinger, Wilhelm (1861) *Die Pathologie und Therapie der psychischen Krankheiten* [Pathology and Therapy of Psychic Diseases], 2nd rev. ed., Stuttgart, Krabbe.

Groddeck, Georg (1917) 'Psychische Bedingtheit und psychoanalytische Behandlung organischer Leiden' [Psychic determination and psychoanalytic treatment of organic illness], reprinted in Günter Clauser, (ed.) (1966) *Georg Groddeck: Psychoanalytische Schriften zur Psychosomatik*, Wiesbaden, Limes Verlag, pp.19–45.

Groddeck, Georg (1921) 'Über die Psychoanalyse des Organischen im Menschen'. *Internationale Zeitschrift für Psychoanalyse*, 7: 252–63.

Hall, Marshall (1836) *Lectures on the Nervous System and Its Diseases*, London, Sherwood.

Halliday, James L. (1943) 'Concept of a Psychosomatic Affection'. *Lancet*, 245:692–6.

Howship, John (1820) *Practical Observations on the Symptoms ... of the Most Important Diseases of the Lower Intestines and Anus*, London, Longman.

Huerkamp, Claudia (1985) *Der Aufstieg der Ärzte im 19. Jahrhundert* [The Rise of the Doctors in the 19th Century], Göttingen, Vandenhoeck & Ruprecht.

Kämpf, Johann (1785) *Für Ärzte und Kranken bestimmte Abhandlung von einer neuen Methode, die hartnäckigsten Krankheiten, die ihren Sitz im Unterleibe haben, besonders die Hypochondrie, sicher und gründlich zu heilen* [A Treatise for Doctors and Patients on How to Heal Successfully the Most Stubborn Diseases, Especially Hypochondria, Having Their Seat in the Abdomen], Frankfurt.

Laycock, Thomas (1840) *A Treatise on the Nervous Diseases of Women*, London, Longman.

Lipowski, Z.J. (1968) 'Review of consultation psychiatry and psychosomatic medicine, part III: theoretical issues'. *Psychosomatic Medicine*, 30:394–422.

Lipowski, Z.J. (1984) 'What does the word "Psychosomatic" really mean?' *Psychosomatic Medicine*, 46:153–71.

Lipowski, Z.J. (1988) 'Somatization: the concept and its clinical application'. *American Journal of Psychiatry*, 145:1358–68.

Lloyd, Geoffrey G. (1986) 'Psychiatric syndromes with a somatic presentation'. *Journal of Psychosomatic Research*, 30: 113–20.

Margetts, Edward L. (1950) 'The early history of the word "Psychosomatic" '. *Canadian Medical Association Journal*, 63:402–4.

Mechanic, David (1962) 'The concept of illness behavior'. *Journal of Chronic Diseases*, 15: 189–94.

Merskey, Harold (1979) *The Analysis of Hysteria*, London, Baillière Tindall.

Merskey, Harold (1981) 'Headache and hysteria'. *Cephalalgia*, 1:109–19.

Merskey, Harold (1991) personal communication.

Meyer, Adolf (1916) 'The scope of psychopathology'. Reprinted in Meyer, A. (1951) *Collected Papers*, Baltimore, Johns Hopkins Press, vol.2, pp.618–23.

Micale, Mark (1990) 'Charcot and the idea of hysteria in the male'. *Medical History*, 34:363–411.

Munthe, Axel (1929) *The Story of San Michele*, London.

Murphy, Henry B.M. (1982) *Comparative Psychiatry: The International and Intercultural Distribution of Mental Illness*, New York, Springer.

Negrier, Charles (1858) *Recueil de faits pour servir à l'histoire des ovaires et des affections hystériques de la femme* [Documentation on the Influence of the Ovaries upon the Hysterical Affections of Women], Angers, Cosnier.

Orelli, Andreas von (1954) 'Der Wandel des Inhaltes der depressiven Ideen bei der reinen Melancholie' [Changes in the content of depressive ideas in pure melancholy]. *Schweizer Archiv für Neurologie und Psychiatrie*, 73:217–87.

Peabody, Francis Weld (1927) *The Care of the Patient*, Cambridge MA.

Pilowsky, I. (1969) 'Abnormal illness behaviour'. *British Journal of Medical Psychology*, 42: 347–51.

Piorry, Pierre-Adolphe (1835) *Clinique Médicale de l'Hôpital de la Pitié et de l'Hospice de la Salpêtrière*, Paris, Baillière.

Porter, Dorothy and Porter, Roy (1989) *Patient's Progress: Doctors and Doctoring in Eighteenth-Century England*, Cambridge, Eng., Polity Press.

Powell, Robert C. (1977) 'Helen Flanders Dunbar (1902–1959) and a holistic approach to psychosomatic problems. I. The rise and fall of a medical philosophy'. *Psychiatric Quarterly*, 49: 133–52.

Romberg, Moritz (1840) *Lehrbuch der Nervenkrankheiten des Menschen* [Textbook of Nervous Diseases in Humans], Berlin, Hirschwald.

Savill, Thomas Dixon (1909) *Lectures on Hysteria and Allied Vaso-motor Conditions*, London.

Schilder, Paul (1925) 'Das Leib-Seelenproblem vom Standpunkt der Philosophie und naturwissenschaftlichen Psychologie' [The mind-body problem from the viewpoints of philosophy and scientific psychology], in Schwarz, 1925, pp.30–69.

Schwarz, Oswald, (ed.) (1925) *Psychogenese und Psychotherapie körperlicher Symptome*, Vienna, Springer.

Shorter, Edward (1985) *Bedside Manners: The Troubled History of Doctors and Patients*, New York, Simon and Schuster. Reprinted in 1991 with a new introduction by the author as *Doctors and Their Patients: A Social History*, New Brunswick USA and London, Eng., Transaction Publishers.

Shorter, Edward (1992) *From Paralysis to Fatigue: A History of Psychosomatic Illness in the Modern Era*, New York, Free Press.

Shorter, Edward (1994) *From the Mind into the Body: the Cultural Origin of Psychosomatic Symptoms*, New York, Free Press.

Sigal, Pierre-André, 1985. *L'homme et le miracle dans la France Médiévale (XIe-XIIe siècle)* [People and Miracles in Medieval France], Paris, Editions du Cerf.

Sims, James (1799) 'Pathological remarks upon various kinds of alienation of the mind'. *Memoirs of the Medical Society of London*, 5: 372–406.

Soll, Andrew H. (1990) 'Pathogenesis of peptic ulcer and implications for therapy'. *New England Journal of Medicine*, 322: 909–16.

Stekel, Wilhelm (1924) 'Der epileptische Symptomenkomplex und seine analytische Bedeutung' [The complex of symptoms of Epilepsy and its analytic significance]. *Fortschritte der Sexualwissenschaft und Psychanalyse*, 1: 17–57.

Stewart, Donna (1990) 'The changing faces of somatization'. *Psychosomatics*, 31: 153–8.

Stilling, Benedict (1840) *Physiologische, pathologische und medicinisch-practische Untersuchungen über die Spinal-Irritation* [Physiological, Pathological, and Clinical Medical Investigations of Spinal Irritation], Leipzig, Wigand.

United States, Department of Health Education and Welfare (1964) *Smoking and Health: Report of the Advisory Committee to the Surgeon General of the Public Health Service*, Washington DC, P.H.S. pub. no. 1103.

Weiss, Edward and English, O. Spurgeon (1943) *Psychosomatic Medicine: The*

Clinical Application of Psychopathology to General Medical Problems, Philadelphia.

Weizsäcker, Viktor von, (1925) 'Randbemerkungen über Aufgabe und Begriff der Nervenheilkunde' [Casual observations on the scope and nature of neurology and psychiatry]. *Deutsche Zeitschrift für Nervenheilkunde*, 87: 1–22.

Wessely, Simon and Powell, R. (1989) ' "Postviral" fatigue with neuromuscular and affective disorders'. *Journal of Neurology, Neurosurgery and Psychiatry*, 52: 940–8.

Wessely, Simon (1990) ' "Old wine in new bottles": Neurasthenia and "M.E" '. *Psychological Medicine*, 20: 35–53.

Will, Herbert (1984) *Die Geburt der Psychosomatik: Georg Groddeck, der Mensch und Wissenschaftler* [The Birth of Psychosomatics: Georg Groddeck, the Man and Scientist], Munich, Urban & Schwarzenberg.

Chapter 19

Post-traumatic Stress Disorder and Shell Shock

Clinical Section

HAROLD MERSKEY

More has been written upon battles and the devastation left in their wake, than upon the long-lasting changes within the survivors. Yet it must always have been recognized that harrowing experiences leave a persisting imprint. Historically, a better understanding of such post-traumatic changes appeared with improvements in knowledge about the distinction between organic and psychological disorders of the central nervous system.

In the second half of the 19th century Charcot paid attention to the way in which emotional stress could produce somatic complaints. Micale (1990) has emphasized that when Charcot wrote of hysteria in men he dealt particularly with the destructive influence of a physical trauma leading to emotional responses. Systems of compensation for the victims of accidents appeared in Western Europe in the 19th century. Charcot and his English and German contemporaries may have been interested in the possibility of compensation for some of their patients. There is evidence that symptoms often do not depend upon compensation (Mendelson, 1982). However, the fact that it existed would engage the doctor's attention.

Some argued that certain untoward events could cause changes on a physical basis. Sir John Erichsen (1866 and 1882) held that disturbance to the nervous system might be physically produced in railway accidents, without haemorrhage, either by temporary disablement of cells or perhaps by the disruption of their connections. He developed a concept of 'concussion of the spine' which resembled the views of Oppenheim (1889) who similarly held that neurosis arising in these circumstances was due to physical changes. Page (1883) objected to the phrase 'concussion of the spine'. He was supported in America, e.g. by Hodges (1881), Putnam (1883), and Walton (1883). Erichsen was probably right however in attributing the complaints of many of his patients to a physical impact and not to emotional causes, as he observed that the passengers with their backs to the direction of impact were the worst affected.

The connection of accidents with psychological symptoms was seen by others. Erichsen's colleague at University College Hospital, Sir John Russell Reynolds (1869) described 'Three cases of paralysis dependent upon idea'. Charcot (1889) said that the idea that symptoms might be caused by the mind had been known for a long time, but gave Reynolds the credit for being the first to study this systematically. Charcot showed further that ideas could be implanted under hypnosis. This reinforced the position which Freud was to develop more strongly that emotional changes could give rise to physical complaints *through ideas*. It had long been accepted that physical changes in the body such as an increase in the pulse rate might be related to emotion. Once it was possible to discern which symptoms depended upon the autonomic nervous system and which upon voluntary functions, it became feasible to distinguish between psychophysiological complaints and purely psychological bodily symptoms.

During the Russo-Japanese War of 1904–1906, Russian doctors described a condition marked by confusional states, and brief hysterical excitement, and going on to irritability, fearfulness, and emotional instability (Baker, 1975). It is perhaps noteworthy that it was the losing side in this war which recognized the occurrence of such battle stress. Armies which are doing well have to contend with it less often. In the First World War concepts of shell shock and battle neurosis were more noticeable first to the British and French who were overrun by the German armies than to the Germans whose literature on the topic developed a little later.

One other source of information was influential before the First World War. In 1907 and 1911 respectively, the ships 'Iéna' and 'Liberté' had exploded at Toulon. Hesnard (1914) eliminated cases in which direct organic causes might have been relevant, and recorded typical symptoms of post-traumatic psychological responses. Many were known previously. They included an initial state of semi-somnambulism, automatic mental activity, absorption in some trivial occupation such as an exclusive pre-occupation with the attempt to save some garment, a strange lucidity and feeling of exaltation and a period of amnesia. The rescuers also showed symptoms of disturbance for several weeks including recapitulation of the scene, terrifying dreams, diffuse anxiety, fatigue, and various minor phobias. This knowledge of emotional change after explosions quickly became part of the contemporary climate of ideas, for example it was abstracted in English (Brown and Williams, 1918). Weisaeth and Eitinger (1991) have drawn attention to the studies by Stierlin of the survivors of the 1908 earthquake in Messina which furnished similar information.

In 1914 the common ideas about post-traumatic responses allowed for both psychological and physical mechanisms in their induction. The way these ideas developed about Shell Shock has been discussed at length elsewhere (Merskey, 1979 & 1991a) and will be summarised here.

SHELL SHOCK

Different Views
In Britain and France cases of Shell Shock emerged gradually. The small British force in France suffered 157 cases of 'shock' or 'shell shock' from August to December 1914 among 520 cases of functional nervous diseases (MacPherson et al, 1923). We do not know just when the term 'Shell Shock' began to be used. The earliest known example relating to it at present is a statement in the *Times* on 6th February 1915 that the War Office was arranging to send soldiers suffering from 'shock' to be treated in special wards at the National Hospital for the Paralysed and Epileptic, Queen Square.

Cases increased steadily to a peak of 16,138 between July and December 1916 with the battle of the Somme. The Royal Society of Medicine held a 'special discussion on shell shock without visible signs of injury' on the 25th of January 1916 in the Section of Psychiatry, presided over by Major F.W. Mott, MD, FRS. Mott who had been the pathologist to the London County Council and its psychiatric hospitals, pointed out that 'The forces producing shell shock are most commonly generated by the explosion of large shells, but also by mines, aerial torpedoes, whiz-bangs, trench mortars, bombs and hand grenades charged with explosives. In a large number of cases, although exhibiting no visible injury, shell shock is accompanied by burial'.

Discussion was animated. Henry Head (Anonymous, 1916) rejected shell shock as a category. He held it to be 'a heterogeneous collection of different nervous affections from concussion to sheer funk which may have merely this much in common that nervous control has at last given way'. One of the most telling pieces of evidence came later from Germany. Lust (1916) observed that among 40,000 war prisoners, hysteric or nervous disturbances 'so common among the soldiers were found only in one among each 8,000'. Mairet and Durante (1917) induced experimental shell shock in rabbits. Minute haemorrhages were found in the lungs, spinal cord and nerve roots, and were held to correspond to the symptomatology of men suffering from shell shock, especially the amnesias, neuralgias and pains at the emerging points of the nerves. Mott (1917) described a microscopic examination of the brains of two men dead of commotio cerebri (concussion or shell shock) without visible injury.

The sceptics noted that men might be blown up without shell shock and men who had not been blown up, but who had been frightened, had similar complaints. They emphasized the part played by suggestibility.

German doctors were sympathetic initially towards the idea of shell shock. Their term (Gaupp, 1915) was 'Granatkontusion' or bomb concussion. This suggested injury due to the effects of an explosion but without an overt lesion, as a result of shaking or the pressure of air or gases. However, Gaupp (1915) dismissed air pressure on the grounds that it only affected the ear drums, and poison gas shells were not being used. Hence, he attributed problems to mechanical injury or to psychological effects. He felt that most of the writing on the topic resembled 'Kraepelin's fright neurosis'. Oppenheim (1915) disagreed.

German discussions were held in September 1916 at a meeting of neuropsychiatrists in Munich (Berlin Letter, 1917). Oppenheim's views were decisively rejected especially by Nonne. The shell explosion neurosis was seen as functional and curable by psychological techniques. Neurasthenia could occur in stable individuals through fatigue and exhaustion. Oppenheim's views were against the economic interests of the state and the therapeutic needs of the patient and most cases were regarded as hysteria.

Overwhelming Stress
In the First World War the numbers of casualties were enormous in the trenches, men often dying over a few yards or a few hundred feet of ground. In four months the Battle of the Somme cost the British 420,000 casualties, the French 194,000 and the Germans 440,000. The rich literature on these topics includes the poetry of Owen, Sassoon, and Graves, and the autobiographical accounts of Graves (1929) and Vaughan (1981). Hynes (1990) concludes that the First

World War has been perhaps the most powerful force in the shaping both of our conceptions of what war is, and of the world we live in. The trenches were its worst feature.

Cases of shell shock rose steeply to a peak of 16,138 from July to December 1916, declining to 7,048 in the next twelve months. By 1917 the British army realised it had to do something about the diagnosis of 'shell shock'. Successive steps were taken which led to the abolition of the term (Report, 1922 and Myers, 1940).

Other 'organic' labels were also available during the First World War. 'Disorderly action of the heart' (DAH) or 'soldier's heart' were popular. Hurst (1940) remarked that 'soldier's heart is nothing more than a manifestation of anxiety neurosis'. But for most of the First World War it was a respectable diagnostic term, often aided by the finding of a cardiac murmur.

Army and Civilian Attitudes

The military and medical authorities wished to recognize whatever might be called genuine illness, and also to keep out of the firing line men whose presence would encourage low morale. They did not wish to penalise men who had served under intolerably dangerous conditions for long periods of time and who had at last broken down, including soldiers who had received the VC, or the DSM, and other medals. Yet they also had to discourage easy complaining. They could not accept that subjective complaints and a wide variety of dramatic symptoms, for example, blindness, deafness, amnesia, mutism, paralysis or tremor, could be allowed to provide a way out of the front line for increasing numbers of individuals. Civilian pressures also existed. With a conscript army there were probably more people in Britain whose relatives were serving involuntarily than voluntarily. The mounting casualty lists and carnage encouraged popular concern that soldiers should not be treated harshly if they broke down in the face of phenomenal stress. Psychological illness had to be recognized. It was easier to keep the numbers down if psychological illness was not called a physical brain disease. In 1917 and 1918, the numbers of patients with shell shock declined, although this may have been in part because of the fall in the rate of slaughter in the trenches, high though that remained.

Most symptoms seen were hysterical and reflected the patient's idea of a symptom, rather than the doctor's knowledge of pathology. This influenced the understanding of hysteria. Such large numbers of people had broken down under acute stress that it was untenable to attribute hysterical symptoms to childhood sexual experience.

As there had been large numbers of casualties so there were large numbers of individuals claiming pensions. MacPherson et al (1923) considered that in Britain in February 1921, 65,000 men were drawing pensions for neurasthenia and allied conditions. There was a fall and then, after that, an apparent increase, despite the downward trend of the initial figures. In March 1939 about 120,000 pensioners were still in receipt of such pensions (Ahrenfeldt, 1958).

Stone (1985) suggested that the clinics of the Ministry of Pensions led to the development of psychiatric services in general hospitals after the First World War. This impression is shared by a number of psychiatrists who qualified before the Second World War (Merskey, 1991). Similar comments have been made about services in Canada (Griffin, 1989). The strength of these claims is uncertain. Some services existed before the First World War even if they were not large and those that emerged between the wars were also not substantial. Nevertheless, the war did demonstrate the relevance of psychotherapeutic skills.

THE SECOND WORLD WAR

The Second World War produced cases of battle neurosis, but not shell shock. Some lessons of the First World War were recognised and quickly applied. Active programs of removal of affected individuals from the firing line and quick treatment of psychiatric casualties, reduced the impact of the stress. In addition during World War II a further theory began to emerge from the observations of mens' reactions to stress (Grinker and Spiegel, 1945; Sargant and Shorvon, 1945). Sargant & Shorvon felt that men who had broken down with gross, uncoordinated, irregular jerking and writhing movements or states of exhaustion, or aphonia, stammer, or slowness of speech, or stupor showed parallels with Pavlov's experimental observations. Treatment by sedation or abreaction was introduced, frequently with good results. However rest and removal from the firing-line and quick sedation might have been as effective. On the other hand the ability of selection processes to identify soldiers who otherwise seem normal but will break down in action is unsettled (Chalke, 1954).

Copp and McAndrew (1990) have described how soldiers had classic psychiatric illnesses produced by stress in the Second World War, both in Italy and in France. Interestingly, a pseudo-organic condition emerged among Norwegian sailors. These men who suffered from sustained stress in conditions of great danger, often developed a syndrome called the 'war sailors' syndrome' which was attributed to an encephalopathy. Sjaastad (1985) concluded that this syndrome was probably due to severe and prolonged stress.

CONCENTRATION CAMPS

Concentration camps have been unquestionably the worst experience of the Second World War. Eitinger (1958 & 1964) identified the overwhelming stress to which Jewish inmates of concentration camps were subjected. Besides the direct observation of unimaginable physical cruelties, Jews and Gypsies singled out for extermination had the misfortune to see their closest relatives being killed in front of them, or sent directly to gas chambers. Their whole personal worlds were destroyed. Concentration camps were survived better by Norwegian resistance workers who had volunteered for dangerous missions, and who were a selected population compared with the Jews who represented an unselected sample of a whole people. Also, the families of the Norwegian resistance workers were still relatively safe. Both groups suffered far-reaching psychological after-effects but these were worse in the Jews. The concentration camp syndrome which has been described mainly comprises the effects of protracted anxiety and depression and some hysterical symptoms. It is a delayed effect of the experience. The initial effect is depression.

Kral (1951) who gave a detailed account of experiences and observations in a relatively benign concentration camp (Theresienstadt) pointed out that overt neurotic symptoms were relatively rare in that camp. One hundred and thirty-nine thousand, six hundred and sixty-six people of both sexes and all ages were sent to Theresienstadt. Thirty-three thousand, four hundred and sixty-eight died there and 86,862 were sent East to other camps in Poland, almost all for extermination. The rest stayed in Theresienstadt until the liberation. Living conditions were poor, epidemics of various infectious diseases raced through the camp and took the lives of thousands of persons, the imprisonment was humiliating without any objective or subjective guilt, there was no possibility to change one's fate no matter how one behaved, the vital drives were deprived of any gratification, there was a complete lack of privacy, combined with forced labour, and above all, there was the constant danger of being sent East to an unknown but certainly worse destination.

The initial response to removal to Theresienstadt was a state of depression and retardation and loss of initiative, accompanied by anorexia, sleeplessness, constipation and in most of the women amenorrhea. Suicidal attempts or panic reactions were not observed. Children and adolescents adjusted quickly, but older people often remained apathetic. Many patients who were known to have had severe chronic psychoneuroses such as phobias and obsessive-compulsive neuroses, improved completely or greatly. Gastric ulcers became rare. However a few hysterical reactions, seizures, pareses and demonstrative suicidal attempts were observed.

Several neurotic and psychotic reactions emerged after liberation. The principal patterns include emotional instability, nervousness, irritability, insomnia, headaches, marked symptoms of anxiety, periods of depression, nightmares, reduced initiative, dysphoria, bitterness and vertigo. Eitinger (1964) provided important individual evidence of persistent paranoid delusional reactions in some patients resulting from the concentration camp experience. Eitinger and Krell (1985) have provided a valuable bibliography of this whole field, and Weisaeth and Eitinger (1991) offer a summary.

Unfortunately, torture did not cease with the Nazi concentration camps and widespread abuses in many countries have made available a pool of information on the effects of physical and psychological torture (Amnesty International, 1977; Rassmussen, 1990). Allodi and Randall (1985) report typical findings from refugees who have been examined in Denmark, Canada or the U.S.A. among other places. Both psychosomatic and psychological effects appear, namely various anxiety symptoms, nervousness, depression, insomnia, tremors, weakness, diarrhoea, fainting and sweating, pains, nightmares, impaired concentration and impaired memory. Guilt and suicidal attempts were found in individuals who were not subject to nervous illness previously (as well as in some who were). Allodi (1991) points out that unlike other forms of stress, torture engenders personal feelings of humiliation and shame, mistrust of friends, neighbours, authorities and institutions, and confusion of values and of the self at a most intimate level.

CIVILIAN ACCIDENTS

In one sort of civilian accident one or two individuals suffer an unpleasant experience such as a collision. In another sort, many are involved simultaneously.

The characteristics of the first sort depend on the severity of the experience, and the premorbid state of the individual. Motor vehicle accidents with persistent physical sequelae commonly yield a proportion of patients who have such a post traumatic stress disorder. The typical patient has been in a minor collision, or worse, of which he or she has been aware immediately prior to its occurrence. Many such patients develop minor phobias of car travel. Some have the full picture of PTSD (post traumatic stress disorder) as defined in DSM-IV (American Psychiatric Association, 1994), which includes severe initial distress, uneasiness or more severe discomfort on passing the site of the accident, unwillingness to travel in cars to a greater or lesser degree, with increasing anxiety as the traffic becomes more thick, unpleasant flashbacks to the time of the accident, and nightmares, both about the accident specifically and about other frightening events, and symptoms of increased arousal. In many cases the condition is hard to disentangle from the effects of chronic pain and unemployment promoting disability and distress. Ultimately, even after pain has been reduced and depression declines, patients are often left with some residual anxiety symptoms which can be de-conditioned by simple measures of greater desensitization in most cases.

Major disasters can affect a group of people simultaneously. The response often includes automatic behaviour and confusion as well as overt panic, anger and guilt (Edwards, 1976). Defensive reactions with hysterical dissociation are likewise recognized (Kinston and Rosser, 1974). More extreme hysterical reactions associated with these events appear to be the result of social upheavals rather than from acute life-threatening disasters or concentration camp experiences. A typical recent report deals with psychological consequences of a bombing incident. Curran et al (1990) described the Enniskillen bombing of November 1987, in which 11 people were killed and 60 injured. They appraised survivors six months and one year after injury. At six months 50 per cent had developed post traumatic stress disorder as defined by DSM-III(R) (American Psychiatric Association, 1987). There was no correlation between psychological injury measured in this fashion and physical injury as measured by an Injury Severity Score. Even in those who did not develop the full scale syndrome of post traumatic stress disorder, all the rest also suffered psychological symptoms such as fear, worry, depression and anger.

VIETNAM

Awareness developed gradually of the prolonged effects of psychological stress in American soldiers returning from Vietnam. Bourne (1978) points out that apart from the fact that the Vietnam War was unique, being unpopular and almost conducted on national television nightly in the United States, it was also unusual in that the soldier knew that if he could survive for 12 months his removal from combat was assured. Thus it seemed that the number of psychiatric casualties in Vietnam in the early years of that war was low. It was only found later that there was an exceptionally high degree of problems in adjustment once the veteran returned to the United States. The soldiers going home were not victorious and did not return with the emotional support of other members of their units (because they had served on rotation). Once they returned home they even encountered vocal opposition and resentment of their service to their country.

Overt American intervention in Vietnam ended on 25th March 1973 with the American evacuation from Saigon. The first comprehensive report of the long-term psychosocial effects of Vietnam on those Americans who fought there was compiled by Figley (1978) building upon the earlier reports of Bourne. Haley (1978) demonstrated that almost all veterans with a post combat stress response syndrome had some form of anxiety or depression or an adult situational reaction. The common phenomena include depression, an explosive aggressive reaction, sleep disturbance with nightmares, startle responses, stimuli associated with previous life-threatening experiences, constriction of ego interests and adaptive functions, and dissociative reactions i.e., flashbacks. The effects of these syndromes in hampering adjustment to civilian life have been explored repeatedly by United States psychiatrists and other psychotherapists. A National Center for Post Traumatic Stress Disorder (PTSD) was mandated by the U.S. Congress in 1984 under Public Law 98–528 to carry out a broad range of multi-disciplinary activities in research, education and training. It has published a PTSD Research Quarterly since 1990. Criteria for PTSD were revised in DSM-III(R) (American Psychiatric Association, 1987) and DSM-IV (American Psychiatric Association, 1994).

Brief details of reports on casualties arising in the Falklands Conflict in 1982 and preparations in Britain for the Gulf Conflict have been noted by Atkinson (1991).

RETROSPECT

The evolution of clinical ideas about PTSD exemplifies three main themes. There is a causal relationship between an event and the immediate symptoms but the explanation of the mechanism of those symptoms has moved to the psychological sphere. Second there are common patterns of anxiety and reliving in almost all types of case, although these vary according to the circumstances of origin. Third, far reaching, slowly emerging effects may be observed which are characteristic of some of the cases of battle neurosis and even more characteristic of the concentration camp and torture cases. Intractable delusional illnesses may even be reasonably attributed to the concentration camp and its effects in a series of patients. At all stages psychotherapy has been provided and may have been influential in the development of psychiatry.

REFERENCES

American Psychiatric Association (1987) Diagnostic and Statistical Manual of Mental Disorders., 3rd Ed. Revised. Washington, D.C., American Psychiatric Association.

American Psychiatric Association (1994) Diagnostic and Statistical Manual of Mental Disorders, 4th Ed. Washington, D.C., American Psychiatric Association.

Ahrenfeldt, R.H. (1958) *Psychiatry in the British Army in the Second World War*, London, Routledge & Kegan Paul.

Allodi, F. (1991) 'Assessment and treatment of torture victims: a critical review'. *Canadian Journal of Psychiatry*, 179:4–11.

Allodi, F. and Randall, G.R. (1985) 'Physical and psychiatric effects of torture'. In Stover, E. and Nightingale, E.O. (eds.) *The Breaking of Bodies and Minds: Torture, Psychiatric Abuse and the Health Professions*, New York, American Association for the Advancement of Science, Chapter 3.

Amnesty International (1977) *Evidence of Torture: Studies by the Amnesty International Danish Medical Group*, London, Amnesty International.

Anonymous (1916) 'A discussion of shell shock'. *Lancet*, I: 306–7.

Atkinson, J.M. (1991) 'The demand for psychiatric services as a result of the Gulf War'. *Psychological Bulletin*, 15:201–3.

Baker, S.L. (1975) 'Military psychiatry'. In Freedman, A.M., Kaplan, H.I. and Sadock, B.J. (eds.) *Comprehensive Textbook of Psychiatry, II*, Baltimore, Williams & Wilkins.

Bourne, P.G. (1978) Foreword in Figley, C.R. (ed.) *Stress Disorders Among Vietnam Veterans: Theory, Research and Treatment*, New York, Brunner/Mazel.

Brown, M.W. and Williams, F.E. (1918) *Neuropsychiatry and The War*, New York, National Committee for Mental Hygiene.

Breuer, J. and Freud, S. (1955) *Studies on Hysteria. Complete Psychological Works of Freud, 1893–1895*, vol.2, London, Hogarth Press.

Chalke, F.C.R. (1954) 'Psychiatric screening of recruits: A review'. *Department of Veterans' Affairs Treatment Services Bull*, 9:273–92.

Charcot, J.M. (1889) *Clinical Lectures on Diseases of the Nervous System*, vol.III. Trans. T. Savill, London, The New Sydenham Society.

Copp, T. and McAndrew, B. (1990) *Battle Exhaustion, Soldiers and Psychiatrists in the Canadian Army, 1939–1945*, Montreal, McGill Queens University Press.

Curran, P.S., Bell, P., Murray, A., Loughrey, G., Roddy, R. and Rocke, E.L.G. (1990) 'Psychological consequences of the Enniskillen bombing'. *British Journal of Psychiatry*, 156:479–82.

DaCosta, J.M. (1871) 'On irritable heart; a clinical study of a form of functional cardiac disorder and its consequences'. *The American Journal of the Medical Sciences*, 61:17–52.

Eitinger, L. (1964) *Concentration Camp Survivors in Norway and Israel*, Oslo, Universitets Forlaget.

Eitinger, L., Krell, R. and Rieck, M. (1985) *The Psychological and Medical Effects of Concentration Camps and Related Persecutions on Survivors of the Holocaust, a Research Bibliography*, Vancouver, University of British Columbia Press.

Erichsen, Sir J.E. (1866, 1867) *On Railway and Other Injuries of the Nervous System*, Philadelphia, Henry C. Lea.

Erichsen, Sir J.E. (1886) *On Concussion of the Spine, Nervous Shock and Other Obscure Injuries to the Nervous System in Their Clinical and Medico-Legal Aspects. A New and Revised Edition*, New York, William Wood & Co.

Figley, C.R. (1978) *Stress Disorders Among Vietnam Veterans. Theory, Research and Treatment*, New York, Brunner/Mazel.

Gaupp, R. (1915) 'Die Granatkontusion'. *Beitrage zur Klin Chirurgie*, 96:277–94.

Graves, R. (1960) *Goodbye to All That, 1929*, Harmondsworth, Penguin.

Griffin, J.D.M. (1989) 'Interview by S. Sussman'. In Blom, D.J. and Sussman, S. (eds.) *Pioneers of Mental Health and Social Change, 1930–89*, London, Canada, Third Eye.

Grinker, R.F. and Spiegel, J.P. (1945) *Men Under Stress*, Philadelphia, Blakiston, McGraw Hill.

Haley, S.A. (1978) 'Treatment implications of post combat stress response syndromes for mental health professionals'. In Figley, C.R. (ed.) *Stress Disorders Among Vietnam Veterans. Theory, Research and Treatment*, New York, Brunner/Mazel, Chap. 12.

Hesnard, A. (1914) 'Les troubles nerveux et psychiques consécutifs aux catastrophes navales'. *Revue de Psychiatrie*, 18:139–51.

Hodges, R.M. (1881) 'So-called concussion of the spinal cord'. *Boston Medical and Surgical Journal*, 104:361–5, 386–9.

Hurst, A.F. (1940) *Medical Diseases of War*, London, Edward Arnold.

Hynes, S. (1990) *A War Imagined, The First World War and English Culture*, London, The Bodley Head, p.469.

Kinston, W. and Rosser, R. (1974) 'Disaster: effects on mental and physical state'. *Journal of Psychosomatic Research*, 18:437–56.

Kral, V.A. (1951) 'Psychiatric observations under severe chronic stress'. *American Journal of Psychiatry*, 108, 3:185–92.

Lewis, Sir T. (1918) *The Soldier's Heart and the Effort Syndrome*, London, Shaw & Sons.

Lust, F. (1916) 'War neuroses among prisoners of war.' *Münch. Med. Woch.*, 63:182; cit *J.A.M.A.*, 69:1386 (1917).

MacPherson, W.G., Herringham, W.P., Elliott, T.R. and Balfour, A. (1923) *History of the Great War Medical Services. Diseases of War, vol.II.*, London, HMSO.

Mairet, A. and Durante, G. (1917) 'Experimental shell-shock.' *Presse Méd. Paris*, 25:478–9.

Mendelson, G. (1982) 'Not "cured by a verdict". Effect of legal settlement on compensation claimants'. *Medical Journal of Australia*, 2:219–30.

Merskey, H. (1979) *The Analysis of Hysteria*, London, Baillière Tindall.

Merskey, H. (1991) 'Shell Shock'. In Berrios, G.E. and Freeman, H.L. (eds.) *150 Years of British Psychiatry. 1841–1991*, London, Gaskell, pp.245–67.

Micale, M. (1990) 'Charcot and the idea of hysteria in the male: Gender, mental science and medical diagnosis in late 19th century France'. *History of Medicine*, 34:363–411.

Mott, F.W. (1916a) 'Special discussion on shell shock without visible signs of injury'. *Proceedings of the Royal Society of Medicine*, Part III, Suppl, 9:1–44.

Mott, F.W. (1919) *War Neuroses and Shell Shock*, London, Henry Frowde and Hodder & Stoughton.

Myers, C.S. (1915) 'A contribution to the study of shell shock'. *Lancet*, 1:316–20.

Oppenheim, H. (1889) *Die traumatischen Neurosen*, Berlin, Hirschwald. See Oppenheim, H. (1911) *Textbook of Nervous Diseases for Physicians and Students*, Trans. A.T.N. Bruce, London, Foulis.

Oppenheim, H. (1915) 'The war and the traumatic neuroses'. *Berliner Klinische Wochenschrift*, 52:257–61.

Page, H.W. (1883) *Injuries of the Spine and Spinal Cord Without Apparent Mechanical Lesion and Nervous Shock in Their Surgical and Medico-Legal Aspects*, London, J. & A. Churchill.

Putnam, J.J. (1883) 'Recent investigations in the pathology of so-called concussion of the spine'. *Boston Medical and Surgical Journal*, 109:217–20.

Rassmussen, O.V. (1990) 'Medical Aspects of Torture'. *Danish Medical Bulletin*, 33:1–88, Suppl 1.

Report of the War Office Committee on Enquiry into 'Shell-Shock' (1922) London, HMSO, Cmd. 1734. (Fortescue, J., page 9; Terrill, W., page 3; Rogers, J.S.Y., page 62).

Reynolds, Sir J.R. (1869) 'Remarks on paralysis and other disorders of motion and sensation, dependent on idea'. *British Medical Journal*, ii:483–5.

Sargant, W. and Shorvon, H.J. (1945) 'Acute war neurosis'. *Archives of Neurology and Psychiatry*, 54:231–40.

Sassoon, S. (1936) *Sherston's Progress*, London, Faber.

Sjaastad, O. (1985) 'The war sailor syndrome: after-effects of extreme mental stress. An organic brain syndrome or pseudodementia?' In Ross, F.C. (ed.) *Modern Approaches to the Dementias Part II: Clinical and Therapeutic Aspects. Interdisciplinary Topics in Gerontology*, 20:94–114, Basel, Karger.

Stone, M. (1985) 'Shell shock and the psychologists'. In Bynum, W.T., Porter, R. and Shepherd, M., (eds.) *The Anatomy of Madness*, London, Tavistock Press, 2:242–71.

Vaughan, E.C. (1981) *Some Desperate Glory. The World War I Diary of a British Officer*, London, F. Warne.

Walton, G.L. (1883) 'Possible cerebral origin of the symptoms usually classed under "railway spine" '. *Boston Medical and Surgical Journal*, 109:337–40.

Weisaeth, L. and Eitinger, L. (1991) 'Research on PTSD and other post-traumatic reactions in European literature'. *Post-traumatic Stress Disorder Research Quarterly*, 2:1–7.

Chapter 19

Post-traumatic Stress Disorder and Shell Shock

Social Section

EDWARD M BROWN

The role of social forces in shaping the construction of disease concepts in psychiatry is particularly clearly demonstrated in the case of the traumatic neuroses. The idea that disturbing experiences affect emotions and cause illnesses is an ancient one. The idea that certain types of traumatic environmental events cause certain specific emotional symptoms, however, developed only during the late nineteenth and early twentieth centuries. This idea emerged out of social conflict over the responsibility of corporations and nations for the suffering of workers and soldiers. Prior to this the psychiatric symptoms of soldiers might be diagnosed as due to insanity or to nostalgia or homesickness but they were not attributed to the effects of battle (Rosen, 1975). Psychiatrists recognized moral causes of insanity, such as fear and grief, as well as physical causes, such as fevers and blows to the head, but they did not develop a causal model in which 'trauma' mediated between circumstance and symptom. Industrialization and the advent of industrial warfare created the social conditions which allowed this model to be constructed. It was not simply that people experienced emotional pain as the result of railway accidents or artillery shellings but that they held corporations and nations responsible for this suffering that gave rise to debate. Neurologists, eager to demonstrate their expertise and enhance the social standing of their young profession, entered into this public debate offering various conflicting explanations for the 'symptoms' of victims. Because different causal explanations had different implications in terms of corporate and national responsibility, the resolution of intellectual differences among doctors was strongly influenced by the social consequences of their ideas.

Controversy over responsibility for the effects of accidents began when passengers started filing damage claims against railway companies. Such claims were a significant source of litigation in England by 1860 and they grew in significance throughout the industrializing world as railroads expanded during the late nineteenth century. Indeed, litigation against railroads became one of the most prominent expressions of the discontents engendered by the process of industrialization. There were a number of reasons for this. Railway corporations were among the most visible of the impersonal corporations which were coming to dominate economic and social life. Railways accidents were frequent, terrifying and highly publicized instances of the capacity of industrial technology to maim and kill. Moreover, railway passengers did not confront the same obstacles to litigation as industrial workers (Brown, 1990).

In 1866 the English surgeon John Eric Erichsen opened the medical debate over the emotional consequences of accidents with his *On Railway and other Injuries of the Nervous System*. What concerned Erichsen was the spectacle of doctors disgracing the profession by disagreeing in court over claims made by accident victims. Erichsen (1866) noted that while 'nineteen-twentieths of all railway or other accidents that are referred to surgeons' provoked no diagnostic controversies, there were many controversies over that small percentage of cases where 'the relation between alleged cause and apparent effect may not always be easy to establish' (Erichsen, 1867 p.19). To resolve these legal controversies Erichsen first argued that the problematic cases were sufficiently similar to constitute a syndrome. He noted that:

> at the time of the occurrence of the injury the sufferer is usually quite unconscious that any serious accident has happened to him. . . . When he reaches his home, the effects of the injury that he has sustained begin to manifest themselves. A revulsion of feelings takes place. He bursts into tears, becomes unusually talkative, and is excited. He cannot sleep, or, if he does, he wakes up suddenly with a vague sense of alarm. The next day he complains of feeling shaken and bruised all over, as if he had been beaten, . . . After a time, which varies much in different cases, from a day or two to a week or more, he finds that he is unfit for exertion and unable to attend to business. He now lays up, and perhaps for the first time seeks surgical assistance. (Erichsen, 1866 p.74)

After presenting 39 case examples, Erichsen went onto explain this syndrome pathologically. He argued that the symptoms of what he called 'concussion of the spine' were 'in reality due to chronic inflammation of the spinal membranes and the cord'. Cerebral symptoms, such as 'headache, confusion of thought, loss of memory, disturbance of the organs of sense, [and] irritability of the eyes and ears', were indirect expressions of the spinal process (Erichsen, 1866, pp.88–91). This was not, at the time, an implausible theory, and given popular sentiment about railway accidents, it was an easy one for many to accept. Indeed while Erichsen insisted that 'concussion of the spine' occurred in a variety of accidents, the growing frequency and importance of railway litigation led virtually everyone to refer to Erichsen's discovery as 'railway spine'.

Throughout the 1870s railway spine reigned without competition as the diagnosis used by plaintiffs seeking damages for emotional symptoms following railway accidents. It was, by all accounts, a highly successful legal strategy (Burry and Andrews, 1888). The success of the diagnosis of railway spine, however, provoked harsh criticism. Erichsen's ideas were vulnerable to such criticism for several reasons. First, while Erichsen had aimed at improving the precision of medical testimony, the diagnosis of railway spine was sufficiently all-inclusive and vague that claims were easy to make. That Erichsen interpreted the clinical findings as due to an inflammation of the spinal cord, for which there was no treatment, implied a poor prognosis and consequently resulted in what many felt were exorbitant awards. Moreover, the fact that victims of railway spine did not die meant that no patho-anatomical findings were available to support the diagnosis. Finally when accident victims were observed to recover after their claims were settled, critics lost patience and cried malingering. According to the Scottish surgeon, James Syme (1867):

> The truth [was] that when juries find the medical evidence is conflicting, not being able to judge for themselves as to the merits of the case, they almost always decide in favor of the claimant. (An accident victim had) merely to go to bed, call in a couple of sympathizing doctors, peruse Mr. Erichsen's . . . work on Railway Injuries [and], go to court on crutches . . . [to be assured a] jury would give large damages.

The first sustained attack on Erichsen's position was that by Herbert W. Page. Although he was a surgeon working for the London and North-Western Railway Company, his influence was great. Presenting 234 cases of his own, Page (1883) argued that Erichsen had been misled by symptoms due to 'injury to the extra-spinal muscular, and ligamentous structures' and had erroneously attributed 'nervous symptoms' to a lesion of the spinal column. In contrast to many railway surgeons, however, he did not claim that all the symptoms of these accident victims represented nothing but compensation seeking. Instead he adopted a psychosomatic position. He argued that 'nervous shock' was a real disorder which could be produced by fear or alarm, but that it had a much better prognosis than concussion of the spine. Erichsen's syndrome, he explained, was produced by 'neuromimesis', an involuntary process, which allowed a functional and curable disorder to mimic an incurable structural lesion. He added skeptically, however, that such 'nervous mimicry' could be brought on and terminated voluntarily, thereby explaining those sudden recoveries which occurred when the matter of compensation was settled.

Because the similarity between Page's nervous shock and the controversial diagnosis of hysteria was immediately apparent, his findings provided support for those neurologists who were attempting to establish the legitimacy of functional explanations for hysteria. During the late nineteenth century efforts to explain all neurological symptoms through the 'anatomo-pathological method of research', which was so central to the legitimacy of the neurological profession, had been blocked by the inability of neurologists to find lesions that would explain hysteria (Levin, 1978). Some neurologists responded to this apparent failure by dismissing hysteria as a disposition 'inherent, if not in all women, at least in the vast majority' (Gowers, 1893, p.985). Others responded by arguing that hysteria was a true, though functional, nervous disorder. In doing so they not only refused to be bound by the nineteenth century obligation to find anatomical correlates for clinical findings but also accorded the emotions a far more substantial explanatory role than they had been accorded previously. Because functionalists were vulnerable to attack on both counts, they found the utility of the notion of traumatic hysteria in resolving disputes over responsibility in cases of railway spine useful in establishing the legitimacy of the diagnosis of hysteria.

Regarding railway spine as a functional, psychosomatic disorder, in which fear produced reversible nervous symptoms, promised to fill the gap between accusations of compensation seeking and crude pathoanatomical explanations. Because traumatic hysteria and the other popular functional diagnosis at the time, traumatic neurasthenia, were considered to be treatable and to have relatively good prognoses, courts could acknowledge the legitimacy of many claims while limiting the damages awarded. Functionally oriented neurologists leaped at the opportunity to expand the utility of their diagnoses. A year after Page published his findings, the American neurologist J.J. Putnam (1883) urged doctors to search cases of apparent railway spine 'carefully for the presence of functional symptoms which may be grouped under the term hysteria'. The eminent French neurologist Jean Martin Charcot (1889, p.99), went even further, concluding that those 'states so grave and tenacious, which present themselves as the sequel of "collisions" . . . are often only hysteria, nothing but hysteria'.

Because of the mediating role played by emotions in these diagnoses, legal controversy surrounded their use in England and the United States. According to common law no compensation could be had for fright or mental anguish caused by simple negligence, unless it was accompanied by another legal injury (Smith and Solomon, 1944). The reason for this rule appears to have been the practical concern that the flood gates of litigation would be opened if complaints about conditions which were not visible were accepted as evidence. In 1888, for example, a train narrowly missed Mary Coultas' wagon. 'In order to prevent the opening of "a wide field . . . for imaginary claims," she was denied compensation for "damages arising from mere sudden terror unaccompanied by any actual physical injury, but occasioning a nervous or mental shock" ' (Victoria Ry. Comm'rs, 1888). By 1901 opinion had shifted. Some argued that 'refusing to admit mental shock or fright . . . as a cause of action (would) result in injustice to many cases of nervous disease', and others insisted that denying all claims for fear of false claims implied 'a certain degree of distrust, . . . in the capacity of legal tribunals to get at the truth in this class of case' (Bailey, 1898–99; Dulieu v. White, 1901). Justice Kennedy expressed the emerging legal view when he argued that while the Privy Council in *Coultas* used the epithets 'nervous' and 'mental' interchangeably, he thought that 'nervous' was 'probably the more correct epithet where terror operates through the parts of the physical organism to produce bodily illnesses' (Dulieu v. White, 1901).

The acceptance of arguments like Justice Kennedy's signaled the acceptance of the utility of the concept of the traumatic nervous disorder, as a tool in resolving conflicts over responsibility in industrial accidents. With the advent of Workers' Compensation laws in England and the United States opinions such as Kennedy's were applied not only to railway passengers but also to industrial workers. While there were special problems involved in establishing claims for emotional injuries under Workers' Compensation laws, the legitimacy of such claims was not a major source of controversy (Brown, 1990).

Extending the concept of the traumatic emotional disorder to the military was another story. Particularly in the British army during World War I, the victims of 'shell shock', like those of railway spine, were initially caught up in controversy over whether they suffered from a form of brain damage or were malingering. The serious and ultimately unacceptable social implications of both of these diagnoses gave advocates of a functional and psychological notion of the traumatic emotional disorder an opportunity to promote the socially more useful compromise suggestion that shell shock was a real disorder but one which could be readily treated by psychological means (Brown, 1988).

The term shell shock was first used in early 1915 by Charles Myers to describe three soldiers suffering from among other things sleeplessness, reduced visual fields, and amnesia. His use of that term was apt considering that the profound negative atmospheric pressure following artillery shell explosions had knocked one off a wall, buried another in a trench and trapped the third in barbed wire (Myers, 1915). His use of the term, however, foreshadowed the confusion and conflict which surrounded it throughout the war. Although Myers saw the close relation of these cases to hysteria as 'fairly certain', the term shell shock itself was more consistent with the pathoanatomical theories of the noted neurologist Fredrick Mott.

Mott (1916) had autopsied soldiers dying without obvious physical injury and found diffuse small hemorrhages throughout their nervous systems. He interpreted these lesions as due either to the effect of the negative atmospheric pressure resulting from artillery explosions or to carbon monoxide poisoning which occurred when a soldier was knocked unconscious and lay at the bottom of a trench. Extrapolating from the autopsy findings, he wondered whether some of the symptoms of soldiers who did not die might be explained along similar lines. While he noted that 'physical shock accompanied by horrifying circumstances . . . has a much more intense and lasting effect on the mind than simple shock has', the thrust of his presentation was clearly to incorporate shell shock within the pathoanatomical model.

Because men with symptoms of shell shock, regardless of how their symptoms were interpreted, would not fight, the existence of such cases demanded that someone establish a boundary between irresponsible action and illness. Problems with Mott's interpretation were soon apparent. Clinically, most cases of shell shock did not occur in the presence of exploding shells or carbon monoxide. Indeed symptoms frequently emerged at some distance from the scene of combat. These limitations of Mott's neuropathological interpretation of shell shock created an opportunity for advocates of functional and psychological interpretations to propose alternatives. These interpretations of shell shock promised to include a far greater array of soldiers within the net of medical explanation. For military authorities, however, the central issue involved in the medical diagnosis of soldiers who would not fight was malingering. For them the signs of genuine neurosis were indistinguishable from those of simulation. Consequently, inclusive functional explanations threatened to allow the problem of malingering to get out of hand (Report of the War Office Committee, 1922, pp.4–8).

The problem of distinguishing malingering from genuine nervous disorders was particularly important and difficult during the First World War. It was a national war involving virtually all of the men and women of the nation in war related activities. Patriotism was actively encouraged and, at least for British soldiers, effective escape was virtually impossible. Press censorship prevented those at home from appreciating the horrifying conditions in the trenches not to mention the discouragement and demoralization of the troops. Moreover, both cowardice and desertion were still capital offenses in the British Army during the First World War. This harsh military code developed during previous centuries, operated on the assumption that soldiers were the uneducated dregs of society (Moore, 1974). This created a particularly bitter irony during World

War I, when patriotic fervor led many working-class and educated middle-class men to volunteer for service (Keegan, 1976, pp.219–29). Nonetheless, traditional military discipline remained in effect. During the war, the British army executed 346 soldiers – mainly for cowardice and desertion (Babington, 1983, p.183). As Charles Myers noted, 'from the standpoint of military discipline', the distinction between intentional and unintentional symptoms was of 'vital importance' (Myers, 1916).

Regardless of whether military authorities treated shell shock as an actual disorder or as a form of malingering what concerned them most was their belief that shell shock could spread through the ranks like an infectious disease. When this occurred panic and a disastrous decline in the effectiveness of fighting units were the likely outcome. In such cases there was general agreement that the behavior of individual soldiers was of less importance than the failure of the commanding officer to maintain morale (Report of the War Office Committee, 1922, p.15). This shift in focus from the responsibility of individual soldiers in isolated cases of shell shock to the responsibility of the commanding officers in situations where whole units were involved, was convenient in that it allowed the authorities to avoid treating the latter as mutinies or acknowledging that the war itself could destroy the morale of so many soldiers. The tactic of blaming commanders was strained to the breaking point, however, by the Somme offensive during the middle of 1916. This enormous and disastrous battle, which involved virtually the whole British army in France, inflicted losses of over 600,000 men on the Allies, two-thirds of them British. It is remembered as having wiped out 'a large part of a generation and much of the best of that generation' (Schmidt and Vedler, 1984). It also resulted in a tremendous increase in the number of British casualties due to war neuroses: these jumped from about 3,000 in the first half of 1916 to 17,000 by the end of that year (Moore, 1974). The battle of the Somme might also be remembered as marking the point where the moral order represented by the dichotomy of courage and cowardice had to make way for a scientific and medical order represented by the idea of neurosis.

As a result of the battle of the Somme two important developments in the treatment of shell-shocked soldiers occurred in early 1917. First, the diagnosis of shell shock itself was officially disallowed. In the face of such massive flight from battle, medical officers were instructed to give soldiers who claimed to be shell-shocked the more ambiguous diagnostic label 'Not Yet Diagnosed – Nervous'. This, it was believed, would prevent soldiers from using the shell shock label to avoid battle. Second, the older system of removing soldiers from the front lines to base hospitals for triage was scrapped in favor of a system, already used by the French, in which triage was performed closer to the front line. While both of these developments were in a sense technical, they had important symbolic significance as well. In dropping the term 'shell shock' the British army was accepting the fact that the phenomenon of shell shock could no longer be treated as peripheral to the war effort. By establishing front line triage stations, the army not only increased its ability to return soldiers to battle, but also put doctors in a much better position to judge why soldiers would not fight. While courts-martial for desertion and cowardice as well as executions, continued until the end of the war, these changes marked the British army's reluctant recognition that their disciplinary system alone could not maintain the fighting force. By more closely integrating doctors into the war effort, they accepted the role of science and medicine as necessary in maintaining morale in industrial warfare.

After the war the notion of the functional nervous disorder in general and the traumatic emotional disorder in particular flourished. Indeed it can be argued that the war finally opened a space for that partly scientific partly moral form of medical discourse that we call the psychological. Psychoanalysis, in particular benefited from a new willingness to accept psychological explanations in place of traditional moral ones. In Britain, as Martin Stone (1985, pp.242,271) has noted, it was probably shell shock more than the writings of Freud, that was responsible for this. After the war, psychological interpretations of war neuroses had become so readily accepted that popularizers of psychoanalysis used examples of shell shock to explain the neuroses in general (Riggs, 1922). Nonetheless experience with shell shock during the war did not prepare governments for the persistence of the symptoms of ex-servicemen in the post war years.

Traumatic emotional disorders continue to be a source of social conflict as recent debate over post traumatic stress disorder among Vietnam veterans and the victims of childhood sexual abuse demonstrates. As the history of railway spine and shell shock suggests such conflict is to be expected because claims of emotional injury inevitably raise questions of responsibility. This history also makes it clear that the process by which our understanding of traumatic emotional disorders has been shaped cannot be completely understood without taking social conflict into consideration.

REFERENCES

Babington, A. (1983) *For the Sake of Example*, New York, St. Martins Press.

Bailey, P. (1898–99) 'The Medico-legal relations of traumatic hysteria'. *The Railway Surgeon*, 5: 555–8.

Brown, E.M. (1988) 'Between cowardice and insanity: Shell shock and the legitimation of the neuroses in Great Britain'. In Mendelsohn, E., Smith, M.R. and Weingart, P. (eds.) *Science Technology and the Military*, Dortrecht, Kluwer Academic Publishers.

Brown, E.M. (1990) 'Regulating damage claims for emotional injuries before the First World War'. *Behavioral Sciences and the Law*, 8: 421–34.

Burry, J. and Andrews, E.W. (1888) 'Medico-legal aspects of some injuries of the spinal cord'. *Journal of the American Medical Association*, 11: 841–84.

Charcot, J.M. (1889) *Clinical Lectures on Diseases of the Nervous System*. Translated by T. Savill, London, New Sydenham Society.

Dulieu v White (1901) 2 Kings Bench 669, 79 Law Journal Kings Bench Decisions 837.

Erichsen, J.E. (1867) *On Railway and other Injuries of the Nervous System*, Philadelphia, Henry C. Lea.

Fischer-Homberger, E. (1971) 'Railway spine und traumatische Neurose-Seele und Ruckenmark'. *Gesnerus*, 67: 96–111.

Gowers, W.R. (1893) *A Manual of Disease of the Nervous System*, London, J. & A. Churchill.

Keegan, J. (1976) *The Face of Battle*, London, Penguin Books.

Levin, K. (1978) *Freud's Early Psychology of the Neuroses*, Pittsburgh, University of Pittsburgh Press.

Moore, W. (1974) *The Thin Yellow Line*, London, Leo Cooper.

Mott, F.W. (1916) 'Effects of high explosives upon the central nervous system'. *Lancet*, Feb. 12, 331–8; Feb. 26, 441–9; March 11, 545–53.

Myers, C.M. (1915) 'Contributions to the study of shell shock'. *Lancet*, Feb. 13, 316–20.

Myers, C.M. (1916) 'Contributions to the study of shell shock'. *Journal of the Royal Army Medical Corps*, 27: 557.

Page, H.W. (1883) *Injuries of the Spine and Spinal Cord, without apparent Mechanical Lesion, and Nervous Shock, in their Surgical and Medico-legal Aspects*, London, J. & A. Churchill.

Putnam, J.J. (1883) 'Recent investigations into the pathology of so-called concussion of the spine'. *Boston Medical and Surgical Journal*, 109: 217–20.

Riggs, A.F. (1922) *Just Nerves*, Boston and New York, Houghton Mifflin Company.

Report of the War Office Committee of Enquiry into 'Shell Shock' (1922), *House of Commons Sessional Papers*, vol.12, London.

Rosen, G. (1975) 'Nostalgia: A "forgotten" psychological disorder'. *Psychological Medicine*, 5: 340–55.

Schivelbusch, W. (1977) *The Railway Journey: The Industrialization of Time and Space in the 19th Century*, Berkeley, University of California Press.

Schmidt, B. and Vedler, H. (1984) *The World in the Crucible*, New York, Harper and Row.

Smith, H.W. and Solomon, H. (1944) 'Relation of emotions to injury and disease; Legal liability for psychic stimuli'. *Virginia Law Review*, 30: 193–249.

Stone, M. (1985) 'Shell shock and the psychologists'. In Bynum, W.F., Porter, R., and Shepherd, M. (eds.) *The Anatomy of Madness*, London and New York, Tavistock Publications.

Syme, J. (1867) 'Compensation for railway injuries'. *Lancet*, Jan. 5, pp.2–3.

Victoria Ry. Comm'rs (1888) Law Reports 13 Appeal Cases 222.

Chapter 20
Neurasthenia and Fatigue Syndromes

Clinical Section
SIMON WESSELY

The New York neurologist George Beard is widely credited with introducing the term neurasthenia in a brief paper presented in the Boston Medical and Surgical Journal in 1869 (Beard, 1869). However, Van Deusen (1869) has an equal claim to the authorship of neurasthenia, as he introduced the term in the American Journal of Insanity in the same year. The rival claims of Van Deusen, an alienist treating farmers in unfashionable Kalamazoo, and Beard, an East Coast neurologist with clients drawn from the Social Register, mirrored the wider confrontation between neurology and psychiatry at that time (Hale, 1987). As with the larger professional conflict, it was Beard who triumphed, and although the American Journal of Insanity would later resurrect Van Deusen's claim, it was the neurologist who became most credited with the 'discovery' of neurasthenia.

The concept of nervous exhaustion was not new, and a few contemporaries took pains to elaborate the history of the disease before Beard, tracing its origins to nervosisme, neurospasm, spinal irritability and so on (ex Huchard, 1883; Arndt, 1892), whilst later historians have pointed out the debt Beard owed hypochondria, spinal irritation and Brownian doctrine of asthenia and esthenia (Fischer-Homberger, 1970; López-Piñero, 1983).

Beard's views were not fully articulated until his two books written towards the end of his life (Beard, 1880, Beard, 1881). In them he drew his ideas from several sources including Marshall Hall's discovery of the spinal reflex arc, Edison's electricity and Du Bois Reymond's electrical nervous impulse, Spencer's Social Darwinism and so on (Rosenberg, 1962). His skill lay in mixing scientific advances with social theory and moral exhortation, and constructing out of these sources a single disease entity, designed to appeal to many of the concerns of the age, but couched in what seemed to many (but by no means all) acceptable scientific terminology.

Whatever the provenance of neurasthenia, its rapid spread and popularity owed much to Beard, especially in France and Germany. By the turn of the century a French doctor wrote that 'everything could be explained by neurasthenia, suicide, decadent art, dress and adultery' (Certhoux, 1961) – 'since the works of George Beard . . . the name of neurasthenia was on everybody's lips, the fashionable disease' (Dubois, 1909), the 'maladie a la mode' (Certhoux, 1961). When Levillain (1891) published his important text he subtitled it 'La

Maladie du Beard'. Many of Charcot's pupils wrote texts on the illness – the most popular was probably that by Adrien Proust, ironically the father of the most famous neurasthenic of the age, Marcel. Bumke later wrote that there was no instance in the history of medicine of a label having the impact of neurasthenia (Bumke, 1925).

Beard's success was because he articulated his ideas to a receptive audience. For example, a series of investigations during the 1880s had revealed the poor health of much of French youth. This was blamed on the alleged excessive mental demands ('surménage') made by the new education system (Rabinbach, 1990) – similar views could be found on the other side of the Atlantic (ex Ely, 1906 and others). Neurasthenia fitted equally well with degeneration (Nye, 1982), as it could be the 'starting point for various kinds of degeneracy' (Bidon, 1899)[1]. It weakened the will, and diminished responsibility (and as such could be used to secure acquittal in murder trials (Castin, 1908)). Neurasthenia allowed medical thought to move away from the outdated doctrines of sentiments and passions no longer suitable for a society preoccupied with 'La Vie Moderne' (Zeldin, 1980).

WHAT WAS NEURASTHENIA?

Neurasthenia was 'a disease of the nervous system, without organic lesion, which may attack any or all parts of the system, and characterized by enfeeblement of the nervous force, which may have all degrees of severity, from slight loosening of these forces down to profound and general prostration' (Bouveret, cited by Deale and Adams, 1894). Authors had their own favourite symptoms – cardiac, gastric, cerebral, ocular, gynaecological and so on, but at the core was 'nervous exhaustion, characterised by undue fatigue on slightest exertion, both physical and mental' (Cobb, 1920) or fatigue and muscular weakness (Berkley, 1901; Mitchell, S. 1908). This fatigue had certain characteristics – it 'comes early, is extreme and lasts long' (Mitchell, 1883). Hence neurasthenics had 'abnormally quick fatigability and slow recuperation' (Jaspers, 1963), their fatigue not being relieved by rest.

Nevertheless, neurasthenia was also 'destitute of the objective signs which experimental medicine of our times more particularly affects' (Blocq, 1894). Sufferers looked normal, and were typically 'well nourished, muscularly well developed' (Ferrier, 1911), despite often profound functional disability. It also had no significant mortality (indeed, some claimed the opposite (Beard, 1880)).

Neurasthenia was an exceptionally broad church. As Shorter (1992) has shown, at least four different strands can be discerned. First, neurasthenia was male hysteria – 'neurasthenia is to men what hysteria is to women' (Gerhardt, 1893). Freud (1888) felt that the 'male nervous system has as preponderant a disposition to neurasthenia as the female to hysteria'. Many of the neurological and popular writings followed this lead. Second, neurasthenia was simply chronic fatigue- the 'fatigue neurosis' (Knapp, 1906; Weiss, 1908). The term should be reserved for 'an enfeeblement or fatigue neurosis, its cardinal characteristics being an inordinate sense of physical or mental fatigue' (Neu, 1920). Third, neurasthenia was depression. Cowles (1893) listed it as a 'first rank symptom' of neurasthenia, and Clouston (1892) viewed it as a 'minor form of melancholia'. Thus could mean depression of 'cortical activity' (ex Hartenburg, 1907) or latterly depression in a more psychological sense. Déjerine and Gauckler (1911) felt that melancholia and neurasthenia could only be distinguished on the basis of history, previous epsiodes of depression or mania favouring the former diagnosis. Many authors equated neurasthenia with a mild melancholia (ex Berkley, 1901), although the differences remained as instructive as the similarities – thus Friedman (1904) stated that whilst both neurasthenics and depressed patients required treatment away from the family, only the latter should be admitted to an asylum. Fourth, Beard himself viewed neurasthenia as the prototype of many diseases, both physical and mental. In particular it was the forerunner of all the mental illnesses, from neurosis to psychosis (Savill, 1894) It was 'the soil from which all mental illnesses spring' (Arndt, 1892) – occupying the 'broad borderland between mental health and outspoken mental disease (insanity)' (Barker & Byrnes, 1913). These intermediate stages are 'the various anomalies usually combined under the common name of neurasthenia' (Durkheim, 1950).

THE AETIOLOGIES OF NEURASTHENIA

Peripheral
During the early years of interest in neurasthenia the prevailing neurological paradigm remained the reflex hypothesis. Excessive irritation of the nervous system led to exhaustion of the peripheral nerves, which could spread to any tissue (see López-Piñero, 1983; Shorter, 1992). One cause of this was over stimulation, which thus fitted easily into Beard's theory. However, the remarkable flourishing of neurophysiology soon discredited the reflex hypothesis, whilst the related belief that female genital reflexes were the cause of nervous disease in women was also under pressure by 1870 (Shorter, 1992). Many of the early advocates of neurasthenia in England, such as Reynolds at University College Hospital, Allbutt at Cambridge and the obstetrician William Playfair at King's College Hospital, were emphatic in their condemnation of reflex theory, and in particular of the practise of 'local treatment' of the female genital organs, although this would survive for several decades. In ridiculing the reflex theory Clifford Allbutt explained that neither muscles nor reflex arc were in a state of exhaustion, nor were the neurasthenic cells too excitable – 'to be excitable is their business' (Allbutt, 1899). All these authorities espoused the new central paradigm of nervous disease, which soon replaced reflex theories.

The central paradigm
As views of the nervous system changed, especially under the impact of the new laws of Thermodynamics and Conservation of Energy (Rosenberg, 1962; Rabinbach, 1982; López-Piñero, 1983) so did the nature of neurasthenia. Doctors were beginning to discuss not only the body, but also the mind in terms of heat and energy before the arrival of neurasthenia – George Johnson, the Chair of Medicine at King's College Hospital, wrote about the mind as a 'set of complex psychological energies' (Johnson, 1875), and it was only a short step to see neurasthenia as an exhaustion of that supply of energy within the central nervous system. The consequence was 'cortical weakness' (Foster, 1900) or

'cortical irritability' (Pershing, 1904). Irritable weakness of the brain permitted some remnants of reflex theory to survive, but many other causes of cerebral exhaustion were identified. These were either local to the brain – a failure of cerebral blood flow or a deficiency in energy sources, or arise from distant sources, such as the effect of toxins. The increased demands on the system could result from overwork, or be the result of toxic, metabolic or infective insults. It was in this manner that masturbation was so deleterious to health, both in men (Cleghorn, 1907) and women (Browning, 1911; Macnaughton-Jones, 1913).

All of the above were acquired in adult life, but individuals could also be predisposed to react to each or all of these factors by hereditary, or could inherit neurasthenia itself. Neurasthenia thus fitted well with concepts of nervous inheritance, or degeneration. As Janet Oppenheim writes neurasthenia could indeed be 'all things to all men' (Oppenheim, 1991).

The social paradigm

The doctrine of overwork and nervous exhaustion linked neurasthenia with a variety of contemporary changes in society. Medical authorities viewed over-work, the agent by which the nervous system became exhausted, (which could be purely physical, mental or a mixture of both) as the inevitable consequence of a host of new social ills. Even before the introduction of neurasthenia, a variety of medical authorities were writing about the dangers of overwork (Poore, 1875; Johnson, 1875; Savage, 1875). Once again, it was Beard, with his facility for similes, who joined together a number of discontents into an explanatory model for his disease. For example, Beard, and many others, ascribed neurasthenia to the new, acquisitive nature of society, singling out, in a famous phrase, wireless telegraphy, science, steam power, newspapers and the education of women, summed up as 'modern civilisation' (Beard, 1881). Much of this was conveyed by metaphors drawn from business life, the exhausted businessman overdrawn on his nervous capital, overspent nervous resources and so on (– see Oppenheim, 1991; Lutz, 1991).

The dramatic rise of neurasthenia seemed to confirm its status as a disease of modern civilisation – indeed, its increasing frequency was 'as certain as the fact of civilization itself' (Ely, 1906). It was both a consequence, and the cause, of numerous social problems. It was the price to be paid for industrialisation, the rise of capitalism, and the consequent strains to which the business and professional classes were exposed (Haller, 1970). It was 'the disease of the century' (Ballet and Proust, 1902; Rankin, 1903; Ash, 1909) or the 'Age of Fatigue' (Rabinbach, 1990).

The psychogenic paradigm

Unfortunately for the organic view of neurasthenia, the central paradigm could not be sustained. Fatigue could only be measured with the greatest of difficulty (White, 1917), if at all (Muscio, 1921), nor could any discrete neuropathological lesion be located. Adolf Meyer later wrote that the 'remarkable changes in the nerve cells' which others had found, which were 'highly fashionable and a matter of pride to both patient and diagnostician . . . could not be replicated. Fatigue exhaustion is no longer tenable' (Meyer, 1919). The consequence was a loss of faith in simple neurological explanations – Donley (1906), in the first issue of the prestigious Journal of Abnormal Psychology, criticised the previous 'mechanical symbolism' of descriptions of neurasthenia, with the false belief that 'for every pathological manifestation there must be an underlying, definite "disease process" ', and the 'futility of the purely anatomical concept' expressing itself in 'apologetic reproductions of nerve cells in a state of fatigue'. Two years later neurasthenia could be described as 'a state of habitual valetudinarianism with no corresponding characteristic organic lesion' (Tanzi, 1909).

Social aetiologies were also changing. It was doubted if neurasthenia really was a disease of modern life (Schofield, 1908), except that 'we had become more tender in our ills' (Dubois, 1909). Neurasthenia was more likely to result from idleness than overwork (Brock, 1913; White, 1921), reflected in the increased emphasis on activity and exercise in place of the classic rest cure. Other aetiologies, considerably less attractive to the potential neurasthenic, were now suggested, such as bad housing (Glorieaux, 1905), and poor dental hygiene, due to the 'fashion of eating ice cream . . . prevalent among the children of the lower classes' (Savill, 1906).

These last quotes suggest a further change, that of class. Neurasthenia had been sustained by the belief that it was a condition of the most successful people in society. 'It is a disease of bright intellects, its victims are leaders and masters of men, each one a captain of industry' (Pritchard, 1905), a view widely shared (Freud, 1887; Kraepelin, 1902). The spread of neurasthenia amongst the male American intelligentsia is well described (see Feinstein, 1981; Kalfus, 1990; Lutz, this volume). One should also point out the large number of doctors afflicted. The importance of the male doctor who, like Beard, Dowse and Mitchell, willingly admitted he had suffered the illness, and of the male sufferer in general, should not be underestimated (Sicherman, 1981; Gay, 1986).

However, the preponderance of the male professional classes amongst sufferers began to alter. As early as 1880 Hutchinson noted that the illness was 'by no means confined to the idle, luxurious classes who have hitherto held a monopoly of functional nerve-derangements', views echoed by Charcot (1889). By 1906 a series of papers were produced describing the illness in the working class (Leubuscher and Bibrowicz, 1905: Iscouesco, 1905; Savill, 1906). The records of the Vanderbilt Clinic in New York (Jelliffe and Clark, 1903) shows that neurasthenia was now mainly a disease of the lower social classes, and, as most of these comprised Jewish immigrants, it could no longer even be called the 'American Disease'. In 1906 Stedman pleaded in his presidential address to the American Neurological Association (Stedman, 1906) for more attention to the need for facilities for the neurasthenic poor, and the illness had become the commonest cause of absenteeism among the garment workers of New York (Schwab, 1911). Cobb (1920) noted sardonically that those who continued to believe the disease was restricted to the upper social echelons were those whose commitment was entirely to private practice. Even the excess of male medical sufferers began to alter – it was the female doctor who was particularly vulnerable, because 'only the strong can survive' (Burr, 1910).

The failure of the organic paradigm, and the change in social class and aetiologies, prepared the way for the psychological model. This took two stages. First, neurasthenia was retained, but viewed as a psychological, rather than a physical illness. The pendulum shifted – rather than psychological symptoms being a consequence of neurasthenia, they first became linked in a vicious circle, with neither having supremacy (ex Tuckey, 1911; Hurry, 1914), and finally were seen as causing the condition – thus Déjerine writes that 'many manifestations [of neurasthenia] are by nature purely phobic in origin' (Déjerine and Gauckler, 1911). Second, the category itself was dismembered, and replaced by new psychiatric diagnoses. It is well known that by 1893 Freud considered sexual exhaustion to be the sole cause of neurasthenia, either directly or indirectly. The following year (Freud, 1894) saw his famous removal of anxiety neurosis from neurasthenia (although he later acknowledged earlier that Hecker had anticipated his work in the previous year in a paper distinguishing anxiety neurosis ('Angstneurose') and neurasthenia). As important was the work of Pierre Janet. He also regarded fatigue as the key to psychological disorder, and, like his contemporaries blamed modern life for fatigue neurosis (Rabinbach, 1990). However, he followed William James in deriding the conventional economic metaphor of the neurasthenic overdrawing on a limited capital of physical energy, but emphasised instead the emotional demands on the psychic economy (Rabinbach, 1990). Janet detached obsessional and phobic neuroses from neurasthenia, via the agency of psychasthenia (see Berrios, 1985). Freud, Bernheim and others continued to believe in a physical neurasthenia, not amenable to psychotherapy, labelled by Freud an 'actual neurosis' in which sexual energy was lost by masturbation, but thought it was rare – Ernest Jones (1961) later wrote that fewer than 1 per cent of neurasthenics were correctly diagnosed. Janet also believed in a physical neurasthenia for a brief period of time, but then abandoned this altogether.

The organicists countered such observations in two ways. First, the present methods of investigation were too crude to detect the organic changes (ex Oppenheim, 1908). Second, psychological symptoms, if present, were part of the physical neurasthenic state (Starr, 1901; De Fleury, 1901), or were an understandable reaction to the illness. In a speech to the American Neurological Association Weir Mitchell (1908) referred to his own early neurasthenia, and pointed out how depression could not be an explanation for his condition, since he had 'no depression that was abnormal or unreasonable'. His own illness, and that of other distinguished contemporary medical men, made it inconceivable that neurasthenia could be 'a malady of the mind alone'.

Nevertheless, these became increasingly minority views. Charles Dana read an influential paper to the Boston Society of Psychiatry and Neurology (Dana, 1904), expounding the 'renaissance' in psychiatric thinking, in contrast to the previous antagonism between neurology and psychiatry, and urging adoption of the new classifications. Only two years later the new President of the Neurological Association described an eminent patient as suffering from 'neurasthenia or mild melancholia' (Stedman, 1906) – the 'or' being unlikely a decade earlier. When the London Medical Society debated neurasthenia in 1913, Kinnier-Wilson wrote that 'it was clear . . . from the discussion that Beard's original description of "American Nervousness" as a physical and not a mental state was evidently not accepted by several of the speakers' (Kinnier Wilson, 1913). Thomas Horder was sceptical about the ability of 'neurasthenia school' to separate it from hypochondriasis, remarking that in his experience the 'mental element' rather overshadowed any physical contribution (Horder, 1903). The

successive editions of one important English psychiatric text show how neurasthenia moved from the neuroses (still an organic neurological diagnosis) to
the psychoneuroses (Stoddart, 1926) – William White's views showed a similar,
albeit less dramatic shift, in only four years (White, 1917; White, 1921).
Neurologists at the Massachusetts General Hospital had already done the same
(Walton, 1906), as did both Dutil and Déjerine, pupils of Charcot, did likewise
– 'Beard's illness must now be seen as of mental origin' (Dutil, 1903).

The change in the nosology of neurasthenia was also influenced by changing
views of treatment. Victorian neurasthenics were treated with a bewildering
variety of pharmacological and electrical treatments, but the mainstay of
treatment was the rest cure. The introduction and extraordinary popularity of
Weir Mitchell's rest cure is well known, and has been described elsewhere
(Olson, 1988; Shorter, 1990; Wessely, 1994a)[2]. The rest cure has attracted many
criticisms over the years. Feminist historians have been influential in highlighting
the influence of male stereotypes of women, especially their moral and physical
weaknesses (see Wood, 1973; Cayleff, 1988). Contemporaries, however, noted
other failings. Principal among these was failure of the somatic model. If there
was no cellular basis to exhaustion, then what was the purpose of rest? The
growing awareness that all the business of the cure, the diet, massage, electricity
etc, were just props for the physician to exhort and encourage the patient, meant
that they could be dispensed with (see Dutil, 1903; Drummond, 1907; Waterman, 1909). It became increasingly difficult to deny the role of suggestion, of
the doctor-patient relationship, upon which 'everything depends' (Déjerine and
Gauckler, 1911), and ultimately of the newer psychotherapies (see Hale, 1981).
Gradually authorities began to suspect that the rest cure might actually make
the patient worse. For example, less than ten years separates two contributions
on neurasthenia made by Dutil, another pupil of Charcot. In the first (Dutil,
1894) he espouses a standard Weir Mitchell approach, but in the second (Dutil,
1903) Mitchell's regime condemned the patient to a life of disability and
hypochondriasis. Similarly, if electrical treatments were effective, it was more
for psychological reasons rather than any 'organic modifications of the nerve
centres' (Proust and Ballet, 1902).

The details of the decline of the rest cure, as it gave way to the new
occupational and psychotherapies, lie outside the scope of this essay. Its descent
into obscurity further weakened the organic models of neurasthenia, and
conversely increased the status of the new psychological schools of thought.
Inevitably, the management of the neurasthenic patient passed from the neurologist to the psychiatrist. By 1944 Karl Menninger's disdainful account of the
rest cure set the seal on this transfer (Menninger, 1944).

THE REACTION AGAINST NEURASTHENIA

What were the consequences of the failures of the simple organic models of
both aetiology and treatment, and the rise of the psychological models?
Physicians could either abandon the concept or concede that the patients were
best cared for by the psychiatric profession. Many neurologists were soon
persuaded that neurasthenia should be abandoned – Browning (1911) wrote
that neurasthenics were rare in his neurological service (although not, he

admitted, in his private practice), because 'Many of our best neurologists do not now recognise such as disease'. Particularly in the United Kingdom, neurology was establishing itself as a scientific speciality and many soon turned their backs on this now discredited diagnosis. This happened with alacrity in the United Kingdom (vide infra), but, although pleas were made for the same process in the USA (ex Dana, 1904), the concept was more deeply entrenched there and in France. As late as 1927 one third of patients seen by American neurologists were still either neurasthenic or psychasthenic (Peterson, 1927). Many physicians retained the diagnosis (and therefore the patients), but began gradually to incorporate the new psychological insights into their treatments – the 'rational psychotherapy' of Paul Dubois being particularly influential, perhaps because it so clearly repudiated notions of the unconscious that were often unpalatable to many neurologists.

The rapid abandonment of neurasthenia by British neurologists was because the illness had never found a fertile soil here anyway. Beard himself had a dismal reception when he visited this country in 1880 and 1881, committing one social gaffe after another[3]. Sir Andrew Clark, an eminent physician at the London Hospital, launched a blistering attack in the Lancet (1886), and, although Playfair made a spirited defence (Playfair, 1886), he was forced to concede that he had been unable to persuade the Collective Investigation Committee of the BMA to take an interest. Neurasthenia was never accepted by the neurological establishment. The giants of the profession, such as Gowers, Gordon Holmes, Ferrier, Buzzard and Kinnier-Wilson based at the National Hospital for Nervous Diseases, declared themselves in various ways against an organic view of neurasthenia, and in favour of psychological interpretations (although hospital records, still readily available, reveal they all made the diagnosis with varying degrees of frequency, whilst contemporary accounts also noted it to be a common diagnosis at the hospital – see Horder, 1903). Gower devoted only one page of his two volume text to the subject (Gowers, 1888), and in the next edition was even briefer – neurasthenia 'occurs especially in those of a neurotic disposition' (Gowers, 1899). This should be contrasted with the extensive coverage given in Oppenheim's equally monumental German neurology text. Unlike the United States, France and Germany, in the United Kingdom the neurasthenic flag was flown by only a few – the most prominent being Clifford Allbutt in Cambridge. Even Allbutt (1899) had to admit that acceptance was at best grudging – in his eight volume textbook Allbutt wrote the section on neurasthenia himself, but felt the necessity of criticising those 'medical men who reject neurasthenia as in part a sham, and in part a figment of complacent physicians'. Despite such efforts a reviewer conceded that neurasthenia had 'not taken deep root in Britain' (Ireland, 1907). The British Medical Journal did not 'take quite so serious a view of the prevalence of neurasthenia in modern life' (Anon, 1909), and by 1913 neurasthenia's 'servicableness as coin of the realm' was doubtful (Anon, 1913).

Issues of class and gender were intimately related to those of aetiology and treatment. The more 'organic' the account, the more likely was the author to insist on the predominance of upper social classes, the distinction from hysteria (the archtypal disease of women – see Oppenheim, 1991), and the over representation of men and 'civilised' races. Physicians were more likely to view sympathetically those whose illnesses had been acquired by praiseworthy rather than contemptible means (as indeed they still do) – neurasthenia, the disease of overwork, came into the former, hysteria the latter (Gosling and Ray, 1986). Groups not subject to such overwork, such as women, lower classes, degenerates, American negroes and all uncivilised races, thus were spared neurasthenia (see Beard, 1881; Althaus, 1898; Mitchell Clarke, 1905; Burr, 1910). Playfair, writing in Tuke's dictionary stated that the difference between neurasthenia and hysteria was that the former 'give all they possess to be well, and heartily long for good health, if only they knew how to obtain it' (Playfair, 1892). Neurasthenics co-operated with the doctor, unlike hysterics (Brill, 1930). The bluntest was Ernest Reynolds, Professor of Medicine in Manchester, who wrote that whereas hysteria was 'purely a mental condition, whose basis is a morbid craving for sympathy and notoriety', neurasthenia was 'entirely different', a functional disorder of chronic overuse of 'neurones' due to 'gross overwork and worry' (Reynolds, 1923).

Even within the sexes, such moral judgements were frequent – thus Mott wrote that 'neurasthenia . . . was more likely to be acquired in *officers of a sound mental constitution than men of the ranks*, because in the former the prolonged stress of responsibility which, in the officer worn out by the prolonged stress of war and want of sleep, causes anxiety less he should fail in his critical duties' [italics in the original].

The consequence was the decline of the diagnosis. This was partially intended, as doctors dismantled the now overstretched concept, that 'mob of incoherent symptoms borrowed from the most diverse disorders' (Clark, 1886). However, as the reception accorded Beard in the journals showed, academic disdain was not new. It now vanished for more practical reasons. Neurasthenia had survived academic dissatisfaction because it was 'useful to the doctor' (Anon, 1913) as a code for non psychotic illnesses for which the only effective treatments were psychologically based. The diagnosis was made 'for the comfort of the relatives and peace of mind of the patient' (Risien Russell, 1913) since it avoided the stigma of psychiatric illness and the necessity to seek treatment in an asylum, where the neurasthenic would 'soon be subject to the usual stigma attached to the abode of mental patients . . . only in a general hospital could the psychic problem be solved under the happiest auspices' (Hallock, 1911). Others commented that even if the symptoms were psychological, it was better to talk about nervous diseases and neurasthenia since 'the patients and the patients friends usually have a horror of mental disease' (Barker and Byrnes, 1913). Several anecdotes attest to the consequences of not keeping to these codes.[4]

For a while it was possible for doctors to maintain the old views in public, but statements such as 'functional illness means pooh poohed illness' (Anon, 1897) and 'neurotic, neurasthenic, hysterical and hypochondriacal are, on the lips of the majority of clinical teachers, terms of opprobrium' (Drummond, 1907) show that the codes were being broken, and the demise of the category a matter of time. In 1868 patients were only too willing to confess to 'weakness of the nerves' (Madden, 1868), but 30 years later the Spectator observed that neurasthenia was no longer 'interesting', it was 'discredited and disgraceful . . . shameful to confess' (Anon, 1894). The changes in social class, and the rise of the psychogenic school, meant that aetiologies had also changed. Infection remained (vide infra), but in place of overwork came laziness, fecklessness, degeneration and poor hygiene. Neurasthenia, once almost a badge of honour[5], was now considerably less praiseworthy – in place of the hard pressed business-man came the stereotype of the work shy labourer, the Jewish garment worker, or the pampered hypochondriacal upper class female invalid (Edes, 1895). Now doctors who had used the rise of neurasthenia as evidence of the advance of both civilisation and medicine made the same observations on its decline – 'the gradual "passing of neurasthenia" is a sign of the times and of the advancement of medical science' (Ramsay Hunt, 1920). It had 'outlived its usefulness' (Clayton, 1926).

Successive editions of the Surgeon General's Index catalogue the decline of the diagnosis. Beard had always argued that neurasthenia was the precursor of a variety of conditions, both mental and physical. As the symptoms were so protean, this was not surprising, but physicians began to see little point in diagnosing neurasthenia in those with conditions adequately covered by other labels (Clayton, 1926). The space devoted to it in the classic neurological texts dwindled, and finally disappeared, or received a brief psychiatric coverage. In the first edition of Cecil's prestigious textbook of medicine neurasthenia has its own chapter (Peterson, 1927). By the third edition it is listed under 'The Neuroses or Psychoneuroses' (Wechsler, 1934), and is reduced to a single sentence in the Seventh Edition (Rennie, 1947). One edition later it disappears from the index.

Only in the context of the effort syndromes (Da Costa's syndrome, Soldier's Heart, neurocirculatory asthenia) did it survive, but even there the same process gradually occurred (Paul, 1987). No figure was more associated with these diagnoses than cardiologist Paul Wood, but by the end of his career he saw them as synonymous with anxiety disorder (Wood, 1968).

Neurasthenia was replaced mainly by the new psychiatric diagnoses. The symptoms were now listed as psychological – painful fatigue became anhedonia (Myerson, 1922) whilst a textbook of anxiety could include the symptom 'fatigue on slightest exertion' (Ross, 1937). For a period of time psychasthenia contained much of obsessional and phobic neuroses (Blumer, 1906), but by 1927 a typical textbook would restrict psychasthenia to illnesses characterised by morbid fears (Peterson, 1927), and soon this concept gave way to the current classifications. The greatest beneficiary was the new concept of depression. Even De Fleury acknowledged the change. In 1901 he used the title 'Les grands symptômes neurasthéniques', but twenty years later this had changed to 'Les états depressifs et la neurasthénie'. With the support of such figures as Jaspers and Bleuler (1924) ('What usually produces the so-called neurasthenia are affective disturbances') the view became widespread that 'all neurasthenic states are in reality depression, – perhaps minor, attenuated, atypical, masked, but always forms of anxious melancholia' (Tinel, 1941). In current neurological practice, neurasthenia, when mentioned at all, is seen as synonymous with depression (Adams and Victor, 1985).

In conclusion there were a number of reasons for the decline in neurasthenia. First, the neuropathological basis of the illness was discredited. Second, rest cure was seen either to be unsuccessful, or to be efficacious principally for psycho-logical reasons. Third, the social class distribution of the illness altered. Finally, the interest and optimism shown by the neurologists was transferred to the new profession of psychiatry.

THE DISEASE THAT DID NOT DISAPPEAR

The consequences of the psychogenic explanations of neurasthenia were not entirely as intended. Buzzard (1930) had warned that although the advances in both neurology and psychiatry had illuminated the plight of the neurasthenic, the same could not be said of the exclusively psychogenic theories, which would lead to a polarisation among doctors. 'On the contrary, Freudian doctrines have produced a reaction in the minds of medical men which has taken the form of a desire to ascribe all mental disorders, including neurasthenia, to some physical or chemical agent the result of disturbed glandular secretions, of septic tonsils or teeth, of intestinal stasis or infection, or of a blood pressure which is too high or too low'.

Buzzard was right. Before the acceptance of the psychogenic paradigm neurasthenia served a purpose – 'At a time when physicians felt comfortable only with clearly organic disorders, a diagnosis of neurasthenia permitted some to address themselves to tangible clinical issues and to provide an essentially psychological therapy under a somatic label' (Sicherman, 1977). With the rise of the psychogenic school, this ability, acquired by physicians with difficulty, was lost. For a time the good physician now 'wanted to study all sides of the question' (Meyer, 1930), which meant attention to emotional issues, but 'without overlooking the possibilities of infective and organic factors'. Conversely, the informed psychiatrist also accepted the possible role of organic factors, hence Tredgold (1911) doubts the existence of a structural basis to neurasthenia, but accepts the probable role of a cerebral 'bio-chemical' abnormality.

However, the introduction of psychoanalysis to the USA, with its exclusive emphasis on mental origins, ended this appropriately labelled 'holistic' approach (Gosling, 1987). Narrow somaticism had failed, but in its place came 'belligerent Freudianism', as illustrated by statements such as 'there is only one certain cure for neurasthenia – viz psychoanalysis' (Stoddart, 1926). Ironically, this treatment attracted criticisms reminiscent of those of the rest cure, namely questionable efficacy, but unquestionable expense (Anon, 1913; Buzzard, 1930; Hale, 1971). Others disliked the new approach because it appeared to encourage introspection, the quality which the neurasthenic apparently already possessed to excess (ex Peterson, 1927).

Paradoxically, it was the solely psychological explanations in the new 'official' consensus on neurasthenia that ensured the survival of a contradictory view familiar to Beard and Mitchell. One reason was financial. Beard had made a virtue out of the predominance of upper classes among his patients, claiming that 'the miseries of the rich, the comfortable and intelligent have been unstudied and unrelieved' (Beard, 1881) – forty years later A. J. Cronin (1952) was still making a decent living in fashionable London by treating society ladies for the illness. American physicians and neurologists were particularly reluctant to abandon it – as late as 1927 Adolf Meyer was writing to Abraham Flexner complaining that neurologists continued to see neurasthenics in their clinics, although it was psychiatrists who had the necessary training (Grob,

1985)[6]. However, as important as the financial rewards was the rejection by sympathetic physicians of what they perceived as the implications of the now ascendant psychological views. Such physicians often endorsed a division between organic and psychological, usually synonymous with a division between real and unreal illnesses. The argument would thus revolve around the status to be accorded neurasthenia. Those continuing to diagnose the condition would thus energetically refute 'the idea, now strongly held that neurasthenia is basically psychiatric, almost imaginary in nature' (de Fleury, 1901). Only by continuing to affirm the organicity of neurasthenia could many doctors continue in their dealings with nervous patients. It was the survival of such attitudes which prolonged the survival of neurasthenia, and prepared the way for its modern re-emergence.

The result was that despite the obituaries, and the consignment of the condition to the 'dump heap' (Browning, 1911), 'garbage can' (Brill, 1930), 'rubbish heap' (Culpin, 1931) or 'waste basket' (Kinnier Wilson, 1913), neurasthenia survived. 'Everywhere we meet with the statements that it is rare . . . yet no name is more often on the lips of both our profession and the laity' (Dicks, 1933). Buzzard (1930) noted with regret that although he felt that most of the patients referred to him were depressed, nearly all came with a label of neurasthenia. Brill (1930) commented 'inspite of all that was said and done about the inadequacy of the name, as well as the concept itself, neurasthenia is still very popular with the medical profession'.

MODERN NEURASTHENIA

Nevertheless, neurasthenia did gradually disappear. In the USA and United Kingdom formal interest had virtually disappeared by 1960 (Chatel and Peele, 1970). However, the term does survive in other parts of the world, and is retained in the International Classification of Diseases (ICD-9 and ICD-10). It is a common neurotic diagnosis in the Netherlands, Eastern Europe and the old Soviet Union and flourishes in parts of Asia, especially China, where it is seen as a physical illness, without stigma, describing what Western observers label as depression (Kleinman, 1982). There are even signs of a revival, perhaps stimulated by the rise of CFS, with a series of recent publications from transcultural psychiatry[7] and the diagnosis has reappeared in modern epidemiological studies (Merikangas and Angst, 1994; Ormel et al, 1994).

After the demise of neurasthenia, general physicians continued to encounter the patient with chronic fatigue, often arising after a variety of insults, including infection. Perhaps mindful of the neurasthenia experience, rather than develop specific nosological entities physicians generally resorted to descriptive labels, such as 'chronic nervous exhaustion' (Macy and Allen, 1934), 'tired, weak and toxic' (Alvarez, 1935), 'fatigue and weakness' (Allan, 1945) or 'fatigue and nervousness' (Wilbur, 1949). However, the main emphasis was on psychological mechanisms. Illnesses closer to classic neurasthenia included the succession of diagnoses such as candidiasis, hypoglycaemia and total allergy syndrome, but none attracted the professional support necessary to become an established part of medical practice. This would not be forthcoming until the recent re-emergence of the post-infective fatigue syndromes (Wessely, 1994a).

Even the first descriptions of neurasthenia included a link with febrile illness. Van Deusen (1869) highlighted malaria, since he worked in an area in which the disease was endemic, whilst Beard drew attention to wasting fevers. The link with infection persisted in the earliest accounts in France (Huchard, 1883), whilst one of the first cases to be treated in this country by the Weir Mitchell regime was a woman with a fourteen year history of neurasthenia, confined to bed in a darkened room, whose illness had begun with a persistent cold (Young, 1884).

By 1914 the observation that neurasthenia frequently followed an infection was widely acknowledged[8]. For most, including Osler, Ely, Oppenheim, Cobb, Horder, Ladova, Clarke, Kraepelin, Althaus and Arndt the principle candidate was influenza, but claims were also made for many others, especially typhoid, and latterly the effects of vaccination (Craig, 1922). As the microbiological revolution spread, each organism was linked with neurasthenia. Everybody had a favourite culprit, until it was conceded that any infective agent could produce the state of chronic exhaustion (Oppenheim, 1908; Dubois, 1909; Dicks, 1933), especially in combination with depression (Lane, 1906) or worry (Ash, 1909). To a generation schooled on Virchow and Koch this was a major hurdle.

Such efforts did not cease after the decline of neurasthenia, since, starting with Reiter's disease (Reiter, 1916), attempts to link infective organisms with previously mysterious clinical conditions had reaped dividends, and the list of bona fide post-infective conditions was growing. Specific post-infective syndromes identical with neurasthenia continued to be described as each new infection was discovered, although many continued to be noticeable for their psychological flavour.

The story of chronic brucellosis is another link between neurasthenia and CFS. Although by 1930 the diagnosis of acute brucellosis was well established, there was less certainty about chronic brucellosis. One of its chief supporters was the public health specialist Alice Evans, who noted the similarities between neurasthenia and chronic brucellosis, but only in order to highlight the plight of the large numbers of those afflicted who suffered the indignity of receiving the erroneous, 'dishonourable' diagnosis of neurasthenia (Evans, 1934). Thirteen years later she was still championing the disease, which remained 'extremely difficult to diagnose . . . however, an unrecognised mild form of brucellosis is a common ailment in this country' (Evans, 1947).

The end of the syndrome encapsulates on a smaller scale the eclipse of neurasthenia. Spinks (1951) studied a series of patients with acute brucella infection, and noted that a proportion failed to recover – the chronic brucellosis group. However, he found no objective evidence of disease, and instead noted high rates of psychological disorder. Researchers from Johns Hopkins Hospital, in the first of a series of papers on the relationship between infection and psychological vulnerability, studied subjects with the label of chronic brucellosis in greater detail. They found no evidence of chronic infection (Cluff et al, 1959), but high levels of psychiatric morbidity, coupled with reluctance to discuss psychological issues and a strong attachment to the 'organic' diagnosis (Imboden et al, 1959). Once this evidence became widely disseminated, chronic brucellosis largely disappeared, reappearing in an editorial on the social construction of mental illness (Eisenberg, 1988).

Chronic brucellosis never made a substantial impact on the medical scene. However, events took a different course with the emergence of the next generation of post-infective syndromes during the mid 1980s, with 'chronic Epstein Barr infection' in the United States, and 'post viral fatigue syndrome' in the United Kingdom, where it is popularly known as 'ME' ('Myalgic Encephalomyelitis'). All these conditions are essentially similar, and are grouped together as 'chronic fatigue syndrome' (CFS).

These illnesses have all the characteristics of neurasthenia in its heyday. All the symptoms, from delayed fatigue, exhaustion after minimal effort, and mental confusion[9]. The earlier forms of 'ME' were divided into cerebral, brainstem and spinal varieties, as in the first series of neurasthenic texts. Upper social classes appear to be over represented among sufferers, and medical and paramedical professionals are particularly affected. These conditions are frequently labelled 'yuppie flu' in the media, reflecting the stereotype of the over stressed, over achieving urban professional, a characterisation more than familiar to the readers of Beard and Kraepelin. Adherents of the conditions emphasise the impeccable moral stature of those afflicted, in order to prove that the illness is not psychological.

The aetiological theories advanced have seen a similar progression from peripheral (neuromuscular), via central (central nervous system) to psychological hypotheses. As with neurasthenia, various medical writers have claimed that CFS is either hysteria, effort syndrome, depression or anxiety, whilst supporters either deny any psychological involvement, or claim that psychiatric disorder is simply the normal reaction to physical disease.

In the popular literature one does not have to search hard for metaphors well known to Beard and the Victorians, as authors use concepts such as limited energy resources, lack of nervous energy, life on a flat battery and so on. Once again, the consequence of such theories is to advocate a treatment not dissimilar to rest cure, with forced inactivity to marshall limited supplies of energy, often accompanied by strict diets, albeit to deal with allergic conditions.

One popular characterisation of neurasthenia was of the body giving way under attack from outside, becoming, as Beard described it, 'overloaded' (Beard, 1881). Contemporary observers ascribed this overload to the deteriorating quality of life, to new organisms, new stresses, new ways of working, the decline of leisure and the increasingly decadent and acquisitive nature of society. All of these ideas reappear in the current theories of immune dysfunction in CFS, and parallels between CFS and AIDS are occasionally drawn in many of the popular books. Abbey and Garfinkel have written that 'just as neurasthenia was a compilation of ideas which captivated the imagination of both public and medical professionals, so too is CFS built upon two of the most interesting themes in modern medicine, infectious disease and immunology' (Abbey and Garfinkel, 1991) in which the new 'overload' is from viruses, pollution, stress and so on. Writers on both neurasthenia and CFS thus use the prevailing scientific discourse to express wider social concerns, but, as Peter Gay observed, 'the symptoms of contemporary culture they liked to adduce in proof were, though plausible villains, not easily demonstrated agents of nervousness' (Gay, 1986).

CONCLUSION

One of the striking features of both neurasthenia and latterly CFS is their capacity to cause dissent. Non-believers have consistently attacked the gullibility of those who willingly accepted neurasthenia or its successors in toto – the reviews that greeted Beard's books between 1880 and 1882 were extraordinarily vituperative[10]. In return believers were hardly less tolerant – Weir Mitchell once reacted to a copy of Freud by saying 'Throw that nonsense on the fire' (Earnest, 1950). The accounts of the 'Congrès des Médicin Aliénists et Neurologist de France'[11], the American Neurological Association on numerous occasions between 1880 and 1914, the American Medical Association in 1944 (Allan, 1944) and many others, including most modern meetings of CFS, were characterised by arguments of varying degrees of intensity. Disputes also split the two camps – on the one hand Dubois and Déjerine devote much space to criticising Bernheim and Freud (and vice versa), whilst on the organic side the arguments between Althaus and Arndt, and between Beard and Hammond, were even more ill tempered. Doctors have always found it easy to disagree about chronic fatigue.

After dissent came dismissal, as the personal scorn about which Beard and Mitchell so often complained became transferred to the patients themselves. Sir Andrew Clark (1886) called neurasthenics 'always ailing, seldom ill' – whilst the 'wealthy neurasthenic will be a useless, frivolous, noxious element of society' (Urquhart, 1889). Charles Beevor (1898) joined Clifford Allbutt in reminding doctors that 'on no account should the patient's symptoms be laughed at', but to little avail. At the Johns Hopkins Hospital 'the neurasthenic patient is treated by physicians . . . with ridicule or a contemptuous summing up of his case in the phrase "there is nothing the matter, he is only nervous" ' (Mitchell, J., 1908), views echoed in the popular press – 'The majority of sufferers have better reason to complain of the weakening of their moral fibres than of either their mental or physical ones' (Anon, 1894). In the USA Jelliffe described them as 'purely mental cases. Laziness, indifference, weakness of mind and supersensitiveness characterise them all. They are . . . ill because of lack of moral courage' (Jelliffe, 1905). Even those sympathetic to neurasthenics could not avoid a note of irritation and condescension. Patients were 'the terror of the busy physician' (Rankin, 1903) 'occupied by their symptoms beyond reason' (Blocq, 1894), going from physician to physician (even Beard called them 'rounders') where they 'write down their sensations in long memoranda which they hasten to read and to explain' (Blocq, 1894).

This dissent largely revolves around differing interpretations of the physical and psychological. The commonest dialectic in both neurasthenia and chronic fatigue syndrome is that these must be physical illnesses, not because of the evidence, which remains inconclusive, but because psychological illnesses are unreal, malingered or imaginary. This tendency of those committed to an exclusively organic view of such illnesses to juxtapose psychiatric and imaginary was criticised by both Dutil (1903) and Tinel (1941), both of whom also denied that neurasthenia was a 'malade imaginaire'. Drummond (1907) attacked with equal vigour those who viewed neurasthenia as a solely physical illness, and those who regarded it as a thinly veiled excuse for malingering. Neurasthenia provided a haven for those uncomfortable with the psychological aspects of illness, who either insist on its solely organic basis, or see it as a refuge for the mentally infirm. Similar themes can be identified in the modern literature of CFS (Wessely, 1994b). The passions that these arguments create are because what is at stake is the issue of legitimacy – what constitutes an acceptable disease, and what is legitimate suffering, deserving of support and sympathy? It is each generation's answers to these questions that permit the survival of neurasthenia, and the survival of the disputes that inevitably accompany it.

ACKNOWLEDGEMENTS

As a clinician and researcher, but only amateur historian, I am extremely grateful for the help I have received from the professionals, including Ned Shorter, Mark Micale, German Berrios and Tom Lutz.

NOTES

1 Although degeneration is frequently linked with French views on neurasthenia, it also enjoyed considerable respect in Britain – see Campbell Smith (1906) for example.

2 It is often forgotten that the cure was originally suggested for the treatment of hysteria (Mitchell, 1875), and it was only as the distinctions between the two became blurred, and perhaps as the financial advantages from treating neurasthenia became clearer, that it became popular for neurasthenia. Thus in 1888 Freud was recommending a combination of Weir Mitchell and Breuer's cathartic treatment for hysteria, adding that 'in the case of the other neuroses, for instance neurasthenia, the success of the treatment is far less certain'.

3 See Fourness-Brice, J. 'Medical Etiquette on Board Ship', British Medical Journal, 1880; i: 238; and Crichton Browne, J. 'Dr. Beard's Experiments in Hypnosis', British Medical Journal, 1881; ii: 378–9.

4 Drummond (1907) describes a scene he witnessed when a 'kindly physician', actually Sir Andrew Clark, during a consultation with a neurasthenic patient, let slip the word 'melancholia'. 'The outcome of that visit was disastrous, involving serious trouble all round, in which even Sir Andrew himself shared, for he was pestered for weeks with letters to know whether in using the term "melancholia" he had the idea of insanity in his mind'.

5 'It is certain that it is chiefly the people who have a neurasthenic constitution who are the most brilliant, original, energetic and influential. It is they who do the intellectual work of the world' (Robertson, 1919). In 'The Guermantes Way', Proust has Dr du Boulbon, the 'alienist and brain doctor', who has 'special competence in cerebral and nervous matters', state that 'Everything we think of as great has come to us from neurotics. It is they and they alone who found religions and create great works of art. The world will never realise how much it owes to them, and what they have suffered in order to bestow their gifts on it'. Marcel Proust, Remembrance of Things Past. Volume 2; The Guermantes Way, trans. C. Scott Moncrieff and Terence Kilmartin, (London, Penguin Modern Classics, 1983), p 315. Haller

(1971) uses contemporary texts to show that neurasthenia was also almost a badge of respect in American 'society' between 1880 and 1900.

6 Nevertheless, neurasthenia was on the decline, albeit with less speed than in Britain. Diller (1917) noted that the between 1894 and 1916 the proportion of neurasthenics and hysterics in his case load had halved, an even more preciptious decline occurring at the New York Neurological Institute. This should be contrasted to the predominance of the diagnosis at the Vanderbilt clinic in the previous decade.

7 A special edition of Transcultural Psychiatric Research Review (Volume 31, Issue 4, 1994) was devoted to the subject.

8 Much the same applied to effort syndromes/Soldier's Heart – see Sir James MacKenzie (1916),

9 The resemblances between chronic fatigue syndrome and neurasthenia have been previously elaborated elsewhere. The current essay is based on two earlier papers, (Wessely, 1990; Wessely, 1991). Wessely (1994a) brings this essay up to the modern era, adding the more recent literature on CFS. Social and epidemiological aspects of modern neurasthenia are discussed in Wessely (1994b). Greenberg (1990) and Abbey & Garfinkel (1991) independently observed similar historical parallels. However, Shorter (1992), contains an analysis critical of the simplistic equation of CFS and neurasthenia.

10 See for example the reviews in the St Louis Clinical Record (1880; 7: 92–94), American J Insanity (1880; 36: 520–526), St Louis Clinical Record (1881; 8: 122–124), J Nervous Mental Dis (1881; 8: 773–777), Medical Record (1881; 20: 296–297), Boston Medical Surgical Journal (1881; 105: 162–163).

11 La Psychothérapie chez les neurasthénique. L'encephale 1907; 2: 266–267, and Pathogenie des état neurasthénique. L'encephale 1908; 3: 525–531.

REFERENCES

Abbey, S. and Garfinkel, P. (1991) 'Neurasthenia and Chronic Fatigue Syndrome: The Role of Culture in the Making of a Diagnosis'. *American Journal of Psychiatry*, 148: 1638–46.

Adams, R. and Victor, M. (1985) *Principles of Neurology* (Third Edition), New York, McGraw-Hill.

Allan, F. (1945) 'The clinical management of weakness and fatigue'. *Journal of the American Medical Association*, 127: 957–60.

Allbutt, T. (1895) 'Nervous Diseases and Modern Life'. *Contemporary Review* 67: 210–17.

Allbutt, T. (1899) 'Neurasthenia'. In Allbutt, T. (ed.) *A System of Medicine*, volume 8, London, Macmillan, pp.134–64.

Althaus, J. (1898) *On Failure of Brain Power (Encephalasthenia); Its Nature and Treatment* (Fifth Edition), London, Longmans, Green and Co.

Alvarez, W. (1935) 'What is wrong with the patient who feels tired, weak and toxic?' *New England Journal of Medicine*, 212: 96–104.

Anon. (1894) 'Nerves and Nervousness'. *The Spectator*, 72: 11–12.

Anon. (1897) 'Review of Otto Binswanger: The Pathology and Treatment of Neurasthenia'. *British Medical Journal*, i: 920–1.

Anon. (1909) 'Neurasthenia and Modern Life'. *British Medical Journal*, iii, 97–8.

526   *A History of Clinical Psychiatry*

Anon. (1913) 'The Definition and Treatment of Neurasthenia'. *Lancet*, ii: 1557–8.

Arndt, R. (1892) 'Neurasthenia'. In Tuke, D. (ed.) *Dictionary of Psychological Medicine*, vol II, London, J Churchill, pp.840–50.

Ash, E. (1909) 'Nervous Breakdown: The Disease of our Age'. *Medical Times*, 37: 35–54.

Ballet, G. and Proust, A. (1902) *The Treatment of Neurasthenia*, London, Henry Kimpton, p.5.

Barker, L. and Byrnes, C. (1913) 'Neurasthenic and Psychasthenic States, including the New Phobias'. In Forcheimer, F. (ed.) *Therapeusis of Internal Diseases*, New York, Appleton, pp.516–81.

Beard, G. (1880) *A Practical Treatise on Nervous Exhaustion (Neurasthenia)*, New York, William Wood.

Beard, G. (1881) *American Nervousness*, New York, G.P. Putnam's.

Beevor, C. (1898) *Diseases of the Nervous System: A Handbook for Students and Practitioners*, London, H K Lewis.

Berrios, G. (1985) 'Obsessional Disorders during the nineteenth century: terminological and classificatory issues'. In Bynum, W., Porter, R. and Shepherd, M. (eds.) *The Anatomy of Madness: Essays in the History of Psychiatry*, London, Tavistock, pp.166–87.

Berkley, H. (1901) *A Treatise on the Mental Diseases*, London, Henry Klimpton, p.445.

Bidon, M. (1899) 'Degenerescence et neurasthenie'. *Archives de Neurologie*, 7: 399–400.

Bleuler, E. (1924) *Textbook of Psychiatry*, trans A. Brill, New York, Macmillan, pp.557–9.

Blocq, P. (1894) 'Neurasthenia'. *Brain*, 14: 306–34.

Blumer, G. (1906) 'The Coming of Psychasthenia'. *Journal of Nervous and Mental Disorder*, 33: 336–53.

Brill, A. (1930) 'Diagnostic Errors in Neurasthenia'. *Medical Review of Reviews*, 36: 122–9.

Browning, W. (1911) 'Is there such a disease as neurasthenia? A discussion and classification of the many conditions that appear to be grouped under that head'. *New York State Journal of Medicine*, 11: 7–17.

Bumke, O. (1925) 'Die Revision der Neurosenfrage'. *Münchener Medizinische Wochenschrift*, 72: 1815–19.

Burr, C. (1910) 'Neurasthenia. The Traumatic neuroses and psychoses'. In Osler, W. and McCrae, T. (eds.) *A System of Medicine*, London, Frowde, pp.721–38.

Buzzard, E.F. (1930) 'The Dumping Ground of Neurasthenia'. *Lancet*, i: 1–4.

Castin, Paul (1908) 'Note clinique de psychopathologie medicolegale, à propos d'un neurasthénique homicide'. *L'encephale*, 3: 215–16.

Cayleff, S. (1988) ' "Prisoners of Their Own Feebleness": Women, Nerves and Western Medicine – A Historical Overview'. *Social Science and Medicine*, 26: 1199–1208.

Certhoux, J. (1961) 'De la neurasthénie aux neuroses: le traitement des neuroses dans le passe'. *Annales Medico-Psychologiques*, 119: 913–30.

Charcot, J. (1889) 'Leçons du Mardi à la Salpêtrière'. *Progrès médical*, Paris, Lecrosniew & Babe.

Clark, A. (1886) 'Some observations concerning what is called neurasthenia'. *Lancet*, i: 1–2.

Clarke, J. Mitchell (1905) *Hysteria and Neurasthenia*, London, The Bodley Head.

Clayton, M. (1926) 'When is the diagnosis of neurasthenia justified?' *United States Veterans Bureau Medical Bulletin*, 2: 61–4.

Cleghorn, C. (1907) 'Notes on Six Thousand Cases of Neurasthenia'. *Medical Record*, 71: 681–4.

Clouston, T. (1892) *Clinical Lectures on Mental Diseases*, Third Edition, London, Churchill.

Cluff, L., Trever, R., Imboden, J. and Canter, A. (1959) Brucellosis II. 'Medical Aspects of Delayed Convalescence'. *Archives Internal Medicine*, 103: 398–405.

Cobb, I. (1920) *A Manual of Neurasthenia (Nervous Exhaustion)*, London, Baillière, Tindall and Cox.

Craig, M. (1922) *Nerve Exhaustion*, London, J Churchill, p.141.

Cronin, A. (1952) *Adventures in Two Worlds*, London, Victor Gollancz.

Culpin, M. (1931) *Recent Advances in the Study of the Psychoneuroses*, London, Churchill.

Dana, C. (1904) 'The Partial Passing of Neurasthenia'. *Boston Medical and Surgical Journal*, 60: 339–44.

De Fleury, M. (1901) *Les Grands Symptômes Neurasthéniques (Pathologie et Traitement)*, Paris, Germer Baillière, p.257.

Deale, H. and Adams, S. (1894) 'Neurasthenia in Young Women'. *American Journal of Obstetrics*, 29: 190–5.

Déjerine, J. and Gauckler, E. (1911) *Les maniféstations functionelles des psychonevroses; leur traitement par la psychothérapie*, Paris, Masson.

Dicks, H. (1933) 'Neurasthenia: Toxic and Traumatic'. *Lancet*, ii: 683–6.

Diller, T. (1917) 'The Psychoneuroses: How Shall We Look at Them Today?' *Journal American Medical Association*, 69: 956–8.

Donley, J. (1906) 'On neurasthenia as a disintegration of personality'. *Journal of Abnormal Psychology*, 1: 55–68.

Drummond, D. (1907) 'The Mental Origin of Neurasthenia, and its Bearing on Treatment'. *British Medical Journal*, ii: 1813–16.

Dubois, P. (1909) *The Psychic Treatment of Nervous Disorders*, 6th Edition, trans S. E. Jelliffe, W. White, New York, Funk and Wagnalls.

Durkheim, E. (1951) *Suicide: A Study in Sociology*, trans J. Spaulding and G. Simpson, Glencoe, Illinois, The Free Press.

Dutil, A. (1894) 'Neurasthénie, ou La Maladie de Beard'. In Charcot, J., Bouchard, E. and Brissaud, E. (eds.) *Traite de Médicine*, volume 6, Paris, G. Masson, 1281–1301.

Dutil, A. (1903) 'Neurasthenie'. In Ballet, G. (ed.) *Traite de Pathologie Mentale*, Paris, Octave Doin, pp.842–50.

Earnest, E. S. (1950) 'Weir Mitchell: Novelist and Physician'. Philadelphia, University of Pennsylvania Press, p.180.

Edes, R. (1895) 'The New England Invalid'. *Boston Medical & Surgical Journal*, 133: 53–7.

Eisenberg, L. (1988) 'The Social Construction of Mental Illness'. *Psychological Medicine*, 18: 1–9.

Ely, T. (1906) 'Neurasthenia as modified by modern conditions; and their prevention'. *Journal of the American Medical Assocation*, 47: 1816–19.

Feinstein, H. (1981) 'The use and abuse of illness in the James Family Circle: A view of neurasthenia as a social phenomenon'. In Brugger, R. (ed.) *Our Selves/Our Past: Psychological Approaches to American History*, Baltimore, Johns Hopkins University Press, pp.228–43.

Fischer-Homberger, E. (1970) 'Hypochondire'. *Melancholie Dis Neurose*, Krankheiten und Zustandbilder, Bern, Hans Huber.

Foster, G. (1900) 'Common Features in Neurasthenia and Insanity: Their Common Basis and Common Treatment'. *American Journal of Insanity*, 56: 395–418.

Freud, S. (1888) 'Hysteria'. In Villaret, A. (ed.) *Handworterbuch der Gesamtem Medizin*, volume 1, Stuttgart, pp.886–92. In (1966) Strachey, J. (ed.) Standard Edition, volume 3, London, Hogarth Press, pp.39–57.

Freud, S. (1895) *On the Grounds for detaching a Particular Syndrome from Neurasthenia under the Description 'Anxiety Neurosis'*. Strachey, J. (ed.) Standard Edition, volume 3, London, Hogarth Press, pp.87–115.

Friedman, M. (1904) 'Uber neurasthenische Melancholie'. *Monatsschrift fur Psychiatrie und Neurologie*, 15: 301–18.

Gay, P. (1986) *The Bourgeois Experience. Victoria to Freud. Volume II; The Tender Passion*, Oxford, Oxford University Press.

Gerhardt, C. (1893) Cited in Fischer-Homberger, op.cit.

Gosling, F. and Ray, J. (1986) 'The Right to be Sick'. *Journal of Social History*, 20: 251–67.

Gosling, F. (1987) *Before Freud: Neurasthenia and the American Medical Community, 1870–1910*, Springfield, University of Illinois Press.

Gowers, W. (1888) *A Manual of Diseases of the Nervous System: Volume II*, Second Edition, London, Churchill, p.960.

Gowers, W. (1899) *A Manual of Diseases of the Nervous System: Volume I*, Third Edition, (Gowers, W. and Taylor, J. eds.), London, Churchill, p.668.

Greenberg, D. (1990) 'Neurasthenia in the 1980s: Chronic Mononucleosis, Chronic Fatigue Syndrome and Anxiety and Depressive Disorders'. *Psychosomatics*, 31: 129–37.

Grob, G. (1985) *The Inner World of American Psychiatry; 1890–1940*, New Jersey, Rutgers University Press.

Hale, H. (1971) *Freud and the Americans: The Beginnings of Psychoanalysis in the United States, 1976–1917*, New York, Oxford University Press.

Haller, J. (1970) 'Neurasthenia: The medical profession and urban "blahs" '. *New York State Journal of Medicine*, 70: 2489–97.

Haller, J. (1971) 'Neurasthenia: The Medical Profession and the "new woman" of the late nineteenth century'. *New York State Journal of Medicine*, 71: 473–82.

Hallock, F. (1911) 'The Sanatorium Treatment of Neurasthenia and the Need of a Colony Sanatorium for the Nervous Poor'. *Boston Medical Surgical Journal*, 44: 73–7.

Hartenberg, P. (1907) 'La Psychothérapie chez les neurasthéniques'. *L'encephale*, 7: 266–7.

Horder, T. (1903) 'Neurasthenia: a critical Inquiry'. *St Bartholomews's Hospital Journal*, February 1903, 67–73.

Huchard, H. (1883) 'Neurasthénie'. In Axenfeld, A. and Huchard, H. (eds.) *Traite des Nevroses*, Paris, Germer Baillière, pp.873–907.

Hutchinson, W. (1880) 'A report of three typical cases of neurasthenia'. *The Medical Record*, 18: 398–401.

Imboden, J., Canter, A. and Cluff, L. (1959) Brucellosis III. 'Psychologic Aspects of Delayed Convalesence'. *Archives of Internal Medicine*, 103: 406–14.

Ireland, W. (1907) 'Review of "The Treatment of Neurasthenia; Proust & Ballet" '. *Journal of Mental Science*, 48: 548–9.

Iscouesco (1905) 'De la Neurasthénie des pauvrès'. *Bulletin Médical 1905*, 19: 359. Reviewed by Feindel, *Revue Neurologique*, 2: 732.

Jaspers, K. (1963) *General Psychopathology*. Trans J. Hoenig and M. Hamilton, Manchester, Manchester University Press, p.441.

Jelliffe, S. and Clark, L. (1903) 'The Work of a Neurological Dispensary Clinic'. *Journal of Nervous Mental Diseases*, 30: 482–8.

Jelliffe, S. (1905) 'Dispensary Work in Nervous Diseases'. *Journal of Nervous & Mental Diseases*, 32: 449–53.

Johnson, G. (1875) 'Lectures on Some Nervous Diseases that Result from Overwork and Anxiety'. *Lancet*, ii: 85–7.

Kalfus, M. (1990) *Frederick Law Olmsted: The Passion of a Public Artist*, New York, New York University Press.

Kinnier Wilson, S. (1913) 'Medical Society of London: Discussion of Neurasthenia'. *Lancet*, ii: 1542–4.

Kleinman, A. (1982) 'Neurasthenia and Depression: A Study of Somatisation and Culture in China'. *Culture, Medicine and Psychiatry*, 6: 117–90.

Lane, C. (1906) 'The Mental Element in the Etiology of Neurasthenia'. *Journal of Nervous and Mental Disease*, 33: 463–6.

Levillain, F. (1891) *La Neurasthenia, maladie de Beard*, (Methodes de Weir-Mitchell et Playfair, traitement de Vigoroux), Paris, A. Malvine.

Leubuscher, P. and Bibrowicz, W. (1905) 'Die Neurasthenie in Arbeitkreisen'. *Deutsche Medizinsche Wochenscrift*, 31: 820–4.

López Piñero, J. (1983) *Historical Origins of the Concept of Neurosis*, Cambridge, Cambridge University Press.

Lutz, T. (1991) *American Nervousness: 1903*, Ithaca, Cornell University Press.

MacKenzie, J. (1916) 'Soldier's Heart'. *British Medical Journal*, i: 117–20.

MacNaughton-Jones, H. (1913) 'The relation of puberty and the menopause to neurasthenia'. *Lancet*, i: 879–81.

Macy, J. and Allen, E. (1933–34) 'Justification of the Diagnosis of Chronic Nervous Exhaustion'. *Annals Intern Med*, 7: 861–7.

Madden, H. (1868) 'On Nervousness'. *Monthly Homeopathic Review*, 12: 211–21.

Menninger, K. (1944) 'The abuse of rest in psychiatry'. *Journal of the American Medical Association*, 125: 1077–83.

Merikangas, K. and Angst, J. (1994) 'Neurasthenia in a Longitudinal Community Survey'. *Psychological Medicine*, 24: 1013–24.

Meyer, A. (1919) 'Discontent – A Psychobiological Problem of Hygiene'. In Winters, E. (ed.) *The Collected Papers of Adolf Meyer*, Baltimore, Johns Hopkins Press, 1962, pp.383–400.

Mitchell, S. (1987) 'Rest in the Treatment of nervous disease'. In Seguin, E. (ed.) *American Clinical Lectures*, vol 1, no 4, New York, GP Putnam's, pp.83–102.

Mitchell, S.W. (1883) *Fat and Blood*, 3rd Edition, Philadelphia, J Lippincott, p.64.

Mitchell, S.W. (1908) 'The treatment by rest, seclusion etc., in relation to psychotherapy'. *Journal of the American Medical Assoc*, 25: 2033–7.

Mitchell, J. (1908) *Diagnosis and Treatment of Neurasthenia*, Johns Hopkins Hospital Bulletin, 19: 41–3.

Mott, F. (1919) *War Neuroses and Shell Shock*, London, Hodder & Stoughton.

Muscio, B. (1921) 'Is a Fatigue Test Possible?' *British Journal of Psychology*, 12: 31–46.

Myerson, A. (1922) 'Anhedonia'. *American Journal of Psychiatry*, 2: 87–103.

Neu, C. (1920) 'Treatment and management of the neurasthenic individual'. *Medical Record*, 97: 341.

Nye, R. (1982) 'Degeneration, Neurasthenia and the Culture of Sport in Belle Epoque France'. *Journal of Contemporary History*, 17: 51–68.

Olson, M. (1988) 'The Weir Mitchell rest cure'. *Pharos*, 50: 30–1.

Oppenheim, H. (1908) *Text-book of Nervous Diseases for Physicians and Students*, volume II, 5th Edition, translated A. Bruce, London, Foulis.

Oppenheim, J. (1991) *'Shattered Nerves': Doctors, Patients and Depression in Victorian England*, London, Oxford University Press.

Ormel, J., VonKorff, M., Ustun, B., Pini, S., Korten, A. and Oldehinkel, T. (1994) 'Common Mental Disorders and Disabilities Across Cultures: Results from the WHO Collaborative Study on Psychological Problems in General Health Care'. *Journal of the American Medical Association*, 272: 1741–8.

Osler, W. (1913) *The Principles and Practice of Medicine*, New York, Appleton, pp.1106–16.

Paul, O. (1987) 'Da Costa's Syndrome or neurocirculatory asthenia'. *British Heart Journal*, 58: 306–15.

Pershing, H. (1904) 'The Treatment of Neurasthenia'. *Medical News*, 84: 637–40.

Peterson, F. (1927) 'Neurasthenia'. In Cecil, R. (ed.) *A Textbook of Medicine*, First Edition, Philadelphia, W Saunders, pp.1419–26.

Playfair, W. (1886) 'Some observations concerning what is called neurasthenia'. *British Medical Journal*, ii: 853–5.

Playfair, W. (1892) 'Neurasthenia – Treatment'. In Tuke, D. (ed.) *Dictionary of Psychological Medicine*, London, J Churchill, pp.850–7.

Pritchard, W. (1905) 'The American Disease: an interpretation'. *Canadian Journal of Medicine Surgery*, 18: 10–22.

Rabinbach, A. (1982) 'The Body Without Fatigue: A Nineteenth Century Utopia'. In Drescher, S., Sabean, D. and Sharlin, A. (eds.) *Political Symbolism in Modern Europe: Essays in Honour of George Mosse*, London, Transaction Books, pp.42–62.

Rabinbach, A. (1990) *The Human Motor: Energy, Fatigue and the Origins of Modernity*, New York, Basic Books.

Ramsay Hunt, J. (1920) 'Neurasthenia'. In *The Medical Annual*, volume 20, Bristol, John Wright & Co., 38: 416–17.

Rankin, G. (1903) 'Neurasthenia: the wear and tear of life'. *British Medical Journal*, i: 1017–20.

Reiter, H. (1916) 'Uber eine bisher unerkannte Spirochateninfection (Spirochaetosis arthritica)'. *Deutsch Med Wochenschrifte*, 42: 1535–47.

Reynolds, E. (1923) 'Hysteria and Neurasthenia'. *British Medical Journal*, ii: 1193–5.

Risien Russell, J. (1913) 'The Treatment of Neurasthenia'. *Lancet*, ii: 1453–6.

Rosenberg, C. (1962) 'The place of George M. Beard in nineteenth-century psychiatry'. *Bulletin of the History of Medicine*, 36: 245–59.

Ross, T. (1937) *The Common Neuroses*, (2nd Edition), London, Edward Arnold, p.31.

Schwab, S. (1911) 'Neurasthenia among the Garment Workers'. *Bulletin of the American Economic Association*, 4th Series, No 2, 265–70.

Shorter, E. (1990) 'Private Clinics in Central Europe 1850–1933'. *Social History of Medicine*, 3: 159–95.

Shorter, E. (1992) *From Paralysis to Fatigue: A History of Psychosomatic Illness in the Modern Era*, New York, Free Press.

Sicherman, B. (1977) 'The Uses of a Diagnosis: Doctors, Patients and Neurasthenia'. *Journal of the History of Medicine*, 32: 33–54.

Smith, P.C. (1906) 'Neurasthenia, Degeneration and Mobile Organs'. *British Medical Journal*, i: 494–6.

Starr, M. (1901) 'The toxic origin of neurasthenia and melancholia'. *Boston Medical and Surgical Journal*, 144: 563.

Stedman, H. (1906) 'The Public Obligations of the Neurologist'. *Journal of Nervous Mental Disease*, 33: 489–99.

Stoddart, W. (1926) *Mind and its Disorders: A Textbook for Students and Practitioners of Medicine*, (5th Edition), London, H Lewis.

Tanzi, E. (1909) *A Textbook of Mental Diseases*, trans Robertson, F. and MacKenzie, T., London, Rebman Ltd, pp.540–57.

Tinel, J. (1941) *Conceptions et Traitement des Etats Neurasthéniques*, Paris, J. B. Baillière et Fils.

Tredgold, A. (1911) 'Neurasthenia and Insanity'. *Practitioner*, 86: 84–95.

Urquhart, A. (1889) 'Austrian Retrospect: Review of the Writings of Professor Benedikt of Vienna'. *Journal of Mental Science*, 34: 276–81.

Van Deusen, E. (1869) 'Observations on a Form of Nervous Prostration (Neurasthenia) Culminating in Insanity'. *American Journal of Insanity; Supplement to the Annual Report for 1867 and 1868*, 25: 445–61.

Walton, O. (1906) 'Proceedings of the Boston Neurological Society'. *J Nerv Mental Disease*, 33: 279.

Waterman, G. (1909) 'The Treatment of Fatigue States'. *Journal of Abnormal Psychology*, 4: 128–39.

Wechsler, I. (1934) 'The Neuroses or Psychoneuroses'. In Cecil, R. (ed.) *A Textbook of Medicine*, Third Edition, Philadelphia, W Saunders, pp.1542–62.

Weiss, E. (1908) 'A Consideration of Neurasthenia in its Relation to Pelvic Symptoms in Women'. *American Journal of Obstetrics*, 57: 230–5.

Wessely, S. (1990) 'Old Wine in New Bottles; Neurasthenia and "ME" '. *Psychological Medicine*, 20: 35–53.

Wessely, S. (1991) 'The History of the Postviral Fatigue Syndrome'. *British Medical Bulletin*, 47: 919–41.

Wessely, S. (1994a) 'The history of chronic fatigue syndrome'. In Straus, S. (ed.) *Chronic Fatigue Syndrome*, New York, Mark Dekker, pp.41–82.

Wessely, S. (1994b) 'Neurasthenia and chronic fatigue syndrome: theory and practice'. *Transcultural Psychiatric Review*, 31: 173–209.

White, W. (1917) *The Principles of Mental Hygiene*, New York, The MacMillan Company, p.225.

White, W. (1921) 'Outlines of Psychiatry'. *Nervous and Mental Disease Publishing Company*, Washington, pp.265–7.

Wilbur, D. (1949) 'Clinical management of the patient with fatigue and nervousness'. *J Am Med Assoc*, 141: 1199–1204.

Wood, P. (1968) *Diseases of the Heart and Circulation*, 3rd Edition, London, Eyre and Spottiswoode, p.1075.

Wood, A. (1973) ' "The Fashionable Diseases": Women's Complaints and Their Treatment in Nineteenth Century America'. *Journal of Interdisciplinary History*, 4: 25–52.

Young, P. (1884) 'Two cases of neurasthenia of long standing successfully treated by the Weir Mitchell method'. *Edinburgh Clinical and Pathological Journal*, 47: 905–9.

Zeldin, T. (1980) *Intellect and Pride*, Oxford, Oxford University Press.

Chapter 20

Neurasthenia and Fatigue Syndromes

Social Section
TOM LUTZ

Neurasthenia had an illustrious and varied career. From its lowly beginnings in secondary medical journals in the 1860s the disease grew in status and stature until it was invited into all the best homes of the industrial nations. By the end of the century, few families in the upper echelons of society in Europe and America had been unaffected by neurasthenia in at least one of its myriad symptomatic forms, and by the 1920s the disease had trickled down to tradesmen, laborers, and farmers as well. Throughout its career as a disease, ideas and metaphors of nervous debility, nervous excitability, and nervous bankruptcy appeared in discussions of economics, politics, religion, art, literature, ethics, sex, work, class – in fact any place writers focussed on the relation of individuals to social process. In its heydey, what I have called neurasthenic discourse (Lutz, 1991) became a prime language for the articulation of social, moral, and cultural debates.

Neurasthenia lent itself readily to these cultural appropriations in part because its earliest theorizers – especially George Beard and S. Weir Mitchell in America – wrote tracts on the disease that argued eloquently and at times vehemently for the importance of understanding the disease in terms of its social and cultural causes and effects. In the last decades of the nineteenth century and the first decades of the twentieth, innumerable essayists and editorialists directly discussed 'our nervous century' or 'our nerve-shaken civilization', and many more strategically deployed a rhetoric of nervous debility to make their arguments.

The medical theory was preceded by and based on prevalent folk theories of bodily energy that were expressly economic. People were assumed to have a certain amount of nerve force or nervous energy which could be wisely spent and reinvested or could be squandered and wasted (Martin, 1981). Sanctioned work and procreation were considered prime examples of nervous expenditure that clearly invested in the future. Masturbation, gambling, and other forms of illicit sexual or financial activity constituted a waste, a drain on nerve force without any corresponding reinvestment (Barker-Benfield, 1976). These notions of nervous economy were already current in the popular etiquette manuals and moral tracts of mid-century where they were deployed along the same moral lines (Haller and Haller, 1974). Fears of 'dissipation' are based on similar notions of dispersed rather than directed nervous energy, spent without any possible return on investment. Dissipation eventually led to 'decadence', the death and decay of nerve centers in the individual and the death and decay of civilization at the social level. The links between medical thinking and economics, and the links to morality, were constantly apparent to both doctors and patients (Fellman and Fellman, 1981), as they were to cultural critics and commentators (Lears, 1981).

According to Beard and other neurologists, the end result of any process of dissipation, or of any unwise (usually meaning immoral) nervous investment, was neurasthenia, literally 'nerve weakness'. Conversely, if patients were sensitive and refined enough to begin with, neurasthenia could be brought on, regardless of the patients' moral probity, by simple exposure to the hectic pace and excessive stimuli of modern life (Douglas, 1973). Life in the technologically transformed, urbanized, industrialized world of the late nineteenth century may not have any discernable effect on the dull-witted or uneducated, but it was enough to thoroughly exhaust the more refined, civilized portion of the population. The disease could thus be a sign of either moral laxity or extreme moral sensitivity.

The medical elaboration of neurasthenia as a disease entity provided a scientific basis and an elaborate lexicon for these general cultural ideas of the relation of bodies to will, of will to value, and of values to the progress of and threats to civilization (Lears, 1981; Rosenberg, 1962; Drinka, 1984; Lutz 1991). As F.G. Gosling (1987) has argued, neurasthenia reached epidemic proportions because it appealed to widely felt and deeply held attitudes. The epidemic in turn helped legitimate and reinforce dominant social theories about class, gender, ethnicity, and economics. And it did so in part by fully appropriating older notions of moral and corporeal economics.

Until 1800, as Peter Gay (1986) has pointed out, the word 'nervous' had connotations of vigor, force, and freedom from debility. A nervous racehorse was one with an oversupply of nerve force, of strength. The older meaning of the term coexisted with its modern connotations of undersupply through the next hundred years, and this doubleness is accounted for in the medical literature. Beard, Mitchell, and the other doctors specializing in neurasthenia assumed that nervous excitability and lethargy, overactivity and underactivity, superb health and debilitating disease were primarily attributable to a patient's nervous economy, to their nervous balance sheet, as it were. And they assumed that one could deduce, from the nervous condition and the patient's testimony, the nature of the patient's moral expenditures.

The medical theory also accounted for the apparent fact that modern debility was outpacing traditional nervous strength: since the stresses and strains of modern, urban life were prime causes of neurasthenia, modernity itself was seen as overtaxing the nervous budgets of the refined urban classes. Neurasthenia was nevertheless, for many doctors and other commentators, the most visible sign of the promise and problems of modern life. '*American nervousness is the product of American civilization*', Beard wrote proudly and emphatically in 1881. 'The Greeks were certainly civilized, but they were not nervous, and in the Greek language there is no word for that term'. Ancient cultures could not have experienced nervousness, Beard thought, because even though only civilized peoples can become neurasthenic, 'civilization alone does not cause nervousness'. Modern civilization differs from the ancient civilizations in five important ways, Beard argued: 'steam power, the periodical press, the telegraph, the sciences, and the mental activity of women. . . . When civilization, plus these five factors, invades any nation, it must carry nervousness and nervous disease along with it'. Steam power had revolutionized transportation, the press and telegraph had revolutionized communication, the sciences had revolutionized metaphysics and ontology, and the mental activity of women had revolutionized both facts and perceptions of the gender system and related social structures. These revolutions, for doctors and patients, constituted the essence of the modern.

Neurasthenia had become epidemic by the late nineteenth century, especially among leisure-class men and women, artists, and 'brain-workers' of various kinds, those most involved with 'the modern'. Henry Adams (1907), the most important American historian from this era, echoes neurasthenic language when he complained that steam power and the changing status of women had combined to break his 'historical neck', another image of the disruption of the nervous system caused by cultural change, if slightly more violent. But while Adams bemoaned the way idealized 'women' had been replaced by machines as the driving force of cultural progress, Beard reconstructed and celebrated the body as a more or less efficient machine, and the doctor as a kind of moral mechanic.

Neurasthenia had innumerable symptoms, such as nervous dyspepsia, insomnia, hysteria, hypochondria, asthma, sick-headache, skin rashes, hay fever, premature baldness, inebriety, hot and cold flashes, nervous exhaustion, brain-collapse, or forms of incipient insanity. The wide swath of symptoms made the diagnosis so widely available, and the theory of exceptional refinement and sensitivity made it so attractive – attractive both to those in elites who felt threatened by cultural change and those upwardly mobile persons who associated nervous feelings with new or desired status positions – that an epidemic was the result.

Beard's emphatic statement of the Americanness of neurasthenia might be read as an indictment of American civilization, especially given the horror with which other writers, often having been diagnosed as neurasthenic themselves, represented the disease. The narrator's growing insanity in Charlotte Perkins Gilman's 'The Yellow Wallpaper' (1892), perhaps the best-known narrative representation of advanced neurasthenia, is just one of many similar representations of the disease. Kate Chopin's *The Awakening* (1899), Frank Norris's *The Pit* (1903), Edith Wharton's *House of Mirth* (1905), Jack London's *Martin Eden* (1909), Theodore Dreiser's *The 'Genius'* (1915) – these are just a few of the many negative narrative representations of neurasthenia. In these books neurasthenia is used to criticize, to excoriate aspects of modern society. 'The Yellow Wallpaper' makes explicit links between woman's estate and ill health and further criticizes S. Weir Mitchell, who is mentioned directly in the text. But Beard and Mitchell were uninterested in any such critical project. Beard's statement is, in fact, a celebration of what he called 'this distinguished malady', made both 'necessary and possible in a new and productive country'. Neurasthenia was 'modern, and originally American; and no age, no country, and no form of civilization, not Greece, nor Rome, nor Spain, nor the Netherlands, in the days of their glory, possessed such maladies'. Beard argued that neurasthenia was caused by the highest levels of civilization and that therefore the epidemic of neurasthenia proved that America was the highest civilization that had ever existed.

The disease was constructed in reference to social boundaries instituted along the fluid but recognizable lines of race, ethnicity, class, and gender. Neurasthenia attacked brain-workers but no laborers. It especially attacked artists and connoisseurs, because they had the most refined sensitivities. It struck only the more 'advanced races', especially the Anglo-Saxon, and not immigrants, blacks, Asian-Americans, Native Americans or laborers, who lacked the requisite 'intelligence' and 'refinement'. Urban elites were more susceptible than rural people because of the increased 'nervous' wear and tear of city life. 'No Catholic country is very nervous', Beard wrote, because neurasthenia preferred the more 'advanced' religious persuasions. Beard's anti-Catholicism is itself an argument about class and ethnicity in America, where the majority of Catholics were lower-class Irish and recent immigrants from Southern and Eastern Europe. Some non-Anglo-Saxon non-protestants have been 'moderately nervous', according to Beard, if they happened to be at one of the 'stopping-places between the strength of the barbarian and the sensitiveness of the highly civilized'. Both neurologists and lay proponents of neurasthenia agreed with Beard that nervousness was a mark of distinction, of class, of status, of refinement. The disease was such a significant status marker, in fact, that it could be coveted: the best thing about neurasthenia, according to William Marrs, M.D., in his *Confessions of a Neurasthenic* (1908), was that it allowed one to 'move in neurasthenic circles'.

Beard was not alone in expressing fear of the possible degeneration of the handful of people who are the caretakers of a fragile civilization. Arguments about race suicide, eugenics, and decadence were a constant feature of the Victorian cultural landscape. The medical discourse lent such theories reality at the personal, corporeal level, and this made the medical discourse an attractive rhetorical device for personalizing polemics of a civilization under siege. The threatening masses themselves, such thinking had it, were as barbaric as they were healthy. The then president of the Reading Railroad, Robert Baer, having been hauled in front of a congressional committee investigating charges that he was mistreating his immigrant laborers, pithily linked the possession of Anglo-American culture to the very ability to suffer: 'They don't suffer', he said of the immigrant laborers he employed. 'They don't even speak English' (Anthracite Coal Commission, 1903, 35). Inversely, neurasthenic suffering was a badge of cultural advancement.

The causes of and the cures for neurasthenia and the conception of health were gender-specific. Women's natural, healthy state differed not in kind, these doctors believed, but only in degree, from their diseased state. Both women and men had been alarmed for years at the number of women – sometimes estimated at half the female population – who were sickly. As early as 1871, William Dean Howells, the novelist and editor, wrote that America sometimes 'seems little better than a hospital for invalid women'. Howells knew at first hand both the force of his statement (his wife was an invalid from the birth of his first child to the end of her life) and the fact that attributing the disease to women was only partially accurate, since he himself was often neurasthenic. Guidebooks for women often accepted sickness as a normal state, as implied by such popular books as *Woman Know Thyself: Female Diseases. Their Prevention and Cure* (Greer, 1902). Rather than anything akin to 'our bodies, ourselves', as feminists later in the century would have it, this declares, 'your body, your disease'. S. Weir Mitchell (1887) most succinctly summed up this view when he wrote, 'He who does not know sick women does not know women'.

Women were, in the Victorian understanding of such things, supposed to be both more sensitive and refined than men and naturally weaker; hence women were more likely to become neurasthenic. They had less 'nerve force' to begin with and were more sensitive to the 'wear and tear' of modern life. (This is according to theory – as far as we can tell more men were actually diagnosed than women; see Gosling, 1987.) Men who were more effeminate – again in theory – tended to get the disease, and were further effeminized by it. Many 'overly active' women needed to be nursed back to a full femininity.

And since women were naturally frail, some neurologists argued, the insistence on education and meaningful work by the New Woman was destroying her health. Because of their limited energy budgets, the argument went, any brain-work combined with women's other duties could leave them in nervous bankruptcy. Mitchell (1887) refers explicitly to these developments, and to the place of neurasthenic treatment in correcting them: 'The woman's desire to be on a level of competition with man and assume his duties is, I am sure, making mischief, for it is my belief that no length of generations of change in her education and modes of activity will ever really alter her characteristics. She is physiologically other than man. I am concerned here with her now as she is, only desiring to help her in my small way to be in wiser and more healthful fashion what I believe her Maker meant her to be'. As Carroll Smith-Rosenberg (1985) has argued in relation to hysteria, the discourse of neurasthenia, in both its assumptions about health and its analysis of the disease, provided legitimation for a traditional definition of femininity based on dependency and passivity. The doctor's job was clear: to help women assume their God-appointed roles, so that, as Mitchell and others argued, they would be able to acquire and distribute the promised dividends of spiritual and cultural advancement.

From neurasthenia's wide variety of symptoms – ranging from lethargy to hyperexcitability, from spermatorreah to impotence, from hysteria to frigidity – and from the understanding of its gendered difference, there developed a wide variety of cures. Prominent cures included exercise cures (primarily for men), rest cures (the majority for women), hydropathy, homeopathy, electricity, diet, and massage. Many of these therapies were used for a variety of ills other than neurasthenia as well, and each has a significant cultural history. Three were developed primarily for nervous debility – rest, exercise, and electricity. Electrical treatments were meant as a technological answer to the problem of drained nervous batteries (Green, 1986). Like the passive rest cure, electrical stimulation was meant to charge the nervous system while allowing the patient to passively avoid expenditure. Rest cures were often conducted at home, sometimes in sanatoriums or at resorts. The most famous of these cures was Mitchell's Rest Cure, adopted by many doctor's including Gilman's own doctor and her narrator's husband. Many prominent women took the rest cure, including Edith Wharton and Virginia Woolf (Poirier, 1983). Exercise cures for men often included sports, hunting, and camp life, all of which required a more active recharging of the system.

The cures aimed at a reconstitution of the individual in terms of gender and class roles. In the Mitchell Rest Cure, the patient was prescribed bed rest for a month or longer, was not allowed visitors or permitted to read or write, and was spoon-fed a diet of milk by a nurse (Olfson, 1989). Mitchell stated clearly that he wanted to infantilize his female patients, since they needed to turn their wills over to him for him to effect a cure (Cayleff, 1988). His regimen of rest, quiet, and seclusion is also obviously related to notions of feminine decorum, the exclusion of women from public spheres, and obedience to paternal authority. In contrast to this infantilization and enforced debilitation, Theodore Roosevelt, who was neurasthenic when young, was cured by his exposure (on doctor's orders) to the rough-riding life of the frontier. Like Roosevelt, Owen Wister the novelist, Frederic Remington the sculptor and artist, and Thomas Eakins the painter were all sent out West as a cure for neurasthenic symptoms (White, 1968). This kind of cure can be seen as a form of occupational therapy; all three of these men were rich kids wandering around wondering what to do. One result was the creation by these very men of the image of the cowboy hero, an image that provided a mythic model for male activity well into the current century.

Other kinds of specifically male activity were encouraged as part of men's cures. Theodore Dreiser, the novelist, was neurasthenic when he experienced reversals on his way up the ladder to literary and financial success. At his most severe career setback, his doctors prescribed sports (this is the origin of medicine ball), horseback expeditions, and physical labor. William James, the premier philosopher and psychologist of his age, was neurasthenic whenever he contemplated changes of direction that involved status and role changes. Novelist and essayist Hamlin Garland's neurasthenia was cured by receiving a job as an English literature instructor, and there are many other cases of men being cured by promotion to or within their professions.

These examples suggest that neurasthenia was available as an explanation for and a place to reidentify with the effects of either upward or downward mobility and a space in which to negotiate whatever other reidentifications were made necessary by changing economic and gender roles. Roosevelt, Eakins, Remington, and Wister all came back from the Dakotas with career tracks. Henry James did the European cure and settled into his profession as a writer. William James continued to become neurasthenic and continued to prescribe vigorous mountain hikes and continental spas for himself until he was in his sixties. Other men congregated at sanitoriums to play sports and to ride for exercise.

The former champion wrestler and boxer William Muldoon directed one such clinic, and regularly organized his patients into a mock cavalry and make them ride in formation behind his white charger. Senators, cabinet members, writers, and other notables all took Muldoon's 'cure'. Muldoon's technique of militaristic discipline, strict moral accountability, and incessant, rigorous exercise provides an obvious model for the manly. Echoes of it can be seen in Roosevelt's championing of the 'strenuous life', his private philosophy that constant, vigorous activity was the only way to stave off depression, and his militarism. Roosevelt, while Secretary of the Navy, energetically built the military machine that made American imperialism possible. Along with his War Secretary Elihu Root, whose own cure was effected by Muldoon, he oversaw the institution of that imperialism in the colonization of the Phillipines and elsewhere. Even William James, an ardent anti-imperialist, wrote (1899) in praise of Roosevelt's strenuous response and (1910) in celebration of martial vigor.

The rest cure cured women (especially 'New Women') of too much exposure to the world, and thus refit them for their basic role in the home. The survivalist, competitive, aggressive exercise cures were explicitly represented as a return to traditional roles. But these cures were not exclusively reactionary. The leisure-class wife was a new role for many women and families, and this largely ornamental and symbolic role seemed to fly in the face of the traditional values of work, asceticism, and motherly and wifely duty. Sometimes medical intervention was necessary to cure the confusion that resulted. Mitchell was clear that the leisure class was his clientele: 'I am reminded as I write that what I say applies and must apply chiefly to the leisure class; but in others there is a good deal of manual work done of necessity, and after all, the leisure class is one which is rapidly increasing in America, and which needs, especially among its new recruits, the very kind of advice I am now giving'. The rest cure was sometimes a form of cultural retraining, teaching women how to consume without producing.

Neurasthenia was also used as a space for transformations not at all in keeping with the old notions of domestic passivity or the more modern notions of leisured consumption. Margaret A. Cleaves, M.D. (1910), for instance, argued that it was only her own work as a doctor of nervous diseases that gave her what few moments of health she had. Her career was impeded by neurasthenia, but somehow made possible by it. Besides, Cleaves wrote, 'It is a recognized fact that the work of the world is largely done by neurasthenes'. To be neurasthenic was to ally and identify oneself with those doing 'the work of the world'. Edith Wharton also became neurasthenic at crisis moments in her movement toward a professional career as a writer. Like Samuel Clemens, another sometime neurasthenic, she dramatized her neurasthenic profession by writing in bed, providing an iconic reversal of the rest cure. Emma Goldman, best known as the anarchist orator who supposedly inspired the assassination of President McKinley, became neurasthenic in 1903 as an embattled anarchist and emerged at the end of the year as a cured socialist. Although not in circumstances of their own choosing, these women constructed their own neurasthenic case histories in ways that made possible a wide variety of assimilations and resistances to a neurasthenic culture.

The exercise cure can also be seen as a progressive rather than traditionalist practice. By the turn of the century, the mid-century image of the refined, civilized, feminized man as the carrier of civilization was replaced by an image of martial entrepreneurialism, an image that responded to and was used to justify the elite pursuit of business success and the related political and economic changes involved with late-century consolidations of industrial and imperial power. The civilized man was being replaced by the civilizing man, by the man whose enterprise was expansion, and neurasthenia and its cures were available as forums for this replacement. Political expansionism is mirrored by the successful man's attempt to increase his bulk through vigorous muscle-building, conspicuous consumption of calories, or the making of 'fat and blood' as prescribed by Mitchell (1878). By late in the century a man's success could often be measured by his girth. The salesman known as Diamond Jim Brady, for instance, was renowned for his business success and his voracious appetite, which combined to swell his midsection to heroic proportions. Roosevelt, like Brady, was constantly trying to expand, and Roosevelt's rhetoric, also expansive, clearly exemplifies a polemic for cultural change, however much presented as a 'return' to heroic, natural, and manly values and an unenervated body.

The brainworkers who were affected by neurasthenia compose a who's who of intellectual and cultural workers on both sides of the Atlantic, and neurasthenic issues pervade their work. American realist novelists in particular, pledged as they were to representing the real life of their contemporaries, peopled their novels with the full range of nervous debilities. Henry James had neurasthenic episodes and his novels are full of neurasthenic characters who go to Europe for rest cures or remain invalids at home (cf. 1878, 1886, 1902, 1903a). In James's later works, claims to neurasthenic debility are sometimes shown to be masks, excuses, or subterfuges. The classic case of this is the opening of *The Ambassadors* (1903b) as Strether and Waymarsh dissemble their symptoms and motives to each other, fully suspecting the other to be falsely claiming the privileges of the ill. Edith Wharton described a social world full of neurasthenics with old money like Mrs. Peniston in *The House of Mirth* (1905), neurasthenics with new money like Mrs. Spragg in *The Custom of the Country* (1913), and neurasthenics with no money like Mrs. Frome in *Ethan Frome* (1911). Theodore Dreiser recorded his own neurasthenic episodes in *An Amateur Laborer* (1904) and *The 'Genius'* (1915) as well as in his autobiographies. William Dean Howells, Frank Norris, Hamlin Garland, Mary Wilkins Freeman, Sarah Orne Jewett, and the other leading fiction writers of the period created neurasthenic characters living in neurasthenic worlds.

European novelists also suffered from neurasthenia and represented it in their work. The most famous of these are perhaps Marcel Proust, whose *Remembrance of Things Past* is a literary monument to neurasthenic ideas about leisure, sickness, sexuality, and social life and Virginia Woolf, who repudiated her own rest cure but continued to pass on Mitchell's advice to drink milk to fortify the nerves. Her portrait of the ineffectual treatment of Septimus Smith's war trauma in *Mrs. Dalloway* (1925) rivals 'The Yellow Wallpaper' as one of the most important deconstructive readings of medical practice. English, French, German, and Russian novelists all played with neurasthenic themes in depicting the life of high society and in validating lower class characters as sensitive and refined.

Sociologists, psychologists, and philosophers were affected by and helped write the disease into their culture. William James had several neurasthenic prostrations and his notion of 'the sick soul' in *Varieties of Religious Experience* (1902) is heavily indebted to neurasthenic understandings of morbid states. He also wrote more directly about the need for better understandings of what one of his articles called 'The Energies of Men' (1906). Josiah Royce, George Santayana, and many of James's other contemporaries in philosophy, also experienced neurasthenia and wrote in its shadow. Max Weber had a neurasthenic breakdown while writing *The Protestant Ethic and the Spirit of Capitalism* (1904) and his understanding of his own morbidity informs the powerful and oft-quoted ending of that text, written after his crisis. Emile Durkheim wrote about neurasthenia as a prime social problem in *Suicide* (1898). Herbert Spencer, whose 'Gospel of Relaxation' was his most often quoted text in America in the late nineteenth century, was a long-suffering neurasthenic. G. Stanley Hall had his bouts and his opinions, as did many of his colleagues in the new academic discipline of psychology.

And writers in several other fields had similar experiences and used the discourse extensively in their work. Muckraking journalists Lincoln Steffens, Ida Tarbell, and Jacob Riis, along with their colleagues in the field better known for their fiction, Jack London, Stephen Crane, Frank Norris, and Theodore Dreiser, all had neurasthenic experiences and produced neurasthenic texts. J.A. Hobson wrote of the 'nervous wear and tear' of modern life in discussing imperialism in *The Psychology of Jingoism* (1901); John Muir used the same phrase to explain the importance of park land in *Our National Parks*, also in 1901. Muir was an early neurasthenic cured by the outdoors and his belief in the possibility of reconciling revelation and science. Other nature writers, such as John Burroughs, Liberty Hyde Bailey, Stewart Edward White, and Theodore Roosevelt used the discourse to discuss the urban problems that were a constant background to their morally-laden descriptions of natural environments.

But these neurasthenic writers account for just a small percentage of the references to the disease in the periodical and book worlds. Popular novelists used the disease as did the elite writers, to mark characters as especially refined, as comically overrefined, or as manipulative or dishonest. Editorial writers made use of the disease to deplore aspects of modern life and to celebrate the progress of civilization. Visual artists, both those working in the publishing world and for the art market, were equally important in imbibing and disseminating ideas of neurasthenia (Dijkstra, 1986). Thomas Eakins and Frederic Remington, both of whom were prescribed the exercise cure in the 1880s, represent the poles: Remington became a staunch depictor of the strenuous, masculine, healthy-minded response to a neurasthenic world while Eakins continued to portray his sitters as more haggard and worn than they really appeared in order to give them a neurasthenic halo of moral heroism (Johns, 1983; Lutz, 1991). And politicians worked both sides of the equation in presenting their platforms and elaborating their polemics. The most famous of the neurasthenic politicians was undoubtedly Theodore Roosevelt, whose story of nervous debility (in the form of asthma and general weakness) conquered through strenuous exertion and will was as famous in his time as George Washington's cherry tree and Abraham Lincoln's log cabin. For Durkhiem, the main cause of neurasthenic anomie was the breakdown of traditional values, and Roosevelt agreed.

Roosevelt was a progressive, believing in the necessity of vast social changes, but he understood the value of arguing for those changes through appeals to the traditional. Neurasthenia, a disease founded in traditional values and explained as an effect of change, provided the language for this cultural double-dealing. His neurasthenic arguments became less convincing by the second decade of the new century and were challenged with more modern rhetorics and discourses. In the elections of 1912 Roosevelt was defeated by Woodrow Wilson, whose most popular campaign speeches declaimed 'the generous energies of the American people' (Wilson, 1913). Like the economic thinkers, who were championing a new economy of surplus, and the advertisers, who were arguing that everyone could and should spend more freely than previous generations, Wilson's rhetoric signals the end of neurasthenic double-consciousness and doubt about spending.

If medically 'neurasthenia was an exceptionally broad church', as Simon Wessely makes clear in his companion piece to this one, culturally the disease was even broader. Neurasthenia entered political and cultural arguments of all kinds, only a fraction of which could be mentioned here. Medical historians argue about the relation between neurasthenia and those obviously similar syndromes now being diagnosed: chronic fatigue syndrome, M.E., and the like.

Gosling (1987), for instance, argues that 'American physicians in the late nineteenth century recognized neuroses and stress disorders' and Oppenheim (1991) argues that neurasthenia was a diagnosis for depression. I would argue in slightly different words that physicians in the late nineteenth and early twentieth centuries recognized neurasthenia when symptoms presented that were very similar to those that call forth diagnoses of stress disorders now (see also Wessely 1990, 1991).

Some of the cultural functions of the two sets of diagnoses also overlap. People clearly 'use' these diagnoses as they make significant life changes, especially changes that impact their sense of gendered social position, their styles of consumption, and their occupational callings. But to say that therefore these entities are the same is to confuse the cultural and the medical where they should perhaps remain distinct. 'Stress' in a late-capitalist culture with a crumbling infrastructure may be analogous to 'nervousness' in a burgeoning and expansive economy making the transition to an ethos of consumer demand. But an analogy is far from an identity; the cultural work of stress begins in a very different space and time and works to different ends. Neurasthenia is extinct in the West because its cultural work is done.

REFERENCES

Adams, H. (1907) *The Education of Henry Adams*, Rpt. (1973) Boston, Houghton Mifflin.

Anthracite Coal Strike Commission (1903) *Report to the President of the Antracite Coal Strike of May-October, 1902*, Washington, D.C., Government Printing Office.

Barker-Benfield, G. (1976) *The Horrors of the Half-Known Life; Male Attitudes toward Women and Sexuality in Nineteenth-Century America*, New York, Harper.

Beard, G.M. (1881) *American Nervousness. Its Causes and Consequences*, New York, G.P. Putnam's Sons.

Cayleff, S.E. (1988) ' "Prisoners of their own feebleness": women, nerves, and western medicine – a historical overview'. *Social Science and Medicine*, 26: 1199–1208.

Chopin, K. (1899) *The Awakening*, Reprint (1976) New York, Norton.

Cleaves, M.A. (1910) *Autobiography of a Neurasthene: As Told by One of Them to Margaret A. Cleaves, M.D.*, Boston, R.G. Badger.

Dijkstra, B. (1986) *Idols of Perversity; Fantasies of Feminine Evil in Fin-de-Siecle Culture*, Oxford, Oxford University Press.

Douglas, A. (1973) ' "The fashionable diseases": women's complaints and their treatment in nineteenth-century America'. *Journal of Interdisciplinary History*, 4: 25–52.

Dreiser, T. (1915) *The 'Genius'*, New York, John Lane.

Dreiser, T. (1904) *An Amateur Laborer*, Reprint (1983) Philadelphia, University of Pennsylvania Press.

Drinka, G. (1984) *The Birth of Neurosis: Myth, Malady, and the Victorians*, New York, Simon & Schuster.

Durkheim, E. (1898) *Le Suicide*, Paris. Translated (1951) as *Suicide: A Study in Sociology*, by Spaulding, J.A. and Simpson, C., Glencoe, Illinois, The Free Press.

Fellman, A.C. and Fellman, M. (1981) *Making Sense of Self: Medical Advice Literature in Late Nineteenth-Century America*, Philadelphia, University of Pennsylvania Press.

Gay, P. (1986) *The Bourgeois Experience, Victoria to Freud: Volume II. The Tender Passion*, Oxford, Oxford University Press.

Gilman, C.P. (1892) 'The Yellow Wallpaper'. Rpt. (1973) Old Westbury, N.Y., The Feminist Press.

Gosling, F.G. (1987) *Before Freud: Neurasthenia and the American Medical Community, 1870–1910*, Urbana, Illinois, University of Illinois Press.

Green, H. (1986) *Fit for America: Health, Fitness, Sport, and American Society*, New York, Pantheon.

Greer, J.H. (1902) *Woman Know Thyself: Female Diseases, Their Prevention and Cure*, Chicago, Columbia Publishing House.

Haller, J.S. and Haller, R.M. (1974) *The Physician and Sexuality in Victorian America*, Urbana, Illinois, University of Illinois Press.

Hobson, J.A. (1901) *The Psychology of Jingoism*, London, G. Richards.

Howells, W.D. (1871) *Suburban Sketches*, New York, Hurd & Houghton.

James, H. (1878) *Daisy Miller*, Reprint (1965) New York, New American Library.

James, H. (1886) *The Bostonians*. Reprint (1956) New York, Modern Library.

James, H. (1902) *The Wings of the Dove*. Reprint (1976) New York, Penguin.

James, H. (1903a) *The Ambassadors*. Reprint (1964) New York, Norton.

James, H. (1903b) *The Better Sort*, New York, Charles Scribner's Sons.

James, W. (1899) 'The gospel of relaxation'. In *Talks to Teachers on Psychology: and to Students on Some of Life's Ideals*, Rpt. (1958) New York, Norton.

James, W. (1902) *Varieties of Religious Experience*, Rpt. (1982) New York, Penguin.

James, W. (1906) 'The energies of men', Rpt (1916) in *On Vital Reserves*, New York, Henry Holt.

James, W. (1910) 'The moral equivalent of war', in (1911) *Memories and Studies*, New York, Longmans, Green.

Johns, E. (1983) *Thomas Eakins: The Heroism of Modern Life*, Princeton, Princeton University Press.

Lears, T.J.J. (1981) *No Place of Grace: Antimodernism and the Transformation of American Culture, 188–1920*, New York, Pantheon.

London, J. (1909) *Martin Eden*, New York, Macmillan.

Marrs, W. (1908) *Confessions of a Neurasthenic*, quoted in Haller and Haller, 1974.

Martin, R. (1981) *American Literature and the Universe of Force*, Durham, N.C., Duke University Press.

Meyer, D. (1980) *The Positive Thinkers: Religion as Pop Psychology from Mary Baker Eddy to Oral Roberts*, New York, Pantheon.

Mitchell, S.W. (1878) *Fat and Blood and How to Make Them*, Philadelphia, Lippincott.

Mitchell, S.W. (1887) *Doctor and Patient*, Philadelphia, Lippincott.

Muir, J. (1901) *Our National Parks*, Boston, Houghton Mifflin.

Norris, F. (1903) *The Pit: A Story of Chicago*, New York, Doubleday, Page.

Olfson, M. (1989) 'The Weir Mitchell rest cure'. *Pharos*, 51: 30–2

Oppenheim, J. (1991) *'Shattered Nerves': Doctors, Patients, and Depression in Victorian England*, Oxford, Oxford University Press.

Poirier, S. (1983) 'The Weir Mitchell rest cure: doctor and patients'. *Women's Studies*, 10: 15–40.

Rosenberg, C. (1962) 'The place of George M. Beard in nineteenth-century psychiatry'. *Bulletin of the History of Medicine*, 36: 245–59.

Smith-Rosenberg, C. (1985) *Disorderly Conduct: Visions of Gender in Victorian America*, Oxford, Oxford University Press.

Weber, M. (1904) *The Protestant Ethic and the Spirit of Capitalism*, translated (1958) Talcott Parsons, New York, Scribners.

Wharton, E. (1905) *House of Mirth*, Reprint (1962), Holt Rinehart & Winston.

Wharton, E. (1911) *Ethan Frome*, New York, Charles Scribner's Sons.

Wharton, E. (1913) *The Custom of the Country*, New York, Charles Scribner's Sons.

Wessely, S. (1990) 'Old wine in new bottles: neurasthenia and "ME"'. *Psychological Medicine*, 20: 35–53.

Wessely, S. (1991) 'History of postviral fatigue syndrome'. *British Medical Bulletin*, 47: 919–41.

White, G.E. (1968) *The Eastern Establishment and the Western Experience: The West of Frederic Remington. Theodore Roosevelt, and Owen Wister*, New Haven, Yale University Press.

Wilson, W. (1913) *The New Freedom: A Call for the Emancipation of the Generous Energies of a People*, New York, Doubleday, Page.

Woolf, V. (1925) *Mrs. Dalloway*. Rpt. (1953) New York, Harcourt, Brace & World.

Chapter 21
Anxiety Disorders

Clinical Section
GE BERRIOS and C LINK

Whilst the history of the neuroses (Raymond, 1911; Cottereau, 1975; López Piñero, 1983; Drinka, 1984; Rosenberg, 1989; Oppenheim, 1991) in general, and that of hysteria (Veith, 1965; Owen, 1971; Roccatagliata, 1990; Trillat, 1986; Bannour, 1992), hypochondria (Michéa, 1843; Guillespie, 1928; Kenyon, 1965; Meister, 1980; Place, 1986) and obsessive-compulsive disorder (Berrios, 1989) in particular, have received historical attention, the evolution of what is nowadays known as 'generalized anxiety disorder', 'panic disorder', and 'phobia' has been relatively neglected (Ey, 1950; Errera, 1962; May, 1968; Sauri, 1979; Boulenger and Uhde, 1987; Zal, 1988; Kuch and Swinson, 1992). This may be due to their relative newness; or to the fact that the historical models used to account for the traditional *nervous disorders* are inappropriate for the *new neuroses*.[1]

This does not mean that the individual symptoms now included under the 'anxiety disorders' are themselves new. Indeed, they have been observed since time immemorial;[2] the only difference being that they were then reported under different psychosocial wrappers. For example, during the eighteenth century individual symptoms were considered to be specific diseases or occasionally included under the syndromic domain of other diseases. The *novelty* has been that during the 1890s these symptoms were rescued from their earlier niches and put together into what was then claimed were *independent* clinical conditions. The notion that these symptoms could all be the *manifestation* of a unitary construct called 'anxiety' was also new, at least alien to pre-Freudian psychiatry. The historical and ideological factors that led to this state of affairs need much disentangling.

Before the final synthesis took place, such symptoms could be found in clinical realms as disparate as cardiovascular, inner ear, gastrointestinal, and neurological medicine. Basically, each symptom seems to have been taken *at face value* and treated as a real 'physical' complaint. This is the reason why they are found mostly reported in *medical* (not psychiatric) journals. Indeed, even the 'treatment' of these disorders had little to do with 'psychiatric' practice, and asylum alienists rarely saw them until the early 20th century.

The symptoms of 'anxiety' are listed under two headings. Subjective ones (i.e. those felt as 'psychological' experiences) include fear, emotional worries, feelings of terror, depersonalisation, etc., and also cognitive mental acts such as obsession-like thoughts concerning the safety of others, fear of dying, etc.

Objective ones, also called somatic, (and sometimes anxiety-equivalents) are referred to a bodily system and include abdominal pain, nausea, vertigo, dizziness, palpitations, dry mouth, hot flushes, hyperventilation, breathlessness, headache, restless legs, and other bodily experiences sometimes indistinguishable from complaints caused by physical disease.

According to personality, culture, social class and other variables not yet identified, subjects may present these symptoms in different combinations. If some of the latter are repetitive and stable enough, they may be called syndromes and even diseases. Sometimes, combinations of such somatic symptoms may mimic heart attacks or inner ear disorder. Others, the subjective symptoms themselves may present as phenocopies of physical diseases such as temporal lobe epilepsy. If the subjective symptoms are more or less continuous they are called generalised anxiety disorder; if paroxysmal, panic attack; the latter are known to be mostly spontaneous; when triggered by a recognisable stimulus (whether heights, or going out, or spiders, etc.) they have been called 'phobias' and taken the name of the stimulus. The current (fashionable) view that 'crisis of anxiety' or 'panic disorder' constitute a separate disease is very new. Since the 1900s, such attacks have been considered as part of the anxiety neurosis; before that they were associated with conditions such as neurasthenia and psychasthenia,[3] and even before considered to be cardiovascular (Krishaber, 1873), or inner ear disorders (Benedikt, 1870).

A historical account of the origin of the modern concept of anxiety disorder and its allied clinical states should deal with questions such as: 1. why were such symptoms and signs – often dissimilar in appearance – brought together under the same banner? 2. Was this the result of clinical observation or of theoretical and social pressures? 3. Were these states considered as exaggerations of 'normal' psychological phenomena, or as 'morbid' forms? 4. How relevant to their inception were late nineteenth century theories of emotion and views on the 'ganglionar' (autonomic) nervous system? It goes without saying that the history of anxiety can also be studied from a metaphysical, social, poetic and religious perspective. This chapter focuses only on its 'medical' aspects.

THE WORD ANXIETY AND COGNATES

The view suggested by Ey (1950) that *anxiété* gained its *medical meaning* at the end of the nineteenth century needs rectification (p.386). 18th century nosologists – including those whose mother tongue was French – already had made use of the Latin term to describe paroxysmal states of 'restlessness' and *inquietude*. For example, *anxietas* is used by Boissier de Sauvages, Linné, Vogel, and Sagar (Cullen, 1803). In addition, *panophobia, vertigo, palpitatio, suspirium*, and *oscitatio* (all redolent of anxiety and panic attacks) were used to refer to states Continental nosologists considered as physical diseases. No one of these clinical categories was ever considered as belonging in the vesanias category (i.e. with the mental disorders). The Scottish McBride and Cullen did not use so many clinical categories, and the nearest the latter got to one was with his *palpitatio melancholica* (Cullen, 1803).

In France, Landré-Beauvais (1813) defined anxiety as: 'a certain malaise, restlessness, excessive agitation' and used the word *angoisse*; he suggested that this state may accompany 'acute' and 'chronic' diseases. There is little doubt that Landré attempted to conceptualise anxiety as a syndrome that included both subjective and somatic components and which could accompany diverse diseases (see below). Littré and Robin (1858) defined *angoisse* as 'feelings of closeness or pressure on the epigastric region, accompanied by a great difficulty in breathing and excessive sadness; it is the most advanced degree of anxiety' (p.77); and *anxiété* as 'troubled and agitated state, with feelings of difficulty in breathing and pressure on the precordial region: inquietude, anxiety and anguish are three stages of the same phenomenon' (p.93).

Lewis (1967) has analysed the way in which the etymology of anxiety, anguish, and anger influenced the clinical conceptualisation of the anxiety states. To this it must be added that, whilst the dichotomy 'anxiety-anguish' has little clinical meaning in Anglo-saxon psychiatry (the term *anguish*, in fact, never gained a place in medical terminology), it found a comfortable niche in France, Germany, and Spain where the terms *Angoisse*, *Angst*, and *Angustia* (respectively) carry distinct meaning, and refer to the paroxysmal and more severe aspects of the disorder. Also playing on the etymology of the term anxiety, Sarbin (1964; 1968) constructed an argument to demonstrate that the symptom was but a metaphor. Unfortunately, historical inaccuracy and loose argument,[4] mar his interesting ideas.[5]

'ANXIETY'-RELATED BEHAVIOURS

Irrespective of the name these states travelled under (i.e. of the history of the words), or of how they were explained (the history of the concepts), *behaviours* recognizable as 'anxiety-related' are found described in the literature of the ages (Errera, 1962). Altschule (1976), for example, reminds us that writers such as Arnold, Locke, Battie, Mead, Smith, and Crichton described medical states of inquietude and uneasiness (pp.119–24). This chapter, however, will only deal with such behaviours, concepts or words as they feature in the clinical theatre of the nineteenth century and after.

Before the 1820s, anxiety symptoms were mostly considered as part of the melancholic states, and rarely, if ever, qualified as diseases in their own right; for example, Pinel (1818) included anxiety symptoms under 'epilepsy' (p.80), melancholia (p.156), rabies (particularly of the 'spontaneous' variety) (p.156), and the 'motility' neuroses (p.159). The same can be said of Georget's book (1820) where some of these symptoms are discussed in the section on 'general and sympathetic symptoms'. Griesinger (1861) – quoting Guislain (1852) – reports that nine per cent of subjects may start their insanity with acute 'fear'.

During this period and generally speaking, the language of psychiatry in Germany and England was not yet ready to assimilate the subtle semiological distinctions rapidly developing in French psychiatry. Thus, where Guislain (1852) had written *craintes* and *frayeurs* (p.45), Griesinger (1861) translated *Shrecken oder Angst* (p.165), and Robertson and Rutherford (the English translators of Griesinger) 'shock or anxiety' (Griesinger, 1967, p.165). A subtle drifting in meaning did thus take place as the translations moved from *frayeur* to *Angst* and anxiety. Indeed, these changes reflect well the evolution of this symptom during the second half of the 19th century. For whilst Guislain (1852) was only referring here to acute fears, Griesinger introduced *Angst*, a term which, after the publication of Kirkegaard's book in 1844 (Kirkegaard, 1959), had acquired a special meaning which went well beyond 'fear'. Apart from reflecting Kirkegaard's own morbid psychology (Jolivet, 1950) the term brought into play the new epistemological and religious dimensions that Kirkegaard had attached to the notion of 'anguish' (McCarty, 1981).

During this period, the term, 'nervousness' seems to have more or less encompassed most of the subjective aspects of the anxiety states. Thus, an anonymous reviewer (1860)[6] of Bouchut's book (1860) on *Nervosisme* complained of the vagueness of the term although accepted that there was no good alternative in the English language. It seems clear both from the points made by the reviewer, and from Bouchut's quotations, that the monograph was *not* only about hysteria or hypochondria (as it would have been expected during this period) but also about anxiety and its somatic accompaniments.[7]

'ANXIETY' AS A CAUSE OF MENTAL DISORDER

Around this same time, and with his usual clinical acumen, Feuchtersleben (1847) wrote: 'Intense anxiety and grief lead us to expect organic affections of the heart and of the larger vessels, fretfulness, dejection, discontent and a disordered digestion' (p.193). The Austrian writer was not discussing, however, diseases as such, but the relationship of body and mind; hence his 'psychosomatic' remark seems to have remained unnoticed. A few years earlier, Prichard (1835) had written along the same lines: 'Care and anxiety, distress, grief, and mental disturbances are by far the most productive causes of insanity' ... 'Anxiety and agitation of mind caused by political events have occasionally produced a very decided effect on the number of persons becoming deranged' (pp.182–3). Bucknill and Tuke (1858) echoed these words in their discussion of the effect of modern civilisation on insanity: 'The very same person is possibly, also, the subject of ever-present anxiety and apprehension, in consequence of a precarious income' (p.38). Amongst the unpublished manuscripts left by Alfred Wigan (1849), there was a rambly piece on 'Anxiety' where the author describes the social difficulties caused by this experience.[8]

Thus, it seems clear that by the mid-nineteenth century the term anxiety was already current in medical writings to describe a mental state that fell within the range of normal human experiences but was able to cause or lead to disease, including insanity.

MODELS AND EXPLANATIONS

After the 1850s, the views that anxiety may be a cause of insanity, but also a disease in its own right become increasingly conflated. Some have suggested that the work of Griesinger led to a period of rampant 'organicism', and that from then on psychiatry had only somatic theories until the work of Janet and Freud. This is inaccurate. It is true that the anatomo-clinical model was influential, but it is also the case that its application to mental illness was governed by what here will be called, for lack of a better name, an 'open causal chain' mechanism; i.e. the belief that although psychiatric symptoms *were*, at some level, the result of brain lesions, the latter could be (and were) caused by psychological trauma (anxiety was a candidate here) and negative life events. In other words, psychological factors could start the causal chain leading to insanity. The analysis of the role played by anxiety during this period may help to correct such misapprehension. After the 1860s, new *physiopathological* mechanisms were marshalled by alienists to explain how stressful events might lead to anatomical changes in the brain.[9]

By the early twentieth century, five views were available to account for the development of mental illness: 1. 'genetic', as expressed by degeneration theory (Genil Perrin, 1913), 2. 'constitutional' as in Dupré (1919) and Duprat (1899), 3. 'chaotic', according to which the breakdown in mental function resulted from total 'hardware' failure,[10] 4. 'hierarchical'[11] or 'ethological' (Houzeau, 1972)[12] models, according to which mental symptoms resulted from the release of lower or atavic functions, and 5. 'software' accounts not dependent upon the anatomo-clinical view.[13] Most of these views originated, in fact, during the nineteenth century, and alienists tended to support combinations thereof.

SYMPTOMS AND SYNDROMES

Morel and his délire emotif

Morel (1866) suggested that pathological changes (or a *neurosis* of) the ganglionic (autonomic) nervous system gave rise to recognisable symptoms which he called 'emotional delusions' (*délire emotif*). Analysis of his clinical reports shows that he had departed from traditional views on fears and anxieties. Morel's cases showed subjective (anxiety, phobias and obsessions) (Berrios, 1989) and objective complaints, the latter referring to the skin, and the cardiovascular, gastrointestinal, and nervous systems. At least two of his patients showed classical 'panic attacks' and generalized anxiety disorder (although in retrospective diagnosis and on account of their age, they were probably secondary to a depressive illness).

Morel combined in his paper recent knowledge on the 'ganglionar system' (started in the work of Bichat and Johnstone) and Willis' useful metaphor of 'sympathy' of functions (Clarke and Jacyna, 1987) to explain the presence and clustering of symptoms which, until then, have been considered as unrelated. By making reference to the ganglionar system he also complied with the anatomo-clinical model of disease. He had asked: what symptoms may the pathology of the ganglionar system engender? His answer was *both* subjective and objective complaints.

Earlier on, Morel (1860) had proposed to substitute symptomatic by aetiological classifications, the idea being that dissimilar symptoms might prove to be related via the same anatomical locus. His 1866 paper provided alienists with the mechanism to bring together disparate symptoms on the grounds that they were all caused by a disturbance of the ganglionic system. But the paper also marks the point of origin of a group of 'neurotic' conditions (here called the 'new neuroses') which were to run parallel to the traditional ones (i.e. hysteria and hypochondriasis). It must be noted that whilst these latter two conditions were beginning to lose their 'organicity' (via the notion of functional lesion and irritability) (López Piñero, 1983) the link with the ganglionar system kept the anxiety and obsessional (Berrios, 1989) disorders linked to the 'organic' model for longer.

Krishaber

Morel's views found expression in Krishaber's 'cerebro-cardiac neurosis'. Maurice Krishaber (1836–1883) was a Hungarian ear-nose-throat specialist, trained and working in France, whose main area of research had, in fact, been the pathology of the larynx, and the physiology of singing (Dechambre, 1889). In 1873, he published a classical monograph reporting 38 cases suffering from 'cerebro-cardiac neurosis'. After criticising the inadequacy of clinical categories such as nervousness, proteiform neuropathy, spasmodic state, etc. to describe his condition, he divided its symptoms into those affecting sensation, movement, circulation, and others. On clinical grounds, he differentiated the new disease from hysteria, hypochondria, chlorosis, cerebrovascular syndromes and toxic states. He also suggested that his illness was due to a pathological instability of the blood vessels and that its symptoms responded to caffeine. His patients showed remarkable homogeneity, with an even incidence (higher than 80 per cent) of anxiety, light-headedness, vertigo, palpitations, tinnitus, tremor, gastrointestinal symptoms (nausea, indigestion and diarrhoea), intolerance to noise, photophobia and inability to concentrate (Krishaber, 1873).

Krishaber died young but his views were influential. Instead of trying to encompass all the symptoms putatively related to the ganglionar system, he chose those seemingly representing a 'lability' of the cardiovascular system. The new 'neurosis' provided internists with a god-sent explanation for the anxiety symptoms, and caffeine became for a while a popular form of treatment.[14]

Vertigo and anxiety

Vertigo had fully been described in Classical times, but during the nineteenth century accounts were produced of its many nosological associations.[15] For example, it features in Axenfeld's treatise where mention is made of the work of Trastour on *vertigo nerveux* and of his cases of subjects experiencing vertigo in social situations or after 'over-exertion' of the intellect (Axenfeld, 1883, p.268). In his award-winning study on vertigo in the insane, Millet also reported cases where vertigo was part of a panic attack. The most illustrative of these being that of an ex-soldier who, on crossing la Place de la Bastille, suddenly felt shaky, dizzy, with vertigo and experienced the irresistible need to run; he became suicidal and had to be admitted after trying to gas himself. Retrospective diagnosis of this case suggests an agoraphobic syndrome secondary to severe depression (Millet, 1884, p.208). Weill (1886) also wrote on the *vertiges des névroses* which may accompany epilepsy, insanity, neurasthenia and the cerebrocardiac neuropathy of Krishaber and include 'anguish, palpitations, and headaches' (p.64). These states are also redolent of typical panic attacks.

In his full review, Leroux reported that vertigo was one of the central symptoms of agoraphobia (as described by Westphal in 1872 and Legrand du Saulle in 1877 – see below), and that this particular form of the symptom had been called by Lasègue *vertige mental*.[16]

Leroux (1889) also suggested that vertigo might accompany severe lypemania (i.e. depressive illness) (pp.152–3). In this case the vertigo included:

sensations of overwhelming pre-cordial and epigastric anxiety, added to a feeling of impending fainting and collapse with weakness of the legs. There was also the sensation that the ground sunk, and that perceptions became misty. Anguish is the predominant component of the attack, and this translates itself in pallor, dyspnoea, cold sweating. The subject cannot reason any more. He knows that there is no danger but is incapable of controlling his worry. He may become paralysed or act in a discontrolled manner. (pp.168–9)

A clearer description of panic attacks cannot be found. It is also likely that Haltenhof's cases of 'paralysing vertigo' were anxiety attacks (Haltenhof, 1887). Grasset (1901) also refers in his treatise to the vertigo of neurasthenia and hysteria (p.203).

Benedikt, Westphal, du Saulle, and agoraphobia

The 'organic' view of the anxiety disorders developed in other directions. For example, Benedikt (1870) related the dizziness of panic attacks to pathology of the inner ear, and Westphal explained agoraphobia as a vertigo of similar origin. Indeed, in his rueful autobiography, Benedikt (1906) claimed that he had been the first to describe the condition of *Platzschwindel*, and that Westphal never acknowledged his idea.[17] Legrand du Saulle, however, with his usual clinical acumen was the first to realize that the feelings reported by these subjects were not, in fact, those of objective vertigo but of fear that they might lose their balance. His description is classical:

by the term *peur des espaces* I refer to a particular neuropathic state, characterised by a feeling of anguish and terror, without loss of consciousness, which occurs in an open space, and which is different from vertigo. . . . This psychological disturbance has not been described in France, except by Perroud's writing on agoraphobia in 1873. This term, accepted by Cordes (1872) and Westphal (1872), seems to me to be too narrow for it does not cover all the many symptoms of the cases described. Patients may fear spaces, but also streets and theatres, travelling by public transport, boats and bridges. (Legrand du Saulle, 1876, pp.405–6)

The clinical status of 'agoraphobia' was not clear at the time. Some, like Ball and Gros (1885) suggested it was a form of psychosis. Others, like Dagonet (1894), regarded it as a hereditary, *sui generis*, mental disorder (pp.424–6).[18] Hartenberg (1901), in turn, suggested that agoraphobia was a learned problem in which anticipation played a major role (p.692). Part of the problem was that, up to this period, phobias and obsessions were not yet distinguished (Leguil, 1979).[19] One of the first to attempt to do so was Ribot who, after criticising the useless coining of 'pseudo-Greek' terms to name each specific phobia, distinguished between *pantophobia* (i.e. generalised anxiety states)[20] and specific phobias, and the latter into two groups: 'the first is connected with fear, and includes all manifestations implying in any degree whatsoever the fear of pain, from that of a fall or the prick of a needle to that of illness or death. The second is directly connected with disgust, and seems to me to include the forms which have sometimes been called *pseudophobia* (Gélineau). Such are the fears of contact, the horror of blood, and of innocuous animals, and many strange and causeless aversions' (Ribot, 1911, p.214). In the event, it was Freud who succeeded in separating phobia from obsession.

Freud and the 'anxiety neurosis'

By the early 1890s, the concept of neurasthenia had become so large that it was threatening to engulf most of 'neurotic' states. Started by US physicians but taken over with some enthusiasm by their European counterparts (less so by alienists), neurasthenia included most if not all the symptoms of anxiety and panic disorder.[21] In 1894, Sigmund Freud (1953) published in French a classical paper entitled 'The justification for detaching from neurasthenia a particular syndrome: the anxiety neurosis' in which he marshalled clinical and theoretical reasons for the creation of the new disease. All symptoms were to revolve around the concept of 'morbid anxiety':

> general irritability, anxious expectation, anxiety attacks, and [somatic] 'equivalents' such as cardiovascular and respiratory symptoms, sweating, tremor, shuddering, ravenous hunger, diarrhoea, vertigo, congestion, paras- thesiae, awakening in fright, obsessional symptoms, agoraphobia, and nausea. The symptoms could be found in various combinations and resulted from 'grave hereditary taint' or from a 'deflection of somatic sexual excitation from the psychical field, and an abnormal use of it, due to this deflection'. (p.97)

A year later, Freud (1953a) published a spirited reply in response to a critical paper by Löwenfeld. A full discussion of changes in Freud's sexual theory of the anxiety neurosis is beyond the scope of this chapter. His suggestion that the anxiety states should constitute a separate condition received little challenge. This is surprising for, as he himself stated in his original paper, he had 'adduced hardly any examples and quoted no statistics' (p.108). In fact, it is likely that his suggestion was accepted less for his aetiological theory than for the fact that similar separatist views had been hinted at by Hecker, Krishaber, Ribot, and others. It should be kept in mind that, at this early stage in its history, anxiety neurosis was considered (by Freud included) *as a disease of the nervous system*: 'The nervous system reacts to an internal source of excitation with a neurosis, just as it reacts to an analogous external one with a corresponding affect' (p.102). At the time Freud, considered 'anxiety neurosis' as an example of 'actual neurosis', i.e. of acquired and reactive conditions unrelated to childhood events (Laplanche and Pontalis, 1973, pp.10–12). Important alienists agreed with Freud's nosological views; for example, Hartenberg (1901) only took issue with the 'sexual aetiology' and preferred the older mechanism of Morel and Krish- aber: 'anxiety neurosis originates in the sympathetic nervous system' (p.699), 'the term anxiety neurosis is useful to differentiate from neurasthenia a distinct group of symptoms that may represent a "primary disorder of the emotions" and which can provide an explanation for the development of phobias'.

But there was also some disagreement. Pitres and Régis in their famous *Les Obsessions et les Impulsions* wrote:

> during recent years German authors have described what they call anxiety neurosis. According to Hecker,[22] this disorder would include all the symp- toms of neurasthenia – the latter term being now reserved for simple spinal

irritation. Freud, on the other hand, considers anxiety neurosis as an independent disorder characterised, in its pure form, by nervous overexcitement,
chronic anxiety and anxious attention, attacks of acute and paroxysmal
anxiety with dyspnoea, palpitations, profuse sweating. (p.250)

Pitres and Régis (1902) believed that: 'This is only a *syndrome* and hence may
be found grafted, whether acutely or chronically, upon any neuropathic or
psychopathic personality.... It is associated with neurasthenia and melancholia
but can also be seen in other neuroses and psychoses.... *There is, therefore, no*
independent disorder called anxiety neuroses' (p.251).

The same criticism was expressed at the Grenoble Congress of 1902, when
Lalanne (1902) presented his oft-quoted historical account. A young Capgras
(1903) sided with the views of Pitres and Régis and reported two cases in their
support. Disagreements on the nature of the anxiety disorders gave rise to a
plethora of treatment approaches; their study is unfortunately beyond the scope
of this chapter (Dubois, 1905; Dejerine and Gauckler, 1911; Thomas, 1913;
Levy, 1917; Janet, 1919).

Janet's views

Janet was at the cross-roads of two French psychological traditions and a foreign
one: positivism, as represented by Ribot, Taine, and Renan (who were his
teachers); the spiritualist and introspective tradition of Maine de Biran, which
had been transmitted to him by his uncle, the philosopher Paul Janet; and
Jacksonism and the hierarchical approach to psychological functions (Rouart,
1950). The spiritualist view had also influenced Royer-Collard, Baillarger,
Moreau de Tours, the so-called 'psychological alienists' (López Piñero and
Morales Meseguer, 1970).

In Janet's model, 'feelings' were 'secondary' mental states, that only served to
guide the expression and termination of behaviours (Fouks et al, 1986). Their
effectiveness depended on the level of energy (*force*) and integrative capacity
(*tension*). Exaggerated energy or reduced integration led to a failure of feelings,
and to the release of primitive behaviours. For Janet, anxiety and anguish were
the main manifestations of such failures. Like Freud, he believed that both were
accompanied by somatic symptoms. His interest was, however, in the description of the 'mental' or 'psychological' component of *l'angoisse*, which he studied
repeatedly (Janet, 1898; 1909; 1919; 1926), starting in 1903 with his work on
psychasthénie (into which category he included all anxiety and panic symptoms)
(Janet, 1919a, pp.220–65).

Féré and 'morbid emotivity'

Féré (1899) published *La Pathologie des Emotions* in 1892. A disciple of Ribot
and collaborator of Binet, he pursued an experimental approach in the study of
emotions and their disorders. Of the twenty-two chapters of his book (covering
all available knowledge on emotions), five are dedicated to 'morbid emotivity'.
By this Féré meant emotivity 'characterised by reactions badly adapted to the
interest of the individual or the species ... [it] presents itself in two forms: 1.
diffuse and permanent morbid emotivity as a pathological character, and 2.
systematic morbid emotivity induced by special conditions always the same for

the same individual' (p.360). Féré's examples of diffuse emotivity exactly correspond to current conceptions of generalised anxiety (what in his time was called pantophobia); likewise, his examples of systematic morbid emotivity refer to phobias (ranging from agoraphobia – which he mentions by name – to specific phobias). Féré believed morbid emotivity to be constitutional, and his view must be regarded as the origin of the idea of *constitution émotive* later on expanded by Dupré (1917).

Brissaud, l'anxiété et l'angoisse

Eduard Brissaud was a neurologist with psychiatric interests (Freeman, 1970). His staunch organic position caused him to break away from Charcot on the issue of the psychogenesis of hysteria. He was equally firm in believing that anguish was not psychological in origin, and that its somatic symptoms resulted from brain stem lesions. Anxiety, on the other hand, was subjective and of cortical origin (Brissaud, 1890, p.410).

Brissaud expressed this view repeatedly. In 1902, he was asked to comment at a meeting of the *Société de Neurologie* on a case of a docker who had anguish without anxiety (*angoisse sans anxiété*), i.e. 'after more than a hundred attacks of severe chest pain, remained philosophical, lived from day to day, and had never developed either sadness (*tristesse*) or panic (*terreur*)' (Souques, 1902). Brissaud re-affirmed his 1890 views that there was a major difference between the two symptoms. Late in 1902, he repeated the performance at the 12th Congress of French Alienists and Neurologists at Grenoble when he confronted Lelanne (1902) and declared: 'Anguish (*l'angoisse*) is a brain stem phenomenon (*phénomène bulbaire*), anxiety is a cortical phenomenon (*phénomène cerebral*): anguish is a physical disorder that expresses itself in a sensation of constriction, of suffocation; anxiety is a psychological disorder that expresses itself in feelings of undefinable insecurity' (Brissaud, 1902). In 1938, Claude and Lévy-Valensi (1938) were still expressing agreement with his view (p.24)! In 1945, in her classical work on *L'Angoisse*, Boutonier (1945)[23] challenged a theory that 'had remained alive up to her time' because 'its clarity and simplicity were more apparent than real' (p.18) and offered an integrated account instead.

Hartenberg, timidité, and social phobia

Social phobia remains a confused construct whose meaning oscillates between avoidance personality disorder and specific social fears. The impression has been given that it was only recognised or defined in 1966 (Liebowitz et al, 1985). This is reinforced by historical accounts showing a gap between the cases purportedly reported by Hippocrates or Burton and the present (Marks, 1969, p.152). This is incorrect as there were two great books on 'Timidity' at the turn of the century. The earliest (*Timidité*) by L. Dugas (1898) (known for his great contribution to the concepts of depersonalisation and déjà vu) is an introspective study, based on the classical psychology tradition. The second, by Paul Hartenberg (1901a) (*Les Timides et la Timidité*) includes much clinical, theoretical and aetiological discussion: indeed, the title of the book alludes to the possible mechanisms involved.

This author specialised in the field of fears and phobias and the same year as his book on social phobias he published another major work on *La Névrose*

D'Angoisse (Hartenberg, 1901). A disciple of Ribot, to whom he paid warm tribute, Hartenberg declared himself a positivist psychologist, interested in behaviour and not in the soul. Like Ribot, he believed in the predominance of the 'affective life' and in the James-Lange theory of emotions. Hartenberg defined timidity as a combination of fear, shame, and embarrassment felt in social situations and which affected psychosocial competence through attacks (*accès*) of fear. From a clinical and experimental perspective, he studied subjective and objective symptoms (including tremor, unsteadiness of gait, dizziness, blushing, etc.). In chapter three of his book he concentrates on the timid personality and their tendency to isolation, misogyny, pessimism, sadness, pride, irritability and suppressed anger. Chapter four is dedicated to the origins, natural history, mechanisms and sub-types of timidity. He distinguished between predisposing (inherited vulnerability), determinant (physical, social or psychological defect – real or imagined), and occasional (learning situations) causes. Chapter five deals with situations in which timidity is phobic and pathological, and Chapter six with treatments which include re-assurance and self-administered behavioural therapies (Hartenberg, 1901a).

Francis Heckel and 'paroxysmal anxiety attacks'

Heckel (1917) was a specialist in nutrition who managed to write one of the great works on *la névrosse de l'angoisse*, particularly on its *formes paroxystiques*, i.e. panic disorder. The book was completed before the Great War started, but only published in 1917. In twelve chapters the author covers issues ranging from history to treatment. The first three chapters are dedicated to *séméiologie* (i.e. clinical presentation) which Heckel divided into paroxysmal and inter-paroxysmal. Then physical signs, mechanisms, and causes are discussed. The paroxysmal states Heckel classified according to the predominance of a particular sign into: cardiovascular, respiratory, digestive, neurological, sensory and secretory or endocrinological. Finally, the association of these states is explored with generalised anxiety, obsessions, phobias, impulsions, and tics.

SUMMARY

Terms and behaviours relating to anxiety were well known before the nineteenth century. After the 1820s, severe forms of anxiety were included with the insanities, but the view remained that anxiety was a form of 'social' stress and a potential *cause* of insanity. In 1867, Morel introduced the view that both subjective and somatic forms of anxiety (together with obsessional disorders) might result from a disorder of the autonomic nervous system.

For the next decades, somatic symptoms were repeatedly considered as separate diseases; for example, typical panic attacks were considered by Krishaber to result from cardiovascular pathology, and by Benedikt from inner ear disease. It was in this medical milieu that the concept of 'agoraphobia' was developed by Benedikt, Westphal, Cordes, and du Saulle. In 1890, Brissaud proposed that generalised anxiety and panic disorder (*angoisse*) were separate symptoms, the one generated in the cortex, the other in the brain stem. For a time, some believed that all the symptoms of anxiety were part of neurasthenia, the new 'disease' that, during the 1880s threatened to engulf most of the neuroses.

In 1895, Freud proposed that 'anxiety neurosis' ought to be separated from neurasthenia and considered as a disease in its own right; and also that phobias and obsessions were different symptoms. In 1902, Hartenberg outlined both the concept of panic disorder (later to be confirmed by Heckel) and also that of social phobia. Soon after, the notion of 'emotive constitution', that had been suggested by Féré, was completed by Dupré.

However, the integrative power of the Freudian view tended to predominate, and all manner of symptoms were brought together under the construct 'anxiety' which by the 1920s was no longer a 'symptom' but had become a full explanation. The view that panic (*angoisse*) was a brain stem disorder managed to last in France up to the Second World War, when Boutonier sounded its death knell.

NOTES

1 By this it is meant here conditions such as the anxiety disorders, vascular neuroses, neurasthenia, obsessive-compulsive disorder and neurotic depression which *were not* included (in name at least) amongst the original 'nervous disorder' of Willis, and which were conceptualised as *neuroses* only during the late nineteenth century.

2 For example Robert Burton (1883) collected many such symptoms in the *Anatomy of Melancholia*.

3 See, for example, Janet's (1919a) work.

4 For example it is inaccurate to claim that 'the word anxiety was hardly used in standard medical and psychological textbooks until the late 1930s. It was a result of Freud's writings about Angst, translated as anxiety' (in Sarbin, 1964).

5 For a good discussion of the etymology involved see López Ibor, 1950.

6 The reviewer was probably Forbes Winslow himself.

7 Zeldin in his historical account of developments in French psychiatry during the middle of the nineteenth century, suggests that 'nervousness' was increasingly recognised as a complaint after the 1850s, and quotes Bouchut in this regard (in Zeldin, 1977, p.833).

8 'Is there a human breast in which this awful word fails to produce an echo? – from the youth who fears to be superseded in the affections of the object of his love, or the parent etc. etc.' (Wigan, 1849).

9 For example, Feuchtersleben's quotation above (1847) illustrates well the use of a 'vascular' model to account for the link between emotion and brain.

10 As in Luys, Meynert, Chaslin, Mairet and many others.

11 As in the work of Jackson and his followers in the Continent such as Ribot and Janet.

12 And in Britain the work of Romanes, Spalding and Morgan.

13 Although both Janet and Freud paid lip service to anatomical explanations, they offered models according to which symptoms resulted from shifts in the level of a putative psychological energy. Both were influenced by Jackson.

14 These observations are likely to have provided the background from which was to emerge the James-Lange theory of emotions (for an account of this theory see pp.295–9 and pp.326–8, Gardiner et al, 1937).

15 It is a pity that the history of the concept of vertigo has been neglected as it

is likely that under its wide umbrella typical cases of anxiety attack were included during the nineteenth century.

16 Leroux (1889) claimed that Lasègue had, *faute de mieux*, included under 'vertigo' the same clinical states that Westphal (1872) (see below) was to call agoraphobia (with *Schwindel* as the central symptom). Lasègue listed his operational criteria: a) somatic symptoms often precede the eruption of acute anxiety, b) the latter is out of proportion to the former, c) the anxiety is overpowering, d) it often has sudden onset and is unprecipitated, and e) once it started it must follow its course.

17 There seems to have been an earlier and typical case: López Ibor (1950), in his excellent historical review, quotes an 1832 paper by Brück in *Huffeland's Journal* reporting the case of a priest who complained of severe vertigo and anxiety as soon as he was outdoors. To feel better, he needed to have a solid top or roof over his head (p.25).

18 A recent French paper on the history of agoraphobia misses the opportunity to study this important problem. For example, it claims that after Legrand de Saulle, agoraphobia 'was forgotten at the beginning of the twentieth century and only retaken in the work of Marks'!! (in Boulenger et al, 1987, p.115).

19 Leguil (1979) quotes Westphal as saying that phobics and obsessives inhabit a borderland (*Grenzgebiet*) between neuroses and psychoses (p.91).

20 'This is a state in which the patient fears everything or nothing, where anxiety, instead of being riveted on one object, floats as in a dream . . .' (in Ribot, 1911, p.214). The best discussion of *panophobie* during this period is to be found in the book by Pitres and Régis (1902) who called it *émotivité diffuse* (see pp.20–34). Devaux and Logre (1917) protested that the term should be 'pantophobic and not panophobic, a word which in good etymology, refers to worshiping the god Pan' (see footnote, p.35).

21 See chapter on history of neurasthenia, this volume.

22 Here Pitres and Régis (1902) were referring to E. Hecker whose 1893 paper is acknowledged by Freud: 'I believed that this conception of the symptoms of the anxiety neurosis had originated with myself until an interesting paper by E. Hecker came into my hands, in which I found the same idea expounded with the most satisfying clearness and completeness. Although Hecker recognises certain symptoms as equivalents or incomplete manifestations of an anxiety attack, he does not separate them from neurasthenia as I propose to do' (in Freud, 1953, p.77). Freud had started thinking about this problem as early as 1983 (in Laplanche and Pontalis, 1973, see p.39). For an excellent treatment of this period see Levin (1978).

23 Juliette Favez-Boutonier was a psychiatrist and psychologist with psychoanalytic interests (Personal Communication by Professor Pierre Pichot, London, September, 1991). Her doctoral thesis in Medicine was on *La Notion d'Ambivalence* (University of Paris, 1938). During the 1960s, and together with Didier Anzieu, Boutonier fought for the independence of clinical psychology from the academic control of philosophy and medicine. This was obtained after the student movement of 1968. She then became director of the *Centre Psychopédagogique Claude-Bernard* (see Parot and Richelle, 1992, pp.255–6). She died in 1994.

REFERENCES

Altschule, M.D. (1976) *The Development of Traditional Psychopathology*, New York, Wiley.

Anonymous (1860) 'Nervousness'. *Journal of Psychological Medicine and Mental Pathology*, 13: 218–33.

Axenfeld, A. (1883) *Traité des Névroses*, 2nd edition, Paris, Baillière.

Bannour, W. (1992) *Jean-Martin Charcot et l'Hystérie*, Paris, Métailié.

Benedikt, M. (1870) 'Über Platzschwindel'. *Allgemeine Wiener Medizinische Zeitung*, 15: 488–90.

Benedikt, M. (1906) *Aus meinem Leben. Erinnerungen und Errterungen*, Wien, Konegen.

Berrios, G.E. (1989) 'Obsessive-Compulsive Disorder: Its Conceptual History in France During the 19th Century'. *Comprehensive Psychiatry*, 30: 283–95.

Bouchut, E. (1860) *De l'État Aigu et Chronique du Névrosisme Appelé Névropathie Aiguë Cérébro-pneumo-gastrique*, Paris, Baillière.

Boulenger, J.P. and Uhde, T.W. (1987) 'Crises aigües d'angoisse et phobies. Aspects historiques et manifestations cliniques du syndrome d'agoraphobie'. *Annales Médico-Psychologiques*, 145: 113–31.

Boutonier, J. (1945) *L'angoisse*, Paris, Presses Universitaires de France.

Brissaud, E. (1890) 'De L'anxiété paroxystique'. *Semaine Médicale*, 9, pp.410–11.

Brissaud, E. (1902) 'Compte Rendu du Xlle Congrès des Médecins Aliénists et Neurologistes'. *Revue Neurologique*, 2: 762–3.

Bucknill, J.C. and Tuke, D.H. (1858) *A Manual of Psychological Medicine*, London, John Churchill.

Burton, R. (1883) *The Anatomy of Melancholy*, London, Chaton and Windus (first edition 1620).

Capgras, J.M.J. (1903) 'Contribution a l'étude de la névrose d'angoisse'. *Annales Médico-Psychologiques*, 61: 397–404.

Clarke, E. and Jacyna, L.S. (1987) *Nineteenth Century Origins of Neuroscientific Concepts*, Berkeley, University of California Press.

Claude, H. and Lévy-Valensi, J. (1938) *Les États Anxieux*, Paris, Maloine.

Cordes, E. (1872) 'Die Platzangst (Agoraphobie), Symptom einer Erschöpfungsparese'. *Archiv für Psychiatrie und Nervenkrankheiten*, 3: 521–74.

Cottereau, M.J. (1975) 'Les nevroses I. Historique des nevroses'. *La Revue de Medicine*, 13: 903–10.

Cullen, W. (1803) *Synopsis nosologiæ methodicæ*, Sixth edition, Edinburgh, W Creech.

Dagonet, H. (1894) *Traité des Maladies Mentales*, Paris, Baillière.

Dechambre, A. (1889) 'Maurice Krishaber'. In Dechambre, A. and Lereboullet, L. (eds.) *Dictionnaire Encyclopédique des Sciences Médicales*, Paris, Masson, p.777.

Dejerine, J. and Gauckler, E. (1911) *Les Manifestations fonctionnelles des Psychonévroses. Leur Traitement par la Psychotherapie*, Paris, Masson.

Devaux and Logre (1917) *Les Anxious. Étude Clinique*, Paris, Masson.

Drinka, G.F. (1984) *The Birth of Neurosis*, New York, Simon and Schuster.

Dubois (no initial) (1905) *Les Psychonévroses et leur Traitement Moral*, Paris, Masson.

Dugas, M. (1898) *Timidité*, Paris, Alcan.

Duprat, G.L. (1899) *L'Instabilité Mentale*, Paris, Alcan.

Dupré, E. (1917) Préface. In Devaux and Logre, *Les Anxieux. Étude Clinique*, Paris, Masson.

Dupré, E. (1919) *Les Désquilibres Constitutionnels du Système Nerveux*, Paris, Baillière.

Errera, P. (1962) 'Some historical aspects of the concept phobia'. *Psychiatric Quarterly*, 36: 325–36.

Ey, H. (1950) 'Anxiété morbide. Etude No15'. In *Etudes Psychiatriques. Aspects sémiologiques*, Paris, Desclée de Brouwer, pp.379–426.

Féré, Ch. (1899) *The Pathology of Emotions*, (rendered into English by R. Park), London, The University Press.

Feuchtersleben, E. von (1847) *The Principles of Medical Psychology*, (translated by Lloyd, H.E. and Babington, B.G.), London, Sydenham Society.

Fouks, L., Potiron, G. and Moukalou, R. (1986) 'L'angoisse et l'anxiété dans la psychopathologie de Pierre Janet'. *Annales Médico-Psychologiques*, 144: 461–71.

Freeman, W. (1970) 'Eduard Brissaud (1852–1909)'. In Haymaker, W. and Schiller, F. (eds.) *The Founders of Neurology*, Springfield, Thomas, pp.417–20.

Freud, S. (1953) 'The justification for detaching from neurasthenia a particular syndrome: the anxiety neurosis'. In *Collected Papers*, vol.1, London, The Hogarth Press, pp.76–106 (first published: 1894).

Freud, S. (1953a) 'A reply to criticisms on the anxiety neurosis'. In *Collected Papers*, vol.1, London, The Hogarth Press, pp.107–27 (First Published: 1895).

Gardiner, H.M., Metcalf, R.C. and Beebe-Center, J.G. (1937) *Feeling and Emotion. A History of Theories*, New York, American Book Company.

Genil Perrin, G. (1913) *L'Idée de Dégénérescence in Médicine Mentale*, Paris, Leclerc.

Georget, E.J. (1820) *De la Folie. Considérations sur cette Maladie: son siége et ses symptômes*, Paris, Crevot.

Grasset, J. (1901) *Les Maladies de l'Orientation et de l'Équilibre*, Paris, Alcan.

Griesinger, W. (1861) *Die Pathologie und Therapie der psychischen Krankheiten für Aerzte und Studirende*, Stuttgart, Adolph Krabbe.

Griesinger, W. (1867) *Mental Pathology and Therapeutics*, London, The New Sydenham Society.

Gros, M. (1885) 'Contribution a l'étude de l'agoraphobie (peur des espaces)'. *Annales Médico-Psychologiques*, 43: 394–407.

Guillespie, R.D. (1928) 'Hypochondria'. *Guy's Hospital Reports*, 78: 408–60.

Guislain, J. (1852) *Leçons orales sur les Phrénopathies*, vol.2, Gand, L. Hebbelynck.

Haltenhof, (1887) 'Vertige Paralysant'. *Bulletin de L'Academie de Médicine*, 51: 334–51.

Hartenberg, P. (1901) 'Le névrose d'angoisse'. *Revue de Médicine*, 21: 464–84; 612–21; 678–99.

Hartenberg, P. (1901a) *Les Timides et la Timidité*, Paris, Alcan.

Heckel, F. (1917) *La Névrose d'Angoisse. Et les Etats d'Emotivité anxieuse*, Paris, Masson.

Houzeau, J.C. (1972) *Etudes sur les Facultés Mentales des Animaux Comparées a Celles de l'Homme*, Paris, Hachette.

Janet, P. (1898) *Névroses et Idées Fixes*, 2 vols., Paris, Alcan.

Janet, P. (1909) *Les Névroses*, Paris, Flammarion.

Janet, P. (1919) *Les Médications Psychologiques*, 3 vols., Paris, Alcan.

Janet, P. (1919a) *Les Obsessions et la Psychasthénie*, third edition, Paris, Alcan (First Edition, 1903).

Janet, P. (1926) *De L'Angoisse a L'Extase*, 2 vols., Paris, Alcan.

Jolivet, R. (1950) *Introducción a Kierkegaard*, Madrid, Gredos.

Kenyon, F.K. (1965) 'Hypochondriasis: a survey of some historical, clinical and social aspects'. *British Journal Medical Psychology*, 38: 117–33.

Kirkegaard, S. (1959) *El concepto de la angustia*, Madrid, Espasa Calpe.

Knapp, T.J. and Schumacher, M.T. (1988) *Westphal's Die Agoraphobie*, Lanham, University Press of America.

Krishaber, M. (1873) 'Cérébro-cardiaque (Névropathie)'. In Dechambre, A. and Lereboullet, L. (eds.) *Dictionnaire Encyclopédique des Sciences Médicales*, Paris, Masson, pp.100–42.

Kuch, K. and Swinson, R.P. (1992) 'Agoraphobia: what Westphal really said'. *Canadian Journal of Psychiatry*, 37: 133–6.

Lalanne, (1902) 'Des États Anxieux dans les Maladies Mentales'. *Revue Neurologique*, 2: 755–62.

Landré-Beauvais, A.J. (1813) *Sémiotique ou Traité des Signes des Maladies*, second edition, Paris, Brosson.

Laplanche, J. and Pontalis, J.B. (1973) *The Language of Psychoanalysis*, London, the Hogarth Press.

Legrand du Saulle, M. (1876) 'De la peur des espaces (agoraphobie des Allemands)'. *Annales Médico-Psychologiques*, 34: 405–33.

Leguil, F. (1979) 'La phobie avant Freud'. *Ornicar?* 17: 88–105.

Leroux (1889) 'Vertige'. In Dechambre, A. and Lereboullet, L. (eds.) *Dictionnaire Encyclopédique des Sciences Médicales*, Paris, Masson, pp.146–88.

Levin, K. (1978) *Freud's Early Psychology of the Neuroses. A Historical Perspective*, Sussex, The Harvester Press.

Levy, P.E. (1917) *Neurasthénie et Névroses. Leur Guérison définitive en cure libre*, Paris, Alcan.

Lewis, A. (1967) 'Problems presented by the ambiguous word "anxiety" as used in psychopathology'. *The Israel Annals of Psychiatry and Related Disciplines*, 5: 105–21.

Liebowitz, M.R., Gorman, J.M., Fier, A.J. and Kein, D. (1985) 'Social Phobia'. *Archives of General Psychiatry*, 42: 729–36.

Littré, E. and Robin, Ch. (1858) *Dictionnaire de Médicine*, Paris, Baillière.

López Ibor, J.J. (1950) *La Angustia Vital*, Madrid, Paz Montalvo, pp.19–33.

López Piñero, J.M. (1983) *Historical Origins of the Concept of Neurosis*, (translated by D. Berrios), Cambridge, Cambridge University Press.

López Piñero, J.M. and Morales Meseguer, J.M. (1970) *Neurosis y psicoterapia*, Madrid, Espasa Calpe.

Marks, I.M. (1969) *Fears and Phobias*, London, Heineman.

May, R. (1968) 'Fundamentos históricos de las modernas teorías de la ansiedad'. In May, R. (ed.) *La Angustia Normal y Patológica*, Paidós, Buenos Aires, pp.7–24.

McCarty, V.A. (1981) ' "Psychological Fragments". Kirkegaard's religious psychology'. In Smith, J.H. (ed.) *Kirkegaard's Truth: The Disclosure of the Self*, New York, Yale University Press, pp.235–65.

Meister, R. (1980) *Hypochondria*, New York, Tapingler.

Michéa, F. (1843) 'Du siége, de la nature intime, des symptomes et du diagnostic de l'hypocondrie'. *Mémoires de l'Académie Royale de Médicine*, 2: 573–654.

Millet, J. (1884) 'Des Vertiges chez les aliénés'. *Annales Médico-Psychologiques*, 42: 38–51; 204–19.

Morel, B.A. (1860) *Traité des Maladies Mentales*, Paris, Masson.

Morel, B. (1866) 'Du délire émotif. Névrose du système nerveux ganglionnaire viscéral'. *Archives Générales de Médecine*, 7: 385–402; 530–51; 700–7.

Oppenheim, J. (1991) *Shattered Nerves*, Oxford, Oxford University Press.

Owen, A.R.G. (1971) *Hysteria, Hypnosis and Healing. The Work of J.M. Charcot*, London, Dobson.

Parot, F. and Richelle, M. (1992) *Psychologues de la Langue Française*, Paris, Presses Universitaires de France.

Pinel, Ph. (1818) *Nosographie Philosophique ou la Méthode de l'Analyse Applique à la Medicine*, sixth edition, vol.1, Paris, Brosson.

Pitres, A. and Régis, E. (1902) *Les Obsessions et les Impulsions*, Paris, Doin.

Place, J.L. (1986) 'L'Hypocondrie: Éloge de Dubois d'Amiens'. *L'Evolution Psychiatrique*, 51: 567–86.

Prichard, J.C. (1835) *A Treatise on Insanity and Other Disorders Affecting the Mind*, London, Sherwood, Gilbert and Piper.

Raymond, F. (1911) 'Névroses et psycho-névroses'. In Marie, A. (ed.) *Traité International de Psychologie Pathologique*, vol.2, Paris, Alcan, pp.1–59.

Ribot, Th. (1911) *The Psychology of Emotions*, 2nd edition, London, Walter Scott, (First Edition: 1896).

Roccatagliata, G. (1990) *Isteria*, Roma, II Pensiero Scientifico.

Rosenberg, C.E. (1989) 'Body and mind in nineteenth century medicine: some clinical origins of the neurosis construct'. *Bulletin of the History of Medicine*, 63: 185–97.

Rouart, J. (1950) 'Janet and Jackson'. *L'Evolution Psychiatrique*, 25: 485–501.

Sarbin, T. (1968) 'Ontology recapitulates philology: the mythic nature of anxiety'. *American Psychologist*, 23: 411–8.

Sarbin, T. (1964) 'Anxiety: Reification of a Metaphor'. *Archives of General Psychiatry*, 10: 630–8.

Sauri, J.J. (ed.) (1979) *Las Fobias*, Buenos Aires, Ediciones Nueva Vision.

Souques, (no initial) (1902) 'Angoisse sans anxiété'. *Revue Neurologique*, 2: 1176.

Thomas, A. (1913) *Psicoterapia*, Barcelona, Salvat.

Trillat, E. (1986) *Histoire de l'Hystérie*, Paris, Seghers.

Veith, I. (1965) *Hysteria. The History of a Disease*, Chicago, University of Chicago Press.

Weill, E. (1886) *Des Vertiges*, Paris, Baillière.

Westphal, C. (1872) 'Die Agoraphobie. Eine neuropathische Erscheinung'. *Archiv für Psychiatrie und Nervenkrankheiten*, 3: 138–61.

Westphal, C. (1872) 'Nachtrag zu dem Aufsatze "Über Agoraphobie" '. *Archiv für Psychiatrie und Nervenkrankheiten*, 3:219–21.

Wigan, A. (1849) 'The Unpublished MSS of the late Alfred Wigan MD'. *The*

Journal of Psychological Medicine and Mental Pathology, 2: 497–513.

Zal, M. (1988) 'From anxiety to panic disorder: a historical perspective'. *Psychiatric Annals*, 18: 367–71.

Zeldin, Th. (1977) *France 1848–1945. Volume 2: Intellect, Taste and Anxiety*, Oxford, Clarendon Press.

Chapter 21

Anxiety Disorders

Social Section
MICHAEL J CLARK

INTRODUCTION

To a greater or lesser extent, all 'clinical' pictures are highly selective abstractions from pre-existing social, psychological and cultural actualities, and the modern clinical syndromes specially characterized by anxiety and panic are no exception. Though anxiety neuroses and panic disorders are comparative newcomers to clinical-psychiatric nosologies, anxiety and panic have long figured prominently in both general-historical and other quasi-factual narratives and in fiction, while even within the much narrower field of psychological medicine, anxiety and panic routinely formed part of the accepted symptomatology of a variety of common conditions, including melancholia, hypochondriasis, neurasthenia and obsessional disorders, long before Freud or anyone else proposed the creation of distinct 'anxiety neuroses' or 'panic disorders' (Jackson, 1986; Oppenheim, 1991). Ever since Biblical times, eye-witness and other quasi-documentary accounts of the psychological effects of war, plague and famine (such as Boccaccio's description in the Introduction to *The Decameron* of the reaction of the Florentines to the Black Death in 1347, or Defoe's *Journal of the Plague Year* (1721)) had contained many striking descriptions of acute anxiety spilling over into panic, and while for the most part such reactions, however bizarre, were comparatively short-lived and without significant effects, occasionally (as, for example, in the French *Grande Peur* of June–July 1789) such events were to have far-reaching consequences (Lefebvre, 1932/1970/1973). In many of these earlier episodes, however, the most striking features were not so much the often bizarre, but seldom overtly psychotic, individual reactions to prolonged stress or fear of imminent death described, for example, by Boccaccio and Defoe, as the often violent outbreaks of mass hysteria and panic in the form of epidemic dancing manias, tarantism, self-flagellation and the like which frequently accompanied major religious, political, economic and social upheavals in mediaeval and early-modern Europe (Rosen, 1962). Though a constant and pervasive aspect of everyday life for the vast majority in an era of almost incessant warfare, plague, and famine, and though already the subject of much medico-moral commentary, individual anxieties did not have the same degree of prominence or attract the same kind of concern that they were to enjoy in the modern era. Anxiety remained as much a matter for the theologian and moralist as for the physician, and some of its most characteristic expressions may be found in the arts and literature of the period rather than in medicine (Huizinga, 1919/1924/1953, Chs.1, 2).

Beginning, however, in the eighteenth century, and coinciding with the rise of the so-called 'nervous complaints', especially hypochondriasis and hysteria, acute and chronic anxiety began to play an increasingly prominent part in the burgeoning symptomatology of both 'nervous' and mental disorders, while individual anxieties, which had for so long been primarily the concern of confessors and moral and pastoral theologians, increasingly came to be looked upon as forming part of the 'psychological' physician's responsibilities. With the coming of industrialisation and the rise of strong national state governments, many of the traditional causes of acute anxiety and panic began to recede, but in the view of many observers the effect of the rise of industrial society was to create new ambitions and passions and multiply many of the lesser and more insidious causes of individual anxiety in such a way that, as Theodore Zeldin has observed with reference to late-nineteenth and early-twentieth-century France, the 'age of progress' might equally well be termed 'the age of fear' – or, rather, an 'age of fear' might be said to have given way to an 'age of anxiety' (Zeldin, 1977/81, p.59). Zeldin goes on to suggest that 'it may be that as [more] serious [and immediate] dangers to life gradually diminished, men [and women] had more leisure to [worry] about less immediate ones' (Zeldin, 1977/81, p. 61). Be that as it may, anxiety certainly acquired a much higher medical, social and cultural profile during this period. From the 1850s and '60s onwards, neuro-logists, psychiatrists and certifying surgeons in every major industrializing nation were forced to contend with a growing number of cases of 'railway spine' and 'traumatic neurasthenia', in which the anxious expectation of incapacity following some trifling or imaginary traumatic injury proved self-fulfilling even in the absence of any physical damage (Fischer-Homberger, 1975; Schivelbusch, 1977/1986; Trimble, 1981); while during the decades prior to the publication of Freud and Breuer's *Studies in Hysteria* (1895), neurologists such as J.M. Charcot were far more apt to ascribe hysteria and hypochondriasis, especially in men, to domestic worries, economic anxieties and stress at work than to sexual neuroses of any kind (Micale, 1991). Around the turn of the century, eminent neurologists and psychiatrists such as George M. Beard, Sigmund Freud and Pierre Janet not only ascribed leading roles to anxiety in the production of neurasthenia, 'anxiety neuroses' and 'psychasthenia'; they and their respective disease concepts came to be seen as archetypically representative of their respective cultures and societies, and their patients' ills as symbolic, or symp-tomatic, of those of society at large (Rosenberg, 1962/1978; Zeldin, 1977/81). In the early decades of the new century, the wartime condition of 'shell-shock' was to undergo a similar process of cultural transformation, as the haunted, anxiety-ridden figure of the shell-shocked soldier became a powerful symbol of the shattered and exhausted state of Western civilization as a whole in the aftermath of the First World War (Showalter, 1985/87, Ch.7). Anxiety and panic are thus woven into the fabric of history and culture, and though their clinical 'recognition' and elevation into distinct psychiatric 'illnesses' or syndromes is itself historically significant, any historical survey whose terms of reference are limited to the classic 'anxiety neuroses' and 'panic disorders' is in danger of passing over much that is of interest and importance for the history of psychiatry in the broadest sense, as well as for the history of society and culture.

ANXIETY AND PANIC – SOME CLINICAL AND HISTORICAL DISTINCTIONS

Though bracketed together for the purposes of this chapter, and, indeed, in up-to-date manuals of psychiatric diagnosis such as DSM-III-R (1989), anxiety and panic in fact differ markedly in many important respects, and their association has been very variable and contingent from both a clinical and historical standpoint. Clinically speaking, in general, both anxiety and panic may form part of the overall symptomatology of major affective disorders such as depression and phobias, or they may form the principal features of distinct clinical syndromes – the so-called 'anxiety neuroses' and 'panic disorders'. Depending on the individual case, anxiety states may be mild or severe, acute or chronic; they may precede or be punctuated by more severe but relatively short-lived panic attacks, or they may become more or less fixed, varying in intensity but more or less indefinite in duration. Both anxiety and panic may, in a certain sense, be regarded as 'contagious', but whereas anxiety tends to communicate itself only very gradually and within a limited range, when panic takes hold it tends to spread very rapidly and affect large numbers of people in a short time. Both in the individual and *en masse*, panic tends to be much more severe, and even more 'primitive' in its manifestations than most forms of anxiety. But whereas panic tends abruptly to subside, and often leaves little or no long-term traces, anxiety tends to be much more insidious, long-lasting and far-reaching in its effects. Thus for all their close modern clinical association, anxiety and panic represent two very different kinds of experience, which the history of clinical psychiatry must take full account of if the origins and development of the modern clinical syndromes of 'anxiety neurosis' and 'panic disorders' are to be seen in their true perspective.

A BRIEF HISTORY OF ANXIETY AS A DISTINCT NEUROSIS

According to one recent survey, 'anxiety has stalked through the last 100 years [of medical history] . . . under a whole rogues' gallery of [clinical-nosological] aliases', many of them more somatic than psychological, including 'irritable heart', DaCosta's syndrome, 'soldier's heart', cardiac neurosis, 'effort syndrome' and panic disorder (Nemiah, 1985, p.883). But the modern elevation of anxiety from a ubiquitous neurotic symptom into a distinct 'neurosis' or syndrome in its own right may effectively be dated from the publication in 1895 of Freud's paper 'On the Grounds for Detaching a Particular Syndrome from Neurasthenia under the Description "Anxiety Neurosis" ' (Freud, ed. Strachey, 1894–95/1962) – though Freud himself generously acknowledged a similar suggestion made by Hecker two years earlier (Freud, ed. Strachey, 1894–95/1962, p.91; Hecker, 1893). In his paper, Freud described a special clinical condition in which severe and persistent 'anxious expectation' or 'neurotic anxiety' was found in conjunction with a complex variety of physical symptoms, including cardiac and respiratory disturbances, tremors, sweating, shivering, auditory hyperaesthesia, paraesthesia, night terrors, sleeplessness and general irritability, and argued strongly on both clinical and aetiological grounds for separating this syndrome off from neurasthenia, on the one hand, and hysteria, on the other. The association of acute anxiety with symptoms of cardiac dysfunction and general nervous irritability was already relatively familiar from existing clinical descriptions of the psychosomatic ailments of combat soldiers and sufferers from neurasthenia, but Freud broke new ground in attributing his 'anxiety neurosis' to 'a set of *noxae* and influences from sexual life', notably sexual frustration and incomplete gratification due as much to the practice of *coitus interruptus* and *coitus reservatus* as to actual sexual abstinence (Freud, ed. Strachey, 1894–95/1962, pp.99–106). Freud's views on the causes of anxiety and its role in the production of the neuroses subsequently underwent several important changes, in the course of which he was to distinguish between 'primary' or traumatic and secondary or 'signal' anxiety and eventually came to regard anxiety less as a product and more as a principal cause of mental repression (Freud, ed. Strachey, 1916–17/1963; idem, 1926/1959; Meares, 1980). As is well known, Freud was eventually forced to abandon his earlier belief in the specifically sexual aetiology of anxiety neurosis (Meares, 1980, pp.42–3; Nemiah, 1985, pp.884–5). But he continued to regard the problem of anxiety as 'a riddle whose solution would . . . throw a flood of light on our whole mental existence' (Freud, ed. Strachey, 1916–17/1963, p.393), and in purely clinical terms his conception of anxiety neurosis remained largely unaltered. Even today, his description of the syndrome remains a standard reference-point for clinicians, and its influence may still clearly be discerned in the description of 'Anxiety Disorders' (or 'Anxiety Phobic Neuroses') with 'Panic Attacks' given in DSM-III-R (1989), not least in the attribution of the condition mainly to intra-psychic conflicts and in the check-list of physical symptoms considered diagnostic of 'Panic Attacks'.

Freud's belief that '. . . the problem of anxiety is a nodal point at which the most varied and important psychological problems converge' (Freud, ed. Strachey, 1916–17/1963, p.393) has attracted widespread support from both psychiatrists and psychoanalysts, many of whom have greatly improved upon Freud's own somewhat elementary analysis of the varieties of anxiety. But seen in a wider perspective, the concept of a distinct 'anxiety neurosis' or group of 'anxiety disorders' has enjoyed very mixed fortunes during the past few decades. As Aubrey Lewis and other, more recent, commentators have noted, while 'Anxiety' has steadily grown in popularity as an explicit focus of clinical-psychiatric and psychoanalytic interest, especially since the Second World War, this interest has not been associated with growing acceptance of a distinct 'anxiety neurosis' but rather with a growing awareness of the clinical importance of anxiety as a symptom across virtually the whole range of neurotic illnesses (Lewis, 1967/1980). In particular, anxiety has become more and more closely associated with depression, and the very large degree of overlap between the diagnosis of anxiety disorders and that of both major and minor depressions revealed by several major clinical and epidemiological studies has increasingly cast doubt upon the validity of the separation of anxiety and panic disorders from depression (Montgomery, 1990). Indeed, whereas DSM-III-R seems to imply a neat separation of anxiety disorders and panic attacks from depression, the even more recent ICD-10 (1990) includes a 'Mixed Anxiety Depression Syndrome', intended more closely to reflect the clinical experience of doctors working in primary care as opposed to specialist psychiatric hospital services. Moreover, differences in diagnostic practice between Britain, Europe and North America are becoming increasingly apparent with respect to anxiety and panic disorders, as with many other psychiatric diagnoses. Thus, according to Montgomery (1990, pp.26–7), many British and European clinicians still regard the diagnostic status of panic disorder with suspicion and though frequently employed in the U.S. since its introduction into DSM-III in 1980, it has yet to gain widespread acceptance on this side of the Atlantic Ocean. Undoubtedly, many psychoanalytically-minded psychiatrists would agree with Freud that '. . . the problem of anxiety occupies a [central] place in the . . . psychology of the neuroses' (Freud, ed. Strachey, 1916–17/1963, p.411). But the very ubiquity of anxiety as a symptom and the aetiological significance frequently ascribed to it make it difficult to do justice to the full complexity of its role in the context of just one or two distinct clinical conditions, while for many philosophers, psychologists and creative writers, as well as psychiatrists and psychoanalysts, it has become increasingly difficult to distinguish the role of anxiety in the psychopathology of the neuroses from its role in the psychopathology of everyday life.

'NORMAL' AND 'ABNORMAL' ANXIETY IN HISTORY

In order for any physical or mental state to be recognised and classified as an 'illness', or at least as having some clinical significance, it must not only be observed, described and delineated by some medical observer, but more or less consistently associated with some definite symptom-complex or pathology in a system of classification of diseases. But the recognition and delineation of anxiety and panic disorders and their incorporation into standard classifications of mental diseases required more than just the existence of an organized medical profession and psychiatric specialty and the presence of free-floating symptomatologies waiting to be appropriated and classified. It required the basic conditions of existence of at least a portion of humanity to change in such a way that, relative to the norms and expectations of that group, anxiety and panic no longer appeared as more or less continuous or recurrent features of common life, but rather as exceptional and to some extent avoidable disturbances to individual mental health and well-being.

In pre-modern and even early-modern times, anxiety, whether about crop failures and famine, epidemic disease, personal security, the threat of war or the end of the world, was a continual and well-nigh universal condition of existence for the mass of mankind, and panic was a frequent occurrence in societies continually at the mercy of war, pestilence and famine. Only in the modern industrial era, and especially during the past century, have anxiety (and, indeed, panic) become more exceptional, more individualized, and even then only for the populations of a few industrialized countries living under especially favourable circumstances for limited periods. Yet this very limited and highly contingent improvement in living standards and conditions for a small minority of mankind, and the greatly enhanced expectations which accompanied them, have been crucial for the recognition of anxiety and panic disorders as distinct clinical conditions. Morbid anxiety had long been regarded as one of the commonest features of melancholia (Macdonald, 1981), but not until society had grown accustomed to significant and lasting improvements in personal well-being, health and security could anxiety and panic be identified and treated as *illnesses*, as conditions which detracted from the maximum level of happiness attainable by individuals as a right. This is not to say that sensitive men and women in earlier times did not often experience intense, morbid anxiety in much the same way and for similar reasons as people during the last 150–200 years – only that, for anxiety and panic to be regarded as distinct clinical conditions or 'syndromes', the general level of 'background' anxiety had to be drastically reduced before such *individual* problems could take on any special clinical significance.

However, even as living standards have become more comfortable and stable, and life expectancy has improved for the bulk of the population of the 'developed' world, so modern man has shown great ingenuity in discovering new, and apparently compelling, causes of anxiety to replace those which 'Progress' has largely or wholly eliminated. Thus, although the immediate threat of poverty and destitution may have receded, even in the midst of affluence the growth of snobbery and pressures to 'keep up appearances' or, more commonly, to increase consumption standards in accordance with one's social status or ambitions have given rise to much anxiety, while the accelerating pace of technical change and the cyclical and highly volatile pattern of economic growth under capitalism has made structural, as well as cyclical, unemployment a recurrent nightmare for much of the work-force. Again, while modern medical science has undoubtedly made great strides towards the elimination, or at least the containment, of major epidemic diseases, the 'discovery' of new and often frightening diseases such as AIDS or Legionnaires' Disease and of many hitherto undreamt-of pathogenic agents such as retroviruses and radon gas, together with the increased availability of diagnostic tests and screening, and the identification of 'risk factors' for many diseases, has simultaneously heightened legitimate public concern with health matters and given many persons with hypochondriac tendencies additional reasons to feel anxious for their health. Finally, the growth of personal affluence and improvements in health and diet, together with increasing individualism, has greatly increased the importance placed upon personal attractiveness as a desirable quality in both men and women, with the result that very many people, especially women, have become desperately anxious about relatively minor, or even imaginary, physical defects such as excess body weight, body odour, hair loss, or breast size and shape, which in previous eras would scarcely have been noticed, much less have given rise to any acute anxiety. Thus, while eliminating or greatly reducing in strength many of the old, global causes of anxiety, modern industrial society has simultaneously tended to aggravate or add to many of the lesser and more partial causes of anxiety, with the result that while the general level of 'background' anxiety has been significantly reduced, at least by comparison with previous eras, doctors are still having to contend with a situation in which, as one psychiatrist has recently put it, 'Patients who are suffering from a variety of complaints loosely grouped under the heading of anxiety disorders make up a large part of the [overall] care load of the general practitioner' (Montgomery, 1990, p.23).

But this apparent proliferation of the lesser forms of anxiety has not been without benefit for society as a whole. Indeed, anxiety – whether about one's health, job security, consumption standards, personal attractiveness, sexual performance, level of cultural awareness or social standing – has become one of the principal economic motors of Western-style capitalist societies, creating new, unsatisfied consumer wants and 'needs' at each successive level of affluence during economic upswings, and disciplining labour forces with the fear of unemployment, homelessness and poverty during downswings. Thus, while 'pathological' or 'morbid anxiety', ascribed mainly to intra-psychic conflicts, has come to be regarded as one of the most ubiquitous features both of depression and of neurotic illness, 'normal' anxiety, the fruit of individual reactions to prevailing social and economic conditions, norms and values, has become one of the principal engines of economic progress and one of the most powerful forces making for economic discipline and social cohesion in the otherwise highly volatile conditions of modern industrial societies. Against this background, 'morbid' anxiety or 'anxiety neuroses' may perhaps best be understood not as a distinct pathological entity foreign to everyday experience, but rather as a kind of developmental disorder, the result of impaired or imperfect development of the individual's capacity to respond positively to the stimulus of 'normal' anxiety, – though whether this should in turn be regarded as a stress-related 'illness', a form of malingering or an unconscious gesture of revolt is, of course, open to debate.

FROM THE 'AGE OF ANXIETY' TO AN ERA OF PANIC?

As for 'Panic', though, the matter is rather different. For the most part, the history of anxiety – even the history of the so-called 'anxiety neuroses' or 'disorders' – is indeed one of *normality*, of the way in which things ordinarily go on relative to the nature and extent of the vicissitudes to which a particular age or society is accustomed. By contrast, though, the history of panic is essentially one of *disaster and catastrophe*, of the sudden, complete breakdown and collapse of individuals and even whole societies in the face of extraordinary and overwhelming pressures. As the historical record of many advanced industrial nations during the past 200 years clearly shows, not only individuals but whole societies and cultures may learn to live with more or less permanently high anxiety levels, and still for the most part function effectively. But panic, whether at the individual or the collective level, is quite incompatible with normal functioning, and must speedily be checked or overcome, if it is not to endanger the affected individual or society's very existence. In the special circumstances of warfare, panic, especially in the form of desertion or refusal to fight, may seem a comprehensible and even rational response to the intolerable stress of combat, the imminent prospect of violent death or the shock of defeat. Yet however understandable such reactions may be, they have normally been regarded as grave derelictions of duty properly subject to collective moral censure and exemplary punishment, rather than as deserving of sympathetic medical attention. On the face of it, the twentieth century has seen a notable relaxation of this attitude, insofar as 'shell-shock' and, more recently, Post-Traumatic Stress Disorder (PTSD) have for the first time been recognised as 'legitimate' psychiatric 'illnesses' requiring urgent and often sustained medical attention, rather than merely being regarded as forms of cowardice (Stone, 1985; Merskey, 1991). But the practice of military psychiatry, whether in the front line or at the base hospital, has always been concerned as much with preserving or restoring *morale* as with the restoration of mental health, and the 'medicalization' of the 'war neuroses' may thus, at least in part, be seen as a continuation of military discipline by other means – as an attempt to check the growth of anxiety and panic in individual soldiers and prevent their spread throughout the ranks by means other than the court-martial and the firing squad. Given the special importance of panic control in warfare, it is hardly surprising that military psychiatry should have been in the forefront of attempts to medicalize panic reactions; but even in the absence of such incentives, broadly similar techniques of psychotherapy and behaviour modification have increasingly been employed in civilian practice to treat agoraphobia and other 'peacetime' forms of panic disorder. In modern times, at least, the medical history of panic has thus been very largely a history of measures taken to prevent or control the spread of panic, rather than a history of 'Panic' itself.

With its stereotypical manifestations and apparent regression to more 'primitive' ways of reacting and behaving, panic often seems to belong more to the sphere of natural than to that of human history. But it would be wrong to dismiss panic as a transient, albeit recurrent, psychopathological aberration of no serious importance in the historical process. Even if panic can scarcely be said to have a history in the same sense or to the same extent as anxiety, the causes of panic – or rather, the significance which society has ascribed to them – have varied considerably according to time and place, while particular instances of widespread panic, such as the *Grande Peur* in the French countryside in June–July 1789, or the reaction of many Americans to Orson Welles' 'War of the Worlds' radio broadcast in October 1938, undoubtedly shed much light upon the fears, terrors, conditions of existence and modes of cultural transmission characteristic of the societies in which they occur. Nor does the history of panic necessarily belong entirely to the past. While in the developed world, at least, the presence of strong national defence forces and public order machinery, effective public health systems and relatively productive and well-managed economies have normally sufficed to prevent or at least contain more than very localized instances of panic, more widespread outbreaks have occurred from time to time in recent years – for example, during the Three Mile Island emergency in 1979, the Gulf War of 1991 and, most recently, during the Los Angeles riots – and nothing in contemporary socio-economic and political conditions suggests that such outbreaks are any less likely to occur in future. In 1947, W.H. Auden aptly dubbed the era of totalitarian dictatorships, nuclear deterrence, Cold War, and economic boom and slump, 'The Age of Anxiety' (Auden, 1947/1976). In an era of collapsing superpowers, nuclear proliferation, reawakened national and religious conflicts, global warming, over-population and economic stagnation or worse, is the 'Age of Anxiety' about to give way to an era of panic?

REFERENCES

This essay owes a great deal to the encouragement and advice of both editors. Thanks are also due to the staffs of the Wellcome Institute and British Medical Association Libraries for help in locating sources, and to Mrs. Marie Williams and Miss Samantha Anderson (Wellcome Trust) for help in preparing this manuscript.

Auden, W.H. (1947/1976) 'The Age of Anxiety (1944–46)' [first published 1947]. In Mendelson, E. (ed.) *Collected Poems*, Pt.IX, London, Faber and Faber.

DSM-III-R (1989) *Diagnostic and Statistical Manual of Mental Disorders* (3rd. Revised Edition), New York, American Psychiatric Press for the American Psychiatric Association.

Fischer-Homberger, E. (1975) *Die Traumatische Neurose: Vom somatischen zum sozialen Leiden*, Berne, Stuttgart and Vienna, Verlag Hans Huber.

Freud, S. (1894–95/1962) 'On the Grounds for Detaching a Particular Syndrome from Neurasthenia under the Description "Anxiety Neurosis" ' (*Uber die Berechtigung, von der Neurasthenie einen Bestimmten Symptomen-Komplex als 'Angst-neurose' Abzutrennen*). In Strachey, J. and Freud, A. (eds.) *The Standard Edition of the Complete Psychological Works of Sigmund Freud*, vol.III, London, Hogarth Press and the Institute of Psychoanalysis, pp.87–115. First published in *Neurologischen Zentralblatt* 14, No.2 (January 1895), 50–66.

Freud, S. (1916–17/1963) *Introductory Lectures on Psychoanalysis*, Pt.III, 'General Theory of the Neuroses', Lecture XXV. In Strachey, J. and Freud, A. (eds.) *The Standard Edition of the Complete Psychological Works of Sigmund Freud*, vol.XVI, London, Hogarth Press and the Institute of Psychoanalysis, pp.392–411.

Freud, S. (1926/1959) *Inhibitions, Symptoms and Anxiety*. In Strachey, J. and Freud, A. (eds.) *The Standard Edition of the Complete Psychological Works of Sigmund Freud*, vol.XX, London, Hogarth Press and the Institute of Psychoanalysis, pp.87–174.

Freud, S. and Breuer, J. (1895) *Studies in Hysteria* (*Studien über Hysterie*), Leipzig and Vienna, Verlag F. Deuticke.

Hecker, E. (1893) 'Uber larvirte und abortive Angstzustände bei Neurasthenie'. *Zentralblatt Nervenheilkunde*, 16: 565.

Huizinga, J. (1919/1924/1953) *The Waning of the Middle Ages: A Study of the Forms of Thought and Art in France and the Netherlands in the Fourteenth and Fifteenth Centuries*. Translated by F. Hopmans (Leiden). Harmondsworth, Middx., Penguin Books.

Jackson, S.W. (1986) *Melancholia and Depression: From Hippocratic Times to Modern Times*, New Haven and London, Yale University Press.

Lefebvre, G. (1932/1970/1973) *La Grande Peur de 1789*, Paris, Librairie Armand Colin. Translated by Joan White as *The Great Fear of 1789: Rural Panic in Revolutionary France*, London, New Left Books.

Lewis, A. (1967/1980). 'Problems presented by the ambiguous word "anxiety" as used in psychopathology'. In Burrows, G.D. and Davies, B. (eds.) *Handbook of Studies on Anxiety*, New York, Amsterdam and Oxford, Elsevier/North Holland Biomedical Press. Reprinted from *Israel Annals of Psychiatry and Related Disciplines*, 5: 105–21.

Macdonald, M. (1981) *Mystical Bedlam: Madness, Anxiety and Healing in Seventeenth-Century England*, Cambridge, London and New York, Cambridge University Press.

Meares, R. (1980) 'A psychodynamic view of anxiety'. In Burrows, G.D. and Davies, B. (eds.) *Handbook of Studies on Anxiety*, New York, Amsterdam and Oxford, Elsevier/North Holland Biomedical Press.

Merskey, H. (1991) 'Shell-Shock'. In Berrios, G.E. and Freeman, H. (eds.) *150 Years of British Psychiatry 1841–1991*, London, Gaskell for Royal College of Psychiatrists, pp.245–67.

Micale, M. (1991) 'Hysteria Male/Hysteria Female; Reflections on Comparative Gender Construction in Nineteenth-Century France and Britain'. In Benjamin, M. (ed.) *Science and Sensibility: Gender and Scientific Enquiry*, Oxford, Basil Blackwell, pp.200–39.

Montgomery, S. (1990) *Anxiety and Depression*, Petersfield, Hants., Wrightson Biomedical.

Nemiah, J.C. (1985) 'Anxiety States (Anxiety Neuroses)'. In Kaplan, H.I. and Sadock, B.J. (eds.) *Comprehensive Textbook of Psychiatry* (4th edn), Baltimore and London, Williams and Wilkins, Ch. 20.1.

Oppenheim, J. (1991) *'Shattered Nerves': Doctors, Patients and Depression in Victorian England*, Oxford and New York, Oxford University Press.

Rosen, G. (1962) 'Psychopathology in the Social Process'. *Bulletin of the History of Medicine*, 36: 13–44.

Rosenberg, C. (1962/1978) 'George M. Beard and American Nervousness'. In Rosenberg, C. *No Other Gods: On Science and American Social Thought*, Baltimore, Johns Hopkins University Press. Reprinted from *Bulletin of the History of Medicine*, 36: 245–59.

Schivelbusch, W. (1977/1986) *Geschichte der Eisenbahnreise*, Munich, Verlag Carl Hanser. Translated as *The Railway Journey: The Industrialization of Time and Space in the Nineteenth Century*, Leamington Spa, Hamburg and New York, Berg Publications, Chs. 8 and 9.

Showalter, E. (1985/87) *The Female Malady: Women, Madness and English Culture, 1830–1980*, Ch.7, 'Male Hysteria: W.H.R. Rivers and the Lessons of Shell-Shock', New York, Pantheon and London, Virago.

Stone, M. (1985) 'Shell-Shock and the Psychologists'. In Bynum, W.F., Porter, Roy and Shepherd, Michael (eds.) *The Anatomy of Madness: Essays in the History of Psychiatry*, vol.II, London, Tavistock Publications, pp.242–71.

Trimble, M.R. (1981) *Post-Traumatic Neurosis. From Railway Spine to the Whiplash*, Chichester, New York, Brisbane and Toronto, John Wiley and Sons Ltd, Chs. 1 and 2.

Zeldin, T. (1977/1981) *France 1848–1945: Anxiety and Hypocrisy*, Ch. 3, 'Worry, Boredom and Hysteria', Oxford, Clarendon Press/Oxford University Press.

Chapter 22

Obsessive-Compulsive Disorder

Clinical Section

GE BERRIOS

'Obsessive-compulsive disorder' only acquired its status of *new neurosis*[1] towards the end of the nineteenth century. As currently defined, it includes interloping and iterative thoughts and actions of a type and severity that fracture behaviour, e.g. DSM IV (APA, 1994) and ICD-10 (WHO, 1992). The condition is accompanied by feelings of distress, and declarations of *resistance* to the abnormal experience. Insight is assumed to be present but it is often belied by bizarre behaviours. Over the years, European scholarship has produced great works on this condition (Pujol and Savy, 1968; Monserrat-Esteve et al, 1971; Beech, 1974; Nagera, 1976; Rachman and Hodgson, 1980). For reasons which remain unclear, the disease has of late elicited great interest in the USA where a life time prevalence of up to 2.5 per cent have been found (APA, 1994, p.420). Interesting differences seem to exist between the classical European and current American definitions of the condition (Berrios and Kan, 1994; Jenike et al, 1986).

Obsessive-compulsive *behaviours* (OCs) have been described in the distant past and often explained in social and religious terms (Mora, 1969). The question of whether these behaviours are expression of the same substratum or underlying invariant is a tantalising one. Before an answer is rehearsed, however, a study must be made of the *terms* employed (historical semantics) to capture these phenomena. The medical *concepts* involved in the current definition of obsessive-compulsive disorder were tooled in France and Germany during the second half of the nineteenth century. This chapter concentrates on the process whereby these behaviours were brought together and transformed into a disease.

OCs BEFORE 1800

In the *Anatomy of Melancholy*, Robert Burton (1883) reported an individual 'who dared not go over a bridge, come near a pool, rock, steep hill, lie in a chamber where cross beams were, for fear he be tempted to hang, drawn or precipitate himself. In a silent auditorium as at a sermon, he [was] afraid he shall speak aloud at unawares, something indecent, unfit to be said' (p.53). Bishop Moore of Norwich described subjects overwhelmed by 'naughty and sometimes blasphemous thoughts' which 'start in their minds while they are exercised in the Worship of God' (Mora, 1969, p.163). David Hartley (1834) described states of 'frequent recurrency of the same ideas' 'When a person applies himself to any particular study, so as to fix his attention deeply on the ideas and terms belonging to it is commonly observed, that he becomes narrow minded . . . the perpetual recurrency of particular ideas and terms makes the vibrations belonging thereto become more than ordinarily vivid, converts associations into strong ones' (p.249).

Terms such as *obsessio*, *compulsio*, and *impulsio* have, since the Medieval period, been use to refer to religious explanations for OCs. Words from the vernacular were also adapted to this purpose: for example, *scruple* (meaning 'small, sharp or pointed stone') (Lewis and Short, 1879) was used since the 1500s (if not earlier) to refer to repetitive thoughts of religious nature. The term appears, for example, in the autobiography of Ignatius of Loyola (the founder of the *Society of Jesus*) describing his (probable) organic obsessional disorder (Sauri, 1983, pp.25–6). In 1660, Bishop Taylor (1660) wrote: 'scruple is a great trouble of minde proceeding from a little motive, and a great indisposition, by which the conscience though sufficiently determined by proper arguments, dares not proceed to action, or if it does, it cannot rest' (p.208) (the concept of scrupulosity has been in use until relatively recently) (Weisner and Riffel, 1961).

Words such as 'superstition' have also been used to refer to OCs. For example, James Boswell (1791) wrote of Dr Johnson:

> He had another particularity . . . it appeared to me some superstitious habit, which had contracted early . . . this was his anxious care to go out or in at a door or passage, by a certain number of steps from a certain point, or at least so that either his right or his left foot (I am not certain which) should constantly make the first actual movement when he came close to the door or passage.

THE NINETEENTH CENTURY

The history of the words
Nineteenth century psychiatric terminology has three origins: classical terms (e.g. mania, melancholia, paranoia); words from the *sermo vulgaris* furnished with technical meaning (e.g. hallucination, obsession, stupor); and neologisms (e.g. lypemania, monomania)

German terminology
In European psychiatry, one of the earliest technical terms to refer to 'irresistible thoughts' was *Zwangsvorstellung*. Coined by Krafft-Ebing (1879) in 1867, it enshrined his views on the aetiology of the disorder: *Zwang* originated from the high German *Dwang* (derived from *Twanc* which in middle high German meant 'to compel, to oppress').[2] During the 1870s, *Vorstellung* meant 'presentation or representation' and had been introduced by Ch. Wolff a century earlier to refer to the concept of 'idea' in Descartes (Abbagnano, 1961). This noble term, important to German psychology and psychiatry, was popularized by J.F. Herbart (Erdmann, 1886; pp.21–5; Ribot, 1885).

It is, therefore, not surprising that Westphal (1877) felt free to equate 'presentation' with the straightforward notion of 'idea' (until then the terms had not been synonymous), and to suggest that obsessional states resulted from a disorder of intellectual function. This 'intellectualistic' interpretation remained influential in German psychiatry until the twentieth century (Schneider, 1918).

Westphal (1877) divided up 'presentations' into 'pure mental experiences' (i.e. obsessive ideas or ruminations) and precursors of actions (i.e. compulsions); this can be seen as the historical point at which compulsions were made parasitical upon thoughts.[3] This created an interesting problem for *Zwangsvorstellung* was translated as 'obsession' in Great Britain and 'compulsion' in the USA, the term 'obsessive-compulsive disorder' emerging as a compromise! (Rado, 1959, p.324). *Zwang* also gave rise to terms such as *Zwangshandlung, Zwangsphenomenen, Zwangszustand* to refer to iterative states and actions of various kinds (Bräutigam, 1973).

Griesinger (1868) introduced *sucht* (meaning 'disease, passion') to refer to states similar to those covered by *Zwangvorstellung*, and coined *Grubelnsucht*[4] for the ruminative behaviour shown by three cases he reported. More terms were soon to accrue. In a lecture before the *Royal Medical Society of Budapest*, Donath (1897) suggested that *Anancasmus* (the Greek term for 'necessity' or 'obligation' ('ἀναγχασμός = Necessitas) (p.214) be used to name the same state that Thomsen (1895) had called 'idiopathic obsessional state' (*idiopathische Zwangsvorgänge*). Anancasmus proved useful as it lent itself to adjectival use (Kahn, 1928; Skoog, 1959; Blakenburg, 1973; Videbech, 1975; ICD-9, 1978); for example, 'anancastic personality' (Schneider, 1950).[5]

French terminology

During the nineteenth century, aspects of OC behaviours were variously referred to in French psychiatry.[6] Early in the century, they were considered as reflecting a for n cf insanity, and hence catalogued under categories meaning 'partial insa it/' (e.g. *manie sans délire, monomanie*, and *folie lucide*). Implicit in the aetiological semantics of these categories was the assumption that OCs were a form of 'intellectual' disorder.[7] During the second half of the century, the possibility that emotions might be involved was introduced with Morel's *délire emotif*. The old word *obsession* arrived late in French medical terminology and it is said to have been first used by Falret (1866)[8]; however, no medical meaning is yet found in Littré's (1877) dictionary. Few years later, Luys (1883) defined *obsessions pathologiques* as 'anomalous and repetitive, subjective events without external source'. Until this period the term obsession had been mostly used in its verbal, 'transitive' sense, to describe the action of an external agent 'besieging' the individual (Jastrow, 1901). Luys' usage was thus a departure in that it rendered obsessions into internal, private affairs. This novel view was soon accepted in French psychiatry (Ball, 1892; Falret, 1889; Eeden, 1892).

British terminology

Terminology in the English language followed a similar path (Berrios, 1977). The word 'obsession' had been in use at least since the sixteenth century to refer to the act of being 'besieged by the devil' (Oxford English Dictionary), but it was incorporated late into medical terminology; indeed, by the end of the nineteenth century, Tuke (1892; 1894) still preferred 'imperative idea', and Mickle (1896) 'mental besetment'. Before this period, a common term had been 'fixed idea'. It was only in his English translation of Legrain's (1892) entry that Tuke (1892) used the French words 'obsession' and 'impulse'. At the beginning of this century, 'mental obsession' was adopted by the *Lancet* (Leader, 1904) and 'morbid impulse' by the *British Medical Journal* (Editorial, 1901). When few years later, Shaw (1904) published a review, he wrote as if the word 'obsession' had been in use for some time. The term also appeared in the American literature around this period (Diller, 1902). In 1906, The Nomenclature of Diseases drawn up by the Joint Committee of the Royal College of Physicians in London (which included George Savage and Percy Smith as the psychiatric members) recognised 'obsessive insanity' (Royal College of Physicians, 1906).

THE HISTORY OF THE CONCEPTS

French Contribution

Esquirol (1772–1840)

Esquirol can be said to have opened a new clinical space for OC when he classified the *délire partiel* of 'Mademoiselle F' as a form of 'reasoning or instinctive monomania' (Esquirol, 1838) defined as 'involuntary, irresistible, and instinctive activity' where the subject was 'chained to actions that neither reason or emotion have originated, that conscience rejects, and will cannot suppress' (p.332). Mademoiselle F.[9] described her thoughts as 'irresistible' and had 'insight'; Esquirol concluded that her experience reflected a weakness in the volitional faculty. Esquirol oscillated between explaining OC as a disorder of ideas or of the will; the view that it might be the latter became important in French psychiatry (Billod, 1847; Ribot, 1904).

Esquirol's view that OC was a form of monomania did not last long as the concept of monomania itself was attacked during the 1850s (Winslow, 1856). Its critics claimed that it: 1. did not respond to clinical observation but resulted from a mechanical application of Faculty Psychology (Falret, 1864), 2. encompassed too many clinical states and hence had little or nothing to say about individual cases (Kageyama, 1984), 3. was based on cross-sectional observation and had no conceptual machinery to deal with longitudinal changes (Linas, 1871), 4. handled badly subjective symptomatology which, since the 1840s, had become important to the mental disorder (Berrios, 1985), and 5. created medico-legal difficulties (Saussure, 1946). All these points were powerful arguments against monomania, and its death knell was sounded at the 1853–54 debate of the *Société Médico-Psychologique* in Paris (SMP, 1854). Its disappearance set OC asunder.

Morel (1809–1873)

Morel was responsible for a major shift in the concept of OC. Until his time, effort had gone into accommodating the disorder into the insanities which rendered it a disorder of intellect. But this was not good enough from the clinical viewpoint: subjects with OC often showed emotional upheaval and this was not being accounted for. Keen as he was on aetiological classifications, Morel (1860) started from a new angle and suggested that OC might be the complex expression of a diseased ganglionar (autonomic) nervous system. *Délire emotif* was to be not 'an insanity but a neurosis, that is, a disease of the emotions' (Morel, 1866): 'What I call *délire emotif*[10] corresponds to a particular type of fixed idea and abnormal act whose existence, however, does not entail an involvement of intellectual faculties'. The drive leading to a compulsion, for example, resulted from a 'heightened affective state'. Retrospective diagnosis of his seven cases shows that his category was broad indeed: it included patients with vasomotor and digestive symptomatology, phobias, dysphoria, unmotivated fears, fixed ideas, and impulsions but none showed cognitive impairment or hallucinations. Almost forty years later, Janet was to use similar clinical boundaries for his notion of psychasthenia (Janet, 1903; Pitman, 1987).

Three reasons explain the success of *délire emotif*. First, the reputation of Morel; second, the fact that it provided an alternative to the German view that OC was a disorder of thinking (Meyer, 1906), and third, its flexibility could fit both subjective and somatic symptoms, including those of generalised and paroxysmal anxiety (Doyen, 1885). Luys disagreed with Morel's view that all vegetative functions were localized in the ganglionar system (Semelaigne, 1932), and suggested that symptoms might originate in the cortex; furthermore, since ideas, emotions and actions had separate cortical localization, 'bizarre ideas', 'involuntary' emotions or compulsive acts could be produced independently.

The reclassification of the OC as a form of 'neuroses' re-opened the possibility that it might result from involvement of brain sites related to cognition, emotions or volition. By this time the concept was in a transitional state: 'neuroses' were considered as 'organic' but no focalised lesion was demanded (López Piñero, 1983). For example, this was the view of Axenfeld (1883).[11]

Dagonet (1823–1902) and *l'impulsion*

In the same way that obsession had to be separated off from 'delusion'[12] compulsion required separation from *impulsion*, a category of behaviour that since early in the nineteenth century (Hoffbauer, 1827; p.37 and pp.270–308; Esquirol, 1838, pp.376–93, vol.1; Griesinger, 1861, p.78)[13] had been used to name all manner of paroxysmal, stereotyped, and (apparently) involuntary actions (Littré, 1877; Dagonet, 1870; Porot, 1975; Pinel 1809, pp.156–60; Georget, 1820, p.49).[14] Impulsion was for Dagonet an irresistible and involuntary act, that imposed itself upon the mind just like hallucinations or fixed ideas (Dagonet, 1870, p.17). Dagonet's view, however, had religious and moralistic connotations; Magnan's (1893) did not: 'Impulsion is a mode of cerebral activity that forces actions that occasionally (*parfois*) the will cannot prevent'. Bourdin (1896) felt this definition to be flawed, and suggested a four-fold classification: conscious and unconscious impulsions, pseudo-impulsions and mixed impulsions. Conscious impulsions were secondary to obsessions and seen in OC; unconscious impulsions follow fleeting ideas but left no memory after the act had been committed (as happened in epileptic patients); pseudo-impulsions followed a delusion or a hallucination and were typical of insanity; finally 'mixed impulsions' combined the other three and were seen in hysterical insanity (pp.238–9). With Bourdin impulsions lost their moral ring and mysterious irresistibility, and were incorporated into the general field of mental disorder. Pitres and Régis completed this process: 'impulsions have no special aetiology and their cause merges with that of insanity . . . impulsivity is a return to elementary reflex action which betrays a form of inferiority, whether innate or acquired' (Pitres and Régis, 1902, p.208).

Dagonet also resuscitated the notion of 'Impulsive insanity' (*folie impulsive*) to include phobias, homicidal and suicidal tendencies, manic behaviour, hypochondriacal preoccupations, and epileptic seizures (Baldwin, 1901; Dagonet, 1870). He offered a clinical and taxonomic analysis and concluded that any subject suffering from insanity might show *impulsions violentes, irrésistibles* which could be primary or secondary to delusions, emotions or hallucinations, and which led to a 'failure of the will' (Dagonet, 1870, p.15). Dagonet included a subtype of disorder redolent of OC: 'the more one tries to discard the idea, the more it becomes imposed upon the mind, the more one tries to get rid of the emotion or tendency, the stronger it becomes' (Dagonet, 1870, p.20).

Legrand du Saulle (1830–1886)
The description of OC achieves its consolidation in the work of Legrand du Saulle who in 1875 reported a series of 27 cases (11 his own) (Legrand du Saulle, 1875). He recognized that patients admitted to hospital tended to be complicated by psychotic symptoms or depression; and was aware of the fluctuating course, insidious onset, and tendency to change that characterise the disease. He classified *la folie de doute avec délire de toucher* as a variety of *folie avec conscience* ('insanity with insight') and reported that it had early onset and was more frequent amongst females, higher social classes, and fastidious and rigid personalities.

He identified three stages: first, 'involuntary, spontaneous and irresistible thoughts without illusions or hallucinations' accompanied by 'feelings of doubt, of brooding', and occasionally, 'mental representations and images' of the thoughts. These symptoms engendered fears and anxieties which led to rituals. second, 'unexpected revelations' were made to relatives or friends of symptoms that might have been afflicting the patient for years. At this stage, depression, anxiety and agitation make their appearance together with suicidal brooding which rarely leads to self-harm. Subjects also develop 'animal phobias', somatic (e.g. vasomotor) symptoms, rituals, fear of touching objects, abnormal cleanliness, handwashing, and 'eccentric behaviour'. Insight was not loss and symptoms fluctuated in severity. During the third stage, rituals and obsessional paralysis severely impair psychosocial competence. On follow up (of, sometimes, 20 years), patients might be house-bound, maintained only a semblance of insight, show a typical 'double book-keeping' type of behaviour, and on examination reveal a darker, psychotic attitude. However, there was no evolution towards dementia.

Legrand du Saulle accepted Morel's concept of *délire emotif*, i.e. that OC was a disorder of emotions. His acute clinical eye, however, identified frequent 'psychotic' symptoms which justifies his use of terms such as *folie* and *délire*.[15] He also included under his category animal phobias, agoraphobia, vasomotor phenomena, panic disorder and probably complex seizures. This might sound strange to modern eyes, particularly to those following DSM IV criteria, but that was exactly the cluster of symptoms that Janet called *psychasthénie* and which, with minor changes, has governed until very recently the European definition of obsessive disease (Monserrat-Esteve, *et al*, 1971; Pujol and Savy, 1968).

Ball (1834–1893)
Ball (1892) offered eight operational criteria for OC: presence of insight, sudden onset (subjects may remember the day the disease started), paroxysmal (severity

varies; winter being a period of calm) and fluctuating course (periods of remission); absence of cognitive impairment; release of tension by the compulsion; frequent somatic and anxiety symptoms; and, family history (although acquired obsessions were common). Ball recognised three subtypes: minor (only obsessions), moderate (presence of anxiety and major hesitations), and major (compulsions). The disease could be brought about by fatigue, major life events, puberty, sexual problems, pregnancy, puerperium and menopause. Although Ball believed that OC resulted from impaired brain circulation, he advised against the use of morphine. Ball also suggested that some symptoms might predominate in OC leading to recognisable types: the metaphysicians, realists, scrupulous, timid, etc. (pp.605–22).

Magnan (1835–1916)

Magnan (1886–1887) classified mental disorders into organic, psychoses (proper), and mental retardations; the second group he subdivided into mania, melancholia, chronic delusional state, intermittent psychosis, and psychosis of degeneration (*folie des dégénérés*). OC was included in the latter category, together with phobias, agoraphobia, sexual perversions, and hypochondriacal states. Magnan believed that OC and its variants *onomatomanie* (the 'repeating obsession'; Ballet, 1881) and *erythromanie* (*facilité extreme à rougir*, blushing; Boucher, 1890) resulted from specific cerebral pathology (p.1109) which 'appeared only in subjects affected by degeneration and [hence] merited to be considered as the psychological stigmata of degeneration psychosis' (p.1109). Ladame (1890) summarized well Magnan's contribution:

> Since Morel, the majority of authors have regarded heredity as an important factor in obsessions. No one had, however, considered the symptoms themselves as a sign of pathological heredity. This is what Magnan has done with success. For him, obsessions and impulsions are but episodic presentations of the psychosis of degeneration, i.e. are psychological stigmata. (p.381)

The German contribution

Griesinger, Westphal and Thomsen

OC were handled differently by German authors, and as mentioned above, their terminology emphasised the 'intellectual' origin of the disorder (Warda, 1905; Schneider, 1918). On 28th March 1868, at a meeting of the *Berlin Medico-Psychological Society*[16], Griesinger (1868)[17] read a paper on 'a little known psychopathic state' which he believed to be similar to the 'so-called *maladie de doute* de Falret' (p.627). He reported the cases of a middle aged woman, a 34 year-old Russian prince, and 21 year-old man, suffering from obsessional ruminations and self-questioning, and proposed that these resulted from an impairment of ideas.

At the 5th March 1877 meeting of the same Society, Westphal (1877) read his paper on: *Über Zwangsvorstellungen* in which he created what is now considered to be the German version of the disease. Westphal knew of du Saulle's and Falret's work, and also of Griesinger's notion of *Grübelsucht*. Obsessions differed from delusions in that they were ego-dystonic (even when the patient carried out bizarre acts) and were divided into: ruminative (insanity of doubt);

compulsive (*délire de toucher*), and impulsive. Obsessions reflected pathology of thinking and not of emotions. This latter conclusion was not accepted by Sander and Jastrowitz who defended the opposite view in the discussion that followed (*Berliner Medicinisch-psychologische Gessellschaft*, 1877).

But the most cogent case against the 'intellectual' thesis was put forward years latter by Wille (1881) who sided with the French in suggesting an emotional origin for OC. Furthermore, Wille believed that the symptoms were changeable and fluctuating, and could, on occasions, turn into insanity[18], particularly of the melancholic type. Based on the analysis of 16 cases, Wille (1881) proposed that OC constituted a transition between neuroses and psychoses, and that, together with the affective psychoses, OC formed a new group, the hereditary psychoses. Following this lead, Thomsen (1895) went on to classify OC into a group secondary to hysteria, phobias, and neurasthenia (*deuteropathische Zwangsvorgänge*) and a primary or idiopathic one in which, in addition to OC, he placed tics, coprolalia, migraine, and somatic sensations. The same year Donath (1897) gave his Budapest lecture coining the term *anacasmus* to refer to Thomsen's idiopathic group; he made, however, a determined effort to reduce its size as he believed it to be overinclusive. The word anacasmus has been used in ways other that his originator intended (Skoog, 1959).

At the very end of the century, in an equally seminal paper, Tuczek suggested that OC only developed when on the fertile ground of a particular personality structure (Tuczek, 1899). This was followed by the important study by Löwenfeld (1904) of 200 'anancastic' patients, 70 per cent of whom showed family history of dissimilar mental illness which led him to conclude that OC symptoms 'do not form a unitary condition but belong to different illnesses'. Lastly, Kraepelin (1915) proposed *Zwangsneurose* to name a 'series of conditions' including the phobic states; he kept impulsive psychosis as a different condition.

The British contribution
British alienists limited themselves to commenting upon Continental views on OC. Ireland (1885) reviewed such ideas and Julius Mickle (1896) dedicated his Presidential address to what he called 'Mental Besetments'. He defined these as the 'state in which the mind is affected by some compulsive thought, of a kind, or irrational and often progressive fear; alone, or conjoined with an impulse which is, or tends to become, irresistible. Also an abulic form (sic)' (p.692). Mickle included under besetments, agoraphobia and other phobic states, tics, the Jumping disease, Myriachit, and Latah. Feeling unable to take sides in the aetiological dispute, he backed all three horses at once: 'But I think that here the proper "organising idea" is that, broadly viewed, besetments invariably tend to, and usually are, a blending of anomalies of all three: thought; feeling; "will" ' (p.699). The term mental besetments never caught on. Few years later, Shaw (1904) wrote a review more sensibly entitled 'Obsessions', and reported a solitary case with contamination fears.

Tuke and Jackson
The most interesting British event during this period is the exchange between Tuke and Jackson on the mechanism of imperative ideas (Berrios, 1977). It started with a paper on 'Imperative Ideas' read by the elderly Tuke before the

Neurological Society in London on 1st March 1894. Tuke (1894) quoted Jackson in his belief that minor departures from mental health were as important as the severe ones seen in asylums (p.179). He regretted that imperative ideas tended to be reported only when complicated by depression or delusions, and embarked on their historical and clinical analysis. He objected to the 'French' word 'obsession' for it evoked demoniacal associations in the patient's mind. His own view was that OC included emotions or impulses, and that, although overwhelming in intensity, the symptoms were not delusional in nature (at least in the early stages). He indicated that family history of epilepsy was high in OC, and that pleading imperative ideas had little value in English law (p.191).

In regards to aetiology, Tuke (1894) stated that although no cortical lesions had been found, it was possible to understand the impulsiveness of OC in terms of 'Laycock's doctrine of the reflex or automatic function of the cerebral cortex' (p.192). According to this doctrine, 'by what is termed the association of ideas, the morbid action of vesicular neurine[19] be brought within the current of his thought he becomes utterly powerless to resist it, as much so as the electro-biologised (hypnotised) to resist the suggestions presented to their minds. The formation of these *substrata* is due to fixity of the mind on one idea or class of ideas, at a time when, from morbid changes, induced in the vesicular neurine (as by undue mental labour, intense emotional excitement, want of repose, the development of a dormant disposition, and the like), it is unusually susceptible to the operation of the unconsciously constructing mind, so that the fixed idea becomes deeply writ, as it were, on the vesicular neurine, in the same way as acquired instincts, habits, etc.; and are, in fact, as difficult to remove'.[20]

Laycock's speculative view on the basis of memory was no longer current in the neurophysiology of the 1890s; however, it provided Tuke (1894) with an almost metaphorical account of how imperative ideas might be acquired whilst preserving his belief that OC were aleatory phenomena. Tuke felt that Laycock's ideas had fallen into desuetude except by the interest shown by H. Jackson. After summarising the latter's ideas Tuke suggested that obsessions were exaggerated forms of behaviour released by the weakening of mental power (i.e. positive symptoms resulting from an abolition or negative symptom):

> With regard to those cases in which there is a morbid dread of dirt, I do not know that we can say more, in many instances, than that there is an exaggeration of the scrupulous cleanliness which in a marked degree characterises some persons who are in perfect health, but the origin of the imperative idea may occasionally be traced to some affection of the skin, which has necessitated the attention being drawn to it, and has at last induced a morbid state of mind, not of introspection but of 'extero-spection'. Should the general mental power be lowered, or a hereditary predisposition exist, this tendency to attend to the state of the skin becomes a passion. (p.195)

To summarise, Tuke's rather nostalgic and valedictory paper (he died of a brain haemorrhage five days after delivering it) attempts to explain how imperative ideas are acquired and remembered (as per Laycock's hypothesis) and why do they manifest themselves as they do (as per Jackson's hierarchical model).

Jackson (1895) had not been present at the meeting but submitted a reply stating that although he had seen cases with imperative ideas as described by

582   A History of Clinical Psychiatry

Tuke, he had 'paid little attention' to them. He felt that the view expressed in his Leeds paper (which Tuke had quoted) (Jackson, 1889) *did not apply to imperative ideas* 'without qualification'. His view was that: 'certain very absurd and persisting delusions are owing to fixation of grotesque fancies or dreams in cases where a morbid change in the brain happens suddenly, during sleep' (p.355). In the case of imperative ideas 'certain obtrusive thoughts which otherwise might be transitory become fixed, become "imperative ideas", consequent on some *very slight morbid change* in the brain occurring during sleep' (my italics) (p.318).

Thus, Jackson seems to be suggesting that the difference between delusion and imperative idea only concerned severity of the morbid change: light in the latter, marked in the former. Jackson felt that the alienist must also: 'have to account for the existence of these quasi-parasitical states in cases where the general mental power is but little lessened' (p.319). The rest of the paper is but a repetition of his views, and those of Monro and Anstie. He agreed with Tuke that 'the scientific study of insanities may be best begun in general hospitals' (p.221).

George Savage, Charles Mercier, and Milne Bramwell also published replies to Tuke's paper. Savage (1895) criticised the use of the term 'imperative' for the 'ideas are not always the spring of action' and, in typical fashion, Mercier (1895) stated that what 'impressed me most was Tuke's complete acceptance of a doctrine that I have long held and preached'. Milne Bramwell (1894) followed with a long paper summarising Continental ideas and reporting 18 cases. He stated that 'in nearly all my cases the condition appears to have had an emotional origin' (p.348) and challenged Tuke's view that OC were automatic:

Are these acts automatic? An automatic act is simply an habitual voluntary one performed inattentively or unconsciously; while the so-called automatic acts of the sufferer from imperative ideas are carried out in opposition to his volition and frequently associated with intense and painful consciousness. Possibly with justice they might be called reflex, seeing that they are 'fatal, unchosen, response to stimulation'. (pp.347–8)

This was a superficial criticism, for the 'automatism' entailed by Tuke, referred, not to the semantics of behaviour, but to the mechanism of acquisition of the imperative idea.

THE AFTERMATH

In the event, the view that OC resulted from disturbances of emotions rather than thinking was to prevail. The reasons for this were less scientific than social as there was no methodology then (as, indeed, there is not now!) to demonstrate that, at such level of abstraction, one hypothesis is superior to the other. Anxiety-based explanations became acceptable because great men were espousing them, and because during the second half of the nineteenth century there was a revival of 'affectivity', emotions, and of interest in the autonomic nervous system.[21] This was encouraged not only by internal conceptual swings, but also by rivalries between Germany and France, and by the work of Ribot who championed the emotions. There was also the 'Zeitgeist' factor: in France, this was a period of heightened social anxiety,[22] and the complaints brought to doctors often fell outside traditional insanity concepts. This is the period when notions such as neurasthenia, psychasthenia, *surmenage*, and phosphate deficiency also make their appearance. Research by psychologists (who, like Ribot and Janet, were also philosophers) took place against a background of changing philosophical fashion in favour of the emotions (Ravaisson, 1885). The predicted outcome was the re-conceptualisation of 'diseases' such as agoraphobia or obsessional disorders in emotional terms. A good illustration of this trend is the work of Janet.

Janet (1859–1947)

Janet owed much to his predecessors, including Pitres and Régis. His work, as his co-worker Raymond (Raymond and Janet, 1908) once said, must be considered as more theoretical than clinical (Raymond, 1911). For Janet, OC resulted from *engourdissement* of the mind (Baruk, 1967); 'obsessions' were the experiential concomitant of a 'feeling of incompletion' resulting from a defect in the 'function of the real'. In *L'Automatisme Psychologique*, Janet (1889) defined obsession as an *idée fixe* which, together with hallucinations, constituted 'simple and rudimentary forms of mental activity' (Janet, 1903).

These descriptions, heavy with the assumptions made by late nineteenth century energetist psychology, amounts to no more than to a metaphorical re-description of what patients say of their inability to bring tasks to completion. Janet carved out 'psychasthenia' from the already inflated category of neurasthenia (Chatel and Peel, 1971; Cobb, 1920); indeed, psychasthenia was itself an over-inclusive category, soon to became the new 'giant of neuropathology' (Dubois, 1909). Psychasthenia had no clear-cut clinical boundaries (Hesnard, 1976) and relied for its meaning on theoretical mechanisms such as 'reduction' of psychological tension (Sjövall, 1967) and 'incompletion' (*inachévement*) (Prevost, 1973a). Schwartz (1955), one of the great biographers of Janet, was right in referring to psychasthenia as 'a cluster of symptoms artificially demarcated to which the predominance of a "typical (causal) mechanism" conferred a particular aspect'. Indeed, analysis of the 236 cases reported by Janet shows that psychasthenia included, in addition to OC, panic, phobic and tic disorder, hypochondriacal and confusional states, and epilepsy (Berrios et al, 1996).

SUMMARY

During the nineteenth century, OC was successively classified as insanity (monomania), neurosis (old definition), psychosis (new definition), and finally placed as a member of the newly formed class of the neurosis. The component symptoms of OC had to be carved out of larger categories: obsession from fixed idea and delusion; compulsion from 'impulsion'. OC was successively explained as a disorder of volition, intellect and emotions; the first and third views being more popular in France, the second in Germany. In the event, the 'emotional' hypothesis prevailed. The description of the disease was completed by Legrand du Saulle in 1875 and not by Janet as it is often claimed. Indeed, his category of psychasthenia was wider than du Saulle's, and constituted a return to Thomsens' views. Obsessions, agoraphobia and other anxiety disorders travelled together until the end of the century when Freud separated them successfully.

NOTES

1 By 'new neuroses' is meant here the group of conditions that acquired such status only after the 1890s (e.g. agoraphobia, neurasthenia, psychasthenia, neurotic depression and obsessive compulsive neurosis).

2 The etymological origin of *Twanc* is the Sanskrit *tvanzkti* ('he pulls together') (Walshe, 1951, pp.260–1).

3 To current writers (particularly psychologists) this is the 'natural' way of understanding a compulsion, i.e. the acting out of a thought; indeed, this view has provided the theoretical basis for its treatment (see Beech, 1974; Rachman and Hodgson, 1980). This is not the only way to conceptualise 'compulsion', and as the French showed during the nineteenth century, it can also be seen as a disorder of the will (see Berrios and Gili, 1995).

4 The term was the nineteenth century version of the old high German *Suht* which was related to *Siech* (sick), and a cognate of the Armenian *hiucanim* ('I am ill'). The term also gained evocative force from *Grubeln*, an old German word for 'racking one's brains' (Walshe, 1951).

5 Schneider (1950) explained: 'As adjectival forms to refer to personality cannot be formed with the German term *Zwang*, we have to use a non-German word. The one I have chosen comes from Donath. Ziehen has objected that it is insufficiently known. The expression *anancastic*, however, is perfectly understandable and certainly less equivocal than "obsessive", borrowed by Ziehen from the French' (p.87).

6 For example, *manie sans délire* (Pinel, 1809); *Folie raisonnante* (Ladame, 1890); *monomanie raisonnante* (Esquirol, 1838); *kleptomanie* (Marc, 1840); *idées fixes* (Parchappe, 1850–1851); *idée irrésistible* (Brierre de Boismont, 1851); *délire avec conscience, délire sans délire* (Guislain, 1852); *idées restrictives or mobiles* (Renaudin, 1854); *pseudomonomanie* (Delasiauve, 1861); *folie lucide* (Trélat, 1861); *folie or monomanie avec conscience* (Ritti, 1879); *délire de toucher* (Legrand du Saulle, 1875; Ritti, 1879); *folie de doute* (Marcé, 1862); *délire emotif* (Morel, 1866); *obsessions pathologiques* (Luys, 1883); *folie des héréditaires dégénéres* (Magnan, 1886–1887); *crainte de souillure* (Eeden, 1892); *onomatomanie* (Charcot and Magnan, 1885; Séglas, 1891); *maladie du doute* (Falret, 1866).

7 The change over to the new category, *folie avec conscience* (insanity with insight) was discussed in a famous debate at the *Société Médico-Psychologique* (Paris) (SMP, 1875) and merits a short comment. It marked the surrender of the 'lack of insight' criterion (which had been central to the concept of insanity), and allowed for disorders such as OC, agoraphobia, panic disorder, and the hypochondriacal and homicidal monomanias to be classified as 'insanities'. By the end of the century, and under the increasing pressure of the narrow Kraepelinian concept of psychosis, the category *folie avec conscience* eventually disintegrated (Berrios and Hauser, 1988). This did not affect OC a great deal for by then it had been given an alternative clinical and aetiological interpretation.

8 However, the present writer has been unable to find the word *obsession* mentioned in this paper (which started the debate on *folie raisonnante* at the *Société Médico-Psychologique*). It, nonetheless, includes a clear description of OC (pp.413–16). It was in this intervention that Falret claimed that 'his

father had coined for this mental disorder the term *maladie du doute'* (p.414).

9   Mademoiselle F. was a tall, happy-go-lucky 34 year-old female accountant, whose illness started suddenly at age 18 with fears that she might take in 'her pockets objects belonging to her aunt'. She worried lest she got the accounts wrong, and that on touching money something of value might get stuck to her fingers. She accepted that her worries were absurd but could not help it. She started to handwash and to fear that 'her clothes might touch anything'; when this happened she would rub her hands as if to get rid of 'some invisible substance'. The fear included food, and she had to be fed by her servant, etc. etc. (Esquirol, 1838, pp.361–4).

10 Morel's use of the word *délire* was unconventional in that it allowed for the presence of insight.

11 Axenfeld (1883) defines neurosis as: 'morbid states frequently apyretic, in which there are changes in cognition, sensibility, or motility (or all combined) which have two important characteristics: that they can occur in the absence of an appreciable lesion, and that they themselves do not cause serious lesions' (Axenfeld, 1883, p.14,).

12 'Fixed idea' was their common ancestor. During the nineteenth century this term referred mainly to persistent thoughts or overvalued ideas, whether or not seen in a pathological situation (e.g., p.74, Griesinger, 1861). It thus served as the parent term for delusions, obsessions, phobias, post-oniric ideas, etc. After the 1880s, all these symptoms were redefined, and for a time 'fixed idea' survived as a synonym for obsession (Buccola, 1880), phobia (Ireland, 1885). In the event, it received a narrow definition posed ambiguously between the normal and the pathological (Valery, 1933).

13 For example, it is fully discussed by Hoffbauer (1827) (pp.270–308). Hoffbauer made the point, which was to re-appear in Magnan at the end of the century, that 'impulsion as an act may be strong without being irresistible. A scale is needed' (p.307). Esquirol (1838) discussed the concept of impulsion in the context of *Monomanie Homicide* (pp.376–93). Griesinger (1861) was also cautious in his discussion of impulsion which he included under 'disorders of the will': 'Whether, and to what extent, certain impulses in the insane, particular those ending up in criminal acts, are irresistible, is unclear. Few insane behaviours can be said to be forced or purely automatic; even in mania and according to reports from subjects who have recovered, many of their wild desires could have been restrained' (p.78).

14 In French, *impulsion* was originally imported from the science of mechanics (Littré, 1877). However, the 'explanatory' force of the concept partially came from its allusion to vestigial behaviours, drives, cravings, and appetites. By the 1860s, *impulsion* was ambiguously poised between two dichotomies: description vs. explanation and internal vs. reactive. From the historical viewpoint, the view that it was of 'inner' origin was the earliest to appear (Dagonet, 1870; Porot, 1975). Versions of 'impulsive or instinctive insanity' had been described under the category *manie sans délire* by Pinel (1809) (pp.156–60), and by Georget (1820) as cases with *impetuosité de penchans* (p.49).

15 Legrand du Saulle's quaint usage of the terms 'neurosis' and *délire* to refer

to OC may cause confusion. His work was transitional between the old and new concept of insanity (Berrios, 1987).

16 For a history of the *Berlin Medico-Psychological Society* see Schultze and Donalies, 1968.

17 Griesinger died of appendicitis, at the young age of 51, on 26th October of the same year. He had been the founder of the *Berlin Medico-Psychological Society* and of the *Archiv für Psychiatrie* in whose First Volume his paper and obituary appeared together (Westphal, 1868).

18 During these years, the question of whether obsessions could become delusions split both German and French psychiatry (see Masselon, 1913).

19 It would be easy to read 'vesicular neurine' anachronistically, i.e. as a forerunner of the concept of neurotransmitter. It was not. During Laycock's time even the notion of neuron did not exist. The word 'vesicular neurine' or 'substance' referred to whatever was the material that constituted the central nervous system. As late as 1876, and in the most popular physiology textbook of the period, it was defined thus: 'the nervous system of Man, like that of all other animals, is composed of ganglionic centres and nerve trunks; the former being essentially composed of "vesicular substance" ' (Carpenter and Power, 1876, p.582). And 'neurine' was defined as 'Term for the matter of which nerves are composed, and which is enveloped in neurilemma' (Mayne, 1860, p.761). On the neurophysiological background during this period see Clarke and Jacyna (1987) and Black (1981); on Laycock and his role in English neurophysiology see Leff (1991).

20 This quotation was taken by Tuke from a paper delivered by Layçock (1845) at the York British Association meeting of 1844. At the time, this great man was still a physician to the York Dispensary.

21 The philosophical reaction against 'materialism' and 'intellectualism' was led by Albert Lemoine and Paul Janet (Pierre Janet's uncle), and started in 1867 with the publication of Lemoine's *Le Cerveau et la Pensée*. Pierre Janet became the standard-bearer of the 'emotive' tradition in French philosophical psychology which had started with Maine de Biran (Dwelshauvers, 1920; Moore, 1970) and kept alive by Royer-Collard (whose brother was a psychiatrist), Cousin, and Jouffroy (Ravaisson, 1885). Feelings and emotions, Pierre Janet declared in his popular Paris lectures, were the 'centre of psychological organization' (Prevost, 1973).

22 Zeldin has suggested that anxiety increased 'in the sense that traditional supports of behaviour were weakened, that people were left facing a larger world and a vastly greater range of problems, with far less certainty as to how they should treat them, and often with sharper sensibilities' (Zeldin, 1977, p.823).

REFERENCES

Abbagnano, N. (1961) *Dizionario di filosofia*, Turin, Unione Tipografico-Editrice.

APA (1994) American Psychiatric Association: *Diagnostic and Statistical Manual of Mental Disorder*, Fourth edition, Washington DC, American Psychiatric Association.

Axenfeld, A. (1883) *Traité des Névroses*, Paris, Baillière.

Baldwin, J.M. (1901) *Dictionary of Philosophy and Psychology*, New York, MacMillan.

Ball, B. (1890) *Leçons sur Les Maladies Mentales*, Paris, Asselin et Houzeau.

Ball, B. (1892) 'Des Obsessions en Pathologie Mentale'. *Annales de Psychiatrie et d'Hypnologie*, 2: 1–15.

Ballet, G. (1881) 'Contribution à l'étude de l'état mental des héréditaires dégénérés'. *Archives Générales de Médecine*, 21: 257–75; 427–41.

Baruk, H. (1967) *La psychiatrie française de Pinel à nos jours*, Paris, Presses Universitaires de France.

Beech, H.R. (ed.) (1974) *Obsessional States*, London, Methuen.

Berliner Medicinisch-psychologische Gesellschaft (1877) *Berliner klinische Wochenschrift*, 14: 706–8; 720–2.

Berrios, G.E. (1977) 'Henri Ey, Jackson, et les idées obsédantes'. *L'Evolution Psychiatrique*, 42: 687–99.

Berrios, G.E. (1985) 'The Psychopathology of Affectivity: conceptual and historical aspects'. *Psychological Medicine*, 15: 745–58.

Berrios, G.E. (1987) 'Historical Aspects of the Psychoses: 19th century issues'. *British Medical Bulletin*, 43: 484–98.

Berrios, G.E. and Hauser, R. (1988) 'The Early Development of Kraepelin's ideas on Classification: A conceptual History'. *Psychological Medicine*, 18: 813–21.

Berrios, G.E. and Kan Chung Sing (1994) 'The neurobiology of Obsessive compulsive disorder'. *Neurology, Psychiatry and Brain Research*, 2: 210–20.

Berrios, G.E. and Gili, M. (1995) 'Will and its disorders: a conceptual history'. *History of Psychiatry*, 6:87–104.

Berrios, G.E., Gairin, I. and Fuentenebro, F. (1996) 'Statistical Analysis of Janet's 234 cases of Psychasthenia'. *History of Psychiatry*, (in the press).

Billod, E. (1847) 'Maladies de la Volonté'. *Annales Médico-Psychologiques*, 10:15–35; 170–202; 317–47.

Black, S.E. (1981) 'Pseudopods and synapses: the amoeboid theories of neuronal mobility and the early formulation of the synapse concept'. *Bulletin of the History of Medicine*, 55: 34–58.

Blakenburg, W. (1973) 'Anankastische Psychopathie'. In Müller, Ch. (ed.) *Lexicon der Psychiatrie*, Berlin, Springer, pp.406–7.

Boswell, J. (1791) *The Life of Dr Johnson*, 2 vols., London, Dent.

Boucher, L. (1890) 'Note sur une forme particulière d'obsession chez une héréditaire'. *Normandie Médicale*, 5: 285–6, 309–10.

Bourdin, V. (1896) 'De L'impulsion'. *Annales Médico-Psychologiques*, iii, 217–39.

Bramwell, J.M. (1894) 'On Imperative Ideas'. *Brain*, 17: 331–51.

Bräutigam, W. (1973) 'Zwang'. In Müller, Ch. (ed.) *Lexicon der Psychiatrie*, Berlin, Springer, pp.586–7.

Brierre de Boismont, A.J.F. (1851) 'De l'état des facultés dans les délires partiels ou monomanies'. *Annales Médico-Psychologiques*, 5: 567–91.

Buccola, G. (1880) 'Le Idee Fisse'. In Tamburini, A. (ed.) *Memorie della Clinica Psichiatrica della R. Univerista di Modena*, Serie II^a, Reggio-Emilia, Calderini, pp.1–29.

Burton, R. (1883) *The Anatomy of Melancholy*, London, Chatto and Windus (First Edition, 1620).

Carpenter, W.B. and Power, H. (1876) *Principles of Human Physiology*, 8th Edition, London, Churchill.

Charcot, J.M. and Magnan, V. (1885) 'De l'Onomatomanie'. *Archives de Neurologie*, 10: 157–68.

Chatel, J.C. and Peel, R. (1971) 'The Concept of Neurasthenia'. *International Journal of Psychiatry*, 9: 36–49.

Clarke, E. and Jacyna, L.S. (1987) *Nineteenth-Century Origins of Neuroscientific Concepts*, Berkeley, University of California Press.

Cobb, I.G. (1920) *A Manual of Neurasthenia (nervous exhaustion)*, London, Baillière, Tindall and Cox.

Dagonet, H. (1870) 'Des Impulsions dans la Folie et de la Folie Impulsive'. *Annales Médico-Psychologiques*, 4: 5–32; 215–59.

Delasiauve, L.J.F. (1861) 'De la monomanie'. *Journal de Médecine Mentale*, 1:348–64.

Diller, T. (1902) 'Obsessions; fixed ideas, indecisions, imperative conceptions, abulias, phobias'. *The Medical News*, 81: 961–8.

Donath, J. (1897) 'Zur Kenntniss des Anancasmus (psychische Zwangszustände)'. *Archiv für Psychiatrie und Nervenkrankeiten*, 29:211–24.

Doyen, E. (1885) 'Quelques considerations sur les terreurs morbides et la délire emotif en général'. *L'Encéphale*, 4: 418–38.

Dubois, P. (1909) *Les Psychonévroses*, Paris, Masson.

Dwelshauvers, G. (1920) *La Psychologie Française Contemporaine*, Paris, Alcan.

Editorial (1901) 'Mental Obsessions' *British Medical Journal*, ii: 100.

Eeden, V. (1892) 'Les Obsessions'. *Revue de l'Hypnotisme*, 6: 5–14.

Erdmann, B. (1886) 'Vorstellung'. *Viertel-jarsch für wissenschaftliche Philosophie*, 10: 307–15.

Esquirol, J.E.D. (1838) *Des Maladies Mentales Considérées sous les Rapports Médical, Hygienique et Médico-legal*, 2 vols., Paris, Baillière.

Falret, J. (1866) 'De la folie raisonnante ou folie morale'. *Annales Médico-Psychologiques*, 7: 382–431.

Falret, J.P. (1864) *Des Maladies Mentales et des Asiles d'Aliénes. Leçons Cliniques et Considérations Générales*, Paris, Baillière, pp.425–48.

Falret, J.P. (1889) 'Obsessions intellectuelles et emotives'. *Archives of Neurology*, 2: 274–93.

Gardiner, H.M., Metcalf, R.C. and Beebe-Center, J.G. (1937) *Feeling and Emotion. A History of Theories*, New York, American Book Company.

Georget, E. (1820) *De la Folie*, Paris, Crevot.

Griesinger, W. (1861) *Die Pathologie und Therapie der psuchischen Krankheiten*, 2nd edition, Stuttgart, Krabbe.

Griesinger, W. (1868) 'Über einen wenig bekannten psychopathischen Zustand'. *Archiv für Psychiatrie und Nervenkrankheiten*, 1: 626–35.

Guislain, J. (1852) *Leçons Orales sur les Phrénopathies ou Traité Théorique et Pratique des Maladies Mentales*, 3 vols., Gand, Hebbelynck.

Hartley, D. (1834) *Observations on Man, his Frame, his Duty and his Expectations*, 6th edition, London, Thomas Tegg and Son (First Edition, 1749).

Hesnard, A. (1976) *De Freud a Lacan*, Barcelona, Ediciones Martinez Roca.

Hoffbauer, J.C. (1827) *Médecine Légale Relative aux Aliénés et aux Sourds-muets*, (translated by A.M. Chambeyron) Paris, Baillière.

ICD-9 (1978) *Mental Disorders: Glossary and Guide to their Classification*, Geneva, World Health Organization.

Ireland, W.W. (1885) 'On fixed ideas'. In *The Blot upon the Brain: Studies in History and Psychology*, Edinburgh, Bell and Bradfute.

Jackson, J.H. (1889) 'On the comparative study of diseases of the nervous system'. *British Medical Journal*, ii: 355–64.

Jackson, J.H. (1895) 'On imperative ideas'. *Brain*, 18: 318–22.

Janet, P. (1889) *L'Automatisme Psychologique*, Paris, Alcan.

Janet, P. (1903) *Les Obsessions et la Psychasthénie*, Paris, Alcan.

Jastrow, J. (1901) 'Obsession'. In Baldwin, J.M. (ed.) *Dictionary of Philosophy and Psychology*, vol.2, London, MacMillan.

Jenike, M.A., Baer, L. and Minichiello, W.E. (eds.) (1986) *Obsessive Compulsive Disorders. Theory and Management*, Massachusetts, PSG Publishing Company.

Kageyama, J. (1984) 'Sur L'histoire de la Monomanie'. *L'Evolution Psychiatrique*, 49: 155–62.

Kahn, E. (1928) 'Die anakastische Psychopathen'. In Bumke, O. (ed.) *Handbuch der Geisteskrankheiten*, vol.5, Part 1 Berlin, Springer.

Kraepelin, E. (1915) *Ein Lehrbuch für Studierende und Ärzte*, vol.4, Klinische Psychiatrie, Lepizig, Barth, pp.1823–901.

Krafft-Ebing, R. (1879) 'Über Geistestörung durch Zwangsvorstellungen'. *Allgemeine Zeitschrift für Psychiatrie*, 35: 303–28.

Ladame, P.L. (1890) 'La folie du doute et le délire du toucher'. *Annales Médico-Psychologiques*, 12: 368–86.

Laycock, T. (1845) 'On the reflex function of the brain'. *British and Foreign Medico-Chirurgical Review*, vol.19: 303.

Leader, (1904) 'Obsessions and morbid impulses'. *Lancet*, i: 1441.

Leff, A. (1991) 'Thomas Laycock and the cerebral reflex: a function arising from and pointing to the unity of nature'. *History of Psychiatry*, 2: 385–408.

Legrain, M. (1892) 'Obsession and impulse'. In Tuke, D.H. (ed.) *Dictionary of Psychological Medicine*, vol.1, London, J. & A. Churchill, pp.866–8.

Legrand du Saulle, H. (1875) *La Folie du Doute (avec délire du toucher)*, Paris, Adrien Delahaye.

Lewis, C.T. and Short, C. (1879) *A Latin Dictionary*, Oxford, Clarendon Press.

Linas, A. (1871) 'Monomanie'. In Dechambre, A. (ed.) *Dictionnaire Encyclopédique des Sciences Médicales*, vol.61, Paris, Mason, pp.146–95.

Littré, E. (1877) *Dictionnaire de la Langue Française*, Paris, Hachette.

López Piñero, J.M. (1983) *Historical Origins of the Concept of Neurosis*, (translated by D. Berrios), Cambridge, Cambridge University Press.

Löwenfeld, L. (1904) *Psychische Zwangserscheinungen*, Wiesbaden, J.F. Bergmann.

Luys, J. (1883) 'Des obsessions pathologiques dans leur rapports avec l'activité automatique des elements nerveux'. *L'Encéphale*, 3: 20–61.

Magnan, V. (1886–1887) 'Considérations générales sur la folie (des héréditaires ou dégénéres'. *Le Progrés Médical*, 14: 1089–90; 1108–12; 15: 187–90; 209–13.

Magnan, V. (1893) 'Recherches sur les Centres Nerveux;' quoted in p.218

Bourdin, V. (1896) 'De L'Impulsion. Sa Définition, ses Formes et sa Valeur Psychologique'. *Annales Médico-Psychologiques*, 54: 317–39.

Marc, C.C.H. (1840) *De la Folie, Considérée dans ses Rapports avec les Questions Médico-judiciaires*, vol.1, Paris, Baillière.

Marcé, L.V. (1862) *Traité Pratique des Maladies Mentales*, Paris, Baillière.

Masselon, R. (1913) 'Délire systématisé à base d'obsessions'. *Annales Médico-Psychologiques*, 71: 513–27.

Mayne, R.G. (1860) *An Expository Lexicon of the terms, Ancient and Modern, in Medical and General Sciences*, London, John Churchill.

Mercier, Ch. (1895) 'On imperative ideas'. *Brain*, 18:328–30.

Meyer, A. (1906) 'The relation of emotional and intellectual functions in paranoia and in obsessions'. *Psychological Bulletin*, 3: 255–74.

Mickle, J. (1896) 'Mental Besetments'. *Journal of Mental Science*, 42: 691–719.

Monserrat-Esteve, S., Costa, J.M. and Ballús, C. (eds.) (1971) *Patologia Obsesiva*, Málaga, Graficasa.

Moore, F.C. (1970) *The Psychology of Maine de Biran*, Oxford, Clarendon Press.

Mora, G. (1969) 'The scrupulosity syndrome'. *International Journal of Clinical Psychology*, 5: 163–74.

Morel, B.A. (1860) *Traité de Maladies Mentales*, Paris, Masson.

Morel, B.A. (1866) 'Du délire emotif. Nevrose du systeme nerveux ganglionaire visceral'. *Archives Générales de Médecine*, 7: 385–402; 530–51; 700–7.

Nagera, H. (1976) *Obsessional Neuroses*, New York, Jason Aronson.

Parchappe, J.B.M. (1850–1851) 'Symptomatologie de la Folie'. *Annales Médico-Psychologiques*, 2: 1–20; 332–50; 3: 40–52; 236–49.

Pinel, Ph. (1809) *Traité Médico-Philosophique de la Aliénation Mentale*, 2nd edition, Paris, Brosson.

Pitman, R.K. (1987) 'Pierre Janet on Obsessive Compulsive Disorder'. *Archives of General Psychiatry*, 44: 226–32.

Pitres, A. and Régis, E. (1902) 'Les impulsions'. *Revue de Psychiatrie*, 9: 208–17.

Porot, A. (1975) *Manuel Alphabétique de Psychiatrie*, Paris, Presses Universitaries de France.

Prevost, C.M. (1973) *La Psycho-philosophie de Pierre Janet*, Paris, Payot.

Prevost, C.M. (1973a) *Janet, Freud et la Psychologie Clinique*, Paris, Payot.

Pujol, R. and Savy, A. (1968) *Le Devenir de L'Obsédé*, Paris, Masson.

Rachman, S.J. and Hodgson, R.J. (1980) *Obsessions and Compulsions*, New Jersey, Prentice-Hall.

Rado, S. (1959) 'Obsessive Behaviour'. In Arieti, S. (ed.) *American Handbook of Psychiatry*, New York, Basic Books.

Ravaisson, F. (1885) *La Philosophie en France au XIXe siècle*, 2nd edition, Paris, Hachette.

Raymond, F. and Janet, P. (1908) *Névroses et Idées Fixes*, vol.2, Paris, Alcan.

Raymond, F. (1911) 'Névroses et psycho-névroses'. In Marie, A. (ed.) *Traité International de Psychologie Pathologique*, Paris, Alcan, pp.1–59.

Renaudin, L.F.E. (1854) 'Observations médico-legales sur la monomanie'. *Annales Médico-Psychologiques*, 6: 236–49.

Ribot, Th. (1885) *La Psychologie Allemande Contemporaine*, 2nd edition, Paris, Alcan.

Ribot, Th. (1904) *Les Maladies de la Volonté*, 18th edition, Paris, Alcan.

Ritti, A. (1879) 'Folie avec conscience'. In Dechambre, A. (ed.) *Dictionnaire Encyclopédique des Sciences Médicales*, vol.39, Paris, Masson, pp.307–20.

Ritti, A. (1879) 'Folie de doute avec délire de toucher'. In Dechambre, A. (ed.) *Dictionnaire Encyclopédique des Sciences Médicales*, vol.39, Paris, Masson, pp.339–48.

Royal College of Physicians (1906) *The Nomenclature of Diseases*, 4th edition, London, His Majesty's Stationary Office.

Sauri, J.J. (ed) (1983) *Las Obsesiones*, Buenos Aires, Nueva Vision.

Saussure, R. de (1946) 'The influence of the concept of Monomania on French Medico-Legal Psychiatry (from 1825–1840)'. *Journal of the History of Medicine*, 1: 365–97.

Savage, G.H. (1895) 'On imperative ideas'. *Brain*, 18:322–8.

Schneider, K. (1918) 'Die Lehre von Zwangsdenken in den letzten zwölf Jahren'. *Zeitschrift für die gesammte Neurologie und Psychiatrie*, 16: 113–251.

Schneider, K. (1950) *Die Psychopathischen Persönlichkeiten*, 9th edition, Vienna, Deuticke.

Schultze, H.A.F. and Donalies, Ch. (1968) '100 Jahre Psychiatrie und Neurologie in Rahmen der Berliner Gesellschaft für Psychiatrie und Neurologie und der Nervenklinik der Charité'. *Wissenschaftsliche Zeitschrift Humboldt Universitäts Berlin*, 17: 5–14.

Schwartz, L. (1955) *Les Névroses et la Psychologie Dynamique de Pierre Janet*, Paris, Presses Universitaires de France.

Séglas, J. (1891) 'Des troubles de la fonction du langage dans l'onomatomanie'. *Médecine Moderne*, 2: 845–7.

Semelaigne, R. (1932) *Les Pionniers de la Psychiatrie Française (Après Pinel)*, vol.2, Paris, Baillière.

Shaw, J. (1904) 'Obsessions'. *Journal of Mental Science*, 50: 234–49.

Sjövall, B. (1967) *Psychology of Tension. An Analysis of Pierre Janet's Concept of 'Tension Psychologique' together with an Historical Aspect*, Stockholm, (no editorial).

Skoog, G. (1959) 'The anacastic syndrome and its relation to personality attitude'. *Acta Psychiatrica Scandinavica*, 34: (Suppl. 134) 5–207.

SMP (1875) Minutes of the *Société Médico-Psychologique*, (Paris) 'Debate on Folie avec conscience'. *Annales Médico-Psychologiques*, vol.33.

SMP (1854) Minutes of the *Société Médico-Psychologique*, (Paris) 'Debate on Monomanie'. *Annales Médico-Psychologiques*, 6: 99–118; 273–98; 464–74; 629–44.

Taylor, J. (1660) *Ductor Dubitantium, or the Rule of Conscience*, 2 vols., London, Royston.

Thomsen, (no initial) (1895) 'Klinische Beiträge zur Lehre von den Zwangsvorstellungen und verwandten psychischen Zuständen'. *Archiv für Psychiatrie und Nervenkrankheiten*, 27: 319–85.

Trélat, U. (1861) *La Folie Lucide*, Paris, Delahaye.

Tuczek (1899) 'Über Zwangsvorstellungen'. *Berliner klinische Wochenschrift*, 36: 117–19; 148–59; 171–4; 195–7; 212–4.

Tuke, D.H. (1892) 'Imperative ideas'. In Tuke, D.H. (ed.) *A Dictionary of Psychological Medicine*, vol.1, London, J. & A. Churchill, pp.678–81.

Tuke, D.H. (1894) 'Imperative ideas'. *Brain*, 17: 179–97.

Valery, P. (1933) *L'Idée Fixe*, Paris, Gallimard.

Vallejo, J. and Berrios, G.E. (eds.) (1995) *Estados Obsesivos*, 2nd Edition, Barcelona, Salvat.

Videbech, Th. (1975) 'The psychopathology of anancastic endogenous depression'. *Acta Psychiatrica Scandinavica*, 52: 336–73.

Walshe, M.O'.C. (1951) *A Concise German Etymological Dictionary*, London, Routledge and Kegan Paul.

Warda, W. (1905) 'Zur Geschichte und Kritik der sogenannten psychischen Zwangszustände'. *Archiv für Psychiatrie und Nervenkrankheiten*, 39: 239–85; 533–85.

Weisner, W.M. and Riffel, P.A. (1961) 'Scrupulosity: religion and obsessive compulsive behavior in children'. *American Journal of Psychiatry*, 117: 314–8.

Westphal, C. (1868) 'Nekrolog für Griesinger'. *Archiv für Psychiatrie und Nervenkrankheiten*, 1: 760–74.

Westphal, K. (1877) 'Über Zwangsvorstellungen'. *Archiv für Psychiatrie und Nervenkrankheiten*, 8: 734–50.

WHO (1992) *The ICD-10 Classification of Mental and Behavioural Disorders*, Geneva, World Health Organization.

Wille, L. (1881) 'Zur Lehre von den Zwangsvorstellungen'. *Archiv für Psychiatrie und Nervenkrankheiten*, 12: 1–43.

Winslow, F. (1856) 'On monomania'. *Journal of Psychological Medicine and Mental Pathology*, 9: 501–21.

Zeldin, T. (1977) *France (1848–1945). Vol.2: Intellect, taste and anxiety*, Oxford, Clarendon Press.

Chapter 23
Eating Disorders

Clinical Section
RON VAN DETH and WALTER VANDEREYCKEN

A complex array of disordered eating has been described for centuries. The phenomenon of rumination for instance, i.e. regurgitation of food into the mouth for a second mastication, has been known for hundreds of years. The craving for bizarre foods or substances unfit for consumption, called pica, has been noted since antiquity. And obesity, the physical manifestation of relative overnutrition, has been identified even in stone age carvings.[1] The vast domain of all these, often badly specified, disturbed patterns of eating cannot be adequately surveyed in this compressed overview. Hence, we will address the historical roots of the two currently most important and clear-cut eating disorders: anorexia nervosa and bulimia nervosa.

ANOREXIA NERVOSA AND THE HISTORY OF FOOD AVOIDANCE

Throughout history food avoidance belonged to the common symptoms in many debilitating physical disorders as well as in a wide variety of psychiatric syndromes. But for centuries this behaviour was not considered primarily a pathological phenomenon. Initially, extreme fasting was part of the penitential or ascetic practice of many pious Christians. Later on, forms of long-lasting food refusal, not attended with symptoms of well-known diseases like tuberculosis, were more likely to stir up speculations about supernatural powers or demonic influences. Ultimately, extreme or unusual forms of food abstinence were looked upon as signs of a mental disorder.

The evolution of the concept of anorexia

The term anorexia nervosa implies that the disorder is rooted in a nervous loss of appetite. References to the word anorexia can be found in medical sources ever since antiquity.[2] In classical times anorexia plainly denoted a state of insufficient 'orexis', i.e. general lassitude. Galen was one of the prominent medical men at the time referring to the term in the more restricted sense of want of appetite or loathing of food. Just like Hippocrates, however, Galen generally used the concept 'asitia' (or inedia) to refer to abstinence from food. The condition was attributed particularly to bad humours.

These conceptions remained unchanged well into the early-modern period, as appears from a considerable number of medical doctoral theses on anorexia. Although emotional factors were not neglected in these monographs, attention was focused on physical causes, particularly on derangements of the stomach. In medical lexicons and works of famous 18th-century nosologists the stomach was also incriminated as the source of the mischief in anorexia. In the first part of the 19th century anorexia was still more likely to be considered a symptom of several gastric complaints than a distinct clinical entity.

Especially in early 19th-century French literature the term nervous anorexia can be traced. In 1840, in a treatise on women's diseases, Fleury Imbert, an almost unknown French physiologist and phrenologist, distinguished, beside bulimia and pica, two kinds of anorexia: 'anorexie gastrique' and 'anorexie nerveuse'. The first is mainly a gastric disorder, whereas in the latter patients refuse to eat because their appetite is not excited by the brain. This 'anorexie nerveuse' is attended with neurotic symptoms like a 'change of ideation', inducing melancholy, anger and anxiety. Imbert's account did not arouse any professional attention from contemporaries and remained forgotten in the annals of medical history. Whereas in France the term 'anorexie mentale' became a standard medical expression from the 1890s on, it was the British physician William Gull who successfully introduced the term anorexia nervosa in 1874. Though clearly a misnomer, for the next 75 years loss of appetite was mistakenly assumed to be a necessary criterion for the syndrome.

Precursors of anorexia nervosa

Although the modern history of anorexia nervosa can only be dated from the 1870s, this does not exclude that the disorder might have existed long before under other names. Food avoidance and emaciation belonged to the common symptoms of ancient diseases like hysteria, love-sickness, mania, melancholy, dementia and all kinds of psychotic disorders. Of particular relevance seems chlorosis or 'green-sickness', which figured prominently in the medical literature of the 18th and 19th century. This disease predominantly afflicted beautiful, young ladies and was characterised by a multitude of symptoms, including paleness, amenorrhoea, emaciation and eating disturbances like lack of appetite and overeating, but especially pica. At the end of the 19th century iron-deficiency was generally known to be the most likely cause and within a few decades chlorosis belonged to the medical curiosities.[3]

Apart from this possible clinical analogue, the long forgotten nervous consumption is relevant to the history of anorexia nervosa because of a lucid description by Richard Morton. In his magnum opus ('Phthisiologia', 1689) this prominent British physician mentions the so-called 'nervous consumption', a wasting due to physical causes as well as emotional turmoil. Particularly Morton's case history of Mr. Duke's daughter immortalised him in the history of medicine as 'the first limner of anorexia nervosa'. This girl suffered in her teens from eating problems, emaciation, amenorrhoea, hypothermia, and recurring fainting fits. Morton was perplexed seeing her wasted condition, for which he could not establish any physical cause. He prescribed her several medicines, but refusing to cooperate with his medical regimen she died. Strikingly, Morton's astute depiction suggesting anorexia nervosa did not open the eyes of contemporaries. Although it appeared in a widely acclaimed and often reprinted and translated book, it has been a white crow in the vast medical literature for about two centuries.[4]

The first unequivocal descriptions of anorexia nervosa
Intriguing as Morton's case report may be, it was not until the second half of
the 19th century that the first unequivocal descriptions of anorexia nervosa
began to appear. In 1859 the chief medical officer of an asylum in Kentucky,
William Stout Chipley described the so-called sitomania, in those days usually
labelled as 'sitophobia'. Apart from this rather well-known form of food refusal
in the insane, he observed another type in emaciated adolescent girls 'belonging
to the higher walks of society', who refused food because of their craving for
attention. He illustrated this with a case of an 'amiable' and 'delicate' young
woman, who 'was not slow in perceiving that wonder and amazement grew
inversely to the amount of food taken'. In spite of every effort 'to wean her from
her folly, she died'.

A year thereafter the French clinician Louis-Victor Marcé published an article
about a specific form of 'hypochondriacal delirium'. He had observed several
young pubertal girls, who became subject to a distaste for food or a painful
digestion. Arriving at the 'delirious' conviction that they cannot eat, some
patients for months abstained almost completely from food and were reduced
to skeletons. Efforts to change the eating pattern were 'opposed with infinite
stratagems and unconquerable resistance'. The French original is enriched with
several case-histories which convincingly confirm that Marcé described early
examples of anorexia nervosa. Yet, however keen his description may be, the
psychiatric community of his day was apparently not ready for it: just like
Chipley's, it attracted hardly any attention.

It took more than a decade before morbid self-starvation became a distinct
clinical entity, recognised as such by the medical establishment. The Parisian
clinician Ernest-Charles Lasègue and the London physician Sir William Withey
Gull must be awarded 'joint parenthood' for the first explicit description of
anorexia nervosa.[5] In April 1873 Lasègue published his article on 'anorexie
hystérique' of which an English translation appeared shortly before Gull read
his paper on 'anorexia hysterica' in October of the same year. This lecture was
published in 1874, now provided with the term 'anorexia nervosa'. According
to both clinicians it was a psychogenic affliction, which occurred predominantly
in girls and young women. The characteristics described by Gull and Lasègue
are still valid today: severe weight loss, amenorrhoea, constipation, restlessness
and no evidence of underlying organic pathology.

The emergence of anorexia nervosa
Despite the accurate description by distinguished medical men, anorexia nervosa
did not yet attract much attention. Even in the countries of the two 'discoverers'
it took another decade before the medical press showed some interest in this
'new' syndrome. In many countries, like the United States, Germany and Italy,
anorexia nervosa remained largely a marginal phenomenon until well into the
20th century.[6]

Initially it was generally looked upon as a mental disorder. However, when
in 1914 the Hamburg pathologist Morris Simmonds found lesions of the
pituitary gland in some emaciated patients, anorexia nervosa became inextricably associated with this 'Simmonds' disease. It took more than two decades
before this erroneous idea was clearly refuted. In the 1940s, under the influence

of psychoanalysis and psychosomatic medicine, anorexia nervosa was rediscovered as a mental disorder. Removing from handbooks of internal medicine to those of psychiatry, a more broad and complex view of anorexia nervosa gradually emerged. From the 1960s on, especially through the influential publications of Hilde Bruch and Mara Selvini Palazzoli, anorexia nervosa established its reputation as a 'modern' and 'enigmatic' illness. Two essential features have been added to the original clinical picture as described by Lasègue and Gull: the relentless pursuit of thinness and a disturbance of the body image. In the most recent decades anorexia nervosa evolved from a rare and little known clinical entity to a 'fashionable' disorder appealing to the general public.

BULIMIA NERVOSA AND THE HISTORY OF OVEREATING

Like food avoidance, its counterpart overeating has an age-old history. No doubt, in the past gluttonous gorging frequently occurred among the privileged elite. Beyond this, at fairs spectacular overeaters incidentally entertained the general public and were exhibited among other freaks. However, apart from these rarities, excessive overeating has been within the physicians' realm from time immemorial.

The evolution of the concept of bulimia

Comparably to the term anorexia, the concept of bulimia has an extensive history.[7] According to Plutarch bulimos referred to an evil demon and originally it would have meant a great famine (pou limos = polys limos). Later philologists, however, claimed that it was taken from the Greek bous (ox) and limos (hunger), denoting hunger of such intensity that a man had the capacity to eat an entire ox. In this sense of morbid hunger the concept can be traced back to the work of the Greek comedy-poet Timokles (4th century BC). However, bulimia also implied weakness and fainting from hunger. In medical sources the aetiology of bulimia was closely connected with dysfunctions or abnormalities of the digestive system.

These various meanings of bulimia and specific explanations from antiquity endured well into the early-modern period. Some 18th-century nosologists distinguished no less than seven forms of bulimia. Four of them were 'symptomatic' and were attended with other symptoms like worms, diarrhoea and convulsions. Primary 'idiopathic' bulimia was divided into three categories: bulimia helluonum (excessive hunger), bulimia syncopalis (fainting from hunger) and bulimia emetica (overeating with vomiting). Emotional factors, like a lowered mood, increasingly were taken into consideration. However, well into the 20th century especially internists from French- and German-speaking countries considered bulimia primarily a sign of gastric dysfunctioning.

It was only recently that a specific form of bulimia achieved the status of a widely accepted psychiatric diagnosis. In 1979 the British psychiatrist Gerald Russell coined the term bulimia nervosa, referring to 'powerful and intractable urges to overeat' in combination with 'a morbid fear of becoming fat' and the avoidance 'of the fattening effects of food by inducing vomiting or abusing purgatives or both' in women with normal body-weight.

Precursors of bulimia nervosa

Although the term bulimia nervosa is of recent origin, reports on morbid hunger may be found under a multitude of different labels as far back as medical records exist. In view of the modern clinical picture of bulimia nervosa, historical accounts of gorging combined with vomiting need special attention. In medicine this eating abnormality was generally known under the label kynorexia or fames canina (canine appetite). From antiquity on until the 19th century it mostly denoted a dog-like insatiable voracity followed by spontaneous vomiting. Again, especially dysfunctions and abnormalities of the stomach were considered to be the cause.

The specific clinical picture of binge eating combined with vomiting was also mentioned in the context of other diseases. Just like food avoidance, overeating was not only a symptom of many organic disorders, but could also be associated with various other conditions like nervous gastric disorders, mania, hypochondriasis and chlorosis. Particularly in accounts on hysteria, overeating and vomiting were frequently mentioned symptoms, sometimes labelled as hysterical vomiting.[8] Nevertheless, a hundred years had to elapse before bulimia nervosa was introduced in the medical literature.

The emergence of bulimia nervosa

In former days overeating was sometimes described in association with anorexia and it was in this context that the clinical entity bulimia nervosa emerged. In his address of 1874 Gull already reported a voracious appetite in one of his anorexic patients, whereas Lasègue observed binge eating in reconvalescent anorexics. By the turn of the century several accounts appeared on patients with compulsive overeating followed by self-induced vomiting. These symptoms were regarded as a neurotic condition or a variant in the eating pattern of anorexic patients rather than a distinct syndrome. No doubt, the most carefully documented case report (although misdiagnosed as schizophrenia) was published by the Swiss psychiatrist Ludwig Binswanger in 1944. It is a moving account of Ellen West's relentless pursuit of thinness and her struggle with bulimia, leading to violent vomiting and excessive abuse of laxatives.

From the early 1970s on a relevant cluster of symptoms was identified, distinguishable from the better known clinical pictures of anorexia nervosa and obesity. Clinicians increasingly reported on women who binged copious quantities of food, but whose weights stayed within normal ranges via induced vomiting, laxatives, diuretics or constant dieting. A multitude of different names like dysorexia, bulimarexia, thin-fat syndrome, binge-purge syndrome and dietary chaos syndrome was proposed. However, only the term bulimia found its way to international classification systems of mental disorders, like DSM-III (American Psychiatric Association, 1980). Its description, however, was confusing and overinclusive, unlike Russell's (1979) notion of bulimia nervosa, which he considered an 'ominous variant of anorexia nervosa'. In the revised version of DSM-III (American Psychiatric Association, 1987), the bulimia diagnosis was brought into line with British terminology and renamed bulimia nervosa. Yet, even today some controversy continues as to whether this disorder is indeed a distinct clinical entity.

EATING DISORDERS: AGE-OLD OR NEW?

Throughout history we can recognise the existence of a heterogeneous manifestation of many disturbed patterns of eating. Whereas the terms bulimia and anorexia have been employed for ages, their nosological status has continuously been challenged. Traditionally, both food avoidance and overeating were almost invariably looked upon as symptoms of a diversity of disorders. They were predominantly viewed to be intimately associated with stomach-ailments. Considering this multifaceted continuum of eating abnormalities the history of eating disorders is age-old. Undoubtedly, disturbed patterns of eating such as food avoidance and gorging followed by spontaneous vomiting have always been with us.

Yet, despite intensified scholarly enquiry into their particular history in recent years, until now clear-cut and explicit descriptions closely matching modern anorexia nervosa or bulimia nervosa have not been discovered prior to about 1850. Symptoms associated with food avoidance or overeating varied considerably over time: preoccupations with weight and shape and the use of weight control strategies like dieting and self-induced vomiting have acquired popular and medical attention relatively recently (and only in Western or westernized countries). Hence, the specific syndromes of anorexia nervosa and bulimia nervosa appear to be relatively 'modern' clinical entities.[9]

In view of this historical variability in the clinical picture, eating disorders apparently belong to those disorders whose features show a remarkable susceptibility over the span of centuries to prevailing economic and socio-cultural conditions as well as to developing medical knowledge. The current constellations of symptoms comprising anorexia nervosa and bulimia nervosa are to be considered the latest – and conceivably not the last – variants in an ever-existing, but constantly changing pattern of disordered eating behaviour.

NOTES

1 For the medical history of pica, rumination and obesity, see respectively Parry-Jones and Parry-Jones (1992), Parry-Jones (1994) and Bray (1990).

2 On the conceptual history of anorexia, see Vandereycken and Van Deth (1988) and Parry-Jones (1991).

3 Exploration of 19th-century British asylum records revealed the frequent incidence of food refusal predominantly related to melancholia, mania and dementia (Parry-Jones, 1985). On the importance of these symptoms in the medical literature on melancholy, hysteria and love-sickness, see Vandereycken and Van Deth (1988). On chlorosis in relation to anorexia nervosa, see especially Loudon (1980; 1984).

4 See for the historical relationship between nervous consumption and anorexia nervosa: Van Deth and Vandereycken (1991).

5 On the respective claims for priority of Gull and Lasègue, see Vandereycken and Van Deth (1989) and on the English translation of Lasègue's text, see Vandereycken and Van Deth (1990). For the emergence of anorexia nervosa in the 19th century, see Vandereycken and Van Deth (1988), Brumberg (1988), Beumont (1991), Shorter (1987; 1994).

6 On national differences in reports of anorexia nervosa at the turn of the

century, see: Vandereycken and Lowenkopf (1990), Vandereycken et al. (1991) and especially Habermas (1991).

7 On the conceptual history of bulimia, see: Baumann (1935), Ziolko and Schrader (1985), Stein and Laakso (1988), Parry-Jones (1991), Parry-Jones and Parry-Jones (1991). The more recent history of bulimia (nervosa) was reviewed by Casper (1983), Habermas (1989; 1990; 1992a), Vandereycken (1994).

8 On the relationship between late 19th-century hysterical vomiting and bulimia nervosa, see: Van Deth and Vandereycken (1995).

9 On the continuous and discontinuous elements of the history of eating disturbances, see DiNicola (1990), Habermas (1992b), Van Deth and Vandereycken (1992; 1994) and Parry-Jones and Parry-Jones (1994).

REFERENCES

American Psychiatric Association (1980) *Diagnostic and Statistical Manual of Mental Disorders – Third edition (DSM-III)*, Washington, D.C., A.P.A.

American Psychiatric Association (1987) *Diagnostic and Statistical Manual of Mental Disorders – Third edition, Revised (DSM-III-R)*, Washington, D.C., A.P.A.

Baumann, E.D. (1935) 'Ueber den boulimos und die fames canina' (On the boulimos and the fames canina). *Janus*, 39: 165–74.

Beumont, P.J.V. (1991) 'The history of eating and dieting disorders'. *Clinics in applied Nutrition*, 1 (2): 9–20.

Binswanger, L. (1944/45) 'Der Fall Ellen West: Eine anthropologisch-klinische Studie'. *Schweizer Archiv für Neurologie und Psychiatrie*, 53: 255–77; 54: 69–117, 330–60; 1945, 55: 16–40. Translation: 'The case of Ellen West: An anthropological-clinical study'. In May, R., Angel, E. and Ellenberger, H.F. (eds.) *Existence*, New York, Basic Books, 1958, 237–364.

Bray, G.A. (1990) 'Obesity: Historical development of scientific and cultural ideas'. *International Journal of Obesity*, 14: 909–26.

Brumberg, J.J. (1988) *Fasting Girls: The Emergence of Anorexia Nervosa as a Modern Disease*, Cambridge (Mass.), Harvard University Press.

Casper, R.C. (1983) 'On the emergence of bulimia nervosa as a syndrome. A historical view'. *International Journal of Eating Disorders*, 2: 3–16.

Chipley, W.S. (1859) 'Sitomania: Its causes and treatment'. *American Journal of Insanity*, 16 (July): 1–42.

DiNicola, V.F. (1990) 'Anorexia multiforme: self-starvation in historical and cultural context'. *Transcultural Psychiatric Research Review*, 27: 165–96, 245–86.

Gull, W.W. (1874) 'Anorexia nervosa (apepsia hysterica, anorexia hysterica)'. *Transactions of the Clinical Society of London*, 7: 22–8.

Habermas, T. (1989) 'The psychiatric history of anorexia nervosa and bulimia nervosa: Weight concerns and bulimic symptoms in early case reports'. *International Journal of Eating Disorders*, 8: 259–73.

Habermas, T. (1990) *Heisshunger. Historische Bedingungen der Bulimia Nervosa*, (Binge eating. Historical conditions of bulimia nervosa), Frankfurt, Fischer.

Habermas, T. (1991) 'The role of psychiatric and medical traditions in the discovery and description of anorexia nervosa in France, Germany, and Italy, 1873–1918'. *Journal of Nervous and Mental Disease*, 179: 360–5.

Habermas, T. (1992a) 'Further evidence on early case descriptions of anorexia nervosa and bulimia nervosa'. *International Journal of Eating Disorders*, 11: 351–9.

Habermas, T. (1992b) 'Historical continuities and discontinuities between religious and medical interpretations of extreme fasting. The background to Giovanni Brugnoli's description of two cases of anorexia nervosa in 1875'. *History of Psychiatry*, 3: 431–55.

Imbert, F. (1840) *Traité Théorique et Pratique des Maladies des Femmes*, (Theoretical and practical treatise on women's diseases), Paris, G. Baillière.

Lasègue, E.C. (1873) 'De l'anorexie hystérique'. *Archives Générales de Médecine*, 21: 385–403. Partial translation: On hysterical anorexia. *Medical Times and Gazette*, 2: 265–6; 367–9.

Loudon, I.S.L. (1980) 'Chlorosis, anaemia and anorexia nervosa'. *British Medical Journal*, 281: 1669–75.

Loudon, I.S.L. (1984) 'The diseases called chlorosis'. *Psychological Medicine*, 14: 27–36.

Marcé, L.-V. (1860) 'Note sur une forme de délire hypochondriaque consécutive aux dyspepsies et caractérisée principalement par le refus d'aliments'. *Annales Médico-Psychologiques*, 6: 15–28. Partial translation in *Journal of Psychological Medicine and Mental Pathology*, 1860, 13: 264–6 and completely translated in *History of Psychiatry*, 1994, 5, 273–83.

Morton, R. (1689) *Phthisiologia seu exercitationes de phthisi*, London, S. Smith.

Parry-Jones, B. (1991) 'Historical terminology of eating disorders'. *Psychological Medicine*, 21: 21–8.

Parry-Jones, B. (1994) 'Merycism or rumination disorder. A historical investigation and current assessment'. *British Journal of Psychiatry*, 165: 303–14.

Parry-Jones, B. and Parry-Jones, W.L. (1991) 'Bulimia: An archival review of its history in psychosomatic medicine'. *International Journal of Eating Disorders*, 10: 129–43.

Parry-Jones, B. and Parry-Jones, W.L. (1992) 'Pica: Symptom or eating disorder? A historical assessment'. *British Journal of Psychiatry*, 160: 341–54.

Parry-Jones, W.L. (1985) 'Archival exploration of anorexia nervosa'. *Journal of Psychiatric Research*, 19: 95–100.

Parry-Jones, W.L. and Parry-Jones, B. (1994) 'Implications of historical evidence for the classification of eating disorders. A dimension overlooked in DSM-III-R and ICD-10'. *British Journal of Psychiatry*, 165: 287–92.

Russell, G.F.M. (1979) 'Bulimia nervosa: An ominous variant of anorexia nervosa'. *Psychological Medicine*, 9: 429–48.

Shorter, E. (1987) 'The first great increase in anorexia nervosa'. *Journal of Social History*, 21: 69–96.

Shorter, E. (1994) *From the Mind into the Body. The Cultural Origins of Psychosomatic Symptoms*, New York, Free Press, pp.149–93.

Simmonds, M. (1914) 'Über Hypophysisschwund mit tödlichem Ausgang'. *Deutsche medizinische Wochenschrift*, 40: 322–3.

Stein, D.M. and Laakso, W. (1988) 'Bulimia: A historical perspective'. *International Journal of Eating Disorders*, 7: 201–10.

Vandereycken, W., (1994) 'Emergence of bulimia nervosa as a separate diagnostic entity: Review of the literature from 1960 to 1979'. *International Journal of Eating Disorders*, 16: 105–16.

Vandereycken, W., Habermas, T., Van Deth, R. and Meermann, R. (1991) 'German publications on anorexia nervosa in the nineteenth century'. *International Journal of Eating Disorders*, 10: 473–90.

Vandereycken, W. and Lowenkopf, E.L. (1990) 'Anorexia nervosa in 19th-century America'. *Journal of Nervous and Mental Disease*, 178: 531–5.

Vandereycken, W. and Van Deth, R. (1988) *Van vastenwonder tot magerzucht. Anorexia nervosa in historisch perspectief*, Meppel-Amsterdam, Boom. German version: (1990) *Hungerkünstler, Fastenwunder, Magersucht. Eine Kulturgeschichte der Ess-störungen*, Zülpich, Biermann. English version: (1994) *From Fasting Saints to Anorexic Girls. The History of Self-Starvation*, London/New York, The Athlone Press/New York University Press.

Vandereycken, W. and Van Deth, R. (1989) 'Who was the first to describe anorexia nervosa: Gull or Lasègue?' *Psychological Medicine*, 19: 837–45.

Vandereycken, W. and Van Deth, R. (1990) 'A tribute to Lasègue's description of anorexia nervosa (1873), with completion of its English translation'. *British Journal of Psychiatry*, 157: 902–8.

Van Deth, R. and Vandereycken, W. (1991) 'Was nervous consumption a precursor of anorexia nervosa?' *Journal of the History of Medicine and Allied Sciences*, 46: 3–19.

Van Deth, R. and Vandereycken, W. (1992) 'What happened to the "fasting girls"? A follow-up in retrospect'. In Herzog, W., Deter, H.-C. and Vandereycken, W. (eds.) *The Course of Eating Disorders*, Berlin-Heidelberg-New York, Springer-Verlag, pp. 348–66.

Van Deth, R. and Vandereycken, W. (1994) 'Continuity and discontinuity in the history of self-starvation'. *Eating Disorders Review*, 2: 47–55.

Van Deth, R. and Vandereycken, W. (1995) 'Was 19th-century hysterical vomiting a variant of bulimia nervosa?' *History of Psychiatry*, (in press).

Ziolko, H.U. and Schrader, H.C. (1985) 'Bulimie' (Bulimia). *Fortschritte der Neurologie und Psychiatrie*, 53: 231–58.

Chapter 23

Eating Disorders

Social Section
WILLIAM LL PARRY-JONES and
BRENDA PARRY-JONES

INTRODUCTION

Although there is some discrepancy between DSM-III-R (American Psychiatric Association, 1987) and ICD-10 (World Health Organisation, 1990) in terms of which conditions carry the full status of eating disorders, there is general consensus that they comprise anorexia nervosa, bulimia nervosa, rumination disorder and pica. These disorders, therefore, form the subject of this chapter, excluding obesity, which is classified as a physical disorder not associated generally with any distinct psychological or behavioural syndrome. The chapter draws upon the findings of on-going studies of published cases, from the 16th century onwards, of self-inflicted starvation, bulimia, rumination disorder and pica, and their consideration in the light of current diagnostic criteria (Parry-Jones, W.Ll. and Parry-Jones, B., 1994). The longitudinal perspective makes it possible to identify continuities and discontinuities between historical presentations of these conditions and their current forms, thereby distinguishing consistent from possibly ephemeral clinical phenomena and causative influences. Such research highlights changes in the form of disorders over time and the degree of symptom overlap between them. In this chapter, consideration is given to historical evidence of socio-cultural variables implicated in the pathogenesis of eating disorders and to social consequences of disorders or some of their components.

ANOREXIA NERVOSA

The term anorexia was first used in English sources in the late-sixteenth century and the specialised form, anorexia nervosa, from 1874 onwards. Observations relating to anorexia nervosa are based chiefly on evidence derived from a series of 360 cases of voluntary self-starvation, or sustained abnormally low weight, from 1500 to 1939 (Parry-Jones, B. and Parry-Jones, W.Ll., unpublished data). These cases were grouped into eight categories, as accurately as the variable historical evidence permitted. The largest category (179 cases) was characterised by abnormal attitudes to food, eating or weight. A striking 85 per cent of this sub-group were female, over half were aged under 20 at the time of fasting and most were unmarried. This group, therefore, forms a discrete entity, which contains certain features strongly suggestive of continuities with modern anorexia nervosa and, conversely, emphasises some important differences.

While extreme caution has to be exercised in retrospective causative speculation, there is evidence which suggests some correlation between socio-cultural
influences and predisposition to, and the precipitation and maintenance of
disordered eating. This is well-illustrated by pressures fostering the pursuit of
holiness by self-starvation, involving the sublimation of sexuality and assertion
of self-control, e.g. St. Catherine of Siena in the 14th century (Rampling, 1985).
Although opinion remains divided among current historians whether ascetic
food-refusal by medieval nuns represented an antecedent form of the modern
eating disorder (Bell, 1985; Bynum, 1986; van Deth and Vandereycken, 1991;
Vandereycken and van Deth, 1994), the appeal of extreme abstinence and
self-denial has endured in presentations of anorexia nervosa in Western culture
(Skrabanek, 1983).

There is little doubt concerning the inter-relationship between socio-cultural
influences and changing concepts of female beauty, relative to body-shape and
weight (Burke, 1810; Fothergill, 1874). The clear association of female attractiveness with a particular body-shape or complexion changed over time, but
reduced food intake and dietary peculiarities remained consistent strategies in
achieving such goals (Schwartz, 1986). Body-shape concern was shown by girls
as early as the mid-seventeenth century (Bulwer, 1653); there were cases in the
18th and 19th century which indicated fears of being or becoming fat, and
restrictive measures such as drinking vinegar, or severely limiting food intake
were initiated (De Valangin, 1768; Brillat-Savarin, 1825). 'Morbid dread of fat'
was sufficiently common to feature in medical journals from the 1880s onwards
(e.g. Editorial, 1880). In the 1870s, there were references to girls' education
being unhealthy and superficial, because it was imbued with 'matrimonial'
aspirations, not to make healthy wives and mothers, but to render pupils
attractive to the male sex (Hime, 1876). In fact, from the 17th century onwards,
maternal ambition to achieve a fashionable 'shape' for daughters perpetuated
the practice of strait-lacing even pre-adolescent girls, with disregard for the perils
of organ-constriction, spinal deformity or even chlorosis (e.g. Dover, 1742).
Marriage eligibility, therefore, provided an enduring social pressure on middle
and upper class females for cultivating the appropriate aesthetic appeal. Although
there is no evidence of body-shape concern in cases described by Gull or Lasègue,
Charcot's entry in Tuke's 'Dictionary of Psychological Medicine' (1892) noted that
patients with anorexia nervosa were 'strongly impressed with the fear of obesity',
and Allbutt (1905) related 'panic fear of obesity' to decreased intake, particularly
of meat. Moreover, it is important to place early evidence of body-shape concern
in juxtaposition with the lack of any historical corroboration to date of
body-image distortion, in terms of personal size perception, in the authors' case
series (Parry-Jones, B. and Parry-Jones W.Ll., unpublished data), although this
does not imply, necessarily, that the latter did not exist (Shorter, 1987).

In addition to the identification of physical factors as likely precipitants of
eating pathology, psychological and social causes have been implicated regularly. Themes, such as lovesickness and sexual frustration, have been consistent
since the 16th century and, regularly, therapeutic recommendations have included marriage or childbearing. Maintaining or perpetuating factors of self-
inflicted fasting effectively demonstrate the role of social influences. The fasting
identity and life-style could be influential, socially and situationally, coupled

with secondary gains from invalidism and prolonged dependency on family or friends. In many cases, personal financial or material gain followed public recognition as a curiosity or a miracle (Lentulus, 1604). Sometimes, there was frank exploitation of abstainers by family, friends or entrepreneurs and, conversely, fasters could exercise considerable control over their personal destiny and, in some cases, over their care-givers. Both processes are well-reflected in the tragic case of Sarah Jacob, the Welsh fasting girl (Fowler, 1871).

Voluntary starvation, especially in the presence of an abundant food supply, has always exerted an emotive and manipulative impact on others. Historical cases confirm the extent to which this behaviour could become, rapidly, the focus of attention in the family, neighbourhood or wider society, and reveal that a sentiment of not being displeased with their situation was evinced by many fasters. From the 'inedia mirabilis' of successive fasting girls of the 16th to the 19th century to the relentless pursuit of thinness of modern anorexics, who are the target of ever-increasing public awareness and media exploitation, the same morbid fascination is manifested by observers. This has to be seen in the context of growing interest in human freaks in the 18th and 19th centuries (Bogdan, 1988), aptly termed 'The Deformito-Mania' (Editorial, 1847). Suspected imposture always attracted public and medical curiosity. Although some claims were frankly fraudulent, alleged abstinence often followed ill-health and periods of genuine fasting, and many proven impostors, such as Ann Moor of Tutbury, survived for years on minute food intake (J-L-, 1809). Diverse features associated with fasting included claims of prophecy, divine or supernatural sustenance, spiritualism and the mysterious ability to live on air, concepts aided by traditional correlation of weightlessness with witchcraft. The potential rewards of fraudulence, usually short-lived, were fame, material gain, and the paradoxical benefits of invalidism. Professional exhibitionists were predominantly male. They included freaks and 'living skeletons', e.g. Claude Seurat (Hone, 1825), maintaining low body-weight with, or without, controlled intake, and touring 'hunger artists', who displayed themselves for money and, increasingly for scientific observation, reflecting rising interest in the physiology and pathology of inanition. Maintenance of low weight, from occupational necessity, was seen historically in jockeys and the same pressure features, currently, in high-risk, anorexic groups e.g. ballet dancers.

The unpublished series of historical cases (Parry-Jones, B. and Parry-Jones, W.Ll.), suggest strongly that the socio-cultural context had an important bearing on the generation and manifestation of self-inflicted starvation, lending support to the modern view of anorexia nervosa as a 'culture reactive', if not 'culture bound', syndrome (Di Nicola 1990a and b). The role of chlorosis in the history of eating abnormalities remains controversial and chloro-anorexic and chloro-anaemic forms have been identified (Loudon, 1984). While the enigmatic disappearance of chlorosis in the early 20th century has been attributed to advances in haematology, socio-cultural factors such as female emancipation, dress reform, exercise and improved nutrition, were contributory also. Placing the modern disorder of anorexia nervosa in historical perspective provides a valuable corrective against over-simplistic assumption that current socio-cultural hypotheses, such as those based on feminist ideology or particular patterns of family dynamics, can provide the final definitive explanation (Brumberg, 1988; Wolf, 1990).

BULIMIA NERVOSA

Bulimia, in the form of pathological voracity, has been reported for over 2000 years (Parry-Jones, B., 1991; Parry-Jones, B. and Parry-Jones, W.Ll., 1995), associated with a wide variety of physical, and some psychological, features. Its pre-twentieth century incidence, however, is difficult to gauge. One early medical commentator (Robinson 1727), who defined bulimia as a 'Ravening, and all devouring Appetite', in which 'the Patient is very uneasy unless he be continually a-cramming', was of the opinion that 'an increased Appetite is a very uncommon Disorder'. Published cases of bulimia or canine appetite were certainly strikingly less numerous than those of self-inflicted starvation and the quality of the descriptive material is highly variable. The findings utilised in this chapter are based chiefly on 40 case reports from the late 17th to the 19th century (Parry-Jones, B. and Parry-Jones, W.Ll., 1991; and 1995).

Among the earliest examples of socio-culturally determined hyperphagia were the traditions of induced vomiting by satiated Roman patricians to make space for further culinary delights, such as were described in the first century by Petronius. Although gluttony was reviled by the medieval Roman Catholic church, societal response to limited life expectancy and insecurity of food supplies led to gross over-eating during times of plenty and, consequently, discussions of 'bulimia' and 'hounds' appetite' featured in a number of early medical texts. A consequence of ecclesiastical censure of over-indulgence was the practice of self-induced vomiting as a penance, which formed part of the austerities of some medieval nuns, notably Catherine of Siena in the 14th century. The life-dominating social effects of gorging followed by vomiting was commented upon as early as the 18th century. From the latter period on, the relationship of bulimia with 'neurotic' and 'hysterical' disorders came to be acknowledged increasingly, and by the early twentieth century its frequent occurrence in 'hysterical' females had gained widespread acceptance. During the 1930s, bulimia was reported as a symptom of emotional deprivation and poor social adaptation among maladjusted juveniles, evacuees and refugees.

Bulimia seems to have been viewed originally as an ailment affecting the stomach or as a structural abnormality, but it began to acquire psychological attributes from the early 18th century onwards, notably lowered mood, and minor self-mutilative behaviour was identified in four of the historical cases (Parry-Jones, B. and Parry-Jones, W.Ll., 1993). Significantly, none of these historical subjects appeared to have body-weight and shape preoccupations, or, indeed, to be affected by related social pressures. Despite enormous food intake, the weight of historical bulimics was described as normal, 'embonpoint', thin or emaciated, and rarely over-weight. Bulimia emetica featured in some historical cases (e.g. Mortimer, 1745), but there is no evidence that the vomiting was ever self-induced. It is indicative of socio-cultural change, in terms of public tolerance, that emesis has now become secretive in bulimia nervosa. Such reticence rarely applied in earlier periods when therapeutic use of emetics was widespread. In fact, Stein and Laakso (1988) suggest that 'apparent social attention for eating large quantities of food . . . may be explanatory in some cases', in that it provided reinforcement for gorging behaviour. Over the centuries, the reported bulimic cases generated considerable medical interest and public fascination, particularly for displays of sensational polyphagic behaviour for financial gain, such as that of the Frenchman, Tarrare, who performed grotesque ingestive feats with a troupe of itinerant jugglers (Lord, 1834).

The increased reporting of bulimia from the mid-20th century on has been widely attributed to changed socio-cultural expectations among young women (Habermas, 1989). Their extreme concerns about body-shape and weight has led to the increasing use of compensatory mechanisms, including self-induced vomiting, diuretic and laxative abuse, which were entirely absent from the historical, predominantly male, cases. By taking a historical perspective, it is possible to view the current form, bulimia nervosa, with its characteristic preoccupation with body-weight and shape and feelings of loss of control over eating, as the 1980s variant in a long line of bulimic disorders, influenced by the prevalence of socio-culturally determined weight-consciousness among young women.

RUMINATION DISORDER

Rumination, or merycism, is a relatively rare disturbance of gastric and oeso-phageal function in man. In this disorder, a bolus of food is regurgitated, without nausea, into the mouth shortly after a meal, and subjected to second mastication, like cattle chewing the cud. The remasticated mass is generally re-swallowed, but sometimes ejected, the latter resulting, particularly in infants or mentally defective subjects, in moderate to severe nutritional deficits. Surprisingly, there is no evidence of the description of human rumination during antiquity or in the Middle Ages and the condition was first identified in 1618, by the Italian anatomist, Fabricius of Aquapendente. Medical interest persisted throughout the 17th century and, in 1685, J.C. Peyer published a detailed treatise, 'Merycologia', dealing exclusively with bovine and human rumination (Kanner, 1936). From its first description, this behaviour was perceived as an atavistic analogy to the cud-chewing of herbivorous animals and carried considerable stigma (Riesman, 1895). Rumination has been recorded over a long time-span and observations made in this chapter are based on the examination of over 100 cases, from the 17th to the 20th century (Parry-Jones, B., 1994).

Ruminators in the historical series were predominantly male and came from a variety of social classes, ranging from peasants and artisans to educated professionals, including a surprising number of medical practitioners. The disorder occurred frequently in the mentally retarded of all ages, especially among understimulated institutionalised populations with limited social contact. Stigma was attached to rumination throughout its history owing to its association with ideas of degeneracy and bestiality, and some ruminators from the 17th to the 20th century suffered considerable embarrassment and resented being viewed as medical curiosities. Their degree of social impairment was variable, but at worst it could amount to complete withdrawal from society. Some of the early causative theories accentuated the degenerate 'bovine' connections, encouraging concealment and secrecy, and making accurate estimates of incidence difficult. Other theories included viewing rumination as an imitative behaviour – copying human or animal ruminators – or the popular 'maternal impressions' theory, which held that continuous observation of, or cohabitation with, ruminating animals during pregnancy could transmit bovine influences to the unborn child, subsequently emerging as rumination. Hereditary influences were commented on frequently (e.g. Brockbank, 1907) and, historically, it is possible to distinguish familial patterns in incidence, including descent through the male line and recurrence in consecutive generations of one family.

Some ruminators utilised their unusual ability to earn their livings as public performers (Long, 1929), while others presented as malingerers, accentuating their medical problems to avoid military or naval service (Nelson, 1876). The occurrence of rumination in young children was first referred to by Heiling, in 1823, and infants were described increasingly from 1907 onwards. Infant cases without physical abnormalities causative of rumination demonstrated consistent correlation with lower socio-economic class, poor nurturing relationships and inadequate stimulation and their rumination generally ceased when a warm, stable relationship with care-givers was achieved. Infant rumination was more common in the early part of the twentieth century and decreased from late 1950s on, a fact attributed to the improved post-war socio-economic conditions, which benefited infant care and nutrition. The influence of socio-cultural factors can be seen clearly in the range of explanations proffered for rumination overtime, including inherited degeneracy; bovine ancestry; aberrant behaviour; digestive disorder; anatomic abnormality; neuroticism; benign, natural habit; under-stimulation and emotional deprivation, and nurturing deficiencies. Although characterised as an eating disorder in DSM-III-R from 1987, there continues to be controversy whether it constitutes a benign condition or habit or a disease entity with potentially fatal outcome.

PICA

Pica has been known for over 2,000 years, as a manifestation of false or craving appetite, the deliberate ingestion of a bizarre selection of foods, non-nutritive substances and non-food items (Parry-Jones, B. and Parry-Jones, W.Ll., 1992). Collective accounts of identified groups of pica sufferers, such as chlorotic girls, predominate over individual case-histories, making numerical estimate of cases difficult. Observations in this chapter are based on descriptions of pica from the mid-sixteenth century to the present. Pica was symptomatic of pregnancy, chlorosis, iron-deficiency, worm infestation and, later, in the case of young children, inadequate stimulation or mothering. Historically, it was heavily female orientated, with some rare male cases from the 17th century on and was found most commonly in chlorotic girls. Lange (1554), credited with the first description of chlorosis, noted the extraordinary pica of young girls, whose surest cure he maintained (as did many subsequent medical men) was marriage. Pregnant women and young children have remained the social groups consist-ently presenting with pica from the mid-sixteenth century to the present and its frequent occurrence in the mentally retarded of all ages has been described from the mid-nineteenth century. Harris (1742) claimed that pregnant pica was social class-related, claiming that it occurred chiefly in idle and fashionable upper-class ladies and only rarely in working women on a plain diet.

It is evident that socio-cultural factors influenced adolescent pica and, as early as the 17th century, girls consumed lime, ashes, plaster, coal, vinegar, raw corn and earth for cosmetic reasons, to make themselves pale and attractive, and showed aversion to normal food (Havers and Davies, 1665). Such abnormal cravings were described graphically in The Spectator (Letter 431, 1712) and the frequency of similar literary references, over a considerable timespan, corroborates the high pre-twentieth century incidence of chlorosis throughout Europe. One astute medical commentator (Calmette, 1706) noted that these 'perversions' could be 'induced by others, as often happens in Maids, that create one another an Appetite to certain things by persuading them, that by taking such things they formerly have made themselves look fair and handsome'. This provides an early, unequivocal statement concerning conformity induced by peer-group pressure to the prevailing pattern of female beauty. The stylised pica of upper-class chlorotic girls perpetuated behaviour which became fashionable for the weaker sex and it was imitated also by lower class females. By the 19th century, therefore, chlorotic pica was seen in maidservants and factory girls, as well as in girls in more genteel society. Similarly, there is evidence of the undesirable influence of some school experiences on eating habits, particularly inadequate diet and lack of open-air exercise, which fostered excessive delicacy, even invalidism, as appropriate female attributes.

Many pica substances were non-nutritive, non-foods or, in modern terms, non-calorific and can be regarded in some circumstances, as implementation of a regime of severe dietary restraint, resembling that in anorexia nervosa. Lièbault (1582), for example, referred to young girls who 'stuffe themselves everie hour' with excessive amounts of cold water, causing menstrual suppression. This was endorsed by Riverius (1668), who described chlorotic girls who drank 'great draughts of water at bed-time, or in the morning fasting, or eat . . . snow or ice'. It seems likely that cultural factors were instrumental in the persistence of such behaviour, a modern variant of which pagophagia (compulsive ice eating), occurs in the USA and Africa (Parry-Jones, B., 1992). Similarly, geophagy, the custom of eating a specific clay or earth, traditionally passed down in primitive communities from generation to generation, provides clear evidence of the continuing influence of cultural traditions on ingestae. The ingestion of substances which appear bizarre in some social contexts, but are seen as the norm in other civilisations and social groups, clearly illustrates the impact of socio-cultural factors.

CONCLUSIONS

There is indisputable evidence of enduring pathological processes concerned with eating behaviour and attitudes to food, body-shape and weight, which have attracted diverse interpretations over time. These disorders have shown varying degrees of overlap and have manifested themselves variously, characterised by the passing prominence of different features, influenced by the pathoplastic effects of prevailing socio-cultural factors. This is particularly well-illustrated by the morphological changes displayed by the antecedent forms of modern anorexia nervosa, or 'anorexia multiforme' (Di Nicola, 1990a), as medieval asceticism gave way to secularisation and medicalisation of fasting behaviour.

The impact of socio-cultural factors is most prominent in self-inflicted starvation and in pica, and the former has spawned the widest descriptive and pictorial representations, providing a considerable resource for social and medical historians. Historical evidence of the significance of changing socio-cultural factors in the pathogenesis and syndromal delineation of eating disorders and their classification raises queries about over-reliance on diagnostic criteria relating to phenomena that have acquired emphasis relatively recently (Parry-Jones, W.Ll. and Parry-Jones, B., 1994). The value of a historical approach lies in the extraction of the enduring core phenomena, such as voluntary food abstention or hyperphagia. Moreover, therapeutic objectives can be jeopardised by the uncritical acceptance of the significance of potentially ephemeral socio-cultural influences. While it is possible to construct some plausible explanatory models linking socio-cultural factors to eating disorders, major problems of interpretation remain, since such factors tend to be inter-related and it is unclear whether they have direct influence, independent of other variables.

REFERENCES

American Psychiatric Association (1987) *Diagnostic and Statistical Manual of Mental Disorders*, 3rd edition revised, Washington DC, American Psychiatric Association.

Bell, R. (1985) *Holy Anorexia*, Chicago, University of Chicago Press.

Bicknell, D.J. (1975) *Pica A Childhood Symptom*, Southampton, Butterworths.

Bogdan, R. (1988) *Freak Show Presenting Human Oddities for Amusement and Profit*, Chicago, University of Chicago Press.

Bourneville, D.M. and Séglas, J. (1883) 'Du Mérycisme'. *Archives de Neurologie*, VI: 86–94, 246–61, 376–402.

Brillat-Savarin, J.A. (1825) *The Philosopher in the Kitchen*, translated (1988), A. Drayton, London, Penguin.

Brockbank, E.M. (1907) 'Merycism or rumination in man'. *British Medical Journal*, 1: 421–7.

Brumberg, J.J. (1988) *Fasting Girls. The Emergence of Anorexia Nervosa as a Modern Disease*, Cambridge, MA, Harvard University Press.

Bulwer, J. (1653) *Anthropometamorphosis: Man transform'd: Or The Artifical Changeling Historically Presented*, London, Printed by W. Hunt.

Burke, E. (1810) *A Philosophical Inquiry into the Origin of our Ideas of the Sublime and Beautiful*, London, Printed for T. Tegg.

Bynum, C.W. (1987) *Holy Feast and Holy Fast The Religious Significance of Food to Medieval Women*, Berkeley & Los Angeles, University of California Press.

Calmette, F. (1706) *Riverius Reformatus or the Modern Riverius, Containing the Modern Practice of Physick*, London, Printed for R. Wellington.

Cooper, M. (1957) *Pica: A Survey of the Historical Literature as well as Reports from the Fields of Veterinary Medicine and Anthropology, the Present Study of Pica in Young Children, and a Discussion of its Pediatric and Psychological Implications*, Springfield, Ill, C.C. Thomas.

De Valangin, F. (1768) *A Treatise on Diet*, London, For the Author.

Di Nicola, V.F. (1990a) 'Anorexia multiforme: Self-starvation in historical and cultural context. Part I: Self-starvation as a historical chameleon'. *Transcultural Psychiatric Research*, 27: 165–96.

Di Nicola, V.F. (1990b) 'Anorexia multiforme. Self-starvation in historical and cultural context. Part II: Anorexia nervosa as a culture-reactive syndrome'. *Transcultural Psychiatric Research*, 27: 245–86.

Dover, T. (1742) *The Ancient Physician's Legacy to his Country. Being What He has Collected Himself in Fifty-eight Years Practice*, London, C. Hitch.

Editorial (1847) 'The Deformito-Mania'. *Punch, or The London Charivari*, XIII: 90.

Editorial (1880) 'The fear of fat'. *Lancet*, 1: 349.

Fothergill, J.M. (1874) *The Maintenance of Health. A Medical Work for Lay Readers*, London, Smith, Elder & Co.

Fowler, R. (1871) *A Complete History of the Welsh Fasting Girl (Sarah Jacob) with Comments thereon and Observations on Death from Starvation*, London, H. Renshaw.

Habermas, T. (1989) 'The psychiatric history of anorexia nervosa and bulimia nervosa: weight concerns and bulimic symptoms in early case reports'. *International Journal of Eating Disorders*, 8: 259–73.

Harris, W. (1742) *A Full View of All the Diseases Incident to Children*, London, For A. Millar.

Havers, G. and Davies, J. (1665) *Another Collection of Philosophical Conferences of the French Virtuosi, upon Questions of All Sorts; for the Improving of Natural Knowledge*, London, T. Dring & J. Starkey.

Hime, T.W. (1876) 'Obstetric medicine: Hysteria'. *British Medical Journal*, 2, 277–8.

Hone, W. (1825) *The Everyday Book*, London, Printed by A. Applegath.

J-L- (1809) *An Account of the Extraordinary Abstinence of Ann Moor . . . giving . . . an Account of the Investigation Instituted on the Occasion . . .*, Uttoxeter, Printed by R. Richards.

Kanner, L. (1936) 'Historical notes on rumination in man'. *Medical Life*, 43: 26–60.

Lange, J. (1554) *Epistolae Medicinales*, Basle.

Lentulus, P. (1604) *Historia Admiranda de Prodigiosa Appolloniae Schreierae virginis in agro Bernensi, Inedia*, Bern.

Letter 431 (1712) *The Spectator*, Ed. (1965) D.F. Bond, vol.IV, pp. 14–17 Oxford, Clarendon Press.

Lièbault, J. (1582) *Trois Livres del la Santé, Fecondité et Maladies des Femmes*, Paris.

Long, C.F. (1929) 'Rumination in man'. *American Journal of Medical Sciences*, 178: 815–22.

Lord, P.B. (1834) *Popular Physiology*, London, J.W. Parker.

Loudon, I.S.L. (1984) 'The diseases called chlorosis'. *Psychological Medicine*, 14: 27–36.

Mortimer, C. (1745) 'Communication of the extract of a letter from Mr. B__ B__ r containing an account in pounds and ounces, of the surprising quantities of food devoured by a boy . . . who labour'd under a canine appetite, at Black Barnsley in Yorkshire'. *Philosophical Transactions of the Royal Society*, XLIII, 366–8.

Nelson, R. (1876) 'Letter to the Editor concerning cases of voluntary vomiting or rumination, frequently in the context of malingering'. *Lancet*, 1: 624.

Parry-Jones, B. (1991) 'Historical terminology of eating disorders'. *Psychological Medicine*, 21: 21–8.

Parry-Jones, B. (1992) 'Pagophagia, or compulsive ice consumption: a historical perspective'. *Psychological Medicine*, 22: 561–71.

Parry-Jones, B. (1994) 'Merycism or rumination disorder: A historical investigation and current assessment'. *British Journal of Psychiatry*, 165: 303–14.

Parry-Jones, B. and Parry-Jones, W.Ll. (1991) 'Bulimia: An archival review of its history in psychosomatic medicine'. *International Journal of Eating Disorders*, 10: 129–43.

Parry-Jones, B. and Parry-Jones, W.Ll. (1992) 'Pica: Symptom or eating disorder? A historical assessment'. *British Journal of Psychiatry*, 160: 341–54.

Parry-Jones, B. and Parry-Jones, W.Ll. (1993) 'Self-mutilation in four historical cases of bulimia'. *British Journal of Psychiatry*, 163: 394–402.

Parry-Jones, B. and Parry-Jones, W.Ll. (1994) 'Implications of historical evidence for the classification of eating disorders. A dimension overlooked in DSM-III-R and ICD-10'. *British Journal of Psychiatry*, 165: 287–92.

Parry-Jones, B. and Parry-Jones, W.Ll. (1995) 'The History of Bulimia and Bulimia Nervosa'. In Brownell, K.D. and Fairburn, C.G. (eds.) *Eating Disorders & Obesity: A Comprehensive Handbook*, pp.145–50, New York, Guilford Press.

Parry-Jones, B. and Parry-Jones, W.Ll. (Unpublished data) 'Cases of voluntary self-starvation or low body weight, 1500–1939'.

Rampling, D. (1985) 'Ascetic ideals and anorexia nervosa'. *Journal of Psychiatric Research*, 19: 89–94.

Riesman, D. (1895) 'Merycism or rumination with a report of two cases'. *Journal of Nervous and Mental Diseases*, 22: 359–69.

Riverius, L. (1668) *The Practice of Physick in Seventeen Several Books*, London, Printed by J. Streater.

Robinson, N. (1727) *A New Method of Treating Consumptions*, London.

Schwartz, H. (1986) *Never Satisfied A Cultural History of Diets, Fantasies and Fat*, New York, The Free Press.

Shorter, E. (1987) 'The first great increase in anorexia nervosa'. *Journal of Social History*, 21: 69–96.

Skrabanek, P. (1983) 'Notes towards the history of anorexia nervosa'. *Janus*, 70: 109–28.

Stein, D.M. and Laakso, W. (1988) 'Bulimia: A historical perspective'. *International Journal of Eating Disorders*, 7: 201–10.

Tuke, D.H. (1892) *A Dictionary of Psychological Medicine*, London, J. & A. Churchill.

Vandereycken, W. and Van Deth, R. (1994) *From Fasting Saints to Anorexic Girls. The History of Self-Starvation*, London, The Athlone Press.

Van Deth, R. and Vandereycken, W. (1991) 'Was nervous consumption a precursor of anorexia nervosa?' *Journal of the History of Medicine and Allied Sciences*, 46: 3–19.

Wolf, N. (1990) *The Beauty Myth*, London, Chatto & Windus.

World Health Organization (1990) *Tenth Revision of the International Classification of Diseases. Chapter V: Mental and Behavioural Disorders*, Geneva, World Health Organization.

Chapter 24
Suicidal Behaviour

Clinical Section
GE BERRIOS and M MOHANNA

Early 19th century views on suicide or self-harm were but a continuation of concepts created in previous centuries (McDonald and Murphy, 1990; McManners, 1985; Rosen, 1971; Crocker, 1952; Doughty, 1926; Bartel, 1960; Sym, 1637). For example, the debate during the Enlightenment reflected a clash between religious views and the new liberalism; a good illustration of this is the work of Madame de Staël (1820) who in her much neglected *Réflexions sur le suicide* wrote: 'In my work on the *Influence of Passions* I defended the act of suicide, but I repent now of having penned those thoughtless words. I was then a proud and vivacious young woman: but what is the use of living but having the hope of improving oneself?' (p.296).[1] Cesare Beccaria (1868)[2] is another representative of the liberal view; in his *Dei delitti e delle pene* he wrote: 'Suicide is a crime that cannot be punished for when punishment is meted out it either falls upon the innocent or upon a corpse. In the latter case it will have no effect upon the living, in the former it is tyrannical and unfair as political rights dictate that punishment must be personal' (p.89).

After the 1820s, this moral debate became medicalised, and shaped by changes in the notion of mental disease, and in psychological theory. As Lanteri-Laura and del Pistoia (1970) have observed: 'at the end of the 18th century [suicide] ceased to be condemned on the basis of religiously inspired tradition: the secularisation of the law no longer made it permissible to punish it as a revolt against God. Nevertheless, it remained a shocking act; so psychiatry was invited to take charge of it, since society still regarded it as a threat to established order' (pp.324–5).

The rise of the anatomo-clinical model of disease transformed the concept of mental illness and this, in turn, led to a disintegration of 'total insanity'. The 'partial' insanities (e.g. monomania and lypemania) offered a new medical way of explaining suicide. Changes in psychological theory were equally important: the rise of faculty psychology made possible the clinical existence of non-intellectual insanities (i.e. insanities whose primary disorder was to be found in the emotions or volition) (Berrios, 1987; 1988). This concept offered the medical establishment a second explanation for self-harm; thus those attempting suicide could now be called 'insane' or 'alienated' without, in fact, having to show delusions or hallucinations. One way or the other, alienists became able to protect families of suicidal persons from religious and legal persecution. In fact, by the end of the 18th century, laws against completed suicide had ceased to be regularly enforced as they caused as much trouble to the enforcers as they did to the families of the deceased (McManners, 1985).

During the first half of the 19th century, the debate on whether all suicidal acts were 'pathological' was finely balanced (Blondel, 1933; Ey, 1950). To explore this further, a definitional baseline of representative 18th century views is needed, and these are nowhere better expressed than in the French Encyclopedia. Diderot and D'Alembert (1765) stated that the imputation of suicide should depend upon the ascertaining of *mental state (situation d'esprit)*; subjects being unimputable when found to be suffering from a brain disorder (*cerveau derange*), depression (*tombe dans une noire melancolie*), or delirium (*phrénesie*). The 'French doctrine', up to the 1760s, seems to have been that at least some amongst the mental ill could not be declared *felo de sè*; and although only three categories of mental disorder are mentioned, it is clear that the first – *cerveau derange* – was meant to include cases without obvious clinical features. The idea that some mental disorders could lead to suicide was not, of course, new: as J.C. Schmitt (1976) has shown, since the Medieval period states such as *accidia, tristitia, desperatio, taedium vitae,* and *frenesia* had been regularly mentioned; the problem, for the historian is to identify these states from a clinical point of view, indeed, some may have not had even recognisable clinical boundaries.

Towards the end of the 18th century, the abuse of the 'psychiatric' view of suicide encouraged some to put forward narrower views: for example, the French protestant Jean Dumas (1773) attacked the defence of suicide contained in Montesquieu's LXXVIth *Letter persane* and in Holbach's *Système de la Nature*.[3] In England, E. Burton (1790), a former Fellow of Trinity College, Cambridge, also worried about the medical excuse and stated: 'where ten destroy themselves through insanity, hundreds destroy themselves coolly and deliberately'; unfortunately, 'a state of lunacy becomes a matter of purchase . . . thus it generally happens that the result of all these public inquiries into the cause of voluntary death is a state of lunacy; which implies that no one can in the full possession of his senses, resolutely and deliberately destroy himself' (pp.15–16). C. Moore (1790), also from Trinity College, in his magnificent two-volume book wrote: 'that suicide implies no necessity of an absolute an permanent madness is agreed on all hands' (p.326) and 'suicide, then, whether deliberate or precipitate, no more "necessarily" implies madness or lunacy that every other great crime can be said to do' (p.329). And even in the case of known madness, Moore claimed, there might be imputability. He was only echoing Blackstone who earlier on had commented: 'if a lunatic can be proved to have committed suicide during a lucid interval he is adjudged in the eye of the law a *felo de se*' (Blackstone, 1775–1779, p.326). Bayet (1922) made similar comments in regard to the French situation.

The view that only a proportion of persons who committed suicide were actually mentally ill, or that mental illness may not be an explanation even when present, was already present during the 18th century (Rosen, 1971). Indeed, the same claim was to continue into the following century, except that, as has been mentioned above, new concepts made the debate drift into other directions. It is, therefore, surprising that at the very end of the 19th century, and with the benefit of hindsight, Émile Durkheim still felt able to say that the 'psychiatric' conception of suicide was an absolute belief amongst 19th century alienists. Since we have elsewhere shown that this was an inaccurate interpretation by Durkheim, the topic will not be touched upon again (Berrios and Mohanna, 1990).

The 19th century debate, however, is interesting in its own right because it generated new questions – some of these still current – such as the relationship between suicide and heredity and brain localisation, and the value of national statistics (Voisin, 1882; Krugelstein, 1841). This issue became particularly important towards the end of the century when, under the influence of degeneration theory, suicide began to be considered as a stigma of 'degeneration' (Saury, 1886, pp.8–9). By the 1880s, much agreement existed between French, German, British, Italian and Spanish alienists on the definition and classification of suicide, and also on the role played by heredity, mental illness, and social factors. This consensus was reached through the publication of some major works, all translated into the main European languages, in which what will here be called the 'standard view' was formulated (e.g. Winslow, 1840; Lisle, 1856; Boismont, 1856; Morselli, 1881). This view was reached by steps, and these will be presently described.

Esquirol: creator of the 'standard view'

Accounts of 19th century psychiatric views on suicide tend to start with Esquirol (1838): 'suicide shows all the features of mental alienation of which is but a symptom. There is no need to search for a special brain site for suicide as it can be found associated with all kinds of clinical situations being, as it is, secondary to both acute delirium and to the chronic delusional states; post-mortem studies have not thrown much light on the subject' (p.639). This quotation comes from his 1838 book, a final summary of his work. The original version of the chapter on suicide, however, was published in 1821, and is different in various ways. This is, perhaps, the reason why Esquirol is quoted both by those who see him as the champion of the 'psychiatric' thesis (e.g. Durkheim (1897), Halbwachs (1930), Achille-Delmas (1932) and Giddens (1978)) and also by those who see him as the representative of the 'standard view' view (Berrios and Mohanna, 1990), namely, that some suicides are caused by mental illness and some are not.[4]

Esquirol (1821) had defined suicide in a very wide fashion: 'this phenomenon is observed in the most varied circumstances . . . and shaped by the same uncertainties that affect mental illness; doubtless, suicide is idiopathic, but it can frequently be *secondary*' (p.269). Amongst the causes of suicide, Esquirol (1821) listed dying: 'for the highest motives', 'for social delusions' (*idées fausses, mais accréditées*), impulsive emotion, organic delirium, mania, hypochondria, lypemania, and *suicide simulé* . . .' 'from what has been said it can be concluded that suicide is a phenomenon that follows a large number of, and has diverse presentations; this phenomenon cannot, therefore, be considered as a disease. The general conclusions drawn from having considered suicide as a *sui generis* disease have been proven wrong by experience' (p.214). By 1838, his definition of suicide had become narrower, and the 'psychiatric' explanation acquired more importance. But even then, his later views were not as absolute as Durkheim presented them. For example, when discussing treatment Esquirol (1838) stated: 'suicide is an act secondary to severe emotional upheaval (*délire de passion*) or insanity (*folie*)' . . . 'treatment should rest on the understanding of causes and determinant motives of suicide' (p.655). It is unlikely, therefore, that for Esquirol suicide was always a form of monomania; indeed, it is unlikely that it was always a form of insanity. A more recent interpretation of Esquirol's view has also given him the benefit of the doubt (Blondel, 1933, pp.35–6) making the point that although Esquirol might have claimed that most suicides entailed some sort of abnormal or upset state of mind, the French alienist was very aware of the role of social factors. Blondel (1933) also accused Esquirol's successors of having hardened his views, particularly neglecting his acceptance of social factors, in order to bolster their own views (p.55). Giddens (1965) has also considered Esquirol's views as more flexible than they appear in Durkheim's version.[5]

Interpretation of what Esquirol really said is bedevilled by the ambiguous meaning of a number of French clinical concepts: *aliénation mentale, folie, délire de passion*, and *symptomatique*. An analysis of these issues is beyond the scope of this chapter. Briefly, however, the word *folie* was a generic term used to refer to various states of madness and hence to long lasting diseases (Cotard, 1878). Things are more complicated in relation to *délire*, which has no direct English rendition. From the beginning of the 19th century, untold confusion has been caused by translators rendering *délire* into the English term 'delirium'. In fact, it very rarely means this (in the sense of organic brain syndrome); almost always it simply means 'delusion' (affecting, however, intellect, motility or affect) (Esquirol, 1814). Hence, the presence of *délire* does not necessarily indicate a diagnosis of *folie* or madness. Spaulding and Simpson (the English translators of Durkheim) rendered 'délire' as 'delirium' throughout, thereby adding to the confusion. In the case of *délire de passion*, however, the meaning is somewhat clearer: Esquirol (1814) believed that *délire* could follow any major emotional upheaval: 'passions (i.e. emotions) can so affect our sensations, ideas, judgements and decisions that is not surprising that violent excitement may cause *délire*: in this case it is sudden in onset and short lived; it can also be the lingering product of lasting emotions (*passion chronique*)' (p.255). This means that both Esquirol and many of his followers would use *délire de passion* to refer to an upset of mind, to a temporary emotional upheaval following a social or personal crisis; this description did not entail at all the presence of a disease (i.e. *folie*).[6]

It can be concluded, therefore, that Esquirol was saying that, during the suicidal act the individual *was always in an altered mental state* but that this might only be a *short lived emotional upheaval*, and *not* insanity. This interpretation is shared by Blondel (1933): 'it is a fact that madmen kill themselves and that such suicides are pathological. It is a different fact that men said to be normal also kill themselves. But they are not normal in the moment of the act. They only do it under the effect of a strong emotion' . . . 'this disorder of the emotions that Esquirol makes the basis of his second category of suicide can be precipitated by life events and the proclivities of the individuals' (pp.42–3). This interpretation is reinforced by the view, expressed by Esquirol himself, that the treatment of suicide must focus on the subject's 'motivations and reasons'.

Other French supporters of the 'standard' view
In a popular book, Brierre de Boismont (1856)[7] presented a balanced view of the association between insanity and suicide. For reasons which are unclear, Durkheim totally ignores Brierre de Boismont's claims that 'suicide is not always

evidence of mental illness' (p.135) and that 'the disease of spleen, when accompanied by tendency to suicide, cannot be considered as a variety of mental illness unless it is accompanied by a disorder of emotions or thinking. To make such state yet another form of insanity is to justify the reproach, oft-times addressed at alienists, that they see their fad every where' . . . 'Spleen has more social than personal origins' (p.181).

Another important representative of the 'standard' view was G-F Etoc-Demazy (1844; 1846),[8] who confessed that he had never been able to convince himself that all suicides were the result of mental illness. He criticized the a priori (and clinically weak) approach taken by Bourdin,[9] and offered instead his notion of *aberration morbid passagère*, (Etoc-Demazy, 1846, p.347) which was but another version of Esquirol's *délire de passion*. He rejected the view that all suicides had mental illness, and concluded: 'the insistence with which some authors want to consider suicide as a form of mental alienation, stems from an exaggerated human fondness for life' (Etoc-Demazy, 1846, p.362).

E. Lisle (1856) also defended the 'standard' view. His book, appeared the same year as Brierre's, was awarded the coveted Imperial Academy Prize of Medicine. Lisle, perhaps unfairly, attacked Esquirol whom he interpreted (wrongly) as defending the psychiatric thesis; he explained the former's shift from moderate to absolutist as resulting from the fact that Esquirol had always worked in mental hospitals and thus lost perspective. Lisle then proceeded to reduce *ad absurdum* the view that all suicide is madness by saying that a similar argument should apply to homicide; he also attacked Falret (1822) for inventing the notion of *melancolie suicide* and made fun of him by claiming that perhaps all the classical suicidal heroes were at the time suffering from melancholia! He also dismissed Bourdin's book as insignificant, and as trying to propagate the doctrine of monomania.[10] More importantly, he criticized his method of reasoning by induction, i.e. trying to demonstrate a point of view from theoretical premises without resorting to empirical evidence. He denied the existence of a 'suicidal monomania' in cases when suicidal behaviour is the only evidence for the existence of the disease, and concluded that if the clinical facts were observed, the view that all suicides are 'pathological' would soon be dispelled.

But not all defenders of the 'standard' view had a medical perspective; Bertrand, for example, wrote from a deeply religious viewpoint, and his award winning book received the imprimatur of Gousset, Archbishop of Reims (Bertrand, 1857; Kushner, 1986). Predictably, Bertrand (1857) started by saying that suicide is an act against God, family and fatherland. He believed that moral freedom must be preserved at all costs, and this led him to accuse Bourdin of believing that man was like a clock, and paradoxically, to deny the view that all suicides must be the result of madness. He concluded that 'to put forward the view that all suicides are the result of mental alienation, and hence not imputable, is a dangerous and serious mistake which can give rise to undesirable moral consequences' (p.56). Interestingly, he again differentiated between acute and chronic suicide (the terminology was Esquirol's) (Esquirol, 1821, p.219) and included amongst the latter alcoholism (this about 100 years before Menninger's identical claim in *Man against himself*).

Non-French supporters of the 'standard' view
The standard view was held by most renowned alienists of the period. For example, Prichard (1835) wrote:

> the prevalent opinion is that insanity is not always the cause of suicide, though the verdict of lunacy is generally brought by juries, owing to the extreme barbarity of the law on this subject. M Fodéré[11] has expressed long ago the opinion that suicide is always the result of madness. Though every one would wish to be of the same sentiment, it seems difficult to maintain it when we consider the frequent and almost ordinary occurrence of suicide in some countries . . . like the impulse to homicide, this propensity to suicide is simply a moral perversion,[12] and therefore neither of these affections fall within the restricted definition of insanity. (pp.400–1)

Griesinger (1861) was equally balanced in his views: 'the pathological and aetiological history of suicide does not belong entirely to psychiatry; in fact, whatever some writers have said, we cannot conclude that suicide is always a symptom or a result of insanity' (pp.256–7). Bucknill and Tuke (1858) wrote:

> We have had occasion, previously, to remark that the act of self-destruction may originate in different, and even opposite conditions of mind. Hence, it is quite clear that the suicide act cannot always be properly referred to disorder of the same group of feelings . . . and here it may be observed, in regard to suicide in general, that the question so often asked *Is suicide the result of cerebromental disease* [italics in original] must be answered both affirmatively and negatively. That the act may be committed in a perfectly healthy state of mind cannot, for a moment, be disputed. (pp.201–3)

Defenders of the 'psychiatric thesis'
During the first half of the 19th century there were, however, some whose views approached the caricature drawn by Durkheim; one was Cazauvieilh on 'rural' suicide.[13] Cazauvieilh (1840) put forward an extreme view: there were three types of suicide and all were psychiatric disorders. In the purest Faculty Psychology tradition he listed suicides resulting from disorders of thought, affection and volition (*délire de intelligence, affections, and actions*). 'Real' suicides he defined as acts accompanied by willingness and clear consciousness. He considered as 'accidental' all deaths in the insane when there was no formed intent to die. Loyal to Esquirol, he defended a concept of monomania that, at the time, had already been called into question (p.v). He dealt with both suicide and homicide as related acts and reported 16 post-mortem studies searching for the *siège de l'organe dont les souffrances portent au meurtre de soi-meme* (p.175).

THE AFTERMATH
By the 1880s, the psychiatric debate on whether suicide was *always* due to mental illness (the 'psychiatric' thesis) had been decided in favour of the view that it was not (the 'standard' view). Most alienists entertained a broad definition of suicide, and consequently all manner of 'social' events were accepted as potential causes (Morselli, 1881; Legoyt, 1884; Ritti, 1884; Strahan, 1893). Of

this view many non-medical men – except perhaps, Durkheim – were aware: for example, Westcott (1885) listed amongst the supporters of the standard view Blandford, Leuret, Gray, Bucknill and Tuke, Des Etangs (1857), and Littré (1881). Morselli (1881), whom no one could accuse of softness (Guarnieri, 1988), expressed a similar sentiment: 'just as madness may go on without any attempt at suicide, so the suicidal determination is formed in the healthiest of minds, which then carry it out with the coolness inspired by the most perfect logic' (p.272). Brouc (1836) discussed suicide as a 'social event', and Legoyt (1884) went as far as discussing the very social variables that played such an important role in Durkheim's argument (Legoyt, 1884).

The 'standard view' was carried without difficulty into the 20th century. In his assessment of the controversy, Viallon (1901–1902) restated that Etoc-Demazy, Cerise, Belhomme, Chereau, Palmer and Gray 'had reacted with force against' the 'psychiatric thesis'; Pilcz (1908) agreed with Kraepelin that only a 30 per cent of suicides seem to be related to diagnosable mental illness; (Pilcz, 1908) and Serin (1926) concluded, after a detailed survey that 'a third [of suicides] were conceived and executed in the absence of psychopathology' (p.358).

Things should have been allowed to rest there. With hindsight, it seems clear that much of the 19th century debate (including Durkheim's contribution), was conceptual rather than empirical, i.e. resulted from confusion in regards to the definition of suicide; but after Durkheim's book, disagreement also resulted from the way in which 'social' was defined. It is beyond dispute that most 19th century alienists manage to include 'social' facts as causes of suicide. However, by the time of Durkheim, and probably as a result of his contribution, 'social fact' had acquired a wider and more abstract meaning (Durkheim, 1894, p.466). Analysis of this shift, which has to do with the gradual development of sociology during the 19th century, is beyond both the scope of this chapter and the ken of its authors. However, it seems as if 'the social' had, by the very end of the century, become accepted as a higher, irreducible, and omnipresent level of explanation (Parain-Vial, 1966; Duverger, 1961). This was good for sociology and for the professionalisation of her practitioners, but created explanatory splits in a number of regions of reality, one of which was mental illness and suicide.

In a way, Durkheim was unfair to accuse early 19th century psychiatrists of not fully accepting the social explanation of suicide for, during this period, such concepts were not yet part of the intellectual fare of alienists. For example, for Esquirol 'social' meant environmental in relation to specific individuals; he had little thought for social laws; for Durkheim, on the other hand, it meant general, the result of objective laws equally applicable to all people. Whilst for Esquirol the 'dependent' variable for social explanations was the behaviour (e.g. suicide) of a given individual, for Durkheim it became the social facts, as expressed in large group statistics.

And these differences became more obvious by the time the controversy flared up again in France in the 1930s. It started with the publication by Maurice de Fleury (1926) of an update of the 'psychiatric thesis' whose only new feature was the incorporation of the 'neuroses'. It must be remembered that up to the 1880s, 'mental disorder' basically referred to the 'insanities' (organic states, melancholia, etc.). Between this time and the 1930s, however, and thanks to the work of Janet, Freud and others, the neuroses (López Piñero and Morales Meseguer, 1970; Oppenheim, 1991) and the personality disorders were included under the rubric 'mental disorder'. When Fleury and Achille-Delmas (1932) claimed that all suicides resulted from mental disorder, they meant both the old insanities and the new neurotic conditions, particularly the anxiety states. This is why, few years later, Deshaies felt able to claim that about one third of the psychiatric causes of suicide fell into this latter category (Deshaies, 1947).

Maurice Halbwachs (1930)[14] replied in 1930 in a classical book that went further than Durkheim's in its re-affirmation of the 'social thesis' of suicide. By Halbwachs's time, the 'social' explanation had become fully consolidated, and he had no difficulty in making the claim that all suicides were socially originated, including those in which alienists might show clear mental illness for, after all, mental illness was also social in origin. This claim, legitimate from the conceptual point of view, did upset alienists then as much as it might upset some today. One reason for the discrepancy of view is that psychiatrists deal with individual cases, and grand social causes are well beyond their perception and remedial manipulation. Consequently, some may deny their existence, or re-define them in simpler and more tangible ways. This was what Achille-Delmas (1932) tried to do in his book which to the sociologist may sound naive and conceptually uncouth; it simply conveys the perplexity of a generation of alienists *vis à vis* the sociological explanation of suicide.

But the obvious thing to do, when faced with multiple levels of explanation, might be to blend them. This is precisely what Blondel (1933) did:[15] after chastising Achille-Demas for 'inventing a phrenology without organology' (p.132) he stated that Halbwachs had resuscitated a conflict, and that both were wrong (*En cette querelle les partis extrêmes semblend tous deux dans leur tort*) (p.3): 'in regards to suicide, it would be dangerous to reject the sociological explanation; but it would be equally dangerous not to acknowledge the role of the pathological which although may have social causes and lead to social effects, *may not be social* at all' (p.4). Whether or not Blondel was successful in his quest remains to be seen. To many current clinicians, old issues such as the definition of suicide, the informational value of suicide statistics, and the ways in which these should be collected and interpreted (Selvin, 1958) have not yet been solved; as has not the crucial question of whether they are susceptible to empirical solution.

NOTES

1 Madame de Staël wrote her apology of suicide in 1796 (and her change of mind in 1812). Esquirol (1821) commented about her change of mind: 'In the enthusiasm of youth, Madame de Staël seemed to have approved of suicide, later she recanted' (p.241). It is unclear whether she was influenced by Hume's liberal *Essays on Suicide* (1783).

2 Cesare Bonesana, Marquis de Beccaria (1733–1781) was educated by the Jesuits and decided on a philosophical career after reading Montesquieu's *Lettres Persans*. He wrote *Dei delitti* when he was 25, and at the instigation of his friends who used to find him boring and sluggish. He had read widely, and was influenced by Diderot, Helvetius, Voltaire, D'Alembert, Buffon, and Hume.

3 Although of French origin, Dumas worked in Leipzig where he died in 1799. He also published literary criticism and poetry.

4 One of the earliest to recognise this was Griesinger (1861) who quoted Esquirol's well known lines: 'I believe that I have proved that an individual will only put an end to his life when he is deluded, and the suicides are mentally diseased' (Esquirol, 1838, p.138) and then commented: 'Esquirol expresses himself *less absolutely* in other parts of the book' (p.256).

5 'Esquirol himself did allow that social factors play a certain role in the aetiology of mental disorder and, consequently, suicide'. (Giddens, 1965, Footnote 26). It is arguable whether Esquirol allowed social factors to be relevant to suicide only through their role in mental disorder. The issue here is whether Esquirol felt that all suicides suffered from mental illness. We do not think he did, although he often stated that, during the act, suicidal persons are in an upset state of mind; unfortunately, – like all alienists during his period – to refer to this he used terms such as delusion, passion, or transient insanity; this gives the impression that he is talking about real madness. For a full analysis of Durkheim's *Le Suicide* see Lester, 1994.

6 On the role of the passions in the aetiology of mental disease see: Berrios, 1985.

7 Alexandre Jacques François Brierre de Boismont (1797–1881) was a prolific writer who published work on homicidal monomania, and hallucinations. In 1840, on account of his political views he lost the opportunity to replace Esquirol at the Charenton.

8 Gustave François Etoc-Demazy (1806–1893) trained under Ferrus and Pariset and wrote on stupor (see Berrios, 1981), monomania, and a number of medico-legal topics.

9 Bourdin (1845) (not a physician) was a rabid defender of the view that suicide was always a form of mental disease, and fits well into Durkheim's stereotypy. However, he was not an alienist, although he also wrote on catalepsy and alcoholism. He claimed that suicide was always a monomania: 'frequently, suicide was the earliest manifestation of monomania' (p.8); thus the view that suicide was not pathological was based on 'incomplete observations' (p.7). He also complained that legislators and philosophers have attached an idea of criminality, or at least of imputability, 'to the act of suicide' (p.20): 'If I showed that suicide constitutes a real disease, that all its aspects, when considered in themselves and in their relationship and origins, are no different from the array of ordinary symptoms [of mental illness], I would have freed suicidal individuals from all culpability . . .' (p.21). Bourdin's book is rambling, sententious, and obsolete in terms of clinical argument.

10 Monomania was a diagnosis invented by Esquirol which achieved certain fashion, particularly in the area of forensic psychiatry. It was never fully accepted by those not belonging to Esquirol's school and after severe attack during the 1950s, it gradually disappeared (see Kageyama, 1984; Debate on Monomanie in *Annales Médico-Psychologiques*, 1854; Falret, 1864 and Linas, 1871).

11 Emmanuel Françoise Fodéré (1764–1835) was a physician in the 18th century mould: he held vitalist principles and his views on insanity were an

offshoot from his medico-legal preoccupations. He defined *délire* as a 'disease in which freedom had been lost'.

12 When used by alienists, 'moral' meant 'psychological', had little moralistic overtones, and carried no implication in regards to duration.

13 A disciple of Esquirol, and organicist au outrance, Cazauvieilh wrote a classical paper on epilepsy (Berrios, 1984). After leaving La Salpêtriere, he worked in various provincial hospitals until he settled in the asylum of Liancourt-Oise. He reported in his book suicide cases from four regions: Gironde, Landes, Seine and Oise.

14 This author (1877–1945) died in a Nazi concentration camp.

15 This great and neglected French writer had since the 1910s shown great sensitivity for the conceptual and the 'sociological'. See for example, his *La conscience morbide* (1914) and *Introduction à la psychologie collective* (1928). The latter book, particularly, shows the awareness that Blondel had of the work of Comte, Durkheim, Tarde, and Halbwachs. He had trained both under Lévy-Bruhl and Deny (the latter one of the great French alienists of the early 20th century).

REFERENCES

Achille-Delmas, F. (1932) *Psychologie Pathologique du Suicide*, Paris, Alcan.

Anonymous (1854) 'Debate on Monomanie'. *Annales Médico-Psychologiques*, 6:99–118; 273–98; 464–74; 629–44.

Bartel, R. (1960) 'Suicide in 18th century England'. *Huntington Library Quarterly*, 23:145–58.

Bayet, A. (1922) *Le Suicide et la Morale*, Paris, Alcan.

Beccaria, C. (1868) *De los delitos y de las penas*, (translated by Juan Antonio de las Casas), Madrid, Alianza (first published in 1764).

Berrios, G.E. (1981) 'Stupor: a conceptual history'. *Psychological Medicine*, 11:677–88.

Berrios, G.E. (1984) 'Epilepsy and insanity during the 19th century. A conceptual history'. *Archives of Neurology*, 41:978–81.

Berrios, G.E. (1985) 'The psychopathology of affectivity: conceptual and historical aspects'. *Psychological Medicine*, 15:745–58.

Berrios, G.E. (1987) 'Historical aspects of the psychosis'. *British Medical Bulletin*, 43:484–98.

Berrios, G.E. (1988) 'Historical background to Abnormal psychology'. In Miller, E. and Cooper, P.J. (eds.) *Adult Abnormal Psychology*, Edinburgh, Churchill and Livingstone, pp.26–51.

Berrios, G.E. and Mohanna, M. (1990) 'Durkheim and French views on suicide during the 19th century: a conceptual history'. *British Journal of Psychiatry*, 156:1–9.

Bertrand, L. (1857) *Traité du Suicide Considéré dans ses Rapports avec la Philosophie, la Théologie, la Médecine, et la Jurisprudence*, Paris, Baillière.

Blackstone, W. (1775–1779) *Commentaries on the Laws of England*, London, Cadell, (reference taken from the 15th Edition).

Blondel, Ch. (1933) *Le Suicide*, Strassbourg, Librairie Universitaire D'Alsace.

Blondel, Ch. (1914) *La Conscience Morbide. Essai de Psycho-pathologie Générale*, Paris, Alcan.

Blondel, Ch. (1964) *Introduction à la Psychologie Collective*, Paris, Colin (first published in 1928).

Bourdin, C.E. (1845) *Du Suicide Considéré Comme Maladie*, Paris, Batignolles, Hennuyer et Turpin.

Brierre de Boismont, A. (1856) *Du Suicide et de la Folie Suicide*, Paris, Baillière.

Brouc, M. (1836) 'Considerations sur le suicide de notre époque'. *Annales d'Hygiène Publique et the Médecine Légale*, 6:223–62.

Bucknill, J.C. and Tuke, D.H. (1858) *A Manual of Psychological Medicine*, London, John Churchill.

Burton, E. (1790) *Suicide, a Dissertation*, London, Vint.

Cazauvieilh, J.B. (1840) *Du Suicide et l'Aliénation Mentale et des Crimes contra les Personnes, Comparés dans leurs Rapports Reciproques. Recherches sur ce Premier Penchant chez les Habitants des Campagnes*, Paris, Baillière.

Cotard, J. (1878) 'Folie'. In Dechambre, A. and Lereboullet, L. (eds.) *Dictionnaire Encyclopédique des Sciences Médicales*, Paris, Masson, vol.39, pp.271–306.

Crocker, L.G. (1952) 'The discussion of suicide in the 18th century'. *Journal of the History of Ideas*, 13:47–52.

Des Etangs, (1857) 'Du Suicide en France. Etudes sur la mort volontaire depuis 1798 jusqu'a nos jours'. *Annales Médico-Pyschologiques*, 3:1–27.

Deshaies, G. (1947) *Psychologie du Suicide*, Paris, Presses Universitaires de France.

Diderot and D'Alembert (eds.) (1765) *Encyclopédie ou Dictionnaire Raisonné des Sciences, des Arts et des Métieres, par Une Societé de gens de Lettres*, vol.14, A. Neufchastel, Samuel Faulche, pp.639–41.

Doughty, O. (1926) 'The English malady of the 18th century'. *Review of English Studies*, 2:257–69.

Dumas, J. (1773) *Traité du suicide ou du Meurtre volontaire de soi-même*, Leipzig.

Durkheim, E. (1894) 'Les règles de la méthode sociologique'. *Revue Philosophique*, 37:465–98.

Durkheim, E. (1897) *Le Suicide*, Paris, Alcan (translated by J.A. Spaulding and G. Simpson as *Suicide. A Study in Sociology*, London, Routledge & Kegan Paul 1952).

Duverger, M. (1961) *Méthodes des Sciences Sociales*, Paris, Presses Universitaires de France.

Esquirol, E. (1814) 'Délire'. In Adelon, Alard, Alibert et al (eds.) *Dictionnaire des Sciences Médicales par une Société de Médecins et de Chirurgiens*, Paris, Panckoucke, pp.251–9.

Esquirol, E. (1821) 'Suicide'. In Adelon, Alard, Alibert et al (eds.) *Dictionnaire des Sciences Médicales par une Société de Médecins et de Chirurgiens*, Paris, Panckoucke, pp.213–83.

Esquirol, E. (1838) *Des Maladies Mentales Considérés sous les Rapports Médical, Hygiénique et Médico-légal*, 2 vols. Paris, JB Baillière.

Etoc-Demazy, G.F. (1844) *Recherches Statistiques sur le Suicide, Appliquées à la Hygiene Publique et à la Médecine legal*, Paris, Bailliére.

Etoc-Demazy, G.F. (1846) 'Sur la folie dans la production du suicide'. *Annales Médico-Psychologiques*, 7:338–62.

Ey, H. (1950) 'Le suicide pathologique'. In Ey, H. *Études Psiquiatriques, Aspects séméiologiques*, vol.2, Paris, Desclée de Brouwer, pp.341–78.

Falret, J.P. (1822) *De l'Hypocondrie et du Suicide. Considérations sur les Causes, sur le Siége et le Traitement de ces Maladies, sur Moyens d'en Arrêter les Progrès et d'en Prévenir le Développement*, Paris, Croullebois.

Falret, J.P. (1854) 'De la non-existence de la monomanie'. In Falret, J.P. *Des Maladies Mentales et des Asiles d'Aliénés. Leçons Cliniques et Considérations Générales*, Paris, Baillière, pp.425–55.

Fedden, H.R. (1938) *Suicide*, London, Peter Davies.

Fleury, M. de (1926) *L'Angoisse Humaine*, Paris, Les Editions de France.

Giddens, A. (1965) 'The suicide problem in French sociology'. *British Journal of Sociology*, 16:3–18.

Giddens, A. (1978) Introduction to the translation by Goldblatt, H. of Halbwachs, M. *The Causes of Suicide*, London, Routledge & Kegan Paul.

Griesinger, W. (1861) *Die Pathologie und Therapie der psychischen Krankheiten*, 2nd edition, Stuttgart, Krabbe.

Guarnieri, P. (1988) 'Between soma and psyche: Morselli and psychiatry in late nineteenth century Italy'. In Bynum, W.F., Porter, R. and Shepherd, M. (eds.) *The Anatomy of Madness*, vol.3, London, Tavistock, pp.102–24.

Halbwachs, M. (1930) *Les Causes du Suicide*, Paris, Alcan.

Hume, D. (1783) *Essays on Suicide and the Inmortality of the Soul*, London, Smith.

Kageyama, J. (1984) 'Sur l'histoire de la monomanie'. *L'Evolution Psychiatrique*, 49:155–62.

Krugelstein, J. (1841) 'Mémoire sur le suicide'. *Annales d'Hygiène Publique et the Médecine Légale*, 25:151–82.

Kushner, H.I. (1986) 'American psychiatry and the cause of suicide 1844–1917'. *Bulletin History of Medicine*, 60:36–57.

Lanteri-Laura, G. and Del Pistoia, L. (1970) 'Structural analysis of suicidal behaviour'. *Social Research*, 37:324–47.

Lester, D. (ed.) (1994) *Emile Durkheim's 'Le suicide'*, Philadelphia, The Charles Press.

Legoyt, A. (1884) 'Suicide'. In Dechambre, A. (ed.) *Dictionnaire Encyclopédique de Sciences Médicales*, vol.13. Paris, Asselin, pp.242–96.

Linas, A. (1871) 'Monomanie'. In Dechambre, A. (ed.) *Dictionnaire Encyclopédique de Sciences Médicales*, vol.5. Paris, Asselin, pp.146–95.

Lisle, E. (1856) *Du Suicide, Statistique, Médecine, Histoire et Legislation*, Paris, Baillière.

Littré, E. (1881) *Dictionnaire de la Langue Française*, Supplément, Paris, Hachette.

López Piñero, J.M. and Morales Meseguer, J.M. (1970) *Neurosis y psicoterapia*, Madrid, Espasa.

McDonald, M. and Murphy, T.R. (1990) *Sleepless Souls. Suicide in Early Modern England*, Oxford, Clarendon Press.

McManners, J. (1985) *Death and the Enlightenment*, Oxford, Oxford University Press.

Moore, C. (1790) *A full Inquiry into the Subject of Suicide*, 2 vols., London, J.F.C. Rivington.

Morselli, H. (1881) *Suicide. An Essay on Comparative Moral Statistics*, London, C Kegan Paul.

Oppenheim, J. (1991) *'Shattered Nerves', Doctors, Patients, and Depression in Victorian England*, Oxford, Oxford University Press.

Parain-Vial, J. (1966) *La Nature du Fait dans les Sciences Humaines*, Paris, Presses Universitaires de France.

Pilcz, A. (1908) 'Contribution à l'étude du suicide'. *Annales Médico-Psychologiques*, 7:193–205.

Prichard, J.C. (1835) *A Treatise on Insanity*, London, Sherwood, Gilbert & Piper.

Ritti, A. (1884) 'Suicide'. In Dechambre, A. (ed.) *Dictionnaire Encyclopédique de Sciences Médicales*, vol.13, Paris, Asselin, pp.296–347.

Ritti, A. (1898) 'A discussion on suicide and its psychiatric aspects'. *Journal of Mental Science*, 45:202–3.

Rosen, G. (1971) 'History in the study of suicide'. *Psychological Medicine*, 4:267–85.

Saury, H. (1886) *Étude Clinique sur la Folie Héréditaire (les Dégénérés)*, Delahaye, Paris.

Schmitt, J.C. (1976) 'Le suicide au moyen âge'. *Annales: Economies, Sociétés, Civilisations*, 31:3–28.

Selvin, H.C. (1958) 'Durkheim's "Suicide" and problems of empirical research'. *American Journal of Sociology*, 63:607–19.

Serin, S. (1926) 'Une enquête médico-sociale sur le suicide à Paris'. *Annales Médico-Psychologiques*, 84:356–63.

Staël, Mme la Baronne de (1820) *De L'Influence des Passions sur le Bonheur des Individues et des Nations*, New Edition, Paris, Treuttel et Würtz.

Strahan, S.A.K. (1893) *Suicide and Insanity*, (a physiological, sociological study), London, Swan Sonnenschein & Co.

Sym, J. (1637) *Life's Preservating against Self-killing*, London, Flesher.

Viallon, A. (1901–1902) 'Suicide et folie'. *Annales Médico-Psychologiques*, 59:19–28; 210–34; 60:21–35; 219–29; 379–92; 235–54; 392–403.

Voisin, A. (1882) 'Idées sur le suicide'. *Progres Médical*, 10:614.

Westcott, W.W. (1885) *Suicide. Its History, Literature, Jurisprudence, Causation, and Prevention*, London, H.K. Lewis.

Winslow, F. (1840) *The Anatomy of Suicide*, London, Henry Renshaw.

Chapter 24
Suicidal Behaviour

Social Section
MICHAEL MACDONALD

Suicide has almost everywhere been regarded as a bad way to die. There are some famous exceptions: cultures that permitted or even demanded self-killing to expiate wrongs, and individuals whose deaths have been hailed as heroic or tragic. But in Europe in particular the sad and solitary act of killing oneself has generally been deplored. As historians have begun more thoroughly to research beliefs about suicide and responses to it, however, it has become clear that the intensity of disapproval has varied from region to region and waxed and waned over time. The Greeks and Romans were famously tolerant of suicide. The Epicureans and the Cynics justified it to escape physical and mental suffering; the Stoics, especially Seneca, practically celebrated it. Roman suicides motivated by political principle or by questions of honour, such as those of Cato and Lucretia, were hailed as heroic. Tolerance was nevertheless neither continuous nor universal. Some of the Greek city-states punished suicide, and the most famous Greek philosophers disapproved of it. Pythagoras, Plato and Aristotle provided some of the most enduring arguments against self-killing. Even the Romans outlawed suicide by certain kinds of people, notably slaves and soldiers, and left the bodies of suicides by hanging unburied (Van Hooff, 1990; Grisé, 1983; Griffin, 1986).

Medieval Christian writers assailed the tolerant views of the ancients. St. Augustine condemned suicide in the *City of God*, and his arguments were developed by St. Thomas Aquinas in the thirteenth century. Together they established the Christian tradition that views it as a violation of divine and natural law. Because it is not explicitly forbidden in the Bible, they argued that it violates the Sixth Commandment and the natural instinct of self-preservation, which God has given to every person. The church also condemned suicide in practice. The early councils that formed Christian doctrine forbade the burial of suicides in consecrated ground and denied them at least some of the normal funerary rites. The clergy also condoned popular, non-Christian rituals for desecrating the bodies of self-murderers. These varied from place to place, but they often involved dragging the corpse on a hurdle and hanging it from a gibbet or burying it in a highway with a stake driven through it, as in England. Secular governments also began to penalize suicide. By the thirteenth century or so many kingdoms called for the forfeiture of a suicide's goods (Schmitt, 1976; Bayet, 1922; MacDonald and Murphy, 1990).

And yet despite harsh condemnations, laws and customs, suicide was in general treated leniently in the Middle Ages. Most historians now agree that suicide was much more common than the documents recording punishments for it suggest. In England, for instance, kindly coroners and their juries often either attributed suicidal deaths to some other cause or returned verdicts of *non compos mentis* (lunacy) that excused the deceased and his or her family from penalty. On the Continent late medieval and early modern casuists found ways to excuse a broad range of kinds of self-killing as justifiable. The law also recognized that there were kinds of self-killing that were not self-murder. Children and lunatics were exempt from punishment everywhere; so were soldiers who cast their lives away on the battlefield and, of course, martyrs. As far as can be told at present medieval attitudes to suicide were a compound of three elements: theological condemnation, popular fears and practical compassion. The church condemned suicide officially. Demotic beliefs that the ghosts of suicides were dangerous generated gruesome burial rituals. But in practice theologians and lawyers looked for loopholes to excuse actual suicides and local officials and the authorities failed to apply the secular, religious and folkloric punishments except in rare instances or brief periods (MacDonald and Murphy, 1990; Murray, forthcoming).

The Reformation prompted more rigorous enforcement of the laws against suicide in England, and it may also have done so elsewhere. Under Henry VII and Henry VIII the English crown encouraged coroners and their juries to convict suicides as culpable self-murderers. The clergy intensified medieval condemnations of suicide and gave them a Protestant cast. They emphasized in particular that self-murder was a terrible sin, caused directly by the Devil. Sermons on this topic heightened and reshaped old popular beliefs that suicide was supernaturally evil and dangerous. As a result of both of these developments, increasing numbers of suicides were convicted and punished as self-murderers. The sixteenth and early seventeenth centuries were an era of unprecedented severity (MacDonald and Murphy, 1990). The rise of severity in England may have been unique, at least in its rigour. In Zurich the law against suicide was enforced with greater intensity in the seventeenth and eighteenth centuries than it had been before, but the religious penalties for it were progressively weakened (Schär, 1985). The story was much the same in Geneva (Haeberli, 1975). In France the complex set of regional laws punishing self-murder was finally codified into a single harsh ordinance in 1670 that applied nationwide, but prosecutors enforced it fitfully. Lawyers manoeuvred successfully in many instances to acquit suicides of guilt for their own deaths (Bayet, 1922; Merrick, 1989). No one yet knows what happened in Italy, Spain, Scandinavia, most of Germany or even Scotland. Although disapproval of suicide seems to have intensified in both Protestant and Catholic nations, there was no single early modern European attitude to it (Delumeau, 1990). What can be asserted confidently is that the treatment of suicide was very different in different countries.

In most of Europe the penalties for suicide were relaxed or repealed during the eighteenth century. English coroner's juries gradually stopped enforcing the law. They were motivated partly by an abiding dislike of the secular penalties for self-murder: forfeiting suicides's goods to the crown impoverished their survivors and placed additional burdens on the community (MacDonald and

Murphy, 1990). There were also broad intellectual movements that promoted this trend toward leniency. Three developments that are usually regarded as central features of the Enlightenment encouraged tolerance in England and elsewhere: the development of secular moral philosophy, the growing prestige of science and the spread of legal humanitarianism. Most of the leading philosophers of the age – d'Holbach, Voltaire, Montesquieu; Hume – offered philosophical justifications for suicide, and so did a host of lesser thinkers. Rousseau offered arguments pro and con, and Diderot ducked the problem. Only Kant condemned it forcefully. Few readers would have accepted the most radical of the philosophers' arguments, but they did encourage a more forgiving attitude. Ironically, this often took the form of a medical explanation for suicide, even though the arguments for rational suicide were obviously inapplicable to irrational suicides (Crocker, 1952; Favre, 1978; McManners, 1981).

Building on a medical tradition that had been largely uninfluential in the Renaissance, Enlightenment laymen began to attribute virtually all suicides to mental illness. Thus Montesquieu attributed an alleged epidemic of suicide in England to its natives's propensity to nervous disease and its bad weather. It was therefore pointless and illogical to punish suicides there. English coroners' juries agreed: the proportion of lunacy verdicts that they returned in cases of suicide grew steadily until by the 1790s almost 98 percent of recorded suicides were said to have been insane (MacDonald and Murphy, 1990). The growing propensity to see suicide as the outcome of a mental disease and hence blameless was also fortified by direct attacks on the old laws against it. The most celebrated legal reformer of the age, Cesare Beccaria, called for their abolition, and other philosophers, such as Voltaire, amplified the cry. In some places these ideas led directly to the repeal or suspension of the laws against suicide. The chief prosecutor in Geneva announced in 1735 that he would no longer enforce a law that was contrary to 'good philosophy'; the French dropped the 1670 ordinance from the revolutionary law code of 1791 (Haeberli, 1975; Bayet, 1922). The trajectory of attitudinal and legal change in America was much the same as in England, except that the new state governments abolished the traditional English penalties earlier, soon after the American Revolution. Reformers such as Thomas Jefferson were strongly influenced by Beccaria (Kushner, 1989).

By the second half of the eighteenth century attitudes to suicide had become sufficiently secularized so that suicides could be depicted as heroic or tragic. Suicides for honour flourished, particularly in England and Germany. During the French Revolution there was an outbreak of political suicides modelled after the death of Cato, who killed himself to protest Caesar's dictatorship (Outram, 1989). Neoclassicism thus revivified the ancient notion of heroic suicide. Romanticism created a new stereotype of sentimental suicide. Goethe's best-selling novel *The Sorrows of Young Werther* (1774) allegedly inspired a brief epidemic of love-suicides. Specific deaths were attributed to its influence, and in at least a few instances suicides themselves compared their exits to Werther's (Atkins, 1949). The Romantics were in fact fascinated by suicide. In England they turned lamentation over the death of Thomas Chatterton, a poetical forger of genius, into a cult. He was compared to Werther and a generation after his death the major Romantic poets – Wordsworth, Coleridge and Keats – eulogized him.

Artists depicted his tragic end in pitiful scenes. There were even souvenir handkerchiefs commemorating his death (Meyerstein, 1930).

Neoclassical and Romantic suicides were viewed as rational or pitiful responses to unendurable situations. At the same time that these traditions were gathering strength, the opinion that suicide was the consequence of individual pathology was also growing stronger. Physicians had paid remarkably little attention to suicide in the Renaissance and even in the Enlightenment. As the psychiatric profession began to emerge as a distinct entity in the nineteenth century, however, medical writers began to emphasize increasingly that suicide was caused by various kinds of mental disease. Thus, for instance, the hugely influential French alienist Esquirol saw suicide as the outcome of monomania. Other physicians offered broader diagnoses of the psychiatric causes of suicide, and attempted suicides were increasingly committed to asylums in England and France and given medical care. As medical study of suicide grew more systematic, however, physicians such as Henry Maudsley in England and Brierre de Boismont in France acknowledged that not all suicides were caused by mental illness. Social factors such as destitution, family problems and alcoholism prompted many deaths (Lieberman, 1987; Anderson, 1987). And in fact at the same time that the physicians were claiming suicide for their own field of expertise, the newly-emergent profession of sociology was starting to claim it for theirs. Throughout the nineteenth century, particularly in France, social scientists conducted statistical investigations into the social causes of suicide (Lieberman, 1987).

The social-scientific investigation of suicide climaxed in 1897 with the publication of Durkheim's *Suicide*. Durkheim rejected the notion that suicide was primarily caused by individual pathology and sought to show instead that it was promoted or discouraged by the strength or weakness of social norms in a society or group. His lead has been followed by many others, the most notable of whom may be Maurice Halbawchs (1978). The starting-point for both Durkheim and Halbwachs was the realization that suicide rates tend to be rather regular over time and that their variations can be correlated with social factors such as religious beliefs and practice and events such as economic depression and war. Both believed that suicide rates had increased and were increasing in the nineteenth and early twentieth centuries. Recently there has been a strong reaction against Durkheimian formulations of the relationship between suicide and social factors. Most of these have been motivated by philosophical objections to the positivist foundation of Durkheim's methods, but their most forceful objection has been that suicide rates are so faulty as to be useless for sociological analysis (Taylor, 1982). Some brave scholars still labor at the computer, and they are joined by some distinguished psychologists, but the trend is definitely away from statistical analyses.

This trend in social-scientific thought has probably been a boon to historical studies of suicide. For the fixation with suicide rates was a perilous attraction for historians. At least until the nineteenth century, national suicide rates measure the extent to which the laws punishing the act were enforced and cannot be used as indicators of the actual frequency of self-killing. We shall never know whether the rate of suicide in England, for instance, increased in the Tudor period as some scholars assert or if contemporaries were right to believe that suicide was epidemical in the eighteenth century. The data are simply too faulty (MacDonald and Murphy, 1990). Similarly, trans-national comparisons of suicide rates for periods prior to about 1800 are very unlikely to be accurate, and their validity is debatable even after that date. Different jurisdictions had different laws, different procedures for identifying deaths as suicides and different attitudes to how rigorously the law should be enforced. For the nineteenth century, some confidence can be placed in statistical findings for particular countries or jurisdictions. Thus Olive Anderson shows that in Victorian and Edwardian England, suicide was not promoted by urbanization, for example, challenging a widely-held contemporary belief. She also argues that there were important differences between the suicide rates of men and women and among different age groups (Anderson, 1987). One of her findings is among the two assertions that can also confidently be made about suicide rates prior to 1800. For every period for which we have data, suicide has been less common among women than men. (The other abiding pattern is that suicides peak in the spring or early summer and fall in the depths of winter [Schmitt, 1976; MacDonald and Murphy, 1990]).

Some researchers have asserted that men's greater propensity to kill themselves is to an extent an illusion. They have found that women are far more likely than men to attempt suicide: they simply succeed much less often. Some historians, particularly feminists, have hypothesized that this must have been true in the past, too. It is notable that men who killed themselves in England prior to this century chose more deadly methods, such as hanging and shooting, than women, who always preferred drowning (MacDonald and Murphy, 1990; Anderson, 1987). Certainly, the psychological burdens that women are forced to bear in patriarchal societies were at least as great and probably much greater in the past. The frustrations caused or heightened by subordination are evident, for example, in the disproportionate number of women who complained of mental afflictions to a seventeenth-century English astrological physician, Richard Napier (MacDonald, 1981). Explicitly suicidal feelings, however, were not more common among Napier's female patients, and his practice is the only, pre-1800 source so far discovered that permits a more or less systematic examination of attempted suicide. The reason why information about attempted suicide is so hard to find is that paradoxically it was not illegal until the later eighteenth or nineteenth centuries. To succeed in killing oneself was a crime; to try and fail was not, and so the act was not systematically recorded. Nor can the rates of admission of suicidal patients to asylums such as Bedlam tell us very much. Criteria for admission and the process of choosing incarceration (as opposed to home care) were different for men and women, and the sheer capacity of wards for males and females shaped the gender profile of early asylums. About all that can be said about attempted suicides is that in England they frequently received medical care even before the nineteenth century, and that suicidal men and women were increasingly confined in private and public asylums as private and public institutions proliferated (Lieberman, 1987; MacDonald and Murphy, 1990). Almost nothing has so far been published on attempted suicide on the Continent in the medieval and early modern periods.

As frustrating as this lacuna is, it underlines a fundamental fact about societal responses to suicide. Prior to the end of the eighteenth century, European cultures relied on moral suasion and the deterrent effects of the terrible punishments for self-murder to prevent suicide. The reluctance of governments to remove laws against suicide from the books even when they were seldom enforced was almost certainly due to the conviction that they did deter suicide. This view was articulated explicitly by opponents to legal reform in eighteenth-century England. It may be that the clergy's lingering aversion to burying suicides with the full Christian rites in France and England owed something to this practical consideration as well as to moral qualms (Lieberman, 1987; MacDonald and Murphy, 1990). The great eighteenth-century historian of suicide, Charles Moore, wanted to reform the law so that desecration would be carried out more often and hence act as a surer deterrent (Moore, 1790). The French actually briefly restored penalties for suicide between 1793 and 1795 to deter political suicides (Outram, 1989). There were calls for the more frequent punishment of suicide in England to deter others even after the formal penalties for self-murder were removed in 1870. But by then there were other schemes of suicide prevention in place, and in England and France there were lively debates about the best ways to discourage self-slaughter. In England the Humane Society, established in 1774, rescued and resuscitated drowning persons, and on both sides of the Channel attempted suicides were turned over to psychiatrists after their arrest (Lieberman, 1987; Anderson, 1987).

The transformation of suicide into a medical and social problem did not remove the stigma from it altogether. The English were shocked in 1822 when the Foreign Secretary, Viscount Castlereagh, was given a state funeral and interred in Westminster Abbey after cutting his own throat (Gates, 1988). Moralists there and in France clung to the belief that suicide was sinful and ought to be punished. But looking back over the centuries, it is clear that there were four broad movements in opinion about suicide. Ancient tolerance gave way to medieval ambivalence. Reformation hostility to self-murder deepened beliefs in its supernatural causes and in the dangers of suicide's ghosts. Suicide was secularized and in practice decriminalized in the Enlightenment. It was only in the eighteenth century that the word 'suicide', began to be widely used in England and spread to France and Italy. The term was less pejorative than its older alternatives, such as 'self-murder' or 'self-slaughter', and reflected the emergence of more tolerant attitudes (MacDonald and Murphy, 1990). Finally, in the nineteenth century suicide came to be regarded as an indication of individual or social pathology. Suicide was still a bad death, but it was no longer a supernaturally evil one.

During each of these stages in the development of opinion about suicide there were dissenters from the prevailing outlook. Philosophers objected to classical tolerance to suicide. Medieval casuists carved out exemptions from theological condemnations for numerous kinds of self-killing. During the era of severity, writers inspired by classical sources adopted much less harsh views than their clerical contemporaries. Indeed, we are now more likely to be familiar with the dissenters than the orthodox. Montaigne's essays and even Donne's *Biathanatos* are more congenial to modern attitudes than a book like John Sym's *Lifes Preservative Against Self-Killing*, which voiced the prevailing hostility to suicide. And certainly the complex and moving portraits of suicides and suicidal people in Shakespeare's plays are far more widely read than, say, the theologically orthodox characterizations of Massinger (Wymer, 1985). Similarly, the powerful objections of traditionalists to increasing tolerance in the eighteenth and nineteenth centuries are today mostly overlooked. They were, however, important in determining the tempo and nature of changing attitudes and practices (Andrew, 1988).

Just as there were cross-currents in the general tide of opinion, so there were differences in attitudes in different classes and regions. Albert Bayet argued two generations ago that harshness toward suicide had its origins in peasant superstitions and ignorance (Bayet, 1922). He believed that in general the upper classes had always held a more nuanced view, and he contrasted clerical severity with aristocratic tolerance. In his view, the interaction of these three different outlooks, linked with three social groups, determined the changing character of opinion in different ages. Bayet's argument is weakened by tendentious anticlericalism, but he was right to argue that different social groups adopted different postures. The rituals of desecrating the corpse did arise from popular beliefs and fears. And in the early modern period those beliefs were strengthened by the clergy, particularly in Protestant countries. It is also true that it was among the lay elite that tolerance spread earliest, after about 1650; the clergy were far more reluctant to abandon old condemnations. The lower classes clung to beliefs about the supernatural dangers of suicide long after they had become unfashionable among the elite. In some parts of Europe there were riots when officials permitted suicides to be buried normally in the eighteenth century. It would be easy, however, to push the equation of harshness with popular ignorance and clerical conservatism and of tolerance with aristocratic and bourgeois enlightenment too far. Medieval men and women feared suicide but they do not seem to have been particularly dismayed that it was seldom punished ritually. Moreover, there were parts of France, for example, where medieval customary law had not proscribed it, and it was only criminalized by the ordinance of 1670. In England, there was a good deal of popular resentment of the secular penalties for self-murder. Changing attitudes to suicide, in other words, were as complex and variable as the very complicated social and cultural systems in which they existed. That is still true today.

REFERENCES

The literature on the history of suicide is expanding fast, but it is still uneven. There are no detailed surveys of long periods for major countries such as Germany, Italy or Spain. Eastern Europe is a blank. England and France are the best-studied nations; hence the emphasis on them above. In the listing below U.P. stands for University Press.

Anderson, O. (1987) *Suicide in Victorian and Edwardian England*, Oxford, Clarendon.

Andrew, D.T. (1988) 'The Secularization of Suicide in England: A Comment'. *Past and Present*, no. 119: 161–4.

Atkins, S.P. (1949) *The Testament of Werther*, Cambridge, Mass., Harvard U.P.

Bayet, A. (1922) *Le Suicide et la Morale*, Paris, Colin.

Crocker, L.G. (1952) 'The Discussion of Suicide in the Eighteenth Century'. *Journal of the History of Ideas*, 13: 47–72.

Delumeau, J. (1990) *Sin and Fear: The Emergence of a Guilt Culture, 13th–18th Centuries*, Trans. E. Nicholson, New York, St. Martin's.

Durkheim, E. (1970) *Suicide: A Study in Sociology*, trans. J.A. Spaulding and G. Simpson, London, Routledge and Kegan Paul.

Favre, R. (1978) *La Mort dans la Littérature et la Pensé Françaises au Siècle des Lumières*, Lyons, Lyon U.P.

Fedden, H.R. (1972) *Suicide: A Social and Historical Study*, New York, B. Blom.

Gates, B. (1988) *Victorian Suicide*, Princeton, Princeton U.P.

Griffin, M. (1986) 'Philosophy, Cato, and Roman Suicide'. *Greece and Rome*, 33: 64–77, 192–202.

Grisé, Y. (1982) *Suicide dans la Rome Antique*, Paris and Montreal, Les Belles Lettres.

Haeberli, L. (1975) 'Le Suicide à Genève au XVIIIe siècle'. In (Anon. ed.) *Pour une Histoire Qualitative*, Geneva, Romandes U.P.

Halbawchs, M. (1978) *The Causes of Suicide*, trans. H. Goldblatt, New York, Free Press.

Kushner, H.I. (1989) *Self-Destruction in the Promised Land*, New Brunswick, N.J., Rutgers U.P.

Lieberman, L.J. (1987) *Une Maladie Epidémique: Suicide and Its Implications in Nineteenth-Century France*, Unpublished Ph.D thesis, Yale University.

MacDonald, M. (1981) *Mystical Bedlam: Madness, Anxiety and Healing in Seventeenth-Century England*, Cambridge, Cambridge U.P.

MacDonald, M. and Murphy, T.R. (1990) *Sleepless Souls: Suicide in Early Modern England*, Oxford, Clarendon.

McManners, J. (1981) *Death and the Enlightenment*, Oxford, Clarendon.

Merrick, J. (1989) 'Patterns and Prosecution of Suicide in Eighteenth-Century Paris'. *Historical Reflections/Réflexions Historiques*, 16: 1–53.

Meyerstein, E.H.W. (1930) *A Life of Thomas Chatterton*, London, Igpen and Grant.

Moore, C. (1790) *A Full Inquiry into the Subject of Suicide*, 2 vols., London, Rivington, et al.

Murray, A. (Forthcoming) *Suicide in the Middle Ages*, Oxford, Clarendon.

Outram, D. (1989) *The Body and the French Revolution*, New Haven, Yale U.P.

Schär, M. (1985) *Seelennöte der Untertanen: Selbstmord, Melancholie und Religion im Alten Zürich, 1500–1800*, Zurich, Chronos.

Schmitt, J.-C. (1976) 'Le Suicide au moyen âge'. *Annales, E.S.C.*, 31: 3–28.

Taylor, S. (1982) *Durkheim and the Study of Suicide*, London, Macmillan.

Van Hooff, A.J.L. (1990) *From Autothanasia to Suicide*, London, Routledge.

Wymer, R. (1986) *Suicide and Despair in Jacobean Drama*, New York, St. Martin.

Chapter 25
Personality Disorders

Clinical Section
H SASS and S HERPERTZ[1]

The concept of Psychopathy results from a confluence of views entertained in the French, German and Anglo-American psychiatric traditions. Well into the twentieth century, socio-cultural factors caused these conceptions of psychopathy to develop more or less independently. This chapter deals with all three traditions.

FRENCH CONCEPTS

Pinel's (1809) concept of a *manie sans délire*[2] includes instances of 'deranged personality' and hence can be looked upon as the beginning of the scientific study of personality disorder as a nosological entity. The eighteenth century had regarded all mental diseases as a fundamental disturbance of intellect. Pinel was one of the first to stress that in some disorders it was the emotions that were primarily involved. In his *Traité médico-philosophique sur l'aliénation mentale* he listed five nosological categories: melancholia, mania without delirium, mania with delirium, dementia and idiotism. One of Pinel's examples of mania without *délire* exhibited emotional instability and social drift, and just about fits present diagnostic criteria. Pinel believed that this behaviour was caused by inadequate education or a perverse, unrestrained constitution and therefore suggested that psychopathy may be a biographical or endogenous development. This notwithstanding, early nineteenth century definitions of madness remained in the main intellectualistic in nature. Indeed, to this day, psychiatric phenomenology neglects the disorders of affect (Berrios, 1985).

Monomania

To deal with the problem of 'total insanity', Esquirol (1838) developed the idea of 'monomania', a diagnostic category which was based on the partial, primary (and independent) involvement of intellectual, emotional or volitional mental functions. Esquirol extended his theory of monomania to the point of circularity to include states in which a single behavioural disturbance became the only diagnostic criterion to diagnose the condition (e.g. Pyromania, Kleptomania, Erotomania and Homicidal Monomania). Not surprisingly, monomania was one of the sources for the notion of psychopathy, and towards the end of the century 'instinctive monomania' had an easy transition to *Impulsives Irresein*.

Since its inception, and both in France and beyond, the concept of monomania was criticised on clinical and medico-legal grounds. For example, Griesinger (1845) emphasized that all 'fixe idées' were the expression of a deranged mind and hence they were better understood as inchoate forms of mania. He also proposed that forensic examination should search for other features of mental disease and not consider the act itself as the only diagnostic criterion for a putative abnormal state of mind.

The Theory of Degeneration

Morel's (1857) idea of degeneration enshrined a religious world view which included a pseudo-biological account of the myth of the Fall. It proposed that: 1) degenerative alterations are pathological deviations from normality, 2) mental diseases are mostly hereditary; i.e. originally caused by external influences, the disorder becomes written into the biology of the subject and is passed on, with ever increasing pathological deviation, from generation to generation; deterioration, however, may also take place within an individual's life time, 3) degeneration is both quantitative and qualitative, i.e. new disorders may appear. According to Morel's model, all types of mental and neurological disorder can be traced back to one common hereditary origin (idea of polymorphic heredity).

Morel's nosology of mental diseases was also grounded on speculative aetiology. *Les folies hereditaires* he divided up according to degree of degeneration. The less disordered group presented eccentricity, unstable emotions, untrustworthiness and sparing of cognitive functions. They suffered from *folie morale* a notion similar to the British concept of 'moral insanity'.

Morel's conception of progressive and polymorphic degeneration was accepted as a source of mental illness. Magnan (1895), a famous representative of the theory of degeneration in France, saw himself as a disciple of Darwin, and did his best to dissociate himself from Morel's overt religious point of view. He formulated the concept of 'predisposition' which could be latent or manifest itself at birth. Mental disorder was thus an expression of degenerational changes affecting cerebro-spinal centres which render the person vulnerable to any stress. In his view, man was persistently threatened by external destructive influences any of which might start the degeneration process. Magnan also distinguished degrees of degeneration. The least damaged group were the *dégénérés superieurs* who only showed emotional vulnerability.

Degeneration theory also influenced the Italian writer Cesare Lombroso (Zambianchi, 1963) who in 1876 developed the notion of the born criminal (*delinquente nato*). Inspired by Darwin's evolutionism, Lombroso regarded criminality as a form of human atavism, a step back in the phylogenesis of mankind. Criminal acts were rooted in biology, and the criminal lacked in the higher nervous centres related to moral behaviour; furthermore he could be recognized by anatomical stigmata of degeneration. Social prognosis was thus very poor. Lombroso's 'social-darwinism' has not altogether disappeared and underlies current negative and moralistic views of mental illness and psychopathy.

After the First World War, the idea of degeneration was replaced by the doctrine of constitution (Delmas, 1943), and with Dupré (1925), degeneration becomes *desequilibration mentale*. The latter is connected with German views on the 'psychopathic constitution'.

ANGLO-AMERICAN VIEWS

Prichard (1835) defined *moral insanity* as 'madness consisting in a morbid perversion of the natural feelings, affections, inclinations, temper habits, moral dispositions, and natural impulses, without any remarkable disorder or defect of the interest or knowing and reasoning faculties, and particularly without any insane illusion or hallucinations' (p.6). Lest 'moral insanity' is interpreted in purely moralistic terms, the reader must be reminded that during the early nineteenth century, the word 'moral' was multivocal, and mainly meant 'psychological' (to refer to the affective and conative in contrast to the intellectual; and in the phrase 'moral treatment' it referred to a set of psychosocial techniques; far less often (in medical parlance), it meant 'ethical'. There is good textual evidence to believe that for Prichard moral simply meant 'psychological'. Like Pinel, he believed that mental functions other than the intellectual could be *primarily* involved (Berrios, 1993). Moral insanity had for Prichard different causes, ranging from more or less typical bipolar disorder, to epilepsy, moral shock and fever (Tuke, 1884, p.80). It would seem, therefore, that *ab initio*, moral insanity was a heterogeneous clinical concept.

Maudsley (1874) attempted to differentiate the mad from the bad. In *Responsibility in Mental Diseases* he argued against those who described moral insanity as a 'groundless medical invention' (p.68), and pleaded for the concept of diminished criminal responsibility. In contrast to his contemporaries, he believed that emotions and impulses alone could drive man to commit criminal acts.

The British Concept of Constitution and the Psychopathic State

The British concept of psychopathy was shaped by D.K. Henderson (1939). A Scottish disciple of A. Meyer (1903), Henderson considered 'psychopathic states' as a condition of 'constitutional abnormality'. In contrast to other (especially German) psychiatrists he conceived of 'constitution' as resulting from both heredity and environment. There were three psychopathic states, the predominantly aggressive, inadequate, and creative. The former two were characterized by antisocial traits and were soon to become part of the Anglo-Saxon concepts of personality disorder. Thus, the concept of 'psychopathic disorder' included in the 'Mental Health Act' is defined on the basis of aggressive and irresponsible behaviour.

Henderson also believed that psychopathic states had prognostic value: 'It is the underlying psychopathic state which constitutes the rock on which our prognosis and treatment in relation to many psychoneurotic and psychotic states becomes shattered' (in Henderson, 1939, p.37). The term 'psychopathic disorder' is also used to refer to aspects of the personality which have special value in forensic psychiatry (Sass and Herpertz, 1994). Thus, it can be concluded that the meaning of the term 'psychopathy' has evolved from his earlier reference to any psychopathological change to a narrow signifier for aggressive, antisocial recidivists.

Psychopathy as Antisocial Disorder

By providing inclusion and exclusion criteria, Craft (1966) formulated the first operational view of psychopathy as an antisocial disorder. The 'primary' features were lack of feeling towards other beings, and a tendency to act on impulse; the 'secondary' features were aggressiveness, absence of shame and remorse, an inability to profit from experience, and a shortage of drive or motivation. The diagnosis of psychopathy could not be made if the subject was suffering from psychoses or serious 'mental disability' or if normal criminal motivation could be demonstrated (p.5).

North America

Rush (1812) was the first Anglo-American psychiatrist to study individuals whose disturbances were primarily characterized by irresponsibility, unscrupulousness and aggressiveness. He spoke of 'perversion of the moral faculties' and of 'moral alienation of mind' and believed that such reprehensible acts were manifestations of mental disease and hence were motiveless and driven 'by a kind of involuntary power' (in Rush, 1827, p.261). Like British views, American ones also emphasize dissocial and amoral behaviour. However, it is Ray's (1838) idea of 'moral mania' that is most closely associated with European concepts of psychopathy. Influenced by phrenological ideas, Ray believed in well-defined cerebral localizations for both intellectual and emotional faculties. This made it easier for him to accept the idea of 'moral insanity'.

Difference between Constitutional Inferiority and Neurosis

Meyer (1903) distinguished neurasthenia, psychasthenia and hysteria (forms of neurosis) from 'constitutional inferiority'. This group included 'psychological inferiors' whose mental state was not sufficiently differentiated to be regarded as falling into the mentally ill category. By the turn of the century, the idea of degeneration was gradually replaced by that of constitution, and by the late 1920's, 'constitutional inferiority' was replaced by 'psychopathic personality'. Partridge (1930) was one of the main advocates of the new concept of psychopathy. He described personalities whose abnormality was expressed in impulsiveness and moral 'deficiency'.

Psychoanalytic views

Following Freud's (1959) work on 'Character and anal erotism', Alexander (1928) and Reich (1933) proposed the concept of 'character neurosis', i.e. the view that 'neurosis' could manifest itself in changes of character as a whole. Alexander limited his definition to those cases who act out their deviance in impulsive behaviour. Reich, in turn, regarded character primarily as a defensive structure against inner pulsions and external stresses, and believed that the neurotic character was at the basis of all neurotic symptoms. This led him to develop a form of analysis focused on character structure (Reich, 1949).

Psychopathy and Sociopathy

As explained above, the conception of psychopathic personality was progressively narrowed down until it basically meant antisocial behaviour. Partridge (1930) defined it as a persistent maladjustment which cannot be corrected by ordinary methods of education or by punishment: 'We might say that pragmatically the psychopath is mainly reduced to types which are of importance from the standpoint of society and the effect of personalities adversely upon the social life seems to be recognized as a justification for a category within the field of the psychopathological in its more individual and subjective aspects' (p.75).

From the time of Partridge on, the emphasis has been on descriptions and aetiological speculation has taken the back seat. To this day, a view of 'psychopathy' as 'sociopathy' has dominated Anglo-Saxon psychiatry; a parallel concept, 'antisocial personality disorder' appeared in DSM III (APA, 1980), and has been kept in DSM-III-R (APA, 1987) and DSM-IV (APA, 1994).

Idiopathic and symptomatic psychopathy

Karpman (1941) suggested a distinction between idiopathic and symptomatic psychopathy. The latter category included reactions which were basically neurotic and therefore could be traced back to intra-psychic conflicts. The small group of true (idiopathic) psychopaths whose behaviour cannot be explained in those terms, Krapman (1941) considered as 'anethopaths' and as lacking in conscience.

Semantic Dementia

Cleckley's (1976) monograph 'The Mask of Sanity' was published in 1941 and went through five editions. Cleckley's 'psychopath' was characterized by antisocial behaviour which could not be derived from psychosis, neurosis or mental handicap. He listed 16 criteria: superficial charm and undisturbed intelligence; unreliability and insincerity; inability to accept blame or shame; failure to learn from experience; pathological egocentricity and incapacity for love; lacking emotions in general; impersonal and poorly integrated sexual relationships; inability to follow one's aim in life.

Indeed, the DSM-IV (APA, 1994) concept of antisocial personality disorder includes most of these criteria. Cleckley was convinced that 'psychopathy' was a 'severe disease', a form of psychosis which had not yet manifested itself. Cleckley also coined the term 'semantic dementia' to refer to the incapacity of the psychopath to 'evaluate or experience life as a totally integrated organism. Although the psychopath can react verbally as though he understood love, pride, grief, shame, or the other emotions, he has no real experience of these human values or connotations' (Cleckley, 1942). A similar picture of the psychopath was offered by the sociologists McCord and McCord (1964) who researched the long-term association between psychopathy and delinquency.

The Concept of Antisocial Personality Disorder

In his well known monograph 'Deviant Children Grown Up', Robins (1966) described a population of more than 500 males who had been followed up for a period of 30 years. These data are the most important database for the current American concept of antisocial personality disorder (Robins, 1979). Robins' general conclusion was that the degree of antisocial and especially aggressive behaviour in childhood and youth remains the main predictor for sociopathic disorder. This finding also supported the wide-spread supposition that disordered personality traits are stable and enduring.

GERMAN CONCEPTS

In Germany, the term and concept of 'psychopathy' embrace most forms of abnormal personality. Up to the 1840's, however, the term was used in its etymological sense: for example, for von Feuchtersleben (1845) 'psychopathy' meant psychological defect, psychosis or disorder of personality. The current German meaning is traceable to Koch (1889) who in his *Leitfaden der Psychiatrie* first applied the term *psychopathische Minderwertigkeiten* to the anomalies of personality.

Koch's monograph *Psychopathische Minderwertigkeiten* (1891–1893) played in Germany the same role in relation to the concept of abnormal personality as the work of Pinel had in France, Rush in the USA and Prichard in Great Britain. German ideas on psychopathy also influenced French and Anglo-American views. This was more noticeable after the 1930's when many German-speaking psychiatrists and psychoanalysts emigrated to the countries in question.

In the 'psychopathic inferiorities', Koch included clinical states characterized by a range of minor 'mental defects', and also definite forms of psychopathic inferiority (the latter in the current sense of psychopathy). It was thus Koch who established the present usage of psychopathy and formulated its definition in terms of typological theory.

Koch divided the 'psychopathic inferiorities' into congenital and acquired, and each category into psychopathic predisposition, defect, and degeneration. He described in some detail many of the psychopathic types which were to re-appear in later writings; for example, he identified individuals with 'psychic brittleness' (*psychische Zartheit*), i.e. those with a weak and vulnerable constitution.

In the 1840s, Griesinger defined 'nervous constitution' or 'sensitive weakness' as that individual vulnerability that might lead to mental suffering and loosing one's balance of mind. This notion was related both to the old French idea of *desequilibration mentale* and to the even earlier concept of 'asthenia'. The German concept was thus wider than the Anglo-American one, and included far more than a dissocial criterion. Although no pejorative or moralizing intention seems apparent in the writings of Koch, the notion of inferiority nonetheless includes a component of amorality and socially harmful behaviour. It is not surprising that the term soon acquired a negative evaluation and moral condemnation.

Psychopathic Constitution

Ziehen (1905–1912) developed Koch's views one step further, and his 'psychopathic constitutions' were also considered as genetic in nature. In a book entitled *Geisteskrankheiten des Kindesalters* (mental diseases of childhood), Ziehen went on to list twelve forms of psychopathic constitutions including hysterical, neurasthenic, hyperthymic, paranoid and obsessive types.

Psychopathic Personalities: Predominantly Social

Kraepelin's concept of psychopathy was influenced by the French theory of degeneration and itself forms the basis of K. Schneider's typology, and through the latter, of today's German doctrine of psychopathy. In successive editions of his textbook, Kraepelin elaborated his concept of 'psychopathic states' as an abnormal personality. The expression *Die psychopathischen Zustände* first appeared in the 5th edition (Kraepelin, 1896) and comprised compulsive states, impulsive insanity, homosexuality and disturbances of the mood (the so-called *konstitutionellen Verstimmungen*. In this regard, it is important to notice that until the 7th edition (Vol.2, Kraepelin, 1904) the anomalies of personality were included under the heading *Entartungsirresein* (i.e. insanity of degeneration).

From then on Kraepelin made a further distinction between *Originäre Krankheitszustände* (original disease states) – the group he had earlier on called psychopathic states – and *Psychopathische Persönlichkeiten*. The latter were regarded as stable psychopathic conditions (i.e. personality defects). Kraepelin employed the term 'psychopathic personalities' in a predominantly socially evaluating sense. In the 7th edition, he also subsumed under this rubric the inborn delinquents, the unstable liars, swindlers and pseudo-querulous.

In the 8th edition (1909–1915), Kraepelin re-named or re-classified some groups, and in addition to the *Gesellschaftsfeind* (the antisocial one) he listed the excitable, the unstable, the *Triebmenschen* (the 'driven' individuals, i.e. those suffering from impulsive insanity), the eccentric, the liars, the swindlers and the querulous. Interestingly enough, the states of disturbed mood – today's sub-affective disorders – he separated from the psychopathic states and re-classified them as mild forms of manic-depressive psychosis. Current classifications of mood disorder do likewise (Akiskal, 1981; Akiskal et al, 1983; Sass et al, 1993).

Birnbaum (1926) also researched into the social aspects of psychopathy, and his *Die psychopathischen Verbrecher* (the psychopathic delinquents) includes a great deal on the forensic aspects of abnormal personality. Inspired in the French theory of degeneration, he also developed the concept of 'abnormal inherited predisposition'.

Relationship between Body Type and Personality
During this period there also appeared various 'systematic' typologies, i.e. proposals to draw 'psychopathic' categories from prototypic personality theories. Foremost amongst these is Kretschmer's *konstitutionstypologisches Modell* (1919). But there were many others. For example, Gruhle (1956) abstracted his categories from fundamental characteristics of human behaviour such as activity, basic mood, affective responsiveness, will power, and so on. Kahn (1928), Schultz (1928), Homburger (1929), and Rothacker (1947) also proposed hierarchical models of personality (*Schichttypologien*). Kretschmer (1919) and Ewald (1924) also introduced the notion of *Reaktionstypologien* to account for specific styles of dealing with experience. Systematic typologies lost influence after the publication of Schneider's monograph (1923).

Kretschmer (1919; 1925) suggested that there was a specific correlation between body type and personality and recognized the pyknic, leptosomic and athletic body types. The pyknic body type was associated with the cyclothymic character which he considered to be in a continuum with the 'abnormal cycloid variant' and with the manic-depressive psychosis. The leptosomic and athletic body types were related to a schizothymic temperament and were also on a continuum with the schizoid form of psychopathy and with schizophrenia.

Abnormal and (value free) Psychopathic Personalities
K. Schneider's famous monograph *Die psychopathischen Persönlichkeiten* (1950) (first published in 1923) finds its roots in his earlier study on *Persönlichkeit und Schicksal eingeschriebener Prostituierter* (1938) (first published in 1921) where he recognized up to 12 characterological types. Schneider made

use of a 'typological approach', and endeavoured to keep his types free from value judgements; for example, he included no anti-social forms of behaviour. 'Abnormal personalities' were statistical deviations from an estimated average norm, but the concept of norm is poorly formulated in his work. Within his model, eminently creative and intelligent individuals were also abnormal; hence, not all abnormal personalities could be said to have psychiatric implications. Schneider defined 'psychopathic personalities [as] those abnormal personalities that suffer from their abnormality or whose abnormality causes society to suffer' (p.6).

Very importantly, for Schneider psychopathy is not a form of mental illness because the latter by definition must be associated with brain lesion or a recognized disease process. In this, he opposed Kretschmer and Bleuler who believed that psychosis and psychopathy were just different degrees on a scale of derangement.

Schneider differentiated ten forms of 'psychopathic' personality: hyperthymic and depressive psychopaths with stable deviation of mood and activity; the insecure divided into sensitive and anankastic psychopaths; the fanatic; the self-assertive; the emotionally unstable; the explosive; the callous; weak-willed; and the aesthenic psychopaths. More recently, Petrilowitsch (1966) has built into Schneider's types a patho-characterological dimension. Schneider's doctrine influenced all subsequent typologies and current classification systems include essential parts of his concept of psychopathy. In an appendix, DSM-IV has even included the 'depressive type' to encourage further research on this topic.

FINAL COMMENTS

As described above, nineteenth and twentieth century concepts of 'personality disorder' include elements taken from the nosology of psychopathological disturbances and value-laden criteria such as social deviation. The later component has dominated Anglo-American views, but it can also be found in the French doctrine of degeneration and in the German tradition. The concept of 'moral insanity' is a good example as its core components (disorders of affectivity and volition) were highly susceptible to ethical evaluation. Similar elements are found in the German doctrine of psychopathy; for example, Kraepelin explicitly combined sociological and psychopathological criteria, and in later editions of his textbook concentrated on the socially harmful forms of psychopathy. He purified the latter category by transferring all personality types based on 'disturbed mood' to the manic-depressive 'circle'.

K. Schneider, in turn, favoured a value-free psychological and characterological point of view and reclaimed the subclinical disorders of affect. By distinguishing two forms of psychopath – those who suffer from their psychic abnormality and those society suffers from – Schneider, however, reintroduced social variables by a backdoor (Sass, 1987). The German tradition can be considered as conceptually wider in that it also included an 'asthenic type', i.e. a feeble form of psychopathy to which later on were added the 'subclinical' abnormalities of affect. This wide compass has added to the popularity of the concept of psychopathy in German-speaking countries.

Personality Disorder and Endogenous Psychosis

'Personality disorder' includes clinical phenomena falling on a borderland between mental health and recognized mental disease. Whilst transitions between normal and slightly abnormal personalities are readily accepted, states falling between the most severe form of pathology of character and the endogenous psychoses cause classificatory difficulty (Sass and Koehler, 1983). The 'idea of a continuum' is especially associated with the German tradition of 'unitary psychosis' (Zeller, 1840; Griesinger, 1845; Sass, 1990). A similar unitary approach, however, can be detected in the French theory of degeneration and polymorphic heredity as according to this view all forms of mental disorder can be traced back to one origin. The French notion of *manie sans délire* is wider and includes proto-concepts for a number of mental derangements.

Two lines can be distinguished in the development of the German concept of psychopathy. One was linked to Kretschmer's putative transitions between normal personality traits, psychopathies and endogenous psychoses; the other to the categorical approach put forward by Schneider (1950), Birnbaum (1909), Jaspers (1959), and Gruhle (1956). (Schneider, for example, enjoined psychiatrists to decide between abnormal personality or endogenous psychosis.)

Empirical research, however, has not confirmed an association between specific personality disorders and schizophrenia (in the sense of Kretschmer's schizoid dimension) although there is some evidence in favour of wider notions such as 'increased psychic vulnerability'. In the field of the affective psychoses, typical premorbid traits of personality have also been described and sometimes conceptualized as *typus melancholicus* (Tellencbach, 1961) and *typus manicus* (von Zerssen, 1992). The debate continues.

NOTES

1 Re-written by G.E.B.
2 Earlier views of mania (up to the 1840s) were coterminous with 'madness'. 'Delirium' on the other hand meant derangement of reason and included confusion, incoherent speech, delusions and hallucinations.

REFERENCES

Akiskal, H.S. (1981) 'Subaffective disorders: dysthymic, cyclothymic and bipolar II disorders in the borderline realm'. *Psychiatr. Clin. North. Am.*, 4: 25–46.

Akiskal, H.S., Hirschfeld, R.M.A. and Yerevanian, B.J. (1983) 'The relationship of personality to affective disorders'. *Arch. Gen. Psychiat.*, 40: 801–10.

Alexander, F. (1928) 'Der neurotische Charakter. Seine Stellung in der Psychopathologie und in der Literatur'. *Int. Z. Psychoanal.*, 14: 26–44.

American Psychiatric Association (1980) *Diagnostic and Statistical Manual of Mental Disorders*, third edition, Washington, D.C., American Psychiatric Press.

American Psychiatric Association (1987) *Diagnostic and Statistical Manual of Mental Disorders*, third edition, revised, Washington, D.C., American Psychiatric Press.

American Psychiatric Association (1994) *Diagnostic and Statistical Manual of*

Mental Disorders, fourth edition, Washington, D.C., American Psychiatric Press.

Berrios, G.E. (1985) 'The psychopathology of affectivity: conceptual and historical aspects'. *Psychological Medicine*, 15: 745–58.

Berrios, G.E. (1993) 'European views on personality disorders: a conceptual history'. *Comprehensive Psychiatry*, 34(1): 14–30.

Birnbaum, K. (1909) 'Über psychopathische Persönlichkeiten. Eine psychopathologische Studie'. In Loewenfeld, L. (ed.) *Grenzfragen des Nerven- und Seelenlebens*, vol.64, Wiesbaden, C.F. Bergmann.

Birnbaum, K. (1926) *Die psychopathischen Verbrecher*, (2nd ed.) Leipzig: Thieme. (1st ed. 1914.)

Bleuler, E. (1896) *Der geborene Verbrecher. Eine kritische Studie*, Munchen, Lehmann.

Cleckley, H. (1942) 'Semantic Dementia'. *Psychiatric Quarterly*, 16: 521.

Cleckley, H. (1976) *The Mask of Sanity: An Attempt to Clarify some Issues about the So-called Psychopathic Personality*, (5th ed.), St Louis, Mosby. (1st ed. 1941.)

Craft, M. (1966) *Psychopathic Disorders and their Assessment*, Oxford, Permagon Press.

Delmas, F. (1943) 'Le Constitutions psychopathiques'. *Ann. Med. Psych.*, 101: 219–32.

Dupré, E. (1925) *Pathologie de l'Imagination et de l'Emotivité*, Paris, Payot.

Esquirol, E. (1838) *Des Maladies Mentales Considerées sous les Rapports Médical. Hygienique et Médico-legal*, Paris, Baillière.

Ewald, G. (1924) *Temperament und Character*, Berlin, Springer.

Feuchtersleben, E. von (1845) *Lehrbuch der arztlichen Seelenkunde*, Wien, Gerold.

Freud, S. (1905) *Drei Abhandlungen zur Sexualtheorie*, GW V, Frankfurt, Fischer.

Freud, S. (1908) *Charakter und Analerotik*, GW VII, Frankfurt, Fischer.

Freud, S. (1953) 'Three essays on sexuality'. In Strachey, J. (ed.) *Standard Edition*, vol.7, London, Hogarth Press.

Freud, S. (1959) 'Character and anal erotism'. In Strachey, J. (ed.) *Standard Edition*, vol.9, London, Hogarth Press.

Griesinger, W. (1845) *Die Pathologie und Therapie der psychischen Krankheiten*, Stuttgart, Krabbe.

Gruhle, H.W. (1956) 'Psychopathie'. In Weygandt, W. (ed.) *Lehrbuch der Nerven- und Geisteskrankheiten*, (2nd ed.) Halle, Marhold, pp.664–86.

Henderson, D. (1939) *Psychopathic States*, New York, Norton.

Homburger, A. (1929) 'Versuch einer Typologie der psychopathischen Konstitution'. *Nervenarzt*, 2: 134–6.

Jaspers, K. (1959) *Allgemeine Psychopathologie*, (7th ed.), Heidelberg, Springer. (1st ed. 1913.)

Kahn, E. (1928) 'Die psychopathischen Persönlichkeiten'. In Bumke, O. (ed.) *Handbuch der Geisteskrankheiten*, vol.5, Berlin, Springer, pp.227–487.

Karpman, B. (1941) 'On the need of separating psychopathy into two distinct clinical types: The symptomatic and the idiopathic'. *J. Crim. Psychopathol.*, 2: 112–37.

Koch, J.L.A. (1889) *Kurzgefalßter Leitfaden der Psychiatrie*, (2nd ed.) Ravensburg, Dorn'schen Buchhandlung.

Koch, J.L.A. (1891–1893) *Die psychopathischen Minderwertigkeiten*, Ravensburg, Maier.

Kolle, K. (1963) 'Hans W. Gruhle'. In Kolle, K. (ed.) *Große Nervenärzte*, vol.3, Stuttgart, Thieme.

Kraepelin, E. (1896) *Psychiatrie. Ein Lehrbuch für Studierende und Ärzte*, (5th ed.) Leipzig, Barth.

Kraepelin, E. (1904) *Psychiatrie. Ein Lehrbuch für Studierende und Ärzte*, vol.2, (7th ed.), Leipzig, Barth.

Kraepelin, E. (1909–1915) *Psychiatrie. Ein Lehrbuch für Studierende und Ärzte*, (8th ed.), Leipzig, Barth.

Kretschmer, E. (1919) *Körperbau und Character*, Berlin, Springer.

Magnan, M. and Legrain, M. (1895) *Les Dégénerés (état mental et syndromes épisodiques)*, Paris, Rueff.

Maudsley, H. (1874) *Responsibility in Mental Disease*, London, King.

McCord, W. and McCord, J. (1964) *The Psychopath. An Essay on the Criminal Mind*, (2nd ed.), New York, Van Norstrand.

Meyer. A. (1903) 'An attempt at analysis of the neurotic constitution'. *Am. J. Psych.*, 14: 354–67.

Morel, B.A. (1857) *Traité des Degénéréscences Physiques, Intellectuelles et Morales de l'Espéce Humaine et des Causes qui Produisent ces Varietés Maladive*, Paris, Bailliére.

Partridge, G.E. (1930) 'Current conceptions of psychopathic personality'. *Am. J. Psychiat.*, 10: 53–99.

Petrilowitsch, N. (1966) *Abnorme Persönlichkeiten*, (3rd ed.) Basel, Karger.

Pichot, P. (1978) 'Psychopathic behaviour: A historical overview'. In Hare, R.D. and Schalling, D. (eds.) *Psychopathic Behaviour: Approaches to Research*, Chichester, Wiley, pp.55–70.

Pinel, P. (1809) *Traité Médico-philosophique sur l'Alienation Mentale*, (2nd ed.) Paris, Brosson.

Prichard, J.C. (1835) *A Treatise on Insanity and other Disorders Affecting the Mind*, London, Sherwood, Gilbert & Piper.

Ray, I. (1838) *A Treatise on the Medical Jurisprudence of Insanity*, Boston, Little.

Reich, W. (1933) *Charakteranalyse. Technik und Grundlagen*, Berlin, Selbstverlag.

Reich, W. (1949) *Character Analysis*, New York, Orgone Institute Press.

Robins, L.N. (1966) *Deviant Children Grown up: A Sociological and Psychiatric Study of Sociopathic Personality*, Baltimore, Williams & Wilkens.

Robins, L.N. (1979) 'Longitudinal methods in the study of normal and pathological development'. In Kisker, K.P. et al (eds.) *Psychiatrie der Gegenwart*, vol.1, (2nd ed.) Heidelberg, Springer, pp.627–84.

Rothacker, E. (1947) *Die Schichten der Persönlichkeit*, (3rd ed.)

Rush, B. (1827) *Medical Inquiries and Observations upon the Diseases of the Mind*, (3rd ed.) Philadelphia, Kimber & Richardson. (1st ed. 1812.)

Sass, H. (1987) *Psychopathie – Soziopathie – Dissozialitat: zur Differentialtypologie der Persönlichkeitsstörungen*, Heidelberg, Springer.

644 A History of Clinical Psychiatry

Sass, H. (1990) 'Einheitspsychose'. In Stephanis, C.N., Soldatos, C.R. and Rabavilas, A.D. (eds.) *Psychiatry: A World Perspective. Proceedings of the 8th World Congress of Psychiatry*, Athens, Congress Series 900, pp.260–6.

Sass, H. and Koehler, K. (1983) 'Borderline-Syndrome: Grenzgebiet oder Niemandsland? Zur klinischpsychiatrischen Relevanz von Borderline-Diagnosen'. *Nervenarzt*, 54: 221–30.

Sass, H., Herpertz, S. and Steinmeyer, E.D. (1993) 'Subaffective personality disorders'. *International Clinical Psychopharmacology*, 8 (Suppl. 1): 39–46.

Sass, H. and Herpertz, S (1994) 'Psychopathic Disorder'. In Felthous, A.R. and Bowden, P., 'Forensic Psychiatry'. *Current Opinion in Psychiatry*, 7(6): 437–41.

Schneider, K. (1938) *Studien uber Persönlichkeit und Schicksal eingeschriebener Prostituierter*, Berlin, Springer.

Schneider, K. (1950) *Die psychopathischen Persönlichkeiten*, (9th ed.), Wien, Deuticke. (1st ed. 1923, Leipzig: Thieme.)

Schneider, K. (1967) *Klinische Psychopathologie*, (8th ed.) Stuttgart, Thieme.

Schultz, J.H. (1928) 'Die konstitutionelle Nervosität'. In Bumke, O. (ed.), *Handbuch der Geisteskrankheiten*, vol.5, Berlin, Springer, pp.28–111.

Tellenbach, H. (1961) *Melancholie*, Heidelberg, Springer.

Tuke, D.H. (1884) *Prichard and Symonds in especial Relation to Mental Science with Chapters on Moral Insanity*, London, J. & A. Churchill.

World Health Organization (1989) *ICD-10*, WHO Division of Mental Health, Geneva.

Zambianchi, A. (1963) 'Cesare Lombroso'. In Kolle, K. (ed.) *Große Nervenärzte*, vol.3, Stuttgart, Thieme.

Zeller, A. (1840) *Med. Korr. Bl. d. Württemb. Medizinvereins* 10, 17.

Zerssen, D. von (1992) 'Der "Typus manicus" – eine Variante der Zyklothymie?' In Marneros, A. and Philipp, M. (eds.) *Persönlichkeit und psychische Erkrankung*, Heidelberg, Springer, pp.72–86.

Ziehen, T.H. (1905, 1907, 1908, 1912) 'Zur Lehre von den psychopathischen Konstitutionen'. *Charité-Annalen*, 29, 31, 32, 36.

Chapter 25
Personality Disorders

Social Section
WALTRAUD ERNST

UNMASKING AN ENIGMA

For at least two centuries the concept of 'personality disorders' has been a close, albeit at times uncomfortable, bedfellow of mayhem and murder. It evoked images of blood baths and of weird, if not emotionally twisted, perpetrators revelling in sanguine pursuits. In addition to violence and crime, eccentricity, vice and genius, have all been closely linked with the personality disorders. Rush (1745–1813) was an early author who initiated the coining of psychiatric labels such as 'moral derangement' for these conditions.

The term 'moral insanity' was used by Prichard (1786–1848) in 1833 and 1835 to refer to those exhibiting an 'unusual prevalence of angry and malicious feelings, which arise without provocation or any of the ordinary incitements', exciting 'the greatest disgust and abhorrence' (Prichard, 1835). Prichard believed that there were 'many individuals living at large' who were of a 'singular, wayward, and eccentric character' and thus good exemplars of 'moral insanity'. A hundred years later, in 1941, Cleckley used the resounding phrase of a 'convincing mask of sanity' to characterise those who – though neither mentally debilitated nor psychotic – are subject to 'irrational or even fantastic' beliefs. Cleckley (1964), of course, admitted that the literary achievements of unorthodox authors such as Sartre, Joyce or Gide remained outside the 'categorial haven' of psychiatric classification. Nevertheless he considered them to come close to 'incomplete manifestations or suggestions' of psychopathic disorders. They showed 'rapt predilection' for 'what is generally regarded as perverse, dispirited, or distastefully unintelligible'.

The concept of what came to be known as 'personality disorders' – and here in particular the sub-group of 'psychopathic' or 'anti-social' personality – has certainly had a chequered career, often embroidered by value judgements and prejudice. Cleckley (1955) sighed in surprising humility in the foreword to the third edition of his acclaimed *Mask of Sanity* that it was still 'not easy to convey this concept', admitting that 'the psychopath presents an important and challenging enigma for which no adequate solution has yet been found'. In a similar vein, the McCords (McCord and McCord, 1964) lamented in 1964, that 'the proliferation of definitions, the tendency to expand the concept to include all deviant behaviour, the discrepancies in judgment between different observers – these pitfalls in the history of the concept – are enough to make a systematic diagnostician weep'.

The framework of the *Diagnostic and Statistical Manual of Mental Disorders* (DSM) in its revised version of 1987 seems to provide a more definitive basis for clinical classification. Psychopathy has now been transformed into the anti-social personality and has become but one of a variety of personality disorders. From a clinician's point of view the various sub-groups of the personality disorders certainly appear at long last more clearly delimited from each other, and from the other main disorders. In the post-modern era clinicians should therefore (despite Rosenhan and Seligman's (1984) view that the documentation of the various types of personality disorders is 'at bottom, anecdotal', and has 'grown out of clinical lore') no longer be reduced to tears.

The history of the concept of 'personality disorder', and here in particular of the narrower category of 'psychopathy', provides ample indication that the stuff of clinical lore can perhaps be related better to social issues and cultural prejudice, than to allegedly pure science and supposedly rigorous clinical knowledge. Rather than assessing the comparative clinical value of different definitions, it may be more illuminating to trace the social and cultural myths which surround and buttress the concept.

THE PSYCHOPATH – MAD OR BAD?

Until very recently, the tendency in Western cultures has been for responsibility for the care and control of the insane to shift away from family, village, and religious or spiritual networks to the state and its different institutions and professional groups. By the end of the nineteenth century, family heads, priests, village councils and healers had been superseded by a medical profession which laid more or less exclusive claim to the care and custody of the mad. Medical supremacy did not, of course, go unchallenged. The question of whether those suffering from 'moral insanity' or 'psychopathy' were bad, and therefore to be subject to legal sanction; or mad, and therefore to be the object of medical treatment or spiritual enlightenment, remained a matter of controversy within and between the legal, medical and religious professions until well into the twentieth century.

Subject to a continual tug-of-war between different professional groups, the anti-social personality emerged as a 'psychiatric wastebasket' (Robins, 1967) among clinical categories. It is to this day distinguished by the *absence* of what is otherwise considered to be the core phenomenon of mental illness: mental derangement. If the mentally ill were to be exempted from criminal culpability on account of their delusions, hallucinations and problems in 'distinguishing and chusing [sic] between good and evil' (Rush, 1786), whilst ordinary criminal deviants who were aware of legal standards had to answer for their actions, why then should the morally insane, who were seen to be in possession of their wits and able to tell right from wrong, be treated as mad rather than as bad?

At the beginning of the nineteenth century, Rush was already aware of this problem and the multifarious nature of what he called the 'total perversion of the moral faculties' (1812). He admitted that the extent to which the morally deranged 'should be considered as responsible to human or divine laws for their actions, and where the line should be drawn which divides free agency from necessity, and vice from disease, I am unable to determine'. He was, however, quite convinced of the vital role of medicine, claiming that in 'whatever manner this question may be settled, it will readily be admitted that such persons are, in pre-eminent degree, objects of compassion, and it is the business of medicine to aid both religion and law in preventing and curing the moral alienation of mind'.

The problem pointed to by Rush became particularly acute during the discussion of the 'McNaughton Rules' (1843) which set out to settle the argument about legal culpability in a period when Victorian England was eager to differentiate various social groups in terms of their eligibility for moral and economic support (Moran, 1983; Smith, 1981). Although these Rules have since remained important diagnostic guidelines, the problem of distinguishing the sick from the healthy delinquent remains. As it is the absence rather than presence of symptoms of mental disorder which make a psychopath, s/he is, as pointed out by Wootton (1959), subject to 'the circular process by which mental abnormality is inferred from anti-social behaviour while antisocial behaviour is explained by mental abnormality'. The issue is further complicated by the usual clinical premise that only those with a history of anti-social behaviour and an inability to feel and express guilt, qualify for the diagnosis of 'psychopathy', which lends itself to the inference that if you are 'wicked enough, you may hope to be excused from responsibility for your misdeeds; but if your wickedness is only moderate or if you show occasional signs of repentance or reform, then you must expect to take the blame for what you do' (Wootton, 1959). Furthermore, if the logic of the psychopathy defence was pushed to its limit a 'good defence of the apparently normal man of previous good character who one day commits a crime of violence could be provided, as does not the fact that such a man has acted out of character in itself create at least as great a presumption of mental aberration as does the psychopath's consistently acting in character?' (Wootton, 1960, quoted in Craft, 1966).

Legal criticism of psychiatric definitions is, in many respects, well-founded. Yet it is silent on the extent to which the definition of psychopathy in terms of its marginal position in regard to crime, mental disorder and sanity, undermines the definitional criteria not only for psychiatry, but also for legal, and, above all, social definitions of health, illness and deviancy. After all, notwithstanding the beguiling crispness of legal logic, and the validity of the accusation that the psychiatric expansionism of the 1950s and 60s tended to identify 'mental health with the moral or cultural ideas of its proponents' (Wootton, 1968), legal expansionism has hardly been less prevalent.

Judgements inherent in both psychiatric and legal definitions of what is ill rather than healthy behaviour are crucially socially determined, being expressions of the morals of the period. Even apparently neutral characteristics attributed to psychopaths (such as the inability to learn from past experiences), as well as the therapeutic goals designed for them (such as becoming well-adapted, honest citizens) are based on social norms rather than scientific impartiality. The view that psychopaths ought to learn that crime and violence do not pay as well as honest endeavour, for example, smacks of hypocracy in the face of the number of unresolved violent crimes in most western countries, the even higher estimated rate for undetected white collar crime, the fact that war and war crimes frequently go unsanctioned, and a general social permissiveness towards 'ordinary' 'honest' citizens who fiddle their tax statements or change the price tag in a super-market.

The question therefore emerges whether those, who have been labelled as lacking moral sense – the 'semantically demented' (Cleckley) and perhaps even the 'embryonic stormtrooper' (Lindner) – have not in fact been adapting particularly well to the moral standards prevalent in society. Krasner (1948, quoted in Harrington, 1972) gave some credence to this when he asserted that 'there are very definite aspects to our culture pattern which give [psychopaths] encouragement. . . . we have very short memories about the origins of some of our great national fortunes, toward the holders of which we hold so much respect'. In similar vein Lieutenant Colonel Grinker and Major Spiegel of the United States Marine Corps point out that whilst psychopathic personalities are often 'heroic figures' on overseas duties, being 'at last . . . well adapted to their social milieu', their return home constituted a 'sad sequel' because their aggressive behaviour was 'no longer adaptive' (quoted in Harrington, 1972). Harrington (1972) concluded that the psychopath 'confronts and affronts the bourgeois and all his values, including those held by middle-class psychiatrists and sociologists'. Even if this 'is not to imply that psychopaths are on the right track, and judgments handed down on them by professional people wrong', the psychopath remains an 'outsider': a perpetual challenge to established social structure, and to medical as well as legal codes.

MEDICAL DISORDER AND SOCIAL ORDER

The discussion as to whether mental illness in general was myth or reality, social construction or a disorder, disease or illness, has, of course, had its effect on the category of personality disorders (Sedgwick, 1982; Schwartz, 1976; Blackburn, 1988). Whilst most psychiatrists agree that in previous centuries and in non-Western cultures the concept may have had resonance as vice, divine or demonic intervention or crime, contemporary opinion is divided about whether the personality disorders are in fact disorders, rather than diseases or medicalised social problems. Certainly, an integrative view of mental illness has emerged in recent decades which allows for personality disorders, too, to be described as syndromes, and for each of the various subgroups to be seen as constituted by a multitude of factors or dimensions rather than being the effect of a single cause (for example Craft, 1966). Yet, the problem of the real nature of personality disorders, and of mental illness in general, has been a perpetual clinical and scientific bugbear for psychiatry since at least the mid-nineteenth century. It has indeed been quite recently suggested that the category of psychopathy, for example, may be 'nothing more than a semantic fiction' (McCord and McCord, 1964), and that 'the disorder in personality disorder is mythical' (Blackburn, 1983).

On the one hand even somatically orientated 'great men' of medicine and psychiatry have seen in insanity 'really a social phenomenon' (Maudsley, 1879; quoted in Shepherd, 1983), attributing 'extraordinary social significance' to it (Kraepelin; quoted in Shepherd, 1983). (Some have even conceived of the doctor as the 'advocate of the poor' (Virchow, 1848; quoted from Shepherd, 1983).) On the other hand, it has been held that the 'only disease to which the moral structure is subject, *is sin*' (Ordronaux, 1873), and that the concepts of moral insanity and psychopathy were attempts 'to return to belief in demon possession'.

For middle-class America the medical interpretation of antisocial behaviour as a manifestation of disease has for decades been seen as an attack on legal concepts of criminal responsibility and Calvinist views of free will. During the Second World War it was even – perhaps even predictably – seen as having been fostered by a 'class of modern German pagans, who are trying with what help they can get in America to break down all the safeguards of our Christian civilization, by destroying, if possible, all grounds for human responsibility' (Elwell, quoted in Maughs, 1941). The morally insane and those who define them as a medical problem would seem to be gnawing away at the very foundations of society – especially at times of war and social upheaval.

The medical professions in countries such as China, the Soviet Union and Eastern Europe have had during this century by decree of 'socialist' doctrine a better time of it. Negative social phenomena were classified as deeply rooted in the 'realities of the social structure' (Uzunov, 1960; quoted in Shepherd, 1983); psychopaths were subject to the 'educative role of the social environment' and 'in need of judicial reformative influence, rather than medical care' (Popov, 1958; quoted in Shepherd, 1983); and the allegedly 'comparatively insignificant percentage of psychopaths' (in the Soviet Union) who happened to be delinquent were – 'as is taught by Marxism-Leninism and demonstrated by practical experience' – 'certain relics of survivals of Capitalism'.

Recent events in some of the 'actually existing socialist' countries may engender some re-writing of medical history there. Having been prevented from conceptualising the anti-social personality as 'a sick person in need of treatment rather than punishment' (Glueck, 1918), as well as having had the dubious advantage of drawing on their own 'practical experience' that politics have a tremendous bearing upon medical concepts, Eastern block psychiatrists could provide a stimulating impetus to their Western colleagues' perpetual debates about the medical, legal, political and social causes and consequences of personality disorders. It can only be hoped that such involvement will lead to more enlightening statements than that by Farrington (1991) who held that it 'may be that psychopathy is an essentially general construct with some elements of specificity superimposed on the predominant generality'.

THE TIME AND THE MORALS

The persistent close affiliation between the personality disorders (especially psychopathy) and sin, vice, and crime has meant that the ethical maxims and social preoccupations of any one period could not but have a significant effect on both medical conceptualisation and the public's perception. Mental disorders, in general, lent themselves admirably to the fostering of ethical presumptions and the inducement, redirection, or expression of irrational fears or *Angst* prevalent in society at large. In 1808, madness was seen to 'stride like a Colossus' (Reid, 1808) in England, and earlier still, the 'English malady' – melancholy – had been described as 'a kind of demon that haunts the island' (Skultans, 1979). The personality disordered and in particular the violent, antisocial or psycho/sociopathic among them tended to capture the public imagination even more, and instilled a fear which went far beyond the actual numbers involved. Today's incidence of psychopathic disorders among the American population, for example, is estimated to be well under five per cent (Rosenhan and Seligman, 1984). However, when moral panic strikes, the image of the 'moral monster' (Campagne, quoted from Werlinder, 1978) seems to creep up on the average citizen to an astonishing degree. Media reports, in particular of lurking violent sexual offenders, cause not a few to bolt their doors at night (in England) or keep the side-arm close at hand (in America).

In the post-war period, Cleckley had warned that the psychopath was 'no rarity in any North American community', yet was by 'an almost universal conspiracy of evasion' ignored by those who have 'sensibly provided courts, operating rooms, tuberculosis sanatoriums, prisons, fire departments, psychiatric hospitals, police forces, and houses for the orphaned, the ill, the psychotic, and the infirm' (Cleckley, 1955). The failure to cater for the psychopath implied a 'potential for social disaster'. The McCords (McCord and McCord, 1964) proclaimed that psychopathy, 'possibly more than other mental disorders, threatens the safety, the serenity, and the security of American life'. In similar vein Lindner (quoted from Harrington, 1972) spoke of the 'psychopathy virus' and a 'plague of psychopathic behaviour', and ruminated upon the rebellious youngsters of the 1950s, those 'young people in a state of mutiny against civilization itself'.

Harrington (1972) located the above statements as typical of the late 1940s and 50s, when a 'sense of menacing strangers', and of 'brilliant, icy intelligence, incapable of love or guilt, with aggressive designs on the rest of the world' existed. As so often when *Angst* pervades society and existing values and morals are seen to be at stake, it is Western civilisation itself which is believed to be under threat. The danger to a nation's or race's womenfolk seemed even more acute: according to Cleckley (1964) 'nearly all psychopaths and part-psychopaths' possess 'the astonishing power' of binding 'forever the devotion of women'.

Admittedly, part of the difficulty in separating vice from crime, and moral insanity or psychopathy from both, may be due to the ever-lasting confusion about, and ambiguity of the word 'moral' – a confusion prevalent not only during the prototypical age of 'morals', the nineteenth century, but also today. Even when the translation of vice to disease seemed complete, and the term was changed from 'moral insanity' to allegedly less prejudicial words such as 'psychopathy', 'moral imbecility', 'moral defectiveness', 'sociopathy', and last but not least 'antisocial personality' and 'personality disorder', a penumbra of obsolete and modern moral connotations hung around the concept. However, the problem is not merely one of finding the right, namely, unprejudiced, impartial or scientific terminology. The above transmutations are proof that, notwithstanding considerable linguistic acrobatics and extensive re-definitions, archaic images of unpredictable danger and horrific acts of violence are easily conjured up for the public, as well as for medical and legal professionals. That the concept of moral insanity and psychopathy appeared to rise like a medically purged Phoenix from the ashes of sin, vice and crime perhaps indicates that Western society long after the Enlightenment is still incapable of abstaining from raking over the dark cinders.

The fear of the unpredictable and irrational which has, according to Foucault (1961), been one of the main factors involved in 'reason's subjugation of unreason' from 1660 right through the Age of Reason and into post-modernity, still feeds the imagination of contemporary man and woman. Research by critical anthropology has shown how this fascinated horror has been mirrored in the Western 'self's' perception of the supposedly primitive 'other' (for example Leiris, 1950, 1969; Kramer, 1977; Parin, 1978). The attempt to identify rationality and predictability with Western civilisation and spiritual superiority has lent itself to colonial and Western-scientific expansionism. The impact of the Enlightenment preoccupation with rationality (and of its problem with 'passions unguided' (Hobbes, 1651) on the conceptualisation of psychiatric notions in general has been well-documented (Porter, 1987). In regard to the personality disorders, however, this important nexus has been but rarely explored.

The link between personality disorders, and the degeneracy concept (Morel, 1857; Magnan, 1893), the eugenics movement and evolutionism (Lombroso, 1876) has been pointed out by some few authors. Their varied impact on medical opinion and racial and colonial ideologies in Britain, the United States, France and Germany, by even less. It is also intriguing to note that the Romantic tradition (in particular the impact of German romanticism) has been somewhat neglected by Anglo-Saxon researchers, and that whilst passion and will have received a great deal of attention in the psychopathy literature, the other concept which is equally central to psychiatric classification – guilt – has not as yet been put into a socio-historical perspective. Yet lack of guilt remains for most twentieth-century clinical authors one of the main indications of psychopathy. What is more, despite the high profile of passion in Romantic medicine, and its controversial – often passionately condemned – position during the Enlightenment, it is not a particularly new concept. Passion, after all, belonged traditionally to the six non-naturals (along with exercise, diet, sleep, food, air). Guilt, in contrast, is said to have emerged – at least in Western Europe – as recently as the sixteenth and seventeenth century (according to Jackson (1986), who sees the rise of Lutheranism and the Reformation closely linked to its appearance in depression).

PSYCHOPATHY AND THE PROGRESS OF CIVILISATION

Notwithstanding the above lacunae, personality disorders have been extensively theorised and researched. Most of the more recent literature however relates almost only to 'psychopathy', which represents but a small fraction of the personality disorders. The persistent fascination exercised by the psychopath may well be due, at least partially, to the 'mutually contradictory inhibitions upon violence and love which civilization has exacted of us' (Mailer, 1957). The very fact that most authors date the emergence of the concept to around 200 years ago – starting with Rush (1786), Pinel (1801), Prichard (1835), or von Feuchtersleben (1845) – may be a further indication that psychopathy and the first hey-day of Western civilisation, as we know it today, are closely bound up. Yet, the assumption that – for better or worse – civilisation exacts its toll is, of course, neither new nor unproblematic. It has in fact lent support to both conservative ideologies and critical theories (see for example Elias' [1969] civilisation theory, and Duerr's [1987, 1990] critique).

Further, clinical definitions of psychopathy remain ethnically and culturally ill-informed. As recently as 1977 West and Farrington, for example, developed a scale of 'antisocial tendency' which included such features as 'being tattooed' and 'sexual promiscuity'. Whilst it may be useful to devise a scale of deviance which is not based on the types of acts committed, the result should not be prejudicial to particular cultural or religious groups, subcultures, and social alternatives (in this case, for example, tattooed Maori revivalist groups in New Zealand, or polygamously orientated African or Muslim groups). Of similar concern are unreflected statements such as that in the *Reference Companion to the History of Abnormal Psychology* (Howells and Osburn, 1984) which describes the behaviour of Indian thugs simply as having been historical examples of 'psychopathy'.

THE NORMAL AND THE PATHOLOGICAL

It appears that to date ethical judgements and Eurocentricity have been part and parcel of the various concepts of personality disorder. This has freely been admitted and regretted by some clinicians, who go on to argue that what has to be done is 'to divest the concept of mental health of ethical and political content' (Shepherd, 1983). Although this suggested segregation of the 'social' from the 'clinical' may at first sight appear to be the only adequate solution, it may be asked whether it does not constitute yet another attempt to make good the promise of the Enlightenment: that rationality could prevail and science be guided by impartial assessment rather than socially-determined and subjective criteria. Despite the appeal of making clinical categories more 'objective', purporting to do so conceals the interrelatedness of what Durkheim (1901) called the 'normal' and the 'pathological'. Crime is normal 'because a society exempt from it is utterly impossible', and therefore it is 'bound up with the fundamental conditions of all social life, and by that very fact it is useful, because these conditions of which it is a part are themselves indispensable to the normal evolution of morality and law'.

If Durkheim is right, it may well be futile, or even damaging, to try to exorcise the social demon from the body of clinical virtue by segregating allegedly 'clinical' issues from their 'social' nexus, or separating the 'anecdotal' and the 'clinical lore' from systematic observation and psychiatric 'fact'. It may be more revealing, and socially and culturally appropriate, to relocate the personality disorders from whence they emerged: their social, political and cultural context. In Durkheim's words: 'If, indeed, crime is a disease, its punishment is its remedy and cannot be otherwise conceived; thus, all the discussions it arouses bear on the point of determining what the punishment must be in order to fulfill this role of remedy. If crime is not pathological at all, the object of punishment cannot be to cure it, and its true function must be sought elsewhere'.

REFERENCES

American Psychiatric Association (1987) *Diagnostic and Statistical Manual of Mental Disorders*, (3rd ed., Revised), Washington D.C.

Blackburn, R. (1988a) 'Are personality disorders treatable?' In Shapland, J. and Williams, T. (eds.) *Mental Disorder and the Law*, Leicester, British Psychological Society.

Blackburn, R. (1988b) 'On moral judgments and personality disorder: the myth of psychopathic personality revisited'. *British Journal of Psychiatry*, 153: 505–12.

Cleckley, H. (1941[1], 1950[2], 1955[3], 1964[4]) *The Mask of Sanity, An attempt to clarify some issues about the so-called psychopathic personality*, Saint Louis, C.V. Mosby Company.

Craft, M. (ed.) (1966) *Psychopathic Disorders and their Assessment*, Oxford, London, etc., Pergamon Press.

Duerr, H.P. (1987) *Nacktheit und Scham*, Frankfurt am Main, Suhrkamp.

Duerr, H.P. (1990) *Intimität, Der Mythos vom Zivilisationsprozess*, Frankfurt am Main, Suhrkamp.

Durkheim, E. (1901) *Les Règles de la méthode sociologique*. Reprinted (1970[2]) as an abstract as *The Normal and the Pathological* in *The Sociology of Crime and Delinquency* (eds. M.E. Wolfgang, L. Savitz and N. Johnston), New York, Wiley.

Elias, N. (1969) *Über den Prozess der Zivilisation*, Köln. Translated (1978) as *The civilizing process*, by E. Jephcott, New York, Urizon Books.

Farrington, D.P. (1991) 'Antisocial Personality from Childhood to Adulthood'. *The Psychologist*, 4: 389–94.

Feuchtersleben, E. von (1845) *Lehrbuch der ärztlichen Seelenkunde*, Wien. Translated (1847) as *The principles of medical psychology being the outlines of a course of lectures by Baron Ernst von Feuchtersleben, M.D.*, by H.E. Lloyd, edited by B.G. Babington, London, Sydenham Society.

Foucault, M. (1961) *La Folie et La Déraison: Histoire de la Folie à l'Age Classique. Civilisations d'Hier et Aujourd'hui*, Paris. Translated in abridged version (1965) as *Madness and Civilization: a History of Insanity in the Age of Reason*, by R. Howard, New York, Patheon Books.

Glueck, B. (1918) 'A Study of 608 Admissions to Sing Sing Prison'. *Mental Hygiene*, 2: 85–151.

Harrington, A. (1972) *Psychopaths*, London, If Books.

Hobbes, T. (1651) *Leviathan: or the matter, forme, & power of a commonwealth, ecclesiasticall and civill*, London. Edited and abridged (1962) with an introduction by J. Plamenatz, London, Fontana.

Howells, J.G. and Osborn, M.L. (1984) *A Reference Companion to the History of Abnormal Psychology*, 2 vols, Westport, Connecticut and London, Greenwood Press.

Jackson, S.W. (1986) *Melancholia and Depression: From Hippocratic Times to Modern Times*, New Haven, Yale University Press.

Koch, J.L.A. (1891) *Die psychopathischen Minderwertigkeiten*, Ravensburg, Otto Maier.

Kramer, F. (1977) *Verkehrte Welten. Zur imaginären Ethnographie des 19. Jahrhunderts*, Frankfurt am Main, Syndikat.

Krasner, W. (1948) 'The Psychopath in Our Society'. *Neurotica*, 2.

Leiris, M. (1950) 'L'Ethnographe devant le colonialisme'. *Les Temps modernes*, 58: 357–74.

Leiris, M. (1969) *Cinq Etudes d'ethnologie*, Paris, Editions Denoel.

Lewis, A. (1974) 'Psychopathic personality: a most elusive category'. *Psychological Medicine*, 4: 133–40.

Lindner, R.M. (1944) *Rebel without a cause: the hypnoanalysis of a criminal psychopath*, New York, Grune and Stratton.

Magnan, V. (1893) *Leçons Cliniques sur les Maladies Mentales*, Paris, Battaille.

Maughs, S.B. (1941) 'A Concept of Psychopathy'. *Journal of Criminal Psychopathology*, 2: 329–56, 465–99.

McCord, W. and McCord, J. (1964) *The Psychopath. An Essay on the Criminal Mind*, New York, Van Nostrand. Revised and abridged version of *Psychopathy and Delinquency* (1956), New York, Grune and Stratton.

Moran, R. (1983) *Knowing Right from Wrong. The Insanity Defense of Daniel McNaughtan*, New York, Free Press.

Morel, B.A. (1839) *Traité des Dégénérescences Physiques, Intellectuelles et Morales de l'Espèce Humaine et des Causes qui produisent ces Variétés Maladives*, Paris, London, New York, Madrid, J.B. Baillière.

Ordronaux, J. 'Moral Insanity'. *American Journal of Insanity*, 29: 313. Abstracted (1874) in *Journal of Mental Science*, 20: 145.

Parin, P. (1978) *Der Widerspruch im Subjekt: ethnopsychoanalytische Studien*, Frankfurt am Main, Syndikat.

Pinel, P. (1801) *Traité médico-philosophique sur l'aliénation mental, ou la manie*, Paris. Translated (1806) as *A treatise on insanity, in which are contained the Principles of a new and more practical nosology of maniacal disorders*, by D.D. Davis, Sheffield, Cadell and Davies.

Porter, R. (1987) *Disease, medicine and society in England, 1550–1860*, Basingstoke, Macmillan Education.

Richard, J.C. (1835) *A treatise on insanity and other disorders affecting the mind*, London, Sherwood et al.

Robins, E. (1967) 'Antisocial and dyssocial personality disorders'. In Freedman, A.M. and Kaplan, H.J. (eds.) *Comprehensive Textbook of Psychiatry*, Baltimore, The William and Wilkins Company.

Rosenhan, D.L. and Seligman, M.E.P. (1984) *Abnormal Psychology*, New York and London, W.W. Norton and Company.

Rush, B. (1786) *An inquiry into the influence of physical causes upon the moral faculty*. Reprinted (1793) in *Medical inquiries and observations upon the diseases of the mind*.

Rush, B. (1812) *Medical inquiries and observations upon the diseases of the mind*, Philadelphia, Kimber & Richardson. Reprinted (1962) New York, Hefner Press.

Sedgwick, P. (1982) *Psycho Politics*, London, Pluto.

Shepherd, M. (1983) *The Psychosocial Matrix of Psychiatry*, London and New York, Tavistock.

Schwartz, R.A. and Schwartz, I.K. (1976) 'Are personality disorders diseases?' *Diseases of the Nervous System*, 86: 613–17.

Skultans, V. (1979) *English madness. Ideas on insanity, 1580–1890*, London, Boston and Henley, Routledge & Kegan Paul.

Smith, R. (1981) 'The Boundary Between Insanity and Criminal Responsibility in Nineteenth Century England'. In Scull, A. (ed.) *Madhouses, Mad-Doctors and Madmen*, London, Athlone Press.

Werlinder, H. (1978) *Psychopathy: a history of the concepts. Analysis of the origin and development of a family of concepts in psychopathology*, Uppsala, Almqvist & Wiksell International.

West, D.J. and Farrington, D.P. (1977) *The Delinquent Way of Life*, London, Heinemann.

Wootton, B. (1959) *Social Science and Social Pathology*, London, Allen & Unwin.

Wootton, B. (1968) 'Social psychiatry and psychopathology; a layman's comments on contemporary developments'. In Zubin, J. and Freyhan, F. (eds.) *Social Psychiatry*, New York, Grune & Stratton.

Chapter 26
Substance Use Disorders

Clinical Section
JS MADDEN

Psychoactive substances have been employed for medical and nonmedical purposes across millenia. The oldest textbook on pharmacology, *The Book of the Yellow Emperor*, which is attributed to a semimythical Chinese emperor and dated to at least two and a half thousand years B.C., refers to cannabis. Herodotus in the fifth century B.C. described cannabis inhalation among the Scythians. Opium was used medically by the Sumerian civilisation; the ancient Egyptians utilised its sedative property to quieten children. An early example of therapeutic dependence involved a distinguished doctor and an exemplary patient. Galen prescribed opium in the form of theriac to the Emperor Marcus Aurelius; the Stoic philosophy of the ruler did not prevent an intractable reliance on the drug for sleep (Birley, 1960).

The Hippocratic writings noted that a high level of wine drinking induced tremors. Aristotle recorded the ill effects of the sudden withdrawal of wine in heavy drinkers, and warned that drinking could be injurious during pregnancy (O'Brien, 1980). The Roman physician Celsus held that dependence on intoxicating drink was a disease. This early establishment of the medical model has battled across the centuries with a moralising and condemnatory approach.

The excess use of alcohol was common in Northern Europe, including Britain, during the Middle Ages. Problem drinking attracted attention from religious authorities and from poets but received little notice in medical writings (Glatt, 1958). The sixteenth century physician Philip Barrough (1953), in accordance with humoral teaching, warned against dark, turgid or old wine in the management of melancholy. The subsequent century saw a warning (albeit by a moralist) that drinking to relieve sadness increases melancholic humor and can induce suicide (Younge, 1638).

Cognitive impairment was emphasised by Thomas Willis (1684). He reported that 'stupidity, moroseness or foolishness' could be caused by 'frequent drunkenness and surfeiting . . . almost by the same reason the frequent use of opiates very much troubles the sharpness of the mind' (available in Berrios, 1987). It is, of course, no longer considered that opiate drugs produce intellectual deficits which persist after the acute effects have subsided. Willis, able physician though he was, confused the short and long term effects of drugs. Later writers, notably the great taxonomist Cullen in 1770, made the same error. Not withstanding his animadversion Willis considered that opiates formed a 'Specifick Remedy' against insanity.

The extensive drinking habits of the eighteenth century, exemplified in Britain (Richardson, 1931) and in Ireland (Walsh, 1972), led to increasing recognition by doctors of the addictive and other harmful effects of alcohol. Thomas Wilson referred to habitual drunkenness as a 'disease' (Porter, 1985). George Cheyne (1733) frankly described his own excess use of wine and spirituous liquors; with time and age his consumption gradually abated.

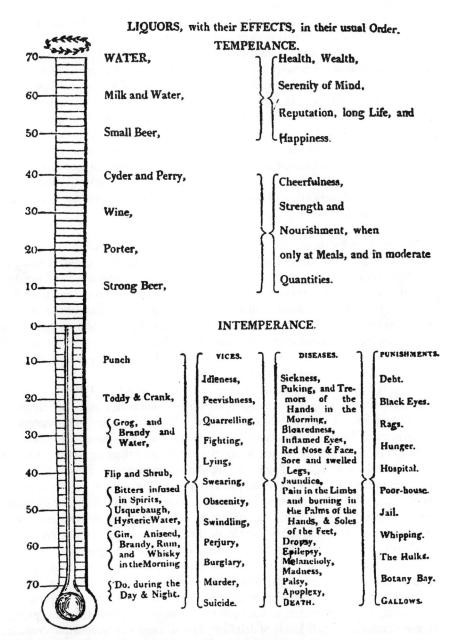

Figure 1: A Moral and Physical Thermometer, Lettsom (1789)

The closing years of the eighteenth century evinced the notable contributions of Lettsom and Rush. John Coakley Lettsom was a tactful reprover of the drinking habits of his acquaintance, the writer James Boswell. Lettsom (1789, 1792) described the clinical courses of what are now recognised as alcoholic cirrhosis and alcoholic neuropathy. Unusually for his period he reported the development of dependence ('compulsion', 'attachment') in females (Rix, 1976). He used the analogy of a thermometer to contrast the tendencies of differing liquors to promote temperance or intemperance (Figure 1). It is typical of his time that the restrained use of wine or beer was portrayed as beneficial while the consumption of spirits was depicted as malevolent.

The thermometer likeness was borrowed from a friend abroad. The colleague was Benjamin Rush, whose publication *An Inquiry into the Effects of Harmful Spirits upon the Human Body and Mind* gained numerous reprints. Rush, who had been a signatory of the American Declaration of Independence, advocated control of the availability of alcoholic beverages, proposed an asylum for drunkards, and was probably the first physician to conduct aversion therapy. He described the concurrent administration of rum and tartar emetic; the resultant nausea and vomiting exerted a prolonged though not permanent aversion to the sight and smell of spirits (Rush, 1793). In less serious mood Rush included in his classification of phobia the categories of rum phobia ('a very rare distemper') and of home phobia, which 'belongs to all those men who prefer tavern, to domestic society'.

The nineteenth century saw at its beginning an epochal text on maladaptive drinking as a disease, shortly followed by the clear delimitation and naming of delirium tremens. The century continued two preceding themes: the contribution of intoxicants to mental disorders, especially to the insanities, and their role in the treatment of psychiatric illnesses. During the second half of the century the doctrine emerged of the mental and physical degeneration of successive family generations, in which alcohol misuse provided a major target for medical abuse. The century closed with seminal descriptions of organic cerebral complications of excessive drinking.

Thomas Trotter, in his book *An Essay on Drunkenness* (1804) firmly declared that excessive drinking is a disease. He described tolerance, abstinence tremors, drinking to relieve withdrawal distress, the advent of anxiety and depression ('ill-grounded fears', 'melancholia'), impotence and fetal damage. In common with an ancient tradition he attributed the results on offspring to the effects of alcohol on the sex organs. Trotter rebuked his contemporary Erasmus Darwin for overstating the harm resulting from inebriety. Perhaps Darwin was prejudiced because his first wife was alcoholic, but Trotter fell into the same common error. Trotter believed in the spontaneous combustion of individuals whose bodies were replete with self-ignitable alcohol; he also claimed that over half of sudden deaths occurred during intoxication. On his more lengthy creditable side Trotter delimited bout and continuous patterns of excessive drinking (the gamma and delta varieties of Jellinek), warned how chronic intemperance can follow the medical prescription of alcohol, outlined a sympathetic approach to treatment, and anticipated contemporary thought on prevention by precise recommendation of safe levels of drinking. His account was widened to consider opium and cannabis ('bang'). Trotter's volume became so influential that it was reprinted three times within its first decade, was published in America in 1813, and was translated into German and Spanish.

The term 'delirium tremens' is, like many of the older descriptive titles for diseases, a vivid and useful mnemonic. Although the condition had been partially recognised from classical times (Leibowitz, 1967) it was fully described and named by Thomas Sutton (1813). Sutton gave an illustration, colourful to the modern reader, of the occupational hazard of working with alcohol by reporting that many of his patients were brandy smugglers. Sutton received advice from William Saunders, who had lectured on the malady at Guy's Hospital; the condition is therefore sometimes known as the Saunders-Sutton syndrome. A contemporary article by John Armstrong (1813) also furnished a clear account of the delirium ('brain fever') produced by chronic intoxication. Armstrong was the first to notice that the disorder was likely to follow the cessation of alcohol intake rather than develop in the course of drinking (Rix, 1979). The writings of Armstrong brought him renown in America as well as in Britain.

Thomas Prichard (1835) referred specifically to Bruonian theory in stating that the excitement of delirium tremens can terminate in weakness and debility. When such collapse threatened he considered that opium 'sustains the vital activities in a degree of energy'. For much of the nineteenth century both alcohol and opium were viewed as stimulants to the body, including the nervous system.

Prichard held that 'intoxicating liquor' is a common cause of mental disease, 'particularly in the lower classes of Europe and America', though he quoted Samuel Tuke as saying that this did not apply amongst members of the Society of Friends who were patients of the Retreat at York. The misapprehension that intoxicants were major contributors to insanity was a long standing belief. During the previous century William Battie (1758) contended that opium as well as the bottle provoked 'continual insanity' though his antagonist John Munro (1758) exonerated substances other than alcohol. Ellis (1838) opined that inebriety was a common cause of madness, while Sir Alexander Morison (1848) wrote:

> Intermittent Mania, and palsy, are frequent effects of drunkenness, as well as that species of temporary insanity which has been denominated delirium tremens, or Mania a Potu, and it is said that cases of Dementia not infrequently occur amongst the Russians from the abuse of intoxicating drinks.

The confusion illustrated by Morison over mania a potu persisted to recent times until the concept of pathological drunkenness was largely discounted (Coid, 1979; Madden, 1984).

Morison's contention that alcohol misuse is a frequent cause of mental illness was not supported by data he provided from his own hospital. Actually the published data showed wide variations in the rates at which intoxicants were held to contribute to asylum admissions. Griesinger (1845) drew attention to the large national differences and observed that the figures additionally varied with respect to the inclusion or exclusion of delirium tremens.

Griesinger and Esquirol (1838) were amongst the many authors who understood that abuse or dependence on alcohol could form a symptom of mental illness. Doctors were also sympathetic to the consideration that reliance on psychoactive agents could follow psychological distress which did not amount to formal mental disease. Bereavement, harsh conditions of work or housing, and poverty were often cited as leading to intemperance.

A concept peculiar to a broad period from the middle of the eighteenth century was that of spontaneous combustion. From time to time burned but largely intact corpses were discovered of persons who had regularly taken large quantities of alcohol, generally as distilled spirits. It was presumed that the alcohol had spontaneously ignited. Cases were reported from 1753 in Holland, France, Germany, England and Canada (Oliver, 1936). The catastrophe was employed in the novels of Dickens and Zola. It is now recognised that bodies which are accidentally and fatally ignited can burn slowly, leaving a corpse that is disfigured yet substantially whole. The combination of intoxication and a flame is a not uncommon source of domestic fires and deaths.

Spontaneous combustion carried the overtone of punishment for the vice of habitual drunkenness. A later and more widely held tenet also evoked expressions of censure. Benedict Morel (1857), in proposing the theory of progressive degeneration of families, included intoxication amongst the prominent features. The habitual use of intoxicants was viewed as a manifestation, as a consequence and in turn as a hastener of the degenerative process.

The influence of Morel was widespread. In England Bucknill and Tuke (1862) believed that a parent who was drunk at conception could beget insane progeny. Maudsley (1868) and Clouston (1993) considered that parental drunkenness evolved into the insanity of offspring. Norman Kerr (1888), who was the first president of the Society for the Study of Inebriety, held that mental instability as well as the craving for drink were transmitted through alcoholic heredity. The French psychiatrist Magnan (1876) reported alcohol intoxication as a contributor to family degeneration. In Germany Griesinger and in Austria Kraft-Ebbing ascribed to the same view. As late as the present century Forel in Switzerland cited animal experiments to show that alcohol damages the gametes within the reproductive organs.

Alcohol was considered to affect the offspring by damage to the germ cells during repeated intoxication, by injury at the moment of conception, and by an effect on the developing fetus within a heavily drinking mother. At the present time, although it is known that alcohol misuse can reduce male fertility by impairment of potency and depletion of spermatoza, only the third mechanism of a direct toxic action on the fetus is accepted.

A lively correspondence in the *Lancet* at the turn of the century proposed imprisonment for drunkards who procreated, or as alternative means castration and spaying (Malcolm, 1984). Fortunately the degeneration theory was at the same period rapidly losing ground, a process aided by the scepticism of Janet (Ellenberger, 1970) and from their different outlooks by Kraepelin and Freud (Bynum, 1984). Maudsley in his 1895 volume no longer referred to parental drunkenness as a cause of degeneracy and insanity in the offspring.

Across the course of the nineteenth century medical authors provided increasing attention to alcoholic disorders. Sometimes they concentrated almost exclusively on delirium tremens, which was the most dramatic complication and the one most readily attributable to alcohol. Hall (1837), in an account of the effects of alcohol, confined his discussion entirely to delirium tremens. Magnan (1876), in his book on alcoholism, devoted almost 150 pages from a text of 254 pages to the condition. Gowers (1888) allotted ten pages to the disorder and only four to other medical aspects of drinking. Writers agreed that delirium tremens could arise in the course of continued alcohol intake, and that it might be precipitated in persons still drinking by means of infections and other disorders. This error was held as late as the 1940s by Haggard and Jellinek (1945). Experimental work eventually led to the realisation that delirium tremens is a severe form of the alcohol withdrawal syndrome, and that other illnesses or trauma act by cutting short the supply or ingestion of alcoholic drinks.

Considerable impetus to medical interest was given through the introduction of the term 'alcoholism' by the Swedish doctor Magnus Huss (1851). The term promoted further the disease concept and expanded theory beyond Esquirol's simple depiction of spells of excessive drinking as a type of monomania. These apparently inexplicable alcoholic recurrences were also known subsequently as dipsomania, oinomania and trunksucht. Dipsomania persisted as a concept well into the present century, receiving demotion from psychosis to 'compulsion neurosis' (Wechsler, 1929). It would now be viewed simply as bout drinking.

Commencing with Huss the classification of alcoholic disorders became more complex. Maudsley (1895) outlined six variants of alcoholic insanity: delirium tremens, dipsomania, alcoholic mania (with hallucinations and paranoid delusions, i.e. an early formulation of alcoholic hallucinosis), mania of exaltation (temporary delusions of grandeur), acute transitory mania (i.e. mania a potu), and alcoholic dementia. Alcoholic hallucinosis began to emerge as a recognised clinical entity during the second half of the nineteenth century (Glass, 1989) and received its title from Bleuler (1916). Defendorf (1902), adapting from Kraepelin, outlined the separate disorder of alcoholic paranoia; he was aware, unlike some more modern authors, that the suspicions and delusions are not restricted to the area of morbid sexual jealousy.

Carl Wernicke published in 1881 the first precise description of the encephalopathy that now bears his name. Two of the three patients he reported were alcoholic. Animal experiments in the following century demonstrated that Wernicke's encephalopathy is due to thiamine deficiency, which can of course result from excessive drinking (Alexander, 1940; Prados and Swank, 1942). The Russian psychiatrist Sergei Sergeievich Korsakoff described in 1887 twenty alcoholic patients with amnesia, and provided subsequent descriptions in Russian and German journals. Bonhoeffer (1904) noticed the presence of amnesia in each of his patients with Wernicke's disease. His finding was crystallised by Victor, Adams and Collins (1971, 1989) into the conclusion that the Wernicke and Korsakoff conditions are the acute and chronic manifestations of the same process.

The Wernicke-Korsakoff lesions are located medially at the base of the brain. Conceptually it has not been easy to disentangle their effects from those of more global cerebral damage, particularly as pathological overlap can occur. The British pathologist Baillie first described ventricular dilatation from any cause in 1795; equally remarkably Wilks in 1864 reported cortical atrophy, which he attributed to syphilis, chronic alcoholism and senile dementia (U'Ren, 1987). Air encephalopathy (Brewer and Pernett, 1971) and later, computerised tomography and magnetic resonance imaging now allow these observations *in vivo* on alcoholic subjects.

Alcoholic dementia was for a long period not clearly distinguished from general paralysis of the insane. Until the spirochaetal nature of paresis was established at the commencement of the present century indulgence in alcohol – and in tobacco (Husband, 1878) – were considered as causes of paresis. Alcoholic pseudoparesis (in fact a blend of cerebral and peripheral nerve damage) was distinguished from dementia paralytica by its benign course (Defendorf, 1902). Alcoholic paraplegia was rightly viewed as usually due to neuritis, yet curiously the neurologist Gowers (1888) felt that although he had never seen an instance alcoholic myelitis probably occurred.

The ready availability of opium in Victorian Britain provoked increasing medical concern which, although not always grounded on facts, led to progressively more severe restrictions on its legal provision (Berridge, 1978; Berridge and Edwards, 1981). Morphine had been isolated in 1805 and the hypodermic needle invented in 1843. The American Civil War produced many wounded who became dependent on morphine. Heroin entered clinical practice in 1898 and was hailed at first as a potent cure for morphinism. A similar mistake took place with cocaine. The enthusiasm of Freud for cocaine led Ernest Jones (1953) to consider that for a while Freud was in danger of becoming a public menace. By 1902 Defendorf was able to warn that cocainism could induce a chronic delusional insanity which resembled alcoholic insanity (i.e. alcoholic hallucinosis) but developed more rapidly, was of greater severity, contained more prominent delusions of jealousy, and included the sensation of objects under the skin.

Opium and alcohol aroused increasing misgivings as remedies for insanity, not so much because of their addictive powers but because of their inutility. Clouston (1883) bluntly affirmed that opium was useless in mania and melancholia. There was awareness of the fatalities induced by sedatives in acute mania. Maudsley in 1868 was prepared to use opium for incipient melancholy, brandy for maniacal excitement, and liberal amounts of wine for chronic insanity. But by 1895 he reflected:

> A bicycle or a game of golf is oftentimes a better sleep-producer than any drug in the pharmacopoeia.

Maudsley added to these enlightened remedies 'the common onion'.

Newer sedatives were introduced. Cannabis (henbane) was employed in mental treatment during the second half of the nineteenth century. It was shortly joined by chloral, bromides and paraldehyde. Barbiturates were added in 1903 as barbitone (Veronal), amphetamines in 1935, and benzodiazepines during the late 1950's. All these preparations were, as with cocaine and heroin, recognised in due course to promote dependence.

The concept of dependence included, as nowadays, not merely pathophysiological features, but also changes of mentation and behaviour. Yet the disease concept did not always incline doctors to take a kindly view. Amongst psychiatrists of eminence the nadir of disapprobation was reached by Thomas Clouston (1883). He deplored the legal impossibility of interference with the liberty of some inveterate drinkers, and continued:

> I say it with deliberation, – the sooner they drink themselves to death the better. They are a curse to all who have to do with them, a nuisance and a danger to society, and propagators of a bad breed.

The modern reader is warned that this attitude could recur. Indeed,. similar sentiments were mooted in the early years of the Aids epidemic.

The temperance movement comprised, as a religious and humanitarian corollary, support and medical help for inebriates (Bynum, 1968). Following the Washingtonian Movement of the 1840s a public treatment system for excessive drinkers expanded in North America (Baumohl, 1990). As in Britain temperance physicians in the United States promoted academic as well as practical activities, which included in both countries a learned society and a journal (Blumberg, 1978; Lender, 1979; Berridge, 1984). Before the end of the nineteenth century temperance societies in the Russian empire opened a hospital in Kazan and an outpatient clinic in Moscow for alcoholics; before its revolution of 1917 Russia possessed fifteen alcoholic clinics (Segal, 1987). Amongst the leading psychiatrists who pressed for preventive measures were Forel and his pupil Eugen Bleuler; they were both personal abstainers from alcohol. Kraepelin was also keen to reduce the general extent of alcohol misuse.

The disease concept of dependence was strongly in favour by the end of the nineteenth century (Levine, 1979; Edwards, 1991). The formulation reached its apogée in the mid-twentieth century with the classic text of Jellinek (1960) *The Disease Concept of Alcoholism*. It should be noted that Jellinek applied the sickness perception only to his gamma (bout) and delta (continuous) patterns of drinking, which are the varieties that show withdrawal features. Subsequently the medical model of dependence surrendered its monopoly when professionals, including doctors, came to realise that other considerations, especially those derived from learning theory, are additionally relevant.

Treatment of alcohol dependence has traditionally concentrated on abstinence until the awareness of the last two decades that some problem drinkers with minimal or no dependence could revert to moderate drinking. Therapy for drug misusers has also been largely confined to abstinence although in some countries, notably Britain, long-term opiates were prescribed, when other measures failed, to persons who had become addicted in the course of treatment for pain or through professional access to drugs. Methadone was synthesised in Germany during the 1940s and given as a prolonged substitute for illicit heroin from 1967 (Dole and Nyswander, 1967). The approach did not gain world-wide favour, while its employment in Britain led to disillusion, but the arrival of HIV infection has brought a swing towards oral methadone employed in varying lengths of treatment.

Practice and preoccupations do not always fluctuate so widely. Constancy of motifs is particularly found with alcohol, largely because the substance is so ingrained in national cultures. Malcolm (1990) has compared an alcoholism congress that took place in 1895 with an international series of conferences held in Liverpool over the past two decades. In both centuries the meetings were absorbed with drinking amongst young people and women, expressed concern at the availability of alcohol in food stores, debated legislative remedies, outlined the role of voluntary agencies, and delineated the impact of excessive drinking on industry. History does not ensure that we profit from our mistakes but can teach us when we are repeating ourselves.

ACKNOWLEDGMENTS
The assistance is gratefully acknowledged of Derek Crook and Susan Floate, who are the librarians respectively of the Liverpool Medical Institution and of the Royal College of Psychiatrists.

REFERENCES

Alexander, L. (1940) 'Wernicke's disease: identity of lesions produced experimentally by B1 avitaminosis in pigeons with haemorrhagic polioencephalitis occurring in chronic alcoholism in man'. *American Journal of Pathology*, 16: 61–70.

Armstrong, J. (1813) 'On the Brain fever produced by intoxication'. *Edinburgh Medical and Surgical Journal*, 9: 58–61.

Barrough, P. (1583) 'The Method of Physicke'. In Hunter, R. and Macalpine, I. (eds.) *Three Hundred Years of Psychiatry 1583–1860*, London, Oxford University Press, p.28.

Battie, W. (1758) *A Treatise on Madness*, first edition, London, Whiston and White. Annotated by Hunter, R. and Macalpine, I. (1962), London, Dawsons of Pall Mall.

Baumohl, J. (1990) 'Inebriate institutions in North America, 1840–1920'. *British Journal of Addiction*, 85: 1181–204.

Berridge, V. (1978) 'Opium eating and the working class in the nineteenth century: the public and official reaction'. *British Journal of Addiction*, 73: 107–12.

Berridge, V. (1984) Editorial. *British Journal of Addiction*, 79: 1–6.

Berridge, V. and Edwards, G. (1981) *Opium and the People. Opiate Use in Nineteenth Century England*, London, Allen Lane.

Berrios, G.E. (1987) 'Dementia during the seventeenth and eighteenth centuries: a conceptual history'. *Psychological Medicine*, 17: 829–37.

Birley, A. (1966) *Marcus Aurelius*, London, Eyre and Spottiswood, p.246.

Bleuler, E.P. (1916) *Textbook of Psychiatry*. Translated Brill, A.A. (1924), reprinted 1951, New York, Dover Publications.

Blumberg, L.V. (1978) 'The American Association for the Study and Cure of Inebriety'. *Alcoholism: Clinical and Experimental Research*, 2: 234–40.

Bonhoeffer, K. (1904) 'Der Korsakowische symptomencomplex in Seinen bezeitungen zu den verschliedenen krankheitsformen'. *Aliggemeine Zeitschrift fuer Psychiatrie*, 61: 744–52.

Brewer, C. and Perrett, L. (1971) 'Brain damage due to alcohol consumption: an air-encephalographic, psychometric and electroencephalographic study'. *British Journal of Addiction*, 66: 170–82.

Bucknill, J.C. and Tuke, D.H. (1862) *A Manual of Psychological Medicine*, 2nd edition, London, John Churchill.

Bynum, W.F. (1968) 'Chronic alcoholism in the first half of the 19th century'. *Bulletin of the History of Medicine*, 42: 160–85.

Bynum, W.F. (1984) 'Alcoholism and degeneration in 19th century European medicine and psychiatry'. *British Journal of Addiction*, 79: 59–70.

Cheyne, G. (1733) *The English Malady: or, a treatise of Nervous Diseases of all Kinds, as Spleen, Vapours, Lowness of Spirits, Hypochondriacal, and Hysterical Distempers, etc.*, London, G. Strahan.

Clouston, T.S. (1883) *Clinical Lectures on Mental Diseases*, London, J. and A. Churchill.

Coid, J. (1979) 'Mania a potu: a critical review of pathological intoxication'. *Psychological Medicine*, 9: 709–19.

Cullen, W. (1800) *Nosology: or a systematic arrangement of diseases*, Edinburgh, Creech. First published 1772 (in Latin).

Defendorf, A.R. (1902) *Clinical Psychiatry: A Textbook for Students and Physicians*, abstracted and adapted from the 6th German edition of Kraepelin's *Lehrbuch der Psychiatrie*, London, Macmillan.

Dole, V.P. and Nyswander, M.E. (1965) 'A medical treatment for diacetylmorphine (heroin) addiction'. *Journal of the American Medical Association*, 193: 646–50.

Edwards, G. (1991) 'Who was Jellinek?' *British Journal of Psychiatry*, 158: 431.

Ellenberger, H.E. (1970) *The Discovery of the Unconscious. The History and Evolution of Dynamic Psychiatry*, London, Allen Lane and New York, Basic Books.

Ellis, W.C. (1838) *A Treatise on the Nature, Symptoms, Causes and Treatment of Insanity*, London, Samuel Holdsworth.

Esquirol, J.E.D. (1838) *Des Maladies Mentales Considerées sous les Rapports Médical, Hygiénique et Médico-legal*, translated by Hunt, E.K. (1945), Philadelphia, Lee and Blanchard.

Glass, I.B. (1989) 'Alcoholic hallucinosis: a psychiatric enigma – 1. The development of an idea'. *British Journal of Addiction*, 84: 29–41.

Glatt, M.M. (1958) 'The English drink problem: its rise and decline through the ages'. *British Journal of Addiction*, 55: 51–67.

Gowers, W.R. (1888) *A Manual of Diseases of the Nervous System*, London, J. and A. Churchill.

Griesinger, W. (1845) *Mental Pathology and Therapeutics*, translated from the second edition by Lockhart Robinson, C. and Rutherford, J. (1867), London, New Sydenham Society.

Haggard, H.W. and Jellinek, E.M. (1945) *Alcohol Explored*, New York, Doubleday, Doran and Company.

Hall, M. (1837) *Principles of the Theory and Practice of Medicine*, London, Sherwood Gilbert and Piper.

Husband, H.A. (1878) *Student's Hand-Book of the Practice of Medicine*, Edinburgh, E. and S. Livingstone.

Huss, M. (1851) *Chronische Alkoholskrankheit oder Alcoholismus chronicus*, translated into German by G. Van Dem Busch (1852), Fritze, Stockholm and Leipzig.

Jellinek, E.M. (1960) *The Disease Concept of Alcoholism*, New Haven, College and University Press.

Jones, E. (1953) *Sigmund Freud, Life and Work. Volume One: The Young Freud 1856–1900*, London, Hogarth.

Kerr, N. (1888) *Inebriety, its Etiology, Pathology, Treatment and Jurisprudence*, London, H.K. Lewis.

Korsakoff, S.S. (1887) 'Disturbance of psychic function in alcoholic paralysis and its relation to the disturbance of the psychic sphere in multiple neuritis of non-alcoholic origin'. *Vestnik Psychiatrie IV*, fascile 2.

Leibowitz, J.O. (1967) 'Acute alcoholism in ancient Greek and Roman medicine'. *British Journal of Addiction*, 62: 82–6.

Lender, M.E. (1979) 'Jellinek's typology of alcoholism: Some historical antecedents'. *Journal of Studies on Alcohol*, 40: 361–5.

Lettsom, J.C. (1789) *History of Some of the Effects of Hard Drinking*, London, C. Dilly.

Lettsom, J.C. (1792) 'Some Remarks on the Effects of Lignum Quassiae Amarae'. *Memoirs of the Medical Society of London*, 1: 128–65.

Levine, H.G. (1978) 'The discovery of addiction: changing conceptions of habitual drunkenness in America'. *Journal of Studies on Alcohol*, 39: 143–74.

Levine, H.G. (1984) 'The alcohol problem in America: from temperance to alcoholism'. *British Journal of Addiction*, 79: 109–19.

Madden, J.S. (1984) 'Psychiatric advances in the understanding and treatment of alcohol dependence'. *Alcohol and Alcoholism*, 19: 339–53.

Magnan, V. (1876) *On Alcoholism, the Various Forms of Alcoholic Delirium and Their Treatment*, translated by Greenfield, W.S., London, H.K. Lewis.

Malcolm, M.T. (1984) 'Fetal alcohol syndrome: historical aspects'. *Alcohol and Alcoholism*, 19: 261–2.

Malcolm, M.T. (1990) 'A century of alcoholism conferences: unchanging themes'. *Alcohol and Alcoholism*, 26: 5–15.

Maudsley, H. (1868) *The Physiology and Pathology of Mind*, 2nd edition, London, MacMillan and Co.

Maudsley, H. (1895) *Pathology of Mind*, 4th edition, London, MacMillan and Co.

Monro, J. (1758) *Remarks on Dr Battie's Treatise on Madness*, first edition, London, John Clarke. Annotated by Hunter, R. and Macalpine, I. (1962), London, Dawsons of Pall Mall.

Morel, B. (1857) *Traité des Degénéréscences Physiques Intellectuelles et Morales de l'Espèce Humaine*, Paris, J.B. Baillière.

Morison, A. (1848) *Outlines of Lectures on the Nature, Causes and Treatment of Insanity*, ed. Morison, T.C., fourth edition, London, Longmans, Brown, Green and Longmans.

O'Brien, J.M. (1980) 'Alexander and Dionysius: the invisible enemy'. *Annals of Scholarship*, 1: 83–105.

Oliver, J.R. (1936) 'Spontaneous combustion – a literary curiosity'. *Bulletin of the History of Medicine*, 4: 559–72.

Oxenbridge, D. (1915) 'General Observations and Prescriptions on the Practice of Physick'. In Hunter, R. and Macalpine, I. (eds.) *Three Hundred Years of Psychiatry 1583–1860*, London, Oxford University Press, pp.122–3.

Porter, R. (1985) 'The drinking man's disease: the "pre-history" of alcoholism in Great Britain'. *British Journal of Addiction*, 80: 385–96.

Prados, M. and Swank, R.L. (1942) 'Vascular and interstitial cell changes in thiamine-deficient animals'. *Archives of Neurology and Psychiatry*, 47: 626–34.

Prichard, T. (1835) *A Treatise on Insanity*, London, Sherwood, Gilbert and Piper.

Richardson, A.E. (1931) *Georgian England*, London, B.T. Batsford, p.28.

Rix, K.J.B. (1976) 'John Coakley Lettsom and Some of the Effects of Hard Drinking'. *Journal of Alcoholism*, 11: 97–103.

Rix, K.J.B. (1978) 'John Armstrong, MD, and the brain fever following intoxication'. *British Journal on Alcoholism*, 13: 111–15.

Rush, B. (1793) *An Enquiry into the Effects of Ardent Spirits upon the Human Body and Mind*. Reprinted in *Medical Inquiries and Observations, Volume 2*, Philadelphia, Kimber and Richardson.

Segal, B.M. (1987) *Russian Drinking: Use and Abuse of Alcohol in Pre-Revolutionary Russia*, Monograph Number 15, New Brunswick, Rutgers Center of Alcohol Studies.

Sutton, T. (1813) *Tracts on Delirium Tremens, on Peritonitis, and on Some Internal Inflammatory Affections, and on the Gout*, London, Underwood.

Trotter, T. (1804) *An Essay, Medical, Philosophical and Chemical on Drunkenness and its Effects on the Human Body*. Edited with an Introduction, Porter, R. (1988), London and New York, Routledge.

U'Ren, R.C. (1987) Introduction. In Pitt, B. (ed.) *Dementia*, London, Melbourne and New York, Churchill Livingstone.

Victor, M., Adams, R.D.D. and Collins, G.H. (1971) *The Wernicke-Korsakoff Syndrome*, Philadelphia, F.A. Davis.

Victor, M., Adams, R.D. and Collins, G.H. (1989) *The Wernicke-Korsakoff Syndrome and Related Neurological Disorders due to Alcoholism and Malnutrition*, 2nd edition, Philadelphia, F.A. Davis.

Walsh, D. (1972) 'Alcoholism and the Irish'. *Journal of Alcoholism*, 7: 40–7.

Wechsler, I.S.S. (1929) *The Neuroses*, Philadelphia and London, W.B. Saunders.

Wernicke, C. (1881) *Lehrbuch der Gehirnkrankheiten fur Aerzte und Studirende. Vol.2*, Kassel, Theodor Fischer.

Willis, T. (1864) *Practice of Physick*, translated by Pordage, S. (1681), London, Dring, Harper and Leigh.

Younge, R. (1638) 'The Drunkard's Character'. London, Latham. In Hunter, R. and Macalpine, I. (eds.) *Three Hundred Years of Psychiatry 1583–1860*, London, Oxford University Press, pp.116–17.

Chapter 26
Substance Use Disorders

Social Section
EDWARD M BROWN

A review of the history of the excessive consumption of alcohol since antiquity makes it clear that until the nineteenth century doctors played a very limited role in the regulation of drinking habits (Sournia, 1990). Indeed doctors contributed to the consumption of alcohol by prescribing it as a treatment for many conditions (Risse, 1970; Warner, 1980). Nonetheless since the late eighteenth century, when the first clear arguments that excessive drinking ought to be regarded as a disease were put forward, doctors have actively sought to provide medical treatment for a condition previously regarded as a vice (Bynum, 1968). As such the history of the emergence of the disease concept of alcoholism might be seen as part of a broader historical process through which medical and scientific explanations have supplanted moral and supernatural descriptions of deviant behavior. While some have looked upon this process as a triumph of progress, others have regarded the growing influence of medical explanations as indicative of medical empire building and the scapegoating of 'victims' (Porter, 1990; Conrad and Schneider, 1980). Debate over these interpretations should not, however, obscure the fact that, in the case of alcoholism, efforts at 'medicalization', at least, during the nineteenth century were not completely successful.

The reasons for this lack of success are complex but in part it resulted from the fact that with alcoholism, unlike many other diseases, it is difficult to separate the disease itself from the actions of the afflicted person. As a result the moral question of whether individual's drinking behavior is voluntary or not has always been critical to deciding whether to treat alcoholism as a disease. Those chiefly interested in holding the drinker responsible for his actions have preferred the language of self-control while those who have regarded alcoholism as a disease have used causal language. In general the former have been advocates of punishment and prohibition while the latter have advocated treatment. One of the most notable ironies in the history of alcoholism, however, is the fact that during the nineteenth century efforts to speak about drinking behavior in purely medical language resulted in the most draconian proposals for social control. Rather than result in the utopian medical solution to the problem of drunkenness that their advocates envisioned, however, these proposals demonstrated the limits of medicalization and, perhaps, the necessity of mixing causal and moral languages when speaking about alcoholism.

Consider, for example, the following summary of the 'scientific methods' of curing the disease of alcoholism written in 1891 by Thomas Davison Crothers for the *North American Review*:

> First legislate for their [alcoholics'] legal control; then organize industrial hospitals in the vicinity of all large towns and cities; tax the spirit traffic to build and maintain such places, . . . arrest and commit all drunkards to such hospitals for an indefinite time, depending on the restoration of the patients; also commit all persons who use spirits to excess and imperil their own lives and the lives of others; put them under exact military, medical, and hygienic care, where all the conditions and circumstances of life and living can be regulated and controlled; make them self-supporting as far as it is possible; and let this treatment be continued for years if necessary. The recent cases will become cured, and the incurable will be protected from themselves and others, and made both useful and self-supporting. (Crothers, 1891)

Baumohl and Room (1987) have suggested that this proposal resulted from the failure of medical approaches to come to terms with urban disorder and represented a 'calculated bargain with the State . . . intended as a plan to institutionalize public responsibility for all habitual drunkards by promising in return the social control of pauper inebriates'. While this interpretation makes sense, it is important not to forget the medical origins of the idea of the 'industrial hospital'. After all while Crothers' rhetoric was harsh, he was not a law and order politician but the highly respected superintendent of the Walnut Lodge inebriate asylum in Hartford, Connecticut, and the editor of the influential *Quarterly Journal of Inebriety*. Beginning his career in the 1860s as an assistant physician at the New York State Inebriate Asylum in Binghamton, New York, he was by the 1880s, widely recognized, both in the United States and abroad, as a leading authority on the 'disease of inebriety' (Brown, 1985).

While the notion that incarceration and discipline might be curative is certainly suspect in a era like ours in which critics frequently call our attention to the social control function of psychiatry, when Crothers began his career, the idea that extended residence in a well run asylum offered hope for the cure of insanity was still a popular idea. Indeed Crothers proposal can be seen as a logical consequence of a union between the idea of asylum treatment and certain popular nineteenth century ideas about alcoholism as a disease.

It had long been recognized that alcohol produced alterations in behavior which resembled insanity. At the beginning of the nineteenth century, alcohol had been considered a plausible cause of mental disturbance in the same manner as trauma, intestinal worms, syphilis and menstrual upsets (Sournia, 1990, p.36). In the early nineteenth century the influential French psychiatrist Jean Etienne Dominique Esquirol (1845, p.355) argued that drunkenness was not only a cause of insanity but 'in many cases it (was) only the first and sometimes the characteristic symptom of a commencing monomania'. Specifically, he insisted, it was a symptom of the instinctive type of monomania, that is, a form of partial insanity in which an individual committed acts which were 'involuntary, instinctive, (and) irresistible' and which 'the conscience rebukes (but) . . . the will has no longer the power to restrain'. This view had much in common with the German physician Bruhl-Cramer's notion of 'periodic dipsomania', which was marked by 'an abnormal, all-consuming and elemental need for alcohol' (Sournia, 1990; Bynum, 1968). By the middle of the nineteenth century, these ideas had wide currency and considerable legitimacy.

In 1853, in his popular discussion of the subject, the eminent British physiologist and temperance advocate William B. Carpenter, for example, quoted psychiatric views at length and without critical comment. According to Carpenter dipsomania was a form of insanity characterized by 'the irresistible propensity to swallow stimulants in enormous doses, whenever and wherever they can be procured . . . (it is an) impulse which drives the unhappy being to do that which he knows to be pernicious and wrong, and which, in the intervals of his paroxysms, he views with loathing and disgust' (Carpenter, 1859). Central to this popular scientific view was the belief that 'the patient is perfectly incapable of self-control'. A corollary of this view of the disease of alcoholism was that extended periods of abstinence were necessary to overcome inebriety. Furthermore, as Carpenter (1859, pp.47–8) argued:

> considering . . . that the individual is irresponsible and dangerous to himself and others – that, if left uncontrolled, he will ruin his family – and that this disease can be treated only in an Asylum, it is not only merciful to him and his relatives, but necessary for the security of the public, that he be deprived of the liberty which he abuses and perverts, and that he should be prevented from committing crimes instead of being punished, or I should rather say, being the object of vindictive infliction after he has perpetrated them.

These ideas achieved popularity during the nineteenth century in part because of the failure of other approaches to come to terms with drunkenness. In England a shift in population from the countryside to industrialized urban areas made public drunkenness as well as poverty a fact of everyday life (MacLeod, 1967). In the United States both urbanization and immigration stirred fears of foreign and pauper drunkards. The temperance movement during the early nineteenth century was generally more concerned with the 'drink question' and the 'liquor traffic' than with the individual drunkard. In the United States the result was a number of state and local prohibition laws (Brown, 1985). Concern with the individual drunkard tended to focus on his disruptive behavior, and short jail sentences were the most common response. Many, however, felt that both prohibitory legislation and jail sentences were inadequate responses to what was perceived as a rising tide of intemperance.

Temperance groups such as the Washingtonian movement, an association of reformed drunkards which flourished in the United States during the 1840s, attempted to respond to the individual drinker with moral suasion and pledges of abstinence. They even established 'homes' where drunkards could go to recover from a debauche (Maxwell, 1950). The limitations of movements such as this, however, left the question of what should be done with the inebriate both pressing and unanswered. The idea that alcoholism was a disease characterized by an irresistible craving for alcohol which could be cured only by enforced abstinence provided one answer.

Some drunkards were treated in insane asylums. This made sense both because of the popularity of such institutions and because of the close parallel between the idea of dipsomania and the diagnosis of monomania. Some argued that the dipsomaniac's 'irresistible desire to indulge in the use of intoxicating substances' rather than the presence of hallucinations or delusions rendered him insane and justified his treatment in an insane asylum. In contrast to their optimism about the curative value of these institutions for the insane, however, asylum superintendents were notably pessimistic about their value for the inebriate. There were two reasons for this. First, the dipsomaniac was not easily distinguished from the common drunkard, and asylum superintendents were not anxious to assume responsibility for the latter. Second, experience with dipsomaniacs demonstrated not only that they did poorly in insane asylums but that they interfered with the treatment of other patients. For these reasons, as well as the fact that by the 1850s insane asylums were already becoming overcrowded, most superintendents of these institutions were unwilling to actively use the concept of dipsomania to extend their authority (Brown, 1985; Baumohl and Room, 1987).

A more promising answer to the question of how to provide treatment for the alcoholic lay in the view that alcoholism was not simply a form of insanity but a specific disease. The intellectual basis for the idea of alcoholism as a specific disease had been laid through the development of the idea of dipsomania. There were, however, a number of problems with the concept of dipsomania. Its associations with the concept of monomania became a liability as the latter term declined in popularity after the middle of the nineteenth century. Dipsomania was a relatively narrowly defined term describing an uncontrolled drinking mania. As such it was not a good tool for a broad based attack on the many forms of problem drunkenness. Other more general terms were suggested. Norman Kerr suggested the term narcomania, referring narrowly to a desire or impulse for relief from discomfort, unrest and pain (Crothers, 1911, p.39). The Swedish physician Magnus Huss suggested the term alcoholism in 1849, but for some this term focused too closely on the toxic effects of alcohol. The most widely used term in the late nineteenth century was inebriety. Adopting the term inebriety, and reducing dipsomania to one form of inebriety, allowed men like Crothers to claim that 'the inebriate although appearing to be in possession of his mind, will always be found on the other side of that mysterious border-line of mental health' (Crothers, 1881). The inebriate was mentally ill even if he was not insane.

If inebriety was to be treated as a specific disease and not merely a form of insanity, institutional support was necessary to fully establish this new idea. For nineteenth century physicians the logical candidate for this task was an asylum specifically for the treatment of inebriety. Asylum treatment for the insane was based on the notion that the insane could be healed only if they could be separated from the baneful influence of their environment and exposed to the healing effects of asylum life for sufficient time. Regarding inebriety as a disease which was caused by an interaction of the toxic effects of alcohol and an individual's hereditary predisposition meant that abstinence was not only a goal of treatment but was also critical to cure. Through abstinence and healthful living the patient's constitution could be strengthened and the risk of passing a weakened constitution on to his offspring minimized. Furthermore, putting an inebriate in such an asylum would remove him from the alcoholic poison that was the exciting cause of his malady and, in the words of a leading advocate of asylum treatment 'put him *at once* in the condition of cure' (Turner, 1858).

The obstacles to establishing such an asylum, however, were many. On the one hand, the view that the drunkard was not sick but merely vicious was widespread and deeply entrenched, even among physicians. According to this view, the alcoholic was likely to abuse the asylum by using it as a place to dry out between debauches. On the other hand, some felt that avoiding such abuse by granting physicians the authority to detain even the inebriate who appeared to be in possession of his mind would lead to a violation of individual liberties. The traditional criteria used to detain the insane did not apply to the alcoholic once he had dried out. As Isaac Ray (1855), the superintendent of the Butler Hospital for the Insane put it, the inebriate:

> while in the paroxysm, or suffering under its immediate effects, may, in any proper sense of the term be called insane, and so long we have an unquestionable right to hold him. When, however, the mind resumes its perfect consciousness, what are we to do? The person claims his liberty, while nobody doubts that he would use it only to advance another step in the road to bodily and mental ruin.

At the outset, however the greatest obstacle was the pessimism, among both lay people and physicians, that surrounded any plan to restore the drunkard. If this was to be overcome, someone with the optimism and zeal of what has been called a 'moral entrepreneur' was needed to promote the idea that asylum treatment could cure the disease of inebriety. In the United States one man with these qualifications was, Crothers mentor, J. Edward Turner. Born in Bath, Maine in 1822, Turner began his study of the treatment of alcoholism in the 1840s with a tour of Glasgow, Edinburgh, London, and Paris. After many years of campaigning, he was finally successful in establishing the first public inebriate asylum in Binghamton New York in 1854 (Crothers, 1889; Turner, 1888). As the superintendent he acquired extensive authority to 'retain' inebriates against their will and to govern their lives through draconian rules which prohibited among other things walking within three hundred feet of public roads, possessing money or postage stamps or receiving uncensored mail (New York State Inebriate Asylum, 1866). In spite of these regulations Binghamton was successful in attracting a middle class clientele (Baumohl and Room, 1987). Indeed when it was converted into an insane asylum in 1879, the governor of New York characterized it as a 'hotel for the entertainment of wealthy inebriates' (Burr, 1881). Though Turner's tenure as superintendent was stormy and short, Binghamton became a model for men like Crothers.

By 1870 a number of similar institutions had been formed and the superintendents of these formed the American Association for the Cure of Inebriety (Blumberg, 1978). A model law that they proposed restated the principles guiding the operation of the Binghamton Asylum. In 1872 two members of the association testified before a select committee of the House of Commons in support of an Habitual Drunkards Bill. British advocates of this bill shared the views of their American counterparts that inebriety was a disease and that extended involuntary treatment was necessary to cure it. British concerns for the 'liberty of the subject' were strong enough, however, to defeat that bill and delay passage of a less coercive bill until 1898 (Macleod, 1967; Brown, 1986). Nonetheless the testimony of American experts before the House of Commons and the establishment of a British Society for the Study and Cure of Inebriety in 1884 signalled the international acceptance of a broad biologically-based concept of inebriety and its corollary the idea of asylum treatment (Berridge, 1990).

Not all the members of the American Association for the Cure of Inebriety, however, shared Turner and Crother's views on the hereditary and toxic nature of inebriety. Influenced by the Washingtonian movement these inebriety specialists were skeptical about the value of medicine in the treatment of inebriety and saw self-control as playing a central role in the inebriate's recovery (Baumohl and Room, 1987). Ironically their therapeutic prescriptions were far less disciplinary than those of advocates of the purely biological view of inebriety. Albert Day, for example, wrote in 1867 that 'the victims [of inebriety], themselves . . . know that self control though weakened is not wholly lost' (Day, 1867, p.49). By taking the position that his patients were sick but suffering from only a partial loss of self-control, Day was able to identify with these people and to encourage them in their struggle with their disease. This allowed him to develop a 'moral treatment' which stressed that 'the patient should be encouraged that his disease can be cured, and at the same time impressed with the belief that it rests mostly with himself . . . [to do so]' (Day, 1867). When Day was brought in to replace Turner as the superintendent of the Binghamton Asylum in 1868, he sought to exclude involuntary patients as far as possible and to treat only patients who would voluntarily submit to mild restraints designed to give them an opportunity to prove their 'courage' and their 'honor' (Day, 1868).

By the 1890s Turner's optimistic belief that alcoholism could be cured by enforced abstinence had resulted in few legislative enactments. In the end his ideas had little appeal. Those concerned with civil liberties were offended by their penal implications, while those interested in penal solutions to the problem of drunkenness found little new in them. One sustained effort to implement his views at the Foxborough Inebriate Asylum in Massachusetts was plagued by escapes, rebellions and the accumulation of chronic cases. It was abandoned as a failure (Brown, 1985).

The voluntary treatment of alcoholism, however, thrived. As early as 1883, for example, on inebriety specialist noted that 94 per cent of all patients treated in American inebriate asylums were treated voluntarily (Parrish, 1883, p.121). By 1902 this success could be seen in the existence of over one hundred such institutions (Editorial, 1902). This was ironically due to the fact that though the public was unwilling to accept broad programs for the legislative control of alcoholic patients, they were increasingly willing to accept the notion that inebriety was a disease. This public acceptance can be graphically seen in the profusion of advertisements for homes and sanitaria for the treatment of inebriety. Many of these were regarded by inebriety specialists as quack establishments which offered quick cures such as the injections of 'bichloride of gold' used by the notorious Dr. Keeley (Lender and Martin, 1982, pp.122–4). Even Crothers, however, found that he could attract a steady stream of patients by advertising his Walnut Lodge as offering 'the best surroundings, and every appointment of an elegant residence' (Advertisement, 1896).

Advocates of the disease concept of alcoholism in the nineteenth century saw that concept as an advance over narrowly moralistic views which held that the alcoholic's behavior was due to moral depravity and deserved punishment. By excluding moral factors from their understanding of alcoholism, however, they denied the alcoholic the status of a moral agent and were able to compare the power to control the alcoholic with the power to quarantine the contagious. What they achieved was a disciplinary treatment that proved both unpalatable and unworkable. Although such extreme paternalism may seem unjustifiable to those critical of medical power, the problem of mixing threats with therapy for the alcoholic has by no means been resolved in the late twentieth century. The most successful form of 'treatment' in the twentieth century, Alcoholics Anonymous, like the 'moral treatment' of the nineteenth, continues to rely on an unstable mix of the language of self-control and the language of disease. What this suggests is that if doctors want to treat alcoholism as a disease, they will have to rethink what they mean by disease.

REFERENCES

Advertisement (1896) *Quarterly Journal of Inebriety*, 18: 208.

Baumohl, J. and Room, R. (1987) 'Inebriety, doctors, and the State: Alcoholism treatment institutions before 1940'. *Recent developments in Alcoholism*, 5: 135–74.

Berridge, V. (1990) 'The Society for the Study of Addiction: 1884–1888'. *British Journal of Addiction*, 85: 993–1085.

Blumberg, L. (1978) 'The American Association for the Study and Cure of Inebriety'. *Alcoholism: Clinical and Experimental Research*, 2: 235–40.

Brown, E.M. (1985) ' "What shall we do with the inebriate?" Asylum treatment and the disease concept of alcoholism in the late nineteenth century'. *Journal of the History of the Behavioral Sciences*, 21: 48–59.

Brown, E.M. (1986) 'British interest in the treatment of alcoholism in the early 1870s'. *British Journal of Addiction*, 81: 545–52.

Burr, G. (1881) 'The New York State Inebriate Asylum – A defense of its management and operations'. *Transactions of the Medical Society of New York*, Syracuse, pp.318.

Bynum, W.F. (1968) 'Chronic alcoholism in the first half of the 19th century'. *Bulletin of the History of Medicine*, 42: 160–85.

Carpenter, W.B. (1859) *On the Use and Abuse of Alcoholic Liquors, in Health and Disease*, Philadelphia, Blanchard and Lea.

Conrad, P. and Schneider, J.W. (1980) *Deviance and Medicalization: From Badness to Sickness*, St. Louis, C.V. Mosby Co.

Crothers, T.D. (1881) 'What shall we do with the inebriate?' *Alienist and Neurologist*, 2: 175.

Crothers, T.D. (1889) 'Sketch of the late Dr. J. Edward Turner: Founder of inebriate asylums'. *Quarterly Journal of Inebriety*, 11: 1–25.

Crothers, T.D. (1891) 'Is inebriety curable?' *North American Review*, 153: 359–60.

Crothers, T.D. (1911) *Inebriety*, Cincinnati, Harvey Publishing Co.

Day, A. (1867) *Methomania*, Boston, James Campbell.

Day, A. (1868) *Superintendent's Report*, Binghamton, New York State Inebriate Asylum.

Editorial (1902) *Quarterly Journal of Inebriety*, 24: 94.

Esquirol, J.E.D. (1845) *Mental Maladies: A Treatise on Insanity*. Translated by Hunt, E.K., facsimile Edition, (1965), New York, Haffner Publishing Co.

Lender, E. and Martin, J.K. (1982) *Drinking in America: A History*, New York, Free Press.

MacLeod, R.M. (1967) 'The edge of hope: social policy and chronic alcoholism'. *Journal of the History of Medicine and Allied Sciences*, 22: 215–45.

Maxwell, M. (1950) 'The Washingtonian Movement'. *Quarterly Journal of Studies on Alcohol*, 11: 310–451.

New York State Inebriate Asylum (1866) *The Charter and Bylaws*, New York, Press of Wynkoop & Hallenbeck.

Parrish, J. (1883) *Alcoholic Inebriety*, Philadelphia, P. Blackiston, Son & Co.

Porter, R. (1990) Introduction. In Sournia, J-C., *A History of Alcoholism*, Oxford, Basil Blackwell.

Ray, I. (1855) 'Hospitals for the Intemperates'. *Journal of Psychological Medicine*, 8: 172.

Risse, G. (1970) 'The Brownian System of Medicine: Its theoretical and practical implications'. *Clio Medica*, 5: 45–51.

Sournia, J-C. (1990) *A History of Alcoholism*, Oxford, Basil Blackwell.

Turner, J.E. (1858) 'A letter of the Corresponding Secretary of the New York State Inebriate Asylum, to Hon. Edwin D. Morgan, Governor Elect of the State of New York'.

Turner, J.E. (1888) *The History of the First Inebriate Asylum in the World by its Founder*, New York.

Warner, J.H. (1980) 'Physiological theory and therapeutic explanation in the 1860s: The British debate on the medical use of alcohol'. *Bulletin of the History of Medicine*, 54: 235–57.

Index

Löwenfeld, L.: obsessive-compulsive
  disorders, 580
Loyola, Ignatius of, 574
Lucid intervals, 318, 388
Lugaro, E.: Alzheimer's disease, 44
Lund, J.C.: Huntington's disease, 131,
  138
Lust: shell shock, 492
Luther, M.: changelings, 244
Luys, J.L.: hypochondriasis, 461;
  obsessive-compulsive disorders, 575,
  577
Lyon, I.W.: chorea, 131, 138–9
Lypemania, 108, 389–90

Macalpine, I.: on Freudians, 120;
  phenothiazine effects, 117
McCord, W. and J.: psychopathy, 645,
  650
McCurdy, J.T., 399
Maclachlan, D.: on J. Parkinson, 115
McNaughton Rules, 647
Mad *vs* bad, 646–8
Magendie, F.: experiments, 196
Magic: for epilepsy, 166
Magnan, J.J.V.: degeneration theory,
  324, 337, 422, 634; delusional
  disorder, 373–9; epilepsy, 155–6;
  impulsions, 577–8;
  obsessive-compulsive disorders, 579
Mairet, A.: cognitive impairment, 40;
  dementia, 57–8
Mairet, A. and Durante, G.: shell shock,
  rabbits, 492
Major disasters, 496
Male: hysteria, 446
Malingering, 505–6
Man: concept of, 246
Mandeville, B. de: hypochondriasis,
  454–5
Mania, 385, 415–16; Aretaeus, 410;
  Maudsley, 396; Plater, 411–12;
  presbyophrenia, 42; Prichard, 395;
  public view, 415
Mania a potu, 659
Manic-depressive illness: Kraepelin, 272
Manie sans délire (Pinel), 633
Mantegna, A. (painter), 249
Mapother, E.: affective disorders, 398–9
Marandon de Montyel, E: opposition to
  Kraepelin, 285
Marcé, L.V.: dementia, 74–5; eating
  disorder, 595
Marchand, L.: Parkinson's disease, 101
Marie, P.: multiple sclerosis, 180
Marlowe, Kit, 416
Marrs, W.: neurasthenia, 536
Masked epilepsy, 147, 150–1
Mass hysteria, 124, 563; dancing mania,
  123–4, 142–4
Masturbation: epilepsy, 170; mental
  retardation, 213
Maternal impressions theory:
  rumination, 606
Maudsley, H., 205; affective disorders,
  395–6; alcohol, 661; alcohol and
  opium, 662; delirium, 26–7;
  dementia, 59; epilepsy, 155; mad *vs*
  bad, 635; pain, 205; social context,
  30
Maudsley hospital, 398
Maury, A.: dreaming, 7
Max-Planck-Institute for Psychiatry. *See*
  German Psychiatric Research
  Institute (Kraepelin)
Mayer-Gross, W.: vascular dementias,
  78–9
Meacher, M.: dementia, 65
Mead, R.: St. Vitus dance, 144
Mean, criterion of, 240–1
Mechanic, D.: 'illness behaviour,' 483
Medical diagnosis: fashions, 480, 482
Medical model, 120; mental retardation
  (*vs* continuum model), 232

Medical Nemesis (Illich), 355
Medicalization: ageing, 61; alcoholism,
  668
Meeus, F.: combined psychoses, 156,
  157–8
Melancholia (*see also*
  Hypochondria/iasis), 385–6, 468;
  cultural views, 416
Melancholic dementia (Mairet), 58
Melancholic stupor, 10
Melzack, R.: pain, 206
Menninger, K.: taxonomy, 327
Mental age, 253–4
Mental besetments (Mickle), 580
Mental illness: causes, 549
Mental pain, 203, 204; Zeller, 319
Mental retardation, 212–58; causation,
  215–18; classifications, 214–15, 247;
  vs madness, 215; management,
  218–20; social aspects, 239–58
Mercier, C.: obsessive-compulsive
  disorders, 582
Merskey, H.: organic symptoms, 483–4;
  somatoform disorders, 476
Merycism (rumination), 593, 606–7
Mesmer, F.-A., 437
Metabolic psychoses (Schröder), 423
Metalanguage, metaperspective, 402
Metamorphosis (Neumann), 321
Metaphor: disease as (Sontag), 164–5
Methadone, 663
Meyer, A.: constitutional inferiority, 636;
  psychosomatic illness, 478
Meynert, Th., 302; *Verwirrtheit*, 8
Micale, M.: hysteria, 445–6
Michéa, C.F.: hypochondriasis, 460
Mickle, J.: obsessive-compulsive
  disorders, 580
Microcephaly, 217
Middle Ages: species membership, 244;
  suicide, 626
Middleton's Dictionary: paralysis, 106
Military psychiatry. *See* Army
Mill, J.S.: confusion, 7–8
Mind/body problem: hysteria, 447
Ministry of Pensions, 493–4
Miracles of Christ: epilepsy, 165
Mistletoe: for epilepsy, 166–7
Mitchell, S.W.: melancholia, 394;
  neurasthenia, 510, 514, 536–8
Modern art, 353
Modern civilization (*see also*
  Industrialization): anxiety, 564,
  567–8; dementia, 58; neurasthenia,
  512, 534; personality disorder,
  651–2; schizophrenia, 356
Mongeri, L.: on Kraepelin, 285
'Mongolian' idiocy, 217–18
Monism: delirium, 25; Kraepelin, 267,
  268
Monomania (*see also* Paranoia), 360–3,
  373, 620, 633–4; alcohol, 669;
  obsessive-compulsive disorder as, 576
Monro, H.: classification, 324
Monsieur C.: stroke case, 88–9
Monsters: idiots as, 228, 233
Montesquieu: suicide, 627
Moore (Bishop of Norwich):
  obsessive-compulsive disorder, 573
Moore, C.: on suicide, 613
Moral defectives, 254
Moral insanity, 635, 645
Morale, 569
Morals, morality: Kraepelin, 268; and
  nervous energy, 533–4; personality
  disorder, 650
Morbid emotivity (Féré), 553–4
Morbid introspection (Clark, M.J.), 197
Morbid species: multiple sclerosis, 187
Mordret, A.E.: combined affective
  disorders, 391
Moreau de Tours, J.-J., 27, 28

Morel, B.A.: alcohol, 660; classification,
  323, 338; degeneracy, 216, 634;
  dementia, 38; dementia praecox,
  337; emotional delusions, 549–50,
  576–7; epilepsy, 150–1;
  hypochondriasis, 460;
  obsessive-compulsive disorder, 576–7
Morer, S.: delirium, misdiagnosis, 24;
  social context, 30
Morgagni, G.B.: apoplexy, 73, 87;
  hypochondriasis, 453
Morison, Sir A.: alcohol, 659
Morphine, 662
Morselli, E.: dysmorphophobia, 465; on
  suicide, 618
Morton, R.: nervous consumption, 594
Motility symptom complex, 423–5
Motor vehicle accidents, 496
Mott, F.: neurasthenia, 517; shell shock,
  492, 505
Muldoon, W.: neurasthenia clinic, 538
Müller, J., 196
Multi-infarct dementia, 79–80
Multiple sclerosis, 174–92; differential
  diagnosis, 178; mental symptoms,
  178–87
Murder: of mental defectives, 255
Muscle-building, 539
Music therapy, 414
Myalgic encephalomyelitis, 522
Myers, C.: shell shock, 505

Napier, R.: on suicide, 629
Napoleonic Code: dementia, 36
Nascher, I.: geriatrics, 59
National Center for Post Traumatic
  Stress Disorder, 497
National Hospital for Nervous Diseases:
  neurasthenia, 516
National Institute of Ageing, 66
National responsibility: trauma, 501
National Schizophrenia Hotline, 349
National Socialists: murder of mental
  defectives, 255; schizophrenia, 344,
  425
Natural *vs* artificial classifications, 314
Naturalism: and Kraepelin, 268, 269
Nature writers: neurasthenia, 541
Neo-Kraepelinians, 273–4, 275
'Nervous': change in meaning, 534
Nervous exhaustion, 512
Nervousness: Bouchut, 548
Netchine, G.: mental retardation, 231
Neumann, H.: taxonomy, 321–2
'Neuralpathology', 176, 456
Neurasthenia, 151, 398, 481, 509–44;
  disputes over, 523; modern, 520–2;
  reaction against, 515–19; social
  aspects, 533–44
Neurasthenic discourse, 533
Neurofibrils: Alzheimer's disease, 43
Neurographs, 132
Neurology, 169, 176, 302; Alzheimer's
  disease, 66
Neuropsychiatric disorders, 3–258
Neuroses, 176; Axenfeld, 585; chronic
  pain without lesion, 194, 195–6; *vs*
  constitutional inferiority, 636;
  epilepsy, 151; Freud, 438–9;
  hypochondria as (18th century),
  455–6; in Parkinson's disease, 103;
  vs Parkinson's disease, 98; *vs*
  psychoses (Mapother), 398
Newington, H.H.: stupor, 11
Newspapers: schizophrenia (term), 350
New York: meeting on multiple sclerosis,
  182–3
New York Neurological Society:
  affective disorders, 394–5
New York *vs* London: dementia
  prevalence, 64
Niemeyer, F. von: epilepsy, 156
Nijinsky (dancer), 353
Nissl staining: Huntington's disease, 132